The
Poetical Works
of
Tennyson

The
Poetical Works
of
Tennyson

❧

Cambridge Edition

Edited by G. Robert Stange

Houghton Mifflin Company Boston

Copyright © 1974 by Houghton Mifflin Company

For information about permission to reproduce selections
from this book, write to Permissions, Houghton Mifflin
Company, 2 Park Street, Boston, Massachusetts 02108.

Library of Congress Cataloging in Publication Data

Tennyson, Alfred Tennyson, Baron, 1809–1892.
The poetical works of Tennyson.
(Cambridge edition of the poets)
Published in 1898 under title: The poetic and
dramatic works of Alfred, Lord Tennyson.
I. Series.
PR5550.F74   821'.8   74-1151
ISBN 0-395-18014-7

Printed in the United States of America

V 14 13 12 11 10 9 8 7 6 5

EDITOR'S NOTE

THE CAMBRIDGE EDITION of Tennyson's poetical works, edited by W. J. Rolfe, first appeared in 1898 and has since been recognized as the best American edition and the most usable one-volume edition of Tennyson's massive and elaborately revised body of poetry. Although Rolfe did not include the poet's posthumous volume, *The Death of Œnone*, he came close to completeness by republishing in the Appendix the early *Poems by Two Brothers*, the thirty-two poems of 1830 which had been suppressed, and a number of discarded and uncollected pieces. As a result, Rolfe's volume had an amplitude which has not until very recently been equaled.

The present edition is a reprint of the text of 1898, excluding the plays *Queen Maud: A Drama; Harold: A Drama; Beckett; The Falcon; The Cup;* and *The Promise of Man;* and with the addition of the twenty-three poems from *The Death of Œnone.* It has been decided to leave Rolfe's Notes and Illustrations in their original form. Though the critical opinions expressed in them may occasionally seem old-fashioned, they have the value of containing a great many variant readings and of quoting copiously from both Tennyson and his contemporaries. The particular virtue of this present edition is that it offers, in the form in which Tennyson himself arranged them, all those poems he wished to leave to posterity. The rejected poems, one or two of which are masterpieces, are easily available to the reader in the Appendix.

The texts of the poems follow the last edition supervised by the poet, but they have been collated with earlier volumes and note made of the most interesting variant readings. In the matter of spelling, American practice has been followed with such words as "honor" and "analyze," but the special flavor of Tennyson's idiosyncratic usage–as in "tho'" and "earn'd"–has been maintained.

G. R. S.

CONTENTS

INTRODUCTION

THE READER OF TENNYSON who looks for critical guidance, or merely for information about the poet and his work, may be bewildered by the copiousness of materials and the diversity of judgments. Tennyson has been taken seriously as a poet for nearly one hundred and fifty years, and the essays and books devoted to his work are in bulk, if not in quality, close behind the studies of Shakespeare. The great and continuing enterprise of Tennyson criticism began impressively with an excellent essay by the poet's closest friend, Arthur Hallam. "On Some of the Characteristics of Modern Poetry, and on the Lyrical Poems of Alfred Tennyson," published in 1831, is both a sensitive appreciation of the young poet's art and a provocative manifesto for a new kind of poetry. From the 1830s onward the stream of critical appreciation (and denigration) has not ceased to flow. With the publication of his *Poems* in 1842 Tennyson was recognized as the leading poet of his time, and before he had reached middle age, his work had become the subject of full-length books.

However, as Tennyson would have been the first to remark, the attention of critics may improve a writer's sales, but it does not always lead to understanding or appreciation. It is a poignant fact that the man who reached a larger audience than had any previous poet, whose publications were rewarded not only by the esteem of critics and notables, but also by cash profits that even now seem staggering, and who was made a baron solely on the basis of his literary achievements, should have nursed a lifelong conviction that the reading public never understood his poetry. When *In Memoriam* was received with universal praise, Tennyson would only remark that it was "the least misunderstood of all my work. I don't mean that the commentators have been more right, but that the general reading public has been less wrong than usual as to my intentions." And though we now speak of the Age of Tennyson with an assurance that we could not bring to such labels as the Age of Arnold, or of Browning, there is reason to suspect that Tennyson himself outlived that age. A critical reaction against his work began as early as the 1860s and continued to gain force until the 1930s. There are many reasons for this reaction, but the simplest way of regarding it is as an inevitable concomitant of the poet laureate's unique success and influence. By the time he died in 1892 his image was associated in the public mind with that of Queen Victoria. As she was transformed into a mystic Imperial Mother, Tennyson was cast as Priest and Sage of the Kingdom. Ministers of the church consulted him on matters of morals, and statesmen on questions of politics. His name was given to a lake in New Zealand and to an Arctic promontory. When a certain Professor Ferrier wrote a history of philosophy, he sent the manuscript to Tennyson, begging to be informed of any errors of reasoning he might have committed. Though Tennyson possessed a sufficient strain of gruff self-mockery to save him from the worst effects of idolatry, and though he went serenely on to write several of his most beautiful poems in the last years of his life, there is some risk of our being unable to perceive the poet in the shadow of the public figure created by — and for — Lord Tennyson.

It was inevitable too that there should be a reaction against a poet who had succeeded in stamping the literature of a half century with the imprint of his diction. Young writers, trying as Tennyson himself had, to create new forms and to find a new poetic language were impelled to revolt, and in doing so necessarily forgot what they owed the old master. Tennyson's extraordinary achievements provoked extraordinary reactions, and much of the criticism of the earlier twentieth century now seems to be based on a willful ignoring of the depth and subtlety of his work, an exaggeration of his role as Household Poet or platitudinous moralizer, and a misinterpretation of his tortuous ambiguities. Tennyson had explored so many possibilities in poetry, had left his magisterial tracks in so many fields of snow, that a young writer could only escape his influence by some form of extreme rejection. The turnabout — equally inevitable as it now seems — did not begin until the 1920s; then the process of restoration began, and Tennyson was raised by degrees — as *poet*, not as eminent Victorian — to the pantheon from which he had been banished.

Among the first of the revisionists was Harold Nicolson, who published a critical biography in 1923. His notions now seem rather quaint and wrong-headed, but he deserves credit for beginning the work of reclamation and for engendering a small family of critical books. It was Nicolson's view that Tennyson was by nature a raging romantic, but that he had overlaid this natural self with his public personality and submitted to the stifling claims of his age. If we were to discard approximately half his poetry (the "Victorian" half, of course), we would be left with a group of wild lyrical verses which are the expression of the poet's true, buried self. For many years after the appearance of this influential study, discriminating readers (as opposed, it must be understood, to those placid souls who had never stopped admiring the Tennyson Queen Victoria knew) were urged to see the poet as a caged eagle or a black-blooded gypsy, an outlaw manqué, fettered by the conventions and repressions of his age.

From this view of Tennyson as psychically damaged lyricist, it was only a step to placing him in the society of the highly acceptable French poets of the late nineteenth century. The laureate may, in his superficial life, have gone yachting with prime ministers and sat down in the presence of royalty, but *au fond* he was what Verlaine had proudly called himself, a *poète maudit*, a self-proclaimed exile from bourgeois society. And once Tennyson was associated with the band of *Symbolistes*, it became evident that the good gray laureate had, in fact, a remarkable understanding of the poetic symbol, that he might even be regarded as the creator of the Symbolist movement in English poetry. One critic who has written that "in the case of Tennyson it is justifiable to interpret his whole career as an advance in the techniques of symbolisms" represents the phase of Tennyson criticism involving studies of the meanings, development and interrelationship of his symbols, a critical approach which began in the 1940s and which has since become dominant.

An indication of Tennyson's new respectability among those with the most advanced literary tastes is his acceptance by modern poets. T. S. Eliot, in two essays, approached his work with a fine discrimination and lent his great authority to the task of assigning Tennyson an exalted place in the English poetic tradition. W. H. Auden dealt with the laureate in a more cavalier manner, calling Tennyson "the stupidest of English poets," but praising him as being preeminently the poet of suffering and pairing him (not very convincingly, it must be said) with the impeccable Baudelaire. The atmosphere of interest created by these re-assessments has stimulated analytic studies which reveal in a modern critical idiom the richness and — *pace* Harold Nicolson — the *wholeness* of Tennyson's achievement; along with this has come a body of fresh biographical interpretation, of newly discovered manuscripts and studies of Tennyson's revisions and methods of composition. The main work of restitution has now been done, and though it is to be expected that each new decade will discover its own Tennyson, it is inconceivable that his reputation should ever sink back to what it was in the early years of our century. Writers and critics have now grown out from under the poet's shadow;

enough time has passed so that we can see his work in perspective, and whatever our personal predilections may suggest about this or that detail, it is clear that his poetry represents one of the major achievements in English literature.

It does not always add to a reader's understanding to be told that X is a great poet and Y a minor one, but in the case of Tennyson our sense of his greatness, of what Mallarmé called "the impression of sublimity," which shines around and through his poetry, becomes an aspect of our experience as we read his work. Even when we are most struck by his unevenness, his willingness to slip into bathos, we must admire his poetic daring and the extraordinary range of his interests. To have a supreme mastery of one's craft, to touch human life at innumerable and continually unexpected points, and with all this to maintain a central core of being, inviolable and mysterious — these are the qualities of a great poet, and these — most certainly — are the qualities of Alfred Tennyson.

G. ROBERT STANGE

CHRONOLOGY OF TENNYSON'S LIFE

1809 Born at the Rectory at Somersby, Lincolnshire, the third son in a family of twelve children.

1817 Sent to school at the nearby town of Louth.

1824 Writes a verse play, *The Devil and the Lady*.

1827 Publishes with his brother Charles *Poems by Two Brothers*, which also includes poems by his brother Frederick.

Enters Trinity College, Cambridge, where he is to stay until the spring of 1829. Forms a close friendship with Arthur Hallam and joins the society of "the Apostles."

1829 Wins the chancellor's gold medal at Cambridge for his poem "Timbuctoo."

1830 Publishes *Poems, Chiefly Lyrical*, his first true volume of poetry.

1831 Tennyson's father dies, leaving his family in financial difficulties.

1832 Publishes *Poems*.

1833 Arthur Hallam, who had become engaged to Tennyson's sister, dies suddenly. Tennyson experiences a grief which lasts for many years.

1833–1834 Begins extensive revision of his earlier poems and starts to write the "swallow-flights of song," which eventually formed *In Memoriam*.

1842 Publishes *Poems* in two volumes, one of which is made up of new poems, and one of selected older poems much revised. The warm reception of the work establishes Tennyson's reputation as the leading poet of his time.

1845 Awarded a government pension of £200 a year.

1847 Publishes *The Princess*.

1850 Tennyson's *magnus annus:* he marries Emily Sellwood, to whom he was first engaged in 1838, is made poet laureate, and publishes *In Memoriam*.

1853 The Tennysons move to Farringford, Isle of Wight, which is to be their home for the rest of the poet's life.

1855 Publishes *Maud, and Other Poems*.

1859 Publishes the first four *Idylls of the King*. Four more idylls are to be published in 1869, two in 1872, and the last, making up the cycle of twelve, in 1885.

1864 Publishes *Enoch Arden*, his greatest commercial success.

1880 Publishes *Ballads and Other Poems*.

1883 Elevated to the peerage as a baron.

1885 Publishes *Tiresias and Other Poems*.

1886   Publishes *Locksley Hall Sixty Years After.*

1889   Publishes *Demeter and Persephone.*

1892   Tennyson dies at Aldworth, his estate in Sussex, and is buried in the Poet's Corner of Westminster Abbey.

Posthumous publication of *The Death of Œnone, Akbar's Dream, and Other Poems.*

The
Poetical Works
of
Tennyson

TO THE QUEEN

This poem was prefixed to the first Laureate Edition (1851), where it included the 'Crystal-Palace' stanza (see Notes) omitted in all subsequent editions. The 4th stanza was inserted in the next edition, and a few slight changes were made elsewhere.

Revered, beloved — O you that hold
A nobler office upon earth
Than arms, or power of brain, or birth
Could give the warrior kings of old,

Victoria, — since your Royal grace
To one of less desert allows
This laurel greener from the brows
Of him that utter'd nothing base;

And should your greatness, and the care
That yokes with empire, yield you time
To make demand of modern rhyme
If aught of ancient worth be there;

Then — while a sweeter music wakes,
And thro' wild March the throstle calls,
Where all about your palace-walls
The sun-lit almond-blossom shakes —

Take, Madam, this poor book of song;
For tho' the faults were thick as dust
In vacant chambers, I could trust
Your kindness. May you rule us long,

And leave us rulers of your blood
As noble till the latest day!
May children of our children say,
' She wrought her people lasting good;

' Her court was pure; her life serene;
God gave her peace; her land reposed;
A thousand claims to reverence closed
In her as Mother, Wife, and Queen;

' And statesmen at her council met
Who knew the seasons when to take
Occasion by the hand, and make
The bounds of freedom wider yet

' By shaping some august decree
Which kept her throne unshaken still,
Broad-based upon her people's will,
And compass'd by the inviolate sea.'

March, 1851.

JUVENILIA

Under this head, in the one-volume and seven-volume editions of 1884 and all subsequent editions, Lord Tennyson included certain poems from the volumes of 1830 and 1833 (some of which were suppressed in 1842), with others that had not appeared in any earlier authorized edition of his works. For those not printed in 1830 (or then printed, and afterwards suppressed for a time) see the prefatory notes to the poems. All those without prefatory notes (or reference in other notes) were printed in 1830 and reprinted in 1842.

CLARIBEL

A MELODY

In 1830 ' callow ' was ' fledgling '.

WHERE Claribel low-lieth
  The breezes pause and die,
    Letting the rose-leaves fall;
But the solemn oak-tree sigheth,
  Thick-leaved, ambrosial,
  With an ancient melody
Of an inward agony,
Where Claribel low-lieth.

At eve the beetle boometh
  Athwart the thicket lone;
At noon the wild bee hummeth
  About the moss'd headstone;
At midnight the moon cometh,
  And looketh down alone.
Her song the lintwhite swelleth,
The clear-voiced mavis dwelleth,
  The callow throstle lispeth,
The slumbrous wave outwelleth,
  The babbling runnel crispeth,
The hollow grot replieth
  Where Claribel low-lieth.

NOTHING WILL DIE

This poem and the two next poems, first published in 1830, were omitted in 1842, but afterwards restored.

WHEN will the stream be aweary of· flow-
  ing
    Under my eye?

When will the wind be aweary of blowing
    Over the sky?
When will the clouds be aweary of fleeting?
When will the heart be aweary of beating?
    And nature die?
Never, O, never, nothing will die;
    The stream flows,
    The wind blows,
    The cloud fleets,
    The heart beats,
      Nothing will die.

  Nothing will die;
  All things will change
  Thro' eternity.
  'T is the world's winter;
  Autumn and summer
  Are gone long ago;
  Earth is dry to the centre,
  But spring, a new comer,
  A spring rich and strange,
  Shall make the winds blow
  Round and round,
  Thro' and thro',
    Here and there,
    Till the air
  And the ground
  Shall be fill'd with life anew.

  The world was never made;
  It will change, but it will not fade.
  So let the wind range;
  For even and morn
    Ever will be
    Thro' eternity.
  Nothing was born;
  Nothing will die;
  All things will change.

ALL THINGS WILL DIE

CLEARLY the blue river chimes in its flowing
      Under my eye;
Warmly and broadly the south winds are
      blowing
      Over the sky.
One after another the white clouds are
      fleeting;
Every heart this May morning in joyance
      is beating
      Full merrily;
      Yet all things must die.
The stream will cease to flow;
The wind will cease to blow;
The clouds will cease to fleet;
The heart will cease to beat;
      For all things must die.
      All things must die.
Spring will come never more.
      O, vanity!
Death waits at the door.
See! our friends are all forsaking
The wine and the merrymaking.
We are call'd — we must go.
Laid low, very low,
In the dark we must lie.
The merry glees are still;
The voice of the bird
Shall no more be heard,
Nor the wind on the hill.
      O, misery!
Hark! death is calling
While I speak to ye,
The jaw is falling,
The red cheek paling,
The strong limbs failing;
Ice with the warm blood mixing;
The eyeballs fixing.
Nine times goes the passing bell:
Ye merry souls, farewell.
      The old earth
      Had a birth,
      As all men know,
      Long ago.
And the old earth must die.
So let the warm winds range,
And the blue wave beat the shore;
For even and morn
Ye will never see
Thro' eternity.
All things were born.
Ye will come never more,
For all things must die.

LEONINE ELEGIACS

LOW-FLOWING breezes are roaming the
      broad valley dimm'd in the gloam-
      ing;
Thoro' the black-stemm'd pines only the
      far river shines.
Creeping thro' blossomy rushes and bowers
      of rose-blowing bushes,
Down by the poplar tall rivulets babble
      and fall.
Barketh the shepherd-dog cheerly; the
      grasshopper carolleth clearly;
Deeply the wood-dove coos; shrilly the
      owlet halloos;
Winds creep; dews fall chilly: in her first
      sleep earth breathes stilly:
Over the pools in the burn water-gnats
      murmur and mourn.
Sadly the far kine loweth; the glimmering
      water outfloweth;
Twin peaks shadow'd with pine slope to the
      dark hyaline.
Low-throned Hesper is stayed between the
      two peaks; but the Naiad
Throbbing in mild unrest holds him be-
      neath in her breast.
The ancient poetess singeth that Hesperus
      all things bringeth,
Smoothing the wearied mind: bring me my
      love, Rosalind.
Thou comest morning or even; she cometh
      not morning or even.
False-eyed Hesper, unkind, where is my
      sweet Rosalind?

SUPPOSED CONFESSIONS

OF A SECOND-RATE SENSITIVE MIND

This poem, published in 1830, was suppressed
for more than fifty years. In 1879 the 'Chris-
tian Signal,' an English journal, announced
that its issue for September 6th would contain
' an early unpublished poem of over two hun-
dred lines by Alfred Tennyson (P. L.), entitled
" Confessions of a Sensitive Mind; " ' but the
publication was prevented by a legal injunc-
tion. In 1884 the poem was included in the
complete edition of the Laureate's works.

O GOD! my God! have mercy now.
I faint, I fall. Men say that Thou
Didst die for me, for such as *me*,

Patient of ill, and death, and scorn,
And that my sin was as a thorn
Among the thorns that girt Thy brow,
Wounding Thy soul. — That even now,
In this extremest misery
Of ignorance, I should require
A sign ! and if a bolt of fire   10
Would rive the slumbrous summer noon
While I do pray to Thee alone,
Think my belief would stronger grow !
Is not my human pride brought low ?
The boastings of my spirit still ?
The joy I had in my free-will
All cold, and dead, and corpse-like grown ?
And what is left to me but Thou,
And faith in Thee ?   Men pass me by;
Christians with happy countenances —   20
And children all seem full of Thee !
And women smile with saint-like glances
Like Thine own mother's when she bow'd
Above Thee, on that happy morn
When angels spake to men aloud,
And Thou and peace to earth were born.
Good-will to me as well as all —
I one of them; my brothers they;
Brothers in Christ — a world of peace
And confidence, day after day;   30
And trust and hope till things should cease,
And then one Heaven receive us all.

How sweet to have a common faith !
To hold a common scorn of death !
And at a burial to hear
The creaking cords which wound and eat
Into my human heart, whene'er
Earth goes to earth, with grief, not fear,
With hopeful grief, were passing sweet !

Thrice happy state again to be   40
The trustful infant on the knee,
Who lets his rosy fingers play
About his mother's neck, and knows
Nothing beyond his mother's eyes !
They comfort him by night and day;
They light his little life alway;
He hath no thought of coming woes;
He hath no care of life or death;
Scarce outward signs of joy arise,
Because the Spirit of happiness   50
And perfect rest so inward is;
And loveth so his innocent heart,
Her temple and her place of birth,
Where she would ever wish to dwell,
Life of the fountain there, beneath
Its salient springs, and far apart,

Hating to wander out on earth,
Or breathe into the hollow air,
Whose chillness would make visible
Her subtil, warm, and golden breath,   60
Which mixing with the infant's blood,
Fulfils him with beatitude.
O, sure it is a special care
Of God, to fortify from doubt,
To arm in proof, and guard about
With triple-mailed trust, and clear
Delight, the infant's dawning year.

Would that my gloomed fancy were
As thine, my mother, when with brows
Propt on thy knees, my hands upheld   70
In thine, I listen'd to thy vows,
For me outpour'd in holiest prayer —
For me unworthy ! — and beheld
Thy mild deep eyes upraised, that knew
The beauty and repose of faith,
And the clear spirit shining thro'.
O, wherefore do we grow awry
From roots which strike so deep ? why dare
Paths in the desert?   Could not I
Bow myself down, where thou hast knelt,
To the earth — until the ice would melt 81
Here, and I feel as thou hast felt ?
What devil had the heart to scathe
Flowers thou hadst rear'd — to brush the
    dew
From thine own lily, when thy grave
Was deep, my mother, in the clay ?
Myself ? Is it thus ? Myself ? Had I
So little love for thee ? But why
Prevail'd not thy pure prayers ? Why
    pray
To one who heeds not, who can save   90
But will not ? Great in faith, and strong
Against the grief of circumstance
Wert thou, and yet unheard. What if
Thou pleadest still, and seest me drive
Thro' utter dark a full-sail'd skiff,
Unpiloted i' the echoing dance
Of reboant whirlwinds, stooping low
Unto the death, not sunk ! I know
At matins and at evensong,
That thou, if thou wert yet alive,   100
In deep and daily prayers wouldst strive
To reconcile me with thy God.
Albeit, my hope is gray, and cold
At heart, thou wouldest murmur still —
' Bring this lamb back into Thy fold,
My Lord, if so it be Thy will.'
Wouldst tell me I must brook the rod
And chastisement of human pride;

That pride, the sin of devils, stood
Betwixt me and the light of God;   110
That hitherto I had defied
And had rejected God — that grace
Would drop from His o'er-brimming love,
As manna on my wilderness,
If I would pray — that God would move
And strike the hard, hard rock, and thence,
Sweet in their utmost bitterness,
Would issue tears of penitence
Which would keep green hope's life. Alas !
I think that pride hath now no place   120
Nor sojourn in me. I am void,
Dark, formless, utterly destroyed.

Why not believe then ? Why not yet
Anchor thy frailty there, where man
Hath moor'd and rested ? Ask the sea
At midnight, when the crisp slope waves
After a tempest rib and fret
The broad-imbased beach, why he
Slumbers not like a mountain tarn ?
Wherefore his ridges are not curls   130
And ripples of an inland mere ?
Wherefore he moaneth thus, nor can
Draw down into his vexed pools
All that blue heaven which hues and paves
The other ? I am too forlorn,
Too shaken: my own weakness fools
My judgment, and my spirit whirls,
Moved from beneath with doubt and fear.

' Yet,' said I, in my morn of youth,
The unsunn'd freshness of my strength, 140
When I went forth in quest of truth,
' It is man's privilege to doubt,
If so be that from doubt at length
Truth may stand forth unmoved of change,
An image with profulgent brows
And perfect limbs, as from the storm
Of running fires and fluid range
Of lawless airs, at last stood out
This excellence and solid form
Of constant beauty. For the ox   150
Feeds in the herb, and sleeps, or fills
The horned valleys all about,
And hollows of the fringed hills
In summer heats, with placid lows
Unfearing, till his own blood flows
About his hoof. And in the flocks
The lamb rejoiceth in the year,
And raceth freely with his fere,
And answers to his mother's calls
From the flower'd furrow. In a time   160
Of which he wots not, run short pains

Thro' his warm heart ; and then, from whence
He knows not, on his light there falls
A shadow; and his native slope,
Where he was wont to leap and climb,
Floats from his sick and filmed eyes,
And something in the darkness draws
His forehead earthward, and he dies.
Shall man live thus, in joy and hope
As a young lamb, who cannot dream,   170
Living, but that he shall live on ?
Shall we not look into the laws
Of life and death, and things that seem,
And things that be, and analyze
Our double nature, and compare
All creeds till we have found the one,
If one there be ? ' Ay me ! I fear
All may not doubt, but everywhere
Some must clasp idols. Yet, my God,
Whom call I idol ? Let Thy dove   180
Shadow me over, and my sins
Be unremember'd, and Thy love
Enlighten me. O, teach me yet
Somewhat before the heavy clod
Weighs on me, and the busy fret
Of that sharp-headed worm begins
In the gross blackness underneath.

O weary life ! O weary death !
O spirit and heart made desolate !
O damned vacillating state !   190

THE KRAKEN

Published in 1830, omitted in 1842, but after-
wards restored, with ' fins ' changed to ' arms.'

BELOW the thunders of the upper deep,
Far, far beneath in the abysmal sea,
His ancient, dreamless, uninvaded sleep
The Kraken sleepeth : faintest sunlights
    flee
About his shadowy sides; above him swell
Huge sponges of millennial growth and
    height;
And far away into the sickly light,
From many a wondrous grot and secret
    cell
Unnumber'd and enormous polypi
Winnow with giant arms the slumbering
    green.
There hath he lain for ages, and will lie
Battening upon huge sea - worms in his
    sleep,

Until the latter fire shall heat the deep;
Then once by man and angels to be seen,
In roaring he shall rise and on the surface
    die.

SONG

In 1830 the title was 'We are Free' and
the two stanzas were printed as one; omitted
in 1842, but afterwards restored.

THE winds, as at their hour of birth,
  Leaning upon the ridged sea,
Breathed low around the rolling earth
  With mellow preludes, 'We are free.'

The streams, through many a lilied row
  Down-carolling to the crisped sea,
Low-tinkled with a bell-like flow
  Atween the blossoms, 'We are free.'

LILIAN

In 1842 'purfled' was changed to 'gathered.'

I

  AIRY, fairy Lilian,
  Flitting, fairy Lilian,
When I ask her if she love me,
Claps her tiny hands above me,
  Laughing all she can;
She 'll not tell me if she love me,
  Cruel little Lilian.

II

  When my passion seeks
  Pleasance in love-sighs,
She, looking thro' and thro' me
Thoroughly to undo me,
  Smiling, never speaks:
So innocent-arch, so cunning-simple,
From beneath her gathered wimple
Glancing with black-beaded eyes,
Till the lightning laughters dimple
  The baby-roses in her cheeks;
  Then away she flies.

III

Prythee weep, May Lilian!
  Gaiety without eclipse
Wearieth me, May Lilian;
Thro' my very heart it thrilleth
  When from crimson-threaded lips
Silver-treble laughter trilleth:
  Prythee weep, May Lilian!

IV

  Praying all I can,
If prayers will not hush thee,
  Airy Lilian,
Like a rose-leaf I will crush thee,
  Fairy Lilian.

ISABEL

Tennyson's mother was the basis of this
portrait.

EYES not down-dropt nor over-bright, but
    fed
  With the clear-pointed flame of chastity,
  Clear, without heat, undying, tended by
    Pure vestal thoughts in the translu-
      cent fane
Of her still spirit; locks not wide-dispread,
Madonna-wise on either side her head;
    Sweet lips whereon perpetually did
      reign
  The summer calm of golden charity,
Were fixed shadows of thy fixed mood,
    Revered Isabel, the crown and head,
The stately flower of female fortitude,
    Of perfect wifehood and pure lowli-
      head.

The intuitive decision of a bright
  And thorough-edged intellect to part
    Error from crime; a prudence to with-
      hold;
    The laws of marriage character'd in
      gold
Upon the blanched tablets of her heart;
A love still burning upward, giving light
To read those laws; an accent very low
In blandishment, but a most silver flow
    Of subtle-paced counsel in distress,
Right to the heart and brain, tho' unde-
    scried,
    Winning its way with extreme gentle-
      ness
Thro' all the outworks of suspicious pride;
A courage to endure and to obey;
A hate of gossip parlance, and of sway,
Crown'd Isabel, thro' all her placid life,
The queen of marriage, a most perfect
    wife.

The mellow'd reflex of a winter moon;
A clear stream flowing with a muddy one,

Till in its onward current it absorbs
  With swifter movement and in purer
    light
  The vexed eddies of its wayward bro-
    ther;
  A leaning and upbearing parasite,
  Clothing the stem, which else had
    fallen quite
  With cluster'd flower-bells and ambrosial
    orbs
  Of rich fruit-bunches leaning on each
    other —
  Shadow forth thee: — the world hath
    not another
(Tho' all her fairest forms are types of
    thee,
And thou of God in thy great charity)
Of such a finish'd chasten'd purity.

MARIANA

'Mariana in the moated grange.'
Measure for Measure.

WITH blackest moss the flower-plots
  Were thickly crusted, one and all;
The rusted nails fell from the knots
  That held the pear to the gable-wall.
The broken sheds look'd sad and strange:
  Unlifted was the clinking latch;
  Weeded and worn the ancient thatch
Upon the lonely moated grange.
    She only said, 'My life is dreary,
      He cometh not,' she said;   10
    She said, 'I am aweary, aweary,
      I would that I were dead!'

Her tears fell with the dews at even;
  Her tears fell ere the dews were dried;
She could not look on the sweet heaven,
  Either at morn or eventide.
After the flitting of the bats,
  When thickest dark did trance the sky,
  She drew her casement-curtain by,
And glanced athwart the glooming flats. 20
    She only said, 'The night is dreary,
      He cometh not,' she said;
    She said, 'I am aweary, aweary,
      I would that I were dead!'

Upon the middle of the night,
  Waking she heard the night-fowl crow;
The cock sung out an hour ere light;.
  From the dark fen the oxen's low

Came to her; without hope of change,
  In sleep she seem'd to walk forlorn,   30
Till cold winds woke the gray-eyed morn
About the lonely moated grange.
    She only said, 'The day is dreary,
      He cometh not,' she said;
    She said, 'I am aweary, aweary,
      I would that I were dead!'

About a stone-cast from the wall
  A sluice with blacken'd waters slept,
And o'er it many, round and small,
  The cluster'd marish-mosses crept.   40
Hard by a poplar shook alway,
  All silver-green with gnarled bark:
  For leagues no other tree did mark
The level waste, the rounding gray.
    She only said, 'My life is dreary,
      He cometh not,' she said;
    She said, 'I am aweary, aweary,
      I would that I were dead!'

And ever when the moon was low,
  And the shrill winds were up and away,
In the white curtain, to and fro,   51
  She saw the gusty shadow sway.
But when the moon was very low,
  And wild winds bound within their cell,
  The shadow of the poplar fell
Upon her bed, across her brow.
    She only said, 'The night is dreary,
      He cometh not,' she said;
    She said, 'I am aweary, aweary,
      I would that I were dead!'   60

All day within the dreamy house,
  The doors upon their hinges creak'd;
The blue fly sung in the pane; the mouse
  Behind the mouldering wainscot shriek'd,
Or from the crevice peer'd about.
  Old faces glimmer'd thro' the doors,
  Old footsteps trod the upper floors,
Old voices called her from without.
    She only said, 'My life is dreary,
      He cometh not,' she said;   70
    She said, 'I am aweary, aweary,
      I would that I were dead!'

The sparrow's chirrup on the roof,
  The slow clock ticking, and the sound
Which to the wooing wind aloof
  The poplar made, did all confound
Her sense; but most she loathed the hour
  When the thick-moted sunbeam lay
  Athwart the chambers, and the day

Was sloping toward his western bower. 80
Then said she, 'I am very dreary,
He will not come,' she said;
She wept, 'I am aweary, aweary,
O God, that I were dead!'

TO ——

I

CLEAR-HEADED friend, whose joyful scorn,
Edged with sharp laughter, cuts atwain
The knots that tangle human creeds,
The wounding cords that bind and strain
The heart until it bleeds,
Ray-fringed eyelids of the morn
Roof not a glance so keen as thine;
If aught of prophecy be mine,
Thou wilt not live in vain.

II

Low-cowering shall the Sophist sit;
Falsehood shall bare her plaited brow;
Fair-fronted Truth shall droop not now
With shrilling shafts of subtle wit.
Nor martyr-flames, nor trenchant swords
Can do away that ancient lie;
A gentler death shall Falsehood die,
Shot thro' and thro' with cunning words.

III

Weak Truth a-leaning on her crutch,
Wan, wasted Truth in her utmost need,
Thy kingly intellect shall feed,
Until she be an athlete bold,
And weary with a finger's touch
Those writhed limbs of lightning speed;
Like that strange angel which of old,
Until the breaking of the light,
Wrestled with wandering Israel,
Past Yabbok brook the livelong night,
And heaven's mazed signs stood still
In the dim tract of Penuel.

MADELINE

I

THOU art not steep'd in golden languors,
No tranced summer calm is thine,
Ever varying Madeline.
Thro' light and shadow thou dost range,
Sudden glances, sweet and strange,
Delicious spites and darling angers,
And airy forms of flitting change.

II

Smiling, frowning, evermore,
Thou art perfect in love-lore.
Revealings deep and clear are thine
Of wealthy smiles; but who may know
Whether smile or frown be fleeter?
Whether smile or frown be sweeter,
Who may know?
Frowns perfect-sweet along the brow
Light-glooming over eyes divine,
Like little clouds sun-fringed, are thine,
Ever varying Madeline.
Thy smile and frown are not aloof
From one another,
Each to each is dearest brother;
Hues of the silken sheeny woof
Momently shot into each other.
All the mystery is thine;
Smiling, frowning, evermore,
Thou art perfect in love-lore,
Ever varying Madeline.

III

A subtle, sudden flame,
By veering passion fann'd,
About thee breaks and dances:
When I would kiss thy hand,
The flush of anger'd shame
O'erflows thy calmer glances,
And o'er black brows drops down
A sudden-curved frown:
But when I turn away,
Thou, willing me to stay,
Wooest not, nor vainly wranglest,
But, looking fixedly the while,
All my bounding heart entanglest
In a golden-netted smile;
Then in madness and in bliss,
If my lips should dare to kiss
Thy taper fingers amorously,
Again thou blushest angrily;
And o'er black brows drops down
A sudden-curved frown.

SONG — THE OWL

I

WHEN cats run home and light is come,
And dew is cold upon the ground,
And the far-off stream is dumb,
And the whirring sail goes round,
And the whirring sail goes round;
Alone and warming his five wits,
The white owl in the belfry sits.

II

When merry milkmaids click the latch,
  And rarely smells the new-mown hay,
And the cock hath sung beneath the thatch
  Twice or thrice his roundelay,
  Twice or thrice his roundelay;
    Alone and warming his five wits,
    The white owl in the belfry sits.

SECOND SONG

TO THE SAME

I

THY tuwhits are lull'd, I wot,
  Thy tuwhoos of yesternight,
Which upon the dark afloat,
  So took echo with delight,
  So took echo with delight,
    That her voice, untuneful grown,
    Wears all day a fainter tone.

II

I would mock thy chaunt anew;
  But I cannot mimic it;
Not a whit of thy tuwhoo,
  Thee to woo to thy tuwhit,
  Thee to woo to thy tuwhit,
    With a lengthen'd loud halloo,
    Tuwhoo, tuwhit, tuwhit, tuwhoo-o-o !

RECOLLECTIONS OF THE ARABIAN NIGHTS

WHEN the breeze of a joyful dawn blew
      free
In the silken sail of infancy,
The tide of time flow'd back with me,
  The forward-flowing tide of time;
And many a sheeny summer-morn,
Adown the Tigris I was borne,
By Bagdat's shrines of fretted gold,
High-walled gardens green and old;
True Mussulman was I and sworn,
  For it was in the golden prime   10
    Of good Haroun Alraschid.

Anight my shallop, rustling thro'
The low and bloomed foliage, drove
The fragrant, glistening deeps, and clove
The citron-shadows in the blue;

By garden porches on the brim,
The costly doors flung open wide,
Gold glittering thro' lamplight dim,
And broider'd sofas on each side.
  In sooth it was a goodly time,   20
  For it was in the golden prime
    Of good Haroun Alraschid.

Often, where clear-stemm'd platans guard
The outlet, did I turn away
The boat-head down a broad canal
From the main river sluiced, where all
The sloping of the moonlit sward
Was damask-work, and deep inlay
Of braided blooms unmown, which crept
Adown to where the water slept.   30
  A goodly place, a goodly time,
  For it was in the golden prime
    Of good Haroun Alraschid.

A motion from the river won
Ridged the smooth level, bearing on
My shallop thro' the star-strown calm,
Until another night in night
I enter'd, from the clearer light,
Imbower'd vaults of pillar'd palm,
Imprisoning sweets, which, as they clomb 40
Heavenward, were stay'd beneath the dome
  Of hollow boughs.   A goodly time,
  For it was in the golden prime
    Of good Haroun Alraschid.

Still onward; and the clear canal
Is rounded to as clear a lake.
From the green rivage many a fall
Of diamond rillets musical,
Thro' little crystal arches low
Down from the central fountain's flow   50
Fallen silver-chiming, seemed to shake
The sparkling flints beneath the prow.
  A goodly place, a goodly time,
  For it was in the golden prime
    Of good Haroun Alraschid.

Above thro' many a bowery turn
A walk with vari-colored shells
Wander'd engrain'd.   On either side
All round about the fragrant marge
From fluted vase, and brazen urn   60
In order, eastern flowers large,
Some dropping low their crimson bells
Half-closed, and others studded wide
  With disks and tiars, fed the time
  With odor in the golden prime
    Of good Haroun Alraschid.

Far off, and where the lemon grove
In closest coverture upsprung,
The living airs of middle night
Died round the bulbul as he sung; 70
Not he, but something which possess'd
The darkness of the world, delight,
Life, anguish, death, immortal love,
Ceasing not, mingled, unrepress'd,
  Apart from place, withholding time,
  But flattering the golden prime
  Of good Haroun Alraschid.

Black the garden-bowers and grots
Slumber'd; the solemn palms were ranged
Above, unwoo'd of summer wind; 80
A sudden splendor from behind
Flush'd all the leaves with rich gold-green,
And, flowing rapidly between
Their interspaces, counterchanged
The level lake with diamond-plots
  Of dark and bright. A lovely time,
  For it was in the golden prime
  Of good Haroun Alraschid.

Dark-blue the deep sphere overhead,
Distinct with vivid stars inlaid, 90
Grew darker from that under-flame;
So, leaping lightly from the boat,
With silver anchor left afloat,
In marvel whence that glory came
Upon me, as in sleep I sank
In cool soft turf upon the bank,
  Entranced with that place and time,
  So worthy of the golden prime
  Of good Haroun Alraschid.

Thence thro' the garden I was drawn —
A realm of pleasance, many a mound, 101
And many a shadow-chequer'd lawn
Full of the city's stilly sound,
And deep myrrh-thickets blowing round
The stately cedar, tamarisks,
Thick rosaries of scented thorn,
Tall orient shrubs, and obelisks
  Graven with emblems of the time,
  In honor of the golden prime
  Of good Haroun Alraschid. 110

With dazed vision unawares
From the long alley's latticed shade
Emerged, I came upon the great
Pavilion of the Caliphat.
Right to the carven cedarn doors,
Flung inward over spangled floors,
Broad-based flights of marble stairs

Ran up with golden balustrade,
After the fashion of the time,
And humor of the golden prime 120
  Of good Haroun Alraschid.

The fourscore windows all alight
As with the quintessence of flame,
A million tapers flaring bright
From twisted silvers look'd to shame
The hollow-vaulted dark, and stream'd
Upon the mooned domes aloof
In inmost Bagdat, till there seem'd
Hundreds of crescents on the roof
  Of night new-risen, that marvellous time
  To celebrate the golden prime 131
  Of good Haroun Alraschid.

Then stole I up, and trancedly
Gazed on the Persian girl alone,
Serene with argent-lidded eyes
Amorous, and lashes like to rays
Of darkness, and a brow of pearl
Tressed with redolent ebony,
In many a dark delicious curl,
Flowing beneath her rose-hued zone; 140
  The sweetest lady of the time,
  Well worthy of the golden prime
  Of good Haroun Alraschid.

Six columns, three on either side,
Pure silver, underpropt a rich
Throne of the massive ore, from which
Down-droop'd, in many a floating fold,
Engarlanded and diaper'd
With inwrought flowers, a cloth of gold.
Thereon, his deep eye laughter-stirr'd 150
With merriment of kingly pride,
  Sole star of all that place and time,
  I saw him — in his golden prime,
  THE GOOD HAROUN ALRASCHID.

ODE TO MEMORY

ADDRESSED TO ——

The 1830 volume, instead of 'Addressed to
——,' has 'Written very Early in Life.'

I

THOU who stealest fire,
From the fountains of the past,
To glorify the present, O, haste,
  Visit my low desire !
Strengthen me, enlighten me !
I faint in this obscurity,
Thou dewy dawn of memory.

II

Come not as thou camest of late,
Flinging the gloom of yesternight
On the white day, but robed in soften'd
    light   10
    Of orient state.
Whilome thou camest with the morning
    mist,
Even as a maid, whose stately brow
The dew-impearled winds of dawn have
    kiss'd,
    When she, as thou,
Stays on her floating locks the lovely freight
Of overflowing blooms, and earliest shoots
Of orient green, giving safe pledge of fruits,
Which in wintertide shall star
The black earth with brilliance rare.   20

III

Whilome thou camest with the morning
    mist,
    And with the evening cloud,
Showering thy gleaned wealth into my
    open breast;
Those peerless flowers which in the rudest
    wind
    Never grow sere,
When rooted in the garden of the mind,
    Because they are the earliest of the year.
    Nor was the night thy shroud.
In sweet dreams softer than unbroken rest
Thou leddest by the hand thine infant
    Hope.   30
The eddying of her garments caught from
    thee
The light of thy great presence ; and the
    cope
    Of the half-attain'd futurity,
    Tho' deep not fathomless,
Was cloven with the million stars which
    tremble
O'er the deep mind of dauntless infancy.
Small thought was there of life's distress;
For sure she deem'd no mist of earth could
    dull
Those spirit-thrilling eyes so keen and
    beautiful;
Sure she was nigher to heaven's spheres, 40
Listening the lordly music flowing from
    The illimitable years.
    O, strengthen me, enlighten me !
    I faint in this obscurity,
    Thou dewy dawn of memory.

IV

Come forth, I charge thee, arise,
Thou of the many tongues, the myriad
    eyes !
Thou comest not with shows of flaunting
    vines
    Unto mine inner eye,
    Divinest Memory !   50
Thou wert not nursed by the waterfall
Which ever sounds and shines
    A pillar of white light upon the wall
Of purple cliffs, aloof descried:
Come from the woods that belt the gray
    hillside,
The seven elms, the poplars four
That stand beside my father's door,
And chiefly from the brook that loves
To purl o'er matted cress and ribbed sand,
Or dimple in the dark of rushy coves,   60
Drawing into his narrow earthen urn,
    In every elbow and turn,
The filter'd tribute of the rough woodland;
    O, hither lead thy feet !
Pour round mine ears the livelong bleat
Of the thick-fleeced sheep from wattled
    folds,
    Upon the ridged wolds,
When the first matin-song hath waken'd
    loud
Over the dark dewy earth forlorn,
What time the amber morn   70
Forth gushes from beneath a low-hung
    cloud.

V

Large dowries doth the raptured eye
    To the young spirit present
    When first she is wed,
    And like a bride of old
    In triumph led,
    With music and sweet showers
    Of festal flowers,
Unto the dwelling she must sway.
Well hast thou done, great artist Memory,
In setting round thy first experiment 81
    With royal framework of wrought
    gold ;
Needs must thou dearly love thy first
    essay,
And foremost in thy various gallery
    Place it, where sweetest sunlight falls
    Upon the storied walls;
    For the discovery

And newness of thine art so pleased thee
That all which thou hast drawn of fairest
Or boldest since but lightly weighs   90
With thee unto the love thou bearest
The first-born of thy genius. Artist-like,
Ever retiring thou dost gaze
On the prime labor of thine early days,
No matter what the sketch might be:
Whether the high field on the bushless
    pike,
Or even a sand-built ridge
Of heaped hills that mound the sea,
Overblown with murmurs harsh,
Or even a lowly cottage whence we see 100
Stretch'd wide and wild the waste enor-
    mous marsh,
Where from the frequent bridge,
Like emblems of infinity,
The trenched waters run from sky to sky;
Or a garden bower'd close
With plaited alleys of the trailing rose,
Long alleys falling down to twilight grots,
Or opening upon level plots
Of crowned lilies, standing near
Purple-spiked lavender: 110
Whither in after life retired
From brawling storms,
From weary wind,
With youthful fancy re-inspired,
We may hold converse with all forms
Of the many-sided mind,
And those whom passion hath not blinded,
Subtle-thoughted, myriad-minded.

My friend, with you to live alone
Were how much better than to own   120
A crown, a sceptre, and a throne !

O, strengthen me, enlighten me !
I faint in this obscurity,
Thou dewy dawn of memory.

SONG

I

A spirit haunts the year's last hours
Dwelling amid these yellowing bowers.
    To himself he talks;
For at eventide, listening earnestly,
At his work you may hear him sob and
    sigh
    In the walks;
  Earthward he boweth the heavy stalks
Of the mouldering flowers.

Heavily hangs the broad sunflower
  Over its grave i' the earth so chilly;
Heavily hangs the hollyhock,
  Heavily hangs the tiger-lily.

II

The air is damp, and hush'd, and close,
As a sick man's room when he taketh
    repose
    An hour before death;
My very heart faints and my whole soul
    grieves
At the moist rich smell of the rotting
    leaves,
    And the breath
Of the fading edges of box beneath,
And the year's last rose.
  Heavily hangs the broad sunflower
    Over its grave i' the earth so chilly;
  Heavily hangs the hollyhock,
    Heavily hangs the tiger-lily.

A CHARACTER

With a half-glance upon the sky
At night he said, ' The wanderings
Of this most intricate Universe
Teach me the nothingness of things; '
Yet could not all creation pierce
Beyond the bottom of his eye.

He spake of beauty: that the dull
Saw no divinity in grass,
Life in dead stones, or spirit in air;
Then looking as 't were in a glass,
He smooth'd his chin and sleek'd his hair,
And said the earth was beautiful.

He spake of virtue: not the gods
More purely when they wish to charm
Pallas and Juno sitting by;
And with a sweeping of the arm,
And a lack-lustre dead-blue eye,
Devolved his rounded periods.

Most delicately hour by hour
He canvass'd human mysteries,
And trod on silk, as if the winds
Blew his own praises in his eyes,
And stood aloof from other minds
In impotence of fancied power.

With lips depress'd as he were meek,
Himself unto himself he sold:

Upon himself himself did feed;
Quiet, dispassionate, and cold,
And other than his form of creed,
With chisell'd features clear and sleek.

THE POET

THE poet in a golden clime was born,
With golden stars above;
Dower'd with the hate of hate, the scorn
of scorn,
The love of love.

He saw thro' life and death, thro' good and
ill,
He saw thro' his own soul.
The marvel of the everlasting will,
An open scroll,

Before him lay; with echoing feet he
threaded
The secretest walks of fame:
The viewless arrows of his thoughts were
headed
And wing'd with flame,

Like Indian reeds blown from his silver
tongue,
And of so fierce a flight,
From Calpe unto Caucasus they sung,
Filling with light

And vagrant melodies the winds which bore
Them earthward till they lit;
Then, like the arrow - seeds of the field
flower,
The fruitful wit

Cleaving took root, and springing forth
anew
Where'er they fell, behold,
Like to the mother plant in semblance,
grew
A flower all gold,

And bravely furnish'd all abroad to fling
The winged shafts of truth,
To throng with stately blooms the breath-
ing spring
Of Hope and Youth.

So many minds did gird their orbs with
beams,
Tho' one did fling the fire;

Heaven flow'd upon the soul in many
dreams
Of high desire.

Thus truth was multiplied on truth, the
world
Like one great garden show'd,
And thro' the wreaths of floating dark up-
curl'd,
Rare sunrise flow'd.

And Freedom rear'd in that august sunrise
Her beautiful bold brow,
When rites and forms before his burning
eyes
Melted like snow.

There was no blood upon her maiden robes
Sunn'd by those orient skies;
But round about the circles of the globes
Of her keen eyes

And in her raiment's hem was traced in
flame
WISDOM, a name to shake
All evil dreams of power — a sacred name.
And when she spake,

Her words did gather thunder as they ran,
And as the lightning to the thunder
Which follows it, riving the spirit of man,
Making earth wonder,

So was their meaning to her words. No
sword
Of wrath her right arm whirl'd,
But one poor poet's scroll, and with *his*
word
She shook the world.

THE POET'S MIND

I

VEX not thou the poet's mind
With thy shallow wit;
Vex not thou the poet's mind,
For thou canst not fathom it.
Clear and bright it should be ever,
Flowing like a crystal river,
Bright as light, and clear as wind.

II

Dark-brow'd sophist, come not anear;
All the place is holy ground;

Hollow smile and frozen sneer
    Come not here.
  Holy water will I pour
  Into every spicy flower
Of the laurel-shrubs that hedge it around.
The flowers would faint at your cruel
    cheer.
  In your eye there is death,
  There is frost in your breath
  Which would blight the plants.
  Where you stand you cannot hear
    From the groves within
    The wild-bird's din.
In the heart of the garden the merry bird
    chants.
It would fall to the ground if you came in.
  In the middle leaps a fountain
    Like sheet lightning,
    Ever brightening
With a low melodious thunder;
All day and all night it is ever drawn
  From the brain of the purple mountain
  Which stands in the distance yonder.
It springs on a level of bowery lawn,
And the mountain draws it from heaven
    above,
And it sings a song of undying love;
And yet, tho' its voice be so clear and full,
You never would hear it, your ears are so
    dull;
So keep where you are; you are foul with
    sin;
It would shrink to the earth if you came in.

THE SEA-FAIRIES

First printed in 1830, but suppressed until
1853, when it appeared, with many changes, in
the 8th edition of the ' Poems.'

SLOW sail'd the weary mariners and saw,
Betwixt the green brink and the running
    foam,
Sweet faces, rounded arms, and bosoms
    prest
To little harps of gold; and while they
    mused,
Whispering to each other half in fear,
Shrill music reach'd them on the middle
    sea.

Whither away, whither away, whither
    away ? fly no more.
Whither away from the high green field,
  and the happy blossoming shore ?

Day and night to the billow the fountain
    calls;
Down shower the gambolling waterfalls 10
From wandering over the lea;
Out of the live-green heart of the dells
They freshen the silvery-crimson shells,
And thick with white bells the clover-hill
    swells
High over the full-toned sea.
O, hither, come hither and furl your sails,
Come hither to me and to me;
Hither, come hither and frolic and play;
Here it is only the mew that wails;
We will sing to you all the day.   20
Mariner, mariner, furl your sails,
For here are the blissful downs and dales,
And merrily, merrily carol the gales,
And the spangle dances in bight and bay,
And the rainbow forms and flies on the
    land
Over the islands free;
And the rainbow lives in the curve of the
    sand;
Hither, come hither and see;
And the rainbow hangs on the poising
    wave,
And sweet is the color of cove and cave, 30
And sweet shall your welcome be.
O, hither, come hither, and be our lords,
For merry brides are we.
We will kiss sweet kisses, and speak sweet
    words;
O, listen, listen, your eyes shall glisten
With pleasure and love and jubilee.
O, listen, listen, your eyes shall glisten
When the sharp clear twang of the golden
    chords
Runs up the ridged sea.
Who can light on as happy a shore   40
All the world o'er, all the world o'er ?
Whither away ? listen and stay; mariner,
    mariner, fly no more.

THE DESERTED HOUSE

First printed in 1830, omitted in 1842, but
afterwards restored without change.

I

LIFE and Thought have gone away
    Side by side,
  Leaving door and windows wide;
Careless tenants they !

II

All within is dark as night:
In the windows is no light;
And no murmur at the door,
So frequent on its hinge before.

III

Close the door, the shutters close,
  Or thro' the windows we shall see
  The nakedness and vacancy
Of the dark deserted house.

IV

Come away; no more of mirth
  Is here or merry-making sound.
The house was builded of the earth,
  And shall fall again to ground.

V

Come away; for Life and Thought
  Here no longer dwell,
But in a city glorious —
A great and distant city — have bought
A mansion incorruptible.
Would they could have stayed with us !

THE DYING SWAN

I

THE plain was grassy, wild and bare,
Wide, wild, and open to the air,
Which had built up everywhere
  An under-roof of doleful gray.
With an inner voice the river ran,
Adown it floated a dying swan,
  And loudly did lament.
It was the middle of the day.
Ever the weary wind went on,
  And took the reed-tops as it went.   10

II

Some blue peaks in the distance rose,
And white against the cold-white sky
Shone out their crowning snows.
  One willow over the river wept,
And shook the wave as the wind did sigh;
Above in the wind was the swallow,
  Chasing itself at its own wild will,
  And far thro' the marish green and
    still
  The tangled water-courses slept,
Shot over with purple, and green, and
    yellow.   20

III

The wild swan's death-hymn took the soul
  Of that waste place with joy
Hidden in sorrow. At first to the ear
The warble was low, and full and clear;
And floating about the under-sky,
Prevailing in weakness, the coronach stole
Sometimes afar, and sometimes anear;
But anon her awful jubilant voice,
With a music strange and manifold,
Flow'd forth on a carol free and bold;   30
As when a mighty people rejoice
With shawms, and with cymbals, and harps
  of gold,
And the tumult of their acclaim is roll'd
Thro' the open gates of the city afar,
To the shepherd who watcheth the evening
  star.
And the creeping mosses and clambering
  weeds,
And the willow-branches hoar and dank,
And the wavy swell of the soughing reeds,
And the wave-worn horns of the echoing
  bank,
And the silvery marish - flowers that
  throng   40
The desolate creeks and pools among,
Were flooded over with eddying song.

A DIRGE

I

Now is done thy long day's work;
Fold thy palms across thy breast,
Fold thine arms, turn to thy rest.
    Let them rave.
Shadows of the silver birk
Sweep the green that folds thy grave.
    Let them rave.

II

Thee nor carketh care nor slander;
Nothing but the small cold worm
Fretteth thine enshrouded form.
    Let them rave.
Light and shadow ever wander
O'er the green that folds thy grave.
    Let them rave.

III

Thou wilt not turn upon thy bed;
Chaunteth not the brooding bee
Sweeter tones than calumny ?
    Let them rave.

Thou wilt never raise thine head
From the green that folds thy grave.
Let them rave.

IV

Crocodiles wept tears for thee;
The woodbine and eglatere
Drip sweeter dews than traitor's tear.
Let them rave.
Rain makes music in the tree
O'er the green that folds thy grave.
Let them rave.

V

Round thee blow, self-pleached deep,
Bramble roses, faint and pale,
And long purples of the dale.
Let them rave.
These in every shower creep
Thro' the green that folds thy grave.
Let them rave.

VI

The gold-eyed kingcups fine,
The frail bluebell peereth over
Rare broidery of the purple clover.
Let them rave.
Kings have no such couch as thine,
As the green that folds thy grave.
Let them rave.

VII

Wild words wander here and there;
God's great gift of speech abused
Makes thy memory confused;
But let them rave.
The balm-cricket carols clear
In the green that folds thy grave.
Let them rave.

LOVE AND DEATH

WHAT time the mighty moon was gathering light
Love paced the thymy plots of Paradise,
And all about him roll'd his lustrous eyes;
When, turning round a cassia, full in view,
Death, walking all alone beneath a yew,
And talking to himself, first met his sight.
'You must begone,' said Death, 'these walks are mine.'
Love wept and spread his sheeny vans for flight;
Yet ere he parted said, 'This hour is thine;

Thou art the shadow of life, and as the tree
Stands in the sun and shadows all beneath,
So in the light of great eternity
Life eminent creates the shade of death.
The shadow passeth when the tree shall fall,
But I shall reign for ever over all.'

THE BALLAD OF ORIANA

MY heart is wasted with my woe,
    Oriana.
There is no rest for me below,
    Oriana.
When the long dun wolds are ribb'd with snow,
And loud the Norland whirlwinds blow,
    Oriana,
Alone I wander to and fro,
    Oriana.

Ere the light on dark was growing,   10
    Oriana,
At midnight the cock was crowing,
    Oriana;
Winds were blowing, waters flowing,
We heard the steeds to battle going,
    Oriana,
Aloud the hollow bugle blowing,
    Oriana.

In the yew-wood black as night,
    Oriana,   20
Ere I rode into the fight,
    Oriana,
While blissful tears blinded my sight
By star-shine and by moonlight,
    Oriana,
I to thee my troth did plight,
    Oriana.

She stood upon the castle wall,
    Oriana;
She watch'd my crest among them all,   30
    Oriana,
She saw me fight, she heard me call,
When forth there stept a foeman tall,
    Oriana,
Atween me and the castle wall,
    Oriana.

The bitter arrow went aside,
    Oriana;

The false, false arrow went aside,
    Oriana;   40
The damned arrow glanced aside,
And pierced thy heart, my love, my bride,
    Oriana !
Thy heart, my life, my love, my bride,
    Oriana !

O, narrow, narrow was the space,
    Oriana !
Loud, loud rung out the bugle's brays,
    Oriana.
O, deathful stabs were dealt apace,   50
The battle deepen'd in its place,
    Oriana;
But I was down upon my face,
    Oriana.

They should have stabb'd me where I lay,
    Oriana !
How could I rise and come away,
    Oriana ?
How could I look upon the day ?
They should have stabb'd me where I lay,
    Oriana —   61
They should have trod me into clay,
    Oriana.

O breaking heart that will not break,
    Oriana !
O pale, pale face so sweet and meek,
    Oriana !
Thou smilest, but thou dost not speak,
And then the tears run down my cheek,
    Oriana.   70
What wantest thou ? whom dost thou seek,
    Oriana ?

I cry aloud; none hear my cries,
    Oriana.
Thou comest atween me and the skies,
    Oriana.
I feel the tears of blood arise
Up from my heart unto my eyes,
    Oriana.
Within thy heart my arrow lies,   80
    Oriana.

O cursed hand ! O cursed blow !
    Oriana !
O happy thou that liest low,
    Oriana !
All night the silence seems to flow
Beside me in my utter woe,
    Oriana.

A weary, weary way I go,
    Oriana !   90

When Norland winds pipe down the sea,
    Oriana,
I walk, I dare not think of thee,
    Oriana.
Thou liest beneath the greenwood tree,
I dare not die and come to thee,
    Oriana.
I hear the roaring of the sea,
    Oriana.

CIRCUMSTANCE

Two children in two neighbor villages
Playing mad pranks along the heathy leas;
Two strangers meeting at a festival;
Two lovers whispering by an orchard wall;
Two lives bound fast in one with golden
    ease;
Two graves grass - green beside a gray
    church-tower,
Wash'd with still rains and daisy - blos-
    somed;
Two children in one hamlet born and bred:
So runs the round of life from hour to
    hour.

THE MERMAN

I

WHO would be
A merman bold,
Sitting alone,
Singing alone
Under the sea,
With a crown of gold,
On a throne ?

II

I would be a merman bold,
I would sit and sing the whole of the day;
I would fill the sea-halls with a voice of
    power;
But at night I would roam abroad and
    play
With the mermaids in and out of the rocks,
Dressing their hair with the white sea-
    flower;
And holding them back by their flowing
    locks
I would kiss them often under the sea,

And kiss them again till they kiss'd me
  Laughingly, laughingly;
And then we would wander away, away,
To the pale-green sea-groves straight and
  high,
  Chasing each other merrily.

III

There would be neither moon nor star;
But the wave would make music above us
  afar —
Low thunder and light in the magic night —
  Neither moon nor star.
We would call aloud in the dreamy dells,
Call to each other and whoop and cry
  All night, merrily, merrily.
They would pelt me with starry spangles
  and shells,
Laughing and clapping their hands be-
  tween,
  All night, merrily, merrily,
But I would throw to them back in mine
Turkis and agate and almondine;
Then leaping out upon them unseen
I would kiss them often under the sea,
And kiss them again till they kiss'd me
  Laughingly, laughingly.
O, what a happy life were mine
Under the hollow-hung ocean green !
Soft are the moss-beds under the sea;
We would live merrily, merrily.

THE MERMAID

I

WHO would be
A mermaid fair,
Singing alone,
Combing her hair
Under the sea,
In a golden curl
With a comb of pearl,
On a throne ?

II

I would be a mermaid fair;
I would sing to myself the whole of the day;
With a comb of pearl I would comb my
  hair;
And still as I comb'd I would sing and say,
' Who is it loves me ? who loves not me ? '
I would comb my hair till my ringlets
  would fall
  Low adown, low adown,

From under my starry sea-bud crown
    Low adown and around,
And I should look like a fountain of gold
    Springing alone
  With a shrill inner sound,
    Over the throne
  In the midst of the hall;
Till that great sea-snake under the sea
From his coiled sleeps in the central deeps
Would slowly trail himself sevenfold
Round the hall where I sate. and look in at
    the gate
With his large calm eyes for the love of
    me.
And all the mermen under the sea
Would feel their immortality
Die in their hearts for the love of me.

III

But at night I would wander away, away,
  I would fling on each side my low-flow-
    ing locks,
And lightly vault from the throne and play
  With the mermen in and out of the
    rocks;
We would run to and fro, and hide and
    seek,
  On the broad sea-wolds in the crimson
    shells,
Whose silvery spikes are nighest the sea.
But if any came near I would call, and
    shriek,
And adown the steep like a wave I would
    leap
  From the diamond-ledges that jut from
    the dells;
For I would not be kiss'd by all who would
    list
Of the bold merry mermen under the sea.
They would sue me, and woo me, and flat-
    ter me,
In the purple twilights under the sea;
But the king of them all would carry me,
Woo me, and win me, and marry me,
In the branching jaspers under the sea.
Then all the dry pied things that be
In the hueless mosses under the sea
Would curl round my silver feet silently,
All looking up for the love of me.
And if I should carol aloud, from aloft
All things that are forked, and horned, and
    soft
Would lean out from the hollow sphere of
    the sea,
All looking down for the love of me.

ADELINE

I

MYSTERY of mysteries,
　Faintly smiling Adeline,
　Scarce of earth nor all divine,
Nor unhappy, nor at rest,
　But beyond expression fair
　With thy floating flaxen hair;
Thy rose-lips and full blue eyes
　Take the heart from out my breast.
Wherefore those dim looks of thine,
Shadowy, dreaming Adeline?

II

Whence that aery bloom of thine,
　Like a lily which the sun
Looks thro' in his sad decline,
　And a rose-bush leans upon,
Thou that faintly smilest still,
　As a Naiad in a well,
　Looking at the set of day,
Or a phantom two hours old
Of a maiden past away,
Ere the placid lips be cold?
Wherefore those faint smiles of thine,
　Spiritual Adeline?

III

What hope or fear or joy is thine?
Who talketh with thee, Adeline?
　For sure thou art not all alone.
　Do beating hearts of salient springs
Keep measure with thine own?
　Hast thou heard the butterflies
　What they say betwixt their wings?
　Or in stillest evenings
With what voice the violet woos
To his heart the silver dews?
　Or when little airs arise,
　How the merry bluebell rings
To the mosses underneath?
Hast thou look'd upon the breath
Of the lilies at sunrise?
Wherefore that faint smile of thine,
Shadowy, dreaming Adeline?

IV

Some honey-converse feeds thy mind,
　Some spirit of a crimson rose
In love with thee forgets to close
　His curtains, wasting odorous sighs
All night long on darkness blind.
What aileth thee? whom waitest thou

With thy soften'd, shadow'd brow,
　And those dew-lit eyes of thine,
　Thou faint smiler, Adeline?

V

Lovest thou the doleful wind
　When thou gazest at the skies?
Doth the low-tongued Orient
　Wander from the side of the morn,
　Dripping with Sabæan spice
On thy pillow, lowly bent
　With melodious airs lovelorn,
Breathing Light against thy face,
While his locks a-drooping twined
Round thy neck in subtle ring
Make a carcanet of rays,
　And ye talk together still,
In the language wherewith Spring
　Letters cowslips on the hill?
Hence that look and smile of thine,
　Spiritual Adeline.

MARGARET

First printed in 1833; reprinted with slight changes (see Notes) in 1842.

I

O SWEET pale Margaret,
O rare pale Margaret,
What lit your eyes with tearful power,
Like moonlight on a falling shower?
Who lent you, love, your mortal dower
　Of pensive thought and aspect pale,
　Your melancholy sweet and frail
As perfume of the cuckoo flower?
From the westward-winding flood,
From the evening-lighted wood,
　From all things outward you have
　　won
A tearful grace, as tho' you stood
　Between the rainbow and the sun.
The very smile before you speak,
That dimples your transparent cheek,
　Encircles all the heart, and feedeth
The senses with a still delight
　Of dainty sorrow without sound,
　Like the tender amber round
　Which the moon about her spreadeth
Moving thro' a fleecy night.

II

You love, remaining peacefully,
　To hear the murmur of the strife,

But enter not the toil of life.
Your spirit is the calmed sea,
  Laid by the tumult of the fight.
You are the evening star, alway
  Remaining betwixt dark and bright;
Lull'd echoes of laborious day
  Come to you, gleams of mellow light
  Float by you on the verge of night.

III

What can it matter, Margaret,
  What songs below the waning stars
The lion-heart, Plantagenet,
  Sang looking thro' his prison bars?
Exquisite Margaret, who can tell
The last wild thought of Chatelet,
  Just ere the falling axe did part
  The burning brain from the true heart,
Even in her sight he loved so well?

IV

A fairy shield your Genius made
  And gave you on your natal day.
Your sorrow, only sorrow's shade,
  Keeps real sorrow far away.
You move not in such solitudes,
  You are not less divine,
But more human in your moods,
  Than your twin-sister, Adeline.
Your hair is darker, and your eyes
  Touch'd with a somewhat darker hue,
  And less aërially blue,
  But ever trembling thro' the dew
Of dainty-woeful sympathies.

V

O sweet pale Margaret,
  O rare pale Margaret,
Come down, come down, and hear me
  speak.
Tie up the ringlets on your cheek.
  The sun is just about to set,
The arching limes are tall and shady,
  And faint, rainy lights are seen,
  Moving in the leavy beech.
Rise from the feast of sorrow, lady,
  Where all day long you sit between
  Joy and woe, and whisper each.
Or only look across the lawn,
  Look out below your bower-eaves,
Look down, and let your blue eyes dawn
  Upon me thro' the jasmine-leaves.

ROSALIND

Printed in 1833, but suppressed until 1884.
See Notes.

I

My Rosalind, my Rosalind,
My frolic falcon, with bright eyes,
Whose free delight, from any height of
    rapid flight,
Stoops at all game that wing the skies,
My Rosalind, my Rosalind,
My bright-eyed, wild-eyed falcon, whither,
Careless both of wind and weather,
Whither fly ye, what game spy ye,
Up or down the streaming wind?

II

The quick lark's closest-caroll'd strains,
The shadow rushing up the sea,
The lightning flash atween the rains,
The sunlight driving down the lea,
The leaping stream, the very wind,
That will not stay, upon his way,
To stoop the cowslip to the plains,
Is not so clear and bold and free
As you, my falcon Rosalind.
You care not for another's pains,
Because you are the soul of joy,
Bright metal all without alloy.
Life shoots and glances thro' your veins,
And flashes off a thousand ways,
Thro' lips and eyes in subtle rays.
Your hawk-eyes are keen and bright,
Keen with triump', watching still
To pierce me thro' with pointed light;
But oftentimes they flash and glitter
Like sunshine on a dancing rill,
And your words are seeming-bitter,
Sharp and few, but seeming-bitter
From excess of swift delight.

III

Come down, come home, my Rosalind,
My gay young hawk, my Rosalind.
Too long you keep the upper skies;
Too long you roam and wheel at will;
But we must hood your random eyes,
That care not whom they kill,
And your cheek, whose brilliant hue
Is so sparkling-fresh to view,
Some red heath-flower in the dew,
Touch'd with sunrise. We must bind
And keep you fast, my Rosalind,
Fast, fast, my wild-eyed Rosalind,

And clip your wings, and make you love.
When we have lured you from above,
And that delight of frolic flight, by day or
    night,
From North to South,
We 'll bind you fast in silken cords,
And kiss away the bitter words
From off your rosy mouth.

ELEÄNORE

Reprinted in 1842 from the 1833 volume.
See Notes.

I

THY dark eyes open'd not,
    Nor first reveal'd themselves to English
        air,
    For there is nothing here
Which, from the outward to the inward
        brought,
Moulded thy baby thought.
Far off from human neighborhood
    Thou wert born, on a summer morn,
A mile beneath the cedar-wood.
Thy bounteous forehead was not fann'd
    With breezes from our oaken glades, 10
But thou wert nursed in some delicious
        land
    Of lavish lights, and floating shades;
And flattering thy childish thought
The oriental fairy brought,
    At the moment of thy birth,
From old well-heads of haunted rills,
And the hearts of purple hills,
And shadow'd coves on a sunny shore,
    The choicest wealth of all the earth,
Jewel or shell, or starry ore,   20
To deck thy cradle, Eleänore.

II

Or the yellow-banded bees,
Thro' half-open lattices
Coming in the scented breeze,
Fed thee, a child, lying alone,
    With whitest honey in fairy gardens
        cull'd —
A glorious child, dreaming alone,
In silk-soft folds, upon yielding down,
With the hum of swarming bees
    Into dreamful slumber lull'd.   30

III

Who may minister to thee ?
Summer herself should minister

To thee, with fruitage golden-rinded
On golden salvers, or it may be,
Youngest Autumn, in a bower
Grape-thicken'd from the light, and blinded
With many a deep-hued bell-like flower
Of fragrant trailers, when the air
Sleepeth over all the heaven,
And the crag that fronts the even,   40
    All along the shadowing shore,
Crimsons over an inland mere,
            Eleänore !

IV

How may full-sail'd verse express,
    How may measured words adore
The full-flowing harmony
Of thy swan-like stateliness,
            Eleänore ?
The luxuriant symmetry
Of thy floating gracefulness,   50
            Eleänore ?
Every turn and glance of thine,
Every lineament divine,
            Eleänore,
    And the steady sunset glow
That stays upon thee ?   For in thee
Is nothing sudden, nothing single;
Like two streams of incense free
From one censer in one shrine,
Thought and motion mingle,   60
Mingle ever.   Motions flow
To one another, even as tho'
They were modulated so
To an unheard melody,
Which lives about thee, and a sweep
    Of richest pauses, evermore
Drawn from each other mellow-deep;
    Who may express thee, Eleänore ?

V

I stand before thee, Eleänore;
    I see thy beauty gradually unfold, 70
Daily and hourly, more and more.
I muse, as in a trance, the while
    Slowly, as from a cloud of gold,
Comes out thy deep ambrosial smile.
I muse, as in a trance, whene'er
    The languors of thy love-deep eyes
Float on to me.   I would I were
    So tranced, so rapt in ecstasies,
To stand apart, and to adore,
Gazing on thee for evermore,   80
Serene, imperial Eleänore !

VI

Sometimes, with most intensity
Gazing, I seem to see
Thought folded over thought, smiling
    asleep,
Slowly awaken'd, grow so full and deep
In thy large eyes that, overpower'd quite,
I cannot veil or droop my sight,
But am as nothing in its light.
As tho' a star, in inmost heaven set,
Even while we gaze on it,   90
Should slowly round his orb, and slowly grow
To a full face, there like a sun remain
Fix'd — then as slowly fade again,
    And draw itself to what it was before;
So full, so deep, so slow,
Thought seems to come and go
    In thy large eyes, imperial Eleänore.

VII

As thunder-clouds that, hung on high,
Roof'd the world with doubt and fear,
Floating thro' an evening atmosphere,   100
Grow golden all about the sky;
In thee all passion becomes passionless,
Touch'd by thy spirit's mellowness,
Losing his fire and active might
    In a silent meditation,
Falling into a still delight,
    And luxury of contemplation.
As waves that up a quiet cove
    Rolling slide, and lying still
    Shadow forth the banks at will,   110
Or sometimes they swell and move,
    Pressing up against the land
    With motions of the outer sea;
And the self-same influence
Controlleth all the soul and sense
Of Passion gazing upon thee.
His bow-string slacken'd, languid Love,
    Leaning his cheek upon his hand,
    Droops both his wings, regarding thee,
And so would languish evermore,   120
Serene, imperial Eleänore.

VIII

But when I see thee roam, with tresses un-
    confined,
While the amorous odorous wind
Breathes low between the sunset and the
    moon;
Or, in a shadowy saloon,
On silken cushions half reclined;
    I watch thy grace, and in its place

My heart a charmed slumber keeps,
    While I muse upon thy face;
And a languid fire creeps   130
    Thro' my veins to all my frame,
Dissolvingly and slowly. Soon
    From thy rose-red lips MY name
Floweth; and then, as in a swoon,
With dinning sound my ears are rife,
    My tremulous tongue faltereth,
    I lose my color, I lose my breath,
    I drink the cup of a costly death,
Brimm'd with delirious draughts of warm-
    est life.
I die with my delight before   140
    I hear what I would hear from thee;
    Yet tell my name again to me,
I *would* be dying evermore,
So dying ever, Eleänore.

KATE

First printed in 1833, but suppressed until
after the poet's death, and not included in any
authorized edition until 1897.

I KNOW her by her angry air,
Her bright black eyes, her bright black
    hair,
    Her rapid laughters wild and shrill,
As laughters of the woodpecker
    From the bosom of a hill.
'T is Kate — she sayeth what she will;
For Kate hath an unbridled tongue,
    Clear as the twanging of a harp.
    Her heart is like a throbbing star.
Kate hath a spirit ever strung
    Like a new bow, and bright and sharp
    As edges of the scimitar.
Whence shall she take a fitting mate ?
    For Kate no common love will feel;
    My woman-soldier, gallant Kate,
    As pure and true as blades of steel.

Kate saith 'the world is void of might.'
Kate saith 'the men are gilded flies.'
    Kate snaps her fingers at my vows;
Kate will not hear of lovers' sighs.
I would I were an armed knight,
Far-famed for well-won enterprise,
    And wearing on my swarthy brows
The garland of new-wreathed emprise;
    For in a moment I would pierce
The blackest files of clanging fight,
And strongly strike to left and right,

In dreaming of my lady's eyes.
  O, Kate loves well the bold and fierce;
But none are bold enough for Kate,
She cannot find a fitting mate.

'MY LIFE IS FULL OF WEARY DAYS'

First printed in 1833, with the heading, ' To
——.' The first two stanzas were not reprinted
until 1865, when they appeared in the volume of
'Selections' in their present form. The next
three stanzas were added later. See Notes.

MY life is full of weary days,
  But good things have not kept aloof,
Nor wander'd into other ways;
  I have not lack'd thy mild reproof,
Nor golden largess of thy praise.

And now shake hands across the brink
  Of that deep grave to which I go,
Shake hands once more; I cannot sink
  So far — far down, but I shall know
Thy voice, and answer from below.

When in the darkness over me
  The four-handed mole shall scrape,
Plant thou no dusky cypress-tree,
  Nor wreathe thy cap with doleful crape,
But pledge me in the flowing grape.

And when the sappy field and wood
  Grow green beneath the showery gray,
And rugged barks begin to bud,
  And thro' damp holts new-flush'd with
    may,
Ring sudden scritches of the jay,

Then let wise Nature work her will,
  And on my clay her darnel grow;
Come only, when the days are still,
  And at my headstone whisper low,
  And tell me if the woodbines blow.

EARLY SONNETS

I

TO ——

This and the third sonnet were in the 1833
volume, but were suppressed in 1842.

As when with downcast eyes we muse and
    brood,
And ebb into a former life, or seem

To lapse far back in some confused dream
To states of mystical similitude,
If one but speaks or hems or stirs his chair,
Ever the wonder waxeth more and more,
So that we say, ' All this hath been before,
All this hath been, I know not when or
    where;'
So, friend, when first I look'd upon your
    face,
Our thought gave answer each to each, so
    true —
Opposed mirrors each reflecting each —
That, tho I knew not in what time or place,
Methought that I had often met with you,
And either lived in either's heart and
    speech.

II

TO J. M. K.

Reprinted in 1842 from the 1830 volume.
Addressed to John Mitchell Kemble (1807–
1857) who was a fellow-student of the poet at
Cambridge.

MY hope and heart is with thee — thou wilt
    be
A latter Luther, and a soldier-priest
To scare church-harpies from the master's
    feast;
Our dusted velvets have much need of
    thee:
Thou art no Sabbath-drawler of old saws,
Distill'd from some worm-canker'd homily;
But spurr'd at heart with fieriest energy
To embattail and to wall about thy cause
With iron-worded proof, hating to hark
The humming of the drowsy pulpit-drone
Half God's good Sabbath, while the worn-
    out clerk
Brow-beats his desk below. Thou from a
    throne
Mounted in heaven wilt shoot into the dark
Arrows of lightnings. I will stand and
    mark.

III

Mine be the strength of spirit, full and
    free,
Like some broad river rushing down alone,
With the selfsame impulse wherewith he
    was thrown
From his loud fount upon the echoing
    lea; —
Which with increasing might doth forward
    flee

By town, and tower, and hill, and cape, and isle,
And in the middle of the green salt sea
Keeps his blue waters fresh for many a mile.
Mine be the power which ever to its sway
Will win the wise at once, and by degrees
May into uncongenial spirits flow;
Even as the warm gulf-stream of Florida
Floats far away into the Northern seas
The lavish growths of southern Mexico.

IV

ALEXANDER

First published in the 'Library Edition' of the 'Poems' in 1872.

WARRIOR of God, whose strong right arm debased
The throne of Persia, when her Satrap bled
At Issus by the Syrian gates, or fled
Beyond the Memmian naphtha-pits, disgraced
For ever — thee (thy pathway sand-erased)
Gliding with equal crowns two serpents led
Joyful to that palm-planted fountain-fed
Ammonian Oasis in the waste.
There in a silent shade of laurel brown
Apart the Chamian Oracle divine
Shelter'd his unapproached mysteries:
High things were spoken there, unhanded down;
Only they saw thee from the secret shrine
Returning with hot cheek and kindled eyes.

V

BUONAPARTE

This sonnet and the next were in the 1833 volume, but were suppressed in 1842.

HE thought to quell the stubborn hearts of oak,
Madman! — to chain with chains, and bind with bands
That island queen who sways the floods and lands
From Ind to Ind, but in fair daylight woke,
When from her wooden walls, — lit by sure hands, —
With thunders, and with lightnings, and with smoke, —

Peal after peal, the British battle broke,
Lulling the brine against the Coptic sands.
We taught him lowlier moods, when Elsinore
Heard the war moan along the distant sea,
Rocking with shatter'd spars, with sudden fires
Flamed over; at Trafalgar yet once more
We taught him; late he learned humility
Perforce, like those whom Gideon school'd with briers.

VI

POLAND

How long, O God, shall men be ridden down,
And trampled under by the last and least
Of men? The heart of Poland hath not ceased
To quiver, tho' her sacred blood doth drown
The fields, and out of every smouldering town
Cries to Thee, lest brute Power be increased,
Till that o'ergrown Barbarian in the East
Transgress his ample bound to some new crown, —
Cries to Thee, 'Lord, how long shall these things be ?
How long this icy-hearted Muscovite
Oppress the region ?' Us, O Just and Good,
Forgive, who smiled when she was torn in three ;
Us, who stand now, when we should aid the right —
A matter to be wept with tears of blood !

VII

This sonnet and the two that follow were first printed in the 'Selections' of 1865, with the heading, 'Three Sonnets to a Coquette.'

CARESS'D or chidden by the slender hand,
And singing airy trifles this or that,
Light Hope at Beauty's call would perch and stand,
And run thro' every change of sharp and flat ;
And Fancy came and at her pillow sat,
When Sleep had bound her in his rosy band,

And chased away the still-recurring gnat,
And woke her with a lay from fairy land.
But now they live with Beauty less and
    less,
For Hope is other Hope and wanders far,
Nor cares to lisp in love's delicious creeds;
And Fancy watches in the wilderness,
Poor Fancy sadder than a single star,
That sets at twilight in a land of reeds.

VIII

THE form, the form alone is eloquent !
A nobler yearning never broke her rest
Than but to dance and sing, be gaily drest,
And win all eyes with all accomplishment;
Yet in the whirling dances as we went,
My fancy made me for a moment blest
To find my heart so near the beauteous
    breast
That once had power to rob it of content.
A moment came the tenderness of tears,
The phantom of a wish that once could
    move,
A ghost of passion that no smiles re-
    store —
For ah ! the slight coquette, she cannot
    love,
And if you kiss'd her feet a thousand
    years,
She still would take the praise, and care no
    more.

IX

WAN Sculptor, weepest thou to take the
    cast
Of those dead lineaments that near thee lie ?
O, sorrowest thou, pale Painter, for the
    past,
In painting some dead friend from mem-
    ory ?
Weep on ; beyond his object Love can
    last.
His object lives; more cause to weep
    have I :
My tears, no tears of love, are flowing fast,
No tears of love, but tears that Love can
    die.
I pledge her not in any cheerful cup,
Nor care to sit beside her where she sits —
Ah ! pity — hint it not in human tones,
But breathe it into earth and close it up
With secret death for ever, in the pits
Which some green Christmas crams with
    weary bones.

X

First printed *Printed in 1833, but suppressed in 1842.*

IF I were loved, as I desire to be,
What is there in the great sphere of the
    earth,
And range of evil between death and birth,
That I should fear, — if I were loved by
    thee ?
All the inner, all the outer world of pain
Clear Love would pierce and cleave, if thou
    wert mine,
As I have heard that, somewhere in the
    main,
Fresh-water springs come up through bitter
    brine.
'T were joy, not fear, claspt hand-in-hand
    with thee,
To wait for death — mute — careless of all
    ills,
Apart upon a mountain, tho' the surge
Of some new deluge from a thousand hills
Flung leagues of roaring foam into the
    gorge
Below us, as far on as eye could see.

XI

THE BRIDESMAID

First printed in 1872.

O BRIDESMAID, ere the happy knot was
    tied,
Thine eyes so wept that they could hardly
    see;
Thy sister smiled and said, ' No tears for
    me !
A happy bridesmaid makes a happy bride.'
And then, the couple standing side by side,
Love lighted down between them full of
    glee,
And over his left shoulder laugh'd at thee,
' O happy bridesmaid, make a happy bride.'
And all at once a pleasant truth I learn'd,
For while the tender service made thee
    weep,
I loved thee for the tear thou couldst not
    hide,
And prest thy hand, and knew the press
    return'd,
And thought, ' My life is sick of single
    sleep:
O happy bridesmaid, make a happy bride !'

THE LADY OF SHALOTT

AND OTHER POEMS

This heading does not represent a separate published volume, but is found as a division of the poems in the editions of 1884 and the more recent ones.

THE LADY OF SHALOTT

First published in 1833, and much altered in 1842. See Notes.

PART I

On either side the river lie
Long fields of barley and of rye,
That clothe the wold and meet the sky;
And thro' the field the road runs by
　　To many-tower'd Camelot;
And up and down the people go,
Gazing where the lilies blow
Round an island there below,
　　The island of Shalott.

Willows whiten, aspens quiver,　　　　　10
Little breezes dusk and shiver
Thro' the wave that runs for ever
By the island in the river
　　Flowing down to Camelot.
Four gray walls, and four gray towers,
Overlook a space of flowers,
And the silent isle imbowers
　　The Lady of Shalott.

By the margin, willow-veil'd,
Slide the heavy barges trail'd　　　　　20
By slow horses; and unhail'd
The shallop flitteth silken-sail'd
　　Skimming down to Camelot:
But who hath seen her wave her hand?
Or at the casement seen her stand?
Or is she known in all the land,
　　The Lady of Shalott?

Only reapers, reaping early
In among the bearded barley,
Hear a song that echoes cheerly　　　　30
From the river winding clearly,
　　Down to tower'd Camelot;
And by the moon the reaper weary,
Piling sheaves in uplands airy,
Listening, whispers ''T is the fairy
　　Lady of Shalott.'

PART II

There she weaves by night and day
A magic web with colors gay.
She has heard a whisper say,
A curse is on her if she stay　　　　　40
　　To look down to Camelot.
She knows not what the curse may be,
And so she weaveth steadily,
And little other care hath she,
　　The Lady of Shalott.

And moving thro' a mirror clear
That hangs before her all the year,
Shadows of the world appear.
There she sees the highway near
　　Winding down to Camelot;　　　　50
There the river eddy whirls,
And there the surly village-churls,
And the red cloaks of market girls,
　　Pass onward from Shalott.

Sometimes a troop of damsels glad,
An abbot on an ambling pad,
Sometimes a curly shepherd-lad,
Or long-hair'd page in crimson clad,
　　Goes by to tower'd Camelot;
And sometimes thro' the mirror blue　　60
The knights come riding two and two:
She hath no loyal knight and true,
　　The Lady of Shalott.

But in her web she still delights
To weave the mirror's magic sights,
For often thro' the silent nights
A funeral, with plumes and lights
　　And music, went to Camelot;
Or when the moon was overhead,
Came two young lovers lately wed:　　70
'I am half sick of shadows,' said
　　The Lady of Shalott.

PART III

A bow-shot from her bower-eaves,
He rode between the barley-sheaves,

The sun came dazzling thro' the leaves,
And flamed upon the brazen greaves
    Of bold Sir Lancelot.
A red-cross knight for ever kneel'd
To a lady in his shield,
That sparkled on the yellow field,   80
    Beside remote Shalott.

The gemmy bridle glitter'd free,
Like to some branch of stars we see
Hung in the golden Galaxy.
The bridle bells rang merrily
    As he rode down to Camelot;
And from his blazon'd baldric slung
A mighty silver bugle hung,
And as he rode his armor rung,
    Beside remote Shalott.   90

All in the blue unclouded weather
Thick-jewell'd shone the saddle-leather,
The helmet and the helmet-feather
Burn'd like one burning flame together,
    As he rode down to Camelot;
As often thro' the purple night,
Below the starry clusters bright,
Some bearded meteor, trailing light,
    Moves over still Shalott.   99

His broad clear brow in sunlight glow'd;
On burnish'd hooves his war-horse trode;
From underneath his helmet flow'd
His coal-black curls as on he rode,
    As he rode down to Camelot.
From the bank and from the river
He flash'd into the crystal mirror,
'Tirra lirra,' by the river
    Sang Sir Lancelot.

She left the web, she left the loom,
She made three paces thro' the room,   110
She saw the water-lily bloom,
She saw the helmet and the plume,
    She look'd down to Camelot.
Out flew the web and floated wide;
The mirror crack'd from side to side;
'The curse is come upon me,' cried
    The Lady of Shalott.

PART IV

In the stormy east-wind straining,
The pale yellow woods were waning,
The broad stream in his banks complaining,
Heavily the low sky raining   121
    Over tower'd Camelot;

Down she came and found a boat
Beneath a willow left afloat,
And round about the prow she wrote
    The Lady of Shalott.

And down the river's dim expanse
Like some bold seër in a trance,
Seeing all his own mischance —
With a glassy countenance   130
    Did she look to Camelot.
And at the closing of the day
She loosed the chain, and down she lay;
The broad stream bore her far away,
    The Lady of Shalott.

Lying, robed in snowy white
That loosely flew to left and right —
The leaves upon her falling light —
Thro' the noises of the night
    She floated down to Camelot;   140
And as the boat-head wound along
The willowy hills and fields among,
They heard her singing her last song,
    The Lady of Shalott.

Heard a carol, mournful, holy,
Chanted loudly, chanted lowly,
Till her blood was frozen slowly,
And her eyes were darken'd wholly,
    Turn'd to tower'd Camelot.
For ere she reach'd upon the tide   150
The first house by the water-side,
Singing in her song she died,
    The Lady of Shalott.

Under tower and balcony,
By garden-wall and gallery,
A gleaming shape she floated by,
Dead-pale between the houses high,
    Silent into Camelot.
Out upon the wharfs they came,
Knight and burgher, lord and dame,   160
And round the prow they read her name,
    The Lady of Shalott.

Who is this? and what is here?
And in the lighted palace near
Died the sound of royal cheer;
And they cross'd themselves for fear,
    All the knights at Camelot:
But Lancelot mused a little space;
He said, 'She has a lovely face;
God in his mercy lend her grace,   170
    The Lady of Shalott.'

MARIANA IN THE SOUTH

First printed in 1833, but changed so much
in 1842 that we give the original form in full
in the Notes.

WITH one black shadow at its feet,
  The house thro' all the level shines,
Close-latticed to the brooding heat,
  And silent in its dusty vines;
A faint-blue ridge upon the right,
  An empty river-bed before,
  And shallows on a distant shore,
In glaring sand and inlets bright.
    But ' Ave Mary,' made she moan,   9
    And ' Ave Mary,' night and morn,
    And ' Ah,' she sang, ' to be all alone,
      To live forgotten, and love forlorn.'

She, as her carol sadder grew,
  From brow and bosom slowly down
Thro' rosy taper fingers drew
  Her streaming curls of deepest brown
To left and right, and made appear
  Still-lighted in a secret shrine
  Her melancholy eyes divine,
The home of woe without a tear.   20
    And ' Ave Mary,' was her moan,
    'Madonna, sad is night and morn,'
    And ' Ah,' she sang, ' to be all alone,
      To live forgotten, and love forlorn.'

Till all the crimson changed, and past
  Into deep orange o'er the sea,
Low on her knees herself she cast,
  Before Our Lady murmur'd she;
Complaining, ' Mother, give me grace
  To help me of my weary load.'   30
And on the liquid mirror glow'd
The clear perfection of her face.
    ' Is this the form,' she made her moan,
    ' That won his praises night and
      morn ? '
    And ' Ah,' she said, ' but I wake alone,
      I sleep forgotten, I wake forlorn.'

Nor bird would sing, nor lamb would bleat,
  Nor any cloud would cross the vault,
But day increased from heat to heat,
  On stony drought and steaming salt;   40
Till now at noon she slept again,
  And seem'd knee - deep in mountain
    grass,
  And heard her native breezes pass,
And runlets babbling down the glen.

She breathed in sleep a lower moan,
  And murmuring, as at night and
    morn,
She thought, ' My spirit is here alone,
  Walks forgotten, and is forlorn.'

Dreaming, she knew it was a dream;
  She felt he was and was not there.   50
She woke; the babble of the stream
  Fell, and, without, the steady glare
Shrank one sick willow sere and small.
  The river-bed was dusty-white;
  And all the furnace of the light
Struck up against the blinding wall.
    She whisper'd, with a stifled moan
    More inward than at night or morn,
    'Sweet Mother, let me not here alone
      Live forgotten and die forlorn.'   60

And, rising, from her bosom drew
  Old letters, breathing of her worth,
For ' Love,' they said, ' must needs be true,
  To what is loveliest upon earth.'
An image seem'd to pass the door,
  To look at her with slight, and say
  ' But now thy beauty flows away,
So be alone for evermore.'
    ' O cruel heart,' she changed her tone,
    ' And cruel love, whose end is scorn,
    Is this the end, to be left alone,   71
      To live forgotten, and die forlorn ? '

But sometimes in the falling day
  An image seem'd to pass the door,
To look into her eyes and say,
  ' But thou sha't be alone no more.'
And flaming downward over all
  From heat to heat the day decreased,
  And slowly rounded to the east
The one black shadow from the wall.   80
    'The day to night,' she made her
      moan,
    'The day to night, the night to
      morn,
    And day and night I am left alone
      To live forgotten, and love forlorn.'

At eve a dry cicala sung,
  There came a sound as of the sea;
Backward the lattice-blind she flung,
  And lean'd upon the balcony.
There all in spaces rosy-bright
  Large Hesper glitter'd on her tears,   90
  And deepening thro' the silent spheres
Heaven over heaven rose the night.

And weeping then she made her moan,
  ' The night comes on that knows not
     morn,
When I shall cease to be all alone,
  To live forgotten, and love forlorn.'

THE TWO VOICES

  Written in a period (1833) of great depression consequent upon the death of his sister.

A STILL small voice spake unto me,
' Thou art so full of misery,
Were it not better not to be ? '

Then to the still small voice I said:
' Let me not cast in endless shade
What is so wonderfully made.'

To which the voice did urge reply:
' To-day I saw the dragon-fly
Come from the wells where he did lie.

' An inner impulse rent the veil   10
Of his old husk; from head to tail
Came out clear plates of sapphire mail.

' He dried his wings; like gauze they grew;
Thro' crofts and pastures wet with dew
A living flash of light he flew.'

I said: ' When first the world began,
Young Nature thro' five cycles ran,
And in the sixth she moulded man.

' She gave him mind, the lordliest
Proportion, and, above the rest,   20
Dominion in the head and breast.'

Thereto the silent voice replied:
' Self-blinded are you by your pride;
Look up thro' night; the world is wide.

  This truth within thy mind rehearse,
That in a boundless universe
Is boundless better, boundless worse.

' Think you this mould of hopes and fears
Could find no statelier than his peers
In yonder hundred million spheres ? '   30

It spake, moreover, in my mind:
' Tho' thou wert scatter'd to the wind,
Yet is there plenty of the kind.'

Then did my response clearer fall:
' No compound of this earthly ball
Is like another, all in all.'

To which he answer'd scoffingly:
' Good soul ! suppose I grant it thee,
Who 'll weep for thy deficiency ?

' Or will one beam be less intense,   40
When thy peculiar difference
Is cancell'd in the world of sense ? '

I would have said, ' Thou canst not know,'
But my full heart, that work'd below,
Rain'd thro' my sight its overflow.

Again the voice spake unto me:
' Thou art so steep'd in misery,
Surely 't were better not to be.

' Thine anguish will not let thee sleep,
Nor any train of reason keep;   50
Thou canst not think, but thou wilt weep.'

I said: ' The years with change advance;
If I make dark my countenance,
I shut my life from happier chance.

' Some turn this sickness yet might take,
Even yet.' But he: ' What drug can make
A wither'd palsy cease to shake ? '

I wept: ' Tho' I should die, I know
That all about the thorn will blow
In tufts of rosy-tinted snow;   60

' And men, thro' novel spheres of thought
Still moving after truth long sought,
Will learn new things when I am not.'

' Yet,' said the secret voice, ' some time,
Sooner or later, will gray prime
Make thy grass hoar with early rime.

' Not less swift souls that yearn for light,
Rapt after heaven's starry flight,
Would sweep the tracts of day and night.

' Not less the bee would range her cells, 70
The furzy prickle fire the dells,
The foxglove cluster dappled bells.'

I said that ' all the years invent;
Each month is various to present
The world with some development.

'Were this not well, to bide mine hour,
Tho' watching from a ruin'd tower
How grows the day of human power?'

'The highest-mounted mind,' he said,
'Still sees the sacred morning spread   80
The silent summit overhead.

'Will thirty seasons render plain'
Those lonely lights that still remain,
Just breaking over land and main?

'Or make that morn, from his cold crown
And crystal silence creeping down,
Flood with full daylight glebe and town?

'Forerun thy peers, thy time, and let
Thy feet, millenniums hence, be set
In midst of knowledge, dream'd not yet. 90

'Thou hast not gain'd a real height,
Nor art thou nearer to the light,
Because the scale is infinite.

''T were better not to breathe or speak,
Than cry for strength, remaining weak,
And seem to find, but still to seek.

'Moreover, but to seem to find
Asks what thou lackest, thought resign'd,
A healthy frame, a quiet mind.'

I said: 'When I am gone away,   100
"He dared not tarry," men will say,
Doing dishonor to my clay.'

'This is more vile,' he made reply,
'To breathe and loathe, to live and sigh,
Than once from dread of pain to die.

'Sick art thou — a divided will
Still heaping on the fear of ill
The fear of men, a coward still.

'Do men love thee?   Art thou so bound
To men that how thy name may sound   110
Will vex thee lying underground?

'The memory of the wither'd leaf
In endless time is scarce more brief
Than of the garner'd autumn-sheaf.

'Go, vexed spirit, sleep in trust;
The right ear that is fill'd with dust
Hears little of the false or just.'

'Hard task, to pluck resolve,' I cried,
'From emptiness and the waste wide
Of that abyss, or scornful pride!   120

'Nay — rather yet that I could raise
One hope that warm'd me in the days
While still I yearn'd for human praise.

'When, wide in soul and bold of tongue,
Among the tents I paused and sung,
The distant battle flash'd and rung.

'I sung the joyful Pæan clear,
And, sitting, burnish'd without fear
The brand, the buckler, and the spear —

'Waiting to strive a happy strife,   130
To war with falsehood to the knife,
And not to lose the good of life —

'Some hidden principle to move,
To put together, part and prove,
And mete the bounds of hate and love —

'As far as might be, to carve out
Free space for every human doubt,
That the whole mind might orb about —

'To search thro' all I felt or saw,
The springs of life, the depths of awe,   140
And reach the law within the law;

'At least, not rotting like a weed,
But, having sown some generous seed,
Fruitful of further thought and deed,

'To pass, when Life her light withdraws,
Not void of righteous self-applause,
Nor in a merely selfish cause —

'In some good cause, not in mine own,
To perish, wept for, honor'd, known,
And like a warrior overthrown;   150

'Whose eyes are dim with glorious tears,
When, soil'd with noble dust, he hears
His country's war-song thrill his ears:

'Then dying of a mortal stroke,
What time the foeman's line is broke,
And all the war is roll'd in smoke.'

'Yea!' said the voice, 'thy dream was good,
While thou abodest in the bud.
It was the stirring of the blood.

'If Nature put not forth her power   160
About the opening of the flower,
Who is it that could live an hour ?

'Then comes the check, the change, the fall,
Pain rises up, old pleasures pall.
There is one remedy for all.

'Yet hadst thou, thro' enduring pain,
Link'd month to month with such a chain
Of knitted purport, all were vain.

'Thou hadst not between death and birth
Dissolved the riddle of the earth.   170
So were thy labor little worth.

'That men with knowledge merely play'd,
I told thee — hardly nigher made,
Tho' scaling slow from grade to grade;

'Much less this dreamer, deaf and blind,
Named man, may hope some truth to find,
That bears relation to the mind.

'For every worm beneath the moon
Draws different threads, and late and soon
Spins, toiling out his own cocoon.   180

'Cry, faint not: either Truth is born
Beyond the polar gleam forlorn,
Or in the gateways of the morn.

'Cry, faint not, climb: the summits slope
Beyond the furthest flights of hope,
Wrapt in dense cloud from base to cope.

'Sometimes a little corner shines,
As over rainy mist inclines
A gleaming crag with belts of pines.

'I will go forward, sayest thou,   190
I shall not fail to find her now.
Look up, the fold is on her brow.

'If straight thy track, or if oblique,
Thou know'st not.   Shadows thou dost
      strike,
Embracing cloud, Ixion-like;

'And owning but a little more
Than beasts, abidest lame and poor,
Calling thyself a little lower

'Than angels.   Cease to wail and brawl !
Why inch by inch to darkness crawl ?   200
There is one remedy for all.'

'O dull, one-sided voice,' said I,
'Wilt thou make everything a lie,
To flatter me that I may die ?

'I know that age to age succeeds,
Blowing a noise of tongues and deeds,
A dust of systems and of creeds.

'I cannot hide that some have striven,
Achieving calm, to whom was given
The joy that mixes man with Heaven;   210

'Who, rowing hard against the stream,
Saw distant gates of Eden gleam,
And did not dream it was a dream;

'But heard, by secret transport led,
Even in the charnels of the dead,
The murmur of the fountain-head —

'Which did accomplish their desire,
Bore and forebore, and did not tire,
Like Stephen, an unquenched fire.

'He heeded not reviling tones,   220
Nor sold his heart to idle moans,
Tho' cursed and scorn'd, and bruised with
      stones;

'But looking upward, full of grace,
He pray'd, and from a happy place
God's glory smote him on the face.'

The sullen answer slid betwixt:
'Not that the grounds of hope were fix'd,
The elements were kindlier mix'd.'

I said: 'I toil beneath the curse,
But, knowing not the universe,   230
I fear to slide from bad to worse;

'And that, in seeking to undo
One riddle, and to find the true,
I knit a hundred others new;

'Or that this anguish fleeting hence,
Unmanacled from bonds of sense,
Be fix'd and frozen to permanence:

'For I go, weak from suffering here;
Naked I go, and void of cheer:
What is it that I may not fear ?'   240

'Consider well,' the voice replied,
'His face, that two hours since hath died;
Wilt thou find passion, pain or pride ?

'Will he obey when one commands ?
Or answer should one press his hands ?
He answers not, nor understands.

'His palms are folded on his breast;
There is no other thing express'd
But long disquiet merged in rest.

'His lips are very mild and meek;   250
Tho' one should smite him on the cheek,
And on the mouth, he will not speak.

'His little daughter, whose sweet face
He kiss'd, taking his last embrace,
Becomes dishonor to her race —

'His sons grow up that bear his name,
Some grow to honor, some to shame, —
But he is chill to praise or blame.

'He will not hear the north-wind rave,
Nor, moaning, household shelter crave   260
From winter rains that beat his grave.

'High up the vapors fold and swim;
About him broods the twilight dim;
The place he knew forgetteth him.'

'If all be dark, vague voice,' I said,
'These things are wrapt in doubt and dread,
Nor canst thou show the dead are dead.

'The sap dries up: the plant declines.
A deeper tale my heart divines.
Know I not death ? the outward signs ?   270

'I found him when my years were few;
A shadow on the graves I knew,
And darkness in the village yew.

'From grave to grave the shadow crept;
In her still place the morning wept;
Touch'd by his feet the daisy slept.

'The simple senses crown'd his head:
"Omega ! thou art Lord," they said,
"We find no motion in the dead !"

'Why, if man rot in dreamless ease,   280
Should that plain fact, as taught by these,
Not make him sure that he shall cease ?

'Who forged that other influence,
That heat of inward evidence,
By which he doubts against the sense ?

'He owns the fatal gift of eyes,
That read his spirit blindly wise,
Not simple as a thing that dies.

'Here sits he shaping wings to fly;
His heart forebodes a mystery;   290
He names the name Eternity.

'That type of Perfect in his mind
In Nature can he nowhere find.
He sows himself on every wind.

'He seems to hear a Heavenly Friend,
And thro' thick veils to apprehend
A labor working to an end.

'The end and the beginning vex
His reason: many things perplex,
With motions, checks, and counterchecks.

'He knows a baseness in his blood   301
At such strange war with something good,
He may not do the thing he would.

'Heaven opens inward, chasms yawn,
Vast images in glimmering dawn,
Half shown, are broken and withdrawn.

'Ah ! sure within him and without,
Could his dark wisdom find it out,
There must be answer to his doubt,

'But thou canst answer not again.   310
With thine own weapon art thou slain,
Or thou wilt answer but in vain.

'The doubt would rest, I dare not solve.
In the same circle we revolve.
Assurance only breeds resolve.'

As when a billow, blown against,
Falls back, the voice with which I fenced
A little ceased, but recommenced:

'Where wert thou when thy father play'd
In his free field, and pastime made,   320
A merry boy in sun and shade ?

'A merry boy they call'd him then,
He sat upon the knees of men
In days that never come again;

'Before the little ducts began
To feed thy bones with lime, and ran
Their course, till thou wert also man:

'Who took a wife, who rear'd his race,
Whose wrinkles gather'd on his face,
Whose troubles number with his days; 330

'A life of nothings, nothing worth,
From that first nothing ere his birth
To that last nothing under earth!'

'These words,' I said, 'are like the rest;
No certain clearness, but at best
A vague suspicion of the breast:

'But if I grant, thou mightst defend
The thesis which thy words intend —
That to begin implies to end;

'Yet how should I for certain hold, 340
Because my memory is so cold,
That I first was in human mould?

'I cannot make this matter plain,
But I would shoot, howe'er in vain,
A random arrow from the brain.

'It may be that no life is found,
Which only to one engine bound
Falls off, but cycles always round.

'As old mythologies relate,
Some draught of Lethe might await 350
The slipping thro' from state to state;

'As here we find in trances, men
Forget the dream that happens then,
Until they fall in trance again;

'So might we, if our state were such
As one before, remember much,
For those two likes might meet and touch.

'But, if I lapsed from nobler place,
Some legend of a fallen race
Alone might hint of my disgrace; 360

'Some vague emotion of delight
In gazing up an Alpine height,
Some yearning toward the lamps of night;

'Or if thro' lower lives I came —
Tho' all experience past became
Consolidate in mind and frame —

'I might forget my weaker lot;
For is not our first year forgot?
The haunts of memory echo not.

'And men, whose reason long was blind,
From cells of madness unconfined, 371
Oft lose whole years of darker mind.

'Much more, if first I floated free,
As naked essence, must I be
Incompetent of memory;

'For memory dealing but with time,
And he with matter, could she climb
Beyond her own material prime?

'Moreover, something is or seems,
That touches me with mystic gleams, 380
Like glimpses of forgotten dreams —

'Of something felt, like something here;
Of something done, I know not where;
Such as no language may declare.'

The still voice laugh'd. 'I talk,' said he,
'Not with thy dreams. Suffice it thee
Thy pain is a reality.'

'But thou,' said I, 'hast missed thy mark,
Who sought'st to wreck my mortal ark,
By making all the horizon dark. 390

'Why not set forth, if I should do
This rashness, that which might ensue
With this old soul in organs new?

'Whatever crazy sorrow saith,
No life that breathes with human breath
Has ever truly long'd for death.

''T is life, whereof our nerves are scant,
O, life, not death, for which we pant;
More life, and fuller, that I want.'

I ceased, and sat as one forlorn. 400
Then said the voice, in quiet scorn,
'Behold, it is the Sabbath morn.'

And I arose, and I released
The casement, and the light increased
With freshness in the dawning east.

Like soften'd airs that blowing steal,
When meres begin to uncongeal,
The sweet church bells began to peal.

On to God's house the people prest;
Passing the place where each must rest,
Each enter'd like a welcome guest. 411

One walk'd between his wife and child,
With measured footfall firm and mild,
And now and then he gravely smiled.

The prudent partner of his blood
Lean'd on him, faithful, gentle, good,
Wearing the rose of womanhood.

And in their double love secure,
The little maiden walk'd demure,
Pacing with downward eyelids pure. 420

These three made unity so sweet,
My frozen heart began to beat,
Remembering its ancient heat.

I blest them, and they wander'd on;
I spoke, but answer came there none;
The dull and bitter voice was gone.

A second voice was at mine ear,
A little whisper silver-clear,
A murmur, ' Be of better cheer.'

As from some blissful neighborhood, 430
A notice faintly understood,
' I see the end, and know the good.'

A little hint to solace woe,
A hint, a whisper breathing low,
' I may not speak of what I know.'

Like an Æolian harp that wakes
No certain air, but overtakes
Far thought with music that it makes;

Such seem'd the whisper at my side:
' What is it thou knowest, sweet voice ? '
    I cried. 440
' A hidden hope,' the voice replied;

So heavenly-toned, that in that hour
From out my sullen heart a power
Broke, like the rainbow from the shower,

To feel, altho' no tongue can prove,
That every cloud, that spreads above
And veileth love, itself is love.

And forth into the fields I went,
And Nature's living motion lent
The pulse of hope to discontent. 450

I wonder'd at the bounteous hours,
The slow result of winter showers;
You scarce could see the grass for flowers.

I wonder'd, while I paced along;
The woods were fill'd so full with song,
There seem'd no room for sense of wrong;

And all so variously wrought,
I marvell'd how the mind was brought
To anchor by one gloomy thought ;

And wherefore rather I made choice 460
To commune with that barren voice,
Than him that said, ' Rejoice ! Rejoice ! '

THE MILLER'S DAUGHTER

First printed in 1833, but much changed in
1842. See Notes.

I SEE the wealthy miller yet,
  His double chin, his portly size,
And who that knew him could forget
  The busy wrinkles round his eyes ?
The slow wise smile that, round about
  His dusty forehead drily curl'd,
Seem'd half-within and half-without,
  And full of dealings with the world ?

In yonder chair I see him sit, 9
  Three fingers round the old silver cup —
I see his gray eyes twinkle yet
  At his own jest — gray eyes lit up
With summer lightnings of a soul
  So full of summer warmth, so glad,
So healthy, sound, and clear and whole,
  His memory scarce can make me sad.

Yet fill my glass; give me one kiss:
  My own sweet Alice, we must die.
There 's somewhat in this world amiss
  Shall be unriddled by and by. 20
There 's somewhat flows to us in life,
  But more is taken quite away.
Pray, Alice, pray, my darling wife,
  That we may die the self-same day.

Have I not found a happy earth ?
  I least should breathe a thought of pain.
Would God renew me from my birth,
  I 'd almost live my life again;

So sweet it seems with thee to walk,
    And once again to woo thee mine —   30
It seems in after-dinner talk
    Across the walnuts and the wine —

To be the long and listless boy
    Late-left an orphan of the squire,
Where this old mansion mounted high
    Looks down upon the village spire;
For even here, where I and you
    Have lived and loved alone so long,
Each morn my sleep was broken thro'
    By some wild skylark's matin song.   40

And oft I heard the tender dove
    In firry woodlands making moan;
But ere I saw your eyes, my love,
    I had no motion of my own.
For scarce my life with fancy play'd
    Before I dream'd that pleasant dream —
Still hither thither idly sway'd
    Like those long mosses in the stream.

Or from the bridge I lean'd to hear
    The milldam rushing down with noise, 50
And see the minnows everywhere
    In crystal eddies glance and poise,
The tall flag-flowers when they sprung
    Below the range of stepping-stones,
Or those three chestnuts near, that hung
    In masses thick with milky cones.

But, Alice, what an hour was that,
    When after roving in the woods
('T was April then), I came and sat
    Below the chestnuts, when their buds 60
Were glistening to the breezy blue;
    And on the slope, an absent fool,
I cast me down, nor thought of you,
    But angled in the higher pool.

A love-song I had somewhere read,
    An echo from a measured strain,
Beat time to nothing in my head
    From some odd corner of the brain.
It haunted me, the morning long,
    With weary sameness in the rhymes, 70
The phantom of a silent song,
    That went and came a thousand times.

Then leapt a trout. In lazy mood
    I watch'd the little circles die;
They past into the level flood,
    And there a vision caught my eye;

The reflex of a beauteous form,
    A glowing arm, a gleaming neck,
As when a sunbeam wavers warm
    Within the dark and dimpled beck. 80

For you remember, you had set,
    That morning, on the casement-edge
A long green box of mignonette,
    And you were leaning from the ledge;
And when I raised my eyes, above
    They met with two so full and bright —
Such eyes! I swear to you, my love,
    That these have never lost their light.

I loved, and love dispell'd the fear
    That I should die an early death; 90
For love possess'd the atmosphere,
    And fill'd the breast with purer breath.
My mother thought, What ails the boy?
    For I was alter'd, and began
To move about the house with joy,
    And with the certain step of man.

I loved the brimming wave that swam
    Thro' quiet meadows round the mill,
The sleepy pool above the dam,
    The pool beneath it never still, 100
The meal-sacks on the whiten'd floor,
    The dark round of the dripping wheel,
The very air about the door
    Made misty with the floating meal.

And oft in ramblings on the wold,
    When April nights began to blow,
And April's crescent glimmer'd cold,
    I saw the village lights below;
I knew your taper far away,
    And full at heart of trembling hope, 110
From off the wold I came, and lay
    Upon the freshly-flower'd slope.

The deep brook groan'd beneath the mill;
    And 'by that lamp,' I thought, 'she sits!'
The white chalk-quarry from the hill
    Gleam'd to the flying moon by fits.
'O, that I were beside her now!
    O, will she answer if I call?
O, would she give me vow for vow,
    Sweet Alice, if I told her all?' 120

Sometimes I saw you sit and spin;
    And, in the pauses of the wind,
Sometimes I heard you sing within;
    Sometimes your shadow cross'd **the**
        blind.

At last you rose and moved the light,
  And the long shadow of the chair
Flitted across into the night,
  And all the casement darken'd there.

But when at last I dared to speak,
  The lanes, you know, were white with
    may;   130
Your ripe lips moved not, but your cheek
  Flush'd like the coming of the day;
And so it was — half-sly, half-shy,
  You would, and would not, little one!
Although I pleaded tenderly,
  And you and I were all alone.

And slowly was my mother brought
  To yield consent to my desire:
She wish'd me happy, but she thought
  I might have look'd a little higher; 140
And I was young — too young to wed:
  'Yet must I love her for your sake;
Go fetch your Alice here,' she said:
  Her eyelid quiver'd as she spake.

And down I went to fetch my bride:
  But, Alice, you were ill at ease;
This dress and that by turns you tried,
  Too fearful that you should not please.
I loved you better for your fears,
  I knew you could not look but well; 150
And dews, that would have fallen in tears,
  I kiss'd away before they fell.

I watch'd the little flutterings,
  The doubt my mother would not see;
She spoke at large of many things,
  And at the last she spoke of me;
And turning look'd upon your face,
  As near this door you sat apart,
And rose, and, with a silent grace 159
  Approaching, press'd you heart to heart.

Ah, well — but sing the foolish song
  I gave you, Alice, on the day
When, arm in arm, we went along,
  A pensive pair, and you were gay
With bridal flowers — that I may seem,
  As in the nights of old, to lie
Beside the mill-wheel in the stream,
  While those full chestnuts whisper by.

  It is the miller's daughter,
    And she is grown so dear, so dear, 170
  That I would be the jewel
    That trembles in her ear;

For hid in ringlets day and night,
I'd touch her neck so warm and white.

And I would be the girdle
  About her dainty dainty waist,
And her heart would beat against me,
  In sorrow and in rest;
And I should know if it beat right,
I'd clasp it round so close and tight. 180

And I would be the necklace,
  And all day long to fall and rise
Upon her balmy bosom,
  With her laughter or her sighs;
And I would lie so light, so light,
I scarce should be unclasp'd at night.

A trifle, sweet! which true love spells —
  True love interprets — right alone.
His light upon the letter dwells,
  For all the spirit is his own. 190
So, if I waste words now, in truth
  You must blame Love. His early rage
Had force to make me rhyme in youth,
  And makes me talk too much in age.

And now those vivid hours are gone,
  Like mine own life to me thou art,
Where Past and Present, wound in one,
  Do make a garland for the heart;
So sing that other song I made,
  Half-anger'd with my happy lot, 200
The day, when in the chestnut shade
  I found the blue forget-me-not.

  Love that hath us in the net,
  Can he pass, and we forget?
  Many suns arise and set;
  Many a chance the years beget;
  Love the gift is Love the debt.
    Even so.
  Love is hurt with jar and fret;
  Love is made a vague regret; 210
  Eyes with idle tears are wet;
  Idle habit links us yet.
  What is love? for we forget:
    Ah, no! no!

Look thro' mine eyes with thine. True
    wife,
  Round my true heart thine arms entwine;
My other dearer life in life,
  Look thro' my very soul with thine!
Untouch'd with any shade of years,
  May those kind eyes for ever dwell! 220
They have not shed a many tears,
  Dear eyes, since first I knew them well.

Yet tears they shed; they had their part
  Of sorrow; for when time was ripe,
The still affection of the heart
  Became an outward breathing type,
That into stillness past again,
  And left a want unknown before;
Although the loss had brought us pain,
  That loss but made us love the more, 230

With farther lookings on. The kiss,
  The woven arms, seem but to be
Weak symbols of the settled bliss,
  The comfort, I have found in thee;
But that God bless thee, dear — who
    wrought
  Two spirits to one equal mind —
With blessings beyond hope or thought,
  With blessings which no words can find.

Arise, and let us wander forth
  To yon old mill across the wolds;   240
For look, the sunset, south and north,
  Winds all the vale in rosy folds,
And fires your narrow casement glass,
  Touching the sullen pool below;
On the chalk-hill the bearded grass
  Is dry and dewless. Let us go.

FATIMA

Reprinted in 1842 from the volume of 1833,
where, instead of the present title, it has for
heading the following quotation :

    Φαινεταί μοι κῆνος ἴσος θεοῖσιν
    Ἔμμεν ἀνήρ. — SAPPHO.

O LOVE, Love, Love ! O withering might !
O sun, that from thy noonday height
Shudderest when I strain my sight,
Throbbing thro' all thy heat and light,
  Lo, falling from my constant mind,
  Lo, parch'd and wither'd, deaf and blind,
I whirl like leaves in roaring wind.

Last night I wasted hateful hours
Below the city's eastern towers;
I thirsted for the brooks, the showers;
I roll'd among the tender flowers;
  I crush'd them on my breast, my mouth;
  I look'd athwart the burning drouth
Of that long desert to the south.

Last night, when some one spoke his name,
From my swift blood that went and came
A thousand little shafts of flame
Were shiver'd in my narrow frame.

O Love, O fire ! once he drew
With one long kiss my whole soul thro'
My lips, as sunlight drinketh dew.

Before he mounts the hill, I know
He cometh quickly; from below
Sweet gales, as from deep gardens, blow
Before him, striking on my brow.
  In my dry brain my spirit soon,
  Down-deepening from swoon to swoon,
Faints like a dazzled morning moon.

The wind sounds like a silver wire,
And from beyond the noon a fire
Is pour'd upon the hills, and nigher
The skies stoop down in their desire;
  And, isled in sudden seas of light,
  My heart, pierced thro' with fierce de-
    light,
Bursts into blossom in his sight.

My whole soul waiting silently,
All naked in a sultry sky,
Droops blinded with his shining eye;
I *will* possess him or will die.
  I will grow round him in his place,
  Grow, live, die looking on his face,
Die, dying clasp'd in his embrace.

ŒNONE

First printed in 1833, but materially altered
in 1842. See Notes.

THERE lies a vale in Ida, lovelier
Than all the valleys of Ionian hills.
The swimming vapor slopes athwart the
    glen,
Puts forth an arm, and creeps from pine to
    pine,
And loiters, slowly drawn. On either
    hand
The lawns and meadow-ledges midway
    down
Hang rich in flowers, and far below them
    roars
The long brook falling thro' the cloven
    ravine
In cataract after cataract to the sea.
Behind the valley topmost Gargarus   10
Stands up and takes the morning; but in
    front
The gorges, opening wide apart, reveal
Troas and Ilion's column'd citadel,
The crown of Troas.

Hither came at noon
Mournful Œnone, wandering forlorn
Of Paris, once her playmate on the hills.
Her cheek had lost the rose, and round her
    neck
Floated her hair or seem'd to float in rest.
She, leaning on a fragment twined with
    vine,
Sang to the stillness, till the mountain-
    shade   20
Sloped downward to her seat from the
    upper cliff.

'O mother Ida, many-fountain'd Ida,
Dear mother Ida, harken ere I die.
For now the noonday quiet holds the hill;
The grasshopper is silent in the grass;
The lizard, with his shadow on the stone,
Rests like a shadow, and the winds are
    dead.
The purple flower droops, the golden bee
Is lily-cradled; I alone awake
My eyes are full of tears, my heart of
    love,   30
My heart is breaking, and my eyes are dim,
And I am all aweary of my life

'O mother Ida, many-fountain'd Ida,
Dear mother Ida, harken ere I die.
Hear me, O earth, hear me, O hills, O caves
That house the cold crown'd snake ! O
    mountain brooks,
I am the daughter of a River-God,
Hear me, for I will speak, and build up all
My sorrow with my song, as yonder walls
Rose slowly to a music slowly breathed, 40
A cloud that gather'd shape; for it may be
That, while I speak of it, a little while
My heart may wander from its deeper woe.

'O mother Ida, many-fountain'd Ida,
Dear mother Ida, harken ere I die.
I waited underneath the dawning hills;
Aloft the mountain lawn was dewy-dark,
And dewy dark aloft the mountain pine.
Beautiful Paris, evil-hearted Paris,
Leading a jet-black goat white-horn'd,
    white-hooved,   50
Came up from reedy Simois all alone.

'O mother Ida, harken ere I die.
Far-off the torrent call'd me from the cleft;
Far up the solitary morning smote
The streaks of virgin snow   With down-
    dropt eyes

I sat alone; white-breasted like a star
Fronting the dawn he moved; a leopard
    skin
Droop'd from his shoulder, but his sunny
    hair
Cluster'd about his temples like a God's;
And his cheek brighten'd as the foam-bow
    brightens   60
When the wind blows the foam, and all my
    heart
Went forth to embrace him coming ere he
    came.

'Dear mother Ida, harken ere I die.
He smiled, and opening out his milk-white
    palm
Disclosed a fruit of pure Hesperian gold,
That smelt ambrosially, and while I look'd
And listen'd, the full-flowing river of
    speech
Came down upon my heart:
    '"My own Œnone,
Beautiful-brow'd Œnone, my own soul,
Behold this fruit, whose gleaming rind
    ingraven   70
'For the most fair,' would seem to award
    it thine,
As lovelier than whatever Oread haunt
The knolls of Ida, loveliest in all grace
Of movement, and the charm of married
    brows."

'Dear mother Ida, harken ere I die.
He prest the blossom of his lips to mine,
And added, "This was cast upon the
    board,
When all the full-faced presence of the
    Gods
Ranged in the halls of Peleus; whereupon
Rose feud, with question unto whom 't were
    due;   80
But light-foot Iris brought it yester-eve,
Delivering, that to me, by common voice
Elected umpire, Herè comes to-day,
Pallas and Aphrodite, claiming each
This meed of fairest. Thou, within the
    cave
Behind yon whispering tuft of oldest pine,
Mayst well behold them unbeheld, unheard
Hear all, and see thy Paris judge of Gods."

'Dear mother Ida, harken ere I die.
It was the deep midnoon; one silvery
    cloud   90
Had lost his way between the piny sides

Of this long glen. Then to the bower they
    came,
Naked they came to that smooth-swarded
    bower,
And at their feet the crocus brake like fire,
Violet, amaracus, and asphodel,
Lotos and lilies; and a wind arose,
And overhead the wandering ivy and vine,
This way and that, in many a wild fes-
    toon
Ran riot, garlanding the gnarled boughs
With bunch and berry and flower thro' and
    thro'.   100

' O mother Ida, harken ere I die.
On the tree-tops a crested peacock lit,
And o'er him flow'd a golden cloud, and
    lean'd
Upon him, slowly dropping fragrant dew.
Then first I heard the voice of her to
    whom
Coming thro' heaven, like a light that
    grows
Larger and clearer, with one mind the Gods
Rise up for reverence. She to Paris made
Proffer of royal power, ample rule
Unquestion'd, overflowing revenue   110
Wherewith to embellish state, " from many
    a vale
And river-sunder'd champaign clothed with
    corn,
Or labor'd mine undrainable of ore.
Honor," she said, " and homage, tax and
    toll,
From many an inland town and haven
    large,
Mast-throng'd beneath her shadowing cita-
    del
In glassy bays among her tallest towers."

' O mother Ida, harken ere I die.
Still she spake on and still she spake of
    power,
" Which in all action is the end of all;   120
Power fitted to the season; wisdom-bred
And throned of wisdom — from all neigh-
    bor crowns
Alliance and allegiance, till thy hand
Fail from the sceptre-staff. Such boon
    from me,
From me, heaven's queen, Paris, to thee
    king-born,
A shepherd all thy life but yet king-born,
Should come most welcome, seeing men, in
    power

Only, are likest Gods, who have attain'd
Rest in a happy place and quiet seats
Above the thunder, with undying bliss   130
In knowledge of their own supremacy."

' Dear mother Ida, harken ere I die.
She ceased, and Paris held the costly fruit
Out at arm's-length, so much the thought
    of power
Flatter'd his spirit ; but Pallas where she
    stood
Somewhat apart, her clear and bared limbs
O'erthwarted with the brazen-headed spear
Upon her pearly shoulder leaning cold,
The while, above, her full and earnest eye
Over her snow - cold breast and angry
    cheek   140
Kept watch, waiting decision, made reply :

' " Self-reverence, self-knowledge, self-
    control,
These three alone lead life to sovereign
    power.
Yet not for power (power of herself
Would come uncall'd for) but to live by
    law,
Acting the law we live by without fear;
And, because right is right, to follow right
Were wisdom in the scorn of consequence."

' Dear mother Ida, harken ere I die.
Again she said: " I woo thee not with
    gifts.   ·150
Sequel of guerdon could not alter me
To fairer. Judge thou me by what I am,
So shalt thou find me fairest.
                  Yet, indeed,
If gazing on divinity disrobed
Thy mortal eyes are frail to judge of fair,
Unbias'd by self-profit, O, rest thee sure
That I shall love thee well and cleave to
    thee,
So that my vigor, wedded to thy blood,
Shall strike within thy pulses, like a
    God's,   159
To push thee forward thro' a life of shocks,
Dangers, and deeds, until endurance grow
Sinew'd with action, and the full-grown
    will,
Circled thro' all experiences, pure law,
Commeasure perfect freedom."
                ' Here she ceas'd,
And Paris ponder'd, and I cried, " O Paris,
Give it to Pallas ! " but he heard me not,
Or hearing would not hear me, woe is me !

'O mother Ida, many-fountain'd Ida,
Dear mother Ida, harken ere I die.
Idalian Aphrodite beautiful,   170
Fresh as the foam, new-bathed in Paphian
    wells,
With rosy slender fingers backward drew
From her warm brows and bosom her deep
    hair
Ambrosial, golden round her lucid throat
And shoulder; from the violets her light
    foot
Shone rosy-white, and o'er her rounded
    form
Between the shadows of the vine-bunches
Floated the glowing sunlights, as she
    moved.

'Dear mother Ida, harken ere I die.
She with a subtle smile in her mild eyes, 180
The herald of her triumph, drawing nigh
Half-whisper'd in his ear, "I promise thee
The fairest and most loving wife in
    Greece."
She spoke and laugh'd; I shut my sight for
    fear;
But when I look'd, Paris had raised his
    arm,
And I beheld great Herè's angry eyes,
As she withdrew into the golden cloud,
And I was left alone within the bower;
And from that time to this I am alone,
And I shall be alone until I die.   190

'Yet, mother Ida, harken ere I die.
Fairest — why fairest wife? am I not fair?
My love hath told me so a thousand times.
Methinks I must be fair, for yesterday,
When I past by, a wild and wanton pard,
Eyed like the evening star, with playful
    tail
Crouch'd fawning in the weed. Most lov-
    ing is she?
Ah me, my mountain shepherd, that my
    arms
Were wound about thee, and my hot lips
    prest
Close, close to thine in that quick-falling
    dew   200
Of fruitful kisses, thick as autumn rains
Flash in the pools of whirling Simois!

'O mother, hear me yet before I die.
They came, they cut away my tallest pines,
My tall dark pines, that plumed the craggy
    ledge

High over the blue gorge, and all between
The snowy peak and snow-white cataract
Foster'd the callow eaglet — from beneath
Whose thick mysterious boughs in the dark
    morn
The panther's roar came muffled, while I
    sat   210
Low in the valley. Never, never more
Shall lone Œnone see the morning mist
Sweep thro' them; never see them over-
    laid
With narrow moonlit slips of silver cloud,
Between the loud stream and the trembling
    stars.

'O mother, hear me yet before I die.
I wish that somewhere in the ruin'd folds,
Among the fragments tumbled from the
    glens,
Or the dry thickets, I could meet with her
The Abominable, that uninvited came   220
Into the fair Peleïan banquet-hall,
And cast the golden fruit upon the board,
And bred this change; that I might speak
    my mind,
And tell her to her face how much I hate
Her presence, hated both of Gods and men.

'O mother, hear me yet before I die.
Hath he not sworn his love a thousand
    times,
In this green valley, under this green hill,
Even on this hand, and sitting on this
    stone?
Seal'd it with kisses? water'd it with
    tears?   230
O happy tears, and how unlike to these!
O happy heaven, how canst thou see my
    face?
O happy earth, how canst thou bear my
    weight?
O death, death, death, thou ever-floating
    cloud,
There are enough unhappy on this earth,
Pass by the happy souls, that love to live;
I pray thee, pass before my light of life,
And shadow all my soul, that I may die.
Thou weighest heavy on the heart within,
Weigh heavy on my eyelids; let me die. 240

'O mother, hear me yet before I die.
I will not die alone, for fiery thoughts
Do shape themselves within me, more and
    more,
Whereof I catch the issue, as I hear

Dead sounds at night come from the in-
    most hills,
Like footsteps upon wool. I dimly see
My far-off doubtful purpose, as a mother
Conjectures of the features of her child
Ere it is born. Her child!—a shudder
    comes
Across me: never child be born of me,   250
Unblest, to vex me with his father's eyes !

'O mother, hear me yet before I die.
Hear me, O earth. I will not die alone,
Lest their shrill happy laughter come to
    me
Walking the cold and starless road of
    death
Uncomforted, leaving my ancient love
With the Greek woman. I will rise and go
Down into Troy, and ere the stars come
    forth
Talk with the wild Cassandra, for she says
A fire dances before her, and a sound   260
Rings ever in her ears of armed men.
What this may be I know not, but I know
That, wheresoe'er I am by night and day,
All earth and air seem only burning fire.'

THE SISTERS

Reprinted in 1842 from the 1833 volume,
with no change except 'and' for 'an'' in 'tur-
ret and tree.'

WE were two daughters of one race;
She was the fairest in the face.
    The wind is blowing in turret and tree.
They were together, and she fell;
Therefore revenge became me well.
    O, the earl was fair to see !

She died; she went to burning flame;
She mix'd her ancient blood with shame.
    The wind is howling in turret and tree.
Whole weeks and months, and early and
    late,
To win his love I lay in wait.
    O, the earl was fair to see !

I made a feast; I bade him come;
I won his love, I brought him home.
    The wind is roaring in turret and tree.
And after supper, on a bed,
Upon my lap he laid his head.
    O, the earl was fair to see !

I kiss'd his eyelids into rest,
His ruddy cheek upon my breast.
    The wind is raging in turret and tree.
I hated him with the hate of hell,
But I loved his beauty passing well.
    O, the earl was fair to see !

I rose up in the silent night;
I made my dagger sharp and bright.
    The wind is raving in turret and tree.
As half-asleep his breath he drew,
Three times I stabb'd him thro' and thro'.
    O, the earl was fair to see !

I curl'd and comb'd his comely head,
He look'd so grand when he was dead.
    The wind is blowing in turret and tree.
I wrapt his body in the sheet,
And laid him at his mother's feet.
    O, the earl was fair to see !

TO ——

WITH THE FOLLOWING POEM

'The Palace of Art' was printed, with this
introduction, in 1833, but was much altered in
1842 and somewhat in more recent editions.
See Notes.

I SEND you here a sort of allegory —
For you will understand it — of a soul,
A sinful soul possess'd of many gifts,
A spacious garden full of flowering weeds,
A glorious devil, large in heart and brain,
That did love beauty only — beauty seen
In all varieties of mould and mind —
And knowledge for its beauty; or if good,
Good only for its beauty, seeing not
That Beauty, Good, and Knowledge are
    three sisters
That doat upon each other, friends to man,
Living together under the same roof,
And never can be sunder'd without tears.
And he that shuts Love out, in turn shall
    be
Shut out from Love, and on her threshold
    lie
Howling in outer darkness. Not for this
Was common clay ta'en from the common
    earth
Moulded by God, and temper'd with the
    tears
Of angels to the perfect shape of man.

THE PALACE OF ART

I BUILT my soul a lordly pleasure-house,
  Wherein at ease for aye to dwell.
I said, ' O Soul, make merry and carouse,
  Dear soul, for all is well.'

A huge crag-platform, smooth as burnish'd
    brass,
  I chose.   The ranged ramparts bright
From level meadow-bases of deep grass
  Suddenly scaled the light.

Thereon I built it firm.   Of ledge or shelf
  The rock rose clear, or winding stair.   10
My soul would live alone unto herself
  In her high palace there.

And ' while the world runs round and
    round,' I said,
  ' Reign thou apart, a quiet king,
Still as, while Saturn whirls, his steadfast
    shade
  Sleeps on his luminous ring.'

To which my soul made answer readily:
  ' Trust me, in bliss I shall abide
In this great mansion, that is built for
    me,
  So royal-rich and wide.'   20
     .   .   .   .   .   .
Four courts I made, East, West and South
    and North,
  In each a squared lawn, wherefrom
The golden gorge of dragons spouted forth
  A flood of fountain-foam.

And round the cool green courts there ran
    a row
  Of cloisters, branch'd like mighty woods,
Echoing all night to that sonorous flow
  Of spouted fountain-floods;

And round the roofs a gilded gallery
  That lent broad verge to distant lands, 30
Far as the wild swan wings, to where the
    sky
  Dipt down to sea and sands.

From those four jets four currents in one
    swell
  Across the mountain stream'd below
In misty folds, that floating as they fell
  Lit up a torrent-bow.

And high on every peak a statue seem'd
  To hang on tiptoe, tossing up
A cloud of incense of all odor steam'd
  From out a golden cup.   40

So that she thought, ' And who shall gaze
    upon
  My palace with unblinded eyes,
While this great bow will waver in the
    sun,
  And that sweet incense rise ? '

For that sweet incense rose and never
    fail'd,
  And, while day sank or mounted higher,
The light aerial gallery, golden-rail'd,
  Burnt like a fringe of fire.

Likewise the deep-set windows, stain'd and
    traced,
  Would seem slow-flaming crimson fires 50
From shadow'd grots of arches interlaced,
  And tipt with frost-like spires.
     .   .   .   .   .   .
Full of long-sounding corridors it was,
  That over-vaulted grateful gloom,
Thro' which the livelong day my soul did
    pass,
  Well-pleased, from room to room.

Full of great rooms and small the palace
    stood,
  All various, each a perfect whole
From living Nature, fit for every mood
  And change of my still soul.   60

For some were hung with arras green and
    blue,
  Showing a gaudy summer-morn,
Where with puff'd cheek the belted hunter
    blew
  His wreathed bugle-horn.

One seem'd all dark and red — a tract of
    sand,
  And some one pacing there alone,
Who paced for ever in a glimmering land,
  Lit with a low large moon.

One show'd an iron coast and angry waves.
  You seem'd to hear them climb and
    fall
And roar rock-thwarted under bellowing
    caves,   7:
  Beneath the windy wall.

And one, a full-fed river winding slow
  By herds upon an endless plain,
The ragged rims of thunder brooding low,
  With shadow-streaks of rain.

And one, the reapers at their sultry toil.
  In front they bound the sheaves. Be-
    hind
Were realms of upland, prodigal in oil,
  And hoary to the wind.   80

And one a foreground black with stones
    and slags;
  Beyond, a line of heights; and higher
All barr'd with long white cloud the scorn-
    ful crags;
  And highest, snow and fire.

And one, an English home — gray twilight
    pour'd
  On dewy pastures, dewy trees,
Softer than sleep — all things in order
    stored,
  A haunt of ancient Peace.

Nor these alone, but every landscape fair,
  As fit for every mood of mind,   90
Or gay, or grave, or sweet, or stern, was
    there,
  Not less than truth design'd.

.   .   .   .

Or the maid-mother by a crucifix,
  In tracts of pasture sunny-warm,
Beneath branch-work of costly sardonyx
  Sat smiling, babe in arm.

Or in a clear-wall'd city on the sea,
  Near gilded organ-pipes, her hair
Wound with white roses, slept Saint Cecily;
  An angel look'd at her.   100

Or thronging all one porch of Paradise
  A group of Houris bow'd to see
The dying Islamite, with hands and eyes
  That said, We wait for thee.

Or mythic Uther's deeply-wounded son
  In some fair space of sloping greens
Lay, dozing in the vale of Avalon,
  And watch'd by weeping queens.

Or hollowing one hand against his ear,
  To list a foot-fall, ere he saw   110

The wood-nymph, stay'd the Ausonian king
    to hear
  Of wisdom and of law.

Or over hills with peaky tops engrail'd,
  And many a tract of palm and rice,
The throne of Indian Cama slowly sail'd
  A summer fann'd with spice.

Or sweet Europa's mantle blew unclasp'd,
  From off her shoulder backward borne;
From one hand droop'd a crocus; one hand
    grasp'd
  The mild bull's golden horn.   120

Or else flush'd Ganymede, his rosy thigh
  Half-buried in the eagle's down,
Sole as a flying star shot thro' the sky
  Above the pillar'd town.

Nor these alone; but every legend fair
  Which the supreme Caucasian mind
Carved out of Nature for itself was there,
  Not less than life design'd.

.   .   .   .

Then in the towers I placed great bells
    that swung,
  Moved of themselves, with silver sound;
And with choice paintings of wise men I
    hung   131
  The royal dais round.

For there was Milton like a seraph strong,
  Beside him Shakespeare bland and mild;
And there the world-worn Dante grasp'd
    his song,
  And somewhat grimly smiled.

And there the Ionian father of the rest;
  A million wrinkles carved his skin;
A hundred winters snow'd upon his breast,
  From cheek and throat and chin.   140

Above, the fair hall-ceiling stately-set
  Many an arch high up did lift,
And angels rising and descending met
  With interchange of gift.

Below was all mosaic choicely plann'd
  With cycles of the human tale
Of this wide world, the times of every
    land
  So wrought they will not fail.

The people here, a beast of burden slow,
   Toil'd onward, prick'd with goads and
      stings;   150
Here play'd, a tiger, rolling to and fro
    The heads and crowns of kings;

Here rose, an athlete, strong to break or
    bind
All force in bonds that might endure,
And here once more like some sick man
    declined,
    And trusted any cure.

But over these she trod; and those great
    bells
Began to chime. She took her throne;
She sat betwixt the shining oriels,
    To sing her songs alone.   160

And thro' the topmost oriels' colored flame
    Two godlike faces gazed below;
Plato the wise, and large-brow'd Verulam,
    The first of those who know.

And all those names that in their motion
    were
Full-welling fountain-heads of change,
Betwixt the slender shafts were blazon'd fair
    In diverse raiment strange;

Thro' which the lights, rose, amber, em-
    erald, blue,
Flush'd in her temples and her eyes, 170
And from her lips, as morn from Memnon,
    drew
    Rivers of melodies.

No nightingale delighteth to prolong
    Her low preamble all alone,
More than my soul to hear her echo'd
    song
    Throb thro' the ribbed stone;

Singing and murmuring in her feastful
    mirth,
    Joying to feel herself alive,
Lord over Nature, lord of the visible earth,
    Lord of the senses five;   180

Communing with herself: 'All these are
    mine,
    And let the world have peace or wars,
'T is one to me.' She — when young night
    divine
    Crown'd dying day with stars,

Making sweet close of his delicious toils —
    Lit light in wreaths and anadems,
And pure quintessences of precious oils
    In hollow'd moons of gems,

To mimic heaven; and clapt her hands and
    cried,
    'I marvel if my still delight   190
In this great house so royal-rich and wide
    Be flatter'd to the height.

'O all things fair to sate my various eyes!
    O shapes and hues that please me well!
O silent faces of the Great and Wise,
    My Gods, with whom I dwell!

'O Godlike isolation which art mine,
    I can but count thee perfect gain,
What time I watch the darkening droves
    of swine
    That range on yonder plain.   200

'In filthy sloughs they roll a prurient
    skin,
    They graze and wallow, breed and sleep;
And oft some brainless devil enters in,
    And drives them to the deep.'

Then of the moral instinct would she prate
    And of the rising from the dead,
As hers by right of full-accomplish'd Fate;
    And at the last she said:

'I take possession of man's mind and deed.
    I care not what the sects may brawl. 210
I sit as God holding no form of creed,
    But contemplating all.'

  .   .   .   .

Full oft the riddle of the painful earth
    Flash'd thro' her as she sat alone,
Yet not the less held she her solemn mirth,
    And intellectual throne.

And so she throve and prosper'd; so three
    years
    She prosper'd; on the fourth she fell,
Like Herod, when the shout was in his
    ears,
    Struck thro' with pangs of hell.   220

Lest she should fail and perish utterly,
    God, before whom ever lie bare
The abysmal deeps of personality,
    Plagued her with sore despair.

When she would think, where'er she turn'd
    her sight
The airy hand confusion wrought,
Wrote, 'Mene, mene,' and divided quite
    The kingdom of her thought.

Deep dread and loathing of her solitude
    Fell on her, from which mood was born
Scorn of herself; again, from out that
    mood   231
    Laughter at her self-scorn.

'What ! is not this my place of strength,'
    she said,
'My spacious mansion built for me,
Whereof the strong foundation-stones were
    laid
    Since my first memory ? '

But in dark corners of her palace stood
    Uncertain shapes; and unawares
On white-eyed phantasms weeping tears of
    blood,
    And horrible nightmares,   240

And hollow shades enclosing hearts of
    flame,
    And, with dim fretted foreheads all,
On corpses three-months-old at noon she
    came,
    That stood against the wall.

A spot of dull stagnation, without light
    Or power of movement, seem'd my soul,
Mid onward-sloping motions infinite
    Making for one sure goal;

A still salt pool, lock'd in with bars of
    sand,
    Left on the shore, that hears all night 250
The plunging seas draw backward from
    the land
    Their moon-led waters white;

A star that with the choral starry dance
    Join'd not, but stood, and standing saw
The hollow orb of moving Circumstance
    Roll'd round by one fix'd law.

Back on herself her serpent pride had
    curl'd.
'No voice,' she shriek'd in that lone hall,
'No voice breaks thro' the stillness of this
    world;
    One deep, deep silence all ! '   260

She, mouldering with the dull earth's
    mouldering sod,
    Inwrapt tenfold in slothful shame,
Lay there exiled from eternal God,
    Lost to her place and name;

And death and life she hated equally,
    And nothing saw, for her despair,
But dreadful time, dreadful eternity,
    No comfort anywhere;

Remaining utterly confused with fears,
    And ever worse with growing time,   270
And ever unrelieved by dismal tears,
    And all alone in crime.

Shut up as in a crumbling tomb, girt round
    With blackness as a solid wall,
Far off she seem'd to hear the dully sound
    Of human footsteps fall:

As in strange lands a traveller walking
    slow,
    In doubt and great perplexity,
A little before moonrise hears the low
    Moan of an unknown sea;   280

And knows not if it be thunder, or a sound
    Of rocks thrown down, or one deep cry
Of great wild beasts; then thinketh, 'I
    have found
    A new land, but I die.'

She howl'd aloud, 'I am on fire within.
    There comes no murmur of reply.
What is it that will take away my sin,
    And save me lest I die ? '

So when four years were wholly finished,
    She threw her royal robes away.   290
'Make me a cottage in the vale,' she said,
    'Where I may mourn and pray.

'Yet pull not down my palace towers, that
    are
So lightly, beautifully built;
Perchance I may return with others there
    When I have purged my guilt.'

LADY CLARA VERE DE VERE

First printed in 1842, but written in 1833.

Lady Clara Vere de Vere,
    Of me you shall not win renown:

You thought to break a country heart
  For pastime, ere you went to town.
At me you smiled, but unbeguiled
  I saw the snare, and I retired;
The daughter of a hundred earls,
  You are not one to be desired.

Lady Clara Vere de Vere,
  I know you proud to bear your name,
Your pride is yet no mate for mine,
  Too proud to care from whence I came.
Nor would I break for your sweet sake
  A heart that dotes on truer charms.
A simple maiden in her flower
  Is worth a hundred coats-of-arms.

Lady Clara Vere de Vere,
  Some meeker pupil you must find,
For, were you queen of all that is,
  I could not stoop to such a mind.
You sought to prove how I could love,
  And my disdain is my reply.
The lion on your old stone gates
  Is not more cold to you than I.

Lady Clara Vere de Vere,
  You put strange memories in my head.
Not thrice your branching limes have
    blown
Since I beheld young Laurence dead.
O, your sweet eyes, your low replies !
  A great enchantress you may be;
But there was that across his throat
  Which you had hardly cared to see.

Lady Clara Vere de Vere,
  When thus he met his mother's view,
She had the passions of her kind,
  She spake some certain truths of you.
Indeed I heard one bitter word
  That scarce is fit for you to hear;
Her manners had not that repose
  Which stamps the caste of Vere de
    Vere.

Lady Clara Vere de Vere,
  There stands a spectre in your hall;
The guilt of blood is at your door;
  You changed a wholesome heart to
    gall.
You held your course without remorse,
  To make him trust his modest worth,
And, last, you fix'd a vacant stare,
  And slew him with your noble birth.

Trust me, Clara Vere de Vere,
  From yon blue heavens above us bent
The gardener Adam and his wife
  Smile at the claims of long descent.
Howe'er it be, it seems to me,
  'T is only noble to be good.
Kind hearts are more than coronets,
  And simple faith than Norman blood.

I know you, Clara Vere de Vere,
  You pine among your halls and towers;
The languid light of your proud eyes
  Is wearied of the rolling hours.
In glowing health, with boundless wealth,
  But sickening of a vague disease,
You know so ill to deal with time,
  You needs must play such pranks as
    these.

Clara, Clara Vere de Vere,
  If time be heavy on your hands,
Are there no beggars at your gate,
  Nor any poor about your lands ?
O, teach the orphan-boy to read,
  Or teach the orphan-girl to sew;
Pray Heaven for a human heart,
  And let the foolish yeoman go.

THE MAY QUEEN

Printed in 1833, with the exception of the
' Conclusion,' which was added in 1842.

You must wake and call me early, call me
    early, mother dear;
To-morrow 'ill be the happiest time of all
    the glad New-year;
Of all the glad New-year, mother, the mad-
    dest merriest day,
For I 'm to be Queen o' the May, mother,
  I 'm to be Queen o' the May.

There 's many a black, black eye, they say,
    but none so bright as mine;
There 's Margaret and Mary, there 's Kate
    and Caroline;
But none so fair as little Alice in all the
    land they say,
So I 'm to be Queen o' the May, mother,
  I 'm to be Queen o' the May.

I sleep so sound all night, mother, that I
    shall never wake,
If you do not call me loud when the day
    begins to break;   10

But I must gather knots of flowers, and
    buds and garlands gay,
For I 'm to be Queen o' the May, mother,
    I 'm to be Queen o' the May.

As I came up the valley whom think ye
    should I see
But Robin leaning on the bridge beneath
    the hazel-tree ?
He thought of that sharp look, mother, I
    gave him yesterday,
But I 'm to be Queen o' the May, mother,
    I 'm to be Queen o' the May.

He thought I was a ghost, mother, for I
    was all in white,
And I ran by him without speaking, like a
    flash of light.
They call me cruel-hearted, but I care not
    what they say,
For I 'm to be Queen o' the May, mother,
    I 'm to be Queen o' the May.   20

They say he 's dying all for love, but that
    can never be;
They say his heart is breaking, mother —
    what is that to me ?
There 's many a bolder lad 'ill woo me any
    summer day,
And I 'm to be Queen o' the May, mother,
    I 'm to be Queen o' the May.

Little Effie shall go with me to-morrow to
    the green,
And you 'll be there, too, mother, to see
    me made the Queen;
For the shepherd lads on every side 'ill come
    from far away,
And I 'm to be Queen o' the May, mother,
    I 'm to be Queen o' the May.

The honeysuckle round the porch has
    woven its wavy bowers,
And by the meadow-trenches blow the faint
    sweet cuckoo-flowers;   30
And the wild marsh-marigold shines like
    fire in swamps and hollows gray,
And I 'm to be Queen o' the May, mother,
    I 'm to be Queen o' the May.

The night-winds come and go, mother, upon
    the meadow-grass,
And the happy stars above them seem to
    brighten as they pass;

There will not be a drop of rain the whole
    of the livelong day,
And I 'm to be Queen o' the May, mother,
    I 'm to be Queen o' the May.

All the valley, mother, 'ill be fresh and
    green and still,
And the cowslip and the crowfoot are over
    all the hill,
And the rivulet in the flowery dale 'ill mer-
    rily glance and play,
For I 'm to be Queen o' the May, mother,
    I 'm to be Queen o' the May.   40

So you must wake and call me early, call
    me early, mother dear,
To-morrow 'ill be the happiest time of all
    the glad New-year;
To-morrow 'ill be of all the year the mad-
    dest merriest day,
For I 'm to be Queen o' the May, mother,
    I 'm to be Queen o' the May.

NEW-YEAR'S EVE

IF you 're waking call me early, call me
    early, mother dear,
For I would see the sun rise upon the glad
    New-year.
It is the last New-year that I shall ever
    see,
Then you may lay me low i' the mould and
    think no more of me.

To-night I saw the sun set; he set and left
    behind
The good old year, the dear old time, and
    all my peace of mind;
And the New-year's coming up, mother,
    but I shall never see
The blossom on the blackthorn, the leaf
    upon the tree.

Last May we made a crown of flowers; we
    had a merry day;
Beneath the hawthorn on the green they
    made me Queen of May;   10
And we danced about the may-pole and in
    the hazel copse,
Till Charles's Wain came out above the tall
    white chimney-tops.

There 's not a flower on all the hills; the
    frost is on the pane.

I only wish to live till the snowdrops come
 again;
I wish the snow would melt and the sun
 come out on high;
I long to see a flower so before the day I die.

The building rook 'll caw from the windy
 tall elm-tree,
And the tufted plover pipe along the fal-
 low lea,
And the swallow 'ill come back again with
 summer o'er the wave,
But I shall lie alone, mother, within the
 mouldering grave.   20

Upon the chancel-casement, and upon that
 grave of mine,
In the early early morning the summer sun
 'ill shine,
Before the red cock crows from the farm
 upon the hill,
When you are warm-asleep, mother, and
 all the world is still.

When the flowers come again, mother, be-
 neath the waning light
You 'll never see me more in the long gray
 fields at night;
When from the dry dark wold the summer
 airs blow cool
On the oat-grass and the sword-grass, and
 the bulrush in the pool.

You 'll bury me, my mother, just beneath
 the hawthorn shade,
And you 'll come sometimes and see me
 where I am lowly laid.   30
I shall not forget you, mother, I shall hear
 you when you pass,
With your feet above my head in the long
 and pleasant grass.

I have been wild and wayward, but you 'll
 forgive me now;
You 'll kiss me, my own mother, and for-
 give me ere I go;
Nay, nay, you must not weep, nor let your
 grief be wild;
You should not fret for me, mother, you
 have another child.

If I can I 'll come again, mother, from out
 my resting-place;
Tho' you 'll not see me, mother, I shall look
 upon your face;

Tho' I cannot speak a word, I shall harken
 what you say,
And be often, often with you when you
 think I 'm far away.   40

Good-night, good-night, when I have said
 good-night for evermore,
And you see me carried out from the
 threshold of the door,
Don't let Effie come to see me till my grave
 be growing green.
She 'll be a better child to you than ever I
 have been.

She 'll find my garden-tools upon the gran-
 ary floor.
Let her take 'em, they are hers; I shall
 never garden more;
But tell her, when I 'm gone, to train the
 rosebush that I set
About the parlor-window and the box of
 mignonette.

Good-night, sweet mother; call me before
 the day is born.
All night I lie awake, but I fall asleep at
 morn;   50
But I would see the sun rise upon the glad
 New-year,
So, if you 're waking, call me, call me
 early, mother dear.

CONCLUSION

I THOUGHT to pass away before, and yet
 alive I am;
And in the fields all round I hear the bleat-
 ing of the lamb.
How sadly, I remember, rose the morning
 of the year !
To die before the snowdrop came, and now
 the violet 's here.

O, sweet is the new violet, that comes be-
 neath the skies,
And sweeter is the young lamb's voice to
 me that cannot rise,
And sweet is all the land about, and all the
 flowers that blow,
And sweeter far is death than life to me
 that long to go.

It seem'd so hard at first, mother, to leave
 the blessed sun,

And now it seems as hard to stay, and yet
   His will be done !   10
But still I think it can't be long before I
   find release;
And that good man, the clergyman, has
   told me words of peace.

O, blessings on his kindly voice and on his
   silver hair !
And blessings on his whole life long, until
   he meet me there !
O, blessings on his kindly heart and on his
   silver head !
A thousand times I blest him, as he knelt
   beside my bed.

He taught me all the mercy, for he show'd
   me all the sin.
Now, tho' my lamp was lighted late, there's
   One will let me in;
Nor would I now be well, mother, again, if
   that could be,
For my desire is but to pass to Him that
   died for me.   20

I did not hear the dog howl, mother, or the
   death-watch beat,
There came a sweeter token when the night
   and morning meet;
But sit beside my bed, mother, and put
   your hand in mine,
And Effie on the other side, and I will tell
   the sign.

All in the wild March-morning I heard the
   angels call;
It was when the moon was setting, and the
   dark was over all;
The trees began to whisper, and the wind
   began to roll,
And in the wild March-morning I heard
   them call my soul.

For lying broad awake I thought of you
   and Effie dear;
I saw you sitting in the house, and I no
   longer here;   30
With all my strength I pray'd for both,
   and so I felt resign'd,
And up the valley came a swell of music
   on the wind.

I thought that it was fancy, and I listen'd
   in my bed,

And then did something speak to me — I
   know not what was said;
For great delight and shuddering took hold
   of all my mind,
And up the valley came again the music on
   the wind.

But you were sleeping; and I said, 'It's
   not for them, it's mine.'
And if it come three times, I thought, I
   take it for a sign.
And once again it came, and close beside
   the window-bars,
Then seem'd to go right up to heaven and
   die among the stars.   40

So now I think my time is near. I trust it
   is. I know
The blessed music went that way my soul
   will have to go.
And for myself, indeed, I care not if I go
   to-day;
But, Effie, you must comfort *her* when I
   am past away.

And say to Robin a kind word, and tell him
   not to fret;
There's many a worthier than I, would
   make him happy yet.
If I had lived — I cannot tell — I might
   have been his wife;
But all these things have ceased to be, with
   my desire of life.

O, look ! the sun begins to rise, the heavens
   are in a glow;
He shines upon a hundred fields, and all of
   them I know.   50
And there I move no longer now, and there
   his light may shine —
Wild flowers in the valley for other hands
   than mine.

O, sweet and strange it seems to me, that
   ere this day is done
The voice, that now is speaking, may be
   beyond the sun —
For ever and for ever with those just souls
   and true —
And what is life, that we should moan ?
   why make we such ado ?

For ever and for ever, all in a blessed
   home —

And there to wait a little while till you
  and Effie come —
To lie within the light of God, as I lie upon
  your breast —
And the wicked cease from troubling, and
  the weary are at rest.   60

THE LOTOS-EATERS

First printed in 1833, but considerably al-
tered in 1842.

'COURAGE !' he said, and pointed toward
  the land,
'This mounting wave will roll us shore-
  ward soon.'
In the afternoon they came unto a land
In which it seemed always afternoon.
All round the coast the languid air did
  swoon,
Breathing like one that hath a weary
  dream.
Full - faced above the valley stood the
  moon;
And, like a downward smoke, the slender
  stream
Along the cliff to fall and pause and fall
  did seem.

A land of streams ! some, like a downward
  smoke,
Slow-dropping veils of thinnest lawn, did
  go;
And some thro' wavering lights and
  shadows broke,
Rolling a slumbrous sheet of foam below.
They saw the gleaming river seaward flow
From the inner land; far off, three moun-
  tain-tops,
Three silent pinnacles of aged snow,
Stood sunset - flush'd; and, dew'd with
  showery drops,
Up-clomb the shadowy pine above the
  woven copse.

The charmed sunset linger'd low adown
In the red West; thro' mountain clefts the
  dale
Was seen far inland, and the yellow down
Border'd with palm, and many a winding
  vale
And meadow, set with slender galingale;
A land where all things always seem'd the
  same !

And round about the keel with faces pale,
Dark faces pale against that rosy flame,
The mild - eyed melancholy Lotos - eaters
  came.

Branches they bore of that enchanted stem,
Laden with flower and fruit, whereof they
  gave
To each, but whoso did receive of them
And taste, to him the gushing of the wave
Far far away did seem to mourn and rave
On alien shores; and if his fellow spake,
His voice was thin, as voices from the
  grave;
And deep-asleep he seem'd, yet all awake,
And music in his ears his beating heart did
  make.

They sat them down upon the yellow sand,
Between the sun and moon upon the shore;
And sweet it was to dream of Fatherland,
Of child, and wife, and slave; but ever-
  more
Most weary seem'd the sea, weary the oar,
Weary the wandering fields of barren
  foam.
Then some one said, 'We will return no
  more;'
And all at once they sang, 'Our island
  home
Is far beyond the wave; we will no longer
  roam.'

CHORIC SONG

I

THERE is sweet music here that softer falls
Than petals from blown roses on the grass,
Or night-dews on still waters between walls
Of shadowy granite, in a gleaming pass;
Music that gentlier on the spirit lies,
Than tired eyelids upon tired eyes;
Music that brings sweet sleep down from
  the blissful skies.
Here are cool mosses deep,
And thro' the moss the ivies creep,
And in the stream the long-leaved flowers
  weep,   10
And from the craggy ledge the poppy
  hangs in sleep.

II

Why are we weigh'd upon with heaviness,
And utterly consumed with sharp distress,

While all things else have rest from weari-
      ness ?
All things have rest: why should we toil
      alone,
We only toil, who are the first of things,
And make perpetual moan,
Still from one sorrow to another thrown;
Nor ever fold our wings,
And cease from wanderings,   20
Nor steep our brows in slumber's holy
      balm;
Nor harken what the inner spirit sings,
'There is no joy but calm !' —
Why should we only toil, the roof and
      crown of things ?

III

Lo ! in the middle of the wood,
The folded leaf is woo'd from out the bud
With winds upon the branch, and there
Grows green and broad, and takes no care,
Sun-steep'd at noon, and in the moon
Nightly dew-fed; and turning yellow   30
Falls, and floats adown the air.
Lo ! sweeten'd with the summer light,
The full-juiced apple, waxing over-mellow,
Drops in a silent autumn night.
All its allotted length of days
The flower ripens in its place,
Ripens and fades, and falls, and hath no
      toil,
Fast-rooted in the fruitful soil.

IV

Hateful is the dark-blue sky,
Vaulted o'er the dark-blue sea.   40
Death is the end of life; ah, why
Should life all labor be ?
Let us alone.   Time driveth onward fast,
And in a little while our lips are dumb.
Let us alone.   What is it that will last ?
All things are taken from us, and become
Portions and parcels of the dreadful past.
Let us alone.   What pleasure can we have
To war with evil ?   Is there any peace
In ever climbing up the climbing wave ? 50
All things have rest, and ripen toward the
      grave
In silence — ripen, fall, and cease :
Give us long rest or death, dark death, or
      dreamful ease.

V

How sweet it were, hearing the downward
      stream,

With half-shut eyes ever to seem
Falling asleep in a half-dream !
To dream and dream, like yonder amber
      light,
Which will not leave the myrrh-bush on
      the height;
To hear each other's whisper'd speech;
Eating the Lotos day by day,   60
To watch the crisping ripples on the beach,
And tender curving lines of creamy spray;
To lend our hearts and spirits wholly
To the influence of mild-minded melan-
      choly;
To muse and brood and live again in mem-
      ory,
With those old faces of our infancy
Heap'd over with a mound of grass,
Two handfuls of white dust, shut in an urn
      of brass !

VI

Dear is the memory of our wedded lives,
And dear the last embraces of our wives
And their warm tears; but all hath suffer'd
      change;   71
For surely now our household hearths are
      cold,
Our sons inherit us, our looks are strange,
And we should come like ghosts to trouble
      joy.
Or else the island princes over-bold
Have eat our substance, and the minstrel
      sings
Before them of the ten years' war in Troy,
And our great deeds, as half - forgotten
      things.
Is there confusion in the little isle ?
Let what is broken so remain.   80
The Gods are hard to reconcile;
'T is hard to settle order once again.
There *is* confusion worse than death,
Trouble on trouble, pain on pain,
Long labor unto aged breath,
Sore task to hearts worn out by many wars
And eyes grown dim with gazing on the
      pilot-stars.

VII

But, propt on beds of amaranth and moly,
How sweet — while warm airs lull us, blow-
      ing lowly —
With half-dropt eyelid still,   90
Beneath a heaven dark and holy,
To watch the long bright river drawing
      slowly

His waters from the purple hill —
To hear the dewy echoes calling
From cave to cave thro' the thick-twined
    vine —
To watch the emerald-color'd water falling
Thro' many a woven acanthus-wreath di-
    vine !
Only to hear and see the far-off sparkling
    brine,
Only to hear were sweet, stretch'd out be-
    neath the pine.   99

VIII

The Lotos blooms below the barren peak,
The Lotos blows by every winding creek;
All day the wind breathes low with mel-
    lower tone;
Thro' every hollow cave and alley lone
Round and round the spicy downs the yel-
    low Lotos-dust is blown.
We have had enough of action, and of
    motion we,
Roll'd to starboard, roll'd to larboard, when
    the surge was seething free,
Where the wallowing monster spouted his
    foam-fountains in the sea.
Let us swear an oath, and keep it with an
    equal mind,
In the hollow Lotos-land to live and lie re-
    clined
On the hills like Gods together, careless of
    mankind.   110
For they lie beside their nectar, and the
    bolts are hurl'd
Far below them in the valleys, and the
    clouds are lightly curl'd
Round their golden houses, girdled with
    the gleaming world;
Where they smile in secret, looking over
    wasted lands,
Blight and famine, plague and earthquake,
    roaring deeps and fiery sands,
Clanging fights, and flaming towns, and
    sinking ships, and praying hands.
But they smile, they find a music centred
    in a doleful song
Steaming up, a lamentation and an ancient
    tale of wrong,
Like a tale of little meaning tho' the
    words are strong;
Chanted from an ill-used race of men that
    cleave the soil,   120
Sow the seed, and reap the harvest with
    enduring toil,

Storing yearly little dues of wheat, and
    wine and oil;
Till they perish and they suffer — some, 't is
    whisper'd — down in hell
Suffer endless anguish, others in Elysian
    valleys dwell,
Resting weary limbs at last on beds of
    asphodel.
Surely, surely, slumber is more sweet than
    toil, the shore
Than labor in the deep mid-ocean, wind and
    wave and oar;
O, rest ye, brother mariners, we will not
    wander more.

A DREAM OF FAIR WOMEN

First printed in 1833, considerably altered in
1842, and again retouched in 1845, 1853, and
(in one passage) in 1884. See Notes.

I read, before my eyelids dropt their
    shade,
    ' The Legend of Good Women,' long ago
Sung by the morning star of song, who
    made
    His music heard below;

Dan Chaucer, the first warbler, whose
    sweet breath
    Preluded those melodious bursts that fill
The spacious times of great Elizabeth
    With sounds that echo still.

And, for a while, the knowledge of his art
    Held me above the subject, as strong
    gales   10
Hold swollen clouds from raining, tho' my
    heart,
    Brimful of those wild tales,

Charged both mine eyes with tears. In
    every land
    I saw, wherever light illumineth,
Beauty and anguish walking hand in hand
    The downward slope to death.

Those far-renowned brides of ancient song
    Peopled the hollow dark, like burning
    stars,
And I heard sounds of insult, shame, and
    wrong,
    And trumpets blown for wars;   20

And clattering flints batter'd with clanging
hoofs;
    And I saw crowds in column'd sanctu-
    aries,
And forms that pass'd at windows and on
roofs
    Of marble palaces;

Corpses across the threshold, heroes tall
    Dislodging pinnacle and parapet
Upon the tortoise creeping to the wall,
    Lances in ambush set;

And high shrine-doors burst thro' with
heated blasts
    That run before the fluttering tongues of
    fire;   30
White surf wind-scatter'd over sails and
masts,
    And ever climbing higher;

Squadrons and squares of men in brazen
plates,
    Scaffolds, still sheets of water, divers
    woes,
Ranges of glimmering vaults with iron
grates,
    And hush'd seraglios.

So shape chased shape as swift as, when to
land
    Bluster the winds and tides the selfsame
    way,
Crisp foam-flakes scud along the level sand,
    Torn from the fringe of spray.   40

I started once, or seem'd to start in pain,
    Resolved on noble things, and strove to
    speak,
As when a great thought strikes along the
brain
    And flushes all the cheek.

And once my arm was lifted to hew down
    A cavalier from off his saddle-bow,
That bore a lady from a leaguer'd town;
    And then, I know not how,

All those sharp fancies, by down-lapsing
thought
    Stream'd onward, lost their edges, and
    did creep   50
Roll'd on each other, rounded, smooth'd,
and brought
    Into the gulfs of sleep.

At last methought that I had wander'd far
    In an old wood; fresh-wash'd in coolest
    dew
The maiden splendors of the morning star
    Shook in the steadfast blue.

Enormous elm-tree boles did stoop and lean
    Upon the dusky brushwood underneath
Their broad curved branches, fledged with
clearest green,
    New from its silken sheath.   60

The dim red Morn had died, her journey
done,
    And with dead lips smiled at the twilight
    plain,
Half-fallen across the threshold of the sun,
    Never to rise again.

There was no motion in the dumb dead air,
    Not any song of bird or sound of rill;
Gross darkness of the inner sepulchre
    Is not so deadly still

As that wide forest.   Growths of jasmine
turn'd
    Their humid arms festooning tree to
    tree,   70
And at the root thro' lush green grasses
burn'd
    The red anemone.

I knew the flowers, I knew the leaves, I
knew
    The tearful glimmer of the languid dawn
On those long, rank, dark wood-walks
drench'd in dew,
    Leading from lawn to lawn.

The smell of violets, hidden in the green,
    Pour'd back into my empty soul and
    frame
The times when I remember to have been
    Joyful and free from blame.   80

And from within me a clear undertone
    Thrill'd thro' mine ears in that unbliss-
    ful clime,
'Pass freely thro'; the wood is all thine
own
    Until the end of time.'

At length I saw a lady within call,
    Stiller than chisell'd marble, standing
    there;

A daughter of the gods, divinely tall,
  And most divinely fair.

Her loveliness with shame and with sur-
    prise
  Froze my swift speech; she turning on
    my face   90
The star-like sorrows of immortal eyes,
  Spoke slowly in her place:

'I had great beauty; ask thou not my
    name:
No one can be more wise than destiny.
Many drew swords and died. Where'er
    I came
  I brought calamity.'

'No marvel, sovereign lady: in fair field
  Myself for such a face had boldly died,'
I answer'd free; and turning I appeal'd
  To one that stood beside.   100

But she, with sick and scornful looks averse,
  To her full height her stately stature
    draws;
'My youth,' she said, 'was blasted with
    a curse:
  This woman was the cause.

'I was cut off from hope in that sad place
  Which men call'd Aulis in those iron
    years:
My father held his hand upon his face;
  I, blinded with my tears,

'Still strove to speak: my voice was thick
    with sighs   109
As in a dream. Dimly I could descry
The stern black-bearded kings with wolf-
    ish eyes,
  Waiting to see me die.

'The high masts flicker'd as they lay afloat;
  The crowds, the temples, waver'd, and
    the shore;
The bright death quiver'd at the victim's
    throat —
  Touch'd — and I knew no more.'

Whereto the other with a downward brow:
  'I would the white cold heavy-plunging
    foam,
Whirl'd by the wind, had roll'd me deep
    below,
  Then when I left my home.'   120

Her slow full words sank thro' the silence
    drear,
  As thunder-drops fall on a sleeping sea:
Sudden I heard a voice that cried, 'Come
    here,
  That I may look on thee.'

I turning saw, throned on a flowery rise,
  One sitting on a crimson scarf unroll'd;
A queen, with swarthy cheeks and bold
    black eyes,
  Brow-bound with burning gold.

She, flashing forth a haughty smile, began:
  'I govern'd men by change, and so I
    sway'd   130
All moods. 'T is long since I have seen
    a man.
  Once, like the moon, I made

The ever-shifting currents of the blood
  According to my humor ebb and flow.
I have no men to govern in this wood:
  That makes my only woe.

'Nay — yet it chafes me that I could not
    bend
  One will; nor tame and tutor with mine
    eye
That dull cold-blooded Cæsar. Prythee,
    friend,
  Where is Mark Antony?   140

'The man, my lover, with whom I rode sub-
    lime
  On Fortune's neck; we sat as God by
    God:
The Nilus would have risen before his time
  And flooded at our nod.

'We drank the Libyan Sun to sleep, and
    lit
  Lamps which out-burn'd Canopus. O,
    my life
In Egypt! O, the dalliance and the wit,
  The flattery and the strife,

'And the wild kiss, when fresh from war's
    alarms,
  My Hercules, my Roman Antony,   150
My mailed Bacchus leapt into my arms,
  Contented there to die!

'And there he died: and when I heard my
    name

Sigh'd forth with life I would not brook
  my fear
Of the other; with a worm I balk'd his
  fame.
  What else was left ? look here ! ' —

With that she tore her robe apart, and
  half
  The polish'd argent of her breast to sight
Laid bare. Thereto she pointed with a
  laugh,
  Showing the aspick's bite. —   160

' I died a Queen. The Roman soldier
  found
  Me lying dead, my crown about my
  brows,
A name for ever ! — lying robed and
  crown'd,
  Worthy a Roman spouse.'

Her warbling voice, a lyre of widest range
  Struck by all passion, did fall down and
  glance
From tone to tone, and glided thro' all
  change
  Of liveliest utterance.

When she made pause I knew not for de-
  light;
  Because with sudden motion from the
  ground   170
She raised her piercing orbs, and fill'd with
  light
  The interval of sound.

Still with their fires Love tipt his keenest
  darts;
  As once they drew into two burning rings
All beams of Love, melting the mighty
  hearts
  Of captains and of kings.

Slowly my sense undazzled. Then I heard
  A noise of some one coming thro' the
  lawn,
And singing clearer than the crested bird
  That claps his wings at dawn: 180

' The torrent brooks of hallow'd Israel
  From craggy hollows pouring, late and
  soon,
Sound all night long, in falling thro' the
  dell,
  Far-heard beneath the moon.

' The balmy moon of blessed Israel
  Floods all the deep-blue gloom with
  beams divine;
All night the splinter'd crags that wall
  the dell
  With spires of silver shine.'

As one that museth where broad sunshine
  laves
  The lawn by some cathedral, thro' the
  door   190
Hearing the holy organ rolling waves
  Of sound on roof and floor

Within, and anthem sung, is charm'd and
  tied
  To where he stands, — so stood I, when
  that flow
Of music left the lips of her that died
  To save her father's vow;

The daughter of the warrior Gileadite,
  A maiden pure; as when she went along
From Mizpeh's tower'd gate with welcome
  light,
  With timbrel and with song.   200

My words leapt forth: 'Heaven heads the
  count of crimes
  With that wild oath.' She render'd
  answer high:
' Not so, nor once alone; a thousand times
  I would be born and die.

' Single I grew, like some green plant,
  whose root
  Creeps to the garden water-pipes be-
  neath,
Feeding the flower; but ere my flower to
  fruit
  Changed, I was ripe for death.

' My God, my land, my father — these did
  move
  Me from my bliss of life that Nature
  gave,   210
Lower'd softly with a threefold cord of love
  Down to a silent grave.

' And I went mourning, " No fair Hebrew
  boy
  Shall smile away my maiden blame
  among
The Hebrew mothers " — emptied of all joy,
  Leaving the dance and song,

'Leaving the olive-gardens far below,
  Leaving the promise of my bridal bower,
The valleys of grape - loaded vines that
    glow
    Beneath the battled tower.   220

'The light white cloud swam over us.
    Anon
We heard the lion roaring from his den;
We saw the large white stars rise one by
    one,
  Or, from the darken'd glen,

'Saw God divide the night with flying
    flame,
  And thunder on the everlasting hills.
I heard Him, for He spake, and grief be-
    came
  A solemn scorn of ills.

'When the next moon was roll'd into the
    sky,
  Strength came to me that equall'd my
    desire.   230
How beautiful a thing it was to die
  For God and for my sire !

'It comforts me in this one thought to
    dwell,
  That I subdued me to my father's will;
Because the kiss he gave me, ere I fell,
  Sweetens the spirit still.

'Moreover it is written that my race
  Hew'd Ammon, hip and thigh, from
    Aroer
On Arnon unto Minneth.' Here her face
  Glow'd, as I look'd at her.   240

She lock'd her lips; she left me where I
    stood:
'Glory to God,' she sang, and past afar,
Thridding the sombre boskage of the wood,
  Toward the morning-star.

Losing her carol I stood pensively,
  As one that from a casement leans his
    head,
When midnight bells cease ringing sud-
    denly,
  And the old year is dead.

'Alas ! alas !' a low voice, full of care,
  Murmur'd beside me: 'Turn and look
    on me;   250

I am that Rosamond, whom men call fair,
  If what I was I be.

'Would I had been some maiden coarse
    and poor !
O me, that I should ever see the light !
Those dragon eyes of anger'd Eleanor
  Do hunt me, day and night.'

She ceased in tears, fallen from hope and
    trust;
  To whom the Egyptian: 'O, you tamely
    died !
You should have clung to Fulvia's waist,
    and thrust
  The dagger thro' her side.'   260

With that sharp sound the white dawn's
    creeping beams,
  Stolen to my brain, dissolved the mys-
    tery
Of folded sleep. The captain of my dreams
  Ruled in the eastern sky.

Morn broaden'd on the borders of the dark
  Ere I saw her who clasp'd in her last
    trance
Her murder'd father's head, or Joan of
    Arc,
  A light of ancient France;

Or her who knew that Love can vanquish
    Death,
  Who kneeling, with one arm about her
    king,   270
Drew forth the poison with her balmy
    breath,
  Sweet as new buds in spring.

No memory labors longer from the deep
  Gold-mines of thought to lift the hidden
    ore
That glimpses, moving up, than I from
    sleep
  To gather and tell o'er

Each little sound and sight. With what
    dull pain
  Compass'd, how eagerly I sought to
    strike
Into that wondrous track of dreams again !
  But no two dreams are like.   280

As when a soul laments, which hath been
    blest,

Desiring what is mingled with past
  years,
In yearnings that can never be exprest
    By signs or groans or tears;

Because all words, tho' cull'd with choicest
    art,
Failing to give the bitter of the sweet,
Wither beneath the palate, and the heart
    Faints, faded by its heat.

THE BLACKBIRD

First published in 1842, but written in 1833.

O BLACKBIRD! sing me something well:
  While all the neighbors shoot thee round,
  I keep smooth plats of fruitful ground,
Where thou mayst warble, eat, and dwell.

The espaliers and the standards all
  Are thine; the range of lawn and park;
  The unnetted black-hearts ripen dark,
All thine, against the garden wall.

Yet, tho' I spared thee all the spring,
  Thy sole delight is, sitting still,
  With that gold dagger of thy bill
To fret the summer jenneting.

A golden bill! the silver tongue,
  Cold February loved, is dry;
  Plenty corrupts the melody
That made thee famous once when young;

And in the sultry garden-squares,
  Now thy flute-notes are changed to
    coarse,
  I hear thee not at all, or hoarse
As when a hawker hawks his wares.

Take warning! he that will not sing
  While yon sun prospers in the blue,
  Shall sing for want, ere leaves are new,
Caught in the frozen palms of Spring.

THE DEATH OF THE OLD YEAR

Reprinted in 1842 from the volume of 1833.

FULL knee-deep lies the winter snow,
  And the winter winds are wearily sighing;

Toll ye the church-bell sad and slow,
And tread softly and speak low,
For the old year lies a-dying.
    Old year, you must not die;
    You came to us so readily,
    You lived with us so steadily,
    Old year, you shall not die.

He lieth still, he doth not move;
He will not see the dawn of day.
He hath no other life above.
He gave me a friend, and a true true-love,
And the New-year will take 'em away.
    Old year, you must not go;
    So long as you have been with us,
    Such joy as you have seen with us,
    Old year, you shall not go.

He froth'd his bumpers to the brim;
A jollier year we shall not see.
But tho' his eyes are waxing dim,
And tho' his foes speak ill of him,
He was a friend to me.
    Old year, you shall not die;
    We did so laugh and cry with you,
    I 've half a mind to die with you,
    Old year, if you must die.

He was full of joke and jest,
But all his merry quips are o'er.
To see him die, across the waste
His son and heir doth ride post-haste,
But he 'll be dead before.
    Every one for his own.
    The night is starry and cold, my
      friend,
    And the New-year blithe and bold,
      my friend,
    Comes up to take his own.

How hard he breathes! over the snow
I heard just now the crowing cock.
The shadows flicker to and fro;
The cricket chirps; the light burns low;
'T is nearly twelve o'clock.
    Shake hands, before you die.
    Old year, we 'll dearly rue for you.
    What is it we can do for you?
    Speak out before you die.

His face is growing sharp and thin.
Alack! our friend is gone.
Close up his eyes; tie up his chin;
Step from the corpse, and let him in
That standeth there alone,

And waiteth at the door.
There 's a new foot on the floor, my
    friend,
And a new face at the door, my friend,
    A new face at the door.

TO J. S.

First printed in 1833, and slightly altered in
1842.

THE wind that beats the mountain blows
    More softly round the open wold,
And gently comes the world to those
    That are cast in gentle mould.

And me this knowledge bolder made,
    Or else I had not dared to flow
In these words toward you, and invade
    Even with a verse your holy woe.

'T is strange that those we lean on most,
    Those in whose laps our limbs are
        nursed,
Fall into shadow, soonest lost;
    Those we love first are taken first.

God gives us love. Something to love
    He lends us; but, when love is grown
To ripeness, that on which it throve
    Falls off, and love is left alone.

This is the curse of time. Alas !
    In grief I am not all unlearn'd;
Once thro' mine own doors Death did pass;
    One went who never hath return'd.

He will not smile — not speak to me
    Once more. Two years his chair is
        seen
Empty before us. That was he
    Without whose life I had not been.

Your loss is rarer; for this star
    Rose with you thro' a little arc
Of heaven, nor having wander'd far
    Shot on the sudden into dark.

I knew your brother; his mute dust
    I honor and his living worth;
A man more pure and bold and just
    Was never born into the earth.

I have not look'd upon you nigh
    Since that dear soul hath fallen asleep.

Great Nature is more wise than I;
    I will not tell you not to weep.

And tho' mine own eyes fill with dew,
    Drawn from the spirit thro' the brain,
I will not even preach to you,
    'Weep, weeping dulls the inward
        pain.'

Let Grief be her own mistress still.
    She loveth her own anguish deep
More than much pleasure. Let her will
    Be done — to weep or not to weep.

I will not say, 'God's ordinance
    Of death is blown in every wind;'
For that is not a common chance
    That takes away a noble mind.

His memory long will live alone
    In all our hearts, as mournful light
That broods above the fallen sun,
    And dwells in heaven half the night.

Vain solace ! Memory standing near
    Cast down her eyes, and in her throat
Her voice seem'd distant, and a tear
    Dropt on the letters as I wrote.

I wrote I know not what. In truth,
    How *should* I soothe you any way,
Who miss the brother of your youth ?
    Yet something I did wish to say;

For he too was a friend to me.
    Both are my friends, and my true
        breast
Bleedeth for both; yet it may be
    That only silence suiteth best.

Words weaker than your grief would make
    Grief more. 'T were better I should
        cease
Although myself could almost take
    The place of him that sleeps in peace.

Sleep sweetly, tender heart, in peace;
    Sleep, holy spirit, blessed soul,
While the stars burn, the moons increase,
    And the great ages onward roll.

Sleep till the end, true soul and sweet.
    Nothing comes to thee new or strange.
Sleep full of rest from head to feet;
    Lie still, dry dust, secure of change.

ON A MOURNER

First printed in the 'Selections' of 1865.

I

NATURE, so far as in her lies,
  Imitates God, and turns her face
To every land beneath the skies,
  Counts nothing that she meets with base,
  But lives and loves in every place;

II

Fills out the homely quickset-screens,
  And makes the purple lilac ripe,
Steps from her airy hill, and greens
  The swamp, where humm'd the drop-
    ping snipe,
  With moss and braided marish-pipe;

III

And on thy heart a finger lays,
  Saying, 'Beat quicker, for the time
Is pleasant, and the woods and ways
  Are pleasant, and the beech and lime
  Put forth and feel a gladder clime.'

IV

And murmurs of a deeper voice,
  Going before to some far shrine,
Teach that sick heart the stronger choice,
  Till all thy life one way incline
  With one wide Will that closes thine.

V

And when the zoning eve has died
  Where yon dark valleys wind forlorn,
Come Hope and Memory, spouse and bride,
  From out the borders of the morn,
  With that fair child betwixt them born.

VI

And when no mortal motion jars
  The blackness round the tombing sod,
Thro' silence and the trembling stars
  Comes Faith from tracts no feet have
    trod,
  And Virtue, like a household god

VII

Promising empire; such as those
  Once heard at dead of night to greet
Troy's wandering prince, so that he rose
  With sacrifice, while all the fleet
  Had rest by stony hills of Crete.

This and the two following poems, written in 1833, were first printed in 1842, and have been altered but slightly. See Notes.

YOU ask me, why, tho' ill at ease,
  Within this region I subsist,
  Whose spirits falter in the mist,
And languish for the purple seas.

It is the land that freemen till,
  That sober-suited Freedom chose,
  The land, where girt with friends or foes
A man may speak the thing he will;

A land of settled government,
  A land of just and old renown,
  Where Freedom slowly broadens down
From precedent to precedent;

Where faction seldom gathers head,
  But, by degrees to fullness wrought,
  The strength of some diffusive thought
Hath time and space to work and spread.

Should banded unions persecute
  Opinion, and induce a time
  When single thought is civil crime,
And individual freedom mute,

Tho' power should make from land to
    land
  The name of Britain trebly great —
  Tho' every channel of the State
Should fill and choke with golden sand —

Yet waft me from the harbor-mouth,
  Wild wind! I seek a warmer sky,
  And I will see before I die
The palms and temples of the South.

OF old sat Freedom on the heights,
  The thunders breaking at her feet;
Above her shook the starry lights;
  She heard the torrents meet.

There in her place she did rejoice,
  Self-gather'd in her prophet-mind,
But fragments of her mighty voice
  Came rolling on the wind.

Then stept she down thro' town and field
  To mingle with the human race,
And part by part to men reveal'd
  The fullness of her face —

Grave mother of majestic works,
  From her isle-altar gazing down,
Who, Godlike, grasps the triple forks,
  And, king-like, wears the crown.

Her open eyes desire the truth.
  The wisdom of a thousand years
Is in them. May perpetual youth
  Keep dry their light from tears;

That her fair form may stand and shine,
  Make bright our days and light our
    dreams,
Turning to scorn with lips divine
  The falsehood of extremes!

———

Love thou thy land, with love far-brought
  From out the storied past, and used
Within the present, but transfused
  Thro' future time by power of thought;

True love turn'd round on fixed poles,
  Love, that endures not sordid ends,
For English natures, freemen, friends,
  Thy brothers and immortal souls.

But pamper not a hasty time,
  Nor feed with crude imaginings   10
  The herd, wild hearts and feeble wings
That every sophister can lime.

Deliver not the tasks of might
  To weakness, neither hide the ray
  From those, not blind, who wait for
    day,
Tho' sitting girt with doubtful light.

Make knowledge circle with the winds;
  But let her herald, Reverence, fly
  Before her to whatever sky
Bear seed of men and growth of minds. 20

Watch what main-currents draw the years;
  Cut Prejudice against the grain.
  But gentle words are always gain;
Regard the weakness of thy peers.

Nor toil for title, place, or touch
  Of pension, neither count on praise —
  It grows to guerdon after-days.
Nor deal in watch-words overmuch;

Not clinging to some ancient saw,
  Not master'd by some modern term,   30

Not swift nor slow to change, but firm;
  And in its season bring the law,

That from Discussion's lip may fall
  With Life that, working strongly, binds —
  Set in all lights by many minds,
To close the interests of all.

For Nature also, cold and warm,
  And moist and dry, devising long,
  Thro' many agents making strong,
Matures the individual form.   40

Meet is it changes should control
  Our being, lest we rust in ease.
  We all are changed by still degrees,
All but the basis of the soul.

So let the change which comes be free
  To ingroove itself with that which flies,
  And work, a joint of state, that plies
Its office, moved with sympathy.

A saying hard to shape in act;
  For all the past of Time reveals   50
  A bridal dawn of thunder-peals,
Wherever Thought hath wedded Fact.

Even now we hear with inward strife
  A motion toiling in the gloom —
  The Spirit of the years to come
Yearning to mix himself with Life.

A slow-develop'd strength awaits
  Completion in a painful school;
  Phantoms of other forms of rule,
New Majesties of mighty States —   60

The warders of the growing hour,
  But vague in vapor, hard to mark;
  And round them sea and air are dark
With great contrivances of Power.

Of many changes, aptly join'd,
  Is bodied forth the second whole.
  Regard gradation, lest the soul
Of Discord race the rising wind;

A wind to puff your idol-fires,
  And heap their ashes on the head;   70
  To shame the boast so often made,
That we are wiser than our sires.

O, yet, if Nature's evil star
  Drive men in manhood, as in youth,

To follow flying steps of Truth
Across the brazen bridge of war —

If New and Old, disastrous feud,
  Must ever shock, like armed foes,
  And this be true, till Time shall close,
That Principles are rain'd in blood;   80

Not yet the wise of heart would cease
  To hold his hope thro' shame and guilt,
  But with his hand against the hilt,
Would pace the troubled land, like Peace;

Not less, tho' dogs of Faction bay,
  Would serve his kind in deed and word,
  Certain, if knowledge bring the sword,
That knowledge takes the sword away —

Would love the gleams of good that broke
  From either side, nor veil his eyes;   90
  And if some dreadful need should rise
Would strike, and firmly, and one stroke.

To-morrow yet would reap to-day,
  As we bear blossom of the dead;
  Earn well the thrifty months, nor wed
Raw Haste, half-sister to Delay.

ENGLAND AND AMERICA IN 1782

First published in the 1874 edition of the 'Poems.'   See Notes.

O THOU that sendest out the man
  To rule by land and sea,
Strong mother of a Lion-line,
Be proud of those strong sons of thine
  Who wrench'd their rights from thee !

What wonder if in noble heat
  Those men thine arms withstood,
Retaught the lesson thou hadst taught,
And in thy spirit with thee fought —
  Who sprang from English blood !

But thou rejoice with liberal joy,
  Lift up thy rocky face,
And shatter, when the storms are black,
In many a streaming torrent back,
  The seas that shock thy base !

Whatever harmonies of law
  The growing world assume,

Thy work is thine — the single note
From that deep chord which **Hampden**
  smote
Will vibrate to the doom.

THE GOOSE

First printed in 1842, and unchanged.

I KNEW an old wife lean and poor,
  Her rags scarce held together;
There strode a stranger to the door,
  And it was windy weather.

He held a goose upon his arm,
  He utter'd rhyme and reason:
' Here, take the goose, and keep you warm,
  It is a stormy season.'

She caught the white goose by the leg,
  A goose — 't was no great matter.
The goose let fall a golden egg
  With cackle and with clatter.

She dropt the goose, and caught the pelf,
  And ran to tell her neighbors,
And bless'd herself, and cursed herself,
  And rested from her labors;

And feeding high, and living soft,
  Grew plump and able-bodied,
Until the grave churchwarden doff'd,
  The parson smirk'd and nodded.

So sitting, served by man and maid,
  She felt her heart grow prouder;
But ah ! the more the white goose laid
  It clack'd and cackled louder.

It clutter'd here, it chuckled there,
  It stirr'd the old wife's mettle;
She shifted in her elbow-chair,
  And hurl'd the pan and kettle.

' A quinsy choke thy cursed note ! '
  Then wax'd her anger stronger.
' Go, take the goose, and wring her throat,
  I will not bear it longer.'

Then yelp'd the cur, and yawl'd the cat,
  Ran Gaffer, stumbled Gammer.
The goose flew this way and flew that,
  And fill'd the house with clamor.

As head and heels upon the floor
　They flounder'd all together,
There strode a stranger to the door,
　And it was windy weather.

He took the goose upon his arm,
　He utter'd words of scorning:
'So keep you cold, or keep you warm,
　It is a stormy morning.'

The wild wind rang from park and plain,
　And round the attics rumbled,

Till all the tables danced again,
　And half the chimneys tumbled.

The glass blew in, the fire blew out,
　The blast was hard and harder.
Her cap blew off, her gown blew up,
　And a whirlwind clear'd the larder;

And while on all sides breaking loose
　Her household fled the danger,
Quoth she, 'The devil take the goose,
　And God forget the stranger ! '

ENGLISH IDYLS

AND OTHER POEMS

A heading adopted in the 1884 and subsequent editions.

THE EPIC

First published in 1842, but written as early as 1835. See Notes.

At Francis Allen's on the Christmas-
　　eve, —
The game of forfeits done — the girls all
　　kiss'd
Beneath the sacred bush and past away —
The parson Holmes, the poet Everard
　　Hall,
The host, and I sat round the wassail-
　　bowl,
Then half-way ebb'd; and there we held
　　a talk,
How all the old honor had from Christmas
　　gone,
Or gone or dwindled down to some odd
　　games
In some odd nooks like this; till I, tired
　　out
With cutting eights that day upon the
　　pond,　　　　　　　　　　10
Where, three times slipping from the outer
　　edge,
I bump'd the ice into three several stars,
Fell in a doze; and half-awake I heard
The parson taking wide and wider sweeps,
Now harping on the church-commissioners,
Now hawking at geology and schism;
Until I woke, and found him settled down
Upon the general decay of faith

Right thro' the world: 'at home was little
　　left,
And none abroad; there was no anchor,
　　none,　　　　　　　　　　20
To hold by.' Francis, laughing, clapt his
　　hand
On Everard's shoulder, with 'I hold by
　　him.'
'And I,' quoth Everard, 'by the wassail-
　　bowl.'
'Why yes,' I said, 'we knew your gift that
　　way
At college; but another which you had —
I mean of verse (for so we held it then),
What came of that ? ' 'You know,' said
　　Frank, ' he burnt
His epic, his King Arthur, some twelve
　　books ' —
And then to me demanding why: ' O, sir,
He thought that nothing new was said, or
　　else　　　　　　　　　　30
Something so said 't was nothing — that
　　a truth
Looks freshest in the fashion of the day;
God knows; he has a mint of reasons; ask.
It pleased me well enough.' 'Nay, nay,'
　　said Hall,
' Why take the style of those heroic times ?
For nature brings not back the mastodon,
Nor we those times; and why should any
　　man
Remodel models ? these twelve books of
　　mine

Were faint Homeric echoes, nothing-worth,
Mere chaff and draff, much better burnt.'
'But I,'   40
Said Francis, 'pick'd the eleventh from
     this hearth,
And have it; keep a thing, its use will
     come.
I hoard it as a sugar-plum for Holmes.'
He laugh'd, and I, tho' sleepy, like a horse
That hears the corn-bin open, prick'd my
     ears;
For I remember'd Everard's college fame
When we were Freshmen.   Then at my
     request
He brought it; and the poet, little urged,
But with some prelude of disparagement,
Read, mouthing out his hollow oes and aes,
Deep-chested music, and to this result.   51

MORTE D'ARTHUR

So all day long the noise of battle roll'd
Among the mountains by the winter sea,
Until King Arthur's table, man by man,
Had fallen in Lyonness about their lord,
King Arthur; then, because his wound was
     deep,
The bold Sir Bedivere uplifted him,
Sir Bedivere, the last of all his knights,
And bore him to a chapel nigh the field,
A broken chancel with a broken cross,   60
That stood on a dark strait of barren land.
On one side lay the ocean, and on one
Lay a great water, and the moon was full.
     Then spake King Arthur to Sir Bedi-
     vere:
'The sequel of to-day unsolders all
The goodliest fellowship of famous knights
Whereof this world holds record.   Such a
     sleep
They sleep — the men I loved.   I think
     that we
Shall never more, at any future time,
Delight our souls with talk of knightly
     deeds,   70
Walking about the gardens and the halls
Of Camelot, as in the days that were.
I perish by this people which I made, —
Tho' Merlin sware that I should come
     again
To rule once more — but let what will be
     be,
I am so deeply smitten thro' the helm
That without help I cannot last till morn.

Thou therefore take my brand Excalibur,
Which was my pride; for thou remember-
     est how
In those old days, one summer noon, an
     arm   80
Rose up from out the bosom of the lake,
Clothed in white samite, mystic, wonderful,
Holding the sword — and how I row'd
     across
And took it, and have worn it, like a king;
And, wheresoever I am sung or told
In aftertime, this also shall be known.
But now delay not; take Excalibur,
And fling him far into the middle mere;
Watch what thou seest, and lightly bring
     me word.'
     To him replied the bold Sir Bedivere: 90
'It is not meet, Sir King, to leave thee
     thus,
Aidless, alone, and smitten thro' the helm.
A little thing may harm a wounded man.
Yet I thy hest will all perform at full,
Watch what I see, and lightly bring thee
     word.'
     So saying, from the ruin'd shrine he
     stept
And in the moon athwart the place of
     tombs,
Where lay the mighty bones of ancient
     men,
Old knights, and over them the sea-wind
     sang
Shrill, chill, with flakes of foam.   He, step-
     ping down   100
By zigzag paths and juts of pointed rock,
Came on the shining levels of the lake.
     There drew he forth the brand Excali-
     bur,
And o'er him, drawing it, the winter moon,
Brightening the skirts of a long cloud, ran
     forth
And sparkled keen with frost against the
     hilt;
For all the haft twinkled with diamond
     sparks,
Myriads of topaz-lights, and jacinth-work
Of subtlest jewellery.   He gazed so long
That both his eyes were dazzled, as he
     stood,   110
This way and that dividing the swift mind,
In act to throw; but at the last it seem'd
Better to leave Excalibur conceal'd
There in the many-knotted water-flags,
That whistled stiff and dry about the
     marge.

So strode he back slow to the wounded
 king.
Then spake King Arthur to Sir Bedivere:
Hast thou perform'd my mission which I
 gave ?
What is it thou hast seen, or what hast
 heard ? '
And answer made the bold Sir Bedi-
 vere: 120
'I heard the ripple washing in the reeds,
And the wild water lapping on the crag.'
To whom replied King Arthur, faint and
 pale:
'Thou hast betray'd thy nature and thy
 name,
Not rendering true answer, as beseem'd
Thy fealty, nor like a noble knight;
For surer sign had follow'd, either hand,
Or voice, or else a motion of the mere.
This is a shameful thing for men to lie. 129
Yet now, I charge thee, quickly go again
As thou art lief and dear, and do the thing
I bade thee, watch, and lightly bring me
 word.'
Then went Sir Bedivere the second time
Across the ridge, and paced beside the
 mere,
Counting the dewy pebbles, fix'd in thought;
But when he saw the wonder of the hilt,
How curiously and strangely chased, he
 smote
His palms together, and he cried aloud:
'And if indeed I cast the brand away,
Surely a precious thing, one worthy note, 140
Should thus be lost forever from the earth,
Which might have pleased the eyes of
 many men.
What good should follow this, if this were
 done ?
What harm, undone ? deep harm to dis-
 obey,
Seeing obedience is the bond of rule.
Were it well to obey then, if a king de-
 mand
An act unprofitable, against himself ?
The king is sick, and knows not what he
 does.
What record, or what relic of my lord
Should be to aftertime, but empty breath 150
And rumors of a doubt ? but were this
 kept,
Stored in some treasure-house of mighty
 kings,
Some one might show it at a joust of arms,
Saying, " King Arthur's sword, Excalibur,

Wrought by the lonely maiden of the lake;
Nine years she wrought it, sitting in the
 deeps
Upon the hidden bases of the hills."
So might some old man speak in the after-
 time
To all the people, winning reverence;
But now much honor and much fame were
 lost.'   160
 So spake he, clouded with his own con-
 ceit,
And hid Excalibur the second time,
And so strode back slow to the wounded
 king.
 Then spoke King Arthur, breathing heav-
 ily:
'What is it thou hast seen, or what hast
 heard ? '
 And answer made the bold Sir Bedivere:
'I heard the water lapping on the crag,
And the long ripple washing in the reeds.'
 To whom replied King Arthur, much in
 wrath:
'Ah, miserable and unkind, untrue, 170
Unknightly, traitor-hearted ! Woe is me !
Authority forgets a dying king,
Laid widow'd of the power in his eye
That bow'd the will. I see thee what thou
 art,
For thou, the latest-left of all my knights,
In whom should meet the offices of all,
Thou wouldst betray me for the precious
 hilt;
Either from lust of gold, or like a girl
Valuing the giddy pleasure of the eyes.
Yet, for a man may fail in duty twice, 180
And the third time may prosper, get thee
 hence;
But, if thou spare to fling Excalibur,
I will arise and slay thee with my hands.'
 Then quickly rose Sir Bedivere, and ran,
And, leaping down the ridges lightly,
 plunged
Among the bulrush-beds, and clutch'd the
 sword,
And strongly wheel'd and threw it. The
 great brand
Made lightnings in the splendor of the
 moon,
And flashing round and round, and whirl'd
 in an arch,
Shot like a streamer of the northern morn,
Seen where the moving isles of winter
 shock   191
By night, with noises of the northern sea.

So flash'd and fell the brand Excalibur;
But ere he dipt the surface, rose an arm
Cloth'd in white samite, mystic, wonderful,
And caught him by the hilt, and brandish'd him
Three times, and drew him under in the mere.
And lightly went the other to the king.
  Then spoke King Arthur, drawing thicker breath:
'Now see I by thine eyes that this is done.   200
Speak out; what is it thou hast heard, or seen ?'
  And answer made the bold Sir Bedivere:
'Sir King, I closed mine eyelids, lest the gems
Should blind my purpose, for I never saw,
Nor shall see, here or elsewhere, till I die,
Not tho' I live three lives of mortal men,
So great a miracle as yonder hilt.
Then with both hands I flung him, wheeling him;
But when I look'd again, behold an arm,
Clothed in white samite, mystic, wonderful,   210
That caught him by the hilt, and brandish'd him
Three times, and drew him under in the mere.'
  And answer made King Arthur, breathing hard:
'My end draws nigh; 't is time that I were gone.
Make broad thy shoulders to receive my weight,
And bear me to the margin; yet I fear
My wound hath taken cold, and I shall die.'
  So saying, from the pavement he half rose,
Slowly, with pain, reclining on his arm,
And looking wistfully with wide blue eyes   220
As in a picture. Him Sir Bedivere
Remorsefully regarded thro' his tears,
And would have spoken, but he found not words,
Then took with care, and kneeling on one knee,
O'er both his shoulders drew the languid hands,
And rising bore him thro' the place of tombs.
  But, as he walk'd, King Arthur panted hard,

Like one that feels a nightmare on his bed
When all the house is mute. So sigh'd the king,
Muttering and murmuring at his ear,
'Quick, quick !   230
I fear it is too late, and I shall die.'
But the other swiftly strode from ridge to ridge,
Clothed with his breath, and looking, as he walk'd,
Larger than human on the frozen hills.
He heard the deep behind him, and a cry
Before. His own thought drove him like a goad.
Dry clash'd his harness in the icy caves
And barren chasms, and all to left and right
The bare black cliff clang'd round him, as he based
His feet on juts of slippery crag that rang   240
Sharp-smitten with the dint of armed heels —
And on a sudden, lo ! the level lake,
And the long glories of the winter moon.
  Then saw they how there hove a dusky barge,
Dark as a funeral scarf from stem to stern,
Beneath them; and descending they were ware
That all the decks were dense with stately forms
Black-stoled, black-hooded, like a dream — by these
Three queens with crowns of gold — and from them rose
A cry that shiver'd to the tingling stars,   250
And, as it were one voice, an agony
Of lamentation, like a wind that shrills
All night in a waste land, where no one comes,
Or hath come, since the making of the world.
  Then murmur'd Arthur, 'Place me in the barge,'
And to the barge they came. There those three queens
Put forth their hands, and took the king, and wept.
But she that rose the tallest of them all
And fairest laid his head upon her lap,
And loosed the shatter'd casque, and chafed his hands,   260
And call'd him by his name, complaining loud,

And dropping bitter tears against his brow
Striped with dark blood; for all his face
 was white
And colorless, and like the wither'd moon
Smote by the fresh beam of the springing
 east;
And all his greaves and cuisses dash'd with
 drops
Of onset; and the light and lustrous curls —
That made his forehead like a rising sun
High from the dais-throne — were parch'd
 with dust;
Or, clotted into points and hanging loose,
Mix'd with the knightly growth that fringed
 his lips.   271
So like a shatter'd column lay the king;
Not like that Arthur who, with lance in
 rest,
From spur to plume a star of tournament,
Shot thro' the lists at Camelot, and charged
Before the eyes of ladies and of kings.
 Then loudly cried the bold Sir Bedivere:
'Ah! my Lord Arthur, whither shall I go?
Where shall I hide my forehead and my
 eyes?
For now I see the true old times are
 dead,   280
When every morning brought a noble
 chance,
And every chance brought out a noble
 knight.
Such times have been not since the light
 that led
The holy Elders with the gift of myrrh.
But now the whole ROUND TABLE is dis-
 solved
Which was an image of the mighty world;
And I, the last, go forth companionless,
And the days darken round me, and the
 years,
Among new men, strange faces, other
 minds.'
 And slowly answer'd Arthur from the
 barge: 290
'The old order changeth, yielding place to
 new,
And God fulfils himself in many ways,
Lest one good custom should corrupt the
 world.
Comfort thyself: what comfort is in me?
I have lived my life, and that which I have
 done
May He within himself make pure! but
 thou,
If thou shouldst never see my face again,

Pray for my soul. More things are wrought
 by prayer
Than this world dreams of. Wherefore,
 let thy voice
Rise like a fountain for me night and
 day.   300
For what are men better than sheep or
 goats
That nourish a blind life within the brain,
If, knowing God, they lift not hands of
 prayer
Both for themselves and those who call
 them friend?
For so the whole round earth is every way
Bound by gold chains about the feet of God.
But now farewell. I am going a long way
With these thou seest — if indeed I go —
For all my mind is clouded with a doubt —
To the island-valley of Avilion;   310
Where falls not hail, or rain, or any snow,
Nor ever wind blows loudly, but it lies
Deep-meadow'd, happy, fair with orchard
 lawns
And bowery hollows crown'd with summer
 sea,
Where I will heal me of my grievous
 wound.'
 So said he, and the barge with oar and
 sail
Moved from the brink, like some full-
 breasted swan
That, fluting a wild carol ere her death,
Ruffles her pure cold plume, and takes the
 flood
With swarthy webs. Long stood Sir Bedi-
 vere   320
Revolving many memories, till the hull
Look'd one black dot against the verge of
 dawn,
And on the mere the wailing died away.

 Here ended Hall, and our last light, that
 long
Had wink'd and threaten'd darkness, flared
 and fell;
At which the parson, sent to sleep with
 sound,
And waked with silence, grunted 'Good!'
 but we
Sat rapt: it was the tone with which he
 read —
Perhaps some modern touches here and
 there
Redeem'd it from the charge of nothing-
 ness —   330

Or else we loved the man, and prized his
    work;
I know not; but we sitting, as I said,
The cock crew loud, as at that time of
    year
The lusty bird takes every hour for dawn.
Then Francis, muttering, like a man ill-
    used,
'There now — that's nothing!' drew a lit-
    tle back,
And drove his heel into the smoulder'd log,
That sent a blast of sparkles up the flue.
And so to bed, where yet in sleep I seem'd
To sail with Arthur under looming shores,
Point after point; till on to dawn, when
    dreams   341
Begin to feel the truth and stir of day,
To me, methought, who waited with the
    crowd,
There came a bark that, blowing forward,
    bore
King Arthur, like a modern gentleman
Of stateliest port; and all the people cried,
'Arthur is come again: he cannot die.'
Then those that stood upon the hills be-
    hind
Repeated — 'Come again, and thrice as
    fair;'
And, further inland, voices echoed —
    'Come   350
With all good things, and war shall be no
    more.'
At this a hundred bells began to peal,
That with the sound I woke, and heard in-
    deed
The clear church-bells ring in the Christ-
    mas morn.

THE GARDENER'S DAUGHTER

OR, THE PICTURES

First printed in 1842.

THIS morning is the morning of the day,
When I and Eustace from the city went
To see the Gardener's daughter; I and he,
Brothers in Art; a friendship so complete
Portion'd in halves between us, that we
    grew
The fable of the city where we dwelt.
    My Eustace might have sat for Her-
    cules;
So muscular he spread, so broad of breast.

He, by some law that holds in love, and
    draws
The greater to the lesser, long desired   10
A certain miracle of symmetry,
A miniature of loveliness, all grace
Summ'd up and closed in little; — Juliet,
    she
So light of foot, so light of spirit — O, she
To me myself, for some three careless
    moons,
The summer pilot of an empty heart
Unto the shores of nothing! Know you
    not
Such touches are but embassies of Love,
To tamper with the feelings, ere he found
Empire for life? but Eustace painted her. 21
And said to me, she sitting with us then,
'When will you paint like this?' and I
    replied —
My words were half in earnest, half in jest:
''Tis not your work, but Love's. Love,
    unperceived,
A more ideal artist he than all,
Came, drew your pencil from you, made
    those eyes
Darker than darkest pansies, and that hair
More black than ashbuds in the front of
    March.'
And Juliet answer'd laughing, 'Go and see
The Gardener's daughter; trust me, after
    that,   30
You scarce can fail to match his master-
    piece.'
And up we rose, and on the spur we went.
    Not wholly in the busy world, nor quite
Beyond it, blooms the garden that I love.
News from the humming city comes to it
In sound of funeral or of marriage bells;
And, sitting muffled in dark leaves, you
    hear
The windy clanging of the minster clock;
Altho' between it and the garden lies
A league of grass, wash'd by a slow broad
    stream,   40
That, stirr'd with languid pulses of the oar,
Waves all its lazy lilies, and creeps on,
Barge-laden, to three arches of a bridge
Crown'd with the minster-towers.
                        The fields between
Are dewy-fresh, browsed by deep-udder'd
    kine,
And all about the large lime feathers
    low —
The lime a summer home of murmurous
    wings.

In that still place she, hoarded in herself,
Grew, seldom seen; not less among us lived
Her fame from lip to lip. Who had not
    heard   50
Of Rose, the Gardener's daughter? Where
    was he,
So blunt in memory, so old at heart,
At such a distance from his youth in grief,
That, having seen, forgot? The common
    mouth,
So gross to express delight, in praise of her
Grew oratory. Such a lord is Love,
And Beauty such a mistress of the world.
    And if I said that Fancy, led by Love,
Would play with flying forms and images,
Yet this is also true, that, long before   60
I look'd upon her, when I heard her name
My heart was like a prophet to my heart,
And told me I should love. A crowd of
    hopes,
That sought to sow themselves like winged
    seeds,
Born out of everything I heard and saw,
Flutter'd about my senses and my soul;
And vague desires, like fitful blasts of
    balm
To one that travels quickly, made the air
Of life delicious, and all kinds of thought,
That verged upon them, sweeter than the
    dream   70
Dream'd by a happy man, when the dark
    East,
Unseen, is brightening to his bridal morn.
    And sure this orbit of the memory folds
For ever in itself the day we went
To see her. All the land in flowery
    squares,
Beneath a broad and equal-blowing wind,
Smelt of the coming summer, as one large
    cloud
Drew downward; but all else of heaven was
    pure
Up to the sun, and May from verge to
    verge,
And May with me from head to heel. And
    now,   80
As tho' 't were yesterday, as tho' it were
The hour just flown, that morn with all its
    sound —
For those old Mays had thrice the life of
    these —
Rings in mine ears. The steer forgot to
    graze,
And, where the hedge-row cuts the path-
    way, stood,

Leaning his horns into the neighbor field
And lowing to his fellows. From the
    woods
Came voices of the well-contented doves.
The lark could scarce get out his notes for
    joy,
But shook his song together as he near'd
His happy home, the ground. To left and
    right,   91
The cuckoo told his name to all the hills;
The mellow ouzel fluted in the elm;
The redcap whistled; and the nightingale
Sang loud, as tho' he were the bird of
    day.
    And Eustace turn'd, and smiling said to
    me:
'Hear how the bushes echo! by my life,
These birds have joyful thoughts. Think
    you they sing
Like poets, from the vanity of song?   99
Or have they any sense of why they sing?
And would they praise the heavens for
    what they have?'
And I made answer: 'Were there nothing
    else
For which to praise the heavens but only
    love,
That only love were cause enough for
    praise.'
    Lightly he laugh'd, as one that read my
    thought,
And on we went; but ere an hour had
    pass'd,
We reach'd a meadow slanting to the
    North,
Down which a well-worn pathway courted
    us
To one green wicket in a privet hedge.
This, yielding, gave into a grassy walk   110
Thro' crowded lilac-ambush trimly pruned;
And one warm gust, full-fed with perfume,
    blew
Beyond us, as we enter'd in the cool.
The garden stretches southward. In the
    midst
A cedar spread his dark-green layers of
    shade.
The garden-glasses shone, and momently
The twinkling laurel scatter'd silver lights.
    'Eustace,' I said, 'this wonder keeps
    the house.'
He nodded, but a moment afterwards
He cried, 'Look! look!' Before he ceased
    I turn'd,   120
And, ere a star can wink, beheld her there.

For up the porch there grew an Eastern
  rose,
That, flowering high, the last night's gale
  had caught
And blown across the walk.   One arm
  aloft —
Gown'd in pure white that fitted to the
  shape —
Holding the bush, to fix it back, she stood,
A single stream of all her soft brown
  hair
Pour'd on one side; the shadow of the flow-
  ers
Stole all the golden gloss, and, wavering
Lovingly lower, trembled on her waist — 130
Ah, happy shade! — and still went wavering
  down,
But, ere it touch'd a foot, that might have
  danced
The greensward into greener circles, dipt,
And mix'd with shadows of the common
  ground.
But the full day dwelt on her brows, and
  sunn'd
Her violet eyes, and all her Hebe bloom,
And doubled his own warmth against her
  lips,
And on the bounteous wave of such a
  breast
As never pencil drew.   Half light, half
  shade,
She stood, a sight to make an old man
  young.   140
  So rapt, we near'd the house; but she, a
    Rose
In roses, mingled with her fragrant toil,
Nor heard us come, nor from her tendance
  turn'd
Into the world without; till close at hand,
And almost ere I knew mine own intent,
This murmur broke the stillness of that
  air
Which brooded round about her :
                ' Ah, one rose,
One rose, but one, by those fair fingers
  cull'd,
Were worth a hundred kisses press'd on
  lips
Less exquisite than thine.'
                She look'd; but all
Suffused with blushes — neither self-pos-
  sess'd   151
Nor startled, but betwixt this mood and
  that,
Divided in a graceful quiet — paused,

And dropt the branch she held, and turn-
  ing wound
Her looser hair in braid, and stirr'd her
  lips
For some sweet answer, tho' no answer
  came,
Nor yet refused the rose, but granted it,
And moved away, and left me, statue-like,
In act to render thanks.
             I, that whole day,
Saw her no more, altho' I linger'd there 160
Till every daisy slept, and Love's white
  star
Beam'd thro' the thicken'd cedar in the
  dusk.
  So home we went, and all the livelong
    way
With solemn gibe did Eustace banter me.
' Now,' said he, ' will you climb the top of
  art.
You cannot fail but work in hues to dim
The Titianic Flora.   Will you match
My Juliet ? you, not you, — the master,
  Love,
A more ideal artist he than all.'
  So home I went, but could not sleep for
    joy,   170
Reading her perfect features in the gloom,
Kissing the rose she gave me o'er and o'er,
And shaping faithful record of the glance
That graced the giving — such a noise of
  life
Swarm'd in the golden present, such a
  voice
Call'd to me from the years to come, and
  such
A length of bright horizon rimm'd the
  dark.
And all that night I heard the watchman
  peal
The sliding season; all that night I heard
The heavy clocks knolling the drowsy
  hours.   180
The drowsy hours, dispensers of all good,
O'er the mute city stole with folded wings,
Distilling odors on me as they went
To greet their fairer sisters of the East.
  Love at first sight, first-born, and heir
    to all,
Made this night thus.   Henceforward squall
  nor storm
Could keep me from that Eden where she
  dwelt.
Light pretexts drew me: sometimes a
  Dutch love

For tulips; then for roses, moss or musk,
To grace my city rooms; or fruits and
  cream 190
Served in the weeping elm; and more and
  more
A word could bring the color to my cheek;
A thought would fill my eyes with happy
  dew;
Love trebled life within me, and with each
The year increased.
          The daughters of the year,
One after one, thro' that still garden
  pass'd;
Each garlanded with her peculiar flower
Danced into light, and died into the shade;
And each in passing touch'd with some
  new grace
Or seem'd to touch her, so that day by
  day, 200
Like one that never can be wholly known,
Her beauty grew; till Autumn brought an
  hour
For Eustace, when I heard his deep 'I
  will,'
Breathed, like the covenant of a God, to
  hold
From thence thro' all the worlds; but I
  rose up
Full of his bliss, and following her dark
  eyes
Felt earth as air beneath me, till I reach'd
The wicket-gate, and found her standing
  there.
    There sat we down upon a garden
      mound,
Two mutually enfolded; Love, the third, 210
Between us, in the circle of his arms
Enwound us both; and over many a range
Of waning lime the gray cathedral towers,
Across a hazy glimmer of the west,
Reveal'd their shining windows. From them
  clash'd
The bells; we listen'd; with the time we
  play'd,
We spoke of other things; we coursed
  about
The subject most at heart, more near and
  near,
Like doves about a dovecote, wheeling
  round
The central wish, until we settled there. 220
  Then, in that time and place, I spoke to
    her,
Requiring, tho' I knew it was mine own,
Yet for the pleasure that I took to hear,

Requiring at her hand the greatest gift,
A woman's heart, the heart of her I loved;
And in that time and place she answer'd me,
And in the compass of three little words,
More musical than ever came in one,
The silver fragments of a broken voice,
Made me most happy, faltering, 'I am
  thine.' 230
  Shall I cease here? Is this enough to
    say
That my desire, like all strongest hopes,
By its own energy fulfill'd itself,
Merged in completion? Would you learn
  at full
How passion rose thro' circumstantial
  grades
Beyond all grades develop'd? and indeed
I had not staid so long to tell you all,
But while I mused came Memory with sad
  eyes,
Holding the folded annals of my youth;
And while I mused, Love with knit brows
  went by, 240
And with a flying finger swept my lips,
And spake, 'Be wise: not easily forgiven
Are those who, setting wide the doors that
  bar
The secret bridal chambers of the heart,
Let in the day.' Here, then, my words
  have end.
  Yet might I tell of meetings, of fare-
    wells —
Of that which came between, more sweet
  than each,
In whispers, like the whispers of the leaves
That tremble round a nightingale — in
  sighs
Which perfect Joy, perplex'd for utter-
  ance, 250
Stole from her sister Sorrow. Might I not
  tell
Of difference, reconcilement, pledges given,
And vows, where there was never need of
  vows,
And kisses, where the heart on one wild
  leap
Hung tranced from all pulsation, as above
The heavens between their fairy fleeces
  pale
Sow'd all their mystic gulfs with fleeting
  stars;
Or while the balmy glooming, crescent-lit,
Spread the light haze along the river-
  shores,
And in the hollows; or as once we met 260

Unheedful, tho' beneath a whispering rain
Night slid down one long stream of sighing wind,
And in her bosom bore the baby, Sleep?
  But this whole hour your eyes have been intent
On that veil'd picture — veil'd, for what it holds
May not be dwelt on by the common day.
This prelude has prepared thee. Raise thy soul,
Make thine heart ready with thine eyes; the time
Is come to raise the veil.
              Behold her there,
As I beheld her ere she knew my heart, 270
My first, last love; the idol of my youth,
The darling of my manhood, and, alas!
Now the most blessed memory of mine age.

DORA

This poem, first printed in 1842, and unaltered since, 'was partly suggested,' as a note in the editions of 1842 and 1843 informs us, 'by one of Miss Mitford's pastorals,' — the story of ' Dora Cresswell ' in ' Our Village.'

WITH farmer Allan at the farm abode
William and Dora. William was his son,
And she his niece. He often look'd at them,
And often thought, ' I 'll make them man and wife.'
Now Dora felt her uncle's will in all,
And yearn'd toward William; but the youth, because
He had been always with her in the house,
Thought not of Dora.
           Then there came a day
When Allan call'd his son, and said: ' My son,
I married late, but I would wish to see   10
My grandchild on my knees before I die;
And I have set my heart upon a match.
Now therefore look to Dora; she is well
To look to; thrifty too beyond her age.
She is my brother's daughter; he and I
Had once hard words, and parted, and he died
In foreign lands; but for his sake I bred
His daughter Dora. Take her for your wife;
For I have wish'd this marriage, night and day,

For many years.' But William answer'd short: 20
' I cannot marry Dora; by my life,
I will not marry Dora!' Then the old man
Was wroth, and doubled up his hands, and said:
' You will not, boy! you dare to answer thus!
But in my time a father's word was law,
And so it shall be now for me. Look to it;
Consider, William, take a month to think,
And let me have an answer to my wish,
Or, by the Lord that made me, you shall pack,   29
And never more darken my doors again.'
But William answer'd madly, bit his lips,
And broke away. The more he look'd at her
The less he liked her; and his ways were harsh;
But Dora bore them meekly. Then before
The month was out he left his father's house,
And hired himself to work within the fields;
And half in love, half spite, he woo'd and wed
A laborer's daughter, Mary Morrison.
  Then, when the bells were ringing, Allan call'd
His niece and said: ' My girl, I love you well;   40
But if you speak with him that was my son,
Or change a word with her he calls his wife,
My home is none of yours. My will is law.'
And Dora promised, being meek. She thought,
' It cannot be; my uncle's mind will change!'
  And days went on, and there was born a boy
To William; then distresses came on him,
And day by day he pass'd his father's gate,
Heart-broken, and his father help'd him not.
But Dora stored what little she could save,   50
And sent it them by stealth, nor did they know
Who sent it; till at last a fever seized
On William, and in harvest time he died.

Then Dora went to Mary. Mary sat
And look'd with tears upon her boy, and
    thought
Hard things of Dora. Dora came and said:
    ' I have obey'd my uncle until now,
And I have sinn'd, for it was all thro' me
This evil came on William at the first.
But, Mary, for the sake of him that 's
    gone,   60
And for your sake, the woman that he
    chose,
And for this orphan, I am come to you.
You know there has not been for these five
    years
So full a harvest. Let me take the boy,
And I will set him in my uncle's eye
Among the wheat; that when his heart is
    glad
Of the full harvest, he may see the boy,
And bless him for the sake of him that 's
    gone.'
    And Dora took the child, and went her
    way
Across the wheat, and sat upon a mound 70
That was unsown, where many poppies
    grew.
Far off the farmer came into the field
And spied her not, for none of all his
    men
Dare tell him Dora waited with the child;
And Dora would have risen and gone to
    him,
But her heart fail'd her; and the reapers
    reap'd,
And the sun fell, and all the land was
    dark.
    But when the morrow came, she rose
    and took
The child once more, and sat upon the
    mound;   79
And made a little wreath of all the flowers
That grew about, and tied it round his hat
To make him pleasing in her uncle's eye.
Then when the farmer pass'd into the
    field
He spied her, and he left his men at work,
And came and said: ' Where were you
    yesterday ? '
Whose child is that ? What are you doing
    here ? '
So Dora cast her eyes upon the ground,
And answer'd softly, ' This is William's
    child ! '
' And did I not,' said Allan, ' did I not
Forbid you, Dora ? ' Dora said again: 90

' Do with me as you will, but take the
    child,
And bless him for the sake of him that 's
    gone ! '
And Allan said: ' I see it is a trick
Got up betwixt you and the woman there.
I must be taught my duty, and by you !
You knew my word was law, and yet you
    dared
To slight it. Well — for I will take the
    boy;
But go you hence, and never see me more.'
    So saying, he took the boy that cried
    aloud
And struggled hard. The wreath of flowers
    fell   100
At Dora's feet. She bow'd upon her hands,
And the boy's cry came to her from the
    field
More and more distant. She bow'd down
    her head,
Remembering the day when first she came,
And all the things that had been. She
    bow'd down
And wept in secret; and the reapers reap'd,
And the sun fell, and all the land was dark.
    Then Dora went to Mary's house, and
    stood
Upon the threshold. Mary saw the boy
Was not with Dora. She broke out in
    praise   110
To God, that help'd her in her widowhood.
And Dora said: ' My uncle took the boy;
But, Mary, let me live and work with you:
He says that he will never see me more.'
Then answer'd Mary: ' This shall never be,
That thou shouldst take my trouble on thy-
    self;
And, now I think, he shall not have the boy,
For he will teach him hardness, and to
    slight
His mother. Therefore thou and I will go,
And I will have my boy, and bring him
    home;   120
And I will beg of him to take thee back.
But if he will not take thee back again,
Then thou and I will live within one house,
And work for William's child, until he
    grows
Of age to help us.'
              So the women kiss'd
Each other, and set out, and reach'd the
    farm.
The door was off the latch; they peep'd,
    and saw

The boy set up betwixt his grandsire's
  knees,
Who thrust him in the hollows of his arm,
And clapt him on the hands and on the
  cheeks,   130
Like one that loved him; and the lad
  stretch'd out
And babbled for the golden seal, that hung
From Allan's watch and sparkled by the
  fire.
Then they came in; but when the boy be-
  held
His mother, he cried out to come to her;
And Allan set him down, and Mary said:
  'O father! — if you let me call you so —
I never came a-begging for myself,
Or William, or this child; but now I come
For Dora; take her back, she loves you
  well.   140
O Sir, when William died, he died at peace
With all men; for I ask'd him, and he said,
He could not ever rue his marrying me —
I had been a patient wife; but, Sir, he said
That he was wrong to cross his father thus.
"God bless him!" he said, "and may he
  never know
The troubles I have gone thro'!" Then
  he turn'd
His face and pass'd — unhappy that I am!
But now, Sir, let me have my boy, for you
Will make him hard, and he will learn to
  slight   150
His father's memory; and take Dora back,
And let all this be as it was before.'
  So Mary said, and Dora hid her face
By Mary. There was silence in the room;
And all at once the old man burst in
  sobs:
  'I have been to blame — to blame. I
  have kill'd my son.
I have kill'd him — but I loved him — my
  dear son.
May God forgive me! — I have been to
  blame.
Kiss me, my children.'
                 Then they clung about
The old man's neck, and kiss'd him many
  times.   160
And all the man was broken with remorse;
And all his love came back a hundred-fold;
And for three hours he sobb'd o'er William's
  child
Thinking of William.
                 So those four abode
Within one house together, and as years

Went forward Mary took another mate;
But Dora lived unmarried till her death.

AUDLEY COURT

First printed in 1842, and unaltered except
for the insertion of lines 77 ('A rolling stone,'
etc.) and 86 ('Sole star,' etc.).

'THE Bull, the Fleece are cramm'd, and not
  a room
For love or money. Let us picnic there
At Audley Court.'
                 I spoke, while Audley feast
Humm'd like a hive all round the narrow
  quay,
To Francis, with a basket on his arm,
To Francis just alighted from the boat
And breathing of the sea. 'With all my
  heart,'
Said Francis. Then we shoulder'd thro'
  the swarm,
And rounded by the stillness of the beach
To where the bay runs up its latest horn. 10
  We left the dying ebb that faintly lipp'd
The flat red granite; so by many a sweep
Of meadow smooth from aftermath we
  reach'd
The griffin-guarded gates, and pass'd thro'
  all
The pillar'd dusk of sounding sycamores,
And cross'd the garden to the gardener's
  lodge,
With all its casements bedded, and its
  walls
And chimneys muffled in the leafy vine.
  There, on a slope of orchard, Francis
  laid
A damask napkin wrought with horse and
  hound,   20
Brought out a dusky loaf that smelt of
  home,
And, half-cut-down, a pasty costly-made,
Where quail and pigeon, lark and leveret
  lay,
Like fossils of the rock, with golden yolks
Imbedded and injellied; last, with these,
A flask of cider from his father's vats,
Prime, which I knew; and so we sat and
  eat
And talk'd old matters over, — who was
  dead,
Who married, who was like to be, and how
The races went, and who would rent the
  hall;   30

Then touch'd upon the game, how scarce it
was
This season; glancing thence, discuss'd the
farm,
The four-field system, and the price of
grain;
And struck upon the corn-laws, where we
split,
And came again together on the king
With heated faces; till he laugh'd aloud,
And, while the blackbird on the pippin
hung
To hear him, clapt his hand in mine and
sang:
'O, who would fight and march and
countermarch,
Be shot for sixpence in a battle-field,   40
And shovell'd up into some bloody trench
Where no one knows? but let me live my
life.
'O, who would cast and balance at a
desk,
Perch'd like a crow upon a three-legg'd
stool,
Till all his juice is dried, and all his joints
Are full of chalk? but let me live my life.
'Who'd serve the state? for if I carved
my name
Upon the cliffs that guard my native land,
I might as well have traced it in the sands;
The sea wastes all; but let me live my life.
'O, who would love? I woo'd a woman
once,   51
But she was sharper than an eastern wind,
And all my heart turn'd from her, as a
thorn
Turns from the sea; but let me live my
life.'
He sang his song, and I replied with
mine.
I found it in a volume, all of songs,
Knock'd down to me, when old Sir Robert's
pride,
His books —the more the pity, so I said —
Came to the hammer here in March — and
this —
I set the words, and added names I knew:
'Sleep, Ellen Aubrey, sleep, and dream
of me: 61
Sleep, Ellen, folded in thy sister's arm,
And sleeping, haply dream her arm · is
mine.
'Sleep, Ellen, folded in Emilia's arm;
Emilia, fairer than all else but thou,
For thou art fairer than all else that is.

'Sleep, breathing health and peace upon
her breast;
Sleep, breathing love and trust against her
lip.
I go to-night; I come to-morrow morn.
'I go, but I return; I would I were   70
The pilot of the darkness and the dream.
Sleep, Ellen Aubrey, love, and dream of
me.'
So sang we each to either, Francis Hale,
The farmer's son, who lived across the bay,
My friend; and I, that having where-
withal,
And in the fallow leisure of my life
A rolling stone of here and everywhere,
Did what I would. But ere the night we
rose
And saunter'd home beneath a moon that,
just
In crescent, dimly rain'd about the leaf   80
Twilights of airy silver, till we reach'd
The limit of the hills; and as we sank
From rock to rock upon the glooming quay,
The town was hush'd beneath us; lower
down
The bay was oily calm; the harbor-buoy,
Sole star of phosphorescence in the calm,
With one green sparkle ever and anon
Dipt by itself, and we were glad at heart.

WALKING TO THE MAIL

First printed in 1842, and afterwards slightly
changed in the opening lines. See Notes.

John. I'm glad I walk'd. How fresh
the meadows look
Above the river, and, but a month ago,
The whole hillside was redder than a fox!
Is yon plantation where this byway joins
The turnpike?
James.   Yes.
John.   And when does this come by?
James. The mail? At one o'clock.
John.   What is it now?
James. A quarter to.
John.   Whose house is that I see?
No, not the County Member's with the
vane.   8
Up higher with the yew-tree by it, and half
A score of gables.
James.   That? Sir Edward Head's.
But he's abroad; the place is to be sold.
John. O, his! He was not broken.

James.   No, sir, he,
Vext with a morbid devil in his blood
That veil'd the world with jaundice, hid his
    face
From all men, and commercing with him-
    self,
He lost the sense that handles daily life —
That keeps us all in order more or less —
And sick of home went overseas for
    change.
   John. And whither ?
   James. Nay, who knows ? he 's here and
    there.
But let him go; his devil goes with him, 20
As well as with his tenant, Jocky Dawes.
   John. What 's that ?
   James. You saw the man — on Monday,
    was it ? —
There by the humpback'd willow; half
    stands up
And bristles, half has fallen and made a
    bridge;
And there he caught the younker tickling
    trout —
Caught *in flagrante* — what 's the Latin
    word ? —
Delicto ; but his house, for so they say,
Was haunted with a jolly ghost, that shook
The curtains, whined in lobbies, tapt at
    doors,
And rummaged like a rat; no servant
    stay'd.   30
The farmer vext packs up his beds and
    chairs,
And all his household stuff; and with his boy
Betwixt his knees, his wife upon the tilt,
Sets out, and meets a friend who hails him,
    ' What !
You 're flitting !' 'Yes, we 're flitting,'
    says the ghost —
For they had pack'd the thing among the
    beds.
'O, well,' says he, 'you flitting with us
    too ! —
Jack, turn the horses' heads and home
    again.'
   John. *He* left *his* wife behind; for so I
    heard.
   James. He left her, yes. I met my
    lady once;   40
A woman like a butt, and harsh as crabs.
   John. O, yet but I remember, ten years
    back —
'T is now at least ten years — and then she
    was —

You could not light upon a sweeter thing;
A body slight and round, and like a pear
In growing, modest eyes, a hand, a foot
Lessening in perfect cadence, and a skin
As clean and white as privet when it flow-
    ers.
   James. Ay, ay, the blossom fades, and
    they that loved
At first like dove and dove were cat and
    dog.   50
She was the daughter of a cottager,
Out of her sphere. What betwixt shame
    and pride,
New things and old, himself and her, she
    sour'd
To what she is; a nature never kind !
Like men, like manners; like breeds like,
    they say.
Kind nature is the best; those manners next
That fit us like a nature second-hand —
Which are indeed the manners of the great.
   John. But I had heard it was this bill
    that past,
And fear of change at home, that drove
    him hence.   60
   James. That was the last drop in the
    cup of gall.
I once was near him, when his bailiff
    brought
A Chartist pike. You should have seen him
    wince
As from a venomous thing; he thought
    himself
A mark for all, and shudder'd, lest a cry
Should break his sleep by night, and his
    nice eyes
Should see the raw mechanic's bloody
    thumbs
Sweat on his blazon'd chairs. But, sir, you
    know
That these two parties still divide the
    world —
Of those that want, and those that have;
    and still   70
The same old sore breaks out from age to
    age
With much the same result. Now I my-
    self,
A Tory to the quick, was as a boy
Destructive, when I had not what I would.
I was at school, — a college in the South.
There lived a flayflint near; we stole his
    fruit,
His hens, his eggs; but there was law for
    us :

We paid in person. He had a sow, sir.
She,
With meditative grunts of much content,
Lay great with pig, wallowing in sun and
mud.   80
By night we dragg'd her to the college
tower
From her warm bed, and up the corkscrew
stair
With hand and rope we haled the groaning
sow,
And on the leads we kept her till she
pigg'd.
Large range of prospect had the mother
sow,
And but for daily loss of one she loved
As one by one we took them — but for
this —
As never sow was higher in this world —
Might have been happy; but what lot is
pure ?
We took them all, till she was left alone 90
Upon her tower, the Niobe of swine,
And so return'd unfarrow'd to her sty.
    John. They found you out ?
    James.   Not they.
    John.   Well — after all —
What know we of the secret of a man ?
His nerves were wrong. What ails us who
are sound,
That we should mimic this raw fool the
world,
Which charts us all in its coarse blacks or
whites,
As ruthless as a baby with a worm,
As cruel as a schoolboy ere he grows 99
To pity — more from ignorance than will.
    But put your best foot forward, or I fear
That we shall miss the mail; and here it
comes
With five at top, as quaint a four-in-hand
As you shall see, — three pyebalds and a
roan.

EDWIN MORRIS

OR, THE LAKE

Written in 1839 during a visit to the Llan-
beris lakes in Wales. Printed in 1851.

O ME, my pleasant rambles by the lake,
My sweet, wild, fresh three quarters of a
year,
My one oasis in the dust and drouth

Of city life ! I was a sketcher then.
See here, my doing: curves of mountain,
bridge,
Boat, island, ruins of a castle, built
When men knew how to build, upon a
rock
With turrets lichen-gilded like a rock;
And here, new-comers in an ancient hold,
New-comers from the Mersey, million-
aires,   10
Here lived the Hills — a Tudor-chimney'd
bulk
Of mellow brickwork on an isle of bowers.
O me, my pleasant rambles by the lake
With Edwin Morris and with Edward Bull
The curate — he was fatter than his cure !
    But Edwin Morris, he that knew the
names,
Long learned names of agaric, moss, and
fern,
Who forged a thousand theories of the
rocks,
Who taught me how to skate, to row, to
swim,
Who read me rhymes elaborately good, 20
His own — I call'd him Crichton, for he
seem'd
All-perfect, finish'd to the finger-nail.
    And once I ask'd him of his early life,
And his first passion; and he answer'd me,
And well his words became him — was he
not
A full-cell'd honeycomb of eloquence
Stored from all flowers ? Poet-like he
spoke:
' My love for Nature is as old as I;
But thirty moons, one honeymoon to that,
And three rich sennights more, my love for
her.   30
My love for Nature and my love for her,
Of different ages, like twin-sisters grew,
Twin-sisters differently beautiful.
To some full music rose and sank the sun,
And some full music seem'd to move and
change
With all the varied changes of the dark,
And either twilight and the day between;
For daily hope fulfill'd, to rise again
Revolving toward fulfilment, made it sweet
To walk, to sit, to sleep, to wake, to
breathe.'   40
    Or this or something like to this he
spoke.
Then said the fat-faced curate Edward
Bull:

'I take it, God made the woman for the man,
And for the good and increase of the world.
A pretty face is well, and this is well,
To have a dame indoors, that trims us up,
And keeps us tight; but these unreal ways
Seem but the theme of writers, and indeed
Worn threadbare. Man is made of solid stuff.
I say, God made the woman for the man, 50
And for the good and increase of the world.'
    'Parson,' said I, 'you pitch the pipe too low.
But I have sudden touches, and can run
My faith beyond my practice into his;
Tho' if, in dancing after Letty Hill,
I do not hear the bells upon my cap,
I scarce have other music — yet say on.
What should one give to light on such a dream ?'
I ask'd him half-sardonically.
                        'Give ?   59
Give all thou art,' he answer'd, and a light
Of laughter dimpled in his swarthy cheek;
'I would have hid her needle in my heart,
To save her little finger from a scratch
No deeper than the skin; my ears could hear
Her lightest breath ; her least remark was worth
The experience of the wise. I went and came;
Her voice fled always thro' the summer land;
I spoke her name alone. Thrice-happy days !
The flower of each, those moments when we met, 69
The crown of all, we met to part no more.'
Were not his words delicious, I a beast
To take them as I did ? but something jarr'd;
Whether he spoke too largely, that there seem'd
A touch of something false, some self-conceit,
Or over-smoothness; howsoe'er it was,
He scarcely hit my humor, and I said:
    'Friend Edwin, do not think yourself alone
Of all men happy. Shall not Love to me,
As in the Latin song I learnt at school,
Sneeze out a full God-bless-you right and left ?   80

But you can talk, yours is a kindly vein;
I have, I think, — Heaven knows, — as much within;
Have, or should have, but for a thought or two,
That like a purple beech among the greens
Looks out of place. 'T is from no want in her;
It is my shyness, or my self-distrust,
Or something of a wayward modern mind
Dissecting passion. Time will set me right.'
    So spoke I, knowing not the things that were.
Then said the fat-faced curate, Edward Bull: 90
    'God made the woman for the use of man,
And for the good and increase of the world.'
And I and Edwin laughed; and now we paused
About the windings of the marge to hear
The soft wind blowing over meadowy holms
And alders, garden-isles; and now we left
The clerk behind us, I and he, and ran
By ripply shallows of the lisping lake,
Delighted with the freshness and the sound.
    But when the bracken rusted on their crags,   100
My suit had wither'd, nipt to death by him
That was a god, and is a lawyer's clerk,
The rent-roll Cupid of our rainy isles.
'T is true, we met; one hour I had, no more:
She sent a note, the seal an *Elle vous suit*,
The close, 'Your Letty, only yours;' and this
Thrice underscored. The friendly mist of morn
Clung to the lake. I boated over, ran
My craft aground, and heard with beating heart
The sweet-gale rustle round the shelving keel;   110
And out I stept, and up I crept. She moved,
Like Proserpine in Enna, gathering flowers.
Then low and sweet I whistled thrice; and she,
She turn'd, we closed, we kiss'd, swore faith, I breathed
In some new planet. A silent cousin stole
Upon us and departed. 'Leave,' she cried,

'O, leave me!' 'Never, dearest, never:
here
I brave the worst;' and while we stood like
fools
Embracing, all at once a score of pugs
And poodles yell'd within, and out they
came,   120
Trustees and aunts and uncles. 'What,
with him!
Go,' shrill'd the cotton - spinning chorus;
'him!'
I choked. Again they shriek'd the burthen,
'Him!'
Again with hands of wild rejection, 'Go!—
Girl, get you in!' She went—and in one
month
They wedded her to sixty thousand pounds,
To lands in Kent and messuages in York,
And slight Sir Robert with his watery
smile
And educated whisker. But for me,
They set an ancient creditor to work;   130
It seems I broke a close with force and
arms:
There came a mystic token from the king
To greet the sheriff, needless courtesy!
I read, and fled by night, and flying turn'd;
Her taper glimmer'd in the lake below;
I turn'd once more, close-button'd to the
storm;
So left the place, left Edwin, nor have seen
Him since, nor heard of her, nor cared to
hear.
    Nor cared to hear? perhaps; yet long
ago
I have pardon'd little Letty; not indeed, 140
It may be, for her own dear sake, but
this,—
She seems a part of those fresh days to me;
For in the dust and drouth of London life
She moves among my visions of the lake,
While the prime swallow dips his wing, or
then
While the gold-lily blows, and overhead
The light cloud smoulders on the summer
crag.

SAINT SIMEON STYLITES

First printed in 1842. In line 201 'brother'
was originally 'mother.'

ALTHO' I be the basest of mankind,
From scalp to sole one slough and crust of
sin,

Unfit for earth, unfit for heaven, scarce
meet
For troops of devils, mad with blasphemy,
I will not cease to grasp the hope I hold
Of saintdom, and to clamor, mourn, and
sob,
Battering the gates of heaven with storms
of prayer,
Have mercy, Lord, and take away my sin!
    Let this avail, just, dreadful, mighty
God,
This not be all in vain, that thrice ten
years,   10
Thrice multiplied by superhuman pangs,
In hungers and in thirsts, fevers and cold,
In coughs, aches, stitches, ulcerous throes
and cramps,
A sign betwixt the meadow and the cloud,
Patient on this tall pillar I have borne
Rain, wind, frost, heat, hail, damp, and
sleet, and snow;
And I had hoped that ere this period closed
Thou wouldst have caught me up into thy
rest,
Denying not these weather-beaten limbs
The meed of saints, the white robe and the
palm.   20
    O, take the meaning, Lord! I do not
breathe,
Not whisper, any murmur of complaint.
Pain heap'd ten-hundred-fold to this, were
still
Less burthen, by ten-hundred-fold, to bear,
Than were those lead-like tons of sin that
crush'd
My spirit flat before thee.
                              O Lord, Lord,
Thou knowest I bore this better at the
first,
For I was strong and hale of body then;
And tho' my teeth, which now are dropt
away,
Would chatter with the cold, and all my
beard   30
Was tagg'd with icy fringes in the moon,
I drown'd the whoopings of the owl with
sound
Of pious hymns and psalms, and sometimes
saw
An angel stand and watch me, as I sang.
Now am I feeble grown; my end draws
nigh.
I hope my end draws nigh; half deaf I am,
So that I scarce can hear the people hum
About the column's base, and almost blind,

And scarce can recognize the fields I know;
And both my thighs are rotted with the
dew; 40
Yet cease I not to clamor and to cry,
While my stiff spine can hold my weary
head,
Till all my limbs drop piecemeal from the
stone,
Have mercy, mercy ! take away my sin !
O Jesus, if thou wilt not save my soul,
Who may be saved ? who is it may be
saved ?
Who may be made a saint if I fail here ?
Show me the man hath suffer'd more than I.
For did not all thy martyrs die one death ?
For either they were stoned, or crucified, 50
Or burn'd in fire, or boil'd in oil, or sawn
In twain beneath the ribs; but I die here
To-day, and whole years long, a life of
death.
Bear witness, if I could have found a way —
And heedfully I sifted all my thought —
More slowly-painful to subdue this home
Of sin, my flesh, which I despise and hate,
I had not stinted practice, O my God !
For not alone this pillar-punishment,
Not this alone I bore; but while I lived 60
In the white convent down the valley there,
For many weeks about my loins I wore
The rope that haled the buckets from the
well,
Twisted as tight as I could knot the noose,
And spake not of it to a single soul,
Until the ulcer, eating thro' my skin,
Betray'd my secret penance, so that all
My brethren marvell'd greatly. More than
this
I bore, whereof, O God, thou knowest all.
Three winters, that my soul might grow
to thee, 70
I lived up there on yonder mountain-side.
My right leg chain'd into the crag, I lay
Pent in a roofless close of ragged stones;
Inswathed sometimes in wandering mist,
and twice
Black'd with thy branding thunder, and
sometimes
Sucking the damps for drink, and eating
not,
Except the spare chance-gift of those that
came
To touch my body and be heal'd, and live.
And they say then that I work'd miracles,
Whereof my fame is loud amongst man-
kind, 80

Cured lameness, palsies, cancers. Thou,
O God,
Knowest alone whether this was or no.
Have mercy, mercy ! cover all my sin !
Then, that I might be more alone with
thee,
Three years I lived upon a pillar, high
Six cubits, and three years on one of
twelve;
And twice three years I crouch'd on one
that rose
Twenty by measure; last of all, I grew
Twice ten long weary, weary years to this,
That numbers forty cubits from the soil. 90
I think that I have borne as much as
this —
Or else I dream — and for so long a time,
If I may measure time by yon slow light,
And this high dial, which my sorrow
crowns —
So much — even so.
And yet I know not well,
For that the evil ones come here, and say,
'Fall down, O Simeon; thou hast suffer'd
long
For ages and for ages !' then they prate
Of penances I cannot have gone thro',
Perplexing me with lies; and oft I fall, 100
Maybe for months, in such blind lethargies
That Heaven, and Earth, and Time are
choked.
But yet
Bethink thee, Lord, while thou and all the
saints
Enjoy themselves in heaven, and men on
earth
House in the shade of comfortable roofs,
Sit with their wives by fires, eat wholesome
food,
And wear warm clothes, and even beasts
have stalls,
I, 'tween the spring and downfall of the
light,
Bow down one thousand and two hundred
times,
To Christ, the Virgin Mother, and the
saints; 110
Or in the night, after a little sleep,
I wake; the chill stars sparkle; I am wet
With drenching dews, or stiff with crack-
ling frost.
I wear an undress'd goatskin on my back;
A grazing iron collar grinds my neck;
And in my weak, lean arms I lift the
cross,

And strive and wrestle with thee till I die.
O, mercy, mercy ! wash away my sin ! 118
  O Lord, thou knowest what a man I am;
A sinful man, conceived and born in sin.
'T is their own doing; this is none of mine;
Lay it not to me. Am I to blame for this,
That here come those that worship me ?
  Ha ! ha !
They think that I am somewhat. What
  am I ?
The silly people take me for a saint,
And bring me offerings of fruit and flow-
  ers;
And I, in truth — thou wilt bear witness
  here —
Have all in all endured as much, and
  more
Than many just and holy men, whose
  names
Are register'd and calendar'd for saints. 130
  Good people, you do ill to kneel to me.
What is it I can have done to merit this ?
I am a sinner viler than you all.
It may be I have wrought some miracles,
And cured some halt and maim'd; but what
  of that ?
It may be no one, even among the saints,
May match his pains with mine; but what
  of that ?
Yet do not rise; for you may look on me,
And in your looking you may kneel to
  God. 139
Speak! is there any of you halt or maim'd ?
I think you know I have some power with
  Heaven
From my long penance; let him speak his
  wish.
  Yes, I can heal him. Power goes forth
    from me.
They say that they are heal'd. Ah, hark !
  they shout
'Saint Simeon Stylites.' Why, if so,
God reaps a harvest in me. O my soul,
God reaps a harvest in thee! If this be,
Can I work miracles and not be saved ?
This is not told of any. They were saints.
It cannot be but that I shall be saved, 150
Yea, crown'd a saint. They shout, ' Behold
  a saint ! '
And lower voices saint me from above.
Courage, Saint Simeon ! This dull chrysalis
Cracks into shining wings, and hope ere
  death
Spreads more and more and more, that
  God hath now

Sponged and made blank of crimeful record
  all
My mortal archives.
                        O my sons, my sons,
I, Simeon of the pillar, by surname
Stylites, among men; I, Simeon,   159
The watcher on the column till the end;
I, Simeon, whose brain the sunshine bakes;
I, whose bald brows in silent hours become
Unnaturally hoar with rime, do now
From my high nest of penance here pro-
  claim
That Pontius and Iscariot by my side
Show'd like fair seraphs. On the coals I
  lay,
A vessel full of sin; all hell beneath
Made me boil over. Devils pluck'd my
  sleeve,
Abaddon and Asmodeus caught at me.
I smote them with the cross; they swarm'd
  again.   170
In bed like monstrous apes they crush'd
  my chest;
They flapp'd my light out as I read; I saw
Their faces grow between me and my
  book;
With coltlike whinny and with hoggish
  whine
They burst my prayer. Yet this way was
  left,
And by this way I 'scaped them. Mortify
Your flesh, like me, with scourges and with
  thorns;
Smite, shrink not, spare not. If it may
  be, fast
Whole Lents, and pray. I hardly, with
  slow steps,
With slow, faint steps, and much exceed-
  ing pain,   180
Have scrambled past those pits of fire,
  that still
Sing in mine ears. But yield not me the
  praise;
God only thro' his bounty hath thought fit,
Among the powers and princes of this
  world,
To make me an example to mankind,
Which few can reach to. Yet I do not say
But that a time may come — yea, even
  now,
Now, now, his footsteps smite the thresh-
  old stairs
Of life — I say, that time is at the doors
When you may worship me without re-
  proach;   190

For I will leave my relics in your land,
And you may carve a shrine about my dust,
And burn a fragrant lamp before my
    bones,
When I am gather'd to the glorious saints.
    While I spake then, a sting of shrewdest
        pain
Ran shrivelling thro' me, and a cloudlike
    change,
In passing, with a grosser film made thick
These heavy, horny eyes. The end! the end!
Surely the end! What 's here ? a shape,
    a shade,
A flash of light. Is that the angel there
That holds a crown ? Come, blessed bro-
    ther, come!   201
I know thy glittering face. I waited long;
My brows are ready. What ! deny it now ?
Nay, draw, draw, draw nigh. So I clutch
    it. Christ!
'T is gone; 't is here again; the crown !
    the crown !
So now 't is fitted on and grows to me,
And from it melt the dews of Paradise,
Sweet! sweet ! spikenard, and balm, and
    frankincense.
Ah ! let me not be fool'd, sweet saints; I
    trust
That I am whole, and clean, and meet for
    Heaven.   210
    Speak, if there be a priest, a man of
        God,
Among you there, and let him presently
Approach, and lean a ladder on the shaft,
And climbing up into my airy home,
Deliver me the blessed sacrament;
For by the warning of the Holy Ghost,
I prophesy that I shall die to-night,
A quarter before twelve.
                    But thou, O Lord,
Aid all this foolish people; let them take
Example, pattern; lead them to thy light.

THE TALKING OAK

'An experiment meant to test the degree in
which it is within the power of poetry to human-
ize external nature' (Tennyson to Aubrey de
Vere).

ONCE more the gate behind me falls;
    Once more before my face
I see the moulder'd Abbey-walls,
    That stand within the chace.

Beyond the lodge the city lies,
    Beneath its drift of smoke;
And ah ! with what delighted eyes
    I turn to yonder oak.

For when my passion first began,
    Ere that which in me burn'd,   10
The love that makes me thrice a man,
    Could hope itself return'd,

To yonder oak within the field
    I spoke without restraint,
And with a larger faith appeal'd
    Than Papist unto Saint.

For oft I talk'd with him apart,
    And told him of my choice,
Until he plagiarized a heart,
    And answer'd with a voice.   20

Tho' what he whisper'd under heaven
    None else could understand,
I found him garrulously given,
    A babbler in the land.

But since I heard him make reply
    Is many a weary hour;
'T were well to question him, and try
    If yet he keeps the power.

Hail, hidden to the knees in fern,
    Broad Oak of Sumner-chace,   30
Whose topmost branches can discern
    The roofs of Sumner-place!

Say thou, whereon I carved her name,
    If ever maid or spouse,
As fair as my Olivia, came
    To rest beneath thy boughs.

'O Walter, I have shelter'd here
    Whatever maiden grace
The good old summers, year by year,
    Made ripe in Sumner-chace;   40

'Old summers, when the monk was fat,
    And, issuing shorn and sleek,
Would twist his girdle tight, and pat
    The girls upon the cheek,

'Ere yet, in scorn of Peter's-pence,
    And number'd bead, and shrift,
Bluff Harry broke into the spence
    And turn'd the cowls adrift.

'And I have seen some score of those
  Fresh faces that would thrive   50
When his man-minded offset rose
  To chase the deer at five;

'And all that from the town would stroll,
  Till that wild wind made work
In which the gloomy brewer's soul
  Went by me, like a stork;

'The slight she-slips of loyal blood,
  And others, passing praise,
Strait-laced, but all-too-full in bud
  For puritanic stays.   60

'And I have shadow'd many a group
  Of beauties that were born
In teacup-times of hood and hoop,
  Or while the patch was worn;

'And, leg and arm with love-knots gay,
  About me leap'd and laugh'd
The modish Cupid of the day,
  And shrill'd his tinsel shaft.

'I swear — and else may insects prick
  Each leaf into a gall ! —   70
This girl, for whom your heart is sick,
  Is three times worth them all;

'For those and theirs, by Nature's law,
  Have faded long ago;
But in these latter springs I saw
  Your own Olivia blow,

'From when she gamboll'd on the greens
  A baby-germ, to when
The maiden blossoms of her teens
  Could number five from ten.   80

'I swear, by leaf, and wind, and rain —
  And hear me with thine ears —
That, tho' I circle in the grain
  Five hundred rings of years,

Yet, since I first could cast a shade,
  Did never creature pass
So slightly, musically made,
  So light upon the grass;

'For as to fairies, that will flit
  To make the greensward fresh,   90
I hold them exquisitely knit,
  But far too spare of flesh.'

O, hide thy knotted knees in fern,
  And overlook the chace,
And from thy topmost branch discern
  The roofs of Sumner-place !

But thou, whereon I carved her name,
  That oft hast heard my vows,
Declare when last Olivia came
  To sport beneath thy boughs.   100

'O, yesterday, you know, the fair
  Was holden at the town;
Her father left his good arm-chair,
  And rode his hunter down.

'And with him Albert came on his.
  I look'd at him with joy;
As cowslip unto oxlip is,
  So seems she to the boy.

'An hour had past — and, sitting straight
  Within the low-wheel'd chaise,   110
Her mother trundled to the gate
  Behind the dappled grays.

'But as for her, she staid at home,
  And on the roof she went,
And down the way you used to come,
  She look'd with discontent.

'She left the novel half-uncut
  Upon the rosewood shelf;
She left the new piano shut;
  She could not please herself.   120

'Then ran she, gamesome as the colt,
  And livelier than a lark
She sent her voice thro' all the holt
  Before her, and the park.

'A light wind chased her on the wing,
  And in the chase grew wild,
As close as might be would he cling
  About the darling child;

'But light as any wind that blows
  So fleetly did she stir,   130
The flower she touch'd on dipt and rose,
  And turn'd to look at her.

'And here she came, and round me play'd,
  And sang to me the whole
Of those three stanzas that you made
  About my " giant bole; "

' And in a fit of frolic mirth
  She strove to span my waist.
Alas ! I was so broad of girth,
  I could not be embraced.   140

' I wish'd myself the fair young beech
  That here beside me stands,
That round me, clasping each in each,
  She might have lock'd her hands.

' Yet seem'd the pressure thrice as sweet
  As woodbine's fragile hold,
Or when I feel about my feet
  The berried briony fold.'

O, muffle round thy knees with fern,
  And shadow Sumner-chace !   150
Long may thy topmost branch discern
  The roofs of Sumner-place !

But tell me, did she read the name
  I carved with many vows
When last with throbbing heart I came
  To rest beneath thy boughs ?

' O, yes, she wander'd round and round
  These knotted knees of mine,
And found, and kiss'd the name she found,
  And sweetly murmur'd thine.   160

' A teardrop trembled from its source,
  And down my surface crept.
My sense of touch is something coarse,
  But I believe she wept.

' Then flush'd her cheek with rosy light,
  She glanced across the plain,
But not a creature was in sight;
  She kiss'd me once again.

' Her kisses were so close and kind
  That, trust me on my word,   170
Hard wood I am, and wrinkled rind,
  But yet my sap was stirr'd;

' And even into my inmost ring
  A pleasure I discern'd,
Like those blind motions of the spring
  That show the year is turn'd.

' Thrice-happy he that may caress
  The ringlet's waving balm —
The cushions of whose touch may press
  The maiden's tender palm.   180

' I, rooted here among the groves,
  But languidly adjust
My vapid vegetable loves
  With anthers and with dust;

' For ah ! my friend, the days were brief
  Whereof the poets talk,
When that which breathes within the leaf
  Could slip its bark and walk.

' But could I, as in times foregone,
  From spray and branch and stem   190
Have suck'd and gather'd into one
  The life that spreads in them,

' She had not found me so remiss;
  But lightly issuing thro',
I would have paid her kiss for kiss,
  With usury thereto.'

O, flourish high, with leafy towers,
  And overlook the lea !
Pursue thy loves among the bowers,
  But leave thou mine to me.   200

O, flourish, hidden deep in fern,
  Old oak, I love thee well !
A thousand thanks for what I learn
  And what remains to tell.

' 'T is little more: the day was warm;
  At last, tired out with play,
She sank her head upon her arm
  And at my feet she lay.

' Her eyelids dropp'd their silken eaves.
  I breathed upon her eyes   210
Thro' all the summer of my leaves
  A welcome mix'd with sighs.

' I took the swarming sound of life —
  The music from the town —
The murmurs of the drum and fife
  And lull'd them in my own.

' Sometimes I let a sunbeam slip,
  To light her shaded eye;
A second flutter'd round her lip
  Like a golden butterfly;   220

' A third would glimmer on her neck
  To make the necklace shine;
Another slid, a sunny fleck,
  From head to ankle fine.

'Then close and dark my arms I spread,
  And shadow'd all her rest —
Dropt dews upon her golden head,
  An acorn in her breast.

'But in a pet she started up,
  And pluck'd it out, and drew   230
My little oakling from the cup,
  And flung him in the dew.

'And yet it was a graceful gift —
  I felt a pang within
As when I see the woodman lift
  His axe to slay my kin.

'I shook him down because he was
  The finest on the tree.
He lies beside thee on the grass.
  O, kiss him once for me !   240

'O, kiss him twice and thrice for me,
  That have no lips to kiss !
For never yet was oak on lea
  Shall grow so fair as this.'

Step deeper yet in herb and fern,
  Look further thro' the chace,
Spread upward till thy boughs discern
  The front of Sumner-place.

This fruit of thine by Love is blest,
  That but a moment lay   250
Where fairer fruit of Love may rest
  Some happy future day.

I kiss it twice, I kiss it thrice,
  The warmth it thence shall win
To riper life may magnetize
  The baby-oak within.

But thou, while kingdoms overset,
  Or lapse from hand to hand,
Thy leaf shall never fail, nor yet
  Thine acorn in the land.   260

May never saw dismember thee,
  Nor wielded axe disjoint,
That art the fairest-spoken tree
  From here to Lizard-point.

O, rock upon thy towery top
  All throats that gurgle sweet !
All starry culmination drop
  Balm-dews to bathe thy feet !

All grass of silky feather grow —
  And while he sinks or swells   270
The full south-breeze around thee blow
  The sound of minster bells !

The fat earth feed thy branchy root,
  That under deeply strikes !
The northern morning o'er thee shoot,
  High up, in silver spikes !

Nor ever lightning char thy grain,
  But, rolling as in sleep,
Low thunders bring the mellow rain,
  That makes thee broad and deep !   280

And hear me swear a solemn oath,
  That only by thy side
Will I to Olive plight my troth,
  And gain her for my bride.

And when my marriage morn may fall,
  She, Dryad-like, shall wear
Alternate leaf and acorn-ball
  In wreath about her hair.

And I will work in prose and rhyme,
  And praise thee more in both   290
Than bard has honor'd beech or lime,
  Or that Thessalian growth

In which the swarthy ringdove sat,
  And mystic sentence spoke;
And more than England honors that,
  Thy famous brother-oak,

Wherein the younger Charles abode
  Till all the paths were dim,
And far below the Roundhead rode,
  And humm'd a surly hymn.   300

LOVE AND DUTY

First printed in 1842, and afterwards altered
but slightly. See Notes.

OF love that never found his earthly close,
What sequel ?   Streaming eyes and break-
      ing hearts ?
Or all the same as if he had not been ?
  Not so.   Shall Error in the round of
      time
Still father Truth ? O, shall the braggart
  shout

For some blind glimpse of freedom work
    itself
Thro' madness, hated by the wise, to law,
System, and empire ?   Sin itself be found
The cloudy porch oft opening on the sun ?
And only he, this wonder, dead, become   10
Mere highway dust ? or year by year alone
Sit brooding in the ruins of a life,
Nightmare of youth, the spectre of him-
    self ?
  If this were thus, if this, indeed, were
    all,
Better the narrow brain, the stony heart,
The staring eye glazed o'er with sapless
    days,
The long mechanic pacings to and fro,
The set gray life, and apathetic end.
But am I not the nobler thro' thy love ?
O, three times less unworthy ! likewise
    thou   20
Art more thro' Love, and greater than thy
    years,
The sun will run his orbit, and the moon
Her circle.   Wait, and Love himself will
    bring
The drooping flower of knowledge changed
    to fruit
Of wisdom.   Wait; my faith is large in
    Time,
And that which shapes it to some perfect
    end.
  Will some one say, Then why not ill for
    good ?
Why took ye not your pastime ?   To that
    man
My work shall answer, since I knew the
    right
And did it; for a man is not as God,   30
But then most Godlike being most a
    man. —
So let me think 't is well for thee and
    me —
Ill-fated that I am, what lot is mine
Whose foresight preaches peace, my heart
    so slow
To feel it !   For how hard it seem'd to
    me,
When eyes, love-languid thro' half tears
    would dwell
One earnest, earnest moment upon mine,
Then not to dare to see ! when thy low
    voice,
Faltering, would break its syllables, to keep
My own full-tuned, — hold passion in a
    leash,   40

And not leap forth and fall about thy neck,
And on thy bosom — deep desired relief ! —
Rain out the heavy mist of tears, that
    weigh'd
Upon my brain, my senses, and my soul !
  For Love himself took part against him-
    self
To warn us off, and Duty loved of Love —
O, this world's curse — beloved but hated
    — came
Like Death betwixt thy dear embrace and
    mine,
And crying, ' Who is this ?   behold thy
    bride,'   49
She push'd me from thee.
                     If the sense is hard
To alien ears, I did not speak to these —
No, not to thee, but to thyself in me.
Hard is my doom and thine; thou knowest
    it all.
  Could Love part thus ? was it not well to
    speak,
To have spoken once ?   It could not but
    be well.
The slow sweet hours that bring us all
    things good,
The slow sad hours that bring us all things
    ill,
And all good things from evil, brought the
    night
In which we sat together and alone,
And to the want that hollow'd all the
    heart   60
Gave utterance by the yearning of an eye,
That burn'd upon its object thro' such tears
As flow but once a life.
                     The trance gave way
To those caresses, when a hundred times
In that last kiss, which never was the last,
Farewell, like endless welcome, lived and
    died.
Then follow'd counsel, comfort, and the
    words
That make a man feel strong in speaking
    truth;
Till now the dark was worn, and over-
    head
The lights of sunset and of sunrise mix'd
In that brief night, the summer night, that
    paused   71
Among her stars to hear us, stars that hung
Love-charm'd to listen; all the wheels of
    Time
Spun round in station, but the end had
    come.

O, then, like those who clench their
   nerves to rush
Upon their dissolution, we two rose,
There — closing like an individual life —
In one blind cry of passion and of pain,
Like bitter accusation even to death,
Caught up the whole of love and utter'd
   it,   80
And bade adieu for ever.
                Live — yet live —
Shall sharpest pathos blight us, knowing
   all
Life needs for life is possible to will ? —
Live happy; tend thy flowers; be tended by
My blessing! Should my Shadow cross
   thy thoughts
Too sadly for their peace, remand it thou
For calmer hours to Memory's darkest
   hold,
If not to be forgotten — not at once —
Not all forgotten. Should it cross thy
   dreams,
O, might it come like one that looks con-
   tent,   90
With quiet eyes unfaithful to the truth,
And point thee forward to a distant light,
Or seem to lift a burthen from thy heart
And leave thee freer, till thou wake re-
   fresh'd
Then when the first low matin-chirp hath
   grown
Full quire, and morning driven her plow
   of pearl
Far furrowing into light the mounded
   rack,
Beyond the fair green field and eastern sea.

THE GOLDEN YEAR

First printed in 1846, in the fourth edition
of the 'Poems,' and unaltered except in one
passage. See Notes.

WELL, you shall have that song which
   Leonard wrote:
It was last summer on a tour in Wales.
Old James was with me; we that day had
   been
Up Snowdon; and I wish'd for Leonard
   there,
And found him in Llanberis. Then we
   crost
Between the lakes, and clamber'd half-way
   up

The counter side; and that same song of
   his
He told me, for I banter'd him and swore
They said he lived shut up within himself,
A tongue-tied poet in the feverous days   10
That, setting the *how much* before the *how*,
Cry, like the daughters of the horseleech,
   'Give,
Cram us with all,' but count not me the
   herd !
To which 'They call me what they will,'
   he said:
'But I was born too late; the fair new
   forms,
That float about the threshold of an age,
Like truths of Science waiting to be
   caught —
Catch me who can, and make the catcher
   crown'd —
Are taken by the forelock. Let it be.
But if you care indeed to listen, hear   20
These measured words, my work of yester-
   morn:
  'We sleep and wake and sleep, but all
   things move;
The sun flies forward to his brother sun;
The dark earth follows wheel'd in her
   ellipse;
And human things returning on themselves
Move onward, leading up the golden year.
  'Ah! tho' the times when some new
   thought can bud
Are but as poets' seasons when they flower,
Yet seas that daily gain upon the shore
Have ebb and flow conditioning their
   march,   30
And slow and sure comes up the golden
   year;
  'When wealth no more shall rest in
   mounded heaps,
But smit with freer light shall slowly melt
In many streams to fatten lower lands,
And light shall spread, and man be liker
   man
Thro' all the season of the golden year.
  'Shall eagles not be eagles? wrens be
   wrens ?
If all the world were falcons, what of that ?
The wonder of the eagle were the less,
But he not less the eagle. Happy days   40
Roll onward, leading up the golden year.
  'Fly, happy, happy sails, and bear the
   Press;
Fly happy with the mission of the Cross;
Knit land to land, and blowing havenward

With silks, and fruits, and spices, clear of
 toll,
Enrich the markets of the golden year.
 ' But we grow old. Ah ! when shall all
 men's good
Be each man's rule, and universal Peace
Lie like a shaft of light across the land, 49
And like a lane of beams athwart the sea,
Thro' all the circle of the golden year ? '
 Thus far he flow'd, and ended; where-
 upon
' Ah, folly ! ' in mimic cadence answer'd
 James —
' Ah, folly ! for it lies so far away,
Not in our time, nor in our children's time,
'T is like the second world to us that live;
'T were all as one to fix our hopes on
 heaven
As on this vision of the golden year.'
 With that he struck his staff against the
 rocks
And broke it, — James, — you know him,
 — old, but full 60
Of force and choler, and firm upon his feet,
And like an oaken stock in winter woods,
O'erflourish'd with the hoary clematis;
Then added, all in heat:
    ' What stuff is this !
Old writers push'd the happy season back, —
The more fools they, — we forward; dream-
 ers both —
You most, that, in an age when every hour
Must sweat her sixty minutes to the death,
Live on, God love us, as if the seedsman,
 rapt
Upon the teeming harvest, should not
 plunge 70
His hand into the bag; but well I know
That unto him who works, and feels he
 works,
This same grand year is ever at the doors.'
 He spoke; and, high above, I heard them
 blast
The steep slate-quarry, and the great echo
 flap
And buffet round the hills, from bluff to
 bluff.

ULYSSES

First printed in 1842, and unaltered.

It little profits that an idle king,
By this still hearth, among these barren
 crags,

Match'd with an aged wife, I mete and
 dole
Unequal laws unto a savage race,
That hoard, and sleep, and feed, and know
 not me.
I cannot rest from travel; I will drink
Life to the lees. All times I have enjoy'd
Greatly, have suffer'd greatly, both with
 those
That loved me, and alone; on shore, and
 when
Thro' scudding drifts the rainy Hyades 10
Vext the dim sea. I am become a name;
For always roaming with a hungry heart
Much have I seen and known, — cities of
 men
And manners, climates, councils, govern-
 ments,
Myself not least, but honor'd of them
 all, —
And drunk delight of battle with my
 peers,
Far on the ringing plains of windy Troy.
I am a part of all that I have met;
Yet all experience is an arch wherethro'
Gleams that untravell'd world whose mar-
 gin fades 20
For ever and for ever when I move.
How dull it is to pause, to make an end,
To rust unburnish'd, not to shine in use !
As tho' to breathe were life ! Life piled
 on life
Were all too little, and of one to me
Little remains; but every hour is saved
From that eternal silence, something more,
A bringer of new things; and vile it were
For some three suns to store and hoard
 myself,
And this gray spirit yearning in desire 30
To follow knowledge like a sinking star,
Beyond the utmost bound of human
 thought.
 This is my son, mine own Telemachus,
To whom I leave the sceptre and the
 isle, —
Well-loved of me, discerning to fulfil
This labor, by slow prudence to make mild
A rugged people, and thro' soft degrees
Subdue them to the useful and the good.
Most blameless is he, centred in the sphere
Of common duties, decent not to fail 40
In offices of tenderness, and pay
Meet adoration to my household gods,
When I am gone. He works his work, I
 mine.

There lies the port; the vessel puffs her sail;
There gloom the dark, broad seas. My mariners,
Souls that have toil'd, and wrought, and thought with me, —
That ever with a frolic welcome took
The thunder and the sunshine, and opposed
Free hearts, free foreheads, — you and I are old;
Old age hath yet his honor and his toil. 50
Death closes all; but something ere the end,
Some work of noble note, may yet be done,
Not unbecoming men that strove with Gods.
The lights begin to twinkle from the rocks;
The long day wanes; the slow moon climbs; the deep
Moans round with many voices. Come, my friends.
'T is not too late to seek a newer world.
Push off, and sitting well in order smite
The sounding furrows; for my purpose holds
To sail beyond the sunset, and the baths 60
Of all the western stars, until I die.
It may be that the gulfs will wash us down;
It may be we shall touch the Happy Isles,
And see the great Achilles, whom we knew.
Tho' much is taken, much abides; and tho'
We are not now that strength which in old days
Moved earth and heaven, that which we are, we are, —
One equal temper of heroic hearts,
Made weak by time and fate, but strong in will
To . strive, to seek, to find, and not to yield. 70

TITHONUS

First printed in the 'Cornhill Magazine' for February, 1860, and afterwards included in the 'Enoch Arden' volume in 1864. See Notes.

THE woods decay, the woods decay and fall,
The vapors weep their burthen to the ground,

Man comes and tills the field and lies beneath,
And after many a summer dies the swan.
Me only cruel immortality
Consumes; I wither slowly in thine arms,
Here at the quiet limit of the world,
A white-hair'd shadow roaming like a dream
The ever-silent spaces of the East,
Far-folded mists, and gleaming halls of morn. 10
Alas! for this gray shadow, once a man —
So glorious in his beauty and thy choice,
Who madest him thy chosen, that he seem'd
To his great heart none other than a God!
I ask'd thee, 'Give me immortality.'
Then didst thou grant mine asking with a smile,
Like wealthy men who care not how they give.
But thy strong Hours indignant work'd their wills,
And beat me down and marr'd and wasted me,
And tho' they could not end me, left me maim'd 20
To dwell in presence of immortal youth,
Immortal age beside immortal youth,
And all I was in ashes. Can thy love,
Thy beauty, make amends, tho' even now,
Close over us, the silver star, thy guide,
Shines in those tremulous eyes that fill with tears
To hear me? Let me go; take back thy gift.
Why should a man desire in any way
To vary from the kindly race of men,
Or pass beyond the goal of ordinance 30
Where all should pause, as is most meet for all?
A soft air fans the cloud apart; there comes
A glimpse of that dark world where I was born.
Once more the old mysterious glimmer steals
From thy pure brows, and from thy shoulders pure,
And bosom beating with a heart renew'd.
Thy cheek begins to redden thro' the gloom,
Thy sweet eyes brighten slowly close to mine,

Ere yet they blind the stars, and the wild
   team
Which love thee, yearning for thy yoke,
   arise,   40
And shake the darkness from their loosen'd
   manes,
And beat the twilight into flakes of fire.
  Lo! ever thus thou growest beautiful
In silence, then before thine answer given
Departest, and thy tears are on my cheek.
  Why wilt thou ever scare me with thy
   tears,
And make me tremble lest a saying learnt,
In days far-off, on that dark earth, be true?
'The Gods themselves cannot recall their
   gifts.'
  Ay me! ay me! with what another
   heart   50
In days far-off, and with what other eyes
I used to watch — if I be he that watch'd —
The lucid outline forming round thee; saw
The dim curls kindle into sunny rings;
Changed with thy mystic change, and felt
   my blood
Glow with the glow that slowly crimson'd
   all
Thy presence and thy portals, while I lay,
Mouth, forehead, eyelids, growing dewy-
   warm
With kisses balmier than half-opening buds
Of April, and could hear the lips that
   kiss'd   60
Whispering I knew not what of wild and
   sweet,
Like that strange song I heard Apollo
   sing,
While Ilion like a mist rose into towers.
  Yet hold me not for ever in thine East;
How can my nature longer mix with thine?
Coldly thy rosy shadows bathe me, cold
Are all thy lights, and cold my wrinkled
   feet
Upon thy glimmering thresholds, when the
   steam
Floats up from those dim fields about the
   homes
Of happy men that have the power to
   die,   70
And grassy barrows of the happier dead.
Release me, and restore me to the ground.
Thou seest all things, thou wilt see my
   grave;
Thou wilt renew thy beauty morn by morn,
I earth in earth forget these empty courts,
And thee returning on thy silver wheels.

LOCKSLEY HALL

First printed in 1842, and slightly altered in
subsequent editions. See Notes.

COMRADES, leave me here a little, while as
   yet 't is early morn;
Leave me here, and when you want me,
   sound upon the bugle-horn.

'T is the place, and all around it, as of old,
   the curlews call,
Dreary gleams about the moorland flying
   over Locksley Hall;

Locksley Hall, that in the distance over-
   looks the sandy tracts,
And the hollow ocean-ridges roaring into
   cataracts.

Many a night from yonder ivied casement,
   ere I went to rest,
Did I look on great Orion sloping slowly
   to the west.

Many a night I saw the Pleiads, rising
   thro' the mellow shade,
Glitter like a swarm of fireflies tangled in
   a silver braid.   10

Here about the beach I wander'd, nour-
   ishing a youth sublime
With the fairy tales of science, and the
   long result of time;

When the centuries behind me like a fruit-
   ful land reposed;
When I clung to all the present for the
   promise that it closed;

When I dipt into the future far as human
   eye could see,
Saw the vision of the world and all the
   wonder that would be. —

In the spring a fuller crimson comes upon
   the robin's breast;
In the spring the wanton lapwing gets him-
   self another crest;

In the spring a livelier iris changes on the
   burnish'd dove;
In the spring a young man's fancy lightly
   turns to thoughts of love.   20

Then her cheek was pale and thinner than
    should be for one so young,
And her eyes on all my motions with a
    mute observance hung.

And I said, 'My cousin Amy, speak, and
    speak the truth to me,
Trust me, cousin, all the current of my
    being sets to thee.'

On her pallid cheek and forehead came a
    color and a light,
As I have seen the rosy red flushing in the
    northern night.

And she turn'd — her bosom shaken with
    a sudden storm of sighs —
All the spirit deeply dawning in the dark
    of hazel eyes —

Saying, 'I have hid my feelings, fearing
    they should do me wrong;'
Saying, 'Dost thou love me, cousin?' weep-
    ing, 'I have loved thee long.'   30

Love took up the glass of Time, and turn'd
    it in his glowing hands;
Every moment, lightly shaken, ran itself
    in golden sands.

Love took up the harp of Life, and smote
    on all the chords with might;
Smote the chord of Self, that, trembling,
    past in music out of sight.

Many a morning on the moorland did we
    hear the copses ring,
And her whisper throng'd my pulses with
    the fulness of the spring.

Many an evening by the waters did we
    watch the stately ships,
And our spirits rush'd together at the
    touching of the lips.

O my cousin, shallow - hearted! O my
    Amy, mine no more!
O the dreary, dreary moorland! O the
    barren, barren shore!   40

Falser than all fancy fathoms, falser than
    all songs have sung,
Puppet to a father's threat, and servile to
    a shrewish tongue!

Is it well to wish thee happy? — having
    known me — to decline
On a range of lower feelings and a nar-
    rower heart than mine!

Yet it shall be; thou shalt lower to his level
    day by day,
What is fine within thee growing coarse to
    sympathize with clay.

As the husband is, the wife is; thou art
    mated with a clown,
And the grossness of his nature will have
    weight to drag thee down.

He will hold thee, when his passion shall
    have spent its novel force,
Something better than his dog, a little
    dearer than his horse.   50

What is this? his eyes are heavy; think
    not they are glazed with wine.
Go to him, it is thy duty; kiss him, take
    his hand in thine.

It may be my lord is weary, that his brain
    is overwrought;
Soothe him with thy finer fancies, touch
    him with thy lighter thought.

He will answer to the purpose, easy things
    to understand —
Better thou wert dead before me, tho' I
    slew thee with my hand!

Better thou and I were lying, hidden from
    the heart's disgrace,
Roll'd in one another's arms, and silent in
    a last embrace.

Cursed be the social wants that sin against
    the strength of youth!
Cursed be the social lies that warp us from
    the living truth!   60

Cursed be the sickly forms that err from
    honest Nature's rule!
Cursed be the gold that gilds the straiten'd
    forehead of the fool!

Well — 't is well that I should bluster! —
    Hadst thou less unworthy proved —
Would to God — for I had loved thee more
    than ever wife was loved.

Am I mad, that I should cherish that
 which bears but bitter fruit?
I will pluck it from my bosom, tho' my
 heart be at the root.

Never, tho' my mortal summers to such
 length of years should come
As the many-winter'd crow that leads the
 clanging rookery home.

Where is comfort? in division of the rec-
 ords of the mind?
Can I part her from herself, and love her,
 as I knew her, kind?   70

I remember one that perish'd; sweetly did
 she speak and move;
Such a one do I remember, whom to look
 at was to love.

Can I think of her as dead, and love her
 for the love she bore?
No — she never loved me truly; love is
 love for evermore.

Comfort? comfort scorn'd of devils! this
 is truth the poet sings,
That a sorrow's crown of sorrow is remem-
 bering happier things.

Drug thy memories, lest thou learn it, lest
 thy heart be put to proof,
In the dead unhappy night, and when the
 rain is on the roof.

Like a dog, he hunts in dreams, and thou
 art staring at the wall,
Where the dying night-lamp flickers, and
 the shadows rise and fall.   80

Then a hand shall pass before thee, pointing
 to his drunken sleep,
To thy widow'd marriage-pillows, to the
 tears that thou wilt weep.

Thou shalt hear the 'Never, never,' whis-
 per'd by the phantom years,
And a song from out the distance in the
 ringing of thine ears;

And an eye shall vex thee, looking ancient
 kindness on thy pain.
Turn thee, turn thee on thy pillow; get
 thee to thy rest again.

Nay, but Nature brings thee solace; for a
 tender voice will cry.
'T is a purer life than thine, a lip to drain
 thy trouble dry.

Baby lips will laugh me down; my latest
 rival brings thee rest.
Baby fingers, waxen touches, press me from
 the mother's breast.   90

O, the child too clothes the father with a
 dearness not his due.
Half is thine and half is his; it will be
 worthy of the two.

O, I see thee old and formal, fitted to thy
 petty part,
With a little hoard of maxims preaching
 down a daughter's heart.

' They were dangerous guides the feelings
 — she herself was not exempt —
Truly, she herself had suffer'd ' — Perish in
 thy self-contempt!

Overlive it — lower yet — be happy! where-
 fore should I care?
I myself must mix with action, lest I
 wither by despair.

What is that which I should turn to, light-
 ing upon days like these?
Every door is barr'd with gold, and opens
 but to golden keys.   100

Every gate is throng'd with suitors, all the
 markets overflow.
I have but an angry fancy; what is that
 which I should do?

I had been content to perish, falling on the
 foeman's ground,
When the ranks are roll'd in vapor, and
 the winds are laid with sound.

But the jingling of the guinea helps the
 hurt that Honor feels,
And the nations do but murmur, snarling at
 each other's heels.

Can I but relive in sadness? I will turn
 that earlier page.
Hide me from my deep emotion, O thou
 wondrous Mother-Age!

Make me feel the wild pulsation that I felt
before the strife,
When I heard my days before me, and the
tumult of my life;   110

Yearning for the large excitement that the
coming years would yield,
Eager-hearted as a boy when first he leaves
his father's field,

And at night along the dusky highway
near and nearer drawn,
Sees in heaven the light of London flaring
like a dreary dawn;

And his spirit leaps within him to be gone
before him then,
Underneath the light he looks at, in among
the throngs of men;

Men, my brothers, men the workers, ever
reaping something new;
That which they have done but earnest of
the things that they shall do.

For I dipt into the future, far as human eye
could see,
Saw the Vision of the world, and all the
wonder that would be;   120

Saw the heavens fill with commerce, argo-
sies of magic sails,
Pilots of the purple twilight, dropping
down with costly bales;

Heard the heavens fill with shouting, and
there rain'd a ghastly dew
From the nations' airy navies grappling in
the central blue;

Far along the world-wide whisper of the
south-wind rushing warm,
With the standards of the peoples plung-
ing thro' the thunder-storm;

Till the war-drum throbb'd no longer, and
the battle-flags were furl'd
In the Parliament of man, the Federation
of the world.

There the common sense of most shall hold
a fretful realm in awe,
And the kindly earth shall slumber, lapt in
universal law.   130

So I triumph'd ere my passion sweeping
thro' me left me dry,
Left me with the palsied heart, and left me
with the jaundiced eye;

Eye, to which all order festers, all things
here are out of joint.
Science moves, but slowly, slowly, creeping
on from point to point;

Slowly comes a hungry people, as a lion,
creeping nigher,
Glares at one that nods and winks behind a
slowly-dying fire.

Yet I doubt not thro' the ages one increas-
ing purpose runs,
And the thoughts of men are widen'd with
the process of the suns.

What is that to him that reaps not harvest
of his youthful joys,
Tho' the deep heart of existence beat for
ever like a boy's ?   140

Knowledge comes, but wisdom lingers, and
I linger on the shore,
And the individual withers, and the world
is more and more.

Knowledge comes, but wisdom lingers, and
he bears a laden breast,
Full of sad experience, moving toward the
stillness of his rest.

Hark, my merry comrades call me, sound-
ing on the bugle-horn,
They to whom my foolish passion were a
target for their scorn.

Shall it not be scorn to me to harp on such
a moulder'd string ?
I am shamed thro' all my nature to have
loved so slight a thing.

Weakness to be wroth with weakness !
woman's pleasure, woman's pain —
Nature made them blinder motions bounded
in a shallower brain.   150

Woman is the lesser man, and all thy
passions, match'd with mine,
Are as moonlight unto sunlight, and as
water unto wine —

Here at least, where nature sickens, nothing.
    Ah, for some retreat
Deep in yonder shining Orient, where my
    life began to beat,

Where in wild Mahratta-battle fell my
    father evil-starr'd; —
I was left a trampled orphan, and a selfish
    uncle's ward.

Or to burst all links of habit — there to
    wander far away,
On from island unto island at the gateways
    of the day.

Larger constellations burning, mellow
    moons and happy skies,
Breadths of tropic shade and palms in clus-
    ter, knots of Paradise.   160

Never comes the trader, never floats an
    European flag,
Slides the bird o'er lustrous woodland,
    swings the trailer from the crag;

Droops the heavy-blossom'd bower, hangs
    the heavy-fruited tree —
Summer isles of Eden lying in dark-purple
    spheres of sea.

There methinks would be enjoyment more
    than in this march of mind,
In the steamship, in the railway, in the
    thoughts that shake mankind.

There the passions cramp'd no longer shall
    have scope and breathing space;
I will take some savage woman, she shall
    rear my dusky race.

Iron-jointed, supple-sinew'd, they shall dive,
    and they shall run,
Catch the wild goat by the hair, and hurl
    their lances in the sun;   170

Whistle back the parrot's call, and leap the
    rainbows of the brooks,
Not with blinded eyesight poring over mis-
    erable books —

Fool, again the dream, the fancy ! but I
    know my words are wild,

But I count the gray barbarian lower than
    the Christian child.

I, to herd with narrow foreheads, vacant of
    our glorious gains,
Like a beast with lower pleasures, like a
    beast with lower pains !

Mated with a squalid savage — what to me
    were sun or clime ?
I the heir of all the ages, in the foremost
    files of time —

I that rather held it better men should per-
    ish one by one,
Than that earth should stand at gaze like
    Joshua's moon in Ajalon !   180

Not in vain the distance beacons. Forward,
    forward let us range,
Let the great world spin for ever down the
    ringing grooves of change.

Thro' the shadow of the globe we sweep
    into the younger day;
Better fifty years of Europe than a cycle
    of Cathay.

Mother-Age, — for mine I knew not, — help
    me as when life begun;
Rift the hills, and roll the waters, flash the
    lightnings, weigh the sun.

O, I see the crescent promise of my spirit
    hath not set.
Ancient founts of inspiration well thro' all
    my fancy yet.

Howsoever these things be, a long farewell
    to Locksley Hall !
Now for me the woods may wither, now for
    me the roof-tree fall.   190

Comes a vapor from the margin, blacken-
    ing over heath and holt,
Cramming all the blast before it, in its
    breast a thunderbolt.

Let it fall on Locksley Hall, with rain or
    hail, or fire or snow;
For the mighty wind arises, roaring sea-
    ward, and I go.

GODIVA

First published in 1842, when line 64 had 'archways.'

I WAITED for the train at Coventry;
I hung with grooms and porters on the bridge,
To watch the three tall spires; and there I shaped
The city's ancient legend into this : —
Not only we, the latest seed of Time,
New men, that in the flying of a wheel
Cry down the past, not only we, that prate
Of rights and wrongs, have loved the people well,
And loathed to see them overtax'd; but she   9
Did more, and underwent, and overcame,
The woman of a thousand summers back,
Godiva, wife to that grim Earl, who ruled
In Coventry; for when he laid a tax
Upon his town, and all the mothers brought
Their children, clamoring, 'If we pay, we starve !'
She sought her lord, and found him, where he strode
About the hall, among his dogs, alone,
His beard a foot before him, and his hair
A yard behind. She told him of their tears,
And pray'd him, 'If they pay this tax, they starve.'   20
Whereat he stared, replying, half-amazed,
'You would not let your little finger ache
For such as *these?*' — 'But I would die,' said she.
He laugh'd, and swore by Peter and by Paul,
Then fillip'd at the diamond in her ear:
'O, ay, ay, ay, you talk !' — 'Alas !' she said,
'But prove me what it is I would not do.'
And from a heart as rough as Esau's hand,
He answer'd, 'Ride you naked thro' the town,   29
And I repeal it;' and nodding, as in scorn,
He parted, with great strides among his dogs.
So left alone, the passions of her mind,
As winds from all the compass shift and blow,
Made war upon each other for an hour,
Till pity won. She sent a herald forth,
And bade him cry, with sound of trumpet, all
The hard condition, but that she would loose
The people; therefore, as they loved her well,
From then till noon no foot should pace the street,   39
No eye look down, she passing, but that all
Should keep within, door shut, and window barr'd.
Then fled she to her inmost bower, and there
Unclasp'd the wedded eagles of her belt,
The grim Earl's gift; but ever at a breath
She linger'd, looking like a summer moon
Half-dipt in cloud. Anon she shook her head,
And shower'd the rippled ringlets to her knee;
Unclad herself in haste; adown the stair
Stole on; and like a creeping sunbeam slid
From pillar unto pillar, until she reach'd   50
The gateway; there she found her palfrey trapt
In purple blazon'd with armorial gold.
Then she rode forth, clothed on with chastity.
The deep air listen'd round her as she rode,
And all the low wind hardly breathed for fear.
The little wide-mouth'd heads upon the spout
Had cunning eyes to see; the barking cur
Made her cheek flame; her palfrey's footfall shot
Light horrors thro' her pulses; the blind walls
Were full of chinks and holes; and overhead   60
Fantastic gables, crowding, stared; but she
Not less thro' all bore up, till, last, she saw
The white-flower'd elder-thicket from the field
Gleam thro' the Gothic archway in the wall.
Then she rode back, clothed on with chastity.
And one low churl, compact of thankless earth,
The fatal byword of all years to come,
Boring a little auger-hole in fear,
Peep'd — but his eyes, before they had their will,

Were shrivell'd into darkness in his head,
And dropt before him. So the Powers,
    who wait   71
On noble deeds, cancell'd a sense misused;
And she, that knew not, pass'd; and all at
    once,
With twelve great shocks of sound, the
    shameless noon
Was clash'd and hammer'd from a hun-
    dred towers,
One after one; but even then she gain'd
Her bower, whence reissuing, robed and
    crown'd,
To meet her lord, she took the tax away
And built herself an everlasting name.

THE DAY-DREAM

The part of this poem entitled 'The Sleep-
ing Beauty' was printed in 1830; the rest was
added in 1842, and a few alterations have since
been made.

PROLOGUE

O LADY FLORA, let me speak;
    A pleasant hour has passed away
While, dreaming on your damask cheek,
    The dewy sister-eyelids lay.
As by the lattice you reclined,
    I went thro' many wayward moods
To see you dreaming — and, behind,
    A summer crisp with shining woods.
And I too dream'd, until at last
    Across my fancy, brooding warm,   10
The reflex of a legend past,
    And loosely settled into form.
And would you have the thought I had,
    And see the vision that I saw,
Then take the broidery-frame, and add
    A crimson to the quaint macaw,
And I will tell it. Turn your face, —
    Nor look with that too-earnest eye —
The rhymes are dazzled from their place
    And order'd words asunder fly.   20

THE SLEEPING PALACE

I

THE varying year with blade and sheaf
    Clothes and reclothes the happy plains,
Here rests the sap within the leaf,
    Here stays the blood along the veins.

Faint shadows, vapors lightly curl'd,
    Faint murmurs from the meadows come,
Like hints and echoes of the world
    To spirits folded in the womb.

II

Soft lustre bathes the range of urns
    On every slanting terrace-lawn.   30
The fountain to his place returns
    Deep in the garden lake withdrawn.
Here droops the banner on the tower,
    On the hall-hearths the festal fires,
The peacock in his laurel bower,
    The parrot in his gilded wires.

III

Roof-haunting martins warm their eggs;
    In these, in those the life is stay'd.
The mantles from the golden pegs
    Droop sleepily; no sound is made,   40
Not even of a gnat that sings.
    More like a picture seemeth all
Than those old portraits of old kings,
    That watch the sleepers from the wall.

IV

Here sits the butler with a flask
    Between his knees, half-drain'd; and
    there
The wrinkled steward at his task,
    The maid-of-honor blooming fair.
The page has caught her hand in his;
    Her lips are sever'd as to speak;   50
His own are pouted to a kiss;
    The blush is fix'd upon her cheek.

V

Till all the hundred summers pass,
    The beams that thro' the oriel shine
Make prisms in every carven glass
    And beaker brimm'd with noble wine.
Each baron at the banquet sleeps,
    Grave faces gather'd in a ring.
His state the king reposing keeps.
    He must have been a jovial king.   60

VI

All round a hedge upshoots, and shows
    At distance like a little wood;
Thorns, ivies, woodbine, mistletoes,
    And grapes with bunches red as blood;
All creeping plants, a wall of green
    Close-matted, bur and brake and brier,
And glimpsing over these, just seen,
    High up, the topmost palace spire.

VII

When will the hundred summers die,
  And thought and time be born again, 70
And newer knowledge, drawing nigh,
  Bring truth that sways the soul of
    men ?
Here all things in their place remain,
  As all were order'd, ages since.
Come, Care and Pleasure, Hope and Pain,
  And bring the fated fairy Prince.

THE SLEEPING BEAUTY

I

YEAR after year unto her feet,
  She lying on her couch alone,
Across the purple coverlet 79
  The maiden's jet-black hair has grown,
On either side her tranced form
  Forth streaming from a braid of pearl;
The slumbrous light is rich and warm,
  And moves not on the rounded curl.

II

The silk star-broider'd coverlid
  Unto her limbs itself doth mould
Languidly ever; and, amid
  Her full black ringlets downward roll'd,
Glows forth each softly-shadow'd arm
  With bracelets of the diamond bright. 90
Her constant beauty doth inform
  Stillness with love, and day with light.

III

She sleeps; her breathings are not heard
  In palace chambers far apart.
The fragrant tresses are not stirr'd
  That lie upon her charmed heart.
She sleeps; on either hand upswells
  The gold-fringed pillow lightly prest;
She sleeps, nor dreams, but ever dwells
  A perfect form in perfect rest. 100

THE ARRIVAL

I

ALL precious things, discover'd late,
  To those that seek them issue forth;
For love in sequel works with fate,
  And draws the veil from hidden worth.
He travels far from other skies —
  His mantle glitters on the rocks —

A fairy Prince, with joyful eyes,
  And lighter-footed than the fox.

II

The bodies and the bones of those
  That strove in other days to pass 110
Are wither'd in the thorny close,
  Or scatter'd blanching on the grass.
He gazes on the silent dead:
  'They perish'd in their daring deeds.'
This proverb flashes thro' his head,
  'The many fail, the one succeeds.'

III

He comes, scarce knowing what he seeks;
  He breaks the hedge; he 'enters there;
The color flies into his cheeks;
  He trusts to light on something fair; 120
For all his life the charm did talk
  About his path, and hover near
With words of promise in his walk,
  And whisper'd voices at his ear.

IV

More close and close his footsteps wind;
  The Magic Music in his heart,
Beats quick and quicker, till he find
  The quiet chamber far apart.
His spirit flutters like a lark,
  He stoops — to kiss her — on his knee.
'Love, if thy tresses be so dark, 131
  How dark those hidden eyes must be !'

THE REVIVAL

I

A TOUCH, a kiss ! the charm was snapt.
  There rose a noise of striking clocks,
And feet that ran, and doors that clapt,
  And barking dogs, and crowing cocks;
A fuller light illumined all,
  A breeze thro' all the garden swept,
A sudden hubbub shook the hall,
  And sixty feet the fountain leapt. 140

II

The hedge broke in, the banner blew,
  The butler drank, the steward scrawl'd,
The fire shot up, the martin flew,
  The parrot scream'd, the peacock squall'd,
The maid and page renew'd their strife,
  The palace bang'd and buzz'd and clackt,
And all the long-pent stream of life
  Dash'd downward in a cataract.

III

And last with these the king awoke,
  And in his chair himself uprear'd,   150
And yawn'd, and rubb'd his face, and
      spoke,
  'By holy rood, a royal beard !
How say you ? we have slept, my lords.
  My beard has grown into my lap.'
The barons swore, with many words,
  'T was but an after-dinner's nap.

IV

'Pardy,' return'd the king, 'but still
  My joints are somewhat stiff or so.
My lord, and shall we pass the bill
  I mention'd half an hour ago ?'   160
The chancellor, sedate and vain,
  In courteous words return'd reply,
But dallied with his golden chain,
  And, smiling, put the question by.

THE DEPARTURE

I

AND on her lover's arm she leant,
  And round her waist she felt it fold,
And far across the hills they went
  In that new world which is the old;
Across the hills, and far away
  Beyond their utmost purple rim,   170
And deep into the dying day
  The happy princess follow'd him.

II

'I 'd sleep another hundred years,
  O love, for such another kiss;'
'O, wake for ever, love,' she hears;
  'O love, 't was such as this and this.'
And o'er them many a sliding star
  And many a merry wind was borne,
And, stream'd thro' many a golden bar,
  The twilight melted into morn.   180

III

'O eyes long laid in happy sleep !'
  'O happy sleep, that lightly fled !'
'O happy kiss, that woke thy sleep !'
  'O love, thy kiss would wake the dead !'
And o'er them many a flowing range
  Of vapor buoy'd the crescent-bark,
And, rapt thro' many a rosy change,
  The twilight died into the dark.

IV

'A hundred summers ! can it be ?
  And whither goest thou, tell me where ?'
'O, seek my father's court with me,   191
  For there are greater wonders there.'
And o'er the hills, and far away
  Beyond their utmost purple rim,
Beyond the night, across the day,
  Thro' all the world she follow'd him.

MORAL

I

So, Lady Flora, take my lay,
  And if you find no moral there,
Go, look in any glass and say,
  What moral is in being fair.   200
O, to what uses shall we put
  The wildweed-flower that simply blows ?
And is there any moral shut
  Within the bosom of the rose ?

II

But any man that walks the mead,
  In bud or blade or bloom, may find,
According as his humors lead,
  A meaning suited to his mind.
And liberal applications lie
  In Art like Nature, dearest friend;   210
So 't were to cramp its use if I
  Should hook it to some useful end.

L'ENVOI

I

YOU shake your head.   A random string
  Your finer female sense offends.
Well — were it not a pleasant thing
  To fall asleep with all one's friends;
To pass with all our social ties
  To silence from the paths of men,
And every hundred years to rise
  And learn the world, and sleep again;   220
To sleep thro' terms of mighty wars,
  And wake on science grown to more,
On secrets of the brain, the stars,
  As wild as aught of fairy lore;
And all that else the years will show,
  The Poet-forms of stronger hours,
The vast Republics that may grow,
  The Federations and the Powers;

Titanic forces taking birth
  In divers seasons, divers climes ?   230
For we are Ancients of the earth,
  And in the morning of the times.

II

So sleeping, so aroused from sleep
  Thro' sunny decads new and strange,
Or gay quinquenniads, would we reap
  The flower and quintessence of change.

III

Ah, yet would I — and would I might !
  So much your eyes my fancy take —
Be still the first to leap to light
  That I might kiss those eyes awake !   240
For, am I right, or am I wrong,
  To choose your own you did not care;
You 'd have *my* moral from the song,
  And I will take my pleasure there;
And, am I right or am I wrong,
  My fancy, ranging thro' and thro',
To search a meaning for the song,
  Perforce will still revert to you,
Nor finds a closer truth than this
  All-graceful head, so richly curl'd,   250
And evermore a costly kiss
  The prelude to some brighter world.

IV

For since the time when Adam first
  Embraced his Eve in happy hour,
And every bird of Eden burst
  In carol, every bud to flower,
What eyes, like thine, have waken'd hopes,
  What lips, like thine, so sweetly join'd ?
Where on the double rosebud droops
  The fulness of the pensive mind;   260
Which, all too dearly self-involved,
  Yet sleeps a dreamless sleep to me, —
A sleep by kisses undissolved,
  That lets thee neither hear nor see:
But break it. In the name of wife,
  And in the rights that name may give,
Are clasp'd the moral of thy life,
  And that for which I care to live.

EPILOGUE

So, Lady Flora, take my lay,
  And if you find a meaning there,   270
O, whisper to your glass, and say,
  ' What wonder if he thinks me fair ? '
What wonder I was all unwise,
  To shape the song for your delight

Like long-tail'd birds of Paradise
  That float thro' heaven, and cannot light?
Or old-world trains, upheld at court
  By Cupid-boys of blooming hue —
But take it — earnest wed with sport,
  And either sacred unto you.   280

AMPHION

First printed in 1842, and altered but
slightly.

My father left a park to me,
  But it is wild and barren,
A garden too with scarce a tree,
  And waster than a warren;
Yet say the neighbors when they call
  It is not bad but good land,
And in it is the germ of all
  That grows within the woodland.

O, had I lived when song was great
  In days of old Amphion,   10
And ta'en my fiddle to the gate,
  Nor cared for seed or scion !
And had I lived when song was great,
  And legs of trees were limber,
And ta'en my fiddle to the gate,
  And fiddled in the timber !

'T is said he had a tuneful tongue,
  Such happy intonation,
Wherever he sat down and sung
  He left a small plantation;   20
Wherever in a lonely grove
  He set up his forlorn pipes,
The gouty oak began to move,
  And flounder into hornpipes.

The mountain stirr'd its bushy crown,
  And, as tradition teaches,
Young ashes pirouetted down
  Coquetting with young beeches;
And briony-vine and ivy-wreath
  Ran forward to his rhyming,   30
And from the valleys underneath
  Came little copses climbing.

The linden broke her ranks and rent
  The woodbine wreaths that bind her,
And down the middle, buzz ! she went
  With all her bees behind her;
The poplars, in long order due,
  With cypress promenaded,

The shock-head willows two and two
By rivers gallopaded.   40

Came wet-shod alder from the wave,
  Came yews, a dismal coterie;
Each pluck'd his one foot from the grave,
  Poussetting with a sloe-tree;
Old elms came breaking from the vine,
  The vine stream'd out to follow,
And, sweating rosin, plump'd the pine
  From many a cloudy hollow.

And was n't it a sight to see,
  When, ere his song was ended,   50
Like some great landslip, tree by tree,
  The country-side descended;
And shepherds from the mountain-eaves
  Look'd down, half-pleased, half-fright-
    en'd,
As dash'd about the drunken leaves
  The random sunshine lighten'd ?

O, Nature first was fresh to men,
  And wanton without measure;
So youthful and so flexile then,
  You moved her at your pleasure.   60
Twang out, my fiddle ! shake the twigs !
  And make her dance attendance;
Blow, flute, and stir the stiff-set sprigs,
  And scirrhous roots and tendons !

'T is vain ! in such a brassy age
  I could not move a thistle;
The very sparrows in the hedge
  Scarce answer to my whistle;
Or at the most, when three-parts-sick
  With strumming and with scraping,   70
A jackass heehaws from the rick,
  The passive oxen gaping.

But what is that I hear ? a sound
  Like sleepy counsel pleading;
O Lord ! — 't is in my neighbor's ground,
  The modern Muses reading.
They read Botanic Treatises,
  And Works on Gardening thro' there,
And Methods of Transplanting Trees
  To look as if they grew there.   80

The wither'd Misses ! how they prose
  O'er books of travell'd seamen,
And show you slips of all that grows
  From England to Van Diemen.
They read in arbors clipt and cut,
  And alleys, faded places,

By squares of tropic summer shut
  And warm'd in crystal cases.

But these, tho' fed with careful dirt,
  Are neither green nor sappy;   90
Half-conscious of the garden-squirt,
  The spindlings look unhappy.
Better to me the meanest weed
  That blows upon its mountain,
The vilest herb that runs to seed
  Beside its native fountain.

And I must work thro' months of toil,
  And years of cultivation,
Upon my proper patch of soil
  To grow my own plantation.   100
I 'll take the showers as they fall,
  I will not vex my bosom;
Enough if at the end of all
  A little garden blossom.

SAINT AGNES' EVE

First published in ' The Keepsake ' for 1837,
and reprinted in 1842.   Until 1855 the title
was ' Saint Agnes.'

DEEP on the convent-roof the snows
  Are sparkling to the moon;
My breath to heaven like vapor goes;
  May my soul follow soon !
The shadows of the convent-towers
  Slant down the snowy sward,
Still creeping with the creeping hours
  That lead me to my Lord.
Make Thou my spirit pure and clear
  As are the frosty skies,
Or this first snowdrop of the year
  That in my bosom lies.

As these white robes are soil'd and dark,
  To yonder shining ground;
As this pale taper's earthly spark,
  To yonder argent round;
So shows my soul before the Lamb,
  My spirit before Thee;
So in mine earthly house I am,
  To that I hope to be.
Break up the heavens, O Lord ! and far,
  Thro' all yon starlight keen,
Draw me, thy bride, a glittering star,
  In raiment white and clean.

He lifts me to the golden doors;
  The flashes come and go;

All heaven bursts her starry floors,
And strows her lights below,
And deepens on and up ! the gates
Roll back, and far within
For me the Heavenly Bridegroom waits,
To make me pure of sin.
The Sabbaths of Eternity,
One Sabbath deep and wide —
A light upon the shining sea —
The Bridegroom with his bride !

SIR GALAHAD

First printed in 1842. In line 15 ' till ' was
originally ' to.'

MY good blade carves the casques of men,
My tough lance thrusteth sure,
My strength is as the strength of ten,
Because my heart is pure.
The shattering trumpet shrilleth high,
The hard brands shiver on the steel,
The splinter'd spear-shafts crack and fly,
The horse and rider reel;
They reel, they roll in clanging lists,
And when the tide of combat stands,   10
Perfume and flowers fall in showers,
That lightly rain from ladies' hands.

How sweet are looks that ladies bend
On whom their favors fall !
For them I battle till the end,
To save from shame and thrall;
But all my heart is drawn above,
My knees are bow'd in crypt and shrine;
I never felt the kiss of love,
Nor maiden's hand in mine.   20
More bounteous aspects on me beam,
Me mightier transports move and thrill;
So keep I fair thro' faith and prayer
A virgin heart in work and will.

When down the stormy crescent goes,
A light before me swims,
Between dark stems the forest glows,
I hear a noise of hymns.
Then by some secret shrine I ride;
I hear a voice, but none are there;   30
The stalls are void, the doors are wide,
The tapers burning fair.
Fair gleams the snowy altar-cloth,
The silver vessels sparkle clean,
The shrill bell rings, the censer swings,
And solemn chaunts resound between.

Sometimes on lonely mountain-meres
I find a magic bark.
I leap on board; no helmsman steers;
I float till all is dark.   40
A gentle sound, an awful light !
Three angels bear the Holy Grail;
With folded feet, in stoles of white,
On sleeping wings they sail.
Ah, blessed vision ! blood of God !
My spirit beats her mortal bars,
As down dark tides the glory slides,
And starlike mingles with the stars.

When on my goodly charger borne
Thro' dreaming towns I go,   50
The cock crows ere the Christmas morn,
The streets are dumb with snow.
The tempest crackles on the leads,
And, ringing, springs from brand and
mail;
But o'er the dark a glory spreads,
And gilds the driving hail.
I leave the plain, I climb the height;
No branchy thicket shelter yields;
But blessed forms in whistling storms
Fly o'er waste fens and windy fields.   60

A maiden knight — to me is given
Such hope, I know not fear;
I yearn to breathe the airs of heaven
That often meet me here.
I muse on joy that will not cease,
Pure spaces clothed in living beams,
Pure lilies of eternal peace,
Whose odors haunt my dreams;
And, stricken by an angel's hand,
This mortal armor that I wear,   70
This weight and size, this heart and eyes,
Are touch'd, are turn'd to finest air.

The clouds are broken in the sky,
And thro' the mountain-walls
A rolling organ-harmony
Swells up and shakes and falls.
Then move the trees, the copses nod,
Wings flutter, voices hover clear:
'O just and faithful knight of God !
Ride on ! the prize is near.'   80
So pass I hostel, hall, and grange;
By bridge and ford, by park and pale,
All-arm'd I ride, whate'er betide,
Until I find the Holy Grail.

EDWARD GRAY

First printed in 1842, and unaltered.

Sweet Emma Moreland of yonder town
  Met me walking on yonder way;
'And have you lost your heart?' she
    said;
  'And are you married yet, Edward
    Gray?'

Sweet Emma Moreland spoke to me;
  Bitterly weeping I turn'd away:
'Sweet Emma Moreland, love no more
  Can touch the heart of Edward Gray.

'Ellen Adair she loved me well,
  Against her father's and mother's will;
To-day I sat for an hour and wept
  By Ellen's grave, on the windy hill.

'Shy she was, and I thought her cold,
  Thought her proud, and fled over the
    sea;
Fill'd I was with folly and spite,
  When Ellen Adair was dying for me.

'Cruel, cruel the words I said!
  Cruelly came they back to-day:
"You're too slight and fickle," I said,
  "To trouble the heart of Edward Gray."

'There I put my face in the grass —
  Whisper'd, "Listen to my despair;
I repent me of all I did;
  Speak a little, Ellen Adair!"

'Then I took a pencil, and wrote
  On the mossy stone, as I lay,
"Here lies the body of Ellen Adair;
  And here the heart of Edward Gray!"

'Love may come, and love may go,
  And fly, like a bird, from tree to tree;
But I will love no more, no more,
  Till Ellen Adair come back to me.

'Bitterly wept I over the stone;
  Bitterly weeping I turn'd away.
There lies the body of Ellen Adair!
  And there the heart of Edward Gray!'

WILL WATERPROOF'S LYRICAL MONOLOGUE

MADE AT THE COCK

First printed in 1842, and slightly altered
since. See Notes.

O plump head-waiter at The Cock,
  To which I most resort,
How goes the time? 'T is five o'clock.
  Go fetch a pint of port;
But let it not be such as that
  You set before chance-comers,
But such whose father-grape grew fat
  On Lusitanian summers.

No vain libation to the Muse,
  But may she still be kind,   10
And whisper lovely words, and use
  Her influence on the mind,
To make me write my random rhymes,
  Ere they be half-forgotten;
Nor add and alter, many times,
  Till all be ripe and rotten.

I pledge her, and she comes and dips
  Her laurel in the wine,
And lays it thrice upon my lips,
  These favor'd lips of mine;   20
Until the charm have power to make
  New life-blood warm the bosom,
And barren commonplaces break
  In full and kindly blossom.

I pledge her silent at the board;
  Her gradual fingers steal
And touch upon the master-chord
  Of all I felt and feel.
Old wishes, ghosts of broken plans,
  And phantom hopes assemble;   30
And that child's heart within the man's
  Begins to move and tremble.

Thro' many an hour of summer suns,
  By many pleasant ways,
Against its fountain upward runs
  The current of my days.
I kiss the lips I once have kiss'd;
  The gaslight wavers dimmer;
And softly, thro' a vinous mist,
  My college friendships glimmer.   40

I grow in worth and wit and sense,
  Unboding critic-pen,
Or that eternal want of pence
  Which vexes public men,
Who hold their hands to all, and cry
  For that which all deny them —
Who sweep the crossings, wet or dry,
  And all the world go by them.

Ah ! yet, tho' all the world forsake,
  Tho' fortune clip my wings,   50
I will not cramp my heart, nor take
  Half-views of men and things.
Let Whig and Tory stir their blood;
  There must be stormy weather;
But for some true result of good
  All parties work together.

Let there be thistles, there are grapes;
  If old things, there are new;
Ten thousand broken lights and shapes,
  Yet glimpses of the true.   60
Let raffs be rife in prose and rhyme,
  We lack not rhymes and reasons,
As on this whirligig of Time
  We circle with the seasons.

This earth is rich in man and maid,
  With fair horizons bound;
This whole wide earth of light and shade
  Comes out a perfect round.
High over roaring Temple-bar,
  And set in heaven's third story,   70
I look at all things as they are,
  But thro' a kind of glory.

Head-waiter, honor'd by the guest
  Half-mused, or reeling ripe,
The pint you brought me was the best
  That ever came from pipe.
But tho' the port surpasses praise,
  My nerves have dealt with stiffer.
Is there some magic in the place ?
  Or do my peptics differ ?   80

For since I came to live and learn,
  No pint of white or red
Had ever half the power to turn
  This wheel within my head,
Which bears a season'd brain about,
  Unsubject to confusion,
Tho' soak'd and saturate, out and out,
  Thro' every convolution.

For I am of a numerous house,
  With many kinsmen gay,   90
Where long and largely we carouse
  As who shall say me nay ?
Each month, a birthday coming on,
  We drink, defying trouble,
Or sometimes two would meet in one,
  And then we drank it double;

Whether the vintage, yet unkept,
  Had relish fiery-new,
Or elbow-deep in sawdust slept,
  As old as Waterloo,   100
Or, stow'd when classic Canning died,
  In musty bins and chambers,
Had cast upon its crusty side
  The gloom of ten Decembers.

The Muse, the jolly Muse, it is !
  She answer'd to my call;
She changes with that mood or this,
  Is all-in-all to all;
She lit the spark within my throat,
  To make my blood run quicker,   110
Used all her fiery will, and smote
  Her life into the liquor.

And hence this halo lives about
  The waiter's hands, that reach
To each his perfect pint of stout,
  His proper chop to each.
He looks not like the common breed
  That with the napkin dally;
I think he came, like Ganymede,
  From some delightful valley.   120

The Cock was of a larger egg
  Than modern poultry drop,
Stept forward on a firmer leg,
  And cramm'd a plumper crop,
Upon an ampler dunghill trod,
  Crow'd lustier late and early,
Sipt wine from silver, praising God,
  And raked in golden barley.

A private life was all his joy,
  Till in a court he saw   130
A something-pottle-bodied boy
  That knuckled at the taw.
He stoop'd and clutch'd him, fair and
    good,
  Flew over roof and casement;
His brothers of the weather stood
  Stock-still for sheer amazement.

But he, by farmstead, thorpe, and spire,
  And follow'd with acclaims,
A sign to many a staring shire,
  Came crowing over Thames.   140
Right down by smoky Paul's they bore,
  Till, where the street grows straiter,
One fix'd for ever at the door,
  And one became head-waiter.

But whither would my fancy go?
  How out of place she makes
The violet of a legend blow
  Among the chops and steaks !
'T is but a steward of the can,
  One shade more plump than common;
As just and mere a serving-man   151
  As any born of woman.

I ranged too high: what draws me down
  Into the common day ?
Is it the weight of that half-crown
  Which I shall have to pay ?
For, something duller than at first,
  Nor wholly comfortable,
I sit, my empty glass reversed,
  And thrumming on the table;   160

Half fearful that, with self at strife,
  I take myself to task,
Lest of the fulness of my life
  I leave an empty flask;
For I had hope, by something rare,
  To prove myself a poet,
But, while I plan and plan, my hair
  Is gray before I know it.

So fares it since the years began,
  Till they be gather'd up;   170
The truth, that flies the flowing can,
  Will haunt the vacant cup;
And others' follies teach us not,
  Nor much their wisdom teaches;
And most, of sterling worth, is what
  Our own experience preaches.

Ah, let the rusty theme alone !
  We know not what we know.
But for my pleasant hour, 't is gone;
  'T is gone, and let it go.   180
'T is gone: a thousand such have slipt
  Away from my embraces,
And fallen into the dusty crypt
  Of darken'd forms and faces.

Go, therefore, thou ! thy betters went
  Long since, and came no more;
With peals of genial clamor sent
  From many a tavern-door,
With twisted quirks and happy hits,
  From misty men of letters;   190
The tavern-hours of mighty wits, —
  Thine elders and thy betters;

Hours when the Poet's words and looks
  Had yet their native glow,
Nor yet the fear of little books
  Had made him talk for show;
But, all his vast heart sherris-warm'd,
  He flash'd his random speeches,
Ere days that deal in ana swarm'd
  His literary leeches.   200

So mix for ever with the past,
  Like all good things on earth !
For should I prize thee, couldst thou last,
  At half thy real worth ?
I hold it good, good things should pass;
  With time I will not quarrel;
It is but yonder empty glass
  That makes me maudlin-moral.

Head-waiter of the chop-house here,
  To which I most resort,   210
I too must part; I hold thee dear
  For this good pint of port.
For this, thou shalt from all things suck
  Marrow of mirth and laughter;
And wheresoe'er thou move, good luck
  Shall fling her old shoe after.

But thou wilt never move from hence,
  The sphere thy fate allots;
Thy latter days increased with pence
  Go down among the pots;   220
Thou battenest by the greasy gleam
  In haunts of hungry sinners,
Old boxes, larded with the steam
  Of thirty thousand dinners.

We fret, we fume, would shift our skins,
  Would quarrel with our lot;
Thy care is, under polish'd tins,
  To serve the hot-and-hot;
To come and go, and come again,
  Returning like the pewit,   230
And watch'd by silent gentlemen,
  That trifle with the cruet.

Live long, ere from thy topmost head
  The thick-set hazel dies;
Long, ere the hateful crow shall tread
  The corners of thine eyes;
Live long, nor feel in head or chest
  Our changeful equinoxes,
Till mellow Death, like some late guest,
  Shall call thee from the boxes.   240

But when he calls, and thou shalt cease
  To pace the gritted floor,
And, laying down an unctuous lease
  Of life, shalt earn no more,
No carved cross-bones, the types of Death,
  Shall show thee past to heaven,
But carved cross-pipes, and, underneath,
  A pint-pot neatly graven.

LADY CLARE

First printed in 1842. A note in that edition
and the next stated that the ballad was 'partly
suggested by the novel of "Inheritance"' (Miss
Ferrier's), the heroine of which is a Miss St.
Clair.

IT was the time when lilies blow,
  And clouds are highest up in air,
Lord Ronald brought a lily-white doe
  To give his cousin, Lady Clare.

I trow they did not part in scorn;
  Lovers long-betroth'd were they;
They two will wed the morrow morn —
  God's blessing on the day!

'He does not love me for my birth,
  Nor for my lands so broad and fair;   10
He loves me for my own true worth,
  And that is well,' said Lady Clare.

In there came old Alice the nurse,
  Said, 'Who was this that went from thee?'
'It was my cousin,' said Lady Clare;
  'To-morrow he weds with me.'

'O, God be thank'd,' said Alice the nurse,
  'That all comes round so just and fair!
Lord Ronald is heir of all your lands,
  And you are *not* the Lady Clare.'   20

'Are ye out of your mind, my nurse, my
    nurse,'
  Said Lady Clare, 'that ye speak so wild?'

'As God's above,' said Alice the nurse,
  'I speak the truth: you are my child.

'The old earl's daughter died at my breast;
  I speak the truth, as I live by bread!
I buried her like my own sweet child,
  And put my child in her stead.'

'Falsely, falsely have ye done,
  O mother,' she said, 'if this be true,   30
To keep the best man under the sun
  So many years from his due.'

'Nay now, my child,' said Alice the nurse,
  'But keep the secret for your life,
And all you have will be Lord Ronald's,
  When you are man and wife.'

'If I 'm a beggar born,' she said,
  'I will speak out, for I dare not lie.
Pull off, pull off, the brooch of gold,
  And fling the diamond necklace by.'   40

'Nay now, my child,' said Alice the nurse,
  'But keep the secret all ye can.'
She said, 'Not so; but I will know
  If there be any faith in man.'

'Nay now, what faith?' said Alice the
    nurse;
  'The man will cleave unto his right.'
'And he shall have it,' the lady replied,
  'Tho' I should die to-night.'

'Yet give one kiss to your mother dear!
  Alas, my child, I sinn'd for thee!'   50
'O mother, mother, mother,' she said,
  'So strange it seems to me.

'Yet here 's a kiss for my mother dear,
  My mother dear, if this be so,
And lay your hand upon my head,
  And bless me, mother, ere I go.'

She clad herself in a russet gown,
  She was no longer Lady Clare;
She went by dale, and she went by down,
  With a single rose in her hair.   60

The lily-white doe Lord Ronald had
    brought
  Leapt up from where she lay,
Dropt her head in the maiden's hand,
  And follow'd her all the way.

Down stept Lord Ronald from his tower:
  'O Lady Clare, you shame your worth!
Why come you drest like a village maid,
  That are the flower of the earth?'

'If I come drest like a village maid,
  I am but as my fortunes are;   70
I am a beggar born,' she said,
  'And not the Lady Clare.'

'Play me no tricks,' said Lord Ronald,
  'For I am yours in word and in deed.
Play me no tricks,' said Lord Ronald,
  'Your riddle is hard to read.'

O, and proudly stood she up!
  Her heart within her did not fail;
She look'd into Lord Ronald's eyes,
  And told him all her nurse's tale.   80

He laugh'd a laugh of merry scorn;
  He turn'd and kiss'd her where she stood;
'If you are not the heiress born,
  And I,' said he, 'the next in blood, —

'If you are not the heiress born,
  And I,' said he, 'the lawful heir,
We two will wed to-morrow morn,
  And you shall still be Lady Clare.'

THE CAPTAIN

A LEGEND OF THE NAVY

First printed in the 'Selections' of 1865,
and unaltered.

HE that only rules by terror
  Doeth grievous wrong.
Deep as hell I count his error.
  Let him hear my song.
Brave the Captain was; the seamen
  Made a gallant crew,
Gallant sons of English freemen,
  Sailors bold and true.
But they hated his oppression;
  Stern he was and rash,
So for every light transgression
  Doom'd them to the lash.
Day by day more harsh and cruel
  Seem'd the Captain's mood.
Secret wrath like smother'd fuel
  Burnt in each man's blood.
Yet he hoped to purchase glory,

Hoped to make the name
  Of his vessel great in story,
  Wheresoe'er he came.
So they past by capes and islands,
  Many a harbor-mouth,
Sailing under palmy highlands
  Far within the South.
On a day when they were going
  O'er the lone expanse,
In the north, her canvas flowing,
  Rose a ship of France.
Then the Captain's color heighten'd,
  Joyful came his speech;
But a cloudy gladness lighten'd
  In the eyes of each.
'Chase,' he said; the ship flew forward,
  And the wind did blow;
Stately, lightly, went she norward,
  Till she near'd the foe.
Then they look'd at him they hated,
  Had what they desired;
Mute with folded arms they waited —
  Not a gun was fired.
But they heard the foeman's thunder
  Roaring out their doom;
All the air was torn in sunder,
  Crashing went the boom,
Spars were splinter'd, decks were shatter'd,
  Bullets fell like rain;
Over mast and deck were scatter'd
  Blood and brains of men.
Spars were splinter'd; decks were broken;
  Every mother's son —
Down they dropt — no word was spoken —
  Each beside his gun.
On the decks as they were lying,
  Were their faces grim.
In their blood, as they lay dying,
  Did they smile on him.
Those in whom he had reliance
  For his noble name
With one smile of still defiance
  Sold him unto shame.
Shame and wrath his heart confounded,
  Pale he turn'd and red,
Till himself was deadly wounded
  Falling on the dead.
Dismal error! fearful slaughter!
  Years have wander'd by;
Side by side beneath the water
  Crew and Captain lie;
There the sunlit ocean tosses
  O'er them mouldering,
And the lonely seabird crosses
  With one waft of the wing.

THE LORD OF BURLEIGH

First printed in 1842, and unaltered.

In her ear he whispers gaily,
   ' If my heart by signs can tell,
Maiden, I have watch'd thee daily,
   And I think thou lov'st me well.'
She replies, in accents fainter,
   ' There is none I love like thee.'
He is but a landscape-painter,
   And a village maiden she.
He to lips that fondly falter
   Presses his without reproof,   10
Leads her to the village altar,
   And they leave her father's roof.
' I can make no marriage present;
   Little can I give my wife.
Love will make our cottage pleasant,
   And I love thee more than life.'
They by parks and lodges going
   See the lordly castles stand;
Summer woods, about them blowing,
   Made a murmur in the land.   20
From deep thought himself he rouses,
   Says to her that loves him well,
' Let us see these handsome houses
   Where the wealthy nobles dwell.'
So she goes by him attended,
   Hears him lovingly converse,
Sees whatever fair and splendid
   Lay betwixt his home and hers;
Parks with oak and chestnut shady,
   Parks and order'd gardens great,   30
Ancient homes of lord and lady,
   Built for pleasure and for state.
All he shows her makes him dearer;
   Evermore she seems to gaze
On that cottage growing nearer,
   Where they twain will spend their days.
O, but she will love him truly !
   He shall have a cheerful home;
She will order all things duly,
   When beneath his roof they come.   40
Thus her heart rejoices greatly,
   Till a gateway she discerns
With armorial bearings stately,
   And beneath the gate she turns,
Sees a mansion more majestic
   Than all those she saw before.
Many a gallant gay domestic
   Bows before him at the door;

And they speak in gentle murmur,
   When they answer to his call,   50
While he treads with footstep firmer,
   Leading on from hall to hall.
And, while now she wonders blindly,
   Nor the meaning can divine,
Proudly turns he round and kindly,
   ' All of this is mine and thine.'
Here he lives in state and bounty,
   Lord of Burleigh, fair and free;
Not a lord in all the county
   Is so great a lord as he.   60
All at once the color flushes
   Her sweet face from brow to chin;
As it were with shame she blushes,
   And her spirit changed within.
Then her countenance all over
   Pale again as death did prove;
But he clasp'd her like a lover,
   And he cheer'd her soul with love.
So she strove against her weakness,
   Tho' at times her spirit sank,   70
Shaped her heart with woman's meekness
   To all duties of her rank;
And a gentle consort made he,
   And her gentle mind was such
That she grew a noble lady,
   And the people loved her much.
But a trouble weigh'd upon her,
   And perplex'd her, night and morn,
With the burthen of an honor
   Unto which she was not born.   80
Faint she grew, and ever fainter,
   And she murmur'd, ' O, that he
Were once more that landscape-painter
   Which did win my heart from me ! '
So she droop'd and droop'd before him,
   Fading slowly from his side;
Three fair children first she bore him,
   Then before her time she died.
Weeping, weeping late and early,
   Walking up and pacing down,   90
Deeply mourn'd the Lord of Burleigh,
   Burleigh-house by Stamford-town.
And he came to look upon her,
   And he look'd at her and said,
' Bring the dress and put it on her,
   That she wore when she was wed.'
Then her people, softly treading,
   Bore to earth her body, drest
In the dress that she was wed in,
   That her spirit might have rest.   100

THE VOYAGE

First printed in the 'Enoch Arden' volume in 1864.
'Life as Energy, in the great ethical sense of the word, — Life as the pursuit of the Ideal, — is figured in this brilliantly descriptive allegory' (Palgrave).

I

We left behind the painted buoy
  That tosses at the harbor-mouth;
And madly danced our hearts with joy,
  As fast we fleeted to the south.
How fresh was every sight and sound
  On open main or winding shore !
We knew the merry world was round,
  And we might sail for evermore.

II

Warm broke the breeze against the brow,
  Dry sang the tackle, sang the sail;   10
The Lady's-head upon the prow
  Caught the shrill salt, and sheer'd the
    gale.
The broad seas swell'd to meet the keel,
  And swept behind; so quick the run,
We felt the good ship shake and reel,
  We seem'd to sail into the sun !

III

How oft we saw the sun retire,
  And burn the threshold of the night,
Fall from his Ocean-lane of fire,
  And sleep beneath his pillar'd light !   20
How oft the purple-skirted robe
  Of twilight slowly downward drawn,
As thro' the slumber of the globe
  Again we dash'd into the dawn !

IV

New stars all night above the brim
  Of waters lighten'd into view;
They climb'd as quickly, for the rim
  Changed every moment as we flew.
Far ran the naked moon across
  The houseless ocean's heaving field,   30
Or flying shone, the silver boss
  Of her own halo's dusky shield.

V

The peaky islet shifted shapes,
  High towns on hills were dimly seen;
We past long lines of Northern capes
  And dewy Northern meadows green.

We came to warmer waves, and deep
  Across the boundless east we drove,
Where those long swells of breaker sweep
  The nutmeg rocks and isles of clove.   40

VI

By peaks that flamed, or, all in shade,
  Gloom'd the low coast and quivering brine
With ashy rains, that spreading made
  Fantastic plume or sable pine;
By sands and steaming flats, and floods
  Of mighty mouth, we scudded fast,
And hills and scarlet-mingled woods
  Glow'd for a moment as we past.

VII

O hundred shores of happy climes,
  How swiftly stream'd ye by the bark !   50
At times the whole sea burn'd, at times
  With wakes of fire we tore the dark;
At times a carven craft would shoot
  From havens hid in fairy bowers,
With naked limbs and flowers and fruit,
  But we nor paused for fruit nor flowers.

VIII

For one fair Vision ever fled
  Down the waste waters day and night,
And still we follow'd where she led,
  In hope to gain upon her flight.   60
Her face was evermore unseen,
  And fixt upon the far sea-line;
But each man murmur'd, 'O my Queen,
  I follow till I make thee mine.'

IX

And now we lost her, now she gleam'd
  Like Fancy made of golden air,
Now nearer to the prow she seem'd
  Like Virtue firm, like Knowledge fair,
Now high on waves that idly burst
  Like Heavenly Hope she crown'd the
    sea,   70
And now, the bloodless point reversed,
  She bore the blade of Liberty.

X

And only one among us — him
  We pleased not — he was seldom pleased;
He saw not far, his eyes were dim,
  But ours he swore were all diseased.
'A ship of fools,' he shriek'd in spite,
  'A ship of fools,' he sneer'd and wept.
And overboard one stormy night
  He cast his body, and on we swept.   80

XI

And never sail of ours was furl'd,
  Nor anchor dropt at eve or morn;
We loved the glories of the world,
  But laws of nature were our scorn.
For blasts would rise and rave and cease,
  But whence were those that drove the
     sail
Across the whirlwind's heart of peace,
  And to and thro' the counter gale ?

XII

Again to colder climes we came,
  For still we follow'd where she led;   90
Now mate is blind and captain lame,
  And half the crew are sick or dead,
But, blind or lame or sick or sound,
  We follow that which flies before;
We know the merry world is round,
  And we may sail for evermore.

SIR LAUNCELOT AND QUEEN GUINEVERE

A FRAGMENT

First printed in 1842. In the 1st stanza ' elm-tree ' was originally ' linden '; and in the 4th ' In ' was ' On,' and ' fleeter now ' was ' still more fleet.'

LIKE souls that balance joy and pain,
With tears and smiles from heaven again
The maiden Spring upon the plain
Came in a sunlit fall of rain.
  In crystal vapor everywhere
Blue isles of heaven laugh'd between,
And far, in forest-deeps unseen,
The topmost elm-tree gather'd green
  From draughts of balmy air.

Sometimes the linnet piped his song;
Sometimes the throstle whistled strong;
Sometimes the sparhawk, wheel'd along,
Hush'd all the groves from fear of wrong;
  By grassy capes with fuller sound
In curves the yellowing river ran,
And drooping chestnut-buds began
To spread into the perfect fan,
  Above the teeming ground.

Then, in the boyhood of the year,
Sir Launcelot and Queen Guinevere

Rode thro' the coverts of the deer,
With blissful treble ringing clear.
  She seem'd a part of joyous Spring;
A gown of grass-green silk she wore,
Buckled with golden clasps before;
A light-green tuft of plumes she bore
  Closed in a golden ring.

Now on some twisted ivy-net,
Now by some tinkling rivulet,
In mosses mixt with violet
Her cream-white mule his pastern set;
  And fleeter now she skimm'd the
    plains
Than she whose elfin prancer springs
By night to eery warblings,
When all the glimmering moorland rings
  With jingling bridle-reins.

As she fled fast thro' sun and shade,
The happy winds upon her play'd,
Blowing the ringlet from the braid.
She look'd so lovely, as she sway'd
  The rein with dainty finger-tips,
A man had given all other bliss,
And all his worldly worth for this,
To waste his whole heart in one kiss
  Upon her perfect lips.

A FAREWELL

First printed in 1842, and unaltered except ' thousand suns ' for ' hundred suns.'

FLOW down, cold rivulet, to the sea,
  Thy tribute wave deliver;
No more by thee my steps shall be,
  For ever and for ever.

Flow, softly flow, by lawn and lea,
  A rivulet, then a river;
Nowhere by thee my steps shall be,
  For ever and for ever.

But here will sigh thine alder-tree,
  And here thine aspen shiver;
And here by thee will hum the bee,
  For ever and for ever.

A thousand suns will stream on thee,
  A thousand moons will quiver;
But not by thee my steps shall be,
  For ever and for ever.

THE BEGGAR MAID

First printed in 1842, and unaltered. It is founded on the old ballad of 'King Cophetua and the Beggar Maid,' which was very popular in its day, and is alluded to by Shakespeare in 'Love's Labour's Lost,' 'Richard II.,' and 'Romeo and Juliet.'

HER arms across her breast she laid;
  She was more fair than words can say;
Barefooted came the beggar maid
  Before the king Cophetua.
In robe and crown the king stept down,
  To meet and greet her on her way;
'It is no wonder,' said the lords,
  'She is more beautiful than day.'

As shines the moon in clouded skies,
  She in her poor attire was seen;
One praised her ankles, one her eyes,
  One her dark hair and lovesome mien.
So sweet a face, such angel grace,
  In all that land had never been.
Cophetua sware a royal oath:
  'This beggar maid shall be my queen!'

THE EAGLE

FRAGMENT

First printed in the edition of 1851.

HE clasps the crag with crooked hands;
Close to the sun in lonely lands,
Ring'd with the azure world, he stands.

The wrinkled sea beneath him crawls;
He watches from his mountain walls,
And like a thunderbolt he falls.

'MOVE EASTWARD, HAPPY EARTH'

First printed in 1842, when the ninth line had 'lightly' instead of 'smoothly.'
The 'silver sister-world' is Venus, the morning-star, not the moon, as some have assumed.

MOVE eastward, happy earth, and leave
  Yon orange sunset waning slow;
From fringes of the faded eve,
  O happy planet, eastward go,
Till over thy dark shoulder glow
  Thy silver sister-world, and rise

To glass herself in dewy eyes
That watch me from the glen below.

Ah, bear me with thee, smoothly borne,
  Dip forward under starry light,
And move me to my marriage-morn,
  And round again to happy night.

'COME NOT, WHEN I AM DEAD'

First printed in 'The Keepsake' for 1851, under the title of 'Stanzas;' included in the seventh edition of the 'Poems' the same year.

COME not, when I am dead,
  To drop thy foolish tears upon my grave,
To trample round my fallen head,
  And vex the unhappy dust thou wouldst
    not save.
There let the wind sweep and the plover
    cry;
    But thou, go by.

Child, if it were thine error or thy crime
  I care no longer, being all unblest:
Wed whom thou wilt, but I am sick of
    time,
  And I desire to rest.
Pass on, weak heart, and leave me where I
    lie;
    Go by, go by.

THE LETTERS

First published with 'Maud' in 1855, and unaltered.

I

STILL on the tower stood the vane,
  A black yew gloom'd the stagnant air;
I peer'd athwart the chancel pane
  And saw the altar cold and bare.
A clog of lead was round my feet,
  A band of pain across my brow;
'Cold altar, heaven and earth shall meet
  Before you hear my marriage vow.'

II

I turn'd and humm'd a bitter song
  That mock'd the wholesome human
    heart,
And then we met in wrath and wrong,
  We met, but only meant to part.
Full cold my greeting was and dry;
  She faintly smiled, she hardly moved;

I saw with half-unconscious eye
She wore the colors I approved.

III

She took the little ivory chest,
  With half a sigh she turn'd the key,
Then raised her head with lips comprest,
  And gave my letters back to me;
And gave the trinkets and the rings,
  My gifts, when gifts of mine could
    please.
As looks a father on the things
  Of his dead son, I look'd on these.

IV

She told me all her friends had said;
  I raged against the public liar;
She talk'd as if her love were dead,
  But in my words were seeds of fire.
'No more of love, your sex is known;
  I never will be twice deceived.
Henceforth I trust the man alone,
  The woman cannot be believed.

V

'Thro' slander, meanest spawn of hell, —
  And women's slander is the worst, —
And you, whom once I loved so well,
  Thro' you my life will be accurst.'
I spoke with heart and heat and force,
  I shook her breast with vague alarms —
Like torrents from a mountain source
  We rush'd into each other's arms.

VI

We parted; sweetly gleam'd the stars,
  And sweet the vapor-braided blue;
Low breezes fann'd the belfry bars,
  As homeward by the church I drew.
The very graves appear'd to smile,
  So fresh they rose in shadow'd swells;
'Dark porch,' I said, 'and silent aisle,
  There comes a sound of marriage bells.'

THE VISION OF SIN

First printed in 1842. Lines 97, 98, 121, 122
at first had 'minute' for 'moment'; 106, 'in'
for 'by'; 128, 'the' for 'a'; 188, 'or' for
'nor'; 208, 'Again' for 'Once more'; and
213, 'said' for 'spake.' In the 'Selections' of
1865 (but only there) the following couplet ap-
pears after line 214: —

> Another answer'd : 'But a crime of sense ?
> Give him new nerves with old experience.'

I

I HAD a vision when the night was late;
A youth came riding toward a palace-gate.
He rode a horse with wings, that would
  have flown,
But that his heavy rider kept him down.
And from the palace came a child of sin,
And took him by the curls, and led him
  in,
Where sat a company with heated eyes,
Expecting when a fountain should arise.
A sleepy light upon their brows and lips —
As when the sun, a crescent of eclipse,   10
Dreams over lake and lawn, and isles and
  capes —
Suffused them, sitting, lying, languid
  shapes,
By heaps of gourds, and skins of wine, and
  piles of grapes.

II

Then methought I heard a mellow sound,
Gathering up from all the lower ground;
Narrowing in to where they sat assem-
  bled,
Low voluptuous music winding trembled,
Woven in circles. They that heard it sigh'd,
Panted hand-in-hand with faces pale,
Swung themselves, and in low tones re-
  plied;   20
Till the fountain spouted, showering wide
Sleet of diamond-drift and pearly hail.
Then the music touch'd the gates and died,
Rose again from where it seem'd to fail,
Storm'd in orbs of song, a growing gale;
Till thronging in and in, to where they
  waited,
As 't were a hundred-throated nightingale,
The strong tempestuous treble throbb'd
  and palpitated;
Ran into its giddiest whirl of sound,
Caught the sparkles, and in circles,   30
Purple gauzes, golden hazes, liquid mazes,
Flung the torrent rainbow round.
Then they started from their places,
Moved with violence, changed in hue,
Caught each other with wild grimaces,
Half-invisible to the view,
Wheeling with precipitate paces
To the melody, till they flew,
Hair and eyes and limbs and faces,
Twisted hard in fierce embraces,   40
Like to Furies, like to Graces,
Dash'd together in blinding dew;

Till, kill'd with some luxurious agony,
The nerve-dissolving melody
Flutter'd headlong from the sky.

III

And then I look'd up toward a mountain-
   tract,
That girt the region with high cliff and
   lawn.
I saw that every morning, far withdrawn
Beyond the darkness and the cataract,
God made Himself an awful rose of dawn,
Unheeded; and detaching, fold by fold, 51
From those still heights, and, slowly draw-
   ing near,
A vapor heavy, hueless, formless, cold,
Came floating on for many a month and
   year,
Unheeded; and I thought I would have
   spoken,
And warn'd that madman ere it grew too
   late,
But, as in dreams, I could not.   Mine was
   broken,
When that cold vapor touch'd the palace-
   gate,
And link'd again.   I saw within my head
A gray and gap-tooth'd man as lean as
   death, 60
Who slowly rode across a wither'd heath,
And lighted at a ruin'd inn, and said:

IV

' Wrinkled ostler, grim and thin !
   Here is custom come your way;
Take my brute, and lead him in,
   Stuff his ribs with mouldy hay.

' Bitter barmaid, waning fast !
   See that sheets are on my bed.
What ! the flower of life is past;
   It is long before you wed. 70

' Slip-shod waiter, lank and sour,
   At the Dragon on the heath !
Let us have a quiet hour,
   Let us hob-and-nob with Death.

' I am old, but let me drink;
   Bring me spices, bring me wine;
I remember, when I think,
   That my youth was half divine.

' Wine is good for shrivell'd lips,
   When a blanket wraps the day, 80

When the rotten woodland drips,
   And the leaf is stamp'd in clay.

' Sit thee down, and have no shame,
   Cheek by jowl, and knee by knee;
What care I for any name ?
   What for order or degree ?

' Let me screw thee up a peg;
   Let me loose thy tongue with wine;
Callest thou that thing a leg ?
   Which is thinnest ? thine or mine ? 90

' Thou shalt not be saved by works,
   Thou hast been a sinner too;
Ruin'd trunks on wither'd forks,
   Empty scarecrows, I and you !

' Fill the cup and fill the can,
   Have a rouse before the morn;
Every moment dies a man,
   Every moment one is born.

' We are men of ruin'd blood;
   Therefore comes it we are wise. 100
Fish are we that love the mud,
   Rising to no fancy-flies.

' Name and fame ! to fly sublime
   Thro' the courts, the camps, the schools,
Is to be the ball of Time,
   Bandied by the hands of fools.

' Friendship ! — to be two in one —
   Let the canting liar pack !
Well I know, when I am gone,
   How she mouths behind my back. 110

' Virtue ! — to be good and just —
   Every heart, when sifted well,
Is a clot of warmer dust,
   Mix'd with cunning sparks of hell.

' O, we two as well can look
   Whited thought and cleanly life
As the priest, above his book
   Leering at his neighbor's wife.

' Fill the cup and fill the can,
   Have a rouse before the morn: 120
Every moment dies a man,
   Every moment one is born.

' Drink, and let the parties rave;
   They are fill'd with idle spleen,

Rising, falling, like a wave,
  For they know not what they mean.

'He that roars for liberty
  Faster binds a tyrant's power,
And the tyrant's cruel glee
  Forces on the freer hour.   130

'Fill the can and fill the cup;
  All the windy ways of men
Are but dust that rises up,
  And is lightly laid again.

'Greet her with applausive breath,
  Freedom, gaily doth she tread;
In her right a civic wreath,
  In her left a human head.

'No, I love not what is new;
  She is of an ancient house,   140
And I think we know the hue
  Of that cap upon her brows.

'Let her go! her thirst she slakes
  Where the bloody conduit runs,
Then her sweetest meal she makes
  On the first-born of her sons.

'Drink to lofty hopes that cool, —
  Visions of a perfect State;
Drink we, last, the public fool,
  Frantic love and frantic hate.   150

'Chant me now some wicked stave,
  Till thy drooping courage rise,
And the glow-worm of the grave
  Glimmer in thy rheumy eyes.

'Fear not thou to loose thy tongue,
  Set thy hoary fancies free;
What is loathsome to the young
  Savors well to thee and me.

'Change, reverting to the years,
  When thy nerves could understand 160
What there is in loving tears,
  And the warmth of hand in hand.

'Tell me tales of thy first love —
  April hopes, the fools of chance —
Till the graves begin to move,
  And the dead begin to dance.

'Fill the can and fill the cup;
  All the windy ways of men

Are but dust that rises up,
  And is lightly laid again.   170

'Trooping from their mouldy dens
  The chap-fallen circle spreads —
Welcome, fellow-citizens,
  Hollow hearts and empty heads!

'You are bones, and what of that?
  Every face, however full,
Padded round with flesh and fat,
  Is but modell'd on a skull.

'Death is king, and Vivat Rex!
  Tread a measure on the stones,   180
Madam — if I know your sex
  From the fashion of your bones.

'No, I cannot praise the fire
  In your eye — nor yet your lip;
All the more do I admire
  Joints of cunning workmanship.

'Lo! God's likeness — the ground-plan —
  Neither modell'd, glazed, nor framed;
Buss me, thou rough sketch of man,
  Far too naked to be shamed!   190

'Drink to Fortune, drink to Chance,
  While we keep a little breath!
Drink to heavy Ignorance!
  Hob-and-nob with brother Death!

'Thou art mazed, the night is long,
  And the longer night is near —
What! I am not all as wrong
  As a bitter jest is dear.

'Youthful hopes, by scores, to all,
  When the locks are crisp and curl'd; 200
Unto me my maudlin gall
  And my mockeries of the world.

'Fill the cup and fill the can;
  Mingle madness, mingle scorn!
Dregs of life, and lees of man;
  Yet we will not die forlorn.'

V

The voice grew faint; there came a further
  change;
Once more uprose the mystic mountain-
  range.
Below were men and horses pierced with
  worms,   209

And slowly quickening into lower forms;
By shards and scurf of salt, and scum of
    dross,
Old plash of rains, and refuse patch'd with
    moss.
Then some one spake: 'Behold! it was a
    crime
Of sense avenged by sense that wore with
    time.'
Another said: 'The crime of sense became
The crime of malice, and is equal blame.'
And one: 'He had not wholly quench'd his
    power;
A little grain of conscience made him sour.'
At last I heard a voice upon the slope   219
Cry to the summit, 'Is there any hope?'
To which an answer peal'd from that high
    land,
But in a tongue no man could understand;
And on the glimmering limit far with-
    drawn
God made Himself an awful rose of dawn.

TO —

AFTER READING A LIFE AND LETTERS

'Cursed be he that moves my bones.'
Shakespeare's Epitaph.

First printed in the 'Examiner' for March 24,
1849, and included in the sixth edition of the
'Poems' in 1850. The second part of the title,
'After Reading a Life and Letters,' was added
in 1853.

You might have won the Poet's name,
    If such be worth the winning now,
    And gain'd a laurel for your brow
Of sounder leaf than I can claim;

But you have made the wiser choice,
    A life that moves to gracious ends
    Thro' troops of unrecording friends,
A deedful life, a silent voice.

And you have miss'd the irreverent doom
    Of those that wear the Poet's crown;
    Hereafter, neither knave nor clown
Shall hold their orgies at your tomb.

For now the Poet cannot die,
    Nor leave his music as of old,
    But round him ere he scarce be cold
Begins the scandal and the cry:

'Proclaim the faults he would not show;
    Break lock and seal, betray the trust;
    Keep nothing sacred, 't is but just
The many-headed beast should know.'

Ah, shameless! for he did but sing
    A song that pleased us from its worth;
    No public life was his on earth,
No blazon'd statesman he, nor king.

He gave the people of his best;
    His worst he kept, his best he gave.
    My Shakespeare's curse on clown and
        knave
Who will not let his ashes rest!

Who make it seem more sweet to be
    The little life of bank and brier,
    The bird that pipes his lone desire
And dies unheard within his tree,

Than he that warbles long and loud
    And drops at Glory's temple-gates,
    For whom the carrion vulture waits
To tear his heart before the crowd!

TO E. L., ON HIS TRAVELS IN GREECE

First printed in 1853, and unaltered. It was
addressed to Edward Lear, the painter, and
refers to his 'Landscape-Painter in Albania
and Illyria,' 1851.

ILLYRIAN woodlands, echoing falls
    Of water, sheets of summer glass,
    The long divine Peneïan pass,
The vast Akrokeraunian walls,

Tomohrit, Athos, all things fair,
    With such a pencil, such a pen,
    You shadow forth to distant men,
I read and felt that I was there.

And trust me while I turn'd the page,
    And track'd you still on classic ground,
    I grew in gladness till I found
My spirits in the golden age.

For me the torrent ever pour'd
    And glisten'd — here and there alone
    The broad-limb'd Gods at random thrown
By fountain-urns; — and Naiads oar'd

A glimmering shoulder under gloom
  Of cavern pillars; on the swell
  The silver lily heaved and fell;
And many a slope was rich in bloom,

From him that on the mountain lea
  By dancing rivulets fed his flocks
  To him who sat upon the rocks
And fluted to the morning sea.

First printed in 1842, and unaltered. Various fanciful accounts of its origin have been published; but, according to the poet himself, 'it was made in a Lincolnshire lane at five o'clock in the morning between blossoming hedges.'

BREAK, break, break,
  On thy cold gray stones, O Sea!
And I would that my tongue could utter
  The thoughts that arise in me.

O, well for the fisherman's boy,
  That he shouts with his sister at play!
O, well for the sailor lad,
  That he sings in his boat on the bay!

And the stately ships go on
  To their haven under the hill;
But O for the touch of a vanish'd hand,
  And the sound of a voice that is still!

Break, break, break,
  At the foot of thy crags, O Sea!

But the tender grace of a day that is dead
Will never come back to me.

THE POET'S SONG

First printed in 1842, and unaltered for more than forty years, when 'fly' was substituted for 'bee' in the first line of the second stanza.

THE rain had fallen, the Poet arose,
  He pass'd by the town and out of the
    street;
A light wind blew from the gates of the
    sun,
  And waves of shadow went over the
    wheat;
And he sat him down in a lonely place,
  And chanted a melody loud and sweet,
That made the wild-swan pause in her
    cloud,
  And the lark drop down at his feet.

The swallow stopt as he hunted the fly,
  The snake slipt under a spray,
The wild hawk stood with the down on his
    beak,
  And stared, with his foot on the prey;
And the nightingale thought, 'I have sung
    many songs,
  But never a one so gay,
For he sings of what the world will be
  When the years have died away.'

THE PRINCESS; A MEDLEY

The poem was first published in 1847, but has since undergone many changes. In the second edition, issued in 1848, the dedication to Henry Lushington was added (omitted in the recent editions), and the text was slightly revised. In the third (1850) the six intercalary songs were inserted, many additions and alterations were made in the body of the poem, and the Prologue and Conclusion were partially rewritten. The most important change in the fourth edition (1851) was the introduction of the passages relating to the 'weird seizures' of the Prince. In the fifth edition (1853) lines 35-49 of the Prologue ('O miracle of women,' etc.) first appeared, and the text was settled in the form which it has since preserved. For the various readings, etc., see the Notes.

PROLOGUE

SIR WALTER VIVIAN all a summer's day
Gave his broad lawns until the set of sun
Up to the people; thither flock'd at noon
His tenants, wife and child, and thither
  half

The neighboring borough with their Institute,
Of which he was the patron. I was there
From college, visiting the son, — the son
A Walter too, — with others of our set,
Five others; we were seven at Vivianplace.

And me that morning Walter show'd the
   house,   10
Greek, set with busts. From vases in the
   hall
Flowers of all heavens, and lovelier than
   their names,
Grew side by side; and on the pavement lay
Carved stones of the Abbey-ruin in the
   park,
Huge Ammonites, and the first bones of
   Time;
And on the tables every clime and age
Jumbled together; celts and calumets,
Claymore and snow-shoe, toys in lava, fans
Of sandal, amber, ancient rosaries,
Laborious orient ivory sphere in sphere, 20
The cursed Malayan crease, and battle-
   clubs
From the isles of palm; and higher on the
   walls,
Betwixt the monstrous horns of elk and
   deer,
His own forefathers' arms and armor hung.

And 'this,' he said, ' was Hugh's at Agin-
   court;
And that was old Sir Ralph's at Ascalon.
A good knight he ! we keep a chronicle
With all about him,' — which he brought,
   and I
Dived in a hoard of tales that dealt with
   knights   29
Half-legend, half-historic, counts and kings
Who laid about them at their wills and
   died;
And mixt with these a lady, one that arm'd
Her own fair head, and sallying thro' the
   gate,
Had beat her foes with slaughter from her
   walls.

'O miracle of women,' said the book,
'O noble heart who, being strait-besieged
By this wild king to force her to his wish,
Nor bent, nor broke, nor shunn'd a soldier's
   death,
But now when all was lost or seem'd as
   lost —   39
Her stature more than mortal in the burst
Of sunrise, her arm lifted, eyes on fire —
Brake with a blast of trumpets from the
   gate,
And, falling on them like a thunderbolt,
She trampled some beneath her horses'
   heels,

And some were whelm'd with missiles of
   the wall,
And some were push'd with lances from
   the rock,
And part were drown'd within the whirling
   brook;
O miracle of noble womanhood !'

So sang the gallant glorious chronicle;
And, I all rapt in this, 'Come out,' he
   said,   50
'To the Abbey; there is Aunt Elizabeth
And sister Lilia with the rest.' We went —
I kept the book and had my finger in
   it —
Down thro' the park. Strange was the sight
   to me;
For all the sloping pasture murmur'd,
   sown
With happy faces and with holiday.
There moved the multitude, a thousand
   heads;
The patient leaders of their Institute
Taught them with facts. One rear'd a font
   of stone   59
And drew, from butts of water on the slope,
The fountain of the moment, playing, now
A twisted snake, and now a rain of pearls,
Or steep-up spout whereon the gilded ball
Danced like a wisp; and somewhat lower
   down
A man with knobs and wires and vials fire
A cannon; Echo answer'd in her sleep
From hollow fields; and here were tele-
   scopes
For azure views; and there a group of girls
In circle waited, whom the electric shock
Dislink'd with shrieks and laughter; round
   the lake   70
A little clock-work steamer paddling plied
And shook the lilies; perch'd about the
   knolls
A dozen angry models jetted steam;
A petty railway ran; a fire-balloon
Rose gem-like up before the dusky groves
And dropt a fairy parachute and past;
And there thro' twenty posts of telegraph
They flash'd a saucy message to and fro
Between the mimic stations; so that sport
Went hand in hand with science; other-
   where   80
Pure sport; a herd of boys with clamor
   bowl'd
And stump'd the wicket; babies roll'd
   about

Like tumbled fruit in grass; and men and
maids
Arranged a country dance, and flew thro'
light
And shadow, while the twangling violin
Struck up with Soldier-laddie, and over-
head
The broad ambrosial aisles of lofty lime
Made noise with bees and breeze from end
to end.

Strange was the sight and smacking of
the time; 89
And long we gazed, but satiated at length
Came to the ruins. High-arch'd and ivy-
claspt,
Of finest Gothic lighter than a fire,
Thro' one wide chasm of time and frost
they gave
The park, the crowd, the house; but all
within
The sward was trim as any garden lawn.
And here we lit on Aunt Elizabeth,
And Lilia with the rest, and lady friends
From neighbor seats; and there was Ralph
himself,
A broken statue propt against the wall,
As gay as any. Lilia, wild with sport, 100
Half child, half woman as she was, had
wound
A scarf of orange round the stony helm,
And robed the shoulders in a rosy silk,
That made the old warrior from his ivied
nook
Glow like a sunbeam. Near his tomb a feast
Shone, silver-set; about it lay the guests,
And there we join'd them; then the maiden
aunt
Took this fair day for text, and from it
preach'd
An universal culture for the crowd,
And all things great. But we, unworthier,
told 110
Of college: he had climb'd across the spikes,
And he had squeezed himself betwixt the
bars,
And he had breathed the Proctor's dogs;
and one
Discuss'd his tutor, rough to common men,
But honeying at the whisper of a lord;
And one the Master, as a rogue in grain
Veneer'd with sanctimonious theory.

But while they talk'd, above their heads
I saw

The feudal warrior lady-clad; which
brought 119
My book to mind, and opening this I read
Of old Sir Ralph a page or two that rang
With tilt and tourney; then the tale of her
That drove her foes with slaughter from
her walls,
And much I praised her nobleness, and
'Where,'
Ask'd Walter, patting Lilia's head—she lay
Beside him—'lives there such a woman
now?'

Quick answer'd Lilia: 'There are thou-
sands now
Such women, but convention beats them
down;
It is but bringing up; no more than that.
You men have done it—how I hate you
all! 130
Ah, were I something great! I wish I were
Some mighty poetess, I would shame you
then,
That love to keep us children! O, I wish
That I were some great princess, I would
build
Far off from men a college like a man's,
And I would teach them all that men are
taught;
We are twice as quick!' And here she
shook aside
The hand that play'd the patron with her
curls.

And one said smiling: 'Pretty were the
sight
If our old halls could change their sex, and
flaunt 140
With prudes for proctors, dowagers for
deans,
And sweet girl-graduates in their golden
hair.
I think they should not wear our rusty
gowns,
But move as rich as Emperor-moths, or
Ralph
Who shines so in the corner; yet I fear,
If there were many Lilias in the brood,
However deep you might embower the nest,
Some boy would spy it.'
At this upon the sward
She tapt her tiny silken-sandall'd foot:
'That's your light way; but I would make
it death 150
For any male thing but to peep at us.'

Petulant she spoke, and at herself she laugh'd;
A rosebud set with little wilful thorns,
And sweet as English air could make her, she!
But Walter hail'd a score of names upon her,
And 'petty Ogress,' and 'ungrateful Puss,'
And swore he long'd at college, only long'd,
All else was well, for she-society.
They boated and they cricketed; they talk'd
At wine, in clubs, of art, of politics;   160
They lost their weeks; they vext the souls of deans;
They rode; they betted; made a hundred friends,
And caught the blossom of the flying terms,
But miss'd the mignonette of Vivian-place,
The little hearth-flower Lilia. Thus he spoke,
Part banter, part affection.
                        'True,' she said,
'We doubt not that. O, yes, you miss'd us much!
I 'll stake my ruby ring upon it you did.'

She held it out; and as a parrot turns
Up thro' gilt wires a crafty loving eye,   170
And takes a lady's finger with all care,
And bites it for true heart and not for harm,
So he with Lilia's. Daintily she shriek'd
And wrung it. 'Doubt my word again!' he said.
'Come, listen! here is proof that you were miss'd:
We seven stay'd at Christmas up to read;
And there we took one tutor as to read.
The hard-grain'd Muses of the cube and square
Were out of season; never man, I think,
So moulder'd in a sinecure as he;   180
For while our cloisters echo'd frosty feet,
And our long walks were stript as bare as brooms,
We did but talk you over, pledge you all
In wassail; often, like as many girls —
Sick for the hollies and the yews of home —
As many little trifling Lilias — play'd
Charades and riddles as at Christmas here,
And *what 's my thought* and *when and where and how*,
And often told a tale from mouth to mouth
As here at Christmas.'

She remember'd that;   190
A pleasant game, she thought. She liked it more
Than magic music, forfeits, all the rest.
But these — what kind of tales did men tell men,
She wonder'd, by themselves?
                        A half-disdain
Perch'd on the pouted blossom of her lips;
And Walter nodded at me: '*He* began,
The rest would follow, each in turn; and so
We forged a sevenfold story. Kind? what kind?
Chimeras, crotchets, Christmas solecisms;
Seven-headed monsters only made to kill
Time by the fire in winter.'
                        'Kill him now,
The tyrant! kill him in the summer too,'
Said Lilia; 'Why not now?' the maiden aunt.   203
'Why not a summer's as a winter's tale?
A tale for summer as befits the time,
And something it should be to suit the place,
Heroic, for a hero lies beneath,
Grave, solemn!'
                        Walter warp'd his mouth at this
To something so mock-solemn, that I laugh'd,
And Lilia woke with sudden-shrilling mirth
An echo like a ghostly woodpecker   211
Hid in the ruins; till the maiden aunt —
A little sense of wrong had touch'd her face
With color — turn'd to me with 'As you will;
Heroic if you will, or what you will,
Or be yourself your hero if you will.'

'Take Lilia, then, for heroine,' clamor'd he,
'And make her some great princess, six feet high,
Grand, epic, homicidal; and be you   219
The prince to win her!'
                        'Then follow me, the prince,
I answer'd, 'each be hero in his turn!
Seven and yet one, like shadows in a dream. —
Heroic seems our princess as required —
But something made to suit with time and place,
A Gothic ruin and a Grecian house,
A talk of college and of ladies' rights,
A feudal knight in silken masquerade,

And, yonder, shrieks and strange experiments
For which the good Sir Ralph had burnt
  them all —
This *were* a medley ! we should have him
  back   230
Who told the " Winter's Tale " to do it for
  us.
No matter; we will say whatever comes.
And let the ladies sing us, if they will,
From time to time, some ballad or a song
To give us breathing-space.'
                      So I began,
And the rest follow'd; and the women
  sang
Between the rougher voices of the men,
Like linnets in the pauses of the wind:
And here I give the story and the songs.

I

A Prince I was, blue-eyed, and fair in face,
Of temper amorous as the first of May,
With lengths of yellow ringlet, like a girl,
For on my cradle shone the Northern star.

There lived an ancient legend in our
  house.
Some sorcerer, whom a far-off grandsire
  burnt
Because he cast no shadow, had foretold,
Dying, that none of all our blood should
  know
The shadow from the substance, and that
  one
Should come to fight with shadows and to
  fall;   10
For so, my mother said, the story ran.
And, truly, waking dreams were, more or
  less,
An old and strange affection of the house.
Myself too had weird seizures, Heaven
  knows what!
On a sudden in the midst of men and day,
And while I walk'd and talk'd as hereto-
  fore,
I seem'd to move among a world of ghosts,
And feel myself the shadow of a dream.
Our great court-Galen poised his gilt-head
  cane,
And paw'd his beard, and mutter'd ' cata-
  lepsy.'   20
My mother pitying made a thousand
  prayers.
My mother was as mild as any saint,

Half-canonized by all that look'd on her,
So gracious was her tact and tenderness;
But my good father thought a king a king.
He cared not for the affection of the house;
He held his sceptre like a pedant's wand
To lash offence, and with long arms and
  hands
Reach'd out and pick'd offenders from the
  mass
For judgment.
              Now it chanced that I had been,
While life was yet in bud and blade, be-
  troth'd   31
To one, a neighboring Princess. She to me
Was proxy-wedded with a bootless calf
At eight years old; and still from time to
  time
Came murmurs of her beauty from the
  South,
And of her brethren, youths of puissance;
And still I wore her picture by my heart,
And one dark tress; and all around them
  both
Sweet thoughts would swarm as bees about
  their queen.

But when the days drew nigh that I
  should wed,   40
My father sent ambassadors with furs
And jewels, gifts, to fetch her. These
  brought back
A present, a great labor of the loom;
And therewithal an answer vague as wind.
Besides, they saw the king; he took the
  gifts;
He said there was a compact; that was
  true;
But then she had a will; was he to blame ?
And maiden fancies; loved to live alone
Among her women; certain, would not wed.

That morning in the presence room I
  stood   50
With Cyril and with Florian, my two
  friends:
The first, a gentleman of broken means —
His father's fault — but given to starts and
  bursts
Of revel; and the last, my other heart,
And almost my half-self, for still we moved
Together, twinn'd as horse's ear and eye.

Now, while they spake, I saw my father's
  face
Grow long and troubled like a rising moon,

Inflamed with wrath. He started on his
    feet,
Tore the king's letter, snow'd it down, and
    rent   60
The wonder of the loom thro' warp and
    woof
From skirt to skirt; and at the last he
    sware
That he would send a hundred thousand
    men,
And bring her in a whirlwind; then he
    chew'd
The thrice-turn'd cud of wrath, and cook'd
    his spleen,
Communing with his captains of the war.

At last I spoke: ' My father, let me go.
It cannot be but some gross error lies
In this report, this answer of a king   69
Whom all men rate as kind and hospitable;
Or, maybe, I myself, my bride once seen,
Whate'er my grief to find her less than
    fame,
May rue the bargain made.' And Florian
    said:
' I have a sister at the foreign court,
Who moves about the Princess; she, you
    know,
Who wedded with a nobleman from thence.
He, dying lately, left her, as I hear,
The lady of three castles in that land;
Thro' her this matter might be sifted
    clean.'
And Cyril whisper'd: ' Take me with you
    too.'   80
Then laughing, ' What if these weird seiz-
    ures come
Upon you in those lands, and no one near
To point you out the shadow from the
    truth !
Take me; I 'll serve you better in a strait;
I grate on rusty hinges here.' But ' No ! '
Roar'd the rough king, ' you shall not; we
    ourself
Will crush her pretty maiden fancies dead
In iron gauntlets; break the council up.'

But when the council broke, I rose and
    past
Thro' the wild woods that hung about the
    town;   90
Found a still place, and pluck'd her like-
    ness out;
Laid it on flowers, and watch'd it lying
    bathed

In the green gleam of dewy-tassell'd trees.
What were those fancies ? wherefore break
    her troth ?
Proud look'd the lips; but while I medi-
    tated
A wind arose and rush'd upon the South,
And shook the songs, the whispers, and the
    shrieks
Of the wild woods together, and a Voice
Went with it, ' Follow, follow, thou shalt
    win.'   99

Then, ere the silver sickle of that month
Became her golden shield, I stole from
    court
With Cyril and with Florian, unperceived,
Cat-footed thro' the town and half in dread
To hear my father's clamor at our backs
With ' Ho ! ' from some bay-window shake
    the night;
But all was quiet. From the bastion'd walls
Like threaded spiders, one by one, we
    dropt,
And flying reach'd the frontier; then we
    crost
To a livelier land; and so by tilth and
    grange,
And vines, and blowing bosks of wilder-
    ness,   110
We gain'd the mother-city thick with
    towers,
And in the imperial palace found the king.

His name was Gama; crack'd and small
    his voice,
But bland the smile that like a wrinkling
    wind
On glassy water drove his cheek in lines;
A little dry old man, without a star,
Not like a king. Three days he feasted us,
And on the fourth I spake of why we came,
And my betroth'd. ' You do us, Prince,'
    he said,
Airing a snowy hand and signet gem,   120
' All honor. We remember love ourself
In our sweet youth. There did a compact
    pass
Long summers back, a kind of ceremony —
I think the year in which our olives fail'd.
I would you had her, Prince, with all my
    heart,
With my full heart; but there were widows
    here,
Two widows, Lady Psyche, Lady Blanche;
They fed her theories, in and out of place

Maintaining that with equal husbandry
The woman were an equal to the man. 130
They harp'd on this; with this our banquets
   rang;
Our dances broke and buzz'd in knots of
   talk;
Nothing but this; my very ears were hot
To hear them. Knowledge, so my daughter
   held,
Was all in all; they had but been, she
   thought,
As children; they must lose the child, as-
   sume
The woman. Then, sir, awful odes she
   wrote,
Too awful, sure, for what they treated of,
But all she is and does is awful; odes 139
About this losing of the child; and rhymes
And dismal lyrics, prophesying change
Beyond all reason. These the women sang;
And they that know such things — I sought
   but peace;
No critic I — would call them master-
   pieces.
They master'd *me*. At last she begg'd a
   boon,
A certain summer-palace which I have
Hard by your father's frontier. I said no,
Yet being an easy man, gave it; and there,
All wild to found an University
For maidens, on the spur she fled; and
   more 150
We know not, — only this: they see no
   men,
Not even her brother Arac, nor the twins
Her brethren, tho' they love her, look upon
   her
As on a kind of paragon; and I —
Pardon me saying it — were much loth to
   breed
Dispute betwixt myself and mine; but
   since —
And I confess with right — you think me
   bound
In some sort, I can give you letters to her;
And yet, to speak the truth, I rate your
   chance 159
Almost at naked nothing.'
            Thus the king;
And I, tho' nettled that he seem'd to slur
With garrulous ease and oily courtesies
Our formal compact, yet, not less — all frets
But chafing me on fire to find my bride —
Went forth again with both my friends.
   We rode

Many a long league back to the North.
   At last
From hills that look'd across a land of
   hope
We dropt with evening on a rustic town
Set in a gleaming river's crescent-curve,
Close at the boundary of the liberties; 170
There, enter'd an old hostel, call'd mine
   host
To council, plied him with his richest wines,
And show'd the late-writ letters of the
   king.

He with a long low sibilation, stared
As blank as death in marble; then ex-
   claim'd,
Averring it was clear against all rules
For any man to go; but as his brain
Began to mellow, 'If the king,' he said,
'Had given us letters, was he bound to
   speak?
The king would bear him out;' and at the
   last — 180
The summer of the vine in all his veins —
'No doubt that we might make it worth
   his while.
She once had past that way; he heard her
   speak;
She scared him; life! he never saw the
   like;
She look'd as grand as doomsday and as
   grave!
And he, he reverenced his liege-lady there;
He always made a point to post with
   mares;
His daughter and his housemaid were the
   boys;
The land, he understood, for miles about
Was till'd by women; all the swine were
   sows, 190
And all the dogs' —
           But while he jested thus,
A thought flash'd thro' me which I clothed
   in act,
Remembering how we three presented
   Maid,
Or Nymph, or Goddess, at high tide of
   feast,
In masque or pageant at my father's court.
We sent mine host to purchase female
   gear;
He brought it, and himself, a sight to shake
The midriff of despair with laughter, holp
To lace us up, till each in maiden plumes
We rustled; him we gave a costly bribe 200

To guerdon silence, mounted our good
    steeds,
And boldly ventured on the liberties.

We follow'd up the river as we rode,
And rode till midnight, when the college
    lights
Began to glitter firefly-like in copse
And linden alley; then we past an arch,
Whereon a woman-statue rose with wings
From four wing'd horses dark against the
    stars,
And some inscription ran along the front,
But deep in shadow. Further on we gain'd
A little street half garden and half house,
But scarce could hear each other speak for
    noise   212
Of clocks and chimes, like silver hammers
    falling
On silver anvils, and the splash and stir
Of fountains spouted up and showering
    down
In meshes of the jasmine and the rose;
And all about us peal'd the nightingale,
Rapt in her song and careless of the snare.

There stood a bust of Pallas for a sign,
By two sphere lamps blazon'd like Heaven
    and Earth   220
With constellation and with continent,
Above an entry. Riding in, we call'd;
A plump-arm'd ostleress and a stable wench
Came running at the call, and help'd us
    down.
Then stept a buxom hostess forth, and sail'd,
Full-blown, before us into rooms which
    gave
Upon a pillar'd porch, the bases lost
In laurel. Her we ask'd of that and this,
And who were tutors. 'Lady Blanche.'
    she said,
'And Lady Psyche.' 'Which was pret-
    tiest,   230
Best natured?' 'Lady Psyche.' 'Hers
    are we,'
One voice, we cried; and I sat down and
    wrote
In such a hand as when a field of corn
Bows all its ears before the roaring East:

'Three ladies of the Northern empire
    pray
Your Highness would enroll them with
    your own,
As Lady Psyche's pupils.'

This I seal'd;
The seal was Cupid bent above a scroll,
And o'er his head Uranian Venus hung,
And raised the blinding bandage from his
    eyes.   240
I gave the letter to be sent with dawn;
And then to bed, where half in doze I
    seem'd
To float about a glimmering night, and
    watch
A full sea glazed with muffled moonlight
    swell
On some dark shore just seen that it was
    rich.

As thro' the land at eve we went,
    And pluck'd the ripen'd ears,
We fell out, my wife and I,
O, we fell out, I know not why,
    And kiss'd again with tears.   250
And blessings on the falling out
    That all the more endears,
When we fall out with those we love
    And kiss again with tears!
For when we came where lies the child
    We lost in other years,
There above the little grave,
O, there above the little grave,
    We kiss'd again with tears.

II

At break of day the College Portress
    came;
She brought us academic silks, in hue
The lilac, with a silken hood to each,
And zoned with gold; and now when these
    were on,
And we as rich as moths from dusk co-
    coons,
She, curtseying her obeisance, let us know
The Princess Ida waited. Out we paced,
I first, and following thro' the porch that
    sang
All round with laurel, issued in a court
Compact of lucid marbles, boss'd with
    lengths   10
Of classic frieze, with ample awnings gay
Betwixt the pillars, and with great urns of
    flowers.
The Muses and the Graces, group'd in
    threes,
Enring'd a billowing fountain in the midst,
And here and there on lattice edges lay
Or book or lute; but hastily we past,
And up a flight of stairs into the hall.

There at a board by tome and paper
    sat,
With two tame leopards couch'd beside
    her throne,
All beauty compass'd in a female form, 20
The Princess; liker to the inhabitant
Of some clear planet close upon the sun,
Than our man's earth; such eyes were in
    her head,
And so much grace and power, breathing
    down
From over her arch'd brows, with every
    turn
Lived thro' her to the tips of her long
    hands,
And to her feet. She rose her height, and
    said:

'We give you welcome; not without re-
    dound
Of use and glory to yourselves ye come,
The first-fruits of the stranger; aftertime,
And that full voice which circles round the
    grave,   31
Will rank you nobly, mingled up with me.
What! are the ladies of your land so
    tall?'
'We of the court,' said Cyril. 'From the
    court,'
She answer'd, 'then ye know the Prince?'
    and he:
'The climax of his age! as tho' there
    were
One rose in all the world, your Highness
    that,
He worships your ideal.' She replied:
'We scarcely thought in our own hall to
    hear   39
This barren verbiage, current among men,
Light coin, the tinsel clink of compliment.
Your flight from out your bookless wilds
    would seem
As arguing love of knowledge and of
    power;
Your language proves you still the child.
    Indeed,
We dream not of him; when we set our
    hand
To this great work, we purposed with our-
    self
Never to wed. You likewise will do well,
Ladies, in entering here, to cast and fling
The tricks which make us toys of men,.
    that so
Some future time, if so indeed you will, 50

You may with those self-styled our lords
    ally
Your fortunes, justlier balanced, scale with
    scale.'

    At those high words, we, conscious of
    ourselves,
Perused the matting; then an officer
Rose up, and read the statutes, such as
    these:
Not for three years to correspond with
    home;
Not for three years to cross the liberties;
Not for three years to speak with any men;
And many more, which hastily subscribed,
We enter'd on the boards. And 'Now,' she
    cried,   60
'Ye are green wood, see ye warp not.
    Look, our hall!
Our statues! — not of those that men de-
    sire,
Sleek Odalisques, or oracles of mode,
Nor stunted squaws of West or East; but
    she
That taught the Sabine how to rule, and
    she
The foundress of the Babylonian wall,
The Carian Artemisia strong in war,
The Rhodope that built the pyramid,
Clelia, Cornelia, with the Palmyrene
That fought Aurelian, and the Roman
    brows   70
Of Agrippina. Dwell with these, and lose
Convention, since to look on noble forms
Makes noble thro' the sensuous organism
That which is higher. O, lift your natures
    up;
Embrace our aims; work out your freedom.
    Girls,
Knowledge is now no more a fountain
    seal'd!
Drink deep, until the habits of the slave,
The sins of emptiness, gossip and spite
And slander, die. Better not be at all
Than not be noble. Leave us; you may
    go.   80
To-day the Lady Psyche will harangue
The fresh arrivals of the week before;
For they press in from all the provinces,
And fill the hive.'
            She spoke, and bowing waved
Dismissal; back again we crost the court
To Lady Psyche's. As we enter'd in,
There sat along the forms, like morning
    doves

That sun their milky bosoms on the thatch,
A patient range of pupils; she herself
Erect behind a desk of satin-wood,   90
A quick brunette, well-moulded, falcon-
  eyed,
And on the hither side, or so she look'd,
Of twenty summers. At her left, a child,
In shining draperies, headed like a star,
Her maiden babe, a double April old,
Aglaïa slept. We sat; the lady glanced;
Then Florian, but no livelier than the
  dame
That whisper'd 'Asses' ears' among the
  sedge,
'My sister.' 'Comely, too, by all that 's
  fair,'   99
Said Cyril. 'O, hush, hush!' and she began.

'This world was once a fluid haze of
  light,
Till toward the centre set the starry tides,
And eddied into suns, that wheeling cast
The planets; then the monster, then the
  man;
Tattoo'd or woaded, winter-clad in skins,
Raw from the prime, and crushing down
  his mate,
As yet we find in barbarous isles, and here
Among the lowest.'
                    Thereupon she took
A bird's-eye view of all the ungracious
  past;
Glanced at the legendary Amazon   110
As emblematic of a nobler age;
Appraised the Lycian custom, spoke of
  those
That lay at wine with Lar and Lucumo;
Ran down the Persian, Grecian, Roman
  lines
Of empire, and the woman's state in each,
How far from just; till warming with her
  theme
She fulmined out her scorn of laws Salique
And little-footed China, touch'd on Ma-
  homet
With much contempt, and came to chiv-
  alry,
When some respect, however slight, was
  paid   120
To woman, superstition all awry.
However, then commenced the dawn; a
  beam
Had slanted forward, falling in a land
Of promise; fruit would follow. Deep,
  indeed,

Their debt of thanks to her who first had
  dared
To leap the rotten pales of prejudice,
Disyoke their necks from custom, and as-
  sert
None lordlier than themselves but that
  which made
Woman and man. She had founded; they
  must build.
Here might they learn whatever men were
  taught.   130
Let them not fear, some said their heads
  were less;
Some men's were small, not they the least
  of men;
For often fineness compensated size.
Besides the brain was like the hand, and
  grew
With using; thence the man's, if more was
  more.
He took advantage of his strength to be
First in the field; some ages had been lost;
But woman ripen'd earlier, and her life
Was longer; and albeit their glorious
  names
Were fewer, scatter'd stars, yet since in
  truth   140
The highest is the measure of the man,
And not the Kaffir, Hottentot, Malay,
Nor those horn-handed breakers of the
  glebe,
But Homer, Plato, Verulam; even so
With woman; and in arts of government
Elizabeth and others, arts of war
The peasant Joan and others, arts of grace
Sappho and others vied with any man;
And, last not least, she who had left her
  place,
And bow'd her state to them, that they
  might grow   150
To use and power on this oasis, lapt
In the arms of leisure, sacred from the
  blight
Of ancient influence and scorn.
                              At last
She rose upon a wind of prophecy
Dilating on the future: 'everywhere
Two heads in council, two beside the
  hearth,
Two in the tangled business of the world,
Two in the liberal offices of life,
Two plummets dropt for one to sound the
  abyss
Of science and the secrets of the mind; 160
Musician, painter, sculptor, critic, more;

And everywhere the broad and bounteous Earth
Should bear a double growth of those rare souls,
Poets, whose thoughts enrich the blood of the world.'

She ended here, and beckon'd us; the rest
Parted; and, glowing full-faced welcome, she
Began to address us, and was moving on
In gratulation, till as when a boat
Tacks and the slacken'd sail flaps, all her voice
Faltering and fluttering in her throat, she cried,   170
'My brother!' 'Well, my sister.' 'O,' she said,
'What do you here? and in this dress? and these?
Why, who are these? a wolf within the fold!
A pack of wolves! the Lord be gracious to me!
A plot, a plot, a plot, to ruin all!'
'No plot, no plot,' he answer'd. 'Wretched boy,
How saw you not the inscription on the gate,
LET NO MAN ENTER IN ON PAIN OF DEATH?'
'And if I had,' he answer'd, 'who could think
The softer Adams of your Academe,   180
O sister, Sirens tho' they be, were such
As chanted on the blanching bones of men?'
'But you will find it otherwise,' she said.
'You jest; ill jesting with edge-tools! my vow
Binds me to speak, and O that iron will,
That axelike edge unturnable, our Head,
The Princess!' 'Well then, Psyche, take my life,
And nail me like a weasel on a grange
For warning; bury me beside the gate,
And cut this epitaph above my bones: 190
Here lies a brother by a sister slain,
All for the common good of womankind.'
'Let me die too,' said Cyril, 'having seen
And heard the Lady Psyche.'
                               I struck in:
'Albeit so mask'd, madam, I love the truth;

Receive it, and in me behold the Prince
Your countryman, affianced years ago
To the Lady Ida. Here, for here she was,
And thus — what other way was left? — I came.'
'O sir, O Prince, I have no country, none;   200
If any, this; but none. Whate'er I was
Disrooted, what I am is grafted here.
Affianced, sir? love-whispers may not breathe
Within this vestal limit, and how should I,
Who am not mine, say, live? The thunderbolt
Hangs silent; but prepare. I speak, it falls.'
'Yet pause,' I said: 'for that inscription there,
I think no more of deadly lurks therein,
Than in a clapper clapping in a garth,
To scare the fowl from fruit; if more there be,   210
If more and acted on, what follows? war;
Your own work marr'd; for this your Academe,
Whichever side be victor, in the halloo
Will topple to the trumpet down, and pass
With all fair theories only made to gild
A stormless summer.' 'Let the Princess judge
Of that,' she said: 'farewell, sir — and to you.
I shudder at the sequel, but I go.'

'Are you that Lady Psyche,' I rejoin'd,
'The fifth in line from that old Florian,   220
Yet hangs his portrait in my father's hall —
The gaunt old baron with his beetle brow
Sun-shaded in the heat of dusty fights —
As he bestrode my grandsire, when he fell,
And all else fled? we point to it, and we say,
The loyal warmth of Florian is not cold,
But branches current yet in kindred veins.'
'Are you that Psyche,' Florian added; 'she
With whom I sang about the morning hills,
Flung ball, flew kite, and raced the purple fly,   230
And snared the squirrel of the glen? are you
That Psyche, wont to bind my throbbing brow,
To smooth my pillow, mix the foaming draught

Of fever, tell me pleasant tales, and read
My sickness down to happy dreams ? are
  you
That brother-sister Psyche, both in one ?
You were that Psyche, but what are you
  now ? '
' You are that Psyche,' Cyril said, ' for
  whom
I would be that forever which I seem,
Woman, if I might sit beside your feet, 240
And glean your scatter'd sapience.'
                          Then once more,
' Are you that Lady Psyche,' I began,
' That on her bridal morn before she past
From all her old companions, when the king
Kiss'd her pale cheek, declared that an-
  cient ties
Would still be dear beyond the southern
  hills;
That were there any of our people there
In want or peril, there was one to hear
And help them ? look ! for such are these
  and I.'
' Are you that Psyche,' Florian ask'd, ' to
  whom,   250
In gentler days, your arrow-wounded fawn
Came flying while you sat beside the well ?
The creature laid his muzzle on your lap
And sobb'd, and you sobb'd with it, and
  the blood
Was sprinkled on your kirtle, and you
  wept.
That was fawn's blood, not brother's, yet
  you wept.
O, by the bright head of my little niece,
You were that Psyche, and what are you
  now ? '
' You are that Psyche,' Cyril said again,
' The mother of the sweetest little maid 260
That ever crow'd for kisses.'
                          ' Out upon it ! '
She answer'd, ' peace ! and why should I
  not play
The Spartan Mother with emotion, be
The Lucius Junius Brutus of my kind ?
Him you call great; he for the common
  weal,
The fading politics of mortal Rome,
As I might slay this child, if good need
  were,
Slew both his sons; and I, shall I, on
  whom
The secular emancipation turns
Of half this world, be swerved from right
  to save   270

A prince, a brother ? a little will I yield.
Best so, perchance, for us, and well for
  you.
O, hard when love and duty clash ! I fear
My conscience will not count me fleckless;
  yet —
Hear my conditions: promise — otherwise
You perish — as you came, to slip away
To-day, to-morrow, soon. It shall be said,
These women were too barbarous, would
  not learn;
They fled, who might have shamed us.
  Promise, all.'

What could we else, we promised each;
  and she,   280
Like some wild creature newly-caged, com-
  menced
A to-and-fro, so pacing till she paused
By Florian; holding out her lily arms
Took both his hands, and smiling faintly
  said:
' I knew you at the first; tho' you have
  grown
You scarce have alter'd. I am sad and
  glad
To see you, Florian. *I* give thee to death,
My brother ! it was duty spoke, not I.
My needful seeming harshness, pardon it.
Our mother, is she well ? '
                          With that she kiss'd
His forehead, then, a moment after, clung
About him, and betwixt them blossom'd
  up   292
From out a common vein of memory
Sweet household talk, and phrases of the
  hearth,
And far allusion, till the gracious dews
Began to glisten and to fall; and while
They stood, so rapt, we gazing, came a
  voice,
' I brought a message here from Lady
  Blanche.'
Back started she, and turning round we
  saw
The Lady Blanche's daughter where she
  stood,   300
Melissa, with her hand upon the lock,
A rosy blonde, and in a college gown,
That clad her like an April daffodilly —
Her mother's color — with her lips apart,
And all her thoughts as fair within her
  eyes,
As bottom agates seen to wave and float
In crystal currents of clear morning seas.

So stood that same fair creature at the
    door.
Then Lady Psyche, ' Ah — Melissa — you !
You heard us ? ' and Melissa, ' O, pardon
    me !   310
I heard, I could not help it, did not wish;
But, dearest lady, pray you fear me not,
Nor think I bear that heart within my
    breast,
To give three gallant gentlemen to death.'
' I trust you,' said the other, ' for we two
Were always friends, none closer, elm and
    vine;
But yet your mother's jealous tempera-
    ment —
Let not your prudence, dearest, drowse, or
    prove
The Danaïd of a leaky vase, for fear
This whole foundation ruin, and I lose   320
My honor, these their lives.' ' Ah, fear me
    not,'
Replied Melissa; ' no — I would not tell,
No, not for all Aspasia's cleverness,
No, not to answer, madam, all those hard
    things
That Sheba came to ask of Solomon.'
' Be it so,' the other, ' that we still may
    lead
The new light up, and culminate in peace,
For Solomon may come to Sheba yet.'
Said Cyril, ' Madam, he the wisest man
Feasted the woman wisest then, in halls 330
Of Lebanonian cedar; nor should you —
Tho', madam, *you* should answer, *we* would
    ask —
Less welcome find among us, if you came
Among us, debtors for our lives to you,
Myself for something more.' He said not
    what,
But ' Thanks,' she answer'd, ' go; we have
    been too long
Together; keep your hoods about the face;
They do so that affect abstraction here.
Speak little; mix not with the rest; and
    hold
Your promise. All, I trust, may yet be
    well.'   340

    We turn'd to go, but Cyril took the
    child,
And held her round the knees against his
    waist,
And blew the swollen cheek of a trumpeter,
While Psyche watch'd them, smiling, and
    the child

Push'd her flat hand against his face and
    laugh'd;
And thus our conference closed.
                        And then we strolled
For half the day thro' stately theatres
Bench'd crescent-wise. In each we sat, we
    heard
The grave professor. On the lecture slate
The circle rounded under female hands 350
With flawless demonstration; follow'd then
A classic lecture, rich in sentiment,
With scraps of thunderous epic lilted out
By violet-hooded Doctors, elegies
And quoted odes, and jewels five-words-
    long
That on the stretch'd forefinger of all
    Time
Sparkle forever. Then we dipt in all
That treats of whatsoever is, the state,
The total chronicles of man, the mind,
The morals, something of the frame, the
    rock,   360
The star, the bird, the fish, the shell, the
    flower,
Electric, chemic laws, and all the rest,
And whatsoever can be taught and known;
Till like three horses that have broken
    fence,
And glutted all night long breast-deep in
    corn,
We issued gorged with knowledge, and I
    spoke:
' Why, sirs, they do all this as well as we.'
' They hunt old trails,' said Cyril, ' very
    well;
But when did woman ever yet invent ? '
' Ungracious ! ' answer'd Florian; ' have you
    learnt   370
No more from Psyche's lecture, you that
    talk'd
The trash that made me sick, and almost
    sad ? '
' O, trash,' he said, ' but with a kernel in it!
Should I not call her wise who made me
    wise ?
And learnt ? I learnt more from her in a
    flash
Than if my brainpan were an empty hull,
And every Muse tumbled a science in.
A thousand hearts lie fallow in these halls,
And round these halls a thousand baby
    loves
Fly twanging headless arrows at the hearts,
Whence follows many a vacant pang;
    but O,   381

With me, sir, enter'd in the bigger boy,
The head of all the golden-shafted firm,
The long-limb'd lad that had a Psyche too;
He cleft me thro' the stomacher. And now
What think you of it, Florian ? do I chase
The substance or the shadow ? will it
    hold ?
I have no sorcerer's malison on me,
No ghostly hauntings like his Highness. I
Flatter myself that always everywhere 390
I know the substance when I see it. Well,
Are castles shadows ? Three of them ?
    Is she
The sweet proprietress a shadow ? If not,
Shall those three castles patch my tatter'd
    coat ?
For dear are those three castles to my wants,
And dear is sister Psyche to my heart,
And two dear things are one of double
    worth;
And much I might have said, but that my
    zone
Unmann'd me. Then the Doctors ! O, to
    hear
The Doctors ! O, to watch the thirsty
    plants   400
Imbibing ! once or twice I thought to roar,
To break my chain, to shake my mane; but
    thou,
Modulate me, soul of mincing mimicry !
Make liquid treble of that bassoon, my
    throat;
Abase those eyes that ever loved to meet
Star - sisters answering under crescent
    brows;
Abate the stride which speaks of man, and
    loose
A flying charm of blushes o'er this cheek,
Where they like swallows coming out of
    time
Will wonder why they came. But hark the
    bell   410
For dinner, let us go ! '
                    And in we stream'd
Among the columns, pacing staid and still
By twos and threes, till all from end to end
With beauties every shade of brown and
    fair
In colors gayer than the morning mist,
The long hall glitter'd like a bed of flow-
    ers.
How might a man not wander from his
    wits
Pierced thro' with eyes, but that I kept
    mine own

Intent on her, who rapt in glorious dreams,
The second-sight of some Astræan age, 420
Sat compass'd with professors; they, the
    while,
Discuss'd a doubt and tost it to and fro.
A clamor thicken'd, mixt with inmost terms
Of art and science; Lady Blanche alone
Of faded form and haughtiest lineaments,
With all her autumn tresses falsely brown,
Shot sidelong daggers at us, a tiger-cat
In act to spring.
                    At last a solemn grace
Concluded, and we sought the gardens.
    There
One walk'd reciting by herself, and one 430
In this hand held a volume as to read,
And smoothed a petted peacock down with
    that.
Some to a low song oar'd a shallop by,
Or under arches of the marble bridge
Hung, shadow'd from the heat; some hid
    and sought
In the orange thickets; others tost a ball
Above the fountain-jets, and back again
With laughter; others lay about the lawns,
Of the older sort, and murmur'd that their
    May
Was passing — what was learning unto
    them ?   440
They wish'd to marry; they could rule a
    house;
Men hated learned women. But we three
Sat muffled like the Fates; and often came
Melissa hitting all we saw with shafts
Of gentle satire, kin to charity,
That harm'd not. Then day droopt; the
    chapel bells
Call'd us; we left the walks; we mixt with
    those
Six hundred maidens clad in purest white,
Before two streams of light from wall to
    wall,
While the great organ almost burst his
    pipes,   450
Groaning for power, and rolling thro' the
    court
A long melodious thunder to the sound
Of solemn psalms and silver litanies,
The work of Ida, to call down from heaven
A blessing on her labors for the world.

        Sweet and low, sweet and low,
            Wind of the western sea,
        Low, low, breathe and blow,
            Wind of the western sea !

Over the rolling waters go,
Come from the dying moon, and blow,
    Blow him again to me ;
While my little one, while my pretty one
    sleeps.

Sleep and rest, sleep and rest,
    Father will come to thee soon ;
Rest, rest, on mother's breast,
    Father will come to thee soon ;
Father will come to his babe in the nest,
Silver sails all out of the west
    Under the silver moon ;
Sleep, my little one, sleep, my pretty one, sleep.

III

Morn in the white wake of the morning
    star
Came furrowing all the orient into gold.
We rose, and each by other drest with
    care
Descended to the court that lay three parts
In shadow, but the Muses' heads were
    touch'd
Above the darkness from their native East.

There while we stood beside the fount,
    and watch'd,
Or seem'd to watch the dancing bubble,
    approach'd
Melissa, tinged with wan from lack of
    sleep,
Or grief, and glowing round her dewy
    eyes   10
The circled Iris of a night of tears ;
And ' Fly,' she cried, ' O fly, while yet you
    may !
My mother knows.' And when I ask'd her
    ' how,'
' My fault,' she wept, ' my fault ! and yet
    not mine ;
Yet mine in part. O, hear me, pardon me !
My mother, 't is her wont from night to
    night
To rail at Lady Psyche and her side.
She says the Princess should have been the
    Head,
Herself and Lady Psyche the two arms ; 19
And so it was agreed when first they came ;
But Lady Psyche was the right hand now,
And she the left, or not or seldom used ;
Hers more than half the students, all the
    love.
And so last night she fell to canvass you,
Her countrywomen ! she did not envy her.

" Who ever saw such wild barbarians ?
Girls ? — more like men ! " and at these
    words the snake,
My secret, seem'd to stir within my breast ;
And O, sirs, could I help it, but my cheek
Began to burn and burn, and her lynx eye
To fix and make me hotter, till she laugh'd :
" O marvellously modest maiden, you ! 32
Men ! girls, like men ! why, if they had
    been men
You need not set your thoughts in rubric
    thus
For wholesale comment." Pardon, I am
    shamed
That I must needs repeat for my excuse
What looks so little graceful : " men " — for
    still
My mother went revolving on the word —
" And so they are, — very like men in-
    deed —
And with that woman closeted for hours ! "
Then came these dreadful words out one
    by one,   41
" Why — these — *are* — men ; " I shud-
    der'd ; " and you know it."
" O, ask me nothing," I said. " And she
    knows too,
And she conceals it." So my mother
    clutch'd
The truth at once, but with no word from
    me ;
And now thus early risen she goes to in-
    form
The Princess. Lady Psyche will be crush'd ;
But you may yet be saved, and therefore
    fly ;
But heal me with your pardon ere you go.'

' What pardon, sweet Melissa, for a
    blush ? '   50
Said Cyril : ' Pale one, blush again ; than
    wear
Those lilies, better blush our lives away.
Yet let us breathe for one hour more in
    heaven,'
He added, ' lest some classic angel speak
In scorn of us, " They mounted, Ganymedes,
To tumble, Vulcans, on the second morn."
But I will melt this marble into wax
To yield us farther furlough ; ' and he went.

Melissa shook her doubtful curls, and
    thought
He scarce would prosper. ' Tell us,' Flo-
    rian ask'd,   60

'How grew this feud betwixt the right and
  left.'
'O, long ago,' she said, ' betwixt these two
Division smoulders hidden; 't is my mother,
Too jealous, often fretful as the wind
Pent in a crevice: much I bear with her.
I never knew my father, but she says —
God help her! — she was wedded to a fool;
And still she rail'd against the state of
  things.
She had the care of Lady Ida's youth,
And from the Queen's decease she brought
  her up.   70
But when your sister came she won the
  heart
Of Ida; they were still together, grew —
For so they said themselves — inosculated;
Consonant chords that shiver to one note;
One mind in all things. Yet my mother still
Affirms your Psyche thieved her theories,
And angled with them for her pupil's love;
She calls her plagiarist, I know not what.
But I must go; I dare not tarry,' and light,
As flies the shadow of a bird, she fled.   80

  Then murmur'd Florian, gazing after
    her:
'An open-hearted maiden, true and pure.
If I could love, why this were she. How
    pretty
Her blushing was, and how she blush'd
    again,
As if to close with Cyril's random wish!
Not like your Princess cramm'd with err-
    ing pride,
Nor like poor Psyche whom she drags in
    tow.'

  'The crane,' I said, 'may chatter of the
    crane,
The dove may murmur of the dove, but I
An eagle clang an eagle to the sphere.   90
My princess, O my princess! true she errs,
But in her own grand way; being herself
Three times more noble than three score of
    men,
She sees herself in every woman else,
And so she wears her error like a crown
To blind the truth and me. For her, and
    her,
Hebes are they to hand ambrosia, mix
The nectar; but — ah, she — whene'er she
    moves
The Samian Herè rises, and she speaks   99
A Memnon smitten with the morning sun.'

So saying from the court we paced, and
    gain'd
The terrace ranged along the northern
    front,
And leaning there on those balusters, high
Above the empurpled champaign, drank
    the gale
That blown about the foliage underneath,
And sated with the innumerable rose,
Beat balm upon our eyelids. Hither came
Cyril, and yawning, 'O hard task,' he cried:
'No fighting shadows here. I forced a way
Thro' solid opposition crabb'd and gnarl'd.
Better to clear prime forests, heave and
    thump   111
A league of street in summer solstice down,
Than hammer at this reverend gentle-
    woman.
I knock'd and, bidden, enter'd; found her
    there
At point to move, and settled in her eyes
The green malignant light of coming storm.
Sir, I was courteous, every phrase well-
    oil'd,
As man's could be; yet maiden-meek I
    pray'd
Concealment. She demanded who we were,
And why we came? I fabled nothing fair,
But, your example pilot, told her all.   121
Up went the hush'd amaze of hand and eye.
But when I dwelt upon your old affiance,
She answer'd sharply that I talk'd astray.
I urged the fierce inscription on the gate,
And our three lives. True — we had limed
    ourselves
With open eyes, and we must take the
    chance.
But such extremes, I told her, well might
    harm
The woman's cause. "Not more than
    now," she said,
"So puddled as it is with favoritism."   130
I tried the mother's heart. Shame might
    befall
Melissa, knowing, saying not she knew;
Her answer was, "Leave me to deal with
    that."
I spoke of war to come and many deaths,
And she replied, her duty was to speak,
And duty duty, clear of consequences.
I grew discouraged, sir; but since I knew
No rock so hard but that a little wave
May beat admission in a thousand years,
I recommended: "Decide not ere you
    pause.   140

I find you here but in the second place,
Some say the third — the authentic foun-
dress you.
I offer boldly; we will seat you highest.
Wink at our advent; help my prince to
gain
His rightful bride, and here I promise you
Some palace in our land, where you shall
reign
The head and heart of all our fair she-
world,
And your great name flow on with broad-
ening time
For ever." Well, she balanced this a lit-
tle, 149
And told me she would answer us to-day,
Meantime be mute; thus much, nor more I
gain'd.'

He ceasing, came a message from the
Head.
' That afternoon the Princess rode to take
The dip of certain strata to the north.
Would we go with her? we should find the
land
Worth seeing, and the river made a fall
Out yonder;' then she pointed on to where
A double hill ran up his furrowy forks
Beyond the thick-leaved platans of the
vale.

Agreed to, this, the day fled on thro'
all 160
Its range of duties to the appointed hour.
Then summon'd to the porch we went. She
stood
Among her maidens, higher by the head,
Her back against a pillar, her foot on one
Of those tame leopards. Kitten-like he
roll'd
And paw'd about her sandal. I drew near;
I gazed. On a sudden my strange seizure
came
Upon me, the weird vision of our house.
The Princess Ida seem'd a hollow show,
Her gay-furr'd cats a painted fantasy, 170
Her college and her maidens empty masks,
And I myself the shadow of a dream,
For all things were and were not. Yet I
felt
My heart beat thick with passion and with
awe;
Then from my breast the involuntary sigh
Brake, as she smote me with the light of
eyes

That lent my knee desire to kneel, and
shook
My pulses, till to horse we got, and so
Went forth in long retinue following up
The river as it narrow'd to the hills. 180

I rode beside her and to me she said:
' O friend, we trust that you esteem'd us
not
Too harsh to your companion yestermorn;
Unwillingly we spake.' ' No — not to her,'
I answer'd, ' but to one of whom we spake
Your Highness might have seem'd the thing
you say.'
' Again?' she cried, 'are you ambassa-
dresses
From him to me? we give you, being
strange,
A license; speak, and let the topic die.'

I stammer'd that I knew him — could
have wish'd — 190
' Our king expects — was there no precon-
tract?
There is no truer-hearted — ah, you seem
All he prefigured, and he could not see
The bird of passage flying south but long'd
To follow. Surely, if your Highness keep
Your purport, you will shock him even to
death,
Or baser courses, children of despair.'

' Poor boy,' she said, ' can he not read —
no books?
Quoit, tennis, ball — no games? nor deals
in that
Which men delight in, martial exercise?
To nurse a blind ideal like a girl, 201
Methinks he seems no better than a girl;
As girls were once, as we ourself have been.
We had our dreams; perhaps he mixt with
them.
We touch on our dead self, nor shun to do
it,
Being other — since we learnt our meaning
here,
To lift the woman's fallen divinity
Upon an even pedestal with man.'

She paused, and added with a haughtier
smile,
' And as to precontracts, we move, my
friend, 210
At no man's beck, but know ourself and
thee,

O Vashti, noble Vashti ! Summon'd out
She kept her state, and left the drunken
    king
To brawl at Shushan underneath the
    palms.'

  ' Alas, your Highness breathes full East,'
    I said,
' On that which leans to you ! I know the
    Prince,
I prize his truth. And then how vast a
    work
To assail this gray preëminence of man !
You grant me license; might I use it ?
    think;
Ere half be done perchance your life may
    fail;   220
Then comes the feebler heiress of your
    plan,
And takes and ruins all; and thus your
    pains
May only make that footprint upon sand
Which old-recurring waves of prejudice
Resmooth to nothing. Might I dread that
    you,
With only Fame for spouse and your great
    deeds
For issue, yet may live in vain, and miss
Meanwhile what every woman counts her
    due,
Love, children, happiness ? '
                              And she exclaim'd,
' Peace, you young savage of the Northern
    wild !   230
What ! tho' your Prince's love were like a
    god's,
Have we not made ourself the sacrifice ?
You are bold indeed; we are not talk'd to
    thus.
Yet will we say for children, would they
    grew
Like field - flowers everywhere ! we like
    them well:
But children die; and let me tell you, girl,
Howe'er you babble, great deeds cannot
    die;
They with the sun and moon renew their
    light
For ever, blessing those that look on them.
Children — that men may pluck them from
    our hearts,   240
Kill us with pity, break us with our-
    selves —
O — children — there is nothing upon earth
More miserable than she that has a son

And sees him err. Nor would we work for
    fame;
Tho' she perhaps might reap the applause
    of Great,
Who learns the one POU STO whence after-
    hands
May move the world, tho' she herself
    effect
But little; wherefore up and act, nor
    shrink
For fear our solid aim be dissipated
By frail successors. Would, indeed, we
    had been,   250
In lieu of many mortal flies, a race
Of giants living each a thousand years,
That we might see our own work out, and
    watch
The sandy footprint harden into stone.'

  I answer'd nothing, doubtful in myself
If that strange poet - princess with her
    grand
Imaginations might at all be won.
And she broke out interpreting my
    thoughts:

  ' No doubt we seem a kind of monster
    to you;
We are used to that; for women, up till
    this   260
Cramp'd under worse than South-sea-isle
    taboo,
Dwarfs of the gynæceum, fail so far
In high desire, they know not, cannot guess
How much their welfare is a passion to us.
If we could give them surer, quicker
    proof —
O, if our end were less achievable
By slow approaches than by single act
Of immolation, any phase of death,
We were as prompt to spring against the
    pikes,
Or down the fiery gulf as talk of it,   270
To compass our dear sisters' liberties.'

  She bow'd as if to veil a noble tear;
And up we came to where the river sloped
To plunge in cataract, shattering on black
    blocks
A breadth of thunder. O'er it shook the
    woods,
And danced the color, and, below, stuck
    out
The bones of some vast bulk that lived
    and roar'd

Before man was. She gazed awhile and said,
'As these rude bones to us, are we to her
That will be.' 'Dare we dream of that,'
  I ask'd,   280
'Which wrought us, as the workman and
  his work,
That practice betters?' 'How,' she cried,
  'you love
The metaphysics! read and earn our prize,
A golden brooch. Beneath an emerald
  plane
Sits Diotima, teaching him that died
Of hemlock — our device, wrought to the
  life —
She rapt upon her subject, he on her;
For there are schools for all.' 'And yet,'
  I said,
'Methinks I have not found among them
  all
One anatomic.' 'Nay, we thought of that,'
She answer'd, 'but it pleased us not; in
  truth   291
We shudder but to dream our maids should
  ape
Those monstrous males that carve the liv-
  ing hound,
And cram him with the fragments of the
  grave,
Or in the dark dissolving human heart,
And holy secrets of this microcosm,
Dabbling a shameless hand with shameful
  jest,
Encarnalize their spirits. Yet we know
Knowledge is knowledge, and this matter
  hangs.
Howbeit ourself, foreseeing casualty,   300
Nor willing men should come among us,
  learnt,
For many weary moons before we came,
This craft of healing. Were you sick, our-
  self
Would tend upon you. To your question
  now,
Which touches on the workman and his
  work.
Let there be light and there was light;
  't is so,
For was, and is, and will be, are but is,
And all creation is one act at once,
The birth of light; but we that are not all,
As parts, can see but parts, now this, now
  that,   310
And live, perforce, from thought to
  thought, and make

One act a phantom of succession. Thus
Our weakness somehow shapes the shadow,
  Time;
But in the shadow will we work, and mould
The woman to the fuller day.'
                              She spake
With kindled eyes: we rode a league be-
  yond,
And, o'er a bridge of pinewood crossing,
  came
On flowery levels underneath the crag,
Full of all beauty. 'O, how sweet,' I said,—
For I was half-oblivious of my mask,— 320
'To linger here with one that loved us!'
                                      'Yea,'
She answer'd, 'or with fair philosophies
That lift the fancy; for indeed these fields
Are lovely, lovelier not the Elysian lawns,
Where paced the demigods of old, and
  saw
The soft white vapor streak the crowned
  towers
Built to the Sun.' Then, turning to her
  maids,
'Pitch our pavilion here upon the sward;
Lay out the viands.' At the word, they
  raised
A tent of satin, elaborately wrought   330
With fair Corinna's triumph; here she
  stood,
Engirt with many a florid maiden-cheek,
The woman-conqueror; woman-conquer'd
  there
The bearded Victor of ten-thousand hymns,
And all the men mourn'd at his side. But
  we
Set forth to climb; then, climbing, Cyril
  kept
With Psyche, with Melissa Florian, I
With mine affianced. Many a little hand
Glanced like a touch of sunshine on the
  rocks,
Many a light foot shone like a jewel set
In the dark crag. And then we turn'd, we
  wound   341
About the cliffs, the copses, out and in,
Hammering and clinking, chattering stony
  names
Of shale and hornblende, rag and trap and
  tuff,
Amygdaloid and trachyte, till the sun
Grew broader toward his death and fell,
  and all
The rosy heights came out above the
  lawns.

The splendor falls on castle walls
And snowy summits old in story;
The long light shakes across the lakes,
And the wild cataract leaps in glory.
Blow, bugle, blow, set the wild echoes flying,
Blow, bugle; answer, echoes, dying, dying,
dying.

O, hark, O, hear! how thin and clear,
And thinner, clearer, farther going!
O, sweet and far from cliff and scar
The horns of Elfland faintly blowing!
Blow, let us hear the purple glens replying,
Blow, bugle; answer, echoes, dying, dying,
dying.

O love, they die in yon rich sky,
They faint on hill or field or river;
Our echoes roll from soul to soul,
And grow for ever and for ever.
Blow, bugle, blow, set the wild echoes flying,
And answer, echoes, answer, dying, dying,
dying.

IV

'There sinks the nebulous star we call the
sun,
If that hypothesis of theirs be sound,'
Said Ida; 'let us down and rest;' and we
Down from the lean and wrinkled preci-
pices,
By every coppice - feather'd chasm and
cleft,
Dropt thro' the ambrosial gloom to where
below
No bigger than a glowworm shone the
tent
Lamp-lit from the inner.   Once she lean'd
on me,
Descending; once or twice she lent her
hand,
And blissful palpitations in the blood   10
Stirring a sudden transport rose and fell.

But when we planted level feet, and
dipt
Beneath the satin dome and enter'd in,
There leaning deep in broider'd down we
sank
Our elbows; on a tripod in the midst
A fragrant flame rose, and before us glow'd
Fruit, blossom, viand, amber wine, and
gold.

Then she, 'Let some one sing to us;
lightlier move

The minutes fledged with music;' and a
maid,
Of those beside her, smote her harp and
sang.   20

'Tears, idle tears, I know not what they
mean,
Tears from the depth of some divine despair
Rise in the heart, and gather to the eyes,
In looking on the happy autumn-fields,
And thinking of the days that are no more.

'Fresh as the first beam glittering on a sail,
That brings our friends up from the underworld,
Sad as the last which reddens over one
That sinks with all we love below the verge;
So sad, so fresh, the days that are no more.   30

'Ah, sad and strange as in dark summer
dawns
The earliest pipe of half-awaken'd birds
To dying ears, when unto dying eyes
The casement slowly grows a glimmering
square;
So sad, so strange, the days that are no more.

'Dear as remember'd kisses after death,
And sweet as those by hopeless fancy feign'd
On lips that are for others; deep as love,
Deep as first love, and wild with all regret;
O Death in Life, the days that are no more!'   40

She ended with such passion that the
tear
She sang of shook and fell, an erring pearl
Lost in her bosom; but with some disdain
Answer'd the Princess: 'If indeed there
haunt
About the moulder'd lodges of the past
So sweet a voice and vague, fatal to men,
Well needs it we should cram our ears with
wool
And so pace by.   But thine are fancies
hatch'd
In silken-folded idleness; nor is it
Wiser to weep a true occasion lost,   50
But trim our sails, and let old bygones be,
While down the streams that float us each
and all
To the issue, goes, like glittering bergs of
ice,
Throne after throne, and molten on the
waste
Becomes a cloud; for all things serve their
time
Toward that great year of equal mights
and rights.

Nor would I fight with iron laws, in the
    end
Found golden. Let the past be past, let be
Their cancell'd Babels; tho' the rough kex
    break
The starr'd mosaic, and the beard-blown
    goat   60
Hang on the shaft, and the wild fig-tree
    split
Their monstrous idols, care not while we
    hear
A trumpet in the distance pealing news
Of better, and Hope, a poising eagle, burns
Above the unrisen morrow.' Then to me,
' Know you no song of your own land,' she
    said,
' Not such as moans about the retrospect,
But deals with the other distance and the
    hues
Of promise; not a death's - head at the
    wine ? '

Then I remember'd one myself had
    made,   70
What time I watch'd the swallow winging
    south
From mine own land, part made long since,
    and part
Now while I sang, and maiden-like as far
As I could ape their treble did I sing.

' O Swallow, Swallow, flying, flying south,
Fly to her, and fall upon her gilded eaves,
And tell her, tell her, what I tell to thee.

' O, tell her, Swallow, thou that knowest each,
That bright and fierce and fickle is the South,
And dark and true and tender is the North. 80

' O Swallow, Swallow, if I could follow, and
    light
Upon her lattice, I would pipe and trill,
And cheep and twitter twenty million loves.

' O, were I thou that she might take me in,
And lay me on her bosom, and her heart
Would rock the snowy cradle till I died !

' Why lingereth she to clothe her heart with
    love,
Delaying as the tender ash delays
To clothe herself, when all the woods are
    green ?

' O, tell her, Swallow, that thy brood is flown ;
Say to her, I do but wanton in the South, 91
But in the North long since my nest is made.

' O, tell her, brief is life but love is long,
And brief the sun of summer in the North,
And brief the moon of beauty in the South.

' O Swallow, flying from the golden woods,
Fly to her, and pipe and woo her, and make
    her mine,
And tell her, tell her, that I follow thee.'

I ceased, and all the ladies, each at each,
Like the Ithacensian suitors in old time, 100
Stared with great eyes, and laugh'd with
    alien lips,
And knew not what they meant; for still
    my voice
Rang false. But smiling, ' Not for thee,'
    she said,
' O Bulbul, any rose of Gulistan
Shall burst her veil; marsh-divers, rather,
    maid,
Shall croak thee sister, or the meadow-
    crake
Grate her harsh kindred in the grass — and
    this
A mere love-poem ! O, for such, my friend,
We hold them slight; they mind us of the
    time
When we made bricks in Egypt. Knaves
    are men,   110
That lute and flute fantastic tenderness,
And dress the victim to the offering up,
And paint the gates of Hell with Paradise,
And play the slave to gain the tyranny.
Poor soul ! I had a maid of honor once;
She wept her true eyes blind for such a
    one,
A rogue of canzonets and serenades.
I loved her. Peace be with her. She is
    dead.
So they blaspheme the muse ! But great
    is song
Used to great ends; ourself have often
    tried   120
Valkyrian hymns, or into rhythm have
    dash'd
The passion of the prophetess; for song
Is duer unto freedom, force and growth
Of spirit, than to junketing and love.
Love is it ? Would this same mock-love,
    and this
Mock-Hymen were laid up like winter bats,
Till all men grew to rate us at our worth,
Not vassals to be beat, nor pretty babes
To be dandled, no, but living wills, and
    sphered

Whole in ourselves and owed to none.
   Enough !   130
But now to leaven play with profit, you,
Know you no song, the true growth of your
   soil,
That gives the manners of your country-
   women ? '

   She spoke and turn'd her sumptuous head
   with eyes
Of shining expectation fixt on mine.
Then while I dragg'd my brains for such a
   song,
Cyril, with whom the bell-mouth'd glass
   had wrought,
Or master'd by the sense of sport, began
To troll a careless, careless tavern-catch
Of Moll and Meg, and strange experi-
   ences   140
Unmeet for ladies.   Florian nodded at
   him,
I frowning; Psyche flush'd and wann'd and
   shook;
The lilylike Melissa droop'd her brows.
'Forbear,' the Princess cried; 'Forbear,
   sir,' I;
And heated thro' and thro' with wrath and
   love,
I smote him on the breast.   He started up;
There rose a shriek as of a city sack'd;
Melissa clamor'd, 'Flee the death;' 'To
   horse !'
Said Ida, 'home ! to horse !' and fled, as
   flies
A troop of snowy doves athwart the dusk
When some one batters at the dovecote
   doors,   151
Disorderly the women.   Alone I stood
With Florian, cursing Cyril, vext at heart
In the pavilion.   There like parting hopes
I heard them passing from me; hoof by
   hoof,
And every hoof a knell to my desires,
Clang'd on the bridge; and then another
   shriek,
'The Head, the Head, the Princess, O the
   Head !'
For blind with rage she miss'd the plank,
   and roll'd
In the river.   Out I sprang from glow to
   gloom;   160
There whirl'd her white robe like a blos-
   som'd branch
Rapt to the horrible fall.   A glance I gave,
No more, but woman-vested as I was

Plunged, and the flood drew; yet I caught
   her; then
Oaring one arm, and bearing in my left
The weight of all the hopes of half the
   world,
Strove to buffet to land in vain.   A tree
Was half-disrooted from his place and
   stoop'd
To drench his dark locks in the gurgling
   wave
Mid-channel.   Right on this we drove and
   caught,   170
And grasping down the boughs I gain'd
   the shore.

   There stood her maidens glimmeringly
   group'd
In the hollow bank.   One reaching forward
   drew
My burthen from mine arms; they cried,
   'She lives.'
They bore her back into the tent: but I,
So much a kind of shame within me
   wrought,
Not yet endured to meet her opening eyes,
Nor found my friends; but push'd alone on
   foot —
For since her horse was lost I left her
   mine —
Across the woods, and less from Indian
   craft   180
Than beelike instinct hiveward, found at
   length
The garden portals.   Two great statues,
   Art
And Science, Caryatids, lifted up
A weight of emblem, and betwixt were
   valves
Of open-work in which the hunter rued
His rash intrusion, manlike, but his brows
Had sprouted, and the branches thereupon
Spread out at top, and grimly spiked the
   gates.

   A little space was left between the
   horns,
Thro' which I clamber'd o'er at top with
   pain,   190
Dropt on the sward, and up the linden
   walks,
And, tost on thoughts that changed from
   hue to hue,
Now poring on the glowworm, now the star,
I paced the terrace, till the Bear had
   wheel'd

Thro' a great arc his seven slow suns.
A step
Of lightest echo, then a loftier form
Than female, moving thro' the uncertain
gloom,
Disturb'd me with the doubt 'if this were
she,'
But it was Florian. 'Hist, O, hist!' he
said,
'They seek us; out so late is out of rules.
Moreover, "Seize the strangers" is the
cry.   201
How came you here?' I told him. 'I,'
said he,
'Last of the train, a moral leper, I,
To whom none spake, half-sick at heart,
return'd.
Arriving all confused among the rest
With hooded brows I crept into the hall,
And, couch'd behind a Judith, underneath
The head of Holofernes peep'd and saw.
Girl after girl was call'd to trial; each
Disclaim'd all knowledge of us; last of
all,   210
Melissa; trust me, sir, I pitied her.
She, question'd if she knew us men, at first
Was silent; closer prest, denied it not,
And then, demanded if her mother knew,
Or Psyche, she affirm'd not, or denied;
From whence the Royal mind, familiar
with her,
Easily gather'd either guilt.   She sent
For Psyche, but she was not there; she
call'd
For Psyche's child to cast it from the
doors;
She sent for Blanche to accuse her face to
face;   220
And I slipt out. But whither will you now?
And where are Psyche, Cyril? both are
fled;
What, if together? that were not so well.
Would rather we had never come! I dread
His wildness, and the chances of the dark.'

'And yet,' I said, 'you wrong him more
than I
That struck him; this is proper to the
clown,
Tho' smock'd, or furr'd and purpled, still
the clown,
To harm the thing that trusts him, and to
shame
That which he says he loves. For Cyril,
howe'er   230

He deal in frolic, as to-night — the song
Might have been worse and sinn'd in
grosser lips
Beyond all pardon — as it is, I hold
These flashes on the surface are not he.
He has a solid base of temperament;
But as the water-lily starts and slides
Upon the level in little puffs of wind,
Tho' anchor'd to the bottom, such is he.'

Scarce had I ceased when from a tama-
risk near
Two Proctors leapt upon us, crying,
'Names!'   240
He, standing still, was clutch'd; but I be-
gan
To thrid the musky-circled mazes, wind
And double in and out the boles, and race
By all the fountains. Fleet I was of foot;
Before me shower'd the rose in flakes; be-
hind
I heard the puff'd pursuer; at mine ear
Bubbled the nightingale and heeded not,
And secret laughter tickled all my soul.
At last I hook'd my ankle in a vine
That claspt the feet of a Mnemosyne,   250
And falling on my face was caught and
known.

They haled us to the Princess where she
sat
High in the hall; above her droop'd a lamp,
And made the single jewel on her brow
Burn like the mystic fire on a mast-head,
Prophet of storm; a handmaid on each
side
Bow'd toward her, combing out her long
black hair
Damp from the river; and close behind her
stood
Eight daughters of the plough, stronger
than men,
Huge women blowzed with health, and
wind, and rain,   260
And labor. Each was like a Druid rock;
Or like a spire of land that stands apart
Cleft from the main, and wail'd about with
mews.

Then, as we came, the crowd dividing
clove
An advent to the throne; and therebeside,
Half-naked as if caught at once from bed
And tumbled on the purple footcloth, lay
The lily-shining child; and on the left,

Bow'd on her palms and folded up from
wrong,
Her round white shoulder shaken with her
sobs,   270
Melissa knelt; but Lady Blanche erect
Stood up and spake, an affluent orator:

'It was not thus, O Princess, in old days;
You prized my counsel, lived upon my lips.
I led you then to all the Castalies;
I fed you with the milk of every Muse;
I loved you like this kneeler, and you me
Your second mother, those were gracious
times.
Then came your new friend; you began to
change —
I saw it and grieved — to slacken and to
cool;   280
Till taken with her seeming openness
You turn'd your warmer currents all to
her,
To me you froze; this was my meed for
all.
Yet I bore up in part from ancient love,
And partly that I hoped to win you back,
And partly conscious of my own deserts,
And partly that you were my civil head,
And chiefly you were born for something
great,
In which I might your fellow-worker be,
When time should serve; and thus a noble
scheme   290
Grew up from seed we two long since had
sown;
In us true growth, in her a Jonah's gourd,
Up in one night and due to sudden sun.
We took this palace; but even from the
first
You stood in your own light and darken'd
mine.
What student came but that you planed her
path
To Lady Psyche, younger, not so wise,
A foreigner, and I your countrywoman,
I your old friend and tried, she new in
all?
But still her lists were swell'd and mine
were lean;   300
Yet I bore up in hope she would be
known.
Then came these wolves; *they* knew her;
they endured,
Long-closeted with her the yestermorn,
To tell her what they were, and she to
hear.

And me none told. Not less to an eye like
mine,
A lidless watcher of the public weal,
Last night, their mask was patent, and my
foot
Was to you. But I thought again; I fear'd
To meet a cold " We thank you, we shall
hear of it
From Lady Psyche;" you had gone to
her,   310
She told, perforce, and winning easy grace,
No doubt, for slight delay, remain'd
among us
In our young nursery still unknown, the
stem
Less grain than touchwood, while my hon-
est heat
Were all miscounted as malignant haste
To push my rival out of place and power.
But public use required she should be
known;
And since my oath was ta'en for public
use,
I broke the letter of it to keep the sense.
I spoke not then at first, but watch'd them
well,   320
Saw that they kept apart, no mischief
done;
And yet this day — tho' you should hate me
for it —
I came to tell you; found that you had gone,
Ridden to the hills, she likewise. Now, I
thought,
That surely she will speak; if not, then I.
Did she? These monsters blazon'd what
they were,
According to the coarseness of their kind,
For thus I hear; and known at last — my
work —
And full of cowardice and guilty shame —
I grant in her some sense of shame — she
flies;   330
And I remain on whom to wreak your rage,
I, that have lent my life to build up yours,
I, that have wasted here health, wealth, and
time,
And talent, I — you know it — I will not
boast;
Dismiss me, and I prophesy your plan,
Divorced from my experience, will be chaff
For every gust of chance, and men will
say
We did not know the real light, but chased
The wisp that flickers where no foot can
tread.'

She ceased; the Princess answer'd coldly,
'Good; 340
Your oath is broken; we dismiss you, go.
For this lost lamb'—she pointed to the
child—
'Our mind is changed; we take it to our-
self.'

Thereat the lady stretch'd a vulture
throat,
And shot from crooked lips a haggard
smile.
'The plan was mine. I built the nest,' she
said,
'To hatch the cuckoo. Rise!' and stoop'd
to updrag
Melissa. She, half on her mother propt,
Half-drooping from her, turn'd her face,
and cast
A liquid look on Ida, full of prayer, 350
Which melted Florian's fancy as she hung,
A Niobeän daughter, one arm out,
Appealing to the bolts of heaven; and
while
We gazed upon her came a little stir
About the doors, and on a sudden rush'd
Among us, out of breath, as one pursued,
A woman-post in flying raiment. Fear
Stared in her eyes, and chalk'd her face,
and wing'd
Her transit to the throne, whereby she fell
Delivering seal'd dispatches which the
Head 360
Took half-amazed, and in her lion's mood
Tore open, silent we with blind surmise
Regarding, while she read, till over brow
And cheek and bosom brake the wrathful
bloom
As of some fire against a stormy cloud,
When the wild peasant rights himself, the
rick
Flames, and his anger reddens in the hea-
vens;
For anger most it seem'd, while now her
breast,
Beaten with some great passion at her
heart, 369
Palpitated, her hand shook, and we heard
In the dead hush the papers that she held
Rustle. At once the lost lamb at her feet
Sent out a bitter bleating for its dam.
The plaintive cry jarr'd on her ire; she
crush'd
The scrolls together, made a sudden turn
As if to speak, but, utterance failing her,

She whirl'd them on to me, as who should
say
'Read,' and I read—two letters—one
her sire's:

'Fair daughter, when we sent the Prince
your way
We knew not your ungracious laws, which
learnt, 380
We, conscious of what temper you are
built,
Came all in haste to hinder wrong, but
fell
Into his father's hand, who has this night,
You lying close upon his territory,
Slipt round and in the dark invested you,
And here he keeps me hostage for his son.'

The second was my father's running
thus:
'You have our son; touch not a hair of his
head;
Render him up unscathed; give him your
hand;
Cleave to your contract—tho' indeed we
hear 390
You hold the woman is the better man;
A rampant heresy, such as if it spread
Would make all women kick against their
lords
Thro' all the world, and which might well
deserve
That we this night should pluck your pal-
ace down;
And we will do it, unless you send us back
Our son, on the instant, whole.'
So far I read;
And then stood up and spoke impetuously:

'O, not to pry and peer on your reserve,
But led by golden wishes, and a hope 400
The child of regal compact, did I break
Your precinct; not a scorner of your sex
But venerator, zealous it should be
All that it might be. Hear me, for I bear,
Tho' man, yet human, whatsoe'er your
wrongs,
From the flaxen curl to the gray lock a life
Less mine than yours. My nurse would tell
me of you;
I babbled for you, as babies for the moon,
Vague brightness; when a boy, you stoop'd
to me
From all high places, lived in all fair
lights, 410

Came in long breezes rapt from inmost
    south
And blown to inmost north; at eve and
    dawn
With Ida, Ida, Ida, rang the woods;
The leader wild-swan in among the stars
Would clang it, and lapt in wreaths of
    glowworm light
The mellow breaker murmur'd Ida. Now,
Because I would have reach'd you, had you
    been
Sphered up with Cassiopeia, or the en-
    throned
Persephone in Hades, now at length,   419
Those winters of abeyance all worn out,
A man I came to see you; but, indeed,
Not in this frequence can I lend full tongue,
O noble Ida, to those thoughts that wait
On you, their centre. Let me say but this,
That many a famous man and woman, town
And landskip, have I heard of, after seen
The dwarfs of presage; tho' when known,
    there grew
Another kind of beauty in detail
Made them worth knowing; but in you I
    found
My boyish dream involved and dazzled
    down   430
And master'd, while that after-beauty
    makes
Such head from act to act, from hour to
    hour,
Within me, that except you slay me here,
According to your bitter statute-book,
I cannot cease to follow you, as they say
The seal does music; who desire you more
Than growing boys their manhood; dying
    lips,
With many thousand matters left to do,
The breath of life; O, more than poor men
    wealth,
Than sick men health — yours, yours, not
    mine — but half   440
Without you; with you, whole; and of those
    halves
You worthiest; and howe'er you block and
    bar
Your heart with system out from mine, I
    hold
That it becomes no man to nurse despair,
But in the teeth of clench'd antagonisms
To follow up the worthiest till he die.
Yet that I came not all unauthorized
Behold your father's letter.'
                 On one knee

Kneeling, I gave it, which she caught, and
    dash'd
Unopen'd at her feet. A tide of fierce   450
Invective seem'd to wait behind her lips,
As waits a river level with the dam
Ready to burst and flood the world with
    foam;
And so she would have spoken, but there
    rose
A hubbub in the court of half the maids
Gather'd together; from the illumined hall
Long lanes of splendor slanted o'er a press
Of snowy shoulders, thick as herded ewes,
And rainbow robes, and gems and gemlike
    eyes,
And gold and golden heads. They to and
    fro   460
Fluctuated, as flowers in storm, some red,
    some pale,
All open-mouth'd, all gazing to the light,
Some crying there was an army in the
    land,
And some that men were in the very walls,
And some they cared not; till a clamor
    grew
As of a new-world Babel, woman-built,
And worse-confounded. High above them
    stood
The placid marble Muses, looking peace.

Not peace she look'd, the Head; but ris-
    ing up
Robed in the long night of her deep hair,
    so   470
To the open window moved, remaining
    there
Fixt like a beacon-tower above the waves
Of tempest, when the crimson-rolling eye
Glares ruin, and the wild birds on the light
Dash themselves dead. She stretch'd her
    arms and call'd
Across the tumult, and the tumult fell.

'What fear ye, brawlers? am not I your
    Head?
On me, me, me, the storm first breaks;
    I dare
All these male thunderbolts; what is it ye
    fear?
Peace! there are those to avenge us and
    they come;   480
If not, — myself were like enough, O girls,
To unfurl the maiden banner of our rights,
And clad in iron burst the ranks of war,
Or, falling, protomartyr of our cause,

Die; yet I blame you not so much for fear;
Six thousand years of fear have made you
  that
From which I would redeem you. But for
  those
That stir this hubbub — you and you — I
  know
Your faces there in the crowd — to-morrow
  morn
We hold a great convention; then shall
  they   490
That love their voices more than duty,
  learn
With whom they deal, dismiss'd in shame
  to live
No wiser than their mothers, household
  stuff,
Live chattels, mincers of each other's fame,
Full of weak poison, turnspits for the
  clown,
The drunkard's football, laughing-stocks
  of Time,
Whose brains are in their hands and in
  their heels,
But fit to flaunt, to dress, to dance, to
  thrum,
To tramp, to scream, to burnish, and to
  scour,   499
For ever slaves at home and fools abroad.'

  She, ending, waved her hands; thereat
  the crowd
Muttering, dissolved; then with a smile,
  that look'd
A stroke of cruel sunshine on the cliff,
When all the glens are drown'd in azure
  gloom
Of thunder-shower, she floated to us and
  said:

'You have done well and like a gentle-
  man,
And like a prince; you have our thanks for
  all.
And you look well too in your woman's
  dress.
Well have you done and like a gentleman.
You saved our life; we owe you bitter
  thanks.   510
Better have died and spilt our bones in the
  flood —
Then men had said — but now — what
  hinders me
To take such bloody vengeance on you
  both ? —

Yet since our father — wasps in our good
  hive,
You would-be quenchers of the light to
  be,
Barbarians, grosser than your native
  bears —
O, would I had his sceptre for one hour !
You that have dared to break our bound,
  and gull'd
Our servants, wrong'd and lied and
  thwarted us —
I wed with thee ! *I* bound by precontract
Your bride, your bondslave ! not tho' all
  the gold   521
That veins the world were pack'd to make
  your crown,
And every spoken tongue should lord you.
  Sir,
Your falsehood and yourself are hateful to
  us;
I trample on your offers and on you.
Begone; we will not look upon you more.
Here, push them out at gates.'
                        In wrath she spake.
Then those eight mighty daughters of the
  plough
Bent their broad faces toward us and ad-
  dress'd
Their motion. Twice I sought to plead my
  cause,   530
But on my shoulder hung their heavy
  hands,
The weight of destiny; so from her face
They push'd us, down the steps, and thro'
  the court,
And with grim laughter thrust us out at
  gates.

  We cross'd the street and gain'd a petty
  mound
Beyond it, whence we saw the lights and
  heard
The voices murmuring. While I listen'd,
  came
On a sudden the weird seizure and the
  doubt.
I seem'd to move among a world of ghosts;
The Princess with her monstrous woman-
  guard,   540
The jest and earnest working side by side,
The cataract and the tumult and the kings
Were shadows; and the long fantastic
  night
With all its doings had and had not been,
And all things were and were not.

This went by
As strangely as it came, and on my spirits
Settled a gentle cloud of melancholy —
Not long; I shook it off; for spite of doubts
And sudden ghostly shadowings I was one
To whom the touch of all mischance but
    came   550
As night to him that sitting on a hill
Sees the midsummer, midnight, Norway sun
Set into sunrise; then we moved away.

INTERLUDE

Thy voice is heard thro' rolling drums
    That beat to battle where he stands;
Thy face across his fancy comes,
    And gives the battle to his hands.
A moment, while the trumpets blow,
    He sees his brood about thy knee;
The next, like fire he meets the foe,
    And strikes him dead for thine and thee.

So Lilia sang. We thought her half-pos-
    sess'd,
She struck such warbling fury thro' the
    words;   10
And, after, feigning pique at what she call'd
The raillery, or grotesque, or false sub-
    lime —
Like one that wishes at a dance to change
The music — clapt her hands and cried for
    war,
Or some grand fight to kill and make an
    end.
And he that next inherited the tale,
Half turning to the broken statue, said,
'Sir Ralph has got your colors; if I prove
Your knight, and fight your battle, what
    for me?'
It chanced, her empty glove upon the tomb
Lay by her like a model of her hand.   21
She took it and she flung it. 'Fight,' she
    said,
'And make us all we would be, great and
    good.'
He knightlike in his cap instead of casque,
A cap of Tyrol borrow'd from the hall,
Arranged the favor, and assumed the
    Prince.

V

Now, scarce three paces measured from
    the mound,
We stumbled on a stationary voice,
And 'Stand, who goes?' 'Two from the
    palace,' I.
'The second two; they wait,' he said, 'pass
    on;
His Highness wakes;' and one, that clash'd
    in arms,
By glimmering lanes and walls of canvas
    led
Threading the soldier-city, till we heard
The drowsy folds of our great ensign shake
From blazon'd lions o'er the imperial tent
Whispers of war.
            Entering, the sudden light
Dazed me half-blind. I stood and seem'd
    to hear,   11
As in a poplar grove when a light wind
    wakes
A lisping of the innumerous leaf and dies,
Each hissing in his neighbor's ear; and
    then
A strangled titter, out of which there brake
On all sides, clamoring etiquette to death,
Unmeasured mirth; while now the two old
    kings
Began to wag their baldness up and down,
The fresh young captains flash'd their glit-
    tering teeth,
The huge bush-bearded barons heaved and
    blew,   20
And slain with laughter roll'd the gilded
    squire.

At length my sire, his rough cheek wet
    with tears,
Panted from weary sides, 'King, you are
    free!
We did but keep you surety for our son,
If this be he, — or a draggled mawkin,
    thou,
That tends her bristled grunters in the
    sludge;'
For I was drench'd with ooze, and torn
    with briers,
More crumpled than a poppy from the
    sheath,
And all one rag, disprinced from head to
    heel.
Then some one sent beneath his vaulted
    palm   30
A whisper'd jest to some one near him,
    'Look,
He has been among his shadows.' 'Satan
    take
The old women and their shadows!'— thus
    the king

Roar'd — 'make yourself a man to fight
with men.
Go; Cyril told us all.'
          As boys that slink
From ferule and the trespass-chiding eye,
Away we stole, and transient in a trice
From what was left of faded woman-slough
To sheathing splendors and the golden scale
Of harness, issued in the sun, that now   40
Leapt from the dewy shoulders of the
    earth,
And hit the Northern hills. Here Cyril
    met us,
A little shy at first, but by and by
We twain, with mutual pardon ask'd and
    given
For stroke and song, resolder'd peace,
    whereon
Follow'd his tale. Amazed he fled away
Thro' the dark land, and later in the night
Had come on Psyche weeping: 'then we
    fell   48
Into your father's hand, and there she lies,
But will not speak nor stir.'
                He show'd a tent
A stone-shot off; we enter'd in, and there
Among piled arms and rough accoutre-
    ments,
Pitiful sight, wrapp'd in a soldier's cloak,
Like some sweet sculpture draped from
    head to foot,
And push'd by rude hands from its pedes-
    tal,
All her fair length upon the ground she
    lay;
And at her head a follower of the camp,
A charr'd and wrinkled piece of woman-
    hood,
Sat watching like a watcher by the dead.

    Then Florian knelt, and 'Come,' he whis-
    per'd to her,   60
'Lift up your head, sweet sister; lie not
    thus.
What have you done but right? you could
    not slay
Me, nor your prince; look up, be com-
    forted.
Sweet is it to have done the thing one
    ought,
When fallen in darker ways.' And like-
    wise I :
'Be comforted; have I not lost her too,
In whose least act abides the nameless
    charm

That none has else for me?' She heard,
    she moved,
She moan'd, a folded voice; and up she
    sat,
And raised the cloak from brows as pale
    and smooth   70
As those that mourn half-shrouded over
    death
In deathless marble. 'Her,' she said, 'my
    friend —
Parted from her — betray'd her cause and
    mine —
Where shall I breathe? why kept ye not
    your faith?
O base and bad! what comfort? none for
    me!'
To whom remorseful Cyril, 'Yet I pray
Take comfort; live, dear lady, for your
    child!'
At which she lifted up her voice and cried:

    'Ah me, my babe, my blossom, ah, my
    child,
My one sweet child, whom I shall see no
    more!   80
For now will cruel Ida keep her back;
And either she will die from want of care,
Or sicken with ill-usage, when they say
The child is hers — for every little fault,
The child is hers; and they will beat my
    girl
Remembering her mother — O my flower!
Or they will take her, they will make her
    hard,
And she will pass me by in after-life
With some cold reverence worse than were
    she dead.   89
Ill mother that I was to leave her there,
To lag behind, scared by the cry they made,
The horror of the shame among them all.
But I will go and sit beside the doors,
And make a wild petition night and day,
Until they hate to hear me like a wind
Wailing for ever, till they open to me,
And lay my little blossom at my feet,
My babe, my sweet Aglaïa, my one child;
And I will take her up and go my way,
And satisfy my soul with kissing her.   100
Ah! what might that man not deserve
    of me
Who gave me back my child?' 'Be com-
    forted,'
Said Cyril, 'you shall have it;' but again
She veil'd her brows, and prone she sank,
    and so,

Like tender things that being caught feign
　　death,
Spoke not, nor stirr'd.
　　　　　　　By this a murmur ran
Thro' all the camp, and inward raced the
　　scouts
With rumor of Prince Arac hard at hand.
We left her by the woman, and without
Found the gray kings at parle; and 'Look
　　you,' cried
My father, 'that our compact be fulfill'd.
You have spoilt this child; she laughs at
　　you and man;
She wrongs herself, her sex, and me, and
　　him.
But red-faced war has rods of steel and
　　fire;
She yields, or war.'
　　　　　　　Then Gama turn'd to me:
'We fear, indeed, you spent a stormy time
With our strange girl; and yet they say
　　that still
You love her.　Give us, then, your mind
　　at large:
How say you, war or not?'
　　　　　　　'Not war, if possible,
O king,' I said, 'lest from the abuse of
　　war,　　　　　　　　　　　　　　120
The desecrated shrine, the trampled year,
The smouldering homestead, and the house-
　　hold flower
Torn from the lintel — all the common
　　wrong —
A smoke go up thro' which I loom to her
Three times a monster.　Now she lightens
　　scorn
At him that mars her plan, but then would
　　hate —
And every voice she talk'd with ratify it,
And every face she look'd on justify it —
The general foe.　More soluble is this knot
By gentleness than war.　I want her love. 130
What were I nigher this altho' we dash'd
Your cities into shards with catapults? —
She would not love — or brought her
　　chain'd, a slave,
The lifting of whose eyelash is my lord?
Not ever would she love, but brooding turn
The book of scorn, till all my flitting chance
Were caught within the record of her
　　wrongs
And crush'd to death; and rather, Sire,
　　than this
I would the old god of war himself were
　　dead,

Forgotten, rusting on his iron hills,　　140
Rotting on some wild shore with ribs of
　　wreck,
Or like an old-world mammoth bulk'd in
　　ice,
Not to be molten out.'
　　　　　　　And roughly spake
My father: 'Tut, you know them not, the
　　girls.
Boy, when I hear you prate I almost think
That idiot legend credible.　Look you, sir!
Man is the hunter; woman is his game.
The sleek and shining creatures of the
　　chase,
We hunt them for the beauty of their skins;
They love us for it, and we ride them
　　down.　　　　　　　　　　　　　150
Wheedling and siding with them!　Out!
　　for shame!
Boy, there's no rose that's half so dear to
　　them
As he that does the thing they dare not do,
Breathing and sounding beauteous battle,
　　comes
With the air of the trumpet round him, and
　　leaps in
Among the women, snares them by the
　　score
Flatter'd and fluster'd, wins, tho' dash'd
　　with death
He reddens what he kisses.　Thus I won
Your mother, a good mother, a good wife,
Worth winning; but this firebrand — gen-
　　tleness　　　　　　　　　　　　160
To such as her! if Cyril spake her true,
To catch a dragon in a cherry net,
To trip a tigress with a gossamer,
Were wisdom to it.'
　　　　　　　'Yea, but, Sire,' I cried,
'Wild natures need wise curbs.　The sol-
　　dier?　No!
What dares not Ida do that she should
　　prize
The soldier?　I beheld her, when she rose
The yesternight, and storming in extremes
Stood for her cause, and flung defiance
　　down
Gagelike to man, and had not shunn'd the
　　death,　　　　　　　　　　　　170
No, not the soldier's; yet I hold her, king,
True woman; but you clash them all in one,
That have as many differences as we.
The violet varies from the lily as far
As oak from elm.　One loves the soldier,
　　one

The silken priest of peace, one this, one that,
And some unworthily; their sinless faith,
A maiden moon that sparkles on a sty,
Glorifying clown and satyr; whence they
    need   179
More breadth of culture. Is not Ida right?
They worth it? truer to the law within?
Severer in the logic of a life?
Twice as magnetic to sweet influences
Of earth and heaven? and she of whom
    you speak,
My mother, looks as whole as some serene
Creation minted in the golden moods
Of sovereign artists; not a thought, a touch,
But pure as lines of green that streak the
    white
Of the first snowdrop's inner leaves; I say,
Not like the piebald miscellany, man, 190
Bursts of great heart and slips in sensual
    mire,
But whole and one; and take them all-in-all,
Were we ourselves but half as good, as
    kind,
As truthful, much that Ida claims as right
Had ne'er been mooted, but as frankly
    theirs
As dues of Nature. To our point; not war,
Lest I lose all.'
       'Nay, nay, you spake but sense,'
Said Gama. 'We remember love ourself
In our sweet youth; we did not rate him
    then   199
This red-hot iron to be shaped with blows.
You talk almost like Ida; *she* can talk;
And there is something in it as you say:
But you talk kindlier; we esteem you for
    it.
He seems a gracious and a gallant Prince,
I would he had our daughter. For the rest,
Our own detention, why, the causes weigh'd,
Fatherly fears – you used us courteously —
We would do much to gratify your Prince —
We pardon it; and for your ingress here 209
Upon the skirt and fringe of our fair land,
You did but come as goblins in the night,
Nor in the furrow broke the ploughman's
    head,
Nor burnt the grange, nor buss'd the milk-
    ing-maid,
Nor robb'd the farmer of his bowl of cream.
But let your Prince — our royal word
    upon it,
He comes back safe — ride with us to our
    lines,
And speak with Arac. Arac's word is thrice

As ours with Ida; something may be done —
I know not what — and ours shall see us
    friends.
You, likewise, our late guests, if so you
    will,   220
Follow us. Who knows? we four may build
    some plan
Foursquare to opposition.'
             Here he reach'd
White hands of farewell to my sire, who
    growl'd
An answer which, half-muffled in his beard,
Let so much out as gave us leave to go.

    Then rode we with the old king across
    the lawns
Beneath huge trees, a thousand rings of
    Spring
In every bole, a song on every spray
Of birds that piped their Valentines, and
    woke
Desire in me to infuse my tale of love 230
In the old king's ears, who promised help,
    and oozed
All o'er with honey'd answer as we rode;
And blossom-fragrant slipt the heavy dews
Gather'd by night and peace, with each
    light air
On our mail'd heads. But other thoughts
    than peace
Burnt in us, when we saw the embattled
    squares
And squadrons of the Prince, trampling
    the flowers
With clamor; for among them rose a cry
As if to greet the king; they made a halt;
The horses yell'd; they clash'd their arms;
    the drum   240
Beat; merrily-blowing shrill'd the martial
    fife;
And in the blast and bray of the long horn
And serpent-throated bugle, undulated
The banner. Anon to meet us lightly
    pranced
Three captains out; c ever had I seen
Such thews of men. The midmost and the
    highest
Was Arac; all about his motion clung
The shadow of his sister, as the beam
Of the East, that play'd upon them, made
    them glance
Like those three stars of the airy Giant's
    zone,   250
That glitter burnish'd by the frosty dark;
And as the fiery Sirius alters hue,

And bickers into red and emerald, shone
Their morions, wash'd with morning, as
   they came.

   And I that prated peace, when first I
     heard
War-music, felt the blind wild-beast of
     force,
Whose home is in the sinews of a man,
Stir in me as to strike. Then took the king
His three broad sons; with now a wander-
     ing hand   259
And now a pointed finger, told them all.
A common light of smiles at our disguise
Broke from their lips, and, ere the windy
     jest
Had labor'd down within his ample lungs,
The genial giant, Arac, roll'd himself
Thrice in the saddle, then burst out in
     words:

'Our land invaded, 'sdeath! and he him-
     self
Your captive, yet my father wills not war!
And, 'sdeath! myself, what care I, war
     or no?
But then this question of your troth re-
     mains;
And there's a downright honest meaning
     in her.   270
She flies too high, she flies too high! and
     yet
She ask'd but space and fair-play for her
     scheme;
She prest and prest it on me — I myself,
What know I of these things? but, life
     and soul!
I thought her half - right talking of her
     wrongs;
I say she flies too high, 'sdeath! what of
     that?
I take her for the flower of womankind,
And so I often told her, right or wrong;
And, Prince, she can be sweet to those she
     loves,   279
And, right or wrong, I care not; this is all,
I stand upon her side; she made me swear
     it —
'Sdeath! — and with solemn rites by can-
     dle-light —
Swear by Saint something — I forget her
     name —
Her that talk'd down the fifty wisest men;
She was a princess too; and so I swore.

Come, this is all; she will not; waive your
     claim.
If not, the foughten field, what else, at
     once
Decides it, 'sdeath! against my father's
     will.'

   I lagg'd in answer, loth to render up 289
My precontract, and loth by brainless war
To cleave the rift of difference deeper yet;
Till one of those two brothers, half aside
And fingering at the hair about his lip,
To prick us on to combat, 'Like to like!
The woman's garment hid the woman's
     heart.'
A taunt that clench'd his purpose like a
     blow!
For fiery-short was Cyril's counter-scoff,
And sharp I answer'd, touch'd upon the
     point
Where idle boys are cowards to their
     shame,
'Decide it here; why not? we are three to
     three.'   300

   Then spake the third: 'But three to
     three? no more?
No more, and in our noble sister's cause?
More, more, for honor! every captain waits
Hungry for honor, angry for his king.
More, more, some fifty on a side, that each
May breathe himself, and quick! by over-
     throw
Of these or those, the question settled die.'

   'Yea,' answer'd I, 'for this wild wreath
     of air,
This flake of rainbow flying on the highest
Foam of men's deeds — this honor, if ye
     will.   310
It needs must be for honor if at all;
Since, what decision? if we fail we fail,
And if we win we fail; she would not keep
Her compact.' ' 'Sdeath! but we will send
     to her,'
Said Arac, 'worthy reasons why she should
Bide by this issue; let our missive thro',
And you shall have her answer by the
     word.'

   'Boys!' shriek'd the old king, but vain-
     lier than a hen
To her false daughters in the pool; for
     none

Regarded; neither seem'd there more to
   say.   320
Back rode we to my father's camp, and
   found
He thrice had sent a herald to the gates,
To learn if Ida yet would cede our claim,
Or by denial flush her babbling wells
With her own people's life; three times he
   went.
The first, he blew and blew, but none ap-
   pear'd;
He batter'd at the doors, none came; the
   next,
An awful voice within had warn'd him
   thence;
The third, and those eight daughters of the
   plough
Came sallying thro' the gates, and caught
   his hair,   .   330
And so belabor'd him on rib and cheek
They made him wild. Not less one glance
   he caught
Thro' open doors of Ida station'd there
Unshaken, clinging to her purpose, firm
Tho' compass'd by two armies and the noise
Of arms; and standing like a stately pine
Set in a cataract on an island-crag,
When storm is on the heights, and right
   and left
Suck'd from the dark heart of the long hills
   roll
The torrents, dash'd to the vale; and yet
   her will   340
Bred will in me to overcome it or fall.

But when I told the king that I was
   pledged
To fight in tourney for my bride, he clash'd
His iron palms together with a cry;
Himself would tilt it out among the lads;
But overborne by all his bearded lords
With reasons drawn from age and state,
   perforce
He yielded, wroth and red, with fierce de-
   mur;
And many a bold knight started up in heat,
And sware to combat for my claim till
   death.   350

All on this side the palace ran the field
Flat to the garden-wall; and likewise here,
Above the garden's glowing blossom-belts,
A column'd entry shone and marble stairs,
And great bronze valves, emboss'd with
   Tomyris

And what she did to Cyrus after fight,
But now fast barr'd. So here upon the flat
All that long morn the lists were hammer'd
   up,
And all that morn the heralds to and fro,
With message and defiance, went and came;
Last, Ida's answer, in a royal hand,   361
But shaken here and there, and rolling
   words
Oration-like. I kiss'd it and I read:

  'O brother, you have known the pangs
   we felt,
What heats of indignation when we heard
Of those that iron-cramp'd their women's
   feet;
Of lands in which at the altar the poor
   bride
Gives her harsh groom for bridal-gift a
   scourge;
Of living hearts that crack within the fire
Where smoulder their dead despots; and of
   those, —   370
Mothers, — that, all prophetic pity, fling
Their pretty maids in the running flood,
   and swoops
The vulture, beak and talon, at the heart
Made for all noble motion. And I saw
That equal baseness lived in sleeker times
With smoother men; the old leaven lea-
   ven'd all;
Millions of throats would bawl for civil
   rights,
No woman named; therefore I set my face
Against all men, and lived but for mine
   own.
Far off from men I built a fold for them;
I stored it full of rich memorial;   381
I fenced it round with gallant institutes,
And biting laws to scare the beasts of prey,
And prosper'd, till a rout of saucy boys
Brake on us at our books, and marr'd our
   peace,
Mask'd like our maids, blustering I know
   not what
Of insolence and love, some pretext held
Of baby troth, invalid, since my will
Seal'd not the bond — the striplings ! —
   for their sport ! —
I tamed my leopards; shall I not tame
   these ?   390
Or you ? or I ? for since you think me
   touch'd
In honor — what ! I would not aught of
   false —

Is not our cause pure ? and whereas I know
Your prowess, Arac, and what mother's
blood
You draw from, fight! You failing, I abide
What end soever; fail you will not. Still,
Take not his life, he risk'd it for my own;
His mother lives. Yet whatsoe'er you do,
Fight and fight well; strike and strike
home. O dear
Brothers, the woman's angel guards you,
you   400
The sole men to be mingled with our cause,
The sole men we shall prize in the after-
time,
Your very armor hallow'd, and your statues
Rear'd, sung to, when, this gadfly brush'd
aside,
We plant a solid foot into the Time,
And mould a generation strong to move
With claim on claim from right to right,
till she
Whose name is yoked with children's
know herself;
And Knowledge in our own land make her
free,
And, ever following those two crowned
twins,   410
Commerce and Conquest, shower the fiery
grain
Of freedom broadcast over all that orbs
Between the Northern and the Southern
morn.'

Then came a postscript dash'd across the
rest:
'See that there be no traitors in your camp.
We seem a nest of traitors — none to trust
Since our arms fail'd — this Egypt-plague
of men !
Almost our maids were better at their
homes,
Than thus man-girdled here. Indeed I
think
Our chiefest comfort is the little child   420
Of one unworthy mother, which she left.
She shall not have it back; the child shall
grow
To prize the authentic mother of her mind.
I took it for an hour in mine own bed
This morning; there the tender orphan
hands
Felt at my heart, and seem'd to charm from
thence
The wrath I nursed against the world.
Farewell.'

I ceased; he said, 'Stubborn, but she
may sit
Upon a king's right hand in thunder-
storms,
And breed up warriors ! See now, tho'
yourself   430
Be dazzled by the wildfire Love to sloughs
That swallow common sense, the spindling
king,
This Gama swamp'd in lazy tolerance.
When the man wants weight, the woman
takes it up,
And topples down the scales; but this is
fixt
As are the roots of earth and base of all, —
Man for the field and woman for the
hearth;
Man for the sword, and for the needle she;
Man with the head, and woman with the
heart;
Man to command, and woman to obey;   440
All else confusion. Look you ! the gray
mare
Is ill to live with, when her whinny shrills
From tile to scullery, and her small good-
man
Shrinks in his arm-chair while the fires of
hell
Mix with his hearth. But you — she's yet
a colt —
Take, break her; strongly groom'd and
straitly curb'd
She might not rank with those detestable
That let the bantling scald at home, and
brawl
Their rights or wrongs like potherbs in the
street.
They say she's comely; there's the fairer
chance.   450
I like her none the less for rating at her!
Besides, the woman wed is not as we,
But suffers change of frame. A lusty brace
Of twins may weed her of her folly. Boy,
The bearing and the training of a child
Is woman's wisdom.'
           Thus the hard old king.
I took my leave, for it was nearly noon;
I pored upon her letter which I held,
And on the little clause, 'take not his life;'
I mused on that wild morning in the woods,
And on the 'Follow, follow, thou shalt
win;'   461
I thought on all the wrathful king had said,
And how the strange betrothment was to
end.

Then I remember'd that burnt sorcerer's
    curse
That one should fight with shadows and
    should fall;
And like a flash the weird affection came.
King, camp, and college turn'd to hollow
    shows;
I seem'd to move in old memorial tilts,
And doing battle with forgotten ghosts,
To dream myself the shadow of a dream;
And ere I woke it was the point of noon,
The lists were ready. Empanoplied and
    plumed   472
We enter'd in, and waited, fifty there
Opposed to fifty, till the trumpet blared
At the barrier like a wild horn in a land
Of echoes, and a moment, and once more
The trumpet, and again; at which the
    storm
Of galloping hoofs bare on the ridge of
    spears
And riders front to front, until they closed
In conflict with the crash of shivering
    points,   480
And thunder. Yet it seem'd a dream, I
    dream'd
Of fighting. On his haunches rose the
    steed,
And into fiery splinters leapt the lance,
And out of stricken helmets sprang the fire.
Part sat like rocks; part reel'd but kept
    their seats;
Part roll'd on the earth and rose again and
    drew;
Part stumbled mixt with floundering horses.
    Down
From those two bulks at Arac's side, and
    down
From Arac's arm, as from a giant's flail,
The large blows rain'd, as here and every-
    where   490
He rode the mellay, lord of the ringing
    lists,
And all the plain — brand, mace, and
    shaft, and shield —
Shock'd, like an iron-clanging anvil bang'd
With hammers; till I thought, can this be he
From Gama's dwarfish loins? if this be so,
The mother makes us most — and in my
    dream
I glanced aside, and saw the palace-front
Alive with fluttering scarfs and ladies' eyes,
And highest, among the statues, statue-like,
Between a cymbal'd Miriam and a Jael,
With Psyche's babe, was Ida watching us,

A single band of gold about her hair,   502
Like a saint's glory up in heaven; but she,
No saint — inexorable — no tenderness —
Too hard, too cruel. Yet she sees me fight,
Yea, let her see me fall. With that I drave
Among the thickest and bore down a
    prince,
And Cyril one. Yea, let me make my
    dream
All that I would. But that large-moulded
    man,
His visage all agrin as at a wake,   510
Made at me thro' the press, and, stagger-
    ing back
With stroke on stroke the horse and
    horseman, came
As comes a pillar of electric cloud,
Flaying the roofs and sucking up the
    drains,
And shadowing down the champaign till it
    strikes
On a wood, and takes, and breaks, and
    cracks, and splits,
And twists the grain with such a roar that
    Earth
Reels, and the herdsmen cry; for every-
    thing
Gave way before him. Only Florian, he
That loved me closer than his own right
    eye,   520
Thrust in between; but Arac rode him
    down.
And Cyril seeing it, push'd against the
    Prince,
With Psyche's color round his helmet,
    tough,
Strong, supple, sinew-corded, apt at arms;
But tougher, heavier, stronger, he that
    smote
And threw him. Last I spurr'd; I felt my
    veins
Stretch with fierce heat; a moment hand to
    hand,
And sword to sword, and horse to horse we
    hung,
Till I struck out and shouted; the blade
    glanced,
I did but shear a feather, and dream and
    truth   530
Flow'd from me; darkness closed me, and
    I fell.

    Home they brought her warrior dead;
      She nor swoon'd nor utter'd cry.
    All her maidens, watching, said,
      'She must weep or she will die.'

Then they praised him, soft and low,
  Call'd him worthy to be loved,
  Truest friend and noblest foe ;
    Yet she neither spoke nor moved.

Stole a maiden from her place,
  Lightly to the warrior stept,
Took the face-cloth from the face ;
    Yet she neither moved nor wept.

Rose a nurse of ninety years,
  Set his child upon her knee —
Like summer tempest came her tears —
    'Sweet my child, I live for thee.'

VI

My dream had never died or lived again;
As in some mystic middle state I lay.
Seeing I saw not, hearing not I heard;
Tho', if I saw not, yet they told me all
So often that I speak as having seen.

  For so it seem'd, or so they said to me,
That all things grew more tragic and more
    strange;
That when our side was vanquish'd and my
    cause
For ever lost, there went up a great cry,
'The Prince is slain!' My father heard
    and ran   10
In on the lists, and there unlaced my
    casque
And grovell'd on my body, and after him
Came Psyche, sorrowing for Aglaïa.

  But high upon the palace Ida stood
With Psyche's babe in arm; there on the
    roofs
Like that great dame of Lapidoth she
    sang.

  'Our enemies have fallen, have fallen : the
    seed,
The little seed they laugh'd at in the dark,
Has risen and cleft the soil, and grown a bulk
Of spanless girth, that lays on every side   20
A thousand arms and rushes to the sun.

  'Our enemies have fallen, have fallen : they
    came ;
The leaves were wet with women's tears ; they
    heard
A noise of songs they would not understand ;
They mark'd it with the red cross to the fall,
And would have strown it, and are fallen them-
    selves.

  'Our enemies have fallen, have fallen : they
    came,
The woodmen with their axes : lo the tree !
But we will make it faggots for the hearth,
And shape it plank and beam for roof and
    floor,   30
And boats and bridges for the use of men.

  'Our enemies have fallen, have fallen ; they
    struck ;
With their own blows they hurt themselves,
    nor knew
There dwelt an iron nature in the grain ;
The glittering axe was broken in their arms,
Their arms were shatter'd to the shoulder
    blade.

  'Our enemies have fallen, but this shall
    grow
A night of Summer from the heat, a breadth
Of Autumn, dropping fruits of power ; and
    roll'd
With music in the growing breeze of Time, 40
The tops shall strike from star to star, the
    fangs
Shall move the stony bases of the world.

  'And now, O maids, behold our sanctu-
    ary
Is violate, our laws broken ; fear we not
To break them more in their behoof, whose
    arms
Champion'd our cause and won it with a
    day
Blanch'd in our annals, and perpetual feast,
When dames and heroines of the golden
    year
Shall strip a hundred hollows bare of
    Spring,
To rain an April of ovation round   50
Their statues, borne aloft, the three ; but
    come,
We will be liberal, since our rights are
    won.
Let them not lie in the tents with coarse
    mankind,
Ill nurses ; but descend, and proffer these
The brethren of our blood and cause, that
    there
Lie bruised and maim'd, the tender minis-
    tries
Of female hands and hospitality.'

  She spoke, and with the babe yet in her
    arms,
Descending, burst the great bronze valves,
    and led   59
A hundred maids in train across the park.

Some cowl'd, and some bare-headed, on
they came,
Their feet in flowers, her loveliest.   By
them went
The enamor'd air sighing, and on their
curls
From the high tree the blossom wavering
fell,
And over them the tremulous isles of light
Slided, they moving under shade; but
Blanche
At distance follow'd.   So they came: anon
Thro' open field into the lists they wound
Timorously; and as the leader of the herd
That holds a stately fretwork to the sun, 70
And follow'd up by a hundred airy does,
Steps with a tender foot, light as on air,
The lovely, lordly creature floated on
To where her wounded brethren lay; there
stay'd,
Knelt on one knee, — the child on one, —
and prest
Their hands, and call'd them dear deliver-
ers,
And happy warriors, and immortal names,
And said, 'You shall not lie in the tents,
but here,
And nursed by those for whom you fought,
and served
With female hands and hospitality.'   80

Then, whether moved by this, or was it
chance,
She past my way.   Up started from my
side
The old lion, glaring with his whelpless eye,
Silent; but when she saw me lying stark,
Dishelm'd and mute, and motionlessly pale,
Cold even to her, she sigh'd; and when she
saw
The haggard father's face and reverend
beard
Of grisly twine, all dabbled with the blood
Of his own son, shudder'd, a twitch of pain
Tortured her mouth, and o'er her forehead
past   90
A shadow, and her hue changed, and she
said:
'He saved my life; my brother slew him
for it.'
No more; at which the king in bitter scorn
Drew from my neck the painting and the
tress,
And held them up.   She saw them, and a
day

Rose from the distance on her memory,
When the good queen, her mother, shore
the tress
With kisses, ere the days of Lady Blanche.
And then once more she look'd at my pale
face;
Till understanding all the foolish work 100
Of Fancy, and the bitter close of all,
Her iron will was broken in her mind;
Her noble heart was molten in her breast;
She bow'd, she set the child on the earth;
she laid
A feeling finger on my brows, and pre-
sently
'O Sire,' she said, 'he lives; he is not
dead!
O, let me have him with my brethren here
In our own palace; we will tend on him
Like one of these; if so, by any means,
To lighten this great clog of thanks, that
make   110
Our progress falter to the woman's goal.'

She said; but at the happy word 'he
lives!'
My father stoop'd, re-father'd o'er my
wounds.
So those two foes above my fallen life,
With brow to brow like night and evening
mixt
Their dark and gray, while Psyche ever
stole
A little nearer, till the babe that by us,
Half - lapt in glowing gauze and golden
brede,
Lay like a new-fallen meteor on the grass,
Uncared for, spied its mother and began
A blind and babbling laughter, and to
dance   121
Its body, and reach its fatling innocent
arms
And lazy lingering fingers.   She the appeal
Brook'd not, but clamoring out 'Mine —
mine — not yours!
It is not yours, but mine; give me the
child !'
Ceased all on tremble; piteous was the
cry.
So stood the unhappy mother open-
mouth'd,
And turn'd each face her way.   Wan was
her cheek
With hollow watch, her blooming mantle
torn,
Red grief and mother's hunger in her eye,

And down dead-heavy sank her curls, and
   half   131
The sacred mother's bosom, panting, burst
The laces toward her babe; but she nor
   cared
Nor knew it, clamoring on, till Ida heard,
Look'd up, and rising slowly from me,
   stood
Erect and silent, striking with her glance
The mother, me, the child. But he that lay
Beside us, Cyril, batter'd as he was,
Trail'd himself up on one knee; then he
   drew
Her robe to meet his lips, and down she
   look'd   140
At the arm'd man sideways, pitying as it
   seem'd,
Or self-involved; but when she learnt his
   face,
Remembering his ill-omen'd song, arose
Once more thro' all her height, and o'er
   him grew
Tall as a figure lengthen'd on the sand
When the tide ebbs in sunshine, and he
   said:

'O fair and strong and terrible! Lioness
That with your long locks play the lion's
   mane!
But Love and Nature, these are two more
   terrible
And stronger. See, your foot is on our
   necks,   150
We vanquish'd, you the victor of your will.
What would you more? give her the child!
   remain
Orb'd in your isolation; he is dead,
Or all as dead: henceforth we let you be.
Win you the hearts of women; and beware
Lest, where you seek the common love of
   these,
The common hate with the revolving wheel
Should drag you down, and some great
   Nemesis
Break from a darken'd future, crown'd
   with fire,
And tread you out for ever. But howso-
   e'er   160
Fixt in yourself, never in your own arms
To hold your own, deny not hers to her,
Give her the child! O, if, I say, you keep
One pulse that beats true woman, if you
   loved
The breast that fed or arm that dandled
   you,

Or own one port of sense not flint to
   prayer,
Give her the child! or if you scorn to lay it,
Yourself, in hands so lately claspt with
   yours,
Or speak to her, your dearest, her one
   fault
The tenderness, not yours, that could not
   kill,   170
Give *me* it; *I* will give it her.'
                              He said.
At first her eye with slow dilation roll'd
Dry flame, she listening; after sank and
   sank
And, into mournful twilight mellowing,
   dwelt
Full on the child. She took it: 'Pretty
   bud!
Lily of the vale! half-open'd bell of the
   woods!
Sole comfort of my dark hour, when a
   world
Of traitorous friend and broken system
   made
No purple in the distance, mystery,   179
Pledge of a love not to be mine, farewell!
These men are hard upon us as of old,
We two must part; and yet how fain was I
To dream thy cause embraced in mine, to
   think
I might be something to thee, when I felt
Thy helpless warmth about my barren
   breast
In the dead prime; but may thy mother
   prove
As true to thee as false, false, false to me!
And, if thou needs must bear the yoke, I
   wish it
Gentle as freedom' — here she kiss'd it;
   then —   189
'All good go with thee! take it, sir,' and so
Laid the soft babe in his hard - mailed
   hands,
Who turn'd half-round to Psyche as she
   sprang
To meet it, with an eye that swum in
   thanks;
Then felt it sound and whole from head
   to foot,
And hugg'd and never hugg'd it close
   enough,
And in her hunger mouth'd and mumbled
   it,
And hid her bosom with it; after that
Put on more calm and added suppliantly:

'We two were friends: I go to mine
own land
For ever. Find some other; as for me 200
I scarce am fit for your great plans: yet
speak to me,
Say one soft word and let me part for-
given.'

But Ida spoke not, rapt upon the child.
Then Arac: ' Ida — 'sdeath ! you blame the
man;
You wrong yourselves — the woman is so
hard
Upon the woman. Come, a grace to me !
I am your warrior ; I and mine have
fought
Your battle. Kiss her; take her hand, she
weeps.
'Sdeath ! I would sooner fight thrice o'er
than see it.'   209

But Ida spoke not, gazing on the ground;
And reddening in the furrows of his chin,
And moved beyond his custom, Gama said:

' I 've heard that there is iron in the
blood,
And I believe it. Not one word ? not
one ?
Whence drew you this steel temper ? not
from me,
Not from your mother, now a saint with
saints.
She said you had a heart — I heard her say
it —
" Our Ida has a heart " — just ere she
died —
" But see that some one with authority
Be near her still;" and I — I sought for
one —   220
All people said she had authority —
The Lady Blanche — much profit ! Not one
word ;
No ! tho' your father sues. See how you
stand
Stiff as Lot's wife, and all the good knights
maim'd,
I trust that there is no one hurt to death,
For your wild whim. And was it then for
this,
Was it for this we gave our palace up,
Where we withdrew from summer heats
and state,
And had our wine and chess beneath the
planes,

And many a pleasant hour with her that 's
gone,   230
Ere you were born to vex us ? Is it kind ?
Speak to her, I say; is this not she of
whom,
When first she came, all flush'd you said to
me,
Now had you got a friend of your own age,
Now could you share your thought, now
should men see
Two women faster welded in one love
Than pairs of wedlock ? she you walk'd
with, she
You talk'd with, whole nights long, up in
the tower,
Of sine and arc, spheroid and azimuth,
And right ascension, heaven knows what;
and now   240
A word, but one, one little kindly word,
Not one to spare her ! Out upon you, flint!
You love nor her, nor me, nor any; nay,
You shame your mother's judgment too.
Not one ?
You will not ? well — no heart have you,
or such
As fancies like the vermin in a nut
Have fretted all to dust and bitterness.'
So said the small king moved beyond his
wont.

But Ida stood nor spoke, drain'd of her
force   249
By many a varying influence and so long.
Down thro' her limbs a drooping languor
wept;
Her head a little bent; and on her mouth
A doubtful smile dwelt like a clouded
moon
In a still water. Then brake out my sire,
Lifting his grim head from my wounds:
' O you,
Woman, whom we thought woman even
now,
And were half fool'd to let you tend our
son,
Because he might have wish'd it — but we
see
The accomplice of your madness unfor-
given,
And think that you might mix his draught
with death,   260
When your skies change again; the rougher
hand
Is safer. On to the tents; take up the
Prince.'

He rose, and while each ear was prick'd
    to attend
A tempest, thro' the cloud that dimm'd her
    broke
A genial warmth and light once more, and
    shone
Thro' glittering drops on her sad friend.
                         'Come hither,
O Psyche,' she cried out, 'embrace me,
    come,
Quick while I melt; make reconcilement
    sure
With one that cannot keep her mind an
    hour;   269
Come to the hollow heart they slander
    so !
Kiss and be friends, like children being
    chid !
I seem no more, *I* want forgiveness too;
I should have had to do with none but
    maids,
That have no links with men. Ah false
    but dear,
Dear traitor, too much loved, why ? —
    why ? — yet see
Before these kings we embrace you yet
    once more
With all forgiveness, all oblivion,
And trust, not love, you less.
                    And now, O Sire,
Grant me your son, to nurse, to wait upon
    him,
Like mine own brother. For my debt to
    him,   280
This nightmare weight of gratitude, I know
    it.
Taunt me no more; yourself and yours
    shall have
Free adit; we will scatter all our maids
Till happier times each to her proper
    hearth.
What use to keep them here — now ? grant
    my prayer.
Help, father, brother, help; speak to the
    king;
Thaw this male nature to some touch of
    that
Which kills me with myself, and drags me
    down
From my fixt height to mob me up with
    all   289
The soft and milky rabble of womankind,
Poor weakling even as they are.'
                      Passionate tears
Follow'd; the king replied not; Cyril said:

'Your brother, lady, — Florian, — ask for
    him
Of your great Head — for he is wounded
    too —
That you may tend upon him with the
    Prince.'
'Ay, so,' said Ida with a bitter smile,
'Our laws are broken; let him enter too.'
Then Violet, she that sang the mournful
    song,
And had a cousin tumbled on the plain,
Petition'd too for him. 'Ay, so,' she
    said,   300
'I stagger in the stream; I cannot keep
My heart an eddy from the brawling hour.
We break our laws with ease, but let it
    be.'
'Ay, so ?' said Blanche: 'Amazed am I to
    hear
Your Highness; but your Highness breaks
    with ease
The law your Highness did not make;
    't was I.
I had been wedded wife, I knew man-
    kind,
And block'd them out; but these men came
    to woo
Your Highness, — verily I think to win.'

So she, and turn'd askance a wintry eye;
But Ida, with a voice that, like a bell   311
Toll'd by an earthquake in a trembling
    tower,
Rang ruin, answer'd full of grief and scorn:

'Fling our doors wide ! all, all, not one,
    but all,
Not only he, but by my mother's soul,
Whatever man lies wounded, friend or foe,
Shall enter, if he will ! Let our girls flit,
Till the storm die ! but had you stood by
    us,
The roar that breaks the Pharos from his
    base
Had left us rock. She fain would sting us
    too,   320
But shall not. Pass, and mingle with your
    likes.
We brook no further insult, but are gone.'

She turn'd; the very nape of her white
    neck
Was rosed with indignation; but the Prince
Her brother came; the king her father
    charm'd

Her wounded soul with words; nor did
mine own
Refuse her proffer, lastly gave his hand.

Then us they lifted up, dead weights,
and bare
Straight to the doors; to them the doors
gave way   329
Groaning, and in the vestal entry shriek'd
The virgin marble under iron heels.
And on they moved and gain'd the hall,
and there
Rested; but great the crush was, and each
base,
To left and right, of those tall columns
drown'd
In silken fluctuation and the swarm
Of female whisperers. At the further end
Was Ida by the throne, the two great cats
Close by her, like supporters on a shield,
Bow-back'd with fear; but in the centre
stood
The common men with rolling eyes;
amazed   340
They glared upon the women, and aghast
The women stared at these, all silent, save
When armor clash'd or jingled, while the
day,
Descending, struck athwart the hall, and
shot
A flying splendor out of brass and steel,
That o'er the statues leapt from head to
head,
Now fired an angry Pallas on the helm,
Now set a wrathful Dian's moon on flame;
And now and then an echo started up,
And shuddering fled from room to room,
and died   350
Of fright in far apartments.
                        Then the voice
Of Ida sounded, issuing ordinance;
And me they bore up the broad stairs, and
thro'
The long-laid galleries past a hundred
doors
To one deep chamber shut from sound, and
due
To languid limbs and sickness, left me
in it;
And others otherwhere they laid; and all
That afternoon a sound arose of hoof
And chariot, many a maiden passing home
Till happier times; but some were left of
those   360
Held sagest, and the great lords out and in,

From those two hosts that lay beside the
wall,
Walk'd at their will, and everything was
changed.

Ask me no more : the moon may draw the sea;
  The cloud may stoop from heaven and take
    the shape,
  With fold to fold, of mountain or of cape;
But O too fond, when have I answer'd thee ?
          Ask me no more.

Ask me no more: what answer should I give ?
  I love not hollow cheek or faded eye:
  Yet, O my friend, I will not have thee die!
Ask me no more, lest I should bid thee live;
          Ask me no more.

Ask me no more : thy fate and mine are seal'd:
  I strove against the stream and all in vain;
  Let the great river take me to the main.
No more, dear love, for at a touch I yield;
          Ask me no more.

                  VII

So was their sanctuary violated,
So their fair college turn'd to hospital,
At first with all confusion; by and by
Sweet order lived again with other laws,
A kindlier influence reign'd, and every-
where
Low voices with the ministering hand
Hung round the sick. The maidens came,
they talk'd,
They sang, they read; till she not fair be-
gan
To gather light, and she that was became
Her former beauty treble; and to and
fro   10
With books, with flowers, with angel offices,
Like creatures native unto gracious act,
And in their own clear element, they
moved.

But sadness on the soul of Ida fell,
And hatred of her weakness, blent with
shame.
Old studies fail'd; seldom she spoke; but
oft
Clomb to the roofs, and gazed alone for
hours
On that disastrous leaguer, swarms of men
Darkening her female field. Void was her
use,
And she as one that climbs a peak to gaze

O'er land and main, and sees a great black
   cloud   21
Drag inward from the deeps, a wall of
   night,
Blot out the slope of sea from verge to
   shore,
And suck the blinding splendor from the
   sand,
And quenching lake by lake and tarn by
   tarn
Expunge the world; so fared she gazing
   there,
So blacken'd all her world in secret, blank
And waste it seem'd and vain; till down
   she came,
And found fair peace once more among the
   sick.

And twilight dawn'd; and morn by morn
   the lark   30
Shot up and shrill'd in flickering gyres,
   but I
Lay silent in the muffled cage of life.
And twilight gloom'd, and broader-grown
   the bowers
Drew the great night into themselves, and
   heaven,
Star after star, arose and fell; but I,
Deeper than those weird doubts could reach
   me, lay
Quite sunder'd from the moving Universe,
Nor knew what eye was on me, nor the
   hand
That nursed me, more than infants in their
   sleep.

But Psyche tended Florian; with her oft 40
Melissa came, for Blanche had gone, but
   left
Her child among us, willing she should
   keep
Court-favor. Here and there the small
   bright head,
A light of healing, glanced about the couch,
Or thro' the parted silks the tender face
Peep'd, shining in upon the wounded man
With blush and smile, a medicine in them-
   selves
To wile the length from languorous hours,
   and draw
The sting from pain; nor seem'd it strange
   that soon   49
He rose up whole, and those fair charities
Join'd at her side; nor stranger seem'd that
   hearts

So gentle, so employ'd, should close in love,
Than when two dewdrops on the petal
   shake
To the same sweet air, and tremble deeper
   down,
And slip at once all-fragrant into one.

Less prosperously the second suit ob-
   tain'd
At first with Psyche. Not tho' Blanche
   had sworn
That after that dark night among the fields
She needs must wed him for her own good
   name;   59
Not tho' he built upon the babe restored;
Not tho' she liked him, yielded she, but
   fear'd
To incense the Head once more; till on a
   day
When Cyril pleaded, Ida came behind
Seen but of Psyche; on her foot she hung
A moment, and she heard, at which her
   face
A little flush'd, and she past on; but each
Assumed from thence a half-consent in-
   volved
In stillness, plighted troth, and were at
   peace.

Nor only these; Love in the sacred halls
Held carnival at will, and flying struck   70
With showers of random sweet on maid and
   man.
Nor did her father cease to press my claim,
Nor did mine own now reconciled; nor yet
Did those twin brothers, risen again and
   whole;
Nor Arac, satiate with his victory.

But I lay still, and with me oft she sat.
Then came a change; for sometimes I
   would catch
Her hand in wild delirium, gripe it hard,
And fling it like a viper off, and shriek,
'You are not Ida;' clasp it once again,   80
And call her Ida, tho' I knew her not,
And call her sweet, as if in irony,
And call her hard and cold, which seem'd a
   truth;
And still she fear'd that I should lose my
   mind,
And often she believed that I should die;
Till out of long frustration of her care,
And pensive tendance in the all-weary
   noons,

And watches in the dead, the dark, when
    clocks
Throbb'd thunder thro' the palace floors, or
    call'd
On flying Time from all their silver
    tongues —   90
And out of memories of her kindlier days,
And sidelong glances at my father's grief,
And at the happy lovers heart in heart —
And out of hauntings of my spoken love,
And lonely listenings to my mutter'd
    dream,
And often feeling of the helpless hands,
And wordless broodings on the wasted
    cheek —
From all a closer interest flourish'd up,
Tenderness touch by touch, and last, to
    these,
Love, like an Alpine harebell hung with
    tears   100
By some cold morning glacier; frail at first
And feeble, all unconscious of itself,
But such as gather'd color day by day.

Last I woke sane, but well-nigh close to
    death
For weakness. It was evening; silent light
Slept on the painted walls, wherein were
    wrought
Two grand designs; for on one side arose
The women up in wild revolt, and storm'd
At the Oppian law. Titanic shapes, they
    cramm'd
The forum, and half-crush'd among the
    rest   110
A dwarf-like Cato cower'd. On the other
    side
Hortensia spoke against the tax; behind,
A train of dames. By axe and eagle sat,
With all their foreheads drawn in Roman
    scowls,
And half the wolf's-milk curdled in their
    veins,
The fierce triumvirs; and before them
    paused
Hortensia, pleading; angry was her face.

I saw the forms; I knew not where I
    was.
They did but look like hollow shows; nor
    more   119
Sweet Ida. Palm to palm she sat; the dew
Dwelt in her eyes, and softer all her shape
And rounder seem'd. I moved, I sigh'd;
    a touch

Came round my wrist, and tears upon my
    hand.
Then all for languor and self-pity ran
Mine down my face, and with what life I
    had,
And like a flower that cannot all unfold,
So drench'd it is with tempest, to the sun,
Yet, as it may, turns toward him, I on
    her
Fixt my faint eyes, and utter'd whisper-
    ingly:

    'If you be what I think you, some sweet
        dream,   130
I would but ask you to fulfil yourself;
But if you be that Ida whom I knew,
I ask you nothing; only, if a dream,
Sweet dream, be perfect. I shall die to-
    night.
Stoop down and seem to kiss me ere I die.'

    I could no more, but lay like one in
    trance,
That hears his burial talk'd of by his friends,
And cannot speak, nor move, nor make one
    sign,
But lies and dreads his doom. She turn'd,
    she paused,   139
She stoop'd; and out of languor leapt a
    cry,
Leapt fiery Passion from the brinks of
    death,
And I believed that in the living world
My spirit closed with Ida's at the lips;
Till back I fell, and from mine arms she
    rose
Glowing all over noble shame; and all
Her falser self slipt from her like a robe,
And left her woman, lovelier in her mood
Than in her mould that other, when she
    came
From barren deeps to conquer all with love,
And down the streaming crystal dropt; and
    she   150
Far-fleeted by the purple island-sides,
Naked, a double light in air and wave,
To meet her Graces, where they deck'd her
    out
For worship without end — nor end of mine,
Stateliest, for thee! but mute she glided
    forth,
Nor glanced behind her, and I sank and
    slept,
Fill'd thro' and thro' with love, a happy
    sleep.

Deep in the night I woke: she, near me, held
A volume of the poets of her land.   159
There to herself, all in low tones, she read:

'Now sleeps the crimson petal, now the white ;
Nor waves the cypress in the palace walk ;
Nor winks the gold fin in the porphyry font.
The fire-fly wakens ; waken thou with me.

'Now droops the milk-white peacock like a ghost,
And like a ghost she glimmers on to me.

'Now lies the Earth all Danaë to the stars,
And all thy heart lies open unto me.

'Now slides the silent meteor on, and leaves
A shining furrow, as thy thoughts in me.   170

'Now folds the lily all her sweetness up,
And slips into the bosom of the lake.
So fold thyself, my dearest, thou, and slip
Into my bosom and be lost in me.'

I heard her turn the page; she found a small
Sweet idyl, and once more, as low, she read:

'Come down, O maid, from yonder mountain height.
What pleasure lives in height (the shepherd sang),
In height and cold, the splendor of the hills ?
But cease to move so near the heavens, and cease   180
To glide a sunbeam by the blasted pine,
To sit a star upon the sparkling spire ;
And come, for Love is of the valley, come,
For Love is of the valley, come thou down
And find him ; by the happy threshold, he,
Or hand in hand with Plenty in the maize,
Or red with spirted purple of the vats,
Or foxlike in the vine ; nor cares to walk
With Death and Morning on the Silver Horns,
Nor wilt thou snare him in the white ravine,
Nor find him dropt upon the firths of ice,   191
That huddling slant in furrow-cloven falls
To roll the torrent out of dusky doors.
But follow ; let the torrent dance thee down
To find him in the valley ; let the wild
Lean-headed eagles yelp alone, and leave
The monstrous ledges there to slope, and spill
Their thousand wreaths of dangling water-smoke,
That like a broken purpose waste in air.   199
So waste not thou, but come ; for all the vales
Await thee ; azure pillars of the hearth

Arise to thee ; the children call, and I
Thy shepherd pipe, and sweet is every sound,
Sweeter thy voice, but every sound is sweet ;
Myriads of rivulets hurrying thro' the lawn,
The moan of doves in immemorial elms,
And murmuring of innumerable bees.'

So she low-toned, while with shut eyes I lay
Listening, then look'd.   Pale was the perfect face;
The bosom with long sighs labor'd; and meek   210
Seem'd the full lips, and mild the luminous eyes,
And the voice trembled and the hand.   She said
Brokenly, that she knew it, she had fail'd
In sweet humility, had fail'd in all;
That all her labor was but as a block
Left in the quarry; but she still were loth,
She still were loth to yield herself to one
That wholly scorn'd to help their equal rights
Against the sons of men and barbarous laws.
She pray'd me not to judge their cause from her   220
That wrong'd it, sought far less for truth than power
In knowledge.   Something wild within her breast,
A greater than all knowledge, beat her down.
And she had nursed me there from week to week;
Much had she learnt in little time.   In part
It was ill counsel had misled the girl
To vex true hearts; yet was she but a girl —
'Ah fool, and made myself a queen of farce !
When comes another such ? never, I think,
Till the sun drop, dead, from the signs.'
                                    Her voice
Choked, and her forehead sank upon her hands,   231
And her great heart thro' all the faultful past
Went sorrowing in a pause I dared not break;
Till notice of a change in the dark world
Was lispt about the acacias, and a bird,
That early woke to feed her little ones,
Sent from a dewy breast a cry for light.
She moved, and at her feet the volume fell.

'Blame not thyself too much,' I said,
'nor blame
Too much the sons of men and barbarous
laws; 240
These were the rough ways of the world till
now.
Henceforth thou hast a helper, me, that
know
The woman's cause is man's; they rise or
sink
Together, dwarf'd or godlike, bond or free.
For she that out of Lethe scales with man
The shining steps of Nature, shares with
man
His nights, his days, moves with him to one
goal,
Stays all the fair young planet in her
hands —
If she be small, slight-natured, miserable,
How shall men grow? but work no more
alone! 250
Our place is much; as far as in us lies
We two will serve them both in aiding
her —
Will clear away the parasitic forms
That seem to keep her up but drag her
down —
Will leave her space to burgeon out of all
Within her — let her make herself her
own
To give or keep, to live and learn and be
All that not harms distinctive womanhood.
For woman is not undevelopt man,
But diverse. Could we make her as the
man, 260
Sweet Love were slain; his dearest bond
is this,
Not like to like, but like in difference.
Yet in the long years liker must they
grow;
The man be more of woman, she of man;
He gain in sweetness and in moral height,
Nor lose the wrestling thews that throw
the world;
She mental breadth, nor fail in childward
care,
Nor lose the childlike in the larger mind;
Till at the last she set herself to man,
Like perfect music unto noble words; 270
And so these twain, upon the skirts of
Time,
Sit side by side, full-summ'd in all their
powers,
Dispensing harvest, sowing the to-be,
Self-reverent each and reverencing each,

Distinct in individualities,
But like each other even as those who love.
Then comes the statelier Eden back to
men;
Then reign the world's great bridals, chaste
and calm;
Then springs the crowning race of human-
kind. 279
May these things be!'
    Sighing she spoke: 'I fear
They will not.'
    'Dear, but let us type them now
In our own lives, and this proud watch-
word rest
Of equal; seeing either sex alone
Is half itself, and in true marriage lies
Nor equal, nor unequal. Each fulfils
Defect in each, and always thought in
thought,
Purpose in purpose, will in will, they grow,
The single pure and perfect animal,
The two-cell'd heart beating, with one full
stroke, 289
Life.'
    And again sighing she spoke: 'A dream
That once was mine! what woman taught
you this?'

'Alone,' I said, 'from earlier than I
know,
Immersed in rich foreshadowings of the
world,
I loved the woman. He, that doth not,
lives
A drowning life, besotted in sweet self,
Or pines in sad experience worse than
death,
Or keeps his wing'd affections clipt with
crime.
Yet was there one thro' whom I loved her,
one
Not learned, save in gracious household
ways,
Not perfect, nay, but full of tender wants,
No angel, but a dearer being, all dipt 301
In angel instincts, breathing Paradise,
Interpreter between the gods and men,
Who look'd all native to her place, and yet
On tiptoe seem'd to touch upon a sphere
Too gross to tread, and all male minds per-
force
Sway'd to her from their orbits as they
moved,
And girdled her with music. Happy he
With such a mother! faith in womankind

Beats with his blood, and trust in all things
  high   310
Comes easy to him, and tho' he trip and fall
He shall not blind his soul with clay.'
                              ' But I,'
Said Ida, tremulously, ' so all unlike —
It seems you love to cheat yourself with
  words;
This mother is your model. I have heard
Of your strange doubts; they well might
  be; I seem
A mockery to my own self. Never, Prince!
You cannot love me.'
                      ' Nay, but thee,' I said,
' From yearlong poring on thy pictured
  eyes,
Ere seen I loved, and loved thee seen, and
  saw   320
Thee woman thro' the crust of iron moods
That mask'd thee from men's reverence
  up, and forced
Sweet love on pranks of saucy boyhood;
  now,
Given back to life, to life indeed, thro'
  thee,
Indeed I love. The new day comes, the
  light
Dearer for night, as dearer thou for faults
Lived over. Lift thine eyes; my doubts are
  dead,
My haunting sense of hollow shows; the
  change,
This truthful change in thee has kill'd it.
  Dear,
Look up, and let thy nature strike on
  mine,   330
Like yonder morning on the blind half-
  world.
Approach and fear not; breathe upon my
  brows;
In that fine air I tremble, all the past
Melts mist-like into this bright hour, and
  this
Is morn to more, and all the rich to-come
Reels, as the golden Autumn woodland
  reels
Athwart the smoke of burning weeds. For-
  give me,
I waste my heart in signs; let be. My
  bride,
My wife, my life! O, we will walk this
  world,
Yoked in all exercise of noble end,   340
And so thro' those dark gates across the
  wild

That no man knows. Indeed I love thee;
  come,
Yield thyself up; my hopes and thine are
  one.
Accomplish thou my manhood and thyself;
Lay thy sweet hands in mine and trust to
  me.'

CONCLUSION

So closed our tale, of which I give you all
The random scheme as wildly as it rose.
The words are mostly mine; for when we
  ceased
There came a minute's pause, and Walter
  said,
' I wish she had not yielded ! ' then to me,
' What if you drest it up poetically ! '
So pray'd the men, the women; I gave
  assent.
Yet how to bind the scatter'd scheme of
  seven
Together in one sheaf ? What style could
  suit ?
The men required that I should give
  throughout   10
The sort of mock-heroic gigantesque,
With which we banter'd little Lilia first;
The women — and perhaps they felt their
  power,
For something in the ballads which they
  sang,
Or in their silent influence as they sat,
Had ever seem'd to wrestle with bur-
  lesque,
And drove us, last, to quite a solemn
  close —
They hated banter, wish'd for something
  real,
A gallant fight, a noble princess — why 19
Not make her true-heroic — true-sublime ?
Or all, they said, as earnest as the close ?
Which yet with such a framework scarce
  could be.
Then rose a little feud betwixt the two,
Betwixt the mockers and the realists;
And I, betwixt them both, to please them
  both,
And yet to give the story as it rose,
I moved as in a strange diagonal,
And maybe neither pleased myself nor
  them.

But Lilia pleased me, for she took no part
In our dispute; the sequel of the tale   30

Had touch'd her, and she sat, she pluck'd
    the grass,
She flung it from her, thinking; last, she
    fixt
A showery glance upon her aunt, and said,
' You — tell us what we are ' — who might
    have told,
For she was cramm'd with theories out of
    books,
But that there rose a shout. The gates were
    closed
At sunset, and the crowd were swarming
    now,
To take their leave, about the garden rails.

So I and some went out to these; we
    climb'd   39
The slope to Vivian - place, and turning
    saw
The happy valleys, half in light, and half
Far-shadowing from the west, a land of
    peace;
Gray halls alone among their massive
    groves;
Trim hamlets; here and there a rustic
    tower
Half-lost in belts of hop and breadths of
    wheat;
The shimmering glimpses of a stream; the
    seas;
A red sail, or a white; and far beyond,
Imagined more than seen, the skirts of
    France.

' Look there, a garden ! ' said my college
    friend,
The Tory member's elder son, ' and there !
God bless the narrow sea which keeps her
    off,   51
And keeps our Britain, whole within her-
    self,
A nation yet, the rulers and the ruled —
Some sense of duty, something of a faith,
Some reverence for the laws ourselves have
    made,
Some patient force to change them when
    we will,
Some civic manhood firm against the
    crowd —
But yonder, whiff ! there comes a sudden
    heat,
The gravest citizen seems to lose his head,
The king is scared, the soldier will not
    fight,   60
The little boys begin to shoot and stab,

A kingdom topples over with a shriek
Like an old woman, and down rolls the
    world
In mock heroics stranger than our own;
Revolts, republics, revolutions, most
No graver than a schoolboys' barring out;
Too comic for the solemn things they are,
Too solemn for the comic touches in them,
Like our wild Princess with as wise a
    dream
As some of theirs — God bless the narrow
    seas !   70
I wish they were a whole Atlantic broad.'

' Have patience,' I replied, ' ourselves are
    full
Of social wrong; and maybe wildest dreams
Are but the needful preludes of the truth.
For me, the genial day, the happy crowd,
The sport half-science, fill me with a faith,
This fine old world of ours is but a child
Yet in the go - cart. Patience ! Give it
    time
To learn its limbs; there is a hand that
    guides.'

In such discourse we gain'd the garden
    rails,   80
And there we saw Sir Walter where he
    stood,
Before a tower of crimson holly-oaks,
Among six boys, head under head, and
    look'd
No little lily-handed baronet he,
A great broad-shoulder'd genial English-
    man,
A lord of fat prize-oxen and of sheep,
A raiser of huge melons and of pine,
A patron of some thirty charities,
A pamphleteer on guano and on grain,
A quarter-sessions chairman, abler none; 90
Fair-hair'd and redder than a windy morn;
Now shaking hands with him, now him, of
    those
That stood the nearest — now address'd to
    speech —
Who spoke few words and pithy, such as
    closed
Welcome, farewell, and welcome for the
    year
To follow. A shout rose again, and made
The long line of the approaching rookery
    swerve
From the elms, and shook the branches of
    the deer

From slope to slope thro' distant ferns, and
   rang   99
Beyond the bourn of sunset — O, a shout
More joyful than the city-roar that hails
Premier or king !   Why should not these
   great sirs
Give up their parks some dozen times a
   year
To let the people breathe ?   So thrice they
   cried,
I likewise, and in groups they stream'd
   away.

  But we went back to the Abbey, and
   sat on,
So much the gathering darkness charm'd;
   we sat

But spoke not, rapt in nameless reverie,
Perchance upon the future man.   The walls
Blacken'd about us, bats wheel'd, and owls
   whoop'd,   110
And gradually the powers of the night,
That range above the region of the wind,
Deepening the courts of twilight broke
   them up
Thro' all the silent spaces of the worlds,
Beyond all thought into the heaven of hea-
   vens.

  Last little Lilia, rising quietly,
Disrobed the glimmering statue of Sir
   Ralph
From those rich silks, and home well-
   pleased we went.

IN MEMORIAM A. H. H.

OBIIT MDCCCXXXIII

'In Memoriam' was first published in 1850.   No changes were made in the second and third editions except the correction of two misprints.   In the fourth edition (1851) the present 59th section ('O Sorrow, wilt thou live with me ? ') was added.   The present 39th section ('Old warder of these buried bones,' etc.) was added in the 'Miniature Edition' of the 'Poems' (1871). Minor changes are recorded in the Notes.

Arthur Henry Hallam, to whose memory the poem is a tribute, was the son of Henry Hallam, the historian, and was born in London, February 1, 1811.   In 1818 he spent some months with his parents in Italy and Switzerland, where he became familiar with the French language, which he had already learned to read with ease.   Latin he also learned to read with facility in little more than a year.   When only eight or nine years old, he began to write tragedies which showed remarkable precocity.

After a brief course in a preparatory school he was sent to Eton, where he remained till 1827. He did not distinguish himself as a classical scholar, being more interested in English literature, especially the earlier dramatists.   He took an active part in the Debating Society, where he showed great power in argumentative discussion ; and during his last year in the school he began to write for the 'Eton Miscellany.'   After leaving Eton he spent eight months with his parents in Italy, where he mastered the language and the works of Dante and Petrarch.

In October, 1829, he went to Trinity College, Cambridge.   There he soon became acquainted with the Tennysons, and thus began the ever-memorable friendship of which 'In Memoriam' is the monument.   Like his friends, he was the pupil of the Rev. William Whewell.   In 1831 he obtained the first prize for an English declamation on the conduct of the Independent party during the Civil War.   In consequence of this success, he was called upon to deliver an oration in the chapel before the Christmas vacation, and chose as a subject the influence of Italian upon English literature.   He also gained a prize for an English essay on the philosophical writings of Cicero.

He left Cambridge on taking his degree in January, 1832.   He resided from that time with his father in London in 67 Wimpole Street, referred to in 'In Memoriam,' vii. : —

> Dark house, by which once more I stand
> Here in the long unlovely street.

Arthur used to say to his friends, 'You know you will always find us at sixes and sevens.'   At the earnest desire of his father he applied himself vigorously to the study of law in the Inner Temple, entering, in the month of October, 1832, the office of an eminent conveyancer, with whom he continued till his departure from England in the following summer.

His father tells the remainder of the sad story very briefly. Arthur accompanied him to Germany in the beginning of August. In returning to Vienna from Pesth, a wet day probably gave rise to an intermittent fever with very slight symptoms, which were apparently subsiding, when a sudden rush of blood to the head caused his death on the 15th of September, 1833. It appeared on examination that the cerebral vessels were weak, and that there was a lack of energy in the heart. In the usual chances of humanity a few more years would probably have been fatal.

His 'loved remains' were brought to England and interred on the 3d of January, 1834, in Clevedon Church, Somersetshire, belonging to his maternal grandfather, Sir Abraham Elton. The place was selected by his father not only from its connection with the family, but also from its sequestered situation on a lone hill overlooking the Bristol Channel.

STRONG Son of God, immortal Love,
  Whom we, that have not seen thy face,
  By faith, and faith alone, embrace,
Believing where we cannot prove;

Thine are these orbs of light and shade;
  Thou madest Life in man and brute;
  Thou madest Death; and lo, thy foot
Is on the skull which thou hast made.

Thou wilt not leave us in the dust:
  Thou madest man, he knows not why,
  He thinks he was not made to die;
And thou hast made him: thou art just.

Thou seemest human and divine,
  The highest, holiest manhood, thou.
  Our wills are ours, we know not how;
Our wills are ours, to make them thine.

Our little systems have their day;
  They have their day and cease to be;
  They are but broken lights of thee,
And thou, O Lord, art more than they.

We have but faith: we cannot know,
  For knowledge is of things we see;
  And yet we trust it comes from thee,
A beam in darkness: let it grow.

Let knowledge grow from more to more,
  But more of reverence in us dwell;
  That mind and soul, according well,
May make one music as before,

But vaster. We are fools and slight;
  We mock thee when we do not fear:
  But help thy foolish ones to bear;
Help thy vain worlds to bear thy light.

Forgive what seem'd my sin in me,
  What seem'd my worth since I began;
  For merit lives from man to man,
And not from man, O Lord, to thee.

Forgive my grief for one removed,
  Thy creature, whom I found so fair.
  I trust he lives in thee, and there
I find him worthier to be loved.

Forgive these wild and wandering cries,
  Confusions of a wasted youth;
  Forgive them where they fail in truth,
And in thy wisdom make me wise.
    1849.

————

I

I held it truth, with him who sings
  To one clear harp in divers tones,
  That men may rise on stepping-stones
Of their dead selves to higher things.

But who shall so forecast the years
  And find in loss a gain to match?
  Or reach a hand thro' time to catch
The far-off interest of tears?

Let Love clasp Grief lest both be drown'd,
  Let darkness keep her raven gloss.
  Ah, sweeter to be drunk with loss,
To dance with Death, to beat the ground,

Than that the victor Hours should scorn
  The long result of love, and boast,
  'Behold the man that loved and lost,
But all he was is overworn.'

II

Old yew, which graspest at the stones
  That name the underlying dead,
  Thy fibres net the dreamless head,
Thy roots are wrapt about the bones.

The seasons bring the flower again,
  And bring the firstling to the flock;
  And in the dusk of thee the clock
Beats out the little lives of men.

O, not for thee the glow, the bloom,
  Who changest not in any gale,
  Nor branding summer suns avail
To touch thy thousand years of gloom;

And gazing on thee, sullen tree,
  Sick for thy stubborn hardihood,
  I seem to fail from out my blood
And grow incorporate into thee.

III

O Sorrow, cruel fellowship,
  O Priestess in the vaults of Death,
  O sweet and bitter in a breath,
What whispers from thy lying lip?

' The stars,' she whispers, ' blindly run;
  A web is woven across the sky;
  From out waste places comes a cry,
And murmurs from the dying sun;

' And all the phantom, Nature, stands —
  With all the music in her tone,
  A hollow echo of my own, —
A hollow form with empty hands.'

And shall I take a thing so blind,
  Embrace her as my natural good;
  Or crush her, like a vice of blood,
Upon the threshold of the mind?

IV

To Sleep I give my powers away;
  My will is bondsman to the dark;
  I sit within a helmless bark,
And with my heart I muse and say:

O heart, how fares it with thee now,
  That thou shouldst fail from thy desire,
  Who scarcely darest to inquire,
' What is it makes me beat so low?'

Something it is which thou hast lost,
  Some pleasure from thine early years.
  Break, thou deep vase of chilling tears,
That grief hath shaken into frost!

Such clouds of nameless trouble cross
  All night below the darken'd eyes;
  With morning wakes the will, and cries,
' Thou shalt not be the fool of loss.'

V

I sometimes hold it half a sin
  To put in words the grief I feel:

For words, like Nature, half reveal
And half conceal the Soul within.

But, for the unquiet heart and brain,
  A use in measured language lies;
  The sad mechanic exercise,
Like dull narcotics, numbing pain.

In words, like weeds, I 'll wrap me o'er,
  Like coarsest clothes against the cold;
  But that large grief which these enfold
Is given in outline and no more.

VI

One writes, that ' other friends remain,'
  That ' loss is common to the race ' —
  And common is the commonplace,
And vacant chaff well meant for grain.

That loss is common would not make
  My own less bitter, rather more.
  Too common! Never morning wore
To evening, but some heart did break.

O father, wheresoe'er thou be,
  Who pledgest now thy gallant son,
  A shot, ere half thy draught be done,
Hath still'd the life that beat from thee.

O mother, praying God will save
  Thy sailor, — while thy head is bow'd,
  His heavy-shotted hammock-shroud
Drops in his vast and wandering grave.

Ye know no more than I who wrought
  At that last hour to please him well;
  Who mused on all I had to tell,
And something written, something thought;

Expecting still his advent home;
  And ever met him on his way
  With wishes, thinking, ' here to-day,'
Or ' here to-morrow will he come.'

O, somewhere, meek, unconscious dove,
  That sittest ranging golden hair;
  And glad to find thyself so fair,
Poor child, that waitest for thy love!

For now her father's chimney glows
  In expectation of a guest;
  And thinking ' this will please him best,'
She takes a riband or a rose;

For he will see them on to-night;
  And with the thought her color burns;
  And, having left the glass, she turns
Once more to set a ringlet right;

And, even when she turn'd, the curse
  Had fallen, and her future lord
  Was drown'd in passing thro' the ford,
Or kill'd in falling from his horse.

O, what to her shall be the end?
  And what to me remains of good?
  To her perpetual maidenhood,
And unto me no second friend.

VII

Dark house, by which once more I stand
  Here in the long unlovely street,
  Doors, where my heart was used to beat
So quickly, waiting for a hand,

A hand that can be clasp'd no more —
  Behold me, for I cannot sleep,
  And like a guilty thing I creep
At earliest morning to the door.

He is not here; but far away
  The noise of life begins again,
  And ghastly thro' the drizzling rain
On the bald street breaks the blank day.

VIII

A happy lover who has come
  To look on her that loves him well,
  Who 'lights and rings the gateway bell,
And learns her gone and far from home;

He saddens, all the magic light
  Dies off at once from bower and hall,
  And all the place is dark, and all
The chambers emptied of delight:

So find I every pleasant spot
  In which we two were wont to meet,
  The field, the chamber, and the street,
For all is dark where thou art not.

Yet as that other, wandering there
  In those deserted walks, may find
  A flower beat with rain and wind,
Which once she foster'd up with care;

So seems it in my deep regret,
  O my forsaken heart, with thee

And this poor flower of poesy
Which, little cared for, fades not yet.

But since it pleased a vanish'd eye,
  I go to plant it on his tomb,
  That if it can it there may bloom,
Or, dying, there at least may die.

IX

Fair ship, that from the Italian shore
  Sailest the placid ocean-plains
  With my lost Arthur's loved remains,
Spread thy full wings, and waft him o'er.

So draw him home to those that mourn
  In vain; a favorable speed
  Ruffle thy mirror'd mast, and lead
Thro' prosperous floods his holy urn.

All night no ruder air perplex
  Thy sliding keel, till Phosphor, bright
  As our pure love, thro' early light
Shall glimmer on the dewy decks.

Sphere all your lights around, above;
  Sleep, gentle heavens, before the prow;
  Sleep, gentle winds, as he sleeps now,
My friend, the brother of my love;

My Arthur, whom I shall not see
  Till all my widow'd race be run;
  Dear as the mother to the son,
More than my brothers are to me.

X

I hear the noise about thy keel;
  I hear the bell struck in the night;
  I see the cabin-window bright;
I see the sailor at the wheel.

Thou bring'st the sailor to his wife,
  And travell'd men from foreign lands;
  And letters unto trembling hands;
And, thy dark freight, a vanish'd life.

So bring him; we have idle dreams;
  This look of quiet flatters thus
  Our home-bred fancies. O, to us,
The fools of habit, sweeter seems

To rest beneath the clover sod,
  That takes the sunshine and the rains,
  Or where the kneeling hamlet drains
The chalice of the grapes of God;

Than if with thee the roaring wells
  Should gulf him fathom-deep in brine,
  And hands so often clasp'd in mine,
Should toss with tangle and with shells.

XI

Calm is the morn without a sound,
  Calm as to suit a calmer grief,
  And only thro' the faded leaf
The chestnut pattering to the ground;

Calm and deep peace on this high wold,
  And on these dews that drench the furze,
  And all the silvery gossamers
That twinkle into green and gold;

Calm and still light on yon great plain
  That sweeps with all its autumn bow-
    ers,
  And crowded farms and lessening towers,
To mingle with the bounding main;

Calm and deep peace in this wide air,
  These leaves that redden to the fall,
  And in my heart, if calm at all,
If any calm, a calm despair;

Calm on the seas, and silver sleep,
  And waves that sway themselves in rest,
  And dead calm in that noble breast
Which heaves but with the heaving deep.

XII

Lo, as a dove when up she springs
  To bear thro' heaven a tale of woe,
  Some dolorous message knit below
The wild pulsation of her wings;

Like her I go, I cannot stay;
  I leave this mortal ark behind,
  A weight of nerves without a mind,
And leave the cliffs, and haste away

O'er ocean-mirrors rounded large,
  And reach the glow of southern skies,
  And see the sails at distance rise,
And linger weeping on the marge,

And saying, ' Comes he thus, my friend ?
  Is this the end of all my care ? '
  And circle moaning in the air,
' Is this the end ?   Is this the end ? '

And forward dart again, and play
  About the prow, and back return

To where the body sits, and learn
That I have been an hour away.

XIII

Tears of the widower, when he sees
  A late-lost form that sleep reveals,
  And moves his doubtful arms, and feels
Her place is empty, fall like these;

Which weep a loss for ever new,
  A void where heart on heart reposed;
  And, where warm hands have prest and
    closed,
Silence, till I be silent too;

Which weep the comrade of my choice,
  An awful thought, a life removed,
  The human-hearted man I loved,
A Spirit, not a breathing voice.

Come, Time, and teach me, many years,
  I do not suffer in a dream;
  For now so strange do these things seem,
Mine eyes have leisure for their tears,

My fancies time to rise on wing,
  And glance about the approaching sails,
  As tho' they brought but merchants' bales,
And not the burthen that they bring.

XIV

If one should bring me this report,
  That thou hadst touch'd the land to-day,
  And I went down unto the quay,
And found thee lying in the port;

And standing, muffled round with woe,
  Should see thy passengers in rank
  Come stepping lightly down the plank,
And beckoning unto those they know;

And if along with these should come
  The man I held as half-divine,
  Should strike a sudden hand in mine,
And ask a thousand things of home;

And I should tell him all my pain,
  And how my life had droop'd of late,
  And he should sorrow o'er my state
And marvel what possess'd my brain;

And I perceived no touch of change,
  No hint of death in all his frame,
  But found him all in all the same,
I should not feel it to be strange.

XV

To-night the winds begin to rise
  And roar from yonder dropping day;
  The last red leaf is whirl'd away,
The rooks are blown about the skies;

The forest crack'd, the waters curl'd,
  The cattle huddled on the lea;
  And wildly dash'd on tower and tree
The sunbeam strikes along the world:

And but for fancies, which aver
  That all thy motions gently pass
  Athwart a plane of molten glass,
I scarce could brook the strain and stir

That makes the barren branches loud;
  And but for fear it is not so,
  The wild unrest that lives in woe
Would dote and pore on yonder cloud

That rises upward always higher,
  And onward drags a laboring breast,
  And topples round the dreary west,
A looming bastion fringed with fire.

XVI

What words are these have fallen from
    me?
  Can calm despair and wild unrest
  Be tenants of a single breast,
Or Sorrow such a changeling be?

Or doth she only seem to take
  The touch of change in calm or storm,
  But knows no more of transient form
In her deep self, than some dead lake

That holds the shadow of a lark
  Hung in the shadow of a heaven?
  Or has the shock, so harshly given,
Confused me like the unhappy bark

That strikes by night a craggy shelf,
  And staggers blindly ere she sink?
  And stunn'd me from my power to think
And all my knowledge of myself;

And made me that delirious man
  Whose fancy fuses old and new,
  And flashes into false and true,
And mingles all without a plan?

XVII

Thou comest, much wept for; such a breeze
  Compell'd thy canvas, and my prayer
  Was as the whisper of an air
To breathe thee over lonely seas.

For I in spirit saw thee move
  Thro' circles of the bounding sky,
  Week after week; the days go by;
Come quick, thou bringest all I love.

Henceforth, wherever thou mayst roam,
  My blessing, like a line of light,
  Is on the waters day and night,
And like a beacon guards thee home.

So may whatever tempest mars
  Mid-ocean spare thee, sacred bark,
  And balmy drops in summer dark
Slide from the bosom of the stars;

So kind an office hath been done,
  Such precious relics brought by thee,
  The dust of him I shall not see
Till all my widow'd race be run.

XVIII

'T is well; 't is something; we may stand
  Where he in English earth is laid,
  And from his ashes may be made
The violet of his native land.

'T is little; but it looks in truth
  As if the quiet bones were blest
  Among familiar names to rest
And in the places of his youth.

Come then, pure hands, and bear the
    head
  That sleeps or wears the mask of sleep,
  And come, whatever loves to weep,
And hear the ritual of the dead.

Ah yet, even yet, if this might be,
  I, falling on his faithful heart,
  Would breathing thro' his lips impart
The life that almost dies in me;

That dies not, but endures with pain,
  And slowly forms the firmer mind,
  Treasuring the look it cannot find,
The words that are not heard again.

XIX

The Danube to the Severn gave
  The darken'd heart that beat no more;
  They laid him by the pleasant shore,
And in the hearing of the wave.

There twice a day the Severn fills;
  The salt sea-water passes by,
  And hushes half the babbling Wye,
And makes a silence in the hills.

The Wye is hush'd nor moved along,
  And hush'd my deepest grief of all,
  When fill'd with tears that cannot fall,
I brim with sorrow drowning song.

The tide flows down, the wave again
  Is vocal in its wooded walls;
  My deeper anguish also falls,
And I can speak a little then.

XX

The lesser griefs that may be said,
  That breathe a thousand tender vows,
  Are but as servants in a house
Where lies the master newly dead;

Who speak their feeling as it is,
  And weep the fulness from the mind.
  'It will be hard,' they say, 'to find
Another service such as this.'

My lighter moods are like to these,
  That out of words a comfort win;
  But there are other griefs within,
And tears that at their fountain freeze;

For by the hearth the children sit
  Cold in that atmosphere of death,
  And scarce endure to draw the breath,
Or like to noiseless phantoms flit;

But open converse is there none,
  So much the vital spirits sink
  To see the vacant chair, and think,
'How good ! how kind ! and he is gone.'

XXI

I sing to him that rests below,
  And, since the grasses round me wave,
  I take the grasses of the grave,
And make them pipes whereon to blow.

The traveller hears me now and then,
  And sometimes harshly will he speak:
  'This fellow would make weakness weak,
And melt the waxen hearts of men.'

Another answers: 'Let him be,
  He loves to make parade of pain,
  That with his piping he may gain
The praise that comes to constancy.'

A third is wroth: 'Is this an hour
  For private sorrow's barren song,
  When more and more the people throng
The chairs and thrones of civil power ?

' A time to sicken and to swoon,
  When Science reaches forth her arms
  To feel from world to world, and charms
Her secret from the latest moon ? '

Behold, ye speak an idle thing;
  Ye never knew the sacred dust.
  I do but sing because I must,
And pipe but as the linnets sing;

And one is glad; her note is gay,
  For now her little ones have ranged;
  And one is sad; her note is changed,
Because her brood is stolen away.

XXII

The path by which we twain did go,
  Which led by tracts that pleased us well,
  Thro' four sweet years arose and fell,
From flower to flower, from snow to snow;

And we with singing cheer'd the way,
  And, crown'd with all the season lent,
  From April on to April went,
And glad at heart from May to May.

But where the path we walk'd began
  To slant the fifth autumnal slope,
  As we descended following Hope,
There sat the Shadow fear'd of man;

Who broke our fair companionship,
  And spread his mantle dark and cold,
  And wrapt thee formless in the fold,
And dull'd the murmur on thy lip,

And bore thee where I could not see
  Nor follow, tho' I walk in haste,
  And think that somewhere in the waste
The Shadow sits and waits for me.

XXIII

Now, sometimes in my sorrow shut,
  Or breaking into song by fits,
  Alone, alone, to where he sits,
The Shadow cloak'd from head to foot,

Who keeps the keys of all the creeds,
  I wander, often falling lame,
  And looking back to whence I came,
Or on to where the pathway leads;

And crying, How changed from where it
      ran
  Thro' lands where not a leaf was dumb,
  But all the lavish hills would hum
The murmur of a happy Pan;

When each by turns was guide to each,
  And Fancy light from Fancy caught,
  And Thought leapt out to wed with
      Thought
Ere Thought could wed itself with Speech;

And all we met was fair and good,
  And all was good that Time could bring,
  And all the secret of the Spring
Moved in the chambers of the blood;

And many an old philosophy
  On Argive heights divinely sang,
  And round us all the thicket rang
To many a flute of Arcady.

XXIV

And was the day of my delight
  As pure and perfect as I say?
  The very source and fount of day
Is dash'd with wandering isles of night.

If all was good and fair we met,
  This earth had been the Paradise
  It never look'd to human eyes
Since our first sun arose and set.

And is it that the haze of grief
  Makes former gladness loom so great?
  The lowness of the present state,
That sets the past in this relief?

Or that the past will always win
  A glory from its being far,
  And orb into the perfect star
We saw not when we moved therein?

XXV

I know that this was Life, — the track
  Whereon with equal feet we fared;
  And then, as now, the day prepared
The daily burden for the back.

But this it was that made me move
  As light as carrier-birds in air;
  I loved the weight I had to bear,
Because it needed help of Love;

Nor could I weary, heart or limb,
  When mighty Love would cleave in
      twain
  The lading of a single pain,
And part it, giving half to him.

XXVI

Still onward winds the dreary way;
  I with it, for I long to prove
  No lapse of moons can canker Love,
Whatever fickle tongues may say.

And if that eye which watches guilt
  And goodness, and hath power to see
  Within the green the moulder'd tree,
And towers fallen as soon as built —

O, if indeed that eye foresee
  Or see — in Him is no before —
  In more of life true life no more
And Love the indifference to be,

Then might I find, ere yet the morn
  Breaks hither over Indian seas,
  That Shadow waiting with the keys,
To shroud me from my proper scorn.

XXVII

I envy not in any moods
  The captive void of noble rage,
  The linnet born within the cage,
That never knew the summer woods;

I envy not the beast that takes
  His license in the field of time,
  Unfetter'd by the sense of crime,
To whom a conscience never wakes;

Nor, what may count itself as blest,
  The heart that never plighted troth
  But stagnates in the weeds of sloth;
Nor any want-begotten rest.

I hold it true, whate'er befall;
   I feel it, when I sorrow most;
   'T is better to have loved and lost
Than never to have loved at all.

XXVIII

The time draws near the birth of Christ.
   The moon is hid, the night is still;
   The Christmas bells from hill to hill
Answer each other in the mist.

Four voices of four hamlets round,
   From far and near, on mead and moor,
   Swell out and fail, as if a door
Were shut between me and the sound;

Each voice four changes on the wind,
   That now dilate, and now decrease,
   Peace and goodwill, goodwill and peace,
Peace and goodwill, to all mankind.

This year I slept and woke with pain,
   I almost wish'd no more to wake,
   And that my hold on life would break
Before I heard those bells again;

But they my troubled spirit rule,
   For they controll'd me when a boy;
   They bring me sorrow touch'd with
      joy,
The merry, merry bells of Yule.

XXIX

With such compelling cause to grieve
   As daily vexes household peace,
   And chains regret to his decease,
How dare we keep our Christmas-eve,

Which brings no more a welcome guest
   To enrich the threshold of the night
   With shower'd largess of delight
In dance and song and game and jest?

Yet go, and while the holly boughs
   Entwine the cold baptismal font,
   Make one wreath more for Use and
      Wont,
That guard the portals of the house;

Old sisters of a day gone by,
   Gray nurses, loving nothing new —
   Why should they miss their yearly
      due
Before their time?   They too will die.

XXX

With trembling fingers did we weave
   The holly round the Christmas hearth;
   A rainy cloud possess'd the earth,
And sadly fell our Christmas-eve.

At our old pastimes in the hall
   We gamboll'd, making vain pretence
   Of gladness, with an awful sense
Of one mute Shadow watching all.

We paused: the winds were in the beech;
   We heard them sweep the winter land;
   And in a circle hand-in-hand
Sat silent, looking each at each.

Then echo-like our voices rang;
   We sung, tho' every eye was dim,
   A merry song we sang with him
Last year; impetuously we sang.

We ceased; a gentler feeling crept
   Upon us: surely rest is meet.
   'They rest,' we said, 'their sleep is
      sweet,'
And silence follow'd, and we wept.

Our voices took a higher range;
   Once more we sang: 'They do not die
   Nor lose their mortal sympathy,
Nor change to us, although they change;

'Rapt from the fickle and the frail
   With gather'd power, yet the same,
   Pierces the keen seraphic flame
From orb to orb, from veil to veil.'

Rise, happy morn, rise, holy morn,
   Draw forth the cheerful day from night:
   O Father, touch the east, and light
The light that shone when Hope was born.

XXXI

When Lazarus left his charnel-cave,
   And home to Mary's house return'd,
   Was this demanded — if he yearn'd
To hear her weeping by his grave?

'Where wert thou, brother, those four
      days?'
   There lives no record of reply,
   Which telling what it is to die
Had surely added praise to praise.

From every house the neighbors met,
  The streets were fill'd with joyful sound,
  A solemn gladness even crown'd
The purple brows of Olivet.

Behold a man raised up by Christ!
  The rest remaineth unreveal'd;
  He told it not, or something seal'd
The lips of that Evangelist.

XXXII

Her eyes are homes of silent prayer,
  Nor other thought her mind admits
  But, he was dead, and there he sits,
And he that brought him back is there.

Then one deep love doth supersede
  All other, when her ardent gaze
  Roves from the living brother's face,
And rests upon the Life indeed.

All subtle thought, all curious fears,
  Borne down by gladness so complete,
  She bows, she bathes the Saviour's feet
With costly spikenard and with tears.

Thrice blest whose lives are faithful
      prayers,
  Whose loves in higher love endure;
  What souls possess themselves so pure,
Or is there blessedness like theirs?

XXXIII

O thou that after toil and storm
  Mayst seem to have reach'd a purer
      air,
  Whose faith has centre everywhere,
Nor cares to fix itself to form,

Leave thou thy sister when she prays
  Her early heaven, her happy views;
  Nor thou with shadow'd hint confuse
A life that leads melodious days.

Her faith thro' form is pure as thine,
  Her hands are quicker unto good.
  O, sacred be the flesh and blood
To which she links a truth divine!

See thou, that countest reason ripe
  In holding by the law within,
  Thou fail not in a world of sin,
And even for want of such a type.

XXXIV

My own dim life should teach me this,
  That life shall live for evermore,
  Else earth is darkness at the core,
And dust and ashes all that is;

This round of green, this orb of flame,
  Fantastic beauty; such as lurks
  In some wild poet, when he works
Without a conscience or an aim.

What then were God to such as I?
  'T were hardly worth my while to choose
  Of things all mortal, or to use
A little patience ere I die;

'T were best at once to sink to peace,
  Like birds the charming serpent draws,
  To drop head-foremost in the jaws
Of vacant darkness and to cease.

XXXV

Yet if some voice that man could trust
  Should murmur from the narrow house,
  'The cheeks drop in, the body bows;
Man dies, nor is there hope in dust;'

Might I not say? 'Yet even here,
  But for one hour, O Love, I strive
  To keep so sweet a thing alive.'
But I should turn mine ears and hear

The moanings of the homeless sea,
  The sound of streams that swift or slow
  Draw down Æonian hills, and sow
The dust of continents to be;

And Love would answer with a sigh,
  'The sound of that forgetful shore
  Will change my sweetness more   and
      more,
Half-dead to know that I shall die.'

O me, what profits it to put
  An idle case?   If Death were seen
  At first as Death, Love had not been,
Or been in narrowest working shut,

Mere fellowship of sluggish moods,
  Or in his coarsest Satyr-shape
  Had bruised the herb and crush'd the
      grape,
And bask'd and batten'd in the woods.

XXXVI

Tho' truths in manhood darkly join,
  Deep-seated in our mystic frame,
  We yield all blessing to the name
Of Him that made them current coin;

For Wisdom dealt with mortal powers,
  Where truth in closest words shall fail,
  When truth embodied in a tale
Shall enter in at lowly doors.

And so the Word had breath, and wrought
  With human hands the creed of creeds
  In loveliness of perfect deeds,
More strong than all poetic thought;

Which he may read that binds the sheaf,
  Or builds the house, or digs the grave,
  And those wild eyes that watch the
    wave
In roarings round the coral reef.

XXXVII

Urania speaks with darken'd brow:
  'Thou pratest here where thou art least;
  This faith has many a purer priest,
And many an abler voice than thou.

'Go down beside thy native rill,
  On thy Parnassus set thy feet,
  And hear thy laurel whisper sweet
About the ledges of the hill.'

And my Melpomene replies,
  A touch of shame upon her cheek:
  'I am not worthy even to speak
Of thy prevailing mysteries;

'For I am but an earthly Muse,
  And owning but a little art
  To lull with song an aching heart,
And render human love his dues;

'But brooding on the dear one dead,
  And all he said of things divine, —
  And dear to me as sacred wine
To dying lips is all he said, —

'I murmur'd, as I came along,
  Of comfort clasp'd in truth reveal'd,
  And loiter'd in the master's field,
And darken'd sanctities with song.'

XXXVIII

With weary steps I loiter on,
  Tho' always under alter'd skies
  The purple from the distance dies,
My prospect and horizon gone.

No joy the blowing season gives,
  The herald melodies of spring,
  But in the songs I love to sing
A doubtful gleam of solace lives.

If any care for what is here
  Survive in spirits render'd free,
  Then are these songs I sing of thee
Not all ungrateful to thine ear.

XXXIX

Old warder of these buried bones,
  And answering now my random stroke
  With fruitful cloud and living smoke,
Dark yew, that graspest at the stones

And dippest toward the dreamless head,
  To thee too comes the golden hour
  When flower is feeling after flower;
But Sorrow, — fixt upon the dead,

And darkening the dark graves of men, —
  What whisper'd from her lying lips ?
  Thy gloom is kindled at the tips,
And passes into gloom again.

XL

Could we forget the widow'd hour
  And look on Spirits breathed away,
  As on a maiden in the day
When first she wears her orange-flower !

When crown'd with blessing she doth rise
  To take her latest leave of home,
  And hopes and light regrets that come
Make April of her tender eyes;

And doubtful joys the father move,
  And tears are on the mother's face,
  As parting with a long embrace
She enters other realms of love;

Her office there to rear, to teach,
  Becoming as is meet and fit
  A link among the days, to knit
The generations each with each;

And, doubtless, unto thee is given
  A life that bears immortal fruit
  In those great offices that suit
The full-grown energies of heaven.

Ay me, the difference I discern !
  How often shall her old fireside
  Be cheer'd with tidings of the bride,
How often she herself return,

And tell them all they would have told,
  And bring her babe, and make her
      boast,
  Till even those that miss'd her most
Shall count new things as dear as old;

But thou and I have shaken hands,
  Till growing winters lay me low;
  My paths are in the fields I know,
And thine in undiscover'd lands.

XLI

Thy spirit ere our fatal loss
  Did ever rise from high to higher,
  As mounts the heavenward altar-fire,
As flies the lighter thro' the gross.

But thou art turn'd to something strange,
  And I have lost the links that bound
  Thy changes; here upon the ground,
No more partaker of thy change.

Deep folly ! yet that this could be —
  That I could wing my will with might
  To leap the grades of life and light,
And flash at once, my friend, to thee!

For tho' my nature rarely yields
  To that vague fear implied in death,
  Nor shudders at the gulfs beneath,
The howlings from forgotten fields;

Yet oft when sundown skirts the moor
  An inner trouble I behold,
  A spectral doubt which makes me cold,
That I shall be thy mate no more,

Tho' following with an upward mind
  The wonders that have come to thee,
  Thro' all the secular to-be,
But evermore a life behind.

XLII

I vex my heart with fancies dim.
  He still outstript me in the race;

It was but unity of place
That made me dream I rank'd with him.

And so may Place retain us still,
  And he the much-beloved again,
  A lord of large experience, train
To riper growth the mind and will;

And what delights can equal those
  That stir the spirit's inner deeps,
  When one that loves, but knows not, reaps
A truth from one that loves and knows ?

XLIII

If Sleep and Death be truly one,
  And every spirit's folded bloom
  Thro' all its intervital gloom
In some long trance should slumber on;

Unconscious of the sliding hour,
  Bare of the body, might it last,
  And silent traces of the past
Be all the color of the flower:

So then were nothing lost to man;
  So that still garden of the souls
  In many a figured leaf enrolls
The total world since life began;

And love will last as pure and whole
  As when he loved me here in Time,
  And at the spiritual prime
Rewaken with the dawning soul.

XLIV

How fares it with the happy dead ?
  For here the man is more and more;
  But he forgets the days before
God shut the doorways of his head.

The days have vanish'd, tone and tint,
  And yet perhaps the hoarding sense
  Gives out at times — he knows not
      whence —
A little flash, a mystic hint;

And in the long harmonious years —
  If Death so taste Lethean springs —
  May some dim touch of earthly things
Surprise thee ranging with thy peers.

If such a dreamy touch should fall,
  O, turn thee round, resolve the doubt;
  My guardian angel will speak out
In that high place, and tell thee all.

XLV

The baby new to earth and sky,
  What time his tender palm is prest
  Against the circle of the breast,
Has never thought that ' this is I; '

But as he grows he gathers much,
  And learns the use of ' I ' and ' me, '
  And finds ' I am not what I see,
And other than the things I touch.'

So rounds he to a separate mind
  From whence clear memory may be-
    gin,
  As thro' the frame that binds him in
His isolation grows defined.

This use may lie in blood and breath,
  Which else were fruitless of their due,
  Had man to learn himself anew
Beyond the second birth of death.

XLVI

We ranging down this lower track,
  The path we came by, thorn and flower,
  Is shadow'd by the growing hour,
Lest life should fail in looking back.

So be it: there no shade can last
  In that deep dawn behind the tomb,
  But clear from marge to marge shall
    bloom
The eternal landscape of the past;

A lifelong tract of time reveal'd,
  The fruitful hours of still increase;
  Days order'd in a wealthy peace,
And those five years its richest field.

O Love, thy province were not large,
  A bounded field, nor stretching far;
  Look also, Love, a brooding star,
A rosy warmth from marge to marge.

XLVII

That each, who seems a separate whole,
  Should move his rounds, and fusing
    all
  The skirts of self again, should fall
Remerging in the general Soul,

Is faith as vague as all unsweet.
  Eternal form shall still divide

The eternal soul from all beside;
  And I shall know him when we meet;

And we shall sit at endless feast,
  Enjoying each the other's good.
  What vaster dream can hit the mood
Of Love on earth ?   He seeks at least

Upon the last and sharpest height,
  Before the spirits fade away,
  Some landing-place, to clasp and say,
' Farewell !   We lose ourselves in light.'

XLVIII

If these brief lays, of Sorrow born,
  Were taken to be such as closed
  Grave doubts and answers here proposed,
Then these were such as men might scorn.

Her care is not to part and prove;
  She takes, when harsher moods remit,
  What slender shade of doubt may flit,
And makes it vassal unto love;

And hence, indeed, she sports with words,
  But better serves a wholesome law,
  And holds it sin and shame to draw
The deepest measure from the chords;

Nor dare she trust a larger lay,
  But rather loosens from the lip
  Short swallow-flights of song, that dip
Their wings in tears, and skim away.

XLIX

From art, from nature, from the schools,
  Let random influences glance,
  Like light in many a shiver'd lance
That breaks about the dappled pools.

The lightest wave of thought shall lisp,
  The fancy's tenderest eddy wreathe,
  The slightest air of song shall breathe
To make the sullen surface crisp.

And look thy look, and go thy way,
  But blame not thou the winds that make
  The seeming-wanton ripple break,
The tender-pencill'd shadow play.

Beneath all fancied hopes and fears
  Ay me, the sorrow deepens down,
  Whose muffled motions blindly drown
The bases of my life in tears.

L

Be near me when my light is low,
  When the blood creeps, and the nerves
    prick
  And tingle; and the heart is sick,
And all the wheels of being slow.

Be near me when the sensuous frame
  Is rack'd with pangs that conquer trust;
  And Time, a maniac scattering dust,
And Life, a Fury slinging flame.

Be near me when my faith is dry,
  And men the flies of latter spring,
  That lay their eggs, and sting and sing
And weave their petty cells and die.

Be near me when I fade away,
  To point the term of human strife,
  And on the low dark verge of life
The twilight of eternal day.

LI

Do we indeed desire the dead
  Should still be near us at our side?
  Is there no baseness we would hide?
No inner vileness that we dread?

Shall he for whose applause I strove,
  I had such reverence for his blame,
  See with clear eye some hidden shame
And I be lessen'd in his love?

I wrong the grave with fears untrue.
  Shall love be blamed for want of faith?
  There must be wisdom with great Death;
The dead shall look me thro' and thro'.

Be near us when we climb or fall;
  Ye watch, like God, the rolling hours
  With larger other eyes than ours,
To make allowance for us all.

LII

I cannot love thee as I ought,
  For love reflects the thing beloved;
  My words are only words, and moved
Upon the topmost froth of thought.

'Yet blame not thou thy plaintive song,'
  The Spirit of true love replied;
  'Thou canst not move me from thy
    side,
Nor human frailty do me wrong.

'What keeps a spirit wholly true
  To that ideal which he bears?
  What record? not the sinless years
That breathed beneath the Syrian blue;

'So fret not, like an idle girl,
  That life is dash'd with flecks of sin.
  Abide; thy wealth is gather'd in,
When Time hath sunder'd shell from
  pearl.'

LIII

How many a father have I seen,
  A sober man, among his boys,
  Whose youth was full of foolish noise,
Who wears his manhood hale and green;

And dare we to this fancy give,
  That had the wild oat not been sown,
  The soil, left barren, scarce had grown
The grain by which a man may live?

Or, if we held the doctrine sound
  For life outliving heats of youth,
  Yet who would preach it as a truth
To those that eddy round and round?

Hold thou the good, define it well;
  For fear divine Philosophy
  Should push beyond her mark, and be
Procuress to the Lords of Hell.

LIV

O, yet we trust that somehow good
  Will be the final goal of ill,
  To pangs of nature, sins of will,
Defects of doubt, and taints of blood;

That nothing walks with aimless feet;
  That not one life shall be destroy'd,
  Or cast as rubbish to the void,
When God hath made the pile complete;

That not a worm is cloven in vain;
  That not a moth with vain desire
  Is shrivell'd in a fruitless fire,
Or but subserves another's gain.

Behold, we know not anything;
  I can but trust that good shall fall
  At last — far off — at last, to all,
And every winter change to spring.

So runs my dream; but what am I?
  An infant crying in the night;

An infant crying for the light,
And with no language but a cry.

LV

The wish, that of the living whole
No life may fail beyond the grave,
Derives it not from what we have
The likest God within the soul?

Are God and Nature then at strife,
That Nature lends such evil dreams?
So careful of the type she seems,
So careless of the single life,

That I, considering everywhere
Her secret meaning in her deeds,
And finding that of fifty seeds
She often brings but one to bear,

I falter where I firmly trod,
And falling with my weight of cares
Upon the great world's altar-stairs
That slope thro' darkness up to God,

I stretch lame hands of faith, and grope,
And gather dust and chaff, and call
To what I feel is Lord of all,
And faintly trust the larger hope.

LVI

'So careful of the type?' but no.
From scarped cliff and quarried stone
She cries, 'A thousand types are gone;
I care for nothing, all shall go.

'Thou makest thine appeal to me:
I bring to life, I bring to death;
The spirit does but mean the breath:
I know no more.' And he, shall he,

Man, her last work, who seem'd so fair,
Such splendid purpose in his eyes,
Who roll'd the psalm to wintry skies,
Who built him fanes of fruitless prayer,

Who trusted God was love indeed
And love Creation's final law —
Tho' Nature, red in tooth and claw
With ravine, shriek'd against his creed —

Who loved, who suffer'd countless ills,
Who battled for the True, the Just,
Be blown about the desert dust,
Or seal'd within the iron hills?

No more? A monster then, a dream,
A discord. Dragons of the prime,
That tare each other in their slime,
Were mellow music match'd with him.

O life as futile, then, as frail!
O for thy voice to soothe and bless!
What hope of answer, or redress?
Behind the veil, behind the veil.

LVII

Peace; come away: the song of woe
Is after all an earthly song.
Peace; come away: we do him wrong
To sing so wildly: let us go.

Come; let us go: your cheeks are pale;
But half my life I leave behind.
Methinks my friend is richly shrined;
But I shall pass, my work will fail.

Yet in these ears, till hearing dies,
One set slow bell will seem to toll
The passing of the sweetest soul
That ever look'd with human eyes.

I hear it now, and o'er and o'er,
Eternal greetings to the dead;
And 'Ave, Ave, Ave,' said,
'Adieu, adieu,' for evermore.

LVIII

In those sad words I took farewell.
Like echoes in sepulchral halls,
As drop by drop the water falls
In vaults and catacombs, they fell;

And, falling, idly broke the peace
Of hearts that beat from day to day,
Half-conscious of their dying clay,
And those cold crypts where they shall
cease.

The high Muse answer'd: 'Wherefore
grieve
Thy brethren with a fruitless tear?
Abide a little longer here,
And thou shalt take a nobler leave.'

LIX

O Sorrow, wilt thou live with me
No casual mistress, but a wife,
My bosom-friend and half of life;
As I confess it needs must be?

O Sorrow, wilt thou rule my blood,
Be sometimes lovely like a bride,
And put thy harsher moods aside,
If thou wilt have me wise and good ?

My centred passion cannot move,
Nor will it lessen from to-day;
But I 'll have leave at times to play
As with the creature of my love;

And set thee forth, for thou art mine,
With so much hope for years to come,
That, howsoe'er I know thee, some
Could hardly tell what name were thine.

LX

He past, a soul of nobler tone;
My spirit loved and loves him yet,
Like some poor girl whose heart is set
On one whose rank exceeds her own.

He mixing with his proper sphere,
She finds the baseness of her lot,
Half jealous of she knows not what,
And envying all that meet him there.

The little village looks forlorn;
She sighs amid her narrow days,
Moving about the household ways,
In that dark house where she was born.

The foolish neighbors come and go,
And tease her till the day draws by;
At night she weeps, ' How vain am I !
How should he love a thing so low ? '

LXI

If, in thy second state sublime,
Thy ransom'd reason change replied
With all the circle of the wise,
The perfect flower of human time;

And if thou cast thine eyes below,
How dimly character'd and slight,
How dwarf'd a growth of cold and night,
How blanch'd with darkness must I grow !

Yet turn thee to the doubtful shore,
Where thy first form was made a man;
I loved thee, Spirit, and love, nor can
The soul of Shakespeare love thee more.

LXII

Tho' if an eye that 's downward cast
Could make thee somewhat blench or fail,

Then be my love an idle tale
And fading legend of the past;

And thou, as one that once declined,
When he was little more than boy,
On some unworthy heart with joy,
But lives to wed an equal mind,

And breathes a novel world, the while
His other passion wholly dies,
Or in the light of deeper eyes
Is matter for a flying smile.

LXIII

Yet pity for a horse o'er-driven,
And love in which my hound has part,
Can hang no weight upon my heart
In its assumptions up to heaven;

And I am so much more than these,
As thou, perchance, art more than I,
And yet I spare them sympathy,
And I would set their pains at ease.

So mayst thou watch me where I weep,
As, unto vaster motions bound,
The circuits of thine orbit round
A higher height, a deeper deep.

LXIV

Dost thou look back on what hath been,
As some divinely gifted man,
Whose life in low estate began
And on a simple village green;

Who breaks his birth's invidious bar,
And grasps the skirts of happy chance,
And breasts the blows of circumstance,
And grapples with his evil star;

Who makes by force his merit known
And lives to clutch the golden keys,
To mould a mighty state's decrees,
And shape the whisper of the throne;

And moving up from high to higher,
Becomes on Fortune's crowning slope
The pillar of a people's hope,
The centre of a world's desire;

Yet feels, as in a pensive dream,
When all his active powers are still,
A distant dearness in the hill,
A secret sweetness in the stream,

The limit of his narrower fate,
　While yet beside its vocal springs
　He play'd at counsellors and kings,
With one that was his earliest mate;

Who ploughs with pain his native lea
　And reaps the labor of his hands,
　Or in the furrow musing stands:
' Does my old friend remember me ? '

LXV

Sweet soul, do with me as thou wilt;
　I lull a fancy trouble-tost
　With ' Love 's too precious to be lost,
A little grain shall not be spilt.'

And in that solace can I sing,
　Till out of painful phases wrought
　There flutters up a happy thought,
Self-balanced on a lightsome wing;

Since we deserved the name of friends,
　And thine effect so lives in me,
　A part of mine may live in thee
And move thee on to noble ends.

LXVI

You thought my heart too far diseased;
　You wonder when my fancies play
　To find me gay among the gay,
Like one with any trifle pleased.

The shade by which my life was crost,
　Which makes a desert in the mind,
　Has made me kindly with my kind,
And like to him whose sight is lost;

Whose feet are guided thro' the land,
　Whose jest among his friends is free,
　Who takes the children on his knee,
And winds their curls about his hand.

He plays with threads, he beats his chair
　For pastime, dreaming of the sky;
　His inner day can never die,
His night of loss is always there.

LXVII

When on my bed the moonlight falls,
　I know that in thy place of rest
　By that broad water of the west
There comes a glory on the walls:

Thy marble bright in dark appears,
　As slowly steals a silver flame

Along the letters of thy name,
And o'er the number of thy years.

The mystic glory swims away,
　From off my bed the moonlight dies;
　And closing eaves of wearied eyes
I sleep till dusk is dipt in gray;

And then I know the mist is drawn
　A lucid veil from coast to coast,
　And in the dark church like a ghost
Thy tablet glimmers in the dawn.

LXVIII

When in the down I sink my head,
　Sleep, Death's twin-brother, times my
　　breath;
　Sleep, Death's twin-brother, knows not
　　Death,
Nor can I dream of thee as dead.

I walk as ere I walk'd forlorn,
　When all our path was fresh with dew,
　And all the bugle breezes blew
Reveillée to the breaking morn.

But what is this ?   I turn about,
　I find a trouble in thine eye,
　Which makes me sad I know not why,
Nor can my dream resolve the doubt;

But ere the lark hath left the lea
　I wake, and I discern the truth;
　It is the trouble of my youth
That foolish sleep transfers to thee.

LXIX

I dream'd there would be Spring no more,
　That Nature's ancient power was lost;
　The streets were black with smoke and
　　frost,
They chatter'd trifles at the door;

I wander'd from the noisy town,
　I found a wood with thorny boughs;
　I took the thorns to bind my brows,
I wore them like a civic crown;

I met with scoffs, I met with scorns
　From youth and babe and hoary hairs:
　They call'd me in the public squares
The fool that wears a crown of thorns.

They call'd me fool, they call'd me child:
　I found an angel of the night;

The voice was low, the look was bright;
He look'd upon my crown and smiled.

He reach'd the glory of a hand,
 That seem'd to touch it into leaf;
 The voice was not the voice of grief,
The words were hard to understand.

LXX

I cannot see the features right,
 When on the gloom I strive to paint
 The face I know; the hues are faint
And mix with hollow masks of night;

Cloud-towers by ghostly masons wrought,
 A gulf that ever shuts and gapes,
 A hand that points, and palled shapes
In shadowy thoroughfares of thought;

And crowds that stream from yawning
  doors,
 And shoals of pucker'd faces drive;
 Dark bulks that tumble half alive,
And lazy lengths on boundless shores;

Till all at once beyond the will
 I hear a wizard music roll,
 And thro' a lattice on the soul
Looks thy fair face and makes it still.

LXXI

Sleep, kinsman thou to death and trance
 And madness, thou hast forged at last
 A night-long present of the past
In which we went thro' summer France.

Hadst thou such credit with the soul?
 Then bring an opiate trebly strong,
 Drug down the blindfold sense of wrong,
That so my pleasure may be whole;

While now we talk as once we talk'd
 Of men and minds, the dust of change,
 The days that grow to something strange,
In walking as of old we walk'd

Beside the river's wooded reach,
 The fortress, and the mountain ridge,
 The cataract flashing from the bridge,
The breaker breaking on the beach.

LXXII

Risest thou thus, dim dawn, again,
 And howlest, issuing out of night,
With blasts that blow the poplar white,
And lash with storm the streaming pane?

Day, when my crown'd estate begun
 To pine in that reverse of doom,
 Which sicken'd every living bloom,
And blurr'd the splendor of the sun;

Who usherest in the dolorous hour
 With thy quick tears that make the rose
 Pull sideways, and the daisy close
Her crimson fringes to the shower;

Who mightst have heaved a windless flame
 Up the deep East, or, whispering, play'd
 A chequer-work of beam and shade
Along the hills, yet look'd the same,

As wan, as chill, as wild as now;
 Day, mark'd as with some hideous crime,
 When the dark hand struck down thro'
  time,
And cancell'd nature's best: but thou,

Lift as thou mayst thy burthen'd brows
 Thro' clouds that drench the morning
  star,
 And whirl the ungarner'd sheaf afar,
And sow the sky with flying boughs,

And up thy vault with roaring sound
 Climb thy thick noon, disastrous day;
 Touch thy dull goal of joyless gray,
And hide thy shame beneath the ground.

LXXIII

So many worlds, so much to do,
 So little done, such things to be,
 How know I what had need of thee,
For thou wert strong as thou wert true?

The fame is quench'd that I foresaw,
 The head hath miss'd an earthly wreath:
 I curse not Nature, no, nor Death;
For nothing is that errs from law.

We pass; the path that each man trod
 Is dim, or will be dim, with weeds.
 What fame is left for human deeds
In endless age? It rests with God.

O hollow wraith of dying fame,
 Fade wholly, while the soul exults,
 And self-infolds the large results
Of force that would have forged a name.

LXXIV

As sometimes in a dead man's face,
  To those that watch it more and more,
  A likeness, hardly seen before,
Comes out — to some one of his race;

So, dearest, now thy brows are cold,
  I see thee what thou art, and know
  Thy likeness to the wise below,
Thy kindred with the great of old.

But there is more than I can see,
  And what I see I leave unsaid,
  Nor speak it, knowing Death has made
His darkness beautiful with thee.

LXXV

I leave thy praises unexpress'd
  In verse that brings myself relief,
  And by the measure of my grief
I leave thy greatness to be guess'd.

What practice howsoe'er expert
  In fitting aptest words to things,
  Or voice the richest-toned that sings,
Hath power to give thee as thou wert?

I care not in these fading days
  To raise a cry that lasts not long,
  And round thee with the breeze of
    song
To stir a little dust of praise.

Thy leaf has perish'd in the green,
  And, while we breathe beneath the sun,
  The world which credits what is done
Is cold to all that might have been.

So here shall silence guard thy fame;
  But somewhere, out of human view,
  Whate'er thy hands are set to do
Is wrought with tumult of acclaim.

LXXVI

Take wings of fancy, and ascend,
  And in a moment set thy face
  Where all the starry heavens of space
Are sharpen'd to a needle's end;

Take wings of foresight; lighten thro'
  The secular abyss to come,
  And lo, thy deepest lays are dumb
Before the mouldering of a yew;

And if the matin songs, that woke
  The darkness of our planet, last,
  Thine own shall wither in the vast,
Ere half the lifetime of an oak.

Ere these have clothed their branchy bow-
    ers
  With fifty Mays, thy songs are vain;
  And what are they when these remain
The ruin'd shells of hollow towers?

LXXVII

What hope is here for modern rhyme
  To him who turns a musing eye
  On songs, and deeds, and lives, that
    lie
Foreshorten'd in the tract of time?

These mortal lullabies of pain
  May bind a book, may line a box,
  May serve to curl a maiden's locks;
Or when a thousand moons shall wane

A man upon a stall may find,
  And, passing, turn the page that tells
  A grief, then changed to something
    else,
Sung by a long-forgotten mind.

But what of that? My darken'd ways
  Shall ring with music all the same;
  To breathe my loss is more than fame,
To utter love more sweet than praise.

LXXVIII

Again at Christmas did we weave
  The holly round the Christmas hearth;
  The silent snow possess'd the earth,
And calmly fell our Christmas-eve.

The yule-clog sparkled keen with frost,
  No wing of wind the region swept,
  But over all things brooding slept
The quiet sense of something lost.

As in the winters left behind,
  Again our ancient games had place,
  The mimic picture's breathing grace,
And dance and song and hoodman-blind.

Who show'd a token of distress?
  No single tear, no mark of pain —
  O sorrow, then can sorrow wane?
O grief, can grief be changed to less?

O last regret, regret can die !
  No — mixt with all this mystic frame,
  Her deep relations are the same,
But with long use her tears are dry.

LXXIX

'More than my brothers are to me,' —
  Let this not vex thee, noble heart !
  I know thee of what force thou art
To hold the costliest love in fee.

But thou and I are one in kind,
  As moulded like in Nature's mint;
  And hill and wood and field did print
The same sweet forms in either mind.

For us the same cold streamlet curl'd
  Thro' all his eddying coves, the same
  All winds that roam the twilight came
In whispers of the beauteous world.

At one dear knee we proffer'd vows,
  One lesson from one book we learn'd,
  Ere childhood's flaxen ringlet turn'd
To black and brown on kindred brows.

And so my wealth resembles thine,
  But he was rich where I was poor,
  And he supplied my want the more
As his unlikeness fitted mine.

LXXX

If any vague desire should rise,
  That holy Death ere Arthur died
  Had moved me kindly from his side,
And dropt the dust on tearless eyes;

Then fancy shapes, as fancy can,
  The grief my loss in him had wrought,
  A grief as deep as life or thought,
But stay'd in peace with God and man.

I make a picture in the brain;
  I hear the sentence that he speaks;
  He bears the burthen of the weeks,
But turns his burthen into gain.

His credit thus shall set me free;
  And, influence-rich to soothe and save,
  Unused example from the grave
Reach out dead hands to comfort me.

LXXXI

Could I have said while he was here,
  'My love shall now no further range;

There cannot come a mellower change,
For now is love mature in ear '?

Love, then, had hope of richer store:
  What end is here to my complaint ?
  This haunting whisper makes me faint,
'More years had made me love thee
    more.'

But Death returns an answer sweet:
  'My sudden frost was sudden gain,
  And gave all ripeness to the grain
It might have drawn from after-heat.'

LXXXII

I wage not any feud with Death
  For changes wrought on form and face;
  No lower life that earth's embrace
May breed with him can fright my faith.

Eternal process moving on,
  From state to state the spirit walks;
  And these are but the shatter'd stalks,
Or ruin'd chrysalis of one.

Nor blame I Death, because he bare
  The use of virtue out of earth;
  I know transplanted human worth
Will bloom to profit, otherwhere.

For this alone on Death I wreak
  The wrath that garners in my heart:
  He put our lives so far apart
We cannot hear each other speak.

LXXXIII

Dip down upon the northern shore,
  O sweet new-year delaying long;
  Thou doest expectant Nature wrong;
Delaying long, delay no more.

What stays thee from the clouded noons,
  Thy sweetness from its proper place ?
  Can trouble live with April days,
Or sadness in the summer moons ?

Bring orchis, bring the foxglove spire,
  The little speedwell's darling blue,
  Deep tulips dash'd with fiery dew,
Laburnums, dropping-wells of fire.

O thou, new-year, delaying long,
  Delayest the sorrow in my blood,
  That longs to burst a frozen bud
And flood a fresher throat with song.

LXXXIV

When I contemplate all alone
  The life that had been thine below,
  And fix my thoughts on all the glow
To which thy crescent would have grown,

I see thee sitting crown'd with good,
  A central warmth diffusing bliss
  In glance and smile, and clasp and kiss,
On all the branches of thy blood;

Thy blood, my friend, and partly mine;
  For now the day was drawing on,
  When thou shouldst link thy life with
    one
Of mine own house, and boys of thine

Had babbled ' Uncle ' on my knee;
  But that remorseless iron hour
  Made cypress of her orange flower,
Despair of hope, and earth of thee.

I seem to meet their least desire,
  To clap their cheeks, to call them mine.
  I see their unborn faces shine
Beside the never-lighted fire.

I see myself an honor'd guest,
  Thy partner in the flowery walk
  Of letters, genial table-talk,
Or deep dispute, and graceful jest;

While now thy prosperous labor fills
  The lips of men with honest praise,
  And sun by sun the happy days
Descend below the golden hills

With promise of a morn as fair;
  And all the train of bounteous hours
  Conduct, by paths of growing powers,
To reverence and the silver hair;

Till slowly worn her earthly robe,
  Her lavish mission richly wrought,
  Leaving great legacies of thought,
Thy spirit should fail from off the globe;

What time mine own might also flee,
  As link'd with thine in love and fate,
  And, hovering o'er the dolorous strait
To the other shore, involved in thee,

Arrive at last the blessed goal,
  And He that died in Holy Land

Would reach us out the shining hand,
And take us as a single soul.

What reed was that on which I leant ?
  Ah, backward fancy, wherefore wake
  The old bitterness again, and break
The low beginnings of content ?

LXXXV

This truth came borne with bier and pall,
  I felt it, when I sorrow'd most,
  'T is better to have loved and lost,
Than never to have loved at all —

O true in word, and tried in deed,
  Demanding, so to bring relief
  To this which is our common grief,
What kind of life is that I lead;

And whether trust in things above
  Be dimm'd of sorrow, or sustain'd;
  And whether love for him have drain'd
My capabilities of love;

Your words have virtue such as draws
  A faithful answer from the breast,
  Thro' light reproaches, half exprest,
And loyal unto kindly laws.

My blood an even tenor kept,
  Till on mine ear this message falls,
  That in Vienna's fatal walls
God's finger touch'd him, and he slept.

The great Intelligences fair
  That range above our mortal state,
  In circle round the blessed gate,
Received and gave him welcome there;

And led him thro' the blissful climes,
  And show'd him in the fountain fresh
  All knowledge that the sons of flesh
Shall gather in the cycled times.

But I remain'd, whose hopes were dim,
  Whose life, whose thoughts were little
    worth,
  To wander on a darken'd earth,
Where all things round me breathed of
  him.

O friendship, equal-poised control,
  O heart, with kindliest motion warm,
  O sacred essence, other form,
O solemn ghost, O crowned soul !

Yet none could better know than I,
    How much of act at human hands
    The sense of human will demands
By which we dare to live or die.

Whatever way my days decline,
    I felt and feel, tho' left alone,
    His being working in mine own,
The footsteps of his life in mine;

A life that all the Muses deck'd
    With gifts of grace, that might express
    All-comprehensive tenderness,
All-subtilizing intellect:

And so my passion hath not swerved
    To works of weakness, but I find
    An image comforting the mind,
And in my grief a strength reserved.

Likewise the imaginative woe,
    That loved to handle spiritual strife,
    Diffused the shock thro' all my life,
But in the present broke the blow.

My pulses therefore beat again
    For other friends that once I met;
    Nor can it suit me to forget
The mighty hopes that make us men.

I woo your love: I count it crime
    To mourn for any overmuch;
    I, the divided half of such
A friendship as had master'd Time;

Which masters Time indeed, and is
    Eternal, separate from fears.
    The all-assuming months and years
Can take no part away from this;

But Summer on the steaming floods,
    And Spring that swells the narrow
        brooks,
    And Autumn, with a noise of rooks,
That gather in the waning woods,

And every pulse of wind and wave
    Recalls, in change of light or gloom,
    My old affection of the tomb,
And my prime passion in the grave.

My old affection of the tomb,
    A part of stillness, yearns to speak:
' Arise, and get thee forth and seek
A friendship for the years to come.

' I watch thee from the quiet shore;
    Thy spirit up to mine can reach;
    But in dear words of human speech
We two communicate no more.'

And I, ' Can clouds of nature stain
    The starry clearness of the free ?
    How is it ? Canst thou feel for me
Some painless sympathy with pain ? '

And lightly does the whisper fall:
    ' 'T is hard for thee to fathom this;
    I triumph in conclusive bliss,
And that serene result of all.'

So hold I commerce with the dead;
    Or so methinks the dead would say;
    Or so shall grief with symbols play
And pining life be fancy-fed.

Now looking to some settled end,
    That these things pass, and I shall prove
    A meeting somewhere, love with love,
I crave your pardon, O my friend;

If not so fresh, with love as true,
    I, clasping brother-hands, aver
    I could not, if I would, transfer
The whole I felt for him to you.

For which be they that hold apart
    The promise of the golden hours ?
    First love, first friendship, equal powers,
That marry with the virgin heart.

Still mine, that cannot but deplore,
    That beats within a lonely place,
    That yet remembers his embrace,
But at his footstep leaps no more,

My heart, tho' widow'd, may not rest
    Quite in the love of what is gone,
    But seeks to beat in time with one
That warms another living breast.

Ah, take the imperfect gift I bring,
    Knowing the primrose yet is dear,
    The primrose of the later year,
As not unlike to that of Spring.

LXXXVI

Sweet after showers, ambrosial air,
    That rollest from the gorgeous gloom
    Of evening over brake and bloom
And meadow, slowly breathing bare

The round of space, and rapt below
　Thro' all the dewy tassell'd wood,
　And shadowing down the horned flood
In ripples, fan my brows and blow

The fever from my cheek, and sigh
　The full new life that feeds thy breath
Throughout　my　frame,　till　Doubt　and
　　　　Death,
Ill brethren, let the fancy fly

From belt to belt of crimson seas
　On leagues of odor streaming far,
　To where in yonder orient star
A hundred spirits whisper ' Peace.'

LXXXVII

I past beside the reverend walls
　In which of old I wore the gown;
　I roved at random thro' the town,
And saw the tumult of the halls;

And heard once more in college fanes
　The storm their high-built organs make,
　And thunder-music, rolling, shake
The prophet blazon'd on the panes;

And caught once more the distant shout,
　The measured pulse of racing oars
　Among the willows; paced the shores
And many a bridge, and all about

The same gray flats again, and felt
　The same, but not the same; and last
　Up that long walk of limes I past
To see the rooms in which he dwelt.

Another name was on the door.
　I linger'd; all within was noise
　Of songs, and clapping hands, and boys
That crash'd the glass and beat the floor;

Where once we held debate, a band
　Of youthful friends, on mind and art,
　And labor, and the changing mart,
And all the framework of the land;

When one would aim an arrow fair,
　But send it slackly from the string;
　And one would pierce an outer ring,
And one an inner, here and there;

And last the master-bowman, he,
　Would cleave the mark.　A willing ear

We lent him.　Who but hung to hear
The rapt oration flowing free

From point to point, with power and grace
　And music in the bounds of law,
　To those conclusions when we saw
The God within him light his face,

And seem to lift the form, and glow
　In azure orbits heavenly-wise;
　And over those ethereal eyes
The bar of Michael Angelo?

LXXXVIII

Wild bird, whose warble, liquid sweet,
　Rings Eden thro' the budded quicks,
　O, tell me where the senses mix,
O, tell me where the passions meet,

Whence radiate: fierce extremes employ
　Thy spirits in the darkening leaf,
　And in the midmost heart of grief
Thy passion clasps a secret joy;

And I — my harp would prelude woe —
　I cannot all command the strings;
　The glory of the sum of things
Will flash along the chords and go.

LXXXIX

Witch-elms that counterchange the floor
　Of this flat lawn with dusk and bright;
　And thou, with all thy breadth and
　　　　height
Of foliage, towering sycamore;

How often, hither wandering down,
　My Arthur found your shadows fair,
　And shook to all the liberal air
The dust and din and steam of town!

He brought an eye for all he saw;
　He mixt in all our simple sports;
　They pleased him, fresh from brawling
　　　　courts
And dusty purlieus of the law.

O joy to him in this retreat,
　Immantled in ambrosial dark,
　To drink the cooler air, and mark
The landscape winking thro' the heat!

O sound to rout the brood of cares,
　The sweep of scythe in morning dew,

The gust that round the garden flew,
And tumbled half the mellowing pears !

O bliss, when all in circle drawn
About him, heart and ear were fed
To hear him, as he lay and read
The Tuscan poets on the lawn!

Or in the all-golden afternoon
A guest, or happy sister, sung,
Or here she brought the harp and flung
A ballad to the brightening moon.

Nor less it pleased in livelier moods,
Beyond the bounding hill to stray,
And break the livelong summer day
With banquet in the distant woods;

Whereat we glanced from theme to theme,
Discuss'd the books to love or hate,
Or touch'd the changes of the state,
Or threaded some Socratic dream;

But if I praised the busy town,
He loved to rail against it still,
For ' ground in yonder social mill
We rub each other's angles down,

' And merge,' he said, ' in form and gloss
The picturesque of man and man.'
We talk'd: the stream beneath us ran,
The wine-flask lying couch'd in moss,

Or cool'd within the glooming wave;
And last, returning from afar,
Before the crimson-circled star
Had fallen into her father's grave,

And brushing ankle-deep in flowers,
We heard behind the woodbine veil
The milk that bubbled in the pail,
And buzzings of the honeyed hours.

XC

He tasted love with half his mind,
Nor ever drank the inviolate spring
Where nighest heaven, who first could
fling
This bitter seed among mankind:

That could the dead, whose dying eyes
Were closed with wail, resume their life,
They would but find in child and wife
An iron welcome when they rise.

'T was well, indeed, when warm with wine,
To pledge them with a kindly tear,
To talk them o'er, to wish them here,
To count their memories half divine;

But if they came who past away,
Behold their brides in other hands;
The hard heir strides about their lands,
And will not yield them for a day.

Yea, tho' their sons were none of these,
Not less the yet-loved sire would make
Confusion worse than death, and shake
The pillars of domestic peace.

Ah, dear, but come thou back to me!
Whatever change the years have wrought,
I find not yet one lonely thought
That cries against my wish for thee.

XCI

When rosy plumelets tuft the larch,
And rarely pipes the mounted thrush,
Or underneath the barren bush
Flits by the sea-blue bird of March;

Come, wear the form by which I know
Thy spirit in time among thy peers;
The hope of unaccomplish'd years
Be large and lucid round thy brow.

When summer's hourly-mellowing change
May breathe, with many roses sweet,
Upon the thousand waves of wheat
That ripple round the lowly grange,

Come; not in watches of the night,
But where the sunbeam broodeth warm,
Come, beauteous in thine after form,
And like a finer light in light.

XCII

If any vision should reveal
Thy likeness, I might count it vain
As but the canker of the brain;
Yea, tho' it spake and made appeal

To chances where our lots were cast
Together in the days behind,
I might but say, I hear a wind
Of memory murmuring the past.

Yea, tho' it spake and bared to view
A fact within the coming year;

And tho' the months, revolving near,
Should prove the phantom-warning true,

They might not seem thy prophecies,
　　But spiritual presentiments,
　　And such refraction of events
As often rises ere they rise.

XCIII

I shall not see thee.　Dare I say
　　No spirit ever brake the band
　　That stays him from the native land
Where first he walk'd when claspt in clay?

No visual shade of some one lost,
　　But he, the Spirit himself, may come
　　Where all the nerve of sense is numb,
Spirit to Spirit, Ghost to Ghost.

O, therefore from thy sightless range
　　With gods in unconjectured bliss,
　　O, from the distance of the abyss
Of tenfold-complicated change,

Descend, and touch, and enter; hear
　　The wish too strong for words to name,
　　That in this blindness of the frame
My Ghost may feel that thine is near.

XCIV

How pure at heart and sound in head,
　　With what divine affections bold
　　Should be the man whose thought would
　　　　hold
An hour's communion with the dead.

In vain shalt thou, or any, call
　　The spirits from their golden day,
　　Except, like them, thou too canst say,
My spirit is at peace with all.

They haunt the silence of the breast,
　　Imaginations calm and fair,
　　The memory like a cloudless air,
The conscience as a sea at rest;

But when the heart is full of din,
　　And doubt beside the portal waits,
　　They can but listen at the gates,
And hear the household jar within.

XCV

By night we linger'd on the lawn,
　　For underfoot the herb was dry;

And genial warmth; and o'er the sky
The silvery haze of summer drawn;

And calm that let the tapers burn
　　Unwavering: not a cricket chirr'd;
　　The brook alone far-off was heard,
And on the board the fluttering urn.

And bats went round in fragrant skies,
　　And wheel'd or lit the filmy shapes
　　That haunt the dusk, with ermine capes
And woolly breasts and beaded eyes;

While now we sang old songs that peal'd
　　From knoll to knoll, where, couch'd at
　　　　ease,
　　The white kine glimmer'd, and the trees
Laid their dark arms about the field.

But when those others, one by one,
　　Withdrew themselves from me and night,
　　And in the house light after light
Went out, and I was all alone,

A hunger seized my heart; I read
　　Of that glad year which once had been,
　　In those fallen leaves which kept their
　　　　green,
The noble letters of the dead.

And strangely on the silence broke
　　The silent-speaking words, and strange
　　Was love's dumb cry defying change
To test his worth; and strangely spoke

The faith, the vigor, bold to dwell
　　On doubts that drive the coward back,
　　And keen thro' wordy snares to track
Suggestion to her inmost cell.

So word by word, and line by line,
　　The dead man touch'd me from the
　　　　past,
　　And all at once it seem'd at last
The living soul was flash'd on mine,

And mine in this was wound, and whirl'd
　　About empyreal heights of thought,
　　And came on that which is, and caught
The deep pulsations of the world,

Æonian music measuring out
　　The steps of Time — the shocks of
　　　　Chance —

The blows of Death. At length my
    trance
Was cancell'd, stricken thro' with doubt.

Vague words! but ah, how hard to frame
    In matter-moulded forms of speech,
    Or even for intellect to reach
Thro' memory that which I became;

Till now the doubtful dusk reveal'd
    The knolls once more where, couch'd at
      ease,
    The white kine glimmer'd, and the trees
Laid their dark arms about the field;

And suck'd from out the distant gloom
    A breeze began to tremble o'er
    The large leaves of the sycamore,
And fluctuate all the still perfume,

And gathering freshlier overhead,
    Rock'd the full-foliaged elms, and swung
    The heavy-folded rose, and flung
The lilies to and fro, and said,

'The dawn, the dawn,' and died away;
    And East and West, without a breath,
    Mixt their dim lights, like life and
      death,
To broaden into boundless day.

XCVI

You say, but with no touch of scorn,
    Sweet-hearted, you, whose light-blue eyes
    Are tender over drowning flies,
You tell me, doubt is Devil-born.

I know not: one indeed I knew
    In many a subtle question versed,
    Who touch'd a jarring lyre at first,
But ever strove to make it true;

Perplext in faith, but pure in deeds,
    At last he beat his music out.
    There lives more faith in honest doubt,
Believe me, than in half the creeds.

He fought his doubts and gather'd strength,
    He would not make his judgment blind,
    He faced the spectres of the mind
And laid them; thus he came at length

To find a stronger faith his own,
    And Power was with him in the night,

Which makes the darkness and the
    light,
And dwells not in the light alone,

But in the darkness and the cloud,
    As over Sinaï's peaks of old,
    While Israel made their gods of gold,
Altho' the trumpet blew so loud.

XCVII

My love has talk'd with rocks and trees;
    He finds on misty mountain-ground
    His own vast shadow glory-crown'd;
He sees himself in all he sees.

Two partners of a married life —
    I look'd on these and thought of thee
    In vastness and in mystery,
And of my spirit as of a wife.

These two — they dwelt with eye on eye,
    Their hearts of old have beat in tune,
    Their meetings made December June,
Their every parting was to die.

Their love has never past away;
    The days she never can forget
    Are earnest that he loves her yet,
Whate'er the faithless people say.

Her life is lone, he sits apart;
    He loves her yet, she will not weep,
    Tho' rapt in matters dark and deep
He seems to slight her simple heart.

He thrids the labyrinth of the mind,
    He reads the secret of the star,
    He seems so near and yet so far,
He looks so cold: she thinks him kind.

She keeps the gift of years before,
    A wither'd violet is her bliss;
    She knows not what his greatness is,
For that, for all, she loves him more.

For him she plays, to him she sings
    Of early faith and plighted vows;
    She knows but matters of the house,
And he, he knows a thousand things.

Her faith is fixt and cannot move,
    She darkly feels him great and wise,
    She dwells on him with faithful eyes,
'I cannot understand; I love.'

XCVIII

You leave us: you will see the Rhine,
  And those fair hills I sail'd below,
  When I was there with him; and go
By summer belts of wheat and vine

To where he breathed his latest breath,
  That city.   All her splendor seems
  No livelier than the wisp that gleams
On Lethe in the eyes of Death.

Let her great Danube rolling fair
  Enwind her isles, unmark'd of me;
  I have not seen, I will not see
Vienna; rather dream that there,

A treble darkness, Evil haunts
  The birth, the bridal; friend from friend
  Is oftener parted, fathers bend
Above more graves, a thousand wants

Gnarr at the heels of men, and prey
  By each cold hearth, and sadness flings
  Her shadow on the blaze of kings.
And yet myself have heard him say,

That not in any mother town
  With statelier progress to and fro
  The double tides of chariots flow
By park and suburb under brown

Of lustier leaves; nor more content,
  He told me, lives in any crowd,
  When all is gay with lamps, and loud
With sport and song, in booth and tent,

Imperial halls, or open plain;
  And wheels the circled dance, and breaks
  The rocket molten into flakes
Of crimson or in emerald rain.

XCIX

Risest thou thus, dim dawn, again,
  So loud with voices of the birds,
  So thick with lowings of the herds,
Day, when I lost the flower of men;

Who tremblest thro' thy darkling red
  On yon swollen brook that bubbles fast
  By meadows breathing of the past,
And woodlands holy to the dead;

Who murmurest in the foliaged eaves
  A song that slights the coming care,

And Autumn laying here and there
  A fiery finger on the leaves;

Who wakenest with thy balmy breath
  To myriads on the genial earth,
  Memories of bridal, or of birth,
And unto myriads more, of death.

O, wheresoever those may be,
  Betwixt the slumber of the poles,
  To-day they count as kindred souls;
They know me not, but mourn with me.

C

I climb the hill: from end to end
  Of all the landscape underneath,
  I find no place that does not breathe
Some gracious memory of my friend;

No gray old grange, or lonely fold,
  Or low morass and whispering reed,
  Or simple stile from mead to mead,
Or sheepwalk up the windy wold;

Nor hoary knoll of ash and haw
  That hears the latest linnet trill,
  Nor quarry trench'd along the hill
And haunted by the wrangling daw;

Nor runlet tinkling from the rock;
  Nor pastoral rivulet that swerves
  To left and right thro' meadowy curves,
That feed the mothers of the flock;

But each has pleased a kindred eye,
  And each reflects a kindlier day;
  And, leaving these, to pass away,
I think once more he seems to die.

CI

Unwatch'd, the garden bough shall sway,
  The tender blossom flutter down,
  Unloved, that beech will gather brown,
This maple burn itself away;

Unloved, the sunflower, shining fair,
  Ray round with flames her disk of
      seed,
  And many a rose-carnation feed
With summer spice the humming air;

Unloved, by many a sandy bar,
  The brook shall babble down the plain,
  At noon or when the Lesser Wain
Is twisting round the polar star;

Uncared for, gird the windy grove,
  And flood the haunts of hern and crake,
  Or into silver arrows break
The sailing moon in creek and cove;

Till from the garden and the wild
  A fresh association blow,
  And year by year the landscape grow
Familiar to the stranger's child;

As year by year the laborer tills
  His wonted glebe, or lops the glades,
  And year by year our memory fades
From all the circle of the hills.

CII

We leave the well-beloved place
  Where first we gazed upon the sky;
  The roofs that heard our earliest cry
Will shelter one of stranger race.

We go, but ere we go from home,
  As down the garden-walks I move,
  Two spirits of a diverse love
Contend for loving masterdom.

One whispers, ' Here thy boyhood sung
  Long since its matin song, and heard
  The low love-language of the bird
In native hazels tassel-hung.'

The other answers, ' Yea, but here
  Thy feet have stray'd in after hours
  With thy lost friend among the bowers,
And this hath made them trebly dear.'

These two have striven half the day,
  And each prefers his separate claim,
  Poor rivals in a losing game,
That will not yield each other way.

I turn to go; my feet are set
  To leave the pleasant fields and farms;
  They mix in one another's arms
To one pure image of regret.

CIII

On that last night before we went
  From out the doors where I was bred,
  I dream'd a vision of the dead,
Which left my after-morn content.

Methought I dwelt within a hall,
  And maidens with me; distant hills

From hidden summits fed with rills
A river sliding by the wall.

The hall with harp and carol rang.
  They sang of what is wise and good
  And graceful. In the centre stood
A statue veil'd, to which they sang;

And which, tho' veil'd, was known to me,
  The shape of him I loved, and love
  For ever. Then flew in a dove
And brought a summons from the sea;

And when they learnt that I must go,
  They wept and wail'd, but led the way
  To where a little shallop lay
At anchor in the flood below;

And on by many a level mead,
  And shadowing bluff that made the
    banks,
  We glided winding under ranks
Of iris and the golden reed;

And still as vaster grew the shore
  And roll'd the floods in grander space,
  The maidens gather'd strength and grace
And presence, lordlier than before;

And I myself, who sat apart
  And watch'd them, wax'd in every limb;
  I felt the thews of Anakim,
The pulses of a Titan's heart;

As one would sing the death of war,
  And one would chant the history
  Of that great race which is to be,
And one the shaping of a star;

Until the forward-creeping tides
  Began to foam, and we to draw
  From deep to deep, to where we saw
A great ship lift her shining sides.

The man we loved was there on deck,
  But thrice as large as man he bent
  To greet us. Up the side I went,
And fell in silence on his neck;

Whereat those maidens with one mind
  Bewail'd their lot; I did them wrong:
  ' We served thee here,' they said, ' so
    long,
And wilt thou leave us now behind ? '

So rapt I was, they could not win
  An answer from my lips, but he
  Replying, 'Enter likewise ye
And go with us:' they enter'd in.

And while the wind began to sweep
  A music out of sheet and shroud,
  We steer'd her toward a crimson cloud
That landlike slept along the deep.

CIV

The time draws near the birth of Christ;
  The moon is hid, the night is still;
  A single church below the hill
Is pealing, folded in the mist.

A single peal of bells below,
  That wakens at this hour of rest
  A single murmur in the breast,
That these are not the bells I know.

Like strangers' voices here they sound,
  In lands where not a memory strays,
  Nor landmark breathes of other days,
But all is new unhallow'd ground.

CV

To-night ungather'd let us leave
  This laurel, let this holly stand:
  We live within the stranger's land,
And strangely falls our Christmas-eve.

Our father's dust is left alone
  And silent under other snows:
  There in due time the woodbine blows,
The violet comes, but we are gone.

No more shall wayward grief abuse
  The genial hour with mask and mime;
  For change of place, like growth of time,
Has broke the bond of dying use.

Let cares that petty shadows cast,
  By which our lives are chiefly proved,
  A little spare the night I loved,
And hold it solemn to the past.

But let no footstep beat the floor,
  Nor bowl of wassail mantle warm;
  For who would keep an ancient form
Thro' which the spirit breathes no more?

Be neither song, nor game, nor feast;
  Nor harp be touch'd, nor flute be blown;

No dance, no motion, save alone
What lightens in the lucid East

Of rising worlds by yonder wood.
  Long sleeps the summer in the seed;
  Run out your measured arcs, and lead
The closing cycle rich in good.

CVI

Ring out, wild bells, to the wild sky,
  The flying cloud, the frosty light:
  The year is dying in the night;
Ring out, wild bells, and let him die.

Ring out the old, ring in the new,
  Ring, happy bells, across the snow:
  The year is going, let him go;
Ring out the false, ring in the true.

Ring out the grief that saps the mind,
  For those that here we see no more;
  Ring out the feud of rich and poor,
Ring in redress to all mankind.

Ring out a slowly dying cause,
  And ancient forms of party strife;
  Ring in the nobler modes of life,
With sweeter manners, purer laws.

Ring out the want, the care, the sin,
  The faithless coldness of the times;
  Ring out, ring out my mournful rhymes,
But ring the fuller minstrel in.

Ring out false pride in place and blood,
  The civic slander and the spite;
  Ring in the love of truth and right,
Ring in the common love of good.

Ring out old shapes of foul disease;
  Ring out the narrowing lust of gold;
  Ring out the thousand wars of old,
Ring in the thousand years of peace.

Ring in the valiant man and free,
  The larger heart, the kindlier hand;
  Ring out the darkness of the land,
Ring in the Christ that is to be.

CVII

It is the day when he was born,
  A bitter day that early sank
  Behind a purple-frosty bank
Of vapor, leaving night forlorn.

The time admits not flowers or leaves
　　To deck the banquet.　Fiercely flies
　　The blast of North and East, and ice
Makes daggers at the sharpen'd eaves,

And bristles all the brakes and thorns
　　To yon hard crescent, as she hangs
　　Above the wood which grides and clangs
Its leafless ribs and iron horns

Together, in the drifts that pass
　　To darken on the rolling brine
　　That breaks the coast.　But fetch the
　　　　wine,
Arrange the board and brim the glass;

Bring in great logs and let them lie,
　　To make a solid core of heat;
　　Be cheerful-minded, talk and treat
Of all things even as he were by;

We keep the day.　With festal cheer,
　　With books and music, surely we
　　Will drink to him, whate'er he be,
And sing the songs he loved to hear.

CVIII

I will not shut me from my kind,
　　And, lest I stiffen into stone,
　　I will not eat my heart alone,
Nor feed with sighs a passing wind:

What profit lies in barren faith,
　　And vacant yearning, tho' with might
　　To scale the heaven's highest height,
Or dive below the wells of death ?

What find I in the highest place,
　　But mine own phantom chanting hymns ?
　　And on the depths of death there swims
The reflex of a human face.

I 'll rather take what fruit may be
　　Of sorrow under human skies:
　　'T is held that sorrow makes us wise,
Whatever wisdom sleep with thee.

CIX

Heart-affluence in discursive talk
　　From household fountains never dry;
　　The critic clearness of an eye
That saw thro' all the Muses' walk;

Seraphic intellect and force
　　To seize and throw the doubts of man;

Impassion'd logic, which outran
The hearer in its fiery course;

High nature amorous of the good,
　　But touch'd with no ascetic gloom;
　　And passion pure in snowy bloom
Thro' all the years of April blood;

A love of freedom rarely felt,
　　Of freedom in her regal seat
　　Of England; not the schoolboy heat,
The blind hysterics of the Celt;

And manhood fused with female grace
　　In such a sort, the child would twine
　　A trustful hand, unask'd, in thine,
And find his comfort in thy face;

All these have been, and thee mine eyes
　　Have look'd on: if they look'd in vain,
　　My shame is greater who remain,
Nor let thy wisdom make me wise.

CX

Thy converse drew us with delight,
　　The men of rathe and riper years;
　　The feeble soul, a haunt of fears,
Forgot his weakness in thy sight.

On thee the loyal-hearted hung,
　　The proud was half disarm'd of pride,
　　Nor cared the serpent at thy side
To flicker with his double tongue.

The stern were mild when thou wert by,
　　The flippant put himself to school
　　And heard thee, and the brazen fool
Was soften'd, and he knew not why;

While I, thy nearest, sat apart,
　　And felt thy triumph was as mine;
　　And loved them more, that they were
　　　　thine,
The graceful tact, the Christian art;

Nor mine the sweetness or the skill,
　　But mine the love that will not tire,
　　And, born of love, the vague desire
That spurs an imitative will.

CXI

The churl in spirit, up or down
　　Along the scale of ranks, thro' all,
　　To him who grasps a golden ball,
By blood a king, at heart a clown, —

The churl in spirit, howe'er he veil
　His want in forms for fashion's sake,
　Will let his coltish nature break
At seasons thro' the gilded pale;

For who can always act? but he,
　To whom a thousand memories call,
　Not being less but more than all
The gentleness he seem'd to be,

Best seem'd the thing he was, and join'd
　Each office of the social hour
　To noble manners, as the flower
And native growth of noble mind;

Nor ever narrowness or spite,
　Or villain fancy fleeting by,
　Drew in the expression of an eye
Where God and Nature met in light;

And thus he bore without abuse
　The grand old name of gentleman,
　Defamed by every charlatan,
And soil'd with all ignoble use.

CXII

High wisdom holds my wisdom less,
　That I, who gaze with temperate eyes
　On glorious insufficiencies,
Set light by narrower perfectness.

But thou, that fillest all the room
　Of all my love, art reason why
　I seem to cast a careless eye
On souls, the lesser lords of doom.

For what wert thou? some novel power
　Sprang up for ever at a touch,
　And hope could never hope too much,
In watching thee from hour to hour,

Large elements in order brought,
　And tracts of calm from tempest made,
　And world-wide fluctuation sway'd
In vassal tides that follow'd thought.

CXIII

'T is held that sorrow makes us wise;
　Yet how much wisdom sleeps with thee
　Which not alone had guided me,
But served the seasons that may rise;

For can I doubt, who knew thee keen
　In intellect, with force and skill

To strive, to fashion, to fulfil —
I doubt not what thou wouldst have been:

A life in civic action warm,
　A soul on highest mission sent,
　A potent voice of Parliament,
A pillar steadfast in the storm,

Should licensed boldness gather force,
　Becoming, when the time has birth,
　A lever to uplift the earth
And roll it in another course,

With thousand shocks that come and go,
　With agonies, with energies,
　With overthrowings, and with cries,
And undulations to and fro.

CXIV

Who loves not Knowledge? Who shall
　　rail
　Against her beauty? May she mix
　With men and prosper! Who shall fix
Her pillars? Let her work prevail.

But on her forehead sits a fire;
　She sets her forward countenance
　And leaps into the future chance,
Submitting all things to desire.

Half-grown as yet, a child, and vain —
　She cannot fight the fear of death.
　What is she, cut from love and faith,
But some wild Pallas from the brain

Of demons? fiery-hot to burst
　All barriers in her onward race
　For power. Let her know her place;
She is the second, not the first.

A higher hand must make her mild,
　If all be not in vain, and guide
　Her footsteps, moving side by side
With Wisdom, like the younger child;

For she is earthly of the mind,
　But Wisdom heavenly of the soul.
　O friend, who camest to thy goal
So early, leaving me behind,

I would the great world grew like thee,
　Who grewest not alone in power
　And knowledge, but by year and hour
In reverence and in charity.

CXV

Now fades the last long streak of snow,
  Now burgeons every maze of quick
  About the flowering squares, and thick
By ashen roots the violets blow.

Now rings the woodland loud and long,
  The distance takes a lovelier hue,
  And drown'd in yonder living blue
The lark becomes a sightless song.

Now dance the lights on lawn and lea,
  The flocks are whiter down the vale,
  And milkier every milky sail
On winding stream or distant sea;

Where now the seamew pipes, or dives
  In yonder greening gleam, and fly
  The happy birds, that change their sky
To build and brood, that live their lives

From land to land; and in my breast
  Spring wakens too, and my regret
  Becomes an April violet,
And buds and blossoms like the rest.

CXVI

Is it, then, regret for buried time
  That keenlier in sweet April wakes,
  And meets the year, and gives and takes
The colors of the crescent prime?

Not all: the songs, the stirring air,
  The life re-orient out of dust,
  Cry thro' the sense to hearten trust
In that which made the world so fair.

Not all regret: the face will shine
  Upon me, while I muse alone,
  And that dear voice, I once have known,
Still speak to me of me and mine.

Yet less of sorrow lives in me
  For days of happy commune dead,
  Less yearning for the friendship fled
Than some strong bond which is to be.

CXVII

O days and hours, your work is this,
  To hold me from my proper plaçe,
  A little while from his embrace,
For fuller gain of after bliss;

That out of distance might ensue
  Desire of nearness doubly sweet,
  And unto meeting, when we meet,
Delight a hundredfold accrue,

For every grain of sand that runs,
  And every span of shade that steals,
  And every kiss of toothed wheels,
And all the courses of the suns.

CXVIII

Contemplate all this work of Time,
  The giant laboring in his youth;
  Nor dream of human love and truth,
As dying Nature's earth and lime;

But trust that those we call the dead
  Are breathers of an ampler day
  For ever nobler ends. They say,
The solid earth whereon we tread

In tracts of fluent heat began,
  And grew to seeming-random forms,
  The seeming prey of cyclic storms,
Till at the last arose the man;

Who throve and branch'd from clime to
      clime,
  The herald of a higher race,
  And of himself in higher place,
If so he type this work of time

Within himself, from more to more;
  Or, crown'd with attributes of woe
  Like glories, move his course, and show
That life is not as idle ore,

But iron dug from central gloom,
  And heated hot with burning fears,
  And dipt in baths of hissing tears,
And batter'd with the shocks of doom

To shape and use. Arise and fly
  The reeling Faun, the sensual feast;
  Move upward, working out the beast,
And let the ape and tiger die.

CXIX

Doors, where my heart was used to beat
  So quickly, not as one that weeps
  I come once more; the city sleeps;
I smell the meadow in the street;

I hear a chirp of birds; I see
  Betwixt the black fronts long-withdrawn

A light-blue lane of early dawn,
And think of early days and thee,

And bless thee, for thy lips are bland,
   And bright the friendship of thine eye;
   And in my thoughts with scarce a sigh
I take the pressure of thine hand.

CXX

I trust I have not wasted breath:
   I think we are not wholly brain,
   Magnetic mockeries; not in vain,
Like Paul with beasts, I fought with Death;

Not only cunning casts in clay:
   Let Science prove we are, and then
   What matters Science unto men,
At least to me? I would not stay.

Let him, the wiser man who springs
   Hereafter, up from childhood shape
   His action like the greater ape,
But I was *born* to other things.

CXXI

Sad Hesper o'er the buried sun
   And ready, thou, to die with him,
   Thou watchest all things ever dim
And dimmer, and a glory done.

The team is loosen'd from the wain,
   The boat is drawn upon the shore;
   Thou listenest to the closing door,
And life is darken'd in the brain.

Bright Phosphor, fresher for the night,
   By thee the world's great work is heard
   Beginning, and the wakeful bird;
Behind thee comes the greater light:

The market boat is on the stream,
   And voices hail it from the brink;
   Thou hear'st the village hammer clink,
And see'st the moving of the team.

Sweet Hesper-Phosphor, double name
   For what is one, the first, the last,
   Thou, like my present and my past,
Thy place is changed; thou art the same.

CXXII

O, wast thou with me, dearest, then,
   While I rose up against my doom,
   And yearn'd to burst the folded gloom,
To bare the eternal heavens again,

To feel once more, in placid awe,
   The strong imagination roll
   A sphere of stars about my soul,
In all her motion one with law?

If thou wert with me, and the grave
   Divide us not, be with me now,
   And enter in at breast and brow,
Till all my blood, a fuller wave,

Be quicken'd with a livelier breath,
   And like an inconsiderate boy,
   As in the former flash of joy,
I slip the thoughts of life and death;

And all the breeze of Fancy blows,
   And every dewdrop paints a bow,
   The wizard lightnings deeply glow,
And every thought breaks out a rose.

CXXIII

There rolls the deep where grew the tree.
   O earth, what changes hast thou seen!
   There where the long street roars hath
      been
The stillness of the central sea.

The hills are shadows, and they flow
   From form to form, and nothing stands;
   They melt like mist, the solid lands,
Like clouds they shape themselves and go.

But in my spirit will I dwell,
   And dream my dream, and hold it true;
   For tho' my lips may breathe adieu,
I cannot think the thing farewell.

CXXIV

That which we dare invoke to bless;
   Our dearest faith; our ghastliest doubt;
   He, They, One, All; within, without;
The Power in darkness whom we guess, —

I found Him not in world or sun,
   Or eagle's wing, or insect's eye,
   Nor thro' the questions men may try,
The petty cobwebs we have spun.

If e'er when faith had fallen asleep,
   I heard a voice, 'believe no more,'
   And heard an ever-breaking shore
That tumbled in the Godless deep,

A warmth within the breast would melt
   The freezing reason's colder part,

And like a man in wrath the heart
Stood up and answer'd, 'I have felt.'

No, like a child in doubt and fear:
But that blind clamor made me wise;
Then was I as a child that cries,
But, crying, knows his father near;

And what I am beheld again
What is, and no man understands;
And out of darkness came the hands
That reach thro' nature, moulding men.

CXXV

Whatever I have said or sung,
Some bitter notes my harp would give,
Yea, tho' there often seem'd to live
A contradiction on the tongue,

Yet Hope had never lost her youth,
She did but look through dimmer eyes;
Or Love but play'd with gracious lies,
Because he felt so fix'd in truth;

And if the song were full of care,
He breathed the spirit of the song;
And if the words were sweet and strong
He set his royal signet there;

Abiding with me till I sail
To seek thee on the mystic deeps,
And this electric force, that keeps
A thousand pulses dancing, fail.

CXXVI

Love is and was my lord and king,
And in his presence I attend
To hear the tidings of my friend,
Which every hour his couriers bring.

Love is and was my king and lord,
And will be, tho' as yet I keep
Within the court on earth, and sleep
Encompass'd by his faithful guard,

And hear at times a sentinel
Who moves about from place to place,
And whispers to the worlds of space,
In the deep night, that all is well.

CXXVII

And all is well, tho' faith and form
Be sunder'd in the night of fear;
Well roars the storm to those that
hear
A deeper voice across the storm,

Proclaiming social truth shall spread,
And justice, even tho' thrice again
The red fool-fury of the Seine
Should pile her barricades with dead.

But ill for him that wears a crown,
And him, the lazar, in his rags!
They tremble, the sustaining crags;
The spires of ice are toppled down,

And molten up, and roar in flood;
The fortress crashes from on high,
The brute earth lightens to the sky,
And the great Æon sinks in blood,

And compass'd by the fires of hell;
While thou, dear spirit, happy star,
O'erlook'st the tumult from afar,
And smilest, knowing all is well.

CXXVIII

The love that rose on stronger wings,
Unpalsied when he met with Death,
Is comrade of the lesser faith
That sees the course of human things.

No doubt vast eddies in the flood
Of onward time shall yet be made,
And throned races may degrade;
Yet, O ye mysteries of good,

Wild Hours that fly with Hope and Fear,
If all your office had to do
With old results that look like new —
If this were all your mission here,

To draw, to sheathe a useless sword,
To fool the crowd with glorious lies,
To cleave a creed in sects and cries,
To change the bearing of a word,

To shift an arbitrary power,
To cramp the student at his desk,
To make old bareness picturesque
And tuft with grass a feudal tower,

Why, then my scorn might well descend
On you and yours. I see in part
That all, as in some piece of art,
Is toil coöperant to an end.

CXXIX

Dear friend, far off, my lost desire,
So far, so near in woe and weal,
O loved the most, when most I feel
There is a lower and a higher;

Known and unknown, human, divine;
  Sweet human hand and lips and eye;
  Dear heavenly friend that canst not
    die,
Mine, mine, for ever, ever mine;

Strange friend, past, present, and to be;
  Loved deeplier, darklier understood;
  Behold, I dream a dream of good,
And mingle all the world with thee.

CXXX

Thy voice is on the rolling air;
  I hear thee where the waters run;
  Thou standest in the rising sun,
And in the setting thou art fair.

What art thou then? I cannot guess;
  But tho' I seem in star and flower
  To feel thee some diffusive power,
I do not therefore love thee less.

My love involves the love before;
  My love is vaster passion now;
  Tho' mix'd with God and Nature thou,
I seem to love thee more and more.

Far off thou art, but ever nigh;
  I have thee still, and I rejoice;
  I prosper, circled with thy voice;
I shall not lose thee tho' I die.

CXXXI

O living will that shalt endure
  When all that seems shall suffer shock,
  Rise in the spiritual rock,
Flow thro' our deeds and make them
    pure,

That we may lift from out of dust
  A voice as unto him that hears,
  A cry above the conquer'd years
To one that with us works, and trust,

With faith that comes of self-control,
  The truths that never can be proved
  Until we close with all we loved,
And all we flow from, soul in soul.

<hr />

O true and tried, so well and long,
  Demand not thou a marriage lay;
  In that it is thy marriage day
Is music more than any song.

Nor have I felt so much of bliss
  Since first he told me that he loved
  A daughter of our house, nor proved
Since that dark day a day like this;

Tho' I since then have number'd o'er
  Some thrice three years; they went and
    came,
  Remade the blood and changed the
    frame,
And yet is love not less, but more;

No longer caring to embalm
  In dying songs a dead regret,
  But like a statue solid-set,
And moulded in colossal calm.

Regret is dead, but love is more
  Than in the summers that are flown,
  For I myself with these have grown
To something greater than before;

Which makes appear the songs I made
  As echoes out of weaker times,
  As half but idle brawling rhymes,
The sport of random sun and shade.

But where is she, the bridal flower,
  That must be made a wife ere noon?
  She enters, glowing like the moon
Of Eden on its bridal bower.

On me she bends her blissful eyes
  And then on thee; they meet thy look
  And brighten like the star that shook
Betwixt the palms of Paradise.

O, when her life was yet in bud,
  He too foretold the perfect rose.
  For thee she grew, for thee she grows
For ever, and as fair as good.

And thou art worthy, full of power;
  As gentle; liberal-minded, great,
  Consistent; wearing all that weight
Of learning lightly like a flower.

But now set out: the noon is near,
  And I must give away the bride;
  She fears not, or with thee beside
And me behind her, will not fear.

For I that danced her on my knee,
  That watch'd her on her nurse's arm,

That shielded all her life from harm,
At last must part with her to thee;

Now waiting to be made a wife,
　Her feet, my darling, on the dead;
　Their pensive tablets round her head,
And the most living words of life

Breathed in her ear. The ring is on,
　The ' Wilt thou ? ' answer'd, and again
　The ' Wilt thou ? ' ask'd, till out of twain
Her sweet ' I will ' has made you one.

Now sign your names, which shall be read,
　Mute symbols of a joyful morn,
　By village eyes as yet unborn.
The names are sign'd, and overhead

Begins the clash and clang that tells
　The joy to every wandering breeze;
　The blind wall rocks, and on the trees
The dead leaf trembles to the bells.

O happy hour, and happier hours
　Await them. Many a merry face
　Salutes them — maidens of the place,
That pelt us in the porch with flowers.

O happy hour, behold the bride
　With him to whom her hand I gave.
　They leave the porch, they pass the grave
That has to-day its sunny side.

To-day the grave is bright for me,
　For them the light of life increased,
　Who stay to share the morning feast,
Who rest to-night beside the sea.

Let all my genial spirits advance
　To meet and greet a whiter sun;
　My drooping memory will not shun
The foaming grape of eastern France.

It circles round, and fancy plays,
　And hearts are warm'd and faces bloom,
　As drinking health to bride and groom
We wish them store of happy days.

Nor count me all to blame if I
　Conjecture of a stiller guest,
　Perchance, perchance, among the rest,
And, tho' in silence, wishing joy.

But they must go, the time draws on,
　And those white-favor'd horses wait;

They rise, but linger; it is late;
Farewell, we kiss, and they are gone.

A shade falls on us like the dark
　From little cloudlets on the grass,
　But sweeps away as out we pass
To range the woods, to roam the park,

Discussing how their courtship grew,
　And talk of others that are wed,
　And how she look'd, and what he said,
And back we come at fall of dew.

Again the feast, the speech, the glee,
　The shade of passing thought, the
　　wealth
　Of words and wit, the double health,
The crowning cup, the three-times-three,

And last the dance; — till I retire.
　Dumb is that tower which spake so
　　loud,
　And high in heaven the streaming cloud,
And on the downs a rising fire:

And rise, O moon, from yonder down,
　Till over down and over dale
　All night the shining vapor sail
And pass the silent-lighted town,

The white-faced halls, the glancing rills,
　And catch at every mountain head,
　And o'er the friths that branch and
　　spread
Their sleeping silver thro' the hills;

And touch with shade the bridal doors,
　With tender gloom the roof, the wall;
　And breaking let the splendor fall
To spangle all the happy shores

By which they rest, and ocean sounds,
　And, star and system rolling past,
　A soul shall draw from out the vast
And strike his being into bounds,

And, moved thro' life of lower phase,
　Result in man, be born and think,
　And act and love, a closer link
Betwixt us and the crowning race

Of those that, eye to eye, shall look
　On knowledge; under whose command
　Is Earth and Earth's, and in their hand
Is Nature like an open book;

No longer half-akin to brute,
  For all we thought and loved and did,
  And hoped, and suffer'd, is but seed
Of what in them is flower and fruit;

Whereof the man that with me trod
  This planet was a noble type

Appearing ere the times were ripe,
That friend of mine who lives in God,

That God, which ever lives and loves,
  One God, one law, one element,
  And one far-off divine event,
To which the whole creation moves.

MAUD, AND OTHER POEMS

This volume, published in 1855, contained in addition to ' Maud ' the following poems: ' The Brook,' ' The Letters,' ' The Daisy,' ' Will,' ' Lines to the Rev. F. D. Maurice ' (all published for the first time); with the ' Ode on the Death of the Duke of Wellington ,' already printed twice (1852, 1853) in pamphlet form, and ' The Charge of the Light Brigade,' reprinted from the ' Examiner ' of December 9, 1854 (also privately reprinted in 1855). A second edition of the volume was published in 1856, when ' Maud ' was considerably enlarged.

MAUD; A MONODRAMA

This poem grew out of the lines, ' O, that 't were possible,' etc., printed in ' The Tribute ' in 1837, and now forming (with some alterations) the fourth section of Part II. of the poem. Sir John Simeon, to whom Tennyson read these lines in the earlier days of their friendship, suggested that something was needed to explain the story. On this hint the poem was founded, and the greater part of it was written under a certain cedar in Sir John's grounds at Swainston. For the additions made in 1856, and minor alterations made afterwards, see the Notes.

The earlier critics of the poem failed to recognize its dramatic character. They ascribed to the author the thoughts and sentiments which he puts into the mouth of the morbid young man who is the *dramatis persona;* for, as in recent editions it has been designated, the poem is a ' monodrama,' and, in that respect, unique. Tennyson, when reading it to Mr. Knowles, said (as in substance he said when reading it to me): ' It should be called " Maud, or the Madness." It is slightly akin to " Hamlet." No other poem (a monotone with plenty of change and no weariness) has been made into a drama where successive phases of passion in one person take the place of successive persons.' At the end of ' Maud ' he declared, ' I've always said that " Maud " and " Guinevere " were the finest things I 've written.'

To Dr. Van Dyke, who in the first edition of ' The Poetry of Tennyson ' had called ' Maud ' a ' splendid failure,' he said: ' I want to read this to you because I want you to feel what the poem means. It is dramatic; it is the story of a man who has a morbid nature, with a touch of inherited insanity, and very selfish. The poem is to show what love does for him. The war is only an episode. You must remember that it is not I myself speaking. It is this man with the strain of madness in his blood, and the memory of a great trouble and wrong that has put him out with the world.'

I felt, when I heard the poet read ' Maud,' that it was the best possible commentary on the poem. I had not misunderstood it, as Dr. Van Dyke did at first, but the reading made me see heights and depths in it of which I had had no conception before. Especially was I amazed, as my friend was, at ' the intensity with which the poet had felt, and the tenacity with which he had pursued, the moral meaning of the poem. It was love, but not love in itself alone, as an emotion, an inward experience, a selfish possession, that he was revealing. It was love as a vital force, love as a part of life, love as an influence, — nay, *the* influence which rescues the soul from the prison, or the madhouse, of self, and leads it into the larger, saner existence. This was the theme of " Maud." And the poet's voice brought it out, and rang the changes on it, so that it was unmistakable and unforgettable, — the history of a man saved from selfish despair by a pure love.' For his last reading of the poem, see the ' Memoir,' vol. i. page 395.

The motto of ' Maud ' might well have been the lines from ' Locksley Hall ' which the poet was fond of copying when friends asked for his autograph: —

Love took up the harp of Life, and smote on all the
    chords with might;
Smote the chord of Self, that, trembling, past in music
    out of sight.

PART I

I

I

I HATE the dreadful hollow behind the
little wood;
Its lips in the field above are dabbled with
blood-red heath,
The red-ribb'd ledges drip with a silent
horror of blood,
And Echo there, whatever is ask'd her, an-
swers ' Death.'

II

For there in the ghastly pit long since a
body was found,
His who had given me life — O father ! O
God ! was it well ? —
Mangled, and flatten'd, and crush'd, and
dinted into the ground;
There yet lies the rock that fell with him
when he fell.

III

Did he fling himself down ? who knows ?
for a vast speculation had fail'd,
And ever he mutter'd and madden'd, and
ever wann'd with despair,   10
And out he walk'd when the wind like a
broken worldling wail'd,
And the flying gold of the ruin'd woodlands
drove thro' the air.

IV

I remember the time, for the roots of my
hair were stirr'd
By a shuffled step, by a dead weight trail'd,
by a whisper'd fright,
And my pulses closed their gates with a
shock on my heart as I heard
The shrill-edged shriek of a mother divide
the shuddering night.

V

Villainy somewhere ! whose ? One says,
we are villains all.
Not he; his honest fame should at least by
me be maintained;
But that old man, now lord of the broad
estate and the Hall,
Dropt off gorged from a scheme that had
left us flaccid and drain'd.   20

VI

Why do they prate of the blessings of
peace ? we have made them a curse,
Pickpockets, each hand lusting for all that
is not its own;
And lust of gain, in the spirit of Cain, is it
better or worse
Than the heart of the citizen hissing in war
on his own hearthstone ?

VII

But these are the days of advance, the
works of the men of mind,
When who but a fool would have faith in a
tradesman's ware or his word ?
Is it peace or war ?   Civil war, as I think,
and that of a kind
The viler, as underhand, not openly bearing
the sword.

VIII

Sooner or later I too may passively take
the print
Of the golden age — why not ?   I have
neither hope nor trust;   30
May make my heart as a millstone, set my
face as a flint,
Cheat and be cheated, and die — who
knows ? we are ashes and dust.

IX

Peace sitting under her olive, and slurring
the days gone by,
When the poor are hovell'd and hustled
together, each sex, like swine,
When only the ledger lives, and when only
not all men lie;
Peace in her vineyard — yes ! — but a com-
pany forges the wine.

X

And the vitriol madness flushes up in the
ruffian's head,
Till the filthy by-lane rings to the yell of
the trampled wife,
And chalk and alum and plaster are sold to
the poor for bread,
And the spirit of murder works in the very
means of life,   40

XI

And Sleep must lie down arm'd, for the vil-
lainous centre-bits
Grind on the wakeful ear in the hush of the
moonless nights,

While another is cheating the sick of a few
    last gasps, as he sits
To pestle a poison'd poison behind his crim-
    son lights.

XII

When a Mammonite mother kills her babe
    for a burial fee,
And Timour-Mammon grins on a pile of
    children's bones,
Is it peace or war? better, war! loud war
    by land and by sea,
War with a thousand battles, and shaking
    a hundred thrones!

XIII

For I trust if an enemy's fleet came yonder
    round by the hill,
And the rushing battle-bolt sang from the
    three-decker out of the foam,   50
That the smooth-faced, snub-nosed rogue
    would leap from his counter and till,
And strike, if he could, were it but with his
    cheating yardwand, home. —

XIV

What! am I raging alone as my father
    raged in his mood?
Must *I* too creep to the hollow and dash
    myself down and die
Rather than hold by the law that I made,
    nevermore to brood
On a horror of shatter'd limbs and a
    wretched swindler's lie?

XV

Would there be sorrow for *me?* there was
    love in the passionate shriek,
Love for the silent thing that had made
    false haste to the grave —
Wrapt in a cloak, as I saw him, and thought
    he would rise and speak
And rave at the lie and the liar, ah God, as
    he used to rave.   60

XVI

I am sick of the Hall and the hill, I am
    sick of the moor and the main.
Why should I stay? can a sweeter chance
    ever come to me here?
O, having the nerves of motion as well as
    the nerves of pain,
Were it not wise if I fled from the place
    and the pit and the fear?

XVII

Workmen up at the Hall! — they are com-
    ing back from abroad;
The dark old place will be gilt by the touch
    of a millionaire.
I have heard, I know not whence, of the
    singular beauty of Maud;
I play'd with the girl when a child; she
    promised then to be fair.

XVIII

Maud, with her venturous climbings and
    tumbles and childish escapes,
Maud, the delight of the village, the ring-
    ing joy of the Hall,   70
Maud, with her sweet purse-mouth when
    my father dangled the grapes,
Maud, the beloved of my mother, the
    moon-faced darling of all, —

XIX

What is she now? My dreams are bad.
    She may bring me a curse.
No, there is fatter game on the moor; she
    will let me alone.
Thanks; for the fiend best knows whether
    woman or man be the worse.
I will bury myself in myself, and the Devil
    may pipe to his own.

II

Long have I sigh'd for a calm; God grant
    I may find it at last!
It will never be broken by Maud; she has
    neither savor nor salt,
But a cold and clear-cut face, as I found
    when her carriage past,
Perfectly beautiful; let it be granted her;
    where is the fault?   80
All that I saw — for her eyes were down-
    cast, not to be seen —
Faultily faultless, icily regular, splendidly
    null,
Dead perfection, no more; nothing more,
    if it had not been
For a chance of travel, a paleness, an hour's
    defect of the rose,
Or an underlip, you may call it a little too
    ripe, too full,
Or the least little delicate aquiline curve
    in a sensitive nose,
From which I escaped heart-free, with the
    least little touch of spleen.

III

Cold and clear-cut face, why come you so
    cruelly meek,
Breaking a slumber in which all spleenful
    folly was drown'd ?
Pale with the golden beam of an eyelash
    dead on the cheek,   90
Passionless, pale, cold face, star-sweet on
    a gloom profound;
Womanlike, taking revenge too deep for a
    transient wrong
Done but in thought to your beauty, and
    ever as pale as before
Growing and fading and growing upon me
    without a sound,
Luminous, gemlike, ghostlike, deathlike,
    half the night long
Growing and fading and growing, till I
    could bear it no more,
But arose, and all by myself in my own
    dark garden ground,
Listening now to the tide in its broad-flung
    shipwrecking roar,
Now to the scream of a madden'd beach
    dragg'd down by the wave,
Walk'd in a wintry wind by a ghastly
    glimmer, and found   100
The shining daffodil dead, and Orion low
    in his grave.

IV

I

A million emeralds break from the ruby-
    budded lime
In the little grove where I sit — ah, where-
    fore cannot I be
Like things of the season gay, like the
    bountiful season bland,
When the far-off sail is blown by the breeze
    of a softer clime,
Half-lost in the liquid azure bloom of a
    crescent of sea,
The silent sapphire-spangled marriage ring
    of the land ?

II

Below me, there, is the village, and looks
    how quiet and small !
And yet bubbles o'er like a city, with gos-
    sip, scandal, and spite;
And Jack on his ale-house bench has as
    many lies as a Czar;   110

And here on the landward side, by a red
    rock, glimmers the Hall;
And up in the high Hall-garden I see her
    pass like a light;
But sorrow seize me if ever that light be
    my leading star !

III

When have I bow'd to her father, the
    wrinkled head of the race ?
I met her to-day with her brother, but not
    to her brother I bow'd;
I bow'd to his lady-sister as she rode by on
    the moor,
But the fire of a foolish pride flash'd over
    her beautiful face.
O child, you wrong your beauty, believe it,
    in being so proud;
Your father has wealth well-gotten, and I
    am nameless and poor.

IV

I keep but a man and a maid, ever ready
    to slander and steal;   120
I know it, and smile a hard-set smile, like
    a stoic, or like
A wiser epicurean, and let the world have
    its way.
For nature is one with rapine, a harm no
    preacher can heal;
The Mayfly is torn by the swallow, the
    sparrow spear'd by the shrike,
And the whole little wood where I sit is a
    world of plunder and prey.

V

We are puppets, Man in his pride, and
    Beauty fair in her flower;
Do we move ourselves, or are moved by an
    unseen hand at a game
That pushes us off from the board, and
    others ever succeed ?
Ah yet, we cannot be kind to each other
    here for an hour;
We whisper, and hint, and chuckle, and
    grin at a brother's shame;   130
However we brave it out, we men are a
    little breed.

VI

A monstrous eft was of old the lord and
    master of earth,
For him did his high sun flame, and his
    river billowing ran,
And he felt himself in his force to be Na-
    ture's crowning race.

As nine months go to the shaping an infant
　　ripe for his birth,
So many a million of ages have gone to the
　　making of man:
He now is first, but is he the last? is he
　　not too base?

VII

The man of science himself is fonder of
　　glory, and vain,
An eye well-practised in nature, a spirit
　　bounded and poor;
The passionate heart of the poet is whirl'd
　　into folly and vice.　　　　140
I would not marvel at either, but keep a
　　temperate brain;
For not to desire or admire, if a man could
　　learn it, were more
Than to walk all day like the sultan of old
　　in a garden of spice.

VIII

For the drift of the Maker is dark, an Isis
　　hid by the veil.
Who knows the ways of the world, how
　　God will bring them about?
Our planet is one, the suns are many, the
　　world is wide.
Shall I weep if a Poland fall? shall I shriek
　　if a Hungary fail?
Or an infant civilization be ruled with rod
　　or with knout?
I have not made the world, and He that
　　made it will guide.

IX

Be mine a philosopher's life in the quiet
　　woodland ways,　　　　150
Where if I cannot be gay let a passionless
　　peace be my lot,
Far-off from the clamor of liars belied in
　　the hubbub of lies;
From the long-neck'd geese of the world
　　that are ever hissing dispraise
Because their natures are little, and,
　　whether he heed it or not,
Where each man walks with his head in a
　　cloud of poisonous flies.

X

And most of all would I flee from the cruel
　　madness of love
The honey of poison-flowers and all the
　　measureless ill.
Ah, Maud, you milk-white fawn, you are
　　all unmeet for a wife.

Your mother is mute in her grave as her
　　image in marble above;
Your father is ever in London, you wander
　　about at your will;　　　160
You have but fed on the roses and lain in
　　the lilies of life.

V

I

A voice by the cedar tree
In the meadow under the Hall!
She is singing an air that is known to me,
A passionate ballad gallant and gay,
A martial song like a trumpet's call!
Singing alone in the morning of life,
In the happy morning of life and of May,
Singing of men that in battle array,
Ready in heart and ready in hand,　　　170
March with banner and bugle and fife
To the death, for their native land.

II

Maud with her exquisite face,
And wild voice pealing up to the sunny sky,
And feet like sunny gems on an English
　　green,
Maud in the light of her youth and her
　　grace,
Singing of Death, and of Honor that can-
　　not die,
Till I well could weep for a time so sordid
　　and mean,
And myself so languid and base.

III

Silence, beautiful voice!　　　180
Be still, for you only trouble the mind
With a joy in which I cannot rejoice,
A glory I shall not find.
Still! I will hear you no more,
For your sweetness hardly leaves me a
　　choice
But to move to the meadow and fall before
Her feet on the meadow grass, and adore,
Not her, who is neither courtly nor kind,
Not her, not her, but a voice.

VI

I

Morning arises stormy and pale,　　　190
No sun, but a wannish glare
In fold upon fold of hueless cloud;

And the budded peaks of the wood are bow'd,
Caught, and cuff'd by the gale:
I had fancied it would be fair.

II

Whom but Maud should I meet
Last night, when the sunset burn'd
On the blossom'd gable-ends
At the head of the village street,
Whom but Maud should I meet ? 200
And she touch'd my hand with a smile so sweet,
She made me divine amends
For a courtesy not return'd.

III

And thus a delicate spark
Of glowing and growing light
Thro' the livelong hours of the dark
Kept itself warm in the heart of my dreams,
Ready to burst in a color'd flame;
Till at last, when the morning came
In a cloud, it faded, and seems 210
But an ashen-gray delight.

IV

What if with her sunny hair,
And smile as sunny as cold,
She meant to weave me a snare
Of some coquettish deceit,
Cleopatra-like as of old
To entangle me when we met,
To have her lion roll in a silken net
And fawn at a victor's feet.

V

Ah, what shall I be at fifty 220
Should Nature keep me alive,
If I find the world so bitter
When I am but twenty-five ?
Yet, if she were not a cheat,
If Maud were all that she seem'd,
And her smile were all that I dream'd,
Then the world were not so bitter
But a smile could make it sweet.

VI

What if, tho' her eye seem'd full
Of a kind intent to me, 230
What if that dandy-despot, he,
That jewell'd mass of millinery,
That oil'd and curl'd Assyrian bull
Smelling of musk and of insolence,
Her brother, from whom I keep aloof,
Who wants the finer politic sense
To mask, tho' but in his own behoof,
With a glassy smile his brutal scorn —
What if he had told her yestermorn
How prettily for his own sweet sake 240
A face of tenderness might be feign'd,
And a moist mirage in desert eyes,
That so, when the rotten hustings shake
In another month to his brazen lies,
A wretched vote may be gain'd ?

VII

For a raven ever croaks, at my side,
Keep watch and ward, keep watch and ward,
Or thou wilt prove their tool.
Yea, too, myself from myself I guard,
For often a man's own angry pride 250
Is cap and bells for a fool.

VIII

Perhaps the smile and tender tone
Came out of her pitying womanhood,
For am I not, am I not, here alone
So many a summer since she died,
My mother, who was so gentle and good ?
Living alone in an empty house,
Here half-hid in the gleaming wood,
Where I hear the dead at midday moan,
And the shrieking rush of the wainscot mouse, 260
And my own sad name in corners cried,
When the shiver of dancing leaves is thrown
About its echoing chambers wide,
Till a morbid hate and horror have grown
Of a world in which I have hardly mixt,
And a morbid eating lichen fixt
On a heart half-turn'd to stone.

IX

O heart of stone, are you flesh, and caught
By that you swore to withstand ? 269
For what was it else within me wrought
But, I fear, the new strong wine of love,
That made my tongue so stammer and trip
When I saw the treasured splendor, her hand,
Come sliding out of her sacred glove,
And the sunlight broke from her lip ?

X

I have play'd with her when a child;
She remembers it now we meet.

Ah, well, well, well, I *may* be beguiled
By some coquettish deceit.
Yet, if she were not a cheat,   280
If Maud were all that she seem'd,
And her smile had all that I dream'd,
Then the world were not so bitter
But a smile could make it sweet.

VII

I

Did I hear it half in a doze
   Long since, I know not where ?
Did I dream it an hour ago,
   When asleep in this arm-chair ?

II

Men were drinking together,
   Drinking and talking of me: 290
' Well, if it prove a girl, the boy
   Will have plenty; so let it be.'

III

Is it an echo of something
   Read with a boy's delight,
Viziers nodding together
   In some Arabian night ?

IV

Strange, that I hear two men,
   Somewhere, talking of me:
' Well, if it prove a girl, my boy
   Will have plenty; so let it be.'   300

VIII

She came to the village church,
And sat by a pillar alone;
An angel watching an urn
Wept over her, carved in stone;
And once, but once, she lifted her eyes,
And suddenly, sweetly, strangely blush'd
To find they were met by my own;
And suddenly, sweetly, my heart beat
   stronger
And thicker, until I heard no longer
The snowy-banded, dilettante,   310
Delicate-handed priest intone;
And thought, is it pride ? and mused and
   sigh'd,
' No surely, now it cannot be pride.'

IX

I was walking a mile,
More than a mile from the shore,
The sun look'd out with a smile
Betwixt the cloud and the moor;
And riding at set of day
Over the dark moor land,
Rapidly riding far away,   320
She waved to me with her hand.
There were two at her side,
Something flash'd in the sun,
Down by the hill I saw them ride,
In a moment they were gone;
Like a sudden spark
Struck vainly in the night,
Then returns the dark
With no more hope of light.

X

I

Sick, am I sick of a jealous dread ?   330
Was not one of the two at her side
This new-made lord, whose splendor plucks
The slavish hat from the villager's head ?
Whose old grandfather has lately died,
Gone to a blacker pit, for whom
Grimy nakedness dragging his trucks
And laying his trams in a poison'd gloom
Wrought, till he crept from a gutted mine
Master of half a servile shire,
And left his coal all turn'd into gold   340
To a grandson, first of his noble line,
Rich in the grace all women desire,
Strong in the power that all men adore,
And simper and set their voices lower,
And soften as if to a girl, and hold
Awe-stricken breaths at a work divine,
Seeing his gewgaw castle shine,
New as his title, built last year,
There amid perky larches and pine,
And over the sullen-purple moor —   350
Look at it — pricking a cockney ear.

II

What, has he found my jewel out ?
For one of the two that rode at her side
Bound for the Hall, I am sure was he;
Bound for the Hall, and I think for a
   bride.
Blithe would her brother's acceptance be.

Maud could be gracious too, no doubt,
To a lord, a captain, a padded shape,
A bought commission, a waxen face,
A rabbit mouth that is ever agape —   360
Bought ? what is it he cannot buy ?
And therefore splenetic, personal, base,
A wounded thing with a rancorous cry,
At war with myself and a wretched race,
Sick, sick to the heart of life, am I.

III

Last week came one to the county town,
To preach our poor little army down,
And play the game of the despot kings,
Tho' the state has done it and thrice as
        well.   369
This broad-brimm'd hawker of holy things,
Whose ear is cramm'd with his cotton, and
        rings
Even in dreams to the chink of his pence,
This huckster put down war ! can he tell
Whether war be a cause or a consequence ?
Put down the passions that make earth
        hell !
Down with ambition, avarice, pride,
Jealousy, down ! cut off from the mind
The bitter springs of anger and fear!
Down too, down at your own fireside,
With the evil tongue and the evil ear,   380
For each is at war with mankind !

IV

I wish I could hear again
The chivalrous battle-song
That she warbled alone in her joy !
I might persuade myself then
She would not do herself this great wrong,
To take a wanton dissolute boy
For a man and leader of men.

V

Ah God, for a man with heart, head,
        hand,
Like some of the simple great ones gone
For ever and ever by,   391
One still strong man in a blatant land,
Whatever they call him — what care I ? —
Aristocrat, democrat, autocrat — one
Who can rule and dare not lie !

VI

And ah for a man to arise in me,
That the man I am may cease to be !

XI

I

O, let the solid ground
    Not fail beneath my feet
Before my life has found   400
    What some have found so sweet !
Then let come what come may,
What matter if I go mad,
I shall have had my day.

II

Let the sweet heavens endure,
    Not close and darken above me
Before I am quite quite sure
    That there is one to love me !
Then let come what come may
To a life that has been so sad,   410
I shall have had my day.

XII

I

Birds in the high Hall-garden
    When twilight was falling,
Maud, Maud, Maud, Maud,
    They were crying and calling.

II

Where was Maud ? in our wood;
    And I — who else ? — was with her,
Gathering woodland lilies,
    Myriads blow together.

III

Birds in our wood sang   420
    Ringing thro' the valleys,
Maud is here, here, here
    In among the lilies.

IV

I kiss'd her slender hand,
    She took the kiss sedately;
Maud is not seventeen,
    But she is tall and stately.

V

I to cry out on pride
    Who have won her favor !
O, Maud were sure of heaven   430
    If lowliness could save her !

VI

I know the way she went
　Home with her maiden posy,
For her feet have touch'd the meadows
　And left the daisies rosy.

VII

Birds in the high Hall-garden
　Were crying and calling to her,
Where is Maud, Maud, Maud ?
　One is come to woo her.

VIII

Look, a horse at the door,　　　440
　And little King Charley snarling !
Go back, my lord, across the moor,
　You are not her darling.

XIII

I

Scorn'd, to be scorn'd by one that I scorn,
Is that a matter to make me fret ?
That a calamity hard to be borne ?
Well, he may live to hate me yet.
Fool that I am to be vext with his pride !
I past him, I was crossing his lands;
He stood on the path a little aside;　450
His face, as I grant, in spite of spite,
Has a broad-blown comeliness, red and
　　white,
And six feet two, as I think, he stands;
But his essences turn'd the live air sick,
And barbarous opulence jewel-thick
Sunn'd itself on his breast and his hands.

II

Who shall call me ungentle, unfair ?
I long'd so heartily then and there
To give him the grasp of fellowship;
But while I past he was humming an air, 460
Stopt, and then with a riding-whip
Leisurely tapping a glossy boot,
And curving a contumelious lip,
Gorgonized me from head to foot
With a stony British stare.

III

Why sits he here in his father's chair ?
That old man never comes to his place;
Shall I believe him ashamed to be seen ?
For only once, in the village street,　469

Last year, I caught a glimpse of his face,
A gray old wolf and a lean.
Scarcely, now, would I call him a cheat;
For then, perhaps, as a child of deceit,
She might by a true descent be untrue;
And Maud is as true as Maud is sweet,
Tho' I fancy her sweetness only due
To the sweeter blood by the other side;
Her mother has been a thing complete,
However she came to be so allied.
And fair without, faithful within,　　480
Maud to him is nothing akin.
Some peculiar mystic grace
Made her only the child of her mother,
And heap'd the whole inherited sin
On that huge scapegoat of the race,
All, all upon the brother.

IV

Peace, angry spirit, and let him be !
Has not his sister smiled on me ?

XIV

I

Maud has a garden of roses
And lilies fair on a lawn;　　　490
There she walks in her state
And tends upon bed and bower,
And thither I climb'd at dawn
And stood by her garden-gate.
A lion ramps at the top,
He is claspt by a passion-flower.

II

Maud's own little oak-room —
Which Maud, like a precious stone
Set in the heart of the carven gloom,
Lights with herself, when alone　500
She sits by her music and books
And her brother lingers late
With a roystering company — looks
Upon Maud's own garden-gate;
And I thought as I stood, if a hand, as
　　white
As ocean-foam in the moon, were laid
On the hasp of the window, and my De-
　　light
Had a sudden desire, like a glorious ghost,
　to glide,
Like a beam of the seventh heaven, down
　to my side,
There were but a step to be made.　510

III

The fancy flatter'd my mind,
And again seem'd overbold;
Now I thought that she cared for me,
Now I thought she was kind
Only because she was cold.

IV

I heard no sound where I stood
But the rivulet on from the lawn
Running down to my own dark wood,
Or the voice of the long sea-wave as it
swell'd
Now and then in the dim-gray dawn; 520
But I look'd, and round, all round the
house I beheld
The death-white curtain drawn,
Felt a horror over me creep,
Prickle my skin and catch my breath,
Knew that the death-white curtain meant
but sleep,
Yet I shudder'd and thought like a fool of
the sleep of death.

XV

So dark a mind within me dwells,
And I make myself such evil cheer,
That if *I* be dear to some one else,
Then some one else may have much to
fear; 530
But if *I* be dear to some one else,
Then I should be to myself more dear.
Shall I not take care of all that I think,
Yea, even of wretched meat and drink,
If I be dear,
If I be dear to some one else ?

XVI

I

This lump of earth has left his estate
The lighter by the loss of his weight;
And so that he find what he went to seek,
And fulsome pleasure clog him, and
drown 540
His heart in the gross mud-honey of town,
He may stay for a year who has gone for a
week.
But this is the day when I must speak,
And I see my Oread coming down,
O, this is the day !

O beautiful creature, what am I
That I dare to look her way ?
Think I may hold dominion sweet,
Lord of the pulse that is lord of her breast,
And dream of her beauty with tender
dread, 550
From the delicate Arab arch of her feet
To the grace that, bright and light as the
crest
Of a peacock, sits on her shining head,
And she knows it not — O, if she knew it,
To know her beauty might half undo it !
I know it the one bright thing to save
My yet young life in the wilds of Time,
Perhaps from madness, perhaps from crime,
Perhaps from a selfish grave.

II

What, if she be fasten'd to this fool lord,
Dare I bid her abide by her word ? 561
Should I love her so well if she
Had given her word to a thing so low ?
Shall I love her as well if she
Can break her word were it even for me ?
I trust that it is not so.

III

Catch not my breath, O clamorous heart,
Let not my tongue be a thrall to my eye,
For I must tell her before we part,
I must tell her, or die. 570

XVII

Go not, happy day,
From the shining fields,
Go not, happy day,
Till the maiden yields.
Rosy is the West,
Rosy is the South,
Roses are her cheeks,
And a rose her mouth.
When the happy Yes
Falters from her lips, 580
Pass and blush the news
Over glowing ships;
Over blowing seas,
Over seas at rest,
Pass the happy news,
Blush it thro' the West;
Till the red man dance
By his red cedar-tree,
And the red man's babe
Leap, beyond the sea. 599

Blush from West to East,
  Blush from East to West,
Till the West is East,
  Blush it thro' the West.
Rosy is the West,
  Rosy is the South,
Roses are her cheeks,
  And a rose her mouth.

XVIII

I

I have led her home, my love, my only
    friend.
There is none like her, none.   600
And never yet so warmly ran my blood
And sweetly, on and on
Calming itself to the long-wish'd-for end,
Full to the banks, close on the promised
    good.

II

None like her, none.
Just now the dry-tongued laurels' pattering
    talk
Seem'd her light foot along the garden
    walk,
And shook my heart to think she comes
    once more.
But even then I heard her close the door;
The gates of heaven are closed, and she is
    gone.   610

III

There is none like her, none,
Nor will be when our summers have de-
    ceased.
O, art thou sighing for Lebanon
In the long breeze that streams to thy de-
    licious East,
Sighing for Lebanon,
Dark cedar, tho' thy limbs have here in-
    creased,
Upon a pastoral slope as fair,
And looking to the South and fed
With honey'd rain and delicate air,
And haunted by the starry head   620
Of her whose gentle will has changed my
    fate,
And made my life a perfumed altar-flame;
And over whom thy darkness must have
    spread
With such delight as theirs of old, thy
    great

Forefathers of the thornless garden, there
Shadowing the snow-limb'd Eve from
    whom she came ?

IV

Here will I lie, while these long branches
    sway,
And you fair stars that crown a happy day
Go in and out as if at merry play,
Who am no more so all forlorn   630
As when it seem'd far better to be born
To labor and the mattock-harden'd hand
Than nursed at ease and brought to under-
    stand
A sad astrology, the boundless plan
That makes you tyrants in your iron skies,
Innumerable, pitiless, passionless eyes,
Cold fires, yet with power to burn and
    brand
His nothingness into man.

V

But now shine on, and what care I,
Who in this stormy gulf have found a
    pearl   640
The countercharm of space and hollow
    sky,
And do accept my madness, and would
    die
To save from some slight shame one sim-
    ple girl ? —

VI

Would die, for sullen-seeming Death may
    give
More life to Love than is or ever was
In our low world, where yet 't is sweet to
    live.
Let no one ask me how it came to pass;
It seems that I am happy, that to me
A livelier emerald twinkles in the grass,
A purer sapphire melts into the sea.   650

VII

Not die, but live a life of truest breath,
And teach true life to fight with mortal
    wrongs.
O, why should Love, like men in drinking-
    songs,
Spice his fair banquet with the dust of
    death ?
Make answer, Maud my bliss,
Maud made my Maud by that long loving
    kiss,
Life of my life, wilt thou not answer this ?

'The dusky strand of Death inwoven here
With dear Love's tie, makes Love himself
   more dear.'

VIII

Is that enchanted moan only the swell   660
Of the long waves that roll in yonder bay ?
And hark the clock within, the silver knell
Of twelve sweet hours that past in bridal
   white,
And died to live, long as my pulses play;
But now by this my love has closed her
   sight
And given false death her hand, and stolen
   away
To dreamful wastes where footless fancies
   dwell
Among the fragments of the golden day.
May nothing there her maiden grace af-
   fright !
Dear heart, I feel with thee the drowsy
   spell.   670
My bride to be, my evermore delight,
My own heart's heart, my ownest own,
   farewell;
It is but for a little space I go.
And ye meanwhile far over moor and fell
Beat to the noiseless music of the night !
Has our whole earth gone nearer to the
   glow
Of your soft splendors that you look so
   bright ?
I have climb'd nearer out of lonely hell.
Beat, happy stars, timing with things be-
   low,
Beat with my heart more blest than heart
   can tell,   680
Blest, but for some dark undercurrent woe
That seems to draw — but it shall not be
   so;
Let all be well, be well.

XIX

I

Her brother is coming back to-night,
Breaking up my dream of delight.

II

My dream ? do I dream of bliss ?
I have walk'd awake with Truth.
O, when did a morning shine
So rich in atonement as this
For my dark-dawning youth,   690

Darken'd watching a mother decline
And that dead man at her heart and mine;
For who was left to watch her but I ?
Yet so did I let my freshness die.

III

I trust that I did not talk
To gentle Maud in our walk —
For often in lonely wanderings
I have cursed him even to lifeless things —
But I trust that I did not talk,
Not touch on her father's sin.   700
I am sure I did but speak
Of my mother's faded cheek
When it slowly grew so thin
That I felt she was slowly dying
Vext with lawyers and harass'd with debt;
For how often I caught her with eyes all
   wet,
Shaking her head at her son and sighing
A world of trouble within !

IV

And Maud too, Maud was moved
To speak of the mother she loved   710
As one scarce less forlorn,
Dying abroad and it seems apart
From him who had ceased to share her
   heart,
And ever mourning over the feud,
The household Fury sprinkled with blood
By which our houses are torn.
How strange was what she said,
When only Maud and the brother
Hung over her dying bed —
That Maud's dark father and mine   720
Had bound us one to the other,
Betrothed us over their wine,
On the day when Maud was born;
Seal'd her mine from her first sweet breath!
Mine, mine by a right, from birth till death!
Mine, mine — our fathers have sworn!

V

But the true blood spilt had in it a heat
To dissolve the precious seal on a bond,
That, if left uncancell'd, had been so sweet;
And none of us thought of a something
   beyond,   730
A desire that awoke in the heart of the
   child,
As it were a duty done to the tomb,
To be friends for her sake, to be recon-
   ciled;
And I was cursing them and my doom,

And letting a dangerous thought run
    wild
While often abroad in the fragrant gloom
Of foreign churches — I see her there,
Bright English lily, breathing a prayer
To be friends, to be reconciled!

VI

But then what a flint is he!   740
Abroad, at Florence, at Rome,
I find whenever she touch'd on me
This brother had laugh'd her down,
And at last, when each came home,
He had darken'd into a frown,
Chid her, and forbid her to speak
To me, her friend of the years before;
And this was what had redden'd her
    cheek
When I bow'd to her on the moor.

VII

Yet Maud, altho' not blind   750
To the faults of his heart and mind,
I see she cannot but love him,
And says he is rough but kind,
And wishes me to approve him,
And tells me, when she lay
Sick once, with a fear of worse,
That he left his wine and horses and
    play,
Sat with her, read to her, night and day,
And tended her like a nurse.

VIII

Kind? but the death-bed desire   760
Spurn'd by this heir of the liar —
Rough but kind? yet I know
He has plotted against me in this,
That he plots against me still.
Kind to Maud? that were not amiss.
Well, rough but kind; why, let it be so,
For shall not Maud have her will?

IX

For, Maud, so tender and true,
As long as my life endures
I feel I shall owe you a debt   770
That I never can hope to pay;
And if ever I should forget
That I owe this debt to you
And for your sweet sake to yours,
O, then, what then shall I say? —
If ever I *should* forget,
May God make me more wretched
Than ever I have been yet!

X

So now I have sworn to bury
All this dead body of hate,   780
I feel so free and so clear
By the loss of that dead weight,
That I should grow light-headed, I fear,
Fantastically merry,
But that her brother comes, like a blight
On my fresh hope, to the Hall to-night.

XX

I

Strange, that I felt so gay,
Strange, that I tried to-day
To beguile her melancholy;
The Sultan, as we name him —   790
She did not wish to blame him —
But he vext her and perplext her
With his worldly talk and folly.
Was it gentle to reprove her
For stealing out of view
From a little lazy lover
Who but claims her as his due?
Or for chilling his caresses
By the coldness of her manners,
Nay, the plainness of her dresses?   800
Now I know her but in two,
Nor can pronounce upon it
If one should ask me whether
The habit, hat, and feather,
Or the frock and gipsy bonnet
Be the neater and completer;
For nothing can be sweeter
Than maiden Maud in either.

II

But to-morrow, if we live,
Our ponderous squire will give   810
A grand political dinner
To half the squirelings near;
And Maud will wear her jewels,
And the bird of prey will hover,
And the titmouse hope to win her
With his chirrup at her ear.

III

A grand political dinner
To the men of many acres,
A gathering of the Tory,
A dinner and then a dance   820
For the maids and marriage-makers,
And every eye but mine will glance
At Maud in all her glory.

IV

For I am not invited,
But, with the Sultan's pardon,
I am all as well delighted,
For I know her own rose-garden,
And mean to linger in it
Till the dancing will be over;
And then, O, then, come out to me 830
For a minute, but for a minute,
Come out to your own true lover,
That your true lover may see
Your glory also, and render
All homage to his own darling,
Queen Maud in all her splendor.

XXI

Rivulet crossing my ground,
And bringing me down from the Hall
This garden-rose that I found,
Forgetful of Maud and me, 840
And lost in trouble and moving round
Here at the head of a tinkling fall,
And trying to pass to the sea;
O rivulet, born at the Hall,
My Maud has sent it by thee —
If I read her sweet will right —
On a blushing mission to me,
Saying in odor and color, ' Ah, be
Among the roses to-night.'

XXII

I

Come into the garden, Maud, 850
For the black bat, night, has flown,
Come into the garden, Maud,
I am here at the gate alone;
And the woodbine spices are wafted abroad,
And the musk of the rose is blown.

II

For a breeze of morning moves,
And the planet of Love is on high,
Beginning to faint in the light that she
loves
On a bed of daffodil sky,
To faint in the light of the sun she loves,
To faint in his light, and to die. 861

III

All night have the roses heard
The flute, violin, bassoon;

All night has the casement jessamine stirr'd
To the dancers dancing in tune;
Till a silence fell with the waking bird,
And a hush with the setting moon.

IV

I said to the lily, ' There is but one,
With whom she has heart to be gay.
When will the dancers leave her alone ? 870
She is weary of dance and play.'
Now half to the setting moon are gone,
And half to the rising day;
Low on the sand and loud on the stone
The last wheel echoes away.

V

I said to the rose, ' The brief night goes
In babble and revel and wine.
O young lord-lover, what sighs are those,
For one that will never be thine ?
But mine, but mine,' so I sware to the
rose, 880
' For ever and ever, mine.'

VI

And the soul of the rose went into my
blood,
As the music clash'd in the hall;
And long by the garden lake I stood,
For I heard your rivulet fall
From the lake to the meadow and on to the
wood,
Our wood, that is dearer than all;

VII

From the meadow your walks have left so
sweet
That whenever a March-wind sighs
He sets the jewel-print of your feet 890
In violets blue as your eyes,
To the woody hollows in which we meet
And the valleys of Paradise.

VIII

The slender acacia would not shake
One long milk-bloom on the tree;
The white lake - blossom fell into the
lake
As the pimpernel dozed on the lea;
But the rose was awake all night for your
sake,
Knowing your promise to me;
The lilies and roses were all awake, 900
They sigh'd for the dawn and thee.

IX

Queen rose of the rosebud garden of girls,
  Come hither, the dances are done,
In gloss of satin and glimmer of pearls,
  Queen lily and rose in one;
Shine out, little head, sunning over with
    curls,
  To the flowers, and be their sun.

X

There has fallen a splendid tear
  From the passion-flower at the gate.
She is coming, my dove, my dear;   910
  She is coming, my life, my fate.
The red rose cries, 'She is near, she is
    near;'
  And the white rose weeps, 'She is late;'
The larkspur listens, 'I hear, I hear;'
  And the lily whispers, 'I wait.'

XI

She is coming, my own, my sweet;
  Were it ever so airy a tread,
My heart would hear her and beat,
  Were it earth in an earthy bed;
My dust would hear her and beat,   920
  Had I lain for a century dead,
Would start and tremble under her feet,
  And blossom in purple and red.

PART II

I

I

'The fault was mine, the fault was mine'—
Why am I sitting here so stunn'd and still,
Plucking the harmless wild-flower on the
    hill?—
It is this guilty hand!—
And there rises ever a passionate cry
From underneath in the darkening land—
What is it, that has been done?
O dawn of Eden bright over earth and sky,
The fires of hell brake out of thy rising
    sun,
The fires of hell and of hate;   10
For she, sweet soul, had hardly spoken a
    word,
When her brother ran in his rage to the
    gate,
He came with the babe-faced lord,
Heap'd on her terms of disgrace;

And while she wept, and I strove to be cool,
He fiercely gave me the lie,
Till I with as fierce an anger spoke,
And he struck me, madman, over the face,
Struck me before the languid fool,
Who was gaping and grinning by;   20
Struck for himself an evil stroke,
Wrought for his house an irredeemable
    woe.
For front to front in an hour we stood,
And a million horrible bellowing echoes
    broke
From the red-ribb'd hollow behind the
    wood,
And thunder'd up into heaven the Christless
    code
That must have life for a blow.
Ever and ever afresh they seem'd to grow.
Was it he lay there with a fading eye?
'The fault was mine,' he whisper'd, 'fly!'
Then glided out of the joyous wood   31
The ghastly Wraith of one that I know,
And there rang on a sudden a passionate
    cry,
A cry for a brother's blood;
It will ring in my heart and my ears, till I
    die, till I die.

II

Is it gone? my pulses beat—
What was it? a lying trick of the brain?
Yet I thought I saw her stand,
A shadow there at my feet,
High over the shadowy land.   40
It is gone; and the heavens fall in a gentle
    rain,
When they should burst and drown with
    deluging storms
The feeble vassals of wine and anger and
    lust,
The little hearts that know not how to for-
    give.
Arise, my God, and strike, for we hold
    Thee just,
Strike dead the whole weak race of venom-
    ous worms,
That sting each other here in the dust;
We are not worthy to live.

II

I

See what a lovely shell,
Small and pure as a pearl,   50

Lying close to my foot,
Frail, but a work divine,
Made so fairily well
With delicate spire and whorl,
How exquisitely minute,
A miracle of design !

II

What is it ? a learned man
Could give it a clumsy name.
Let him name it who can,
The beauty would be the same.   60

III

The tiny cell is forlorn,
Void of the little living will
That made it stir on the shore.
Did he stand at the diamond door
Of his house in a rainbow frill ?
Did he push, when he was uncurl'd,
A golden foot or a fairy horn
Thro' his dim water-world ?

IV

Slight, to be crush'd with a tap
Of my finger-nail on the sand,   70
Small, but a work divine,
Frail, but of force to withstand,
Year upon year, the shock
Of cataract seas that snap
The three-decker's oaken spine
Athwart the ledges of rock,
Here on the Breton strand !

V

Breton, not Briton; here
Like a shipwreck'd man on a coast
Of ancient fable and fear —   80
Plagued with a flitting to and fro,
A disease, a hard mechanic ghost
That never came from on high
Nor ever arose from below,
But only moves with the moving eye,
Flying along the land and the main —
Why should it look like Maud ?
Am I to be overawed
By what I cannot but know
Is a juggle born of the brain ?   90

VI

Back from the Breton coast,
Sick of a nameless fear,
Back to the dark sea-line
Looking, thinking of all I have lost;

An old song vexes my ear,
But that of Lamech is mine.

VII

For years, a measureless ill,
For years, for ever, to part —
But she, she would love me still;
And as long, O God, as she   100
Have a grain of love for me,
So long, no doubt, no doubt,
Shall I nurse in my dark heart,
However weary, a spark of will
Not to be trampled out.

VIII

Strange, that the mind, when fraught
With a passion so intense
One would think that it well
Might drown all life in the eye, —   109
That it should, by being so overwrought,
Suddenly strike on a sharper sense
For a shell, or a flower, little things
Which else would have been past by !
And now I remember, I,
When he lay dying there,
I noticed one of his many rings —
For he had many, poor worm — and
          thought,
It is his mother's hair.

IX

Who knows if he be dead ?
Whether I need have fled ?   120
Am I guilty of blood ?
However this may be,
Comfort her, comfort her, all things good,
While I am over the sea !
Let me and my passionate love go by,
But speak to her all things holy and high,
Whatever happen to me !
Me and my harmful love go by;
But come to her waking, find her asleep,
Powers of the height, Powers of the deep,
And comfort her tho' I die !   131

III

Courage, poor heart of stone !
I will not ask thee why
Thou canst not understand
That thou art left for ever alone;
Courage, poor stupid heart of stone ! —
Or if I ask thee why,

Care not thou to reply:
She is but dead, and the time is at hand
When thou shalt more than die.　　140

IV

I

O that 't were possible
After long grief and pain
To find the arms of my true love
Round me once again !

II

When I was wont to meet her
In the silent woody places
By the home that gave me birth,
We stood tranced in long embraces
Mixt with kisses sweeter, sweeter
Than anything on earth.　　150

III

A shadow flits before me,
Not thou, but like to thee.
Ah, Christ, that it were possible
For one short hour to see
The souls we loved, that they might tell
us
What and where they be !

IV

It leads me forth at evening,
It lightly winds and steals
In a cold white robe before me,
When all my spirit reels　　160
At the shouts, the leagues of lights,
And the roaring of the wheels.

V

Half the night I waste in sighs,
Half in dreams I sorrow after
The delight of early skies;
In a wakeful doze I sorrow
For the hand, the lips, the eyes,
For the meeting of the morrow,
The delight of happy laughter,
The delight of low replies.　　170

VI

'T is a morning pure and sweet,
And a dewy splendor falls
On the little flower that clings
To the turrets and the walls;
'T is a morning pure and sweet,
And the light and shadow fleet.

She is walking in the meadow,
And the woodland echo rings;
In a moment we shall meet.
She is singing in the meadow,　　180
And the rivulet at her feet
Ripples on in light and shadow
To the ballad that she sings.

VII

Do I hear her sing as of old,
My bird with the shining head,
My own dove with the tender eye ?
But there rings on a sudden a passionate
cry,
There is some one dying or dead,
And a sullen thunder is roll'd;
For a tumult shakes the city,　　190
And I wake, my dream is fled.
In the shuddering dawn, behold,
Without knowledge, without pity,
By the curtains of my bed
That abiding phantom cold !

VIII

Get thee hence, nor come again,
Mix not memory with doubt,
Pass, thou deathlike type of pain,
Pass and cease to move about !
'T is the blot upon the brain　　200
That *will* show itself without.

IX

Then I rise, the eave-drops fall,
And the yellow vapors choke
The great city sounding wide;
The day comes, a dull red ball
Wrapt in drifts of lurid smoke
On the misty river-tide.

X

Thro' the hubbub of the market
I steal, a wasted frame;
It crosses here, it crosses there,　　210
Thro' all that crowd confused and loud,
The shadow still the same;
And on my heavy eyelids
My anguish hangs like shame.

XI

Alas for her that met me,
That heard me softly call,
Came glimmering thro' the laurels
At the quiet evenfall,
In the garden by the turrets
Of the old manorial hall !　　220

XII

Would the happy spirit descend
From the realms of light and song,
In the chamber or the street,
As she looks among the blest,
Should I fear to greet my friend
Or to say ' Forgive the wrong,'
Or to ask her, ' Take me, sweet,
To the regions of thy rest ' ?

XIII

But the broad light glares and beats,
And the shadow flits and fleets   230
And will not let me be;
And I loathe the squares and streets,
And the faces that one meets,
Hearts with no love for me.
Always I long to creep
Into some still cavern deep,
There to weep, and weep, and weep
My whole soul out to thee.

V

I

Dead, long dead,
Long dead !   240
And my heart is a handful of dust,
And the wheels go over my head,
And my bones are shaken with pain,
For into a shallow grave they are thrust,
Only a yard beneath the street,
And the hoofs of the horses beat, beat,
The hoofs of the horses beat,
Beat into my scalp and my brain,
With never an end to the stream of passing
     feet,
Driving, hurrying, marrying, burying,   250
Clamor and rumble, and ringing and clat-
     ter;
And here beneath it is all as bad,
For I thought the dead had peace, but it is
     not so.
To have no peace in the grave, is that not
     sad ?
But up and down and to and fro,
Ever about me the dead men go;
And then to hear a dead man chatter
Is enough to drive one mad.

II

Wretchedest age, since Time began,
They cannot even bury a man;   260

And tho' we paid our tithes in the days
     that are gone,
Not a bell was rung, not a prayer was read.
It is that which makes us loud in the
     world of the dead;
There is none that does his work, not one.
A touch of their office might have sufficed,
But the churchmen fain would kill their
     church,
As the churches have kill'd their Christ.

III

See, there is one of us sobbing,
No limit to his distress;   269
And another, a lord of all things, praying
To his own great self, as I guess;
And another, a statesman there, betraying
His party-secret, fool, to the press;
And yonder a vile physician, blabbing
The case of his patient — all for what ?
To tickle the maggot born in an empty
     head,
And wheedle a world that loves him not,
For it is but a world of the dead.

IV

Nothing but idiot gabble !
For the prophecy given of old   280
And then not understood,
Has come to pass as foretold;
Not let any man think for the public good,
But babble, merely for babble.
For I never whisper'd a private affair
Within the hearing of cat or mouse,
No, not to myself in the closet alone,
But I heard it shouted at once from the
     top of the house;
Everything came to be known.
Who told *him* we were there ?   290

V

Not that gray old wolf, for he came not
     back
From the wilderness, full of wolves, where
     he used to lie;
He has gather'd the bones for his o'ergrown
     whelp to crack —
Crack them now for yourself, and howl, and
     die.

VI

Prophet, curse me the blabbing lip,
And curse me the British vermin, the rat;
I know not whether he came in the Han-
     over ship,

But I know that he lies and listens mute
In an ancient mansion's crannies and holes.
Arsenic, arsenic, sure, would do it,   300
Except that now we poison our babes, poor
    souls !
It is all used up for that.

VII

Tell him now: she is standing here at my
    head;
Not beautiful now, not even kind;
He may take her now; for she never speaks
    her mind,
But is ever the one thing silent here.
She is not *of* us, as I divine;
She comes from another stiller world of the
    dead,
Stiller, not fairer than mine.

VIII

But I know where a garden grows,   310
Fairer than aught in the world beside,
All made up of the lily and rose
That blow by night, when the season is
    good,
To the sound of dancing music and flutes:
It is only flowers, they had no fruits,
And I almost fear they are not roses, but
    blood;
For the keeper was one, so full of pride,
He linkt a dead man there to a spectral
    bride;
For he, if he had not been a Sultan of
    brutes,
Would he have that hole in his side ?   320

IX

But what will the old man say ?
He laid a cruel snare in a pit
To catch a friend of mine one stormy
    day;
Yet now I could even weep to think of
    it;
For what will the old man say
When he comes to the second corpse in the
    pit ?

X

Friend, to be struck by the public foe,
Then to strike him and lay him low,
That were a public merit, far,
Whatever the Quaker holds, from sin;   330
But the red life spilt for a private blow —
I swear to you, lawful and lawless war
Are scarcely even akin.

XI

O me, why have they not buried me deep
    enough ?
Is it kind to have made me a grave so
    rough,
Me, that was never a quiet sleeper ?
Maybe still I am but half-dead;
Then I cannot be wholly dumb.
I will cry to the steps above my head
And somebody, surely, some kind heart
    will come   340
To bury me, bury me
Deeper, ever so little deeper.

PART III

I

My life has crept so long on a broken wing
Thro' cells of madness, haunts of horror
    and fear,
That I come to be grateful at last for a lit-
    tle thing.
My mood is changed, for it fell at a time
    of year
When the face of night is fair on the dewy
    downs,
And the shining daffodil dies, and the
    Charioteer
And starry Gemini hang like glorious
    crowns
Over Orion's grave low down in the west,
That like a silent lightning under the stars
She seem'd to divide in a dream from a
    band of the blest,   10
And spoke of a hope for the world in the
    coming wars —
'And in that hope, dear soul, let trouble
    have rest,
Knowing I tarry for thee,' and pointed to
    Mars
As he glow'd like a ruddy shield on the
    Lion's breast.

II

And it was but a dream, yet it yielded a
    dear delight
To have look'd, tho' but in a dream, upon
    eyes so fair,
That had been in a weary world my one
    thing bright;
And it was but a dream, yet it lighten'd
    my despair

When I thought that a war would arise in
    defence of the right,
That an iron tyranny now should bend or
    cease,   20
The glory of manhood stand on his ancient
    height,
Nor Britain's one sole God be the million-
    aire.
No more shall commerce be all in all, and
    Peace
Pipe on her pastoral hillock a languid note,
And watch her harvest ripen, her herd
    increase,
Nor the cannon-bullet rust on a slothful
    shore,
And the cobweb woven across the cannon's
    throat
Shall shake its threaded tears in the wind
    no more.

III

And as months ran on and rumor of battle
    grew,
'It is time, it is time, O passionate heart,'
    said I, —   30
For I cleaved to a cause that I felt to be
    pure and true, —
'It is time, O passionate heart and morbid
    eye,
That old hysterical mock-disease should
    die.'
And I stood on a giant deck and mixt my
    breath
With a loyal people shouting a battle-
    cry,
Till I saw the dreary phantom arise and
    fly
Far into the North, and battle, and seas of
    death.

IV

Let it go or stay, so I wake to the higher
    aims
Of a land that has lost for a little her lust
    of gold,
And love of a peace that was full of wrongs
    and shames,   40
Horrible, hateful, monstrous, not to be
    told;
And hail once more to the banner of battle
    unroll'd !
Tho' many a light shall darken, and many
    shall weep
For those that are crush'd in the clash of
    jarring claims,

Yet God's just wrath shall be wreak'd on a
    giant liar,
And many a darkness into the light shall
    leap,
And shine in the sudden making of splen-
    did names,
And noble thought be freer under the
    sun,
And the heart of a people beat with one
    desire;
For the peace, that I deem'd no peace, is
    over and done,   50
And now by the side of the Black and the
    Baltic deep,
And deathful-grinning mouths of the for-
    tress, flames
The blood-red blossom of war with a heart
    of fire.

V

Let it flame or fade, and the war roll down
    like a wind,
We have proved we have hearts in a cause,
    we are noble still,
And myself have awaked, as it seems, to
    the better mind.
It is better to fight for the good than to
    rail at the ill;
I have felt with my native land, I am one
    with my kind,
I embrace the purpose of God, and the
    doom assign'd.

THE BROOK

'Here by this brook we parted, I to the
    East
And he for Italy — too late — too late:
One whom the strong sons of the world de-
    spise;
For lucky rhymes to him were scrip and
    share,
And mellow metres more than cent for
    cent.
Nor could he understand how money breeds,
Thought it a dead thing; yet himself could
    make
The thing that is not as the thing that is.
O, had he lived ! In our schoolbooks we
    say
Of those that held their heads above the
    crowd,   10
They flourish'd then or then; but life in
    him

Could scarce be said to flourish, only
    touch'd
On such a time as goes before the leaf,
When all the wood stands in a mist of
    green,
And nothing perfect. Yet the brook he
    loved,
For which, in branding summers of Ben-
    gal,
Or even the sweet half-English Neilgherry
    air,
I panted, seems, as I re-listen to it,
Prattling the primrose fancies of the boy
To me that loved him; for " O brook," he
    says,   20
" O babbling brook," says Edmund in his
    rhyme,
" Whence come you ? " and the brook —
    why not ? — replies:

        I come from haunts of coot and hern,
            I make a sudden sally,
        And sparkle out among the fern,
            To bicker down a valley.

        By thirty hills I hurry down,
            Or slip between the ridges,
        By twenty thorps, a little town,
            And half a hundred bridges.   30

        Till last by Philip's farm I flow
            To join the brimming river,
        For men may come and men may go,
            But I go on for ever.

' Poor lad, he died at Florence, quite worn
    out,
Travelling to Naples. There is Darnley
    bridge,
It has more ivy; there the river; and there
Stands Philip's farm where brook and river
    meet.

        I chatter over stony ways,
            In little sharps and trebles,   40
        I bubble into eddying bays,
            I babble on the pebbles.

        With many a curve my banks I fret
            By many a field and fallow,
        And many a fairy foreland set
            With willow-weed and mallow.

        I chatter, chatter, as I flow
            To join the brimming river,
        For men may come and men may go,
            But I go on for ever.   50

' But Philip chatter'd more than brook
    or bird,
Old Philip; all about the fields you caught
His weary daylong chirping, like the
    dry
High-elbow'd grigs that leap in summer
    grass.

        I wind about, and in and out,
            With here a blossom sailing,
        And here and there a lusty trout,
            And here and there a grayling,

        And here and there a foamy flake
            Upon me, as I travel   60
        With many a silvery water-break
            Above the golden gravel,

        And draw them all along, and flow
            To join the brimming river,
        For men may come and men may go,
            But I go on for ever.

' O darling Katie Willows, his one child !
A maiden of our century, yet most meek;
A daughter of our meadows, yet not coarse;
Straight, but as lissome as a hazel wand;
Her eyes a bashful azure, and her hair   71
In gloss and hue the chestnut, when the
    shell
Divides threefold to show the fruit within.

' Sweet Katie, once I did her a good
    turn,
Her and her far-off cousin and betrothed,
James Willows, of one name and heart
    with her.
For here I came, twenty years back — the
    week
Before I parted with poor Edmund — crost
By that old bridge which, half in ruins
    then,   79
Still makes a hoary eyebrow for the gleam
Beyond it, where the waters marry — crost,
Whistling a random bar of Bonny Doon,
And push'd at Philip's garden-gate. The
    gate,
Half-parted from a weak and scolding
    hinge,
Stuck; and he clamor'd from a casement,
    " Run,"
To Katie somewhere in the walks below,
" Run, Katie ! " Katie never ran; she
    moved
To meet me, winding under woodbine bow-
    ers,

A little flutter'd, with her eyelids down, 89
Fresh apple-blossom, blushing for a boon.

'What was it? less of sentiment than
    sense
Had Katie; not illiterate, nor of those
Who dabbling in the fount of fictive tears,
And nursed by mealy-mouth'd philanthro-
    pies,
Divorce the Feeling from her mate the
    Deed.

'She told me. She and James had
    quarrell'd. Why?
What cause of quarrel? None, she said,
    no cause;
James had no cause: but when I prest the
    cause,
I learnt that James had flickering jealousies
Which anger'd her. Who anger'd James?
    I said. 100
But Katie snatch'd her eyes at once from
    mine,
And sketching with her slender pointed
    foot
Some figure like a wizard pentagram
On garden gravel, let my query pass
Unclaim'd, in flushing silence, till I ask'd
If James were coming. "Coming every
    day,"
She answer'd, "ever longing to explain,
But evermore her father came across
With some long-winded tale, and broke
    him short;
And James departed vext with him and
    her." 110
How could I help her? "Would I — was
    it wrong?" —
Claspt hands and that petitionary grace
Of sweet seventeen subdued me ere she
    spoke —
"O, would I take her father for one hour,
For one half-hour, and let him talk to me!"
And even while she spoke, I saw where
    James
Made toward us, like a wader in the surf,
Beyond the brook, waist-deep in meadow-
    sweet.

'O Katie, what I suffer'd for your sake!
For in I went, and call'd old Philip out 120
To show the farm. Full willingly he rose;
He led me thro' the short sweet-smelling
    lanes
Of his wheat-suburb, babbling as he went.

He praised his land, his horses, his ma-
    chines;
He praised his ploughs, his cows, his hogs,
    his dogs;
He praised his hens, his geese, his guinea-
    hens,
His pigeons, who in session on their roofs
Approved him, bowing at their own deserts.
Then from the plaintive mother's teat he
    took
Her blind and shuddering puppies, naming
    each, 130
And naming those, his friends, for whom
    they were;
Then crost the common into Darnley chase
To show Sir Arthur's deer. In copse and
    fern
Twinkled the innumerable ear and tail.
Then, seated on a serpent-rooted beech,
He pointed out a pasturing colt, and said,
"That was the four-year-old I sold the
    Squire."
And there he told a long, long-winded tale
Of how the Squire had seen the colt at
    grass,
And how it was the thing his daughter
    wish'd, 140
And how he sent the bailiff to the farm
To learn the price, and what the price he
    ask'd,
And how the bailiff swore that he was mad,
But he stood firm, and so the matter
    hung;
He gave them line; and five days after
    that
He met the bailiff at the Golden Fleece,
Who then and there had offer'd something
    more,
But he stood firm, and so the matter hung;
He knew the man, the colt would fetch its
    price;
He gave them line; and how by chance at
    last — 150
It might be May or April, he forgot,
The last of April or the first of May —
He found the bailiff riding by the farm,
And, talking from the point, he drew him in,
And there he mellow'd all his heart with
    ale,
Until they closed a bargain, hand in hand.

'Then, while I breathed in sight of haven,
    he —
Poor fellow, could he help it? — recom-
    menced,

And ran thro' all the coltish chronicle,   159
Wild Will, Black Bess, Tantivy, Tallyho,
Reform, White Rose, Bellerophon, the
    Jilt,
Arbaces, and Phenomenon, and the rest,
Till, not to die a listener, I arose,
And with me Philip, talking still; and so
We turn'd our foreheads from the falling
    sun,
And following our own shadows thrice as
    long
As when they follow'd us from Philip's
    door,
Arrived, and found the sun of sweet con-
    tent
Re - risen in Katie's eyes, and all things
    well.

I steal by lawns and grassy plots,   170
    I slide by hazel covers ;
I move the sweet forget-me-nots
    That grow for happy lovers.

I slip, I slide, I gloom, I glance,
    Among my skimming swallows ;
I make the netted sunbeam dance
    Against my sandy shallows.

I murmur under moon and stars
    In brambly wildernesses ;
I linger by my shingly bars,   180
    I loiter round my cresses ;

And out again I curve and flow
    To join the brimming river,
For men may come and men may go,
    But I go on for ever.

Yes, men may come and go; and these are
    gone,
All gone. My dearest brother, Edmund,
    sleeps,
Not by the well-known stream and rustic
    spire,
But unfamiliar Arno, and the dome
Of Brunelleschi, sleeps in peace; and he,
Poor Philip, of all his lavish waste of
    words   191
Remains the lean P. W. on his tomb;
I scraped the lichen from it. Katie walks
By the long wash of Australasian seas
Far off, and holds her head to other
    stars,
And breathes in April-autumns. All are
    gone.'

So Lawrence Aylmer, seated on a stile
In the long hedge, and rolling in his mind
Old waifs of rhyme, and bowing o'er the
    brook
A tonsured head in middle age forlorn,   200
Mused, and was mute. On a sudden a low
    breath
Of tender air made tremble in the hedge
The fragile bindweed - bells and briony
    rings;
And he look'd up. There stood a maiden
    ·near,
Waiting to pass. In much amaze he stared
On eyes a bashful azure, and on hair
In gloss and hue the chestnut, when the
    shell
Divides threefold to show the fruit with-
    in;
Then, wondering, ask'd her, 'Are you from
    the farm ? '
'Yes,' answer'd she. 'Pray stay a little;
    pardon me,   210
What do they call you ? ' ' Katie.' ' That
    were strange.
What surname ? ' 'Willows.' 'No !' 'That
    is my name.'
'Indeed !' and here he look'd so self-
    perplext,
That Katie laugh'd, and laughing blush'd,
    till he
Laugh'd also, but as one before he wakes,
Who feels a glimmering strangeness in his
    dream.
Then looking at her: 'Too happy, fresh
    and fair,
Too fresh and fair in our sad world's best
    bloom,
To be the ghost of one who bore your
    name   219
About these meadows, twenty years ago.'

'Have you not heard ? ' said Katie, ' we
    came back.
We bought the farm we tenanted be-
    fore.
Am I so like her ? so they said on board.
Sir, if you knew her in her English days,
My mother, as it seems you did, the
    days
That most she loves to talk of, come with
    me.
My brother James is in the harvest-field;
But she — you will be welcome — O, come
    in !'

THE DAISY

WRITTEN AT EDINBURGH

'A tender dream of the poet; musing in a
murky street in Edinburgh over a daisy picked
on the "Snowy Splügen" gives him oppor-
tunity for many varied sketches of Southern
life, full of color and spirit and movement'
(Waugh, ' Alfred Lord Tennyson,' 1892). The
Italian journey was made in 1851, the year
after the poet's marriage.

O LOVE, what hours were thine and
mine,
In lands of palm and southern pine;
  Iu lands of palm, or orange-blossom,
Of olive, aloe, and maize and vine!

What Roman strength Turbìa show'd
In ruin, by the mountain road;
  How like a gem, beneath, the city
Of little Monaco, basking, glow'd!

How richly down the rocky dell
The torrent vineyard streaming fell   10
  To meet the sun and sunny waters,
That only heaved with a summer swell!

What slender campanili grew
By bays, the peacock's neck in hue;
  Where, here and there, on sandy beaches
A milky-bell'd amaryllis blew!

How young Columbus seem'd to rove,
Yet present in his natal grove,
  Now watching high on mountain cor-
  nice,
And steering, now, from a purple cove,   20

Now pacing mute by ocean's rim;
Till, in a narrow street and dim,
  I stay'd the wheels at Cogoletto,
And drank, and loyally drank to him!

Nor knew we well what pleased us most;
Not the clipt palm of which they boast,
  But distant color, happy hamlet,
A moulder'd citadel on the coast,

Or tower, or high hill-convent, seen
A light amid its olives green;   30
  Or olive-hoary cape in ocean;
Or rosy blossom in hot ravine,

Where oleanders flush'd the bed
Of silent torrents, gravel-spread;
  And, crossing, oft we saw the glisten
Of ice, far up on a mountain head.

We loved that hall, tho' white and cold,
Those niched shapes of noble mould,
  A princely people's awful princes,
The grave, severe Genovese of old.   40

At Florence too what golden hours;
In those long galleries, were ours;
  What drives about the fresh Cascinè,
Or walks in Boboli's ducal bowers!

In bright vignettes, and each complete,
Of tower or duomo, sunny-sweet,
  Or palace, how the city glitter'd,
Thro' cypress avenues, at our feet!

But when we crost the Lombard plain
Remember what a plague of rain;   50
  Of rain at Reggio, rain at Parma,
At Lodi rain, Piacenza rain.

And stern and sad — so rare the smiles
Of sunlight — look'd the Lombard piles;
  Porch-pillars on the lion resting,
And sombre, old, colonnaded aisles.

O Milan, O the chanting quires,
The giant windows' blazon'd fires,
  The height, the space, the gloom, the
  glory !
A mount of marble, a hundred spires !   60

I climb'd the roofs at break of day;
Sun-smitten Alps before me lay.
  I stood among the silent statues,
And statued pinnacles, mute as they.

How faintly-flush'd, how phantom-fair,
Was Monte Rosa, hanging there
  A thousand shadowy-pencill'd valleys
And snowy dells in a golden air !

Remember how we came at last
To Como; shower and storm and blast   70
  Had blown the lake beyond his limit,
And all was flooded; and how we past

From Como, when the light was gray,
And in my head, for half the day,
  The rich Virgilian rustic measure
Of 'Lari Maxume,' all the way,

Like ballad-burthen music, kept,
As on the Lariano crept
   To that fair port below the castle
Of Queen Theodolind, where we slept;   80

Or hardly slept, but watch'd awake
A cypress in the moonlight shake,
   The moonlight touching o'er a terrace
One tall agave above the lake.

What more ? we took our last adieu,
And up the snowy Splügen drew;
   But ere we reach'd the highest summit
I pluck'd a daisy, I gave it you.

It told of England then to me,
And now it tells of Italy.   90
   O love, we two shall go no longer
To lands of summer across the sea,

So dear a life your arms enfold
Whose crying is a cry for gold;
   Yet here to-night in this dark city,
When ill and weary, alone and cold,

I found, tho' crush'd to hard and dry,
This nursling of another sky
   Still in the little book you lent me,
And where you tenderly laid it by;   100

And I forgot the clouded Forth,
The gloom that saddens heaven and earth,
   The bitter east, the misty summer
And gray metropolis of the North.

Perchance to lull the throbs of pain,
Perchance to charm a vacant brain,
   Perchance to dream you still beside
     me,
My fancy fled to the South again.

TO THE REV. F. D. MAURICE

Come, when no graver cares employ,
Godfather, come and see your boy;
   Your presence will be sun in winter,
Making the little one leap for joy.

For, being of that honest few
Who give the Fiend himself his due,
   Should eighty thousand college-councils
Thunder ' Anathema,' friend, at you,

Should all our churchmen foam in spite
At you, so careful of the right,   10
   Yet one lay-hearth would give you wel-
     come —
Take it and come — to the Isle of Wight;

Where, far from noise and smoke of
     town,
I watch the twilight falling brown
   All round a careless-order'd garden
Close to the ridge of a noble down.

You 'll have no scandal while you dine,
But honest talk and wholesome wine,
   And only hear the magpie gossip
Garrulous under a roof of pine;   20

For groves of pine on either hand,
To break the blast of winter, stand,
   And further on, the hoary Channel
Tumbles a billow on chalk and sand;

Where, if below the milky steep
Some ship of battle slowly creep,
   And on thro' zones of light and shadow
Glimmer away to the lonely deep,

We might discuss the Northern sin
Which made a selfish war begin,   30
   Dispute the claims, arrange the
     chances, —
Emperor, Ottoman, which shall win;

Or whether war's avenging rod
Shall lash all Europe into blood;
   Till you should turn to dearer matters,
Dear to the man that is dear to God, —

How best to help the slender store,
How mend the dwellings, of the poor,
   How gain in life, as life advances,
Valor and charity more and more.   40

Come, Maurice, come; the lawn as yet
Is hoar with rime or spongy-wet,
   But when the wreath of March has blos-
     som'd, —
Crocus, anemone, violet, —

Or later, pay one visit here,
For those are few we hold as dear;
   Nor pay but one, but come for many,
Many and many a happy year.

January, 1854.

WILL

I

O, WELL for him whose will is strong!
He suffers, but he will not suffer long;
He suffers, but he cannot suffer wrong.
For him nor moves the loud world's random
    mock,
Nor all Calamity's hugest waves confound,
Who seems a promontory of rock,
That, compass'd round with turbulent
    sound,
In middle ocean meets the surging shock,
Tempest-buffeted, citadel-crown'd.

II

But ill for him who, bettering not with
    time,
Corrupts the strength of heaven-descended
    Will,
And ever weaker grows thro' acted crime,
Or seeming-genial venial fault,
Recurring and suggesting still!
He seems as one whose footsteps halt,
Toiling in immeasurable sand,
And o'er a weary sultry land,
Far beneath a blazing vault,
Sown in a wrinkle of the monstrous hill,
The city sparkles like a grain of salt.

ODE ON THE DEATH OF THE DUKE OF WELLINGTON

This poem, originally published on the day of the Duke's funeral in 1852, was probably written in some haste. It underwent considerable revision before it was reprinted in 1853, and was further retouched before it appeared with 'Maud' in 1855. The variations of the present text from the first edition are given in the Notes.

Shepherd ('Tennysoniana.' 1879), in his chapter on 'Tennyson's Versification,' remarks: 'In the "Ode on the Death of the Duke of Wellington," he has soared to lyric heights to which, perhaps, even Pindar never attained. The tolling of the bell, the solemn and slow funeral march, the quick rush of battle, and the choral chant of the cathedral all succeed one another, and the verse sinks and swells, rises and falls to every alternation with equal power.'

I

BURY the Great Duke
  With an empire's lamentation;
Let us bury the Great Duke
  To the noise of the mourning of a mighty
    nation;
Mourning when their leaders fall,
Warriors carry the warrior's pall,
And sorrow darkens hamlet and hall.

II

Where shall we lay the man whom we de-
    plore?
Here, in streaming London's central roar.
Let the sound of those he wrought for,   10
And the feet of those he fought for,
Echo round his bones for evermore.

III

Lead out the pageant: sad and slow,
As fits an universal woe,
Let the long, long procession go,
And let the sorrowing crowd about it grow,
And let the mournful martial music blow;
The last great Englishman is low.

IV

Mourn, for to us he seems the last,   19
Remembering all his greatness in the past.
No more in soldier fashion will he greet
With lifted hand the gazer in the street.
O friends, our chief state-oracle is mute!
Mourn for the man of long-enduring blood,
The statesman-warrior, moderate, resolute,
Whole in himself, a common good.
Mourn for the man of amplest influence,
Yet clearest of ambitious crime,
Our greatest yet with least pretence,
Great in council and great in war,   30
Foremost captain of his time,
Rich in saving common-sense,
And, as the greatest only are,
In his simplicity sublime.
O good gray head which all men knew,
O voice from which their omens all men
    drew,
O iron nerve to true occasion true,
O fallen at length that tower of strength
Which stood four-square to all the winds
    that blew!
Such was he whom we deplore.   40
The long self-sacrifice of life is o'er.
The great World-victor's victor will be
    seen no more.

V

All is over and done.
Render thanks to the Giver,

England, for thy son.
Let the bell be toll'd.
Render thanks to the Giver,
And render him to the mould.
Under the cross of gold
That shines over city and river, 50
There he shall rest for ever
Among the wise and the bold.
Let the bell be toll'd,
And a reverent people behold
The towering car, the sable steeds.
Bright let it be with its blazon'd deeds,
Dark in its funeral fold.
Let the bell be toll'd,
And a deeper knell in the heart be knoll'd;
And the sound of the sorrowing anthem
roll'd 60
Thro' the dome of the golden cross;
And the volleying cannon thunder his loss;
He knew their voices of old.
For many a time in many a clime
His captain's-ear has heard them boom
Bellowing victory, bellowing doom.
When he with those deep voices wrought,
Guarding realms and kings from shame,
With those deep voices our dead captain
taught
The tyrant, and asserts his claim 70
In that dread sound to the great name
Which he has worn so pure of blame,
In praise and in dispraise the same,
A man of well-attemper'd frame.
O civic muse, to such a name,
To such a name for ages long,
To such a name,
Preserve a broad approach of fame,
And ever-echoing avenues of song!

VI

'Who is he thàt cometh, like an honor'd
guest, 80
With banner and with music, with soldier
and with priest,
With a nation weeping, and breaking on
my rest?'—
Mighty Seaman, this is he
Was great by land as thou by sea.
Thine island loves thee well, thou famous
man,
The greatest sailor since our world began.
Now, to the roll of muffled drums,
To thee the greatest soldier comes;
For this is he
Was great by land as thou by sea. 90
His foes were thine; he kept us free;

O, give him welcome, this is he
Worthy of our gorgeous rites,
And worthy to be laid by thee;
For this is England's greatest son,
He that gain'd a hundred fights,
Nor ever lost an English gun;
This is he that far away
Against the myriads of Assaye
Clash'd with his fiery few and won; 100
And underneath another sun,
Warring on a later day,
Round affrighted Lisbon drew
The treble works, the vast designs
Of his labor'd rampart-lines,
Where he greatly stood at bay,
Whence he issued forth anew,
And ever great and greater grew,
Beating from the wasted vines
Back to France her banded swarms, 110
Back to France with countless blows,
Till o'er the hills her eagles flew
Beyond the Pyrenean pines,
Follow'd up in valley and glen
With blare of bugle, clamor of men,
Roll of cannon and clash of arms,
And England pouring on her foes.
Such a war had such a close.
Again their ravening eagle rose
In anger, wheel'd on Europe-shadowing
wings, 120
And barking for the thrones of kings;
Till one that sought but Duty's iron crown
On that loud Sabbath shook the spoiler
down;
A day of onsets of despair!
Dash'd on every rocky square,
Their surging charges foam'd themselves
away;
Last, the Prussian trumpet blew;
Thro' the long-tormented air
Heaven flash'd a sudden jubilant ray,
And down we swept and charged and over-
threw. 130
So great a soldier taught us there
What long-enduring hearts could do
In that world-earthquake, Waterloo!
Mighty Seaman, tender and true,
And pure as he from taint of craven guile,
O saviour of the silver-coasted isle,
O shaker of the Baltic and the Nile,
If aught of things that here befall
Touch a spirit among things divine, 139
If love of country move thee there at all,
Be glad, because his bones are laid by
thine!

And thro' the centuries let a people's voice
In full acclaim,
A people's voice,
The proof and echo of all human fame,
A people's voice, when they rejoice
At civic revel and pomp and game,
Attest their great commander's claim
With honor, honor, honor, honor to him,
Eternal honor to his name.   150

VII

A people's voice! we are a people yet.
Tho' all men else their nobler dreams for-
      get,
Confused by brainless mobs and lawless
      Powers,
Thank Him who isled us here, and roughly
      set
His Briton in blown seas and storming
      showers,
We have a voice with which to pay the
      debt
Of boundless love and reverence and regret
To those great men who fought, and kept
      it ours.
And keep it ours, O God, from brute con-
      trol!
O Statesmen, guard us, guard the eye, the
      soul   160
Of Europe, keep our noble England whole,
And save the one true seed of freedom
      sown
Betwixt a people and their ancient throne,
That sober freedom out of which there
      springs
Our loyal passion for our temperate kings!
For, saving that, ye help to save mankind
Till public wrong be crumbled into dust,
And drill the raw world for the march of
      mind,
Till crowds at length be sane and crowns
      be just.
But wink no more in slothful overtrust. 170
Remember him who led your hosts;
He bade you guard the sacred coasts.
Your cannons moulder on the seaward
      wall;
His voice is silent in your council-hall
For ever; and whatever tempests lour
For ever silent; even if they broke
In thunder, silent; yet remember all
He spoke among you, and the Mán who
      spoke;
Who never sold the truth to serve the
      hour,   179

Nor palter'd with Eternal God for power;
Who let the turbid streams of rumor flow
Thro' either babbling world of high and
      low;
Whose life was work, whose language
      rife
With rugged maxims hewn from life;
Who never spoke against a foe;
Whose eighty winters freeze with one
      rebuke
All great self-seekers trampling on the
      right.
Truth-teller was our England's Alfred
      named;
Truth-lover was our English Duke;
Whatever record leap to light   190
He never shall be shamed.

VIII

Lo! the leader in these glorious wars
Now to glorious burial slowly borne,
Follow'd by the brave of other lands,
He, on whom from both her open hands
Lavish Honor shower'd all her stars,
And affluent Fortune emptied all her horn
Yea, let all good things await
Him who cares not to be great
But as he saves or serves the state.   200
Not once or twice in our rough island-
      story
The path of duty was the way to glory.
He that walks it, only thirsting
For the right, and learns to deaden
Love of self, before his journey closes,
He shall find the stubborn thistle bursting
Into glossy purples, which outredden
All voluptuous garden-roses.
Not once or twice in our fair island-story
The path of duty was the way to glory. 210
He, that ever following her commands,
On with toil of heart and knees and hands,
Thro' the long gorge to the far light has
      won
His path upward, and prevail'd,
Shall find the toppling crags of Duty
      scaled
Are close upon the shining table-lands
To which our God Himself is moon and
      sun.
Such was he: his work is done.
But while the races of mankind endure
Let his great example stand   220
Colossal, seen of every land,
And keep the soldier firm, the statesman
      pure;

Till in all lands and thro' all human story
The path of duty be the way to glory.
And let the land whose hearths he saved
    from shame
For many and many an age proclaim
At civic revel and pomp and game,
And when the long-illumined cities flame,
Their ever-loyal iron leader's fame,
With honor, honor, honor, honor to him,
Eternal honor to his name.   231

IX

Peace, his triumph will be sung
By some yet unmoulded tongue
Far on in summers that we shall not see.
Peace, it is a day of pain
For one about whose patriarchal knee
Late the little children clung.
O peace, it is a day of pain
For one upon whose hand and heart and
    brain
Once the weight and fate of Europe hung.
Ours the pain, be his the gain !   241
More than is of man's degree
Must be with us, watching here
At this, our great solemnity.
Whom we see not we revere;
We revere, and we refrain
From talk of battles loud and vain,
And brawling memories all too free
For such a wise humility
As befits a solemn fane: 250
We revere, and while we hear
The tides of Music's golden sea
Setting toward eternity,
Uplifted high in heart and hope are we,
Until we doubt not that for one so true
There must be other nobler work to do
Than when he fought at Waterloo,
And Victor he must ever be.
For tho' the Giant Ages heave the hill
And break the shore, and evermore   260
Make and break, and work their will,
Tho' world on world in myriad myriads
    roll
Round us, each with different powers,
And other forms of life than ours,
What know we greater than the soul ?
On God and Godlike men we build our
    trust.
Hush, the Dead March wails in the people's
    ears;
The dark crowd moves, and there are sobs
    and tears;

The black earth yawns; the mortal disap-
    pears;
Ashes to ashes, dust to dust;   270
He is gone who seem'd so great. —
Gone, but nothing can bereave him
Of the force he made his own
Being here, and we believe him
Something far advanced in State,
And that he wears a truer crown
Than any wreath that man can weave him.
Speak no more of his renown,
Lay your earthly fancies down,
And in the vast cathedral leave him,   280
God accept him, Christ receive him !
    1852.

THE CHARGE OF THE LIGHT BRIGADE

For the successive versions of this lyric, see
the Notes.

I

HALF a league, half a league,
Half a league onward,
All in the valley of Death
    Rode the six hundred.
'Forward the Light Brigade !
Charge for the guns ! ' he said.
Into the valley of Death
    Rode the six hundred.

II

'Forward, the Light Brigade !'
Was there a man dismay'd ?
Not tho' the soldier knew
    Some one had blunder'd.
Theirs not to make reply,
Theirs not to reason why,
Theirs but to do and die.
Into the valley of Death
    Rode the six hundred.

III

Cannon to right of them,
Cannon to left of them,
Cannon in front of them
    Volley'd and thunder'd;
Storm'd at with shot and shell,
Boldly they rode and well,
Into the jaws of Death,
Into the mouth of hell
    Rode the six hundred.

IV

Flash'd all their sabres bare,
Flash'd as they turn'd in air
Sabring the gunners there,
Charging an army, while
 All the world wonder'd.
Plunged in the battery-smoke
Right thro' the line they broke;
Cossack and Russian
Reel'd from the sabre-stroke
 Shatter'd and sunder'd.
Then they rode back, but not,
 Not the six hundred.

V

Cannon to right of them,
Cannon to left of them,

Cannon behind them
 Volley'd and thunder'd;
Storm'd at with shot and shell,
While horse and hero fell,
They that had fought so well
Came thro' the jaws of Death,
Back from the mouth of hell,
All that was left of them,
 Left of six hundred.

VI

When can their glory fade?
O the wild charge they made!
 All the world wonder'd.
Honor the charge they made!
Honor the Light Brigade,
 Noble six hundred!

ENOCH ARDEN

AND OTHER POEMS

This was the title of the volume, published in 1864, containing, besides 'Enoch Arden,' the following poems: 'Aylmer's Field,' 'Sea Dreams,' 'Ode sung at Opening of International Exhibition,' 'The Grandmother,' 'The Northern Farmer (Old Style),' 'Tithonus,' 'The Voyage,' 'In the Valley of Cauteretz, 'The Flower,' 'Requiescat,' 'The Sailor Boy,' 'The Islet,' 'The Ringlet' (afterwards suppressed), 'Welcome to Alexandra,' 'Dedication,' 'Attempts at Classic Metres in Quantity,' and 'Specimen of Blank Verse Translation of the Iliad.' The list given under the title of this volume in the English editions is misleading, as it includes only two of the above poems, with two ('The Brook' and 'Lucretius') published in other volumes.

ENOCH ARDEN

'Enoch Arden' has been one of the most popular of the poet's works, not only in English-speaking countries, but also on the continent of Europe. Mr. Eugene Parsons, in his pamphlet on 'Tennyson's Life and Poetry' (2d edition, 1893), enumerates no less than twenty-four translations: nine in German, two in Dutch, one in Danish, one in Bohemian, eight in French, one in Spanish, and two in Italian. There is also a Latin version by Mr. W. Selwyn (London, 1867).

According to the 'British Quarterly Review' for October, 1880, the stories of both 'Enoch Arden' and 'Aylmer's Field' were 'told by a friend to the poet, who, struck by their aptitude for versification, requested to have them at length in writing. When they were thus supplied, the poetic versions were made as we now have them.' This is confirmed by the 'Memoir' (vol. ii. p. 7), where we learn that the 'friend' was Woolner the sculptor.

LONG lines of cliff breaking have left a
 chasm;
And in the chasm are foam and yellow
 sands;
Beyond, red roofs about a narrow wharf
In cluster; then a moulder'd church; and
 higher
A long street climbs to one tall-tower'd
 mill;
And high in heaven behind it a gray down
With Danish barrows; and a hazel-wood,
By autumn nutters haunted, flourishes
Green in a cuplike hollow of the down.
Here on this beach a hundred years ago, 10
Three children of three houses, Annie Lee,
The prettiest little damsel in the port,
And Philip Ray, the miller's only son,
And Enoch Arden, a rough sailor's lad
Made orphan by a winter shipwreck, play'd
Among the waste and lumber of the shore,
Hard coils of cordage, swarthy fishing-nets,

Anchors of rusty fluke, and boats updrawn;
And built their castles of dissolving sand
To watch them overflow'd, or following up
And flying the white breaker, daily left   21
The little footprint daily wash'd away.

A narrow cave ran in beneath the cliff;
In this the children play'd at keeping
    house.
Enoch was host one day, Philip the next,
While Annie still was mistress; but at
    times
Enoch would hold possession for a week:
' This is my house and this my little wife.'
' Mine too,' said Philip; ' turn and turn
    about;'
When, if they quarrell'd, Enoch stronger-
    made   30
Was master.   Then would Philip, his blue
    eyes
All flooded with the helpless wrath of tears,
Shriek out, ' I hate you, Enoch,' and at this
The little wife would weep for company,
And pray them not to quarrel for her sake,
And say she would be little wife to both.

But when the dawn of rosy childhood
    past,
And the new warmth of life's ascending
    sun
Was felt by either, either fixt his heart
On that one girl; and Enoch spoke his
    love,   40
But Philip loved in silence; and the girl
Seem'd kinder unto Philip than to him;
But she loved Enoch, tho' she knew it not,
And would if ask'd deny it.   Enoch set
A purpose evermore before his eyes,
To hoard all savings to the uttermost,
To purchase his own boat, and make a
    home
For Annie; and so prosper'd that at last
A luckier or a bolder fisherman,
A carefuller in peril, did not breathe   50
For leagues along that breaker - beaten
    coast
Than Enoch.   Likewise had he served a
    year
On board a merchantman, and made him-
    self
Full sailor; and he thrice had pluck'd a
    life
From the dread sweep of the down-stream-
    ing seas,
And all men look'd upon him favorably.

And ere he touch'd his one-and-twentieth
    May
He purchased his own boat, and made a
    home
For Annie, neat and nestlike, halfway up
The narrow street that clamber'd toward
    the mill.   60

Then, on a golden autumn eventide,
The younger people making holiday,
With bag and sack and basket, great and
    small,
Went nutting to the hazels.   Philip stay'd —
His father lying sick and needing him —
An hour behind; but as he climb'd the hill,
Just where the prone edge of the wood be-
    gan
To feather toward the hollow, saw the pair,
Enoch and Annie, sitting hand-in-hand,
His large gray eyes and weather-beaten
    face   70
All-kindled by a still and sacred fire,
That burn'd as on an altar.   Philip look'd,
And in their eyes and faces read his doom;
Then, as their faces drew together, groan'd,
And slipt aside, and like a wounded life
Crept down into the hollows of the wood;
There, while the rest were loud in merry-
    making,
Had his dark hour unseen, and rose and
    past
Bearing a lifelong hunger in his heart.

So these were wed, and merrily rang the
    bells,   80
And merrily ran the years, seven happy
    years,
Seven happy years of health and compe-
    tence,
And mutual love and honorable toil,
With children, first a daughter.   In him
    woke,
With his first babe's first cry, the noble
    wish
To save all earnings to the uttermost,
And give his child a better bringing-up
Than his had been, or hers; a wish re-
    new'd,
When two years after came a boy to be
The rosy idol of her solitudes,   90
While Enoch was abroad on wrathful seas,
Or often journeying landward; for in truth
Enoch's white horse, and Enoch's ocean-
    spoil
In ocean-smelling osier, and his face,

Rough-redden'd with a thousand winter
    gales,
Not only to the market-cross were known,
But in the leafy lanes behind the down,
Far as the portal-warding lion-whelp
And peacock yew-tree of the lonely Hall,
Whose Friday fare was Enoch's minister-
    ing.   100

    Then came a change, as all things human
      change.
Ten miles to northward of the narrow port
Open'd a larger haven. Thither used
Enoch at times to go by land or sea;
And once when there, and clambering on a
    mast
In harbor, by mischance he slipt and fell.
A limb was broken when they lifted him;
And while he lay recovering there, his wife
Bore him another son, a sickly one.
Another hand crept too across his trade 110
Taking her bread and theirs; and on him
    fell,
Altho' a grave and staid God-fearing man,
Yet lying thus inactive, doubt and gloom.
He seem'd, as in a nightmare of the night,
To see his children leading evermore
Low miserable lives of hand-to-mouth,
And her he loved a beggar. Then he pray'd,
' Save them from this, whatever comes
    to me.'
And while he pray'd, the master of that
    ship
Enoch had served in, hearing his mis-
    chance,   120
Came, for he knew the man and valued
    him,
Reporting of his vessel China-bound,
And wanting yet a boatswain. Would
    he go ?
There yet were many weeks before she
    sail'd,
Sail'd from this port. Would Enoch have
    the place ?
And Enoch all at once assented to it,
Rejoicing at that answer to his prayer.

    So now that shadow of mischance ap-
      pear'd
No graver than as when some little cloud
Cuts off the fiery highway of the sun,   130
And isles a light in the offing. Yet the
    wife —
When he was gone — the children — what
    to do ?

Then Enoch lay long-pondering on his
    plans:
To sell the boat — and yet he loved her
    well —
How many a rough sea had he weather'd
    in her !
He knew her, as a horseman knows his
    horse —
And yet to sell her — then with what she
    brought
Buy goods and stores — set Annie forth in
    trade
With all that seamen needed or their
    wives —
So might she keep the house while he was
    gone.   140
Should he not trade himself out yonder ?
    go
This voyage more than once ? yea, twice
    or thrice —
As oft as needed — last, returning rich,
Become the master of a larger craft,
With fuller profits lead an easier life,
Have all his pretty young ones educated,
And pass his days in peace among his own.

    Thus Enoch in his heart determined all;
Then moving homeward came on Annie
    pale,
Nursing the sickly babe, her latest-born. 150
Forward she started with a happy cry,
And laid the feeble infant in his arms;
Whom Enoch took, and handled all his
    limbs,
Appraised his weight and fondled father-
    like,
But had no heart to break his purposes
To Annie, till the morrow, when he spoke.

    Then first since Enoch's golden ring had
      girt
Her finger, Annie fought against his will;
Yet not with brawling opposition she,
But manifold entreaties, many a tear,   160
Many a sad kiss by day, by night, renew'd —
Sure that all evil would come out of it —
Besought him, supplicating, if he cared
For her or his dear children, not to go.
He not for his own self caring, but her,
Her and her children, let her plead in vain;
So grieving held his will, and bore it thro'.

    For Enoch parted with his old sea-friend,
Bought Annie goods and stores, and set his
    hand

To fit their little streetward sitting-room
With shelf and corner for the goods and
    stores.   171
So all day long till Enoch's last at home,
Shaking their pretty cabin, hammer and
    axe,
Auger and saw, while Annie seem'd to
    hear
Her own death-scaffold raising, shrill'd and
    rang,
Till this was ended, and his careful hand, —
The space was narrow, — having order'd
    all
Almost as neat and close as Nature packs
Her blossom or her seedling, paused; and
    he,
Who needs would work for Annie to the
    last,   180
Ascending tired, heavily slept till morn.

And Enoch faced this morning of fare-
    well
Brightly and boldly. All his Annie's fears,
Save as his Annie's, were a laughter to
    him.
Yet Enoch as a brave God-fearing man
Bow'd himself down, and in that mystery
Where God-in-man is one with man-in-
    God,
Pray'd for a blessing on his wife and babes,
Whatever came to him; and then he said:
'Annie, this voyage by the grace of God
Will bring fair weather yet to all of us. 191
Keep a clean hearth and a clear fire for me,
For I'll be back, my girl, before you
    know it;'
Then lightly rocking baby's cradle, 'and
    he,
This pretty, puny, weakly little one, —
Nay — for I love him all the better for
    it —
God bless him, he shall sit upon my knees
And I will tell him tales of foreign parts,
And make him merry, when I come home
    again.   199
Come, Annie, come, cheer up before I go.'

Him running on thus hopefully she
    heard,
And almost hoped herself; but when he
    turn'd
The current of his talk to graver things
In sailor fashion roughly sermonizing
On providence and trust in heaven, she
    heard,

Heard and not heard him; as the village
    girl,
Who sets her pitcher underneath the
    spring,
Musing on him that used to fill it for her,
Hears and not hears, and lets it overflow.

At length she spoke: 'O Enoch, you are
    wise;   210
And yet for all your wisdom well know I
That I shall look upon your face no more.'

'Well, then,' said Enoch, 'I shall look
    on yours.
Annie, the ship I sail in passes here ' —
He named the day; — 'get you a seaman's
    glass,
Spy out my face, and laugh at all your
    fears.'

But when the last of those last moments
    came:
'Annie, my girl, cheer up, be comforted,
Look to the babes, and till I come again
Keep everything shipshape, for I must
    go.   220
And fear no more for me; or if you fear,
Cast all your cares on God; that anchor
    holds.
Is He not yonder in those uttermost
Parts of the morning? if I flee to these,
Can I go from Him? and the sea is His,
The sea is His; He made it.'

                    Enoch rose,
Cast his strong arms about his drooping
    wife,
And kiss'd his wonder-stricken little ones;
But for the third, the sickly one, who slept
After a night of feverous wakefulness, 230
When Annie would have raised him Enoch
    said,
'Wake him not, let him sleep; how should
    the child
Remember this?' and kiss'd him in his
    cot.
But Annie from her baby's forehead clipt
A tiny curl, and gave it; this he kept
Thro' all his future, but now hastily caught
His bundle, waved his hand, and went his
    way.

She, when the day that Enoch mention'd
    came,
Borrow'd a glass, but all in vain. Perhaps

She could not fix the glass to suit her eye;
Perhaps her eye was dim, hand tremulous;
She saw him not, and while he stood on
    deck   242
Waving, the moment and the vessel past.

Even to the last dip of the vanishing sail
She watch'd it, and departed weeping for
    him;
Then, tho' she mourn'd his absence as his
    grave,
Set her sad will no less to chime with his,
But throve not in her trade, not being bred
To barter, nor compensating the want
By shrewdness, neither capable of lies, 250
Nor asking overmuch and taking less,
And still foreboding 'what would Enoch
    say ? '
For more than once, in days of difficulty
And pressure, had she sold her wares for
    less
Than what she gave in buying what she
    sold.
She fail'd and sadden'd knowing it; and
    thus,
Expectant of that news which never came,
Gain'd for her own a scanty sustenance,
And lived a life of silent melancholy.

Now the third child was sickly-born and
    grew   260
Yet sicklier, tho' the mother cared for it
With all a mother's care; nevertheless,
Whether her business often call'd her
    from it,
Or thro' the want of what it needed most,
Or means to pay the voice who best could
    tell
What most it needed — howsoe'er it was,
After a lingering, — ere she was aware, —
Like the caged bird escaping suddenly,
The little innocent soul flitted away.

In that same week when Annie buried
    it,   270
Philip's true heart, which hunger'd for her
    peace, —
Since Enoch left he had not look'd upon
    her, —
Smote him, as having kept aloof so long.
'Surely,' said Philip, 'I may see her now,
May be some little comfort;' therefore
    went,
Past thro' the solitary room in front,
Paused for a moment at an inner door,

Then struck it thrice, and, no one opening,
Enter'd, but Annie, seated with her grief,
Fresh from the burial of her little one, 280
Cared not to look on any human face,
But turn'd her own toward the wall and
    wept.
Then Philip standing up said falteringly,
'Annie, I came to ask a favor of you.'

He spoke; the passion in her moan'd re-
    ply,
'Favor from one so sad and so forlorn
As I am !' half abash'd him; yet unask'd,
His bashfulness and tenderness at war,
He set himself beside her, saying to her:

'I came to speak to you of what he
    wish'd,   290
Enoch, your husband. I have ever said
You chose the best among us — a strong
    man;
For where he fixt his heart he set his hand
To do the thing he will'd, and bore it thro'.
And wherefore did he go this weary way,
And leave you lonely ? not to see the
    world —
For pleasure ? — nay, but for the where-
    withal
To give his babes a better bringing up
Than his had been, or yours; that was his
    wish.
And if he come again, vext will he be 300
To find the precious morning hours were
    lost.
And it would vex him even in his grave,
If he could know his babes were running
    wild
Like colts about the waste. So, Annie,
    now —
Have we not known each other all our
    lives ?
I do beseech you by the love you bear
Him and his children not to say me nay —
For, if you will, when Enoch comes again
Why then he shall repay me — if you will,
Annie — for I am rich and well-to-do. 310
Now let me put the boy and girl to school;
This is the favor that I came to ask.'

Then Annie with her brows against the
    wall
Answer'd, 'I cannot look you in the face;
I seem so foolish and so broken down.
When you came in my sorrow broke me
    down;

And now I think your kindness breaks me
down.
But Enoch lives; that is borne in on me;
He will repay you. Money can be repaid,
Not kindness such as yours.'

                    And Philip ask'd,
' Then you will let me, Annie ? '

                    There she turn'd,
She rose, and fixt her swimming eyes upon
him,   322
And dwelt a moment on his kindly face,
Then calling down a blessing on his head
Caught at his hand, and wrung it passion-
ately,
And past into the little garth beyond.
So lifted up in spirit he moved away.

  Then Philip put the boy and girl to
school,
And bought them needful books, and every
way,
Like one who does his duty by his own, 330
Made himself theirs; and tho' for Annie's
sake,
Fearing the lazy gossip of the port,
He oft denied his heart his dearest wish,
And seldom crost her threshold, yet he
sent
Gifts by the children, garden - herbs and
fruit,
The late and early roses from his wall,
Or conies from the down, and now and
then,
With some pretext of fineness in the meal
To save the offence of charitable, flour
From his tall mill that whistled on the
waste.   340

  But Philip did not fathom Annie's mind;
Scarce could the woman, when he came
upon her,
Out of full heart and boundless gratitude
Light on a broken word to thank him with.
But Philip was her children's all-in-all;
From distant corners of the street they ran
To greet his hearty welcome heartily;
Lords of his house and of his mill were
they,
Worried his passive ear with petty wrongs
Or pleasures, hung upon him, play'd with
him   350
And call'd him Father Philip. Philip
gain'd

As Enoch lost, for Enoch seem'd to them
Uncertain as a vision or a dream,
Faint as a figure seen in early dawn
Down at the far end of an avenue,
Going we know not where; and so ten
years,
Since Enoch left his hearth and native land,
Fled forward, and no news of Enoch came.

  It chanced one evening Annie's children
long'd
To go with others nutting to the wood, 360
And Annie would go with them; then they
begg'd
For Father Philip, as they call'd him, too.
Him, like the working bee in blossom-dust,
Blanch'd with his mill, they found; and
saying to him,
' Come with us, Father Philip,' he denied;
But when the children pluck'd at him to go,
He laugh'd, and yielded readily to their
wish,
For was not Annie with them ? and they
went.

  But after scaling half the weary down,
Just where the prone edge of the wood
began   370
To feather toward the hollow, all her force
Fail'd her; and sighing, ' Let me rest,' she
said.
So Philip rested with her well-content;
While all the younger ones with jubilant
cries
Broke from their elders, and tumultuously
Down thro' the whitening hazels made a
plunge
To the bottom, and dispersed, and bent or
broke
The lithe reluctant boughs to tear away
Their tawny clusters, crying to each other
And calling, here and there, about the
wood.   380

  But Philip sitting at her side forgot
Her presence, and remember'd one dark
hour
Here in this wood, when like a wounded
life
He crept into the shadow. At last he said,
Lifting his honest forehead, ' Listen, Annie,
How merry they are down yonder in the
wood.
Tired, Annie ? ' for she did not speak a
word.

'Tired?' but her face had fallen upon her
   hands;
At which, as with a kind of anger in him,
'The ship was lost,' he said, 'the ship was
   lost! 390
No more of that! why should you kill
   yourself
And make them orphans quite?' And
   Annie said,
'I thought not of it; but — I know not
   why —
Their voices make me feel so solitary.'

Then Philip coming somewhat closer
   spoke:
'Annie, there is a thing upon my mind,
And it has been upon my mind so long
That, tho' I know not when it first came
   there,
I know that it will out at last. O Annie,
It is beyond all hope, against all chance,
That he who left you ten long years ago
Should still be living; well, then — let me
   speak. 402
I grieve to see you poor and wanting help;
I cannot help you as I wish to do
Unless — they say that women are so
   quick —
Perhaps you know what I would have you
   know —
I wish you for my wife. I fain would
   prove
A father to your children; I do think
They love me as a father; I am sure
That I love them as if they were mine
   own; 410
And I believe, if you were fast my wife,
That after all these sad uncertain years
We might be still as happy as God grants
To any of his creatures. Think upon it;
For I am well-to-do — no kin, no care,
No burthen, save my care for you and
   yours,
And we have known each other all our lives,
And I have loved you longer than you
   know.'

Then answer'd Annie — tenderly she
   spoke:
'You have been as God's good angel in our
   house. 420
God bless you for it, God reward you for it,
Philip, with something happier than my-
   self.
Can one love twice? can you be ever loved

As Enoch was? what is it that you ask?'
'I am content,' he answer'd, 'to be loved
A little after Enoch.' 'O,' she cried,
Scared as it were, 'dear Philip, wait a
   while.
If Enoch comes — but Enoch will not
   come —
Yet wait a year, a year is not so long.
Surely I shall be wiser in a year. 430
O, wait a little!' Philip sadly said,
'Annie, as I have waited all my life
I well may wait a little.' 'Nay,' she cried,
'I am bound: you have my promise — in a
   year.
Will you not bide your year as I bide
   mine?'
And Philip answer'd, 'I will bide my year.'

Here both were mute, till Philip glancing
   up
Beheld the dead flame of the fallen day
Pass from the Danish barrow overhead;
Then, fearing night and chill for Annie,
   rose 440
And sent his voice beneath him thro' the
   wood.
Up came the children laden with their
   spoil;
Then all descended to the port, and there
At Annie's door he paused and gave his
   hand,
Saying gently, 'Annie, when I spoke to you,
That was your hour of weakness. I was
   wrong,
I am always bound to you, but you are
   free.'
Then Annie weeping answer'd, 'I am
   bound.'

She spoke; and in one moment as it were,
While yet she went about her household
   ways, 450
Even as she dwelt upon his latest words,
That he had loved her longer than she
   knew,
That autumn into autumn flash'd again,
And there he stood once more before her
   face,
Claiming her promise. 'Is it a year?'
   she ask'd.
'Yes, if the nuts,' he said, 'be ripe again;
Come out and see.' But she — she put him
   off —
So much to look to — such a change — a
   month —

Give her a month — she knew that she was
      bound —
A month — no more.   Then Philip with his
      eyes   460
Full of that lifelong hunger, and his voice
Shaking a little like a drunkard's hand,
'Take your own time, Annie, take your own
      time.'
And Annie could have wept for pity of him;
And yet she held him on delayingly
With many a scarce-believable excuse,
Trying his truth and his long-sufferance,
Till half another year had slipt away.

By this the lazy gossips of the port,
Abhorrent of a calculation crost,   470
Began to chafe as at a personal wrong.
Some thought that Philip did but trifle
      with her;
Some that she but held off to draw him on;
And others laugh'd at her and Philip too,
As simple folk that knew not their own
      minds;
And one, in whom all evil fancies clung
Like serpent eggs together, laughingly
Would hint at worse in either.   Her own son
Was silent, tho' he often look'd his wish;
But evermore the daughter prest upon her
To wed the man so dear to all of them   481
And lift the household out of poverty;
And Philip's rosy face contracting grew
Careworn and wan; and all these things
      fell on her
Sharp as reproach.

                  At last one night it chanced
That Annie could not sleep, but earnestly
Pray'd for a sign, 'My Enoch, is he gone?'
Then compass'd round by the blind wall of
      night
Brook'd not the expectant terror of her
      heart,
Started from bed, and struck herself a
      light,   490
Then desperately seized the holy Book,
Suddenly set it wide to find a sign,
Suddenly put her finger on the text,
'Under the palm-tree.'   That was nothing
      to her,
No meaning there; she closed the Book and
      slept.
When lo! her Enoch sitting on a height,
Under a palm-tree, over him the sun.
'He is gone,' she thought, 'he is happy, he
      is singing

Hosanna in the highest; yonder shines
The Sun of Righteousness, and these be
      palms   500
Whereof the happy people strowing cried
"Hosanna in the highest!"'   Here she
      woke,
Resolved, sent for him and said wildly to
      him,
'There is no reason why we should not wed.'
'Then for God's sake,' he answer'd, 'both
      our sakes,
So you will wed me, let it be at once.'

So these were wed, and merrily rang the
      bells,
Merrily rang the bells, and they were wed.
But never merrily beat Annie's heart.   509
A footstep seem'd to fall beside her path,
She knew not whence; a whisper on her ear,
She knew not what; nor loved she to be
      left
Alone at home, nor ventured out alone.
What ail'd her then that, ere she enter'd,
      often
Her hand dwelt lingeringly on the latch,
Fearing to enter?   Philip thought he knew:
Such doubts and fears were common to her
      state,
Being with child; but when her child was
      born,
Then her new child was as herself renew'd,
Then the new mother came about her heart,
Then her good Philip was her all-in-all, 521
And that mysterious instinct wholly died.

And where was Enoch?   Prosperously
      sail'd
The ship 'Good Fortune,' tho' at setting
      forth
The Biscay, roughly ridging eastward,
      shook
And almost overwhelm'd her, yet unvext
She slipt across the summer of the world,
Then after a long tumble about the Cape
And frequent interchange of foul and fair,
She passing thro' the summer world again,
The breath of heaven came continually 531
And sent her sweetly by the golden isles,
Till silent in her oriental haven.

There Enoch traded for himself, and
      bought
Quaint monsters for the market of those
      times,
A gilded dragon also for the babes.

Less lucky her home - voyage: at first
  indeed
Thro' many a fair sea-circle, day by day,
Scarce-rocking, her full-busted figure-head
Stared o'er the ripple feathering from her
  bows: 540
Then follow'd calms, and then winds vari-
  able,
Then baffling, a long course of them; and
  last
Storm, such as drove her under moonless
  heavens
Till hard upon the cry of 'breakers' came
The crash of ruin, and the loss of all
But Enoch and two others. Half the
  night,
Buoy'd upon floating tackle and broken
  spars,
These drifted, stranding on an isle at morn
Rich, but the loneliest in a lonely sea.

No want was there of human suste-
  nance,   550
Soft fruitage, mighty nuts, and nourishing
  roots;
Nor save for pity was it hard to take
The helpless life so wild that it was tame.
There in a seaward-gazing mountain-gorge
They built, and thatch'd with leaves of
  palm, a hut,
Half hut, half native cavern. So the three,
Set in this Eden of all plenteousness,
Dwelt with eternal summer, ill-content.
For one, the youngest, hardly more than
  boy,
Hurt in that night of sudden ruin and
  wreck,   560
Lay lingering out a five-years' death-in-
  life.
They could not leave him. After he was
  gone,
The two remaining found a fallen stem;
And Enoch's comrade, careless of himself,
Fire-hollowing this in Indian fashion, fell
Sun-stricken, and that other lived alone.
In those two deaths he read God's warning
  ' wait.'

The mountain wooded to the peak, the
  lawns
And winding glades high up like ways to
  heaven,
The slender coco's drooping crown of
  plumes,   570
The lightning flash of insect and of bird,
The lustre of the long convolvuluses
That coil'd around the stately stems, and
  ran
Even to the limit of the land, the glows
And glories of the broad belt of the
  world, —
All these he saw; but what he fain had
  seen
He could not see, the kindly human face,
Nor ever hear a kindly voice, but heard
The myriad shriek of wheeling ocean-fowl,
The league-long roller thundering on the
  reef,   580
The moving whisper of huge trees that
  branch'd
And blossom'd in the zenith, or the sweep
Of some precipitous rivulet to the wave,
As down the shore he ranged, or all day
  long
Sat often in the seaward-gazing gorge,
A shipwreck'd sailor, waiting for a sail.
No sail from day to day, but every day
The sunrise broken into scarlet shafts
Among the palms and ferns and precipices;
The blaze upon the waters to the east; 590
The blaze upon his island overhead;
The blaze upon the waters to the west;
Then the great stars that globed them-
  selves in heaven,
The hollower-bellowing ocean, and again
The scarlet shafts of sunrise — but no sail.

There often as he watch'd or seem'd to
  watch,
So still the golden lizard on him paused,
A phantom made of many phantoms moved
Before him haunting him, or he himself
Moved haunting people, things, and places,
  known   600
Far in a darker isle beyond the line;
The babes, their babble, Annie, the small
  house,
The climbing street, the mill, the leafy
  lanes,
The peacock yew-tree and the lonely Hall,
The horse he drove, the boat he sold, the
  chill
November dawns and dewy - glooming
  downs,
The gentle shower, the smell of dying
  leaves,
And the low moan of leaden-color'd seas.

Once likewise, in the ringing of his ears,
Tho' faintly, merrily — far and far away —

He heard the pealing of his parish bells; 611
Then, tho' he knew not wherefore, started up
Shuddering, and when the beauteous hateful isle
Return'd upon him, had not his poor heart
Spoken with That which being everywhere
Lets none who speaks with Him seem all alone,
Surely the man had died of solitude.

Thus over Enoch's early-silvering head
The sunny and rainy seasons came and went
Year after year.   His hopes to see his own, 620
And pace the sacred old familiar fields,
Not yet had perish'd, when his lonely doom
Came suddenly to an end.   Another ship —
She wanted water — blown by baffling winds,
Like the 'Good Fortune,' from her destined course,
Stay'd by this isle, not knowing where she lay;
For since the mate had seen at early dawn
Across a break on the mist-wreathen isle
The silent water slipping from the hills, 629
They sent a crew that landing burst away
In search of stream or fount, and fill'd the shores
With clamor.   Downward from his mountain gorge
Stept the long-hair'd, long-bearded solitary,
Brown, looking hardly human, strangely clad,
Muttering and mumbling, idiot-like it seem'd,
With inarticulate rage, and making signs
They knew not what; and yet he led the way
To where the rivulets of sweet water ran,
And ever as he mingled with the crew,
And heard them talking, his long-bounden tongue 640
Was loosen'd, till he made them understand;
Whom, when their casks were fill'd, they took aboard.
And there the tale he utter'd brokenly,
Scarce-credited at first but more and more,
Amazed and melted all who listen'd to it;
And clothes they gave him and free passage home,

But oft he work'd among the rest and shook
His isolation from him.   None of these
Came from his country, or could answer him,
If question'd, aught of what he cared to know. 650
And dull the voyage was with long delays,
The vessel scarce sea-worthy; but evermore
His fancy fled before the lazy wind
Returning, till beneath a clouded moon
He like a lover down thro' all his blood
Drew in the dewy meadowy morning-breath
Of England, blown across her ghostly wall.
And that same morning offcers and men
Levied a kindly tax upon themselves,
Pitying the lonely man, and gave him it;
Then moving up the coast they landed him, 661
Even in that harbor whence he sail'd before.

There Enoch spoke no word to any one,
But homeward — home — what home? had he a home? —
His home, he walk'd.   Bright was that afternoon,
Sunny but chill; till drawn thro' either chasm,
Where either haven open'd on the deeps,
Roll'd a sea-haze and whelm'd the world in gray,
Cut off the length of highway on before,
And left but narrow breadth to left and right 670
Of wither'd holt or tilth or pasturage.
On the nigh-naked tree the robin piped
Disconsolate, and thro' the dripping haze
The dead weight of the dead leaf bore it down.
Thicker the drizzle grew, deeper the gloom;
Last, as it seem'd, a great mist-blotted light
Flared on him, and he came upon the place.

Then down the long street having slowly stolen,
His heart foreshadowing all calamity,
His eyes upon the stones, he reach'd the home 680
Where Annie lived and loved him, and his babes

In those far-off seven happy years were
    born;
But finding neither light nor murmur
    there —
A bill of sale gleam'd thro' the drizzle —
    crept
Still downward thinking, 'dead or dead to
    me!'

Down to the pool and narrow wharf he
    went,
Seeking a tavern which of old he knew,
A front of timber-crost antiquity,
So propt, worm-eaten, ruinously old,
He thought it must have gone; but he was
    gone   690
Who kept it, and his widow Miriam Lane,
With daily - dwindling profits held the
    house;
A haunt of brawling seamen once, but
    now
Stiller, with yet a bed for wandering men.
There Enoch rested silent many days.

But Miriam Lane was good and garru-
    lous,
Nor let him be, but often breaking in,
Told him, with other annals of the port,
Not knowing — Enoch was so brown, so
    bow'd,
So broken — all the story of his house: 700
His baby's death, her growing poverty,
How Philip put her little ones to school,
And kept them in it, his long wooing her,
Her slow consent and marriage, and the
    birth
Of Philip's child; and o'er his countenance
No shadow past, nor motion. Any one,
Regarding, well had deem'd he felt the
    tale
Less than the teller; only when she closed,
'Enoch, poor man, was cast away and
    lost,'
He, shaking his gray head pathetically, 710
Repeated muttering, 'cast away and lost;'
Again in deeper inward whispers, 'lost!'

But Enoch yearn'd to see her face again:
'If I might look on her sweet face again,
And know that she is happy.' So the
    thought
Haunted and harass'd him, and drove him
    forth,
At evening when the dull November day
Was growing duller twilight, to the hill.

There he sat down gazing on all below;
There did a thousand memories roll upon
    him,   720
Unspeakable for sadness. By and by
The ruddy square of comfortable light,
Far-blazing from the rear of Philip's house,
Allured him, as the beacon-blaze allures
The bird of passage, till he madly strikes
Against it and beats out his weary life.

For Philip's dwelling fronted on the
    street,
The latest house to landward; but behind,
With one small gate that open'd on the
    waste,
Flourish'd a little garden square and
    wall'd,   730
And in it throve an ancient evergreen,
A yew-tree, and all round it ran a walk
Of shingle, and a walk divided it.
But Enoch shunn'd the middle walk and
    stole
Up by the wall, behind the yew; and
    thence
That which he better might have shunn'd,
    if griefs
Like his have worse or better, Enoch saw.

For cups and silver on the burnish'd
    board
Sparkled and shone; so genial was the
    hearth;
And on the right hand of the hearth he
    saw   740
Philip, the slighted suitor of old times,
Stout, rosy, with his babe across his knees;
And o'er her second father stoopt a girl,
A later but a loftier Annie Lee,
Fair-hair'd and tall, and from her lifted
    hand
Dangled a length of ribbon and a ring
To tempt the babe, who rear'd his creasy
    arms,
Caught at and ever miss'd it, and they
    laugh'd;
And on the left hand of the hearth he
    saw
The mother glancing often toward her
    babe,   750
But turning now and then to speak with
    him,
Her son, who stood beside her tall and
    strong,
And saying that which pleased him, for he
    smiled.

Now when the dead man come to life beheld
His wife his wife no more, and saw the babe
Hers, yet not his, upon the father's knee,
And all the warmth, the peace, the happiness,
And his own children tall and beautiful,
And him, that other, reigning in his place,
Lord of his rights and of his children's
 love —   760
Then he, tho' Miriam Lane had told him
 all,
Because things seen are mightier than things
 heard,
Stagger'd and shook, holding the branch,
 and fear'd
To send abroad a shrill and terrible cry,
Which in one moment, like the blast of
 doom,
Would shatter all the happiness of the
 hearth.

He therefore turning softly like a thief,
Lest the harsh shingle should grate underfoot,
And feeling all along the garden-wall,
Lest he should swoon and tumble and be
 found,   770
Crept to the gate, and open'd it and
 closed,
As lightly as a sick man's chamber-door,
Behind him, and came out upon the waste.

And there he would have knelt, but that
 his knees
Were feeble, so that falling prone he dug
His fingers into the wet earth, and pray'd:

'Too hard to bear ! why did they take
 me thence ?
O God Almighty, blessed Saviour, Thou
That didst uphold me on my lonely isle,
Uphold me, Father, in my loneliness 780
A little longer ! aid me, give me strength
Not to tell her, never to let her know.
Help me not to break in upon her peace.
My children too ! must I not speak to
 these ?
They know me not. I should betray myself.
Never ! no father's kiss for me — the girl
So like her mother, and the boy, my son.'

There speech and thought and nature
 fail'd a little,

And he lay tranced; but when he rose and
 paced
Back toward his solitary home again, 790
All down the long and narrow street he
 went
Beating it in upon his weary brain,
As tho' it were the burthen of a song,
'Not to tell her, never to let her know.'

He was not all unhappy. His resolve
Upbore him, and firm faith, and evermore
Prayer from a living source within the
 will,
And beating up thro' all the bitter world,
Like fountains of sweet water in the sea,
Kept him a living soul. 'This miller's
 wife,'   800
He said to Miriam, 'that you spoke about,
Has she no fear that her first husband
 lives ?'
'Ay, ay, poor soul,' said Miriam, 'fear
 enow !
If you could tell her you had seen him
 dead,
Why, that would be her comfort;' and he
 thought,
'After the Lord has call'd me she shall
 know,
I wait His time;' and Enoch set himself,
Scorning an alms, to work whereby to live.
Almost to all things could he turn his
 hand.
Cooper he was and carpenter, and wrought
To make the boatmen fishing - nets, or
 help'd   811
At lading and unlading the tall barks
That brought the stinted commerce of
 those days,
Thus earn'd a scanty living for himself.
Yet since he did but labor for himself,
Work without hope, there was not life in
 it
Whereby the man could live; and as the
 year
Roll'd itself round again to meet the day
When Enoch had return'd, a languor came
Upon him, gentle sickness, gradually 820
Weakening the man, till he could do no
 more,
But kept the house, his chair, and last his
 bed.
And Enoch bore his weakness cheerfully.
For sure no gladlier does the stranded
 wreck
See thro' the gray skirts of a lifting squall

The boat that bears the hope of life approach
To save the life despair'd of, than he saw
Death dawning on him, and the close of all.

For thro' that dawning gleam'd a kindlier hope
On Enoch thinking, 'after I am gone,   830
Then may she learn I loved her to the last.'
He call'd aloud for Miriam Lane and said:
'Woman, I have a secret — only swear,
Before I tell you — swear upon the book
Not to reveal it, till you see me dead.'
'Dead,' clamor'd the good woman, 'hear him talk!
I warrant, man, that we shall bring you round.'
'Swear,' added Enoch sternly, 'on the book;'
And on the book, half-frighted, Miriam swore.
Then Enoch rolling his gray eyes upon her,   840
'Did you know Enoch Arden of this town?'
'Know him?' she said, 'I knew him far away.
Ay, ay, I mind him coming down the street;
Held his head high, and cared for no man, he.'
Slowly and sadly Enoch answer'd her:
'His head is low, and no man cares for him.
I think I have not three days more to live;
I am the man.'   At which the woman gave
A half-incredulous, half-hysterical cry:
'You Arden, you! nay, — sure he was a foot   850
Higher than you be.'   Enoch said again:
'My God has bow'd me down to what I am;
My grief and solitude have broken me;
Nevertheless, know you that I am he
Who married — but that name has twice been changed —
I married her who married Philip Ray.
Sit, listen.'   Then he told her of his voyage,
His wreck, his lonely life, his coming back,
His gazing in on Annie, his resolve,   859
And how he kept it.   As the woman heard,
Fast flow'd the current of her easy tears,
While in her heart she yearn'd incessantly

To rush abroad all round the little haven,
Proclaiming Enoch Arden and his woes;
But awed and promise-bounden she forbore,
Saying only, 'See your bairns before you go!
Eh, let me fetch 'em, Arden,' and arose
Eager to bring them down, for Enoch hung
A moment on her words, but then replied:

'Woman, disturb me not now at the last,   870
But let me hold my purpose till I die.
Sit down again; mark me and understand,
While I have power to speak.   I charge you now,
When you shall see her, tell her that I died
Blessing her, praying for her, loving her;
Save for the bar between us, loving her
As when she laid her head beside my own.
And tell my daughter Annie, whom I saw
So like her mother, that my latest breath
Was spent in blessing her and praying for her.   880
And tell my son that I died blessing him.
And say to Philip that I blest him too;
He never meant us anything but good.
But if my children care to see me dead,
Who hardly knew me living, let them come,
I am their father; but she must not come,
For my dead face would vex her after-life.
And now there is but one of all my blood
Who will embrace me in the world-to-be.
This hair is his, she cut it off and gave it,
And I have borne it with me all these years,   891
And thought to bear it with me to my grave;
But now my mind is changed, for I shall see him,
My babe in bliss.   Wherefore when I am gone,
Take, give her this, for it may comfort her;
It will moreover be a token to her
That I am he.'

He ceased; and Miriam Lane
Made such a voluble answer promising all,
That once again he roll'd his eyes upon her
Repeating all he wish'd, and once again   900
She promised.

Then the third night after this,
While Enoch slumber'd motionless and
    pale,
And Miriam watch'd. and dozed at inter-
    vals,
There came so loud a calling of the sea
That all the houses in the haven rang.
He woke, he rose, he spread his arms
    abroad,
Crying with a loud voice, ' A sail ! a sail !
I am saved;' and so fell back and spoke
    no more.

So past the strong heroic soul away.
And when they buried him the little port
Had seldom seen a costlier funeral.   911

AYLMER'S FIELD

1793

This poem, first published with ' Enoch Ar-
den,' was less favorably received than the lat-
ter by the English critics, on account of what
' Blackwood ' calls ' Tennyson's old infelicity
in dealing with the higher orders.' That re-
viewer also finds fault with the construction
of the story : ' The incidents are somewhat trite,
and its characters more than somewhat im-
probable. Its heroine is a model of every
Christian virtue ; yet she deceives her father,
and carries on a clandestine correspondence
with her lover. Her pastor is an excellent
clergyman ; yet when two of his parishioners
seek the sanctuary for the first time after their
daughter's death, he seizes the opportunity to
preach publicly against them — an act surely
unbefitting the pulpit of any period or of any
country, but simply impossible in that of a de-
cent rector in the decorous Church of England
of the eighteenth century. . . . Averill's ser-
mon doubtless contains what a man, situated as
he was, could not help thinking ; but no less
certainly what a gentleman and a Christian
would, when the mischief was done and the
punishment had fallen, have scrupulously re-
frained from publicly expressing. Why pour
the molten lead of those fierce denunciations
into wounds yet deeper than his own ? Why
smite those afresh whom God had smitten so
terribly already ? The preacher, arising from
his own desolate hearth, like a prophet of old,
to denounce the crime which has laid it waste,
is unquestionably a grandly tragic figure. But
a deeper sense of the proprieties of character
might have enabled its possessor to attain this
fine effect without that perilous approach to
the unreal and to the theatrical, by which, as it

appears to us, it has been purchased in the pre-
sent instance.'

The ' Quarterly Review ' says of the poem:
' Full of wonderful beauty in places, and writ-
ten throughout as Mr. Tennyson alone can
write, we must, by the standard of his former
work, pronounce it a comparative failure. The
story does not bear the marks of such careful
thought, in its design, nor in the grouping of
its parts. After the simple and clear effect of
" Enoch Arden," " Aylmer's Field " gives an
uncertain impression, and wants a like repose.
Nor is there the same continuous unfolding of
probabilities in the action, nor the same pure
and noble feeling in the persons. . . . Sir Ayl-
mer Aylmer is drawn with no kindly insight;
he is a stupid ruffian, and being so is no type
of an English gentleman. His wife is a mere
shadow upon the page, and the author writes
throughout more in the spirit of a radical pam-
phleteer than of the poet laureate.'

Peter Bayne, on the other hand, remarks:
' " Aylmer's Field " seems to me the compan-
ion picture to " Locksley Hall." It is one of
the most tragic of Tennyson's pieces — one of
the saddest, sternest, and I might almost add
mightiest, poems in the world. In " Locksley
Hall " we see desecrated affection making two
persons unhappy ; in " Aylmer's Field " the
blight is more deadly and more comprehensive.
I know nothing of Tennyson's in which the
moral earnestness is so prophet-like as in this
great poem. With all the might of his genius
in its maturity, he pours a molten torrent of in-
dignation and of scorn upon that pride which
is, perhaps, the central vice of England, that
pride which displays itself in many ways — in
pride of birth, in pride of gold, in pride of in-
sular superiority, and which is always desolat-
ing and deadly. Pride, in this instance, tram-
pling love under its feet, provides exquisite pain
for all the chief personages in the poem, and
obliterates two ancient families from the face
of the earth. . . .

' In this poem Tennyson has reaped the high-
est honor man can attain, namely, that of add-
ing to the Scripture of his country ; nor should
I think it a much less dark or pernicious error
than the pride which caused all this woe, to
hold that the Almighty could speak only
through or to Jewish seers, and that there is
no true inspiration in such writing as this.'

The fact (see page 227 above) that the story
of the poem is true is a sufficient reply to the
criticisms of ' Blackwood ' and the ' Quarterly '
upon what seems ' improbable ' in it.

The present Lord Tennyson says, in the
' Memoir ' (vol. ii. p. 9): ' The opening lines of
" Aylmer's Field " unfold the moral of that
poem. The sequel describes the Nemesis which
fell upon Sir Aylmer Aylmer in his pride of

wealth. My father always felt a prophet's righteous wrath against this form of selfishness; and no one can read his terrible denunciations of such pride trampling on a holy human love, without being aware that the poet's heart burnt within him while at work on this tale of wrong.'

Dust are our frames; and, gilded dust, our pride
Looks only for a moment whole and sound,
Like that long-buried body of the king,
Found lying with his urns and ornaments,
Which at a touch of light, an air of heaven,
Slipt into ashes, and was found no more.

Here is a story which in rougher shape
Came from a grizzled cripple, whom I saw
Sunning himself in a waste field alone —
Old, and a mine of memories — who had
served,   10
Long since, a bygone rector of the place,
And been himself a part of what he told.

Sir Aylmer Aylmer, that almighty man,
The county God — in whose capacious hall,
Hung with a hundred shields, the family tree
Sprang from the midriff of a prostrate king —
Whose blazing wyvern weathercock'd the spire,
Stood from his walls and wing'd his entry-gates,
And swang besides on many a windy sign —
Whose eyes from under a pyramidal head
Saw from his windows nothing save his own —   21
What lovelier of his own had he than her,
His only child, his Edith, whom he loved
As heiress and not heir regretfully?
But 'he that marries her marries her name.'
This fiat somewhat soothed himself and wife,
His wife a faded beauty of the Baths,
Insipid as the queen upon a card;
Her all of thought and bearing hardly more
Than his own shadow in a sickly sun.   30

A land of hops and poppy-mingled corn,
Little about it stirring save a brook!
A sleepy land, where under the same wheel
The same old rut would deepen year by year;

Where almost all the village had one name;
Where Aylmer followed Aylmer at the Hall
And Averill Averill at the Rectory
Thrice over; so that Rectory and Hall,
Bound in an immemorial intimacy,
Were open to each other; tho' to dream   40
That Love could bind them closer well had made
The hoar hair of the baronet bristle up
With horror, worse than had he heard his priest
Preach an inverted scripture, sons of men,
Daughters of God; so sleepy was the land.

And might not Averill, had he will'd it so,
Somewhere beneath his own low range of roofs,
Have also set his many-shielded tree?
There was an Aylmer-Averill marriage once,
When the red rose was redder than itself,
And York's white rose as red as Lancaster's,   51
With wounded peace which each had prick'd to death.
'Not proven,' Averill said, or laughingly,
'Some other race of Averills'—proven or no,
What cared he? what, if other or the same?
He lean'd not on his fathers but himself.
But Leolin, his brother, living oft
With Averill, and a year or two before
Call'd to the bar, but ever call'd away
By one low voice to one dear neighborhood,
Would often, in his walks with Edith claim
A distant kinship to the gracious blood
That shook the heart of Edith hearing him.

Sanguine he was; a but less vivid hue
Than of that islet in the chestnut-bloom
Flamed in his cheek; and eager eyes, that still
Took joyful note of all things joyful, beam'd,
Beneath a mane-like mass of rolling gold,
Their best and brightest when they dwelt on hers,
Edith, whose pensive beauty, perfect else,
But subject to the season or the mood,   71
Shone like a mystic star between the less
And greater glory varying to and fro,

We know not wherefore; bounteously made,
And yet so finely, that a troublous touch
Thinn'd, or would seem to thin her in a day,
A joyous to dilate, as toward the light.
And these had been together from the first.
Leolin's first nurse was, five years after,
hers.
So much the boy foreran; but when his
date   80
Doubled her own, for want of playmates,
he —
Since Averill was a decad and a half
His elder, and their parents underground —
Had tost his ball and flown his kite, and
roll'd
His hoop to pleasure Edith, with her dipt
Against the rush of the air in the prone
swing,
Made blossom-ball or daisy-chain, arranged
Her garden, sow'd her name and kept it
green
In living letters, told her fairy-tales,
Show'd her the fairy footings on the grass,
The little dells of cowslip, fairy palms,   91
The petty mare's-tail forest, fairy pines,
Or from the tiny pitted target blew
What look'd a flight of fairy arrows aim'd
All at one mark, all hitting, make-believes
For Edith and himself; or else he forged,
But that was later, boyish histories
Of battle, bold adventure, dungeon, wreck,
Flights, terrors, sudden rescues, and true
love
Crown'd after trial; sketches rude and
faint,   100
But where a passion yet unborn perhaps
Lay hidden as the music of the moon
Sleeps in the plain eggs of the nightingale.
And thus together, save for college-times
Or Temple-eaten terms, a couple, fair
As ever painter painted, poet sang,
Or heaven in lavish bounty moulded, grew.
And more and more, the maiden woman-
grown,
He wasted hours with Averill; there, when
first
The tented winter-field was broken up   110
Into that phalanx of the summer spears
That soon should wear the garland; there
again
When burr and bine were gather'd; lastly
there
At Christmas; ever welcome at the Hall,
On whose dull sameness his full tide of
youth

Broke with a phosphorescence charming
even
My lady, and the baronet yet had laid
No bar between them. Dull and self-in-
volved,
Tall and erect, but bending from his height
With half-allowing smiles for all the world,
And mighty courteous in the main — his
pride   121
Lay deeper than to wear it as his ring —
He, like an Aylmer in his Aylmerism,
Would care no more for Leolin's walking
with her
Than for his old Newfoundland's, when they
ran
To loose him at the stables, for he rose
Two-footed at the limit of his chain,
Roaring to make a third; and how should
Love,
Whom the cross-lightnings of four chance-
met eyes
Flash into fiery life from nothing, follow
Such dear familiarities of dawn ?   131
Seldom, but when he does, master of all.

So these young hearts, not knowing that
they loved,
Not she at least, nor conscious of a bar
Between them, nor by plight or broken
ring
Bound, but an immemorial intimacy,
Wander'd at will, and oft accompanied
By Averill; his, a brother's love, that hung
With wings of brooding shelter o'er her
peace,
Might have been other, save for Leolin's —
Who knows ? but so they wander'd, hour
by hour   141
Gather'd the blossom that re-bloom'd, and
drank
The magic cup that fill'd itself anew.

A whisper half reveal'd her to herself.
For out beyond her lodges, where the brook
Vocal, with here and there a silence, ran
By sallowy rims, arose the laborers' homes,
A frequent haunt of Edith, on low knolls
That dimpling died into each other, huts
At random scatter'd, each a nest in bloom.
Her art, her hand, her counsel, all had
wrought   151
About them. Here was one that, summer-
blanch'd,
Was parcel-bearded with the traveller's-
joy

In autumn, parcel ivy-clad; and here
The warm-blue breathings of a hidden
  hearth
Broke from a bower of vine and honey-
  suckle.
One look'd all rose-tree, and another wore
A close-set robe of jasmine sown with stars.
This had a rosy sea of gillyflowers
About it; this, a milky-way on earth,   160
Like visions in the Northern dreamer's
  heavens,
A lily-avenue climbing to the doors;
One, almost to the martin-haunted eaves
A summer burial deep in hollyhocks;
Each, its own charm; and Edith's every-
  where;
And Edith ever visitant with him,
He but less loved than Edith, of her poor.
For she — so lowly-lovely and so loving,
Queenly responsive when the loyal hand
Rose from the clay it work'd in as she
  past,   170
Not sowing hedgerow texts and passing by,
Nor dealing goodly counsel from a height
That makes the lowest hate it, but a voice
Of comfort and an open hand of help,
A splendid presence flattering the poor
  roofs
Revered as theirs, but kindlier than them-
  selves
To ailing wife or wailing infancy
Or old bedridden palsy, — was adored;
He, loved for her and for himself. A grasp
Having the warmth and muscle of the
  heart,   180
A childly way with children, and a laugh
Ringing like proven golden coinage true,
Were no false passport to that easy realm,
Where once with Leolin at her side the girl,
Nursing a child, and turning to the warmth
The tender pink five-beaded baby-soles,
Heard the good mother softly whisper,
  'Bless,
God bless 'em! marriages are made in
  heaven.'

A flash of semi-jealousy clear'd it to her.
My lady's Indian kinsman unannounced   190
With half a score of swarthy faces came.
His own, tho' keen and bold and soldierly,
Sear'd by the close ecliptic, was not fair;
Fairer his talk, a tongue that ruled the
  hour,
Tho' seeming boastful. So when first he
  dash'd

Into the chronicle of a deedful day,
Sir Aylmer half forgot his lazy smile
Of patron, 'Good! my lady's kinsman
  good!'
My lady with her fingers interlock'd,
And rotatory thumbs on silken knees,   200
Call'd all her vital spirits into each ear
To listen; unawares they flitted off,
Busying themselves about the flowerage
That stood from out a stiff brocade in
  which,
The meteor of a splendid season, she,
Once with this kinsman, ah! so long ago,
Stept thro' the stately minuet of those
  days.
But Edith's eager fancy hurried with him
Snatch'd thro' the perilous passes of his life;
Till Leolin, ever watchful of her eye,   210
Hated him with a momentary hate.
Wife-hunting, as the rumor ran, was he.
I know not, for he spoke not, only show-
  er'd
His oriental gifts on every one
And most on Edith. Like a storm he came,
And shook the house, and like a storm he
  went.

Among the gifts he left her — possibly
He flow'd and ebb'd uncertain, to return
When others had been tested — there was
  one,   219
A dagger, in rich sheath with jewels on it
Sprinkled about in gold that branch'd itself
Fine as ice-ferns on January panes
Made by a breath. I know not whence at
  first,
Nor of what race, the work; but as he told
The story, storming a hill-fort of thieves
He got it; for their captain after fight,
His comrades having fought their last be-
  low,
Was climbing up the valley, at whom he
  shot.
Down from the beetling crag to which he
  clung
Tumbled the tawny rascal at his feet,   230
This dagger with him, which, when now
  admired
By Edith whom his pleasure was to please,
At once the costly Sahib yielded to her.

And Leolin, coming after he was gone,
Tost over all her presents petulantly;
And when she show'd the wealthy scabbard,
  saying,

'Look what a lovely piece of workman-
  ship !'
Slight was his answer, 'Well — I care not
  for it.'
Then playing with the blade he prick'd his
  hand,
'A gracious gift to give a lady, this !'   240
'But would it be more gracious,' ask'd the
  girl,
'Were I to give this gift of his to one
That is no lady ?' 'Gracious ? No,' said
  he.
'Me ? — but I cared not for it. O, par-
  don me,
I seem to be ungraciousness itself.'
'Take it,' she added sweetly, 'tho' his gift;
For I am more ungracious even than you,
I care not for it either;' and he said,
'Why, then I love it;' but Sir Aylmer
  past,
And neither loved nor liked the thing he
  heard.   250

  The next day came a neighbor. Blues
  and reds
They talk'd of; blues were sure of it, he
  thought;
Then of the latest fox — where started —
  kill'd
In such a bottom. '.Peter had the brush,
My Peter, first;' and did Sir Aylmer know
That great pock-pitten fellow had been
  caught ?
Then made his pleasure echo, hand to hand,
And rolling as it were the substance of it
Between his palms a moment up and
  down —
'The birds were warm, the birds were
  warm upon him;   260
We have him now;' and had Sir Aylmer
  heard —
Nay, but he must — the land was ringing
  of it —
This blacksmith border - marriage — one
  they knew —
Raw from the nursery — who could trust a
  child ?
That cursed France with her egalities !
And did Sir Aylmer — deferentially
With nearing chair and lower'd accent —
  think —
For people talk'd — that it was wholly wise
To let that handsome fellow Averill walk
So freely with his daughter ? people
  talk'd —   270

The boy might get a notion into him;
The girl might be entangled ere she knew.
Sir Aylmer Aylmer slowly stiffening spoke:
'The girl and boy, sir, know their differ-
  ences !'
'Good,' said his friend, 'but watch !' and
  he, 'Enough,
More than enough, sir ! I can guard my
  own.'
They parted, and Sir Aylmer Aylmer
  watch'd.

  Pale, for on her the thunders of the
  house
Had fallen first, was Edith that same night;
Pale as the Jephtha's daughter, a rough
  piece   280
Of early rigid color, under which
Withdrawing by the counter door to that
Which Leolin open'd, she cast back upon
  him
A piteous glance, and vanish'd. He, as one
Caught in a burst of unexpected storm,
And pelted with outrageous epithets,
Turning beheld the Powers of the House
On either side the hearth, indignant; her,
Cooling her false cheek with a feather fan,
Him, glaring, by his own stale devil
  spurr'd,   290
And, like a beast hard-ridden, breathing
  hard.
'Ungenerous, dishonorable, base,
Presumptuous ! trusted as he was with her,
The sole succeeder to their wealth, their
  lands,
The last remaining pillar of their house,
The one transmitter of their ancient name,
Their child.' 'Our child !' 'Our heiress !'
  'Ours !' for still,
Like echoes from beyond a hollow, came
Her sicklier iteration. Last he said:
'Boy, mark me ! for your fortunes are to
  make.   300
I swear you shall not make them out of
  mine.
Now inasmuch as you have practised on her,
Perplext her, made her half forget herself,
Swerve from her duty to herself and us —
Things in an Aylmer deem'd impossible,
Far as we track ourselves — I say that
  this —
Else I withdraw favor and countenance
From you and yours for ever — shall you do.
Sir, when you see her — but you shall not
  see her —

No, you shall write, and not to her, but
 me; 310
And you shall say that having spoken with
 me,
And after look'd into yourself, you find
That you meant nothing — as indeed you
 know
That you meant nothing. Such a match as
 this !
Impossible, prodigious !' These were
 words,
As meted by his measure of himself,
Arguing boundless forbearance: after
 which,
And Leolin's horror-stricken answer, ' I
So foul a traitor to myself and her !
Never, O, never !' for about as long 320
As the wind - hover hangs in balance,
 paused
Sir Aylmer reddening from the storm
 within,
Then broke all bonds of courtesy, and cry-
 ing,
' Boy, should I find you by my doors again,
My men shall lash you from them like a
 dog;
Hence !' with a sudden execration drove
The footstool from before him, and arose;
So, stammering ' scoundrel ' out of teeth
 that ground 328
As in a dreadful dream, while Leolin still
Retreated half-aghast, the fierce old man
Follow'd, and under his own lintel stood
Storming with lifted hands, a hoary face
Meet for the reverence of the hearth, but
 now,
Beneath a pale and unimpassion'd moon,
Vext with unworthy madness, and de-
 form'd.

 Slowly and conscious of the rageful eye
That watch'd him, till he heard the pon-
 derous door
Close, crashing with long echoes thro' the
 land,
Went Leolin; then, his passions all in flood
And masters of his motion, furiously 340
Down thro' the bright lawns to his bro-
 ther's ran,
And foam'd away his heart at Averill's
 ear;
Whom Averill solaced as he might,
 amazed:
The man was his, had been his father's,
 friend;

He must have seen, himself had seen it
 long;
He must have known, himself had known;
 besides,
He never yet had set his daughter forth
Here in the woman-markets of the west,
Where our Caucasians let themselves be
 sold.
Some one, he thought, had slander'd Leo-
 lin to him. 350
' Brother, for I have loved you more as
 son
Than brother, let me tell you: I myself —
What is their pretty saying ? jilted, is it ?
Jilted I was; I say it for your peace.
Pain'd, and, as bearing in myself the
 shame
The woman should have borne, humiliated,
I lived for years a stunted sunless life;
Till after our good parents past away
Watching your growth, I seem'd again to
 grow.
Leolin, I almost sin in envying you. 360
The very whitest lamb in all my fold
Loves you; I know her; the worst thought
 she has
Is whiter even than her pretty hand.
She must prove true; for, brother, where
 two fight
The strongest wins, and truth and love are
 strength,
And you are happy; let her parents be.'

 But Leolin cried out the more upon
 them —
Insolent, brainless, heartless ! heiress,
 wealth,
Their wealth, their heiress ! wealth enough
 was theirs
For twenty matches. Were he lord of
 this, 370
Why, twenty boys and girls should marry
 on it,
And forty blest ones bless him, and him-
 self
Be wealthy still, ay, wealthier. He be-
 lieved
This filthy marriage-hindering Mammon
 made
The harlot of the cities; Nature crost
Was mother of the foul adulteries
That saturate soul with body. Name, too !
 name,
Their ancient name ! they *might* be proud;
 its worth

Was being Edith's.   Ah, how pale she had
   look'd
Darling, to-night ! they must have rated
   her   380
Beyond all tolerance.   These old pheasant-
   lords,
These partridge - breeders of a thousand
   years,
Who had mildew'd in their thousands, do-
   ing nothing
Since Egbert — why, the greater their dis-
   grace !
Fall back upon a name ! rest, rot in that !
Not *keep* it noble, make it nobler ? fools,
With such a vantage - ground for noble-
   ness !
He had known a man, a quintessence of
   man,
The life of all — who madly loved — and
   he,   389
Thwarted by one of these old father-fools,
Had rioted his life out, and made an end.
He would not do it ! her sweet face and
   faith
Held him from that; but he had powers,
   he knew it.
Back would he to his studies, make a
   name,
Name, fortune too; the world should ring
   of him,
To shame these mouldy Aylmers in their
   graves.
Chancellor, or what is greatest would he
   be —
' O brother, I am grieved to learn your
   grief —
Give me my fling, and let me say my say.'

At which, like one that sees his own ex-
   cess,   400
And easily forgives it as his own,
He laugh'd, and then was mute, but pre-
   sently
Wept like a storm; and honest Averill,
   seeing
How low his brother's mood had fallen,
   fetch'd
His richest bee's-wing from a binn reserved
For banquets, praised the waning red, and
   told
The vintage — when *this* Aylmer came of
   age —
Then drank and past it; till at length the
   two,
Tho' Leolin flamed and fell again, agreed

That much allowance must be made for
   men.   410
After an angry dream this kindlier glow
Faded with morning, but his purpose held.

Yet once by night again the lovers met,
A perilous meeting under the tall pines
That darken'd all the northward of her
   Hall.
Him, to her meek and modest bosom prest
In agony, she promised that no force,
Persuasion, no, nor death could alter her;
He, passionately hopefuller, would go,
Labor for his own Edith, and return   420
In such a sunlight of prosperity
He should not be rejected. ' Write to me !
They loved me, and because I love their
   child
They hate me.   There is war between us,
   dear,
Which breaks all bonds but ours; we must
   remain
Sacred to one another.' So they talk'd,
Poor children, for their comfort. The wind
   blew,
The rain of heaven and their own bitter
   tears,
Tears and the careless rain of heaven,
   mixt   429
Upon their faces, as they kiss'd each other
In darkness, and above them roar'd the
   pine.

So Leolin went; and as we task our-
   selves
To learn a language known but smatter-
   ingly
In phrases here and there at random, toil'd
Mastering the lawless science of our law,
That codeless myriad of precedent,
That wilderness of single instances,
Thro' which a few, by wit or fortune led,
May beat a pathway out to wealth and
   fame.
The jests, that flash'd about the pleader's
   room,   440
Lightning of the hour, the pun, the scurri-
   lous tale, —
Old scandals buried now seven decads deep
In other scandals that have lived and died,
And left the living scandal that shall die —
Were dead to him already; bent as he was
To make disproof of scorn, and strong in
   hopes,
And prodigal of all brain-labor he,

Charier of sleep, and wine, and exercise,
Except when for a breathing-while at eve,
Some niggard fraction of an hour, he ran
Beside the river-bank. And then indeed 451
Harder the times were, and the hands of power
Were bloodier, and the according hearts of men
Seem'd harder too; but the soft river-breeze,
Which fann'd the gardens of that rival rose
Yet fragrant in a heart remembering
His former talks with Edith, on him breathed
Far purelier in his rushings to and fro,
After his books, to flush his blood with air,
Then to his books again. My lady's cousin, 460
Half-sickening of his pension'd afternoon,
Drove in upon the student once or twice,
Ran a Malayan amuck against the times,
Had golden hopes for France and all mankind,
Answer'd all queries touching those at home
With a heaved shoulder and a saucy smile,
And fain had haled him out into the world,
And air'd him there. His nearer friend would say,
'Screw not the chord too sharply lest it snap.'
Then left alone he pluck'd her dagger forth 470
From where his worldless heart had kept it warm,
Kissing his vows upon it like a knight.
And wrinkled benchers often talk'd of him
Approvingly, and prophesied his rise;
For heart, I think, help'd head. Her letters too,
Tho' far between, and coming fitfully
Like broken music, written as she found
Or made occasion, being strictly watch'd,
Charm'd him thro' every labyrinth till he saw
An end, a hope, a light breaking upon him. 480

But they that cast her spirit into flesh,
Her worldly-wise begetters, plagued themselves
To sell her, those good parents, for her good.
Whatever eldest-born of rank or wealth

Might lie within their compass, him they lured
Into their net made pleasant by the baits
Of gold and beauty, wooing him to woo.
So month by month the noise about their doors,
And distant blaze of those dull banquets, made 489
The nightly wirer of their innocent hare
Falter before he took it. All in vain.
Sullen, defiant, pitying, wroth, return'd
Leolin's rejected rivals from their suit
So often, that the folly taking wings
Slipt o'er those lazy limits down the wind
With rumor, and became in other fields
A mockery to the yeomen over ale,
And laughter to their lords. But those at home,
As hunters round a hunted creature draw
The cordon close and closer toward the death, 500
Narrow'd her goings out and comings in;
Forbade her first the house of Averill,
Then closed her access to the wealthier farms,
Last from her own home-circle of the poor
They barr'd her. Yet she bore it, yet her cheek
Kept color — wondrous! but, O mystery!
What amulet drew her down to that old oak,
So old, that twenty years before, a part
Falling had let appear the brand of John —
Once grove-like, each huge arm a tree, but now 510
The broken base of a black tower, a cave
Of touchwood, with a single flourishing spray.
There the manorial lord too curiously
Raking in that millennial touchwood-dust
Found for himself a bitter treasure-trove;
Burst his own wyvern on the seal, and read
Writhing a letter from his child, for which
Came at the moment Leolin's emissary,
A crippled lad, and coming turn'd to fly,
But scared with threats of jail and halter gave 520
To him that fluster'd his poor parish wits
The letter which he brought, and swore besides
To play their go-between as heretofore
Nor let them know themselves betray'd;
and then,
Soul-stricken at their kindness to him, went
Hating his own lean heart and miserable.

Thenceforward oft from out a despot
   dream
The father panting woke, and oft, as dawn
Aroused the black republic on his elms,
Sweeping the froth-fly from the fescue
   brush'd   530
Thro' the dim meadow toward his treasure-
   trove,
Seized it, took home, and to my lady, —
   who made
A downward crescent of her minion mouth,
Listless in all despondence, — read; and
   tore,
As if the living passion symboll'd there
Were living nerves to feel the rent; and
   burnt,
Now chafing at his own great self defied,
Now striking on huge stumbling-blocks of
   scorn
In babyisms and dear diminutives
Scatter'd all over the vocabulary   540
Of such a love as like a chidden child,
After much wailing, hush'd itself at last
Hopeless of answer.   Then tho' Averill
   wrote
And bade him with good heart sustain him-
   self —
All would be well — the lover heeded not,
But passionately restless came and went,
And rustling once at night about the place,
There by a keeper shot at, slightly hurt,
Raging return'd.   Nor was it well for her
Kept to the garden now, and grove of
   pines,   550
Watch'd even there; and one was set to
   watch
The watcher, and Sir Aylmer watch'd them
   all,
Yet bitterer from his readings.   Once in-
   deed,
Warm'd with his wines, or taking pride in
   her,
She look'd so sweet, he kiss'd her tenderly,
Not knowing what possess'd him.   That one
   kiss
Was Leolin's one strong rival upon earth;
Seconded, for my lady follow'd suit,
Seem'd hope's returning rose; and then en-
   sued
A Martin's summer of his faded love,   560
Or ordeal by kindness.   After this
He seldom crost his child without a sneer;
The mother flow'd in shallower acrimonies,
Never one kindly smile, one kindly word;
So that the gentle creature shut from all

Her charitable use, and face to face
With twenty months of silence, slowly lost,
Nor greatly cared to lose, her hold on life.
Last some low fever ranging round to spy
The weakness of a people or a house,   570
Like flies that haunt a wound, or deer, or
   men,
Or almost all that is, hurting the hurt —
Save Christ as we believe him — found the
   girl
And flung her down upon a couch of fire,
Where careless of the household faces
   near,
And crying upon the name of Leolin,
She, and with her the race of Aylmer,
   past.

Star to star vibrates light; may soul to
   soul
Strike thro' a finer element of her own?
So, — from afar, — touch as at once? or
   why   580
That night, that moment, when she named
   his name,
Did the keen shriek, 'Yes, love, yes, Edith,
   yes,'
Shrill, till the comrade of his chambers
   woke,
And came upon him half-arisen from sleep,
With a weird bright eye, sweating and
   trembling,
His hair as it were crackling into flames,
His body half flung forward in pursuit,
And his long arms stretch'd as to grasp a
   flyer.
Nor knew he wherefore he had made the
   cry;
And being much befool'd and idioted   590
By the rough amity of the other, sank
As into sleep again.   The second day,
My lady's Indian kinsman rushing in,
A breaker of the bitter news from home,
Found a dead man, a letter edged with
   death
Beside him, and the dagger which himself
Gave Edith, redden'd with no bandit's
   blood;
'From Edith' was engraven on the blade.

Then Averill went and gazed upon his
   death.
And when he came again, his flock be-
   lieved —   600
Beholding how the years which are not
   Time's

Had blasted him — that many thousand days
Were clipt by horror from his term of life.
Yet the sad mother, for the second death
Scarce touch'd her thro' that nearness of the first,
And being used to find her pastor texts,
Sent to the harrow'd brother, praying him
To speak before the people of her child,
And fixt the Sabbath. Darkly that day rose.
Autumn's mock sunshine of the faded woods 610
Was all the life of it; for hard on these,
A breathless burthen of low - folded hea-vens
Stifled and chill'd at once; but every roof
Sent out a listener. Many too had known
Edith among the hamlets round, and since
The parents' harshness and the hapless loves
And double death were widely murmur'd, left
Their own gray tower, or plain-faced tab-ernacle,
To hear him; all in mourning these, and those 619
With blots of it about them, ribbon, glove,
Or kerchief; while the church, — one night, except
For greenish glimmerings thro' the lancets, — made
Still paler the pale head of him, who tow-er'd
Above them, with his hopes in either grave.

Long o'er his bent brows linger'd Aver-ill,
His face magnetic to the hand from which
Livid he pluck'd it forth, and labor'd thro'
His brief prayer-prelude, gave the verse, 'Behold,
Your house is left unto you desolate ! '
But lapsed into so long a pause again 630
As half amazed, half frighted, all his flock;
Then from his height and loneliness of grief
Bore down in flood, and dash'd his angry heart
Against the desolations of the world.

Never since our bad earth became one sea,
Which rolling o'er the palaces of the proud,

And all but those who knew the living God —
Eight that were left to make a purer world —
When since had flood, fire, earthquake, thunder, wrought
Such waste and havoc as the idolatries 640
Which from the low light of mortality
Shot up their shadows to the heaven of heavens,
And worshipt their own darkness in the Highest ?
'Gash thyself, priest, and honor thy brute Baäl,
And to thy worst self sacrifice thyself,
For with thy worst self hast thou clothed thy God.
Then came a Lord in no wise like to Baäl.
The babe shall lead the lion. Surely now
The wilderness shall blossom as the rose.
Crown thyself, worm, and worship thine own lusts ! — 650
No coarse and blockish God of acreage
Stands at thy gate for thee to grovel to —
Thy God is far diffused in noble groves
And princely halls, and farms, and flowing lawns,
And heaps of living gold that daily grow,
And title-scrolls and gorgeous heraldries.
In such a shape dost thou behold thy God.
Thou wilt not gash thy flesh for *him;* for thine
Fares richly, in fine linen, not a hair
Ruffled upon the scarfskin, even while 660
The deathless ruler of thy dying house
Is wounded to the death that cannot die;
And tho' thou numberest with the follow-ers
Of One who cried, "Leave all and follow me."
Thee therefore with His light about thy feet,
Thee with His message ringing in thine ears,
Thee shall thy brother man, the Lord from heaven,
Born of a village girl, carpenter's son,
Wonderful, Prince of Peace, the Mighty God,
Count the more base idolater of the two; 670
Crueller, as not passing thro' the fire
Bodies, but souls — thy children's — thro' the smoke,
The blight of low desires — darkening thine own

To thine own likeness; or if one of these,
Thy better born unhappily from thee,
Should, as by miracle, grow straight and
    fair —
Friends, I was bid to speak of such a one
By those who most have cause to sorrow
    for her —
Fairer than Rachel by the palmy well,   679
Fairer than Ruth among the fields of corn,
Fair as the Angel that said "Hail!" she
    seem'd,
Who entering fill'd the house with sudden
    light.
For so mine own was brighten'd — where
    indeed
The roof so lowly but that beam of heaven
Dawn'd sometime thro' the doorway? whose the babe
Too ragged to be fondled on her lap,
Warm'd at her bosom? The poor child of
    shame,
The common care whom no one cared for,
    leapt
To greet her, wasting his forgotten heart,
As with the mother he had never known, 690
In gambols; for her fresh and innocent eyes
Had such a star of morning in their blue,
That all neglected places of the field
Broke into nature's music when they saw
    her.
Low was her voice, but won mysterious
    way
Thro' the seal'd ear to which a louder one
Was all but silence — free of alms her
    hand —
The hand that robed your cottage-walls
    with flowers
Has often toil'd to clothe your little ones;
How often placed upon the sick man's
    brow   700
Cool'd it, or laid his feverish pillow smooth!
Had you one sorrow and she shared it not?
One burthen and she would not lighten it?
One spiritual doubt she did not soothe?
Or when some heat of difference sparkled
    out,
How sweetly would she glide between your
    wraths,
And steal you from each other! for she
    walk'd
Wearing the light yoke of that Lord of love
Who still'd the rolling wave of Galilee!
And one — of him I was not bid to speak —
Was always with her, whom you also
    knew.   711

Him too you loved, for he was worthy
    love.
And these had been together from the
    first;
They might have been together till the last.
Friends, this frail bark of ours, when sorely
    tried,
May wreck itself without the pilot's guilt,
Without the captain's knowledge; hope
    with me.
Whose shame is that, if he went hence with
    shame?
Nor mine the fault, if losing both of these
I cry to vacant chairs and widow'd walls,
"My house is left unto me desolate."'   721

While thus he spoke, his hearers wept;
    but some,
Sons of the glebe, with other frowns than
    those
That knit themselves for summer shadow,
    scowl'd
At their great lord. He, when it seem'd
    he saw
No pale sheet-lightnings from afar, but
    fork'd
Of the near storm, and aiming at his head,
Sat anger-charm'd from sorrow, soldier-
    like,
Erect; but when the preacher's cadence
    flow'd
Softening thro' all the gentle attributes   730
Of his lost child, the wife, who watch'd his
    face,
Paled at a sudden twitch of his iron mouth;
And 'O, pray God that he hold up!' she
    thought,
'Or surely I shall shame myself and him.'

'Nor yours the blame — for who beside
    your hearths
Can take her place — if echoing me you
    cry
"Our house is left unto us desolate"?
But thou, O thou that killest, hadst thou
    known,
O thou that stonest, hadst thou understood
The things belonging to thy peace and
    ours!   740
Is there no prophet but the voice that calls
Doom upon kings, or in the waste "Re-
    pent"?
Is not our own child on the narrow way,
Who down to those that saunter in the
    broad

Cries, " Come up hither," as a prophet to
   us ?
Is there no stoning save with flint and
   rock ?
Yes, as the dead we weep for testify —
No desolation but by sword and fire ?   748
Yes, as your moanings witness, and myself
Am lonelier, darker, earthlier for my loss.
Give me your prayers, for he is past your
   prayers,
Not past the living fount of pity in heaven.
But I that thought myself long-suffering,
   meek,
Exceeding "poor in spirit" — how the
   words
Have twisted back upon themselves, and
   mean
Vileness, we are grown so proud — I wish'd
   my voice
A rushing tempest of the wrath of God
To blow these sacrifices thro' the world —
Sent like the twelve-divided concubine
To inflame the tribes; but there — out
   yonder — earth   760
Lightens from her own central hell — O,
   there
The red fruit of an old idolatry —
The heads of chiefs and princes fall so fast,
They cling together in the ghastly sack —
The land all shambles — naked marriages
Flash from the bridge, and ever-murder'd
   France,
By shores that darken with the gathering
   wolf,
Runs in a river of blood to the sick sea.
Is this a time to madden madness then ?
Was this a time for these to flaunt their
   pride ?   770
May Pharaoh's darkness, folds as dense as
   those
Which hid the Holiest from the people's
   eyes
Ere the great death, shroud this great sin
   from all !
Doubtless our narrow world must canvass
   it.
O, rather pray for those and pity them,
Who, thro' their own desire accomplish'd,
   bring
Their own gray hairs with sorrow to the
   grave
Who broke the bond which they desired to
   break,
Which else had link'd their race with times
   to come —   779

Who wove coarse webs to snare her purity,
Grossly contriving their dear daughter's
   good —
Poor souls, and knew not what they did,
   but sat
Ignorant, devising their own daughter's
   death !
May not that earthly chastisement suffice ?
Have not our love and reverence left them
   bare ?
Will not another take their heritage ?
Will there be children's laughter in their
   hall
For ever and for ever, or one stone
Left on another, or is it a li ht thing
That I, their guest, their host, their ancient
   friend,   790
I made by these the last of all my race,
Must cry to these the last of theirs, as cried
Christ ere His agony to those that swore
Not by the temple but the gold, and made
Their own traditions God, and slew the
   Lord,
And left their memories a world's curse —
   " Behold,
Your house is left unto you desolate " ? '

   Ended he had not, but she brook'd no
   more;
Long since her heart had beat remorse-
   lessly,
Her crampt-up sorrow pain'd her, and a
   sense   800
Of meanness in her unresisting life.
Then their eyes vext her; for on entering
He had cast the curtains of their seat
   aside —
Black velvet of the costliest — she herself
Had seen to that. Fain had she closed them
   now,
Yet dared not stir to do it, only near'd
Her husband inch by inch, but when she laid,
Wifelike, her hand in one of his, he veil'd
His face with the other, and at once, as
   falls
A creeper when the prop is broken, fell   810
The woman shrieking at his feet, and
   swoon'd.
Then her own people bore along the nave
Her pendent hands, and narrow meagre
   face
Seam'd with the shallow cares of fifty
   years.
And her the lord of all the landscape
   round

Even to its last horizon, and of all
Who peer'd at him so keenly, follow'd out
Tall and erect, but in the middle aisle
Reel'd, as a footsore ox in crowded ways
Stumbling across the market to his death,
Unpitied; for he groped as blind, and
    seem'd   821
Always about to fall, grasping the pews
And oaken finials till he touch'd the door;
Yet to the lychgate, where his chariot
    stood,
Strode from the porch, tall and erect
    again.

But nevermore did either pass the gate
Save under pall with bearers. In one
    month,
Thro' weary and yet ever wearier hours,
The childless mother went to seek her
    child;
And when he felt the silence of his house
About him, and the change and not the
    change,   831
And those fixt eyes of painted ancestors
Staring for ever from their gilded walls
On him their last descendant, his own head
Began to droop, to fall. The man became
Imbecile; his one word was 'desolate.'
Dead for two years before his death was
    he;
But when the second Christmas came, es-
    caped
His keepers, and the silence which he felt,
To find a deeper in the narrow gloom   840
By wife and child; nor wanted at his end
The dark retinue reverencing death
At golden thresholds; nor from tender
    hearts,
And those who sorrow'd o'er a vanish'd
    race,
Pity, the violet on the tyrant's grave.
Then the great Hall was wholly broken
    down,
And the broad woodland parcell'd into
    farms;
And where the two contrived their daugh-
    ter's good,
Lies the hawk's cast, the mole has made his
    run,
The hedgehog underneath the plantain
    bores,   850
The rabbit fondles his own harmless face,
The slow-worm creeps, and the thin weasel
    there
Follows the mouse, and all is open field.

SEA DREAMS

This poem was first printed in 'Macmillan's
Magazine' for January, 1860, and afterwards
included in the 'Enoch Arden' volume.
'The grace of the poem,' says the 'Quarterly
Review,' 'is equalled by the winning kindli-
ness of it.' Stedman calls it 'a poem of mea-
sureless satire and much idyllic beauty.'

A CITY clerk, but gently born and bred;
His wife, an unknown artist's orphan
    child —
One babe was theirs, a Margaret, three
    years old.
They, thinking that her clear germander
    eye
Droopt in the giant-factoried city-gloom,
Came, with a month's leave given them, to
    the sea;
For which his gains were dock'd, however
    small.
Small were his gains, and hard his work;
    besides,
Their slender household fortunes — for the
    man   9
Had risk'd his little — like the little thrift,
Trembled in perilous places o'er a deep.
And oft, when sitting all alone, his face
Would darken, as he cursed his credulous-
    ness,
And that one unctuous mouth which lured
    him, rogue,
To buy strange shares in some Peruvian
    mine.
Now seaward-bound for health they gain'd
    a coast,
All sand and cliff and deep-inrunning cave,
At close of day; slept, woke, and went the
    next,
The Sabbath, pious variers from the church,
To chapel; where a heated pulpiteer,   20
Not preaching simple Christ to simple
    men,
Announced the coming doom, and fulmi-
    nated
Against the Scarlet Woman and her creed.
For sideways up he swung his arms, and
    shriek'd
'Thus, thus with violence,' even as if he
    held
The Apocalyptic millstone, and himself
Were that great angel; 'Thus with vio-
    lence
Shall Babylon be cast into the sea;

Then comes the close.' The gentle-hearted
    wife
Sat shuddering at the ruin of a world,   30
He at his own; but when the wordy storm
Had ended, forth they came and paced the
    shore,
Ran in and out the long sea-framing caves,
Drank the large air, and saw, but scarce
    believed —
The soot-flake of so many a summer still
Clung to their fancies — that they saw, the
    sea.
So now on sand they walk'd, and now on
    cliff,
Lingering about the thymy promontories,
Till all the sails were darken'd in the west,
And rosed in the east, then homeward and
    to bed;   40
Where she, who kept a tender Christian
    hope,
Haunting a holy text, and still to that
Returning, as the bird returns, at night,
'Let not the sun go down upon your
    wrath,'
Said, 'Love, forgive him.' But he did not
    speak;
And silenced by that silence lay the wife,
Remembering her dear Lord who died for
    all,
And musing on the little lives of men,
And how they mar this little by their
    feuds.

But while the two were sleeping, a full
    tide   50
Rose with ground - swell, which, on the
    foremost rocks
Touching, upjetted in spirts of wild sea-
    smoke,
And scaled in sheets of wasteful foam, and
    fell
In vast sea-cataracts — ever and anon
Dead claps of thunder from within the
    cliffs
Heard thro' the living roar. At this the
    babe,
Their Margaret cradled near them, wail'd
    and woke
The mother, and the father suddenly cried,
'A wreck, a wreck!' then turn'd and
    groaning said:

'Forgive! How many will say, "for-
    give," and find   60
A sort of absolution in the sound

To hate a little longer! No; the sin
That neither God nor man can well for-
    give,
Hypocrisy, I saw it in him at once.
Is it so true that second thoughts are best?
Not first, and third, which are a riper
    first?
Too ripe, too late! they come too late for
    use.
Ah, love, there surely lives in man and
    beast
Something divine to warn them of their
    foes;
And such a sense, when first I fronted him,
Said, "Trust him not;" but after, when I
    came   71
To know him more, I lost it, knew him
    less,
Fought with what seem'd my own un-
    charity,
Sat at his table, drank his costly wines,
Made more and more allowance for his
    talk;
Went further, fool! and trusted him with
    all,
All my poor scrapings from a dozen years
Of dust and desk-work. There is no such
    mine,
None; but a gulf of ruin, swallowing gold,
Not making. Ruin'd! ruin'd! the sea
    roars   80
Ruin — a fearful night!'

               'Not fearful; fair,'
Said the good wife, 'if every star in heaven
Can make it fair; you do but hear the tide.
Had you ill dreams?'

             'O, yes,' he said, 'I dream'd
Of such a tide swelling toward the land,
And I from out the boundless outer deep
Swept with it to the shore, and enter'd one
Of those dark caves that run beneath the
    cliffs.
I thought the motion of the boundless deep
Bore thro' the cave, and I was heaved upon
    it   90
In darkness; then I saw one lovely star
Larger and larger. "What a world," I
    thought,
"To live in!" but in moving on I found
Only the landward exit of the cave,
Bright with the sun upon the stream be-
    yond;
And near the light a giant woman sat,

All over earthy, like a piece of earth,
A pickaxe in her hand.   Then out I slipt
Into a land all sun and blossom, trees
As high as heaven, and every bird that
   sings;   100
And here the night-light flickering in my
   eyes
Awoke me.'

     'That was then your dream,' she said,
' Not sad, but sweet.'

               ' So sweet, I lay,' said he,
' And mused upon it, drifting up the stream
In fancy, till I slept again, and pieced
The broken vision; for I dream'd that
   still
The motion of the great deep bore me
   on,
And that the woman walk'd upon the
   brink.
I wonder'd at her strength, and ask'd her
   of it.
" It came," she said, " by working in the
   mines."   110
O, then to ask her of my shares, I thought;
And ask'd; but not a word; she shook her
   head.
And then the motion of the current ceased,
And there was rolling thunder; and we
   reach'd
A mountain, like a wall of burs and thorns;
But she with her strong feet up the steep
   hill
Trod out a path.   I follow'd, and at top
She pointed seaward; there a fleet of glass,
That seem'd a fleet of jewels under me,
Sailing along before a gloomy cloud   120
That not one moment ceased to thunder,
   past
In sunshine.   Right across its track there
   lay,
Down in the water, a long reef of gold,
Or what seem'd gold; and I was glad at
   first
To think that in our often-ransack'd world
Still so much gold was left; and then I
   fear'd
Lest the gay navy there should splinter
   on it,
And fearing waved my arm to warn them
   off;
An idle signal, for the brittle fleet —
I thought I could have died to save it —
   near'd,   130

Touch'd, clink'd, and clash'd, and vanish'd,
   and I woke,
I heard the clash so clearly.   Now I see
My dream was Life, the woman honest
   Work,
And my poor venture but a fleet of glass
Wreck'd on a reef of visionary gold.'

   ' Nay,' said the kindly wife to comfort
   him,
' You raised your arm, you tumbled down
   and broke
The glass with little Margaret's medicine
   in it;
And, breaking that, you made and broke
   your dream.
A trifle makes a dream, a trifle breaks.' 140

   ' No trifle,' groan'd the husband; ' yester-
   day
I met him suddenly in the street, and ask'd
That which I ask'd the woman in my dream.
Like her, he shook his head.   " Show me
   the books ! "
He dodged me with a long and loose ac-
   count.
" The books, the books ! " but he, he could
   not wait,
Bound on a matter he of life and death;
When the great Books — see Daniel seven
   and ten —
Were open'd, I should find he meant me
   well;   149
And then began to bloat himself, and ooze
All over with the fat affectionate smile
That makes the widow lean.   " My dearest
   friend,
Have faith, have faith ! We live by faith,"
   said he;
" And all things work together for the
   good
Of those " — it makes me sick to quote
   him — last
Gript my hand hard, and with God-bless-
   you went.
I stood like one that had received a blow.
I found a hard friend in his loose accounts,
A loose one in the hard grip of his hand,
A curse in his God-bless-you; then my
   eyes   160
Pursued him down the street, and far
   away,
Among the honest shoulders of the crowd,
Read rascal in the motions of his back,
And scoundrel in the supple-sliding knee.'

'Was he so bound, poor soul?' said the
  good wife;
'So are we all; but do not call him, love,
Before you prove him, rogue, and proved,
  forgive.
His gain is loss; for he that wrongs his
  friend
Wrongs himself more, and ever bears
  about
A silent court of justice in his breast,   170
Himself the judge and jury, and himself
The prisoner at the bar, ever condemn'd.
And that drags down his life; then comes
  what comes
Hereafter; and he meant, he said he meant,
Perhaps he meant, or partly meant, you
  well.'

  ' "With all his conscience and one eye
    askew" —
Love, let me quote these lines, that you
  may learn
A man is likewise counsel for himself,
Too often, in that silent court of yours —
"With all his conscience and one eye
  askew,   180
So false, he partly took himself for true;
Whose pious talk, when most his heart was
  dry,
Made wet the crafty crowsfoot round his eye;
Who, never naming God except for gain,
So never took that useful name in vain,
Made Him his catspaw and the Cross his
  tool,
And Christ the bait to trap his dupe and
  fool;
Nor deeds of gift, but gifts of grace he
  forged,
And snake-like slimed his victim ere he
  gorged;
And oft at Bible meetings, o'er the rest   190
Arising, did his holy oily best,
Dropping the too rough H in Hell and
  Heaven,
To spread the Word by which himself had
  thriven."
How like you this old satire?'

                    'Nay,' she said,
'I loathe it; he had never kindly heart,
Nor ever cared to better his own kind,
Who first wrote satire, with no pity in it.
But will you hear my dream, for I had one
That altogether went to music? Still
It awed me.'

Then she told it, having dream'd   200
Of that same coast. —

              But round the North, a light,
A belt, it seem'd, of luminous vapor, lay,
And ever in it a low musical note
Swell'd up and died; and, as it swell'd, a
  ridge
Of breaker issued from the belt, and still
Grew with the growing note, and when the
  note
Had reach'd a thunderous fulness, on those
  cliffs
Broke, mixt with awful light — the same as
  that
Living within the belt — whereby she saw
That all those lines of cliffs were cliffs no
  more,   210
But huge cathedral fronts of every age,
Grave, florid, stern, as far as eye could see,
One after one; and then the great ridge
  drew,
Lessening to the lessening music, back,
And past into the belt and swell'd again
Slowly to music. Ever when it broke
The statues, king, or saint, or founder
  fell;
Then from the gaps and chasms of ruin
  left
Came men and women in dark clusters
  round,
Some crying, 'Set them up! they shall not
  fall!'   220
And others, 'Let them lie, for they have
  fallen.'
And still they strove and wrangled; and
  she grieved
In her strange dream, she knew not why,
  to find
Their wildest wailings never out of tune
With that sweet note; and ever as their
  shrieks
Ran highest up the gamut, that great wave
Returning, while none mark'd it, on the
  crowd
Broke, mixt with awful light, and show'd
  their eyes
Glaring, and passionate looks, and swept
  away
The men of flesh and blood, and men of
  stone,   230
To the waste deeps together.

                        'Then I fixt
My wistful eyes on two fair images,

Both crown'd with stars and high among
   the stars, —
The Virgin Mother standing with her child
High up on one of those dark minster-
   fronts —
Till she began to totter, and the child
Clung to the mother, and sent out a cry
Which mixt with little Margaret's, and I
   woke,
And my dream awed me; — well — but
   what are dreams?
Yours came but from the breaking of a
   glass,   240
And mine but from the crying of a child.'

   'Child? No!' said he, 'but this tide's
   roar, and his,
Our Boanerges with his threats of doom
And loud-lung'd Antibabylonianisms —
Altho' I grant but little music there —
Went both to make your dream; but if
   there were
A music harmonizing our wild cries,
Sphere-music such as that you dream'd
   about,
Why, that would make our passions far too
   like
The discords dear to the musician. No —
One shriek of hate would jar all the hymns
   of heaven.   251
True devils with no ear, they howl in tune
With nothing but the devil!'

                   '"True" indeed!
One of our town, but later by an hour
Here than ourselves, spoke with me on the
   shore;
While you were running down the sands,
   and made
The dimpled flounce of the sea-furbelow
   flap,
Good man, to please the child. She brought
   strange news.
Why were you silent when I spoke to-
   night?   259
I had set my heart on your forgiving him
Before you knew. We *must* forgive the
   dead.'

   'Dead! who is dead?'

               'The man your eye pursued.
A little after you had parted with him,
He suddenly dropt dead of heart-disease.'

'Dead? he? of heart-disease? what
   heart had he
To die of? dead!'

            'Ah, dearest, if there be
A devil in man, there is an angel too,
And if he did that wrong you charge him
   with,
His angel broke his heart. But your rough
   voice —
You spoke so loud — has roused the child
   again.   270
Sleep, little birdie, sleep! will she not
   sleep
Without her "little birdie"? well, then,
   sleep,
And I will sing you "birdie."'

                     Saying this,
The woman half turn'd round from him
   she loved,
Left him one hand, and reaching thro' the
   night
Her other, found — for it was close beside —
And half-embraced the basket cradle-
   head
With one soft arm, which, like the pliant
   bough
That moving moves the nest and nestling,
   sway'd   279
The cradle, while she sang this baby-song:

   What does little birdie say
   In her nest at peep of day?
   Let me fly, says little birdie,
   Mother, let me fly away.
   Birdie, rest a little longer,
   Till the little wings are stronger,
   So she rests a little longer,
   Then she flies away.

   What does little baby say,
   In her bed at peep of day?   290
   Baby says, like little birdie,
   Let me rise and fly away.
   Baby, sleep a little longer,
   Till the little limbs are stronger;
   If she sleeps a little longer,
   Baby too shall fly away.

   'She sleeps; let us too, let all evil, sleep.
He also sleeps — another sleep than ours.
He can do no more wrong; forgive him,
   dear,
And I shall sleep the sounder!'

Then the man,
'His deeds yet live, the worst is yet to
   come.   301
Yet let your sleep for this one night be
   sound;
I do forgive him!'

      'Thanks, my love,' she said,
' Your own will be the sweeter,' and they
   slept.

ODE SUNG AT THE OPENING OF THE INTERNATIONAL EXHIBITION

Originally entitled : ' May the First, 1862,'
and first printed, incorrectly and with omis-
sions, in the ' Times,' April 24, 1862. A cor-
rect version appeared in ' Fraser's Magazine,'
for June, 1862.
A Greek translation of the Ode, signed
W. G. C., appeared in the ' Times,' July 14,
1862 (when the original poem was reprinted
with errors that called forth a letter from the
poet to the editor) ; and a Latin verse trans-
lation, signed W., in the same journal, Jul
1862.

I

UPLIFT a thousand voices full and sweet,
   In this wide hall with earth's invention
      stored,
   And praise the invisible universal Lord,
Who lets once more in peace the nations
   meet,
   Where Science, Art, and Labor have out-
      pour'd
Their myriad horns of plenty at our feet.

II

O silent father of our Kings to be,
Mourn'd in this golden hour of jubilee,
For this, for all, we weep our thanks
   thee !

III

The world-compelling plan was thine, —
And, lo ! the long laborious miles
Of Palace; lo ! the giant aisles,
Rich in model and design;
Harvest-tool and husbandry,
Loom and wheel and enginery,
Secrets of the sullen mine,
Steel and gold, and corn and wine,
Fabric rough, or fairy-fine,

Sunny tokens of the Line,
Polar marvels, and a feast
Of wonder, out of West and East,
And shapes and hues of Art divine !
All of beauty, all of use,
That one fair planet can produce,
   Brought from under every star,
Blown from over every main,
And mixt, as life is mixt with pain,
   The works of peace with works of war.

IV

   Is the goal so far away ?
   Far, how far no tongue can say,
   Let us dream our dream to-day.

V

O ye, the wise who think, the wise who
   reign,
From growing Commerce loose her latest
   chain,
And let the fair white-wing'd peacemaker
   fly
To happy havens under all the sky,
And mix the seasons and the golden
   hours;
Till each man find his own in all men's
   good,
And all men work in noble brotherhood,
Breaking their mailed fleets and armed
   towers,
And ruling by obeying Nature's powers,
And gathering all the fruits of earth and
   crown'd with all her flowers.

A WELCOME TO ALEXANDRA

MARCH 7, 1863

Written on the arrival of the Princess Al-
exandra in England just before her marriage
to the Prince of Wales on the 10th of March,
1863 ; published separately the same month ;
and afterwards included in the ' Enoch Arden '
volume. Thackeray, in the ' Cornhill Maga-
zine,' compared the poem to the waving of a
flaring pine-tree torch on a windy headland.

SEA-KINGS' daughter from over the sea,
               Alexandra !
Saxon and Norman and Dane are we,
But all of us Danes in our welcome of
   thee,
               Alexandra !

Welcome her, thunders of fort and of fleet !
Welcome her, thundering cheer of the
    street !
Welcome her, all things youthful and
    sweet,
Scatter the blossom under her feet !
Break, happy land, into earlier flowers !
Make music, O bird, in the new - budded
    bowers !
Blazon your mottoes of blessing and prayer !
Welcome her, welcome her, all that is
    ours !
Warble, O bugle, and trumpet, blare !
Flags, flutter out upon turrets and towers !
Flames, on the windy headland flare !
Utter your jubilee, steeple and spire !
Clash, ye bells, in the merry March air !
Flash, ye cities, in rivers of fire !
Rush to the roof, sudden rocket, and
    higher
Melt into stars for the land's desire !
Roll and rejoice, jubilant voice,
Roll as a ground - swell dash'd on the
    strand,
Roar as the sea when he welcomes the land,
And welcome her, welcome the land's de-
    sire,
The sea-kings' daughter as happy as fair,
Blissful bride of a blissful heir,
Bride of the heir of the kings of the sea —
O joy to the people and joy to the throne,
Come to us, love us and make us your
    own;
For Saxon or Dane or Norman we,
Teuton or Celt, or whatever we be,
We are each all Dane in our welcome of
    thee,
                    Alexandra !

THE GRANDMOTHER

First printed in ' Once a Week,' July 16,
1859, with the title, ' The Grandmother's Apo-
logy,' and an illustration by Millais.

I

AND Willy, my eldest-born, is gone, you
    say, little Anne ?
Ruddy and white, and strong on his legs,
    he looks like a man.
And Willy's wife has written; she never
    was over-wise,
Never the wife for Willy; he would n't
    take my advice.

II

For, Annie, you see, her father was not the
    man to save,
Had n't a head to manage, and drank him-
    self into his grave.
Pretty enough, very pretty ! but I was
    against it for one.
Eh ! — but he would n't hear me — and
    Willy, you say, is gone.

III

Willy, my beauty, my eldest - born, the
    flower of the flock;
Never a man could fling him, for Willy
    stood like a rock.   10
' Here 's a leg for a babe of a week !' says
    Doctor; and he would be bound
There was not his like that year in twenty
    parishes round.

IV

Strong of his hands, and strong on his legs,
    but still of his tongue !
I ought to have gone before him; I wonder
    he went so young.
I cannot cry for him, Annie; I have not
    long to stay.
Perhaps I shall see him the sooner, for he
    lived far away.

V

Why do you look at me, Annie ? you think
    I am hard and cold;
But all my children have gone before me,
    I am so old.
I cannot weep for Willy, nor can I weep
    for the rest;
Only at your age, Annie, I could have wept
    with the best.   20

VI

For I remember a quarrel I had with your
    father, my dear,
All for a slanderous story, that cost me
    many a tear.
I mean your grandfather, Annie; it cost
    me a world of woe,
Seventy years ago, my darling, seventy
    years ago.

VII

For Jenny, my cousin, had come to the
    place, and I knew right well
That Jenny had tript in her time; I knew,
    but I would not tell.

And she to be coming and slandering me,
  the base little liar !
But the tongue is a fire, as you know, my
  dear, the tongue is a fire.

VIII

And the parson made it his text that week,
  and he said likewise
That a lie which is half a truth is ever the
  blackest of lies,   30
That a lie which is all a lie may be met and
  fought with outright,
But a lie which is part a truth is a harder
  matter to fight.

IX

And Willy had not been down to the farm
  for a week and a day;
And all things look'd half-dead, tho' it was
  the middle of May.
Jenny, to slander me, who knew what
  Jenny had been !
But soiling another, Annie, will never
  make oneself clean.

X

And I cried myself well-nigh blind, and all
  of an evening late
I climb'd to the top of the garth, and stood
  by the road at the gate.
The moon like a rick on fire was rising
  over the dale,
And whit, whit, whit, in the bush beside
  me chirrupt the nightingale.   40

XI

All of a sudden he stopt; there past by the
  gate of the farm
Willy, — he did n't see me, — and Jenny
  hung on his arm.
Out into the road I started, and spoke I
  scarce knew how;
Ah, there 's no fool like the old one — it
  makes me angry now.

XII

Willy stood up like a man, and look'd the
  thing that he meant;
Jenny, the viper, made me a mocking curt-
  sey and went.
And I said, 'Let us part; in a hundred
  years it 'll all be the same.
You cannot love me at all, if you love not
  my good name.'

XIII

And he turn'd, and I saw his eyes all wet,
  in the sweet moonshine:
'Sweetheart, I love you so well that your
  good name is mine.   50
And what do I care for Jane, let her speak
  of you well or ill;
But marry me out of hand; we two shall be
  happy still.'

XIV

'Marry you, Willy !' said I, 'but I needs
  must speak my mind,
And I fear you 'll listen to tales, be jealous
  and hard and unkind.'
But he turn'd and claspt me in his arms,
  and answer'd, 'No, love, no;'
Seventy years ago, my darling, seventy
  years ago.

XV

So Willy and I were wedded. I wore a
  lilac gown;
And the ringers rang with a will, and he
  gave the ringers a crown.
But the first that ever I bare was dead be-
  fore he was born;
Shadow and shine is life, little Annie,
  flower and thorn.   60

XVI

That was the first time, too, that ever I
  thought of death.
There lay the sweet little body that never
  had drawn a breath.
I had not wept, little Anne, not since I had
  been a wife;
But I wept like a child that day, for the
  babe had fought for his life.

XVII

His dear little face was troubled, as if with
  anger or pain;
I look'd at the still little body — his trouble
  had all been in vain.
For Willy I cannot weep, I shall see him
  another morn;
But I wept like a child for the child that
  was dead before he was born.

XVIII

But he cheer'd me, my good man, for he
  seldom said me nay.
Kind, like a man, was he; like a man, too,
  would have his way;   70

Never jealous — not he. We had many a
    happy year;
And he died, and I could not weep — my
    own time seem'd so near.

XIX

But I wish'd it had been God's will that I,
    too, then could have died;
I began to be tired a little, and fain had
    slept at his side.
And that was ten years back, or more, if I
    don't forget;
But as to the children, Annie, they 're all
    about me yet.

XX

Pattering over the boards, my Annie who
    left me at two,
Patter she goes, my own little Annie, an
    Annie like you;
Pattering over the boards, she comes and
    goes at her will,
While Harry is in the five-acre and Charlie
    ploughing the hill.   80

XXI

And Harry and Charlie, I hear them too
    — they sing to their team;
Often they come to the door in a pleasant
    kind of a dream.
They come and sit by my chair, they hover
    about my bed —
I am not always certain if they be alive or
    dead.

XXII

And yet I know for a truth there 's none of
    them left alive,
For Harry went at sixty, your father at
    sixty-five;
And Willy, my eldest-born, at nigh three-
    score and ten.
I knew them all as babies, and now they 're
    elderly men.

XXIII

For mine is a time of peace, it is not often
    I grieve;
I am oftener sitting at home in my father's
    farm at eve;   90
And the neighbors come and laugh and
    gossip, and so do I;
I find myself often laughing at things that
    have long gone by.

XXIV

To be sure the preacher says, our sins
    should make us sad;
But mine is a time of peace, and there is
    Grace to be had;
And God, not man, is the Judge of us all
    when life shall cease;
And in this Book, little Annie, the message
    is one of peace.

XXV

And age is a time of peace, so it be free
    from pain,
And happy has been my life; but I would
    not live it again.
I seem to be tired a little, that 's all, and
    long for rest;
Only at your age, Annie, I could have wept
    with the best.   100

XXVI

So Willy has gone, my beauty, my eldest-
    born, my flower;
But how can I weep for Willy, he has but
    gone for an hour, —
Gone for a minute, my son, from this room
    into the next;
I, too, shall go in a minute. What time
    have I to be vext?

XXVII

And Willy's wife has written, she never
    was over-wise.
Get me my glasses, Annie; thank God that
    I keep my eyes.
There is but a trifle left you, when I shall
    have past away.
But stay with the old woman now; you can-
    not have long to stay.

NORTHERN FARMER

OLD STYLE

The 'Northern Farmer, Old Style,' appeared
in the 'Enoch Arden' volume, 1864; the
'Northern Farmer, New Style,' in the 'Holy
Grail' volume, 1870.

Stopford Brooke ('Tennyson,' London, 1894)
says of it: 'It is a vivid piece out of the great
comedy of man, not of its mere mirth, but of
that elemental humorousness of things which
belongs to the lives of the brutes as well as to

ourselves, that steady quaintness of the ancient earth and all who are born of her, which first made men smile, and which has enabled us to bear our pain better, and to love one another more, than might appear possible in a world where Nature generally seems to be doing her best to hurt us first, and then to kill us. . . . There never was a more superbly hewn piece of rough and vital sculpture.'

I

WHEER 'asta beän saw long and meä liggin' 'ere aloän ?
Noorse ? thoort nowt o' a noorse; whoy, Doctor 's abeän an' agoän;
Says that I moänt 'a naw moor aäle, but I beänt a fool;
Git ma my aäle, fur I beänt a-gawin' to breäk my rule.

II

Doctors, they knaws nowt, fur a says what 's nawways true;
Naw soort o' koind o' use to saäy the things that a do.
I 've 'ed my point o' aäle ivry noight sin' I beän 'ere.
An' I 've 'ed my quart ivry market-noight for foorty year.

III

Parson 's a beän loikewoise, an' a sittin' ere o' my bed.
'The Amoighty 's a taäkin o' you[1] to 'issén, my friend,' a said,
An' a towd ma my sins, an' 's toithe were due, an' I gied it in hond;
I done moy duty boy 'um, as I 'a done boy the lond.

IV

Larn'd a ma' beä. I reckons I 'annot sa mooch to larn.
But a cast oop, thot a did, 'bout Bessy Marris's barne.
Thaw a knaws I hallus voäted wi' Squoire an' choorch an' staäte,
An' i' the woost o' toimes I wur niver agin the raäte.

V

An' I hallus coom'd to 's choorch afoor moy Sally wur deäd,
An' 'eärd 'um a bummin' awaäy loike a buzzard-clock[2] ower my 'eäd,

---

An' I niver knaw'd whot a meän'd but I thowt a 'ad summut to saäy,
An' I thowt a said whot a owt to 'a said, an' I coom'd awaäy.

VI

Bessy Marris's barne ! tha knaws she laäid it to meä.
Mowt a beän, mayhap, for she wur a bad un, sheä.
'Siver, I kep 'um, I kep 'um, my lass, tha mun understond;
I done moy duty boy 'um, as I 'a done boy the lond.

VII

But Parson a cooms an' a goäs, an' a says it eäsy an' freeä:
'The Amoighty 's a taäkin o' you to 'issén, my friend,' says 'eä.
I weänt saäy men be loiars, thaw summun said it in 'aäste;
But 'e reäds wonn sarmin a weeäk, an' I 'a stubb'd Thurnaby waäste.

VIII

D' ya moind the waäste, my lass ? naw, naw, tha was not born then;
Theer wur a boggle in it, I often 'eärd 'um mysén;
Moäst loike a butter-bump,[1] fur I 'eärd 'um about an' about,
But I stubb'd 'um oop wi' the lot, an' raäved an' rembled 'um out.

IX

Keäper's it wur; fo' they fun 'um theer a-laäid of 'is faäce
Down i' the woild 'enemies[2] afoor I coom'd to the plaäce.
Noäks or Thimbleby — toäner[3] 'ed shot 'um as deäd as a naäil.
Noäks wur 'ang'd for it oop at 'soize — but git ma my aäle.

X

Dubbut looök at the waäste; theer warn't not feeäd for a cow;
Nowt at all but bracken an' fuzz, an' looök at it now —
Warn't worth nowt a haäcre, an' now theer 's lots o' feeäd,
Fourscoor[4] yows upon it, an' some on it down i' seeäd.[5]

---

[1] *ou* as in *hour*. [2] Cockchafer.

[1] Bittern. [2] Anemones. [3] One or other.
[4] *ou* as in *hour*. [5] Clover.

XI

Nobbut a bit on it 's left, an' I meän'd to 'a
    stubb'd it at fall,
Done it ta-year I meän'd, an' runn'd plow
    thruff it an' all,
If Godamoighty an' parson 'ud nobbut let
    ma aloän, —
Meä, wi' haäte hoonderd haäcre o' Squoire's,
    an' lond o' my oän.

XII

Do Godamoighty knaw what a 's doing
    a-taäkin' o' meä ?
I beänt wonn as saws 'ere a beän an' yon-
    der a peä;
An' Squoire 'ull be sa mad an' all — a' dear,
    a' dear !
And I 'a managed for Squoire coom
    Michaelmas thutty year.

XIII

A mowt 'a taäen owd Joänes, as 'ant not a
    'aäpoth o' sense,
Or a mowt 'a taäen young Robins — a niver
    mended a fence;
But Godamoighty a moost taäke meä an'
    taäke ma now,
Wi' aäf the cows to cauve an' Thurnaby
    hoälms to plow !

XIV

Looök 'ow quoloty smoiles when they seeäs
    ma a passin' boy,
Says to thessén, naw doubt, ' What a man
    a beä sewer-loy ! '
Fur they knaws what I beän to Squoire sin'
    fust a coom'd to the 'All;
I done moy duty by Squoire an' I done
    moy duty boy hall.

XV

Squoire 's i' Lunnon, an' summun I reckons
    'ull 'a to wroite,
For whoä 's to howd the lond ater meä thot
    muddles ma quoit;
Sartin-sewer I beä thot a weänt niver give
    it to Joänes,
Naw, nor a moänt to Robins — a niver rem-
    bles the stoäns.

XVI

But summun 'ull come ater meä mayhap
    wi' 'is kittle o' steäm
Huzzin' an' maäzin' the blessed feälds wi'
    the divil's oän teäm.

Sin' I mun doy I mun doy, thaw loife they
    says is sweet,
But sin' I mun doy I mun doy, for I couldn
    abeär to see it.

XVII

What atta stannin' theer fur, an' doesn
    bring ma the aäle ?
Doctor 's a 'toättler, lass, an a 's hallus i'
    the owd taäle;
I weänt breäk rules fur Doctor, a knaws
    naw moor nor a floy;
Git ma my aäle, I tell tha, an' if I mun doy
    I mun doy.

NORTHERN FARMER

NEW STYLE

I

Dosn't thou 'ear my 'erse's legs, as they
    canters awaäy ?
Proputty, proputty, proputty — that 's what
    I 'ears 'em saäy.
Proputty, proputty, proputty — Sam, thou 's
    an ass for thy païns;
Theer 's moor sense i' one o' 'is legs, nor in
    all thy braïns.

II

Woä — theer 's a craw to pluck wi' tha,
    Sam: yon 's parson's 'ouse —
Dosn't thou knaw that a man mun be
    eäther a man or a mouse ?
Time to think on it then; for thou 'll be
    twenty to weeäk.[1]
Proputty, proputty — woä then, woä — let
    ma 'ear mysén speäk.

III

Me an' thy muther, Sammy, 'as beän
    a-talkin' o' thee;
Thou 's beän talkin' to muther, an' she beän
    a-tellin' it me.
Thou 'll not marry for munny — thou 's
    sweet upo' parson's lass —
Noä — thou 'll marry for luvv — an' we
    boäth on us thinks tha an ass.

IV

Seeä'd her to-daäy goä by — Saäint's-daäy
    — they was ringing the bells.
She 's a beauty, thou thinks — an' soä is
    scoors o' gells,

[1] This week.

Them as 'as munny an' all — wot 's a
beauty ? — the flower as blaws.
But proputty, proputty sticks, an' pro-
putty, proputty graws.

V

Do'ant be stunt;[1] taäke time. I knaws
what maäkes tha sa mad.
Warn't I craäzed fur the lasses mysén
when I wur a lad ?
But I knaw'd a Quaäker feller as often 'as
towd ma this:
'Doänt thou marry for munny, but goä
wheer munny is !'

VI

An' I went wheer munny war; an' thy
muther coom to 'and,
Wi' lots o' munny laaïd by, an' a nicetish
bit o' land.
Maäybe she warn't a beauty — I niver giv
it a thowt —
But warn't she as good to cuddle an' kiss
as a lass as 'ant nowt ?

VII

Parson's lass 'ant nowt, an' she weänt 'a
nowt when 'e 's deäd,
Mun be a guvness, lad, or summut, and ad-
dle[2] her breäd.
Why ? fur 'e 's nobbut a curate, an' weänt
niver get hissén clear,
An' 'e maäde the bed as 'e ligs on afoor 'e
coom'd to the shere.

VIII

An' thin 'e coom'd to the parish wi' lots o'
Varsity debt,
Stook to his taaïl they did, an' 'e 'ant got
shut on 'em yet.
An' 'e ligs on 'is back i' the grip, wi' noän
to lend 'im a shove,
Woorse nor a far-welter'd[3] yowe; fur,
Sammy, 'e married fur luvv.

IX

Luvv ? what 's luvv ? thou can luvv thy
lass an' 'er munny too,
Maäkin' 'em goä togither, as they 've good
right to do.

[1] Obstinate.   [2] Earn.
[3] Or, fow-welter'd, — said of a sheep lying
on its back in the furrow.

Couldn I luvv thy muther by cause o' 'er
munny laaïd by ?
Naäy — fur I luvv'd 'er a vast sight moor
fur it; reäson why.

X

Ay, an' thy muther says thou wants to
marry the lass,
Cooms of a gentleman burn; an' we boäth
on us thinks tha an ass.
Woä then, proputty, wiltha ? — an ass as
near as mays nowt[1] —
Woä then, wiltha ? dangtha ! — the bees is
as fell as owt.[2]

XI

Breäk me a bit o' the esh for his 'eäd, lad,
out o' the fence !
Gentleman burn ! what 's gentleman burn ?
is it shillins an' pence ?
Proputty, proputty 's ivrything 'ere, an',
Sammy, I 'm blest
If it is n't the saäme oop yonder, fur them
as 'as it 's the best.

XII

Tis 'n them as 'as munny as breäks into
'ouses an' steäls,
Them as 'as coäts to their backs an' taäkes
their regular meäls.
Noä, but it 's them as niver knaws wheer a
meäl 's to be 'ad.
Taäke my word for it, Sammy, the poor in
a loomp is bad.

XIII

Them or thir feythers, tha sees, mun 'a
beän a laäzy lot,
Fur work mun 'a gone to the gittin' whin-
iver munny was got.
Feyther 'ad ammost nowt; leästways 'is
munny was 'id.
But 'e tued an' moil'd issén deäd, an' 'e died
a good un, 'e did.

XIV

Looök thou theer wheer Wrigglesby beck
cooms out by the 'ill !
Feyther run oop to the farm, an' I runs
oop to the mill;

[1] Makes nothing.
[2] The flies are as fierce as anything.

An' I 'll run oop to the brig, an' that thou 'll
　　live to see;
And if thou marries a good un I 'll leäve
　　the land to thee.

XV

Thim 's my noätions, Sammy, wheerby I
　　meäns to stick;
But if thou marries a bad un, I 'll leäve
　　the land to Dick. —
Coom oop, proputty, proputty — that 's
　　what I 'ears 'im saäy —
Proputty, proputty, proputty — canter an'
　　canter awaäy.

IN THE VALLEY OF CAUTERETZ

Written in September, 1861, but not pub-
lished until 1864 in the 'Enoch Arden' vol-
ume.
　　Cauteretz is a beautiful valley in the French
Pyrenees. The visit of Tennyson and Arthur
Hallam to the place, here commemorated, took
place in 1830. The date of the second visit
has sometimes been given as 1862, but Arthur
Hugh Clough's diary, in which he refers to
meeting Tennyson there, makes it 1861. Un-
der date of September 1, at Mont Dore-les-
Bains, he writes: 'The Tennysons arrived at
6.30 yesterday. Tennyson was here with Ar-
thur Hallam thirty-one years ago, and really
finds great pleasure in the place; they stayed
here and at Cauteretz. "Œnone," he said,
was written on the inspiration of the Pyrenees,
which stood for Ida.' The poet probably wrote
'two and thirty' in the verses for the sake of
euphony. 'I walk'd with one I loved one and
thirty years ago' would have offended his sen-
sitive ear.

ALL along the valley, stream that flashest
　　white,
Deepening thy voice with the deepening of
　　the night,
All along the valley, where thy waters
　　flow,
I walk'd with one I loved two and thirty
　　years ago.
All along the valley, while I walk'd to-day,
The two and thirty years were a mist that
　　rolls away;
For all along the valley, down thy rocky
　　bed,
Thy living voice to me was as the voice of
　　the dead,

And all along the valley, by rock and cave
　　and tree,
The voice of the dead was a living voice to
　　me.

THE FLOWER

First printed in the 'Enoch Arden' volume,
and unaltered.
　　The poem has been supposed to have some
personal reference, but Lord Tennyson himself
assured me that it had not. According to the
'Memoir' (vol. ii. p. 10), he described it in his
manuscript notes as 'an universal apologue.'

ONCE in a golden hour
　　I cast to earth a seed.
Up there came a flower,
　　The people said, a weed.

To and fro they went
　　Thro' my garden-bower,
And muttering discontent
　　Cursed me and my flower.

Then it grew so tall
　　It wore a crown of light,
But thieves from o'er the wall
　　Stole the seed by night:

Sow'd it far and wide
　　By every town and tower,
Till all the people cried,
　　'Splendid is the flower.'

Read my little fable:
　　He that runs may read.
Most can raise the flowers now
　　For all have got the seed.

And some are pretty enough,
　　And some are poor indeed;
And now again the people
　　Call it but a weed.

REQUIESCAT

First printed in the 'Enoch Arden' volume,
and unaltered.

FAIR is her cottage in its place,
　　Where yon broad water sweetly, slowly
　　glides.

It sees itself from thatch to base
Dream in the sliding tides.

And fairer she, but ah, how soon to die!
Her quiet dream of life this hour may
cease.
Her peaceful being slowly passes by
To some more perfect peace.

THE SAILOR BOY

First printed in the 'Victoria Regia,' Christmas, 1861 (edited by Miss Emily Faithfull), and afterwards included in the 'Enoch Arden' volume.

HE rose at dawn and, fired with hope,
Shot o'er the seething harbor-bar,
And reach'd the ship and caught the rope,
And whistled to the morning star.

And while he whistled long and loud
He heard a fierce mermaiden cry,
'O boy, tho' thou art young and proud,
I see the place where thou wilt lie.

'The sands and yeasty surges mix
In caves about the dreary bay,
And on thy ribs the limpet sticks,
And in thy heart the scrawl shall play.'

'Fool,' he answer'd, 'death is sure
To those that stay and those that roam,
But I will nevermore endure
To sit with empty hands at home.

'My mother clings about my neck,
My sisters crying, "Stay for shame;"
My father raves of death and wreck, —
They are all to blame, they are all to
blame.

'God help me! save I take my part
Of danger on the roaring sea,
A devil rises in my heart,
Far worse than any death to me.'

THE ISLET

First printed in the 'Enoch Arden' volume, and unaltered.

'WHITHER, O whither, love, shall we go,
For a score of sweet little summers or so?'
The sweet little wife of the singer said,

On the day that follow'd the day she was
wed,
'Whither, O whither, love, shall we go?'
And the singer shaking his curly head
Turn'd as he sat, and struck the keys
There at his right with a sudden crash,
Singing, 'And shall it be over the seas
With a crew that is neither rude nor rash,
But a bevy of Eroses apple-cheek'd,
In a shallop of crystal ivory-beak'd,
With a satin sail of a ruby glow,
To a sweet little Eden on earth that I know,
A mountain islet pointed and peak'd;
Waves on a diamond shingle dash,
Cataract brooks to the ocean run,
Fairily-delicate palaces shine
Mixt with myrtle and clad with vine,
And overstream'd and silvery-streak'd
With many a rivulet high against the sun
The facets of the glorious mountain flash
Above the valleys of palm and pine.'

'Thither, O thither, love, let us go.'

'No, no, no!
For in all that exquisite isle, my dear,
There is but one bird with a musical throat,
And his compass is but of a single note,
That it makes one weary to hear.'

'Mock me not! mock me not! love, let us
go.'

'No, love, no.
For the bud ever breaks into bloom on the
tree,
And a storm never wakes on the lonely
sea,
And a worm is there in the lonely wood,
That pierces the liver and blackens the
blood,
And makes it a sorrow to be.'

A DEDICATION

Addressed to the poet's wife, and first printed in the 'Enoch Arden' volume. The only alteration is in the sixth line, which originally read: 'and spite of praise and scorn.'

DEAR, near and true, — no truer Time
himself
Can prove you, tho' he make you evermore
Dearer and nearer, as the rapid of life

Shoots to the fall, — take this and pray
that he
Who wrote it, honoring your sweet faith in
him,
May trust himself; and after praise and
scorn,
As one who feels the immeasurable world,
Attain the wise indifference of the wise;
And after autumn past — if left to pass
His autumn into seeming-leafless days —
Draw toward the long frost and longest
night,
Wearing his wisdom lightly, like the fruit
Which in our winter woodland looks a
flower.[1]

EXPERIMENTS

BOÄDICÉA

First published in the ' Enoch Arden ' vol-
ume. The only change since made is in the
19th line, which originally read : ' There the
hive of Roman liars worship a gluttonous em-
peror-idiot.'

WHILE about the shore of Mona those Ne-
ronian legionaries
Burnt and broke the grove and altar of the
Druid and Druidess,
Far in the East Boädicéa, standing loftily
charioted,
Mad and maddening all that heard her in
her fierce volubility,
Girt by half the tribes of Britain, near the
colony Cámulodúne,
Yell'd and shriek'd between her daughters
o'er a wild confederacy.

' They that scorn the tribes and call us
Britain's barbarous populaces,
Did they hear me, would they listen, did
they pity me supplicating ?
Shall I heed them in their anguish ? shall
I brook to be supplicated ?
Hear, Icenian, Catieuchlanian, hear, Cori-
tanian, Trinobant !
Must their ever-ravening eagle's beak and
talon annihilate us ?
Tear the noble heart of Britain, leave it
gorily quivering ?

[1] The fruit of the Spindle-tree (*Euonymus
Europœus*).

Bark an answer, Britain's raven ! bark and
blacken innumerable,
Blacken round the Roman carrion, make
the carcase a skeleton,
Kite and kestrel, wolf and wolfkin, from
the wilderness, wallow in it,
Till the face of Bel be brighten'd, Taranis
be propitiated.
Lo their colony half-defended ! lo their
colony, Cámulodúne !
There the horde of Roman robbers mock
at a barbarous adversary.
There the hive of Roman liars worship an
emperor-idiot.
Such is Rome, and this her deity; hear it,
Spirit of Cássivëlaún !

' Hear it, Gods ! the Gods have heard it,
O Icenian, O Coritanian !
Doubt not ye the Gods have answer'd,
Catieuchlanian, Trinobant !
These have told us all their anger in mir-
aculous utterances,
Thunder, a flying fire in heaven, a murmur
heard aërially,
Phantom sound of blows descending, moan
of an enemy massacred,
Phantom wail of women and children, mul-
titudinous agonies.
Bloodily flow'd the Tamesa rolling phan-
tom bodies of horses and men;
Then a phantom colony smoulder'd on the
refluent estuary;
Lastly yonder yester-even, suddenly giddily
tottering —
There was one who watch'd and told me —
down their statue of Victory fell.
Lo their precious Roman bantling, lo the
colony Cámulodúne,
Shall we teach it a Roman lesson ? shall
we care to be pitiful ?
Shall we deal with it as an infant ? shall
we dandle it amorously ?

' Hear, Icenian, Catieuchlanian, hear,
Coritanian, Trinobant !
While I roved about the forest, long and
bitterly meditating,
There I heard them in the darkness, at the
mystical ceremony;
Loosely robed in flying raiment, sang the
terrible prophetesses:
" Fear not, isle of blowing woodland, isle
of silvery parapets !

Tho' the Roman eagle shadow thee, tho'
the gathering enemy narrow thee,
Thou shalt wax and he shall dwindle, thou
shalt be the mighty one yet !
Thine the liberty, thine the glory, thine the
deeds to be celebrated,
Thine the myriad-rolling ocean, light and
shadow illimitable,
Thine the lands of lasting summer, many-
blossoming Paradises,
Thine the North and thine the South and
thine the battle-thunder of God."
So they chanted: how shall Britain light
upon auguries happier ?
So they chanted in the darkness, and there
cometh a victory now.

'Hear, Icenian, Catieuchlanian, hear,
Coritanian, Trinobant !
Me the wife of rich Prasútagus, me the
lover of liberty,
Me they seized and me they tortured, me
they lash'd and humiliated,
Me the sport of ribald Veterans, mine of
ruffian violators !
See, they sit, they hide their faces, miser-
able in ignominy !
Wherefore in me burns an anger, not by
blood to be satiated.
Lo the palaces and the temple, lo the col-
ony Cámulodúne !
There they ruled, and thence they wasted
all the flourishing territory,
Thither at their will they haled the yellow-
ringleted Britoness —
Bloodily, bloodily fall the battle-axe, unex-
hausted, inexorable.
Shout, Icenian, Catieuchlanian, shout, Cori-
tanian, Trinobant,
Till the victim hear within and yearn to
hurry precipitously,
Like the leaf in a roaring whirlwind, like
the smoke in a hurricane whirl'd.
Lo the colony, there they rioted in the city
of Cúnobelíne !
There they drank in cups of emerald, there
at tables of ebony lay,
Rolling on their purple couches in their
tender effeminacy.
There they dwelt and there they rioted;
there — there — they dwell no more.
Burst the gates, and burn the palaces, break
the works of the statuary,
Take the hoary Roman head and shatter it,
hold it abominable,

Cut the Roman boy to pieces in his lust
and voluptuousness,
Lash the maiden into swooning, me they
lash'd and humiliated,
Chop the breasts from off the mother, dash
the brains of the little one out,
Up, my Britons ! on, my chariot ! on, my
chargers, trample them under us !'

So the Queen Boädicéa, standing loftily
charioted,
Brandishing in her hand a dart and rolling
glances lioness-like,
Yell'd and shriek'd between her daughters
in her fierce volubility.
Till her people all around the royal chariot
agitated,
Madly dash'd the darts together, writhing
barbarous lineaments,
Made the noise of frosty woodlands, when
they shiver in January,
Roar'd as when the roaring breakers boom
and blanch on the precipices,
Yell'd as when the winds of winter tear an
oak on a promontory.
So the silent colony, hearing her tumultu-
ous adversaries
Clash the darts and on the buckler beat
with rapid unanimous hand,
Thought on all her evil tyrannies, all her
pitiless avarice,
Till she felt the heart within her fall and
flutter tremulously,
Then her pulses at the clamoring of her
enemy fainted away.
Out of evil evil flourishes, out of tyranny
tyranny buds.
Ran the land with Roman slaughter, mul-
titudinous agonies.
Perish'd many a maid and matron, many a
valorous legionary,
Fell the colony, city, and citadel, **London,**
Verulam, Cámulodúne.

IN QUANTITY

ON TRANSLATIONS OF HOMER

(HEXAMETERS AND PENTAMETERS)

This and the three following 'experiments
in quantity' appeared in the 'Cornhill Maga-
zine' for December, 1863. This was not
printed with the others in the 'Enoch Arden'

volume, but was finally included in the edition of 1884.

The 'Milton' and the 'Hendecasyllabics' have not been altered.

The 'Specimen of a Translation of the Iliad in Blank Verse' was prefaced in the 'Cornhill Magazine' with the following note : —

'Some, and among these one at least of our best and greatest, have endeavored to give us the "Iliad" in English hexameters, and by what appears to me their failures have gone far to prove the impossibility of the task. I have long held by our blank verse in this matter, and now after having spoken so disrespectfully here of these hexameters, I venture, or rather feel bound, to subjoin a specimen, however brief and with whatever demerits, of a blank verse translation.'

THESE lame hexameters the strong-wing'd
  music of Homer !
  No — but a most burlesque barbarous
    experiment.
When was a harsher sound ever heard, ye
  Muses, in England ?
  When did a frog coarser croak upon our
    Helicon ?
Hexameters no worse than daring Germany
  gave us,
  Barbarous experiment, barbarous hexa-
    meters.

MILTON

(ALCAICS)

O MIGHTY-MOUTH'D inventor of harmonies,
O skill'd to sing of Time or Eternity,
  God-gifted organ-voice of England,
    Milton, a name to resound for ages;
Whose Titan angels, Gabriel, Abdiel,
Starr'd from Jehovah's gorgeous armories,
  Tower, as t\.e deep-domed empyrean
    Rings to the roar of an angel onset !
Me rather all that bowery loneliness,
The brooks of Eden mazily murmuring,
  And bloom profuse and cedar arches
    Charm, as a wanderer out in ocean,
Where some refulgent sunset of India
Streams o'er a rich ambrosial ocean isle,
  And crimson-hued the stately palm-woods
    Whisper in odorous heights of even.

(HENDECASYLLABICS)

O you chorus of indolent reviewers,
Irresponsible, indolent reviewers,
Look, I come to the test, a tiny poem
All composed in a metre of Catullus,
All in quantity, careful of my motion,
Like the skater on ice that hardly bears
  him,
Lest I fall unawares before the people,
Waking laughter in indolent reviewers.
Should I flounder awhile without a tumble
Thro' this metrification of Catullus,
They should speak to me not without a
  welcome,
All that chorus of indolent reviewers.
Hard, hard, hard is it, only not to tumble,
So fantastical is the dainty metre.
Wherefore slight me not wholly, nor be-
  lieve me
Too presumptuous, indolent reviewers.
O blatant Magazines, regard me rather —
Since I blush to belaud myself a moment —
As some rare little rose, a piece of inmost
Horticultural art, or half coquette-like
Maiden, not to be greeted unbenignly.

SPECIMEN OF A TRANSLATION OF THE ILIAD IN BLANK VERSE

[ILIAD, VIII. 542–561]

So Hector spake; the Trojans roar'd ap-
  plause;
Then loosed their sweating horses from the
  yoke,
And each beside his chariot bound his own;
And oxen from the city, and goodly sheep
In haste they drove, and honey-hearted
  wine
And bread from out the houses brought,
  and heap'd
Their firewood, and the winds from off the
  plain
Roll'd the rich vapor far into the heaven.
And these all night upon the bridge [1] of
  war
Sat glorying; many a fire before them
  blazed.
As when in heaven the stars about the moon
Look beautiful, when all the winds are
  laid,
And every height comes out, and jutting
  peak
And valley, and the immeasurable heavens
Break open to their highest, and all the
  stars

[1] Or, ridge.

Shine, and the shepherd gladdens in his
    heart;
So many a fire between the ships and stream
Of Xanthus blazed before the towers of
    Troy,
A thousand on the plain; and close by each
Sat fifty in the blaze of burning fire;
And eating hoary grain and pulse the
    steeds,
Fixt by their cars, waited the golden dawn.

THE THIRD OF FEBRUARY, 1852

This poem is one of three inspired by the
excitement in England which followed the
coup d'état of Louis Napoleon in December,
1851. It was 'a powerful rebuke to the House
of Lords for having deprecated the free criti-
cism expressed in newspapers and in speeches
against the author of that crime.' It appeared
in the 'Examiner' for February 7, 1852, and
was signed 'Merlin.' The patriotic lyric, 'Hands
all round,' was printed in the same number
of the 'Examiner;' and 'Britons, guard your
own,' in the preceding number (January 31,
1852).

The poem was first acknowledged and in-
cluded in the collected works in 1872.

My Lords, we heard you speak: you told
    us all
  That England's honest censure went too
    far,
That our free press should cease to brawl,
  Not sting the fiery Frenchman into war.
It was our ancient privilege, my Lords,
To fling whate'er we felt, not fearing, into
    words.

We love not this French God, the child of
    hell,
  Wild War, who breaks the converse of
    the wise;
But though we love kind Peace so well,
  We dare not even by silence sanction lies.
It might be safe our censures to withdraw,
And yet, my Lords, not well; there is a
    higher law.

As long as we remain, we must speak free,
  Tho' all the storm of Europe on us break.
No little German state are we,
  But the one voice in Europe; we *must*
    speak,

That if to-night our greatness were struck
    dead,
There might be left some record of the
    things we said.

If you be fearful, then must we be bold.
  Our Britain cannot salve a tyrant o'er.
Better the waste Atlantic roll'd
  On her and us and ours for evermore.
What! have we fought for Freedom from
    our prime,
At last to dodge and palter with a public
    crime?

Shall we fear *him?* our own we never
    fear'd.
  From our first Charles by force we wrung
    our claims.
Prick'd by the Papal spur, we rear'd,
  We flung the burthen of the second
    James.
I say, we *never* fear'd! and as for these,
We broke them on the land, we drove them
    on the seas.

And you, my Lords, you make the people
    muse
  In doubt if you be of our Barons' breed —
Were those your sires who fought at
    Lewes?
Is this the manly strain of Runnymede?
O fallen nobility that, overawed,
Would lisp in honey'd whispers of this
    monstrous fraud!

We feel, at least, that silence here were
    sin,
  Not ours the fault if we have feeble
    hosts —
If easy patrons of their kin
  Have left the last free race with naked
    coasts!
They knew the precious things they had to
    guard;
For us, we will not spare the tyrant one
    hard word.

Tho' niggard throats of Manchester may
    bawl,
  What England was, shall her true sons
    forget?
We are not cotton-spinners all,
  But some love England and her honor
    yet.

And these in our Thermopylæ shall stand,
And hold against the world this honor of
    the land.

A WELCOME TO HER ROYAL HIGHNESS MARIE ALEXANDROVNA, DUCHESS OF EDINBURGH

MARCH 7, 1874

Written to welcome Marie to England after
her marriage to the Duke of Edinburgh, January 23, 1874. Printed in the 'Times,' and
afterwards included in the collected editions.

I

THE Son of him with whom we strove for
    power —
  Whose will is lord thro' all his world-
    domain —
  Who made the serf a man, and burst his
    chain —
Has given our Prince his own imperial
    Flower,
          Alexandrovna.
And welcome, Russian flower, a people's
    pride,
  To Britain, when her flowers begin to
    blow!
From love to love, from home to home
    you go,
From mother unto mother, stately bride,
          Marie Alexandrovna !

II

The golden news along the steppes is
    blown,
  And at thy name the Tartar tents are
    stirr'd;
  Elburz and all the Caucasus have heard;
And all the sultry palms of India known,
          Alexandrovna.
The voices of our universal sea
  On capes of Afric as on cliffs of Kent,
  The Maoris and that Isle of Continent,
And loyal pines of Canada murmur thee,
          Marie Alexandrovna !

III

Fair empires branching, both, in lusty
    life ! —
  Yet Harold's England fell to Norman
    swords;

Yet thine own land has bow'd to Tartar
    hordes
Since English Harold gave its throne a
    wife,
          Alexandrovna !
For thrones and peoples are as waifs that
    swing,
  And float or fall, in endless ebb and
    flow;
  But who love best have best the grace to
    know
That Love by right divine is deathless
    king,
          Marie Alexandrovna !

IV

And Love has led thee to the stranger
    land,
  Where men are bold and strongly say
    their say ; —
  See, empire upon empire smiles to-day,
As thou with thy young lover hand in hand,
          Alexandrovna !
So now thy fuller life is in the west,
  Whose hand at home was gracious to thy
    poor;
  Thy name was blest within the narrow
    door;
Here also, Marie, shall thy name be blest,
          Marie Alexandrovna !

V

Shall fears and jealous hatreds flame again ?
  Or at thy coming, Princess, everywhere,
  The blue heaven break, and some diviner
    air
Breathe thro' the world and change the
    hearts of men,
          Alexandrovna ?
But hearts that change not, love that can-
    not cease,
  And peace be yours, the peace of soul in
    soul !
And howsoever this wild world may roll,
Between your peoples truth and manful
    peace,
          Alfred — Alexandrovna !

IN THE GARDEN AT SWAINSTON

Written in 1870, and first printed in the
'Cabinet Edition,' 1874.
Swainston was the seat of the late Sir John

Simeon, in the Isle of Wight. Here the greater part of 'Maud' was written (Waugh). Sir John died at Fribourg in Switzerland in 1870. The body was brought home for burial, and this poem was written in the garden at Swainston during the week that elapsed before the funeral. See the 'Memoir,' vol. ii. p. 97.

NIGHTINGALES warbled without,
  Within was weeping for thee;
Shadows of three dead men
  Walk'd in the walks with me,
  Shadows of three dead men, and thou
    wast one of the three.

Nightingales sang in his woods,
  The Master was far away;
Nightingales warbled and sang
  Of a passion that lasts but a day;
  Still in the house in his coffin the Prince
    of courtesy lay.

Two dead men have I known
  In courtesy like to thee;
Two dead men have I loved
  With a love that ever will be;
  Three dead men have I loved, and thou
    art last of the three.

CHILD SONGS

First printed in 'St. Nicholas' (N. Y.) for February, 1880. Set to music by Mrs. Tennyson in the same number and that for March, 1880. Reprinted in the collected edition of 1884.

I

THE CITY CHILD

DAINTY little maiden, whither would you
    wander?
  Whither from this pretty home, the home
    where mother dwells?
'Far and far away,' said the dainty little
    maiden,
' All among the gardens, auriculas, anemones,
  Roses and lilies and Canterbury bells.'

Dainty little maiden, whither would you
    wander?
  Whither from this pretty house, this city-
    house of ours?

' Far and far away,' said the dainty little
    maiden,
' All among the meadows, the clover and
    the clematis,
  Daisies and kingcups and honeysuckle-
    flowers.'

II

MINNIE AND WINNIE

MINNIE and Winnie
  Slept in a shell.
Sleep, little ladies!
  And they slept well.

Pink was the shell within,
  Silver without;
Sounds of the great sea
  Wander'd about.

Sleep, little ladies!
  Wake not soon!
Echo on echo
  Dies to the moon.

Two bright stars
  Peep'd into the shell.
' What are they dreaming of?
  Who can tell?'

Started a green linnet
  Out of the croft;
Wake, little ladies!
  The sun is aloft!

THE SPITEFUL LETTER

Contributed to 'Once a Week' in January, 1868, and reprinted in 1884.

Attempts have been made to identify the writer of the letter; but the poet wrote to the editor of 'Once a Week': 'It is no particular letter that I meant. I have had dozens of them from one quarter and another.'

HERE, it is here, the close of the year,
  And with it a spiteful letter.
My name in song has done him much wrong,
  For himself has done much better.

O little bard, is your lot so hard,
  If men neglect your pages?
I think not much of yours or of mine,
  I hear the roll of the ages.

Rhymes and rhymes in the range of the
    times !
Are mine for the moment stronger ?
Yet hate me not, but abide your lot;
    I last but a moment longer.

This faded leaf, our names are as brief;
    What room is left for a hater ?
Yet the yellow leaf hates the greener
    leaf,
For it hangs one moment later.

Greater than I — is that your cry ?
    And men will live to see it.
Well — if it be so — so it is, you know;
    And if it be so, so be it.

Brief, brief is a summer leaf,
    But this is the time of hollies.
O hollies and ivies and evergreens,
    How I hate the spites and the follies !

LITERARY SQUABBLES

Originally printed in 'Punch,' March 7, 1846,
where it was entitled 'After-thought.' It was
included, with its present title, in the 'Library
Edition' of the 'Poems,' 1872–73. See p. 791.

Ah God ! the petty fools of rhyme
    That shriek and sweat in pigmy wars
Before the stony face of Time,
    And look'd at by the silent stars;

Who hate each other for a song,
    And do their little best to bite
And pinch their brethren in the throng,
    And scratch the very dead for spite;

And strain to make an inch of room
    For their sweet selves, and cannot hear
The sullen Lethe rolling doom
    On them and theirs and all things here;

When one small touch of Charity
    Could lift them nearer Godlike state
Than if the crowded Orb should cry
    Like those who cried Diana great.

And I too talk, and lose the touch
    I talk of.   Surely, after all,
The noblest answer unto such
    Is perfect stillness when they brawl.

THE VICTIM

Printed in 1867 at the private press of Sir
Ivor Bertie Guest, at Canford Manor, near
Wimborne; contributed to 'Good Words' for
January, 1868; and included in the 'Holy
Grail' volume, 1870.

I

A PLAGUE upon the people fell,
    A famine after laid them low;
Then thorpe and byre arose in fire,
    For on them brake the sudden foe;
So thick they died the people cried,
    'The Gods are moved against the land.'
The Priest in horror about his altar
    To Thor and Odin lifted a hand:
      'Help us from famine
      And plague and strife !
      What would you have of us ?
      Human life ?
      Were it our nearest,
      Were it our dearest, —
      Answer, O answer! —
      We give you his life.'

II

But still the foeman spoil'd and burn'd,
    And cattle died, and deer in wood,
And bird in air, and fishes turn'd
    And whiten'd all the rolling flood;
And dead men lay all over the way,
    Or down in a furrow scathed with flame;
And ever and aye the Priesthood moan'd,
    Till at last it seem'd that an answer
    came:
      'The King is happy
      In child and wife;
      Take you his dearest,
      Give us a life.'

III

The Priest went out by heath and hill;
    The King was hunting in the wild;
They found the mother sitting still;
    She cast her arms about the child.
The child was only eight summers old,
    His beauty still with his years increased,
His face was ruddy, his hair was gold;
    He seem'd a victim due to the priest.
      The Priest beheld him,
      And cried with joy,
      'The Gods have answer'd;
      We give them the boy.'

IV

The King return'd from out the wild,
He bore but little game in hand;
The mother said, 'They have taken the
     child
To spill his blood and heal the land.
The land is sick, the people diseased,
And blight and famine on all the lea;
The holy Gods, they must be appeased,
So I pray you tell the truth to me.
          They have taken our son,
          They will have his life.
          Is *he* your dearest?
          Or I, the wife?'

V

The King bent low, with hand on brow,
He stay'd his arms upon his knee:
'O wife, what use to answer now?
For now the Priest has judged for me.'
The King was shaken with holy fear;
'The Gods,' he said, 'would have chosen
     well;
Yet both are near, and both are dear,
And which the dearest I cannot tell!'
          But the Priest was happy,
          His victim won:
          'We have his dearest,
          His only son!'

VI

The rites prepared, the victim bared,
The knife uprising toward the blow,
To the altar-stone she sprang alone:
'Me, not my darling, no!'
He caught her away with a sudden cry;
Suddenly from him brake his wife,
And shrieking, '*I* am his dearest, I —
I am his dearest!' rush'd on the knife.
          And the Priest was happy:
          'O Father Odin,
          We give you a life.
          Which was his nearest?
          Who was his dearest?
          The Gods have answer'd;
          We give them the wife!'

WAGES

Contributed to 'Macmillan's Magazine' for
February, 1868; and reprinted in the 'Holy
Grail' volume.

GLORY of warrior, glory of orator, glory of
     song,
Paid with a voice flying by to be lost
     on an endless sea —
Glory of Virtue, to fight, to struggle, to
     right the wrong —
Nay, but she aim'd not at glory, no lover
     of glory she;
Give her the glory of going on, and still to be.

The wages of sin is death: if the wages of
     Virtue be dust,
Would she have heart to endure for the
     life of the worm and the fly?
She desires no isles of the blest, no quiet
     seats of the just,
To rest in a golden grove, or to bask in
     a summer sky;
Give her the wages of going on, and not to
     die.

THE HIGHER PANTHEISM

First published in the 'Holy Grail' volume.

THE sun, the moon, the stars, the seas, the
     hills and the plains, —
Are not these, O Soul, the Vision of Him
     who reigns?

Is not the Vision He, tho' He be not that
     which He seems?
Dreams are true while they last, and do we
     not live in dreams?

Earth, these solid stars, this weight of body
     and limb,
Are they not sign and symbol of thy divi-
     sion from Him?

Dark is the world to thee; thyself art the
     reason why,
For is He not all but thou, that hast power
     to feel 'I am I'?

Glory about thee, without thee; and thou
     fulfillest thy doom,
Making Him broken gleams and a stifled
     splendor and gloom.

Speak to Him, thou, for He hears, and
     Spirit with Spirit can meet —
Closer is He than breathing, and nearer
     than hands and feet.

God is law, say the wise; O Soul, and let
us rejoice,
For if He thunder by law the thunder is
yet His voice.

Law is God, say some; no God at all, says
the fool,
For all we have power to see is a straight
staff bent in a pool;

And the ear of man cannot hear, and the
eye of man cannot see;
But if we could see and hear, this Vision —
were it not He ?

THE VOICE AND THE PEAK

First published in the 'Cabinet Edition' of
the 'Poems,' 1874.

I

THE voice and the Peak
Far over summit and lawn,
The lone glow and long roar
Green-rushing from the rosy thrones of
dawn !

II

All night have I heard the voice
Rave over the rocky bar,
But thou wert silent in heaven,
Above thee glided the star.

III

Hast thou no voice, O Peak,
That standest high above all ?
' I am the voice of the Peak,
I roar and rave, for I fall.

IV

' A thousand voices go
To North, South, East, and West;
They leave the heights and are troubled,
And moan and sink to their rest.

V

' The fields are fair beside them,
The chestnut towers in his bloom;
But they — they feel the desire of the
deep —
Fall, and follow their doom.

VI

' The deep has power on the height,
And the height has power on the deep;

They are raised for ever and ever,
And sink again into sleep.'

VII

Not raised for ever and ever,
But when their cycle is o'er,
The valley, the voice, the peak, the star
Pass, and are found no more.

VIII

The Peak is high and flush'd
At his highest with sunrise fire;
The Peak is high, and the stars are high,
And the thought of a man is higher.

IX

A deep below the deep,
And a height beyond the height !
Our hearing is not hearing,
And our seeing is not sight.

X

The voice and the Peak
Far into heaven withdrawn,
The lone glow and long roar
Green-rushing from the rosy thrones of
dawn !

———

First published in the 'Holy Grail' volume.

FLOWER in the crannied wall,
I pluck you out of the crannies,
I hold you here, root and all, in my hand,
Little flower — but *if* I could understand
What you are, root and all, and all in all,
I should know what God and man is.

LUCRETIUS

First published in 'Macmillan's Magazine'
for May, 1868, and afterwards included in the
'Holy Grail' volume of 1869.

The story on which the poem is founded is
taken from Jerome's additions to the 'Euse-
bian Chronicle,' under the year B. C. 94: ' Titus
Lucretius poeta nascitur ; postea amatorio po-
culo in furorem versus, cum aliquot libellos per
intervalla insaniae conscripsisset, quos postea
Cicero emendavit, propria se manu interfecit
anno aetatis xliii.'

LUCILIA, wedded to Lucretius, found
Her master cold; for when the morning
flush

Of passion and the first embrace had died
Between them, tho' he loved her none the
    less,
Yet often when the woman heard his foot
Return from pacings in the field, and ran
To greet him with a kiss, the master took
Small notice, or austerely, for — his mind
Half buried in some weightier argument,
Or fancy-borne perhaps upon the rise   10
And long roll of the hexameter — he past
To turn and ponder those three hundred
    scrolls
Left by the Teacher, whom he held divine.
She brook'd it not, but wrathful, petulant,
Dreaming some rival, sought and found a
    witch
Who brew'd the philtre which had power,
    they said,
To lead an errant passion home again.
And this, at times, she mingled with his
    drink,
And this destroy'd him; for the wicked
    broth
Confused the chemic labor of the blood,   20
And tickling the brute brain within the
    man's
Made havoc among those tender cells, and
    check'd
His power to shape. He loathed himself,
    and once
After a tempest woke upon a morn
That mock'd him with returning calm, and
    cried:

'Storm in the night! for thrice I heard
    the rain
Rushing; and once the flash of a thunder-
    bolt —
Methought I never saw so fierce a fork —
Struck out the streaming mountain-side,
    and show'd
A riotous confluence of watercourses   30
Blanching and billowing in a hollow of it,
Where all but yester-eve was dusty-dry.

'Storm, and what dreams, ye holy Gods,
    what dreams!
For thrice I waken'd after dreams. Per-
    chance
We do but recollect the dreams that come
Just ere the waking. Terrible: for it seem'd
A void was made in Nature; all her bonds
Crack'd; and I saw the flaring atom-streams
And torrents of her myriad universe,
Ruining along the illimitable inane,   40

Fly on to clash together again, and make
Another and another frame of things
For ever. That was mine, my dream, I
    knew it —
Of and belonging to me, as the dog
With inward yelp and restless forefoot
    plies
His function of the woodland; but the
    next!
I thought that all the blood by Sylla shed
Came driving rainlike down again on earth,
And where it dash'd the reddening meadow,
    sprang   49
No dragon warriors from Cadmean teeth,
For these I thought my dream would show
    to me,
But girls, Hetairai, curious in their art,
Hired animalisms, vile as those that made
The mulberry-faced Dictator's orgies worse
Than aught they fable of the quiet Gods.
And hands they mixt, and yell'd and round
    me drove
In narrowing circles till I yell'd again
Half-suffocated, and sprang up, and saw —
Was it the first beam of my latest day?

'Then, then, from utter gloom stood out
    the breasts,   60
The breasts of Helen, and hoveringly a
    sword
Now over and now under, now direct,
Pointed itself to pierce, but sank down
    shamed
At all that beauty; and as I stared, a
    fire,
The fire that left a roofless Ilion,
Shot out of them, and scorch'd me that I
    woke.

'Is this thy vengeance, holy Venus,
    thine,
Because I would not one of thine own
    doves,
Not even a rose, were offer'd to thee?
    thine,
Forgetful how my rich proœmion makes   70
Thy glory fly along the Italian field,
In lays that will outlast thy deity?

'Deity? nay, thy worshippers. My
    tongue
Trips, or I speak profanely. Which of
    these
Angers thee most, or angers thee at all?
Not if thou be'st of those who, far aloof

From envy, hate and pity, and spite and
    scorn,
Live the great life which all our greatest fain
Would follow, centred in eternal calm.

' Nay, if thou canst, O Goddess, like our-
    selves   80
Touch, and be touch'd, then would I cry to
    thee
To kiss thy Mavors, roll thy tender arms
Round him, and keep him from the lust of
    blood
That makes a steaming slaughter-house of
    Rome.

' Ay, but I meant not thee; I meant not
    her
Whom all the pines of Ida shook to see
Slide from that quiet heaven of hers, and
    tempt
The Trojan, while his neatherds were
    abroad;
Nor her that o'er her wounded hunter wept
Her deity false in human-amorous tears; 90
Nor whom her beardless apple-arbiter
Decided fairest. Rather, O ye Gods,
Poet-like, as the great Sicilian called
Calliope to grace his golden verse —
Ay, and this Kypris also — did I take
That popular name of thine to shadow
    forth
The all-generating powers and genial heat
Of Nature, when she strikes thro' the
    thick blood
Of cattle, and light is large, and lambs are
    glad   99
Nosing the mother's udder, and the bird
Makes his heart voice amid the blaze of
    flowers;
Which things appear the work of mighty
    Gods.

' The Gods ! and if I go *my* work is left
Unfinish'd — *if* I go. The Gods, who haunt
The lucid interspace of world and world,
Where never creeps a cloud, or moves a
    wind,
Nor ever falls the least white star of snow,
Nor ever lowest roll of thunder moans,
Nor sound of human sorrow mounts to mar
Their sacred everlasting calm ! and such,
Not all so fine, nor so divine a calm,   111
Not such, nor all unlike it, man may gain
Letting his own life go. The Gods, the
    Gods !

If all be atoms, how then should the Gods
Being atomic not be dissoluble,
Not follow the great law ? My master
    held
That Gods there are, for all men so believe.
I prest my footsteps into his, and meant
Surely to lead my Memmius in a train
Of flowery clauses onward to the proof 120
That Gods there are, and deathless.
    Meant ? I meant ?
I have forgotten what I meant; my mind
Stumbles, and all my faculties are lamed.

' Look where another of our Gods, the
    Sun,
Apollo, Delius, or of older use
All-seeing Hyperion — what you will —
Has mounted yonder; since he never sware,
Except his wrath were wreak'd on wretched
    man,
That he would only shine among the dead
Hereafter — tales ! for never yet on earth
Could dead flesh creep, or bits of roasting
    ox   131
Moan round the spit — nor knows he what
    he sees;
King of the East altho' he seem, and girt
With song and flame and fragrance, slowly
    lifts
His golden feet on those empurpled stairs
That climb into the windy halls of heaven.
And here he glances on an eye new-born,
And gets for greeting but a wail of pain;
And here he stays upon a freezing orb
That fain would gaze upon him to the last;
And here upon a yellow eyelid fallen   141
And closed by those who mourn a friend
    in vain,
Not thankful that his troubles are no more.
And me, altho' his fire is on my face
Blinding, he sees not, nor at all can tell
Whether I mean this day to end myself,
Or lend an ear to Plato where he says,
That men like soldiers may not quit the
    post
Allotted by the Gods. But he that holds
The Gods are careless, wherefore need he
    care   150
Greatly for them, nor rather plunge at
    once,
Being troubled, wholly out of sight, and
    sink
Past earthquake — ay, and gout and stone,
    that break
Body toward death, and palsy, death-in-life,

And wretched age — and worst disease of
    all,
These prodigies of myriad nakednesses,
And twisted shapes of lust, unspeakable,
Abominable, strangers at my hearth
Not welcome, harpies miring every dish,
The phantom husks of something foully
    done,   160
And fleeting thro' the boundless universe,
And blasting the long quiet of my breast
With animal heat and dire insanity ?

   'How should the mind, except it loved
      them, clasp
These idols to herself ? or do they fly
Now thinner, and now thicker, like the
    flakes
In a fall of snow, and so press in, perforce
Of multitude, as crowds that in an hour
Of civic tumult jam the doors, and bear
The keepers down, and throng, their rags
    and they   170
The basest, far into that council-hall
Where sit the best and stateliest of the
    land ?

   ' Can I not fling this horror off me again,
Seeing with how great ease Nature can
    smile,
Balmier and nobler from her bath of storm,
At random ravage ? and how easily
The mountain there has cast his cloudy
    slough,
Now towering o'er him in serenest air,
A mountain o'er a mountain, — ay, and
    within   179
All hollow as the hopes and fears of men ?

   ' But who was he that in the garden
      snared
Picus and Faunus, rustic Gods ? a tale
To laugh at — more to laugh at in my-
    self —
For look ! what is it ? there ? yon arbutus
Totters; a noiseless riot underneath
Strikes through the wood, sets all the tops
    quivering —
The mountain quickens into Nymph and
    Faun;
And here an Oread — how the sun delights
To glance and shift about her slippery
    sides,
And rosy knees and supple roundedness, 190
And budded bosom-peaks — who this way
    runs

Before the rest! — A satyr, a satyr, see,
Follows; but him I proved impossible;
Twy-natured is no nature. Yet he draws
Nearer and nearer, and I scan him now
Beastlier than any phantom of his kind
That ever butted his rough brother-brute
For lust or lusty blood or provender.
I hate, abhor, spit, sicken at him; and she
Loathes him as well; such a precipitate
    heel,   200
Fledged as it were with Mercury's ankle-
    wing,
Whirls her to me — but will she fling herself
Shameless upon me ? Catch her, goat-
    foot! nay,
Hide, hide them, million-myrtled wilder-
    ness,
And cavern-shadowing laurels, hide ! do I
    wish —
What ? — that the bush were leafless ? or
    to whelm
All of them in one massacre ? O ye Gods,
I know you careless, yet, behold, to you
From childly wont and ancient use I call —
I thought I lived securely as yourselves —
No lewdness, narrowing envy, monkey-
    spite,   211
No madness of ambition, avarice, none;
No larger feast than under plane or pine
With neighbors laid along the grass, to
    take
Only such cups as left us friendly-warm,
Affirming each his own philosophy —
Nothing to mar the sober majesties
Of settled, sweet, Epicurean life.
But now it seems some unseen monster
    lays
His vast and filthy hands upon my will, 220
Wrenching it backward into his, and spoils
My bliss in being; and it was not great,
For save when shutting reasons up in
    rhythm,
Or Heliconian honey in living words,
To make a truth less harsh, I often grew
Tired of so much within our little life,
Or of so little in our little life —
Poor little life that toddles half an hour
Crown'd with a flower or two, and there an
    end —   229
And since the nobler pleasure seems to fade,
Why should I, beastlike as I find myself,
Not manlike end myself ? — our privi-
    lege —
What beast has heart to do it ? And what
    man,

What Roman would be dragg'd in triumph
    thus?
Not I; not he, who bears one name with
    her
Whose death-blow struck the dateless doom
    of kings,
When, brooking not the Tarquin in her
    veins,
She made her blood in sight of Collatine
And all his peers, flushing the guiltless air,
Spout from the maiden fountain in her
    heart.   240
And from it sprang the Commonwealth,
    which breaks
As I am breaking now !

                        'And therefore now
Let her, that is the womb and tomb of all,
Great Nature, take, and forcing far apart
Those blind beginnings that have made me
    man,
Dash them anew together at her will
Thro' all her cycles — into man once more,
Or beast or bird or fish, or opulent flower.
But till this cosmic order everywhere
Shatter'd into one earthquake in one day
Cracks all to pieces, — and that hour per-
    haps   251
Is not so far when momentary man
Shall seem no more a something to himself,
But he, his hopes and hates, his homes and
    fanes,
And even his bones long laid within the
    grave,
The very sides of the grave itself shall
    pass,

Vanishing, atom and void, atom and void,
Into the unseen for ever, — till that hour,
My golden work in which I told a truth
That stays the rolling Ixionian wheel,   260
And numbs the Fury's ringlet-snake, and
    plucks
The mortal soul from out immortal hell,
Shall stand.   Ay, surely; then it fails at
    last
And perishes as I must; for O Thou,
Passionless bride, divine Tranquillity,
Yearn'd after by the wisest of the wise,
Who fail to find thee, being as thou art
Without one pleasure and without one
    pain,
Howbeit I know thou surely must be mine
Or soon or late, yet out of season, thus 270
I woo thee roughly, for thou carest not
How roughly men may woo thee so they
    win —
Thus — thus — the soul flies out and dies in
    the air.'

    With that he drove the knife into his
        side.
She heard him raging, heard him fall, ran
    in,
Beat breast, tore hair, cried out upon her-
    self
As having fail'd in duty to him, shriek'd
That she but meant to win him back, fell
    on him,
Clasp'd, kiss'd him, wail'd.   He answer'd,
    'Care not thou !
Thy duty?   What is duty?   Fare thee
    well !'   280

THE WINDOW; OR, THE SONG OF THE WRENS

First printed in 1867 at the private press of Sir Ivor Bertie Guest, at Canford Manor, near Wimborne.   Only a few copies were printed, and one is rarely found in the market.   Reprinted, with variations in the text, and with music by Sir Arthur Sullivan, in December, 1870.   This edition had the following preface, which was retained in the edition of 1884, when the poems next appeared : —

Four years ago Mr. Sullivan requested me to write a little song-cycle, German fashion, for him to exercise his art upon.   He had been very successful in setting such old songs, as 'Orpheus with his lute,' and I drest up for him, partly in the old style, a puppet, whose almost only merit is, perhaps, that it can dance to Mr. Sullivan's instrument.   I am sorry that my four-year-old puppet should have to dance at all in the dark shadow of these days; but the music is now completed, and I am bound by my promise.

                                                            A. TENNYSON.

December, 1870.

THE WINDOW

ON THE HILL

THE lights and shadows fly !
Yonder it brightens and darkens down on
    the plain.
A jewel, a jewel dear to a lover's eye !
O, is it the brook, or a pool, or her window-
    pane,
    When the winds are up in the morn-
        ing ?

Clouds that are racing above,
And winds and lights and shadows that
    cannot be still,
    All running on one way to the home of
      my love,
You are all running on, and I stand on the
    slope of the hill,   9
    And the winds are up in the morning !

Follow, follow the chase !
And my thoughts are as quick and as quick,
    ever on, on, on.
    O lights, are you flying over her sweet
      little face ?
And my heart is there before you are come,
    and gone,
    When the winds are up in the morn-
        ing !

Follow them down the slope !
And I follow them down to the window-
    pane of my dear,
    And it brightens and darkens and bright-
      ens like my hope,
And it darkens and brightens and darkens
    like my fear,   19
    And the winds are up in the morning !

AT THE WINDOW

Vine, vine and eglantine,
Clasp her window, trail and twine !
Rose, rose and clematis,
Trail and twine and clasp and kiss,
Kiss, kiss; and make her a bower
    All of flowers, and drop me a flower,
      Drop me a flower.

Vine, vine and eglantine,
Cannot a flower, a flower, be mine ?
Rose, rose and clematis,   30

Drop me a flower, a flower, to kiss,
Kiss, kiss — and out of her bower
    All of flowers, a flower, a flower,
    Dropt, a flower.

GONE

Gone !
Gone, till the end of the year,
Gone, and the light gone with her, and left
    me in shadow here !
        Gone — flitted away,
Taken the stars from the night and the
    sun from the day !
Gone, and a cloud in my heart, and a storm
    in the air !   40
Flown to the east or the west, flitted I
    know not where !
Down in the south is a flash and a groan:
    she is there ! she is there !

WINTER

The frost is here,
And fuel is dear,
And woods are sear,
And fires burn clear,
And frost   here
And has bitten the heel of the going year.

Bite, frost, bite !
You roll up away from the light   50
The blue wood-louse and the plump dor-
    mouse,
And the bees are still'd, and the flies are
    kill'd,
And you bite far into the heart of the
    house,
But not into mine.

Bite, frost, bite !
The woods are all the searer,
The fuel is all the dearer,
The fires are all the clearer,
My spring is all the nearer,
You have bitten into the heart of the
    earth,   60
But not into mine.

SPRING

Birds' love and birds' song
    Flying here and there,
Birds' song and birds' love,
    And you with gold for hair !

Birds' song and birds' love,
　　Passing with the weather,
Men's song and men's love,
　　To love once and for ever.

Men's love and birds' love,　　　　　70
　　And women's love and men's !
And you my wren with a crown of gold,
　　You my queen of the wrens !
You the queen of the wrens —
　　We 'll be birds of a feather,
I 'll be King of the Queen of the wrens,
　　And all in a nest together.

THE LETTER

Where is another sweet as my sweet,
　　Fine of the fine, and shy of the shy ?
Fine little hands, fine little feet —　　　80
　　Dewy blue eye.
Shall I write to her ? shall I go ?
　　Ask her to marry me by and by ?
Somebody said that she 'd say no;
　　Somebody knows that she 'll say ay !

Ay or no, if ask'd to her face ?
　　Ay or no, from shy of the shy ?
Go, little letter, apace, apace,
　　Fly;
Fly to the light in the valley below —　　90
　　Tell my wish to her dewy blue eye.
Somebody said that she 'd say no;
　　Somebody knows that she 'll say ay !

NO ANSWER

The mist and the rain, the mist and the
　　rain !
　　Is it ay or no ? is it ay or no ?
And never a glimpse of her window-pane !
　　And I may die but the grass will grow,
And the grass will grow when I am gone,
And the wet west wind and the world will
　　go on.

Ay is the song of the wedded spheres,　100
　　No is trouble and cloud and storm,
Ay is life for a hundred years,
　　No will push me down to the worm,
And when I am there and dead and gone,
The wet west wind and the world will go on.

The wind and the wet, the wind and the wet!
　　Wet west wind, how you blow, you blow !

And never a line from my lady yet !
　　Is it ay or no ? is it ay or no ?
Blow then, blow, and when I am gone,　110
The wet west wind and the world may go
　　on.

NO ANSWER

Winds are loud and you are dumb,
Take my love, for love will come,
　　Love will come but once a life.
Winds are loud and winds will pass !
Spring is here with leaf and grass;
　　Take my love and be my wife.
After-loves of maids and men
Are but dainties drest again.
Love me now, you 'll love me then;　120
　　Love can love but once a life.

THE ANSWER

Two little hands that meet,
Claspt on her seal, my sweet !
Must I take you and break you,
Two little hands that meet ?
I must take you, and break you,
And loving hands must part —
Take, take — break, break —
Break — you may break my heart.
　　Faint heart never won —　　　　130
　　Break, break, and all 's done.

AY

Be merry, all birds, to-day,
　　Be merry on earth as you never were
　　　merry before,
Be merry in heaven, O larks, and far
　　away,
　　And merry for ever and ever, and one day
　　more.
　　　　Why ?
　　For it 's easy to find a rhyme.
Look, look, how he flits,
　　The fire-crown'd king of the wrens, from
　　　out of the pine !
Look how they tumble the blossom, the
　　mad little tits !　　　　　　　140
　　' Cuck-oo ! Cuck-oo !' was ever a May
　　so fine ?
　　　　Why ?
　　For it 's easy to find a rhyme.
O merry the linnet and dove,
　　And swallow and sparrow and throstle,
　　and have your desire !

O merry my heart, you have gotten the
    wings of love,
And flit like the king of the wrens with
    a crown of fire.
        Why?
    For it's ay ay, ay ay.

WHEN

Sun comes, moon comes,   150
    Time slips away.
Sun sets, moon sets,
    Love, fix a day.

'A year hence, a year hence.'
    'We shall both be gray.'
'A month hence, a month hence.'
    'Far, far away.'

'A week hence, a week hence.'
    'Ah, the long delay!'
'Wait a little, wait a little,   160
    You shall fix a day.'

'To-morrow, love, to-morrow,
    And that's an age away.'
Blaze upon her window, sun,
    And honor all the day.

MARRIAGE MORNING

Light, so low upon earth,
    You send a flash to the sun.
Here is the golden close of love,
    All my wooing is done.
O, the woods and the meadows,   170
    Woods where we hid from the wet,
Stiles where we stay'd to be kind,
    Meadows in which we met!

Light, so low in the vale
    You flash and lighten afar,
For this is the golden morning of love,
    And you are his morning star.
Flash, I am coming, I come,
    By meadow and stile and wood,
O, lighten into my eyes and my heart, 180
    Into my heart and my blood!

Heart, are you great enough
    For a love that never tires?
O heart, are you great enough for love?
    I have heard of thorns and briers.
Over the thorns and briers,
    Over the meadows and stiles,
Over the world to the end of it
    Flash for a million miles.

THE LOVER'S TALE

This poem (written in 1828) was printed in 1833, but withdrawn before publication for reasons which the author gives in the following preface to the reprint of 1879: —

The original Preface to 'The Lover's Tale' states that it was composed in my nineteenth year. Two only of the three parts then written were printed, when, feeling the imperfection of the poem, I withdrew it from the press. One of my friends, however, who, boylike, admired the boy's work, distributed among our common associates of that hour some copies of these two parts, without my knowledge, without the omissions and amendments which I had in contemplation, and marred by the many misprints of the compositor. Seeing that these two parts have of late been mercilessly pirated, and that what I had deemed scarce worthy to live is not allowed to die, may I not be pardoned if I suffer the whole poem at last to come into the light — accompanied with a reprint of the sequel — a work of my mature life — 'The Golden Supper'?

May, 1879.

ARGUMENT

Julian, whose cousin and foster-sister, Camilla, has been wedded to his friend and rival, Lionel, endeavors to narrate the story of his own love for her, and the strange sequel. He speaks (in Parts II. and III.) of having been haunted by visions and the sound of bells, tolling for a funeral, and at last ringing for a marriage; but he breaks away, overcome, as he approaches the Event, and a witness to it completes the tale.

I

HERE far away, seen from the topmost
    cliff,
Filling with purple gloom the vacancies
Between the tufted hills, the sloping seas
Hung in mid-heaven, and half-way down
    rare sails,
White as white clouds, floated from sky to
    sky.

O pleasant breast of waters, quiet bay,
Like to a quiet mind in the loud world,
Where the chafed breakers of the outer
      sea
Sank powerless, as anger falls aside
And withers on the breast of peaceful
      love !   10
Thou didst receive the growth of pines
      that fledged
The hills that watch'd thee, as Love watch-
      eth Love,
In thine own essence, and delight thyself
To make it wholly thine on sunny days.
Keep thou thy name of 'Lover's Bay.'
      See, sirs,
Even now the Goddess of the Past, that
      takes
The heart, and sometimes touches but one
      string
That quivers and is silent, and sometimes
Sweeps suddenly all its half - moulder'd
      chords
To some old melody, begins to play   20
That air which pleased her first. I feel thy
      breath;
I come, great Mistress of the ear and
      eye;
Thy breath is of the pine-wood, and tho'
      years
Have hollow'd out a deep and stormy strait
Betwixt the native land of Love and me,
Breathe but a little on me, and the sail
Will draw me to the rising of the sun,
The lucid chambers of the morning star,
And East of Life.

                    Permit me, friend, I prythee,
To pass my hand across my brows, and
      muse   30
On those dear hills, that nevermore will
      meet
The sight that throbs and aches beneath
      my touch,
As tho' there beat a heart in either eye;
For when the outer lights are darken'd
      thus,
The memory's vision hath a keener edge.
It grows upon me now — the semicircle
Of dark-blue waters and the narrow fringe
Of curving beach — its wreaths of drip-
      ping green —
Its pale pink shells — the summer-house
      aloft
That open'd on the pines with doors of
      glass,   40

A mountain nest — the pleasure-boat that
      rock'd,
Light-green with its own shadow, keel to
      keel,
Upon the dappled dimplings of the wave
That blanch'd upon its side.

                              O Love, O Hope !
They come, they crowd upon me all at
      once —
Moved from the cloud of unforgotten
      things,
That sometimes on the horizon of the mind
Lies folded, often sweeps athwart in
      storm —
Flash upon flash they lighten thro' me —
      days
Of dewy dawning and the amber eves   50
When thou and I, Camilla, thou and I
Were borne about the bay or safely moor'd
Beneath a low-brow'd cavern, where the
      tide
Plash'd, sapping its worn ribs; and all
      without
The slowly-ridging rollers on the cliffs
Clash'd, calling to each other, and thro' the
      arch
Down those loud waters, like a setting star,
Mixt with the gorgeous west the lighthouse
      shone,
And silver-smiling Venus ere she fell
Would often loiter in her balmy blue,   60
To crown it with herself.

                              Here, too, my love
Waver'd at anchor with me, when day
      hung
From his mid-dome in heaven's airy halls;
Gleams of the water-circles as they broke
Flicker'd like doubtful smiles about her
      lips,
Quiver'd a flying glory on her hair,
Leapt like a passing thought across her
      eyes;
And mine with one that will not pass, till
      earth
And heaven pass too, dwelt on my heaven,
      a face
Most starry-fair, but kindled from within
As 't were with dawn. She was dark-
      hair'd, dark-eyed —   71
O, such dark eyes ! a single glance of
      them
Will govern a whole life from birth to
      death,

Careless of all things else, led on with light
In trances and in visions.   Look at them,
You lose yourself in utter ignorance;
You cannot find their depth; for they go back,
And farther back, and still withdraw themselves
Quite into the deep soul, that evermore
Fresh springing from her fountains in the brain,   80
Still pouring thro', floods with redundant life
Her narrow portals.

          Trust me, long ago
I should have died, if it were possible
To die in gazing on that perfectness
Which I do bear within me.   I had died,
But from my farthest lapse, my latest ebb,
Thine image, like a charm of light and strength
Upon the waters, push'd me back again
On these deserted sands of barren life.
Tho' from the deep vault where the heart of Hope   90
Fell into dust, and crumbled in the dark —
Forgetting how to render beautiful
Her countenance with quick and healthful blood —
Thou didst not sway me upward; could I perish
While thou, a meteor of the sepulchre,
Didst swathe thyself all round Hope's quiet urn
For ever ?   He that saith it hath o'er-stept
The slippery footing of his narrow wit,
And fallen away from judgment.   Thou art light,
To which my spirit leaneth all her flowers,
And length of days, and immortality   101
Of thought, and freshness ever self-re-new'd.
For Time and Grief abode too long with Life,
And, like all other friends i' the world, at last
They grew aweary of her fellowship.
So Time and Grief did beckon unto Death,
And Death drew nigh and beat the doors of Life;
But thou didst sit alone in the inner house,
A wakeful portress, and didst parle with Death, —

'This is a charmed dwelling which I hold;'   110
So Death gave back, and would no further come.
Yet is my life nor in the present time,
Nor in the present place.   To me alone,
Push'd from his chair of regal heritage,
The Present is the vassal of the Past:
So that, in that I *have* lived, do I live,
And cannot die, and am, in having been —
A portion of the pleasant yesterday,
Thrust forward on to-day and out of place;
A body journeying onward, sick with toil,
The weight as if of age upon my limbs,   121
The grasp of hopeless grief about my heart,
And all the senses weaken'd, save in that,
Which long ago they had glean'd and gar-ner'd up
Into the granaries of memory —
The clear brow, bulwark of the precious brain,
Chink'd as you see, and seam'd — and all the while
The light soul twines and mingles with the growths
Of vigorous early days, attracted, won,   129
Married, made one with, molten into all
The beautiful in Past of act or place,
And like the all-enduring camel, driven
Far from the diamond fountain by the palms,
Who toils across the middle moonlit nights,
Or when the white heats of the blinding noons
Beat from the concave sand; yet in him keeps
A draught of that sweet fountain that he loves,
To stay his feet from falling and his spirit
From bitterness of death.

          Ye ask me, friends,
When I began to love.   How should I tell you ?   140
Or from the after-fulness of my heart,
Flow back again unto my slender spring
And first of love, tho' every turn and depth
Between is clearer in my life than all
Its present flow.   Ye know not what ye ask.
How should the broad and open flower tell
What sort of bud it was, when, prest to-gether

In its green sheath, close-lapt in silken
    folds,
It seem'd to keep its sweetness to itself,
Yet was not the less sweet for that it
    seem'd ?   150
For young Life knows not when young
    Life was born,
But takes it all for granted: neither Love,
Warm in the heart, his cradle, can remem-
    ber
Love in the womb, but resteth satisfied,
Looking on her that brought him to the
    light;
Or as men know not when they fall asleep
Into delicious dreams, our other life,
So know I not when I began to love.
This is my sum of knowledge — that my love
Grew with myself — say rather, was my
    growth,   160
My inward sap, the hold I have on earth,
My outward circling air wherewith I
    breathe,
  hich yet upholds my life, and evermore
Is to me daily life and daily death.
For how should I have lived and not have
    loved ?
Can ye take off the sweetness from the
    flower,
The color and the sweetness from the rose,
And place them by themselves; or set
    apart
Their motions and their brightness from
    the stars,   169
And then point out the flower or the star ?
Or build a wall betwixt my life and love,
And tell me where I am ? 'T is even thus:
In that I live I love; because I love
I live. Whate'er is fountain to the one
Is fountain to the other; and whene'er
Our God unknits the riddle of the one,
There is no shade or fold of mystery
Swathing the other.

                        Many, many years —
For they seem many and my most of life,
And well I could have linger'd in that
    porch,   180
So unproportion'd to the dwelling-place, —
In the May-dews of childhood, opposite
The flush and dawn of youth, we lived to-
    gether,
Apart, alone together on those hills.

Before he saw my day my father died,
And he was happy that he saw it not;

But I and the first daisy on his grave
From the same clay came into light at
    once.
As Love and I do number equal years,
So she, my love, is of an age with me.   190
How like each other was the birth of each !
On the same morning, almost the same
    hour,
Under the selfsame aspect of the stars —
O, falsehood of all star-craft ! — we were
    born.
How like each other was the birth of each !
The sister of my mother — she that bore
Camilla close beneath her beating heart,
Which to the imprison'd spirit of the child,
With its true-touched pulses in the flow
And hourly visitation of the blood,   200
Sent notes of preparation manifold,
And mellow'd echoes of the outer world —
My mother's sister, mother of my love,
Who had a twofold claim upon my heart,
One twofold mightier than the other was,
In giving so much beauty to the world,
And so much wealth as God had charged
    her with —
Loathing to put it from herself for ever,
Left her own life with it; and dying thus,
Crown'd with her highest act the placid
    face   210
And breathless body of her good deeds
    past.

  So were we born, so orphan'd. She was
    motherless,
And I without a father. So from each
Of those two pillars which from earth up-
    hold
Our childhood, one had fallen away, and all
The careful burthen of our tender years
Trembled upon the other. He that gave
Her life, to me delightedly fulfill'd
All loving kindnesses, all offices
Of watchful care and trembling tenderness.
He waked for both, he pray'd for both, he
    slept   221
Dreaming of both; nor was his love the
    less
Because it was divided, and shot forth
Boughs on each side, laden with wholesome
    shade,
Wherein we nested sleeping or awake,
And sang aloud the matin-song of life.

  She was my foster-sister. On one arm
The flaxen ringlets of our infancies

Wander'd, the while we rested; one soft lap
Pillow'd us both; a common light of eyes
Was on us as we lay; our baby lips,   231
Kissing one bosom, ever drew from thence
The stream of life, one stream, one life,
    one blood,
One sustenance, which, still as thought
    grew large,
Still larger moulding all the house of
    thought,
Made all our tastes and fancies like, per-
    haps —
All — all but one; and strange to me, and
    sweet,
Sweet thro' strange years to know that
    whatsoe'er
Our general mother meant for me alone,
Our mutual mother dealt to both of us.   240
So what was earliest mine in earliest life,
I shared with her in whom myself remains.

As was our childhood, so our infancy,
They tell me, was a very miracle
Of fellow-feeling and communion.
They tell me that we would not be alone, —
We cried when we were parted; when I
    wept,
Her smile lit up the rainbow on my tears,
Stay'd on the cloud of sorrow; that we
    loved
The sound of one another's voices more 250
Than the gray cuckoo loves his name, and
    learn'd
To lisp in tune together; that we slept
In the same cradle always, face to face,
Heart beating time to heart, lip pressing
    lip,
Folding each other, breathing on each other,
Dreaming together — dreaming of each
    other,
They should have added, — till the morning
    light
Sloped thro' the pines, upon the dewy pane
Falling, unseal'd our eyelids, and we woke
To gaze upon each other. If this be true,
At thought of which my whole soul lan-
    guishes   261
And faints, and hath no pulse, no breath
    — as tho'
A man in some still garden should infuse
Rich atar in the bosom of the rose,
Till, drunk with its own wine, and overfull
Of sweetness, and in smelling of itself,
It fall on its own thorns — if this be true —
And that way my wish leads me evermore

Still to believe it, 't is so sweet a thought —
Why in the utter stillness of the soul   270
Doth question'd memory answer not, nor
    tell
Of this our earliest, our closest-drawn,
Most loveliest, earthly - heavenliest har-
    mony ?

O blossom'd portal of the lonely house,
Green prelude, April promise, glad new-
    year
Of being, which with earliest violets
And lavish carol of clear-throated larks
Fill'd all the March of life ! — I will not
    speak of thee,
These have not seen thee, these can never
    know thee,
They cannot understand me. Pass we
    then   280
A term of eighteen years. Ye would but
    laugh
If I should tell you how I hoard in thought
The faded rhymes and scraps of ancient
    crones,
Gray relics of the nurseries of the world,
Which are as gems set in my memory,
Because she learnt them with me; or what
    use
To know her father left us just before
The daffodil was blown ? or how we found
The dead man cast upon the shore ? All
    this
Seems to the quiet daylight of your minds
But cloud and smoke, and in the dark of
    mine   291
Is traced with flame. Move with me to the
    event.

There came a glorious morning, such a
    one
As dawns but once a season. Mercury
On such a morning would have flung him-
    self
From cloud to cloud, and swum with bal-
    anced wings
To some tall mountain. When I said to her,
' A day for gods to stoop,' she answered,
    ' Ay,
And men to soar; ' for as that other gazed,
Shading his eyes till all the fiery cloud,   300
The prophet and the chariot and the steeds,
Suck'd into oneness like a little star
Were drunk into the inmost blue, we stood,
When first we came from out the pines at
    noon,

With hands for eaves, uplooking and al-
most
Waiting to see some blessed shape in hea-
ven,
So bathed we were in brilliance. Never yet
Before or after have I known the spring
Pour with such sudden deluges of light
Into the middle summer; for that day   310
Love, rising, shook his wings, and charged
the winds
With spiced May - sweets from bound to
bound, and blew
Fresh fire into the sun, and from within
Burst thro' the heated buds, and sent his
soul
Into the songs of birds, and touch'd far-off
His mountain-altars, his high hills, with
flame
Milder and purer.

                Thro' the rocks we wound;
The great pine shook with lonely sounds
of joy
That came on the sea-wind. As mountain
streams
Our bloods ran free; the sunshine seem'd
to brood   320
More warmly on the heart than on the
brow.
We often paused, and, looking back, we saw
The clefts and openings in the mountains
fill'd
With the blue valley and the glistening
brooks,
And all the low dark groves, a land of love!
A land of promise, a land of memory,
A land of promise flowing with the milk
And honey of delicious memories !
And down to sea, and far as eye could ken,
Each way from verge to verge a Holy
Land,   330
Still growing holier as you near'd the bay,
For there the Temple stood.

                When we had reach'd
The grassy platform on some hill, I stoop'd,
I gather'd the wild herbs, and for her brows
And mine made garlands of the selfsame
flower,
Which she took smiling, and with my work
thus
Crown'd her clear forehead. Once or twice
she told me —
For I remember all things — to let grow
The flowers that run poison in their veins.

She said, ' The evil flourish in the world.'
Then playfully she gave herself the lie —
' Nothing in nature is unbeautiful;   342
So, brother, pluck and spare not.' So I
wove
Even the dull-blooded poppy-stem, ' whose
flower,
[ued with the scarlet of a fierce sunrise,
Like to the wild youth of an evil prince,
Is without sweetness, but who crowns him-
self
Above the naked poisons of his heart
In his old age.' A graceful thought of
hers
Graven on my fancy ! And O, how like a
nymph,   350
A stately mountain nymph she look'd ! how
native
Unto the hills she trod on ! While I gazed
My coronal slowly disentwined itself
And fell between us both; tho' while I
gazed
My spirit leap'd as with those thrills of bliss
That strike across the soul in prayer, and
show us
That we are surely heard. Methought a
light
Burst from the garland I had woven, and
stood
A solid glory on her bright black hair;
A light methought broke from her dark,
dark eyes,   360
And shot itself into the singing winds;
A mystic light flash'd even from her white
robe
As from a glass in the sun, and fell about
My footsteps on the mountains.

                            Last we came
To what our people call ' The Hill of Woe.'
A bridge is there, that, look'd at from be-
neath,
Seems but a cobweb filament to link
The yawning of an earthquake - cloven
chasm.
And thence one night, when all the winds
were loud,
A woful man — for so the story went—   370
Had thrust his wife and child and dash'd
himself
Into the dizzy depth below. Below,
Fierce in the strength of far descent, a
stream
Flies with a shatter'd foam along the
chasm.

The path was perilous, loosely strown
     with crags.
We mounted slowly; yet to both there
     came
The joy of life in steepness overcome,
And victories of ascent, and looking down
On all that had look'd down on us; and joy
In breathing nearer heaven; and joy to me,
High over all the azure-circled earth,   381
To breathe with her as if in heaven itself;
And more than joy that I to her became
Her guardian and her angel, raising her
Still higher, past all peril, until she saw
Beneath her feet the region far away,
Beyond the nearest mountain's bosky brows,
Arise in open prospect — heath and hill,
And hollow lined and wooded to the lips,
And steep - down walls of battlemented
     rock   390
Gilded with broom, or shatter'd into spires,
And glory of broad waters interfused,
Whence rose as it were breath and steam
     of gold,
And over all the great wood rioting
And climbing, streak'd or starr'd at inter-
     vals
With falling brook or blossom'd bush —
     and last,
Framing the mighty landscape to the west,
A purple range of mountain-cones, between
Whose interspaces gush'd in blinding bursts
The incorporate blaze of sun and sea.

                              At length
Descending from the point, and standing
     both   401
There on the tremulous bridge, that from
     beneath
Had seem'd a gossamer filament up in air,
We paused amid the splendor. All the
     west
And even unto the middle south was ribb'd
And barr'd with bloom on bloom. The sun
     below,
Held for a space 'twixt cloud and wave,
     shower'd down
Rays of a mighty circle, weaving over
That various wilderness a tissue of light
Unparallel'd. On the other side, the
     moon,   410
Half-melted into thin blue air, stood still,
And pale and fibrous as a wither'd leaf,
Nor yet endured in presence of His eyes
To indue his lustre; most unloverlike,
Since in his absence full of light and joy,

And giving light to others. But this most,
Next to her presence whom I loved so well,
Spoke loudly even into my inmost heart 418
As to my outward hearing. The loud
     stream,
Forth issuing from his portals in the crag, —
A visible link unto the home of my heart, —
Ran amber toward the west, and nigh the
     sea
Parting my own loved mountains was re-
     ceived,
Shorn of its strength, into the sympathy
Of that small bay, which out to open main
Glow'd intermingling close beneath the sun.
Spirit of Love ! that little hour was bound,
Shut in from Time, and dedicate to thee;
Thy fires from heaven had touch'd it, and
     the earth
They fell on became hallow'd evermore. 430

     We turn'd, our eyes met; hers were
          bright, and mine
Were dim with floating tears, that shot the
     sunset
In lightnings round me, and my name was
     borne
Upon her breath. Henceforth my name
     has been
A hallow'd memory like the names of old,
A centred, glory-circled memory,
And a peculiar treasure, brooking not
Exchange or currency; and in that hour
A hope flow'd round me, like a golden mist
Charm'd amid eddies of melodious airs, 440
A moment, ere the onward whirlwind
     shatter it,
Waver'd and floated — which was less than
     Hope,
Because it lack'd the power of perfect
     Hope;
But which was more and higher than all
     Hope,
Because all other Hope had lower aim;
Even that this name to which her gracious
     lips
Did lend such gentle utterance, this one
     name,
In some obscure hereafter, might in-
     wreathe —
How lovelier, nobler then ! — her life, her
     love,
With my life, love, soul, spirit, and heart
     and strength.   450
'Brother,' she said, 'let this be call'd hence-
     forth

The Hill of Hope;' and I replied, 'O sister,
My will is one with thine; the Hill of
    Hope.'
Nevertheless, we did not change the name.

I did not speak; I could not speak my
    love.
Love lieth deep, Love dwells not in lip-
    depths.
Love wraps his wings on either side the
    heart,
Constraining it with kisses close and warm,
Absorbing all the incense of sweet thoughts
So that they pass not to the shrine of
    sound.   460
Else had the life of that delighted hour
Drunk in the largeness of the utterance
Of Love; but how should earthly measure
    mete
The heavenly - unmeasured or unlimited
    Love,
Who scarce can tune his high majestic
    sense
Unto the thunder - song that wheels the
    spheres,
Scarce living in the Æolian harmony,
And flowing odor of the spacious air,
Scarce housed within the circle of this
    earth,
Be cabin'd up in words and syllables,   470
Which pass with that which breathes them ?
    Sooner earth
Might go round heaven, and the strait
    girth of Time
Inswathe the fulness of Eternity,
Than language grasp the infinite of Love.

O day which did enwomb that happy
    hour,
Thou art blessed in the years, divinest day !
O Genius of that hour which dost uphold
Thy coronal of glory like a god,
Amid thy melancholy mates far-seen,   479
Who walk before thee, ever turning round
To gaze upon thee till their eyes are dim
With dwelling on the light and depth of
    thine,
Thy name is ever worshipp'd among hours !
Had I died then, I had not seem'd to die,
For bliss stood round me like the light of
    heaven, —
Had I died then, I had not known the
    death;
Yea, had the Power from whose right hand
    the light

Of Life issueth, and from whose left hand
    floweth
The Shadow of Death, perennial effluences,
Whereof to all that draw the wholesome air,
Somewhile the one must overflow the
    other —   491
Then had he stemm'd my day with night,
    and driven
My current to the fountain whence it
    sprang, —
Even his own abiding excellence —
On me, methinks, that shock of gloom had
    fallen
Unfelt, and in this glory I had merged
The other, like the sun I gazed upon,
Which seeming for the moment due to
    death,
And dipping his head low beneath the
    verge,   499
Yet bearing round about him his own day,
In confidence of unabated strength,
Steppeth from heaven to heaven, from light
    to light,
And holdeth his undimmed forehead far
Into a clearer zenith, pure of cloud.

We trod the shadow of the downward hill;
We past from light to dark. On the other
    side
Is scoop'd a cavern and a mountain hall,
Which none have fathom'd. If you go
    far in —
The country people rumor — you may hear
The moaning of the woman and the child,
Shut in the secret chambers of the rock. 511
I too have heard a sound — perchance of
    streams
Running far on within its inmost halls,
The home of darkness; but the cavern-
    mouth,
Half overtrailed with a wanton weed,
Gives birth to a brawling brook, that pass-
    ing lightly
Adown a natural stair of tangled roots,
Is presently received in a sweet grave
Of eglantines, a place of burial
Far lovelier than its cradle; for unseen, 520
But taken with the sweetness of the place,
It makes a constant bubbling melody
That drowns the nearer echoes. Lower
    down
Spreads out a little lake, that, flooding,
    leaves
Low banks of yellow sand; and from the
    woods

That belt it rise three dark, tall cy-
    presses, —
Three cypresses, symbols of mortal woe,
That men plant over graves.

             Hither we came,
And sitting down upon the golden moss,
Held converse sweet and low — low con-
    verse sweet,   530
In which our voices bore least part. The
    wind
Told a love-tale beside us, how he woo'd
The waters, and the waters answering
    lisp'd
To kisses of the wind, that, sick with love,
Fainted at intervals, and grew again
To utterance of passion. Ye cannot shape
Fancy so fair as is this memory.
Methought all excellence that ever was
Had drawn herself from many thousand
    years,   539
And all the separate Edens of this earth,
To centre in this place and time. I lis-
    ten'd,
And her words stole with most prevailing
    sweetness
Into my heart, as thronging fancies come
To boys and girls when summer days are
    new,
And soul and heart and body are all at
    ease.
What marvel my Camilla told me all ?
It was so happy an hour, so sweet a place,
And I was as the brother of her blood,
And by that name I moved upon her
    breath;
Dear name, which had too much of near-
    ness in it   550
And heralded the distance of this time !
At first her voice was very sweet and low,
As if she were afraid of utterance;
But in the onward current of her speech, —
As echoes of the hollow-banked brooks
Are fashion'd by the channel which they
    keep, —
Her words did of their meaning borrow
    sound,
Her cheek did catch the color of her words.
I heard and trembled, yet I could but
    hear;
My heart paused — my raised eyelids would
    not fall,   560
But still I kept my eyes upon the sky.
I seem'd the only part of Time stood still,
And saw the motion of all other things;

While her words, syllable by syllable,
Like water, drop by drop, upon my ear
Fell, and I wish'd, yet wish'd her not to
    speak;
But she spake on, for I did name no wish.
What marvel my Camilla told me all
Her maiden dignities of Hope and Love —
' Perchance,' she said, ' return'd ' ? Even
    then the stars   570
Did tremble in their stations as I gazed;
But she spake on, for I did name no wish,
No wish — no hope. Hope was not wholly
    dead,
But breathing hard at the approach of
    death, —
Camilla, my Camilla, who was mine
No longer in the dearest sense of mine —
For all the secret of her inmost heart,
And all the maiden empire of her mind,
Lay like a map before me, and I saw
There, where I hoped myself to reign as
    king,   580
There, where that day I crown'd myself as
    king,
There in my realm and even on my throne,
Another! Then it seem'd as tho' a link
Of some tight chain within my inmost
    frame
Was riven in twain; that life I heeded not
Flow'd from me, and the darkness of the
    grave,
The darkness of the grave and utter night,
Did swallow up my vision; at her feet,
Even the feet of her I loved, I fell,
Smit with exceeding sorrow unto death. 590

Then had the earth beneath me yawning
    cloven
With such a sound as when an iceberg
    splits
From cope to base — had Heaven from all
    her doors,
With all her golden thresholds clashing,
    roll'd
Her heaviest thunder — I had lain as dead,
Mute, blind, and motionless as then I lay;
Dead, for henceforth there was no life for
    me !
Mute, for henceforth what use were words
    to me ?
Blind, for the day was as the night to me !
The night to me was kinder than the day;
The night in pity took away my day,   601
Because my grief as yet was newly born
Of eyes too weak to look upon the light;

And thro' the hasty notice of the ear
Frail Life was startled from the tender
　　love
Of him she brooded over.　Would I had
　　lain
Until the plaited ivy-tress had wound
Round my worn limbs, and the wild brier
　　had driven
Its knotted thorns thro' my unpaining
　　brows,
Leaning its roses on my faded eyes.　　610
The wind had blown above me, and the
　　rain
Had fallen upon me, and the gilded snake
Had nestled in this bosom-throne of Love,
But I had been at rest for evermore.

　　Long time entrancement held me.　All
　　　too soon
Life — like a wanton, too-officious friend,
Who will not *hear* denial, vain and rude
With proffer of unwish'd-for services —
Entering all the avenues of sense
Past thro' into his citadel, the brain,　　620
With hated warmth of apprehensiveness.
And first the chillness of the sprinkled
　　brook
Smote on my brows, and then I seem'd to
　　hear
Its murmur, as the drowning seaman hears,
Who with his head below the surface dropt
Listens the muffled booming indistinct
Of the confused floods, and dimly knows
His head shall rise no more; and then came
　　in
The white light of the weary moon above,
Diffused and molten into flaky cloud.　　630
Was my sight drunk that it did shape to
　　me
Him who should own that name?　Were
　　it not well
If so be that the echo of that name
Ringing within the fancy had updrawn
A fashion and a phantasm of the form
It should attach to?　Phantom! — had the
　　ghastliest
That ever lusted for a body, sucking
The foul steam of the grave to thicken by
　　it,
There in the shuddering moonlight brought
　　its face　　　　　　　　　　　　　　639
And what it has for eyes as close to mine
As he did — better that than his, than he
The friend, the neighbor, Lionel, the be-
　　loved.

The loved, the lover, the happy Lionel,
The low-voiced, tender-spirited Lionel,
All joy, to whom my agony was a joy.
O, how her choice did leap forth from his
　　eyes !
O, how her love did clothe itself in smiles
About his lips ! and — not one moment's
　　grace —
Then when the effect weigh'd seas upon
　　my head
To come my way ! to twit me with the
　　cause !　　　　　　　　　　　　　　650

　　Was not the land as free thro' all her
　　　ways
To him as me ?　Was not his wont to
　　walk
Between the going light and growing
　　night ?
Had I not learnt my loss before he came ?
Could that be more because he came my
　　way ?
Why should he not come my way if he
　　would ?
And yet to-night, to-night — when all my
　　wealth
Flash'd from me in a moment and I fell
Beggar'd for ever — why *should* he come
　　my way
Robed in those robes of light I must not
　　wear,　　　　　　　　　　　　　　660
With that great crown of beams about his
　　brows —
Come like an angel to a damned soul,
To tell him of the bliss he had with God —
Come like a careless and a greedy heir
That scarce can wait the reading of the
　　will
Before he takes possession ?　Was mine a
　　mood
To be invaded rudely, and not rather
A sacred, secret, unapproached woe,
Unspeakable ?　I was shut up with Grief;
She took the body of my past delight,　　670
Narded and swathed and balm'd it for her-
　　self,
And laid it in a sepulchre of rock
Never to rise again.　I was led mute
Into her temple like a sacrifice;
I was the High Priest in her holiest place,
Not to be loudly broken in upon.

　　O friend, thoughts deep and heavy as
　　　these well-nigh
O'erbore the limits of my brain: but he

Bent o'er me, and my neck his arm up-
    stay'd.
I thought it was an adder's fold, and once
I strove to disengage myself, but fail'd,   681
Being so feeble. She bent above me, too;
Wan was her cheek, for whatsoe'er of
    blight
Lives in the dewy touch of pity had made
The red rose there a pale one — and her
    eyes —
I saw the moonlight glitter on their tears —
And some few drops of that distressful rain
Fell on my face, and her long ringlets
    moved,
Drooping and beaten by the breeze, and
    brush'd
My fallen forehead in their to and fro,   690
For in the sudden anguish of her heart
Loosed from their simple thrall they had
    flow'd abroad,
And floated on and parted round her neck,
Mantling her form halfway. She, when I
    woke,
Something she ask'd, I know not what, and
    ask'd,
Unanswer'd, since I spake not; for the
    sound
Of that dear voice so musically low,
And now first heard with any sense of pain,
As it had taken life away before,   699
Choked all the syllables that strove to rise
From my full heart.

                    The blissful lover, too,
From his great hoard of happiness dis-
    till'd
Some drops of solace; like a vain rich
    man,
That, having always prosper'd in the world,
Folding his hands, deals comfortable words
To hearts wounded for ever; yet, in truth,
Fair speech was his and delicate of phrase,
Falling in whispers on the sense, address'd
More to the inward than the outward ear,
As rain of the midsummer midnight soft,
Scarce-heard, recalling fragrance and the
    green   711
Of the dead spring: but mine was wholly
    dead,
No bud, no leaf, no flower, no fruit for me.
Yet who had done, or who had suffer'd
    wrong?
And why was I to darken their pure love?
If, as I found, they two did love each
    other.

Because my own was darken'd?   Why
    was I
To cross between their happy star and
    them?
To stand a shadow by their shining doors,
And vex them with my darkness? Did I
    love her?   720
Ye know that I did love her; to this pre-
    sent
My full-orb'd love has waned not. Did I
    love her,
And could I look upon her tearful eyes?
What had *she* done to weep? Why should
    she weep?
O innocent of spirit — let my heart
Break rather — whom the gentlest airs of
    heaven
Should kiss with an unwonted gentleness.
Her love did murder mine? What then?
    She deem'd
I wore a brother's mind; she call'd me
    brother.
She told me all her love; she shall not
    weep.   730

    The brightness of a burning thought,
    awhile
In battle with the glooms of my dark will,
Moonlike emerged, and to itself lit up
There on the depth of an unfathom'd woe
Reflex of action. Starting up at once,
As from a dismal dream of my own death,
I, for I loved her, lost my love in Love;
I, for I loved her, graspt the hand she
    loved,
And laid it in her own, and sent my cry
Thro' the blank night to Him who loving
    made   740
The happy and the unhappy love, that He
Would hold the hand of blessing over
    them,
Lionel, the happy, and her, and her, his
    bride!
Let them so love that men and boys may
    say,
'Lo! how they love each other!' till their
    love
Shall ripen to a proverb, unto all
Known, when their faces are forgot in the
    land —
One golden dream of love, from which may
    death
Awake them with heaven's music in a life
More living to some happier happiness,   750
Swallowing its precedent in victory.

And as for me, Camilla, as for me, —
The dew of tears is an unwholesome dew,
They will but sicken the sick plant the
    more.
Deem that I love thee but as brothers do,
So shalt thou love me still as sisters do;
Or if thou dream aught farther, dream but
    how
I could have loved thee, had there been
    none else
To love as lovers, loved again by thee.

    Or this, or somewhat like to this, I
        spake,   760
When I beheld her weep so ruefully;
For sure my love should ne'er indue the
    front
And mask of Hate, who lives on others'
    moans.
Shall Love pledge Hatred in her bitter
    draughts,
And batten on her poisons? Love forbid!
Love passeth not the threshold of cold
    Hate,
And Hate is strange beneath the roof of
    Love.
O Love, if thou be'st Love, dry up these
    tears
Shed for the love of Love; for tho' mine
    image,
The subject of thy power, be cold in her,
Yet, like cold snow, it melteth in the
    source   771
Of these sad tears, and feeds their down-
    ward flow.
So Love, arraign'd to judgment and to
    death,
Received unto himself a part of blame,
Being guiltless, as an innocent prisoner,
Who, when the woful sentence hath been
    past,
And all the clearness of his fame hath
    gone
Beneath the shadow of the curse of man,
First falls asleep in swoon, wherefrom
    awaked,
And looking round upon his tearful friends,
Forthwith and in his agony conceives   781
A shameful sense as of a cleaving crime —
For whence without some guilt should such
    grief be?

    So died that hour, and fell into the
        abysm
Of forms outworn, but not to me outworn,

Who never hail'd another — was there
    one?
There might be one — one other, worth the
    life
That made it sensible. So that hour died
Like odor rapt into the winged wind
Borne into alien lands and far away.   790

    There be some hearts so airily built, that
        they,
They — when their love is wreck'd — if
    Love can wreck —
On that sharp ridge of utmost doom ride
    highly
Above the perilous seas of Change and
    Chance,
Nay, more, hold out the lights of cheerful-
    ness;
As the tall ship, that many a dreary year
Knit to some dismal sandbank far at sea,
All thro' the livelong hours of utter dark,
Showers slanting light upon the dolorous
    wave.
For me — what light, what gleam on those
    black ways   800
Where Love could walk with banish'd Hope
    no more?

    It was ill-done to part you, sisters fair;
Love's arms were wreath'd about the neck
    of Hope,
And Hope kiss'd Love, and Love drew in
    her breath
In that close kiss, and drank her whisper'd
    tales.
They said that Love would die when Hope
    was gone,
And Love mourn'd long, and sorrow'd after
    Hope;
At last she sought out Memory, and they
    trod
The same old paths where Love had walk'd
    with Hope,
And Memory fed the soul of Love with
    tears.   810

II

From that time forth I would not see her
    more;
But many weary moons I lived alone —
Alone, and in the heart of the great forest.
Sometimes upon the hills beside the sea
All day I watch'd the floating isles of
    shade,

And sometimes on the shore, upon the
  sands
Insensibly I drew her name, until
The meaning of the letters shot into
My brain; anon the wanton billow wash'd
Them over, till they faded like my love.
The hollow caverns heard me — the black
  brooks   11
Of the mid-forest heard me — the soft
  winds,
Laden with thistle - down and seeds of
  flowers,
Paused in their course to hear me, for my
  voice
Was all of thee; the merry linnet knew
  me,
The squirrel knew me, and the dragon-fly
Shot by me like a flash of purple fire.
The rough brier tore my bleeding palms;
  the hemlock,
Brow - high, did strike my forehead as I
  past;   19
Yet trod I not the wild-flower in my path,
Nor bruised the wild-bird's egg.

Was this the end ?
Why grew we then together in one plot ?
Why fed we from one fountain ? drew one
  sun ?
Why were our mothers branches of one
  stem ?
Why were we one in all things, save in
  that
Where to have been one had been the cope
  and crown
Of all I hoped and fear'd ? — if that same
  nearness
Were father to this distance, and that *one*
Vauntcourier to this *double ?* if Affection
Living slew Love, and Sympathy hew'd
  out   30
The bosom-sepulchre of Sympathy ?

Chiefly I sought the cavern and the hill
Where last we roam'd together, for the
  sound
Of the loud stream was pleasant, and the
  wind
Came wooingly with woodbine smells.
  Sometimes
All day I sat within the cavern-mouth,
Fixing my eyes on those three cypress-
  cones
That spired above the wood; and with
  mad hand

Tearing the bright leaves of the ivy-screen,
I cast them in the noisy brook beneath,   40
And watch'd them till they vanish'd from
  my sight
Beneath the bower of wreathed eglantines.
And all the fragments of the living rock, —
Huge blocks, which some old trembling of
  the world
Had loosen'd from the mountain, till they
  fell
Half-digging their own graves, — these in
  my agony
Did I make bare of all the golden moss,
Wherewith the dashing runnel in the spring
Had liveried them all over.   In my brain
The spirit seem'd to flag from thought to
  thought,   50
As moonlight wandering thro' a mist; my
  blood
Crept like marsh drains thro' all my lan-
  guid limbs;
The motions of my heart seem'd far within
  me,
Unfrequent, low, as tho' it told its pulses;
And yet it shook me, that my frame would
  shudder,
As if 't were drawn asunder by the rack.
But over the deep graves of Hope and
  Fear,
And all the broken palaces of the past,
Brooded one master-passion evermore,
Like to a low-hung and a fiery sky   60
Above some fair metropolis, earth-
  shock'd, —
Hung round with ragged rims and burning
  folds, —
Embathing all with wild and woful hues,
Great hills of ruins, and collapsed masses
Of thunder-shaken columns indistinct,
And fused together in the tyrannous
  light —
Ruins, the ruin of all my life and me !

Sometimes I thought Camilla was no
  more;
Some one had told me she was dead, and
  ask'd
If I would see her burial.   Then I seem'd
To rise, and through the forest - shadow
  borne   71
With more than mortal swiftness, I ran
  down
The steepy sea-bank, till I came upon
The rear of a procession, curving round
The silver-sheeted bay, in front of which

Six stately virgins, all in white, upbare
A broad earth-sweeping pall of whitest
   lawn,
Wreathed round the bier with garlands. In
   the distance,
From out the yellow woods upon the hill
Look'd forth the summit and the pinnacles
Of a gray steeple — thence at intervals 81
A low bell tolling. All the pageantry,
Save those six virgins which upheld the
   bier,
Were stoled from head to foot in flowing
   black;
One walk'd abreast with me, and veil'd his
   brow,
And he was loud in weeping and in praise
Of her we follow'd. A strong sympathy
Shook all my soul; I flung myself upon him
In tears and cries. I told him all my love,
How I had loved her from the first;
   whereat 90
He shrank and howl'd, and from his brow
   drew back
His hand to push me from him, and the
   face,
The very face and form of Lionel
Flash'd thro' my eyes into my innermost
   brain,
And at his feet I seem'd to faint and fall,
To fall and die away. I could not rise,
Albeit I strove to follow. They past on,
The lordly phantasms! in their floating
   folds
They past and were no more; but I had
   fallen 99
Prone by the dashing runnel on the grass.

Alway the inaudible, invisible thought,
Artificer and subject, lord and slave,
Shaped by the audible and visible,
Moulded the audible and visible.
All crisped sounds of wave and leaf and
   wind
Flatter'd the fancy of my fading brain;
The cloud-pavilion'd element, the wood,
The mountain, the three cypresses, the
   cave,
Storm, sunset, glows and glories of the
   moon
Below black firs, when silent - creeping
   winds 110
Laid the long night in silver streaks and
   bars,
Were wrought into the tissue of my dream.
The moanings in the forest, the loud brook,

Cries of the partridge like a rusty key
Turn'd in a lock, owl-whoop and dorhawk-
   whirr
Awoke me not, but were a part of sleep,
And voices in the distance calling to me
And in my vision bidding me dream on,
Like sounds without the twilight realm of
   dreams,
Which wander round the bases of the hills,
And murmur at the low-dropt eaves of
   sleep, 121
Half-entering the portals. Oftentimes
The vision had fair prelude, in the end
Opening on darkness, stately vestibules
To caves and shows of death — whether the
   mind,
With some revenge — even to itself un-
   known —
Made strange division of its suffering
With her, whom to have suffering view'd
   had been
Extremest pain; or that the clear-eyed
   Spirit,
Being blunted in the present, grew at
   length 130
Prophetical and prescient of whate'er
The future had in store; or that which
   most
Enchains belief, the sorrow of my spirit
Was of so wide a compass it took in
All I had loved, and my dull agony,
Ideally to her transferr'd, became
Anguish intolerable.

              The day waned;
Alone I sat with her. About my brow
Her warm breath floated in the utterance
Of silver - chorded tones; her lips were
   sunder'd 140
With smiles of tranquil bliss, which broke
   in light
Like morning from her eyes — her eloquent
   eyes —
As I have seen them many a hundred
   times —
Fill'd all with pure clear fire, thro' mine
   down rain'd
Their spirit-searching splendors. As a
   vision
Unto a haggard prisoner, iron-stay'd
In damp and dismal dungeons underground,
Confined on points of faith, when strength
   is shock'd
With torment, and expectancy of worse
Upon the morrow, thro' the ragged walls,

All unawares before his half-shut eyes, 151
Comes in upon him in the dead of night,
And with the excess of sweetness and of
    awe,
Makes the heart tremble, and the sight run
    over
Upon his steely gyves; so those fair eyes
Shone on my darkness, forms which ever
    stood
Within the magic cirque of memory,
Invisible but deathless, waiting still
The edict of the will to reassume
The semblance of those rare realities   160
Of which they were the mirrors.   Now the
    light
Which was their life burst through the
    cloud of thought
Keen, irrepressible.

                    It was a room
Within the summer-house of which I spake,
Hung round with paintings of the sea, and
    one
A vessel in mid-ocean, her heaved prow
Clambering, the mast bent and the ravin
    wind
In her sail roaring.   From the outer day,
Betwixt the close-set ivies came a broad
And solid beam of isolated light,   170
Crowded with driving atomies, and fell
Slanting upon that picture, from prime
    youth
Well-known, well-loved.   She drew it long
    ago
Forthgazing on the waste and open sea,
One morning when the upblown billow
    ran
Shoreward beneath red clouds, and I had
    pour'd
Into the shadowing pencil's naked forms
Color and life.   It was a bond and seal
Of friendship, spoken of with tearful smiles;
A monument of childhood and of love;   180
The poesy of childhood, my lost love
Symboll'd in storm.   We gazed on it to-
    gether
In mute and glad remembrance, and each
    heart
Grew closer to the other, and the eye
Was riveted and charm-bound, gazing like
The Indian on a still-eyed snake, low-
    couch'd —
A beauty which is death; when all at once
That painted vessel, as with inner life,
Began to heave upon that painted sea.

An earthquake, my loud heart-beats, made
    the ground   190
Reel under us, and all at once, soul, life
And breath and motion, past and flow'd
    away
To those unreal billows.   Round and round
A whirlwind caught and bore us; mighty
    gyres
Rapid and vast, of hissing spray wind-
    driven
Far thro' the dizzy dark.   Aloud she
    shriek'd;
My heart was cloven with pain; I wound
    my arms
About her; we whirl'd giddily; the wind
Sung, but I clasp'd her without fear.   Her
    weight
Shrank in my grasp, and over my dim
    eyes,   200
And parted lips which drank her breath,
    down-hung
The jaws of Death.   I, groaning, from me
    flung
Her empty phantom; all the sway and
    whirl
Of the storm dropt to windless calm, and I
Down welter'd thro' the dark ever and
    ever.

III

I came one day and sat among the stones
Strewn in the entry of the moaning cave;
A morning air, sweet after rain, ran over
The rippling levels of the lake, and blew
Coolness and moisture and all smells of
    bud
And foliage from the dark and dripping
    woods
Upon my fever'd brows that shook and
    throbb'd
From temple unto temple.   To what height
The day had grown I know not.   Then
    came on me
The hollow tolling of the bell, and all   10
The vision of the bier.   As heretofore
I walk'd behind with one who veil'd his
    brow.
Methought by slow degrees the sullen bell
Toll'd quicker, and the breakers on the
    shore
Sloped into louder surf.   Those that went
    with me,
And those that held the bier before my
    face,

Moved with one spirit round about the bay,
Trod swifter steps; and while I walk'd
  with these
In marvel at that gradual change, I thought
Four bells instead of one began to ring, 20
Four merry bells, four merry marriage-
  bells,
In clanging cadence jangling peal on
  peal —
A long loud clash of rapid marriage-bells.
Then those who led the van, and those in
  rear,
Rush'd into dance, and like wild Baccha-
  nals
Fled onward to the steeple in the woods.
I, too, was borne along and felt the blast
Beat on my heated eyelids. All at once
The front rank made a sudden halt; the
  bells
Lapsed into frightful stillness; the surge
  fell   30
From thunder into whispers; those six
  maids
With shrieks and ringing laughter on the
  sand
Threw down the bier; the woods upon the
  hill
Waved with a sudden gust that sweeping
  down
Took the edges of the pall, and blew it far
Until it hung, a little silver cloud
Over the sounding seas. I turn'd; my
  heart
Shrank in me, like a snowflake in the hand,
Waiting to see the settled countenance 39
Of her I loved, adorn'd with fading flowers.
But she from out her death-like chrysalis,
She from her bier, as into fresher life,
My sister, and my cousin, and my love,
Leapt lightly clad in bridal white — her
  hair
Studded with one rich Provence rose — a
  light
Of smiling welcome round her lips — her
  eyes
And cheeks as bright as when she climb'd
  the hill.
One hand she reach'd to those that came
  behind,
And while I mused nor yet endured to
  take
So rich a prize, the man who stood with
  me   50
Stept gaily forward, throwing down his
  robes,

And claspt her hand in his. Again the bells
Jangled and clang'd; again the stormy surf
Crash'd in the shingle; and the whirling
  rout
Led by those two rush'd into dance, and
  fled
Wind-footed to the steeple in the woods,
Till they were swallow'd in the leafy
  bowers,
And I stood sole beside the vacant bier.

There, there, my latest vision — then the
  event !

IV

THE GOLDEN SUPPER [1]

(Another speaks)

He flies the event; he leaves the event to
  me.
Poor Julian — how he rush'd away; the
  bells,
Those marriage-bells, echoing in ear and
  heart —
But cast a parting glance at me, you saw,
As who should say 'Continue.' Well, he
  had
One golden hour — of triumph shall I say ?
Solace at least — before he left his home.

  Would you had seen him in that hour of
    his !
He moved thro' all of it majestically —
Restrain'd himself quite to the close — but
  now —   10
Whether they *were* his lady's marriage-
  bells,
Or prophets of them in his fantasy,
I never ask'd; but Lionel and the girl
Were wedded, and our Julian came again
Back to his mother's house among the
  pines.
But these, their gloom, the mountains and
  the Bay,
The whole land weigh'd him down as Ætna
  does
The Giant of Mythology; he would go,
Would leave the land for ever, and had
  gone

[1] This poem is founded upon a story in Boc-
caccio. See Introduction, p. 281.

Surely, but for a whisper, 'Go not yet,' 20
Some warning — sent divinely — as it seem'd
By that which follow'd — but of this I deem
As of the visions that he told — the event
Glanced back upon them in his after life,
And partly made them — tho' he knew it not.

And thus he stay'd and would not look at her —
No, not for months; but, when the eleventh moon
After their marriage lit the lover's Bay,
Heard yet once more the tolling bell, and said,
'Would you could toll me out of life!' but found — 30
All softly as his mother broke it to him —
A crueller reason than a crazy ear
For that low knell tolling his lady dead —
Dead — and had lain three days without a pulse;
All that look'd on her had pronounced her dead.
And so they bore her — for in Julian's land
They never nail a dumb head up in elm —
Bore her free-faced to the free airs of heaven,
And laid her in the vault of her own kin.

What did he then? not die — he is here and hale — 40
Not plunge headforemost from the mountain there,
And leave the name of Lover's Leap, not he.
He knew the meaning of the whisper now,
Thought that he knew it. 'This, I stay'd for this;
O Love, I have not seen you for so long!
Now, now, will I go down into the grave,
I will be all alone with all I love,
And kiss her on the lips. She is his no more;
The dead returns to me, and I go down 49
To kiss the dead.'

The fancy stirr'd him so
He rose and went, and, entering the dim vault
And making there a sudden light, beheld
All round about him that which all will be.

The light was but a flash, and went again.
Then at the far end of the vault he saw
His lady with the moonlight on her face;
Her breast as in a shadow-prison, bars
Of black and bands of silver, which the moon
Struck from an open grating overhead
High in the wall, and all the rest of her 60
Drown'd in the gloom and horror of the vault.

'It was my wish,' he said, 'to pass, to sleep,
To rest, to be with her — till the great day
Peal'd on us with that music which rights all,
And raised us hand in hand.' And kneeling there
Down in the dreadful dust that once was man,
'Dust,' as he said, 'that once was loving hearts,
Hearts that had beat with such a love as mine —
Not such as mine, no, nor for such as her, —
He softly put his arm about her neck 70
And kiss'd her more than once, till helpless death
And silence made him bold — nay, but I wrong him,
He reverenced his dear lady even in death;
But, placing his true hand upon her heart,
'O you warm heart,' he moan'd, 'not even death
Can chill you all at once' — then, starting, thought
His dreams had come again. 'Do I wake or sleep?
Or am I made immortal, or my love
Mortal once more?' It beat — the heart — it beat; 79
Faint — but it beat; at which his own began
To pulse with such a vehemence that it drown'd
The feebler motion underneath his hand.
But when at last his doubts were satisfied
He raised her softly from the sepulchre,
And, wrapping her all over with the cloak
He came in, and now striding fast, and now
Sitting awhile to rest, but evermore
Holding his golden burthen in his arms,
So bore her thro' the solitary land
Back to the mother's house where she was born. 90

There the good mother's kindly minister-
    ing,
With half a night's appliances, recall'd
Her fluttering life. She rais'd an eye that
    ask'd
'Where?' till the things familiar to her
    youth
Had made a silent answer; then she spoke
'Here! and how came I here?' and learn-
    ing it —
They told her somewhat rashly, as I
    think —
At once began to wander and to wail,
'Ay, but you know that you must give me
    back.
Send! bid him come;' but Lionel was
    away —   100
Stung by his loss had vanish'd, none knew
    where.
'He casts me out,' she wept, 'and goes' —
    a wail
That, seeming something, yet was nothing,
    born
Not from believing mind but shatter'd
    nerve,
Yet haunting Julian, as her own reproof
At some precipitance in her burial.
Then, when her own true spirit had return'd,
'O, yes, and you,' she said, 'and none but
    you?
For you have given me life and love again,
And none but you yourself shall tell him
    of it,   110
And you shall give me back when he re-
    turns.'
' Stay then a little,' answer'd Julian, 'here,
And keep yourself, none knowing, to your-
    self;
And I will do your will. I may not stay,
No, not an hour; but send me notice of
    him
When he returns, and then will I return,
And I will make a solemn offering of you
To him you love.' And faintly she re-
    plied,
'And I will do your will, and none shall
    know.'

    Not know? with such a secret to be
        known.   120
But all their house was old and loved them
    both,
And all the house had known the loves of
    both,
Had died almost to serve them any way,

And all the land was waste and solitary.
And then he rode away; but after this,
An hour or two, Camilla's travail came
Upon her, and that day a boy was born,
Heir of his face and land, to Lionel.

    And thus our lonely lover rode away,
And pausing at a hostel in a marsh,   130
There fever seized upon him. Myself was
    then
Travelling that land, and meant to rest an
    hour;
And sitting down to such a base repast,
It makes me angry yet to speak of it —
I heard a groaning overhead, and climb'd
The moulder'd stairs — for everything was
    vile —
And in a loft, with none to wait on him,
Found, as it seem'd, a skeleton alone,
Raving of dead men's dust and beating
    hearts.

    A dismal hostel in a dismal land,   140
A flat malarian world of reed and rush!
But there from fever and my care of him
Sprang up a friendship that may help us
    yet.
For while we roam'd along the dreary
    coast,
And waited for her message, piece by
    piece
I learnt the drearier story of his life;
And, tho' he loved and honor'd Lionel,
Found that the sudden wail his lady made
Dwelt in his fancy. Did he know her worth,
Her beauty even? should he not be taught,
Even by the price that others set upon it, 151
The value of that jewel he had to guard?

    Suddenly came her notice and we past,
I with our lover to his native Bay.

    This love is of the brain, the mind, the
        soul;
That makes the sequel pure, tho' some of
    us
Beginning at the sequel know no more.
Not such am I; and yet I say the bird
That will not hear my call, however sweet
But if my neighbor whistle answers him —
What matter? there are others in the
    wood.   161
Yet when I saw her — and I thought him
    crazed,
Tho' not with such a craziness as needs

A cell and keeper — those dark eyes of
    hers —
O, such dark eyes ! and not her eyes alone,
But all from these to where she touch'd on
    earth,
For such a craziness as Julian's look'd
No less than one divine apology.

So sweetly and so modestly she came   169
To greet us, her young hero in her arms !
'Kiss him,' she said. 'You gave me life
    again.
He, but for you, had never seen it once.
His other father you ! Kiss him, and
    then
Forgive him, if his name be Julian too.'

Talk of lost hopes and broken heart ! his
    own
Sent such a flame into his face, I knew
Some sudden vivid pleasure hit him there.

But he was all the more resolved to go,
And sent at once to Lionel, praying him,
By that great love they both had borne the
    dead,   180
To come and revel for one hour with him
Before he left the land for evermore;
And then to friends — they were not many
    — who lived
Scatteringly about that lonely land of his,
And bade them to a banquet of farewells.

And Julian made a solemn feast; I never
Sat at a costlier, for all round his hall
From column on to column, as in a wood,
Not such as here — an equatorial one,
Great garlands swung and blossom'd; and
    beneath,   190
Heirlooms, and ancient miracles of art,
Chalice and salver, wines that, heaven knows
    when,
Had suck'd the fire of some forgotten sun,
And kept it thro' a hundred years of
    gloom,
Yet glowing in a heart of ruby — cups
Where nymph and god ran ever round in
    gold —
Others of glass as costly — some with gems
Movable and resettable at will,
And trebling all the rest in value — Ah
    heavens !
Why need I tell you all ? — suffice to say
That whatsoever such a house as his,   201
And his was old, has in it rare or fair

Was brought before the guest.   And they,
    the guests,
Wonder'd at some strange light in Julian's
    eyes —
I told you that he had his golden hour —
And such a feast, ill-suited as it seem'd
To such a time, to Lionel's loss and his
And that resolved self-exile from a land
He never would revisit, such a feast
So rich, so strange, and stranger even than
    rich,   210
But rich as for the nuptials of a king.

And stranger yet, at one end of the
    hall
Two great funereal curtains, looping down,
Parted a little ere they met the floor,
About a picture of his lady, taken
Some years before, and falling hid the
    frame.
And just above the parting was a lamp;
So the sweet figure folded round with night
Seem'd stepping out of darkness with a
    smile.

Well, then — our solemn feast — we ate
    and drank,   220
And might — the wines being of such no-
    bleness —
Have jested also, but for Julian's eyes,
And something weird and wild about it
    all.
What was it ? for our lover seldom spoke,
Scarce touch'd the meats, but ever and
    anon
A priceless goblet with a priceless wine
Arising show'd he drank beyond his use;
And when the feast was near an end, he
    said:

'There is a custom in the Orient,
    friends —
I read of it in Persia — when a man   230
Will honor those who feast with him, he
    brings
And shows them whatsoever he accounts
Of all his treasures the most beautiful,
Gold, jewels, arms, whatever it may be.
This custom — '

                Pausing here a moment, all
The guests broke in upon him with meeting
    hands
And cries about the banquet — 'Beautiful !
Who could desire more beauty at a feast ?'

The lover answer'd: 'There is more than
     one   239
Here sitting who desires it. Laud me not
Before my time, but hear me to the close.
This custom steps yet further when the
     guest
Is loved and honor'd to the uttermost.
For after he hath shown him gems or gold,
He brings and sets before him in rich
     guise
That which is thrice as beautiful as these,
The beauty that is dearest to his heart —
" O my heart's lord, would I could show
     you," he says,
" Even my heart too."   And I propose to-
     night   249
To show you what is dearest to my heart,
And my heart too.

               'But solve me first a doubt.
I knew a man, nor many years ago;
He had a faithful servant, one who loved
His master more than all on earth beside.
He falling sick, and seeming close on
     death,
His master would not wait until he died,
But bade his menials bear him from the
     door,
And leave him in the public way to die.
I knew another, not so long ago,
Who found the dying servant, took him
     home,   260
And fed, and cherish'd him, and saved his
     life.
I ask you now, should this first master
     claim
His service, whom does it belong to ? him
Who thrust him out, or him who saved his
     life ? '

     This question, so flung down before the
          guests,
And balanced either way by each, at
     length
When some were doubtful how the law
     would hold,
Was handed over by consent of all
To one who had not spoken, Lionel.

     Fair speech was his, and delicate of
          phrase.   270
And he, beginning languidly — his loss
Weigh'd on him yet — but warming as he
     went,
Glanced at the point of law, to pass it by,

Affirming that as long as either lived,
By all the laws of love and gratefulness,
The service of the one so saved was due
All to the saver — adding, with a smile,
The first for many weeks — a semi-smile
As at a strong conclusion — ' body and soul
And life and limbs, all his to work his
     will.'   280

     Then Julian made a secret sign to me
To bring Camilla down before them all.
And crossing her own picture as she came,
And looking as much lovelier than herself
Is lovelier than all others — on her head
A diamond circlet, and from under this
A veil, that seem'd no more than gilded
     air,
Flying by each fine ear, an Eastern gauze
With seeds of gold — so, with that grace of
     hers,   289
Slow-moving as a wave against the wind,
That flings a mist behind it in the sun —
And bearing high in arms the mighty babe,
The younger Julian, who himself was
     crown'd
With roses, none so rosy as himself —
And over all her babe and her the jewels
Of many generations of his house
Sparkled and flash'd, for he had deck'd
     them out
As for a solemn sacrifice of love —
So she came in — I am long in telling it,
I never yet beheld a thing so strange,   300
Sad, sweet, and strange together — floated
     in —
While all the guests in mute amazement
     rose —
And slowly pacing to the middle hall,
Before the board, there paused and stood,
     her breast
Hard-heaving, and her eyes upon her feet,
Not daring yet to glance at Lionel.
But him she carried, him nor lights nor
     feast
Dazed or amazed, nor eyes of men; who
     cared
Only to use his own, and staring wide
And hungering for the gilt and jewell'd
     world   310
About him, look'd, as he is like to prove,
When Julian goes, the lord of all he saw.

     'My guests,' said Julian, 'you are hon-
          or'd now
Even to the uttermost; in her behold

Of all my treasures the most beautiful,
Of all things upon earth the dearest to
  me;'
Then waving us a sign to seat ourselves,
Led his dear lady to a chair of state.
And I, by Lionel sitting, saw his face
Fire, and dead ashes and all fire again   320
Thrice in a second, felt him tremble too,
And heard him muttering, 'So like, so
  like;
She never had a sister. I knew none.
Some cousin of his and hers — O God, so
  like!'
And then he suddenly ask'd her if she
  were.
She shook, and cast her eyes down, and was
  dumb.
And then some other question'd if she
  came
From foreign lands, and still she did not
  speak.
Another, if the boy were hers; but she   329
To all their queries answer'd not a word,
Which made the amazement more, till one
  of them
Said, shuddering, 'Her spectre!' But his
  friend
Replied, in half a whisper, 'Not at least
The spectre that will speak if spoken to.
Terrible pity, if one so beautiful
Prove, as I almost dread to find her,
  dumb!'

  But Julian, sitting by her, answer'd
  all:
'She is but dumb, because in her you
  see
That faithful servant whom we spoke
  about,
Obedient to her second master now;   340
Which will not last. I have here to-night
  a guest
So bound to me by common love and loss —
What! shall I bind him more? in his be-
  half,
Shall I exceed the Persian, giving him
That which of all things is the dearest to
  me,
Not only showing? and he himself pro-
  nounced
That my rich gift is wholly mine to give.

  'Now all be dumb, and promise all of
  you
Not to break in on what I say by word

Or whisper, while I show you all my
  heart.'   350
And then began the story of his love
As here to-day, but not so wordily —
The passionate moment would not suffer
  that —
Past thro' his visions to the burial; thence
Down to this last strange hour in his own
  hall;
And then rose up, and with him all his
  guests
Once more as by enchantment; all but
  he,
Lionel, who fain had risen, but fell again,
And sat as if in chains — to whom he said:

  'Take my free gift, my cousin, for your
  wife;   360
And were it only for the giver's sake,
And tho' she seem so like the one you
  lost,
Yet cast her not away so suddenly,
Lest there be none left here to bring her
  back.
I leave this land for ever.' Here he ceased.

  Then taking his dear lady by one hand,
And bearing on one arm the noble babe,
He slowly brought them both to Lionel.
And there the widower husband and dead
  wife
Rush'd each at each with a cry that rather
  seem'd   370
For some new death than for a life re-
  new'd;
Whereat the very babe began to wail.
At once they turn'd, and caught and
  brought him in
To their charm'd circle, and, half killing
  him
With kisses, round him closed and claspt
  again.
But Lionel, when at last he freed himself
From wife and child, and lifted up a face
All over glowing with the sun of life,
And love, and boundless thanks — the sight
  of this
So frighted our good friend that, turning
  to me   380
And saying, 'It is over; let us go' —
There were our horses ready at the doors —
We bade them no farewell, but mounting
  these
He past for ever from his native land;
And I with him, my Julian, back to mine.

IDYLLS OF THE KING

IN TWELVE BOOKS

'Flos Regum Arthurus.' — JOSEPH OF EXETER

The poet became interested in the Arthurian story long before the first series of the 'Idylls' was published. 'The Lady of Shalott,' which appeared in 1832, is founded upon the legend which was later made the subject of 'Lancelot and Elaine.' 'The Palace of Art' in the same volume contained an allusion to 'that deep-wounded child of Pendragon,' or 'mythic Uther's deeply wounded son,' as it now reads. 'Sir Galahad' and 'Sir Lancelot and Queen Guinevere' were printed in 1842, when the 'Morte d'Arthur' was also given to the world. This latter poem, afterwards incorporated in 'The Passing of Arthur,' must have been written as early as 1835, when Fitzgerald heard it read from manuscript ('Memoir,' vol. i. p. 194). Landor also writes under date of December 9, 1837: 'Yesterday a Mr. Moreton, a young man of rare judgment, read to me a manuscript by Mr. Tennyson, very different in style from his printed poems. The subject is the death of Arthur. It is more Homeric than any poem of our time, and rivals some of the noblest parts of the Odyssea' (Forster's 'Life of Landor,' ii. 323).

In 1857 the poet printed 'six trial-copies' of 'Enid and Nimuë: the True and the False,' containing the stories of 'Enid' and 'Vivien,' afterwards revised for the edition of 1859. The copy of this book in the library of the British Museum is believed to be the 'sole survivor' of the six.

There is a still earlier form of 'Enid' in the Forster Bequest Library of the South Kensington Museum, London, which appears to be a first proof of the poem as printed in the 1857 volume. In the same collection there is a volume of proof-sheets, the title-page of which reads: 'The True and the False. Four Idylls of the King,' with the date 1859. It contains the four Idylls which, after further revision, were published the same year with the simpler title of 'Idylls of the King.'

This first instalment of the 'Idylls' as finally published in July, 1859, included 'Enid,' 'Vivien,' 'Elaine,' and 'Guinevere,' as they were then entitled. Ten thousand copies were sold in about six weeks, and the critics were almost unanimous in their praise of the book. Among its warmest admirers was Prince Albert, who sent his copy to the poet, asking him to write his name in it. The note continued : —

'You would thus add a peculiar interest to the book containing those beautiful songs, from the perusal of which I derived the greatest enjoyment. They quite rekindle the feeling with which the legends of King Arthur must have inspired the chivalry of old, whilst the graceful form in which they are presented blends those feelings with the softer tone of our present age.'

In 1862, a new edition of the 'Idylls' appeared, with the dedication to the memory of the Prince, who died in December, 1861.

In 1869, four more Idylls were brought out, — 'The Coming of Arthur,' 'The Holy Grail,' 'Pelleas and Ettarre,' and 'The Passing of Arthur,' in which, as already mentioned, the 'Morte d'Arthur' of 1842 is incorporated.

In 1872, 'The Last Tournament' (contributed to the 'Contemporary Review' for December, 1871) and 'Gareth and Lynette' appeared ; and in 1885 'Balin and Balan,' the last of the series, was included in 'Tiresias and Other Poems.'

In 1884, 'Enid,' already entitled 'Geraint and Enid,' was divided into two parts (numbered I. and II.), and in 1888 these parts received their present titles. The poems were now described as 'twelve books,' and arranged in the order in which the author intended they should be read.

In the order of *publication* the last Idyll (or the portion of it included in the 'Morte d'Arthur' of 1842) was the first, followed successively by the third, fourth (these two, as just explained, being originally one), sixth, seventh, eleventh (as the five were arranged in 1859), first, eighth, ninth, twelfth) as arranged in 1869, the twelfth being the amplification of the 'Morte d'Arthur'), second, tenth, and fifth. 'Nave and transept, aisle after aisle, the Gothic minster has extended, until, with the addition of a cloister here and a chapel yonder, the structure stands complete.' Stedman, from whose 'Victorian Poets' we quote this, adds : —

'It has grown insensibly, under the hands of one man who has given it the best years of his life, — but somewhat as Wolf conceived the Homeric poems to have grown, chant by chant, until the time came for the whole to be welded together in heroic form. . . . It is the epic of chivalry, — the Christian ideal of chivalry which we have deduced from a barbaric source, —

our conception of what knighthood should be, rather than what it really was; but so skilfully wrought of high imaginings, faery spells, fantastic legends, and mediæval splendors, that the whole work, suffused with the Tennysonian glamor of golden mist, seems like a chronicle illuminated by saintly hands, and often blazes with light like that which flashed from the holy wizard's book when the covers were unclasped. And, indeed, if this be not the greatest narrative poem since "Paradise Lost," what other English production are you to name in its place? Never so lofty as the grander portions of Milton's epic, it is more evenly sustained and has no long prosaic passages; while "Paradise Lost" is justly declared to be a work of superhuman genius impoverished by dreary wastes of theology.'

For the origin and development of the story of the 'Idylls,' see 'Studies in the Arthurian Legend,' by John Rhys, M. A. (Oxford, 1891), 'Tennyson's Idylls of the King and Arthurian Story from the 16th Century,' by M. W. Maccallum, M. A. (London, 1894), 'Essays on Lord Tennyson's Idylls of the King,' by Harold Littledale, M. A. (London, 1893), 'The Growth of the Idylls of the King,' by Richard Jones, Ph. D. (Philadelphia, 1895), 'King Arthur and the Table Round,' by W. W. Newell (Boston, 1897), etc. For the allegory in the poems, see 'Studies in the Idylls,' by Henry Elsdale (London, 1878), and the articles in the 'Contemporary Review' for January, 1870 (by Dean Alford), and May, 1873 (by the editor), both of which were based on the poet's own explanations. For general criticism, see particularly 'Tennyson, his Art and Relation to Modern Life,' by Rev. Stopford A. Brooke (London and New York, 1894), in which pp. 255–391 are devoted to the 'Idylls,' and 'The Poetry of Tennyson,' by Rev. Dr. Henry van Dyke (3d ed., New York, 1892, pp. 133–196). For bibliographical and miscellaneous information, see the 'Handbook to the Works of Alfred Lord Tennyson,' by Morton Luce (London, 1895), 'A Tennyson Primer,' by William M. Dixon, Litt. D. (London and New York, 1896), and Nicoll and Wise's 'Literary Anecdotes of the Nineteenth Century,' vol. ii. (London, 1896). The 'Bibliography of Tennyson,' by the author of 'Tennysoniana' (R. H. Shepherd), published by subscription (London, 1896), though the most complete up to the present time (1898), is sometimes inaccurate. Malory's 'Morte Darthur,' from which the poet drew much of his material, is accessible in the 'Globe' edition (London and New York, revised ed. 1893), and in the 'Temple Classics' edition (London, 1897).

DEDICATION

THESE to His Memory — since he held them dear,
Perchance as finding there unconsciously
Some image of himself — I dedicate,
I dedicate, I consecrate with tears —
These Idylls.

And indeed he seems to me
Scarce other than my king's ideal knight,
'Who reverenced his conscience as his king;
Whose glory was, redressing human wrong;
Who spake no slander, no, nor listen'd to it;
Who loved one only and who clave to her —'   10
Her — over all whose realms to their last isle,
Commingled with the gloom of imminent war,
The shadow of his loss drew like eclipse,
Darkening the world. We have lost him; he is gone.
We know him now; all narrow jealousies
Are silent, and we see him as he moved,

How modest, kindly, all-accomplish'd, wise,
With what sublime repression of himself,
And in what limits, and how tenderly;
Not swaying to this faction or to that;   20
Not making his high place the lawless perch
Of wing'd ambitions, nor a vantage-ground
For pleasure; but thro' all this tract of years
Wearing the white flower of a blameless life,
Before a thousand peering littlenesses,
In that fierce light which beats upon a throne
And blackens every blot; for where is he
Who dares foreshadow for an only son
A lovelier life, a more unstain'd, than his?
Or how should England dreaming of *his* sons   30
Hope more for these than some inheritance
Of such a life, a heart, a mind as thine,
Thou noble Father of her Kings to be,
Laborious for her people and her poor —
Voice in the rich dawn of an ampler day —
Far-sighted summoner of War and Waste
To fruitful strifes and rivalries of peace –

Sweet nature gilded by the gracious gleam
Of letters, dear to Science, dear to Art,
Dear to thy land and ours, a Prince in-
   deed,   40
Beyond all titles, and a household name,
Hereafter, thro' all times, Albert the Good.

Break not, O woman's - heart, but still
   endure;
Break not, for thou art royal, but endure,
Remembering all the beauty of that star
Which shone so close beside thee that ye
   made
One light together, but has past and leaves
The Crown a lonely splendor.

                   May all love,
His love, unseen but felt, o'ershadow thee,
The love of all thy sons encompass thee, 50
The love of all thy daughters cherish thee,
The love of all thy people comfort thee,
Till God's love set thee at his side again !

THE COMING OF ARTHUR

LEODOGRAN, the king of Cameliard,
Had one fair daughter, and none other
   child;
And she was fairest of all flesh on earth,
Guinevere, and in her his one delight.

For many a petty king ere Arthur came
Ruled in this isle and, ever waging war
Each upon other, wasted all the land;
And still from time to time the heathen
   host
Swarm'd over-seas, and harried what was
   left.
And so there grew great tracts of wilder-
   ness,   10
Wherein the beast was ever more and
   more,
But man was less and less, till Arthur came.
For first Aurelius lived and fought and
   died,
And after him King Uther fought and died,
But either fail'd to make the kingdom
   one.
And after these King Arthur for a space,
And thro' the puissance of his Table
   Round,
Drew all their petty princedoms under him,
Their king and head, and made a realm and
   reign'd.

And thus the land of Cameliard was
   waste,   20
Thick with wet woods, and many a beast
   therein,
And none or few to scare or chase the
   beast;
So that wild dog and wolf and boar and
   bear
Came night and day, and rooted in the
   fields,
And wallow'd in the gardens of the King.
And ever and anon the wolf would steal
The children and devour, but now and then,
Her own brood lost or dead, lent her fierce
   teat
To human sucklings; and the children,
   housed
In her foul den, there at their meat would
   growl,   30
And mock their foster-mother on four feet,
Till, straighten'd, they grew up to wolf-like
   men,
Worse than the wolves. And King Leo-
   dogran
Groan'd for the Roman legions here again
And Cæsar's eagle. Then his brother king,
Urien, assail'd him; last a heathen horde,
Reddening the sun with smoke and earth
   with blood,
And on the spike that split the mother's
   heart
Spitting the child, brake on him, till,
   amazed,   39
He knew not whither he should turn for aid.

But — for he heard of Arthur newly
   crown'd,
Tho' not without an uproar made by those
Who cried, ' He is not Uther's son ' — the
   King
Sent to him, saying, ' Arise, and help us
   thou !
For here between the man and beast we
   die.'

And Arthur yet had done no deed of
   arms,
But heard the call and came; and Guine-
   vere
Stood by the castle walls to watch him pass;
But since he neither wore on helm or shield
The golden symbol of his kinglihood, 50
But rode a simple knight among his knights,
And many of these in richer arms than he,
She saw him not, or mark'd not, if she saw,

One among many, tho' his face was bare.
But Arthur, looking downward as he past,
Felt the light of her eyes into his life
Smite on the sudden, yet rode on, and pitch'd
His tents beside the forest. Then he drave
The heathen; after, slew the beast, and fell'd
The forest, letting in the sun, and made 60
Broad pathways for the hunter and the knight,
And so return'd.

       For while he linger'd there,
A doubt that ever smoulder'd in the hearts
Of those great lords and barons of his realm
Flash'd forth and into war; for most of these,
Colleaguing with a score of petty kings,
Made head against him, crying: ' Who is he
That he should rule us ? who hath proven him
King Uther's son ? for lo ! we look at him,
And find nor face nor bearing, limbs nor voice, 70
Are like to those of Uther whom we knew.
This is the son of Gorloïs, not the King;
This is the son of Anton, not the King.'

And Arthur, passing thence to battle, felt
Travail, and throes and agonies of the life,
Desiring to be join'd with Guinevere,
And thinking as he rode: ' Her father said
That there between the man and beast they die.
Shall I not lift her from this land of beasts
Up to my throne and side by side with me ?
What happiness to reign a lonely king, 81
Vext — O ye stars that shudder over me,
O earth that soundest hollow under me,
Vext with waste dreams ? for saving I be join'd
To her that is the fairest under heaven,
I seem as nothing in the mighty world,
And cannot will my will nor work my work
Wholly, nor make myself in mine own realm
Victor and lord. But were I join'd with her,
Then might we live together as one life, 90
And reigning with one will in everything
Have power on this dark land to lighten it,
And power on this dead world to make it live.'

Thereafter — as he speaks who tells the tale —
When Arthur reach'd a field of battle bright
With pitch'd pavilions of his foe, the world
Was all so clear about him that he saw
The smallest rock far on the faintest hill,
And even in high day the morning star. 99
So when the King had set his banner broad,
At once from either side, with trumpet-blast,
And shouts, and clarions shrilling unto blood,
The long-lanced battle let their horses run.
And now the barons and the kings prevail'd,
And now the King, as here and there that war
Went swaying; but the Powers who walk the world
Made lightnings and great thunders over him,
And dazed all eyes, till Arthur by main might,
And mightier of his hands with every blow,
And leading all his knighthood threw the kings, 110
Carádos, Urien, Cradlemont of Wales,
Claudius, and Clariance of Northumberland,
The King Brandagoras of Latangor,
With Anguisant of Erin, Morganore,
And Lot of Orkney. Then, before a voice
As dreadful as the shout of one who sees
To one who sins, and deems himself alone
And all the world asleep, they swerved and brake
Flying, and Arthur call'd to stay the brands
That hack'd among the flyers, 'Ho ! they yield !' 120
So like a painted battle the war stood
Silenced, the living quiet as the dead,
And in the heart of Arthur joy was lord.
He laugh'd upon his warrior whom he loved
And honor'd most. ' Thou dost not doubt me King,
So well thine arm hath wrought for me to-day.'
' Sir and my liege,' he cried, ' the fire of God
Descends upon thee in the battle-field.
I know thee for my King !' Whereat the two,
For each had warded either in the fight,

Sware on the field of death a deathless
love. 131
And Arthur said, 'Man's word is God in
man;
Let chance what will, I trust thee to the
death.'

Then quickly from the foughten field he
sent
Ulfius, and Brastias, and Bedivere,
His new-made knights, to King Leodogran,
Saying, 'If I in aught have served thee
well,
Give me thy daughter Guinevere to wife.'

Whom when he heard, Leodogran in
heart
Debating — 'How should I that am a king,
However much he holp me at my need, 141
Give my one daughter saving to a king,
And a king's son ?' — lifted his voice, and
call'd
A hoary man, his chamberlain, to whom
He trusted all things, and of him required
His counsel: 'Knowest thou aught of Ar-
thur's birth ?'

Then spake the hoary chamberlain and
said:
'Sir King, there be but two old men that
know;
And each is twice as old as I; and one 149
Is Merlin, the wise man that ever served
King Uther thro' his magic art, and one
Is Merlin's master — so they call him —
Bleys,
Who taught him magic; but the scholar
ran
Before the master, and so far that Bleys
Laid magic by, and sat him down, and
wrote
All things and whatsoever Merlin did
In one great annal-book, where after-years
Will learn the secret of our Arthur's birth.'

To whom the King Leodogran replied:
'O friend, had I been holpen half as well
By this King Arthur as by thee to-day, 161
Then beast and man had had their share of
me;
But summon here before us yet once more
Ulfius, and Brastias, and Bedivere.'

Then, when they came before him, the
king said:

'I have seen the cuckoo chased by lesser
fowl,
And reason in the chase; but wherefore
now
Do these your lords stir up the heat of war,
Some calling Arthur born of Gorloïs,
Others of Anton ? Tell me, ye yourselves,
Hold ye this Arthur for King Uther's
son ?' 171

And Ulfius and Brastias answer'd, 'Ay.'
Then Bedivere, the first of all his knights
Knighted by Arthur at his crowning,
spake —
For bold in heart and act and word was he,
Whenever slander breathed against the
King —

'Sir, there be many rumors on this head;
For there be those who hate him in their
hearts,
Call him baseborn, and since his ways are
sweet,
And theirs are bestial, hold him less than
man; 180
And there be those who deem him more
than man,
And dream he dropt from heaven. But my
belief
In all this matter — so ye care to learn —
Sir, for ye know that in King Uther's time
The prince and warrior Gorloïs, he that
held
Tintagil castle by the Cornish sea,
Was wedded with a winsome wife, Ygerne;
And daughters had she borne him, — one
whereof,
Lot's wife, the Queen of Orkney, Bellicent,
Hath ever like a loyal sister cleaved 190
To Arthur, — but a son she had not borne.
And Uther cast upon her eyes of love;
But she, a stainless wife to Gorloïs,
So loathed the bright dishonor of his love
That Gorloïs and King Uther went to war,
And overthrown was Gorloïs and slain.
Then Uther in his wrath and heat besieged
Ygerne within Tintagil, where her men,
Seeing the mighty swarm about their walls,
Left her and fled, and Uther enter'd in, 200
And there was none to call to but himself.
So, compass'd by the power of the king,
Enforced she was to wed him in her tears,
And with a shameful swiftness; afterward,
Not many moons, King Uther died him-
self,

Moaning and wailing for an heir to rule
After him, lest the realm should go to
wrack.
And that same night, the night of the new
year,
By reason of the bitterness and grief 209
That vext his mother, all before his time
Was Arthur born, and all as soon as born
Deliver'd at a secret postern-gate
To Merlin, to be holden far apart
Until his hour should come, because the
lords
Of that fierce day were as the lords of
this,
Wild beasts, and surely would have torn
the child
Piecemeal among them, had they known;
for each
But sought to rule for his own self and
hand,
And many hated Uther for the sake
Of Gorloïs. Wherefore Merlin took the
child, 220
And gave him to Sir Anton, an old knight
And ancient friend of Uther; and his wife
Nursed the young prince, and rear'd him
with her own;
And no man knew. And ever since the
lords
Have foughten like wild beasts among
themselves,
So that the realm has gone to wrack; but
now,
This year, when Merlin — for his hour had
come —
Brought Arthur forth, and set him in the
hall,
Proclaiming, " Here is Uther's heir, your
king,"
A hundred voices cried: " Away with
him ! 230
No king of ours ! a son of Gorloïs he,
Or else the child of Anton, and no king,
Or else baseborn." Yet Merlin thro' his
craft,
And while the people clamor'd for a king,
Had Arthur crown'd; but after, the great
lords
Banded, and so brake out in open war.'

Then while the king debated with him-
self
If Arthur were the child of shamefulness,
Or born the son of Gorloïs after death, 239
Or Uther's son and born before his time,

Or whether there were truth in anything
Said by these three, there came to Came-
liard,
With Gawain and young Modred, her two
sons,
Lot's wife, the Queen of Orkney, Belli-
cent;
Whom as he could, not as he would, the
king
Made feast for, saying, as they sat at
meat:
' A doubtful throne is ice on summer seas.
Ye come from Arthur's court. Victor his
men
Report him ! Yea, but ye — think ye this
king —
So many those that hate him, and so
strong, 250
So few his knights, however brave they
be —
Hath body enow to hold his foemen
down ? '

' O King,' she cried, ' and I will tell
thee: few,
Few, but all brave, all of one mind with
him;
For I was near him when the savage yells
Of Uther's peerage died, and Arthur sat
Crowned on the daïs, and his warriors
cried,
" Be thou the king, and we will work thy
will
Who love thee." Then the King in low
deep tones,
And simple words of great authority, 260
Bound them by so strait vows to his own
self
That when they rose, knighted from kneel-
ing, some
Were pale as at the passing of a ghost,
Some flush'd, and others dazed, as one who
wakes
Half-blinded at the coming of a light.

' But when he spake, and cheer'd his
Table Round
With large, divine, and comfortable words,
Beyond my tongue to tell thee — I beheld
From eye to eye thro' all their Order flash
A momentary likeness of the King; 270
And ere it left their faces, thro' the cross
And those around it and the Crucified,
Down from the casement over Arthur,
smote

Flame-color, vert, and azure, in three rays,
One falling upon each of three fair queens
Who stood in silence near his throne, the
 friends
Of Arthur, gazing on him, tall, with bright
Sweet faces, who will help him at his need.

 'And there I saw mage Merlin, whose
  vast wit   279
And hundred winters are but as the hands
Of loyal vassals toiling for their liege.

 'And near him stood the Lady of the
  Lake,
Who knows a subtler magic than his
  own —
Clothed in white samite, mystic, wonderful.
She gave the King his huge cross-hilted
  sword,
Whereby to drive the heathen out. A mist
Of incense curl'd about her, and her face
Wellnigh was hidden in the minster gloom;
But there was heard among the holy hymns
A voice as of the waters, for she dwells 290
Down in a deep — calm, whatsoever storms
May shake the world — and when the sur-
  face rolls,
Hath power to walk the waters like our
  Lord.

 'There likewise I beheld Excalibur
Before him at his crowning borne, the
  sword
That rose from out the bosom of the lake,
And Arthur row'd across and took it —
  rich
With jewels, elfin Urim, on the hilt,
Bewildering heart and eye — the blade so
  bright   299
That men are blinded by it — on one side,
Graven in the oldest tongue of all this
  world,
"Take me," but turn the blade and ye
  shall see,
And written in the speech ye speak your-
  self,
"Cast me away!" And sad was Arthur's
  face
Taking it, but old Merlin counsell'd him,
"Take thou and strike! the time to cast
  away
Is yet far-off." So this great brand the
  king
Took, and by this will beat his foemen
  down.'

Thereat Leodogran rejoiced, but thought
To sift his doubtings to the last, and ask'd,
Fixing full eyes of question on her face, 311
'The swallow and the swift are near akin,
But thou art closer to this noble prince,
Being his own dear sister;' and she said,
'Daughter of Gorloïs and Ygerne am I;'
'And therefore Arthur's sister?' ask'd the
  king.
She answer'd, 'These be secret things,'
  and sign'd
To those two sons to pass, and let them be.
And Gawain went, and breaking into song
Sprang out, and follow'd by his flying hair
Ran like a colt, and leapt at all he saw; 321
But Modred laid his ear beside the doors,
And there half-heard — the same that after-
  ward
Struck for the throne, and striking found
  his doom.

And then the Queen made answer:
 'What know I?
For dark my mother was in eyes and hair,
And dark in hair and eyes am I; and dark
Was Gorloïs; yea, and dark was Uther
  too,
Wellnigh to blackness; but this king is
  fair
Beyond the race of Britons and of men. 330
Moreover, always in my mind I hear
A cry from out the dawning of my life,
A mother weeping, and I hear her say,
"O that ye had some brother, pretty one,
To guard thee on the rough ways of the
  world."'

 'Ay,' said the king, 'and hear ye such
  a cry?
But when did Arthur chance upon thee
  first?'

 'O King!' she cried, 'and I will tell
  thee true.
He found me first when yet a little maid.
Beaten I had been for a little fault 340
Whereof I was not guilty; and out I ran
And flung myself down on a bank of heath,
And hated this fair world and all therein,
And wept, and wish'd that I were dead;
  and he —
I know not whether of himself he came,
Or brought by Merlin, who, they say, can
  walk
Unseen at pleasure — he was at my side,

And spake sweet words, and comforted my
  heart, 348
And dried my tears, being a child with me.
And many a time he came, and evermore
As I grew greater grew with me; and sad
At times he seem'd, and sad with him was I,
Stern too at times, and then I loved him
  not,
But sweet again, and then I loved him well.
And now of late I see him less and less,
But those first days had golden hours for
  me,
For then I surely thought he would be
  king.

'But let me tell thee now another tale:
For Bleys, our Merlin's master, as they
  say,
Died but of late, and sent his cry to me, 360
To hear him speak before he left his life.
Shrunk like a fairy changeling lay the
  mage;
And when I enter'd told me that himself
And Merlin ever served about the king,
Uther, before he died; and on the night
When Uther in Tintagil past away
Moaning and wailing for an heir, the two
Left the still king, and passing forth to
  breathe,
Then from the castle gateway by the chasm
Descending thro' the dismal night — a
  night 370
In which the bounds of heaven and earth
  were lost —
Beheld, so high upon the dreary deeps
It seem'd in heaven, a ship, the shape
  thereof
A dragon wing'd, and all from stem to
  stern
Bright with a shining people on the decks,
And gone as soon as seen. And then the
  two
Dropt to the cove, and watch'd the great
  sea fall,
Wave after wave, each mightier than the
  last,
Till last, a ninth one, gathering half the
  deep 379
And full of voices, slowly rose and plunged
Roaring, and all the wave was in a flame;
And down the wave and in the flame was
  borne
A naked babe, and rode to Merlin's feet,
Who stoopt and caught the babe, and cried,
  "The King!

Here is an heir for Uther!" And the
  fringe
Of that great breaker, sweeping up the
  strand,
Lash'd at the wizard as he spake the word,
And all at once all round him rose in fire,
So that the child and he were clothed in
  fire.
And presently thereafter follow'd calm, 390
Free sky and stars. "And this same child,"
  he said,
"Is he who reigns; nor could I part in
  peace
Till this were told." And saying this the
  seer
Went thro' the strait and dreadful pass of
  death,
Not ever to be question'd any more
Save on the further side; but when I met
Merlin, and ask'd him if these things were
  truth —
The shining dragon and the naked child
Descending in the glory of the seas —
He laugh'd as is his wont, and answer'd
  me 400
In riddling triplets of old time, and said: —

  '"Rain, rain, and sun! a rainbow in the
    sky!
A young man will be wiser by and by;
An old man's wit may wander ere he die.

  '"Rain, rain, and sun! a rainbow on the
    lea!
And truth is this to me, and that to thee;
And truth or clothed or naked let it be.

  '"Rain, sun, and rain! and the free blossom
    blows;
Sun, rain, and sun! and where is he who
    knows?
From the great deep to the great deep he
    goes." 410

 'So Merlin riddling anger'd me; but
  thou
Fear not to give this King thine only
  child,
Guinevere; so great bards of him will sing
Hereafter, and dark sayings from of old
Ranging and ringing thro' the minds of
  men,
And echo'd by old folk beside their fires
For comfort after their wage-work is done,
Speak of the King; and Merlin in our time
Hath spoken also, not in jest, and sworn

Tho' men may wound him that he will not
die, 420
But pass, again to come, and then or now
Utterly smite the heathen underfoot,
Till these and all men hail him for their
king.'

She spake and King Leodogran rejoiced,
But musing 'Shall I answer yea or nay?'
Doubted, and drowsed, nodded and slept,
and saw,
Dreaming, a slope of land that ever grew,
Field after field, up to a height, the peak
Haze-hidden, and thereon a phantom king,
Now looming, and now lost; and on the
slope 430
The sword rose, the hind fell, the herd was
driven,
Fire glimpsed; and all the land from roof
and rick,
In drifts of smoke before a rolling wind,
Stream'd to the peak, and mingled with
the haze
And made it thicker; while the phantom
king
Sent out at times a voice; and here or there
Stood one who pointed toward the voice,
the rest
Slew on and burnt, crying, 'No king of
ours,
No son of Uther, and no king of ours;'
Till with a wink his dream was changed,
the haze 440
Descended, and the solid earth became
As nothing, but the King stood out in hea-
ven,
Crown'd. And Leodogran awoke, and sent
Ulfius, and Brastias, and Bedivere,
Back to the court of Arthur answering
yea.

Then Arthur charged his warrior whom
he loved
And honor'd most, Sir Lancelot, to ride
forth
And bring the Queen, and watch'd him
from the gates;
And Lancelot past away among the flow-
ers — 449
For then was latter April — and return'd
Among the flowers, in May, with Guine-
vere.
To whom arrived, by Dubric the high
saint,

Chief of the church in Britain, and before
The stateliest of her altar-shrines, the
King
That morn was married, while in stainless
white,
The fair beginners of a nobler time,
And glorying in their vows and him, his
knights
Stood round him, and rejoicing in his joy.
Far shone the fields of May thro' open
door,
The sacred altar blossom'd white with
May, 460
The sun of May descended on their King,
They gazed on all earth's beauty in their
Queen,
Roll'd incense, and there past along the
hymns
A voice as of the waters, while the two
Sware at the shrine of Christ a deathless
love.
And Arthur said, 'Behold, thy doom is
mine.
Let chance what will, I love thee to the
death!'
To whom the Queen replied with drooping
eyes,
'King and my lord, I love thee to the
death!'
And holy Dubric spread his hands and
spake: 470
'Reign ye, and live and love, and make the
world
Other, and may thy Queen be one with
thee,
And all this Order of thy Table Round
Fulfil the boundless purpose of their King!'

So Dubric said; but when they left the
shrine
Great lords from Rome before the portal
stood,
In scornful stillness gazing as they past;
Then while they paced a city all on fire
With sun and cloth of gold, the trumpets
blew,
And Arthur's knighthood sang before the
King: — 480

'Blow trumpet, for the world is white with
May!
Blow trumpet, the long night hath roll'd away!
Blow thro' the living world — "Let the King
reign!"

'Shall Rome or Heathen rule in Arthur's
  realm ?
Flash brand and lance, fall battle-axe upon
  helm,
Fall battle-axe, and flash brand! Let the
  King reign!

'Strike for the King and live! his knights
  have heard
That God hath told the King a secret word.
Fall battle-axe, and flash brand! Let the
  King reign!

'Blow trumpet! he will lift us from the
  dust.   490
Blow trumpet! live the strength, and die the
  lust!
Clang battle-axe, and clash brand! Let the
  King reign!

'Strike for the King and die! and if thou
  diest,
The King is king, and ever wills the high-
  est.
Clang battle-axe, and clash brand! Let the
  King reign!

' Blow, for our Sun is mighty in his May!
Blow, for our Sun is mightier day by day!
Clang battle-axe, and clash brand! Let the
  King reign!

'The King will follow Christ, and we the
  King,
In whom high God hath breathed a secret
  thing.   500

Fall battle-axe, and clash brand! Let the
  King reign! '

So sang the knighthood, moving to their
  hall.
There at the banquet those great lords from
  Rome,
The slowly-fading mistress of the world,
Strode in and claim'd their tribute as of
  yore.
But Arthur spake: ' Behold, for these have
  sworn
To wage my wars, and worship me their
  King;
The old order changeth, yielding place to
  new,
And we that fight for our fair father
  Christ,   509
Seeing that ye be grown too weak and old
To drive the heathen from your Roman wall,
No tribute will we pay.' So those great
  lords
Drew back in wrath, and Arthur strove
  with Rome.

And Arthur and his knighthood for a
  space
Were all one will, and thro' that strength
  the King
Drew in the petty princedoms under him,
Fought, and in twelve great battles over-
  came
The heathen hordes, and made a realm and
  reign'd.

THE ROUND TABLE

GARETH AND LYNETTE

THE last tall son of Lot and Bellicent,
And tallest, Gareth, in a showerful spring
Stared at the spate. A slender - shafted
  pine
Lost footing, fell, and so was whirl'd away.
' How he went down,' said Gareth, ' as a
  false knight
Or evil king before my lance, if lance

Were mine to use — O senseless cataract,
Bearing all down in thy precipitancy —
And yet thou art but swollen with cold
  snows
And mine is living blood. Thou dost His
  will,   10
The Maker's, and not knowest, and I that
  know,
Have strength and wit, in my good mother's
  hall

Linger with vacillating obedience,
Prison'd, and kept and coax'd and whistled
   to —
Since the good mother holds me still a
   child !
Good mother is bad mother unto me !
A worse were better; yet no worse would I.
Heaven yield her for it, but in me put force
To weary her ears with one continuous
   prayer,
Until she let me fly discaged to sweep   20
In ever-highering eagle-circles up
To the great Sun of Glory, and thence
   swoop
Down upon all things base, and dash them
   dead,
A knight of Arthur, working out his will,
To cleanse the world. Why, Gawain, when
   he came
With Modred hither in the summer-time,
Ask'd me to tilt with him, the proven
   knight.
Modred for want of worthier was the judge.
Then I so shook him in the saddle, he said,
" Thou hast half prevail'd against me," said
   so — he —   30
Tho' Modred biting his thin lips was mute,
For he is alway sullen — what care I ? '

And Gareth went, and hovering round
   her chair
Ask'd, ' Mother, tho' ye count me still the
   child,
Sweet mother, do ye love the child ? ' She
   laugh'd,
' Thou art but a wild-goose to question it.'
' Then, mother, an ye love the child,' he
   said,
' Being a goose and rather tame than wild,
Hear the child's story.' ' Yea, my well-
   beloved,
An 't were but of the goose and golden
   eggs.'   40

And Gareth answer'd her with kindling
   eyes:
' Nay, nay, good mother, but this egg of
   mine
Was finer gold than any goose can lay;
For this an eagle, a royal eagle, laid
Almost beyond eye-reach, on such a palm
As glitters gilded in thy Book of Hours.
And there was ever haunting round the
   palm
A lusty youth, but poor, who often saw

The splendor sparkling from aloft, and
   thought,
" An I could climb and lay my hand upon
   it,   50
Then were I wealthier than a leash of
   kings."
But ever when he reach'd a hand to climb,
One that had loved him from his childhood
   caught
And stay'd him, " Climb not lest thou break
   thy neck,
I charge thee by my love," and so the boy,
Sweet mother, neither clomb nor brake his
   neck,
But brake his very heart in pining for it,
And past away.'

                 To whom the mother said,
' True love, sweet son, had risk'd himself
   and climb'd,
And handed down the golden treasure to
   him.'   60

And Gareth answer'd her with kindling
   eyes:
' Gold ? said I gold ? — ay then, why he, or
   she,
Or whosoe'er it was, or half the world
Had ventured — *had* the thing I spake of
   been
Mere gold — but this was all of that true
   steel
Whereof they forged the brand Excalibur,
And lightnings play'd about it in the storm,
And all the little fowl were flurried at it,
And there were cries and clashings in the
   nest,
That sent him from his senses. Let me
   go.'   70

Then Bellicent bemoan'd herself and
   said:
' Hast thou no pity upon my loneliness ?
Lo, where thy father Lot beside the hearth
Lies like a log, and all but smoulder'd out!
For ever since when traitor to the King
He fought against him in the barons' war,
And Arthur gave him back his territory,
His age hath slowly droopt, and now lies
   there
A yet-warm corpse, and yet unburiable,
No more; nor sees, nor hears, nor speaks,
   nor knows.   80
And both thy brethren are in Arthur's hall,
Albeit neither loved with that full love

I feel for thee, nor worthy such a love.
Stay therefore thou; red berries charm the bird,
And thee, mine innocent, the jousts, the wars,
Who never knewest finger-ache, nor pang
Of wrench'd or broken limb — an often chance
In those brain-stunning shocks, and tourney-falls,
Frights to my heart. But stay; follow the deer 89
By these tall firs and our fast-falling burns;
So make thy manhood mightier day by day.
Sweet is the chase; and I will seek thee out
Some comfortable bride and fair, to grace
Thy climbing life, and cherish my prone year,
Till falling into Lot's forgetfulness
I know not thee, myself, nor anything.
Stay, my best son! ye are yet more boy than man.'

Then Gareth: 'An ye hold me yet for child,
Hear yet once more the story of the child.
For, mother, there was once a king, like ours. 100
The prince his heir, when tall and marriageable,
Ask'd for a bride; and thereupon the king
Set two before him. One was fair, strong, arm'd —
But to be won by force — and many men
Desired her; one, good lack, no man desired.
And these were the conditions of the king:
That save he won the first by force, he needs
Must wed that other, whom no man desired,
A red-faced bride who knew herself so vile 109
That evermore she long'd to hide herself,
Nor fronted man or woman, eye to eye —
Yea — some she cleaved to, but they died of her.
And one — they call'd her Fame; and one — O mother,'
How can ye keep me tether'd to you ? — Shame.
Man am I grown, a man's work must I do.
Follow the deer ? follow the Christ, the King,

Live pure, speak true, right wrong, follow the King —
Else, wherefore born ? '

To whom the mother said:
'Sweet son, for there be many who deem him not,
Or will not deem him, wholly proven king — 120
Albeit in mine own heart I knew him King
When I was frequent with him in my youth,
And heard him kingly speak, and doubted him
No more than he, himself; but felt him mine,
Of closest kin to me. Yet — wilt thou leave
Thine easeful biding here, and risk thine all,
Life, limbs, for one that is not proven king ?
Stay, till the cloud that settles round his birth
Hath lifted but a little. Stay, sweet son.'

And Gareth answer'd quickly: 'Not an hour, 130
So that ye yield me — I will walk thro' fire,
Mother, to gain it — your full leave to go.
Not proven, who swept the dust of ruin'd Rome
From off the threshold of the realm, and crush'd
The idolaters, and made the people free ?
Who should be king save him who makes us free ?'

So when the Queen, who long had sought in vain
To break him from the intent to which he grew,
Found her son's will unwaveringly one,
She answer'd craftily: 'Will ye walk thro' fire ? 140
Who walks thro' fire will hardly heed the smoke.
Ay, go then, an ye must; only one proof,
Before thou ask the King to make thee knight,
Of thine obedience and thy love to me,
Thy mother, — I demand.'

And Gareth cried:
'A hard one, or a hundred, so I go.
Nay — quick ! the proof to prove me to the quick !'

But slowly spake the mother looking at
    him:
'Prince, thou shalt go disguised to Arthur's
    hall,
And hire thyself to serve for meats and
    drinks   150
Among the scullions and the kitchen-
    knaves,
And those that hand the dish across the
    bar.
Nor shalt thou tell thy name to any one.
And thou shalt serve a twelvemonth and a
    day.'

For so the Queen believed that when her
    son
Beheld his only way to glory lead
Low down thro' villain kitchen-vassalage,
Her own true Gareth was too princely-
    proud
To pass thereby; so should he rest with her,
Closed in her castle from the sound of
    arms.   160

Silent awhile was Gareth, then replied:
'The thrall in person may be free in soul,
And I shall see the jousts. Thy son am I,
And, since thou art my mother, must obey.
I therefore yield me freely to thy will;
For hence will I, disguised, and hire myself
To serve with scullions and with kitchen-
    knaves;
Nor tell my name to any — no, not the
    King.'

Gareth awhile linger'd. The mother's
    eye
Full of the wistful fear that he would go,
And turning toward him wheresoe'er he
    turn'd,   171
Perplext his outward purpose, till an hour
When, waken'd by the wind which with
    full voice
Swept bellowing thro' the darkness on to
    dawn,
He rose, and out of slumber calling two
That still had tended on him from his
    birth,
Before the wakeful mother heard him,
    went.

The three were clad like tillers of the
    soil.
Southward they set their faces. The birds
    made

Melody on branch and melody in mid air.
The damp hill-slopes were quicken'd into
    green,   181
And the live green had kindled into flow-
    ers,
For it was past the time of Easter-day.

So, when their feet were planted on the
    plain
That broaden'd toward the base of Came-
    lot,
Far off they saw the silver-misty morn
Rolling her smoke about the royal mount,
That rose between the forest and the field.
At times the summit of the high city
    flash'd;
At times the spires and turrets half-way
    down   190
Prick'd thro' the mist; at times the great
    gate shone
Only, that open'd on the field below;
Anon, the whole fair city had disappear'd.

Then those who went with Gareth were
    amazed,
One crying, 'Let us go no further, lord;
Here is a city of enchanters, built
By fairy kings.' The second echo'd him,
'Lord, we have heard from our wise man
    at home
To northward, that this king is not the
    King,
But only changeling out of Fairyland,   200
Who drave the heathen hence by sorcery
And Merlin's glamour.' Then the first
    again,
'Lord, there is no such city anywhere,
But all a vision.'

               Gareth answer'd them
With laughter, swearing he had glamour
    enow
In his own blood, his princedom, youth,
    and hopes,
To plunge old Merlin in the Arabian sea;
So push'd them all unwilling toward the
    gate.
And there was no gate like it under
    heaven.
For barefoot on the keystone, which was
    lined   210
And rippled like an ever-fleeting wave,
The Lady of the Lake stood; all her dress
Wept from her sides as water flowing
    away;

But like the cross her great and goodly
  arms
Stretch'd under all the cornice and up-
  held.
And drops of water fell from either hand;
And down from one a sword was hung,
  from one
A censer, either worn with wind and storm;
And o'er her breast floated the sacred
  fish;
And in the space to left of her, and
  right, 220
Were Arthur's wars in weird devices done,
New things and old co-twisted, as if Time
Were nothing, so inveterately that men
Were giddy gazing there; and over all
High on the top were those three queens,
  the friends
Of Arthur, who should help him at his
  need.

Then those with Gareth for so long a
  space
Stared at the figures that at last it seem'd
The dragon-boughts and elvish emblem-
  ings
Began to move, seethe, twine, and curl.
  They call'd 230
To Gareth, 'Lord, the gateway is alive.'

And Gareth likewise on them fixt his
  eyes
So long that even to him they seem'd to
  move.
Out of the city a blast of music peal'd.
Back from the gate started the three, to
  whom
From out thereunder came an ancient man,
Long-bearded, saying, 'Who be ye, my
  sons?'

Then Gareth: 'We be tillers of the soil,
Who leaving share in furrow come to
  see
The glories of our King; but these, my
  men,— 240
Your city moved so weirdly in the mist —
Doubt if the King be king at all, or come
From Fairyland; and whether this be built
By magic, and by fairy kings and queens;
Or whether there be any city at all,
Or all a vision; and this music now
Hath scared them both, but tell thou these
  the truth.'

Then that old Seer made answer, playing
  on him
And saying: 'Son, I have seen the good
  ship sail
Keel upward, and mast downward, in the
  heavens, 250
And solid turrets topsy-turvy in air;
And here is truth, but an it please thee
  not,
Take thou the truth as thou hast told it me.
For truly, as thou sayest, a fairy king
And fairy queens have built the city, son;
They came from out a sacred mountain-
  cleft
Toward the sunrise, each with harp in
  hand,
And built it to the music of their harps.
And, as thou sayest, it is enchanted, son,
For there is nothing in it as it seems 260
Saving the King; tho' some there be that
  hold
The King a shadow, and the city real.
Yet take thou heed of him, for, so thou
  pass
Beneath this archway, then wilt thou be-
  come
A thrall to his enchantments, for the King
Will bind thee by such vows as is a shame
A man should not be bound by, yet the
  which
No man can keep; but, so thou dread to
  swear,
Pass not beneath this gateway, but abide
Without, among the cattle of the field. 270
For an ye heard a music, like enow
They are building still, seeing the city is
  built
To music, therefore never built at all,
And therefore built for ever.'

Gareth spake
Anger'd: 'Old master, reverence thine own
  beard
That looks as white as utter truth, and
  seems
Wellnigh as long as thou art statured tall!
Why mockest thou the stranger that hath
  been
To thee fair-spoken?'

But the Seer replied:
'Know ye not then the Riddling of the
  Bards: 280
"Confusion, and illusion, and relation,

Elusion, and occasion, and evasion " ?
I mock thee not but as thou mockest me,
And all that see thee, for thou art not who
Thou seemest, but I know thee who thou
    art.
And now thou goest up to mock the King,
Who cannot brook the shadow of any lie.'

Unmockingly the mocker ending here
Turn'd to the right, and past along the
    plain;
Whom Gareth looking after said: ' My
    men,   290
Our one white lie sits like a little ghost
Here on the threshold of our enterprise.
Let love be blamed for it, not she, nor I.
Well, we will make amends.'

                    With all good cheer
He spake and laugh'd, then enter'd with his
    twain
Camelot, a city of shadowy palaces
And stately, rich in emblem and the work
Of ancient kings who did their days in
    stone;
Which Merlin's hand, the Mage at Arthur's
    court,
Knowing all arts, had touch'd, and every-
    where,   300
At Arthur's ordinance, tipt with lessening
    peak
And pinnacle, and had made it spire to
    heaven.
And ever and anon a knight would pass
Outward, or inward to the hall; his arms
Clash'd, and the sound was good to Gar-
    eth's ear.
And out of bower and casement shyly
    glanced
Eyes of pure women, wholesome stars of
    love;
And all about a healthful people stept
As in the presence of a gracious king.

Then into hall Gareth ascending heard
A voice, the voice of Arthur, and beheld 311
Far over heads in that long-vaulted hall
The splendor of the presence of the King
Throned, and delivering doom — and
    look'd no more —
But felt his young heart hammering in his
    ears,
And thought, ' For this half-shadow of a lie
The truthful King will doom me when I
    speak.'

Yet pressing on, tho' all in fear to find
Sir Gawain or Sir Modred, saw nor one
Nor other, but in all the listening eyes 320
Of those tall knights that ranged about
    the throne
Clear honor shining like the dewy star
Of dawn, and faith in their great King,
    with pure
Affection, and the light of victory,
And glory gain'd, and evermore to gain.

Then came a widow crying to the King:
' A boon, Sir King ! Thy father, Uther,
    reft
From my dead lord a field with violence;
For howsoe'er at first he proffer'd gold, 329
Yet, for the field was pleasant in our eyes,
We yielded not; and then he reft us of it
Perforce and left us neither gold nor field.'

Said Arthur, ' Whether would ye ? gold
    or field ? '
To whom the woman weeping, ' Nay, my
    lord,
The field was pleasant in my husband's
    eye.'

And Arthur: ' Have thy pleasant field
    again,
And thrice the gold for Uther's use thereof,
According to the years.   No boon is here,
But justice, so thy say be proven true.
Accursed, who from the wrongs his father
    did   340
Would shape himself a right ! '

                    And while she past,
Came yet another widow crying to him:
' A boon, Sir King ! Thine enemy, King,
    am I.
With thine own hand thou slewest my dear
    lord,
A knight of Uther in the barons' war,
When Lot and many another rose and
    fought
Against thee, saying thou wert basely born.
I held with these, and loathe to ask thee
    aught.
Yet lo ! my husband's brother had my son
Thrall'd in his castle, and hath starved him
    dead,   350
And standeth seized of that inheritance
Which thou that slewest the sire hast left
    the son.
So, tho' I scarce can ask it thee for hate,

Grant me some knight to do the battle for
    me,
Kill the foul thief, and wreak me for my
    son.'

Then strode a good knight forward, cry-
    ing to him,
'A boon, Sir King! I am her kinsman, I.
Give me to right her wrong, and slay the
    man.'

Then came Sir Kay, the seneschal, and
    cried,
'A boon, Sir King! even that thou grant
    her none,   360
This railer, that hath mock'd thee in full
    hall —
None; or the wholesome boon of gyve and
    gag.'

But Arthur: 'We sit King, to help the
    wrong'd
Thro' all our realm. The woman loves her
    lord.
Peace to thee, woman, with thy loves and
    hates!
The kings of old had doom'd thee to the
    flames;
Aurelius Emrys would have scourged thee
    dead,
And Uther slit thy tongue; but get thee
    hence —   368
Lest that rough humor of the kings of old
Return upon me! Thou that art her kin,
Go likewise; lay him low and slay him not,
But bring him here, that I may judge the
    right,
According to the justice of the King.
Then, be he guilty, by that deathless King
Who lived and died for men, the man shall
    die.'

Then came in hall the messenger of
    Mark,
A name of evil savor in the land,
The Cornish king. In either hand he bore
What dazzled all, and shone far-off as
    shines
A field of charlock in the sudden sun   380
Between two showers, a cloth of palest gold,
Which down he laid before the throne, and
    knelt,
Delivering that his lord, the vassal king,
Was even upon his way to Camelot;
For having heard that Arthur of his grace

Had made his goodly cousin Tristram
    knight,
And, for himself was of the greater state,
Being a king, he trusted his liege-lord
Would yield him this large honor all the
    more;
So pray'd him well to accept this cloth of
    gold,   390
In token of true heart and fealty.

Then Arthur cried to rend the cloth, to
    rend
In pieces, and so cast it on the hearth.
An oak-tree smoulder'd there. 'The
    goodly knight!
What! shall the shield of Mark stand
    among these?'
For, midway down the side of that long
    hall,
A stately pile, — whereof along the front,
Some blazon'd, some but carven, and some
    blank,
There ran a treble range of stony shields, —
Rose, and high-arching overbrow'd the
    hearth.   400
And under every shield a knight was
    named.
For this was Arthur's custom in his hall:
When some good knight had done one
    noble deed,
His arms were carven only; but if twain,
His arms were blazon'd also; but if none,
The shield was blank and bare, without a
    sign
Saving the name beneath. And Gareth saw
The shield of Gawain blazon'd rich and
    bright,
And Modred's blank as death; and Arthur
    cried   409
To rend the cloth and cast it on the hearth.

'More like are we to reave him of his
    crown
Than make him knight because men call
    him king.
The kings we found, ye know we stay'd
    their hands
From war among themselves, but left them
    kings;
Of whom were any bounteous, merciful,
Truth-speaking, brave, good livers, them
    we enroll'd
Among us, and they sit within our hall.
But Mark hath tarnish'd the great name of
    king,

As Mark would sully the low state of churl;
And, seeing he hath sent us cloth of gold,
Return, and meet, and hold him from our
    eyes,   421
Lest we should lap him up in cloth of
    lead,
Silenced for ever — craven — a man of
    plots,
Craft, poisonous counsels, wayside ambush-
    ings —
No fault of thine; let Kay the seneschal
Look to thy wants, and send thee satis-
    fied —
Accursed, who strikes nor lets the hand be
    seen !'

And many another suppliant crying came
With noise of ravage wrought by beast and
    man,   429
And evermore a knight would ride away.

Last, Gareth leaning both hands heavily
Down on the shoulders of the twain, his
    men,
Approach'd between them toward the King,
    and ask'd,
'A boon, Sir King,' — his voice was all
    ashamed, —
'For see ye not how weak and hunger-
    worn
I seem — leaning on these ? grant me to
    serve
For meat and drink among thy kitchen-
    knaves
A twelvemonth and a day, nor seek my
    name.
Hereafter I will fight.'

                        To him the King:
'A goodly youth and worth a goodlier
    boon !   440
But so thou wilt no goodlier, then must
    Kay,
The master of the meats and drinks, be
    thine.'

He rose and past; then Kay, a man of
    mien
Wan-sallow as the plant that feels itself
Root-bitten by white lichen:

                            'Lo ye now !
This fellow hath broken from some abbey,
    where,
God wot, he had not beef and brewis enow,

However that might chance ! but an he
    work,
Like any pigeon will I cram his crop,   449
And sleeker shall he shine than any hog.'

Then Lancelot standing near: 'Sir Senes-
    chal,
Sleuth-hound thou knowest, and gray, and
    all the hounds;
A horse thou knowest, a man thou dost not
    know.
Broad brows and fair, a fluent hair and
    fine,
High nose, a nostril large and fine, and
    hands
Large, fair, and fine ! — Some young lad's
    mystery —
But, or from sheepcot or king's hall, the
    boy
Is noble-natured. Treat him with all grace,
Lest he should come to shame thy judging
    of him.'

Then Kay: 'What murmurest thou of
    mystery ?   460
Think ye this fellow will poison the King's
    dish ?
Nay, for he spake too fool-like — mystery !
Tut, an the lad were noble, he had ask'd
For horse and armor. Fair and fine, for-
    sooth !
Sir Fine-face, Sir Fair-hands ? but see thou
    to it
That thine own fineness, Lancelot, some
    fine day
Undo thee not — and leave my man to
    me.'

So Gareth all for glory underwent
The sooty yoke of kitchen-vassalage,
Ate with young lads his portion by the
    door,   470
And couch'd at night with grimy kitchen-
    knaves.
And Lancelot ever spake him pleasantly,
But Kay the seneschal, who loved him not,
Would hustle and harry him, and labor
    him
Beyond his comrade of the hearth, and set
To turn the broach, draw water, or hew
    wood,
Or grosser tasks; and Gareth bow'd him-
    self
With all obedience to the King, and
    wrought

All kind of service with a noble ease
That graced the lowliest act in doing it.   480
And when the thralls had talk among
    themselves,
And one would praise the love that linkt
    the King
And Lancelot — how the King had saved
    his life
In battle twice, and Lancelot once the
    King's —
For Lancelot was first in the tournament,
But Arthur mightiest on the battle-field —
Gareth was glad.   Or if some other told
How once the wandering forester at dawn,
Far over the blue tarns and hazy seas,   489
On Caer-Eryri's highest found the King,
A naked babe, of whom the Prophet spake,
' He passes to the Isle Avilion,
He passes and is heal'd and cannot die ' —
Gareth was glad.   But if their talk were
    foul,
Then would he whistle rapid as any lark,
Or carol some old roundelay, and so loud
That first they mock'd, but, after, rever-
    enced him.
Or Gareth, telling some prodigious tale
Of knights who sliced a red life-bubbling
    way   499
Thro' twenty folds of twisted dragon, held
All in a gap-mouth'd circle his good mates
Lying or sitting round him, idle hands,
Charm'd; till Sir Kay, the seneschal, would
    come
Blustering upon them, like a sudden wind
Among dead leaves, and drive them all
    apart.
Or when the thralls had sport among them-
    selves,
So there were any trial of mastery,
He, by two yards in casting bar or stone,
Was counted best; and if there chanced a
    joust,   509
So that Sir Kay nodded him leave to go,
Would hurry thither, and when he saw the
    knights
Clash like the coming and retiring wave,
And the spear spring, and good horse reel,
    the boy
Was half beyond himself for ecstasy.

So for a month he wrought among the
    thralls;
But in the weeks that follow'd, the good
    Queen,

Repentant of the word she made him
    swear,
And saddening in her childless castle, sent,
Between the in-crescent and de-crescent
    moon,
Arms for her son, and loosed him from his
    vow.   520

This, Gareth hearing from a squire of
    Lot
With whom he used to play at tourney
    once,
When both were children, and in lonely
    haunts
Would scratch a ragged oval on the sand,
And each at either dash from either end —
Shame never made girl redder than Gareth
    joy.
He laugh'd, he sprang.   ' Out of the smoke,
    at once
I leap from Satan's foot to Peter's knee —
These news be mine, none other's — nay,
    the King's —
Descend into the city; ' whereon he sought
The King alone, and found, and told him
    all.   531

' I have stagger'd thy strong Gawain in
    a tilt
For pastime; yea, he said it; joust can I.
Make me thy knight — in secret! let my
    name
Be hidden, and give me the first quest, I
    spring
Like flame from ashes.'

                    Here the King's calm eye
Fell on, and check'd, and made him flush,
    and bow
Lowly, to kiss his hand, who answer'd him:
' Son, the good mother let me know thee
    here,
And sent her wish that I would yield thee
    thine.   540
Make thee my knight ? my knights are
    sworn to vows
Of utter hardihood, utter gentleness,
And, loving, utter faithfulness in love,
And uttermost obedience to the King.'

Then Gareth, lightly springing from his
    knees:
' My King, for hardihood I can promise
    thee.
For uttermost obedience make demand

Of whom ye gave me to, the Seneschal,
No mellow master of the meats and drinks !
And as for love, God wot, I love not yet,
But love I shall, God willing.'

And the King:
' Make thee my knight in secret ? yea, but
    he,   552
Our noblest brother, and our truest man,
And one with me in all, he needs must
    know.'

' Let Lancelot know, my King, let Lance-
    lot know,
Thy noblest and thy truest ! '

And the King:
' But wherefore would ye men should won-
    der at you ?
Nay, rather for the sake of me, their King,
And the deed's sake my knighthood do the
    deed,   559
Than to be noised of.'

Merrily Gareth ask'd:
' Have I not earn'd my cake in baking of it ?
Let be my name until I make my name !
My deeds will speak; it is but for a day.'
So with a kindly hand on Gareth's arm
Smiled the great King, and half-unwill-
    ingly
Loving his lusty youthhood yielded to him.
Then, after summoning Lancelot privily:
' I have given him the first quest; he is not
    proven.
Look therefore, when he calls for this in
    hall,
Thou get to horse and follow him far
    away.   570
Cover the lions on thy shield, and see,
Far as thou mayest, he be nor ta'en nor
    slain.'

Then that same day there past into the
    hall
A damsel of high lineage, and a brow
May-blossom, and a cheek of apple-blossom,
Hawk-eyes; and lightly was her slender
    nose
Tip-tilted like the petal of a flower.
She into hall past with her page and cried:

' O King, for thou hast driven the foe
    without,   579
See to the foe within ! bridge, ford, beset

By bandits, every one that owns a tower
The lord for half a league. Why sit ye
    there ?
Rest would I not, Sir King, an I were
    king,
Till even the lonest hold were all as free
From cursed bloodshed as thine altar-cloth
From that best blood it is a sin to spill.'

' Comfort thyself,' said Arthur, ' I nor
    mine
Rest; so my knighthood keep the vows
    they swore,
The wastest moorland of our realm shall
    be
Safe, damsel, as the centre of this hall. 590
What is thy name ? thy need ? '

' My name ? ' she said —
' Lynette, my name; noble; my need, a
    knight
To combat for my sister, Lyonors,
A lady of high lineage, of great lands,
And comely, yea, and comelier than my-
    self.
She lives in Castle Perilous. A river
Runs in three loops about her living-place;
And o'er it are three passings, and three
    knights
Defend the passings, brethren, and a fourth,
And of that four the mightiest, holds her
    stay'd   600
In her own castle, and so besieges her
To break her will, and make her wed with
    him;
And but delays his purport till thou send
To do the battle with him thy chief man
Sir Lancelot, whom he trusts to overthrow,
Then wed, with glory; but she will not
    wed
Save whom she loveth, or a holy life.
Now therefore have I come for Lancelot.'

Then Arthur mindful of Sir Gareth
    ask'd: 609
' Damsel, ye know this Order lives to crush
All wrongers of the realm. But say, these
    four,
Who be they ? What the fashion of the
    men ? '

' They be of foolish fashion, O Sir King,
The fashion of that old knight-errantry
Who ride abroad, and do but what they
    will;

Courteous or bestial from the moment,
such
As have nor law nor king; and three of
these
Proud in their fantasy call themselves the
Day,
Morning-Star, and Noon-Sun, and Evening-
Star,
Being strong fools; and never a whit more
wise 620
The fourth, who alway rideth arm'd in
black,
A huge man-beast of boundless savagery.
He names himself the Night and oftener
Death,
And wears a helmet mounted with a skull,
And bears a skeleton figured on his arms,
To show that who may slay or scape the
three,
Slain by himself, shall enter endless night.
And all these four be fools, but mighty
men,
And therefore am I come for Lancelot.'

Hereat Sir Gareth call'd from where he
rose, 630
A head with kindling eyes above the
throng,
'A boon, Sir King — this quest!' then —
for he mark'd
Kay near him groaning like a wounded
bull —
'Yea, King, thou knowest thy kitchen-
knave am I,
And mighty thro' thy meats and drinks
am I,
And I can topple over a hundred such.
Thy promise, King,' and Arthur glancing
at him,
Brought down a momentary brow. 'Rough,
sudden,
And pardonable, worthy to be knight — 639
Go therefore,' and all hearers were amazed.

But on the damsel's forehead shame,
pride, wrath
Slew the may-white. She lifted either
arm,
'Fie on thee, King! I ask'd for thy chief
knight,
And thou hast given me but a kitchen-
knave.'
Then ere a man in hall could stay her,
turn'd,

Fled down the lane of access to the King,
Took horse, descended the slope street, and
past
The weird white gate, and paused without,
beside
The field of tourney, murmuring 'kitchen-
knave!'

Now two great entries open'd from the
hall, 650
At one end one that gave upon a range
Of level pavement where the King would
pace
At sunrise, gazing over plain and wood;
And down from this a lordly stairway
sloped
Till lost in blowing trees and tops of
towers;
And out by this main doorway past the
King.
But one was counter to the hearth, and
rose
High that the highest-crested helm could
ride
Therethro' nor graze; and by this entry
fled
The damsel in her wrath, and on to this 660
Sir Gareth strode, and saw without the door
King Arthur's gift, the worth of half a
town,
A war-horse of the best, and near it stood
The two that out of north had follow'd
him.
This bare a maiden shield, a casque; that
held
The horse, the spear; whereat Sir Gareth
loosed
A cloak that dropt from collar-bone to
heel,
A cloth of roughest web, and cast it down,
And from it, like a fuel-smother'd fire
That lookt half-dead, brake bright, and
flash'd as those 670
Dull-coated things, that making slide apart
Their dusk wing-cases, all beneath there
burns
A jewell'd harness, ere they pass and fly.
So Gareth ere he parted flash'd in arms.
Then as he donn'd the helm, and took the
shield
And mounted horse and graspt a spear, of
grain
Storm-strengthen'd on a windy site, and
tipt

With trenchant steel, around him slowly
    prest
The people, while from out of kitchen
    came
The thralls in throng, and seeing who had
    work'd   680
Lustier than any, and whom they could but
    love,
Mounted in arms, threw up their caps and
    cried,
'God bless the King, and all his fellow-
    ship !'
And on thro' lanes of shouting Gareth rode
Down the slope street, and past without the
    gate.

So Gareth past with joy; but as the cur
Pluckt from the cur he fights with, ere his
    cause
Be cool'd by fighting, follows, being
    named,   688
His owner, but remembers all, and growls
Remembering, so Sir Kay beside the door
Mutter'd in scorn of Gareth whom he used
To harry and hustle.

                'Bound upon a quest
With horse and arms — the King hath past
    his time —
My scullion knave ! Thralls, to your work
    again,
For an your fire be low ye kindle mine !
Will there be dawn in West and eve in
    East ?
Begone ! — my knave ! — belike and like
    enow
Some old head - blow not heeded in his
    youth
So shook his wits they wander in his
    prime —
Crazed ! How the villain lifted up his
    voice,   700
Nor shamed to bawl himself a kitchen-
    knave !
Tut, he was tame and meek enow with me,
Till peacock'd up with Lancelot's noticing.
Well — I will after my loud knave, and
    learn
Whether he know me for his master yet.
Out of the smoke he came, and so my
    lance
Hold, by God's grace, he shall into the
    mire —
Thence, if the King awaken from his craze,
Into the smoke again.'

                But Lancelot said:
'Kay, wherefore wilt thou go against the
    King,   710
For that did never he whereon ye rail,
But ever meekly served the King in thee ?
Abide; take counsel, for this lad is great
And lusty, and knowing both of lance and
    sword.'
'Tut, tell not me,' said Kay, 'ye are over-
    fine
To mar stout knaves with foolish courte-
    sies;'
Then mounted, on thro' silent faces rode
Down the slope city, and out beyond the
    gate.

But by the field of tourney lingering yet
Mutter'd the damsel: 'Wherefore did the
    King   720
Scorn me ? for, were Sir Lancelot lackt, at
    least
He might have yielded to me one of those
Who tilt for lady's love and glory here,
Rather than — O sweet heaven ! O, fie
    upon him ! —
His kitchen-knave.'

              To whom Sir Gareth drew —
And there were none but few goodlier
    than he —
Shining in arms, 'Damsel, the quest is
    mine.
Lead, and I follow.' She thereat, as one
That smells a foul-flesh'd agaric in the
    holt,
And deems it carrion of some woodland
    thing,   730
Or shrew or weasel, nipt her slender nose
With petulant thumb and finger, shrilling,
    'Hence !
Avoid, thou smellest all of kitchen-grease.
And look who comes behind;' for there
    was Kay.
'Knowest thou not me ? thy master ? I
    am Kay.
We lack thee by the hearth.'

                And Gareth to him,
'Master no more ! too well I know thee,
    ay —
The most ungentle knight in Arthur's hall.'
'Have at thee then,' said Kay; they shock'd,
    and Kay   739
Fell shoulder-slipt, and Gareth cried again,
'Lead, and I follow,' and fast away she fled.

But after sod and shingle ceased to fly
Behind her, and the heart of her good
   horse
Was nigh to burst with violence of the
   beat,
Perforce she stay'd, and overtaken spoke:

   ' What doest thou, scullion, in my fellow-
     ship ?
Deem'st thou that I accept thee aught the
   more
Or love thee better, that by some device
Full cowardly, or by mere unhappiness,
Thou hast overthrown and slain thy master
   — thou ! —   750
Dish-washer and broach-turner, loon ! — to
   me
Thou smellest all of kitchen as before.'

   ' Damsel,' Sir Gareth answer'd gently, ' say
Whate'er ye will, but whatsoe'er ye say,
I leave not till I finish this fair quest,
Or die therefore.'

               ' Ay, wilt thou finish it ?
Sweet lord, how like a noble knight he
   talks !
The listening rogue hath caught the man-
   ner of it.
But, knave, anon thou shalt be met with,
   knave,
And then by such a one that thou for all
The kitchen brewis that was ever supt 761
Shalt not once dare to look him in the face.'

   ' I shall assay,' said Gareth with a smile
That madden'd her, and away she flash'd
   again
Down the long avenues of a boundless
   wood ;
And Gareth following was again beknaved:

   ' Sir Kitchen-knave, I have miss'd the
     only way
Where Arthur's men are set along the
   wood;
The wood is nigh as full of thieves as
   leaves.   769
If both be slain, I am rid of thee ; but
   yet,
Sir Scullion, canst thou use that spit of
   thine ?
Fight, an thou canst ; I have miss'd the only
   way.'

So till the dusk that follow'd evensong
Rode on the two, reviler and reviled;
Then after one long slope was mounted,
   saw,
Bowl-shaped, thro' tops of many thousand
   pines
A gloomy-gladed hollow slowly sink
To westward — in the deeps whereof a
   mere,
Round as the red eye of an eagle-owl,
Under the half-dead sunset glared; and
   shouts   780
Ascended, and there brake a servingman
Flying from out of the black wood, and
   crying,
' They have bound my lord to cast him in
   the mere.'
Then Gareth, ' Bound am I to right the
   wrong'd,
But straitlier bound am I to bide with
   thee.'
And when the damsel spake contemptu-
   ously,
' Lead, and I follow,' Gareth cried again,
' Follow, I lead !' so down among the
   pines
He plunged; and there, black-shadow'd
   nigh the mere,   789
And mid-thigh-deep in bulrushes and reed,
Saw six tall men haling a seventh along,
A stone about his neck to drown him in it.
Three with good blows he quieted, but
   three
Fled thro' the pines; and Gareth loosed the
   stone
From off his neck, then in the mere beside
Tumbled it; oilily bubbled up the mere.
Last, Gareth loosed his bonds and on free
   feet
Set him, a stalwart baron, Arthur's friend.

   ' Well that ye came, or else these caitiff
     rogues
Had wreak'd themselves on me; good cause
   is theirs   800
To hate me, for my wont hath ever been
To catch my thief, and then like vermin
   here
Drown him, and with a stone about his
   neck;
And under this wan water many of them
Lie rotting, but at night let go the stone,
And rise, and flickering in a grimly light
Dance on the mere. Good now, ye have
   saved a life

Worth somewhat as the cleanser of this
    wood.
And fain would I reward thee worshipfully.
What guerdon will ye ? '

                   Gareth sharply spake:
' None ! for the deed's sake have I done the
    deed,   811
In uttermost obedience to the King.
But wilt thou yield this damsel harbor-
    age ? '

    Whereat the baron saying, ' I well be-
    lieve
You be of Arthur's Table,' a light laugh
Broke from Lynette: ' Ay, truly of a truth,
And in a sort, being Arthur's kitchen-
    knave ! —
But deem not I accept thee aught the more,
Scullion, for running sharply with thy spit
Down on a rout of craven foresters.   820
A thresher with his flail had scatter'd them.
Nay — for thou smellest of the kitchen
    still.
But an this lord will yield us harborage,
Well.'

    So she spake.   A league beyond the
    wood,
All in a full-fair manor and a rich,
His towers, where that day a feast had
    been
Held in high hall, and many a viand left,
And many a costly cate, received the three.
And there they placed a peacock in his
    pride
Before the damsel, and the baron set   830
Gareth beside her, but at once she rose.

    ' Meseems, that here is much discourtesy,
Setting this knave, Lord Baron, at my side.
Hear me — this morn I stood in Arthur's
    hall,
And pray'd the King would grant me
    Lancelot
To fight the brotherhood of Day and
    Night —
The last a monster unsubduable
Of any save of him for whom I call'd —
Suddenly bawls this frontless kitchen-
    knave,
" The quest is mine; thy kitchen-knave
    am I,   840
And mighty thro' thy meats and drinks
    am I."

Then Arthur all at once gone mad replies,
" Go therefore," and so gives the quest to
    him —
Him — here — a villain fitter to stick swine
Than ride abroad redressing women's
    wrong,
Or sit beside a noble gentlewoman.'

    Then half-ashamed and part-amazed, the
    lord
Now look'd at one and now at other, left
The damsel by the peacock in his pride,
And, seating Gareth at another board,   850
Sat down beside him, ate and then began:

    ' Friend, whether thou be kitchen-knave,
    or not,
Or whether it be the maiden's fantasy,
And whether she be mad, or else the King,
Or both or neither, or thyself be mad,
I ask not; but thou strikest a strong stroke,
For strong thou art and goodly therewithal,
And saver of my life; and therefore now,
For here be mighty men to joust with,
    weigh
Whether thou wilt not with thy damsel
    back   860
To crave again Sir Lancelot of the King.
Thy pardon; I but speak for thine avail,
The saver of my life.'

                   And Gareth said,
' Full pardon, but I follow up the quest,
Despite of Day and Night and Death and
    Hell.'

    So when, next morn, the lord whose life
    he saved
Had, some brief space, convey'd them on
    their way
And left them with God-speed, Sir Gareth
    spake,
' Lead, and I follow.' Haughtily she re-
    plied:

    ' I fly no more; I allow thee for an hour.
Lion and stoat have isled together, knave,
In time of flood. Nay, furthermore, me-
    thinks   872
Some ruth is mine for thee. Back wilt
    thou, fool ?
For hard by here is one will overthrow
And slay thee; then will I to court again,
And shame the King for only yielding me
My champion from the ashes of his hearth.'

To whom Sir Gareth answer'd courteously:
'Say thou thy say, and I will do my deed.
Allow me for mine hour, and thou wilt
find   880
My fortunes all as fair as hers who lay
Among the ashes and wedded the King's
son.'

Then to the shore of one of those long
loops
Wherethro' the serpent river coil'd, they
came.
Rough-thicketed were the banks and steep;
the stream
Full, narrow; this a bridge of single arc
Took at a leap; and on the further side
Arose a silk pavilion, gay with gold
In streaks and rays, and all Lent-lily in hue,
Save that the dome was purple, and above,
Crimson, a slender banneret fluttering. 891
And therebefore the lawless warrior paced
Unarm'd, and calling, 'Damsel, is this he,
The champion thou hast brought from Arthur's hall,
For whom we let thee pass?' 'Nay, nay,'
she said,
'Sir Morning-Star. The King in utter
scorn
Of thee and thy much folly hath sent thee
here
His kitchen-knave; and look thou to thyself.
See that he fall not on thee suddenly,
And slay thee unarm'd; he is not knight
but knave.'   900

Then at his call, 'O daughters of the
Dawn,
And servants of the Morning-Star, approach,
Arm me,' from out the silken curtain-folds
Bare-footed and bare-headed three fair
girls
In gilt and rosy raiment came. Their feet
In dewy grasses glisten'd; and the hair
All over glanced with dewdrop or with
gem
Like sparkles in the stone Avanturine.
These arm'd him in blue arms, and gave a
shield   909
Blue also, and thereon the morning star.
And Gareth silent gazed upon the knight,
Who stood a moment, ere his horse was
brought,

Glorying; and in the stream beneath him
shone,
Immingled with heaven's azure waveringly,
The gay pavilion and the naked feet,
His arms, the rosy raiment, and the star.

Then she that watch'd him: 'Wherefore
stare ye so?
Thou shakest in thy fear. There yet is
time;
Flee down the valley before he get to horse.
Who will cry shame? Thou art not knight
but knave.'   920

Said Gareth: 'Damsel, whether knave or
knight,
Far liefer had I fight a score of times
Than hear thee so missay me and revile.
Fair words were best for him who fights
for thee;
But truly foul are better, for they send
That strength of anger thro' mine arms, I
know
That I shall overthrow him.'

                            And he that bore
The star, when mounted, cried from o'er
the bridge:
'A kitchen-knave, and sent in scorn of
me!
Such fight not I, but answer scorn with
scorn.   930
For this were shame to do him further
wrong
Than set him on his feet, and take his
horse
And arms, and so return him to the King.
Come, therefore, leave thy lady lightly,
knave.
Avoid; for it beseemeth not a knave
To ride with such a lady.'

                            'Dog, thou liest!
I spring from loftier lineage than thine
own.'
He spake; and all at fiery speed the two
Shock'd on the central bridge, and either
spear
Bent but not brake, and either knight at
once,   940
Hurl'd as a stone from out of a catapult
Beyond his horse's crupper and the bridge,
Fell, as if dead; but quickly rose and drew,
And Gareth lash'd so fiercely with his
brand

He drave his enemy backward down the
  bridge,
The damsel crying, 'Well-stricken, kitch-
  en-knave!'
Till Gareth's shield was cloven; but one
  stroke
Laid him that clove it grovelling on the
  ground.

  Then cried the fallen, 'Take not my life;
    I yield.'
And Gareth, 'So this damsel ask it of me
Good — I accord it easily as a grace.'   951
She reddening, 'Insolent scullion! I of
  thee?
I bound to thee for any favor ask'd!'
'Then shall he die.'   And Gareth there
  unlaced
His helmet as to slay him, but she shriek'd,
'Be not so hardy, scullion, as to slay
One nobler than thyself.'   'Damsel, thy
  charge
Is an abounding pleasure to me.   Knight,
Thy life is thine at her command.   Arise
And quickly pass to Arthur's hall, and say
His kitchen-knave hath sent thee.   See thou
  crave   961
His pardon for thy breaking of his laws.
Myself when I return will plead for thee.
Thy shield is mine — farewell; and, dam-
  sel, thou,
Lead, and I follow.'

                  And fast away she fled;
Then when he came upon her, spake:
  'Methought,
Knave, when I watch'd thee striking on the
  bridge,
The savor of thy kitchen came upon me
A little faintlier; but the wind hath
  changed,
I scent it twenty-fold.   And then she sang,
'"O morning star" — not that tall felon
  there   971
Whom thou, by sorcery or unhappiness
Or some device, hast foully overthrown, —

"O morning star that smilest in the blue,
O star, my morning dream hath proven true,
Smile sweetly, thou! my love hath smiled on
  me."

  'But thou begone, take counsel, and
    away,
For hard by here is one that guards a
  ford —

The second brother in their fool's para-
  ble —
Will pay thee all thy wages, and to boot.
Care not for shame; thou art not knight
  but knave.'   981

  To whom Sir Gareth answer'd, laugh-
    ingly:
'Parables?   Hear a parable of the knave.
When I was kitchen-knave among the
  rest,
Fierce was the hearth, and one of my co-
  mates
Own'd a rough dog, to whom he cast his
  coat,
"Guard it," and there was none to meddle
  with it.
And such a coat art thou, and thee the
  King
Gave me to guard, and such a dog am I,
To worry, and not to flee — and — knight
  or knave —   990
The knave that doth thee service as full
  knight
Is all as good, meseems, as any knight
Toward thy sister's freeing.'

                    'Ay, Sir Knave!
Ay, knave, because thou strikest as a
  knight,
Being but knave, I hate thee all the more.'

  'Fair damsel, you should worship me the
    more,
That, being but knave, I throw thine ene-
  mies.'

  'Ay, ay,' she said, 'but thou shalt meet
    thy match.'

So when they touch'd the second river-
  loop,   999
Huge on a huge red horse, and all in mail
Burnish'd to blinding, shone the Noonday
  Sun
Beyond a raging shallow.   As if the flower
That blows a globe of after arrowlets
Ten-thousand-fold had grown, flash'd the
  fierce shield,
All sun; and Gareth's eyes had flying blots
Before them when he turn'd from watch-
  ing him.
He from beyond the roaring shallow roar'd,
'What doest thou, brother, in my marches
  here?'

And she athwart the shallow shrill'd again,
'Here is a kitchen-knave from Arthur's
　　hall　　　　　　　　　　　　　　1010
Hath overthrown thy brother, and hath his
　　arms.'
'Ugh!' cried the Sun, and, vizoring up a
　　red
And cipher face of rounded foolishness,
Push'd horse across the foamings of the
　　ford,
Whom Gareth met mid-stream; no room
　　was there
For lance or tourney-skill.　Four strokes
　　they struck
With sword, and these were mighty, the
　　new knight
Had fear he might be shamed; but as the
　　Sun
Heaved up a ponderous arm to strike the
　　fifth,
The hoof of his horse slipt in the stream,
　　the stream　　　　　　　　　　　1020
Descended, and the Sun was wash'd away.

Then Gareth laid his lance athwart the
　　ford;
So drew him home; but he that fought no
　　more,
As being all bone-batter'd on the rock,
Yielded, and Gareth sent him to the King.
'Myself when I return will plead for thee.
Lead, and I follow.'　Quietly she led.
'Hath not the good wind, damsel, changed
　　again?'
'Nay, not a point; nor art thou victor
　　here.　　　　　　　　　　　　　1029
There lies a ridge of slate across the ford;
His horse thereon stumbled — ay, for I
　　saw it.

'"O sun" — not this strong fool whom
　　thou, Sir Knave,
Hast overthrown thro' mere unhappiness —

"O sun, that wakenest all to bliss or pain,
O moon, that layest all to sleep again,
Shine sweetly; twice my love hath smiled on
　　me."

'What knowest thou of love-song or of
　　love?
Nay, nay, God wot, so thou wert nobly
　　born,
Thou hast a pleasant presence.　Yea, per-
　　chance, —

'"O dewy flowers that open to the sun,
O dewy flowers that close when day is
　　done,　　　　　　　　　　　　　1041
Blow sweetly; twice my love hath smiled
　　on me."

'What knowest thou of flowers, except,
　　belike,
To garnish meats with? hath not our good
　　King
Who lent me thee, the flower of kitchendom,
A foolish love for flowers? what stick ye
　　round
The pasty? wherewithal deck the boar's
　　head?
Flowers? nay, the boar hath rosemaries
　　and bay.

'"O birds that warble to the morning
　　sky,　　　　　　　　　　　　　1049
O birds that warble as the day goes by,
Sing sweetly; twice my love hath smiled on
　　me."

'What knowest thou of birds, lark, mavis,
　　merle,
Linnet? what dream ye when they utter
　　forth
May-music growing with the growing light,
Their sweet sun-worship? these be for the
　　snare —
So runs thy fancy — these be for the spit,
Larding and basting.　See thou have not
　　now
Larded thy last, except thou turn and fly.
There stands the third fool of their alle-
　　gory.'

For there beyond a bridge of treble
　　bow,　　　　　　　　　　　　　1060
All in a rose-red from the west, and all
Naked it seem'd, and glowing in the broad
Deep - dimpled current underneath, the
　　knight
That named himself the Star of Evening
　　stood.

And Gareth, 'Wherefore waits the mad-
　　man there
Naked in open dayshine?'　'Nay,' she
　　cried,
'Not naked, only wrapt in harden'd skins
That fit him like his own; and so ye cleave
His armor off him, these will turn the
　　blade.'

Then the third brother shouted o'er the
    bridge,   1070
' O brother-star, why shine ye here so low ?
Thy ward is higher up; but have ye slain
The damsel's champion ? ' and the damsel
    cried:

' No star of thine, but shot from Arthur's
    heaven
With all disaster unto thine and thee !
For both thy younger brethren have gone
    down
Before this youth; and so wilt thou, Sir
    Star.
Art thou not old ? '

        ' Old, damsel, old and hard,
Old, with the might and breath of twenty
    boys.'
Said Gareth, ' Old, and over-bold in brag !
But that same strength which threw the
    Morning Star   1081
Can throw the Evening.'

        Then that other blew
A hard and deadly note upon the horn.
' Approach and arm me ! '   With slow
    steps from out
An old storm-beaten, russet, many-stain'd
Pavilion, forth a grizzled damsel came,
And arm'd him in old arms, and brought a
    helm
With but a drying evergreen for crest,
And gave a shield whereon the star of
    even
Half-tarnish'd and half-bright, his emblem,
    shone.   1090
But when it glitter'd o'er the saddle-bow,
They madly hurl'd together on the bridge;
And Gareth overthrew him, lighted, drew,
There met him drawn, and overthrew him
    again,
But up like fire he started; and as oft
As Gareth brought him grovelling on his
    knees,
So many a time he vaulted up again;
Till Gareth panted hard, and his great
    heart,
Foredooming all his trouble was in vain,
Labor'd within him, for he seem'd as one
That all in later, sadder age begins   1101
To war against ill uses of a life,
But these from all his life arise, and cry,
' Thou hast made us lords, and canst not
    put us down ! '

He half despairs; so Gareth seem'd to
    strike
Vainly, the damsel clamoring all the while,
' Well done, knave-knight, well stricken, O
    good knight-knave —
O knave, as noble as any of all the
    knights —
Shame me not, shame me not. I have
    prophesied —
Strike, thou art worthy of the Table
    Round —   1110
His arms are old, he trusts the harden'd
    skin —
Strike — strike — the wind will never
    change again.'
And Gareth hearing ever stronglier smote,
And hew'd great pieces of his armor off
    him,
But lash'd in vain against the harden'd
    skin,
And could not wholly bring him under,
    more
Than loud Southwesterns, rolling ridge on
    ridge,
The buoy that rides at sea, and dips and
    springs
For ever; till at length Sir Gareth's brand
Clash'd his, and brake it utterly to the
    hilt.   1120
' I have thee now; ' but forth that other
    sprang,
And, all unknightlike, writhed his wiry
    arms
Around him, till he felt, despite his mail,
Strangled, but straining even his utter-
    most
Cast, and so hurl'd him headlong o'er the
    bridge
Down to the river, sink or swim, and cried,
' Lead, and I follow.'

        But the damsel said:
' I lead no longer; ride thou at my side;
Thou art the kingliest of all kitchen-
    knaves.

    ' " O   trefoil, sparkling on the rainy
    plain,   1130
O rainbow with three colors after rain,
Shine sweetly; thrice my love hath smiled on
    me."

    ' Sir, — and, good faith, I fain had added
    — Knight,
But that I heard thee call thyself a knave, —

Shamed am I that I so rebuked, reviled,
Missaid thee. Noble I am, and thought the
  King
Scorn'd me and mine; and now thy pardon,
  friend,
For thou hast ever answer'd courteously,
And wholly bold thou art, and meek withal
As any of Arthur's best, but, being knave,
Hast maz'd my wit. I marvel what thou
  art.' 1141

'Damsel,' he said, 'you be not all to
  blame,
Saving that you mistrusted our good King
Would handle scorn, or yield you, asking,
  one
Not fit to cope your quest. You said your
  say;
Mine answer was my deed. Good sooth!
  I hold
He scarce is knight, yea but half-man, nor
  meet
To fight for gentle damsel, he, who lets
His heart be stirr'd with any foolish heat
At any gentle damsel's waywardness. 1150
Shamed? care not! thy foul sayings fought
  for me;
And seeing now thy words are fair, me-
  thinks
There rides no knight, not Lancelot, his
  great self,
Hath force to quell me.'

                      Nigh upon that hour
When the lone hern forgets his melan-
  choly,
Lets down his other leg, and stretching
  dreams
Of goodly supper in the distant pool,
Then turn'd the noble damsel smiling at
  him,
And told him of a cavern hard at hand,
Where bread and baken meats and good
  red wine 1160
Of Southland, which the Lady Lyonors
Had sent her coming champion, waited
  him.

  Anon they past a narrow comb wherein
Were slabs of rock with figures, knights on
  horse
Sculptured, and deckt in slowly-waning
  hues.
'Sir Knave, my knight, a hermit once was
  here,

Whose holy hand hath fashion'd on the
  rock
The war of Time against the soul of man.
And yon four fools have suck'd their alle-
  gory
From these damp walls, and taken but the
  form. 1170
Know ye not these?' and Gareth lookt
  and read —
In letters like to those the vexillary
Hath left crag-carven o'er the streaming
  Gelt —
'Phosphorus,' then 'Meridies,' — 'Hes-
  perus '—
'Nox' — 'Mors,' beneath five figures,
  armed men,
Slab after slab, their faces forward all,
And running down the Soul, a shape that
  fled
With broken wings, torn raiment, and loose
  hair,
For help and shelter to the hermit's cave.
'Follow the faces, and we find it. Look,
Who comes behind?'

                      For one — delay'd at first
Thro' helping back the dislocated Kay 1182
To Camelot, then by what thereafter
  chanced,
The damsel's headlong error thro' the
  wood —
Sir Lancelot, having swum the river-
  loops —
His blue shield-lions cover'd — softly drew
Behind the twain, and when he saw the star
Gleam, on Sir Gareth's turning to him,
  cried,
'Stay, felon knight, I avenge me for my
  friend.'
And Gareth crying prick'd against the
  cry; 1190
But when they closed — in a moment — at
  one touch
Of that skill'd spear, the wonder of the
  world —
Went sliding down so easily, and fell,
That when he found the grass within his
  hands
He laugh'd. The laughter jarr'd upon Ly-
  nette.
Harshly she ask'd him, 'Shamed and over-
  thrown,
And tumbled back into the kitchen-knave,
Why laugh ye? that ye blew your boast in
  vain?'

'Nay, noble damsel, but that I, the son
Of old King Lot and good Queen Belli-
    cent,   1200
And victor of the bridges and the ford,
And knight of Arthur, here lie thrown by
    whom
I know not, all thro' mere unhappiness —
Device and sorcery and unhappiness —
Out, sword; we are thrown!' And Lance-
    lot answer'd: 'Prince,
O Gareth — thro' the mere unhappiness
Of one who came to help thee, not to harm,
Lancelot, and all as glad to find thee whole
As on the day when Arthur knighted him.'

Then Gareth: 'Thou — Lancelot! —
    thine the hand   1210
That threw me? An some chance to mar
    the boast
Thy brethren of thee make — which could
    not chance —
Had sent thee down before a lesser spear,
Shamed had I been, and sad — O Lance-
    lot — thou!'

Whereat the maiden, petulant: 'Lance-
    lot,
Why came ye not, when call'd? and where-
    fore now
Come ye, not call'd? I gloried in my
    knave,
Who being still rebuked would answer still
Courteous as any knight — but now, if
    knight,
The marvel dies, and leaves me fool'd and
    trick'd,   1220
And only wondering wherefore play'd
    upon;
And doubtful whether I and mine be
    scorn'd.
Where should be truth if not in Arthur's
    hall,
In Arthur's presence? Knight, knave,
    prince and fool,
I hate thee and forever.'

               And Lancelot said:
'Blessed be thou, Sir Gareth! knight art
    thou
To the King's best wish. O damsel, be
    you wise,
To call him shamed who is but over-
    thrown?
Thrown have I been, nor once, but many a
    time.   1229

Victor from vanquish'd issues at the last,
And overthrower from being overthrown.
With sword we have not striven, and thy
    good horse
And thou are weary; yet not less I felt
Thy manhood thro' that wearied lance of
    thine.
Well hast thou done; for all the stream is
    freed,
And thou hast wreak'd his justice on his
    foes,
And when reviled hast answer'd graciously,
And makest merry when overthrown.
    Prince, knight,
Hail, knight and prince, and of our Table
    Round!'

And then when turning to Lynette he
    told   1240
The tale of Gareth, petulantly she said:
'Ay, well — ay, well — for worse than be-
    ing fool'd
Of others, is to fool one's self. A cave,
Sir Lancelot, is hard by, with meats and
    drinks
And forage for the horse, and flint for fire.
But all about it flies a honeysuckle.
Seek, till we find.' And when they sought
    and found,
Sir Gareth drank and ate, and all his life
Past into sleep; on whom the maiden
    gazed:
'Sound sleep be thine! sound cause to
    sleep hast thou.   1250
Wake lusty! Seem I not as tender to him
As any mother? Ay, but such a one
As all day long hath rated at her child,
And vext his day, but blesses him asleep —
Good lord, how sweetly smells the honey-
    suckle
In the hush'd night, as if the world were one
Of utter peace, and love, and gentleness!
O Lancelot, Lancelot,' — and she clapt her
    hands —
'Full merry am I to find my goodly knave
Is knight and noble. See now, sworn
    have I,   1260
Else yon black felon had not let me pass,
To bring thee back to do the battle with
    him.
Thus an thou goest, he will fight thee first;
Who doubts thee victor? so will my knight-
    knave
Miss the full flower of this accomplish-
    ment.'

Said Lancelot: 'Peradventure he you name
May know my shield. Let Gareth, an he will,
Change his for mine, and take my charger, fresh,
Not to be spurr'd, loving the battle as well
As he that rides him.' 'Lancelot-like,' she said,   1270
'Courteous in this, Lord Lancelot, as in all.'

And Gareth, wakening, fiercely clutch'd the shield:
'Ramp, ye lance-splintering lions, on whom all spears
Are rotten sticks! ye seem agape to roar!
Yea, ramp and roar at leaving of your lord! —
Care not, good beasts, so well I care for you.
O noble Lancelot, from my hold on these
Streams virtue — fire — thro' one that will not shame
Even the shadow of Lancelot under shield.
Hence; let us go.'

Silent the silent field
They traversed. Arthur's Harp tho' summer-wan,   1281
In counter motion to the clouds, allured
The glance of Gareth dreaming on his liege.
A star shot: 'Lo,' said Gareth, 'the foe falls!'
An owl whoopt: 'Hark the victor pealing there!'
Suddenly she that rode upon his left
Clung to the shield that Lancelot lent him, crying:
'Yield, yield him this again; 't is he must fight:
I curse the tongue that all thro' yesterday
Reviled thee, and hath wrought on Lancelot now   1290
To lend thee horse and shield. Wonders ye have done,
Miracles ye cannot. Here is glory enow
In having flung the three. I see thee maim'd,
Mangled; I swear thou canst not fling the fourth.'

'And wherefore, damsel? tell me all ye know.
You cannot scare me; nor rough face, or voice,
Brute bulk of limb, or boundless savagery
Appal me from the quest.'

'Nay, prince,' she cried,
'God wot, I never look'd upon the face,
Seeing he never rides abroad by day,   1300
But watch'd him have I like a phantom pass
Chilling the night; nor have I heard the voice.
Always he made his mouthpiece of a page
Who came and went, and still reported him
As closing in himself the strength of ten,
And when his anger tare him, massacring
Man, woman, lad, and girl — yea, the soft babe!
Some hold that he hath swallow'd infant flesh,
Monster! O prince, I went for Lancelot first,
The quest is Lancelot's; give him back the shield.'   1310

Said Gareth laughing, 'An he fight for this,
Belike he wins it as the better man;
Thus — and not else!'

But Lancelot on him urged
All the devisings of their chivalry
When one might meet a mightier than himself;
How best to manage horse, lance, sword, and shield,
And so fill up the gap where force might fail
With skill and fineness. Instant were his words.

Then Gareth: 'Here be rules. I know but one —
To dash against mine enemy and to win.   1320
Yet have I watch'd thee victor in the joust,
And seen thy way.' 'Heaven help thee!' sigh'd Lynette.

Then for a space, and under cloud that grew
To thunder-gloom palling all stars, they rode
In converse till she made her palfrey halt,
Lifted an arm, and softly whisper'd, 'There.'

And all the three were silent seeing, pitch'd
Beside the Castle Perilous on flat field,
A huge pavilion like a mountain peak 1329
Sunder the glooming crimson on the marge,
Black, with black banner, and a long black
horn
Beside it hanging; which Sir Gareth graspt,
And so, before the two could hinder him,
Sent all his heart and breath thro' all the
horn.
Echo'd the walls; a light twinkled; anon
Came lights and lights, and once again he
blew;
Whereon were hollow tramplings up and
down
And muffled voices heard, and shadows
past;
Till high above him, circled with her maids,
The Lady Lyonors at a window stood, 1340
Beautiful among lights, and waving to
him
White hands and courtesy. But when the
prince
Three times had blown — after long hush
— at last —
The huge pavilion slowly yielded up,
Thro' those black foldings, that which
housed therein.
High on a night-black horse, in night-black
arms,
With white breast-bone, and barren ribs of
Death,
And crown'd with fleshless laughter —
some ten steps —
In the half-light — thro' the dim dawn —
advanced
The monster, and then paused, and spake
no word. 1350

But Gareth spake and all indignantly:
'Fool, for thou hast, men say, the strength
of ten,
Canst thou not trust the limbs thy God
hath given,
But must, to make the terror of thee more,
Trick thyself out in ghastly imageries
Of that which Life hath done with, and the
clod,
Less dull than thou, will hide with man-
tling flowers
As if for pity?' But he spake no word;
Which set the horror higher. A maiden
swoon'd;
The Lady Lyonors wrung her hands and
wept, 1360

As doom'd to be the bride of Night and
Death;
Sir Gareth's head prickled beneath his
helm;
And even Sir Lancelot thro' his warm
blood felt
Ice strike, and all that mark'd him were
aghast.

At once Sir Lancelot's charger fiercely
neigh'd,
And Death's dark war-horse bounded for-
ward with him.
Then those that did not blink the terror
saw
That Death was cast to ground, and slowly
rose.
But with one stroke Sir Gareth split the
skull. 1369
Half fell to right and half to left and
lay.
Then with a stronger buffet he clove the
helm
As throughly as the skull; and out from
this
Issued the bright face of a blooming boy
Fresh as a flower new-born, and crying,
'Knight,
Slay me not; my three brethren bade me
do it,
To make a horror all about the house,
And stay the world 'from Lady Lyonors.
They never dream'd the passes would be
past.'
Answer'd Sir Gareth graciously to one
Not many a moon his younger, 'My fair
child, 1380
What madness made thee challenge the
chief knight
Of Arthur's hall?' 'Fair Sir, they bade
me do it.
They hate the King and Lancelot, the
King's friend;
They hoped to slay him somewhere on the
stream,
They never dream'd the passes could be
past.'

Then sprang the happier day from under-
ground;
And Lady Lyonors and her house, with
dance
And revel and song, made merry over
Death,
As being after all their foolish fears 1389

And horrors only proven a blooming boy.
So large mirth lived, and Gareth won the
    quest.

And he that told the tale in older times
Says that Sir Gareth wedded Lyonors,
But he that told it later says Lynette.

THE MARRIAGE OF GERAINT

THE brave Geraint, a knight of Arthur's
    court,
A tributary prince of Devon, one
Of that great Order of the Table Round,
Had married Enid, Yniol's only child,
And loved her as he loved the light of
    heaven.
And as the light of heaven varies, now
At sunrise, now at sunset, now by night
With moon and trembling stars, so loved
    Geraint
To make her beauty vary day by day,
In crimsons and in purples and in gems. 10
And Enid, but to please her husband's eye,
Who first had found and loved her in a
    state
Of broken fortunes, daily fronted him
In some fresh splendor; and the Queen
    herself,
Grateful to Prince Geraint for service
    done,
Loved her, and often with her own white
    hands
Array'd and deck'd her, as the loveliest,
Next after her own self, in all the court.
And Enid loved the Queen, and with true
    heart
Adored her, as the stateliest and the best 20
And loveliest of all women upon earth.
And seeing them so tender and so close,
Long in their common love rejoiced Ge-
    raint.
But when a rumor rose about the Queen,
Touching her guilty love for Lancelot,
Tho' yet there lived no proof, nor yet was
    heard
The world's loud whisper breaking into
    storm,
Not less Geraint believed it; and there
    fell
A horror on him lest his gentle wife, 29
Thro' that great tenderness for Guinevere,
Had suffer'd or should suffer any taint
In nature. Wherefore, going to the King,

He made this pretext, that his princedom lay
Close on the borders of a territory
Wherein were bandit earls, and caitiff
    knights,
Assassins, and all flyers from the hand
Of Justice, and whatever loathes a law;
And therefore, till the King himself should
    please
To cleanse this common sewer of all his
    realm,
He craved a fair permission to depart, 40
And there defend his marches. And the
    King
Mused for a little on his plea, but, last,
Allowing it, the prince and Enid rode,
And fifty knights rode with them, to the
    shores
Of Severn, and they past to their own
    land;
Where, thinking that, if ever yet was wife
True to her lord, mine shall be so to me,
He compass'd her with sweet observances
And worship, never leaving her, and grew
Forgetful of his promise to the King, 50
Forgetful of the falcon and the hunt,
Forgetful of the tilt and tournament,
Forgetful of his glory and his name,
Forgetful of his princedom and its cares.
And this forgetfulness was hateful to her.
And by and by the people, when they met
In twos and threes, or fuller companies,
Began to scoff and jeer and babble of him
As of a prince whose manhood was all
    gone,
And molten down in mere uxoriousness. 60
And this she gather'd from the people's
    eyes;
This too the women who attired her head,
To please her, dwelling on his boundless
    love,
Told Enid, and they sadden'd her the more;
And day by day she thought to tell Geraint,
But could not out of bashful delicacy,
While he, that watch'd her sadden, was
    the more
Suspicious that her nature had a taint.

At last, it chanced that on a summer
    morn —
They sleeping each by either — the new
    sun 70
Beat thro' the blindless casement of the
    room,
And heated the strong warrior in his
    dreams;

Who, moving, cast the coverlet aside,
And bared the knotted column of his throat,
The massive square of his heroic breast,
And arms on which the standing muscle sloped,
As slopes a wild brook o'er a little stone,
Running too vehemently to break upon it.
And Enid woke and sat beside the couch,
Admiring him, and thought within herself,
Was ever man so grandly made as he? 81
Then, like a shadow, past the people's talk
And accusation of uxoriousness
Across her mind, and, bowing over him,
Low to her own heart piteously she said:

'O noble breast and all-puissant arms,
Am I the cause, I the poor cause that men
Reproach you, saying all your force is gone?
I *am* the cause, because I dare not speak
And tell him what I think and what they say. 90
And yet I hate that he should linger here;
I cannot love my lord and not his name.
Far liefer had I gird his harness on him,
And ride with him to battle and stand by,
And watch his mightful hand striking great blows
At caitiffs and at wrongers of the world.
Far better were I laid in the dark earth,
Not hearing any more his noble voice,
Not to be folded more in these dear arms,
And darken'd from the high light in his eyes, 100
Than that my lord thro' me should suffer shame.
Am I so bold, and could I so stand by,
And see my dear lord wounded in the strife,
Or maybe pierced to death before mine eyes,
And yet not dare to tell him what I think,
And how men slur him, saying all his force
Is melted into mere effeminacy?
O me, I fear that I am no true wife!'

Half inwardly, half audibly she spoke,
And the strong passion in her made her weep 110
True tears upon his broad and naked breast,
And these awoke him, and by great mischance
He heard but fragments of her later words,
And that she fear'd she was not a true wife.

And then he thought, 'In spite of all my care,
For all my pains, poor man, for all my pains,
She is not faithful to me, and I see her
Weeping for some gay knight in Arthur's hall.'
Then, tho' he loved and reverenced her too much
To dream she could be guilty of foul act,
Right thro' his manful breast darted the pang 121
That makes a man, in the sweet face of her
Whom he loves most, lonely and miserable.
At this he hurl'd his huge limbs out of bed,
And shook his drowsy squire awake and cried,
'My charger and her palfrey;' then to her,
'I will ride forth into the wilderness,
For, tho' it seems my spurs are yet to win,
I have not fallen so low as some would wish.
And thou, put on thy worst and meanest dress 130
And ride with me.' And Enid ask'd, amazed,
'If Enid errs, let Enid learn her fault.'
But he, 'I charge thee, ask not, but obey.'
Then she bethought her of a faded silk,
A faded mantle and a faded veil,
And moving toward a cedarn cabinet,
Wherein she kept them folded reverently
With sprigs of summer laid between the folds,
She took them, and array'd herself therein,
Remembering when first he came on her
Drest in that dress, and how he loved her in it, 141
And all her foolish fears about the dress,
And all his journey to her, as himself
Had told her, and their coming to the court.

For Arthur on the Whitsuntide before
Held court at old Caerleon upon Usk.
There on a day, he sitting high in hall,
Before him came a forester of Dean,
Wet from the woods, with notice of a hart
Taller than all his fellows, milky-white,
First seen that day; these things he told the King. 151
Then the good King gave order to let blow
His horns for hunting on the morrow morn,
And when the Queen petition'd for his leave
To see the hunt, allow'd it easily.

So with the morning all the court were
     gone.
But Guinevere lay late into the morn,
Lost in sweet dreams, and dreaming of her
     love
For Lancelot, and forgetful of the hunt,
But rose at last, a single maiden with her,
Took horse, and forded Usk, and gain'd the
     wood;   161
There, on a little knoll beside it, stay'd
Waiting to hear the hounds, but heard in-
     stead
A sudden sound of hoofs, for Prince Ge-
     raint,
Late also, wearing neither hunting-dress
Nor weapon save a golden-hilted brand,
Came quickly flashing thro' the shallow
     ford
Behind them, and so gallop'd up the knoll.
A purple scarf, at either end whereof
There swung an apple of the purest gold,
Sway'd round about him, as he gallop'd
     up   171
To join them, glancing like a dragon-fly
In summer suit and silks of holiday.
Low bow'd the tributary prince, and she,
Sweetly and statelily, and with all grace
Of womanhood and queenhood, answer'd
     him:
' Late, late, Sir Prince,' she said, ' later
     than we ! '
' Yea, noble Queen,' he answer'd, ' and so
     late
That I but come like you to see the hunt,
Not join it.' ' Therefore wait with me,'
     she said;   180
' For on this little knoll, if anywhere,
There is good chance that we shall hear the
     hounds:
Here often they break covert at our feet.'

     And while they listen'd for the distant
          hunt,
And chiefly for the baying of Cavall,
King Arthur's hound of deepest mouth,
     there rode
Full slowly by a knight, lady, and dwarf;
Whereof the dwarf lagg'd latest, and the
     knight
Had vizor up, and show'd a youthful face,
Imperious, and of haughtiest lineaments.
And Guinevere, not mindful of his face 191
In the King's hall, desired his name, and
     sent
Her maiden to demand it of the dwarf,

Who being vicious, old, and irritable,
And doubling all his master's vice of pride,
Made answer sharply that she should not
     know.
' Then will I ask it of himself,' she said.
' Nay, by my faith, thou shalt not,' cried
     the dwarf;
' Thou art not worthy even to ¦ peak of
     him; '
And when she put her horse toward the
     knight,   200
Struck at her with his whip, and she re-
     turn'd
Indignant to the Queen; whereat Geraint
Exclaiming, ' Surely I will learn the name,'
Made sharply to the dwarf, and ask'd it of
     him,
Who answer'd as before; and when the
     prince
Had put his horse in motion toward the
     knight,
Struck at him with his whip, and cut his
     cheek.
The prince's blood spirted upon the scarf,
Dyeing it; and his quick, instinctive hand
Caught at the hilt, as to abolish him: 210
But he, from his exceeding manfulness
And pure nobility of temperament,
Wroth to be wroth at such a worm, re-
     frain'd
From even a word, and so returning said:

' I will avenge this insult, noble Queen,
Done in your maiden's person to yourself,
And I will track this vermin to their earths;
For tho' I ride unarm'd, I do not doubt
To find, at some place I shall come at,
     arms
On loan, or else for pledge; and, being
     found,   220
Then will I fight him, and will break his
     pride,
And on the third day will again be here,
So that I be not fallen in fight. Farewell.'

' Farewell, fair prince,' answer'd the
     stately Queen.
' Be prosperous in this journey, as in all;
And may you light on all things that you
     love,
And live to wed with her whom first you
     love.
But ere you wed with any, bring your
     bride,
And I, were she the daughter of a king,

Yea, tho' she were a beggar from the hedge,   230
Will clothe her for her bridals like the sun.'

And Prince Geraint, now thinking that he heard
The noble hart at bay, now the far horn,
A little vext at losing of the hunt,
A little at the vile occasion, rode,
By ups and downs, thro' many a grassy glade
And valley, with fixt eye following the three.
At last they issued from the world of wood,
And climb'd upon a fair and even ridge,
And show'd themselves against the sky, and sank.   240
And thither came Geraint, and underneath
Beheld the long street of a little town
In a long valley, on one side whereof,
White from the mason's hand, a fortress rose;
And on one side a castle in decay,
Beyond a bridge that spann'd a dry ravine.
And out of town and valley came a noise
As of a broad brook o'er a shingly bed
Brawling, or like a clamor of the rooks
At distance, ere they settle for the night.

And onward to the fortress rode the three,   251
And enter'd, and were lost behind the walls.
'So,' thought Geraint, 'I have track'd him to his earth.'
And down the long street riding wearily,
Found every hostel full, and everywhere
Was hammer laid to hoof, and the hot hiss
And bustling whistle of the youth who scour'd
His master's armor; and of such a one
He ask'd, 'What means the tumult in the town?'
Who told him, scouring still, 'The sparrow-hawk!'   260
Then riding close behind an ancient churl,
Who, smitten by the dusty sloping beam,
Went sweating underneath a sack of corn,
Ask'd yet once more what meant the hub-bub here?
Who answer'd gruffly, 'Ugh! the sparrow-hawk!'

Then riding further past an armorer's,
Who, with back turn'd, and bow'd above his work,
Sat riveting a helmet on his knee,
He put the selfsame query, but the man
Not turning round, nor looking at him, said: 270
'Friend, he that labors for the sparrow-hawk
Has little time for idle questioners.'
Whereat Geraint flash'd into sudden spleen:
'A thousand pips eat up your sparrow-hawk!
Tits, wrens, and all wing'd nothings peck him dead!
Ye think the rustic cackle of your bourg
The murmur of the world! What is it to me?
O wretched set of sparrows, one and all,
Who pipe of nothing but of sparrow-hawks!
Speak, if ye be not like the rest, hawk-mad,   280
Where can I get me harborage for the night?
And arms, arms, arms to fight my enemy? Speak!'
Whereat the armorer turning all amazed
And seeing one so gay in purple silks,
Came forward with the helmet yet in hand
And answer'd: 'Pardon me, O stranger knight;
We hold a tourney here to-morrow morn,
And there is scantly time for half the work.
Arms? truth! I know not; all are wanted here.
Harborage? truth, good truth, I know not, save,   290
It may be, at Earl Yniol's, o'er the bridge
Yonder.' He spoke and fell to work again.

Then rode Geraint, a little spleenful yet,
Across the bridge that spann'd the dry ravine.
There musing sat the hoary-headed earl —
His dress a suit of fray'd magnificence,
Once fit for feasts of ceremony — and said:
'Whither, fair son?' to whom Geraint replied,
'O friend, I seek a harborage for the night.'
Then Yniol, 'Enter therefore and partake
The slender entertainment of a house   301
Once rich, now poor, but ever open-door'd.'

'Thanks, venerable friend,' replied Geraint;
'So that ye do not serve me sparrow-hawks
For supper, I will enter, I will eat
With all the passion of a twelve hours'
 fast.'
Then sigh'd and smiled the hoary-headed
 earl,
And answer'd, 'Graver cause than yours is
 mine
To curse this hedgerow thief, the sparrow-
 hawk.
But in, go in; for save yourself desire it, 310
We will not touch upon him even in jest.'

Then rode Geraint into the castle court,
His charger trampling many a prickly
 star
Of sprouted thistle on the broken stones.
He look'd and saw that all was ruinous.
Here stood a shatter'd archway plumed
 with fern;
And here had fallen a great part of a
 tower,
Whole, like a crag that tumbles from the
 cliff,
And like a crag was gay with wilding flow-
 ers;
And high above a piece of turret stair, 320
Worn by the feet that now were silent,
 wound
Bare to the sun, and monstrous ivy-stems
Claspt the gray walls with hairy-fibred
 arms,
And suck'd the joining of the stones, and
 look'd
A knot, beneath, of snakes, aloft, a grove.

And while he waited in the castle court,
The voice of Enid, Yniol's daughter, rang
Clear thro' the open casement of the hall,
Singing; and as the sweet voice of a bird,
Heard by the lander in a lonely isle, 330
Moves him to think what kind of bird it
 is
That sings so delicately clear, and make
Conjecture of the plumage and the form,
So the sweet voice of Enid moved Ge-
 raint,
And made him like a man abroad at morn
When first the liquid note beloved of men
Comes flying over many a windy wave
To Britain, and in April suddenly
Breaks from a coppice gemm'd with green
 and red, 339
And he suspends his converse with a friend,

Or it may be the labor of his hands,
To think or say, 'There is the nightin-
 gale:'
So fared it with Geraint, who thought and
 said,
'Here, by God's grace, is the one voice for
 me.'

It chanced the song that Enid sang was
 one
Of Fortune and her wheel, and Enid sang:

'Turn, Fortune, turn thy wheel, and lower
 the proud;
Turn thy wild wheel thro' sunshine, storm, and
 cloud;
Thy wheel and thee we neither love nor hate.

'Turn, Fortune, turn thy wheel with smile or
 frown; 350
With that wild wheel we go not up or down;
Our hoard is little, but our hearts are great.

'Smile and we smile, the lords of many
 lands;
Frown and we smile, the lords of our own
 hands;
For man is man and master of his fate.

'Turn, turn thy wheel above the staring
 crowd;
Thy wheel and thou are shadows in the cloud;
Thy wheel and thee we neither love nor hate.'

'Hark, by the bird's song ye may learn
 the nest,'
Said Yniol; 'enter quickly.' Entering
 then, 360
Right o'er a mount of newly-fallen stones,
The dusky-rafter'd many-cobweb'd hall,
He found an ancient dame in dim bro-
 cade;
And near her, like a blossom vermeil-white
That lightly breaks a faded flower-sheath,
Moved the fair Enid, all in faded silk,
Her daughter. In a moment thought Ge-
 raint,
'Here, by God's rood, is the one maid for
 me.'
But none spake word except the hoary
 earl:
'Enid, the good knight's horse stands in the
 court; 370
Take him to stall, and give him corn, and
 then
Go to the town and buy us flesh and wine;

And we will make us merry as we may.
Our hoard is little, but our hearts are
   great.'

   He spake; the prince, as Enid past him,
   fain
To follow, strode a stride, but Yniol caught
His purple scarf, and held, and said, 'For-
   bear !
Rest ! the good house, tho' ruin'd, O my
   son,
Endures not that her guest should serve
   himself.'   379
And reverencing the custom of the house
Geraint, from utter courtesy, forebore.

   So Enid took his charger to the stall,
And after went her way across the bridge,
And reach'd the town, and while the prince
   and earl
Yet spoke together, came again with one,
A youth that, following with a costrel,
   bore
The means of goodly welcome, flesh and
   wine.
And Enid brought sweet cakes to make
   them cheer,
And, in her veil enfolded, manchet bread.
And then, because their hall must also
   serve   390
For kitchen, boil'd the flesh, and spread
   the board,
And stood behind, and waited on the three.
And, seeing her so sweet and serviceable,
Geraint had longing in him evermore
To stoop and kiss the tender little thumb
That crost the trencher as she laid it
   down.
But after all had eaten, then Geraint,
For now the wine made summer in his
   veins,
Let his eye rove in following, or rest
On Enid at her lowly handmaid-work,   400
Now here, now there, about the dusky
   hall;
Then suddenly addrest the hoary earl:

   'Fair host and earl, I pray your cour-
   tesy;
This sparrow-hawk, what is he ? tell me of
   him.
His name ? but no, good faith, I will not
   have it;
For if he be the knight whom late I saw
Ride into that new fortress by your town,

White from the mason's hand, then have I
   sworn
From his own lips to have it — I am Ge-
   raint
Of Devon — for this morning when the
   Queen   410
Sent her own maiden to demand the name,
His dwarf, a vicious under-shapen thing,
Struck at her with his whip, and she re-
   turn'd
Indignant to the Queen; and then I swore
That I would track this caitiff to his hold,
And fight and break his pride, and have it
   of him.
And all unarm'd I rode, and thought to
   find
Arms in your town, where all the men are
   mad;
They take the rustic murmur of their
   bourg
For the great wave that echoes round the
   world.   420
They would not hear me speak; but if ye
   know
Where I can light on arms, or if yourself
Should have them, tell me, seeing I have
   sworn
That I will break his pride and learn his
   name,
Avenging this great insult done the Queen.'

   Then cried Earl Yniol: 'Art thou he in-
   deed,
Geraint, a name far-sounded among men
For noble deeds ? and truly I, when first
I saw you moving by me on the bridge,
Felt ye were somewhat, yea, and by your
   state   430
And presence might have guess'd you one
   of those
That eat in Arthur's hall at Camelot.
Nor speak I now from foolish flattery;
For this dear child hath often heard me
   praise
Your feats of arms, and often when I
   paused
Hath ask'd again, and ever loved to hear;
So grateful is the noise of noble deeds
To noble hearts who see but acts of wrong.
O, never yet had woman such a pair   439
Of suitors as this maiden; first Limours,
A creature wholly given to brawls and
   wine,
Drunk even when he woo'd; and be he
   dead

I know not, but he past to the wild land.
The second was your foe, the sparrow-
          hawk,
My curse, my nephew — I will not let his
          name
Slip from my lips if I can help it — he,
When I that knew him fierce and turbu-
          lent
Refused her to him, then his pride awoke;
And since the proud man often is the
          mean,   449
He sow'd a slander in the common ear,
Affirming that his father left him gold,
And in my charge, which was not render'd
          to him;
Bribed with large promises the men who
          served
About my person, the more easily
Because my means were somewhat broken
          into
Thro' open doors and hospitality;
Raised my own town against me in the
          night
Before my Enid's birthday, sack'd my
          house;
From mine own earldom foully ousted me;
Built that new fort to overawe my friends,
For truly there are those who love me yet; 461
And keeps me in this ruinous castle here,
Where doubtless he would put me soon to
          death
But that his pride too much despises me.
And I myself sometimes despise myself;
For I have let men be and have their way,
Am much too gentle, have not used my
          power;
Nor know I whether I be very base
Or very manful, whether very wise
Or very foolish; only this I know,   470
That whatsoever evil happen to me,
I seem to suffer nothing heart or limb,
But can endure it all most patiently.'

'Well said, true heart,' replied Geraint,
     'but arms,
That if the sparrow-hawk, this nephew,
          fight
In next day's tourney I may break his
          pride.'

And Yniol answer'd: 'Arms, indeed, but
          old
And rusty, old and rusty, Prince Geraint,
Are mine, and therefore, at thine asking,
          thine.   479

But in this tournament can no man tilt,
Except the lady he loves best be there.
Two forks are fixt into the meadow ground,
And over these is placed a silver wand,
And over that a golden sparrow-hawk,
The prize of beauty for the fairest there.
And this, what knight soever be in field
Lays claim to for the lady at his side,
And tilts with my good nephew thereupon,
Who being apt at arms and big of bone
Has ever won it for the lady with him, 490
And toppling over all antagonism
Has earn'd himself the name of sparrow-
          hawk.
But thou, that hast no lady, canst not
          fight.'

To whom Geraint with eyes all bright
          replied,
Leaning a little toward him: 'Thy leave !
Let *me* lay lance in rest, O noble host,
For this dear child, because I never saw,
Tho' having seen all beauties of our time,
Nor can see elsewhere, anything so fair.
And if I fall her name will yet remain   500
Untarnish'd as before; but if I live,
So aid me heaven when at mine utter-
          most
As I will make her truly my true wife !'

Then, howsoever patient, Yniol's heart
Danced in his bosom, seeing better days.
And looking round he saw not Enid there —
Who hearing her own name had stolen
          away —
But that old dame, to whom full tenderly
And fondling all her hand in his he said:
'Mother, a maiden is a tender thing,   510
And best by her that bore her under-
          stood.
Go thou to rest, but ere thou go to rest
Tell her, and prove her heart toward the
          prince.'

So spake the kindly-hearted earl, and
          she
With frequent smile and nod departing
          found,
Half disarray'd as to her rest, the girl;
Whom first she kiss'd on either cheek, and
          then
On either shining shoulder laid a hand,
And kept her off and gazed upon her face,
And told her all their converse in the
          hall,   520

Proving her heart. But never light and shade
Coursed one another more on open ground
Beneath a troubled heaven than red and pale
Across the face of Enid hearing her;
While slowly falling as a scale that falls,
When weight is added only grain by grain,
Sank her sweet head upon her gentle breast;
Nor did she lift an eye nor speak a word,
Rapt in the fear and in the wonder of it.
So moving without answer to her rest   530
She found no rest, and ever fail'd to draw
The quiet night into her blood, but lay
Contemplating her own unworthiness;
And when the pale and bloodless east began
To quicken to the sun, arose, and raised
Her mother too, and hand in hand they moved
Down to the meadow where the jousts were held,
And waited there for Yniol and Geraint.

And thither came the twain, and when Geraint
Beheld her first in field, awaiting him,   540
He felt, were she the prize of bodily force,
Himself beyond the rest pushing could move
The Chair of Idris. Yniol's rusted arms
Were on his princely person, but thro' these
Prince-like his bearing shone; and errant knights
And ladies came, and by and by the town
Flow'd in and settling circled all the lists.
And there they fixt the forks into the ground,
And over these they placed the silver wand,
And over that the golden sparrow-hawk. 550
Then Yniol's nephew, after trumpet blown,
Spake to the lady with him and proclaim'd,
'Advance and take, the fairest of the fair,
What I these two years past have won for thee,
The prize of beauty.' Loudly spake the prince,
'Forbear; there is a worthier,' and the knight
With some surprise and thrice as much disdain

Turn'd, and beheld the four, and all his face
Glow'd like the heart of a great fire at Yule,
So burnt he was with passion, crying out,
'Do battle for it then,' no more; and thrice   561
They clash'd together, and thrice they brake their spears.
Then each, dishorsed and drawing, lash'd at each
So often and with such blows that all the crowd
Wonder'd, and now and then from distant walls
There came a clapping as of phantom hands.
So twice they fought, and twice they breathed, and still
The dew of their great labor and the blood
Of their strong bodies, flowing, drain'd their force.
But either's force was match'd till Yniol's cry,   570
'Remember that great insult done the Queen,'
Increased Geraint's, who heaved his blade aloft,
And crack'd the helmet thro', and bit the bone,
And fell'd him, and set foot upon his breast,
And said, 'Thy name?' To whom the fallen man
Made answer, groaning: 'Edyrn, son of Nudd!
Ashamed am I that I should tell it thee.
My pride is broken; men have seen my fall.'
'Then, Edyrn, son of Nudd,' replied Geraint,
'These two things shalt thou do, or else thou diest.   580
First, thou thyself, with damsel and with dwarf,
Shalt ride to Arthur's court and, coming there,
Crave pardon for that insult done the Queen,
And shalt abide her judgment on it; next,
Thou shalt give back their earldom to thy kin.
These two things shalt thou do, or thou shalt die.'

And Edyrn answer'd, ' These things will I
      do,
For I have never yet been overthrown,
And thou hast overthrown me, and my
      pride   589
Is broken down, for Enid sees my fall ! '
And rising up he rode to Arthur's court,
And there the Queen forgave him easily.
And, being young, he changed and came to
      loathe
His crime of traitor, slowly drew himself
Bright from his old dark life, and fell at
      last
In the great battle fighting for the King.

But when the third day from the hunt-
      ing-morn
Made a low splendor in the world, and
      wings
Moved in her ivy, Enid, for she lay
With her fair head in the dim - yellow
      light,   600
Among the dancing shadows of the birds,
Woke and bethought her of her promise
      given
No later than last eve to Prince Geraint —
So bent he seem'd on going the third day,
He would not leave her till her promise
      given —
To ride with him this morning to the court,
And there be made known to the stately
      Queen,
And there be wedded with all ceremony.
At this she cast her eyes upon her dress,
And thought it never yet had look'd so
      mean.   610
For as a leaf in mid-November is
To what it was in mid-October, seem'd
The dress that now she look'd on to the
      dress
She look'd on ere the coming of Geraint.
And still she look'd, and still the terror
      grew
Of that strange bright and dreadful thing,
      a court,
All staring at her in her faded silk;
And softly to her own sweet heart she
      said:

' This noble prince who won our earldom
      back,
So splendid in his acts and his attire,   620
Sweet heaven, how much I shall discredit
      him !
Would he could tarry with us here awhile,

But being so beholden to the prince,
It were but little grace in any of us,
Bent as he seem'd on going this third day,
To seek a second favor at his hands.
Yet if he could but tarry a day or two,
Myself would work eye dim and finger
      lame
Far liefer than so much discredit him.'

And Enid fell in longing for a dress   630
All branch'd and flower'd with gold, a
      costly gift
Of her good mother, given her on the night
Before her birthday, three sad years ago,
That night of fire, when Edyrn sack'd their
      house
And scatter'd all they had to all the winds;
For while the mother show'd it, and the
      two
Were turning and admiring it, the work
To both appear'd so costly, rose a cry
That Edyrn's men were on them, and they
      fled
With little save the jewels they had on,   640
Which being sold and sold had bought
      them bread.
And Edyrn's men had caught them in their
      flight,
And placed them in this ruin; and she
      wish'd
The prince had found her in her ancient.
      home;
Then let her fancy flit across the past,
And roam the goodly places that she knew,
And last bethought her how she used to
      watch,
Near that old home, a pool of golden carp;
And one was patch'd and blurr'd and lustre-
      less
Among his burnish'd brethren of the pool;
And half asleep she made comparison   651
Of that and these to her own faded self
And the gay court, and fell asleep again,
And dreamt herself was such a faded form
Among her burnish'd sisters of the pool.
But this was in the garden of a king,
And tho' she lay dark in the pool she knew
That all was bright; that all about were
      birds
Of sunny plume in gilded trellis-work;
That all the turf was rich in plots that
      look'd   660
Each like a garnet or a turkis in it;
And lords and ladies of the high court
      went

In silver tissue talking things of state;
And children of the King in cloth of gold
Glanced at the doors or gambol'd down the walks.
And while she thought, 'They will not see me,' came
A stately queen whose name was Guinevere,
And all the children in their cloth of gold
Ran to her, crying, 'If we have fish at all
Let them be gold; and charge the gardeners now   670
To pick the faded creature from the pool,
And cast it on the mixen that it die.'
And therewithal one came and seized on her,
And Enid started waking, with her heart
All overshadowed by the foolish dream,
And lo! it was her mother grasping her
To get her well awake; and in her hand
A suit of bright apparel, which she laid
Flat on the couch, and spoke exultingly:

'See here, my child, how fresh the colors look,   680
How fast they hold, like colors of a shell
That keeps the wear and polish of the wave.
Why not? It never yet was worn, I trow:
Look on it, child, and tell me if ye know it.'

And Enid look'd, but, all confused at first,
Could scarce divide it from her foolish dream.
Then suddenly she knew it and rejoiced,
And answer'd, 'Yea, I know it; your good gift,
So sadly lost on that unhappy night;
Your own good gift!' 'Yea, surely,' said the dame,   690
'And gladly given again this happy morn.
For when the jousts were ended yesterday,
Went Yniol thro' the town, and everywhere
He found the sack and plunder of our house
All scatter'd thro' the houses of the town,
And gave command that all which once was ours
Should now be ours again; and yester-eve,
While ye were talking sweetly with your prince,
Came one with this and laid it in my hand,

For love or fear, or seeking favor of us,   700
Because we have our earldom back again.
And yester-eve I would not tell you of it,
But kept it for a sweet surprise at morn.
Yea, truly is it not a sweet surprise?
For I myself unwillingly have worn
My faded suit, as you, my child, have yours,
And, howsoever patient, Yniol his.
Ah, dear, he took me from a goodly house,
With store of rich apparel, sumptuous fare,
And page, and maid, and squire, and seneschal,   710
And pastime both of hawk and hound, and all
That appertains to noble maintenance.
Yea, and he brought me to a goodly house;
But since our fortune swerved from sun to shade,
And all thro' that young traitor, cruel need
Constrain'd us, but a better time has come.
So clothe yourself in this, that better fits
Our mended fortunes and a prince's bride;
For tho' ye won the prize of fairest fair,
And tho' I heard him call you fairest fair,
Let never maiden think, however fair,   721
She is not fairer in new clothes than old.
And should some great court-lady say, the prince
Hath pick'd a ragged-robin from the hedge,
And like a madman brought her to the court,
Then were ye shamed, and, worse, might shame the prince
To whom we are beholden; but I know,
When my dear child is set forth at her best,
That neither court nor country, tho' they sought
Thro' all the provinces like those of old   730
That lighted on Queen Esther, has her match.'

Here ceased the kindly mother out of breath,
And Enid listen'd brightening as she lay;
Then, as the white and glittering star of morn
Parts from a bank of snow, and by and by
Slips into golden cloud, the maiden rose,
And left her maiden couch, and robed herself,
Help'd by the mother's careful hand and eye,
Without a mirror, in the gorgeous gown;
Who, after, turn'd her daughter round, and said   740

She never yet had seen her half so fair;
And call'd her like that maiden in the tale,
Whom Gwydion made by glamour out of
flowers,
And sweeter than the bride of Cassivelaun,
Flur, for whose love the Roman Cæsar first
Invaded Britain: 'But we beat him back,
As this great prince invaded us, and we,
Not beat him back, but welcomed him with
joy.
And I can scarcely ride with you to court,
For old am I, and rough the ways and
wild; 750
But Yniol goes, and I full oft shall dream
I see my princess as I see her now,
Clothed with my gift and gay among the
gay.'

But while the women thus rejoiced, Ge-
raint
Woke where he slept in the high hall, and
call'd
For Enid, and when Yniol made report
Of that good mother making Enid gay
In such apparel as might well beseem
His princess, or indeed the stately Queen,
He answer'd: 'Earl, entreat her by my
love, 760
Albeit I give no reason but my wish,
That she ride with me in her faded silk.'
Yniol with that hard message went; it fell
Like flaws in summer laying lusty corn;
For Enid, all abash'd she knew not why,
Dared not to glance at her good mother's
face,
But silently, in all obedience,
Her mother silent too, nor helping her,
Laid from her limbs the costly-broider'd
gift, 769
And robed them in her ancient suit again,
And so descended. Never man rejoiced
More than Geraint to greet her thus at-
tired;
And glancing all at once as keenly at her
As careful robins eye the delver's toil,
Made her cheek burn and either eyelid fall,
But rested with her sweet face satisfied;
Then seeing cloud upon the mother's brow,
Her by both hands he caught, and sweetly
said:

'O my new mother, be not wroth or
grieved
At thy new son, for my petition to her. 780
When late I left Caerleon, our great Queen,

In words whose echo lasts, they were so
sweet,
Made promise that, whatever bride I
brought,
Herself would clothe her like the sun in
heaven.
Thereafter, when I reach'd this ruin'd hall,
Beholding one so bright in dark estate,
I vow'd that, could I gain her, our fair
Queen,
No hand but hers, should make your Enid
burst
Sunlike from cloud — and likewise thought
perhaps, 789
That service done so graciously would bind
The two together; fain I would the two
Should love each other. How can Enid find
A nobler friend? Another thought was
mine:
I came among you here so suddenly
That tho' her gentle presence at the lists
Might well have served for proof that I
was loved,
I doubted whether daughter's tenderness,
Or easy nature, might not let itself
Be moulded by your wishes for her weal;
Or whether some false sense in her own
self 800
Of my contrasting brightness overbore
Her fancy dwelling in this dusky hall,
And such a sense might make her long for
court
And all its perilous glories; and I thought,
That could I someway prove such force in
her
Link'd with such love for me that at a
word,
No reason given her, she could cast aside
A splendor dear to women, new to her,
And therefore dearer; or if not so new,
Yet therefore tenfold dearer by the power
Of intermitted usage; then I felt 811
That I could rest, a rock in ebbs and flows,
Fixt on her faith. Now, therefore, I do
rest,
A prophet certain of my prophecy,
That never shadow of mistrust can cross
Between us. Grant me pardon for my
thoughts;
And for my strange petition I will make
Amends hereafter by some gaudy-day,
When your fair child shall wear your costly
gift
Beside your own warm hearth, with, on her
knees, 820

Who knows? another gift of the high God,
Which, maybe, shall have learn'd to lisp
  you thanks.'

  He spoke; the mother smiled, but half
    in tears,
Then brought a mantle down and wrapt her
    in it,
And claspt and kiss'd her, and they rode
    away.

  Now thrice that morning Guinevere had
    climb'd
The giant tower, from whose high crest,
    they say,
Men saw the goodly hills of Somerset,
And white sails flying on the yellow sea;
But not to goodly hill or yellow sea   830
Look'd the fair Queen, but up the vale of
    Usk,
By the flat meadow, till she saw them
    come;
And then descending met them at the gates,
Embraced her with all welcome as a friend,
And did her honor as the prince's bride,
And clothed her for her bridals like the
    sun;
And all that week was old Caerleon gay,
For by the hands of Dubric, the high saint,
They twain were wedded with all ceremony.

  And this was on the last year's Whitsun-
    tide.   840
But Enid ever kept the faded silk,
Remembering how first he came on her
Drest in that dress, and how he loved her
    in it,
And all her foolish fears about the dress,
And all his journey toward her, as himself
Had told her, and their coming to the
    court.

  And now this morning when he said to
    her,
' Put on your worst and meanest dress,' she
    found
And took it, and array'd herself therein.

GERAINT AND ENID

O PURBLIND race of miserable men,
How many among us at this very hour
Do forge a lifelong trouble for ourselves,
By taking true for false, or false for true;
Here, thro' the feeble twilight of this
    world
Groping, how many, until we pass and
    reach
That other where we see as we are seen!

  So fared it with Geraint, who issuing
    forth
That morning, when they both had got to
    horse,   9
Perhaps because he loved her passionately,
And felt that tempest brooding round his
    heart
Which, if he spoke at all, would break per-
    force
Upon a head so dear in thunder, said:
' Not at my side. I charge thee ride before
Ever a good way on before; and this
I charge thee, on thy duty as a wife,
Whatever happens, not to speak to me,
No, not a word!' and Enid was aghast;
And forth they rode, but scarce three paces
    on,
When crying out, ' Effeminate as I am,   20
I will not fight my way with gilded arms,
All shall be iron;' he loosed a mighty
    purse,
Hung at his belt, and hurl'd it toward the
    squire.
So the last sight that Enid had of home
Was all the marble threshold flashing,
    strown
With gold and scatter'd coinage, and the
    squire
Chafing his shoulder.   Then he cried again,
' To the wilds!' and Enid leading down the
    tracks
Thro' which he bade her lead him on, they
    past   29
The marches, and by bandit-haunted holds,
Gray swamps and pools, waste places of
    the hern,
And wildernesses, perilous paths, they rode.
Round was their pace at first, but slacken'd
    soon.
A stranger meeting them had surely
    thought,
They rode so slowly and they look'd so pale,
That each had suffer'd some exceeding
    wrong.
For he was ever saying to himself,
' O, I that wasted time to tend upon her,
To compass her with sweet observances,
To dress her beautifully and keep her
    true' —   40

And there he broke the sentence in his
    heart
Abruptly, as a man upon his tongue
May break it when his passion masters
    him.
And she was ever praying the sweet hea-
    vens
To save her dear lord whole from any
    wound.
And ever in her mind she cast about
For that unnoticed failing in herself
Which made him look so cloudy and so
    cold;
Till the great plover's human whistle
    amazed
Her heart, and glancing round the waste
    she fear'd   50
In every wavering brake an ambuscade;
Then thought again, 'If there be such in
    me,
I might amend it by the grace of Heaven,
If he would only speak and tell me of it.'

But when the fourth part of the day was
    gone,
Then Enid was aware of three tall knights
On horseback, wholly arm'd, behind a rock
In shadow, waiting for them, caitiffs all;
And heard one crying to his fellow, 'Look,
Here comes a laggard hanging down his
    head,   60
Who seems no bolder than a beaten hound;
Come, we will slay him and will have his
    horse
And armor, and his damsel shall be ours.'

Then Enid ponder'd in her heart, and
    said:
'I will go back a little to my lord,
And I will tell him all their caitiff talk;
For, be he wroth even to slaying me,
Far liefer by his dear hand had I die
Than that my lord should suffer loss or
    shame.'

Then she went back some paces of re-
    turn,   70
Met his full frown timidly firm, and said:
'My lord, I saw three bandits by the rock
Waiting to fall on you, and heard them
    boast
That they would slay you, and possess your
    horse
And armor, and your damsel should be
    theirs.'

He made a wrathful answer: 'Did I
    wish
Your warning or your silence? one com-
    mand
I laid upon you, not to speak to me,
And thus ye keep it! Well then, look —
    for now,
Whether ye wish me victory or defeat,   80
Long for my life or hunger for my death,
Yourself shall see my vigor is not lost.'

Then Enid waited pale and sorrowful,
And down upon him bare the bandit three.
And at the midmost charging, Prince Ge-
    raint
Drave the long spear   cubit thro' his
    breast
And out beyond; and then against his
    brace
Of comrades, each of whom had broken on
    him
A lance that splinter'd like an icicle,
Swung from his brand a windy buffet out   90
Once, twice, to right, to left, and stunn'd
    the twain
Or slew them, and dismounting, like a
    man
That skins the wild beast after slaying
    him,
Stript from the three dead wolves of woman
    born
The three gay suits of armor which they
    wore,
And let the bodies lie, but bound the suits
Of armor on their horses, each on each,
And tied the bridle-reins of all the three
Together, and said to her, 'Drive them on
Before you;' and she drove them thro' the
    waste.   100

He follow'd nearer; ruth began to work
Against his anger in him, while he watch'd
The being he loved best in all the world,
With difficulty in mild obedience
Driving them on. He fain had spoken to
    her,
And loosed in words of sudden fire the
    wrath
And smoulder'd wrong that burnt him all
    within;
But evermore it seem'd an easier thing
At once without remorse to strike her dead
Than to cry 'Halt,' and to her own bright
    face   110
Accuse her of the least immodesty:

And thus tongue-tied, it made him wroth
the more
That she *could* speak whom his own ear
had heard
Call herself false, and suffering thus he
made
Minutes an age; but in scarce longer time
Than at Caerleon the full-tided Usk,
Before he turn to fall seaward again,
Pauses, did Enid, keeping watch, behold
In the first shallow shade of a deep wood,
Before a gloom of stubborn-shafted oaks,
Three other horsemen waiting, wholly
arm'd,   121
Whereof one seem'd far larger than her
lord,
And shook her pulses, crying, 'Look, a
prize !
Three horses and three goodly suits of
arms,
And all in charge of whom? a girl! set
on.'
'Nay,' said the second, 'yonder comes a
knight.'
The third, 'A craven; how he hangs his
head !'
The giant answer'd merrily, 'Yea, but
one ?
Wait here, and when he passes fall upon
him !'

And Enid ponder'd in her heart and said:
'I will abide the coming of my lord,   131
And I will tell him all their villany.
My lord is weary with the fight before,
And they will fall upon him unawares.
I needs must disobey him for his good;
How should I dare obey him to his harm ?
Needs must I speak, and tho' he kill me
for it,
I save a life dearer to me than mine.'

And she abode his coming, and said to
him
With timid firmness, 'Have I leave to
speak ?'   140
He said, 'Ye take it, speaking,' and she
spoke:

'There lurk three villains yonder in the
wood,
And each of them is wholly arm'd, and one
Is larger-limb'd than you are, and they say
That they will fall upon you while ye
pass.'

To which he flung a wrathful answer
back:
'And if there were an hundred in the
wood,
And every man were larger-limb'd than I,
And all at once should sally out upon me,
I swear it would not ruffle me so much   150
As you that not obey me. Stand aside,
And if I fall, cleave to the better man.'

And Enid stood aside to wait the event,
Not dare to watch the combat, only breathe
Short fits of prayer, at every stroke a
breath.
And he she dreaded most bare down upon
him.
Aim'd at the helm, his lance err'd; but
Geraint's,
A little in the late encounter strain'd,
Struck thro' the bulky bandit's corselet
home,
And then brake short, and down his enemy
roll'd,   160
And there lay still; as he that tells the
tale
Saw once a great piece of a promontory,
That had a sapling growing on it, slide
From the long shore-cliff's windy walls to
the beach,
And there lie still, and yet the sapling
grew;
So lay the man transfixt. His craven pair
Of comrades making slowlier at the prince,
When now they saw their bulwark fallen,
stood;
On whom the victor, to confound them
more,
Spurr'd with his terrible war-cry; for as
one,   170
That listens near a torrent mountain-brook,
All thro' the crash of the near cataract
hears
The drumming thunder of the huger fall
At distance, were the soldiers wont to hear
His voice in battle, and be kindled by it,
And foemen scared, like that false pair
who turn'd
Flying, but, overtaken, died the death
Themselves had wrought on many an in-
nocent.

Thereon Geraint, dismounting, pick'd the
lance
That pleased him best, and drew from
those dead wolves   180

Their three gay suits of armor, each from
    each,
And bound them on their horses, each on
    each,
And tied the bridle-reins of all the three
Together, and said to her, 'Drive them on
Before you,' and she drove them thro' the
    wood.

He follow'd nearer still. The pain she
    had
To keep them in the wild ways of the
    wood,
Two sets of three laden with jingling arms,
Together, served a little to disedge   189
The sharpness of that pain about her heart;
And they themselves, like creatures gently
    born
But into bad hands fallen, and now so
    long
By bandits groom'd, prick'd their light
    ears, and felt
Her low firm voice and tender government.

So thro' the green gloom of the wood
    they past,
And issuing under open heavens beheld
A little town with towers, upon a rock,
And close beneath, a meadow gemlike
    chased
In the brown wild, and mowers mowing
    in it;   199
And down a rocky pathway from the place
There came a fair-hair'd youth, that in his
    hand
Bare victual for the mowers; and Geraint
Had ruth again on Enid looking pale.
Then, moving downward to the meadow
    ground,
He, when the fair-hair'd youth came by
    him, said,
'Friend, let her eat; the damsel is so faint.'
'Yea, willingly,' replied the youth; 'and
    thou,
My lord, eat also, tho' the fare is coarse,
And only meet for mowers;' then set down
His basket, and dismounting on the sward
They let the horses graze, and ate them-
    selves.   211
And Enid took a little delicately,
Less having stomach for it than desire
To close with her lord's pleasure, but Ge-
    raint
Ate all the mowers' victual unawares,
And when he found all empty was amazed;

And 'Boy,' said he, 'I have eaten all, but
    take
A horse and arms for guerdon; choose the
    best.'
He, reddening in extremity of delight,
'My lord, you overpay me fifty-fold.'   220
'Ye will be all the wealthier,' cried the
    prince.
'I take it as free gift, then,' said the boy,
'Not guerdon; for myself can easily,
While your good damsel rests, return and
    fetch
Fresh victual for these mowers of our earl;
For these are his, and all the field is his,
And I myself am his; and I will tell him
How great a man thou art. He loves to
    know
When men of mark are in his territory;
And he will have thee to his palace here, 230
And serve thee costlier than with mowers'
    fare.'

Then said Geraint: 'I wish no better fare;
I never ate with angrier appetite
Than when I left your mowers dinnerless.
And into no earl's palace will I go.
I know, God knows, too much of palaces!
And if he want me, let him come to me.
But hire us some fair chamber for the
    night,
And stalling for the horses, and return
With victual for these men, and let us
    know.'   240

'Yea, my kind lord,' said the glad youth,
    and went,
Held his head high, and thought himself a
    knight,
And up the rocky pathway disappear'd,
Leading the horse, and they were left alone.

But when the prince had brought his
    errant eyes
Home from the rock, sideways he let them
    glance
At Enid, where she droopt. His own false
    doom,
That shadow of mistrust should never cross
Betwixt them, came upon him, and he
    sigh'd;
Then with another humorous ruth remark'd
The lusty mowers laboring dinnerless, 251
And watch'd the sun blaze on the turning
    scythe,
And after nodded sleepily in the heat.

But she, remembering her old ruin'd hall,
And all the windy clamor of the daws
About her hollow turret, pluck'd the grass
There growing longest by the meadow's
　　edge,
And into many a listless annulet,
Now over, now beneath her marriage ring,
Wove and unwove it, till the boy return'd
And told them of a chamber, and they
　　went;　　　　　261
Where, after saying to her, ' If ye will,
Call for the woman of the house,' to which
She answer'd, ' Thanks, my lord;' the two
　　remain'd
Apart by all the chamber's width, and mute
As creatures voiceless thro' the fault of
　　birth,
Or two wild men supporters of a shield,
Painted, who stare at open space, nor
　　glance
The one at other, parted by the shield.

On a sudden, many a voice along the
　　street,　　　　　270
And heel against the pavement echoing,
　　burst
Their drowse; and either started while the
　　door,
Push'd from without, drave backward to
　　the wall,
And midmost of a rout of roisterers,
Femininely fair and dissolutely pale,
Her suitor in old years before Geraint
Enter'd, the wild lord of the place, Li-
　　mours.
He moving up with pliant courtliness
Greeted Geraint full face, but stealthily,
In the mid-warmth of welcome and graspt
　　hand,　　　　　280
Found Enid with the corner of his eye,
And knew her sitting sad and solitary.
Then cried Geraint for wine and goodly
　　cheer
To feed the sudden guest, and sumptu-
　　ously,
According to his fashion, bade the host
Call in what men soever were his friends,
And feast with these in honor of their
　　earl;
' And care not for the cost; the cost is
　　mine.'

And wine and food were brought, and
　　Earl Limours
Drank till he jested with all ease, and told

Free tales, and took the word and play'd
　　upon it,　　　　　291
And made it of two colors; for his talk,
When wine and free companions kindled
　　him,
Was wont to glance and sparkle like a
　　gem
Of fifty facets; thus he moved the prince
To laughter and his comrades to applause.
Then, when the prince was merry, ask'd
　　Limours,
' Your leave, my lord, to cross the room,
　　and speak
To your good damsel there who sits apart,
And seems so lonely ? ' ' My free leave,'
　　he said;　　　　　300
' Get her to speak; she doth not speak to
　　me.'
Then rose Limours, and looking at his feet,
Like him who tries the bridge he fears may
　　fail,
Crost and came near, lifted adoring eyes,
Bow'd at her side and utter'd whisper-
　　ingly:

' Enid, the pilot star of my lone life,
Enid, my early and my only love,
Enid, the loss of whom hath turn'd me
　　wild —
What chance is this ? how is it I see you
　　here ?
Ye are in my power at last, are in my
　　power.　　　　　310
Yet fear me not; I call mine own self wild,
But keep a touch of sweet civility
Here in the heart of waste and wilderness.
I thought, but that your father came be-
　　tween,
In former days you saw me favorably.
And if it were so do not keep it back.
Make me a little happier; let me know it.
Owe you me nothing for a life half-lost ?
Yea, yea, the whole dear debt of all you
　　are.
And, Enid, you and he, I see with joy,　　320
Ye sit apart, you do not speak to him,
You come with no attendance, page or
　　maid,
To serve you — doth he love you as of
　　old ?
For, call it lovers' quarrels, yet I know
Tho' men may bicker with the things they
　　love,
They would not make them laughable in
　　all eyes,

Not while they loved them; and your
    wretched dress,
A wretched insult on you, dumbly speaks
Your story, that this man loves you no
    more.
Your beauty is no beauty to him now.   330
A common chance — right well I know it
    — pall'd —
For I know men; nor will ye win him back,
For the man's love once gone never re-
    turns.
But here is one who loves you as of old;
With more exceeding passion than of old.
Good, speak the word; my followers ring
    him round.
He sits unarm'd; I hold a finger up;
They understand.   Nay, I do not mean
    blood;
Nor need ye look so scared at what I say.
My malice is no deeper than a moat,   340
No stronger than a wall.   There is the
    keep;
He shall not cross us more; speak but the
    word.
Or speak it not; but then by Him that
    made me
The one true lover whom you ever own'd,
I will make use of all the power I have.
O, pardon me ! the madness of that hour
When first I parted from thee moves me
    yet.'

At this the tender sound of his own voice
And sweet self-pity, or the fancy of it,
Made his eye moist; but Enid fear'd his
    eyes,   350
Moist as they were, wine-heated from the
    feast,
And answer'd with such craft as women
    use,
Guilty or guiltless, to stave off a chance
That breaks upon them perilously, and
    said:

' Earl, if you love me as in former years,
And do not practise on me, come with
    morn,
And snatch me from him as by violence.
Leave me to-night; I am weary to the
    death.'

Low at leave-taking, with his brandish'd
    plume
Brushing his instep, bow'd the all-amorous
    earl,   360

And the stout prince bade him a loud good-
    night.
He moving homeward babbled to his men,
How Enid never loved a man but him,
Nor cared a broken egg-shell for her lord.

But Enid left alone with Prince Geraint,
Debating his command of silence given,
And that she now perforce must violate it,
Held commune with herself, and while she
    held
He fell asleep, and Enid had no heart
To wake him, but hung o'er him, wholly
    pleased   370
To find him yet unwounded after fight,
And hear him breathing low and equally.
Anon she rose and, stepping lightly, heap'd
The pieces of his armor in one place,
All to be there against a sudden need;
Then dozed awhile herself, but, overtoil'd
By that day's grief and travel, evermore
Seem'd catching at a rootless thorn, and
    then
Went slipping down horrible precipices,
And strongly striking out her limbs awoke;
Then thought she heard the wild earl at
    the door,   381
With all his rout of random followers,
Sound on a dreadful trumpet, summoning
    her;
Which was the red cock shouting to the
    light,
As the gray dawn stole o'er the dewy world
And glimmer'd on his armor in the room.
And once again she rose to look at it,
But touch'd it unawares; jangling, the
    casque
Fell, and he started up and stared at her.
Then breaking his command of silence
    given,   390
She told him all that Earl Limours had
    said,
Except the passage that he loved her not;
Nor left untold the craft herself had used,
But ended with apology so sweet,
Low - spoken, and of so few words, and
    seem'd
So justified by that necessity,
That tho' he thought, ' Was it for him she
    wept
In Devon ? ' he but gave a wrathful groan,
Saying, ' Your sweet faces make good fel-
    lows fools
And traitors.   Call the host and bid him
    bring   400

Charger and palfrey.' So she glided out
Among the heavy breathings of the house,
And like a household spirit at the walls
Beat, till she woke the sleepers, and re-
turn'd;
Then tending her rough lord, tho' all un-
ask'd,
In silence, did him service as a squire;
Till issuing arm'd he found the host and
cried,
'Thy reckoning, friend ? ' and ere he learnt
it, 'Take
Five horses and their armors;' and the
host,
Suddenly honest, answer'd in amaze,   410
'My lord, I scarce have spent the worth of
one !'
'Ye will be all the wealthier,' said the
prince,
And then to Enid, 'Forward ! and to-day
I charge you, Enid, more especially,
What thing soever ye may hear, or see,
Or fancy — tho' I count it of small use
To charge you — that ye speak not but
obey.'

And Enid answer'd: 'Yea, my lord, I
know
Your wish and would obey; but, riding
first,
I hear the violent threats you do not hear,
I see the danger which you cannot see.   421
Then not to give you warning, that seems
hard,
Almost beyond me; yet I would obey.'

'Yea so,' said he, 'do it; be not too wise,
Seeing that ye are wedded to a man,
Not all mismated with a yawning clown,
But one with arms to guard his head and
yours,
With eyes to find you out however far,
And ears to hear you even in his dreams.'

With that he turn'd and look'd as keenly
at her   430
As careful robins eye the delver's toil;
And that within her which a wanton fool
Or hasty judger would have call'd her guilt
Made her cheek burn and either eyelid fall.
And Geraint look'd and was not satisfied.

Then forward by a way which, beaten
broad,
Led from the territory of false Limours

To the waste earldom of another earl,
Doorm, whom his shaking vassals call'd the
Bull,
Went Enid with her sullen follower on. 440
Once she look'd back, and when she saw
him ride
More near by many a rood than yester-
morn,
It wellnigh made her cheerful; till Geraint,
Waving an angry hand as who should say,
'Ye watch me,' sadden'd all her heart
again.
But while the sun yet beat a dewy blade,
The sound of many a heavily-galloping
hoof
Smote on her ear, and turning round she
saw
Dust, and the points of lances bicker in it.
Then, not to disobey her lord's behest, 450
And yet to give him warning, for he rode
As if he heard not, moving back she held
Her finger up, and pointed to the dust.
At which the warrior in his obstinacy,
Because she kept the letter of his word,
Was in a manner pleased, and turning
stood.
And in the moment after, wild Limours,
Borne on a black horse, like a thunder-
cloud
Whose skirts are loosen'd by the breaking
storm,   459
Half ridden off with by the thing he rode,
And all in passion uttering a dry shriek,
Dash'd on Geraint, who closed with him,
and bore
Down by the length of lance and arm be-
yond
The crupper, and so left him stunn'd or
dead,
And overthrew the next that follow'd him,
And blindly rush'd on all the rout behind.
But at the flash and motion of the man
They vanish'd panic-stricken, like a shoal
Of darting fish, that on a summer morn
Adown the crystal dykes at Camelot   470
Come slipping o'er their shadows on the
sand,
But if a man who stands upon the brink
But lift a shining hand against the sun,
There is not left the twinkle of a fin
Betwixt the cressy islets white in flower;
So, scared but at the motion of the man,
Fled all the boon companions of the earl,
And left him lying in the public way;
So vanish friendships only made in wine.

Then like a stormy sunlight smiled Ge-
raint, 480
Who saw the chargers of the two that fell
Start from their fallen lords and wildly fly,
Mixt with the flyers. 'Horse and man,' he
said,
'All of one mind and all right - honest
friends !
Not a hoof left ! and I methinks till now
Was honest — paid with horses and with
arms;
I cannot steal or plunder, no, nor beg.
And so what say ye, shall we strip him
there,
Your lover ? has your palfrey heart enough
To bear his armor ? shall we fast or dine ?
No ? — then do thou, being right honest,
pray 491
That we may meet the horsemen of Earl
Doorm;
I too would still be honest.' Thus he said;
And sadly gazing on her bridle-reins,
And answering not one word, she led the
way.

But as a man to whom a dreadful loss
Falls in a far land and he knows it not,
But coming back he learns it, and the loss
So pains him that he sickens nigh to death;
So fared it with Geraint, who, being
prick'd 500
In combat with the follower of Limours,
Bled underneath his armor secretly,
And so rode on, nor told his gentle wife
What ail'd him, hardly knowing it him-
self,
Till his eye darken'd and his helmet
wagg'd;
And at a sudden swerving of the road,
Tho' happily down on a bank of grass,
The prince, without a word, from his horse
fell.

And Enid heard the clashing of his fall,
Suddenly came, and at his side all pale 510
Dismounting loosed the fastenings of his
arms,
Nor let her true hand falter, nor blue eye
Moisten, till she had lighted on his wound,
And tearing off her veil of faded silk
Had bared her forehead to the blistering
sun,
And swathed the hurt that drain'd her dear
lord's life.
Then, after all was done that hand could do,

She rested, and her desolation came
Upon her, and she wept beside the way.

And many past, but none regarded her,
For in that realm of lawless turbulence 521
A woman weeping for her murder'd mate
Was cared as much for as a summer
shower.
One took him for a victim of Earl Doorm,
Nor dared to waste a perilous pity on him.
Another hurrying past, a man-at-arms,
Rode on a mission to the bandit earl;
Half whistling and half singing a coarse
song,
He drove the dust against her veilless
eyes. 529
Another, flying from the wrath of Doorm
Before an ever-fancied arrow, made
The long way smoke beneath him in his
fear;
At which her palfrey whinnying lifted heel,
And scour'd into the coppices and was lost,
While the great charger stood, grieved like
a man.

But at the point of noon the huge Earl
Doorm,
Broad-faced with under-fringe of russet
beard,
Bound on a foray, rolliug eyes of prey,
Came riding with a hundred lances up;
But ere he came, like one that hails a
ship, 540
Cried out with a big voice, 'What, is he
dead ? '
'No, no, not dead !' she answer'd in all
haste.
'Would some of your kind people take
him up,
And bear him hence out of this cruel sun ?
Most sure am I, quite sure, he is not dead.'

Then said Earl Doorm: 'Well, if he be
not dead,
Why wail ye for him thus ? ye seem a
child.
And be he dead, I count you for a fool;
Your wailing will not quicken him; dead
or not,
Ye mar a comely face with idiot tears. 550
Yet, since the face is comely — some of you,
Here, take him up, and bear him to our
hall.
An if he live, we will have him of our
band;

And if he die, why earth has earth enough
To hide him. See ye take the charger too,
A noble one.'
          He spake and past away,
But left two brawny spearmen, who advanced,
Each growling like a dog, when his good
    bone   558
Seems to be pluck'd at by the village boys
Who love to vex him eating, and he fears
To lose his bone, and lays his foot upon it,
Gnawing and growling; so the ruffians
    growl'd,
Fearing to lose, and all for a dead man,
Their chance of booty from the morning's
    raid,
Yet raised and laid him on a litter-bier,
Such as they brought upon their forays out
For those that might be wounded; laid
    him on it
All in the hollow of his shield, and took
And bore him to the naked hall of Doorm —
His gentle charger following him unled —
And cast him and the bier in which he
    lay
Down on an oaken settle in the hall,   572
And then departed, hot in haste to join
Their luckier mates, but growling as before,
And cursing their lost time, and the dead
    man,
And their own earl, and their own souls,
    and her.
They might as well have blest her; she
    was deaf
To blessing or to cursing save from one.

    So for long hours sat Enid by her lord
There in the naked hall, propping his
    head,   580
And chafing his pale hands, and calling to
    him,
Till at the last he waken'd from his swoon,
And found his own dear bride propping his
    head,
And chafing his faint hands, and calling to
    him;
And felt the warm tears falling on his face,
And said to his own heart, 'She weeps for
    me;'
And yet lay still, and feign'd himself as
    dead,
That he might prove her to the uttermost,
And say to his own heart, 'She weeps for
    me.'

But in the falling afternoon return'd 590
The huge Earl Doorm with plunder to the
    hall.
His lusty spearmen follow'd him with
    noise:
Each hurling down a heap of things that
    rang
Against the pavement, cast his lance aside,
And doff'd his helm; and then there flutter'd in,
Half-bold, half-frighted, with dilated eyes,
A tribe of women, dress'd in many hues,
And mingled with the spearmen; and Earl
    Doorm
Struck with a knife's haft hard against the
    board,
And call'd for flesh and wine to feed his
    spears.   600
And men brought in whole hogs and quarter beeves,
And all the hall was dim with steam of
    flesh.
And none spake word, but all sat down at
    once,
And ate with tumult in the naked hall,
Feeding like horses when you hear them
    feed;
Till Enid shrank far back into herself,
To shun the wild ways of the lawless tribe.
But when Earl Doorm had eaten all he
    would,
He roll'd his eyes about the hall, and found
A damsel drooping in a corner of it. 610
Then he remember'd her and how she
    wept,
And out of her there came a power upon
    him;
And rising on the sudden he said: 'Eat!
I never yet beheld a thing so pale.
God's curse, it makes me mad to see you
    weep.
Eat! Look yourself. Good luck had your
    good man,
For were I dead who is it would weep for
    me?
Sweet lady, never since I first drew breath
Have I beheld a lily like yourself.
And so there lived some color in your
    cheek,   620
There is not one among my gentlewomen
Were fit to wear your slipper for a glove.
But listen to me, and by me be ruled,
And I will do the thing I have not done,
For ye shall share my earldom with me,
    girl,

And we will live like two birds in one nest,
And I will fetch you forage from all fields,
For I compel all creatures to my will.'

He spoke; the brawny spearman let his cheek
Bulge with the unswallow'd piece, and turning stared; 630
While some, whose souls the old serpent long had drawn
Down, as the worm draws in the wither'd leaf
And makes it earth, hiss'd each at other's ear
What shall not be recorded — women they,
Women, or what had been those gracious things,
But now desired the humbling of their best,
Yea, would have help'd him to it; and all at once
They hated her, who took no thought of them,
But answer'd in low voice, her meek head yet
Drooping, 'I pray you of your courtesy, 640
He being as he is, to let me be.'

She spake so low he hardly heard her speak,
But like a mighty patron, satisfied
With what himself had done so graciously,
Assumed that she had thank'd him, adding, 'Yea,
Eat and be glad, for I account you mine.'

She answer'd meekly, 'How should I be glad
Henceforth in all the world at anything,
Until my lord arise and look upon me?'

Here the huge earl cried out upon her talk, 650
As all but empty heart and weariness
And sickly nothing; suddenly seized on her,
And bare her by main violence to the board,
And thrust the dish before her, crying, 'Eat.'

'No, no,' said Enid, vext, 'I will not eat
Till yonder man upon the bier arise,
And eat with me.' 'Drink, then,' he answer'd. 'Here!'—
And fill'd a horn with wine and held it to her,—

'Lo! I, myself, when flush'd with fight or hot, 659
God's curse, with anger — often I myself,
Before I well have drunken, scarce can eat;
Drink therefore, and the wine will change your will.'

'Not so,' she cried, 'by Heaven, I will not drink
Till my dear lord arise and bid me do it,
And drink with me; and if he rise no more,
I will not look at wine until I die.'

At this he turn'd all red and paced his hall,
Now gnaw'd his under, now his upper lip,
And coming up close to her, said at last:
'Girl, for I see ye scorn my courtesies, 670
Take warning; yonder man is surely dead,
And I compel all creatures to my will.
Not eat nor drink? And wherefore wail for one
Who put your beauty to this flout and scorn
By dressing it in rags? Amazed am I,
Beholding how ye butt against my wish,
That I forbear you thus; cross me no more.
At least put off to please me this poor gown,
This silken rag, this beggar-woman's weed.
I love that beauty should go beautifully;
For see ye not my gentlewomen here, 681
How gay, how suited to the house of one
Who loves that beauty should go beautifully?
Rise therefore; robe yourself in this; obey.'

He spoke, and one among his gentlewomen
Display'd a splendid silk of foreign loom,
Where like a shoaling sea the lovely blue
Play'd into green, and thicker down the front
With jewels than the sward with drops of dew,
When all night long a cloud clings to the hill, 690
And with the dawn ascending lets the day
Strike where it clung; so thickly shone the gems.

But Enid answer'd, harder to be moved
Than hardest tyrants in their day of power,

With lifelong injuries burning unavenged,
And now their hour has come; and Enid
　　said:

'In this poor gown my dear lord found
　　me first,
And loved me serving in my father's hall;
In this poor gown I rode with him to
　　court,
And there the Queen array'd me like the
　　sun;　　　　　　　　　　　　　　　700
In this poor gown he bade me clothe my-
　　self,
When now we rode upon this fatal quest
Of honor, where no honor can be gain'd;
And this poor gown I will not cast aside
Until himself arise a living man,
And bid me cast it. I have griefs enough;
Pray you be gentle, pray you let me be.
I never loved, can never love but him.
Yea, God, I pray you of your gentleness,
He being as he is, to let me be.'　　　710

Then strode the brute earl up and down
　　his hall,
And took his russet beard between his
　　teeth;
Last, coming up quite close, and in his
　　mood
Crying, 'I count it of no more avail,
Dame, to be gentle than ungentle with
　　you;
Take my salute,' unknightly with flat hand,
However lightly, smote her on the cheek.

Then Enid, in her utter helplessness,
And since she thought, 'He had not dared
　　to do it,　　　　　　　　　　　　719
Except he surely knew my lord was dead,'
Sent forth a sudden sharp and bitter cry,
As of a wild thing taken in the trap,
Which sees the trapper coming thro' the
　　wood.

This heard Geraint, and grasping at his
　　sword, —
It lay beside him in the hollow shield, —
Made but a single bound, and with a sweep
　　of it
Shore thro' the swarthy neck, and like a
　　ball
The russet-bearded head roll'd on the floor.
So died Earl Doorm by him he counted
　　dead.
And all the men and women in the hall　730

Rose when they saw the dead man rise, and
　　fled
Yelling as from a spectre, and the two
Were left alone together, and he said:

'Enid, I have used you worse than that
　　dead man,
Done you more wrong; we both have un-
　　dergone
That trouble which has left me thrice your
　　own.
Henceforward I will rather die than doubt.
And here I lay this penance on myself,
Not, tho' mine own ears heard you yester-
　　morn —
You thought me sleeping, but I heard you
　　say,　　　　　　　　　　　　　　740
I heard you say, that you were no true
　　wife,
I swear I will not ask your meaning in it.
I do believe yourself against yourself,
And will henceforward rather die than
　　doubt.'

And Enid could not say one tender
　　word,
She felt so blunt and stupid at the heart.
She only pray'd him, 'Fly, they will return
And slay you; fly, your charger is without,
My palfrey lost.' 'Then, Enid, shall you
　　ride　　　　　　　　　　　　　　749
Behind me.' 'Yea,' said Enid, 'let us go.'
And moving out they found the stately
　　horse,
Who now no more a vassal to the thief,
But free to stretch his limbs in lawful fight,
Neigh'd with all gladness as they came, and
　　stoop'd
With a low whinny toward the pair; and
　　she
Kiss'd the white star upon his noble front,
Glad also; then Geraint upon the horse
Mounted, and reach'd a hand, and on his
　　foot
She set her own and climb'd; he turn'd his
　　face
And kiss'd her climbing, and she cast her
　　arms　　　　　　　　　　　　　760
About him, and at once they rode away.

And never yet, since high in Paradise
O'er the four rivers the first roses blew,
Came purer pleasure unto mortal kind
Than lived thro' her who in that perilous
　　hour

Put hand to hand beneath her husband's
    heart,
And felt him hers again. She did not weep,
But o'er her meek eyes came a happy
    mist
Like that which kept the heart of Eden
    green
Before the useful trouble of the rain.   770
Yet not so misty were her meek blue eyes
As not to see before them on the path,
Right in the gateway of the bandit hold,
A knight of Arthur's court, who laid his
    lance
In rest and made as if to fall upon him.
Then, fearing for his hurt and loss of
    blood,
She, with her mind all full of what had
    chanced,
Shriek'd to the stranger, 'Slay not a dead
    man!'
'The voice of Enid,' said the knight; but
    she,
Beholding it was Edyrn, son of Nudd,   780
Was moved so much the more, and shriek'd
    again,
'O cousin, slay not him who gave you life.'
And Edyrn moving frankly forward spake:
'My lord Geraint, I greet you with all
    love;
I took you for a bandit knight of Doorm;
And fear not, Enid, I should fall upon
    him,
Who love you, prince, with something of
    the love
Wherewith we love the Heaven that chas-
    tens us.   788
For once, when I was up so high in pride
That I was halfway down the slope to hell,
By overthrowing me you threw me higher.
Now, made a knight of Arthur's Table
    Round,
And since I knew this earl when I myself
Was half a bandit in my lawless hour,
I come the mouthpiece of our King to
    Doorm —
The King is close behind me — bidding
    him
Disband himself, and scatter all his powers,
Submit, and hear the judgment of the
    King.'

'He hears the judgment of the King of
    kings,'
Cried the wan prince; 'and lo, the powers
    of Doorm   800

Are scatter'd!' and he pointed to the field,
Where, huddled here and there on mound
    and knoll,
Were men and women staring and aghast,
While some yet fled; and then he plainlier
    told
How the huge earl lay slain within his
    hall.
But when the knight besought him, 'Fol-
    low me,
Prince, to the camp, and in the King's own
    ear
Speak what has chanced; ye surely have
    endured
Strange chances here alone;' that other
    flush'd,
And hung his head, and halted in reply,   810
Fearing the mild face of the blameless
    King,
And after madness acted question ask'd;
Till Edyrn crying, 'If ye will not go
To Arthur, then will Arthur come to you,'
'Enough,' he said, 'I follow,' and they
    went.
But Enid in their going had two fears,
One from the bandit scatter'd in the field,
And one from Edyrn. Every now and
    then,
When Edyrn rein'd his charger at her
    side,
She shrank a little. In a hollow land,   820
From which old fires have broken, men
    may fear
Fresh fire and ruin. He, perceiving, said:

'Fair and dear cousin, you that most
    had cause
To fear me, fear no longer, I am changed.
Yourself were first the blameless cause to
    make
My nature's prideful sparkle in the blood
Break into furious flame; being repulsed
By Yniol and yourself, I schemed and
    wrought
Until I overturn'd him; then set up —   829
With one main purpose ever at my heart —
My haughty jousts, and took a paramour;
Did her mock-honor as the fairest fair,
And, toppling over all antagonism,
So wax'd in pride that I believed myself
Unconquerable, for I was wellnigh mad;
And, but for my main purpose in these
    jousts,
I should have slain your father, seized
    yourself.

I lived in hope that sometime you would
    come
To these my lists with him whom best you
    loved,
And there, poor cousin, with your meek
    blue eyes,   840
The truest eyes that ever answer'd heaven,
Behold me overturn and trample on him.
Then, had you cried, or knelt, or pray'd to
    me,
I should not less have kill'd him. And
    you came, —
But once you came, — and with your own
    true eyes
Beheld the man you loved — I speak as one
Speaks of a service done him — overthrow
My proud self, and my purpose three years
    old,
And set his foot upon me, and give me life.
There was I broken down, there was I
    saved;   850
Tho' thence I rode all-shamed, hating the
    life
He gave me, meaning to be rid of it.
And all the penance the Queen laid upon
    me
Was but to rest awhile within her court;
Where first as sullen as a beast new-caged,
And waiting to be treated like a wolf,
Because I knew my deeds were known, I
    found,
Instead of scornful pity or pure scorn,
Such fine reserve and noble reticence,
Manners so kind, yet stately, such a grace
Of tenderest courtesy, that I began   861
To glance behind me at my former life,
And find that it had been the wolf's in-
    deed.
And oft I talk'd with Dubric, the high
    saint,
Who, with mild heat of holy oratory,
Subdued me somewhat to that gentleness
Which, when it weds with manhood, makes
    a man.
And you were often there about the Queen,
But saw me not, or mark'd not if you saw;
Nor did I care or dare to speak with you, 870
But kept myself aloof till I was changed;
And fear not, cousin, I am changed in-
    deed.'

He spoke, and Enid easily believed,
Like simple noble natures, credulous
Of what they long for, good in friend or
    foe,

There most in those who most have done
    them ill.
And when they reach'd the camp the King
    himself
Advanced to greet them, and beholding her
Tho' pale, yet happy, ask'd her not a word,
But went apart with Edyrn, whom he held
In converse for a little, and return'd,   881
And, gravely smiling, lifted her from horse,
And kiss'd her with all pureness, brother-
    like,
And show'd an empty tent allotted her,
And glancing for a minute, till he saw
    her
Pass into it, turn'd to the prince, and said:

'Prince, when of late ye pray'd me for
    my leave
To move to your own land and there defend
Your marches, I was prick'd with some
    reproof,   889
As one that let foul wrong stagnate and be,
By having look'd too much thro' alien eyes,
And wrought too long with delegated hands,
Not used mine own; but now behold me
    come
To cleanse this common sewer of all my
    realm,
With Edyrn and with others. Have ye
    look'd
At Edyrn? have ye seen how nobly
    changed?
This work of his is great and wonderful.
His very face with change of heart is
    changed.
The world will not believe a man repents;
And this wise world of ours is mainly right.
Full seldom doth a man repent, or use 901
Both grace and will to pick the vicious
    quitch
Of blood and custom wholly out of him,
And make all clean, and plant himself
    afresh.
Edyrn has done it, weeding all his heart
As I will weed this land before I go.
I, therefore, made him of our Table Round,
Not rashly, but have proved him every way
One of our noblest, our most valorous,
Sanest and most obedient; and indeed 910
This work of Edyrn, wrought upon himself
After a life of violence, seems to me
A thousand-fold more great and wonderful
Than if some knight of mine, risking his
    life,
My subject with my subjects under him,

Should make an onslaught single on a realm
Of robbers, tho' he slew them one by one,
And were himself nigh wounded to the death.'

So spake the King; low bow'd the prince, and felt   919
His work was neither great nor wonderful,
And past to Enid's tent; and thither came
The King's own leech to look into his hurt;
And Enid tended on him there; and there
Her constant motion round him, and the breath
Of her sweet tendance hovering over him,
Fill'd all the genial courses of his blood
With deeper and with ever deeper love,
As the Southwest that blowing Bala lake
Fills all the sacred Dee. So past the days.

But while Geraint lay healing of his hurt,
The blameless King went forth and cast his eyes   931
On each of all whom Uther left in charge
Long since, to guard the justice of the King.
He look'd and found them wanting; and as now
Men weed the White Horse on the Berkshire hills,
To keep him bright and clean as heretofore,
He rooted out the slothful officer
Or guilty, which for bribe had wink'd at wrong,
And in their chairs set up a stronger race
With hearts and hands, and sent a thousand men   940
To till the wastes, and moving everywhere
Clear'd the dark places and let in the law,
And broke the bandit holds and cleansed the land.

Then, when Geraint was whole again, they past
With Arthur to Caerleon upon Usk.
There the great Queen once more embraced her friend,
And clothed her in apparel like the day.
And tho' Geraint could never take again
That comfort from their converse which he took
Before the Queen's fair name was breathed upon,   950
He rested well content that all was well.

Thence after tarrying for a space they rode,
And fifty knights rode with them to the shores
Of Severn, and they past to their own land.
And there he kept the justice of the King
So vigorously yet mildly that all hearts
Applauded, and the spiteful whisper died;
And being ever foremost in the chase,
And victor at the tilt and tournament,
They call'd him the great prince and man of men.   960
But Enid, whom her ladies loved to call
Enid the Fair, a grateful people named
Enid the Good; and in their halls arose
The cry of children, Enids and Geraints
Of times to be; nor did he doubt her more,
But rested in her fealty till he crown'd
A happy life with a fair death, and fell
Against the heathen of the Northern Sea
In battle, fighting for the blameless King.

BALIN AND BALAN

PELLAM the king, who held and lost with Lot
In that first war, and had his realm restored
But render'd tributary, fail'd of late
To send his tribute; wherefore Arthur call'd
His treasurer, one of many years, and spake:
'Go thou with him and him and bring it to us,
Lest we should set one truer on his throne.
Man's word is God in man.'

His baron said:
'We go, but harken: there be two strange knights
Who sit near Camelot at a fountain side   10
A mile beneath the forest, challenging
And overthrowing every knight who comes.
Wilt thou I undertake them as we pass,
And send them to thee?'

Arthur laugh'd upon him:
'Old friend, too old to be so young, depart,
Delay not thou for aught, but let them sit,
Until they find a lustier than themselves.'

So these departed. Early, one fair dawn,
The light-wing'd spirit of his youth return'd

On Arthur's heart; he arm'd himself and
went,   20
So coming to the fountain-side beheld
Balin and Balan sitting statue-like,
Brethren, to right and left the spring, that
down,
From underneath a plume of lady-fern,
Sang, and the sand danced at the bottom
of it.
And on the right of Balin Balin's horse
Was fast beside an alder, on the left
Of Balan Balan's near a poplar-tree.
'Fair sirs,' said Arthur, 'wherefore sit ye
here?'
Balin and Balan answer'd: 'For the sake
Of glory; we be mightier men than all   31
In Arthur's court; that also have we
proved,
For whatsoever knight against us came
Or I or he have easily overthrown.'
'I too,' said Arthur, 'am of Arthur's hall,
But rather proven in his Paynim wars
Than famous jousts; but see, or proven or
not,
Whether me likewise ye can overthrow.'
And Arthur lightly smote the brethren
down,   39
And lightly so return'd, and no man knew.

Then Balin rose, and Balan, and beside
The carolling water set themselves again,
And spake no word until the shadow
turn'd;
When from the fringe of coppice round
them burst
A spangled pursuivant, and crying, 'Sirs,
Rise, follow! ye be sent for by the King,'
They follow'd; whom when Arthur seeing
ask'd,
'Tell me your names; why sat ye by the
well?'
Balin the stillness of a minute broke
Saying, 'An unmelodious name to thee,   50
Balin, " the Savage " — that addition
thine —
My brother and my better, this man here,
Balan. I smote upon the naked skull
A thrall of thine in open hall; my hand
Was gauntleted, half slew him, for I heard
He had spoken evil of me; thy just wrath
Sent me a three-years' exile from thine
eyes.
I have not lived my life delightsomely;
For I that did that violence to thy thrall,
Had often wrought some fury on myself,

Saving for Balan. Those three kingless
years   61
Have past — were wormwood-bitter to me.
King,
Methought that if we sat beside the well,
And hurl'd to ground what knight soever
spurr'd
Against us, thou would'st take me gladlier
back,
And make, as ten times worthier to be
thine
Than twenty Balins, Balan knight. I have
said.
Not so — not all. A man of thine to-day
Abash'd us both, and brake my boast. Thy
will?'
Said Arthur: 'Thou hast ever spoken
truth;   70
Thy too fierce manhood would not let thee
lie.
Rise, my true knight. As children learn,
be thou
Wiser for falling! walk with me, and
move
To music with thine Order and the King.
Thy chair, a grief to all the brethren,
stands
Vacant, but thou retake it, mine again!'

Thereafter, when Sir Balin enter'd hall,
The lost one found was greeted as in
heaven
With joy that blazed itself in woodland
wealth   79
Of leaf, and gayest garlandage of flowers,
Along the walls and down the board; they
sat,
And cup clash'd cup; they drank, and some
one sang,
Sweet-voiced, a song of welcome, where-
upon
Their common shout in chorus, mounting,
made
Those banners of twelve battles overhead
Stir as they stirr'd of old, when Arthur's
host
Proclaim'd him victor and the day was won.

Then Balan added to their Order lived
A wealthier life than heretofore with these
And Balin, till their embassage return'd.   90

'Sir King,' they brought report, 'we
hardly found,
So bush'd about it is with gloom, the hall

Of him to whom ye sent us, Pellam, once
A Christless foe of thine as ever dash'd
Horse against horse; but seeing that thy
    realm
Hath prosper'd in the name of Christ, the
    King
Took, as in rival heat, to holy things,
And finds himself descended from the
    Saint
Arimathæan Joseph, him who first
Brought the great faith to Britain over
    seas.   100
He boasts his life as purer than thine
    own;
Eats scarce enow to keep his pulse a-beat;
Hath push'd aside his faithful wife, nor
    lets
Or dame or damsel enter at his gates
Lest he should be polluted. This gray
    king
Show'd us a shrine wherein were wonders
    — yea,
Rich arks with priceless bones of martyr-
    dom,
Thorns of the crown and shivers of the
    cross,
And therewithal, — for thus he told us, —
    brought   109
By holy Joseph hither, that same spear
Wherewith the Roman pierced the side of
    Christ.
He much amazed us; after, when we sought
The tribute, answer'd, "I have quite fore-
    gone
All matters of this world. Garlon, mine
    heir,
Of him demand it," which this Garlon
    gave
With much ado, railing at thine and thee.

'But when we left, in those deep woods
    we found
A knight of thine spear-stricken from be-
    hind,
Dead, whom we buried; more than one of
    us   119
Cried out on Garlon, but a woodman there
Reported of some demon in the woods
Was once a man, who, driven by evil
    tongues
From all his fellows, lived alone, and came
To learn black magic, and to hate his
    kind
With such a hate that when he died his
    soul

Became a fiend, which, as the man in life
Was wounded by blind tongues he saw not
    whence,
Strikes from behind. This woodman show'd
    the cave
From which he sallies and wherein he
    dwelt.
We saw the hoof - print of a horse, no
    more.'   130

    Then Arthur, 'Let who goes before me
        see
He do not fall behind me. Foully slain
And villainously! who will hunt for me
This demon of the woods?' Said Balan,
    'I!'
So claim'd the quest and rode away, but
    first,
Embracing Balin: 'Good my brother, hear!
Let not thy moods prevail when I am gone
Who used to lay them! hold them outer
    fiends,
Who leap at thee to tear thee; shake them
    aside,
Dreams ruling when wit sleeps! yea, but
    to dream   140
That any of these would wrong thee wrongs
    thyself.
Witness their flowery welcome. Bound are
    they
To speak no evil. Truly, save for fears,
My fears for thee, so rich a fellowship
Would make me wholly blest; thou one of
    them,
Be one indeed. Consider them, and all
Their bearing in their common bond of
    love,
No more of hatred than in heaven itself,
No more of jealousy than in Paradise.'

    So Balan warn'd, and went; Balin re-
        main'd,   150
Who — for but three brief moons had
    glanced away
From being knighted till he smote the
    thrall,
And faded from the presence into years
Of exile — now would strictlier set him-
    self
To learn what Arthur meant by courtesy,
Manhood, and knighthood; wherefore hov-
    er'd round
Lancelot, but when he mark'd his high
    sweet smile
In passing, and a transitory word

Make knight or churl or child or damsel
    seem
From being smiled at happier in them-
    selves —   160
Sigh'd, as a boy, lame - born beneath a
    height
That glooms his valley, sighs to see the
    peak
Sun-flush'd or touch at night the northern
    star;
For one from out his village lately climb'd
And brought report of azure lands and
    fair,
Far seen to left and right; and he himself
Hath hardly scaled with help a hundred
    feet
Up from the base. So Balin, marvelling
    oft
How far beyond him Lancelot seem'd to
    move,
Groan'd, and at times would mutter:
    'These be gifts,   170
Born with the blood, not learnable, divine,
Beyond *my* reach. Well had I foughten
    — well —
In those fierce wars, struck hard — and
    had I crown'd
With my slain self the heaps of whom I
    slew —
So — better! — But this worship of the
    Queen,
That honor too wherein she holds him —
    this,
This was the sunshine that hath given the
    man
A growth, a name that branches o'er the
    rest,
And strength against all odds, and what
    the King
So prizes — overprizes — gentleness.   180
Her likewise would I worship an I might.
I never can be close with her, as he
That brought her hither. Shall I pray the
    King
To let me bear some token of his Queen
Whereon to gaze, remembering her — for-
    get
My heats and violences? live afresh?
What if the Queen disdain'd to grant it!
    nay,
Being so stately-gentle, would she make
My darkness blackness? and with how
    sweet grace   189
She greeted my return! Bold will I be —
Some goodly cognizance of Guinevere,

In lieu of this rough beast upon my shield,
Langued gules, and tooth'd with grinning
    savagery.'

    And Arthur, when Sir Balin sought him,
    said,
'What wilt thou bear?' Balin was bold,
    and ask'd
To bear her own crown-royal upon shield,
Whereat she smiled and turn'd her to the
    King,
Who answer'd: 'Thou shalt put the crown
    to use.
The crown is but the shadow of the king,
And this a shadow's shadow, let him have
    it,   200
So this will help him of his violences!'
'No shadow,' said Sir Balin, 'O my Queen,
But light to me! no shadow, O my King,
But golden earnest of a gentler life!'

So Balin bare the crown, and all the
    knights
Approved him, and the Queen; and all the
    world
Made music, and he felt his being move
In music with his Order and the King.

The nightingale, full-toned in middle
    May,
Hath ever and anon a note so thin   210
It seems another voice in other groves;
Thus, after some quick burst of sudden
    wrath,
The music in him seem'd to change and
    grow
Faint and far-off.
         And once he saw the thrall
His passion half had gauntleted to death,
That causer of his banishment and shame,
Smile at him, as he deem'd, presumptu-
    ously.
His arm half rose to strike again, but fell;
The memory of that cognizance on shield
Weighted it down, but in himself he
    moan'd: 220

    'Too high this mount of Camelot for
    me;
These high-set courtesies are not for me.
Shall I not rather prove the worse for
    these?
Fierier and stormier from restraining, break
Into some madness even before the
    Queen?'

Thus, as a hearth lit in a mountain home,
And glancing on the window, when the gloom
Of twilight deepens round it, seems a flame
That rages in the woodland far below,
So when his moods were darken'd, court and king   230
And all the kindly warmth of Arthur's hall
Shadow'd an angry distance; yet he strove
To learn the graces of their Table, fought
Hard with himself, and seem'd at length in peace.

Then chanced, one morning, that Sir Balin sat
Close-bower'd in that garden nigh the hall.
A walk of roses ran from door to door,
A walk of lilies crost it to the bower;
And down that range of roses the great Queen
Came with slow steps, the morning on her face;   240
And all in shadow from the counter door
Sir Lancelot as to meet her, then at once,
As if he saw not, glanced aside, and paced
The long white walk of lilies toward the bower.
Follow'd the Queen; Sir Balin heard her ' Prince,
Art thou so little loyal to thy Queen
As pass without good morrow to thy Queen ? '
To whom Sir Lancelot with his eyes on earth,
' Fain would I still be loyal to the Queen.'
' Yea, so,' she said; ' but so to pass me by —   250
So loyal scarce is loyal to thyself,
Whom all men rate the king of courtesy.
Let be; ye stand, fair lord, as in a dream.'

Then Lancelot with his hand among the flowers:
' Yea — for a dream. Last night methought I saw
That maiden Saint who stands with lily in hand
In yonder shrine. All round her prest the dark,
And all the light upon her silver face
Flow'd from the spiritual lily that she held.
Lo ! these her emblems drew mine eyes — away;   260

For see, how perfect-pure ! As light a flush
As hardly tints the blossom of the quince
Would mar their charm of stainless maidenhood.'

' Sweeter to me,' she said, ' this garden rose
Deep-hued and many-folded ! sweeter still
The wild-wood hyacinth and the bloom of May !
Prince, we have ridden before among the flowers
In those fair days — not all as cool as these,
Tho' season-earlier. Art thou sad ? or sick ?
Our noble King will send thee his own leech —   270
Sick ? or for any matter anger'd at me ? '

Then Lancelot lifted his large eyes; they dwelt
Deep-tranced on hers, and could not fall. Her hue
Changed at his gaze; so turning side by side
They past, and Balin started from his bower.

' Queen ? subject ? but I see not what I see.
Damsel and lover ? hear not what I hear.
My father hath begotten me in his wrath.
I suffer from the things before me, know,
Learn nothing; am not worthy to be knight —   280
A churl, a clown ! ' and in him gloom on gloom
Deepen'd; he sharply caught his lance and shield,
Nor stay'd to crave permission of the King,
But mad for strange adventure, dash'd away.

He took the selfsame track as Balan, saw
The fountain where they sat together, sigh'd,
' Was I not better there with him ? ' and rode
The skyless woods, but under open blue
Came on the hoar - head woodman at a bough
Wearily hewing. ' Churl, thine axe ! ' he cried,   290

Descended, and disjointed it at a blow;
To whom the woodman utter'd wonder-
   ingly,
'Lord, thou couldst lay the devil of these
   woods
If arm of flesh could lay him!' Balin cried,
'Him, or the viler devil who plays his part;
To lay that devil would lay the devil in me.'
'Nay,' said the churl, 'our devil is a truth,
I saw the flash of him but yester-even.
And some *do* say that our Sir Garlon too
Hath learn'd black magic, and to ride un-
   seen.   300
Look to the cave.' But Balin answer'd
   him,
'Old fabler, these be fancies of the churl;
Look to thy woodcraft,' and so leaving him,
Now with slack rein and careless of him-
   self,
Now with dug spur and raving at himself,
Now with droopt brow down the long glades
   he rode;
So mark'd not on his right a cavern-chasm
Yawn over darkness, where, nor far within,
The whole day died, but, dying, gleam'd on
   rocks
Roof-pendent, sharp; and others from the
   floor,   310
Tusklike, arising, made that mouth of night
Whereout the demon issued up from hell.
He mark'd not this, but, blind and deaf to all
Save that chain'd rage which ever yelpt
   within,
Past eastward from the falling sun. At
   once
He felt the hollow-beaten mosses thud
And tremble, and then the shadow of a
   spear,
Shot from behind him, ran along the
   ground.
Sideways he started from the path, and
   saw,   319
With pointed lance as if to pierce, a shape,
A light of armor by him flash, and pass
And vanish in the woods; and follow'd this,
But all so blind in rage that unawares
He burst his lance against a forest bough,
Dishorsed himself, and rose again, and fled
Far, till the castle of a king, the hall
Of Pellam, lichen-bearded, grayly draped
With streaming grass, appear'd, low-built
   but strong;
The ruinous donjon as a knoll of moss,
The battlement overtopt with ivy-tods, 330
A home of bats, in every tower an owl.

Then spake the men of Pellam crying,
   'Lord,
Why wear ye this crown - royal upon
   shield?'
Said Balin, 'For the fairest and the best
Of ladies living gave me this to bear.'
So stall'd his horse, and strode across the
   court,
But found the greetings both of knight and
   king
Faint in the low dark hall of banquet.
   Leaves
Laid their green faces flat against the
   panes,
Sprays grated, and the canker'd boughs
   without   340
Whined in the wood; for all was hush'd
   within,
Till when at feast Sir Garlon likewise
   ask'd,
'Why wear ye that crown-royal?.' Balin
   said,
'The Queen we worship, Lancelot, I, and
   all,
As fairest, best, and purest, granted me
To bear it!' Such a sound — for Arthur's
   knights
Were hated strangers in the hall — as
   makes
The white swan-mother, sitting, when she
   hears
A strange knee rustle thro' her secret
   reeds,
Made Garlon, hissing; then he sourly
   smiled: 350
'Fairest I grant her — I have seen; but
   best,
Best, purest? *thou* from Arthur's hall, and
   yet
So simple! hast thou eyes, or if, are these
So far besotted that they fail to see
This fair wife - worship cloaks a secret
   shame?
Truly, ye men of Arthur be but babes.'

A goblet on the board by Balin, boss'd
With holy Joseph's legend, on his right
Stood, all of massiest bronze. One side had
   sea
And ship and sail and angels blowing on
   it;   360
And one was rough with wattling, and the
   walls
Of that low church he built at Glastonbury.
This Balin graspt, but while in act to hurl,

Thro' memory of that token on the shield
Relax'd his hold. 'I will be gentle,' he
    thought,
'And passing gentle;' caught his hand
    away,
Then fiercely to Sir Garlon: 'Eyes have I
That saw to-day the shadow of a spear,
Shot from behind me, run along the ground;
Eyes too that long have watch'd how Lance-
    lot draws   370
From homage to the best and purest,
    might,
Name, manhood, and a grace, but scantly
    thine
Who, sitting in thine own hall, canst en-
    dure
To mouth so huge a foulness — to thy guest,
Me, me of Arthur's Table. Felon talk!
Let be! no more!'

                    But not the less by night
The scorn of Garlon, poisoning all his rest,
Stung him in dreams. At length, and dim
    thro' leaves
Blinkt the white morn, sprays grated, and
    old boughs
Whined in the wood. He rose, descended,
    met   380
The scorner in the castle court, and fain,
For hate and loathing, would have past
    him by;
But when Sir Garlon utter'd mocking-wise,
'What, wear ye still that same crown-
    scandalous?'
His countenance blacken'd, and his fore-
    head veins
Bloated and branch'd; and tearing out of
    sheath
The brand, Sir Balin with a fiery, 'Ha!
So thou be shadow, here I make thee
    ghost,'
Hard upon helm smote him, and the blade
    flew
Splintering in six, and clinkt upon the
    stones.   390
Then Garlon, reeling slowly backward, fell,
And Balin by the banneret of his helm
Dragg'd him, and struck, but from the
    castle a cry
Sounded across the court, and — men-at-
    arms,
A score with pointed lances, making at
    him —
He dash'd the pummel at the foremost
    face,

Beneath a low door dipt, and made his feet
Wings thro' a glimmering gallery, till he
    mark'd
The portal of King Pellam's chapel wide
And inward to the wall; he stept behind·
Thence in a moment heard them pass like
    wolves   401
Howling; but while he stared about the
    shrine,
In which he scarce could spy the Christ
    for Saints,
Beheld before a golden altar lie
The longest lance his eyes had ever seen,
Point-painted red; and seizing thereupon
Push'd thro' an open casement down, lean'd
    on it,
Leapt in a semicircle, and lit on earth;
Then hand at ear, and harkening from
    what side
The blindfold rummage buried in the walls
Might echo, ran the counter path, and
    found   411
His charger, mounted on him and away.
An arrow whizz'd to the right, one to the
    left,
One overhead; and Pellam's feeble cry,
'Stay, stay him! he defileth heavenly
    things
With earthly uses!' made him quickly
    dive
Beneath the boughs, and race thro' many a
    mile
Of dense and open, till his goodly horse,
Arising wearily at a fallen oak,
Stumbled headlong, and cast him face to
    ground.   420

    Half-wroth he had not ended, but all
        glad,
Knightlike, to find his charger yet un-
    lamed,
Sir Balin drew the shield from off his neck,
Stared at the priceless cognizance, and
    thought,
'I have shamed thee so that now thou
    shamest me,
Thee will I bear no more,' high on a branch
Hung it, and turn'd aside into the woods,
And there in gloom cast himself all along,
Moaning, 'My violences, my violences!'

    But now the wholesome music of the
        wood   430
Was dumb'd by one from out the hall of
    Mark,

A damsel-errant, warbling, as she rode
The woodland alleys, Vivien, with her
    squire.

'The fire of heaven has kill'd the barren
    cold,
And kindled all the plain and all the wold.
The new leaf ever pushes off the old.
The fire of heaven is not the flame of hell.

'Old priest, who mumble 'worship in your
    quire —
Old monk and nun, ye scorn the world's desire,
Yet in your frosty cells ye feel the fire!   440
The fire of heaven is not the flame of hell.

'The fire of heaven is on the dusty ways.
The wayside blossoms open to the blaze.
The whole wood-world is one full peal of
    praise.
The fire of heaven is not the flame of hell.

'The fire of heaven is lord of all things
    good,
And starve not thou this fire within thy blood,
But follow Vivien thro' the fiery flood!
The fire of heaven is not the flame of hell!'

Then turning to her squire, 'This fire of
    heaven,   450
This old sun-worship, boy, will rise again,
And beat the Cross to earth, and break the
    King
And all his Table.'

                    Then they reach'd a glade,
Where under one long lane of cloudless air
Before another wood, the royal crown
Sparkled, and swaying upon a restless elm
Drew the vague glance of Vivien and her
    squire.
Amazed were these; 'Lo there,' she cried —
    'a crown —
Borne by some high lord-prince of Arthur's
    hall,
And there a horse! the rider? where is
    he?   460
See, yonder lies one dead within the wood.
Not dead; he stirs!— but sleeping. I will
    speak.
Hail, royal knight, we break on thy sweet
    rest,
Not, doubtless, all unearn'd by noble deeds.
But bounden art thou, if from Arthur's
    hall,
To help the weak. Behold, I fly from
    shame,

A lustful king, who sought to win my love
Thro' evil ways. The knight with whom I
    rode
Hath suffer'd misadventure, and my squire
Hath in him small defence; but thou, Sir
    Prince,   470
Wilt surely guide me to the warrior King,
Arthur the blameless, pure as any maid,
To get me shelter for my maidenhood.
I charge thee by that crown upon thy
    shield,
And by the great Queen's name, arise and
    hence.'

And Balin rose: 'Thither no more! nor
    prince
Nor knight am I, but one that hath de-
    famed
The cognizance she gave me. Here I dwell
Savage among the savage woods, here
    die —
Die — let the wolves' black maws ensepul-
    chre   480
Their brother beast, whose anger was his
    lord!
O me, that such a name as Guinevere's,
Which our high Lancelot hath so lifted up,
And been thereby uplifted, should thro' me,
My violence, and my villainy, come to
    shame!'

Thereat she suddenly laugh'd and shrill,
    anon
Sigh'd all as suddenly. Said Balin to her:
'Is this thy courtesy — to mock me, ha?
Hence, for I will not with thee.' Again
    she sigh'd:
'Pardon, sweet lord! we maidens often
    laugh   490
When sick at heart, when rather we should
    weep.
I knew thee wrong'd. I brake upon thy
    rest,
And now full loth am I to break thy dream,
But thou art man, and canst abide a truth,
Tho' bitter. Hither, boy — and mark me
    well.
Dost thou remember at Caerleon once —
A year ago — nay, then I love thee not —
Ay, thou rememberest well — one summer
    dawn —
By the great tower — Caerleon upon Usk —
Nay, truly we were hidden — this fair lord,
The flower of all their vestal knighthood,
    knelt   501

In amorous homage — knelt — what else ?
— O, ay,
Knelt, and drew down from out his night-
black hair
And mumbled that white hand whose ring'd
caress
Had wander'd from her own King's golden
head,
And lost itself in darkness, till she cried —
I thought the great tower would crash down
on both —
" Rise, my sweet King, and kiss me on the
lips,
Thou art my King." This lad, whose
lightest word
Is mere white truth in simple nakedness,
Saw them embrace; he reddens, cannot
speak,   511
So bashful, he ! but all the maiden Saints,
The deathless mother-maidenhood of hea-
ven,
Cry out upon her. Up then, ride with me !
Talk not of shame ! thou canst not, an
thou wouldst,
Do these more shame than these have done
themselves.'

She lied with ease; but horror-stricken
he,
Remembering that dark bower at Camelot,
Breathed in a dismal whisper, 'It is truth.'

Sunnily she smiled: ' And even in this
lone wood,   520
Sweet lord, ye do right well to whisper this.
Fools prate, and perish traitors. Woods
have tongues,
As walls have ears; but thou shalt go with
me,
And we will speak at first exceeding low.
Meet is it the good King be not deceived.
See now, I set thee high on vantage ground,
From whence to watch the time, and eagle-
like
Stoop at thy will on Lancelot and the
Queen.'

She ceased; his evil spirit upon him
leapt,
He ground his teeth together, sprang with
a yell,   530
Tore from the branch and cast on earth the
shield,
Drove his mail'd heel athwart the royal
crown,

Stampt all into defacement, hurl'd it from
him
Among the forest weeds, and cursed the
tale,
The told-of, and the teller.

                                That weird yell,
Unearthlier than all shriek of bird or beast,
Thrill'd thro' the woods; and Balan lurk-
ing there —
His quest was unaccomplish'd — heard and
thought
' The scream of that wood-devil I came to
quell !'
Then nearing: 'Lo ! he hath slain some
brother-knight,   540
And tramples on the goodly shield to show
His loathing of our Order and the Queen.
My quest, meseems, is here. Or devil or
man,
Guard thou thine head.' Sir Balin spake
not word,
But snatch'd a sudden buckler from the
squire,
And vaulted on his horse, and so they
crash'd
In onset, and King Pellam's holy spear,
Reputed to be red with sinless blood,
Redden'd at once with sinful, for the point
Across the maiden shield of Balan prick'd
The hauberk to the flesh; and Balin's
horse   551
Was wearied to the death, and, when they
clash'd,
Rolling back upon Balin, crush'd the man
Inward, and either fell and swoon'd away.

Then to her squire mutter'd the damsel:
' Fools !
This fellow hath wrought some foulness
with his Queen;
Else never had he borne her crown, nor
raved
And thus foam'd over at a rival name.
But thou, Sir Chick, that scarce hast
broken shell,
Art yet half - yolk, not even come to
down —   560
Who never sawest Caerleon upon Usk —
And yet hast often pleaded for my love —
See what I see, be thou where I have been,
Or else, Sir Chick — dismount and loose
their casques;
I fain would know what manner of men
they be.'

And when the squire had loosed them,
    'Goodly ! — look !
They might have cropt the myriad flower
    of May,
And butt each other here, like brainless
    bulls,
Dead for one heifer !'

                Then the gentle squire:
'I hold them happy, so they died for love;
And, Vivien, tho' ye beat me like your
    dog,   571
I too could die, as now I live, for thee.'

    'Live on, Sir Boy,' she cried; 'I better
        prize
The living dog than the dead lion. Away !
I cannot brook to gaze upon the dead.'
Then leapt her palfrey o'er the fallen
    oak,
And bounding forward, 'Leave them to the
    wolves.'

    But when their foreheads felt the cooling
        air,
Balin first woke, and seeing that true face,
Familiar up from cradle-time, so wan,   580
Crawl'd slowly with low moans to where he
    lay,
And on his dying brother cast himself
Dying; and *he* lifted faint eyes; he felt
One near him; all at once they found the
    world,
Staring wild-wide; then with a childlike
    wail,
And drawing down the dim disastrous brow
That o'er him hung, he kiss'd it, moan'd,
    and spake:

'O Balin, Balin, I that fain had died
To save thy life, have brought thee to thy
    death.
Why had ye not the shield I knew ? and
    why   590
Trampled ye thus on that which bare the
    crown ?'

    Then Balin told him brokenly and in
        gasps
All that had chanced, and Balan moan'd
    again:

'Brother, I dwelt a day in Pellam's hall;
This Garlon mock'd me, but I heeded not.
And one said, "Eat in peace ! a liar is he,

And hates thee for the tribute !" This
    good knight
Told me that twice a wanton damsel came,
And sought for Garlon at the castle-gates,
Whom Pellam drove away with holy heat.
I well believe this damsel, and the one   601
Who stood beside thee even now, the same.
"She dwells among the woods," he said,
    "and meets
And dallies with him in the Mouth of
    Hell."
Foul are their lives, foul are their lips;
    they lied.
Pure as our own true mother is our Queen.'

    'O brother,' answer'd Balin, 'woe is me !
My madness all thy life has been thy doom,
Thy curse, and darken'd all thy day; and
    now
The night has come. I scarce can see thee
    now.   610
Good night ! for we shall never bid again
Good morrow — Dark my doom was here,
    and dark
It will be there. I see thee now no more.
I would not mine again should darken
    thine;
Good night, true brother.'

                Balan answer'd low,
'Good night, true brother, here ! good mor-
    row there !
We two were born together, and we die
Together by one doom:' and while he spoke
Closed his death-drowsing eyes, and slept
    the sleep   619
With Balin, either lock'd in either's arm.

MERLIN AND VIVIEN

A STORM was coming, but the winds were
    still,
And in the wild woods of Broceliande,
Before an oak, so hollow, huge, and old
It look'd a tower of ivied masonwork,
At Merlin's feet the wily Vivien lay.

    For he that always bare in bitter grudge
The slights of Arthur and his Table, Mark
The Cornish King, had heard a wandering
    voice,
A minstrel of Caerleon by strong storm
Blown into shelter at Tintagil, say   10
That out of naked knight-like purity

Sir Lancelot worshipt no unmarried girl,
But the great Queen herself, fought in her
 name,
Sware by her — vows like theirs that high
 in heaven
Love most, but neither marry nor are given
In marriage, angels of our Lord's report.

He ceased, and then — for Vivien
 sweetly said —
She sat beside the banquet nearest Mark, —
'And is the fair example follow'd, sir,
In Arthur's household?' — answer'd inno-
 cently: 20

'Ay, by some few — ay, truly — youths
 that hold
It more beseems the perfect virgin knight
To worship woman as true wife beyond
All hopes of gaining, than as maiden girl.
They place their pride in Lancelot and the
 Queen.
So passionate for an utter purity
Beyond the limit of their bond are these,
For Arthur bound them not to singleness.
Brave hearts and clean! and yet — God
 guide them! — young.'

Then Mark was half in heart to hurl his
 cup   30
Straight at the speaker, but forbore. He
 rose
To leave the hall, and, Vivien following him,
Turn'd to her: 'Here are snakes within the
 grass;
And you methinks, O Vivien, save ye fear
The monkish manhood, and the mask of
 pure
Worn by this court, can stir them till they
 sting.'

And Vivien answer'd, smiling scornfully:
'Why fear? because that foster'd at thy
 court
I savor of thy — virtues? fear them? no,
As love, if love be perfect, casts out
 fear,   40
So hate, if hate be perfect, casts out fear.
My father died in battle against the King,
My mother on his corpse in open field;
She bore me there, for born from death
 was I
Among the dead and sown upon the wind —
And then on thee! and shown the truth
 betimes,

That old true filth, and bottom of the well,
Where Truth is hidden. Gracious lessons
 thine,
And maxims of the mud! "This Arthur
 pure!
Great Nature thro' the flesh herself hath
 made
Gives him the lie! There is no being pure,   50
My cherub; saith not Holy Writ the
 same?" —
If I were Arthur, I would have thy blood.
Thy blessing, stainless King! I bring thee
 back,
When I have ferreted out their burrow-
 ings,
The hearts of all this Order in mine
 hand —
Ay — so that fate and craft and folly
 close,
Perchance, one curl of Arthur's golden
 beard.
To me this narrow grizzled fork of thine
Is cleaner-fashion'd — Well, I loved thee
 first;   60
That warps the wit.'

        Loud laugh'd the graceless Mark.
But Vivien, into Camelot stealing, lodged
Low in the city, and on a festal day
When Guinevere was crossing the great
 hall
Cast herself down, knelt to the Queen, and
 wail'd.

'Why kneel ye there? What evil have
 ye wrought?
Rise!' and the damsel bidden rise arose
And stood with folded hands and down-
 ward eyes
Of glancing corner and all meekly said:
'None wrought, but suffer'd much, an or-
 phan maid!   70
My father died in battle for thy King,
My mother on his corpse — in open field,
The sad sea-sounding wastes of Lyon-
 nesse —
Poor wretch — no friend! — and now by
 Mark the king,
For that small charm of feature mine, pur-
 sued —
If any such be mine — I fly to thee.
Save, save me thou! Woman of women
 — thine
The wreath of beauty, thine the crown of
 power,

Be thine the balm of pity, O heaven's own
    white
Earth - angel, stainless bride of stainless
    King — 80
Help, for he follows ! take me to thyself !
O yield me shelter for mine innocency
Among thy maidens !'

                    Here her slow sweet eyes
Fear-tremulous, but humbly hopeful, rose
Fixt on her hearer's, while the Queen who
    stood
All glittering like May sunshine on May
    leaves
In green and gold, and plumed with green
    replied:
'Peace, child ! of over-praise and over-
    blame
We choose the last. Our noble Arthur,
    him
Ye scarce can overpraise, will hear and
    know. 90
Nay — we believe all evil of thy Mark —
Well, we shall test thee farther; but this
    hour
We ride a-hawking with Sir Lancelot.
He hath given us a fair falcon which he
    train'd;
We go to prove it. Bide ye here the
    while.'

    She past; and Vivien murmur'd after,
    'Go !
I bide the while.' Then thro' the portal-
    arch
Peering askance, and muttering broken-
    wise,
As one that labors with an evil dream,
Beheld the Queen and Lancelot get to
    horse. 100

'Is that the Lancelot ? goodly — ay, but
    gaunt;
Courteous — amends for gauntness — takes
    her hand —
That glance of theirs, but for the street,
    had been
A clinging kiss — how hand lingers in
    hand !
Let go at last ! — they ride away — to
    hawk
For waterfowl. Royaller game is mine.
For such a supersensual sensual bond
As that gray cricket chirpt of at our
    hearth —

Touch flax with flame — a glance will serve
    — the liars !
Ah little rat that borest in the dyke 110
Thy hole by night to let the boundless deep
Down upon far-off cities while they dance —
Or dream — of thee they dream'd not —
    nor of me
These — ay, but each of either; ride, and
    dream
The mortal dream that never yet was
    mine —
Ride, ride and dream until ye wake — to
    me !
Then, narrow court and lubber King, fare-
    well !
For Lancelot will be gracious to the rat,
And our wise Queen, if knowing that I
    know,
Will hate, loathe, fear — but honor me the
    more.' 120

    Yet while they rode together down the
    plain,
Their talk was all of training, terms of art,
Diet and seeling, jesses, leash and lure.
'She is too noble,' he said, 'to check at
    pies,
Nor will she rake: there is no baseness in
    her.'
Here when the Queen demanded as by
    chance,
'Know ye the stranger woman ?' 'Let her
    be,'
Said Lancelot, and unhooded casting off
The goodly falcon free; she tower'd; her
    bells,
Tone under tone, shrill'd; and they lifted
    up 130
Their eager faces, wondering at the
    strength,
Boldness, and royal knighthood of the bird,
Who pounced her quarry and slew it.
    Many a time
As once — of old — among the flowers —
    they rode.

But Vivien half-forgotten of the Queen
Among her damsels broidering sat, heard,
    watch'd,
And whisper'd. Thro' the peaceful court
    she crept
And whisper'd; then, as Arthur in the
    highest
Leaven'd the world, so Vivien in the low-
    est,

Arriving at a time of golden rest,   140
And sowing one ill hint from ear to ear,
While all the heathen lay at Arthur's feet,
And no quest came, but all was joust and play,
Leaven'd his hall. They heard and let her be.

Thereafter, as an enemy that has left
Death in the living waters and withdrawn,
The wily Vivien stole from Arthur's court.

She hated all the knights, and heard in thought
Their lavish comment when her name was named.   149
For once, when Arthur walking all alone,
Vext at a rumor issued from herself
Of some corruption crept among his knights,
Had met her, Vivien, being greeted fair,
Would fain have wrought upon his cloudy mood
With reverent eyes mock - loyal, shaken voice,
And flutter'd adoration, and at last
With dark sweet hints of some who prized him more
Than who should prize him most; at which the King
Had gazed upon her blankly and gone by.
But one had watch'd, and had not held his peace;   160
It made the laughter of an afternoon
That Vivien should attempt the blameless King.
And after that, she set herself to gain
Him, the most famous man of all those times,
Merlin, who knew the range of all their arts,
Had built the King his havens, ships, and halls,
Was also bard, and knew the starry heavens,
The people call'd him wizard; whom at first
She play'd about with slight and sprightly talk,
And vivid smiles, and faintly - venom'd points   170
Of slander, glancing here and grazing there;
And yielding to his kindlier moods, the seer

Would watch her at her petulance and play,
Even when they seem'd unlovable, and laugh
As those that watch a kitten. Thus he grew
Tolerant of what he half disdain'd, and she,
Perceiving that she was but half disdain'd,
Began to break her sports with graver fits,
Turn red or pale, would often when they met
Sigh fully, or all-silent gaze upon him   180
With such a fixt devotion that the old man,
Tho' doubtful, felt the flattery, and at times
Would flatter his own wish in age for love,
And half believe her true; for thus at times
He waver'd, but that other clung to him,
Fixt in her will, and so the seasons went.

Then fell on Merlin a great melancholy;
He walk'd with dreams and darkness, and he found
A doom that ever poised itself to fall,
An ever-moaning battle in the mist,   190
World-war of dying flesh against the life,
Death in all life and lying in all love,
The meanest having power upon the highest,
And the high purpose broken by the worm.

So leaving Arthur's court he gain'd the beach,
There found a little boat and stept into it;
And Vivien follow'd; but he mark'd her not.
She took the helm and he the sail; the boat
Drave with a sudden wind across the deeps,
And, touching Breton sands, they disembark'd.   200
And then she follow'd Merlin all the way,
Even to the wild woods of Broceliande.
For Merlin once had told her of a charm,
The which if any wrought on any one
With woven paces and with waving arms,
The man so wrought on ever seem'd to lie
Closed in the four walls of a hollow tower,
From which was no escape for evermore;
And none could find that man for evermore,
Nor could he see but him who wrought the charm   210

Coming and going, and he lay as dead
And lost to life and use and name and
    fame.
And Vivien ever sought to work the charm
Upon the great enchanter of the time,
As fancying that her glory would be great
According to his greatness whom she
    quench'd.

    There lay she all her length and kiss'd his
    feet,
As if in deepest reverence and in love.
A twist of gold was round her hair; a robe
Of samite without price, that more ex-
    prest   220
Than hid her, clung about her lissome
    limbs,
In color like the satin-shining palm
On sallows in the windy gleams of March.
And while she kiss'd them, crying, 'Tram-
    ple me,
Dear feet, that I have follow'd thro' the
    world,
And I will pay you worship; tread me
    down
And I will kiss you for it;' he was mute.
So dark a forethought roll'd about his
    brain,
As on a dull day in an ocean cave
The blind wave feeling round his long sea-
    hall   230
In silence; wherefore, when she lifted up
A face of sad appeal, and spake and said,
'O Merlin, do ye love me?' and again,
'O Merlin, do ye love me?' and once
    more,
'Great Master, do ye love me?' he was
    mute.
And lissome Vivien, holding by his heel,
Writhed toward him, slided up his knee
    and sat,
Behind his ankle twined her hollow feet
Together, curved an arm about his neck,
Clung like a snake; and letting her left
    hand   240
Droop from his mighty shoulder, as a leaf,
Made with her right a comb of pearl to
    part
The lists of such a beard as youth gone out
Had left in ashes. Then he spoke and said,
Not looking at her, 'Who are wise in love
Love most, say least,' and Vivien answer'd
    quick:
'I saw the little elf-god eyeless once
In Arthur's arras hall at Camelot;

But neither eyes nor tongue — O stupid
    child!
Yet you are wise who say it; let me think
Silence is wisdom. I am silent then,   251
And ask no kiss;' then adding all at once,
'And lo, I clothe myself with wisdom,'
    drew
The vast and shaggy mantle of his beard
Across her neck and bosom to her knee,
And call'd herself a gilded summer fly
Caught in a great old tyrant spider's web,
Who meant to eat her up in that wild
    wood
Without one word. So Vivien call'd her-
    self,
But rather seem'd a lovely baleful star   260
Veil'd in gray vapor; till he sadly smiled:
'To what request for what strange boon,'
    he said,
'Are these your pretty tricks and fooleries,
O Vivien, the preamble? yet my thanks,
For these have broken up my melancholy.'

    And Vivien answer'd smiling saucily:
'What, O my Master, have ye found your
    voice?
I bid the stranger welcome. Thanks at
    last!
But yesterday you never open'd lip,   269
Except indeed to drink. No cup had we;
In mine own lady palms I cull'd the spring
That gather'd trickling dropwise from the
    cleft,
And made a pretty cup of both my hands
And offer'd you it kneeling. Then you
    drank
And knew no more, nor gave me one poor
    word;
O, no more thanks than might a goat have
    given
With no more sign of reverence than a
    beard.
And when we halted at that other well,
And I was faint to swooning, and you
    lay
Foot-gilt with all the blossom-dust of those
Deep meadows we had traversed, did you
    know   281
That Vivien bathed your feet before her
    own?
And yet no thanks; and all thro' this wild
    wood
And all this morning when I fondled you.
Boon, ay, there was a boon, one not so
    strange —

How had I wrong'd you ? surely ye are
  wise,
But such a silence is more wise than kind.'

And Merlin lock'd his hand in hers and
  said:
'O, did ye never lie upon the shore,
And watch the curl'd white of the coming
  wave   290
Glass'd in the slippery sand before it
  breaks ?
Even such a wave, but not so pleasurable,
Dark in the glass of some presageful mood,
Had I for three days seen, ready to fall.
And then I rose and fled from Arthur's
  court
To break the mood.   You follow'd me un-
  ask'd;
And when I look'd, and saw you following
  still,
My mind involved yourself the nearest
  thing
In that mind-mist — for shall I tell you
  truth ?
You seem'd that wave about to break upon
  me   300
And sweep me from my hold upon the
  world,
My use and name and fame. Your pardon,
  child.
Your pretty sports have brighten'd all
  again.
And ask your boon, for boon I owe you
  thrice,
Once for wrong done you by confusion,
  next
For thanks it seems till now neglected, last
For these your dainty gambols; wherefore
  ask,
And take this boon so strange and not so
  strange.'

And Vivien answer'd smiling mourn-
  fully:
'O, not so strange as my long asking it, 310
Not yet so strange as you yourself are
  strange,
Nor half so strange as that dark mood of
  yours.
I ever fear'd ye were not wholly mine;
And see, yourself have own'd ye did me
  wrong.
The people call you prophet; let it be;
But not of those that can expound them-
  selves.

Take Vivien for expounder; she will call
That three-days-long presageful gloom of
  yours
No presage, but the same mistrustful mood
That makes you seem less noble than your-
  self,   320
Whenever I have ask'd this very boon,
Now ask'd again; for see you not, dear
  love,
That such a mood as that which lately
  gloom'd
Your fancy when ye saw me following
  you
Must make me fear still more you are not
  mine,
Must make me yearn still more to prove
  you mine,
And make me wish still more to learn this
  charm
Of woven paces and of waving hands,
As proof of trust. O Merlin, teach it me !
The charm so taught will charm us both to
  rest.   330
For, grant me some slight power upon your
  fate,
I, feeling that you felt me worthy trust,
Should rest and let you rest, knowing you
  mine.
And therefore be as great as ye are named,
Not muffled round with selfish reticence.
How hard you look and how denyingly !
O, if you think this wickedness in me,
That I should prove it on you unawares,
That makes me passing wrathful; then our
  bond
Had best be loosed for ever; but think or
  not,   340
By Heaven that hears, I tell you the clean
  truth,
As clean as blood of babes, as white as
  milk !
O Merlin, may this earth, if ever I,
If these unwitty wandering wits of mine,
Even in the jumbled rubbish of a dream,
Have tript on such conjectural treachery —
May this hard earth cleave to the nadir
  hell
Down, down, and close again and nip me
  flat,
If I be such a traitress !   Yield my boon,
Till which I scarce can yield you all I am;
And grant my re-reiterated wish,   351
The great proof of your love; because I
  think,
However wise, ye hardly know me yet.'

And Merlin loosed his hand from hers
    and said:
'I never was less wise, however wise,
Too curious Vivien, tho' you talk of trust,
Than when I told you first of such a charm.
Yea, if ye talk of trust I tell you this,
Too much I trusted when I told you that,
And stirr'd this vice in you which ruin'd
    man   360
Thro' woman the first hour; for howsoe'er
In children a great curiousness be well,
Who have to learn themselves and all the
    world,
In you, that are no child, for still I find
Your face is practised when I spell the
    lines,
I call it, — well, I will not call it vice;
But since you name yourself the summer
    fly,
I well could wish a cobweb for the gnat
That settles beaten back, and beaten back
Settles, till one could yield for weariness. 370
But since I will not yield to give you power
Upon my life and use and name and fame,
Why will ye never ask some other boon?
Yea, by God's rood, I trusted you too
    much!'

And Vivien, like the tenderest-hearted
    maid
That ever bided tryst at village stile,
Made answer, either eyelid wet with tears:
'Nay, Master, be not wrathful with your
    maid;
Caress her, let her feel herself forgiven
Who feels no heart to ask another boon. 380
I think ye hardly know the tender rhyme
Of "trust me not at all or all in all."
I heard the great Sir Lancelot sing it once,
And it shall answer for me.   Listen to it.

  '"In love, if love be love, if love be ours,
Faith and unfaith can ne'er be equal powers:
Unfaith in aught is want of faith in all.

  '"It is the little rift within the lute,
That by and by will make the music mute,
And ever widening slowly silence all.   390

  '"The little rift within the lover's lute,
Or little pitted speck in garner'd fruit,
That rotting inward slowly moulders all.

  '"It is not worth the keeping; let it go:
But shall it? answer, darling, answer, no.
And trust me not at all or all in all."

'O master, do ye love my tender rhyme?'

  And Merlin look'd and half believed her
    true,
So tender. was her voice, so fair her face,
So sweetly gleam'd her eyes behind her
    tears   400
Like sunlight on the plain behind a shower;
And yet he answer'd half indignantly:

  'Far other was the song that once I heard
By this huge oak, sung nearly where we
    sit;
For here we met, some ten or twelve of us,
To chase a creature that was current then
In these wild woods, the hart with golden
    horns.
It was the time when first the question
    rose
About the founding of a Table Round,
That was to be, for love of God and men 410
And noble deeds, the flower of all the
    world;
And each incited each to noble deeds.
And while we waited, one, the youngest
    of us,
We could not keep him silent, out he
    flash'd,
And into such a song, such fire for fame,
Such trumpet-blowings in it, coming down
To such a stern and iron-clashing close,
That when he stopt we long'd to hurl to-
    gether,
And should have done it, but the beauteous
    beast   419
Scared by the noise upstarted at our feet,
And like a silver shadow slipt away
Thro' the dim land.   And all day long we
    rode
Thro' the dim land against a rushing wind,
That glorious roundel echoing in our ears,
And chased the flashes of his golden horns
Until they vanish'd by the fairy well
That laughs at iron — as our warriors
    did —
Where children cast their pins and nails,
    and cry,
"Laugh, little well!" but touch it with a
    sword,
It buzzes fiercely round the point; and
    there   430
We lost him — such a noble song was that.
But, Vivien, when you sang me that sweet
    rhyme,
I felt as tho' you knew this cursed charm,

Were proving it on me, and that I lay
And felt them slowly ebbing, name and
    fame.'

And Vivien answer'd smiling mournfully:
'O, mine have ebb'd away for evermore,
And all thro' following you to this wild
    wood,
Because I saw you sad, to comfort you.
Lo now, what hearts have men! they never
    mount   440
As high as woman in her selfless mood.
And touching fame, howe'er ye scorn my
    song,
Take one verse more — the lady speaks it
    — this:

    ' " My name, once mine, now thine, is close-
        lier mine,
For fame, could fame be mine, that fame were
    thine,
And shame, could shame be thine, that shame
    were mine.
So trust me not at all or all in all."

'Says she not well? and there is more
    — this rhyme
Is like the fair pearl-necklace of the Queen,
That burst in dancing and the pearls were
    spilt;   450
Some lost, some stolen, some as relics
    kept;
But nevermore the same two sister pearls
Ran down the silken thread to kiss each
    other
On her white neck — so is it with this
    rhyme.
It lives dispersedly in many hands,
And every minstrel sings it differently;
Yet is there one true line, the pearl of
    pearls:
"Man dreams of fame while woman wakes
    to love."
Yea! love, tho' love were of the grossest,
    carves
A portion from the solid present, eats   460
And uses, careless of the rest; but fame,
The fame that follows death is nothing to
    us;
And what is fame in life but half-disfame
And counterchanged with darkness? ye
    yourself
Know well that envy calls you devil's son,
And since ye seem the master of all art,
They fain would make you master of all
    vice.'

And Merlin lock'd his hand in hers and
    said:
'I once was looking for a magic weed,
And found a fair young squire who sat
    alone,   470
Had carved himself a knightly shield of
    wood,
And then was painting on it fancied arms,
Azure, an eagle rising or, the sun
In dexter chief; the scroll, "I follow
    fame."
And speaking not, but leaning over him,
I took his brush and blotted out the bird,
And made a gardener putting in a graff,
With this for motto, "Rather use than
    fame."
You should have seen him blush; but after-
    wards
He made a stalwart knight. O Vivien, 480
For you, methinks you think you love me
    well;
For me, I love you somewhat. Rest; and
    Love
Should have some rest and pleasure in him-
    self,
Not ever be too curious for a boon,
Too prurient for a proof against the grain
Of him ye say ye love. But Fame with
    men,
Being but ampler means to serve mankind,
Should have small rest or pleasure in her-
    self,
But work as vassal to the larger love   489
That dwarfs the petty love of one to one.
Use gave me fame at first, and fame again
Increasing gave me use. Lo, there my
    boon!
What other? for men sought to prove me
    vile,
Because I fain had given them greater wits;
And then did envy call me devil's son;
The sick weak beast, seeking to help herself
By striking at her better, miss'd, and
    brought
Her own claw back, and wounded her own
    heart.
Sweet were the days when I was all un-
    known,   499
But when my name was lifted up the storm
Brake on the mountain and I cared not
    for it.
Right well know I that fame is half-dis-
    fame,
Yet needs must work my work. That
    other fame,

To one at least who hath not children
    vague,
The cackle of the unborn about the grave,
I cared not for it. A single misty star,
Which is the second in a line of stars
That seem a sword beneath a belt of three,
I never gazed upon it but I dreamt
Of some vast charm concluded in that star
To make fame nothing. Wherefore, if I
    fear,   511
Giving you power upon me thro' this charm,
That you might play me falsely, having
    power,
However well ye think ye love me now —
As sons of kings loving in pupilage
Have turn'd to tyrants when they came to
    power —
I rather dread the loss of use than fame;
If you — and not so much from wicked-
    ness,
As some wild turn of anger, or a mood
Of overstrain'd affection, it may be,   520
To keep me all to your own self, — or else
A sudden spurt of woman's jealousy, —
Should try this charm on whom ye say ye
    love.'

    And Vivien answer'd smiling as in wrath:
' Have I not sworn ? I am not trusted.
    Good !
Well, hide it, hide it; I shall find it out,
And being found take heed of Vivien.
A woman and not trusted, doubtless I
Might feel some sudden turn of anger
    born
Of your misfaith; and your fine epithet 530
Is accurate too, for this full love of mine
Without the full heart back may merit
    well
Your term of overstrain'd. So used as I,
My daily wonder is, I love at all.
And as to woman's jealousy, O, why not ?
O, to what end, except a jealous one,
And one to make me jealous if I love,
Was this fair charm invented by yourself ?
I well believe that all about this world 539
Ye cage a buxom captive here and there,
Closed in the four walls of a hollow tower
From which is no escape for evermore.'

    Then the great master merrily answer'd
    her.
' Full many a love in loving youth was
    mine;
I needed then no charm to keep them mine

But youth and love; and that full heart of
    yours
Whereof ye prattle, may now assure you
    mine;
So live uncharm'd. For those who wrought
    it first,
The wrist is parted from the hand that
    waved,
The feet unmortised from their ankle-
    bones   550
Who paced it, ages back — but will ye hear
The legend as in guerdon for your rhyme ?

    ' There lived a king in the most eastern
    East,
Less old than I, yet older, for my blood
Hath earnest in it of far springs to be.
A tawny pirate anchor'd in his port,
Whose bark had plunder'd twenty name-
    less isles;
And passing one, at the high peep of dawn,
He saw two cities in a thousand boats
All fighting for a woman on the sea.   560
And pushing his black craft among them
    all,
He lightly scatter'd theirs and brought her
    off,
With loss of half his people arrow-slain;
A maid so smooth, so white, so wonderful,
They said a light came from her when she
    moved.
And since the pirate would not yield her
    up,
The king impaled him for his piracy,
Then made her queen. But those isle-nur-
    tured eyes
Waged such unwilling tho' successful war
On all the youth, they sicken'd; councils
    thinn'd,   570
And armies waned, for magnet-like she
    drew
The rustiest iron of old fighters' hearts;
And beasts themselves would worship;
    camels knelt
Unbidden, and the brutes of mountain
    back
That carry kings in castles bow'd black
    knees
Of homage, ringing with their serpent
    hands,
To make her smile, her golden ankle-bells.
What wonder, being jealous,. that he sent
His horns of proclamation out thro' all
The hundred under - kingdoms that he
    sway'd   580

To find a wizard who might teach the king
Some charm which, being wrought upon the queen,
Might keep her all his own. To such a one
He promised more than ever king has given,
A league of mountain full of golden mines,
A province with a hundred miles of coast,
A palace and a princess, all for him;
But on all those who tried and fail'd the king
Pronounced a dismal sentence, meaning by it 589
To keep the list low and pretenders back,
Or, like a king, not to be trifled with —
Their heads should moulder on the city gates.
And many tried and fail'd, because the charm
Of nature in her overbore their own;
And many a wizard brow bleach'd on the walls,
And many weeks a troop of carrion crows
Hung like a cloud above the gateway towers.'

And Vivien breaking in upon him, said:
'I sit and gather honey; yet, methinks,
Thy tongue has tript a little; ask thyself. 600
The lady never made *unwilling* war
With those fine eyes; she had her pleasure in it,
And made her good man jealous with good cause.
And lived there neither dame nor damsel then
Wroth at a lover's loss? were all as tame,
I mean, as noble, as their queen was fair?
Not one to flirt a venom at her eyes,
Or pinch a murderous dust into her drink,
Or make her paler with a poison'd rose?
Well, those were not our days — but did they find 610
A wizard? Tell me, was he like to thee?'

She ceased, and made her lithe arm round his neck
Tighten, and then drew back, and let her eyes
Speak for her, glowing on him, like a bride's
On her new lord, her own, the first of men.

He answer'd laughing: 'Nay, not like to me.
At last they found — his foragers for charms —
A little glassy-headed hairless man,
Who lived alone in a great wild on grass,
Read but one book, and ever reading grew 620
So grated down and filed away with thought,
So lean his eyes were monstrous; while the skin
Clung but to crate and basket, ribs and spine.
And since he kept his mind on one sole aim,
Nor ever touch'd fierce wine, nor tasted flesh,
Nor own'd a sensual wish, to him the wall
That sunders ghosts and shadow-casting men
Became a crystal, and he saw them thro' it,
And heard their voices talk behind the wall, 629
And learnt their elemental secrets, powers
And forces; often o'er the sun's bright eye
Drew the vast eyelid of an inky cloud,
And lash'd it at the base with slanting storm;
Or in the noon of mist and driving rain,
When the lake whiten'd and the pinewood roar'd,
And the cairn'd mountain was a shadow, sunn'd
The world to peace again. Here was the man;
And so by force they dragg'd him to the king.
And then he taught the king to charm the queen
In such-wise that no man could see her more, 640
Nor saw she save the king, who wrought the charm,
Coming and going, and she lay as dead,
And lost all use of life. But when the king
Made proffer of the league of golden mines,
The province with a hundred miles of coast,
The palace and the princess, that old man
Went back to his old wild, and lived on grass,
And vanish'd, and his book came down to me.'

And Vivien answer'd smiling saucily:
'Ye have the book; the charm is written
in it.   650
Good! take my counsel, let me know it at
once;
For keep it like a puzzle chest in chest,
With each chest lock'd and padlock'd thir-
ty-fold,
And whelm all this beneath as vast a
mound
As after furious battle turfs the slain
On some wild down above the windy deep,
I yet should strike upon a sudden means
To dig, pick, open, find and read the charm;
Then, if I tried it, who should blame me
then?'

And smiling as a master smiles at one 660
That is not of his school, nor any school
But that where blind and naked Igno-
rance
Delivers brawling judgments, unashamed,
On all things all day long, he answer'd her:

'Thou read the book, my pretty Vivien!
O, ay, it is but twenty pages long,
But every page having an ample marge,
And every marge enclosing in the midst
A square of text that looks a little blot, 669
The text no larger than the limbs of fleas;
And every square of text an awful charm,
Writ in a language that has long gone
by,
So long that mountains have arisen since
With cities on their flanks — thou read the
book!
And every margin scribbled, crost, and
cramm'd
With comment, densest condensation, hard
To mind and eye; but the long sleepless
nights
Of my long life have made it easy to me.
And none can read the text, not even I;
And none can read the comment but my-
self;   680
And in the comment did I find the charm.
O, the results are simple; a mere child
Might use it to the harm of any one,
And never could undo it.   Ask no more;
For tho' you should not prove it upon me,
But keep that oath ye sware, ye might,
perchance,
Assay it on some one of the Table Round,
And all because ye dream they babble of
you.'

And Vivien, frowning in true anger, said:
'What dare the full-fed liars say of me?
They ride abroad redressing human
wrongs!   691
They sit with knife in meat and wine in
horn.
They bound to holy vows of chastity!
Were I not woman, I could tell a tale.
But you are man, you well can understand
The shame that cannot be explain'd for
. shame.
Not one of all the drove should touch me
— swine!'

Then answer'd Merlin careless of her
words:
'You breathe but accusation vast and vague,
Spleen-born, I think, and proofless.   If ye
know,   700
Set up the charge ye know, to stand or
fall!'

And Vivien answer'd frowning wrath-
fully:
'O, ay, what say ye to Sir Valence, him
Whose kinsman left him watcher o'er his
wife
And two fair babes, and went to distant
lands,
Was one year gone, and on returning found
Not two but three? there lay the reckling,
one
But one hour old!   What said the happy
sire?
A seven-months' babe had been a truer
gift.
Those twelve sweet moons confused his
fatherhood.'   710

Then answer'd Merlin: 'Nay, I know
the tale.
Sir Valence wedded with an outland dame;
Some cause had kept him sunder'd from
his wife.
One child they had; it lived with her; she
died.
His kinsman travelling on his own affair
Was charged by Valence to bring home the
child.
He brought, not found it therefore; take
the truth.'

'O, ay,' said Vivien, 'over-true a tale!
What say ye then to sweet Sir Sagra-
more,

That ardent man ? " To pluck the flower
in season," 720
So says the song, " I trow it is no treason."
O Master, shall we call him over-quick
To crop his own sweet rose before the
hour ? '

And Merlin answer'd: ' Over-quick art
thou
To catch a loathly plume fallen from the
wing
Of that foul bird of rapine whose whole
prey
Is man's good name. He never wrong'd
his bride.
I know the tale. An angry gust of wind
Puff'd out his torch among the myriad-
room'd
And many-corridor'd complexities 730
Of Arthur's palace. Then he found a door,
And darkling felt the sculptured ornament
That wreathen round it made it seem his
own,
And wearied out made for the couch and
slept,
A stainless man beside a stainless maid;
And either slept, nor knew of other there,
Till the high dawn piercing the royal rose
In Arthur's casement glimmer'd chastely
down,
Blushing upon them blushing, and at once
He rose without a word and parted from
her. 740
But when the thing was blazed about the
court,
The brute world howling forced them into
bonds,
And as it chanced they are happy, being
pure.'

' O, ay,' said Vivien, ' that were likely
too !
What say ye then to fair Sir Percivale
And of the horrid foulness that he wrought,
The saintly youth, the spotless lamb of
Christ,
Or some black wether of Saint Satan's
fold ? 748
What, in the precincts of the chapel-yard,
Among the knightly brasses of the graves,
And by the cold Hic Jacets of the dead !'

And Merlin answer'd careless of her
charge:
' A sober man is Percivale and pure,

But once in life was fluster'd with new wine,
Then paced for coolness in the chapel-yard,
Where one of Satan's shepherdesses caught
And meant to stamp him with her master's
mark.
And that he sinn'd is not believable;
For, look upon his face ! — but if he sinn'd,
The sin that practice burns into the blood,
And not the one dark hour which brings
remorse, 761
Will brand us, after, of whose fold we be;
Or else were he, the holy king whose hymns
Are chanted in the minster, worse than all.
But is your spleen froth'd out, or have ye
more ? '

And Vivien answer'd frowning yet in
wrath:
' O, ay; what say ye to Sir Lancelot, friend,
Traitor or true ? that commerce with the
Queen,
I ask you, is it clamor'd by the child,
Or whisper'd in the corner ? do ye know
it ? ' 770

To which he answer'd sadly: ' Yea, I
know it.
Sir Lancelot went ambassador, at first,
To fetch her, and she watch'd him from her
walls.
A rumor runs, she took him for the King,
So fixt her fancy on him; let them be.
But have ye no one word of loyal praise
For Arthur, blameless king and stainless
man ?'

She answer'd with a low and chuckling
laugh:
' Man ! is he man at all, who knows and
winks ?
Sees what his fair bride is and does, and
winks ? 780
By which the good King means to blind
himself,
And blinds himself and all the Table
Round
To all the foulness that they work. Myself
Could call him — were it not for woman-
hood —
The pretty, popular name such manhood
earns,
Could call him the main cause of all their
crime,
Yea, were he not crown'd king, coward and
fool.'

Then Merlin to his own heart, loathing,
    said:
'O true and tender! O my liege and
    King!
O selfless man and stainless gentleman, 790
Who wouldst against thine own eye-witness
    fain
Have all men true and leal, all women
    pure!
How, in the mouths of base interpreters,
From over-fineness not intelligible
To things with every sense as false and
    foul
As the poach'd filth that floods the middle
    street,
Is thy white blamelessness accounted
    blame!'

But Vivien, deeming Merlin overborne
By instance, recommenced, and let her
    tongue
Rage like a fire among the noblest names,
Polluting, and imputing her whole self, 801
Defaming and defacing, till she left
Not even Lancelot brave nor Galahad
    clean.

Her words had issue other than she
    will'd.
He dragg'd his eyebrow bushes down, and
    made
A snowy pent-house for his hollow eyes,
And mutter'd in himself: 'Tell *her* the
    charm!
So, if she had it, would she rail on me
To snare the next, and if she have it not
So will she rail. What did the wanton
    say? 810
"Not mount as high!" we scarce can sink
    as low;
For men at most differ as heaven and earth,
But women, worst and best, as heaven and
    hell.
I know the Table Round, my friends of
    old;
All brave, and many generous, and some
    chaste.
She cloaks the scar of some repulse with
    lies.
I well believe she tempted them and fail'd,
Being so bitter; for fine plots may fail,
Tho' harlots paint their talk as well as
    face
With colors of the heart that are not
    theirs. 820

I will not let her know; nine tithes of
    times
Face-flatterer and backbiter are the same.
And they, sweet soul, that most impute a
    crime
Are pronest to it, and impute themselves,
Wanting the mental range, or low desire
Not to feel lowest makes them level all;
Yea, they would pare the mountain to the
    plain,
To leave an equal baseness; and in this
Are harlots like the crowd that if they find
Some stain or blemish in a name of note,
Not grieving that their greatest are so
    small, 831
Inflate themselves with some insane de-
    light,
And judge all nature from her feet of
    clay,
Without the will to lift their eyes, and see
Her godlike head crown'd with spiritual fire,
And touching other worlds. I am weary
    of her.'

He spoke in words part heard, in whis-
    pers part,
Half-suffocated in the hoary fell
And many-winter'd fleece of throat and
    chin.
But Vivien, gathering somewhat of his
    mood, 840
And hearing 'harlot' mutter'd twice or
    thrice,
Leapt from her session on his lap, and
    stood
Stiff as a viper frozen; loathsome sight,
How from the rosy lips of life and love
Flash'd the bare-grinning skeleton of
    death!
White was her cheek; sharp breaths of
    anger puff'd
Her fairy nostril out; her hand half-
    clench'd
Went faltering sideways downward to her
    belt,
And feeling. Had she found a dagger
    there —
For in a wink the false love turns to hate —
She would have stabb'd him; but she found
    it not. 851
His eye was calm, and suddenly she took
To bitter weeping like a beaten child,
A long, long weeping, not consolable.
Then her false voice made way, broken
    with sobs:

'O crueller than was ever told in tale
Or sung in song ! O vainly lavish'd love !
O cruel, there was nothing wild or strange,
Or seeming shameful — for what shame in
 love,
So love be true, and not as yours is ? —
 nothing   860
Poor Vivien had not done to win his trust
Who call'd her what he call'd her — all her
 crime,
All — all — the wish to prove him wholly
 hers.'

She mused a little, and then clapt her
 hands
Together with a wailing shriek, and said:
'Stabb'd through the heart's affections to
 the heart !
Seethed like the kid in its own mother's
 milk !
Kill'd with a word worse than a life of
 blows !
I thought that he was gentle, being great;
O God, that I had loved a smaller man !
I should have found in him a greater
 heart.   871
O, I, that flattering my true passion, saw
The knights, the court, the King, dark in
 your light,
Who loved to make men darker than they
 are,
Because of that high pleasure which I had
To seat you sole upon my pedestal
Of worship — I am answer'd, and hence-
 forth
The course of life that seem'd so flowery
 to me
With you for guide and master, only you,
Becomes the sea - cliff pathway broken
 short,   880
And ending in a ruin — nothing left
But into some low cave to crawl, and
 there,
If the wolf spare me, weep my life away,
Kill'd with inutterable unkindliness.'

She paused, she turn'd away, she hung
 her head,
The snake of gold slid from her hair, the
 braid
Slipt and uncoil'd itself, she wept afresh,
And the dark wood grew darker toward
 the storm
In silence, while his anger slowly died
Within him, till he let his wisdom go 890

For ease of heart, and half believed her
 true;
Call'd her to shelter in the hollow oak,
'Come from the storm,' and having no
 reply,
Gazed at the heaving shoulder and the
 face
Hand-hidden, as for utmost grief or shame;
Then thrice essay'd, by tenderest-touching
 terms,
To sleek her ruffled peace of mind, in vain.
At last she let herself be conquer'd by him,
And as the cageling newly flown returns,
The seeming-injured simple-hearted thing
Came to her old perch back, and settled
 there.   901
There while she sat, half-falling from his
 knees,
Half-nestled at his heart, and since he saw
The slow tear creep from her closed eyelid
 yet,
About her, more in kindness than in love,
The gentle wizard cast a shielding arm.
But she dislink'd herself at once and rose,
Her arms upon her breast across, and
 stood,
A virtuous gentlewoman deeply wrong'd,
Upright and flush'd before him; then she
 said: 910

'There must be now no passages of love
Betwixt us twain henceforward evermore;
Since, if I be what I am grossly call'd,
What should be granted which your own
 gross heart
Would reekon worth the taking ? I will
 go.
In truth, but one thing now — better have
 died
Thrice than have ask'd it once — could
 make me stay —
That proof of trust — so often ask'd in
 vain !
How justly, after that vile term of yours,
I find with grief ! I might believe you
 then,   920
Who knows ? once more. Lo ! what was
 once to me
Mere matter of the fancy, now hath grown
The vast necessity of heart and life.
Farewell; think gently of me, for I fear
My fate or folly, passing gayer youth
For one so old, must be to love thee still.
But ere I leave thee let me swear once
 more

That if I schemed against thy peace in
    this,
May yon just heaven, that darkens o'er me,
    send
One flash that, missing all things else, may
    make   930
My scheming brain a cinder, if I lie.'

Scarce had she ceased, when out of heaven
    a bolt —
For now the storm was close above them —
    struck,
Furrowing a giant oak, and javelining
With darted spikes and splinters of the
    wood
The dark earth round. He raised his eyes
    and saw
The tree that shone white-listed thro' the
    gloom.
But Vivien, fearing heaven had heard her
    oath,
And dazzled by the livid-flickering fork,
And deafen'd with the stammering cracks
    and claps   940
That follow'd, flying back and crying out,
'O Merlin, tho' you do not love me, save,
Yet save me!' clung to him and hugg'd
    him close;
And call'd him dear protector in her fright,
Nor yet forgot her practice in her fright,
But wrought upon his mood and hugg'd
    him close.
The pale blood of the wizard at her touch
Took gayer colors, like an opal warm'd.
She blamed herself for telling hearsay
    tales;
She shook from fear, and for her fault she
    wept   950
Of petulancy; she call'd him lord and liege,
Her seer, her bard, her silver star of
    eve,
Her God, her Merlin, the one passionate
    love
Of her whole life; and ever overhead
Bellow'd the tempest, and the rotten branch
Snapt in the rushing of the river-rain
Above them; and in change of glare and
    gloom
Her eyes and neck glittering went and
    came;
Till now the storm, its burst of passion
    spent,
Moaning and calling out of other lands,   960
Had left the ravaged woodland yet once
    more

To peace; and what should not have been
    had been,
For Merlin, overtalk'd and overworn,
Had yielded, told her all the charm, and
    slept.

Then, in one moment, she put forth the
    charm
Of woven paces and of waving hands,
And in the hollow oak he lay as dead,
And lost to life and use and name and
    fame.

Then crying, 'I have made his glory
    mine,'
And shrieking out, 'O fool!' the harlot
    leapt   970
Adown the forest, and the thicket closed
Behind her, and the forest echo'd 'fool.'

LANCELOT AND ELAINE

ELAINE the fair, Elaine the lovable,
Elaine, the lily maid of Astolat,
High in her chamber up a tower to the
    east
Guarded the sacred shield of Lancelot;
Which first she placed where morning's
    earliest ray
Might strike it, and awake her with the
    gleam;
Then fearing rust or soilure fashion'd for
    it
A case of silk, and braided thereupon
All the devices blazon'd on the shield
In their own tinct, and added, of her wit,
A border fantasy of branch and flower,   11
And yellow-throated nestling in the nest.
Nor rested thus content, but day by day,
Leaving her household and good father,
    climb'd
That eastern tower, and entering barr'd her
    door,
Stript off the case, and read the naked
    shield,
Now guess'd a hidden meaning in his arms,
Now made a pretty history to herself
Of every dint a sword had beaten in it,
And every scratch a lance had made upon
    it,   20
Conjecturing when and where: this cut is
    fresh,
That ten years back; this dealt him at
    Caerlyle,

That at Caerleon — this at Camelot —
And ah, God's mercy, what a stroke was
there !
And here a thrust that might have kill'd,
but God
Broke the strong lance, and roll'd his enemy
down,
And saved him: so she lived in fantasy.

How came the lily maid by that good
shield
Of Lancelot, she that knew not even his
name ?
He left it with her, when he rode to tilt 30
For the great diamond in the diamond
jousts,
Which Arthur had ordain'd, and by that
name
Had named them, since a diamond was the
prize.

For Arthur, long before they crown'd
him king,
Roving the trackless realms of Lyonnesse,
Had found a glen, gray boulder and black
tarn.
A horror lived about the tarn, and clave
Like its own mists to all the mountain
side;
For here two brothers, one a king, had
met
And fought together, but their names were
lost; 40
And each had slain his brother at a blow;
And down they fell and made the glen ab-
horr'd.
And there they lay till all their bones were
bleach'd,
And lichen'd into color with the crags.
And he that once was king had on a crown
Of diamonds, one in front and four aside.
And Arthur came, and laboring up the
pass,
All in a misty moonshine, unawares
Had trodden that crown'd skeleton, and
the skull
Brake from the nape, and from the skull
the crown 50
Roll'd into light, and turning on its rims
Fled like a glittering rivulet to the tarn.
And down the shingly scaur he plunged,
and caught,
And set it on his head, and in his heart
Heard murmurs, 'Lo, thou likewise shalt
be king.'

Thereafter, when a king, he had the
gems
Pluck'd from the crown, and show'd them
to his knights
Saying: 'These jewels, whereupon I
chanced
Divinely, are the kingdom's, not the
King's — 59
For public use. Henceforward let there be,
Once every year, a joust for one of these;
For so by nine years' proof we needs must
learn
Which is our mightiest, and ourselves shall
grow
In use of arms and manhood, till we drive
The heathen, who, some say, shall rule the
land
Hereafter, which God hinder ! ' Thus he
spoke.
And eight years past, eight jousts had been,
and still
Had Lancelot won the diamond of the
year,
With purpose to present them to the Queen
When all were won; but, meaning all at
once 70
To snare her royal fancy with a boon
Worth half her realm, had never spoken
word.

Now for the central diamond and the
last
And largest, Arthur, holding then his court
Hard on the river nigh the place which
now
Is this world's hugest, let proclaim a joust
At Camelot, and when the time drew nigh
Spake — for she had been sick — to Guine-
vere:
'Are you so sick, my Queen, you cannot
move
To these fair jousts ? ' 'Yea, lord,' she
said, ' ye know it.' 80
'Then will ye miss,' he answer'd, ' the
great deeds
Of Lancelot, and his prowess in the lists,
A sight ye love to look on.' And the
Queen
Lifted her eyes, and they dwelt languidly
On Lancelot, where he stood beside the
King.
He, thinking that he read her meaning
there,
'Stay with me, I am sick; my love is more
Than many diamonds,' yielded; and a heart

Love-loyal to the least wish of the Queen —
However much he yearn'd to make com-
  plete   90
The tale of diamonds for his destined
  boon —
Urged him to speak against the truth, and
  say,
'Sir King, mine ancient wound is hardly
  whole,
And lets me from the saddle;' and the
  King
Glanced first at him, then her, and went his
  way.
No sooner gone than suddenly she began:

  'To blame, my lord Sir Lancelot, much
  to blame !
Why go ye not to these fair jousts ? the
  knights
Are half of them our enemies, and the
  crowd
Will murmur, " Lo the shameless ones,
  who take   100
Their pastime now the trustful King is
  gone !" '
Then Lancelot, vext at having lied in vain:
' Are ye so wise ? ye were not once so wise,
My Queen, that summer when ye loved me
  first.
Then of the crowd ye took no more account
Than of the myriad cricket of the mead,
When its own voice clings to each blade of
  grass,
And every voice is nothing. As to knights,
Them surely can I silence with all ease.
But now my loyal worship is allow'd   110
Of all men; many a bard, without offence,
Has link'd our names together in his lay,
Lancelot, the flower of bravery, Guinevere,
The pearl of beauty; and our knights at
  feast
Have pledged us in this union, while the
  King
Would listen smiling. How then ? is there
  more ?
Has Arthur spoken aught ? or would your-
  self,
Now weary of my service and devoir,
Henceforth be truer to your faultless lord ? '

  She broke into a little scornful laugh: 120
' Arthur, my lord, Arthur, the faultless
  King,
That passionate perfection, my good lord —
But who can gaze upon the sun in heaven ?

He never spake word of reproach to me,
He never had a glimpse of mine untruth,
He cares not for me. Only here to-day
There gleamed a vague suspicion in his
  eyes;
Some meddling rogue has tamper'd with
  him — else
Rapt in this fancy of his Table Round,
And swearing men to vows impossible, 130
To make them like himself; but, friend, to
  me
He is all fault who hath no fault at all.
For who loves me must have a touch of
  earth;
The low sun makes the color. I am yours,
Not Arthur's, as ye know, save by the
  bond.
And therefore hear my words: go to the
  jousts;
The tiny-trumpeting gnat can break our
  dream
When sweetest; and the vermin voices
  here
May buzz so loud — we scorn them, but
  they sting.'

  Then answer'd Lancelot, the chief of
  knights: 140
' And with what face, after my pretext
  made,
Shall I appear, O Queen, at Camelot, I
Before a king who honors his own word
As if it were his God's ? '

                      ' Yea,' said the Queen,
' A moral child without the craft to rule,
Else had he not lost me; but listen to me,
If I must find you wit. We hear it said
That men go down before your spear at a
  touch,
But knowing you are Lancelot; your great
  name,
This conquers. Hide it therefore; go un-
  known.   150
Win ! by this kiss you will; and our true
  King
Will then allow your pretext, O my knight,
As all for glory; for to speak him true,
Ye know right well, how meek soe'er he
  seem,
No keener hunter after glory breathes.
He loves it in his knights more than him-
  self;
They prove to him his work. Win and re-
  turn.'

Then got Sir Lancelot suddenly to horse,
Wroth at himself. Not willing to be
    known,   159
He left the barren-beaten thoroughfare,
Chose the green path that show'd the rarer
    foot,
And there among the solitary downs,
Full often lost in fancy, lost his way;
Till as he traced a faintly-shadow'd track,
That all in loops and links among the dales
Ran to the Castle of Astolat, he saw
Fired from the west, far on a hill, the tow-
    ers.
Thither he made, and blew the gateway
    horn.
Then came an old, dumb, myriad-wrinkled
    man,
Who let him into lodging and disarm'd. 170
And Lancelot marvell'd at the wordless
    man;
And issuing found the Lord of Astolat
With two strong sons, Sir Torre and Sir
    Lavaine,
Moving to meet him in the castle court;
And close behind them stept the lily maid
Elaine, his daughter; mother of the house
There was not. Some light jest among
    them rose
With laughter dying down as the great
    knight
Approach'd them; then the Lord of Astolat:
'Whence comest thou, my guest, and by
    what name   180
Livest between the lips? for by thy state
And presence I might guess thee chief of
    those,
After the King, who eat in Arthur's halls.
Him have I seen; the rest, his Table
    Round,
Known as they are, to me they are un-
    known.'

Then answer'd Lancelot, the chief of
    knights:
'Known am I, and of Arthur's hall, and
    known,
What I by mere mischance have brought,
    my shield.
But since I go to joust as one unknown
At Camelot for the diamond, ask me not;
Hereafter ye shall know me — and the
    shield —   191
I pray you lend me one, if such you have,
Blank, or at least with some device not
    mine.'

Then said the Lord of Astolat: 'Here is
    Torre's:
Hurt in his first tilt was my son, Sir Torre,
And so, God wot, his shield is blank enough.
His ye can have.' Then added plain Sir
    Torre,
'Yea, since I cannot use it, ye may have it.'
Here laugh'd the father saying: 'Fie, Sir
    Churl,
Is that an answer for a noble knight?   200
Allow him! but Lavaine, my younger here,
He is so full of lustihood, he will ride,
Joust for it, and win, and bring it in an
    hour,
And set it in this damsel's golden hair,
To make her thrice as wilful as before.'

'Nay, father, nay, good father, shame me
    not
Before this noble knight,' said young La-
    vaine,
'For nothing. Surely I but play'd on
    Torre,
He seem'd so sullen, vext he could not go;
A jest, no more! for, knight, the maiden
    dreamt   210
That some one put this diamond in her
    hand,
And that it was too slippery to be held,
And slipt and fell into some pool or stream,
The castle-well, belike; and then I said
That *if* I went and *if* I fought and won
    it —
But all was jest and joke among our-
    selves —
Then must she keep it safelier. All was
    jest.
But, father, give me leave, an if he will,
To ride to Camelot with this noble knight.
Win shall I not, but do my best to win; 220
Young as I am, yet would I do my best.'

'So ye will grace me,' answer'd Lance-
    lot,
Smiling a moment, 'with your fellowship
O'er these waste downs whereon I lost my-
    self,
Then were I glad of you as guide and
    friend;
And you shall win this diamond, — as I
    hear,
It is a fair large diamond, — if ye may,
And yield it to this maiden, if ye will.'
'A fair large diamond,' added plain Sir
    Torre,

'Such be for queens, and not for simple
 maids.'   230
Then she, who held her eyes upon the
 ground,
Elaine, and heard her name so tost about,
Flush'd slightly at the slight disparage-
 ment
Before the stranger knight, who, looking at
 her,
Full courtly, yet not falsely, thus return'd:
'If what is fair be but for what is fair,
And only queens are to be counted so,
Rash were my judgment then, who deem
 this maid
Might wear as fair a jewel as is on earth,
Not violating the bond of like to like.'   240

 He spoke and ceased; the lily maid
  Elaine,
Won by the mellow voice before she look'd,
Lifted her eyes and read his lineaments.
The great and guilty love he bare the
 Queen,
In battle with the love he bare his lord,
Had marr'd his face, and mark'd it ere his
 time.
Another sinning on such heights with one,
The flower of all the west and all the world,
Had been the sleeker for it; but in him   249
His mood was often like a fiend, and rose
And drove him into wastes and solitudes
For agony, who was yet a living soul.
Marr'd as he was, he seem'd the goodliest
 man
That ever among ladies ate in hall,
And noblest, when she lifted up her eyes.
However marr'd, of more than twice her
 years,
Seam'd with an ancient sword-cut on the
 cheek,
And bruised and bronzed, she lifted up her
 eyes
And loved him, with that love which was
 her doom.

 Then the great knight, the darling of the
  court,   260
Loved of the loveliest, into that rude hall
Stept with all grace, and not with half dis-
 dain
Hid under grace, as in a smaller time,
But kindly man moving among his kind;
Whom they with meats and vintage of their
 best
And talk and minstrel melody entertain'd.

And much they ask'd of court and Table
 Round,
And ever well and readily answer'd he;
But Lancelot, when they glanced at Guine-
 vere,
Suddenly speaking of the wordless man,   270
Heard from the baron that, ten years be-
 fore,
The heathen caught and reft him of his
 tongue.
'He learnt and warn'd me of their fierce
 design
Against my house, and him they caught
 and maim'd;
But I, my sons, and little daughter fled
From bonds or death, and dwelt among the
 woods
By the great river in a boatman's hut.
Dull days were those, till our good Arthur
 broke
The Pagan yet once more on Badon hill.'

 'O, there, great lord, doubtless,' Lavaine
  said, rapt   280
By all the sweet and sudden passion of
 youth
Toward greatness in its elder, 'you have
 fought.
O, tell us — for we live apart — you know
Of Arthur's glorious wars.' And Lancelot
 spoke
And answer'd him at full, as having been
With Arthur in the fight which all day
 long
Rang by the white mouth of the violent
 Glem;
And in the four loud battles by the shore
Of Duglas; that on Bassa; then the war
That thunder'd in and out the gloomy
 skirts   290
Of Celidon the forest; and again
By Castle Gurnion, where the glorious
 King
Had on his cuirass worn our Lady's Head,
Carved of one emerald centred in a sun
Of silver rays, that lighten'd as he breathed;
And at Caerleon had he help'd his lord,
When the strong neighings of the wild
 White Horse
Set every gilded parapet shuddering;
And up in Agned-Cathregonion too,
And down the waste sand-shores of Trath
 Treroit,   300
Where many a heathen fell; 'and on the
 mount

Of Badon I myself beheld the King
Charge at the head of all his Table Round,
And all his legions crying Christ and him,
And break them; and I saw him, after, stand
High on a heap of slain, from spur to plume
Red as the rising sun with heathen blood,
And seeing me, with a great voice he cried,
"They are broken, they are broken!" for the King, 309
However mild he seems at home, nor cares
For triumph in our mimic wars, the jousts —
For if his own knight casts him down, he laughs,
Saying his knights are better men than he —
Yet in this heathen war the fire of God
Fills him. I never saw his like; there lives
No greater leader.'

    While he utter'd this,
Low to her own heart said the lily maid,
'Save your great self, fair lord;' and when he fell 318
From talk of war to traits of pleasantry —
Being mirthful he, but in a stately kind —
She still took note that when the living smile
Died from his lips, across him came a cloud
Of melancholy severe, from which again,
Whenever in her hovering to and fro
The lily maid had striven to make him cheer,
There brake a sudden-beaming tenderness
Of manners and of nature; and she thought
That all was nature, all, perchance, for her.
And all night long his face before her lived,
As when a painter, poring on a face, 330
Divinely thro' all hindrance finds the man
Behind it, and so paints him that his face,
The shape and color of a mind and life,
Lives for his children, ever at its best
And fullest; so the face before her lived,
Dark-splendid, speaking in the silence, full
Of noble things, and held her from her sleep,
Till rathe she rose, half-cheated in the thought
She needs must bid farewell to sweet Lavaine.
First as in fear, step after step, she stole
Down the long tower-stairs, hesitating. 341
Anon, she heard Sir Lancelot cry in the court,
'This shield, my friend, where is it?' and Lavaine
Past inward, as she came from out the tower.
There to his proud horse Lancelot turn'd, and smooth'd
The glossy shoulder, humming to himself.
Half-envious of the flattering hand, she drew
Nearer and stood. He look'd, and, more amazed
Than if seven men had set upon him, saw
The maiden standing in the dewy light. 350
He had not dream'd she was so beautiful.
Then came on him a sort of sacred fear,
For silent, tho' he greeted her, she stood
Rapt on his face as if it were a god's.
Suddenly flash'd on her a wild desire
That he should wear her favor at the tilt.
She braved a riotous heart in asking for it.
'Fair lord, whose name I know not — noble it is,
I well believe, the noblest — will you wear
My favor at this tourney?' 'Nay,' said he, 360
'Fair lady, since I never yet have worn
Favor of any lady in the lists.
Such is my wont, as those who know me know.'
'Yea, so,' she answer'd; 'then in wearing mine
Needs must be lesser likelihood, noble lord,
That those who know should know you.'
    And he turn'd
Her counsel up and down within his mind,
And found it true, and answer'd: 'True, my child.
Well, I will wear it; fetch it out to me.
What is it?' and she told him, 'A red sleeve 370
Broider'd with pearls,' and brought it.
    Then he bound
Her token on his helmet, with a smile
Saying, 'I never yet have done so much
For any maiden living,' and the blood
Sprang to her face and fill'd her with delight;
But left her all the paler when Lavaine
Returning brought the yet-unblazon'd shield,
His brother's, which he gave to Lancelot,
Who parted with his own to fair Elaine:

'Do me this grace, my child, to have my
  shield   380
In keeping till I come.' 'A grace to me,'
She answer'd, 'twice to-day. I am your
  squire!'
Whereat Lavaine said laughing: 'Lily
  maid,
For fear our people call you lily maid
In earnest, let me bring your color back;
Once, twice, and thrice. Now get you hence
  to bed;'
So kiss'd her, and Sir Lancelot his own
  hand,
And thus they moved away. She staid a
  minute,
Then made a sudden step to the gate, and
  there —
Her bright hair blown about the serious
  face   390
Yet rosy-kindled with her brother's kiss —
Paused by the gateway, standing near the
  shield
In silence, while she watch'd their arms
  far-off
Sparkle, until they dipt below the downs.
Then to her tower she climb'd, and took
  the shield,
There kept it, and so lived in fantasy.

Meanwhile the new companions past
  away
Far o'er the long backs of the bushless
  downs,
To where Sir Lancelot knew there lived a
  knight   399
Not far from Camelot, now for forty years
A hermit, who had pray'd, labor'd and
  pray'd,
And ever laboring had scoop'd himself
In the white rock a chapel and a hall
On massive columns, like a shore-cliff cave,
And cells and chambers. All were fair
  and dry;
The green light from the meadows under-
  neath
Struck up and lived along the milky roofs;
And in the meadows tremulous aspen-trees
And poplars made a noise of falling showers.
And thither wending there that night they
  bode.   410

But when the next day broke from under-
  ground,
And shot red fire and shadows thro' the
  cave,

They rose, heard mass, broke fast, and rode
  away.
Then Lancelot saying, 'Hear, but hold my
  name
Hidden, you ride with Lancelot of the
  Lake,'
Abash'd Lavaine, whose instant reverence,
Dearer to true young hearts than their own
  praise,
But left him leave to stammer, 'Is it in-
  deed?'
And after muttering, 'The great Lancelot,'
At last he got his breath and answer'd:
  'One,   420
One have I seen — that other, our liege
  lord,
The dread Pendragon, Britain's King of
  kings,
Of whom the people talk mysteriously,
He will be there — then were I stricken
  blind
That minute, I might say that I had seen.'

So spake Lavaine, and when they reach'd
  the lists
By Camelot in the meadow, let his eyes
Run thro' the peopled gallery which half
  round
Lay like a rainbow fallen upon the grass,
Until they found the clear-faced King, who
  sat   430
Robed in red samite, easily to be known,
Since to his crown the golden dragon clung,
And down his robe the dragon writhed in
  gold,
And from the carven-work behind him
  crept
Two dragons gilded, sloping down to make
Arms for his chair, while all the rest of
  them
Thro' knots and loops and folds innumera-
  ble
Fled ever thro' the woodwork, till they
  found
The new design wherein they lost them-
  selves,   439
Yet with all ease, so tender was the work;
And, in the costly canopy o'er him set,
Blazed the last diamond of the nameless
  king.

Then Lancelot answer'd young Lavaine
  and said:
'Me you call great; mine is the firmer seat,
The truer lance; but there is many a youth

Now crescent, who will come to all I am
And overcome it; and in me there dwells
No greatness, save it be some far-off touch
Of greatness to know well I am not great.
There is the man.' And Lavaine gaped
    upon him   450
As on a thing miraculous, and anon
The trumpets blew; and then did either
    side,
They that assail'd, and they that held the
    lists,
Set lance in rest, strike spur, suddenly
    move,
Meet in the midst, and there so furiously
Shock that a man far-off might well per-
    ceive,
If any man that day were left afield,
The hard earth shake, and a low thunder
    of arms.
And Lancelot bode a little, till he saw
Which were the weaker; then he hurl'd
    into it   460
Against the stronger. Little need to speak
Of Lancelot in his glory ! King, duke, earl,
Count, baron — whom he smote, he over-
    threw.

But in the field were Lancelot's kith and
    kin,
Ranged with the Table Round that held
    the lists,
Strong men, and wrathful that a stranger
    knight
Should do and almost overdo the deeds
Of Lancelot; and one said to the other,
    'Lo !
What is he ? I do not mean the force
    alone —
The grace and versatility of the man !   470
Is it not Lancelot ? ' ' When has Lancelot
    worn
Favor of any lady in the lists ?
Not such his wont, as we that know him
    know.'
' How then ? who then ? ' a fury seized
    them all,
A fiery family passion for the name
Of Lancelot, and a glory one with theirs.
They couch'd their spears and prick'd their
    steeds, and thus,
Their plumes driven backward by the wind
    they made
In moving, all together down upon him
Bare, as a wild wave in the wide North
    Sea,   480

Green - glimmering toward the summit,
    bears, with all
Its stormy crests that smoke against the
    skies,
Down on a bark, and overbears the bark
And him that helms it; so they overbore
Sir Lancelot and his charger, and a spear
Down-glancing lamed the charger, and a
    spear
Prick'd sharply his own cuirass, and the
    head
Pierced thro' his side, and there snapt and
    remain'd.

Then Sir Lavaine did well and worship-
    fully.
He bore a knight of old repute to the
    earth,   490
And brought his horse to Lancelot where
    he lay.
He up the side, sweating with agony,
    got,
But thought to do while he might yet en-
    dure,
And being lustily holpen by the rest,
His party, — tho' it seem'd half-miracle
To those he fought with, — drave his kith
    and kin,
And all the Table Round that held the lists,
Back to the barrier; then the trumpets
    blew
Proclaiming his the prize who wore the
    sleeve
Of scarlet and the pearls; and all the
    knights,   500
His party, cried, ' Advance and take thy
    prize
The diamond; ' but he answer'd: ' Diamond
    me
No diamonds ! for God's love, a little air !
Prize me no prizes, for my prize is death !
Hence will I, and I charge you, follow me
    not.'

He spoke, and vanish'd suddenly from
    the field
With young Lavaine into the poplar grove.
There from his charger down he slid, and
    sat,
Gasping to Sir Lavaine, ' Draw the lance-
    head.'
' Ah, my sweet lord Sir Lancelot,' said La-
    vaine,   510
' I dread me, if I draw it, you will die.'
But he, ' I die already with it; draw —

Draw,' — and Lavaine drew, and Sir
Lancelot gave
A marvellous great shriek and ghastly
groan,
And half his blood burst forth, and down
he sank
For the pure pain, and wholly swoon'd
away.
Then came the hermit out and bare him
in,
There stanch'd his wound; and there, in
daily doubt
Whether to live or die, for many a week
Hid from the wild world's rumor by the
grove   520
Of poplars with their noise of falling show-
ers,
And ever-tremulous aspen-trees, he lay.

But on that day when Lancelot fled the
lists,
His party, knights of utmost North and
West,
Lords of waste marshes, kings of desolate
isles,
Came round their great Pendragon, saying
to him,
'Lo, Sire, our knight, thro' whom we won
the day,
Hath gone sore wounded, and hath left his
prize
Untaken, crying that his prize is death.'
'Heaven hinder,' said the King, 'that such
an one,   530
So great a knight as we have seen to-day —
He seem'd to me another Lancelot —
Yea, twenty times I thought him Lance-
lot —
He must not pass uncared for. Wherefore
rise,
O Gawain, and ride forth and find the
knight.
Wounded and wearied, needs must he be
near.
I charge you that you get at once to horse.
And, knights and kings, there breathes not
one of you
Will deem this prize of ours is rashly given;
His prowess was too wondrous. We will
do him   540
No customary honor; since the knight
Came not to us, of us to claim the prize,
Ourselves will send it after. Rise and
take
This diamond, and deliver it, and return,

And bring us where he is, and how he fares,
And cease not from your quest until ye
find.'

So saying, from the carven flower above,
To which it made a restless heart, he took
And gave the diamond. Then from where
he sat
At Arthur's right, with smiling face arose,
With smiling face and frowning heart, a
prince   551
In the mid might and flourish of his May,
Gawain, surnamed the Courteous, fair and
strong,
And after Lancelot, Tristram, and Geraint,
And Gareth, a good knight, but there-
withal
Sir Modred's brother, and the child of Lot,
Nor often loyal to his word, and now
Wroth that the King's command to sally
forth
In quest of whom he knew not, made him
leave
The banquet and concourse of knights and
kings.   560

So all in wrath he got to horse and went;
While Arthur to the banquet, dark in mood,
Past, thinking, 'Is it Lancelot who hath
come
Despite the wound he spake of, all for gain
Of glory, and hath added wound to wound,
And ridden away to die?' So fear'd the
King,
And, after two days' tarriance there, re-
turn'd.
Then when he saw the Queen, embracing
ask'd,
'Love, are you yet so sick?' 'Nay, lord,'
she said.
'And where is Lancelot?' Then the Queen
amazed,   570
'Was he not with you? won he not your
prize?'
'Nay, but one like him.' 'Why, that like
was he.'
And when the King demanded how she
knew,
Said: 'Lord, no sooner had ye parted from
us
Than Lancelot told me of a common talk
That men went down before his spear at a
touch,
But knowing he was Lancelot; his great
name

Conquer'd; and therefore would he hide
    his name
From all men, even the King, and to this
    end
Had made the pretext of a hindering
    wound, 580
That he might joust unknown of all, and
    learn
If his old prowess were in aught decay'd;
And added, " Our true Arthur, when he
    learns,
Will well allow my pretext, as for gain
Of purer glory." '

                Then replied the King:
' Far lovelier in our Lancelot had it been,
In lieu of idly dallying with the truth,
To have trusted me as he hath trusted
    thee.
Surely his King and most familiar friend
Might well have kept his secret. True,
    indeed, 590
Albeit I know my knights fantastical,
So fine a fear in our large Lancelot
Must needs have moved my laughter; now
    remains
But little cause for laughter. His own
    kin —
Ill news, my Queen, for all who love him,
    this ! —
His kith and kin, not knowing, set upon
    him;
So that he went sore wounded from the
    field.
Yet good news too; for goodly hopes are
    mine
That Lancelot is no more a lonely heart.
He wore, against his wont, upon his helm
A sleeve of scarlet, broider'd with great
    pearls, 601
Some gentle maiden's gift.'

             ' Yea, lord,' she said,
' Thy hopes are mine,' and saying that, she
    choked,
And sharply turn'd about to hide her
    face,
Past to her chamber, and there flung her-
    self
Down on the great King's couch, and
    writhed upon it,
And clench'd her fingers till they bit the
    palm,
And shriek'd out ' Traitor ! ' to the unhear-
    ing wall,

Then flash'd into wild tears, and rose
    again,
And moved about her palace, proud and
    pale. 610

    Gawain the while thro' all the region
    round
Rode with his diamond, wearied of the
    quest,
Touch'd at all points except the poplar
    grove,
And came at last, tho' late, to Astolat;
Whom glittering in enamell'd arms the
    maid
Glanced at, and cried, ' What news from
    Camelot, lord ?
What of the knight with the red sleeve ? '
    ' He won.'
' I knew it,' she said. ' But parted from
    the jousts
Hurt in the side; ' whereat she caught her
    breath.
Thro' her own side she felt the sharp lance
    go. 620
Thereon she smote her hand; wellnigh she
    swoon'd.
And, while he gazed wonderingly at her,
    came
The Lord of Astolat out, to whom the
    prince
Reported who he was, and on what quest
Sent, that he bore the prize and could not
    find
The victor, but had ridden a random round
To seek him, and had wearied of the
    search.
To whom the Lord of Astolat: ' Bide with
    us,
And ride no more at random, noble prince !
Here was the knight, and here he left a
    shield; 630
This will he send or come for. Further-
    more
Our son is with him; we shall hear anon,
Needs must we hear.' To this the courte-
    ous prince
Accorded with his wonted courtesy,
Courtesy with a touch of traitor in it,
And staid; and cast his eyes on fair
    Elaine;
Where could be found face daintier ? then
    her shape
From forehead down to foot, perfect —
    again
From foot to forehead exquisitely turn'd.

'Well — if I bide, lo! this wild flower for
me!'   640
And oft they met among the garden yews,
And there he set himself to play upon her
With sallying wit, free flashes from a
height
Above her, graces of the court, and songs,
Sighs, and low smiles, and golden elo-
quence
And amorous adulation, till the maid
Rebell'd against it, saying to him: 'Prince,
O loyal nephew of our noble King,
Why ask you not to see the shield he left,
Whence you might learn his name? Why
slight your King,   650
And lose the quest he sent you on, and
prove
No surer than our falcon yesterday,
Who lost the hern we slipt her at, and
went
To all the winds?' 'Nay, by mine head,'
said he,
'I lose it, as we lose the lark in heaven,
O damsel, in the light of your blue eyes;
But an ye will it let me see the shield.'
And when the shield was brought, and Ga-
wain saw
Sir Lancelot's azure lions, crown'd with
gold,
Ramp in the field, he smote his thigh, and
mock'd: 660
'Right was the King! our Lancelot! that
true man!'
'And right was I,' she answer'd merrily, 'I,
Who dream'd my knight the greatest
knight of all.'
'And if I dream'd,' said Gawain, 'that you
love
This greatest knight, your pardon! lo, ye
know it!
Speak therefore; shall I waste myself in
vain?'
Full simple was her answer: 'What know
I?
My brethren have been all my fellowship;
And I, when often they have talk'd of
love,
Wish'd it had been my mother, for they
talk'd,   670
Meseem'd, of what they knew not; so my-
self —
I know not if I know what true love is,
But if I know, then, if I love not him,
I know there is none other I can love.'

'Yea, by God's death,' said he, 'ye love
him well,
But would not, knew ye what all others
know,
And whom he loves.' 'So be it,' cried
Elaine,
And lifted her fair face and moved away;
But he pursued her, calling, 'Stay a little!
One golden minute's grace! he wore your
sleeve.   680
Would he break faith with one I may not
name?
Must our true man change like a leaf at
last?
Nay — like enow. Why then, far be it
from me
To cross our mighty Lancelot in his loves!
And, damsel, for I deem you know full
well
Where your great knight is hidden, let me
leave
My quest with you; the diamond also —
here!
For if you love, it will be sweet to give it;
And if he love, it will be sweet to have it
From your own hand; and whether he love
or not,   690
A diamond is a diamond. Fare you well
A thousand times! — a thousand times
farewell!
Yet, if he love, and his love hold, we two
May meet at court hereafter! there, I
think,
So ye will learn the courtesies of the court,
We two shall know each other.'

                                Then he gave,
And slightly kiss'd the hand to which he
gave,
The diamond, and all wearied of the quest
Leapt on his horse, and carolling as he
went
A true-love ballad, lightly rode away.   700

   Thence to the court he past; there told
the King
What the King knew, 'Sir Lancelot is the
knight.'
And added, 'Sire, my liege, so much I
learnt,
But fail'd to find him, tho' I rode all round
The region; but I lighted on the maid
Whose sleeve he wore. She loves him;
and to her,
Deeming our courtesy is the truest law,

I gave the diamond. She will render it;
For by mine head she knows his hiding-
place.'

The seldom-frowning King frown'd, and
replied, 710
'Too courteous truly ! ye shall go no more
On quest of mine, seeing that ye forget
Obedience is the courtesy due to kings.'

He spake and parted. Wroth, but all in
awe,
For twenty strokes of the blood, without a
word,
Linger'd that other, staring after him;
Then shook his hair, strode off, and buzz'd
abroad
About the maid of Astolat, and her love.
All ears were prick'd at once, all tongues
were loosed:
' The maid of Astolat loves Sir Lancelot,
Sir Lancelot loves the maid of Astolat.' 721
Some read the King's face, some the
Queen's, and all
Had marvel what the maid might be, but
most
Predoom'd her as unworthy. One old
dame
Came suddenly on the Queen with the
sharp news.
She, that had heard the noise of it before,
But sorrowing Lancelot should have stoop'd
so low,
Marr'd her friend's aim with pale tran-
quillity.
So ran the tale like fire about the court,
Fire in dry stubble a nine-days' wonder
flared; 730
Till even the knights at banquet twice or
thrice
Forgot to drink to Lancelot and the Queen,
And pledging Lancelot and the lily maid
Smiled at each other, while the Queen, who
sat
With lips severely placid, felt the knot
Climb in her throat, and with her feet un-
seen
Crush'd the wild passion out against the floor
Beneath the banquet, where the meats be-
came
As wormwood and she hated all who
pledged.

But far away the maid in Astolat, 740
Her guiltless rival, she that ever kept

The one-day-seen Sir Lancelot in her heart,
Crept to her father, while he mused alone,
Sat on his knee, stroked his gray face and
said:
' Father, you call me wilful, and the fault
Is yours who let me have my will, and
now,
Sweet father, will you let me lose my
wits ? '
' Nay,' said he, 'surely.' ' Wherefore, let
me hence,'
She answer'd, 'and find out our dear La-
vaine.'
' Ye will not lose your wits for dear La-
vaine. 750
Bide,' answer'd he: ' we needs must hear
anon
Of him, and of that other.' ' Ay,' she said,
' And of that other, for I needs must hence
And find that other, wheresoe'er he be,
And with mine own hand give his diamond
to him,
Lest I be found as faithless in the quest
As yon proud prince who left the quest to
me.
Sweet father, I behold him in my dreams
Gaunt as it were the skeleton of himself,
Death-pale, for the lack of gentle maiden's
aid. 760
The gentler-born the maiden, the more
bound,
My father, to be sweet and serviceable
To noble knights in sickness, as ye know,
When these have worn their tokens. Let
me hence,
I pray you.' Then her father nodding
said:
' Ay, ay, the diamond. Wit ye well, my
child,
Right fain were I to learn this knight were
whole,
Being our greatest. Yea, and you must
give it —
And sure I think this fruit is hung too
high
For any mouth to gape for save a
queen's — 770
Nay, I mean nothing; so then, get you
gone,
Being so very wilful you must go.'

Lightly, her suit allow'd, she slipt away,
And while she made her ready for her ride
Her father's latest word humm'd in her
ear,

'Being so very wilful you must go,'
And changed itself and echo'd in her heart,
'Being so very wilful you must die.'
But she was happy enough and shook it
    off,   779
As we shake off the bee that buzzes at us;
And in her heart she answer'd it and said,
'What matter, so I help him back to life?'
Then far away with good Sir Torre for
    guide
Rode o'er the long backs of the bushless
    downs
To Camelot, and before the city-gates
Came on her brother with a happy face
Making a roan horse caper and curvet
For pleasure all about a field of flowers;
Whom when she saw, 'Lavaine,' she cried,
    'Lavaine,
How fares my lord Sir Lancelot?' He
    amazed,   790
'Torre and Elaine! why here? Sir Lance-
    lot!
How know ye my lord's name is Lancelot?'
But when the maid had told him all her
    tale,
Then turn'd Sir Torre, and being in his
    moods
Left them, and under the strange-statued
    gate,
Where Arthur's wars were render'd mysti-
    cally,
Past up the still rich city to his kin,
His own far blood, which dwelt at Came-
    lot;
And her, Lavaine across the poplar grove
Led to the caves. There first she saw the
    casque   800
Of Lancelot on the wall; her scarlet sleeve,
Tho' carved and cut, and half the pearls
    away,
Stream'd from it still; and in her heart she
    laugh'd,
Because he had not loosed it from his
    helm,
But meant once more perchance to tourney
    in it.
And when they gain'd the cell wherein he
    slept,
His battle-writhen arms and mighty hands
Lay naked on the wolf-skin, and a dream
Of dragging down his enemy made them
    move.
Then she that saw him lying unsleek, un-
    shorn,   810
Gaunt as it were the skeleton of himself,

Utter'd a little tender dolorous cry.
The sound not wonted in a place so still
Woke the sick knight, and while he roll'd
    his eyes
Yet blank from sleep, she started to him,
    saying,
'Your prize the diamond sent you by the
    King.'
His eyes glisten'd; she fancied, 'Is it for
    me?'
And when the maid had told him all the
    tale
Of king and prince, the diamond sent, the
    quest
Assign'd to her not worthy of it, she knelt
Full lowly by the corners of his bed,   821
And laid the diamond in his open hand.
Her face was near, and as we kiss the child
That does the task assign'd, he kiss'd her
    face.
At once she slipt like water to the floor.
'Alas,' he said, 'your ride hath wearied
    you.
Rest must you have.' 'No rest for me,'
    she said;
'Nay, for near you, fair lord, I am at rest.'
What might she mean by that? his large
    black eyes,
Yet larger thro' his leanness, dwelt upon
    her,   830
Till all her heart's sad secret blazed itself
In the heart's colors on her simple face;
And Lancelot look'd and was perplext in
    mind,
And being weak in body said no more,
But did not love the color; woman's love,
Save one, he not regarded, and so turn'd
Sighing, and feign'd a sleep until he slept.

Then rose Elaine and glided thro' the
    fields,
And past beneath the weirdly-sculptured
    gates
Far up the dim rich city to her kin;   840
There bode the night, but woke with dawn,
    and past
Down thro' the dim rich city to the fields,
Thence to the cave. So day by day she past
In either twilight ghost-like to and fro
Gliding, and every day she tended him,
And likewise many a night; and Lancelot
Would, tho' he call'd his wound a little
    hurt
Whereof he should be quickly whole, at
    times

Brain-feverous in his heat and agony, seem
Uncourteous, even he. But the meek maid
Sweetly forbore him ever, being to him 851
Meeker than any child to a rough nurse,
Milder than any mother to a sick child,
And never woman yet, since man's first
 fall,
Did kindlier unto man, but her deep love
Upbore her; till the hermit, skill'd in all
The simples and the science of that time,
Told him that her fine care had saved his
 life.
And the sick man forgot her simple blush,
Would call her friend and sister, sweet
 Elaine,
 860
Would listen for her coming and regret
Her parting step, and held her tenderly,
And loved her with all love except the
 love
Of man and woman when they love their
 best,
Closest and sweetest, and had died the
 death
In any knightly fashion for her sake.
And peradventure had he seen her first
She might have made this and that other
 world
Another world for the sick man; but now
The shackles of an old love straiten'd him,
His honor rooted in dishonor stood, 871
And faith unfaithful kept him falsely true.

Yet the great knight in his mid-sickness
 made
Full many a holy vow and pure resolve.
These, as but born of sickness, could not
 live;
For when the blood ran lustier in him
 again,
Full often the bright image of one face,
Making a treacherous quiet in his heart,
Dispersed his resolution like a cloud.
Then if the maiden, while that ghostly
 grace 880
Beam'd on his fancy, spoke, he answer'd
 not,
Or short and coldly, and she knew right
 well
What the rough sickness meant, but what
 this meant
She knew not, and the sorrow dimm'd her
 sight,
And drave her ere her time across the
 fields
Far into the rich city, where alone

She murmur'd, 'Vain, in vain! it cannot be.
He will not love me. How then? must I
 die?'
Then as a little helpless innocent bird, 889
That has but one plain passage of few notes,
Will sing the simple passage o'er and o'er
For all an April morning, till the ear
Wearies to hear it, so the simple maid
Went half the night repeating, 'Must I
 die?'
And now to right she turn'd, and now to
 left,
And found no ease in turning or in rest;
And 'Him or death,' she mutter'd, 'death
 or him,'
Again and like a burthen, 'Him or death.'

But when Sir Lancelot's deadly hurt was
 whole,
To Astolat returning rode the three. 900
There morn by morn, arraying her sweet
 self
In that wherein she deem'd she look'd her
 best,
She came before Sir Lancelot, for she
 thought,
'If I be loved, these are my festal robes,
If not, the victim's flowers before he fall.'
And Lancelot ever prest upon the maid
That she should ask some goodly gift of
 him
For her own self or hers: 'and do not
 shun
To speak the wish most near to your true
 heart; 909
Such service have ye done me that I make
My will of yours, and prince and lord am I
In mine own land, and what I will I can.'
Then like a ghost she lifted up her face,
But like a ghost without the power to
 speak.
And Lancelot saw that she withheld her
 wish,
And bode among them yet a little space
Till he should learn it; and one morn it
 chanced
He found her in among the garden yews,
And said, 'Delay no longer, speak your
 wish, 919
Seeing I go to-day.' Then out she brake:
'Going? and we shall never see you more.
And I must die for want of one bold word.'
'Speak; that I live to hear,' he said, 'is
 yours.'
Then suddenly and passionately she spoke:

'I have gone mad. I love you; let me die.'
'Ah, sister,' answer'd Lancelot, 'what is
  this?'
And innocently extending her white arms,
'Your love,' she said, 'your love — to be
  your wife.'
And Lancelot answer'd, 'Had I chosen to
  wed,   929
I had been wedded earlier, sweet Elaine;
But now there never will be wife of mine.'
'No, no,' she cried, 'I care not to be wife,
But to be with you still, to see your face,
To serve you, and to follow you thro' the
  world.'
And Lancelot answer'd: 'Nay, the world,
  the world,
All ear and eye, with such a stupid heart
To interpret ear and eye, and such a tongue
To blare its own interpretation — nay,
Full ill then should I quit your brother's
  love,
And your good father's kindness.' And
  she said,   940
'Not to be with you, not to see your face —
Alas for me then, my good days are done!'
'Nay, noble maid,' he answer'd, 'ten times
  nay!
This is not love, but love's first flash in
  youth,
Most common; yea, I know it of mine own
  self,
And you yourself will smile at your own self
Hereafter, when you yield your flower of
  life
To one more fitly yours, not thrice your
  age.
And then will I, for true you are and sweet
Beyond mine old belief in womanhood,   950
More specially should your good knight
  be poor,
Endow you with broad land and territory
Even to the half my realm beyond the seas,
So that would make you happy; further-
  more,
Even to the death, as tho' ye were my
  blood,
In all your quarrels will I be your knight.
This will I do, dear damsel, for your sake,
And more than this I cannot.'

                              While he spoke
She neither blush'd nor shook, but deathly-
  pale
Stood grasping what was nearest, then re-
  plied,   960

'Of all this will I nothing;' and so fell,
And thus they bore her swooning to her
  tower.

  Then spake, to whom thro' those black
  walls of yew
Their talk had pierced, her father: 'Ay, a
  flash,
I fear me, that will strike my blossom dead.
Too courteous are ye, fair Lord Lancelot.
I pray you, use some rough discourtesy
To blunt or break her passion.'

                              Lancelot said,
'That were against me; what I can I will;'
And there that day remain'd, and toward
  even   970
Sent for his shield. Full meekly rose the
  maid,
Stript off the case, and gave the naked
  shield;
Then, when she heard his horse upon the
  stones,
Unclasping flung the casement back, and
  look'd
Down on his helm, from which her sleeve
  had gone.
And Lancelot knew the little clinking
  sound;
And she by tact of love was well aware
That Lancelot knew that she was looking
  at him.
And yet he glanced not up, nor waved his
  hand,
Nor bade farewell, but sadly rode away. 980
This was the one discourtesy that he used.

  So in her tower alone the maiden sat.
His very shield was gone; only the case,
Her own poor work, her empty labor, left.
But still she heard him, still his picture
  form'd
And grew between her and the pictured
  wall.
Then came her father, saying in low tones,
'Have comfort,' whom she greeted quietly.
Then came her brethren saying, 'Peace to
  thee,
Sweet sister,' whom she answer'd with all
  calm.   990
But when they left her to herself again,
Death, like a friend's voice from a distant
  field
Approaching thro' the darkness, call'd; the
  owls

Wailing had power upon her, and she mixt
Her fancies with the sallow-rifted glooms
Of evening and the moanings of the wind.

And in those days she made a little song,
And call'd her song 'The Song of Love
    and Death,'
And sang it; sweetly could she make and
    sing.

'Sweet is true love tho' given in vain, in
    vain;
And sweet is death who puts an end to pain.   1000
I know not which is sweeter, no, not I.

'Love, art thou sweet? then bitter death
    must be.
Love, thou art bitter; sweet is death to me.
O Love, if death be sweeter, let me die.

'Sweet love, that seems not made to fade
    away;
Sweet death, that seems to make us loveless
    clay;
I know not which is sweeter, no, not I.

'I fain would follow love, if that could be;
I needs must follow death, who calls for me;
Call and I follow, I follow! let me die.'   1011

High with the last line scaled her voice,
    and this,
All in a fiery dawning wild with wind
That shook her tower, the brothers heard,
    and thought
With shuddering, 'Hark the Phantom of
    the house
That ever shrieks before a death,' and
    call'd
The father, and all three in hurry and fear
Ran to her, and lo! the blood-red light of
    dawn
Flared on her face, she shrilling, 'Let me
    die!'

As when we dwell upon a word we
    know,   1020
Repeating, till the word we know so well
Becomes a wonder, and we know not why,
So dwelt the father on her face, and thought,
'Is this Elaine?' till back the maiden fell,
Then gave a languid hand to each, and lay,
Speaking a still good-morrow with her
    eyes.
At last she said: 'Sweet brothers, yester-
    night
I seem'd a curious little maid again,

As happy as when we dwelt among the
    woods,
And when ye used to take me with the
    flood
Up the great river in the boatman's boat.   1030
Only ye would not pass beyond the cape
That has the poplar on it; there ye fixt
Your limit, oft returning with the tide.
And yet I cried because ye would not pass
Beyond it, and far up the shining flood
Until we found the palace of the King.
And yet ye would not; but this night I
    dream'd
That I was all alone upon the flood,
And then I said, "Now shall I have my
    will;"   1040
And there I woke, but still the wish re-
    main'd.
So let me hence that I may pass at last
Beyond the poplar and far up the flood,
Until I find the palace of the King.
There will I enter in among them all,
And no man there will dare to mock at me;
But there the fine Gawain will wonder at
    me,
And there the great Sir Lancelot muse at
    me;
Gawain, who bade a thousand farewells to
    me,
Lancelot, who coldly went, nor bade me
    one.   1050
And there the King will know me and my
    love,
And there the Queen herself will pity me,
And all the gentle court will welcome me,
And after my long voyage I shall rest!'

'Peace,' said her father, 'O my child, ye
    seem
Light-headed, for what force is yours to go
So far, being sick? and wherefore would
    ye look
On this proud fellow again, who scorns us
    all?'

Then the rough Torre began to heave
    and move,
And bluster into stormy sobs and say: 1060
'I never loved him; an I meet with him,
I care not howsoever great he be,
Then will I strike at him and strike him
    down.
Give me good fortune, I will strike him
    dead,
For this discomfort he hath done the house.'

To whom the gentle sister made reply:
' Fret not yourself, dear brother, nor be
     wroth,
Seeing it is no more Sir Lancelot's fault
Not to love me than it is mine to love
Him of all men who seems to me the high-
     est.'   1070

' Highest ? ' the father answer'd, echoing
     ' highest ? '—
He meant to break the passion in her —
     ' nay,
Daughter, I know not what you call the
     highest;
But this I know, for all the people know it,
He loves the Queen, and in an open shame,
And she returns his love in open shame;
If this be high, what is it to be low ? '

Then spake the lily maid of Astolat:
' Sweet father, all too faint and sick am I
For anger.   These are slanders; never yet
Was noble man but made ignoble talk.   1081
He makes no friend who never made a foe.
But now it is my glory to have loved
One peerless, without stain; so let me pass,
My father, howsoe'er I seem to you,
Not all unhappy, having loved God's best
And greatest, tho' my love had no return.
Yet, seeing you desire your child to live,
Thanks, but you work against your own
     desire,
For if I could believe the things you say
I should but die the sooner; wherefore
     cease,   1091
Sweet father, and bid call the ghostly man
Hither, and let me shrive me clean and
     die.'

So when the ghostly man had come and
     gone,
She, with a face bright as for sin forgiven,
Besought Lavaine to write as she devised
A letter, word for word; and when he
     ask'd,
' Is it for Lancelot, is it for my dear lord ?
Then will I bear it gladly; ' she replied,
' For Lancelot and the Queen and all the
     world,   1100
But I myself must bear it.'   Then he wrote
The letter she devised; which being writ
And folded, ' O sweet father, tender and
     true,
Deny me not,' she said — ' ye never yet
Denied my fancies — this, however strange,

My latest.   Lay the letter in my hand
A little ere I die, and close the hand
Upon it; I shall guard it even in death.
And when the heat has gone from out my
     heart,   1109
Then take the little bed on which I died
For Lancelot's love, and deck it like the
     Queen's
For richness, and me also like the Queen
In all I have of rich, and lay me on it.
And let there be prepared a chariot-bier
To take me to the river, and a barge
Be ready on the river, clothed in black.
I go in state to court, to meet the Queen.
There surely I shall speak for mine own
     self,
And none of you can speak for me so well.
And therefore let our dumb old man alone
Go with me; he can steer and row, and
     he   1121
Will guide me to that palace, to the doors.'

She ceased.   Her father promised; where-
     upon
She grew so cheerful that they deem'd her
     death
Was rather in the fantasy than the blood.
But ten slow mornings past, and on the
     eleventh
Her father laid the letter in her hand,
And closed the hand upon it, and she died.
So that day there was dole in Astolat.

But when the next sun brake from un-
     derground,   1130
Then, those two brethren slowly with bent
     brows
Accompanying, the sad chariot-bier
Past like a shadow thro' the field, that
     shone
Full-summer, to that stream whereon the
     barge,
Pall'd all its length in blackest samite, lay.
There sat the lifelong creature of the
     house,
Loyal, the dumb old servitor, on deck,
Winking his eyes, and twisted all his face.
So those two brethren from the chariot
     took
And on the black decks laid her in her
     bed,   1140
Set in her hand a lily, o'er her hung
The silken case with braided blazonings,
And kiss'd her quiet brows, and saying to
     her,

'Sister, farewell forever,' and again,
' Farewell, sweet sister,' parted all in tears.
Then rose the dumb old servitor, and the
    dead,
Oar'd by the dumb, went upward with the
    flood —
In her right hand the lily, in her left
The letter — all her bright hair streaming
    down —
And all the coverlid was cloth of gold   1150
Drawn to her waist, and she herself in
    white
All but her face, and that clear-featured
    face
Was lovely, for she did not seem as dead,
But fast asleep, and lay as tho' she smiled.

That day Sir Lancelot at the palace
    craved
Audience of Guinevere, to give at last
The price of half a realm, his costly gift,
Hard-won and hardly won with bruise and
    blow,
With deaths of others, and almost his own,
The nine-years-fought-for diamonds; for
    he saw   1160
One of her house, and sent him to the
    Queen
Bearing his wish, whereto the Queen agreed
With such and so unmoved a majesty
She might have seem'd her statue, but that
    he,
Low-drooping till he wellnigh kiss'd her
    feet
For loyal awe, saw with a sidelong eye
The shadow of some piece of pointed lace,
In the Queen's shadow, vibrate on the
    walls,
And parted, laughing in his courtly heart.

All in an oriel on the summer side,   1170
Vine-clad, of Arthur's palace toward the
    stream,
They met, and Lancelot kneeling utter'd:
' Queen,
Lady, my liege, in whom I have my joy,
Take, what I had not won except for you,
These jewels, and make me happy, making
    them
An armlet for the roundest arm on earth,
Or necklace for a neck to which the swan's
Is tawnier than her cygnet's. These are
    words;
Your beauty is your beauty, and I sin
In speaking, yet O, grant my worship of it

Words, as we grant grief tears. Such sin
    in words   1181
Perchance, we both can pardon; but, my
    Queen,
I hear of rumors flying thro' your court.
Our bond, as not the bond of man and wife,
Should have in it an absoluter trust
To make up that defect: let rumors be.
When did not rumors fly? these, as I
    trust
That you trust me in your own nobleness,
I may not well believe that you believe.'

While thus he spoke, half turn'd away,
    the Queen   1190
Brake from the vast oriel-embowering vine
Leaf after leaf, and tore, and cast them
    off,
Till all the place whereon she stood was
    green;
Then, when he ceased, in one cold passive
    hand
Received at once and laid aside the gems
There on a table near her, and replied:

' It may be I am quicker of belief
Than you believe me, Lancelot of the Lake.
Our bond is not the bond of man and
    wife.
This good is in it, whatsoe'er of ill,   1200
It can be broken easier. I for you
This many a year have done despite and
    wrong
To one whom ever in my heart of hearts
I did acknowledge nobler. What are
    these ?
Diamonds for me ! they had been thrice
    their worth
Being your gift, had you not lost your own.
To loyal hearts the value of all gifts
Must vary as the giver's. Not for me !
For her ! for your new fancy. Only this
Grant me, I pray you; have your joys
    apart.   1210
I doubt not that, however changed, you
    keep
So much of what is graceful; and myself
Would shun to break those bounds of cour-
    tesy
In which as Arthur's Queen I move and
    rule,
So cannot speak my mind. An end to this !
A strange one ! yet I take it with Amen.
So pray you, add my diamonds to her
    pearls;

Deck her with these; tell her, she shines
    me down:
An armlet for an arm to which the Queen's
Is haggard, or a necklace for a neck   1220
O, as much fairer — as a faith once fair
Was richer than these diamonds — hers not
    mine —
Nay, by the mother of our Lord himself,
Or hers or mine, mine now to work my
    will —
She shall not have them.'

                Saying which she seized,
And, thro' the casement standing wide for
    heat,
Flung them, and down they flash'd, and
    smote the stream.
Then from the smitten surface flash'd, as it
    were,
Diamonds to meet them, and they past
    away.
Then while Sir Lancelot leant, in half dis-
    dain   1230
At love, life, all things, on the window
    ledge,
Close underneath his eyes, and right across
Where these had fallen, slowly past the
    barge
Whereon the lily maid of Astolat
Lay smiling, like a star in blackest night.

  But the wild Queen, who saw not, burst
    away
To weep and wail in secret; and the barge,
On to the palace-doorway sliding, paused.
There two stood arm'd, and kept the door;
    to whom,
All up the marble stair, tier over tier,   1240
Were added mouths that gaped, and eyes
    that ask'd,
'What is it?' but that oarsman's haggard
    face,
As hard and still as is the face that men
Shape to their fancy's eye from broken
    rocks
On some cliff-side, appall'd them, and they
    said:
'He is enchanted, cannot speak — and she,
Look how she sleeps — the Fairy Queen, so
    fair!
Yea, but how pale! what are they? flesh
    and blood?
Or come to take the King to Fairyland?
For some do hold our Arthur cannot die,
But that he passes into Fairyland.'   1251

While thus they babbled of the King, the
    King
Came girt with knights.   Then turn'd the
    tongueless man
From the half-face to the full eye, and rose
And pointed to the damsel and the doors.
So Arthur bade the meek Sir Percivale
And pure Sir Galahad to uplift the maid;
And reverently they bore her into hall.
Then came the fine Gawain and wonder'd
    at her,   1259
And Lancelot later came and mused at her,
And last the Queen herself, and pitied her;
But Arthur spied the letter in her hand,
Stoopt, took, brake seal, and read it; this
    was all:

'Most noble lord, Sir Lancelot of the
    Lake,
I, sometime call'd the maid of Astolat,
Come, for you left me taking no farewell,
Hither, to take my last farewell of you.
I loved you, and my love had no return,
And therefore my true love has been my
    death.
And therefore to our Lady Guinevere,   1270
And to all other ladies, I make moan:
Pray for my soul, and yield me burial.
Pray for my soul thou too, Sir Lancelot,
As thou art a knight peerless.'

                Thus he read;
And ever in the reading lords and dames
Wept, looking often from his face who read
To hers which lay so silent, and at times,
So touch'd were they, half-thinking that her
    lips
Who had devised the letter moved again.

Then freely spoke Sir Lancelot to them
    all: 1280
'My lord liege Arthur, and all ye that hear,
Know that for this most gentle maiden's
    death
Right heavy am I; for good she was and
    true,
But loved me with a love beyond all love
In women, whomsoever I have known.
Yet to be loved makes not to love again;
Not at my years, however it hold in youth.
I swear by truth and knighthood that I
    gave
No cause, not willingly, for such a love.
To this I call my friends in testimony,   1290
Her brethren, and her father, who himself

Besought me to be plain and blunt, and use,
To break her passion, some discourtesy
Against my nature; what I could, I did.
I left her and I bade her no farewell;
Tho', had I dreamt the damsel would have died,
I might have put my wits to some rough use,
And help'd her from herself.'

Then said the Queen —
Sea was her wrath, yet working after storm:
'Ye might at least have done her so much grace,   1300
Fair lord, as would have help'd her from her death.'
He raised his head, their eyes met and hers fell,
He adding: 'Queen, she would not be content
Save that I wedded her, which could not be.
Then might she follow me thro' the world, she ask'd;
It could not be. I told her that her love
Was but the flash of youth, would darken down,
To rise hereafter in a stiller flame
Toward one more worthy of her — then would I,   1309
More specially were he she wedded poor,
Estate them with large land and territory
In mine own realm beyond the narrow seas,
To keep them in all joyance. More than this
I could not; this she would not, and she died.'

He pausing, Arthur answer'd: 'O my knight,
It will be to thy worship, as my knight,
And mine, as head of all our Table Round,
To see that she be buried worshipfully.'

So toward that shrine which then in all the realm
Was richest, Arthur leading, slowly went
The marshall'd Order of their Table Round,   1321
And Lancelot sad beyond his wont, to see
The maiden buried, not as one unknown,
Nor meanly, but with gorgeous obsequies,
And mass, and rolling music, like a queen.

And when the knights had laid her comely head
Low in the dust of half-forgotten kings,
Then Arthur spake among them: 'Let her tomb
Be costly, and her image thereupon,   1329
And let the shield of Lancelot at her feet
Be carven, and her lily in her hand.
And let the story of her dolorous voyage
For all true hearts be blazon'd on her tomb
In letters gold and azure!' which was wrought
Thereafter; but when now the lords and dames
And people, from the high door streaming, brake
Disorderly, as homeward each, the Queen,
Who mark'd Sir Lancelot where he moved apart,
Drew near, and sigh'd in passing, 'Lancelot,
Forgive me; mine was jealousy in love.'   1340
He answer'd with his eyes upon the ground,
'That is love's curse; pass on, my Queen, forgiven.'
But Arthur, who beheld his cloudy brows,
Approach'd him, and with full affection said:

'Lancelot, my Lancelot, thou in whom I have
Most joy and most affiance, for I know
What thou hast been in battle by my side,
And many a time have watch'd thee at the tilt
Strike down the lusty and long practised knight   1349
And let the younger and unskill'd go by
To win his honor and to make his name,
And loved thy courtesies and thee, a man
Made to be loved; but now I would to God,
Seeing the homeless trouble in thine eyes,
Thou couldst have loved this maiden, shaped, it seems,
By God for thee alone, and from her face,
If one may judge the living by the dead,
Delicately pure and marvellously fair,
Who might have brought thee, now a lonely man   1359
Wifeless and heirless, noble issue, sons
Born to the glory of thy name and fame,
My knight, the great Sir Lancelot of the Lake.'

Then answer'd Lancelot: 'Fair she was,
    my King,
Pure, as you ever wish your knights to be.
To doubt her fairness were to want an eye,
To doubt her pureness were to want a
    heart —
Yea, to be loved, if what is worthy love
Could bind him, but free love will not be
    bound.'

'Free love, so bound, were freest,' said
    the King.   1369
'Let love be free; free love is for the best.
And, after heaven, on our dull side of
    death,
What should be best, if not so pure a love
Clothed in so pure a loveliness? yet thee
She fail'd to bind, tho' being, as I think,
Unbound as yet, and gentle, as I know.'

And Lancelot answer'd nothing, but he
    went,
And at the inrunning of a little brook
Sat by the river in a cove, and watch'd
The high reed wave, and lifted up his eyes
And saw the barge that brought her mov-
    ing down,   1380
Far-off, a blot upon the stream, and said
Low in himself: 'Ah, simple heart and
    sweet,
Ye loved me, damsel, surely with a love
Far tenderer than my Queen's. Pray for
    thy soul?
Ay, that will I. Farewell too — now at
    last —
Farewell, fair lily. "Jealousy in love?"
Not rather dead love's harsh heir, jealous
    pride?
Queen, if I grant the jealousy as of love,
May not your crescent fear for name and
    fame
Speak, as it waxes, of a love that wanes?
Why did the King dwell on my name to
    me?   1391
Mine own name shames me, seeming a re-
    proach,
Lancelot, whom the Lady of the Lake
Caught from his mother's arms — the won-
    drous one
Who passes thro' the vision of the night —
She chanted snatches of mysterious hymns
Heard on the winding waters, eve and
    morn
She kiss'd me saying, "Thou art fair, my
    child,

As a king's son," and often in her arms
She bare me, pacing on the dusky mere.
Would she had drown'd me in it, where'er
    it be!   1401
For what am I? what profits me my name
Of greatest knight? I fought for it, and
    have it.
Pleasure to have it, none; to lose it, pain;
Now grown a part of me; but what use in
    it?
To make men worse by making my sin
    known?
Or sin seem less, the sinner seeming great?
Alas for Arthur's greatest knight, a man
Not after Arthur's heart! I needs must
    break
These bonds that so defame me. Not with-
    out   1410
She wills it — would I, if she will'd it?
    nay,
Who knows? but if I would not, then may
    God,
I pray him, send a sudden angel down
To seize me by the hair and bear me far,
And fling me deep in that forgotten mere,
Among the tumbled fragments of the
    hills.'

So groan'd Sir Lancelot in remorseful
    pain,
Not knowing he should die a holy man.

THE HOLY GRAIL

FROM noiseful arms, and acts of prowess
    done
In tournament or tilt, Sir Percivale
Whom Arthur and his knighthood call'd
    the Pure,
Had past into the silent life of prayer,
Praise, fast, and alms; and leaving for the
    cowl
The helmet in an abbey far away
From Camelot, there, and not long after,
    died.

And one, a fellow-monk among the rest,
Ambrosius, loved him much beyond the
    rest,
And honor'd him, and wrought into his
    heart   10
A way by love that waken'd love within,
To answer that which came; and as they
    sat

Beneath a world-old yew-tree, darkening half
The cloisters, on a gustful April morn
That puff'd the swaying branches into smoke
Above them, ere the summer when he died,
The monk Ambrosius question'd Percivale:

'O brother, I have seen this yew-tree smoke,
Spring after spring, for half a hundred years;
For never have I known the world without,
Nor ever stray'd beyond the pale. But thee,   20
When first thou camest — such a courtesy
Spake thro' the limbs and in the voice — I knew
For one of those who eat in Arthur's hall;
For good ye are and bad, and like to coins,
Some true, some light, but every one of you
Stamp'd with the image of the King; and now
Tell me, what drove thee from the Table Round,
My brother ? was it earthly passion crost ? '

'Nay,' said the knight; 'for no such passion mine.   30
But the sweet vision of the Holy Grail
Drove me from all vainglories, rivalries,
And earthly heats that spring and sparkle out
Among us in the jousts, while women watch
Who wins, who falls, and waste the spiritual strength
Within us, better offer'd up to heaven.'

To whom the monk: 'The Holy Grail !
— I trust
We are green in Heaven's eyes; but here too much
We moulder — as to things without I mean —
Yet one of your own knights, a guest of ours,   40
Told us of this in our refectory,
But spake with such a sadness and so low
We heard not half of what he said. What is it ?
The phantom of a cup that comes and goes ? '

'Nay, monk ! what phantom ? ' answer'd Percivale.
'The cup, the cup itself, from which our Lord
Drank at the last sad supper with his own.
This, from the blessed land of Aromat —
After the day of darkness, when the dead
Went wandering o'er Moriah — the good saint   50
Arimathæan Joseph, journeying brought
To Glastonbury, where the winter thorn
Blossoms at Christmas, mindful of our Lord.
And there awhile it bode; and if a man
Could touch or see it, he was heal'd at once,
By faith, of all his ills. But then the times
Grew to such evil that the holy cup
Was caught away to heaven, and disappear'd.'

To whom the monk: 'From our old books I know
That Joseph came of old to Glastonbury,   60
And there the heathen Prince, Arviragus,
Gave him an isle of marsh whereon to build;
And there he built with wattles from the marsh
A little lonely church in days of yore,
For so they say, these books of ours, but seem
Mute of this miracle, far as I have read.
But who first saw the holy thing to-day ? '

'A woman,' answer'd Percivale, 'a nun,
And one no further off in blood from me
Than sister; and if ever holy maid   70
With knees of adoration wore the stone,
A holy maid; tho' never maiden glow'd,
But that was in her earlier maidenhood,
With such a fervent flame of human love,
Which, being rudely blunted, glanced and shot
Only to holy things; to prayer and praise
She gave herself, to fast and alms. And yet,
Nun as she was, the scandal of the Court,
Sin against Arthur and the Table Round,
And the strange sound of an adulterous race,   80
Across the iron grating of her cell
Beat, and she pray'd and fasted all the more.

'And he to whom she told her sins, or
  what
Her all but utter whiteness held for sin,
A man wellnigh a hundred winters old,
Spake often with her of the Holy Grail,
A legend handed down thro' five or six,
And each of these a hundred winters old,
From our Lord's time. And when King
  Arthur made
His Table Round, and all men's hearts be-
  came   90
Clean for a season, surely he had thought
That now the Holy Grail would come
  again;
But sin broke out. Ah, Christ, that it
  would come,
And heal the world of all their wicked-
  ness !
"O Father !" ask'd the maiden, "might it
  come
To me by prayer and fasting ?" "Nay,"
  said he,
"I know not, for thy heart is pure as
  snow."
And so she pray'd and fasted, till the sun
Shone, and the wind blew, thro' her, and I
  thought
She might have risen and floated when I
  saw her.   100

'For on a day she sent to speak with me.
And when she came to speak, behold her
  eyes
Beyond my knowing of them, beautiful,
Beyond all knowing of them, wonderful,
Beautiful in the light of holiness !
And "O my brother Percivale," she said,
"Sweet brother, I have seen the Holy
  Grail;
For, waked at dead of night, I heard a
  sound
As of a silver horn from o'er the hills   109
Blown, and I thought, 'It is not Arthur's
  use
To hunt by moonlight.' And the slender
  sound
As from a distance beyond distance grew
Coming upon me — O never harp nor horn,
Nor aught we blow with breath, or touch
  with hand,
Was like that music as it came; and then
Stream'd thro' my cell a cold and silver
  beam,
And down the long beam stole the Holy
  Grail,

Rose-red with beatings in it, as if alive,
Till all the white walls of my cell were
  dyed
With rosy colors leaping on the wall;   120
And then the music faded, and the Grail
Past, and the beam decay'd, and from the
  walls
The rosy quiverings died into the night.
So now the Holy Thing is here again
Among us, brother, fast thou too and pray,
And tell thy brother knights to fast and
  pray,
That so perchance the vision may be seen
By thee and those, and all the world be
  heal'd."

'Then leaving the pale nun, I spake of
  this   129
To all men; and myself fasted and pray'd
Always, and many among us many a week
Fasted and pray'd even to the uttermost,
Expectant of the wonder that would be.

'And one there was among us, ever
  moved
Among us in white armor, Galahad.
"God make thee good as thou art beauti-
  ful !"
Said Arthur, when he dubb'd him knight,
  and none
In so young youth was ever made a knight
Till Galahad; and this Galahad, when he
  heard
My sister's vision, fill'd me with amaze; 140
His eyes became so like her own, they
  seem'd
Hers, and himself her brother more than I.

'Sister or brother none had he; but some
Call'd him a son of Lancelot, and some
  said
Begotten by enchantment — chatterers
  they,
Like birds of passage piping up and down,
That gape for flies — we know not whence
  they come;
For when was Lancelot wanderingly lewd ?

'But she, the wan sweet maiden, shore
  away
Clean from her forehead all that wealth of
  hair   150
Which made a silken mat-work for her
  feet;
And out of this she plaited broad and long

A strong sword-belt, and wove with silver
    thread
And crimson in the belt a strange device,
A crimson grail within a silver beam;
And saw the bright boy-knight, and bound
    it on him,
Saying: "My knight, my love, my knight
    of heaven,
O thou, my love, whose love is one with
    mine,
I, maiden, round thee, maiden, bind my
    belt.
Go forth, for thou shalt see what I have
    seen,   160
And break thro' all, till one will crown thee
    king
Far in the spiritual city;" and as she spake
She sent the deathless passion in her eyes
Thro' him, and made him hers, and laid
    her mind
On him, and he believed in her belief.

'Then came a year of miracle. O bro-
    ther,
In our great hall there stood a vacant
    chair,
Fashion'd by Merlin ere he past away,
And carven with strange figures; and in
    and out
The figures, like a serpent, ran a scroll 170
Of letters in a tongue no man could read.
And Merlin call'd it "the Siege Peril-
    ous,"
Perilous for good and ill; "for there," he
    said,
"No man could sit but he should lose him-
    self."
And once by misadvertence Merlin sat
In his own chair, and so was lost; but
    he,
Galahad, when he heard of Merlin's doom,
Cried, "If I lose myself, I save myself!"

'Then on a summer night it came to
    pass,
While the great banquet lay along the
    hall,   180
That Galahad would sit down in Merlin's
    chair.

'And all at once, as there we sat, we
    heard
A cracking and a riving of the roofs,
And rending, and a blast, and overhead
Thunder and in the thunder was a cry.

And in the blast there smote along the hall
A beam of light seven times more clear
    than day;
And down the long beam stole the Holy
    Grail
All over cover'd with a luminous cloud,
And none might see who bare it, and it
    past.   190
But every knight beheld his fellow's face
As in a glory, and all the knights arose,
And staring each at other like dumb men
Stood, till I found a voice and sware a
    vow.

'I sware a vow before them all, that I,
Because I had not seen the Grail, would
    ride
A twelvemonth and a day in quest of it,
Until I found and saw it, as the nun
My sister saw it; and Galahad sware the
    vow,
And good Sir Bors, our Lancelot's cousin,
    sware,   200
And Lancelot sware, and many among the
    knights,
And Gawain sware, and louder than the
    rest.'

Then spake the monk Ambrosius, asking
    him,
'What said the King? Did Arthur take
    the vow?

'Nay, for my lord,' said Percivale, 'the
    King,
Was not in hall; for early that same day,
Scaped thro' a cavern from a bandit bold,
An outraged maiden sprang into the hall
Crying on help; for all her shining hair
Was smear'd with earth, and either milky
    arm   210
Red-rent with hooks of bramble, and all
    she wore
Torn as a sail that leaves the rope is torn
In tempest. So the King arose and went
To smoke the scandalous hive of those
    wild bees
That made such honey in his realm. How-
    beit
Some little of this marvel he too saw,
Returning o'er the plain that then began
To darken under Camelot; whence the
    King
Look'd up, calling aloud, "Lo, there! the
    roofs

Of our great hall are roll'd in thunder-
    smoke !   220
Pray heaven, they be not smitten by the
    bolt ! "
For dear to Arthur was that hall of ours,
As having there so oft with all his knights
Feasted, and as the stateliest under heaven.

  'O brother, had you known our mighty
    hall,
Which Merlin built for Arthur long ago !
For all the sacred mount of Camelot,
And all the dim rich city, roof by roof,
Tower after tower, spire beyond spire,
By grove, and garden - lawn, and rushing
    brook,   230
Climbs to the mighty hall that Merlin
    built.
And four great zones of sculpture, set be-
    twixt
With many a mystic symbol, gird the hall;
And in the lowest beasts are slaying men,
And in the second men are slaying beasts,
And on the third are warriors, perfect
    men,
And on the fourth are men with growing
    wings,
And over all one statue in the mould
Of Arthur, made by Merlin, with a crown,
And peak'd wings pointed to the Northern
    Star.   240
And eastward fronts the statue, and the
    crown
And both the wings are made of gold, and
    flame
At sunrise till the people in far fields,
Wasted so often by the heathen hordes,
Behold it, crying, " We have still a king."

  'And, brother, had you known our hall
    within,
Broader and higher than any in all the
    lands !
Where twelve great windows blazon Ar-
    thur's wars,
And all the light that falls upon the board
Streams thro' the twelve great battles of
    our King.   250
Nay, one there is, and at the eastern end,
Wealthy with wandering lines of mount
    and mere,
Where Arthur finds the brand Excalibur.
And also one to the west, and counter to it,
And blank; and who shall blazon it ? when
    and how ? —

O, there, perchance, when all our wars are
    done,
The brand Excalibur will be cast away !

  'So to this hall full quickly rode the
    King,
In horror lest the work by Merlin wrought,
Dreamlike, should on the sudden vanish,
    wrapt   260
In unremorseful folds of rolling fire.
And in he rode, and up I glanced, and
    saw
The golden dragon sparkling over all;
And many of those who burnt the hold,
    their arms
Hack'd, and their foreheads grimed with
    smoke and sear'd,
Follow'd, and in among bright faces, ours,
Full of the vision, prest; and then the King
Spake to me, being nearest, " Percivale,"—
Because the hall was all in tumult — some
Vowing, and some protesting, — " what is
    this ? "   270

  'O brother, when I told him what had
    chanced,
My sister's vision and the rest, his face
Darken'd, as I have seen it more than once,
When some brave deed seem'd to be done
    in vain,
Darken; and " Woe is me, my knights,"
    he cried,
" Had I been here, ye had not sworn the
    vow."
Bold was mine answer, " Had thyself been
    here,
My King, thou wouldst have sworn." " Yea,
    yea," said he,
" Art thou so bold and hast not seen the
    Grail ? "

  '" Nay, lord, I heard the sound, I saw
    the light,   280
But since I did not see the holy thing,
I sware a vow to follow it till I saw."

  'Then when he ask'd us, knight by
    knight, if any
Had seen it, all their answers were as one:
" Nay, lord, and therefore have we sworn
    our vows."

  '" Lo, now," said Arthur, " have ye seen
    a cloud ?
What go ye into the wilderness to see ? "

'Then Galahad on the sudden, and in a
voice
Shrilling along the hall to Arthur, call'd,
"But I, Sir Arthur, saw the Holy Grail,   290
I saw the Holy Grail and heard a cry —
'O Galahad, and O Galahad, follow me!'"'

'"Ah, Galahad, Galahad," said the King,
"for such
As thou art is the vision, not for these.
Thy holy nun and thou have seen a sign —
Holier is none, my Percivale, than she —
A sign to maim this Order which I made.
But ye that follow but the leader's bell,"—
Brother, the King was hard upon his
knights, —
"Taliessin is our fullest throat of song,   300
And one hath sung and all the dumb will
sing.
Lancelot is Lancelot, and hath overborne
Five knights at once, and every younger
knight,
Unproven, holds himself as Lancelot,
Till overborne by one, he learns — and ye,
What are ye? Galahads? — no, nor Per-
civales"—
For thus it pleased the King to range me
close
After Sir Galahad; — "nay," said he, "but
men
With strength and will to right the wrong'd,
of power
To lay the sudden heads of violence flat,   310
Knights that in twelve great battles
splash'd and dyed
The strong White Horse in his own heathen
blood —
But one hath seen, and all the blind will
see.
Go, since your vows are sacred, being made.
Yet — for ye know the cries of all my
realm
Pass thro' this hall — how often, O my
knights,
Your places being vacant at my side,
This chance of noble deeds will come and
go
Unchallenged, while ye follow wandering
fires
Lost in the quagmire! Many of you, yea
most,   320
Return no more. Ye think I show myself
Too dark a prophet. Come now, let us meet
The morrow morn once more in one full
field

Of gracious pastime, that once more the
King,
Before ye leave him for this quest, may
count
The yet-unbroken strength of all his
knights,
Rejoicing in that Order which he made."

'So when the sun broke next from under-
ground,
All the great Table of our Arthur closed
And clash'd in such a tourney and so full,
So many lances broken — never yet   331
Had Camelot seen the like since Arthur
came;
And I myself and Galahad, for a strength
Was in us from the vision, overthrew
So many knights that all the people cried,
And almost burst the barriers in their heat,
Shouting, "Sir Galahad and Sir Perci-
vale!"

'But when the next day brake from un-
derground —
O brother, had you known our Camelot,
Built by old kings, age after age, so old
The King himself had fears that it would
fall,   341
So strange, and rich, and dim; for where
the roofs
Totter'd toward each other in the sky,
Met foreheads all along the street of those
Who watch'd us pass; and lower, and where
the long
Rich galleries, lady-laden, weigh'd the
necks
Of dragons clinging to the crazy walls,
Thicker than drops from thunder, showers
of flowers
Fell as we past; and men and boys astride
On wyvern, lion, dragon, griffin, swan,   350
At all the corners, named us each by name,
Calling "God speed!" but in the ways be-
low
The knights and ladies wept, and rich and
poor
Wept, and the King himself could hardly
speak
For grief, and all in middle street the
Queen,
Who rode by Lancelot, wail'd and shriek'd
aloud,
"This madness has come on us for our sins."
So to the Gate of the Three Queens we
came,

Where Arthur's wars are render'd mystically,
And thence departed every one his way. 360

'And I was lifted up in heart, and thought
Of all my late-shown prowess in the lists,
How my strong lance had beaten down the knights,
So many and famous names; and never yet
Had heaven appear'd so blue, nor earth so green,
For all my blood danced in me, and I knew
That I should light upon the Holy Grail.

'Thereafter, the dark warning of our King,
That most of us would follow wandering fires,
Came like a driving gloom across my mind. 370
Then every evil word I had spoken once,
And every evil thought I had thought of old,
And every evil deed I ever did,
Awoke and cried, "This quest is not for thee."
And lifting up mine eyes, I found myself
Alone, and in a land of sand and thorns,
And I was thirsty even unto death;
And I, too, cried, "This quest is not for thee."

'And on I rode, and when I thought my thirst
Would slay me, saw deep lawns, and then a brook, 380
With one sharp rapid, where the crisping white
Play'd ever back upon the sloping wave
And took both ear and eye; and o'er the brook
Were apple-trees, and apples by the brook
Fallen, and on the lawns. "I will rest here,"
I said, "I am not worthy of the quest;"
But even while I drank the brook, and ate
The goodly apples, all these things at once
Fell into dust, and I was left alone 389
And thirsting in a land of sand and thorns.

'And then behold a woman at a door
Spinning; and fair the house whereby she sat,

And kind the woman's eyes and innocent,
And all her bearing gracious; and she rose
Opening her arms to meet me, as who should say,
"Rest here;" but when I touch'd her, lo ! she, too,
Fell into dust and nothing, and the house
Became no better than a broken shed,
And in it a dead babe; and also this
Fell into dust, and I was left alone. 400

'And on I rode, and greater was my thirst.
Then flash'd a yellow gleam across the world,
And where it smote the plowshare in the field
The plowman left his plowing and fell down
Before it; where it glitter'd on her pail
The milkmaid left her milking and fell down
Before it, and I knew not why, but thought
"The sun is rising," tho' the sun had risen.
Then was I ware of one that on me moved
In golden armor with a crown of gold 410
About a casque all jewels, and his horse
In golden armor jewelled everywhere;
And on the splendor came, flashing me blind,
And seem'd to me the lord of all the world,
Being so huge. But when I thought he meant
To crush me, moving on me, lo ! he, too,
Open'd his arms to embrace me as he came,
And up I went and touch'd him, and he, too,
Fell into dust, and I was left alone 419
And wearying in a land of sand and thorns.

'And I rode on and found a mighty hill,
And on the top a city wall'd; the spires
Prick'd with incredible pinnacles into heaven.
And by the gateway stirr'd a crowd; and these
Cried to me climbing, "Welcome, Percivale !
Thou mightiest and thou purest among men !"
And glad was I and clomb, but found at top
No man, nor any voice. And thence I past

Far thro' a ruinous city, and I saw
That man had once dwelt there; but there
    I found   430
Only one man of an exceeding age.
" Where is that goodly company," said I,
" That so cried out upon me ? " and he
    had
Scarce any voice to answer, and yet gasp'd,
" Whence and what art thou ? " and even
    as he spoke
Fell into dust and disappear'd, and I
Was left alone once more and cried in
    grief,
" Lo, if I find the Holy Grail itself
And touch it, it will crumble into dust ! "

  ' And thence I dropt into a lowly vale,
Low as the hill was high, and where the
    vale   441
Was lowest found a chapel, and thereby
A holy hermit in a hermitage,
To whom I told my phantoms, and he
    said:

  ' " O son, thou hast not true humility,
The highest virtue, mother of them all;
For when the Lord of all things made
    Himself
Naked of glory for His mortal change,
' Take thou my robe,' she said, ' for all is
    thine,'
And all her form shone forth with sudden
    light   450
So that the angels were amazed, and she
Follow'd Him down, and like a flying star
Led on the gray-hair'd wisdom of the east.
But her thou hast not known; for what is
    this
Thou thoughtest of thy prowess and thy
    sins ?
Thou hast not lost thyself to save thyself
As Galahad." When the hermit made an
    end,
In silver armor suddenly Galahad shone
Before us, and against the chapel door
Laid lance and enter'd, and we knelt in
    prayer.   460
And there the hermit slaked my burning
    thirst,
And at the sacring of the mass I saw
The holy elements alone; but he,
" Saw ye no more ? I, Galahad, saw the
    Grail,
The Holy Grail, descend upon the shrine.
I saw the fiery face as of a child

That smote itself into the bread and went;
And hither am I come; and never yet
Hath what thy sister taught me first to
    see,
This holy thing, fail'd from my side, nor
    come   470
Cover'd, but moving with me night and
    day,
Fainter by day, but always in the night
Blood-red, and sliding down the blacken'd
    marsh
Blood-red, and on the naked mountain top
Blood-red, and in the sleeping mere below
Blood-red. And in the strength of this I
    rode,
Shattering all evil customs everywhere,
And past thro' Pagan realms, and made
    them mine,
And clash'd with Pagan hordes, and bore
    them down,
And broke thro' all, and in the strength of
    this   480
Come victor. But my time is hard at
    hand,
And hence I go, and one will crown me
    king
Far in the spiritual city; and come thou,
    too,
For thou shalt see the vision when I go."

  ' While thus he spake, his eye, dwelling
    on mine,
Drew me, with power upon me, till I grew
One with him, to believe as he believed.
Then, when the day began to wane, we
    went.

  ' There rose a hill that none but man
    could climb,
Scarr'd with a hundred wintry water-
    courses —   490
Storm at the top, and when we gain'd it,
    storm
Round us and death; for every moment
    glanced
His silver arms and gloom'd, so quick and
    thick
The lightnings here and there to left and
    right
Struck, till the dry old trunks about us,
    dead,
Yea, rotten with a hundred years of death,
Sprang into fire. And at the base we found
On either hand, as far as eye could see,
A great black swamp and of an evil smell,

Part black, part whiten'd with the bones of
men,   500
Not to be crost, save that some ancient
king
Had built a way, where, link'd with many
a bridge,
A thousand piers ran into the great Sea.
And Galahad fled along them bridge by
bridge,
And every bridge as quickly as he crost
Sprang into fire and vanish'd, tho' I
yearn'd
To follow; and thrice above him all the
heavens
Open'd and blazed with thunder such as
seem'd
Shoutings of all the sons of God. And first
At once I saw him far on the great Sea,
In silver-shining armor starry-clear; 511
And o'er his head the Holy Vessel hung
Clothed in white samite or a luminous
cloud.
And with exceeding swiftness ran the boat,
If boat it were — I saw not whence it
came.
And when the heavens open'd and blazed
again
Roaring, I saw him like a silver star —
And had he set the sail, or had the boat
Become a living creature clad with wings?
And o'er his head the Holy Vessel hung
Redder than any rose, a joy to me, 521
For now I knew the veil had been with-
drawn.
Then in a moment when they blazed again
Opening, I saw the least of little stars
Down on the waste, and straight beyond
the star
I saw the spiritual city and all her spires
And gateways in a glory like one pearl —
No larger, tho' the goal of all the saints —
Strike from the sea; and from the star
there shot 529
A rose-red sparkle to the city, and there
Dwelt, and I knew it was the Holy Grail,
Which never eyes on earth again shall
see.
Then fell the floods of heaven drowning
the deep,
And how my feet recrost the deathful
ridge
No memory in me lives; but that I touch'd
The chapel-doors at dawn I know, and
thence
Taking my war-horse from the holy man,

Glad that no phantom vext me more, re-
turn'd
To whence I came, the gate of Arthur's
wars.'

  ' O brother,' ask'd Ambrosius, — ' for in
sooth 540
These ancient books — and they would win
thee — teem,
Only I find not there this Holy Grail,
With miracles and marvels like to these,
Not all unlike; which oftentime I read,
Who read but on my breviary with ease,
Till my head swims, and then go forth and
pass
Down to the little thorpe that lies so close,
And almost plaster'd like a martin's nest
To these old walls — and mingle with our
folk; 549
And knowing every honest face of theirs
As well as ever shepherd knew his sheep,
And every homely secret in their hearts,
Delight myself with gossip and old wives,
And ills and aches, and teethings, lyings
in,
And mirthful sayings, children of the place,
That have no meaning half a league away;
Or lulling random squabbles when they
rise,
Chafferings and chatterings at the market-
cross,
Rejoice, small man, in this small world of
mine,
Yea, even in their hens and in their eggs —
O brother, saving this Sir Galahad, 561
Came ye on none but phantoms in your
quest,
No man, no woman ? '

                    Then Sir Percivale:
' All men, to one so bound by such a vow,
And women were as phantoms. O, my
brother,
Why wilt thou shame me to confess to
thee
How far I falter'd from my quest and
vow ?
For after I had lain so many nights,
A bed-mate of the snail and eft and snake,
In grass and burdock, I was changed to
wan 570
And meagre, and the vision had not come;
And then I chanced upon a goodly town
With one great dwelling in the middle of
it.

Thither I made, and there was I disarm'd
By maidens each as fair as any flower;
But when they led me into hall, behold,
The princess of that castle was the one,
Brother, and that one only, who had ever
Made my heart leap; for when I moved of
old
A slender page about her father's hall, 580
And she a slender maiden, all my heart
Went after her with longing, yet we twain
Had never kiss'd a kiss or vow'd a vow.
And now I came upon her once again,
And one had wedded her, and he was dead,
And all his land and wealth and state were
hers.
And while I tarried, every day she set
A banquet richer than the day before
By me, for all her longing and her will
Was toward me as of old; till one fair
morn, 590
I walking to and fro beside a stream
That flash'd across her orchard underneath
Her castle-walls, she stole upon my walk,
And calling me the greatest of all knights,
Embraced me, and so kiss'd me the first
time,
And gave herself and all her wealth to
me.
Then I remember'd Arthur's warning word,
That most of us would follow wandering
fires,
And the quest faded in my heart. Anon,
The heads of all her people drew to me,
With supplication both of knees and
tongue: 601
"We have heard of thee; thou art our
greatest knight,
Our Lady says it, and we well believe.
Wed thou our Lady, and rule over us,
And thou shalt be as Arthur in our land."
O me, my brother! but one night my vow
Burnt me within, so that I rose and fled,
But wail'd and wept, and hated mine own
self,
And even the holy quest, and all but her;
Then after I was join'd with Galahad 610
Cared not for her nor anything upon earth.'

Then said the monk: 'Poor men, when
yule is cold,
Must be content to sit by little fires.
And this am I, so that ye care for me
Ever so little; yea, and blest be heaven
That brought thee here to this poor house
of ours

Where all the brethren are so hard, to
warm
My cold heart with a friend; but O the
pity
To find thine own first love once more — to
hold,
Hold her a wealthy bride within thine
arms, 620
Or all but hold, and then — cast her aside,
Foregoing all her sweetness, like a weed!
For we that want the warmth of double
life,
We that are plagued with dreams of some-
thing sweet
Beyond all sweetness in a life so rich, —
Ah, blessed Lord, I speak too earthly-wise,
Seeing I never stray'd beyond the cell,
But live like an old badger in his earth,
With earth about him everywhere, despite
All fast and penance. Saw ye none be-
side, 630
None of your knights?'

'Yea, so,' said Percivale:
'One night my pathway swerving east, I
saw
The pelican on the casque of our Sir Bors
All in the middle of the rising moon,
And toward him spurr'd, and hail'd him,
and he me,
And each made joy of either. Then he
ask'd:
"Where is he? hast thou seen him —
Lancelot? — Once,"
Said good Sir Bors, "he dash'd across me
— mad,
And maddening what he rode; and when
I cried,
'Ridest thou then so hotly on a quest 640
So holy?' Lancelot shouted, 'Stay me
not!
I have been the sluggard, and I ride apace,
For now there is a lion in the way!'
So vanish'd."

'Then Sir Bors had ridden on
Softly, and sorrowing for our Lancelot,
Because his former madness, once the talk
And scandal of our table, had return'd;
For Lancelot's kith and kin so worship him
That ill to him is ill to them, to Bors
Beyond the rest. He well had been content
Not to have seen, so Lancelot might have
seen, 651
The Holy Cup of healing; and, indeed,

Being so clouded with his grief and love,
Small heart was his after the holy quest.
If God would send the vision, well; if not,
The quest and he were in the hands of
    Heaven.

  ' And then, with small adventure met,
    Sir Bors
Rode to the lonest tract of all the realm,
And found a people there among their
    crags,
Our race and blood, a remnant that were
    left   660
Paynim amid their circles, and the stones
They pitch up straight to heaven; and their
    wise men
Were strong in that old magic which can
    trace
The wandering of the stars, and scoff'd at
    him
And this high quest as at a simple thing,
Told him he follow'd — almost Arthur's
    words —
A mocking fire: " what other fire than he
Whereby the blood beats, and the blossom
    blows,
And the sea rolls, and all the world is
    warm'd ? "
And when his answer chafed them, the
    rough crowd,   670
Hearing he had a difference with their
    priests,
Seized him, and bound and plunged him
    into a cell
Of great piled stones; and lying bounden
    there
In darkness thro' innumerable hours
He heard the hollow-ringing heavens sweep
Over him till by miracle — what else ? —
Heavy as it was, a great stone slipt and
    fell,
Such as no wind could move; and thro' the
    gap
Glimmer'd the streaming scud. Then came
    a night
Still as the day was loud, and thro' the
    gap   680
The seven clear stars of Arthur's Table
    Round —
For, brother, so one night, because they roll
Thro' such a round in heaven, we named
    the stars,
Rejoicing in ourselves and in our King —
And these, like bright eyes of familiar
    friends,

In on him shone: " And then to me, to
    me,"
Said good Sir Bors, " beyond all hopes of
    mine,
Who scarce had pray'd or ask'd it for my-
    self —
Across the seven clear stars — O grace to
    me ! —
In color like the fingers of a hand   690
Before a burning taper, the sweet Grail
Glided and past, and close upon it peal'd
A sharp quick thunder." Afterwards, a
    maid,
Who kept our holy faith among her kin
In secret, entering, loosed and let him go.'

  To whom the monk: ' And I remember
    now
That pelican on the casque. Sir Bors it was
Who spake so low and sadly at our board,
And mighty reverent at our grace was he;
A square-set man and honest, and his eyes,
An outdoor sign of all the warmth within,
Smiled with his lips — a smile beneath a
    cloud,   702
But heaven had meant it for a sunny one.
Ay, ay, Sir Bors, who else ? But when ye
    reach'd
The city, found ye all your knights re-
    turn'd,
Or was there sooth in Arthur's prophecy,
Tell me, and what said each, and what the
    King ? '

  Then answer'd Percivale: ' And that
    can I,   708
Brother, and truly; since the living words
Of so great men as Lancelot and our King
Pass not from door to door and out again,
But sit within the house. O, when we
    reach'd
The city, our horses stumbling as they
    trode
On heaps of ruin, hornless unicorns,
Crack'd basilisks, and splinter'd cocka-
    trices,
And shatter'd talbots, which had left the
    stones
Raw that they fell from, brought us to the
    hall.

  ' And there sat Arthur on the dais-throne,
And those that had gone out upon the
    quest,
Wasted and worn, and but a tithe of them,

And those that had not, stood before the
   King,   721
Who, when he saw me, rose and bade me
   hail,
Saying: " A welfare in thine eyes reproves
Our fear of some disastrous chance for
   thee
On hill or plain, at sea or flooding ford.
So fierce a gale made havoc here of late
Among the strange devices of our kings,
Yea, shook this newer, stronger hall of ours,
And from the statue Merlin moulded for
   us
Half-wrench'd a golden wing; but now —
   the quest,   730
This vision — hast thou seen the Holy Cup
That Joseph brought of old to Glaston-
   bury ? "

   ' So when I told him all thyself hast
      heard,
Ambrosius, and my fresh but fixt resolve
To pass away into the quiet life,
He answer'd not, but, sharply turning,
   ask'd
Of Gawain, " Gawain, was this quest for
   thee ? "

   ' " Nay, lord," said Gawain, " not for
      such as I.
Therefore I communed with a saintly man,
Who made me sure the quest was not for
   me;   740
For I was much a-wearied of the quest,
But found a silk pavilion in a field,
And merry maidens in it; and then this
   gale
Tore my pavilion from the tenting-pin,
And blew my merry maidens all about
With all discomfort; yea, and but for this,
My twelvemonth and a day were pleasant
   to me."

   ' He ceased; and Arthur turn'd to whom
      at first
He saw not, for Sir Bors, on entering,
   push'd
Athwart the throng to Lancelot, caught his
   hand,   750
Held it, and there, half-hidden by him,
   stood,
Until the King espied him, saying to him,
" Hail, Bors ! if ever loyal man and true
Could see it, thou hast seen the Grail; "
   and Bors,

" Ask me not, for I may not speak of it;
I saw it; " and the tears were in his eyes.

   ' Then there remain'd but Lancelot, for
      the rest
Spake but of sundry perils in the storm.
Perhaps, like him of Cana in Holy Writ,
Our Arthur kept his best until the last; 760
" Thou, too, my Lancelot," ask'd the King,
   " my friend,
Our mightiest, hath this quest avail'd for
   thee ? "

   ' " Our mightiest ! " answer'd Lancelot,
      with a groan;
" O King ! " — and when he paused me-
   thought I spied
A dying fire of madness in his eyes —
" O King, my friend, if friend of thine I be,
Happier are those that welter in their sin,
Swine in the mud, that cannot see for
   slime,   768
Slime of the ditch; but in me lived a sin
So strange, of such a kind, that all of pure,
Noble, and knightly in me twined and clung
Round that one sin, until the wholesome
   flower
And poisonous grew together, each as each,
Not to be pluck'd asunder; and when thy
   knights
Sware, I sware with them only in the hope
That could I touch or see the Holy Grail
They might be pluck'd asunder. Then I
   spake
To one most holy saint, who wept and said
That, save they could be pluck'd asunder,
   all
My quest were but in vain; to whom I
   vow'd   780
That I would work according as he will'd.
And forth I went, and while I yearn'd and
   strove
To tear the twain asunder in my heart,
My madness came upon me as of old,
And whipt me into waste fields far away.
There was I beaten down by little men,
Mean knights, to whom the moving of my
   sword
And shadow of my spear had been enow
To scare them from me once; and then I
   came
All in my folly to the naked shore,   790
Wide flats, where nothing but coarse
   grasses grew;
But such a blast, my King, began to blow,

So loud a blast along the shore and sea,
Ye could not hear the waters for the blast,
Tho' heapt in mounds and ridges all the sea
Drove like a cataract, and all the sand
Swept like a river, and the clouded heavens
Were shaken with the motion and the sound.
And blackening in the sea-foam sway'd a
          boat,   799
Half-swallow'd in it, anchor'd with a chain;
And in my madness to myself I said,
'I will embark and I will lose myself,
And in the great sea wash away my sin.'
I burst the chain, I sprang into the boat.
Seven days I drove along the dreary deep,
And with me drove the moon and all the
          stars;
And the wind fell, and on the seventh night
I heard the shingle grinding in the surge,
And felt the boat shock earth, and looking
          up,
Behold, the enchanted towers of Carbonek,
A castle like a rock upon a rock,   811
With chasm-like portals open to the sea,
And steps that met the breaker! There
          was none
Stood near it but a lion on each side
That kept the entry, and the moon was full.
Then from the boat I leapt, and up the
          stairs,
There drew my sword. With sudden-
          flaring manes
Those two great beasts rose upright like a
          man,
Each gript a shoulder, and I stood between,
And, when I would have smitten them,
          heard a voice,   820
'Doubt not, go forward; if thou doubt, the
          beasts
Will tear thee piecemeal.' Then with vio-
          lence
The sword was dash'd from out my hand,
          and fell.
And up into the sounding hall I past;
But nothing in the sounding hall I saw,
No bench nor table, painting on the wall
Or shield of knight, only the rounded moon
Thro' the tall oriel on the rolling sea.
But always in the quiet house I heard,
Clear as a lark, high o'er me as a lark, 830
A sweet voice singing in the topmost
          tower
To the eastward. Up I climb'd a thousand
          steps
With pain; as in a dream I seem'd to
          climb

For ever; at the last I reach'd a door,
A light was in the crannies, and I heard,
'Glory and joy and honor to our Lord
And to the Holy Vessel of the Grail!'
Then in my madness I essay'd the door;
It gave, and thro' a stormy glare, a heat
As from a seven-times-heated furnace, I,
Blasted and burnt, and blinded as I was,
With such a fierceness that I swoon'd
          away —   842
O, yet methought I saw the Holy Grail,
All pall'd in crimson samite, and around
Great angels, awful shapes, and wings and
          eyes!
And but for all my madness and my sin,
And then my swooning, I had sworn I saw
That which I saw; but what I saw was
          veil'd
And cover'd, and this quest was not for me.'

'So speaking, and here ceasing, Lancelot
          left   850
The hall long silent, till Sir Gawain — nay,
Brother, I need not tell thee foolish
          words, —
A reckless and irreverent knight was he,
Now bolden'd by the silence of his King, —
Well, I will tell thee: "O King, my liege,"
          he said,
"Hath Gawain fail'd in any quest of thine?
When have I stinted stroke in foughten
          field?
But as for thine, my good friend Percivale,
Thy holy nun and thou have driven men
          mad,
Yea, made our mightiest madder than our
          least.   860
But by mine eyes and by mine ears I
          swear,
I will be deafer than the blue-eyed cat,
And thrice as blind as any noonday owl,
To holy virgins in their ecstasies,
Henceforward."

          '"Deafer," said the blameless King,
"Gawain, and blinder unto holy things,
Hope not to make thyself by idle vows,
Being too blind to have desire to see.
But if indeed there came a sign from
          heaven,
Blessed are Bors, Lancelot, and Perci-
          vale,   870
For these have seen according to their
          sight.
For every fiery prophet in old times,

And all the sacred madness of the bard,
When God made music thro' them, could
  but speak
His music by the framework and the chord;
And as ye saw it ye have spoken truth.

  '"Nay — but thou errest, Lancelot;
    never yet
Could all of true and noble in knight and
  man
Twine round one sin, whatever it might be,
With such a closeness but apart there
  grew,   880
Save that he were the swine thou spakest
  of,
Some root of knighthood and pure noble-
  ness;
Whereto see thou, that it may bear its
  flower.

  '"And spake I not too truly, O my
    knights ?
Was I too dark a prophet when I said
To those who went upon the Holy Quest,
That most of them would follow wander-
  ing fires,
Lost in the quagmire ? — lost to me and
  gone,
And left me gazing at a barren board,
And a lean Order — scarce return'd a
  tithe —   890
And out of those to whom the vision came
My greatest hardly will believe he saw.
Another hath beheld it afar off,
And, leaving human wrongs to right them-
  selves,
Cares but to pass into the silent life.
And one hath had the vision face to face,
And now his chair desires him here in vain,
However they may crown him otherwhere.

  '"And some among you held that if the
    King
Had seen the sight he would have sworn
  the vow.   900
Not easily, seeing that the King must
  guard
That which he rules, and is but as the hind
To whom a space of land is given to plow,
Who may not wander from the allotted
  field
Before his work be done, but, being done,
Let visions of the night or of the day
Come as they will; and many a time they
  come,

Until this earth he walks on seems not
  earth,
This light that strikes his eyeball is not
  light,
This air that smites his forehead is not
  air   910
But vision — yea, his very hand and foot —
In moments when he feels he cannot die,
And knows himself no vision to himself,
Nor the high God a vision, nor that One
Who rose again. Ye have seen what ye
  have seen."

  'So spake the King; I knew not all he
    meant.'

PELLEAS AND ETTARRE

KING ARTHUR made new knights to fill
  the gap
Left by the Holy Quest; and as he sat
In hall at old Caerleon, the high doors
Were softly sunder'd, and thro' these a
  youth,
Pelleas, and the sweet smell of the fields
Past, and the sunshine came along with
  him.

  'Make me thy knight, because I know,
    Sir King,
All that belongs to knighthood, and I love.'
Such was his cry; for having heard the
  King
Had let proclaim a tournament — the
  prize   10
A golden circlet and a knightly sword,
Full fain had Pelleas for his lady won
The golden circlet, for himself the sword.
And there were those who knew him near
  the King,
And promised for him; and Arthur made
  him knight.

  And this new knight, Sir Pelleas of the
  Isles —
But lately come to his inheritance,
And lord of many a barren isle was he —
Riding at noon, a day or twain before,
Across the forest call'd of Dean, to find   20
Caerleon and the King, had felt the sun
Beat like a strong knight on his helm and
  reel'd
Almost to falling from his horse, but saw
Near him a mound of even-sloping side

Whereon a hundred stately beeches grew,
And here and there great hollies under
    them;
But for a mile all round was open space
And fern and heath. And slowly Pelleas
    drew
To that dim day, then, binding his good
    horse
To a tree, cast himself down; and as he
    lay   30
At random looking over the brown earth
Thro' that green-glooming twilight of the
    grove,
It seem'd to Pelleas that the fern without
Burnt as a living fire of emeralds,
So that his eyes were dazzled looking at
    it.
Then o'er it crost the dimness of a cloud
Floating, and once the shadow of a bird
Flying, and then a fawn; and his eyes
    closed.
And since he loved all maidens, but no
    maid
In special, half - awake he whisper'd:
    'Where ?   40
O, where ? I love thee, tho' I know thee
    not.
For fair thou art and pure as Guinevere,
And I will make thee with my spear and
    sword
As famous — O my Queen, my Guinevere,
For I will be thine Arthur when we meet.'

    Suddenly waken'd with a sound of talk
And laughter at the limit of the wood,
And glancing thro' the hoary boles, he saw,
Strange as to some old prophet might have
    seem'd
A vision hovering on a sea of fire,   50
Damsels in divers colors like the cloud
Of sunset and sunrise, and all of them
On horses, and the horses richly trapt
Breast-high in that bright line of bracken
    stood;
And all the damsels talk'd confusedly,
And one was pointing this way and one
    that,
Because the way was lost.

               And Pelleas rose,
And loosed his horse, and led him to the
    light.
There she that seem'd the chief among
    them said:
'In happy time behold our pilot-star !   60

Youth, we are damsels-errant, and we ride,
Arm'd as ye see, to tilt against the knights
There at Caerleon, but have lost our way.
To right ? to left ? straight forward ? back
    again ?
Which ? tell us quickly.'

               Pelleas gazing thought,
'Is Guinevere herself so beautiful ? '
For large her violet eyes look'd, and her
    bloom
A rosy dawn kindled in stainless heavens,
And round her limbs, mature in woman-
    hood;
And slender was her hand and small her
    shape;   70
And but for those large eyes, the haunts of
    scorn,
She might have seem'd a toy to trifle with,
And pass and care no more. But while he
    gazed
The beauty of her flesh abash'd the boy,
As tho' it were the beauty of her soul;
For as the base man, judging of the good,
Puts his own baseness in him by default
Of will and nature, so did Pelleas lend
All the young beauty of his own soul to
    hers,   79
Believing her, and when she spake to him
Stammer'd, and could not make her a re-
    ply.
For out of the waste islands had he come,
Where saving his own sisters he had
    known
Scarce any but the women of his isles,
Rough wives, that laugh'd and scream'd
    against the gulls,
Makers of nets, and living from the sea.

    Then with a slow smile turn'd the lady
    round
And look'd upon her people; and, as when
A stone is flung into some sleeping tarn
The circle widens till it lip the marge,   90
Spread the slow smile thro' all her com-
    pany.
Three knights were thereamong, and they
    too smiled,
Scorning him; for the lady was Ettarre,
And she was a great lady in her land.

    Again she said: 'O wild and of the
    woods,
Knowest thou not the fashion of our
    speech ?

Or have the Heavens but given thee a fair
    face,
Lacking a tongue ? '

          ' O damsel,' answer'd he,
' I woke from dreams, and coming out of
    gloom
Was dazzled by the sudden light, and
    crave   100
Pardon; but will ye to Caerleon ? I
Go likewise; shall I lead you to the King ? '

    ' Lead then,' she said; and thro' the
    woods they went.
And while they rode, the meaning in his
    eyes,
His tenderness of manner, and chaste awe,
His broken utterances and bashfulness,
Were all a burthen to her, and in her heart
She mutter'd, ' I have lighted on a fool,
Raw, yet so stale ! ' But since her mind
    was bent   109
On hearing, after trumpet blown, her name
And title, ' Queen of Beauty,' in the lists
Cried — and beholding him so strong she
    thought
That peradventure he will fight for me,
And win the circlet — therefore flatter'd
    him,
Being so gracious that he wellnigh deem'd
His wish by hers was echo'd; and her
    knights
And all her damsels too were gracious to
    him,
For she was a great lady.

          And when they reach'd
Caerleon, ere they past to lodging, she,
Taking his hand, ' O the strong hand,' she
    said,   120
' See ! look at mine ! but wilt thou fight for
    me,
And win me this fine circlet, Pelleas,
That I may love thee ? '

          Then his helpless heart
Leapt, and he cried, ' Ay ! wilt thou if I
    win ? '
' Ay, that will I,' she answer'd, and she
    laugh'd,
And straitly nipt the hand, and flung it
    from her;
Then glanced askew at those three knights
    of hers,
Till all her ladies laugh'd along with her.

' O happy world,' thought Pelleas, ' all,
    meseems,
Are happy; I the happiest of them all ! ' 130
Nor slept that night for pleasure in his
    blood,
And green wood-ways, and eyes among the
    leaves;
Then being on the morrow knighted, sware
To love one only. And as he came away,
The men who met him rounded on their
    heels
And wonder'd after him, because his face
Shone like the countenance of a priest of
    old
Against the flame about a sacrifice
Kindled by fire from heaven; so glad was he.

Then Arthur made vast banquets, and
    strange knights   140
From the four winds came in; and each
    one sat,
Tho' served with choice from air, land,
    stream, and sea,
Oft in mid-banquet measuring with his
    eyes
His neighbor's make and might; and Pel-
    leas look'd
Noble among the noble, for he dream'd
His lady loved him, and he knew himself
Loved of the King; and him his new-made
    knight
Worshipt, whose lightest whisper moved
    him more
Than all the ranged reasons of the world.

Then blush'd and brake the morning of
    the jousts,   150
And this was call'd ' The Tournament of
    Youth; '
For Arthur, loving his young knight, with-
    held
His older and his mightier from the lists,
That Pelleas might obtain his lady's love,
According to her promise, and remain
Lord of the tourney. And Arthur had the
    jousts
Down in the flat field by the shore of Usk
Holden; the gilded parapets were crown'd
With faces, and the great tower fill'd with
    eyes   159
Up to the summit, and the trumpets blew.
There all day long Sir Pelleas kept the
    field
With honor; so by that strong hand of his
The sword and golden circlet were achieved.

Then rang the shout his lady loved; the heat
Of pride and glory fired her face, her eye
Sparkled; she caught the circlet from his lance,
And there before the people crown'd herself.
So for the last time she was gracious to him.

Then at Caerleon for a space — her look
Bright for all others, cloudier on her knight —   170
Linger'd Ettarre; and, seeing Pelleas droop,
Said Guinevere, ' We marvel at thee much,
O damsel, wearing this unsunny face
To him who won thee glory !' And she said,
' Had ye not held your Lancelot in your bower,
My Queen, he had not won.' Whereat the Queen,
As one whose foot is bitten by an ant,
Glanced down upon her, turn'd and went her way.

But after, when her damsels, and herself,
And those three knights all set their faces home,   180
Sir Pelleas follow'd. She that saw him cried:
' Damsels — and yet I should be shamed to say it —
I cannot bide Sir Baby. Keep him back
Among yourselves. Would rather that we had
Some rough old knight who knew the worldly way,
Albeit grizzlier than a bear, to ride
And jest with ! Take him to you, keep him off,
And pamper him with papmeat, if ye will,
Old milky fables of the wolf and sheep,
Such as the wholesome mothers tell their boys.   190
Nay, should ye try him with a merry one
To find his mettle, good; and if he fly us,
Small matter ! let him.' This her damsels heard,
And, mindful of her small and cruel hand,
They, closing round him thro' the journey home,
Acted her hest, and always from her side
Restrain'd him with all manner of device,

So that he could not come to speech with her.
And when she gain'd her castle, upsprang the bridge,
Down rang the grate of iron thro' the groove,   200
And he was left alone in open field.

' These be the ways of ladies,' Pelleas thought,
' To those who love them, trials of our faith.
Yea, let her prove me to the uttermost,
For loyal to the uttermost am I.'
So made his moan, and, darkness falling, sought
A priory not far off, there lodged, but rose
With morning every day, and, moist or dry,
Full-arm'd upon his charger all day long
Sat by the walls, and no one open'd to him.   210

And this persistence turn'd her scorn to wrath.
Then, calling her three knights, she charged them, ' Out !
And drive him from the walls.' And out they came,
But Pelleas overthrew them as they dash'd
Against him one by one; and these return'd,
But still he kept his watch beneath the wall.

Thereon her wrath became a hate; and once,
A week beyond, while walking on the walls
With her three knights, she pointed downward, ' Look,
He haunts me — I cannot breathe — besieges me !   220
Down ! strike him ! put my hate into your strokes,
And drive him from my walls.' And down they went,
And Pelleas overthrew them one by one;
And from the tower above him cried Ettarre,
' Bind him, and bring him in.'
                        He heard her voice;
Then let the strong hand, which had overthrown
Her minion-knights, by those he overthrew
Be bounden straight, and so they brought him in.

Then when he came before Ettarre, the
    sight   229
Of her rich beauty made him at one glance
More bondsman in his heart than in his
    bonds.
Yet with good cheer he spake: 'Behold
    me, lady,
A prisoner, and the vassal of thy will;
And if thou keep me in thy donjon here,
Content am I so that I see thy face
But once a day; for I have sworn my vows,
And thou hast given thy promise, and I
    know
That all these pains are trials of my faith,
And that thyself, when thou hast seen me
    strain'd
And sifted to the utmost, wilt at length 240
Yield me thy love and know me for thy
    knight.'

Then she began to rail so bitterly,
With all her damsels, he was stricken
    mute,
But, when she mock'd his vows and the
    great King,
Lighted on words: 'For pity of thine own
    self,
Peace, lady, peace; is he not thine and
    mine?'
'Thou fool,' she said, 'I never heard his
    voice
But long'd to break away. Unbind him
    now,
And thrust him out of doors; for save he
    be
Fool to the midmost marrow of his bones,
He will return no more.' And those, her
    three,   251
Laugh'd, and unbound, and thrust him
    from the gate.

And after this, a week beyond, again
She call'd them, saying: 'There he watches
    yet,
There like a dog before his master's door!
Kick'd, he returns; do ye not hate him,
    ye?
Ye know yourselves; how can ye bide at
    peace,
Affronted with his fulsome innocence?
Are ye but creatures of the board and bed,
No men to strike? Fall on him all at
    once,   260
And if ye slay him I reck not; if ye fail,
Give ye the slave mine order to be bound,

Bind him as heretofore, and bring him
    in.
It may be ye shall slay him in his bonds.'

She spake, and at her will they couch'd
    their spears,
Three against one; and Gawain passing by,
Bound upon solitary adventure, saw
Low down beneath the shadow of those
    towers
A villainy, three to one; and thro' his
    heart
The fire of honor and all noble deeds 270
Flash'd, and he call'd, 'I strike upon thy
    side —
The caitiffs!' 'Nay,' said Pelleas, 'but
    forbear;
He needs no aid who doth his lady's will.'

So Gawain, looking at the villainy done,
Forbore, but in his heat and eagerness
Trembled and quiver'd, as the dog, with-
    held
A moment from the vermin that he sees
Before him, shivers ere he springs and
    kills.

And Pelleas overthrew them, one to
    three;
And they rose up, and bound, and brought
    him in.   280
Then first her anger, leaving Pelleas,
    burn'd
Full on her knights in many an evil name
Of craven, weakling, and thrice-beaten
    hound:
'Yet, take him, ye that scarce are fit to
    touch,
Far less to bind, your victor, and thrust
    him out,
And let who will release him from his
    bonds.
And if he comes again' — there she brake
    short;
And Pelleas answer'd: 'Lady, for indeed
I loved you and I deem'd you beautiful,
I cannot brook to see your beauty marr'd
Thro' evil spite; and if ye love me not, 291
I cannot bear to dream you so forsworn.
I had liefer ye were worthy of my love
Than to be loved again of you — fare-
    well;
And tho' ye kill my hope, not yet my
    love,
Vex not yourself; ye will not see me more.'

While thus he spake, she gazed upon the man
Of princely bearing, tho' in bonds, and thought:
'Why have I push'd him from me? this man loves,
If love there be; yet him I loved not. Why? 300
I deem'd him fool? yea, so? or that in him
A something — was it nobler than myself? —
Seem'd my reproach? He is not of my kind.
He could not love me, did he know me well.
Nay, let him go — and quickly.' And her knights
Laugh'd not, but thrust him bounden out of door.

Forth sprang Gawain, and loosed him from his bonds,
And flung them o'er the walls; and afterward,
Shaking his hands, as from a lazar's rag,
'Faith of my body,' he said, 'and art thou not — 310
Yea thou art he, whom late our Arthur made
Knight of his table; yea, and he that won
The circlet? wherefore hast thou so defamed
Thy brotherhood in me and all the rest
As let these caitiffs on thee work their will?'

And Pelleas answer'd: 'O, their wills are hers
For whom I won the circlet; and mine, hers,
Thus to be bounden, so to see her face,
Marr'd tho' it be with spite and mockery now, 319
Other than when I found her in the woods;
And tho' she hath me bounden but in spite,
And all to flout me, when they bring me in,
Let me be bounden, I shall see her face;
Else must I die thro' mine unhappiness.'

And Gawain answer'd kindly tho' in scorn:
'Why, let my lady bind me if she will,
And let my lady beat me if she will;
But an she send her delegate to thrall
These fighting hands of mine — Christ kill me then 329
But I will slice him handless by the wrist,
And let my lady sear the stump for him,
Howl as he may! But hold me for your friend.
Come, ye know nothing; here I pledge my troth,
Yea, by the honor of the Table Round,
I will be leal to thee and work thy work,
And tame thy jailing princess to thine hand.
Lend me thine horse and arms, and I will say
That I have slain thee. She will let me in
To hear the manner of thy fight and fall;
Then, when I come within her counsels, then 340
From prime to vespers will I chant thy praise
As prowest knight and truest lover, more
Than any have sung thee living, till she long
To have thee back in lusty life again,
Not to be bound, save by white bonds and warm,
Dearer than freedom. Wherefore now thy horse
And armor; let me go; be comforted.
Give me three days to melt her fancy, and hope
The third night hence will bring thee news of gold.'

Then Pelleas lent his horse and all his arms, 350
Saving the goodly sword, his prize, and took
Gawain's, and said, 'Betray me not, but help —
Art thou not he whom men call light-of-love?'

'Ay,' said 'Gawain, 'for women be so light;'
Then bounded forward to the castle walls,
And raised a bugle hanging from his neck,
And winded it, and that so musically
That all the old echoes hidden in the wall
Rang out like hollow woods at hunting-tide. 359

Up ran a score of damsels to the tower;
'Avaunt,' they cried, 'our lady loves thee not!'
But Gawain lifting up his vizor said:

'Gawain am I, Gawain of Arthur's court,
And I have slain this Pelleas whom ye hate.
Behold his horse and armor. Open gates,
And I will make you merry.'

         And down they ran,
Her damsels, crying to their lady, 'Lo !
Pelleas is dead — he told us — he that hath
His horse and armor; will ye let him in ?
He slew him ! Gawain, Gawain of the court,   370
Sir Gawain — there he waits below the wall,
Blowing his bugle as who should say him nay.'

  And so, leave given, straight on thro' open door
Rode Gawain, whom she greeted courteously.
'Dead, is it so ?' she ask'd. 'Ay, ay,' said he,
'And oft in dying cried upon your name.'
'Pity on him,' she answer'd, 'a good knight,
But never let me bide one hour at peace.'
'Ay,' thought Gawain, 'and you be fair enow;
But I to your dead man have given my troth,   380
That whom ye loathe, him will I make you love.'

  So those three days, aimless about the land,
Lost in a doubt, Pelleas wandering
Waited, until the third night brought a moon
With promise of large light on woods and ways.

  Hot was the night and silent; but a sound
Of Gawain ever coming, and this lay —
Which Pelleas had heard sung before the Queen,
And seen her sadden listening — vext his heart,
And marr'd his rest — 'A worm within the rose.'   390

'A rose, but one, none other rose had I,
A rose, one rose, and this was wondrous fair,
One rose, a rose that gladden'd earth and sky,
One rose, my rose, that sweeten'd all mine air —
I cared not for the thorns; the thorns were there.

'One rose, a rose to gather by and by,
One rose, a rose, to gather and to wear,
No rose but one — what other rose had I ?
One rose, my rose; a rose that will not die, —
He dies who loves it, — if the worm be there.'

  This tender rhyme, and evermore the doubt,   401
'Why lingers Gawain with his golden news ?'
So shook him that he could not rest, but rode
Ere midnight to her walls, and bound his horse
Hard by the gates. Wide open were the gates,
And no watch kept; and in thro' these he past,
And heard but his own steps, and his own heart
Beating, for nothing moved but his own self
And his own shadow. Then he crost the court,
And spied not any light in hall or bower,
But saw the postern portal also wide   411
Yawning; and up a slope of garden, all
Of roses white and red, and brambles mixt
And overgrowing them, went on, and found,
Here too, all hush'd below the mellow moon,
Save that one rivulet from a tiny cave
Came lightening downward, and so spilt itself
Among the roses and was lost again.

  Then was he ware of three pavilions rear'd
Above the bushes, gilden-peakt. In one,
Red after revel, droned her lurdane knights   421
Slumbering, and their three squires across their feet;
In one, their malice on the placid lip
Frozen by sweet sleep, four of her damsels lay;
And in the third, the circlet of the jousts
Bound on her brow, were Gawain and Ettarre.

  Back, as a hand that pushes thro' the leaf
To find a nest and feels a snake, he drew;

Back, as a coward slinks from what he
    fears
To cope with, or a traitor proven, or hound
Beaten, did Pelleas in an utter shame   431
Creep with his shadow thro' the court again,
Fingering at his sword - handle until he
    stood
There on the castle-bridge once more, and
    thought,
' I will go back, and slay them where they
    lie.'

    And so went back, and seeing them yet
    in sleep
Said, ' Ye, that so dishallow the holy sleep,
Your sleep is death,' and drew the sword,
    and thought,
' What ! slay a sleeping knight ? the King
    hath bound   439
And sworn me to this brotherhood;' again,
' Alas that ever a knight should be so
    false ! '
Then turn'd, and so return'd, and groaning
    laid
The naked sword athwart their naked
    throats,
There left it, and them sleeping; and she
    lay,
The circlet of the tourney round her brows,
And the sword of the tourney across her
    throat.

    And forth he past, and mounting on his
    horse
Stared at her towers that, larger than
    themselves
In their own darkness, throng'd into the
    moon;
Then crush'd the saddle with his thighs,
    and clench'd   450
His hands, and madden'd with himself and
    moan'd:

    ' Would they have risen against me in
    their blood
At the last day ? I might have answer'd
    them
Even before high God. O towers so strong,
Huge, solid, would that even while I gaze
The crack of earthquake shivering to your
    base
Split you, and hell burst up your harlot
    roofs
Bellowing, and charr'd you thro' and thro'
    within,

Black as the harlot's heart — hollow as a
    skull !
Let the fierce east scream thro' your eye-
    let-holes,   460
And whirl the dust of harlots round and
    round
In dung and nettles ! hiss, snake — I saw
    him there —
Let the fox bark, let the wolf yell ! Who
    yells
Here in the still sweet summer night but
    I —
I, the poor Pelleas whom she call'd her
    fool ?
Fool, beast — he, she, or I ? myself most
    fool;
Beast too, as lacking human wit — dis-
    graced,
Dishonor'd all for trial of true love —
Love ? — we be all alike; only the King
Hath made us fools and liars. O noble
    vows !   470
O great and sane and simple race of brutes
That own no lust because they have no law !
For why should I have loved her to my
    shame ?
I loathe her, as I loved her to my shame.
I never loved her, I but lusted for her —
Away ! ' —

    He dash'd the rowel into his horse,
And bounded forth and vanish'd thro' the
    night.

    Then she, that felt the cold touch on her
    throat,
Awaking knew the sword, and turn'd her-
    self
To Gawain: ' Liar, for thou hast not slain
This Pelleas ! here he stood, and might
    have slain   481
Me and thyself.' And he that tells the tale
Says that her ever-veering fancy turn'd
To Pelleas, as the one true knight on earth
And only lover; and thro' her love her life
Wasted and pined, desiring him in vain.

    But he by wild and way, for half the
    night,
And over hard and soft, striking the sod
From out the soft, the spark from off the
    hard,
Rode till the star above the wakening sun,
Beside that tower where Percivale was
    cowl'd,   491

Glanced from the rosy forehead of the
  dawn.
For so the words were flash'd into his
  heart
He knew not whence or wherefore: ' O
  sweet star,
Pure on the virgin forehead of the dawn ! '
And there he would have wept, but felt his
  eyes
Harder and drier than a fountain bed
In summer. Thither came the village girls
And linger'd talking, and they come no
  more
Till the sweet heavens have fill'd it from
  the heights   500
Again with living waters in the change
Of seasons. Hard his eyes, harder his heart
Seem'd; but so weary were his limbs that
  he,
Gasping, ' Of Arthur's hall am I, but here,
Here let me rest and die,' cast himself
  down,
And gulf'd his griefs in inmost sleep; so
  lay,
Till shaken by a dream, that Gawain fired
The hall of Merlin, and the morning star
Reel'd in the smoke, brake into flame, and
  fell.

He woke, and being ware of some one
  nigh,   510
Sent hands upon him, as to tear him, crying,
' False ! and I held thee pure as Guine-
  vere.'

But Percivale stood near him and replied,
' Am I but false as Guinevere is pure ?
Or art thou mazed with dreams ? or being
  one
Of our free-spoken Table hast not heard
That Lancelot ' — there he check'd himself
  and paused.

Then fared it with Sir Pelleas as with one
Who gets a wound in battle, and the sword
That made it plunges thro' the wound again,
And pricks it deeper; and he shrank and
  wail'd,   521
' Is the Queen false ? ' and Percivale was
  mute.
' Have any of our Round Table held their
  vows ? '
And Percivale made answer not a word.
' Is the King true ? ' ' The King ! ' said
  Percivale.

' Why, then let men couple at once with
  wolves.
What ! art thou mad ? '

            But Pelleas, leaping up,
Ran thro' the doors and vaulted on his horse
And fled. Small pity upon his horse had he,
Or on himself, or any, and when he met 530
A cripple, one that held a hand for alms —
Hunch'd as he was, and like an old dwarf-
  elm
That turns its back on the salt blast, the boy
Paused not, but overrode him, shouting,
  ' False,
And false with Gawain ! ' and so left him
  bruised
And batter'd, and fled on, and hill and
  wood
Went ever streaming by him till the gloom
That follows on the turning of the world
Darken'd the common path. He twitch'd
  the reins,
And made his beast, that better knew it,
  swerve   540
Now off it and now on; but when he saw
High up in heaven the hall that Merlin
  built,
Blackening against the dead-green stripes
  of even,
' Black nest of rats,' he groan'd, ' ye build
  too high.'

Not long thereafter from the city gates
Issued Sir Lancelot riding airily,
Warm with a gracious parting from the
  Queen,
Peace at his heart, and gazing at a star
And marvelling what it was; on whom the
  boy,
Across the silent seeded meadow-grass
Borne, clash'd; and Lancelot, saying,
  ' What name hast thou   551
That ridest here so blindly and so hard ? '
' No name, no name,' he shouted, ' a scourge
  am I
To lash the treasons of the Table Round.'
' Yea, but thy name ? ' ' I have many
  names,' he cried:
' I am wrath and shame and hate and evil
  fame,
And like a poisonous wind I pass to blast
And blaze the crime of Lancelot and the
  Queen.'
' First over me,' said Lancelot, ' shalt thou
  pass.'

'Fight therefore,' yell'd the youth, and
  either knight   560
Drew back a space, and when they closed,
  at once
The weary steed of Pelleas floundering
  flung
His rider, who call'd out from the dark
  field,
'Thou art false as hell; slay me, I have no
  sword.'
Then Lancelot, 'Yea, between thy lips —
  and sharp;
But here will I disedge it by thy death.'
'Slay then,' he shriek'd, 'my will is to be
  slain,'
And Lancelot, with his heel upon the
  fallen,
Rolling his eyes, a moment stood, then
  spake:
'Rise, weakling; I am Lancelot; say thy
  say.'   570

    And Lancelot slowly rode his war-horse
  back
To Camelot, and Sir Pelleas in brief while
Caught his unbroken limbs from the dark
  field,
And follow'd to the city. It chanced that
  both
Brake into hall together, worn and pale.
There with her knights and dames was
  Guinevere.
Full wonderingly she gazed on Lancelot
So soon return'd, and then on Pelleas, him
Who had not greeted her, but cast himself
Down on a bench, hard-breathing. 'Have
  ye fought?'   580
She ask'd of Lancelot. 'Ay, my Queen,'
  he said.
'And thou hast overthrown him?' 'Ay,
  my Queen.'
Then she, turning to Pelleas, 'O young
  knight,
Hath the great heart of knighthood in thee
  fail'd
So far thou canst not bide, unfrowardly,
A fall from *him?*' Then, for he answer'd
  not,
'Or hast thou other griefs? If I, the
  Queen,
May help them, loose thy tongue, and let
  me know.'
But Pelleas lifted up an eye so fierce
She quail'd; and he, hissing 'I have no
  sword,'   590

Sprang from the door into the dark. The
  Queen
Look'd hard upon her lover, he on her,
And each foresaw the dolorous day to be;
And all talk died, as in a grove all song
Beneath the shadow of some bird of prey.
Then a long silence came upon the hall,
And Modred thought, 'The time is hard at
  hand.'

THE LAST TOURNAMENT

DAGONET, the fool, whom Gawain in his
  mood
Had made mock-knight of Arthur's Table
  Round,
At Camelot, high above the yellowing
  woods,
Danced like a wither'd leaf before the hall.
And toward him from the hall, with harp
  in hand,
And from the crown thereof a carcanet
Of ruby swaying to and fro, the prize
Of Tristram in the jousts of yesterday,
Came Tristram, saying, 'Why skip ye so,
  Sir Fool?'

    For Arthur and Sir Lancelot riding once
Far down beneath a winding wall of rock 11
Heard a child wail. A stump of oak half-
  dead,
From roots like some black coil of carven
  snakes,
Clutch'd at the crag, and started thro' mid
  air
Bearing an eagle's nest; and thro' the tree
Rush'd ever a rainy wind, and thro' the
  wind
Pierced ever a child's cry; and crag and tree
Scaling, Sir Lancelot from the perilous
  nest,
This ruby necklace thrice around her neck,
And all unscarr'd from beak or talon,
  brought   20
A maiden babe, which Arthur pitying took,
Then gave it to his Queen to rear. The
  Queen,
But coldly acquiescing, in her white arms
Received, and after loved it tenderly,
And named it Nestling; so forgot herself
A moment, and her cares; till that young
  life
Being smitten in mid heaven with mortal
  cold

Past from her, and in time the carcanet
Vext her with plaintive memories of the
    child.
So she, delivering it to Arthur, said,   30
'Take thou the jewels of this dead inno-
    cence,
And make them, an thou wilt, a tourney-
    prize.'

To whom the King: 'Peace to thine eagle-
    borne
Dead nestling, and this honor after death,
Following thy will! but, O my Queen, I
    muse
Why ye not wear on arm, or neck, or zone
Those diamonds that I rescued from the
    tarn,
And Lancelot won, methought, for thee to
    wear.'

'Would rather you had let them fall,'
    she cried,
'Plunge and be lost — ill-fated as they
    were,   40
A bitterness to me! — ye look amazed,
Not knowing they were lost as soon as
    given —
Slid from my hands when I was leaning
    out
Above the river — that unhappy child
Past in her barge; but rosier luck will go
With these rich jewels, seeing that they
    came
Not from the skeleton of a brother-slayer,
But the sweet body of a maiden babe.
Perchance — who knows? — the purest of
    thy knights   49
May win them for the purest of my maids.'

She ended, and the cry of a great jousts
With trumpet-blowings ran on all the ways
From Camelot in among the faded fields
To furthest towers; and everywhere the
    knights
Arm'd for a day of glory before the King.

But on the hither side of that loud morn
Into the hall stagger'd, his visage ribb'd
From ear to ear with dogwhip-weals, his
    nose
Bridge-broken, one eye out, and one hand
    off,
And one with shatter'd fingers dangling
    lame,   60
A churl, to whom indignantly the King:

'My churl, for whom Christ died, what
    evil beast
Hath drawn his claws athwart thy face?
    or fiend?
Man was it who marr'd heaven's image in
    thee thus?'

Then, sputtering thro' the hedge of
    splinter'd teeth,
Yet strangers to the tongue, and with blunt
    stump
Pitch-blacken'd sawing the air, said the
    maim'd churl:

'He took them and he drave them to his
    tower —
Some hold he was a table-knight of thine —
A hundred goodly ones — the Red Knight,
    he —   70
Lord, I was tending swine, and the Red
    Knight
Brake in upon me and drave them to his
    tower;
And when I call'd upon thy name as one
That doest right by gentle and by churl,
Maim'd me and maul'd, and would out-
    right have slain,
Save that he sware me to a message, say-
    ing:
"Tell thou the King and all his liars that I
Have founded my Round Table in the
    North,
And whatsoever his own knights have sworn
My knights have sworn the counter to it —
    and say   80
My tower is full of harlots, like his court,
But mine are worthier, seeing they profess
To be none other than themselves — and
    say
My knights are all adulterers like his own,
But mine are truer, seeing they profess
To be none other; and say his hour is come,
The heathen are upon him, his long lance
Broken, and his Excalibur a straw." '

Then Arthur turn'd to Kay the senes-
    chal:
'Take thou my churl, and tend him curi-
    ously   90
Like a king's heir, till all his hurts be
    whole.
The heathen — but that ever-climbing wave,
Hurl'd back again so often in empty foam,
Hath lain for years at rest — and rene-
    gades,

Thieves, bandits, leavings of confusion,
    whom
The wholesome realm is purged of other-
    where,
Friends, thro' your manhood and your
    fealty, — now
Make their last head like Satan in the
    North.
My younger knights, new-made, in whom
    your flower
Waits to be solid fruit of golden deeds, 100
Move with me toward their quelling, which
    achieved,
The loneliest ways are safe from shore to
    shore.
But thou, Sir Lancelot, sitting in my place
Enchair'd to-morrow, arbitrate the field;
For wherefore shouldst thou care to mingle
    with it,
Only to yield my Queen her own again?
Speak, Lancelot, thou art silent; is it
    well?'

    Thereto Sir Lancelot answer'd: 'It is
    well;
Yet better if the King abide, and leave 109
The leading of his younger knights to me.
Else, for the King has will'd it, it is well.'

    Then Arthur rose and Lancelot follow'd
    him,
And while they stood without the doors,
    the King
Turn'd to him saying: 'Is it then so well?
Or mine the blame that oft I seem as he
Of whom was written, "A sound is in his
    ears"?
The foot that loiters, bidden go, — the
    glance
That only seems half-loyal to command, —
A manner somewhat fallen from rever-
    ence —
Or have I dream'd the bearing of our
    knights   120
Tells of a manhood ever less and lower?
Or whence the fear lest this my realm, up-
    rear'd,
By noble deeds at one with noble vows,
From flat confusion and brute violences,
Reel back into the beast, and be no more?'

    He spoke, and taking all his younger
    knights,
Down the slope city rode, and sharply
    turn'd

North by the gate.   In her high bower the
    Queen,
Working a tapestry, lifted up her head,
Watch'd her lord pass, and knew not that
    she sigh'd.   130
Then ran across her memory the strange
    rhyme
Of bygone Merlin, 'Where is he who
    knows?
From the great deep to the great deep he
    goes.'

    But when the morning of a tournament,
By these in earnest those in mockery call'd
The Tournament of the Dead Innocence,
Brake with a wet wind blowing, Lancelot,
Round whose sick head all night, like birds
    of prey,
The words of Arthur flying shriek'd, arose,
And down a streetway hung with folds of
    pure   140
White samite, and by fountains running
    wine,
Where children sat in white with cups of
    gold,
Moved to the lists, and there, with slow sad
    steps
Ascending, fill'd his double-dragon'd chair.

    He glanced and saw the stately galleries,
Dame, damsel, each thro' worship of their
    Queen
White-robed in honor of the stainless child,
And some with scatter'd jewels, like a bank
Of maiden snow mingled with sparks of
    fire.
He look'd but once, and vail'd his eyes
    again.   150

    The sudden trumpet sounded as in a
    dream
To ears but half-awaked, then one low roll
Of autumn thunder, and the jousts began;
And ever the wind blew, and yellowing leaf,
And gloom and gleam, and shower and
    shorn plume
Went down it.   Sighing weariedly, as one
Who sits and gazes on a faded fire,
When all the goodlier guests are past
    away,
Sat their great umpire looking o'er the
    lists.
He saw the laws that ruled the tournament
Broken, but spake not; once, a knight cast
    down   161

Before his throne of arbitration cursed
The dead babe and the follies of the King;
And once the laces of a helmet crack'd,
And show'd him, like a vermin in its hole,
Modred, a narrow face. Anon he heard
The voice that billow'd round the barriers
    roar
An ocean-sounding welcome to one knight,
But newly-enter'd, taller than the rest, 169
And armor'd all in forest green, whereon
There tript a hundred tiny silver deer,
And wearing but a holly-spray for crest,
With ever-scattering berries, and on shield
A spear, a harp, a bugle — Tristram — late
From over-seas in Brittany return'd,
And marriage with a princess of that
    realm,
Isolt the White — Sir Tristram of the
    Woods —
Whom Lancelot knew, had held sometime
    with pain
His own against him, and now yearn'd to
    shake
The burthen off his heart in one full shock
With Tristram even to death. His strong
    hands gript   181
And dinted the gilt dragons right and
    left,
Until he groan'd for wrath — so many of
    those
That ware their ladies' colors on the casque
Drew from before Sir Tristram to the
    bounds,
And there with gibes and flickering mock-
    eries
Stood, while he mutter'd, 'Craven crests !
    O shame !
What faith have these in whom they sware
    to love ?
The glory of our Round Table is no more.'

So Tristram won, and Lancelot gave, the
    gems,   190
Not speaking other word than, 'Hast thou
    won ?
Art thou the purest, brother ? See, the
    hand
Wherewith thou takest this is red !' to
    whom
Tristram, half plagued by Lancelot's lan-
    guorous mood,
Made answer: 'Ay, but wherefore toss me
    this
Like a dry bone cast to some hungry
    hound ?

Let be thy fair Queen's fantasy. Strength
    of heart
And might of limb, but mainly use and
    skill,
Are winners in this pastime of our King.
My hand — belike the lance hath dript
    upon it —   200
No blood of mine, I trow; but O chief
    knight,
Right arm of Arthur in the battle-field,
Great brother, thou nor I have made the
    world;
Be happy in thy fair Queen as I in mine.'

    And Tristram round the gallery made
    his horse
Caracole; then bow'd his homage, bluntly
    saying,
'Fair damsels, each to him who worships
    each
Sole Queen of Beauty and of love, behold
This day my Queen of Beauty is not here.'
And most of these were mute, some an-
    ger'd, one   210
Murmuring, 'All courtesy is dead,' and
    one,
'The glory of our Round Table is no more.'

Then fell thick rain, plume droopt and
    mantle clung,
And pettish cries awoke, and the wan day
Went glooming down in wet and weari-
    ness;
But under her black brows a swarthy one
Laugh'd shrilly, crying: 'Praise the patient
    saints,
Our one white day of Innocence hath past,
Tho' somewhat draggled at the skirt. So
    be it.
The snowdrop only, flowering thro' the
    year,   220
Would make the world as blank as winter-
    tide.
Come — let us gladden their sad eyes, our
    Queen's
And Lancelot's, at this night's solemnity
With all the kindlier colors of the field.'

    So dame and damsel glitter'd at the
    feast
Variously gay; for he that tells the tale
Liken'd them, saying, as when an hour of
    cold
Falls on the mountain in midsummer
    snows,

And all the purple slopes of mountain
flowers
Pass under white, till the warm hour re-
turns   230
With veer of wind and all are flowers
again,
So dame and damsel cast the simple white,
And glowing in all colors, the live grass,
Rose-campion, bluebell, kingcup, poppy,
glanced
About the revels, and with mirth so loud
Beyond all use, that, half - amazed, the
Queen,
And wroth at Tristram and the lawless
jousts,
Brake up their sports, then slowly to her
bower   238
Parted, and in her bosom pain was lord.

And little Dagonet on the morrow morn,
High over all the yellowing autumn-tide,
Danced like a wither'd leaf before the hall.
Then Tristram saying, 'Why skip ye so,
Sir Fool ? '
Wheel'd round on either heel, Dagonet re-
plied,
'Belike for lack of wiser company;
Or being fool, and seeing too much wit
Makes the world rotten, why, belike I skip
To know myself the wisest knight of all.'
' Ay, fool,' said Tristram, 'but 't is eating
dry
To dance without a catch, a roundelay   250
To dance to.' Then he twangled on his
harp,
And while he twangled little Dagonet
stood
Quiet as any water-sodden log
Stay'd in the wandering warble of a brook,
But when the twangling ended, skipt again;
And being ask'd, 'Why skipt ye not, Sir
Fool ? '
Made answer, 'I had liefer twenty years
Skip to the broken music of my brains
Than any broken music thou canst make.'
Then Tristram, waiting for the quip to
come,   260
'Good now, what music have I broken,
fool ? '
And little Dagonet, skipping, 'Arthur, the
King's;
For when thou playest that air with Queen
Isolt,
Thou makest broken music with thy bride,
Her daintier namesake down in Brittany —

And so thou breakest Arthur's music too.'
' Save for that broken music in thy brains,
Sir Fool,' said Tristram, 'I would break
thy head.
Fool, I came late, the heathen wars were
o'er,
The life had flown, we sware but by the
shell —   270
I am but a fool to reason with a fool —
Come, thou art crabb'd and sour; but lean
me down,
Sir Dagonet, one of thy long asses' ears,
And harken if my music be not true.

' " Free love — free field — we love but while
we may.
The woods are hush'd, their music is no more ;
The leaf is dead, the yearning past away.
New leaf, new life — the days of frost are
o'er ;
New life, new love, to suit the newer day ;
New loves are sweet as those that went be-
fore.   280
Free love — free field — we love but while we
may."

' Ye might have moved slow-measure to
my tune,
Not stood stock-still. I made it in the
woods,
And heard it ring as true as tested gold.'

But Dagonet with one foot poised in his
hand:
' Friend, did ye mark that fountain yester-
day,
Made to run wine ? — but this had run
itself
All out like a long life to a sour end —
And them that round it sat with golden
cups   289
To hand the wine to whosoever came —
The twelve small damosels white as Inno-
cence,
In honor of poor Innocence the babe,
Who left the gems which Innocence the
Queen
Lent to the King, and Innocence the King
Gave for a prize — and one of those white
slips
Handed her cup and piped, the pretty
one,
" Drink, drink, Sir Fool," and thereupon I
drank,
Spat — pish — the cup was gold, the draught
was mud.'

And Tristram: 'Was it muddier than
thy gibes ?
Is all the laughter gone dead out of
thee ? —   300
Not marking how the knighthood mock
thee, fool —
"Fear God: honor the King — his one
true knight —
Sole follower of the vows " — for here be
they
Who knew thee swine enow before I came,
Smuttier than blasted grain. But when the
King
Had made thee fool, thy vanity so shot
up
It frighted all free fool from out thy
heart;
Which left thee less than fool, and less
than swine,
A naked aught — yet swine I hold thee
still,
For I have flung thee pearls and find thee
swine.'   310

And little Dagonet mincing with his
feet:
'Knight, an ye fling those rubies round my
neck
In lieu of hers, I 'll hold thou hast some
touch
Of music, since I care not for thy pearls.
Swine ? I have wallow'd, I have wash'd —
the world
Is flesh and shadow — I have had my
day.
The dirty nurse, Experience, in her kind
Hath foul'd me — an I wallow'd, then I
wash'd —
I have had my day and my philosophies —
And thank the Lord I am King Arthur's
fool.   320
Swine, say ye ? swine, goats, asses, rams,
and geese
Troop'd round a Paynim harper once, who
thrumm'd
On such a wire as musically as thou
Some such fine song — but never a king's
fool.'

And Tristram, ' Then were swine, goats,
asses, geese
The wiser fools, seeing thy Paynim bard
Had such a mastery of his mystery
That he could harp his wife up out of
hell.'

Then Dagonet, turning on the ball of his
foot,
' And whither harp'st thou thine ? down !
and thyself   330
Down ! and two more; a helpful harper
thou,
That harpest downward ! Dost thou know
the star
We call the Harp of Arthur up in heaven ?'

And Tristram, ' Ay, Sir Fool, for when
our King
Was victor wellnigh day by day, the
knights,
Glorying in each new glory, set his name
High on all hills and in the signs of
heaven.'

And Dagonet answer'd: ' Ay, and when
the land
Was freed, and the Queen false, ye set
yourself
To babble about him, all to show your
wit —   340
And whether he were king by courtesy,
Or king by right — and so went harping
down
The black king's highway, got so far and
grew
So witty that ye play'd at ducks and
drakes
With Arthur's vows on the great lake of fire.
Tuwhoo ! do ye see it ? do ye see the
star ?'

' Nay, fool,' said Tristram, ' not in open
day.'
And Dagonet: ' Nay, nor will; I see it and
hear.
It makes a silent music up in heaven,
And I and Arthur and the angels hear, 350
And then we skip.' ' Lo, fool,' he said,
' ye talk
Fool's treason; is the King thy brother
fool ?'
Then little Dagonet clapt his hands and
shrill'd:
' Ay, ay, my brother fool, the king of
fools !
Conceits himself as God that he can make
Figs out of thistles, silk from bristles, milk
From burning spurge, honey from hornet-
combs,
And men from beasts — Long live the king
of fools !'

And down the city Dagonet danced
  away;
But thro' the slowly-mellowing avenues   360
And solitary passes of the wood
Rode Tristram toward Lyonnesse and the
  west.
Before him fled the face of Queen Isolt
With ruby-circled neck, but evermore
Past, as a rustle or twitter in the wood
Made dull his inner, keen his outer eye
For all that walk'd, or crept, or perch'd, or
  flew.
Anon the face, as, when a gust hath blown,
Unruffling waters re-collect the shape
Of one that in them sees himself, re-
  turn'd;   370
But at the slot or fewmets of a deer,
Or even a fallen feather, vanish'd again.

So on for all that day from lawn to lawn
Thro' many a league-long bower he rode.
  At length
A lodge of intertwisted beechen-boughs,
Furze - cramm'd and bracken - rooft, the
  which himself
Built for a summer day with Queen Isolt
Against a shower, dark in the golden grove
Appearing, sent his fancy back to where
She lived a moon in that low lodge with
  him;   380
Till Mark her lord had past, the Cornish
  King,
With six or seven, when Tristram was
  away,
And snatch'd her thence, yet, dreading
  worse than shame
Her warrior Tristram, spake not any word,
But bode his hour, devising wretchedness.

And now that desert lodge to Tristram
  lookt
So sweet that, halting, in he past and sank
Down on a drift of foliage random-blown;
But could not rest for musing how to
  smooth   389
And sleek his marriage over to the queen.
Perchance in lone Tintagil far from all
The tonguesters of the court she had not
  heard.
But then what folly had sent him over-seas
After she left him lonely here ? a name ?
Was it the name of one in Brittany,
Isolt, the daughter of the king ? ' Isolt .
Of the White Hands' they call'd her: the
  sweet name

Allured him first, and then the maid her-
  self,
Who served him well with those white
  hands of hers,
And loved him well, until himself had
  thought   400
He loved her also, wedded easily,
But left her all as easily, and return'd.
The black-blue Irish hair and Irish eyes
Had drawn him home — what marvel ?
  then he laid
His brows upon the drifted leaf and
  dream'd.

He seem'd to pace the strand of Brittany
Between Isolt of Britain and his bride,
And show'd them both the ruby-chain, and
  both
Began to struggle for it, till his queen
Graspt it so hard that all her hand was
  red.   410
Then cried the Breton, ' Look, her hand is
  red !
These be no rubies, this is frozen blood,
And melts within her hand — her hand is hot
With ill desires, but this I gave thee, look,
Is all as cool and white as any flower.'
Follow'd a rush of eagle's wings, and then
A whimpering of the spirit of the child,
Because the twain had spoil'd her carcanet.

He dream'd; but Arthur with a hundred
  spears
Rode far, till o'er the illimitable reed,   420
And many a glancing plash and sallowy
  isle,
The wide-wing'd sunset of the misty marsh
Glared on a huge machicolated tower
That stood with open doors, whereout was
  roll'd
A roar of riot, as from men secure
Amid their marshes, ruffians at their ease
Among their harlot-brides, an evil song.
' Lo there,' said one of Arthur's youth, for
  there,
High on a grim dead tree before the tower,
A goodly brother of the Table Round   430
Swung by the neck; and on the boughs a
  shield
Showing a shower of blood in a field noir,
And therebeside a horn, inflamed the
  knights
At that dishonor done the gilded spur,
Till each would clash the shield and blow
  the horn.

But Arthur waved them back. Alone he
rode.
Then at the dry harsh roar of the great
horn,
That sent the face of all the marsh aloft
An ever upward-rushing storm and cloud
Of shriek and plume, the Red Knight
heard, and all,   440
Even to tipmost lance and topmost helm,
In blood-red armor sallying, howl'd to the
King:

'The teeth of Hell flay bare and gnash
thee flat! —
Lo! art thou not that eunuch-hearted king
Who fain had clipt free manhood from the
world —
The woman-worshipper? Yea, God's curse,
and I!
Slain was the brother of my paramour
By a knight of thine, and I that heard her
whine
And snivel, being eunuch-hearted too,
Sware by the scorpion-worm that twists in
hell   450
And stings itself to everlasting death,
To hang whatever knight of thine I fought
And tumbled. Art thou king? — Look to
thy life!'

He ended. Arthur knew the voice; the
face
Wellnigh was helmet-hidden, and the name
Went wandering somewhere darkling in
his mind.
And Arthur deign'd not use of word or
sword,
But let the drunkard, as he stretch'd from
horse
To strike him, overbalancing his bulk,
Down from the causeway heavily to the
swamp   460
Fall, as the crest of some slow-arching
wave,
Heard in dead night along that table-shore,
Drops flat, and after the great waters break
Whitening for half a league, and thin
themselves,
Far over sands marbled with moon and
cloud,
From less and less to nothing; thus he fell
Head-heavy. Then the knights, who
watch'd him, roar'd
And shouted and leapt down upon the
fallen,

There trampled out his face from being
known,
And sank his head in mire, and slimed
themselves;   470
Nor heard the King for their own cries,
but sprang
Thro' open doors, and swording right and
left
Men, women, on their sodden faces, hurl'd
The tables over and the wines, and slew
Till all the rafters rang with woman-yells,
And all the pavement stream'd with massa-
cre.
Then, echoing yell with yell, they fired the
tower,
Which half that autumn night, like the live
North,
Red-pulsing up thro' Alioth and Alcor,
Made all above it, and a hundred meres
About it, as the water Moab saw   481
Come round by the east, and out beyond
them flush'd
The long low dune and lazy-plunging sea.

So all the ways were safe from shore to
shore,
But in the heart of Arthur pain was lord.

Then, out of Tristram waking, the red
dream
Fled with a shout, and that low lodge re-
turn'd,
Mid-forest, and the wind among the boughs.
He whistled his good war-horse left to
graze   489
Among the forest greens, vaulted upon him,
And rode beneath an ever-showering leaf,
Till one lone woman, weeping near a cross,
Stay'd him. 'Why weep ye?' 'Lord,'
she said, 'my man
Hath left me or is dead;' whereon he
thought —
'What, if she hate me now? I would not
this.
What, if she love me still? I would not
that.
I know not what I would'— but said to her,
'Yet weep not thou, lest, if thy mate re-
turn,
He find thy favor changed and love thee
not'—
Then pressing day by day thro' Lyonnesse
Last in a roky hollow, belling, heard   501
The hounds of Mark, and felt the goodly
hounds

Yelp at his heart, but, turning, past and
    gain'd
Tintagil, half in sea and high on land,
A crown of towers.

                        Down in a casement sat,
A low sea-sunset glorying round her hair
And glossy-throated grace, Isolt the queen.
And when she heard the feet of Tristram
    grind
The spiring stone that scaled about her
    tower,
Flush'd, started, met him at the doors, and
    there   510
Belted his body with her white embrace,
Crying aloud: 'Not Mark — not Mark, my
    soul !
The footstep flutter'd me at first — not he !
Catlike thro' his own castle steals my Mark,
But warrior - wise thou stridest thro' his
    halls
Who hates thee, as I him — even to the
    death.
My soul, I felt my hatred for my Mark
Quicken within me, and knew that thou
    wert nigh.'
To whom Sir Tristram smiling, 'I am here;
Let be thy Mark, seeing he is not thine.'

    And drawing somewhat backward she
    replied: 521
'Can he be wrong'd who is not even his
    own,
But save for dread of thee had beaten me,
Scratch'd, bitten, blinded, marr'd me some-
    how — Mark ?
What rights are his that dare not strike for
    them ?
Not lift a hand — not, tho' he found me
    thus !
But harken ! have ye met him ? hence he
    went
To-day for three days' hunting — as he
    said —
And so returns belike within an hour.
Mark's way, my soul ! — but eat not thou
    with Mark,   530
Because he hates thee even more than fears,
Nor drink; and when thou passest any
    wood
Close vizor, lest an arrow from the bush
Should leave me all alone with Mark and
    hell.
My God, the measure of my hate for Mark
Is as the measure of my love for thee !'

So, pluck'd one way by hate and one by
    love,
Drain'd of her force, again she sat, and
    spake
To Tristram, as he knelt before her, say-
    ing:
'O hunter, and O blower of the horn,   540
Harper, and thou hast been a rover too,
For, ere I mated with my shambling king,
Ye twain had fallen out about the bride
Of one — his name is out of me — the prize,
If prize she were — what marvel ? — she
    could see —
Thine, friend; and ever since my craven
    seeks
To wreck thee villainously — but, O Sir
    Knight,
What dame or damsel have ye kneel'd to
    last ?'

    And Tristram, 'Last to my Queen Para-
    mount,   549
Here now to my queen paramount of love
And loveliness — ay, lovelier than when
    first
Her light feet fell on our rough Lyonnesse,
Sailing from Ireland.'

                        Softly laugh'd Isolt:
'Flatter me not, for hath not our great
    Queen
My dole of beauty trebled ?' and he said:
'Her beauty is her beauty, and thine thine,
And thine is more to me — soft, gracious,
    kind —
Save when thy Mark is kindled on thy lips
Most gracious; but she, haughty, even to
    him,   559
Lancelot; for I have seen him wan enow
To make one doubt if ever the great Queen
Have yielded him her love.'

                        To whom Isolt:
'Ah, then, false hunter and false harper,
    thou
Who brakest thro' the scruple of my bond,
Calling me thy white hind, and saying to me
That Guinevere had sinn'd against the
    highest,
And I — misyoked with such a want of
    man —
That I could hardly sin against the lowest.'

    He answer'd: 'O my soul, be comforted !
If this be sweet, to sin in leading-strings,

If here be comfort, and if ours be sin,   571
Crown'd warrant had we for the crowning
    sin
That made us happy; but how ye greet me
    — fear
And fault and doubt — no word of that
    fond tale —
Thy deep heart-yearnings, thy sweet mem-
    ories
Of Tristram in that year he was away.'

And, saddening on the sudden, spake
    Isolt:
'I had forgotten all in my strong joy
To see thee — yearnings? — ay! for, hour
    by hour,
Here in the never-ended afternoon,   580
O, sweeter than all memories of thee,
Deeper than any yearnings after thee
Seem'd those far-rolling, westward-smiling
    seas,
Watch'd from this tower. Isolt of Britain
    dash'd
Before Isolt of Brittany on the strand,
Would that have chill'd her bride-kiss?
    Wedded her?
Fought in her father's battles? wounded
    there?
The King was all fulfill'd with grateful-
    ness,
And she, my namesake of the hands, that
    heal'd
Thy hurt and heart with unguent and ca-
    ress —   590
Well — can I wish her any huger wrong
Than having known thee? her too hast
    thou left
To pine and waste in those sweet memories.
O, were I not my Mark's, by whom all
    men
Are noble, I should hate thee more than
    love.'

And Tristram, fondling her light hands,
    replied:
'Grace, queen, for being loved; she loved
    me well.
Did I love her? the name at least I loved.
Isolt? — I fought his battles, for Isolt!
The night was dark; the true star set.
    Isolt!   600
The name was ruler of the dark — Isolt?
Care not for her! patient, and prayerful,
    meek,
Pale-blooded, she will yield herself to God.'

And Isolt answer'd: 'Yea, and why not
    I?
Mine is the larger need, who am not meek,
Pale-blooded, prayerful. Let me tell thee
    now.
Here one black, mute midsummer night I
    sat,
Lonely, but musing on thee, wondering
    where,
Murmuring a light song I had heard thee
    sing,
And once or twice I spake thy name aloud.
Then flash'd a levin-brand; and near me
    stood,   611
In fuming sulphur blue and green, a fiend —
Mark's way to steal behind one in the
    dark —
For there was Mark: "He has wedded
    her," he said,
Not said, but hiss'd it; then this crown of
    towers
So shook to such a roar of all the sky,
That here in utter dark I swoon'd away,
And woke again in utter dark, and cried,
"I will flee hence and give myself to
    God" —
And thou wert lying in thy new leman's
    arms.'   620

Then Tristram, ever dallying with her
    hand,
'May God be with thee, sweet, when old
    and gray,
And past desire!' a saying that anger'd
    her.
'"May God be with thee, sweet, when
    thou art old,
And sweet no more to me!" I need Him
    now.
For when had Lancelot utter'd aught so
    gross
Even to the swineherd's malkin in the
    mast?
The greater man the greater courtesy.
Far other was the Tristram, Arthur's
    knight!
But thou, thro' ever harrying thy wild
    beasts —   630
Save that to touch a harp, tilt with a
    lance
Becomes thee well — art grown wild beast
    thyself.
How darest thou, if lover, push me even
In fancy from thy side, and set me far
In the gray distance, half a life away,

Her to be loved no more ?   Unsay it, un-
    swear !
Flatter me rather, seeing me so weak,
Broken with Mark and hate and solitude,
Thy marriage and mine own, that I should
    suck   639
Lies like sweet wines.   Lie to me ; I believe.
Will ye not lie ? not swear, as there ye
    kneel,
And solemnly as when ye sware to him,
The man of men, our King — My God, the
    power
Was once in vows when men believed the
    King !
They lied not then who sware, and thro'
    their vows
The King prevailing made his realm — I
    say,
Swear to me thou wilt love me even when
    old,
Gray - hair'd, and past desire, and in de-
    spair.'

    Then Tristram, pacing moodily up and
        down:
' Vows ! did you keep the vow you made
    to Mark   650
More than I mine ? Lied, say ye ? Nay,
    but learnt,
The vow that binds too strictly snaps it-
    self —
My knighthood taught me this — ay, being
    snapt —
We run more counter to the soul thereof
Than had we never sworn.   I swear no
    more.
I swore to the great King, and am for-
    sworn.
For once — even to the height — I honor'd
    him.
" Man, is he man at all ? " methought,
    when first
I rode from our rough Lyonnesse, and be-
    held
That victor of the Pagan throned in
    hall —   660
His hair, a sun that ray'd from off a brow
Like hill-snow high in heaven, the steel-
    blue eyes,
The golden beard that clothed his lips with
    light —
Moreover, that weird legend of his birth,
With Merlin's mystic babble about his
    end
Amazed me; then, his foot was on a stool

Shaped as a dragon; he seem'd to me no
    man,
But Michael trampling Satan; so I sware,
Being amazed.   But this went by — The
    vows !
O, ay — the wholesome madness of an
    hour —   670
They served their use, their time; for every
    knight
Believed himself a greater than himself,
And every follower eyed him as a God;
Till he, being lifted up beyond himself,
Did mightier deeds than elsewise he had
    done,
And so the realm was made.   But then
    their vows —
First mainly thro' that sullying of our
    Queen —
Began to gall the knighthood, asking
    whence
Had Arthur right to bind them to himself ?
Dropt down from heaven ? wash'd up from
    out the deep ?   680
They fail'd to trace him thro' the flesh and
    blood
Of our old kings.   Whence then ? a doubt-
    ful lord
To bind them by inviolable vows,
Which flesh and blood perforce would vio-
    late;
For feel this arm of mine — the tide
    within
Red with free chase and heather-scented
    air,
Pulsing full man.   Can Arthur make me
    pure
As any maiden child ? lock up my tongue
From uttering freely what I freely hear ?
Bind me to one ?   The wide world laughs
    at it.   690
And worldling of the world am I, and
    know
The ptarmigan that whitens ere his hour
Woos his own end; we are not angels here
Nor shall be.   Vows — I am woodman of
    the woods,
And hear the garnet-headed yaffingale
Mock them — my soul, we love but while
    we may;
And therefore is my love so large for thee,
Seeing it is not bounded save by love.'

    Here ending, he moved toward her, and
        she said:
' Good; an I turn'd away my love for thee

To some one thrice as courteous as thy-
self —   701
For courtesy wins woman all as well
As valor may, but he that closes both
Is perfect, he is Lancelot — taller indeed,
Rosier and comelier, thou — but say I loved
This knightliest of all knights, and cast
thee back
Thine own small saw, "We love but while
we may,"
Well then, what answer?'

He that while she spake,
Mindful of what he brought to adorn her
with,
The jewels, had let one finger lightly touch
The warm white apple of her throat, re-
plied,   711
'Press this a little closer, sweet, until —
Come, I am hunger'd and half-anger'd —
meat,
Wine, wine — and I will love thee to the
death,
And out beyond into the dream to come.'

So then, when both were brought to full
accord,
She rose, and set before him all he will'd;
And after these had comforted the blood
With meats and wines, and satiated their
hearts —
Now talking of their woodland paradise, 720
The deer, the dews, the fern, the founts,
the lawns;
Now mocking at the much ungainliness,
And craven shifts, and long crane legs of
Mark —
Then Tristram laughing caught the harp
and sang:

'Ay, ay, O, ay — the winds that bend the
brier!
A star in heaven, a star within the mere!
Ay, ay, O, ay — a star was my desire,
And one was far apart and one was near.
Ay, ay, O, ay — the winds that bow the grass!
And one was water and one star was fire, 730
And one will ever shine and one will pass.
Ay, ay, O, ay — the winds that move the
mere!'

Then in the light's last glimmer Tris-
tram show'd
And swung the ruby carcanet. She cried,
The collar of some Order, which our
King

Hath newly founded, all for thee, my soul,
For thee, to yield thee grace beyond thy
peers.'

'Not so, my queen,' he said, 'but the
red fruit
Grown on a magic oak-tree in mid-heaven,
And won by Tristram as a tourney-prize,
And hither brought by Tristram for his
last   741
Love-offering and peace-offering unto thee.'

He spoke, he turn'd, then, flinging round
her neck,
Claspt it, and cried, 'Thine Order, O my
queen!'
But, while he bow'd to kiss the jewell'd
throat,
Out of the dark, just as the lips had
touch'd,
Behind him rose a shadow and a shriek —
'Mark's way,' said Mark, and clove him
thro' the brain.

That night came Arthur home, and while
he climb'd,
All in a death-dumb autumn-dripping
gloom,   750
The stairway to the hall, and look'd and
saw
The great Queen's bower was dark, — about
his feet
A voice clung sobbing till he question'd
it,
'What art thou?' and the voice about his
feet
Sent up an answer, sobbing, 'I am thy
fool,
And I shall never make thee smile again.'

GUINEVERE

QUEEN GUINEVERE had fled the court, and
sat
There in the holy house at Almesbury
Weeping, none with her save a little maid,
A novice. One low light betwixt them
burn'd
Blurr'd by the creeping mist, for all abroad,
Beneath a moon unseen albeit at full,
The white mist, like a face-cloth to the
face,
Clung to the dead earth, and the land was
still.

For hither had she fled, her cause of
    flight
Sir Modred; he that like a subtle beast   10
Lay couchant with his eyes upon the throne,
Ready to spring, waiting a chance. For this
He chill'd the popular praises of the King
With silent smiles of slow disparagement;
And tamper'd with the Lords of the White
    Horse,
Heathen, the brood by Hengist left; and
    sought
To make disruption in the Table Round
Of Arthur, and to splinter it into feuds
Serving his traitorous end; and all his
    aims
Were sharpen'd by strong hate for Lance-
    lot.   20

For thus it chanced one morn when all
    the court,
Green-suited, but with plumes that mock'd
    the may,
Had been — their wont — a-maying and
    return'd,
That Modred still in green, all ear and eye,
Climb'd to the high top of the garden-wall
To spy some secret scandal if he might,
And saw the Queen who sat betwixt her
    best
Enid and lissome Vivien, of her court
The wiliest and the worst; and more than
    this
He saw not, for Sir Lancelot passing by   30
Spied where he couch'd, and as the gar-
    dener's hand
Picks from the colewort a green cater-
    pillar,
So from the high wall and the flowering
    grove
Of grasses Lancelot pluck'd him by the
    heel,
And cast him as a worm upon the way;
But when he knew the prince tho' marr'd
    with dust,
He, reverencing king's blood in a bad man,
Made such excuses as he might, and these
Full knightly without scorn. For in those
    days
No knight of Arthur's noblest dealt in
    scorn;   40
But, if a man were halt, or hunch'd, in
    him
By those whom God had made full-limb'd
    and tall,
Scorn was allow'd as part of his defect,

And he was answer'd softly by the King
And all his Table. So Sir Lancelot holp
To raise the prince, who rising twice or
    thrice
Full sharply smote his knees, and smiled,
    and went;
But, ever after, the small violence done
Rankled in him and ruffled all his heart,
As the sharp wind that ruffles all day long
A little bitter pool about a stone   51
On the bare coast.

            But when Sir Lancelot told
This matter to the Queen, at first she
    laugh'd
Lightly, to think of Modred's dusty fall,
Then shudder'd, as the village wife who
    cries,
'I shudder, some one steps across my
    grave;'
Then laugh'd again, but faintlier, for in-
    deed
She half-foresaw that he, the subtle beast,
Would track her guilt until he found, and
    hers
Would be for evermore a name of scorn. 60
Henceforward rarely could she front in
    hall,
Or elsewhere, Modred's narrow foxy face,
Heart - hiding smile, and gray persistent
    eye.
Henceforward too, the Powers that tend
    the soul,
To help it from the death that cannot die,
And save it even in extremes, began
To vex and plague her. Many a time for
    hours,
Beside the placid breathings of the King,
In the dead night, grim faces came and
    went
Before her, or a vague spiritual fear —   70
Like to some doubtful noise of creaking
    doors,
Heard by the watcher in a haunted house,
That keeps the rust of murder on the
    walls —
Held her awake; or if she slept she dream'd
An awful dream, for then she seem'd to
    stand
On some vast plain before a setting sun,
And from the sun there swiftly made at
    her
A ghastly something, and its shadow flew
Before it till it touch'd her, and she
    turn'd —

When lo ! her own, that broadening from
   her feet, 80
And blackening, swallow'd all the land,
   and in it
Far cities burnt, and with a cry she woke.
And all this trouble did not pass but grew,
Till even the clear face of the guileless
   King,
And trustful courtesies of household life,
Became her bane ; and at the last she
   said :
'O Lancelot, get thee hence to thine own
   land,
For if thou tarry we shall meet again,
And if we meet again some evil chance
Will make the smouldering scandal break
   and blaze 90
Before the people and our lord the King.'
And Lancelot ever promised, but remain'd,
And still they met and met. Again she
   said,
'O Lancelot, if thou love me get thee
   hence.'
And then they were agreed upon a night —
When the good King should not be there
   — to meet
And part for ever. Vivien, lurking, heard.
She told Sir Modred. Passion-pale they
   met
And greeted. Hands in hands, and eye to
   eye,
Low on the border of her couch they sat 100
Stammering and staring. It was their last
   hour,
A madness of farewells. And Modred
   brought
His creatures to the basement of the tower
For testimony; and crying with full voice,
'Traitor, come out, ye are trapt at last,'
   aroused
Lancelot, who rushing outward lionlike
Leapt on him, and hurl'd him headlong,
   and he fell
Stunn'd, and his creatures took and bare
   him off,
And all was still. Then she, 'The end is
   come, 109
And I am shamed for ever;' and he said:
'Mine be the shame, mine was the sin;
   but rise,
And fly to my strong castle over-seas.
There will I hide thee till my life shall
   end,
There hold thee with my life against the
   world.'

She answer'd: 'Lancelot, wilt thou hold me
   so ?
Nay, friend, for we have taken our fare-
   wells.
Would God that thou couldst hide me from
   myself !
Mine is the shame, for I was wife, and thou
Unwedded; yet rise now, and let us fly,
For I will draw me into sanctuary, 120
And bide my doom.' So Lancelot got her
   horse,
Set her thereon, and mounted on his own,
And then they rode to the divided way,
There kiss'd, and parted weeping; for he
   past,
Love-loyal to the least wish of the Queen,
Back to his land; but she to Almesbury
Fled all night long by glimmering waste
   and weald,
And heard the spirits of the waste and
   weald
Moan as she fled, or thought she heard
   them moan.
And in herself she moan'd, 'Too late, too
   late ! ' 130
Till in the cold wind that foreruns the
   morn,
A blot in heaven, the raven, flying high,
Croak'd, and she thought, 'He spies a field
   of death;
For now the heathen of the Northern Sea,
Lured by the crimes and frailties of the
   court,
Begin to slay the folk and spoil the land.'

And when she came to Almesbury she
   spake
There to the nuns, and said, 'Mine ene-
   mies
Pursue me, but, O peaceful Sisterhood,
Receive and yield me sanctuary, nor ask 140
Her name to whom ye yield it till her time
To tell you;' and her beauty, grace, and
   power
Wrought as a charm upon them, and they
   spared
To ask it.

     So the stately Queen abode
For many a week, unknown, among the
   nuns,
Nor with them mix'd, nor told her name,
   nor sought,
Wrapt in her grief, for housel or for shrift,
But communed only with the little maid,

Who pleased her with a babbling heedless-
ness
Which often lured her from herself; but
now,   150
This night, a rumor wildly blown about
Came that Sir Modred had usurp'd the
realm
And leagued him with the heathen, while
the King
Was waging war on Lancelot.   Then she
thought,
'With what a hate the people and the
King
Must hate me,' and bow'd down upon her
hands
Silent, until the little maid, who brook'd
No silence, brake it, uttering 'Late! so
late!
What hour, I wonder now?' and when she
drew
No answer, by and by began to hum   160
An air the nuns had taught her: 'Late, so
late!'
Which when she heard, the Queen look'd
up, and said,
'O maiden, if indeed ye list to sing,
Sing, and unbind my heart that I may
weep.'
Whereat full willingly sang the little maid.

'Late, late, so late! and dark the night and
chill!
Late, late, so late! but we can enter still.
Too late, too late! ye cannot enter now.

'No light had we; for that we do repent,
And learning this, the bridegroom will relent.
Too late, too late! ye cannot enter now.   171

'No light! so late! and dark and chill the
night!
O, let us in, that we may find the light!
Too late, too late! ye cannot enter now.

'Have we not heard the bridegroom is so
sweet?
O, let us in, tho' late, to kiss his feet!
No, no, too late! ye cannot enter now.'

So sang the novice, while full passion-
ately,
Her head upon her hands, remembering
Her thought when first she came, wept the
sad Queen.   180
Then said the little novice prattling to
her:

'O pray you, noble lady, weep no more;
But let my words — the words of one so
small,
Who knowing nothing knows but to obey,
And if I do not there is penance given —
Comfort your sorrows, for they do not
flow
From evil done; right sure am I of that,
Who see your tender grace and stateli-
ness.
But weigh your sorrows with our lord the
King's,
And weighing find them less; for gone is
he   190
To wage grim war against Sir Lancelot
there,
Round that strong castle where he holds
the Queen;
And Modred whom he left in charge of
all,
The traitor — Ah, sweet lady, the King's
grief
For his own self, and his own Queen, and
realm,
Must needs be thrice as great as any of
ours!
For me, I thank the saints, I am not great;
For if there ever come a grief to me
I cry my cry in silence, and have done;
None knows it, and my tears have brought
me good.   200
But even were the griefs of little ones
As great as those of great ones, yet this
grief
Is added to the griefs the great must bear,
That, howsoever much they may desire
Silence, they cannot weep behind a cloud;
As even here they talk at Almesbury
About the good King and his wicked Queen,
And were I such a King with such a Queen,
Well might I wish to veil her wickedness,
But were I such a King it could not be.' 210

Then to her own sad heart mutter'd the
Queen,
'Will the child kill me with her innocent
talk?'
But openly she answer'd, 'Must not I,
If this false traitor have displaced his lord,
Grieve with the common grief of all the
realm?'

'Yea,' said the maid, 'this all is woman's
grief,
That *she* is woman, whose disloyal life

Hath wrought confusion in the Table
Round
Which good King Arthur founded, years
ago,
With signs and miracles and wonders,
there   220
At Camelot, ere the coming of the Queen.'

Then thought the Queen within herself
again,
' Will the child kill me with her foolish
prate ? '
But openly she spake and said to her,
' O little maid, shut in by nunnery walls,
What canst thou know of Kings and Tables
Round,
Or what of signs and wonders, but the signs
And simple miracles of thy nunnery ? '

To whom the little novice garrulously:
' Yea, but I know; the land was full of
signs   230
And wonders ere the coming of the Queen.
So said my father, and himself was knight
Of the great Table — at the founding of
it,
And rode thereto from Lyonnesse; and he
said
That as he rode, an hour or maybe twain
After the sunset, down the coast, he heard
Strange music, and he paused, and turning
— there,
All down the lonely coast of Lyonnesse,
Each with a beacon-star upon his head,
And with a wild sea-light about his feet, 240
He saw them — headland after headland
flame
Far on into the rich heart of the west.
And in the light the white mermaiden
swam,
And strong man-breasted things stood from
the sea,
And sent a deep sea-voice thro' all the
land,
To which the little elves of chasm and
cleft
Made answer, sounding like a distant horn.
So said my father — yea, and furthermore,
Next morning, while he past the dim-lit
woods   249
Himself beheld three spirits mad with joy
Come dashing down on a tall wayside
flower,
That shook beneath them as the thistle
shakes

When three gray linnets wrangle for the
seed.
And still at evenings on before his horse
The flickering fairy - circle wheel'd and
broke
Flying, and link'd again, and wheel'd and
broke
Flying, for all the land was full of life.
And when at last he came to Camelot,
A wreath of airy dancers hand-in-hand
Swung round the lighted lantern of the
hall;   260
And in the hall itself was such a feast
As never man had dream'd; for every
knight
Had whatsoever meat he long'd for served
By hands unseen; and even as he said
Down in the cellars merry bloated things
Shoulder'd the spigot, straddling on the
butts
While the wine ran; so glad were spirits
and men
Before the coming of the sinful Queen.'

Then spake the Queen and somewhat
bitterly,
' Were they so glad ? ill prophets were
they all,   270
Spirits and men. Could none of them fore-
see,
Not even thy wise father with his signs
And wonders, what has fallen upon the
realm ? '

To whom the novice garrulously again:
' Yea, one, a bard, of whom my father
said,
Full many a noble war-song had he sung,
Even in the presence of an enemy's fleet,
Between the steep cliff and the coming
wave;
And many a mystic lay of life and death
Had chanted on the smoky mountain-
tops,   280
When round him bent the spirits of the
hills
With all their dewy hair blown back like
flame.
So said my father — and that night the
bard
Sang Arthur's glorious wars, and sang the
King
As wellnigh more than man, and rail'd at
those
Who call'd him the false son of Gorloïs.

For there was no man knew from whence
he came;
But after tempest, when the long wave
broke
All down the thundering shores of Bude
and Bos,
There came a day as still as heaven, and
then   290
They found a naked child upon the sands
Of dark Tintagil by the Cornish sea,
And that was Arthur, and they foster'd
him
Till he by miracle was approven King;
And that his grave should be a mystery
From all men, like his birth; and could he
find
A woman in her womanhood as great
As he was in his manhood, then, he sang,
The twain together well might change the
world.
But even in the middle of his song   300
He falter'd, and his hand fell from the
harp,
And pale he turn'd, and reel'd, and would
have fallen,
But that they stay'd him up; nor would he
tell
His vision; but what doubt that he fore-
saw
This evil work of Lancelot and the Queen?'

Then thought the Queen, 'Lo! they have
set her on,
Our simple-seeming abbess and her nuns,
To play upon me,' and bow'd her head nor
spake.
Whereat the novice crying, with clasp'd
hands,   309
Shame on her own garrulity garrulously,
Said the good nuns would check her gad-
ding tongue
Full often, 'and, sweet lady, if I seem
To vex an ear too sad to listen to me,
Unmannerly, with prattling and the tales
Which my good father told me, check me
too
Nor let me shame my father's memory,
one
Of noblest manners, tho' himself would
say
Sir Lancelot had the noblest; and he died,
Kill'd in a tilt, come next, five summers
back,   319
And left me; but of others who remain,
And of the two first-famed for courtesy —

And pray you check me if I ask amiss —
But pray you, which had noblest, while
you moved
Among them, Lancelot or our lord the
King?'

Then the pale Queen look'd up and an-
swer'd her:
'Sir Lancelot, as became a noble knight,
Was gracious to all ladies, and the same
In open battle or the tilting-field
Forbore his own advantage, and the King
In open battle or the tilting-field   330
Forbore his own advantage, and these
two
Were the most nobly-manner'd men of
all;
For manners are not idle, but the fruit
Of loyal nature and of noble mind.'

'Yea,' said the maid, 'be manners such
fair fruit?
Then Lancelot's needs must be a thousand-
fold
Less noble, being, as all rumor runs,
The most disloyal friend in all the world.'

To which a mournful answer made the
Queen:
'O, closed about by narrowing nunnery-
walls,   340
What knowest thou of the world and all its
lights
And shadows, all the wealth and all the
woe?
If ever Lancelot, that most noble knight,
Were for one hour less noble than himself,
Pray for him that he scape the doom of
fire,
And weep for her who drew him to his
doom.'

'Yea,' said the little novice, 'I pray for
both;
But I should all as soon believe that his,
Sir Lancelot's, were as noble as the King's,
As I could think, sweet lady, yours would
be   350
Such as they are, were you the sinful
Queen.'

So she, like many another babbler, hurt
Whom she would soothe, and harm'd where
she would heal;
For here a sudden flush of wrathful heat

Fired all the pale face of the Queen, who
   cried:
' Such as thou art be never maiden more
For ever ! thou their tool, set on to plague
And play upon and harry me, petty spy
And traitress ! ' When that storm of an-
   ger brake
From Guinevere, aghast the maiden rose,
White as her veil, and stood before the
   Queen   361
As tremulously as foam upon the beach
Stands in a wind, ready to break and fly,
And when the Queen had added, ' Get
   thee hence ! '
Fled frighted. Then that other left alone
Sigh'd, and began to gather heart again,
Saying in herself: ' The simple, fearful
   child
Meant nothing, but my own too-fearful
   guilt,
Simpler than any child, betrays itself.
But help me, Heaven, for surely I re-
   pent !   370
For what is true repentance but in
   thought —
Not even in inmost thought to think again
The sins that made the past so pleasant to
   us ?
And I have sworn never to see him more,
To see him more.'

                 And even in saying this,
Her memory from old habit of the mind
Went slipping back upon the golden days
In which she saw him first, when Lancelot
   came,
Reputed the best knight and goodliest
   man,
Ambassador, to yield her to his lord   380
Arthur, and led her forth, and far ahead
Of his and her retinue moving, they,
Rapt in sweet talk or lively, all on love
And sport and tilts and pleasure, — for
   the time
Was may - time, and as yet no sin was
   dream'd, —
Rode under groves that look'd a paradise
Of blossom, over sheets of hyacinth
That seem'd the heavens upbreaking thro'
   the earth,
And on from hill to hill, and every day
Beheld at noon in some delicious dale   390
The silk pavilions of King Arthur raised
For brief repast or afternoon repose
By couriers gone before; and on again,

Till yet once more ere set of sun they saw
The Dragon of the great Pendragonship,
That crown'd the state pavilion of the
   King,
Blaze by the rushing brook or silent well.

   But when the Queen immersed in such a
   trance,
And moving thro' the past unconsciously,
Came to that point where first she saw the
   King   400
Ride toward her from the city, sigh'd to
   find
Her journey done, glanced at him, thought
   him cold,
High, self - contain'd, and passionless, not
   like him,
' Not like my Lancelot ' — while she
   brooded thus
And grew half - guilty in her thoughts
   again,
There rode an armed warrior to the doors.
A murmuring whisper thro' the nunnery
   ran,
Then on a sudden a cry, ' The King ! ' She
   sat
Stiff-stricken, listening; but when armed
   feet
Thro' the long gallery from the outer doors
Rang coming, prone from off her seat she
   fell,   411
And grovell'd with her face against the
   floor.
There with her milk-white arms and shad-
   owy hair
She made her face a darkness from the
   King,
And in the darkness heard his armed feet
Pause by her; then came silence, then a
   voice,
Monotonous and hollow like a ghost's
Denouncing judgment, but, tho' changed,
   the King's:

   ' Liest thou here so low, the child of one
I honor'd, happy, dead before thy shame ?
Well is it that no child is born of thee. 421
The children born of thee are sword and
   fire,
Red ruin, and the breaking up of laws,
The craft of kindred and the godless hosts
Of heathen swarming o'er the Northern
   Sea;
Whom I, while yet Sir Lancelot, my right
   arm,

The mightiest of my knights, abode with
   me,
Have everywhere about this land of Christ
In twelve great battles ruining overthrown.
And knowest thou now from whence I come
   — from him,   430
From waging bitter war with him; and he,
That did not shun to smite me in worse
   way,
Had yet that grace of courtesy in him left,
He spared to lift his hand against the King
Who made him knight. But many a knight
   was slain;
And many more and all his kith and kin
Clave to him, and abode in his own land.
And many more when Modred raised revolt,
Forgetful of their troth and fealty, clave
To Modred, and a remnant stays with me.
And of this remnant will I leave a part, 441
True men who love me still, for whom I
   live,
To guard thee in the wild hour coming on,
Lest but a hair of this low head be harm'd.
Fear not; thou shalt be guarded till my
   death.
Howbeit I know, if ancient prophecies
Have err'd not, that I march to meet my
   doom.
Thou hast not made my life so sweet to me,
That I the King should greatly care to
   live;   449
For thou hast spoilt the purpose of my life.
Bear with me for the last time while I
   show,
Even for thy sake, the sin which thou hast
   sinn'd.
For when the Roman left us, and their law
Relax'd its hold upon us, and the ways
Were fill'd with rapine, here and there a
   deed
Of prowess done redress'd a random wrong.
But I was first of all the kings who drew
The knighthood-errant of this realm and all
The realms together under me, their Head,
In that fair Order of my Table Round, 460
A glorious company, the flower of men,
To serve as model for the mighty world,
And be the fair beginning of a time.
I made them lay their hands in mine and
   swear
To reverence the King, as if he were
Their conscience, and their conscience as
   their King,
**To break the heathen and uphold. the
   Christ,**

To ride abroad redressing human wrongs,
To speak no slander, no, nor listen to it,
To honor his own word as if his God's, 470
To lead sweet lives in purest chastity,
To love one maiden only, cleave to her,
And worship her by years of noble deeds,
Until they won her; for indeed I knew
Of no more subtle master under heaven
Than is the maiden passion for a maid,
Not only to keep down the base in man,
But teach high thought, and amiable words
And courtliness, and the desire of fame,
And love of truth, and all that makes a
   man.   480
And all this throve before I wedded thee,
Believing, " Lo, mine helpmate, one to feel
My purpose and rejoicing in my joy ! "
Then came thy shameful sin with Lance-
   lot;
Then came the sin of Tristram and Isolt;
Then others, following these my mightiest
   knights,
And drawing foul ensample from fair
   names,
Sinn'd also, till the loathsome opposite
Of all my heart had destined did obtain,
And all thro' thee ! so that this life of
   mine   490
I guard as God's high gift from scathe and
   wrong,
Not greatly care to lose; but rather think
How sad it were for Arthur, should he
   live,
To sit once more within his lonely hall,
And miss the wonted number of my knights,
And miss to hear high talk of noble deeds
As in the golden days before thy sin.
For which of us who might be left could
   speak
Of the pure heart, nor seem to glance at
   thee ?
And in thy bowers of Camelot or of Usk
Thy shadow still would glide from room to
   room,   501
And I should evermore be vext with thee
In hanging robe or vacant ornament,
Or ghostly footfall echoing on the stair.
For think not, tho' thou wouldst not love
   thy lord,
Thy lord has wholly lost his love for thee.
I am not made of so slight elements.
Yet must I leave thee, woman, to thy
   shame.
I hold that man the worst of public foes
Who either for his own or children's sake,

To save his blood from scandal, lets the
wife 511
Whom he knows false abide and rule the
house:
For being thro' his cowardice allow'd
Her station, taken everywhere for pure,
She like a new disease, unknown to men,
Creeps, no precaution used, among the
crowd,
Makes wicked lightnings of her eyes, and
saps
The fealty of our friends, and stirs the
pulse
With devil's leaps, and poisons half the
young.
Worst of the worst were that man he that
reigns! 520
Better the King's waste hearth and aching
heart
Than thou reseated in thy place of light,
The mockery of my people and their
bane!'

He paused, and in the pause she crept an
inch
Nearer, and laid her hands about his feet.
Far off a solitary trumpet blew.
Then waiting by the doors the war-horse
neigh'd
As at a friend's voice, and he spake again:

'Yet think not that I come to urge thy
crimes; 529
I did not come to curse thee, Guinevere,
I, whose vast pity almost makes me die
To see thee, laying there thy golden head,
My pride in happier summers, at my feet.
The wrath which forced my thoughts on
that fierce law,
The doom of treason and the flaming
death, —
When first I learnt thee hidden here, — is
past.
The pang — which, while I weigh'd thy
heart with one
Too wholly true to dream untruth in thee,
Made my tears burn — is also past — in
part.
And all is past, the sin is sinn'd, and I, 540
Lo, I forgive thee, as Eternal God
Forgives! do thou for thine own soul the
rest.
But how to take last leave of all I loved?
O golden hair, with which I used to play
Not knowing! O imperial-moulded form,

And beauty such as never woman wore,
Until it came a kingdom's curse with
thee —
I cannot touch thy lips, they are not mine,
But Lancelot's; nay, they never were the
King's.
I cannot take thy hand; that too is flesh,
And in the flesh thou hast sinn'd; and mine
own flesh, 551
Here looking down on thine polluted, cries,
"I loathe thee;" yet not less, O Guinevere,
For I was ever virgin save for thee,
My love thro' flesh hath wrought into my
life
So far that my doom is, I love thee still.
Let no man dream but that I love thee
still.
Perchance, and so thou purify thy soul,
And so thou lean on our fair father Christ,
Hereafter in that world where all are pure
We two may meet before high God, and
thou 561
Wilt spring to me, and claim me thine, and
know
I am thine husband — not a smaller soul,
Nor Lancelot, nor another. Leave me that,
I charge thee, my last hope. Now must I
hence.
Thro' the thick night I hear the trumpet
blow.
They summon me their King to lead mine
hosts
Far down to that great battle in the west,
Where I must strike against the man they
call
My sister's son — no kin of mine, who
leagues 570
With Lords of the White Horse, heathen,
and knights,
Traitors — and strike him dead, and meet
myself
Death, or I know not what mysterious
doom.
And thou remaining here wilt learn the
event;
But hither shall I never come again,
Never lie by thy side, see thee no more —
Farewell!'

And while she grovell'd at his feet,
She felt the King's breath wander o'er her
neck,
And in the darkness o'er her fallen head
Perceived the waving of his hands that
blest. 580

Then, listening till those armed steps
    were gone,
Rose the pale Queen, and in her anguish
    found
The casement: 'peradventure,' so she
    thought,
'If I might see his face, and not be seen.'
And lo, he sat on horseback at the door!
And near him the sad nuns with each a
    light
Stood, and he gave them charge about the
    Queen,
To guard and foster her for evermore.
And while he spake to these his helm was
    lower'd,
To which for crest the golden dragon
    clung   590
Of Britain; so she did not see the face,
Which then was as an angel's, but she saw,
Wet with the mists and smitten by the
    lights,
The Dragon of the great Pendragonship
Blaze, making all the night a steam of fire.
And even then he turn'd; and more and
    more
The moony vapor rolling round the King,
Who seem'd the phantom of a giant in it,
Enwound him fold by fold, and made him
    gray
And grayer, till himself became as mist 600
Before her, moving ghostlike to his doom.

Then she stretch'd out her arms and
    cried aloud,
'O Arthur!' there her voice brake sud-
    denly,
Then — as a stream that spouting from a
    cliff
Fails in mid air, but gathering at the base
Re - makes itself, and flashes down the
    vale —
Went on in passionate utterance:

              'Gone — my lord!
Gone thro' my sin to slay and to be slain!
And he forgave me, and I could not speak.
Farewell? I should have answer'd his
    farewell.   610
His mercy choked me. Gone, my lord the
    King,
My own true lord! how dare I call him
    mine?
The shadow of another cleaves to me,
And makes me one pollution. He, the King,
Call'd me polluted. Shall I kill myself?

What help in that? I cannot kill my sin,
If soul be soul, nor can I kill my shame;
No, nor by living can I live it down.
The days will grow to weeks, the weeks to
    months,
The months will add themselves and make
    the years,   620
The years will roll into the centuries,
And mine will ever be a name of scorn.
I must not dwell on that defeat of fame.
Let the world be; that is but of the
    world —
What else? what hope? I think there was
    a hope,
Except he mock'd me when he spake of
    hope;
His hope he call'd it; but he never mocks,
For mockery is the fume of little hearts.
And blessed be the King, who hath for-
    given
My wickedness to him, and left me hope 630
That in mine own heart I can live down
    sin
And be his mate hereafter in the heavens
Before high God! Ah great and gentle
    lord,
Who wast, as is the conscience of a saint
Among his warring senses, to thy knights —
To whom my false voluptuous pride, that
    took
Full easily all impressions from below,
Would not look up, or half-despised the
    height
To which I would not or I could not
    climb —
I thought I could not breathe in that fine
    air,   640
That pure severity of perfect light —
I yearn'd for warmth and color which I
    found
In Lancelot — now I see thee what thou
    art,
Thou art the highest and most human too,
Not Lancelot, nor another. Is there none
Will tell the King I love him tho' so late?
Now — ere he goes to the great battle?
    none!
Myself must tell him in that purer life,
But now it were too daring. Ah my God,
What might I not have made of thy fair
    world,   650
Had I but loved thy highest creature
    here?
It was my duty to have loved the highest;
It surely was my profit had I known;

It would have been my pleasure had I
    seen.
We needs must love the highest when we
    see it,
Not Lancelot, nor another.'

               Here her hand
Grasp'd made her vail her eyes. She look'd
    and saw
The novice, weeping, suppliant, and said to
    her,
' Yea, little maid, for am *I* not forgiven ? '
Then glancing up beheld the holy nuns 660
All round her, weeping; and her heart was
    loosed
Within her, and she wept with these and
    said:

  ' Ye know me then, that wicked one, who
    broke
The vast design and purpose of the King.
O, shut me round with narrowing nunnery-
    walls,
Meek maidens, from the voices crying,
    " Shame ! "
I must not scorn myself; he loves me still.
Let no one dream but that he loves me
    still.
So let me, if you do not shudder at me,
Nor shun to call me sister, dwell with you;
Wear black and white, and be a nun like
    you,   671
Fast with your fasts, not feasting with
    your feasts;
Grieve with your griefs, not grieving at
    your joys,
But not rejoicing; mingle with your rites;
Pray and be pray'd for; lie before your
    shrines;
Do each low office of your holy house;
Walk your dim cloister, and distribute
    dole
To poor sick people, richer in His eyes
Who ransom'd us, and haler too than I;
And treat their loathsome hurts and heal
    mine own;   680
And so wear out in alms - deed and in
    prayer
The sombre close of that voluptuous day
Which wrought the ruin of my lord the
    King.'

  She said. They took her to themselves;
    and she
Still hoping, fearing ' Is it yet too late ? '

Dwelt with them, till in time their abbess
    died.
Then she, for her good deeds and her pure
    life,
And for the power of ministration in her,
And likewise for the high rank she had
    borne,
Was chosen abbess, there, an abbess, lived
For three brief years, and there, an abbess,
    past   691
To where beyond these voices there is
    peace.

THE PASSING OF ARTHUR

THAT story which the bold Sir Bedivere,
First made and latest left of all the knights,
Told, when the man was no more than a
    voice
In the white winter of his age, to those
With whom he dwelt, new faces, other
    minds.

For on their march to westward, Bedi-
    vere,
Who slowly paced among the slumbering
    host,
Heard in his tent the moanings of the
    King:

  ' I found Him in the shining of the stars,
I mark'd Him in the flowering of His
    fields,   10
But in His ways with men I find Him not.
I waged His wars, and now I pass and
    die.
O me ! for why is all around us here
As if some lesser god had made the world,
But had not force to shape it as he would,
Till the High God behold it from beyond,
And enter it, and make it beautiful ?
Or else as if the world were wholly fair,
But that these eyes of men are dense and
    dim,
And have not power to see it as it is —   20
Perchance, because we see not to the
    close; —
For I, being simple, thought to work His
    will,
And have but stricken with the sword in
    vain,
And all whereon I lean'd in wife and friend
Is traitor to my peace, and all my realm
Reels back into the beast, and is no more.

My God, thou hast forgotten me in my
    death !
Nay — God my Christ — I pass but shall
    not die.'

Then, ere that last weird battle in the
    west,
There came on Arthur sleeping, Gawain
    kill'd   30
In Lancelot's war, the ghost of Gawain
    blown
Along a wandering wind, and past his ear
Went shrilling: 'Hollow, hollow all de-
    light !
Hail, King ! to-morrow thou shalt pass
    away.
Farewell ! there is an isle of rest for thee.
And I am blown along a wandering wind,
And hollow, hollow, hollow all delight ! '
And fainter onward, like wild birds that
    change
Their season in the night and wail their
    way
From cloud to cloud, down the long wind
    the dream   40
Shrill'd; but in going mingled with dim
    cries
Far in the moonlit haze among the hills,
As of some lonely city sack'd by night,
When all is lost, and wife and child with
    wail
Pass to new lords; and Arthur woke and
    call'd:
'Who spake ? A dream. O, light upon
    the wind,
Thine, Gawain, was the voice — are these
    dim cries
Thine ? or doth all that haunts the waste
    and wild
Mourn, knowing it will go along with me ? '

This heard the bold Sir Bedivere and
    spake: 50
'O me, my King, let pass whatever will,
Elves, and the harmless glamour of the
    field;
But in their stead thy name and glory
    cling
To all high places like a golden cloud
For ever; but as yet thou shalt not pass.
Light was Gawain in life, and light in death
Is Gawain, for the ghost is as the man;
And care not thou for dreams from him,
    but rise —
I hear the steps of Modred in the west,

And with him many of thy people, and
    knights   60
Once thine, whom thou hast loved, but
    grosser grown
Than heathen, spitting at their vows and
    thee.
Right well in heart they know thee for the
    King.
Arise, go forth and conquer as of old.'

Then spake King Arthur to Sir Bedivere:
'Far other is this battle in the west
Whereto we move than when we strove in
    youth,
And brake the petty kings, and fought with
    Rome,
Or thrust the heathen from the Roman
    wall,
And shook him thro' the north. Ill doom
    is mine   70
To war against my people and my knights.
The king who fights his people fights him-
    self.
And they my knights, who loved me once,
    the stroke
That strikes them dead is as my death to
    me.
Yet let us hence, and find or feel a way
Thro' this blind haze which, ever since I
    saw
One lying in the dust at Almesbury,
Hath folded in the passes of the world.'

Then rose the King and moved his host
    by night,
And ever push'd Sir Modred, league by
    league,   80
Back to the sunset bound of Lyonnesse —
A land of old upheaven from the abyss
By fire, to sink into the abyss again;
Where fragments of forgotten peoples
    dwelt,
And the long mountains ended in a coast
Of ever-shifting sand, and far away
The phantom circle of a moaning sea.
There the pursuer could pursue no more,
And he that fled no further fly the King;
And there, that day when the great light
    of heaven   90
Burn'd at his lowest in the rolling year,
On the waste sand by the waste sea they
    closed.
Nor ever yet had Arthur fought a fight
Like this last, dim, weird battle of the west.
A death-white mist slept over sand and sea,

Whereof the chill, to him who breathed it,
   drew
Down with his blood, till all his heart was
   cold
With formless fear; and even on Arthur
   fell
Confusion, since he saw not whom he
   fought.
For friend and foe were shadows in the
   mist,   100
And friend slew friend not knowing whom
   he slew;
And some had visions out of golden youth,
And some beheld the faces of old ghosts
Look in upon the battle; and in the mist
Was many a noble deed, many a base,
And chance and craft and strength in single
   fights,
And ever and anon with host to host
Shocks, and the splintering spear, the hard
   mail hewn,
Shield-breakings, and the clash of brands,
   the crash
Of battle - axes on shatter'd helms, and
   shrieks   110
After the Christ, of those who falling down
Look'd up for heaven, and only saw the
   mist;
And shouts of heathen and the traitor
   knights,
Oaths, insult, filth, and monstrous blasphe-
   mies,
Sweat, writhings, anguish, laboring of the
   lungs
In that close mist, and cryings for the
   light,
Moans of the dying, and voices of the dead.

Last, as by some one death-bed after wail
Of suffering, silence follows, or thro' death
Or death-like swoon, thus over all that
   shore,   120
Save for some whisper of the seething seas,
A dead hush fell; but when the dolorous
   day
Grew drearier toward twilight falling,
   came
A bitter wind, clear from the north, and
   blew
The mist aside, and with that wind the tide
Rose, and the pale King glanced across the
   field
Of battle. But no man was moving there;
Nor any cry of Christian heard thereon,
Nor yet of heathen; only the wan wave

Brake in among dead faces, to and fro 130
Swaying the helpless hands, and up and
   down
Tumbling the hollow helmets of the fallen,
And shiver'd brands that once had fought
   with Rome,
And rolling far along the gloomy shores
The voice of days of old and days to be.

Then spake King Arthur to Sir Bedivere,
And whiter than the mist that all day long
Had held the field of battle was the King:

'Hearest thou this great voice that
   shakes the world,
And wastes the narrow realm whereon we
   move,   140
And beats upon the faces of the dead,
My dead, as tho' they had not died for
   me ? —
O Bedivere, for on my heart hath fallen
Confusion, till I know not what I am,
Nor whence I am, nor whether I be king;
Behold, I seem but king among the dead.'

Then spake the bold Sir Bedivere: 'My
   King !
King everywhere ! and so the dead have
   kings,
There also will I worship thee as king.
Yet still thy life is whole, and still I live
Who love thee; but who hates thee, he that
   brought   151
The heathen back among us, yonder stands,
Modred, unharm'd, the traitor of thine
   house.'

Then spake the King: 'My house hath
   been my doom.
But call not thou this traitor of my house
Who hath but dwelt beneath one roof with
   me.
My house are rather they who sware my
   vows,
Yea, even while they brake them, own'd
   me king.
And well for thee, saying in my dark hour,
When all the purport of my throne hath
   fail'd,   160
That quick or dead thou holdest me for
   king.
King am I, whatsoever be their cry;
And one last act of kinghood shalt thou see
Yet, ere I pass.' And uttering this the
   King

Made at the man. Then Modred smote his
    liege
Hard on that helm which many a heathen
    sword
Had beaten thin; while Arthur at one blow,
Striking the last stroke with Excalibur,
Slew him, and, all but slain himself, he
    fell.   169

So all day long the noise of battle roll'd
Among the mountains by the winter sea,
Until King Arthur's Table, man by man,
Had fallen in Lyonnesse about their lord,
King Arthur; then, because his wound was
    deep,
The bold Sir Bedivere uplifted him,
And bore him to a chapel nigh the field,
A broken chancel with a broken cross,
That stood on a dark strait of barren land.
On one side lay the Ocean, and on one   179
Lay a great water, and the moon was full.

Then spake King Arthur to Sir Bedivere:
' The sequel of to-day unsolders all
The goodliest fellowship of famous knights
Whereof this world holds record. Such a
    sleep
They sleep — the men I loved. I think
    that we
Shall never more, at any future time,
Delight our souls with talk of knightly
    deeds,
Walking about the gardens and the halls
Of Camelot, as in the days that were.   189
I perish by this people which I made, —
Tho' Merlin sware that I should come
    again
To rule once more — but let what will be
    be,
I am so deeply smitten thro' the helm
That without help I cannot last till morn.
Thou therefore take my brand Excalibur,
Which was my pride; for thou remember-
    est how
In those old days, one summer noon, an
    arm
Rose up from out the bosom of the lake,
Clothed in white samite, mystic, wonder-
    ful,
Holding the sword — and how I row'd
    across   200
And took it, and have worn it, like a king;
And, wheresoever I am sung or told
In aftertime, this also shall be known.
But now delay not; take Excalibur,

And fling him far into the middle mere;
Watch what thou seest, and lightly bring
    me word.'

To him replied the bold Sir Bedivere:
' It is not meet, Sir King, to leave thee
    thus,
Aidless, alone, and smitten thro' the
    helm —
A little thing may harm a wounded man;
Yet I thy hest will all perform at full, 211
Watch what I see, and lightly bring thee
    word.'

So saying, from the ruin'd shrine he
    stept,
And in the moon athwart the place of
    tombs,
Where lay the mighty bones of ancient
    men,
Old knights, and over them the sea-wind
    sang
Shrill, chill, with flakes of foam. He, step-
    ping down
By zigzag paths and juts of pointed rock,
Came on the shining levels of the lake.

There drew he forth the brand Excali-
    bur,   220
And o'er him, drawing it, the winter moon,
Brightening the skirts of a long cloud, ran
    forth
And sparkled keen with frost against the
    hilt;
For all the haft twinkled with diamond
    sparks,
Myriads of topaz-lights, and jacinth-work
Of subtlest jewellery. He gazed so long
That both his eyes were dazzled as he
    stood,
This way and that dividing the swift mind,
In act to throw; but at the last it seem'd
Better to leave Excalibur conceal'd   230
There in the many-knotted water-flags,
That whistled stiff and dry about the
    marge.
So strode he back slow to the wounded
    King.

Then spake King Arthur to Sir Bedi-
    vere:
' Hast thou perform'd my mission which I
    gave ?
What is it thou hast seen ? or what hast
    heard ? '

And answer made the bold Sir Bedivere:
'I heard the ripple washing in the reeds,
And the wild water lapping on the crag.'

To whom replied King Arthur, faint and pale: 240
'Thou hast betray'd thy nature and thy name,
Not rendering true answer, as beseem'd
Thy fealty, nor like a noble knight;
For surer sign had follow'd, either hand,
Or voice, or else a motion of the mere.
This is a shameful thing for men to lie.
Yet now, I charge thee, quickly go again,
As thou art lief and dear, and do the thing
I bade thee, watch, and lightly bring me word.'

Then went Sir Bedivere the second time
Across the ridge, and paced beside the mere, 251
Counting the dewy pebbles, fixt in thought;
But when he saw the wonder of the hilt,
How curiously and strangely chased, he smote
His palms together, and he cried aloud:

'And if indeed I cast the brand away,
Surely a precious thing, one worthy note,
Should thus be lost for ever from the earth,
Which might have pleased the eyes of many men.
What good should follow this, if this were done? 260
What harm, undone? Deep harm to disobey,
Seeing obedience is the bond of rule.
Were it well to obey then, if a king demand
An act unprofitable, against himself?
The King is sick, and knows not what he does.
What record or what relic of my lord
Should be to aftertime, but empty breath
And rumors of a doubt? But were this kept,
Stored in some treasure-house of mighty kings,
Some one might show it at a joust of arms, 270
Saying: "King Arthur's sword, Excalibur,
Wrought by the lonely Maiden of the Lake.

Nine years she wrought it, sitting in the deeps
Upon the hidden bases of the hills."
So might some old man speak in the aftertime
To all the people, winning reverence.
But now much honor and much fame were lost.'

So spake he, clouded with his own conceit,
And hid Excalibur the second time,
And so strode back slow to the wounded King. 280

Then spoke King Arthur, breathing heavily:
'What is it thou hast seen? or what hast heard?'

And answer made the bold Sir Bedivere:
'I heard the water lapping on the crag,
And the long ripple washing in the reeds.'

To whom replied King Arthur, much in wrath:
'Ah miserable, and unkind, untrue,
Unknightly, traitor-hearted! Woe is me!
Authority forgets a dying king,
Laid widow'd of the power in his eye 290
That bow'd the will. I see thee what thou art,
For thou, the latest-left of all my knights,
In whom should meet the offices of all,
Thou wouldst betray me for the precious hilt;
Either from lust of gold, or like a girl
Valuing the giddy pleasure of the eyes.
Yet, for a man may fail in duty twice,
And the third time may prosper, get thee hence;
But, if thou spare to fling Excalibur, 299
I will arise and slay thee with my hands.'

Then quickly rose Sir Bedivere, and ran,
And, leaping down the ridges lightly, plunged
Among the bulrush beds, and clutch'd the sword,
And strongly wheel'd and threw it. The great brand
Made lightnings in the splendor of the moon,

And flashing round and round, and whirl'd in an arch,
Shot like a streamer of the northern morn,
Seen where the moving isles of winter shock
By night, with noises of the Northern Sea.   309
So flash'd and fell the brand Excalibur;
But ere he dipt the surface, rose an arm
Clothed in white samite, mystic, wonderful,
And caught him by the hilt, and brandish'd him
Three times, and drew him under in the mere.
And lightly went the other to the King.

Then spoke King Arthur, drawing thicker breath:
' Now see I by thine eyes that this is done.
Speak out; what is it thou hast heard, or seen ? '

And answer made the bold Sir Bedivere:
' Sir King, I closed mine eyelids, lest the gems   320
Should blind my purpose, for I never saw,
Nor shall see, here or elsewhere, till I die,
Not tho' I live three lives of mortal men,
So great a miracle as yonder hilt.
Then with both hands I flung him, wheeling him;
But when I look'd again, behold an arm,
Clothed in white samite, mystic, wonderful,
That caught him by the hilt, and brandish'd him
Three times, and drew him under in the mere.'

And answer made King Arthur, breathing hard: 330
' My end draws nigh; 't is time that I were gone.
Make broad thy shoulders to receive my weight,
And bear me to the margin; yet I fear
My wound hath taken cold, and I shall die.'

So saying, from the pavement he half rose,
Slowly, with pain, reclining on his arm,
And looking wistfully with wide blue eyes
As in a picture. Him Sir Bedivere
Remorsefully regarded thro' his tears,

And would have spoken, but he found not words;   340
Then took with care, and kneeling on one knee,
O'er both his shoulders drew the languid hands,
And rising bore him thro' the place of tombs.

But, as he walk'd, King Arthur panted hard,
Like one that feels a nightmare on his bed
When all the house is mute. So sigh'd the King,
Muttering and murmuring at his ear,
' Quick, quick !
I fear it is too late, and I shall die.'
But the other swiftly strode from ridge to ridge,
Clothed with his breath, and looking, as he walk'd,   350
Larger than human on the frozen hills.
He heard the deep behind him, and a cry
Before. His own thought drove him like a goad.
Dry clash'd his harness in the icy caves
And barren chasms, and all to left and right
The bare black cliff clang'd round him, as he based
His feet on juts of slippery crag that rang
Sharp - smitten with the dint of armed heels —
And on a sudden, lo, the level lake,   359
And the long glories of the winter moon !

Then saw they how there hove a dusky barge,
Dark as a funeral scarf from stem to stern,
Beneath them; and descending they were ware
That all the decks were dense with stately forms,
Black-stoled, black-hooded, like a dream — by these
Three queens with crowns of gold — and from them rose
A cry that shiver'd to the tingling stars,
And, as it were one voice, an agony
Of lamentation, like a wind that shrills
All night in a waste land, where no one comes,   370
Or hath come, since the making of the world.

Then murmur'd Arthur, 'Place me in
  the barge.'
So to the barge they came. There those
  three queens
Put forth their hands, and took the King,
  and wept.
But she that rose the tallest of them all
And fairest laid his head upon her lap,
And loosed the shatter'd casque, and chafed
  his hands,
And call'd him by his name, complaining
  loud,
And dropping bitter tears against a brow
Striped with dark blood; for all his face
  was white   380
And colorless, and like the wither'd moon
Smote by the fresh beam of the springing
  east;
And all his greaves and cuisses dash'd with
  drops
Of onset; and the light and lustrous curls —
That made his forehead like a rising sun
High from the dais-throne — were parch'd
  with dust,
Or, clotted into points and hanging loose,
Mixt with the knightly growth that fringed
  his lips.
So like a shatter'd column lay the King;
Not like that Arthur who, with lance in
  rest,   390
From spur to plume a star of tournament,
Shot thro' the lists at Camelot, and charged
Before the eyes of ladies and of kings.

Then loudly cried the bold Sir Bedivere:
'Ah! my Lord Arthur, whither shall I
  go?
Where shall I hide my forehead and my
  eyes?
For now I see the true old times are dead,
When every morning brought a noble
  chance,
And every chance brought out a noble
  knight.
Such times have been not since the light
  that led   400
The holy Elders with the gift of myrrh.
But now the whole Round Table is dis-
  solved
Which was an image of the mighty world;
And I, the last, go forth companionless,
And the days darken round me, and the
  years,
Among new men, strange faces, other
  minds.'

And slowly answer'd Arthur from the
  barge:
'The old order changeth, yielding place to
  new,
And God fulfils himself in many ways,
Lest one good custom should corrupt the
  world.   410
Comfort thyself; what comfort is in me?
I have lived my life, and that which I have
  done
May He within himself make pure! but
  thou
If thou shouldst never see my face again,
Pray for my soul. More things are wrought
  by prayer
Than this world dreams of. Wherefore,
  let thy voice
Rise like a fountain for me night and
  day.
For what are men better than sheep or
  goats
That nourish a blind life within the brain,
If, knowing God, they lift not hands of
  prayer   420
Both for themselves and those who call
  them friend?
For so the whole round earth is every way
Bound by gold chains about the feet of
  God.
But now farewell. I am going a long way
With these thou seest — if indeed I go —
For all my mind is clouded with a doubt —
To the island-valley of Avilion;
Where falls not hail, or rain, or any snow,
Nor ever wind blows loudly; but it lies
Deep-meadow'd, happy, fair with orchard
  lawns   430
And bowery hollows crown'd with summer
  sea,
Where I will heal me of my grievous
  wound.'

So said he, and the barge with oar and
  sail
Moved from the brink, like some full-
  breasted swan
That, fluting a wild carol ere her death,
Ruffles her pure cold plume, and takes the
  flood
With swarthy webs. Long stood Sir Bedi-
  vere
Revolving many memories, till the hull
Look'd one black dot against the verge of
  dawn,
And on the mere the wailing died away.   440

But when that moan had past for ever-
more,
The stillness of the dead world's winter
dawn
Amazed him, and he groan'd, 'The King
is gone.'
And therewithal came on him the weird
rhyme,
'From the great deep to the great deep he
goes.'

Whereat he slowly turn'd and slowly
clomb
The last hard footstep of that iron crag,
Thence mark'd the black hull moving yet,
and cried:
'He passes to be king among the dead, 449
And after healing of his grievous wound
He comes again; but — if he come no
more —
O me, be yon dark queens in yon black boat,
Who shriek'd and wail'd, the three whereat
we gazed
On that high day, when, clothed with living
light,
They stood before his throne in silence,
friends
Of Arthur, who should help him at his
need?'

Then from the dawn it seem'd there
came, but faint
As from beyond the limit of the world,
Like the last echo born of a great cry,
Sounds, as if some fair city were one voice
Around a king returning from his wars. 461

Thereat once more he moved about, and
clomb
Even to the highest he could climb, and saw,
Straining his eyes beneath an arch of hand,
Or thought he saw, the speck that bare the
King,
Down that long water opening on the deep
Somewhere far off, pass on and on, and go
From less to less and vanish into light.
And the new sun rose bringing the new
year.

TO THE QUEEN

O LOYAL to the royal in thyself,
And loyal to thy land, as this to thee —
Bear witness, that rememberable day,

When, pale as yet and fever-worn, the
Prince
Who scarce had pluck'd his flickering life
again
From halfway down the shadow of the
grave
Past with thee thro' thy people and their
love,
And London roll'd one tide of joy thro'
all
Her trebled millions, and loud leagues of
man
And welcome! witness, too, the silent cry,
The prayer of many a race and creed, and
clime —   11
Thunderless lightnings striking under sea
From sunset and sunrise of all thy realm,
And that true North, whereof we lately
heard
A strain to shame us, 'Keep you to your-
selves;
So loyal is too costly! friends — your love
Is but a burthen; loose the bond, and go.'
Is this the tone of empire? here the faith
That made us rulers? this, indeed, her
voice
And meaning whom the roar of Hougou-
mont   20
Left mightiest of all peoples under heaven?
What shock has fool'd her since, that she
should speak
So feebly? wealthier — wealthier — hour
by hour!
The voice of Britain, or a sinking land,
Some third-rate isle half-lost among her
seas?
There rang her voice, when the full city
peal'd
Thee and thy Prince! The loyal to their
crown
Are loyal to their own far sons, who love
Our ocean-empire with her boundless homes
For ever - broadening England, and her
throne   30
In our vast Orient, and one isle, one isle,
That knows not her own greatness; if she
knows
And dreads it we are fallen. — But thou,
my Queen,
Not for itself, but thro' thy living love
For one to whom I made it o'er his grave
Sacred, accept this old imperfect tale,
New-old, and shadowing Sense at war with
Soul,
Ideal manhood closed in real man,

Rather than that gray king whose name, a
    ghost,
Streams like a cloud, man-shaped, from
    mountain peak,   40
And cleaves to cairn and cromlech still; or
    him
Of Geoffrey's book, or him of Malleor's,
    one
Touch'd by the adulterous finger of a time
That hover'd between war and wantonness,
And crownings and dethronements. Take
    withal
Thy poet's blessing, and his trust that
    Heaven
Will blow the tempest in the distance back
From thine and ours; for some are scared,
    who mark,
Or wisely or unwisely, signs of storm,
Waverings of every vane with every wind,
And wordy trucklings to the transient
    hour,   51
And fierce or careless looseners of the
    faith,

And Softness breeding scorn of simple life,
Or Cowardice, the child of lust for gold,
Or Labor, with a groan and not a voice,
Or Art with poisonous honey stolen from
    France,
And that which knows, but careful for it-
    self,
And that which knows not, ruling that
    which knows
To its own harm. The goal of this great
    world
Lies beyond sight; yet — if our slowly-
    grown   60
And crown'd Republic's crowning common-
    sense,
That saved her many times, not fail —
    their fears
Are morning shadows huger than the
    shapes
That cast them, not those gloomier which
    forego
The darkness of that battle in the west
Where all of high and holy dies away.

BALLADS

AND OTHER POEMS

The volume with this title appeared in 1880, and contained the poems that follow, as far as the lines ' To Dante ' inclusive. It was dedicated to the eldest son (Alfred Browning Stanley Tennyson, born in 1878) of Lionel Tennyson, the second son of the poet.

Mr. Stedman ('Victorian Poets,' revised ed., 1887, p. 419 fol.) pays a fitting tribute to the ' Ballads ' when, after commenting with qualified praise on the dramas, he goes on to say : ' In striking contrast, Tennyson's recent lyrical poetry is the afterglow of a still radiant genius. Here we see undimmed the fire and beauty of his natural gift, and wisdom increased with age. What a collection, short as it is, forms the volume of " Ballads " issued in his seventy-first year ! It opens with the thoroughly English story of " The First Quarrel," with its tragic culmination, — " And the boat went down that night, — the boat went down that night ! " Country life is what he has observed, and he reflects it with truth of action and dialect. " The Northern Cobbler " and " The Village Wife " could be written only by the idyllist whose Yorkshire ballads delighted us in 1866. But here are greater things, two or three at his highest mark. The passion and lyrical might of " Rizpah " never have been exceeded by the author, nor, I think, by any other poet of his day. " The Revenge " and " Lucknow " are magnificent ballads. . . . " The Voyage of Maeldune " is a weird and vocal fantasy, unequally poetic, with the well-known touch in every number.'

TO ALFRED TENNYSON

MY GRANDSON

Golden-hair'd Ally whose name is one
    with mine,
Crazy with laughter and babble and earth's
    new wine,
Now that the flower of a year and a half is
    thine,

O little blossom, O mine, and mine of
    mine,
Glorious poet who never hast written a
    line,
Laugh, for the name at the head of my
    verse is thine.
Mayst thou never be wrong'd by the name
    that is mine !

THE FIRST QUARREL

(IN THE ISLE OF WIGHT)

This poem, founded on fact ('Memoir,' vol. ii. p. 249), was first published in the 'Ballads,' 1880; as were the poems that follow, unless otherwise stated in the prefatory notes.

I

'WAIT a little,' you say, 'you are sure it 'll
  all come right,'
But the boy was born i' trouble, an' looks
  so wan an' so white;
Wait! an' once I ha' waited — I had n't
  to wait for long.
Now I wait, wait, wait for Harry. — No,
  no, you are doing me wrong!
Harry and I were married; the boy can
  hold up his head,
The boy was born in wedlock, but after my
  man was dead;
I ha work'd for him fifteen years, an' I
  work an' I wait to the end.
I am all alone in the world, an' you are my
  only friend.

II

Doctor, if *you* can wait, I 'll tell you the
  tale o' my life.
When Harry an' I were children, he call'd
  me his own little wife;   10
I was happy when I was with him, an' sorry
  when he was away,
An' when we play'd together, I loved him
  better than play;
He workt me the daisy chain — he made
  me the cowslip ball,
He fought the boys that were rude, an' I
  loved him better than all.
Passionate girl tho' I was, an' often at
  home in disgrace,
I never could quarrel with Harry — I had
  but to look in his face.

III

There was a farmer in Dorset of Harry's
  kin, that had need
Of a good stout lad at his farm; he sent,
  an' the father agreed;
So Harry was bound to the Dorsetshire
  farm for years an' for years;
I walk'd with him down to the quay, poor
  lad, an' we parted in tears.   20

The boat was beginning to move, we heard
  them a-ringing the bell,
'I 'll never love any but you, God bless you,
  my own little Nell.'

IV

I was a child, an' he was a child, an' he
  came to harm;
There was a girl, a hussy, that workt with
  him up at the farm,
One had deceived her an' left her alone
  with her sin an' her shame,
And so she was wicked with Harry; the
  girl was the most to blame.

V

And years went over till I that was little
  had grown so tall
The men would say of the maids, 'Our
  Nelly 's the flower of 'em all.'
I did n't take heed o' *them*, but I taught
  myself all I could
To make a good wife for Harry, when
  Harry came home for good.   30

VI

Often I seem'd unhappy, and often as happy
  too,
For I heard it abroad in the fields, 'I 'll
  never love any but you;'
'I 'll never love any but you,' the morning
  song of the lark;
'I 'll never love any but you,' the nightin-
  gale's hymn in the dark.

VII

And Harry came home at last, but he
  look'd at me sidelong and shy,
Vext me a bit, till he told me that so many
  years had gone by,
I had grown so handsome and tall — that I
  might ha' forgot him somehow —
For he thought — there were other lads —
  he was fear'd to look at me now.

VIII

Hard was the frost in the field, we were
  married o' Christmas day,
Married among· the red berries, an' all as
  merry as May —   40
Those were the pleasant times, my house
  an' my man were my pride,
We seem'd like ships i' the Channel a-sail-
  ing with wind an' tide.

IX

But work was scant in the Isle, tho' he tried
   the villages round,
So Harry went over the Solent to see if
   work could be found;
An' he wrote: 'I ha' six weeks' work, little
   wife, so far as I know;
I 'll come for an hour to-morrow, an' kiss
   you before I go.'

X

So I set to righting the house, for was n't
   he coming that day ?
An' I hit on an old deal-box that was
   push'd in a corner away,
It was full of old odds an' ends, an' a letter
   along wi' the rest,
I had better ha' put my naked hand in a
   hornets' nest.   50

XI

' Sweetheart,' — this was the letter — this
   was the letter I read —
' You promised to find me work near you,
   an' I wish I was dead —
Did n't you kiss me an' promise ? you
   have n't done it, my lad,
An' I almost died o' your going away, an' I
   wish that I had.'

XII

I too wish that I had — in the pleasant
   times that had past,
Before I quarrell'd with Harry — *my* quar-
   rel — the first an' the last.

XIII

For Harry came in, an' I flung him the
   letter that drove me wild,
An' he told it me all at once, as simple as
   any child,
' What can it matter, my lass, what I did
   wi' my single life ?
I ha' been as true to you as ever a man to
   his wife;   60
An' *she* was n't one o' the worst.' ' Then,'
   I said, ' I 'm none o' the best.'
An' he smiled at me, ' Ain't you, my love ?
   Come, come, little wife, let it rest !
The man is n't like the woman, no need to
   make such a stir.'
But he anger'd me all the more, an' I said,
   ' You were keeping with her,

When I was a-loving you all along an'
   the same as before.'
An' he did n't speak for a while, an' he
   anger'd me more and more.
Then he patted my hand in his gentle way,
   ' Let bygones be !'
' Bygones ! you kept yours hush'd,' I said,
   ' when you married me !
By-gones ma' be come-agains; an' *she* — in
   her shame an' her sin —
You 'll have her to nurse my child, if I die
   o' my lying in !   70
You 'll make her its second mother ! I
   hate her — an' I hate you !'
Ah, Harry, my man, you had better ha'
   beaten me black an' blue
Than ha' spoken as kind as you did, when
   I were so crazy wi' spite,
' Wait a little, my lass, I am sure it 'ill all
   come right.'

XIV

An' he took three turns in the rain, an' I
   watch'd him, an' when he came in
I felt that my heart was hard; he was all
   wet thro' to the skin,
An' I never said, ' off wi' the wet,' I never
   said, ' on wi' the dry,'
So I knew my heart was hard, when he
   came to bid me good-bye.
' You said that you hated me, Ellen, but
   that is n't true, you know;
I am going to leave you a bit — you 'll kiss
   me before I go ?'   80

XV

' Going ! you 're going to her — kiss her —
   if you will,' I said —
I was near my time wi' the boy, I must ha'
   been light i' my head —
' I had sooner be cursed than kiss'd !' — I
   did n't know well what I meant,
But I turn'd my face from *him*, an' he
   turn'd *his* face an' he went.

XVI

And then he sent me a letter, ' I 've gotten
   my work to do;
You would n't kiss me, my lass, an' I never
   loved any but you;
I am sorry for all the quarrel an' sorry for
   what she wrote,
I ha' six weeks' work in Jersey an' go to-
   night by the boat.'

XVII

An' the wind began to rise, an' I thought
    of him out at sea,
An' I felt I had been to blame; he was al-
    ways kind to me.   90
'Wait a little, my lass, I am sure it 'ill all
    come right' —
An' the boat went down that night — the
    boat went down that night.

RIZPAH

17—

Founded on an incident related in a penny
magazine called 'Old Brighton.' See the
'Memoir' (vol. ii. pp. 249–251) for interesting
particulars. For the suggestion of the title of
the poem, see 2 Samuel, xxi. 1–14.

I

WAILING, wailing, wailing, the wind over
    land and sea —
And Willy's voice in the wind, 'O mother,
    come out to me !'
Why should he call me to-night, when he
    knows that I cannot go ?
For the downs are as bright as day, and the
    full moon stares at the snow.

II

We should be seen, my dear; they would
    spy us out of the town.
The loud black nights for us, and the storm
    rushing over the down,
When I cannot see my own hand, but am
    led by the creak of the chain,
And grovel and grope for my son till I find
    myself drenched with the rain.

III

Anything fallen again ? nay — what was
    there left to fall ?
I have taken them home, I have number'd
    the bones, I have hidden them all. 10
What am I saying ? and what are *you*?
    do you come as a spy ?
Falls ? what falls ? who knows ? As the
    tree falls so must it lie.

IV

Who let her in ? how long has she been ?
    you — what have you heard ?
Why did you sit so quiet ? you never have
    spoken a word.

O — to pray with me — yes — a lady —
    none of their spies —
But the night has crept into my heart, and
    begun to darken my eyes.

V

Ah — you, that have lived so soft, what
    should *you* know of the night,
The blast and the burning shame and the
    bitter frost and the fright ?
I have done it, while you were asleep —
    you were only made for the day.
I have gather'd my baby together — and
    now you may go your way.   20

VI

Nay — for it 's kind of you, madam, to sit
    by an old dying wife.
But say nothing hard of my boy, I have
    only an hour of life.
I kiss'd my boy in the prison, before he
    went out to die.
'They dared me to do it,' he said, and he
    never has told me a lie.
I whipt him for robbing an orchard once
    when he was but a child —
'The farmer dared me to do it,' he said; he
    was always so wild —
And idle — and could n't be idle — my
    Willy — he never could rest.
The King should have made him a soldier,
    he would have been one of his best.

VII

But he lived with a lot of wild mates, and
    they never would let him be good;
They swore that he dare not rob the mail,
    and he swore that he would;   30
And he took no life, but he took one purse,
    and when all was done
He flung it among his fellows — 'I 'll none
    of it,' said my son.

VIII

I came into court to the judge and the
    lawyers. I told them my tale,
God's own truth — but they kill'd him, they
    kill'd him for robbing the mail.
They hang'd him in chains for a show — we
    had always borne a good name —
To be hang'd for a thief — and then put
    away — is n't that enough shame ?
Dust to dust — low down — let us hide !
    but they set him so high

That all the ships of the world could stare
at him, passing by.
God 'ill pardon the hell-black raven and
horrible fowls of the air,
But not the black heart of the lawyer who
kill'd him and hang'd him there.   40

IX

And the jailer forced me away. I had bid
him my last good-bye;
They had fasten'd the door of his cell. 'O
mother!' I heard him cry.
I couldn't get back tho' I tried, he had
something further to say,
And now I never shall know it. The jailer
forced me away.

X

Then since I couldn't but hear that cry of
my boy that was dead,
They seized me and shut me up: they fas-
ten'd me down on my bed.
'Mother, O mother!'—he call'd in the
dark to me year after year—
They beat me for that, they beat me—
you know that I couldn't but hear;
And then at the last they found I had
grown so stupid and still
They let me abroad again—but the crea-
tures had worked their will.   50

XI

Flesh of my flesh was gone, but bone of
my bone was left—
I stole them all from the lawyers—and
you, will you call it a theft?—
My baby, the bones that had suck'd me,
the bones that had laughed and had
cried—
Theirs? O, no! they are mine—not theirs
—they had moved in my side.

XII

Do you think I was scared by the bones?
I kiss'd 'em, I buried 'em all—
I can't dig deep, I am old—in the night
by the churchyard wall.
My Willy 'ill rise up whole when the trum-
pet of judgment 'ill sound,
But I charge you never to say that I laid
him in holy ground.

XIII

They would scratch him up—they would
hang him again on the cursed tree.

Sin? O, yes, we are sinners, I know—let
all that be,   60
And read me a Bible verse of the Lord's
goodwill toward men—
'Full of compassion and mercy, the Lord'
—let me hear it again;
'Full of compassion and mercy—long-suf-
fering.' Yes, O, yes!
For the lawyer is born but to murder—
the Saviour lives but to bless.
He 'll never put on the black cap except
for the worst of the worst,
And the first may be last—I have heard
it in church—and the last may be
first.
Suffering—O, long-suffering—yes, as the
Lord must know,
Year after year in the mist and the wind
and the shower and the snow.

XIV

Heard, have you? what? they have told
you he never repented his sin.
How do they know it? are they his mother?
are you of his kin?   70
Heard! have you ever heard, when the
storm on the downs began,
The wind that 'ill wail like a child and the
sea that 'ill moan like a man?

XV

Election, Election, and Reprobation—it 's
all very well.
But I go to-night to my boy, and I shall
not find him in hell.
For I cared so much for my boy that the
Lord has look'd into my care,
And He means me I 'm sure to be happy
with Willy, I know not where.

XVI

And if he be lost—but to save my soul,
that is all your desire—
Do you think that I care for my soul if my
boy be gone to the fire?
I have been with God in the dark—go, go,
you may leave me alone—
You never have borne a child—you are
just as hard as a stone.   80

XVII

Madam, I beg your pardon! I think that
you mean to be kind,
But I cannot hear what you say for my
Willy's voice in the wind—

The snow and the sky so bright — he used
   but to call in the dark,
And he calls to me now from the church
   and not from the gibbet — for hark !
Nay — you can hear it yourself — it is
   coming — shaking the walls —
Willy — the moon 's in a cloud —— Good-
   night. I am going. He calls.

THE NORTHERN COBBLER

Founded on a fact which the poet heard in
early youth. The footnotes are his own.

I

Waäit till our Sally cooms in, fur thou
   mun a' sights [1] to tell.
Eh, but I be maäin glad to sceä tha sa 'arty
   an' well.
'Cast awaäy on a disolut land wi' a vartical
   soon [2] !'
Strange fur to goä fur to think what saäilors
   a' seëan an' a' doon;
'Summat to drink — sa 'ot ?'   I 'a nowt
   but Adam's wine:
What 's the 'eät o' this little 'ill-side to the
   'eät o' the line ?

II

'What 's i' tha bottle a-stanning theer ?'
   I 'll tell tha.   Gin.
But if thou wants thy grog, tha mun goä
   fur it down to the inn.
Naäy — fur I be maäin-glad, but thaw tha
   was iver sa dry,
Thou gits naw gin fro' the bottle theer, an'
   I 'll tell tha why.   10

III

Meä an' thy sister was married, when wur
   it ? back-end o' June,
Ten year sin', and wa 'greed as well as a
   fiddle i' tune.
I could fettle and clump owd booöts and
   shoes wi' the best on 'em all,

[1] The vowels *aï*, pronounced separately
though in the closest conjunction, best render
the sound of the long *i* and *y* in this dialect.
But since such words as *craïin'*, *daïin'*, *whaï*,
aï (I), etc., look awkward except in a page of
express phonetics, I have thought it better to
leave the simple *i* and *y*, and to trust that my
readers will give them the broader pronuncia-
tion.
[2] The *oo* short, as in ' wood.'

As fer as fro' Thursby thurn hup to
   Harmsby and Hutterby Hall.
We was busy as beeäs i' the bloom an' as
   'appy as 'art could think,
An' then the babby wur burn, and then I
   taäkes to the drink.

IV

An' I weänt gaäinsaäy it, my lad, thaw I
   be hafe shaämed on it now,
We could sing a good song at the Plow, we
   could sing a good song at the Plow;
Thaw once of a frosty night I slither'd an'
   hurted my huck,[1]
An' I coom'd neck-an-crop soomtimes slaäpe
   down i' the squad an' the muck: 20
An' once I fowt wi' the taäilor — not hafe
   ov a man, my lad —
Fur he scrawm'd an' scratted my faäce like
   a cat, an' it maäde 'er sa mad
That Sally she turn'd a tongue-banger,[2] an'
   raäted ma, ' Sottin' thy braäins
Guzzlin' an' soäkin' an' smoäkin' an' hawm-
   in'[3] about i' the laänes,
Soä sow-droonk that thou doesn not touch
   thy 'at to the Squire;'
An' I looök'd cock-eyed at my noäse an' I
   seeäd 'im a-gittin' o' fire;
But sin' I wur hallus i' liquor an' hallus as
   droonk as a king,
Foälks' coostom flitted awaäy like a kite
   wi' a brokken string.

V

An' Sally she wesh'd foälks' cloäths to keep
   the wolf fro' the door,
Eh, but the moor she riled me, she druv
   me to drink the moor,   30
Fur I fun', when 'er back wur turn'd,
   wheer Sally's owd stockin' wur 'id,
An' I grabb'd the munny she maäde, and I
   weär'd it o' liquor, I did.

VI

An' one night I cooms 'oäm like a bull
   gotten loose at a faäir,
An' she wur a-waäitin' fo'mma, an' cryin'
   and teärin' 'er aäir,
An' I tummled athurt the craädle an'
   sweär'd as I 'd breäk ivry stick
O' furnitur 'ere i' the 'ouse, an' I gied our
   Sally a kick,

[1] Hip.   [2] Scold.
[3] Lounging.

An' I mash'd the taäbles an' chairs, an' she
an' the babby beäl'd,[1]
Fur I knaw'd naw moor what I did nor a
mortal beäst o' the feäld.

VII

An' when I waäked i' the murnin' I seeäd
that our Sally went laämed
Cos' o' the kick as I gied 'er, an' I wur
dreädful ashaämed;
An' Sally wur sloomy[2] an' draggle-taäil'd
in an owd turn gown,
An' the babby's faäce wurn't wesh'd, an'
the 'ole 'ouse hupside down.

VIII

An' then I minded our Sally sa pratty an'
neät an' swccät,
Straät as a pole an' cleän as a flower fro'
'eäd to feeät:
An' then I minded the fust kiss I gied 'er
by Thursby thurn;
Theer wur a lark a-singin' 'is best of a
Sunday at murn,
Could n't see 'im, we 'eärd 'im a-mountin'
oop 'igher an' 'igher,
An' the.. 'e turn'd to the sun, an' 'e shined
like a sparkle o' fire.
' Does n't tha see 'im? ' she axes, ' fur I can
see 'im; ' an' I
Seeäd nobbut the smile o' the sun as danced
in 'er pratty blue eye;   50
An' I says, ' I mun gie tha a kiss,' an'
Sally says, ' Noä, thou moänt,'
But I gied 'er a kiss, an' then anoother, an'
Sally says, ' doänt ! '

IX

An' when we coom'd into meeätin', at fust
she wur all in a tew,
But, arter, we sing'd the 'ymn togither like
birds on a beugh;
An' Muggins 'e preäch'd o' hell-fire an' the
loov o' God fur men,
An' then upo' coomin' awaäy Sally gied me
a kiss ov 'ersen.

X

Heer wur a fall fro' a kiss to a kick like
Saätan as fell
Down out o' heaven i' hell - fire — thaw
theer 's naw drinkin' i' hell;

---

[1] Bellowed, cried out.
[2] Sluggish, out of spirits.

Meä fur to kick our Sally as kep the wolf
fro' the door,
All along o' the drink, fur I loov'd 'er as
well as afoor.   60

XI

Sa like a graät num-cumpus I blubber'd
awaäy o' the bed —
' Weänt niver do it naw moor; ' an' Sally
looökt up an' she said,
' I 'll upowd it [1] tha weänt; thou 'rt like the
rest o' the men,
Thou 'll goä sniffin' about the tap till tha
does it ageän.
Theer 's thy hennemy, man, an' I knaws,
as knaws tha sa well,
That, if tha seeäs 'im an' smells 'im tha 'll
foller 'im slick into hell.'

XII

' Naäy,' says I, ' fur I weänt goä sniffin'
about the tap.'
' Weänt tha ? ' she says, an' mysen I thowt
i' mysen ' mayhap.'
' Noä : ' an' I started awaäy like a shot, an'
down to the hinn,
An' I browt what tha seeäs stannin' theer,
yon big black bottle o' gin.   70

XIII

' That caps owt,'[2] says Sally, an' saw she
begins to cry,
But I puts it inter 'er 'ands an' I says to
'er, ' Sally,' says I,
' Stan' 'im theer i' the naäme o' the Lord
an' the power ov 'is graäce,
Stan' 'im theer, fur I 'll looök my hennemy
straäit i' the faäce,
Stan' 'im theer i' the winder, an' let ma
looök at 'im then,
'E seeäms naw moor nor watter, an' 'e 's the
divil's oän sen.'

XIV

An' I wur down i' tha mouth, could n't do
naw work an' all,
Nasty an' snaggy an' shaäky, an' poonch'd
my 'and wi' the hawl,
But she wur a power o' coomfut, an' sat-
tled 'ersen o' my knee,
An' coäxd an' coodled me oop till ageän I
feel'd mysen free.   80

---

[1] I 'll uphold it.
[2] That 's beyond everything.

XV

An' Sally she tell'd it about, an' foälk stood
    a-gawmin'[1] in,
As thaw it wur summat bewitch'd istead
    of a quart o' gin;
An' some on 'em said it wur watter — an'
    I wur chousin' the wife,
Fur I could n't 'owd 'ands off gin, wur it
    nobbut to saäve my life;
An' blacksmith 'e strips me the thick ov 'is
    airm, an' 'e shaws it to me,
'Feëal thou this! thou can't graw this upo'
    watter!' says he.
An' Doctor 'e calls o' Sunday an' just as
    candles was lit,
'Thou moänt do it,' he says, 'tha mun
    breäk 'im off bit by bit.'
'Thou 'rt but a Methody-man,' says Par-
    son, and laäys down 'is 'at,
Au' 'e points to the bottle o' gin, 'but I re-
    specks tha fur that;'   90
An Squire, his oän very sen, walks down
    fro' the 'All to see,
An' 'e spanks 'is 'and into mine, 'fur I re-
    specks tha,' says 'e;
An' coostom ageän draw'd in like a wind
    fro' far an' wide,
And browt me the booöts to be cobbled fro'
    hafe the coontryside.

XVI

An' theer 'e stans an' theer 'e shall stan' to
    my dying daäy;
I 'a gotten to loov 'im agean in anoother
    kind of a waäy,
Proud on 'im, like, my lad, an' I keeäps
    'im cleän an' bright,
Loovs 'im, an' roobs 'im, an' doosts 'im, an'
    puts 'im back i' the light.

XVII

Would n't a pint a' sarved as well as a
    quart? Naw doubt;
But I liked a bigger feller to fight wi' an'
    fowt it out.   100
Fine an' meller 'e mun be by this, if I cared
    to taäste,
But I moänt, my lad, and I weänt, fur I 'd
    feäl mysen cleän disgraäced.

XVIII

An' once I said to the Missis, 'My lass,
    when I cooms to die,

[1] Staring vacantly.

Smash the bottle to smithers, the divil's
    in 'im,' said I.
But arter I chaänged my mind, an' if Sally
    be left aloän,
I 'll hev 'im a-buried wi'mma an' taäke 'im
    afoor the Throän.

XIX

Coom thou 'eer — yon laädy a-steppin'
    along the streeät,
Does n't tha knaw 'er — sa pratty, an' feät,
    an' neät, an' sweeät?
Look at the cloäths on 'er back, thebbe
    ammost spick-span-new,
An' Tommy's faäce be as fresh as a codlin
    wesh'd i' the dew.   110

XX

'Ere be our Sally an' Tommy, an' we be
    a-goin to dine,
Baäcon an' taätes, an' a beslings-puddin'[1]
    an' Adam's wine;
But if tha wants ony grog tha mun goä fur
    it down to the Hinn,
Fur I weänt shed a drop on 'is blood, noä,
    not fur Sally's oän kin.

THE REVENGE

A BALLAD OF THE FLEET

First published in 'The Nineteenth Century'
for March, 1878, with the title, 'Sir Richard
Grenville, a Ballad of the Fleet;' afterwards
included in the 'Ballads,' 1880, with the pre-
sent title.

According to Sir Walter Raleigh, who wrote
a 'Report of the truth about the fight about the
Iles of Açores this last Sommer,' the engage-
ment began at 3 P. M. on the 31st of August,
Old Style, or the 10th of September. New
Style, in the year 1591. Gervase Markham,
who commemorated the event in a poem en-
titled 'The Most Honorable Tragedie of Sir
Richard Grinuile, Knight' (1595), gives the
main facts in his 'Argument,' or introduction,
as follows: —

'Sir Richard *Grinuile*, lying at anchor neere
vnto *Flores*, one of the westerlie Ilands of the
Azores, the last of August in the after noone,
had intelligence by one Captayne *Midleton* of
the aproch of the Spanish *Armada*, beeing in
number fiftie three saile of great ships, and
fifteene thousand men to man them. Sir *Rich-*

[1] A pudding made with the first milk of the
cow after calving.

ard, staying to recouer his men which were vpon the Iland, and disdayning to flie from his Countries enemy, not beeing able to recouer the winde, was instantlie inuironed with that hudge Nauie, betweene whom began a dreadfull fight, continuing the space of fifteene howers, in which conflict, Sir *Richard* sunck the great *San Phillip* of *Spaine*, the *Ascention* of *Siuel*, the Admirall of the *Hulks*, and two other great *Armados;* about midnight Sir *Richard* receiued a wound through the bodie, and as he was dressing, was shot againe into the head, and his Surgion slaine. Sir *Richard* mayntained the fight, till he had not one corne of powder left, nor one whole pike, nor fortie lyuing men; which seeing, hee would haue sunke his owne ship, but that was gaine-stood by the Maister thereof, who contrarie to his will came to composition with the *Spanyards*, and so saued those which were left aliue. Sir *Richard* dyed aboard the Admyrall of *Spayne*, about the fourth day after the battaile, and was mightlie bewaild of all men.'

A Dutch writer, Jan Huygen van Linschoten, whose book was translated into English in 1598, gives the following account of Sir Richard's death : —

'All the rest of the Captaines and Gentlemen went to visite hym, and to comfort him in his hard fortune, wondring at his courage, and stout hart, for that he shewed not any signe of faintnes nor changing of colour. But feeling the hower of death to approch, hee spake these wordes in Spanish and said : Heere die I, *Richard Greenfield*, with a ioyfull and quiet mind, for that I haue ended my life as a true soldier ought to do, yat hath fought for his countrey, Queene, religion, and honor, whereby my soule most ioyfull departeth out of this bodie, and shall alwaies leaue behinde it an euerlasting fame of a valiant and true soldier that hath done his dutie, as he was bound to doe. When he had finished these or such other like words, hee gaue vp the ghost, with great and stout courage, and no man could perceiue any true signe of heauinesse in him.'

I

At Flores in the Azores Sir Richard Grenville lay,
And a pinnace, like a flutter'd bird, came flying from far away:
'Spanish ships of war at sea! we have sighted fifty-three!'
Then sware Lord Thomas Howard: ' 'Fore God I am no coward;
But I cannot meet them here, for my ships are out of gear,

And the half my men are sick. I must fly, but follow quick.
We are six ships of the line; can we fight with fifty-three ?'

II

Then spake Sir Richard Grenville: 'I know you are no coward;
You fly them for a moment to fight with them again.
But I 've ninety men and more that are lying sick ashore.   10
I should count myself the coward if I left them, my Lord Howard,
To these Inquisition dogs and the devildoms of Spain.'

III

So Lord Howard past away with five ships of war that day,
Till he melted like a cloud in the silent summer heaven;
But Sir Richard bore in hand all his sick men from the land
Very carefully and slow,
Men of Bideford in Devon,
And we laid them on the ballast down below;
For we brought them all aboard,
And they blest him in their pain, that they were not left to Spain,   20
To the thumb-screw and the stake, for the glory of the Lord.

IV

He had only a hundred seamen to work the ship and to fight,
And he sailed away from Flores till the Spaniard came in sight,
With his huge sea-castles heaving upon the weather bow.
'Shall we fight or shall we fly ?
Good Sir Richard, tell us now,
For to fight is but to die !
There 'll be little of us left by the time this sun be set.'
And Sir Richard said again: 'We be all good English men.
Let us bang these dogs of Seville, the children of the devil,   30
For I never turn'd my back upon Don or devil yet.'

V

Sir Richard spoke and he laugh'd, and we
    roar'd a hurrah, and so
The little Revenge ran on sheer into the
    heart of the foe,
With her hundred fighters on deck, and her
    ninety sick below;
For half of their fleet to the right and half
    to the left were seen,
And the little Revenge ran on thro' the long
    sea-lane between.

VI

Thousands of their soldiers look'd down
    from their decks and laugh'd,
Thousands of their seamen made mock at
    the mad little craft
Running on and on, till delay'd
By their mountain-like San Philip that, of
    fifteen hundred tons,   40
And up-shadowing high above us with her
    yawning tiers of guns,
Took the breath from our sails, and we
    stay'd.

VII

And while now the great San Philip hung
    above us like a cloud
Whence the thunderbolt will fall
Long and loud,
Four galleons drew away
From the Spanish fleet that day,
And two upon the larboard and two upon
    the starboard lay,
And the battle-thunder broke from them
    all.

VIII

But anon the great San Philip, she be-
    thought herself and went,   50
Having that within her womb that had left
    her ill content;
And the rest they came aboard us, and they
    fought us hand to hand,
For a dozen times they came with their
    pikes and musqueteers,
And a dozen times we shook 'em off as a
    dog that shakes his ears
When he leaps from the water to the land.

IX

And the sun went down, and the stars came
    out far over the summer sea,
But never a moment ceased the fight of the
    one and the fifty-three.

Ship after ship, the whole night long, their
    high-built galleons came,
Ship after ship, the whole night long, with
    her battle-thunder and flame;   59
Ship after ship, the whole night long, drew
    back with her dead and her shame.
For some were sunk and many were shat-
    ter'd, and so could fight us no more —
God of battles, was ever a battle like this
    in the world before?

X

For he said, 'Fight on! fight on!'
Tho' his vessel was all but a wreck;
And it chanced that, when half of the short
    summer night was gone,
With a grisly wound to be drest he had
    left the deck,
But a bullet struck him that was dressing
    it suddenly dead,
And himself he was wounded again in the
    side and the head,
And he said, 'Fight on! fight on!'

XI

And the night went down, and the sun
    smiled out far over the summer sea,
And the Spanish fleet with broken sides lay
    round us all in a ring;   71
But they dared not touch us again, for they
    fear'd that we still could sting,
So they watch'd what the end would
    be.
And we had not fought them in vain,
But in perilous plight were we,
Seeing forty of our poor hundred were
    slain,
And half of the rest of us maim'd for
    life
In the crash of the cannonades and the
    desperate strife;
And the sick men down in the hold were
    most of them stark and cold,
And the pikes were all broken or bent, and
    the powder was all of it spent;   80
And the masts and the rigging were lying
    over the side;
But Sir Richard cried in his English pride:
'We have fought such a fight for a day
    and a night
As may never be fought again!
We have won great glory, my men!
And a day less or more
At sea or ashore,
We die — does it matter when?

Sink me the ship, Master Gunner — sink
  her, split her in twain !
Fall into the hands of God, not into the
  hands of Spain ! ' 90

XII

And the gunner said, ' Ay, ay,' but the sea-
  men made reply:
' We have children, we have wives,
And the Lord hath spared our lives.
We will make the Spaniard promise, if we
  yield, to let us go;
We shall live to fight again and to strike
  another blow.'
And the lion there lay dying, and they
  yielded to the foe.

XIII

And the stately Spanish men to their flag-
  ship bore him then,
Where they laid him by the mast, old Sir
  Richard caught at last,
And they praised him to his face with their
  courtly foreign grace; 99
But he rose upon their decks, and he cried:
' I have fought for Queen and Faith like
  a valiant man and true;
I have only done my duty as a man is
  bound to do.
With a joyful spirit I Sir Richard Gren-
  ville die ! '
And he fell upon their decks, and he died.

XIV

And they stared at the dead that had been
  so valiant and true,
And had holden the power and glory of
  Spain so cheap
That he dared her with one little ship and
  his English few;
Was he devil or man ? He was devil for
  aught they knew,
But they sank his body with honor down
  into the deep,
And they mann'd the Revenge with a
  swarthier alien crew, 110
And away she sail'd with her loss and
  long'd for her own;
When a wind from the lands they had
  rum'd awoke from sleep,
And the water began to heave and the
  weather to moan,
And or ever that evening ended a great
  gale blew,

And a wave like the wave that is raised by
  an earthquake grew,
Till it smote on their hulls and their sails
  and their masts and their flags,
And the whole sea plunged and fell on the
  shot-shatter'd navy of Spain,
And the little Revenge herself went down
  by the island crags
To be lost evermore in the main.

THE SISTERS

According to the ' Memoir ' (vol. ii. p. 253),
the poem was ' partly founded on the story
known to him [Tennyson] of a girl who con-
sented to be bridesmaid to her sister, although
she secretly loved the bridegroom.'

THEY have left the doors ajar; and by
  their clash,
And prelude on the keys, I know the song,
Their favorite — which I call ' The Tables
  Turn'd.'
Evelyn begins it, ' O diviner Air.'

EVELYN

O diviner Air,
  Thro' the heat, the drowth, the dust, the
    glare,
Far from out the west in shadowing showers,
  Over all the meadow baked and bare,
  Making fresh and fair
All the bowers and the flowers, 10
  Fainting flowers, faded bowers,
  Over all this weary world of ours,
Breathe, diviner Air !

A sweet voice that — you scarce could bet-
  ter that !
Now follows Edith echoing Evelyn.

EDITH

O diviner light,
  Thro' the cloud that roofs our noon with
    night,
Thro' the blotting mist, the blinding showers,
  Far from out a sky for ever bright,
  Over all the woodland's flooded bowers, 20
  Over all the meadow's drowning flowers,
  Over all this ruin'd world of ours,
Break, diviner light !

Marvellously like, their voices — and them-
  selves !
Tho' one is somewhat deeper than the
  other,

As one is somewhat graver than the
   other —
Edith than Evelyn. Your good uncle,
   whom
You count the father of your fortune,
   longs
For this alliance. Let me ask you then,
Which voice most takes you ? for I do not
   doubt,   30
Being a watchful parent, you are taken
With one or other; tho' sometimes I fear
You may be flickering, fluttering in a
   doubt
Between the two — which must not be —
   which might
Be death to one. They both are beautiful:
Evelyn is gayer, wittier, prettier, says
The common voice, if one may trust it,
   she ?
No ! but the paler and the graver, Edith.
Woo her and gain her then; no wavering,
   boy !
The graver is perhaps the one for you   40
Who jest and laugh so easily and so well.
For love will go by contrast, as by likes.

No sisters ever prized each other more.
Not so; their mother and her sister loved
More passionately still.
                But that my best
And oldest friend, your uncle, wishes it,
And that I know you worthy every way
To be my son, I might, perchance, be
   loath
To part them, or part from them; and yet
   one
Should marry, or all the broad lands in
   your view   50
From this bay-window — which our house
   has held
Three hundred years — will pass collater-
   ally.

My father with a child on either knee,
A hand upon the head of either child,
Smoothing their locks, as golden as his
   own
Were silver, 'get them wedded' would he
   say.
And once my prattling Edith ask'd him
   ' why ?'
' Ay, why ?' said he, ' for why should I go
   lame ?'
Then told them of his wars, and of his
   wound.

For see — this wine — the grape from
   whence it flow'd   60
Was blackening on the slopes of Portugal,
When that brave soldier, down the terrible
   ridge
Plunged in the last fierce charge at Water-
   loo,
And caught the laming bullet. He left me
   this,
Which yet retains a memory of its youth,
As I of mine, and my first passion. Come !
Here 's to your happy union with my
   child !

Yet must you change your name — no
   fault of mine !
You say that you can do it as willingly   69
As birds make ready for their bridal-time
By change of feather; for all that, my boy,
Some birds are sick and sullen when they
   moult.
An old and worthy name ! but mine that
   stirr'd
Among our civil wars and earlier too
Among the Roses, the more venerable.
I care not for a name — no fault of mine.
Once more — a happier marriage than my
   own !

You see yon Lombard poplar on the
   plain.
The highway running by it leaves a breadth
Of sward to left and right, where, long
   ago,   80
One bright May morning in a world of
   song,
I lay at leisure, watching overhead
The aerial poplar wave, an amber spire.

I dozed; I woke. An open landaulet
Whirl'd by, which, after it had past me,
   show'd
Turning my way, the loveliest face on
   earth.
The face of one there sitting opposite,
On whom I brought a strange unhappiness,
That time I did not see.
                Love at first sight
May seem — with goodly rhyme and rea-
   son for it —   90
Possible — at first glimpse, and for a face
Gone in a moment — strange. Yet once,
   when first
I came on lake Llanberris in the dark,

A moonless night with storm — one light-
   ning-fork
Flash'd out the lake; and tho' I loiter'd
   there
The full day after, yet in retrospect
That less than momentary thunder-sketch
Of lake and mountain conquers all the day.

   The sun himself has limn'd the face for
      me.
Not quite so quickly, no, nor half as well.
For look you here — the shadows are too
   deep,   101
And like the critic's blurring comment
   make
The veriest beauties of the work appear
The darkest faults; the sweet eyes frown,
   the lips
Seem but a gash. My sole memorial
Of Edith — no, the other, — both indeed.

   So that bright face was flash'd thro'
      sense and soul
And by the poplar vanish'd — to be found
Long after, as it seem'd, beneath the tall
Tree - bowers, and those long - sweeping
   beechen boughs   110
Of our New Forest. I was there alone.
The phantom of the whirling landaulet
For ever past me by; when one quick peal
Of laughter drew me thro' the glimmering
   glades
Down to the snowlike sparkle of a cloth
On fern and foxglove. Lo, the face again,
My Rosalind in this Arden — Edith — all
One bloom of youth, health, beauty, happi-
   ness,
And moved to merriment at a passing jest.

   There one of those about her knowing
      me   120
Call'd me to join them; so with these I
   spent
What seem'd my crowning hour, my day
   of days.

   I woo'd her then, nor unsuccessfully,
The worse for her, for me ! Was I con-
   tent ?
Ay — no, not quite; for now and then I
   thought
Laziness, vague love-longings, the bright
   May,
Had made a heated haze to magnify
The charm of Edith — that a man's ideal

Is high in heaven, and lodged with Plato's
   God,
Not findable here — content, and not con-
   tent,   130
In some such fashion as a man may be
That having had the portrait of his friend
Drawn by an artist, looks at it, and says,
'Good ! very like ! not altogether he.'

   As yet I had not bound myself by words,
Only, believing I loved Edith, made
Edith love me. Then came the day when I,
Flattering myself that all my doubts were
   fools
Born of the fool this Age that doubts of
   all —   139
Not I that day of Edith's love or mine —
Had braced my purpose to declare my-
   self.
I stood upon the stairs of Paradise.
The golden gates would open at a word.
I spoke it — told her of my passion, seen
And lost and found again, had got so far,
Had caught her hand, her eyelids fell — I
   heard
Wheels, and a noise of welcome at the
   doors —
·On a sudden after two Italian years
Had set the blossom of her health again,
The younger sister, Evelyn, enter'd —
   there,   150
There was the face, and altogether she.
The mother fell about the daughter's
   neck,
The sisters closed in one another's arms,
Their people throng'd about them from the
   hall,
And in the thick of question and reply
I fled the house, driven by one angel face,
And all the Furies.

                     I was bound to her;
I could not free myself in honor — bound
Not by the sounded letter of the word, 159
But counter-pressures of the yielded hand
That timorously and faintly echoed mine,
Quick blushes, the sweet dwelling of her
   eyes
Upon me when she thought I did not see —
Were these not bonds ? nay, nay, but could
   I wed her
Loving the other ? do her that great
   wrong ?
Had I not dream'd I loved her yester-
   morn ?

Had I not known where Love, at first a fear,
Grew after marriage to full height and
　　form ?
Yet after marriage, that mock - sister
　　there —
Brother-in-law — the fiery nearness of it —
Unlawful and disloyal brotherhood — 171
What end but darkness could ensue from
　　this
For all the three ?　So Love and Honor
　　jarr'd,
Tho' Love and Honor join'd to raise the full
High-tide of doubt that sway'd me up and
　　down
Advancing nor retreating.

　　　　　　　　　　　Edith wrote:
'My mother bids me ask' — I did not tell
　　you —
A widow with less guile than many a child.
God help the wrinkled children that are
　　Christ's
As well as the plump cheek — she wrought
　　us harm,　　　　　　　　　　180
Poor soul, not knowing ! — 'Are you ill ?'
　　— so ran
The letter — 'you have not been here of
　　late.
You will not find me here.　At last I go
On that long-promised visit to the North.
I told your wayside story to my mother
And Evelyn.　She remembers you.　Fare-
　　well.
Pray come and see my mother.　Almost
　　blind
With ever-growing cataract, yet she thinks
She sees you when she hears.　Again fare-
　　well.'

　Cold words from one I had hoped to
　　warm so far　　　　　　　　　190
That I could stamp my image on her
　　heart !
'Pray come and see my mother, and fare-
　　well.'
Cold, but as welcome as free airs of heaven
After a dungeon's closeness.　Selfish,
　　strange !
What dwarfs are men ! my strangled van-
　　ity
Utter'd a stifled cry — to have vext myself
And all in vain for her — cold heart or
　　none —
No bride for me.　Yet so my path was clear
To win the sister.

　　　　　　　Whom I woo'd and won.
For Evelyn knew not of my former suit,
Because the simple mother work'd upon 201
By Edith pray'd me not to whisper of it.
And Edith would be bridesmaid on the day.
　But on that day, not being all at ease,
I from the altar glancing back upon her,
Before the first 'I will' was utter'd, saw
The bridesmaid pale, statue-like, passion-
　　less —
'No harm, no harm' — I turn'd again, and
　　placed
My ring upon the finger of my bride.

　So, when we parted, Edith spoke no
　　word,　　　　　　　　　　210
She wept no tear, but round my Evelyn
　　clung
In utter silence for so long, I thought,
'What, will she never set her sister free ?'

　We left her, happy each in each, and
　　then,
As tho' the happiness of each in each
Were not enough, must fain have torrents,
　　lakes,
Hills, the great things of Nature and the
　　fair,
To lift us as it were from commonplace,
And help us to our joy.　Better have sent
Our Edith thro' the glories of the earth, 220
To change with her horizon, if true Love
Were not his own imperial all-in-all.

　Far off we went.　My God, I would not
　　live
Save that I think this gross hard-seeming
　　world
Is our misshaping vision of the Powers
Behind the world, that make our griefs our
　　gains.

　For on the dark night of our marriage-
　　day
The great tragedian, that had quench'd
　　herself
In that assumption of the bridesmaid —
　　she
That loved me — our true Edith — her
　　brain broke　　　　　　　　　230
With over-acting, till she rose and fled
Beneath a pitiless rush of autumn rain
To the deaf church — to be let in — to
　　pray
Before *that* altar — so I think ; and there

They found her beating the hard Protes-
tant doors.
She died and she was buried ere we knew.

I learnt it first. I had to speak. At
once
The bright quick smile of Evelyn, that had
sunn'd
The morning of our marriage, past away.
And on our home-return the daily want 240
Of Edith in the house, the garden, still
Haunted us like her ghost; and by and by,
Either from that necessity for talk
Which lives with blindness, or plain inno-
cence
Of nature, or desire that her lost child
Should earn from both the praise of hero-
ism,
The mother broke her promise to the dead,
And told the living daughter with what
love
Edith had welcomed my brief wooing of
her,   249
And all her sweet self-sacrifice and death.

Henceforth that mystic bond betwixt the
twins —
Did I not tell you they were twins? — pre-
vail'd
So far that no caress could win my wife
Back to that passionate answer of full
heart
I had from her at first. Not that her
love,
Tho' scarce as great as Edith's power of
love,
Had lessen'd, but the mother's garrulous
wail
For ever woke the unhappy Past again,
Till that dead bridesmaid, meant to be my
bride,
Put forth cold hands between us, and I
fear'd   260
The very fountains of her life were chill'd;
So took her thence, and brought her here,
and here
She bore a child, whom reverently we
call'd
Edith; and in the second year was born
A second — this I named from her own
self,
Evelyn; then two weeks — no more — she
join'd,
In and beyond the grave, that one she
loved.

Now in this quiet of declining life,
Thro' dreams by night and trances of the
day,   269
The sisters glide about me hand in hand,
Both beautiful alike, nor can I tell
One from the other, no, nor care to tell
One from the other, only know they come,
They smile upon me, till, remembering all
The love they both have borne me, and the
love
I bore them both — divided as I am
From either by the stillness of the grave —
I know not which of these I love the best.

But *you* love Edith; and her own true
eyes   279
Are traitors to her; our quick Evelyn —
The merrier, prettier, wittier, as they talk,
And not without good reason, my good
son —
Is yet untouch'd. And I that hold them
both
Dearest of all things — well, I am not
sure
But if there lie a preference either way,
And in the rich vocabulary of Love
' Most dearest ' be a true superlative —
I think *I* likewise love your Edith most.

THE VILLAGE WIFE; OR, THE ENTAIL [1]

The footnotes are the poet's own.

I

'OUSE-KEEPER sent tha, my lass, fur new
Squire coom'd last night.
Butter an' heggs — yis — yis. I 'll goä wi'
tha back; all right;
Butter I warrants be prime, an' I warrants
the heggs be as well,
Hafe a pint o' milk runs out when ya breäks
the shell.

II

Sit thysen down fur a bit; hev a glass o'
cowslip wine !
I liked the owd Squire an' 'is gells as thaw
they was gells o' mine,
Fur then we was all es one, the Squire an'
'is darters an' me,
Hall but Miss Annie, the heldest, I niver
not took to she.

[1] See note on pronunciation, p. 456.

But Nelly, the last of the cletch,[1] I liked
  'er the fust on 'em all,
Fur hoffens we talkt o' my darter es died
  o' the fever at fall;   10
An' I thowt 't wur the will o' the Lord,
  but Miss Annie she said it wur
  draäins,
Fur she hed n't naw coomfut in 'er, an'
  arn'd naw thanks fur 'er paäins.
Eh! thebbe all wi' the Lord, my childer, I
  han't gotten none!
Sa new Squire 's coom'd wi' 'is taäil in 'is
  'and, an' owd Squire 's gone.

III

Fur 'staäte be i' taäil, my lass — tha dosn'
  knaw what that be?
But I knaws the law, I does, for the lawyer
  ha towd it me.
'When theer 's naw 'eäd to a 'Ouse by
  the fault o' that ere maäle —
The gells they counts fur nowt, and the
  next un he taäkes the taäil.'

IV

What be the next un like? can tha tell
  ony harm on 'im, lass? —
Naäy sit down — naw 'urry — sa cowd! —
  hev another glass!   20
Straänge an' cowd fur the time! we may
  happen a fall o' snaw —
Not es I cares fur to hear ony harm, but
  I likes to knaw.
An' I oäps es 'e beänt boöklarn'd; but 'e
  dosn' not coom fro' the shere;
We 'd anew o' that wi' the Squire, an' we
  haätes boöklarnin' ere.

V

Fur Squire wur a Varsity scholard, an
  niver lookt arter the land —
Whoäts or turmuts or taätes — 'e 'd hallus
  a boök i' 'is 'and,
Hallus aloän wi' 'is boöks, thaw nigh upo'
  seventy year.
An' boöks, what 's boöks? thou knaws
  thebbe neyther 'ere nor theer.

VI

An' the gells, they hed n't naw taäils, an'
  the lawyer he towd it me
That 'is taäil were soä tied up es he
  could n't cut down a tree!   30

[1] A brood of chickens.

"Drat the trees," says I, to be sewer I
  haätes 'em, my lass,
Fur we puts the muck o' the land, an' they
  sucks the muck fro' the grass.

VII

An' Squire wur hallus a-smilin', an' gied
  to the tramps goin' by —
An' all o' the wust i' the parish — wi' hof-
  fens a drop in 'is eye.
An' ivry darter o' Squire 's hed her awn
  ridin-erse to 'ersen,
An' they rampaged about wi' their grooms,
  an' wus 'untin' arter the men,
An' hallus a-dallackt[1] an' dizen'd out, an'
  a-buyin' new cloäthes,
While 'e sit like a greät glimmer-gowk[2]
  wi' 'is glasses athurt 'is noäse,
An' 'is noäse sa grufted wi' snuff as it
  could n't be scroob'd awaäy,
Fur 'atween 'is readin' an' writin' 'e snifft
  up a box in a daäy,   40
An' 'e niver runn'd arter the fox, nor arter
  the birds wi' 'is gun,
An' 'e niver not shot one 'are, but 'e leäved
  it to Charlie 'is son,
An 'e niver not fish'd 'is awn ponds, but
  Charlie 'e cotch'd the pike,
Fur 'e warn't not burn to the land, an' 'e
  did n't take kind to it like;
But I eärs es 'e 'd gie fur a howry[3] owd
  book thutty pound an' moor,
An' 'e 'd wrote an' owd book, his awn sen,
  sa I knaw'd es 'e 'd coom to be poor;
An' 'e gied — I be fear'd fur to tell tha 'ow
  much — fur an owd scratted stoän,
An' 'e digg'd up a loomp i' the land an' 'e
  got a brown pot an' a boän,
An' 'e bowt owd money, es would n't goä,
  wi' good gowd o' the Queen,
An' 'e bowt little statutes all-naäkt an'
  which was a shaäme to be seen;   50
But 'e niver looökt ower a bill, nor 'e niver
  not seed to owt,
An' 'e niver knawd nowt but boöks, an'
  boöks, as thou knaws, beänt nowt.

VIII

But owd Squire's laädy es long es she lived
  she kep' 'em all clear,
Thaw es long es she lived I niver hed none
  of 'er darters 'ere;

[1] Overdrest in gay colors.
[2] Owl.
[3] Filthy.

But arter she died we was all es one, the
    childer an' me,
An' sarvints runn'd in an' out, an' offens we
    hed 'em to tea.
Lawk! 'ow I laugh'd when the lasses 'ud
    talk o' their Missis's waäys,
An' the Missisis talk'd o' the lasses. — I 'll
    tell tha some o' these daäys.
Hoänly Miss Annie were saw stuck oop,
    like 'er mother afoor —
'Er an' 'er blessed darter — they niver
    derken'd my door.   60

IX

An' Squire 'e smiled an' 'e smiled till 'e 'd
    gotten a fright at last,
An' 'e calls fur 'is son, fur the 'turney's let-
    ters they foller'd sa fast;
But Squire wur afear'd o' 'is son, an' 'e
    says to 'im, meek as a mouse,
'Lad, thou mun cut off thy taäil, or the
    gells 'ull goä to the 'Ouse,
Fur I finds es I be that i' debt, es I 'oäps es
    thou 'll 'elp me a bit,
An' if thou 'll 'gree to cut off thy taäil I
    may saäve mysen yit.'

X

But Charlie 'e sets back 'is ears, an' 'e
    sweärs, an' 'e says to 'im, ' Noä.
I 've gotten the 'staäte by the taäil an' be
    dang'd if I iver let goä !
Coom! coom! feyther,' 'e says, ' why
    should n't thy booöks be sowd !
I hears es soom o' thy booöks mebbe worth
    their weight i' gowd.'   70

XI

Heäps an' heäps o' booäks, I ha' seed 'em,
    belong'd to the Squire,
But the lasses 'ed teärd out leäves i' the
    middle to kindle the fire;
Sa moäst on 'is owd big booöks fetch'd nigh
    to nowt at the saäle,
And Squire were at Charlie ageän to git
    'im to cut off 'is taäil.

XII

Ya would n't find Charlie's likes — 'e were
    that outdacious at 'oäm,
Not thaw ya went fur to raäke out hell wi'
    a small-tooth coämb —
Droonk wi' the Quoloty's wine, an' droonk
    wi' the farmer's aäle,
Mad wi' the lasses an' all — an' 'e would n't
    cut off the taäil.

XIII

Thou 's coom'd oop by the beck; and a
    thurn be a-grawin' theer,
I niver ha seed it sa white wi' the maäy es
    I seed it to-year —   80
Theerabouts Charlie joompt — and it gied
    me a scare tother night,
Fur I thowt it wur Charlie's ghoäst i' the
    derk, fur it looökt sa white.
'Billy,' says 'e, ' hev a joomp !' — thaw the
    banks o' the beck be sa high,
Fur he ca'd 'is 'erse Billy-rough-un, thaw
    niver a hair wur awry;
But Billy fell bakkuds o' Charlie, an'
    Charlie 'e brok 'is neck,
Sa theer wur a hend o' the taäil, fur 'e lost
    'is taäil i' the beck.

XIV

Sa 'is taäil wur lost an' 'is booöks wur gone
    an' 'is boy wur deäd,
An' Squire 'e smiled an' 'e smiled, but, 'e
    niver not lift oop 'is 'eäd.
Hallus a soft un, Squire ! an' 'e smiled, fur
    'e hed n't naw friend,
Sa feyther an' son was buried togither, an'
    this wur the hend.   90

XV

An' Parson as hes n't the call, nor the
    mooney, but hes the pride,
'E reäds of a sewer an' sartan 'oäp o' the
    tother side;
But I beänt that sewer es the Lord, how-
    siver they praäy'd an' praäy'd,
Lets them inter 'eaven eäsy es leäves their
    debts to be paäid.
Siver the mou'ds rattled down upo' poor
    owd Squire i' the wood,
An' I cried along wi' the gells, fur they
    weänt niver coom to naw good.

XVI

Fur Molly the long un she walkt awaäy wi'
    a hofficer lad,
An' nawbody 'eärd on 'er sin', sa o' coorse
    she be gone to the bad !
An' Lucy wur laäme o' one leg, sweet'arts
    she niver 'ed none —
Straänge an' unheppen [1] Miss Lucy ! we
    naämed her ' Dot an' gaw one !'   100
An' Hetty wur weak i' the hattics, wi'out
    ony harm i' the legs,

---

[1] Ungainly, awkward.

An' the fever 'ed baäked Jinny's 'eäd as
    bald as one o' them heggs,
An' Nelly wur up fro' the craädle as big i'
    the mouth as a cow,
An' saw she mun hammergrate,[1] lass, or
    she weänt git a maäte onyhow !
An' es for Miss Annie es call'd me afoor
    my awn foälks to my faäce,
'A hignorant village wife es 'ud hev to be
    larn'd her awn plaäce,'
Hes fur Miss Hannie the heldest hes now
    be a-grawin' sa howd,
I knaws that mooch o' sheä, es it beänt not
    fit to be towd !

XVII

Sa I did n't not taäke it kindly ov owd
    Miss Annie to saäy
Es I should be talkin' ageän 'em, es soon
    es they went awaäy,   110
Fur lawks ! 'ow I cried when they went,
    an' our Nelly she gied me 'er 'and,
Fur I 'd ha done owt for the Squire an' 'is
    gells es belong'd to the land;
Boooks, es I said afoor, thebbe neyther
    'ere nor theer !
But I sarved 'em wi' butter an' heggs fur
    huppuds o' twenty year.

XVIII

An' they hallus paäid what I hax'd, sa I
    hallus deal'd wi' the Hall,
An' they knaw'd what butter wur, an' they
    knaw'd what a hegg wur an' all;
Hugger-mugger they lived, but they was n't
    that eäsy to pleäse,
Till I gied 'em Hinjian curn, an' they
    laäid big heggs es tha seeäs;
An' I niver puts saäme [2] i' my butter —
    they does it at Willis's farm;
Taäste another drop o' the wine — tweänt
    do tha naw harm.   120

XIX

Sa new Squire 's coom'd wi' 'is taäil in 'is
    'and, an' owd Squire 's gone;
I heard 'im a roomlin' by, but arter my
    night-cap wur on;
Sa I han't clapt eyes on 'im yit, fur he
    coom'd last night sa laäte —
Pluksh ! ! ! [3] the hens i' the peäs ! why
    did n't tha hesp the gaäte ?

[1] Emigrate.   [2] Lard.
[3] A cry accompanied by a clapping of hands
to scare trespassing fowl.

IN THE CHILDREN'S HOSPITAL

EMMIE

This poem has been criticised as 'marred a
little by the needlessly harsh attack on the
practice of modern surgery, as exhibited by
one of the hospital staff;' but Mr. Palgrave
('Lyrical Poems of Tennyson,' London, 1885)
says: 'It should be remembered that this is a
little drama, in which the Hospital Nurse, not
the Poet, is supposed to be speaking through-
out. The two children, whose story was pub-
lished in a Parish Magazine, are the only char-
acters here described from actual life.' He
adds that 'this is the most absolutely pathetic
poem' known to him. See also the 'Memoir,'
vol. ii. p. 253.

I

Our doctor had call'd in another, I never
    had seen him before,
But he sent a chill to my heart when I saw
    him come in at the door,
Fresh from the surgery-schools of France
    and of other lands —
Harsh red hair, big voice, big chest, big
    merciless hands !
Wonderful cures he had done, O, yes, but
    they said too of him
He was happier using the knife than in try-
    ing to save the limb,
And that I can well believe, for he look'd
    so coarse and so red,
I could think he was one of those who would
    break their jests on the dead,
And mangle the living dog that had loved
    him and fawn'd at his knee —
Drench'd with the hellish oorali — that
    ever such things should be !

II

Here was a boy — I am sure that some of
    our children would die
But for the voice of love, and the smile,
    and the comforting eye —
Here was a boy in the ward, every bone
    seem'd out of its place —
Caught in a mill and crush'd — it was all
    but a hopeless case:
And he handled him gently enough; but his
    voice and his face were not kind,
And it was but a hopeless case, he had seen
    it and made up his mind,
And he said to me roughly, 'The lad will
    need little more of your care.'

'All the more need,' I told him, 'to seek
    the Lord Jesus in prayer;
They are all His children here, and I pray
    for them all as my own.'
But he turn'd to me, 'Ay, good woman,
    can prayer set a broken bone?'
Then he mutter'd half to himself, but I
    know that I heard him say,
'All very well — but the good Lord Jesus
    has had his day.'

III

Had? has it come? It has only dawn'd.
    It will come by and by.
O, how could I serve in the wards if the
    hope of the world were a lie?
How could I bear with the sights and the
    loathsome smells of disease
But that He said, 'Ye do it to me, when ye
    do it to these'?

IV

So he went. And we past to this ward
    where the younger children are laid.
Here is the cot of our orphan, our darling,
    our meek little maid;
Empty, you see, just now! We have lost
    her who loved her so much —
Patient of pain tho' as quick as a sensitive
    plant to the touch.
Hers was the prettiest prattle, it often
    moved me to tears,
Hers was the gratefullest heart I have
    found in a child of her years —
Nay you remember our Emmie; you used
    to send her the flowers.
How she would smile at 'em, play with 'em,
    talk to 'em hours after hours!
They that can wander at will where the
    works of the Lord are reveal'd
Little guess what joy can be got from a
    cowslip out of the field;
Flowers to these 'spirits in prison' are all
    they can know of the spring,
They freshen and sweeten the wards like
    the waft of an angel's wing.
And she lay with a flower in one hand and
    her thin hands crost on her breast —
Wan, but as pretty as heart can desire, and
    we thought her at rest,
Quietly sleeping — so quiet, our doctor said,
    'Poor little dear,
Nurse, I must do it to-morrow; she 'll
    never live thro' it, I fear.'

V

I walk'd with our kindly old doctor as far
    as the head of the stair,
Then I return'd to the ward; the child
    did n't see I was there.

VI

Never since I was nurse had I been so
    grieved and so vext!
Emmie had heard him. Softly she call'd
    from her cot to the next,
'He says I shall never live thro' it; O An-
    nie, what shall I do?'
Annie consider'd. 'If I,' said the wise
    little Annie, 'was you,
I should cry to the dear Lord Jesus to help
    me, for, Emmie, you see,
It 's all in the picture there: "Little chil-
    dren should come to me"'—
Meaning the print that you gave us, I
    find that it always can please
Our children, the dear Lord Jesus with
    children about his knees.
'Yes, and I will,' said Emmie, 'but then if
    I call to the Lord,
How should he know that it 's me? such a
    lot of beds in the ward!'
That was a puzzle for Annie. Again she
    consider'd and said:
'Emmie, you put out your arms, and you
    leave 'em outside on the bed —
The Lord has so *much* to see to! but, Em-
    mie, you tell it him plain,
It 's the little girl with her arms lying out
    on the counterpane.'

VII

I had sat three nights by the child — I
    could not watch her for four —
My brain had begun to reel — I felt I
    could do it no more.
That was my sleeping-night, but I thought
    that it never would pass.
There was a thunderclap once, and a clatter
    of hail on the glass,
And there was a phantom cry that I heard
    as I tost about,
The motherless bleat of a lamb in the
    storm and the darkness without;
My sleep was broken besides with dreams
    of the dreadful knife
And fears for our delicate Emmie who
    scarce would escape with her life;

Then in the gray of the morning it seem'd
   she stood by me and smiled,
And the doctor came at his hour, and we
   went to see to the child.

VIII

He had brought his ghastly tools; we be-
   lieved her asleep again —
Her dear, long, lean, little arms lying out
   on the counterpane —
Say that His day is done ! Ah, why should
   we care what they say ?
The Lord of the children had heard her,
   and Emmie had past away.

DEDICATORY POEM TO THE PRINCESS ALICE

Contributed to ' The Nineteenth Century ' for
April, 1879, and afterwards included in the
' Ballads and Other Poems.' It is a dedica-
tion of the poem that follows, ' The Defence
of Lucknow.'

The Princess Alice, Grand Duchess of Hesse-
Darmstadt, died on the 14th of December,
1878, aged thirty-five years.

DEAD PRINCESS, living Power, if that
   which lived
True life live on — and if the fatal kiss,
Born of true life and love, divorce thee not
From earthly love and life — if what we
   call
The spirit flash not all at once from out
This shadow into Substance — then per-
   haps
The mellow'd murmur of the people's
   praise
From thine own State, and all our breadth
   of realm,
Where Love and Longing dress thy deeds
   in light,
Ascends to thee; and this March morn that
   sees
Thy Soldier-brother's bridal orange-bloom
Break thro' the yews and cypress of thy
   grave,
And thine Imperial mother smile again,
May send one ray to thee ! and who can
   tell —
Thou — England's England-loving daugh-
   ter — thou
Dying so English thou wouldst have her
   flag

Borne on thy coffin — where is he can
   swear
But that some broken gleam from our poor
   earth
May touch thee, while, remembering thee,
   I lay
At thy pale feet this ballad of the deeds
Of England, and her banner in the East ?

THE DEFENCE OF LUCKNOW

First printed in ' The Nineteenth Century '
for April, 1879, and included in the ' Ballads,'
1880.

The events recorded in the poem occurred
during the Sepoy Rebellion in British India,
in 1857. ' Sir Henry Lawrence took charge of
Lucknow as Resident in March of that year.
The spread of rebellion in June confined him
to the defence of the city, where he died of
wounds on July 4. Brigadier Inglis, in suc-
cession, then defended Lucknow for twelve
weeks until it was relieved on September 25
by General Havelock, to whom Sir James Out-
ram (who accompanied as volunteer) had gen-
erously ceded the exploit ' (Palgrave).

I

BANNER of England, not for a season, O
   banner of Britain, hast thou
Floated in conquering battle or flapt to the
   battle-cry !
Never with mightier glory than when we
   had rear'd thee on high
Flying at top of the roofs in the ghastly
   siege of Lucknow —
Shot thro' the staff or the halyard, but ever
   we raised thee anew,
And ever upon the topmost roof our banner
   of England blew.

II

Frail were the works that defended the
   hold that we held with our lives —
Women and children among us, God help
   them, our children and wives!
Hold it we might — and for fifteen days or
   for twenty at most.
' Never surrender, I charge you, but every
   man die at his post ! '   10
Voice of the dead whom we loved, our
   Lawrence the best of the brave;
Cold were his brows when we kiss'd him —
   we laid him that night in his grave.

'Every man die at his post!' and there
    hail'd on our houses and halls
Death from their rifle-bullets, and death
    from their cannon-balls,
Death in our innermost chamber, and death
    at our slight barricade,
Death while we stood with the musket, and
    death while we stoopt to the spade,
Death to the dying, and wounds to the
    wounded, for often there fell,
Striking the hospital wall, crashing thro'
    it, their shot and their shell,
Death — for their spies were among us,
    their marksmen were told of our
    best,
So that the brute bullet broke thro' the
    brain that could think for the rest; 20
Bullets would sing by our foreheads, and
    bullets would rain at our feet —
Fire from ten thousand at once of the rebels
    that girdled us round —
Death at the glimpse of a finger from over
    the breadth of a street,
Death from the heights of the mosque and
    the palace, and death in the ground !
Mine ? yes, a mine ! Countermine ! down,
    down ! and creep thro' the hole !
Keep the revolver in hand ! you can hear
    him — the murderous mole !
Quiet, ah ! quiet — wait till the point of the
    pickaxe be thro' !
Click with the pick, coming nearer and
    nearer again than before —
Now let it speak, and you fire, and the
    dark pioneer is no more;
And ever upon the topmost roof our banner
    of England blew ! 30

III

Ay, but the foe sprung his mine many
    times, and it chanced on a day
Soon as the blast of that underground
    thunder-clap echo'd away,
Dark thro' the smoke and the sulphur like
    so many fiends in their hell —
Cannot-shot, musket-shot, volley on volley,
    and yell upon yell —
Fiercely on all the defences our myriad
    enemy fell.
What have they done ? where is it ? Out
    yonder. Guard the Redan !
Storm at the Water-gate ! storm at the
    Bailey-gate ! storm, and it ran
Surging and swaying all round us, as ocean
    on every side

Plunges and heaves at a bank that is daily
    drown'd by the tide —
So many thousands that, if they be bold
    enough, who shall escape ? 40
Kill or be kill'd, live or die, they shall
    know we are soldiers and men !
Ready ! take aim at their leaders — their
    masses are gapp'd with our grape —
Backward they reel like the wave, like the
    wave flinging forward again,
Flying and foil'd at the last by the handful
    they could not subdue;
And ever upon the topmost roof our banner
    of England blew.

IV

Handful of men as we were, we were Eng-
    lish in heart and in limb,
Strong with the strength of the race to
    command, to obey, to endure,
Each of us fought as if hope for the garri-
    son hung but on him;
Still — could we watch at all points ? we
    were every day fewer and fewer.
There was a whisper among us, but only a
    whisper that past: 50
'Children and wives — if the tigers leap
    into the fold unawares —
Every man die at his post — and the foe
    may outlive us at last —
Better to fall by the hands that they love,
    than to fall into theirs !'
Roar upon roar in a moment two mines by
    the enemy sprung
Clove into perilous chasms our walls and
    our poor palisades.
Rifleman, true is your heart, but be sure
    that your hand be as true !
Sharp is the fire of assault, better aimed
    are your flank fusillades —
Twice do we hurl them to earth from the
    ladders to which they had clung,
Twice from the ditch where they shelter
    we drive them with hand-grenades;
And ever upon the topmost roof our banner
    of England blew. 60

V

Then on another wild morning another wild
    earthquake out-tore
Clean from our lines of defence ten or
    twelve good paces or more.
Rifleman, high on the roof, hidden there
    from the light of the sun —

One has leapt up on the breach, crying out:
    ' Follow me, follow me ! ' —
Mark him — he falls ! then another, and
    him too, and down goes he.
Had they been bold enough then, who can
    tell but the traitors had won ?
Boardings and rafters and doors — an em-
    brasure ! make way for the gun !
Now double-charge it with grape ! It is
    charged and we fire, and they run.
Praise to our Indian brothers, and let the
    dark face have his due !
Thanks to the kindly dark faces who
    fought with us, faithful and few, 70
Fought with the bravest among us, and
    drove them, and smote them, and
    slew,
That ever upon the topmost roof our banner
    in India blew.

VI

Men will forget what we suffer and not
    what we do. We can fight !
But to be soldier all day, and be sentinel
    all thro' the night —
Ever the mine and assault, our sallies, their
    lying alarms,
Bugles and drums in the darkness, and
    shoutings and soundings to arms,
Ever the labor of fifty that had to be done
    by five,
Ever the marvel among us that one should
    be left alive,
Ever the day with its traitorous death from
    the loopholes around,
Ever the night with its coffinless corpse to
    be laid in the ground, 80
Heat like the mouth of a hell, or a deluge
    of cataract skies,
Stench of old offal decaying, and infinite
    torment of flies,
Thoughts of the breezes of May blowing
    over an English field,
Cholera, scurvy, and fever, the wound that
    would not be heal'd,
Lopping away of the limb by the pitiful-
    pitiless knife, —
Torture and trouble in vain, — for it never
    could save us a life.
Valor of delicate women who tended the
    hospital bed,
Horror of women in travail among the
    dying and dead,
Grief for our perishing children, and never
    a moment for grief,

Toil and ineffable weariness, faltering hopes
    of relief, 90
Havelock baffled, or beaten, or butcher'd
    for all that we knew —
Then day and night, day and night, coming
    down on the still-shatter'd walls
Millions of musket-bullets, and thousands
    of cannon-balls —
But ever upon the topmost roof our banner
    of England blew.

VII

Hark cannonade, fusillade ! is it true what
    was told by the scout,
Outram and Havelock breaking their way
    through the fell mutineers ?
Surely the pibroch of Europe is ringing
    again in our ears !
All on a sudden the garrison utter a jubi-
    lant shout,
Havelock's glorious Highlanders answer
    with conquering cheers,
Sick from the hospital echo them, women
    and children come out, 100
Blessing the wholesome white faces of
    Havelock's good fusileers,
Kissing the war-harden'd hand of the High-
    lander wet with their tears !
Dance to the pibroch ! — saved ! we are
    saved ! — is it you ? is it you ?
Saved by the valor of Havelock, saved by
    the blessing of heaven !
' Hold it for fifteen days ! ' we have held it
    for eighty-seven !
And ever aloft on the palace roof the old
    banner of England blew.

SIR JOHN OLDCASTLE, LORD COBHAM

(IN WALES)

Sir John Oldcastle, known in his time as ' the good Lord Cobham,' was born in the reign of Edward III., but in what year is unknown. He was an ardent Wiclifite, and took part in the presentation of a remonstrance to Parliament on the corruption of the church. In the reign of Henry V., he was accused of heresy and imprisoned in the Tower, whence he escaped and hid himself in Wales. A bill of attainder was passed against him, and a reward of a thousand marks offered for his capture. Four years later he was taken, and, being reckoned a traitor as well as a heretic, was

hung up alive in chains, and burned to death
by a fire kindled under the gallows.

My friend should meet me somewhere
    hereabout
To take me to that hiding in the hills.

    I have broke their cage, no gilded one, I
      trow —
I read no more the prisoner's mute wail
Scribbled or carved upon the pitiless
    stone;
I find hard rocks, hard life, hard cheer, or
    none,
For I am emptier than a friar's brains;
But God is with me in this wilderness,
These wet black passes and foam-churning
    chasms —
And God's free air, and hope of better
    things.   10

    I would I knew their speech; not now to
      glean,
Not now — I hope to do it — some scat-
    ter'd ears,
Some ears for Christ in this wild field of
    Wales —
But, bread, merely for bread. This tongue
    that wagg'd
They said with such heretical arrogance
Against the proud archbishop Arundel —
So much God's cause was fluent in it — is
    here
But as a Latin Bible to the crowd;
'Bara!' — what use? The shepherd, when
    I speak,
Vailing a sudden eyelid with his hard   20
'Dim Saesneg,' passes, wroth at things of
    old —
No fault of mine. Had he God's word in
    Welsh
He might be kindlier; happily come the
    day!

    Not least art thou, thou little Bethlehem
In Judah, for in thee the Lord was born;
Nor thou in Britain, little Lutterworth,
Least, for in thee the word was born again.

    Heaven-sweet Evangel, ever-living word,
Who whilome spakest to the South in Greek
About the soft Mediterranean shores,   30
And then in Latin to the Latin crowd,
As good need was — thou hast come to talk
    our isle.

Hereafter thou, fulfilling Pentecost,
Must learn to use the tongues of all the
    world.
Yet art thou thine own witness that thou
    bringest
Not peace, a sword, a fire.
                What did he say,
My frighted Wiclif - preacher whom I
    crost
In flying hither? that one night a crowd
Throng'd the waste field about the city
    gates;
The king was on them suddenly with a
    host.   40
Why there? they came to hear their
    preacher. Then
Some cried on Cobham, on the good Lord
    Cobham;
Ay, for they love me! but the king — nor
    voice
Nor finger raised against him — took and
    hang'd,
Took, hang'd and burnt — how many —
    thirty-nine —
Call'd it rebellion — hang'd, poor friends,
    as rebels
And burn'd alive as heretics! for your
    priest
Labels — to take the king along with
    him —
All heresy, treason; but to call men trai-
    tors
May make men traitors.
                  Rose of Lancaster,
Red in thy birth, redder with household
    war,   51
Now reddest with the blood of holy men,
Redder to be, red rose of Lancaster —
If somewhere in the North, as Rumor
    sang
Fluttering the hawks of this crown-lusting
    line —
By firth and loch thy silver sister grow,[1]
That were my rose, there my allegiance
    due.
Self - starved, they say — nay, murder'd,
    doubtless dead.
So to this king I cleaved. My friend was
    he,
Once my fast friend; I would have given
    my life   60
To help his own from scathe, a thousand
    lives

[1] Richard II.

To save his soul. He might have come to
   learn
Our Wiclif's learning; but the worldly
   priests,
Who fear the king's hard common-sense
   should find
What rotten piles uphold their mason-
   work,
Urge him to foreign war. O, had he
   will'd
I might have stricken a lusty stroke for
   him,
But he would not; far liever led my friend
Back to the pure and universal church,
But he would not — whether that heirless
   flaw   70
In his throne's title make him feel so frail,
He leans on Antichrist; or that his mind,
So quick, so capable in soldiership,
In matters of the faith, alas the while !
More worth than all the kingdoms of this
   world,
Runs in the rut, a coward to the priest.

Burnt — good Sir Roger Acton, my dear
   friend !
Burnt too, my faithful preacher, Bever-
   ley !
Lord, give thou power to thy two wit-
   nesses,
Lest the false faith make merry over
   them !   80
Two — nay, but thirty-nine have risen and
   stand,
Dark with the smoke of human sacrifice,
Before thy light, and cry continually —
Cry — against whom ?
          Him, who should bear the sword
Of Justice — what ! the kingly, kindly
   boy ;
Who took the world so easily heretofore,
My boon companion, tavern-fellow — him
Who jibed and japed — in many a merry
   tale
That shook our sides — at pardoners, sum-
   moners,
Friars, absolution-sellers, monkeries   90
And nunneries, when the wild hour and the
   wine
Had set the wits aflame.
          Harry of Monmouth,
Or Amurath of the East ?
          Better to sink
Thy fleurs-de-lys in slime again, and fling
Thy royalty back into the riotous fits

Of wine and harlotry — thy shame, and
   mine,
Thy comrade — than to persecute the
   Lord,
And play the Saul that never will be Paul.

Burnt, burnt ! and while this mitred
   Arundel
Dooms our unlicensed preacher to the
   flame,   100
The mitre - sanction'd harlot draws his
   clerks
Into the suburb — their hard celibacy,
Sworn to be veriest ice of pureness, molten
Into adulterous living, or such crimes
As holy Paul — a shame to speak of
   them —
Among the heathen —
          Sanctuary granted
To bandit, thief, assassin — yea, to him
Who hacks his mother's throat — denied to
   him
Who finds the Saviour in his mother
   tongue.
The Gospel, the priest's pearl, flung down
   to swine —   110
The swine, lay-men, lay-women, who will
   come,
God willing, to outlearn the filthy friar.
Ah, rather, Lord, than that thy Gospel,
   meant
To course and range thro' all the world,
   should be
Tether'd to these dead pillars of the
   Church —
Rather than so, if thou wilt have it so,
Burst vein, snap sinew, and crack heart,
   and life
Pass in the fire of Babylon ! but how long,
O Lord, how long !
          My friend should meet me here.
Here is the copse, the fountain and — a
   cross !   120
To thee, dead wood, I bow not head nor
   knees.
Rather to thee, green boscage, work of
   God,
Black holly, and white-flower'd wayfaring-
   tree !
Rather to thee, thou living water, drawn
By this good Wiclif mountain down from
   heaven,
And speaking clearly in thy native tongue—
No Latin — He that thirsteth, come and
   drink !

Eh ! how I anger'd Arundel asking me
To worship Holy Cross ! I spread mine
arms,
God's work, I said, a cross of flesh and
blood   130
And holier. That was heresy. — My good
friend
By this time should be with me. — 'Im-
ages ? '
'Bury them as God's truer images
Are daily buried.' 'Heresy. — Penance ? '
'Fast,
Hair-shirt and scourge — nay, let a man
repent,
Do penance in his heart, God hears him.'
'Heresy —
Not shriven, not saved ? ' 'What profits
an ill priest
Between me and my God ? I would not
spurn
Good counsel of good friends, but shrive
myself —
No, not to an Apostle.' 'Heresy.' —   140
My friend is long in coming. — 'Pilgrim-
ages ? '
'Drink, bagpipes, revelling, devil's-dances,
vice.
The poor man's money gone to fat the
friar.
Who reads of begging saints in Scripture ? '
— 'Heresy' —
Hath he been here — not found me — gone
again ?
Have I mislearnt our place of meeting ? —
'Bread —
Bread left after the blessing ? ' how they
stared,
That was their main test-question — glared
at me !
'He veil'd Himself in flesh, and now He
veils
His flesh in bread, body and bread to-
gether.'   150
Then rose the howl of all the cassock'd
wolves,
'No bread, no bread. God's body ! ' Arch-
bishop, bishop,
Priors, canons, friars, bell-ringers, parish-
clerks —
'No bread, no bread ! ' — 'Authority of
the Church,
Power of the keys ! ' — Then I, God help
me, I
So mock'd, so spurn'd, so baited two whole
days —

I lost myself and fell from evenness,
And rail'd at all the Popes that, ever since
Sylvester shed the venom of world-wealth
Into the church, had only proven them-
selves   160
Poisoners, murderers. Well — God pardon
all —
Me, them, and all the world — yea, that
proud priest,
That mock-meek mouth of utter Antichrist,
That traitor to King Richard and the
truth,
Who rose and doom'd me to the fire.
                                   Amen !
Nay, I can burn, so that the Lord of life
Be by me in my death.
                     Those three ! the fourth
Was like the Son of God ! Not burnt
were they.
On *them* the smell of burning had not
past.
That was a miracle to convert the king. 170
These Pharisees, this Caiaphas-Arundel
What miracle could turn ? *He* here again,
He thwarting their traditions of Himself,
He would be found a heretic to Himself,
And doom'd to burn alive.
                     So, caught, I burn.
Burn ? heathen men have borne as much
as this,
For freedom, or the sake of those they
loved,
Or some less cause, some cause far less
than mine;
For every other cause is less than mine.
The moth will singe her wings, and singed
return,   180
Her love of light quenching her fear of
pain —
How now, my soul, we do not heed the
fire ?
Faint - hearted ? tut ! — faint - stomach'd !
faint as I am,
God willing, I will burn for Him.
                          Who comes ?
A thousand marks are set upon my head.
Friend ? — foe perhaps — a tussle for it
then !
Nay, but my friend. Thou art so well dis-
guised,
I knew thee not. Hast thou brought bread
with thee ?
I have not broken bread for fifty hours.
None ? I am damn'd already by the
priest   190

For holding there was bread where bread
    was none —
No bread. My friends await me yonder ?
    Yes.
Lead on then. *Up* the mountain ? Is it
    far ?
Not far. Climb first and reach me down
    thy hand.
I am not like to die for lack of bread,
For I must live to testify by fire.[1]

COLUMBUS

Founded on a passage in Irving's 'Life of
Columbus.' 'It was written after repeated
entreaties from certain prominent Americans
that he would commemorate the discovery of
America in verse' ('Memoir,' vol. ii. p. 255).

CHAINS, my good lord ! In your raised
    brows I read
Some wonder at our chamber ornaments.
We brought this iron from our isles of
    gold.

Does the King know you deign to visit him
Whom once he rose from off his throne to
    greet
Before his people, like his brother king ?
I saw your face that morning in the crowd.

At Barcelona — tho' you were not then
So bearded. Yes. The city deck'd herself
To meet me, roar'd my name; the King,
    the Queen,   10
Bade me be seated, speak, and tell them all
The story of my voyage, and while I spoke
The crowd's roar fell as at the 'Peace, be
    still !'
And when I ceased to speak, the King, the
    Queen,
Sank from their thrones, and melted into
    tears,
And knelt, and lifted hand and heart and
    voice
In praise to God who led me thro' the
    waste.
And then the great 'Laudamus' rose to
    heaven.

Chains for the Admiral of the Ocean !
    chains
For him who gave a new heaven, a new
    earth,   20

[1] He was burnt on Christmas Day, 1417.

As holy John had prophesied of me,
Gave glory and more empire to the kings
Of Spain than all their battles ! chains for
    him
Who push'd his prows into the setting sun,
And made West East, and sail'd the
    Dragon's Mouth,
And came upon the Mountain of the World,
And saw the rivers roll from Paradise !

Chains ! we are Admirals of the Ocean,
    we,
We and our sons for ever. Ferdinand
Hath sign'd it and our Holy Catholic
    Queen —   30
Of the Ocean — of the Indics — Admirals
    we —
Our title, which we never mean to yield,
Our guerdon not alone for what we did,
But our amends for all we might have
    done —
The vast occasion of our stronger life —
Eighteen long years of waste, seven in
    your Spain,
Lost, showing courts and kings a truth the
    babe
Will suck in with his milk hereafter —
    earth
A sphere.

    Were *you* at Salamanca ? No.
We fronted there the learning of all Spain,
All their cosmogonies, their astronomies. 41
Guess-work *they* guess'd it, but the golden
    guess
Is morning-star to the full round of truth.
No guess-work ! I was certain of my
    goal;
Some thought it heresy, but that would not
    hold.
King David call'd the heavens a hide, a
    tent
Spread over earth, and so this earth was flat.
Some cited old Lactantius; could it be
That trees grew downward, rain fell up-
    ward, men
Walk'd like the fly on ceilings ? and be-
    sides,   50
The great Augustine wrote that none could
    breathe
Within the zone of heat; so might there be
Two Adams, two mankinds, and that was
    clean
Against God's word. Thus was I beaten
    back,

And chiefly to my sorrow by the Church,
And thought to turn my face from Spain,
    appeal
Once more to France or England; but our
    Queen
Recall'd me, for at last their Highnesses
Were half-assured this earth might be a
    sphere.

All glory to the all-blessed Trinity,   60
All glory to the mother of our Lord,
And Holy Church, from whom I never
    swerved
Not even by one hair's-breadth of heresy,
I have accomplish'd what I came to do.

Not yet — not all — last night a dream
    — I sail'd
On my first voyage, harass'd by the frights
Of my first crew, their curses and their
    groans.
The great flame-banner borne by Teneriffe,
The compass, like an old friend false at
    last
In our most need, appall'd them, and the
    wind   70
Still westward, and the weedy seas — at
    length
The land-bird, and the branch with berries
    on it,
The carven staff — and last the light, the
    light
On Guanahani ! but I changed the name;
San Salvador I call'd it; and the light
Grew as I gazed, and brought out a broad
    sky
Of dawning over — not those alien palms,
The marvel of that fair new nature — not
That Indian isle, but our most ancient East,
Moriah with Jerusalem; and I saw   80
The glory of the Lord flash up, and beat
Thro' all the homely town from jasper,
    sapphire,
Chalcedony, emerald, sardonyx, sardius,
Chrysolite, beryl, topaz, chrysoprase,
Jacynth, and amethyst — and those twelve
    gates,
Pearl — and I woke, and thought — death
    — I shall die —
I am written in the Lamb's own Book of
    Life
To walk within the glory of the Lord
Sunless and moonless, utter light — but no !
The Lord had sent this bright, strange
    dream to me   90

To mind me of the secret vow I made
When Spain was waging war against the
    Moor —
I strove myself with Spain against the
    Moor.
There came two voices from the Sepulchre,
Two friars crying that, if Spain should oust
The Moslem from her limit, he, the fierce
Soldan of Egypt, would break down and
    raze
The blessed tomb of Christ; whereon I
    vow'd
That, if our princes harken'd to my prayer,
Whatever wealth I brought from that new
    world   100
Should, in this old, be consecrate to lead
A new crusade against the Saracen,
And free the Holy Sepulchre from thrall.

Gold ?   I had brought your princes gold
    enough
If left alone !   Being but a Genovese,
I am handled worse than had I been a
    Moor,
And breach'd the belting wall of Cambalu,
And given the Great Khan's palaces to the
    Moor,
Or clutch'd the sacred crown of Prester
    John,   109
And cast it to the Moor. But had I brought
From Solomon's now-recover'd Ophir all
The gold that Solomon's navies carried
    home,
Would that have gilded me ?   Blue blood
    of Spain,
Tho' quartering your own royal arms of
    Spain,
I have not; blue blood and black blood of
    Spain,
The noble and the convict of Castile,
Howl'd me from Hispaniola. For you know
The flies at home, that ever swarm about
And cloud the highest heads, and murmur
    down
Truth in the distance — these outbuzz'd
    me so   120
That even our prudent King, our righteous
    Queen —
I pray'd them being so calumniated
They would commission one of weight and
    worth
To judge between my slander'd self and
    me —
Fonseca my main enemy at their court,
They sent me out his tool, Bovadilla, one

As ignorant and impolitic as a beast —
Blockish irreverence, brainless greed — who
    sack'd
My dwelling, seized upon my papers, loosed
My captives, feed the rebels of the crown,
Sold the crown-farms for all but nothing,
    gave   131
All but free leave for all to work the mines,
Drove me and my good brothers home in
    chains,
And gathering ruthless gold — a single
    piece
Weigh'd nigh four thousand Castillanos —
    so
They tell me — weigh'd him down into the
    abysm —
The hurricane of the latitude on him fell,
The seas of our discovering over-roll
Him and his gold; the frailer caravel,
With what was mine, came happily to the
    shore.   140
There was a glimmering of God's hand.

                                    And God
Hath more than glimmer'd on me.   O my
    lord,
I swear to you I heard His voice between
The thunders in the black Veragua nights,
'O soul of little faith, slow to believe !
Have I not been about thee from thy birth ?
Given thee the keys of the great Ocean-
    sea ?
Set thee in light till time shall be no more ?
Is it I who have deceived thee or the
    world ?
Endure ! thou hast done so well for men,
    that men   150
Cry out against thee.   Was it otherwise
With mine own Son ? '

                        And more than once in days
Of doubt and cloud and storm, when
    drowning hope
Sank all but out of sight, I heard His
    voice,
'Be not cast down.   I lead thee by the
    hand,
Fear not.'   And I shall hear His voice
    again —
I know that He has led me all my life,
I am not yet too old to work His will —
His voice again.

                        Still for all that, my lord,
I lying here bedridden and alone,   160

Cast off, put by, scouted by court and
    king —
The first discoverer starves — his followers,
    all
Flower into fortune — our world's way —
    and I,
Without a roof that I can call mine own,
With scarce a coin to buy a meal withal,
And seeing what a door for scoundrel scum
I open'd to the West, thro' which the lust,
Villainy, violence, avarice, of your Spain
Pour'd in on all those happy naked isles —
Their kindly native princes slain or slaved,
Their wives and children Spanish concu-
    bines,   171
Their innocent hospitalities quench'd in
    blood,
Some dead of hunger, some beneath the
    scourge,
Some over-labor'd, some by their own
    hands, —
Yea, the dear mothers, crazing Nature, kill
Their babies at the breast for hate of
    Spain —
Ah God, the harmless people whom we
    found
In Hispaniola's island-Paradise !
Who took us for the very gods from hea-
    ven,
And we have sent them very fiends from
    hell;   180
And I myself, myself not blameless, I
Could sometimes wish I had never led the
    way.

    Only the ghost of our great Catholic
        Queen
Smiles on me, saying, 'Be thou com-
    forted !
This creedless people will be brought to
    Christ
And own the holy governance of Rome.'

    But who could dream that we, who bore
        the Cross
Thither, were excommunicated there,
For curbing crimes that scandalized the
    Cross,
By him, the Catalonian Minorite,   190
Rome's Vicar in our Indies ? who believe
These hard memorials of our truth to Spain
Clung closer to us for a longer term
Than any friend of ours at Court ? and yet
Pardon — too harsh, unjust.   I am rack'd
    with pains.

You see that I have hung them by my
    bed,
And I will have them buried in my grave.

Sir, in that flight of ages which are God's
Own voice to justify the dead — perchance
Spain, once the most chivalric race on earth,
Spain, then the mightiest, wealthiest realm
    on earth,   201
So made by me, may seek to unbury me,
To lay me in some shrine of this old Spain,
Or in that vaster Spain I leave to Spain.
Then some one standing by my grave will
    say,
'Behold the bones of Christopher Co-
    lòn ' —
'Ay, but the chains, what do *they* mean —
    the chains ? ' —
I sorrow for that kindly child of Spain
Who then will have to answer, ' These
    same chains
Bound these same bones back thro' the
    Atlantic sea,   210
Which he unchain'd for all the world to
    come.'

O Queen of Heaven who seest the souls
    in hell
And purgatory, I suffer all as much
As they do — for the moment. Stay, my
    son
Is here anon; my son will speak for me
Ablier than I can in these spasms that
    grind
Bone against bone. You will not. One
    last word.

You move about the Court; I pray you
    tell
King Ferdinand who plays with me, that
    one
Whose life has been no play with him and
    his   220
Hidalgos — shipwrecks, famines, fevers,
    fights,
Mutinies, treacheries — wink'd at, and con-
    doned —
That I am loyal to him till the death,
And ready — tho' our Holy Catholic Queen,
Who fain had pledged her jewels on my
    first voyage,
Whose hope was mine to spread the Catho-
    lic faith,
Who wept with me when I return'd in
    chains,

Who sits beside the blessed Virgin now,
To whom I send my prayer by night and
    day —
She is gone — but you will tell the King,
    that I,   230
Rack'd as I am with gout, and wrench'd
    with pains
Gain'd in the service of His Highness, yet
Am ready to sail forth on one last voyage,
And readier, if the King would hear, to
    lead
One last crusade against the Saracen,
And save the Holy Sepulchre from thrall.

Going ? I am old and slighted; you
    have dared
Somewhat perhaps in coming ? my poor
    thanks !
I am but an alien and a Genovese.

THE VOYAGE OF MAELDUNE

(FOUNDED ON AN IRISH LEGEND. A. D. 700)

The original story may be found in P. W.
Joyce's ' Old Celtic Romances ' (London, 1879).
According to the tale, Maildun (*Mail Duin*,
chief of the fort) sets forth with sixty chosen
men, to seek the murderer of his father. They
come, as in the poem, to an island where the
man lives, but are driven away by a tempest.
After three days they arrive at ' the island of
the monstrous ants,' each ' as large as a foal ; '
but, not liking the ' eager and hungry look ' of
the insects, they do not land. Three days later
they reach ' the terraced island of birds,' of
which they take great numbers, and then sail
away to a large sandy island, from whose shores
they are frightened by a monster ' somewhat
like a horse in shape,' but with legs like a dog
and blue claws. On the next island they see a
' demon horse-race,' and continue their voyage
to another, whereon is a magnificent palace.
Here they find ' abundance of food and ale,'
but see no inhabitants ; so after eating and
drinking their fill, they thank God and put to
sea again. The ' island of the wonderful apple-
tree,' a single apple from which serves to sup-
ply the travellers with food and drink for
forty days, and successive islands infested with
' blood-thirsty quadrupeds,' strange monsters,
and ' red-hot animals,' are visited in turn ; also
an island where a ' little cat,' living in a splen-
did palace, kills one of Maildun's brothers ;
another island that ' dyed white and black '
— everything on one side of a wall across it

becoming black, and on the other side white; the island 'of the burning river,' and that 'of the miller of hell,' who grinds up all the good things that men complain of, and all that they 'try to conceal from God;' with the isles of 'weeping,' of 'the four precious walls,' of 'the crystal bridge,' of 'speaking birds,' of 'the aged hermit,' and of 'the big blacksmiths,' who remind one of the Cyclops of old. The voyagers also sail over 'the crystal sea,' and another transparent sea beneath whose waters they see a country beautiful indeed, but infested with strange and monstrous animals. Later they come to another island, about which the sea rose up, forming, 'as it were, a wall all round it;' and to another spanned by a stream of water in the form of a rainbow, 'and they hooked down from it many large salmon.' A mighty 'silver pillar standing in the sea' and an 'island standing on one pillar' are other wonders they encounter before arriving at a lovely island, the queen of which detains them long by her magic arts. Escaping at last, they visit 'the isle of intoxicating wine-fruits' and that of 'the mystic lake,' whose waters renewed the youth of the bather, and a third where the people were 'all continually laughing.' They pass 'the isle of the blest' without venturing to land, and soon see a lonely rock whereon a holy hermit dwelt, who, after telling the wonderful story of his life, said to them : 'You shall all reach your own country in safety ; and you, Maildun, you shall find in an island on your way the very man that slew your father; but you are neither to kill him nor take revenge on him in any way. As God has delivered you from the many dangers you have passed through, though you were very guilty and well deserved death at His hands, so do you forgive your enemy the crime he committed against you.' Sailing away, the voyagers come again to the island where this enemy dwelt. It is evening, and the man is at supper with his friends. Maildun and his companions stand outside the house and listen to the conversation going on within. The people happen to be talking of Maildun, and one asks, 'Supposing he came now, what should we do ?' 'I can easily answer that,' said the man of the house ; 'Maildun has been for a long time suffering great afflictions and hardships; and if he were to come now, though we were enemies once, I should certainly give him a welcome and a kind reception.' Maildun at once knocked at the door and made himself known. The wanderers were invited to enter, and 'were joyfully welcomed by the whole household ; new garments were given to them ; and they feasted and rested, till they forgot their weariness and their hardships.'

It will be seen that while the old Celtic tale has suggested to Tennyson a few of the main incidents in the poem, the details are almost entirely of his own invention. The date which he assigns to the legend (A. D. 700) is that which Joyce and others, from internal evidence, accept for the events on which it is founded.

I

I was the chief of the race — he had
    stricken my father dead —
But I gather'd my fellows together, I swore
    I would strike off his head.
Each of them look'd like a king, and was
    noble in birth as in worth,
And each of them boasted he sprang from
    the oldest race upon earth.
Each was as brave in the fight as the bravest hero of song,
And each of them liefer had died than
    have done one another a wrong.
He lived on an isle in the ocean — we sail'd
    on a Friday morn —
He that had slain my father the day before
    I was born.

II

And we came to the isle in the ocean, and
    there on the shore was he.
But a sudden blast blew us out and away
    thro' a boundless sea.   10

III

And we came to the Silent Isle that we
    never had touch'd at before,
Where a silent ocean always broke on a
    silent shore,
And the brooks glitter'd on in the light
    without sound, and the long waterfalls
Pour'd in a thunderless plunge to the base
    of the mountain walls,
And the poplar and cypress unshaken by
    storm flourish'd up beyond sight,
And the pine shot aloft from the crag to an
    unbelievable height,
And high in the heaven above it there
    flicker'd a songless lark,
And the cock could n't crow, and the bull
    could n't low, and the dog could n't
    bark.
And round it we went, and thro' it, but
    never a murmur, a breath —
It was all of it fair as life, it was all of it
    quiet as death,   20
And we hated the beautiful isle, for whenever we strove to speak

Our voices were thinner and fainter than
   any flittermouse-shriek;
And the men that were mighty of tongue
   and could raise such a battle-cry
That a hundred who heard it would rush
   on a thousand lances and die —
O, they to be dumb'd by the charm ! —
   so fluster'd with anger were they
They almost fell on each other; but after
   we sail'd away.

IV

And we came to the Isle of Shouting; we
   landed, a score of wild birds
Cried from the topmost summit with hu-
   man voices and words.
Once in an hour they cried, and whenever
   their voices peal'd
The steer fell down at the plow and the
   harvest died from the field,   30
And the men dropt dead in the valleys and
   half of the cattle went lame,
And the roof sank in on the hearth, and the
   dwelling broke into flame;
And the shouting of these wild birds ran
   into the hearts of my crew,
Till they shouted along with the shouting
   and seized one another and slew.
But I drew them the one from the other;
   I saw that we could not stay,
And we left the dead to the birds, and we
   sail'd with our wounded away.

V

And we came to the Isle of Flowers; their
   breath met us out on the seas,
For the Spring and the middle Summer sat
   each on the lap of the breeze;
And the red passion-flower to the cliffs, and
   the dark-blue clematis, clung,
And starr'd with a myriad blossom the
   long convolvulus hung;   40
And the topmost spire of the mountain was
   lilies in lieu of snow,
And the lilies like glaciers winded down,
   running out below
Thro' the fire of the tulip and poppy, the
   blaze of gorse, and the blush
Of millions of roses that sprang without
   leaf or a thorn from the bush;
And the whole isle-side flashing down from
   the peak without ever a tree
Swept like a torrent of gems from the sky
   to the blue of the sea.

And we roll'd upon capes of crocus and
   vaunted our kith and our kin,
And we wallow'd in beds of lilies, and
   chanted the triumph of Finn,
Till each like a golden image was pollen'd
   from head to feet
And each was as dry as a cricket, with
   thirst in the middle-day heat.   50
Blossom and blossom, and promise of blos-
   som, but never a fruit !
And we hated the Flowering Isle, as we
   hated the isle that was mute,
And we tore up the flowers by the million
   and flung them in bight and bay,
And we left but a naked rock, and in anger
   we sail'd away.

VI

And we came to the Isle of Fruits; all
   round from the cliffs and the capes,
Purple or amber, dangled a hundred
   fathom of grapes,
And the warm melon lay like a little sun
   on the tawny sand,
And the fig ran up from the beach and
   rioted over the land,
And the mountain arose like a jewell'd
   throne thro' the fragrant air,
Glowing with all-color'd plums and with
   golden masses of pear,   60
And the crimson and scarlet of berries that
   flamed upon bine and vine,
But in every berry and fruit was the poison-
   ous pleasure of wine;
And the peak of the mountain was apples,
   the hugest that ever were seen,
And they prest, as they grew, on each
   other, with hardly a leaflet between,
And all of them redder than rosiest health
   or than utterest shame,
And setting, when Even descended, the
   very sunset aflame.
And we stay'd three days, and we gorged
   and we madden'd, till every one
   drew
His sword on his fellow to slay him, and
   ever they struck and they slew;
And myself, I had eaten but sparely, and
   fought till I sunder'd the fray,
Then I bade them remember my father's
   death, and we sail'd away.   70

VII

And we came to the Isle of Fire; we were
   lured by the light from afar,

For the peak sent up one league of fire to
the Northern Star;
Lured by the glare and the blare, but
scarcely could stand upright,
For the whole isle shudder'd and shook like
a man in a mortal affright.
We were giddy besides with the fruits we
had gorged, and so crazed that at last
There were some leap'd into the fire; and
away we sail'd, and we past
Over that undersea isle, where the water is
clearer than air.
Down we look'd — what a garden ! O bliss,
what a Paradise there !
Towers of a happier time, low down in a
rainbow deep   79
Silent palaces, quiet fields of eternal sleep !
And three of the gentlest and best of my
people, whate'er I could say,
Plunged head - down in the sea, and the
Paradise trembled away.

VIII

And we came to the Bounteous Isle, where
the heavens lean low on the land,
And ever at dawn from the cloud glitter'd
o'er us a sun-bright hand,
Then it open'd and dropt at the side of
each man, as he rose from his rest,
Bread enough for his need till the laborless
day dipt under the west;
And we wander'd about it and thro' it. O,
never was time so good !
And we sang of the triumphs of Finn, and
the boast of our ancient blood,
And we gazed at the wandering wave as we
sat by the gurgle of springs,
And we chanted the songs of the Bards and
the glories of fairy kings.   90
But at length we began to be weary, to
sigh, and to stretch and yawn,
Till we hated the Bounteous Isle and the
sun-bright hand of the dawn,
For there was not an enemy near, but the
whole green isle was our own,
And we took to playing at ball, and we took
to throwing the stone,
And we took to playing at battle, but that
was a perilous play,
For the passion of battle was in us, we slew
and we sail'd away.

IX

And we came to the Isle of Witches and
heard their musical cry —

'Come to us, O, come, come !' in the
stormy red of a sky
Dashing the fires and the shadows of dawn
on the beautiful shapes,
For a wild witch naked as heaven stood on
each of the loftiest capes,   100
And a hundred ranged on the rock like
white sea-birds in a row,
And a hundred gamboll'd and pranced on
the wrecks in the sand below,
And a hundred splash'd from the ledges,
and bosom'd the burst of the spray;
But I knew we should fall on each other,
and hastily sail'd away.

X

And we came in an evil time to the Isle of
the Double Towers,
One was of smooth-cut stone, one carved
all over with flowers,
But an earthquake always moved in the
hollows under the dells,
And they shock'd on each other and butted
each other with clashing of bells,
And the daws flew out of the towers and
jangled and wrangled in vain,
And the clash and boom of the bells rang
into the heart and the brain,   110
Till the passion of battle was on us, and all
took sides with the towers,
There were some for the clean-cut stone,
there were more for the carven
flowers,
And the wrathful thunder of God peal'd
over us all the day,
For the one half slew the other, and after
we sail'd away.

XI

And we came to the Isle of a Saint who
had sail'd with Saint Brendan of
yore,
He had lived ever since on the isle and his
winters were fifteen score,
And his voice was low as from other worlds,
and his eyes were sweet,
And his white hair sank to his heels, and
his white beard fell to his feet,
And he spake to me: 'O Maeldune, let be
this purpose of thine !·
Remember the words of the Lord when he
told us, " Vengeance is mine ! "   120
His fathers have slain thy fathers in war or
in single strife,

Thy fathers have slain his fathers, each
    taken a life for a life,
Thy father had slain his father, how long
    shall the murder last ?
Go back to the Isle of Finn and suffer the
    Past to be Past.'
And we kiss'd the fringe of his beard, and
    we pray'd as we heard him pray,
And the holy man he assoil'd us, and sadly
    we sail'd away.

XII

And we came to the isle we were blown
    from, and there on the shore was he,
The man that had slain my father. I saw
    him and let him be.
O, weary was I of the travel, the trouble,
    the strife, and the sin,
When I landed again with a tithe of my
    men, on the Isle of Finn !   130

DE PROFUNDIS:

THE TWO GREETINGS

First published in the 'Ballads' volume of
1880; but, according to Stopford Brooke
('Tennyson,' London, 1894), it was written on
the birth of the poet's eldest son, Hallam
(August 11, 1852), and is 'far the finest of his
speculative poems. Its stately and majestic
sublimity is warmed by the profound emotion
of his fatherhood.'

I

OUT of the deep, my child, out of the
    deep,
Where all that was to be, in all that was,
Whirl'd for a million æons thro' the vast
Waste dawn of multitudinous - eddying
    light —
Out of the deep, my child, out of the
    deep,
Thro' all this changing world of changeless
    law,
And every phase of ever-heightening life,
And nine long months of antenatal gloom,
With this last moon, this crescent — her
    dark orb
Touch'd with earth's light — thou comest,
    darling boy;
Our own; a babe in lineament and limb
Perfect; and prophet of the perfect man;
Whose face and form are hers and mine in
    one,

Indissolubly married like our love.
Live, and be happy in thyself, and serve
This mortal race thy kin so well that men
May bless thee as we bless thee, O young
    life
Breaking with laughter from the dark; and
    may
The fated channel where thy motion lives
Be prosperously shaped, and sway thy
    course
Along the years of haste and random youth
Unshatter'd; then full - current thro' full
    man;
And last in kindly curves, with gentlest fall,
By quiet fields, a slowly-dying power,
To that last deep where we and thou are
    still.

II

I

Out of the deep, my child, out of the
    deep,
From that great deep, before our world be-
    gins,
Whereon the Spirit of God moves as he
    will —
Out of the deep, my child, out of the
    deep,
From that true world within the world we
    see,
Whereof our world is but the bounding
    shore —
Out of the deep, Spirit, out of the deep,
With this ninth moon, that sends the hid-
    den sun
Down yon dark sea, thou comest, darling
    boy.

II

For in the world which is not ours They
    said,
'Let us make man,' and that which should
    be man,
From that one light no man can look upon,
Drew to this shore lit by the suns and
    moons
And all the shadows. O dear Spirit, half-
    lost
In thine own shadow and this fleshly sign
That thou art thou — who wailest being
    born
And banish'd into mystery, and the pain
Of this divisible-indivisible world

Among the numerable-innumerable
Sun, sun, and sun, thro' finite-infinite space
In finite-infinite Time — our mortal veil
And shatter'd phantom of that infinite One,
Who made thee unconceivably Thyself
Out of His whole World-self and all in
   all —
Live thou ! and of the grain and husk, the
   grape
And ivy-berry, choose; and still depart
From death to death thro' life and life, and
   find
Nearer and ever nearer Him, who wrought
Not matter, nor the finite-infinite,
But this main-miracle, that thou art thou,
With power on thine own act and on the
   world.

THE HUMAN CRY

I

HALLOWED be Thy name — Halleluiah ! —
   Infinite Ideality !
   Immeasurable Reality !
   Infinite Personality !
Hallowed be Thy name — Halleluiah !

II

We feel we are nothing — for all is Thou
   and in Thee;
We feel we are something — *that* also has
   come from Thee;
We know we are nothing — but Thou wilt
   help us to be.
Hallowed be Thy name — Halleluiah !

SONNETS

PREFATORY SONNET

TO ' THE NINETEENTH CENTURY '

Contributed to the first number of ' The
Nineteenth Century,' March, 1877, and after-
wards included in the ' Ballads ' volume.

THOSE that of late had fleeted far and fast
To touch all shores, now leaving to the
   skill
Of others their old craft seaworthy still,
Have charter'd this; where, mindful of the
   past,
Our true co-mates regather round the mast;
Of diverse tongue, but with a common will

Here, in this roaring moon of daffodil
And crocus, to put forth and brave the
   blast,
For some, descending from the sacred
   peak
Of hoar high-templed Faith, have leagued
   again
Their lot with ours to rove the world
   about;
And some are wilder comrades, sworn to
   seek
If any golden harbor be for men
In seas of Death and sunless gulfs of
   Doubt.

TO THE REV. W. H. BROOK-FIELD

First printed in Lord Lyttleton's Memoir
(1869) prefixed to Brookfield's ' Sermons,' and
afterwards in the ' Ballads ' volume. Brook-
field was one of the poet's college friends.

BROOKS, for they call'd you so that knew
   you best,
Old Brooks, who loved so well to mouth
   my rhymes,
How oft we two have heard Saint Mary's
   chimes !
How oft the Cantab supper, host and guest,
Would echo helpless laughter to your jest !
How oft with him we paced that walk of
   limes,
Him, the lost light of those dawn-golden
   times,
Who loved you well !   Now both are gone
   to rest.
You man of humorous-melancholy mark,
Dead of some inward agony — is it so ?
Our kindlier, trustier Jaques, past away !
I cannot laud this life, it looks so dark.
Σκιᾶς ὄναρ — dream of a shadow, go —
God bless you !   I shall join you in a day.

MONTENEGRO

First printed in ' The Nineteenth Century,'
March, 1877.

THEY rose to where their sovran eagle
   sails,
They kept their faith, their freedom, on
   the height,

Chaste, frugal, savage, arm'd by day and
    night
Against the Turk; whose inroad nowhere
    scales
Their headlong passes, but his footstep
    fails,
And red with blood the Crescent reels
    from fight
Before their dauntless hundreds, in prone
    flight
By thousands down the crags and thro' the
    vales.
O smallest among peoples! rough rock-
    throne
Of Freedom! warriors beating back the
    swarm
Of Turkish Islam for five hundred years,
Great Tsernogora! never since thine own
Black ridges drew the cloud and brake the
    storm
Has breathed a race of mightier mountain-
    eers.

TO VICTOR HUGO

Contributed to 'The Nineteenth Century'
for June, 1877. It was written after a visit of
Lionel Tennyson to the French poet, who after-
wards thanked the author for the sonnet in a
letter printed in the 'Memoir' (vol. ii. p. 218).

VICTOR in Drama, Victor in Romance,
Cloud - weaver of phantasmal hopes and
    fears,
French of the French, and Lord of human
    tears;
Child-lover; Bard whose fame-lit laurels
    glance
Darkening the wreaths of all that would
    advance,
Beyond our strait, their claim to be thy
    peers;
Weird Titan by thy winter weight of years
As yet unbroken, stormy voice of France!
Who dost not love our England — so they
    say;
I know not — England, France, all man to
    be
Will make one people ere man's race be
    run:
And I, desiring that diviner day,
Yield thee full thanks for thy full cour-
    tesy
To younger England in the boy my son.

TRANSLATIONS, ETC.

BATTLE OF BRUNANBURH

A translation from the Anglo-Saxon, first
printed in the 'Ballads' volume, with the fol-
lowing prefatory note : —
'Constantinus, King of the Scots, after hav-
ing sworn allegiance to Athelstan, allied him-
self with the Danes of Ireland under Anlaf,
and invading England, was defeated by Ath-
elstan and his brother Edmund with great
slaughter at Brunanburh in the year 937.'

I

[1] ATHELSTAN King,
Lord among Earls,
Bracelet-bestower and
Baron of Barons,
He with his brother,
Edmund Atheling,
Gaining a lifelong
Glory in battle,
Slew with the sword-edge
There by Brunanburh,
Brake the shield-wall,
Hew'd the linden-wood,[2]
Hack'd the battle-shield,
Sons of Edward with hammer'd brands.

II

Theirs was a greatness
Got from their grandsires —
Theirs that so often in
Strife with their enemies
Struck for their hoards and their hearths
    and their homes.

III

Bow'd the spoiler,
Bent the Scotsman,
Fell the ship-crews
Doom'd to the death.
All the field with blood of the fighters
Flow'd, from when first the great
Sun-star of morning-tide,
Lamp of the Lord God
Lord everlasting,
Glode over earth till the glorious creature
Sank to his setting.

[1] I have more or less availed myself of my
son's prose translation of this poem in the
'Contemporary Review' (November, 1876).
[2] Shields of lindenwood.

IV

There lay many a man
Marr'd by the javelin,
Men of the Northland
Shot over shield.
There was the Scotsman
Weary of war.

V

We the West-Saxons,
Long as the daylight
Lasted, in companies
Troubled the track of the host that we
    hated;
Grimly with swords that were sharp from
    the grindstone,
Fiercely we hack'd at the flyers before us.

VI

Mighty the Mercian,
Hard was his hand-play,
Sparing not any of
Those that with Anlaf,
Warriors over the
Weltering waters
Borne in the bark's-bosom,
Drew to this island —
Doom'd to the death.

VII

Five young kings put asleep by the sword-
    stroke,
Seven strong earls of the army of Anlaf
Fell on the war-field, numberless numbers,
Shipmen and Scotsmen.

VIII

Then the Norse leader —
Dire was his need of it,
Few were his following —
Fled to his war-ship;
Fleeted his vessel to sea with the king in
    it,
Saving his life on the fallow flood.

IX

Also the crafty one,
Constantinus,
Crept to his North again,
Hoar-headed hero !

X

Slender warrant had
He to be proud of

The welcome of war-knives —
He that was reft of his
Folk and his friends that had
Fallen in conflict,
Leaving his son too
Lost in the carnage,
Mangled to morsels,
A youngster in war !

XI

Slender reason had
He to be glad of
The clash of the war-glaive —
Traitor and trickster
And spurner of treaties —
He nor had Anlaf
With armies so broken
A reason for bragging
That they had the better
In perils of battle
On places of slaughter —
The struggle of standards,
The rush of the javelins,
The crash of the charges,[1]
The wielding of weapons —
The play that they play'd with
The children of Edward.

XII

Then with their nail'd prows
Parted the Norsemen, a
Blood-redden'd relic of
Javelins over
The jarring breaker, the deep-sea billow,
Shaping their way toward Dyflen [2] again,
Shamed in their souls.

XIII

Also the brethren,
King and Atheling,
Each in his glory,
Went to his own in his own West-Saxon-
    land,
Glad of the war.

XIV

Many a carcase they left to be carrion,
Many a livid one, many a sallow-skin —
Left for the white-tail'd eagle to tear it,
    and
Left for the horny-nibb'd raven to rend it,
    and

---

[1] Lit. ' the gathering of men.'
[2] Dublin.

Gave to the garbaging war-hawk to gorge
  it, and
That gray beast, the wolf of the weald.

XV

Never had huger
Slaughter of heroes
Slain by the sword-edge —
Such as old writers
Have writ of in histories —
Hapt in this isle, since
Up from the East hither
Saxon and Angle from
Over the broad billow
Broke into Britain with
Haughty war-workers who
Harried the Welshman, when
Earls that were lured by the
Hunger of glory gat
Hold of the land.

ACHILLES OVER THE TRENCH

[ILIAD, XVIII. 202]

First printed in 'The Nineteenth Century'
for August, 1877.

So saying, light-foot Iris pass'd away.
Then rose Achilles dear to Zeus; and
  round
The warrior's puissant shoulders Pallas
  flung
Her fringed ægis, and around his head
The glorious goddess wreath'd a golden
  cloud,
And from it lighted an all-shining flame.
As when a smoke from a city goes to heaven
Far off from out an island girt by foes,
All day the men contend in grievous war
From their own city, but with set of sun
Their fires flame thickly, and aloft the glare
Flies streaming, if perchance the neighbors
  round
May see, and sail to help them in the war;
So from his head the splendor went to hea-
  ven.
From wall to dyke he stept, he stood, nor
  join'd
The Achæans — honoring his wise mother's
  word —
There standing, shouted, and Pallas far
  away
Call'd; and a boundless panic shook the foe.

For like the clear voice when a trumpet
  shrills,
Blown by the fierce beleaguerers of a town,
So rang the clear voice of Æakidês;
And when the brazen cry of Æakidês
Was heard among the Trojans, all their
  hearts
Were troubled, and the full-maned horses
  whirl'd
The chariots backward, knowing griefs at
  hand;
And sheer-astounded were the charioteers
To see the dread, unweariable fire
That always o'er the great Peleion's head
Burn'd, for the bright-eyed goddess made
  it burn.
Thrice from the dyke he sent his mighty
  shout,
Thrice backward reel'd the Trojans and
  allies;
And there and then twelve of their noblest
  died
Among their spears and chariots.

TO PRINCESS FREDERICA ON HER MARRIAGE

Written on the marriage of Princess Freder-
ica of Hanover to Baron Alphonse de Pawel-
Rammingen at Windsor, April 24, 1880; and
included in the 'Ballads' volume.

The Princess was the daughter of George V.
of Hanover, who died June 12, 1878.

O YOU that were eyes and light to the
  King till he past away
  From the darkness of life —
He saw not his daughter — he blest her:
  the blind King sees you to-day,
  He blesses the wife.

SIR JOHN FRANKLIN

ON THE CENOTAPH IN WESTMINSTER ABBEY

Written in 1877, and included in the 'Bal-
lads' volume.

NOT here! the white North has thy bones;
  and thou,
  Heroic sailor-soul,
Art passing on thine happier voyage now
  Toward no earthly pole.

TO DANTE

(WRITTEN AT REQUEST OF THE FLOREN-
TINES)

Written for the festival in honor of Dante, opened by the King of Italy on the 14th of May, 1865, the six hundredth anniversary of the birth of the poet; and printed in the 'Ballads' volume. Tennyson did not go to Florence at the time, but sent the lines by Lord Houghton. For some curious facts concerning them, see the 'Memoir,' vol. ii. p. 255.

KING, that hast reign'd six hundred years, and grown
In power, and ever growest, since thine own
Fair Florence honoring thy nativity,
Thy Florence now the crown of Italy,
Hath sought the tribute of a verse from me,
I, wearing but the garland of a day,
Cast at thy feet one flower that fades away.

TIRESIAS

AND OTHER POEMS

This volume was published in 1885, with the following dedication : —

TO MY GOOD FRIEND
ROBERT BROWNING
WHOSE GENIUS AND GENIALITY
WILL BEST APPRECIATE WHAT MAY BE BEST
AND MAKE MOST ALLOWANCE FOR WHAT MAY BE WORST
THIS VOLUME
IS
AFFECTIONATELY DEDICATED

Mr. Arthur Waugh ('Alfred Lord Tennyson,' 2d ed., London, 1893), remarks : 'It is characteristic of a certain shyness in Tennyson that he never told Browning of the dedication, and it was not until the book was in the hands of the public that the latter learned the circumstance from a friend.'

The poems that follow, as far as the lines 'To H. R. H. Princess Beatrice,' were included in the 'Tiresias' volume. The Idyll, 'Balin and Balan,' also appeared in this volume for the first time.

TO E. FITZGERALD

This introduction to the poem that follows was apparently written on or about March 31, 1883, when Fitzgerald was seventy-five years of age. He was rather more than a year older than Tennyson, who was born August 6, 1809. He died June 14, 1883, before the volume containing the poem was published.

OLD FITZ, who from your suburb grange,
  Where once I tarried for a while,
Glance at the wheeling orb of change,
  And greet it with a kindly smile;
Whom yet I see as there you sit
  Beneath your sheltering garden-tree,
And watch your doves about you flit,
  And plant on shoulder, hand, and knee,

Or on your head their rosy feet,
  As if they knew your diet spares
Whatever moved in that full sheet
  Let down to Peter at his prayers;
Who live on milk and meal and grass;
  And once for ten long weeks I tried
Your table of Pythagoras,
  And seem'd at first 'a thing enskied,'
As Shakespeare has it, airy-light
  To float above the ways of men,
Then fell from that half-spiritual height
  Chill'd, till I tasted flesh again
One night when earth was winter-black,
  And all the heavens flash'd in frost;
And on me, half-asleep, came back
  That wholesome heat the blood had lost,
And set me climbing icy capes
  And glaciers, over which there roll'd

To meet me long-arm'd vines with grapes
Of Eshcol hugeness; for the cold
Without, and warmth within me, wrought
To mould the dream; but none can say
That Lenten fare makes Lenten thought
Who reads your golden Eastern lay,
Than which I know no version done
In English more divinely well;
A planet equal to the sun
Which cast it, that large infidel
Your Omar; and your Omar drew
Full-handed plaudits from our best
In modern letters, and from two,
Old friends outvaluing all the rest,
Two voices heard on earth no more;
But we old friends are still alive,
And I am nearing seventy-four,
While you have touch'd at seventy-five,
And so I send a birthday line
Of greeting; and my son, who dipt
In some forgotten book of mine
With sallow scraps of manuscript,
And dating many a year ago,
Has hit on this, which you will take,
My Fitz, and welcome, as I know,
Less for its own than for the sake
Of one recalling gracious times,
When, in our younger London days,
You found some merit in my rhymes,
And I more pleasure in your praise.

TIRESIAS

First published in 1885, though written
much earlier, as we learn from the dedicatory
poem.

I WISH I were as in the years of old,
While yet the blessed daylight made itself
Ruddy thro' both the roofs of sight, and
woke
These eyes, now dull, but then so keen to
seek
The meanings ambush'd under all they
saw,
The flight of birds, the flame of sacrifice,
What omens may foreshadow fate to man
And woman, and the secret of the Gods.
My son, the Gods, despite of human
prayer,
Are slower to forgive than human kings. 10
The great God Arês burns in anger still
Against the guiltless heirs of him from
Tyre,
Our Cadmus, out of whom thou art, who
found
Beside the springs of Dircê, smote, and
still'd
Thro' all its folds the multitudinous beast,
The dragon, which our trembling fathers
call'd
The God's own son.
                    A tale, that told to me,
When but thine age, by age as winter-
white
As mine is now, amazed, but made me
yearn
For larger glimpses of that more than
man
Which rolls the heavens, and lifts and lays
the deep,   20
Yet loves and hates with mortal hates and
loves,
And moves unseen among the ways of
men.
   Then, in my wanderings all the lands
that lie
Subjected to the Heliconian ridge
Have heard this footstep fall, altho' my
wont
Was more to scale the highest of the
heights
With some strange hope to see the nearer
God.
One naked peak — the sister of the Sun
Would climb from out the dark, and linger
there   30
To silver all the valleys with her shafts —
There once, but long ago, five-fold thy
term
Of years, I lay; the winds were dead for
heat;
The noonday crag made the hand burn;
and sick
For shadow — not one bush was near — I
rose,
Following a torrent till its myriad falls
Found silence in the hollows underneath.
   There in a secret olive-glade I saw
Pallas Athene climbing from the bath 39
In anger; yet one glittering foot disturb'd
The lucid well; one snowy knee was prest
Against the margin flowers; a dreadful
light
Came from her golden hair, her golden
helm
And all her golden armor on the grass,
And from her virgin breast, and virgin
eyes

Remaining fixt on mine, till mine grew
    dark
For ever, and I heard a voice that said,
'Henceforth be blind, for thou hast seen
    too much,
And speak the truth that no man may be-
    lieve.'
    Son, in the hidden world of sight that
      lives   50
Behind this darkness, I behold her still,
Beyond all work of those who carve the
    stone,
Beyond all dreams of Godlike womanhood,
Ineffable beauty, out of whom, at a glance,
And as it were, perforce, upon me flash'd
The power of prophesying — but to me
No power — so chain'd and coupled with
    the curse
Of blindness and their unbelief who heard
And heard not, when I spake of famine,
    plague,
Shrine - shattering earthquake, fire, flood,
    thunderbolt,   60
And angers of the Gods for evil done
And expiation lack'd — no power on Fate
Theirs, or mine own ! for when the crowd
    would roar
For blood, for war, whose issue was their
    doom,
To cast wise words among the multitude
Was flinging fruit to lions; nor, in hours
Of civil outbreak, when I knew the twain
Would each waste each, and bring on both
    the yoke
Of stronger states, was mine the voice to
    curb   69
The madness of our cities and their kings.
    Who ever turn'd upon his heel to hear
My warning that the tyranny of one
Was prelude to the tyranny of all ?
My counsel that the tyranny of all
Led backward to the tyranny of one ?
    This power hath work'd no good to aught
    that lives,
And these blind hands were useless in their
    wars.
O, therefore, that the unfulfill'd desire,
The grief for ever born from griefs to be,
The boundless yearning of the prophet's
    heart —   80
Could *that* stand forth, and like a statue,
    rear'd
To some great citizen, win all praise from
    all
Who past it, saying, ' That was he ! '

              In vain !
Virtue must shape itself in deed, and those
Whom weakness or necessity have cramp'd
Within themselves, immerging, each, his
    urn
In his own well, draws solace as he may.
    Menœceus, thou hast eyes, and I can hear
Too plainly what full tides of onset sap
Our seven high gates, and what a weight
    of war   90
Rides on those ringing axles ! jingle of
    bits,
Shouts, arrows, tramp of the horn-footed
    horse
That grind the glebe to powder ! Stony
    showers
Of that ear-stunning hail of Arês crash
Along the sounding walls. Above, below,
Shock after shock, the song-built towers
    and gates
Reel, bruised and butted with the shudder-
    ing
War-thunder of iron rams; and from within
The city comes a murmur void of joy,
Lest she be taken captive — maidens,
    wives,   100
And mothers with their babblers of the
    dawn,
And oldest age in shadow from the night,
Falling about their shrines before their
    Gods,
And wailing, ' Save us.'
              And they wail to thee !
These eyeless eyes, that cannot see thine
    own,
See this, that only in thy virtue lies
The saving of our Thebes; for, yesternight,
To me, the great God Arês, whose one
    bliss
Is war and human sacrifice — himself
Blood-red from battle, spear and helmet
    tipt   110
With stormy light as on a mast at sea,
Stood out before a darkness, crying,
    ' Thebes,
Thy Thebes shall fall and perish, for I
    loathe
The seed of Cadmus — yet if one of these
By his own hand — if one of these —'
              My son,
No sound is breathed so potent to coerce,
And to conciliate, as their names who dare
For that sweet mother land which gave
    them birth
Nobly to do, nobly to die. Their names,

Graven on memorial columns, are a song 120
Heard in the future; few, but more than
    wall
And rampart, their examples reach a hand
Far thro' all years, and everywhere they
    meet
And kindle generous purpose, and the
    strength
To mould it into action pure as theirs.
    Fairer thy fate than mine, if life's best
    end
Be to end well! and thou refusing this,
Unvenerable will thy memory be
While men shall move the lips; but if thou
    dare —
Thou, one of these, the race of Cadmus —
    then 130
No stone is fitted in yon marble girth
Whose echo shall not tongue thy glorious
    doom,
Nor in this pavement but shall ring thy
    name
To every hoof that clangs it, and the
    springs
Of Dircê laving yonder battle-plain,
Heard from the roofs by night, will mur-
    mur thee
To thine own Thebes, while Thebes thro'
    thee shall stand
Firm-based with all her Gods.
             The Dragon's cave
Half hid, they tell me, now in flowing
    vines —
Where once he dwelt and whence he roll'd
    himself 140
At dead of night — thou knowest, and that
    smooth rock
Before it, altar-fashion'd, where of late
The woman-breasted Sphinx, with wings
    drawn back,
Folded her lion paws, and look'd to Thebes.
There blanch the bones of whom she slew,
    and these
Mixt with her own, because the fierce beast
    found
A wiser than herself, and dash'd herself
Dead in her rage; but thou art wise
    enough,
Tho' young, to love thy wiser, blunt the
    curse 149
Of Pallas, hear, and tho' I speak the truth
Believe I speak it, let thine own hand
    strike
Thy youthful pulses into rest and quench
The red God's anger, fearing not to plunge

Thy torch of life in darkness, rather — thou
Rejoicing that the sun, the moon, the stars
Send no such light upon the ways of men
As one great deed.
           Thither, my son, and there
Thou, that hast never known the embrace
    of love, 158
Offer thy maiden life.
           This useless hand!
I felt one warm tear fall upon it. Gone!
He will achieve his greatness.
           But for me,
I would that I were gather'd to my rest,
And mingled with the famous kings of old,
On whom about their ocean-islets flash
The faces of the Gods — the wise man's
    word,
Here trampled by the populace underfoot,
There crown'd with worship — and these
    eyes will find
The men I knew, and watch the chariot
    whirl
About the goal again, and hunters race 169
The shadowy lion, and the warrior-kings,
In height and prowess more than human,
    strive
Again for glory, while the golden lyre
Is ever sounding in heroic ears
Heroic hymns, and every way the vales
Wind, clouded with the grateful incense-
    fume
Of those who mix all odor to the Gods
On one far height in one far-shining fire.

'One height and one far-shining fire!'
    And while I fancied that my friend
For this brief idyll would require 180
    A less diffuse and opulent end,
And would defend his judgment well,
    If I should deem it over nice —
The tolling of his funeral bell
    Broke on my Pagan Paradise,
And mixt the dream of classic times,
    And all the phantoms of the dream,
With present grief, and made the rhymes,
    That miss'd his living welcome, seem
Like would-be guests an hour too late, 190
    Who down the highway moving on
With easy laughter find the gate
    Is bolted, and the master gone.
Gone into darkness, that full light
    Of friendship! past, in sleep, away
By night, into the deeper night!
    The deeper night? A clearer day

Than our poor twilight dawn on earth —
　If night, what barren toil to be !
What life, so maim'd . by night, were
　　worth　　　　　　　　　　　　200
　Our living out ?　Not mine to me
Remembering all the golden hours
　Now silent, and so many dead,
And him the last; and laying flowers,
　This wreath, above his honor'd head,
And praying that, when I from hence
　Shall fade with him into the unknown,
My close of earth's experience
　May prove as peaceful as his own.

THE WRECK

This and the poems that follow were printed
for the first time in the 'Tiresias' volume,
unless otherwise explained in the prefatory
notes.
'The Wreck,' as the 'Memoir' (vol. ii. p. 318)
informs us, was 'suggested by a catastrophe
which happened to an Italian vessel, named the
Rosina, bound from Catania for New York.'

I

HIDE me, mother ! my fathers belong'd to
　　the church of old,
I am driven by storm and sin and death to
　　the ancient fold,
I cling to the Catholic Cross once more, to
　　the Faith that saves.
My brain is full of the crash of wrecks,
　　and the roar of waves,
My life itself is a wreck, I have sullied a
　　noble name,
I am flung from the rushing tide of the
　　world as a waif of shame,
I am roused by the wail of a child, and
　　awake to a livid light,
And a ghastlier face than ever has haunted
　　a grave by night,
I would hide from the storm without, I
　　would flee from the storm within,
I would make my life one prayer for a soul
　　that died in his sin,　　　　　　　10
I was the tempter, mother, and mine was
　　the deeper fall;
I will sit at your feet, I will hide my face,
　　I will tell you all.

II

He that they gave me to, mother, a heed-
　　less and innocent bride —

I never have wrong'd his heart, I have only
　　wounded his pride —
Spain in his blood and the Jew — dark-vis-
　　aged, stately and tall —
A princelier-looking man never stept thro'
　　a prince's hall.
And who, when his anger was kindled,
　　would venture to give him the nay ?
And a man men fear is a man to be loved
　　by the women, they say.
And I could have loved him too, if the
　　blossom can dote on the blight,
Or the young green leaf rejoice in the frost
　　that sears it at night;　　　　　　20
He would open the books that I prized, and
　　toss them away with a yawn,
Repell'd by the magnet of Art to the which
　　my nature was drawn,
The word of the Poet by whom the deeps
　　of the world are stirr'd,
The music that robes it in language be-
　　neath and beyond the word !
My Shelley would fall from my hands when
　　he cast a contemptuous glance
From where he was poring over his Tables
　　of Trade and Finance;
My hands, when I heard him coming, would
　　drop from the chords or the keys,
But ever I fail'd to please him, however I
　　strove to please —
All day long far-off in the cloud of the city,
　　and there
Lost, head and heart, in the chances of
　　dividend, consol, and share —　　30
And at home if I sought for a kindly ca-
　　ress, being woman and weak,
His formal kiss fell chill as a flake of snow
　　on the cheek.
And so, when I bore him a girl, when I
　　held it aloft in my joy,
He look'd at it coldly, and said to me,
　　' Pity it is n't a boy.'
The one thing given me, to love and to live
　　for, glanced at in scorn !
The child that I felt I could die for — as
　　if she were basely born !
I had lived a wild-flower life, I was planted
　　now in a tomb;
The daisy will shut to the shadow, I closed
　　my heart to the gloom;
I threw myself all abroad — I would play
　　my part with the young　　　　　39
By the low foot-lights of the world — and
　　I caught the wreath that was flung.

III

Mother, I have not — however their tongues
    may have babbled of me —
Sinn'd thro' an animal vileness, for all but
    a dwarf was he,
And all but a hunchback too; and I look'd
    at him, first, askance,
With pity — not he the knight for an am-
    orous girl's romance !
Tho' wealthy enough to have bask'd in the
    light of a dowerless smile,
Having lands at home and abroad in a rich
    West-Indian isle;
But I came on him once at a ball, the heart
    of a listening crowd —
Why, what a brow was there ! he was
    seated — speaking aloud
To women, the flower of the time, and men
    at the helm of state —
Flowing with easy greatness and touching
    on all things great,   50
Science, philosophy song — till I felt my-
    self ready to weep
For I knew not what, when I heard that
    voice, — as mellow and deep
As a psalm by a mighty master and peal'd
    from an organ, — roll
Rising and falling — for, mother, the voice
    was the voice of the soul;
And the sun of the soul made day in the
    dark of his wonderful eyes.
Here was the hand that would help me,
    would heal me — the heart that was
    wise !
And he, poor man, when he learnt that I
    hated the ring I wore,
He helpt me with death, and he heal'd me
    with sorrow for evermore.

IV

For I broke the bond.   That day my nurse
    had brought me the child.
The small sweet face was flush'd, but it
    coo'd to the mother and smiled.   60
'Anything ailing,' I ask'd her, ' with baby ?'
    She shook her head,
And the motherless mother kiss'd it, and
    turn'd in her haste and fled.

V

Low warm winds had gently breathed us
    away from the land —
Ten long sweet summer days upon deck,
    sitting hand in hand —

When he clothed a naked mind with the
    wisdom and wealth of his own,
And I bow'd myself down as a slave to his
    intellectual throne,
When he coin'd into English gold some
    treasure of classical song,
When he flouted a statesman's error, or
    flamed at a public wrong,
When he rose as it were on the wings of an
    eagle beyond me, and past
Over the range and the change of the
    world from the first to the last,   70
When he spoke of his tropical home in the
    canes by the purple tide,
And the high star-crowns of his palms on
    the deep-wooded mountain-side,
And cliffs all robed in lianas that dropt to
    the brink of his bay,
And trees like the towers of a minster, the
    sons of a winterless day.
' Paradise there ! ' so he said, but I seem'd
    in Paradise then
With the first great love I had felt for the
    first and greatest of men;
Ten long days of summer and sin — if it
    must be so —
But days of a larger light than I ever again
    shall know —
Days that will glimmer, I fear, thro' life to
    my latest breath;
' No frost there,' so he said, ' as in truest
    love no death.'   80

VI

Mother, one morning a bird with a warble
    plaintively sweet
Perch'd on the shrouds, and then fell flut-
    tering down at my feet;
I took it, he made it a cage, we fondled it,
    Stephen and I,
But it died, and I thought of the child for
    a moment, I scarce know why.

VII

But if sin be sin, not inherited fate, as
    many will say,
My sin to my desolate little one found me
    at sea on a day,
When her orphan wail came borne in the
    shriek of a growing wind,
And a voice rang out in the thunders of
    ocean and heaven, ' Thou hast sinn'd.'
And down in the cabin were we, for the
    towering crest of the tides

Plunged on the vessel and swept in a cata-
   ract off from her sides,   90
And ever the great storm grew with a howl
   and a hoot of the blast
In the rigging, voices of hell — then came
   the crash of the mast.
'The wages of sin is death,' and there I
   began to weep,
'I am the Jonah, the crew should cast me
   into the deep,
For, ah, God! what a heart was mine to
   forsake her even for you!'
'Never the heart among women,' he said,
   'more tender and true.'
'The heart! not a mother's heart, when I
   left my darling alone.'
'Comfort yourself, for the heart of the
   father will care for his own.'
'The heart of the father will spurn her,' I
   cried, 'for the sin of the wife,
The cloud of the mother's shame will enfold
   her and darken her life.'   100
Then his pale face twitch'd. 'O Stephen,
   I love you, I love you, and yet' —
As I lean'd away from his arms — 'would
   God, we had never met!'
And he spoke not — only the storm; till
   after a little, I yearn'd
For his voice again, and he call'd to me,
   'Kiss me!' and there — as I
   turn'd —
'The heart, the heart!' I kiss'd him, I
   clung to the sinking form,
And the storm went roaring above us, and
   he — was out of the storm.

VIII

And then, then, mother, the ship stagger'd
   under a thunderous shock,
That shook us asunder, as if she had struck
   and crash'd on a rock;
For a huge sea smote every soul from the
   decks of the Falcon but one;
All of them, all but the man that was
   lash'd to the helm had gone;   110
And I fell — and the storm and the days
   went by, but I knew no more —
Lost myself — lay like the dead by the
   dead on the cabin floor,
Dead to the death beside me, and lost to
   the loss that was mine,
With a dim dream, now and then, of a
   hand giving bread and wine,

Till I woke from the trance, and the ship
   stood still, and the skies were blue,
But the face I had known, O mother, was
   not the face that I knew.

IX

The strange misfeaturing mask that I saw
   so amazed me that I
Stumbled on deck, half mad. I would fling
   myself over and die!
But one — he was waving a flag — the one
   man left on the wreck —
'Woman,' — he graspt at my arm, — 'stay
   there!' — I crouch'd upon deck —
'We are sinking, and yet there's hope:
   look yonder,' he cried, 'a sail!' 121
In a tone so rough that I broke into pas-
   sionate tears, and the wail
Of a beaten babe, till I saw that a boat was
   nearing us — then
All on a sudden I thought, I shall look on
   the child again.

X

They lower'd me down the side, and there
   in the boat I lay
With sad eyes fixt on the lost sea-home, as
   we glided away,
And I sigh'd as the low dark hull dipt
   under the smiling main,
'Had I stay'd with *him*, I had now — with
   him — been out of my pain.'

XI

They took us aboard. The crew were gentle,
   the captain kind,
But *I* was the lonely slave of an often-
   wandering mind;   130
For whenever a rougher gust might tumble
   a stormier wave,
'O Stephen,' I moan'd, 'I am coming to
   thee in thine ocean-grave.'
And again, when a balmier breeze curl'd
   over a peacefuller sea,
I found myself moaning again, 'O child, I
   am coming to thee.'

XII

The broad white brow of the isle — that
   bay with the color'd sand —
Rich was the rose of sunset there, as we
   drew to the land;
All so quiet the ripple would hardly blanch
   into spray

At the feet of the cliff; and I pray'd —
  'My child,'— for I still could pray,—
'May her life be as blissfully calm, be
  never gloom'd by the curse   139
Of a sin, not hers!'
        Was it well with the child?
          I wrote to the nurse
Who had borne my flower on her hireling
  heart; and an answer came
Not from the nurse — nor yet to the wife
  — to her maiden name!
I shook as I open'd the letter — I knew
  that hand too well —
And from it a scrap, clipt out of the
  'deaths' in a paper, fell.
'Ten long sweet summer days' of fever,
  and want of care!
And gone — that day of the storm — O
  mother, she came to me there!

DESPAIR

First printed in 'The Nineteenth Century'
for November, 1881, with the following pre-
face: 'A man and his wife having lost faith in
a God, and hope of a life to come, and being
utterly miserable in this, resolve to end them-
selves by drowning. The woman is drowned,
but the man rescued by a minister of the sect
he had abandoned.'

I

Is it you, that preach'd in the chapel there
  looking over the sand?
Follow'd us too that night, and dogg'd us,
  and drew me to land?

II

What did I feel that night? You are
  curious. How should I tell?
Does it matter so much what I felt? You
  rescued me — yet — was it well
That you came unwish'd for, uncall'd, be-
  tween me and the deep and my
  doom,
Three days since, three more dark days of
  the Godless gloom
Of a life without sun, without health, with-
  out hope, without any delight
In anything here upon earth? but, ah,
  God! that night, that night
When the rolling eyes of the lighthouse
  there on the fatal neck   9

Of land running out into rock — they had
  saved many hundreds from wreck —
Glared on our way toward death, I remem-
  ber I thought, as we past,
Does it matter how many they saved? we
  are all of us wreck'd at last —
'Do you fear?' and there came thro' the
  roar of the breaker a whisper, a
  breath,
'Fear? am I not with you? I am frighted
  at life, not death.'

III

And the suns of the limitless universe
  sparkled and shone in the sky,
Flashing with fires as of God, but we knew
  that their light was a lie —
Bright as with deathless hope — but, how-
  ever they sparkled and shone,
The dark little worlds running round them
  were worlds of woe like our own —
No soul in the heaven above, no soul on
  the earth below,
A fiery scroll written over with lamentation
  and woe.   20

IV

See, we were nursed in the drear nightfold
  of your fatalist creed,
And we turn'd to the growing dawn, we had
  hoped for a dawn indeed,
When the light of a sun that was coming
  would scatter the ghosts of the past,
And the cramping creeds that had mad-
  den'd the peoples would vanish at
  last,
And we broke away from the Christ, our
  human brother and friend,
For He spoke, or it seem'd that He spoke,
  of a hell without help, without end.

V

Hoped for a dawn, and it came, but the
  promise had faded away;
We had past from a cheerless night to the
  glare of a 'drearier day;
He is only a cloud and a smoke who was
  once a pillar of fire,
The guess of a worm in the dust and the
  shadow of its desire —   30
Of a worm as it writhes in a world of the
  weak trodden down by the strong,
Of a dying worm in a world, all massacre,
  murder, and wrong.

VI

O, we poor orphans of nothing — alone on
   that lonely shore —
Born of the brainless Nature who knew not
   that which she bore !
Trusting no longer that earthly flower
   would be heavenly fruit —
Come from the brute, poor souls — no souls
   — and to die with the brute —

VII

Nay, but I am not claiming your pity; I
   know you of old —
Small pity for those that have ranged
   from the narrow warmth of your
   fold,
Where you bawl'd the dark side of your
   faith and a God of eternal rage,
Till you flung us back on ourselves, and the
   human heart, and the Age.   40

VIII

But pity — the Pagan held it a vice — was
   in her and in me,
Helpless, taking the place of the pitying
   God that should be !
Pity for all that aches in the grasp of an
   idiot power,
And pity for our own selves on an earth
   that bore not a flower;
Pity for all that suffers on land or in air or
   the deep,
And pity for our own selves till we long'd
   for eternal sleep.

IX

'Lightly step over the sands ! the waters
   — you hear them call !
Life with its anguish, and horrors, and
   errors — away with it all !'
And she laid her hand in my own — she
   was always loyal and sweet —
Till the points of the foam in the dusk
   came playing about our feet.   50
There was a strong sea-current would sweep
   us out to the main.
'Ah, God !' tho' I felt as I spoke I was
   taking the name in vain —
'Ah, God !' and we turn'd to each other,
   we kiss'd, we embraced, she and I,
Knowing the love we were used to believe
   everlasting would die.
We had read their know-nothing books, and
   we lean'd to the darker side —

Ah, God, should we find Him, perhaps, per-
   haps, if we died, if we died;
We never had found Him on earth, this
   earth is a fatherless hell —
'Dear love, for ever and ever, for ever
   and ever farewell !'
Never a cry so desolate, not since the world
   began,
Never a kiss so sad, no, not since the com-
   ing of man !   60

X

But the blind wave cast me ashore, and
   you saved me, a valueless life.
Not a grain of gratitude mine ! You have
   parted the man from the wife.
I am left alone on the land, she is all alone
   in the sea;
If a curse meant aught, I would curse you
   for not having let me be.

XI

Visions of youth — for my brain was drunk
   with the water, it seems;
I had past into perfect quiet at length out
   of pleasant dreams,
And the transient trouble of drowning —
   what was it when match'd with the
   pains
Of the hellish heat of a wretched life rush-
   ing back thro' the veins ?

XII

Why should I live ? one son had forged on
   his father and fled,
And if I believed in a God, I would thank
   Him, the other is dead,   70
And there was a baby-girl, that had never
   look'd on the light;
Happiest she of us all, for she past from
   the night to the night.

XIII

But the crime, if a crime, of her eldest-
   born, her glory, her boast,
Struck hard at the tender heart of the
   mother, and broke it almost;
Tho', glory and shame dying out for ever in
   endless time,
Does it matter so much whether crown'd
   for a virtue, or hang'd for a crime ?

XIV

And ruin'd by *him*, by *him*, I stood there,
   naked, amazed

In a world of arrogant opulence, fear'd my-
self turning crazed,
And I would not be mock'd in a mad-
house ! and she, the delicate wife,
With a grief that could only be cured, if
cured, by the surgeon's knife, — 80

XV

Why should we bear with an hour of tor-
ture, a moment of pain,
If every man die for ever, if all his griefs
are in vain,
And the homeless planet at length will be
wheel'd thro' the silence of space,
Motherless evermore of an ever-vanishing
race,
When the worm shall have writhed its last,
and its last brother-worm will have
fled
From the dead fossil skull that is left in
the rocks of an earth that is dead ?

XVI

Have I crazed myself over their horrible
infidel writings ? O, yes,
For these are the new dark ages, you see,
of the popular press,
When the bat comes out of his cave, and
the owls are whooping at noon,
And Doubt is the lord of this dunghill and
crows to the sun and the moon, 90
Till the sun and the moon of our science
are both of them turn'd into blood,
And Hope will have broken her heart, run-
ning after a shadow of good;
For their knowing and know-nothing books
are scatter'd from hand to hand —
We have knelt in your know-all chapel too,
looking over the sand.

XVII

What ! I should call on that Infinite Love
that has served us so well ?
Infinite cruelty rather that made everlast-
ing hell,
Made us, foreknew us, foredoom'd us, and
does what he will with his own;
Better our dead brute mother .who never
has heard us groan !

XVIII

Hell ? if the souls of men were immortal,
as men have been told, 99
The lecher would cleave to his lusts, and
the miser would yearn for his gold,

And so there were hell for ever ! but were
there a God, as you say,
His love would have power over hell till it
utterly vanish'd away.

XIX

Ah, yet — I have had some glimmer, at
times, in my gloomiest woe,
Of a God behind all — after all — the great
God, for aught that I know;
But the God of love and of hell together —
they cannot be thought,
If there be such a God, may the Great God
curse him and bring him to nought !

XX

Blasphemy ! whose is the fault ? is it
mine ? for why would you save
A madman to vex you with wretched words,
who is best in his grave ?
Blasphemy ! ay, why not, being damn'd be-
yond hope of grace ? 109
O, would I were yonder with her, and
away from your faith and your face !
Blasphemy ! true ! I have scared you pale
with my scandalous talk,
But the blasphemy to *my* mind lies all in
the way that you walk.

XXI

Hence ! she is gone ! can I stay ? can I
breathe divorced from the past ?
You needs must have good lynx-eyes if I
do not escape you at last.
Our orthodox coroner doubtless will find it
a felo-de-se,
And the stake and the cross-road, fool, if
you will, does it matter to me ?

THE ANCIENT SAGE

The 'Memoir' (vol. ii. p. 319) quotes from
the poet's MS.: 'The whole poem is very per-
sonal. The passages about "Faith" and the
"Passion of the Past" were more especially
my own personal feelings. This "Passion of
the Past" I used to feel when a boy.'

A THOUSAND summers ere the time of
Christ,
From out his ancient city came a Seer
Whom one that loved and honor'd him, and
yet
Was no disciple, richly garb'd, but worn

From wasteful living, follow'd — in his
 hand
A scroll of verse — till that old man before
A cavern whence an affluent fountain
 pour'd
From darkness into daylight, turn'd and
 spoke:

 'This wealth of waters might but seem
  to draw
From yon dark cave, but, son, the source is
 higher,   10
Yon summit half - a - league in air — and
 higher
The cloud that hides it — higher still the
 heavens
Whereby the cloud was moulded, and
 whereout
The cloud descended. Force is from the
 heights.
I am wearied of our city, son, and go
To spend my one last year among the hills.
What hast thou there? Some death-song
 for the Ghouls
To make their banquet relish? let me read.

 ' " How far thro' all the bloom and brake
  That nightingale is heard! 20
  What power but the bird's could make
  This music in the bird?
  How summer-bright are yonder skies,
  And earth as fair in hue!
  And yet what sign of aught that lies
  Behind the green and blue?
  But man to-day is fancy's fool
  As man hath ever been.
  The nameless Power, or Powers, that rule
  Were never heard or seen." 30

If thou wouldst hear the Nameless, and
 wilt dive
Into the temple-cave of thine own self,
There, brooding by the central altar, thou
Mayst haply learn the Nameless hath a
 voice,
By which thou wilt abide, if thou be wise,
As if thou knewest, tho' thou canst not
 know;
For Knowledge is the swallow on the lake
That sees and stirs the surface-shadow there
But never yet hath dipt into the abysm, 39
The abysm of all abysms, beneath, within
The blue of sky and sea, the green of earth,
And in the million-millionth of a grain
Which cleft and cleft again for evermore,
And ever vanishing, never vanishes,

To me, my son, more mystic than myself,
Or even than the Nameless is to me.
 'And when thou sendest thy free soul
  thro' heaven,
Nor understandest bound nor boundless-
 ness,
Thou seest the Nameless of the hundred
 names.
 'And if the Nameless should withdraw
  from all   50
Thy frailty counts most real, all thy world
Might vanish like thy shadow in the dark.

 ' " And since — from when this earth began —
  The Nameless never came
  Among us, never spake with man,
  And never named the Name " —

Thou canst not prove the Nameless, O my
 son,
Nor canst thou prove the world thou mov-
 est in,
Thou canst not prove that thou art body
 alone,
Nor canst thou prove that thou art spirit
 alone,   60
Nor canst thou prove that thou art both in
 one.
Thou canst not prove thou art immortal,
 no,
Nor yet that thou art mortal — nay, my
 son,
Thou canst not prove that I, who speak
 with thee,
Am not thyself in converse with thyself,
For nothing worthy proving can be proven,
Nor yet disproven. Wherefore thou be
 wise,
Cleave ever to the sunnier side of doubt,
And cling to Faith beyond the forms of
 Faith!
She reels not in the storm of warring
 words,   70
She brightens at the clash of " Yes " and
 " No,"
She sees the best that glimmers thro' the
 worst,
She feels the sun is hid but for a night,
She spies the summer thro' the winter
 bud,
She tastes the fruit before the blossom
 falls,
She hears the lark within the songless egg,
She finds the fountain where they wail'd
 " Mirage! "

' " What Power ? aught akin to Mind,
 The mind in me and you ?
 Or power as of the Gods gone blind   80
 Who see not what they do ? "

But some in yonder city hold, my son,
That none but gods could build this house
 of ours,
So beautiful, vast, various, so beyond
All work of man, yet, like all work of man,
A beauty with defect — till That which
 knows,
And is not known, but felt thro' what we
 feel
Within ourselves is highest, shall descend
On this half-deed, and shape it at the last
According to the Highest in the High-
 est.   90

' " What Power but the Years that make
 And break the vase of clay,
 And stir the sleeping earth, and wake
 The bloom that fades away ?
 What rulers but the Days and Hours
 That cancel weal with woe,
 And wind the front of youth with flowers,
 And cap our age with snow ? "

The days and hours are ever glancing by,
And seem to flicker past thro' sun and
 shade,   100
Or short, or long, as Pleasure leads, or
 Pain,
But with the Nameless is nor day nor hour;
Tho' we, thin minds, who creep from
 thought to thought,
Break into " Thens " and " Whens " the
 Eternal Now —
This double seeming of the single world! —
My words are like the babblings in a
 dream
Of nightmare, when the babblings break
 the dream.
But thou be wise in this dream-world of
 ours,
Nor take thy dial for thy deity,
But make the passing shadow serve thy
 will.   110

' " The years that made the stripling wise
 Undo their work again,
 And leave him, blind of heart and eyes,
 The last and least of men ;
 Who clings to earth, and once would dare
 Hell-heat or Arctic cold,
 And now one breath of cooler air
 Would loose him from his hold.

 His winter chills him to the root,
 He withers marrow and mind ;   120
 The kernel of the shrivell'd fruit
 Is jutting thro' the rind ;
 The tiger spasms tear his chest,
 The palsy wags his head ;
 The wife, the sons, who love him best
 Would fain that he were dead ;
 The griefs by which he once was wrung
 Were never worth the while " —

Who knows ? or whether this earth-narrow
 life   129
Be yet but yolk, and forming in the shell ?

' " The shaft of scorn that once had stung
 But wakes a dotard smile."

The placid gleam of sunset after storm !

' " The statesman's brain that sway'd the past
 Is feebler than his knees ;
 The passive sailor wrecks at last
 In ever-silent seas ;
 The warrior hath forgot his arms,
 The learned all his lore ;
 The changing market frets or charms   140
 The merchant's hope no more :
 The prophet's beacon burn'd in vain,
 And now is lost in cloud ;
 The plowman passes, bent with pain,
 To mix with what he plow'd ;
 The poet whom his age would quote
 As heir of endless fame —
 He knows not even the book he wrote,
 Not even his own name.
 For man has overlived his day,   150
 And, darkening in the light,
 Scarce feels the senses break away
 To mix with ancient Night."

The shell must break before the bird can
 fly.

' " The years that when my youth began
 Had set the lily and rose
 By all my ways where'er they ran,
 Have ended mortal foes ;
 My rose of love for ever gone,
 My lily of truth and trust —   160
 They made her lily and rose in one,
 And changed her into dust.
 O rose-tree planted in my grief,
 And growing on her tomb,
 Her dust is greening in your leaf,
 Her blood is in your bloom.
 O slender lily waving there,
 And laughing back the light,
 In vain you tell me   Earth is fair '
 When all is dark as night."   170

My son, the world is dark with griefs and
   graves,
So dark that men cry out against the hea-
   vens.
Who knows but that the darkness is in
   man ?
The doors of Night may be the gates of
   Light;
For wert thou born or blind or deaf, and
   then
Suddenly heal'd, how wouldst thou glory
   in all
The splendors and the voices of the world !
And we, the poor earth's dying race, and
   yet
No phantoms, watching from a phantom
   shore   179
Await the last and largest sense to make
The phantom walls of this illusion fade,
And show us that the world is wholly fair.

  ' " But vain the tears for darken'd years
     As laughter over wine,
    And vain the laughter as the tears,
     O brother, mine or thine,
    For all that laugh, and all that weep
    And all that breathe are one
    Slight ripple on the boundless deep
     That moves, and all is gone."   190

But that one ripple on the boundless deep
Feels that the deep is boundless, and it-
   self
For ever changing form, but evermore
One with the boundless motion of the deep.

  ' " Yet wine and laughter, friends ! and set
     The lamps alight, and call
    For golden music, and forget
     The darkness of the pall."

If utter darkness closed the day, my
   son —
But earth's dark forehead flings athwart
   the heavens   200
Her shadow crown'd with stars — and yon-
   der — out
To northward — some that never set, but
   pass
From sight and night to lose themselves in
   day.
I hate the black negation of the bier,
And wish the dead, as happier than our-
   selves
And higher, having climb'd one step be-
   yond

Our village miseries, might be borne in
   white
To burial or to burning, hymn'd from
   hence
With songs in praise of death, and crown'd
   with flowers !

  ' " O worms and maggots of to-day   210
     Without their hope of wings ! "

But louder than thy rhyme the silent Word
Of that world-prophet in the heart of man.

  ' " Tho' some have gleams, or so they say,
     Of more than mortal things."

To-day ? but what of yesterday ? for oft
On me, when boy, there came what then I
   call'd,
Who knew no books and no philosophies,
In my boy-phrase, " The Passion of the
   Past."
The first gray streak of earliest summer-
   dawn,   220
The last long strife of waning crimson
   gloom,
As if the late and early were but one —
A height, a broken grange, a grove, a
   flower
Had murmurs, " Lost and gone, and lost
   and gone ! "
A breath, a whisper — some divine fare-
   well —
Desolate sweetness — far and far away —
What had he loved, what had he lost, the
   boy ?
I know not, and I speak of what has been.
  ' And more, my son ! for more than once
   when I
Sat all alone, revolving in myself   230
The word that is the symbol of myself,
The mortal limit of the Self was loosed,
And past into the Nameless, as a cloud
Melts into heaven. I touch'd my limbs,
   the limbs
Were strange, not mine — and yet no shade
   of doubt,
But utter clearness, and thro' loss of self
The gain of such large life as match'd with
   ours
Were sun to spark — unshadowable in
   words,
Themselves but shadows of a shadow-
   world.

  ' " And idle gleams will come and go,   240
     But still the clouds remain ; "

The clouds themselves are children of the Sun.

‘ “ And Night and Shadow rule below
    When only Day should reign.”

And Day and Night are children of the Sun,
And idle gleams to thee are light to me.
Some say, the Light was father of the Night,
And some, the Night was father of the Light,
No night, no day ! — I touch thy world again —
No ill, no good ! such counter-terms, my son,   250
Are border-races, holding each its own
By endless war. But night enough is there
In yon dark city. Get thee back; and since
The key to that weird casket, which for thee
But holds a skull, is neither thine nor mine,
But in the hand of what is more than man,
Or in man’s hand when man is more than man,
Let be thy wail, and help thy fellow-men,
And make thy gold thy vassal, not thy king,   259
And fling free alms into the beggar’s bowl,
And send the day into the darken’d heart;
Nor list for guerdon in the voice of men,
A dying echo from a falling wall;
Nor care — for Hunger hath the evil eye —
To vex the noon with fiery gems, or fold
Thy presence in the silk of sumptuous looms;
Nor roll thy viands on a luscious tongue,
Nor drown thyself with flies in honeyed wine;
Nor thou be rageful, like a handled bee,
And lose thy life by usage of thy sting; 270
Nor harm an adder thro’ the lust for harm,
Nor make a snail’s horn shrink for wantonness.
And more — think well ! Do-well will follow thought,
And in the fatal sequence of this world
An evil thought may soil thy children’s blood;
But curb the beast would cast thee in the mire,
And leave the hot swamp of voluptuousness,
A cloud between the Nameless and thyself,

And lay thine uphill shoulder to the wheel,
And climb the Mount of Blessing, whence, if thou   280
Look higher, then — perchance — thou mayest — beyond
A hundred ever-rising mountain lines,
And past the range of Night and Shadow — see
The high-heaven dawn of more than mortal day
Strike on the Mount of Vision !
                          So, farewell.’

THE FLIGHT

A very early poem, as we learn from the ‘ Memoir,’ though not printed until 1885.

I

ARE you sleeping ? have you forgotten ? do not sleep, my sister dear !
How *can* you sleep ? the morning brings the day I hate and fear;
The cock has crow’d already once, he crows before his time;
Awake ! the creeping glimmer steals, the hills are white with rime.

II

Ah, clasp me in your arms, sister, ah, fold me to your breast !
Ah, let me weep my fill once more, and cry myself to rest !
To rest ? to rest and wake no more were better rest for me,
Than to waken every morning to that face. I loathe to see.

III

I envied your sweet slumber, all night so calm you lay;
The night was calm, the morn is calm, and like another day;   10
But I could wish you moaning sea would rise and burst the shore,
And such a whirlwind blow these woods as never blew before.

IV

For, one by one, the stars went down across the gleaming pane,
And project after project rose, and all of them were vain;

The blackthorn-blossom fades and falls and
leaves the bitter sloe,
The hope I catch at vanishes, and youth is
turn'd to woe.

V

Come, speak a little comfort ! all night I
pray'd with tears,
And yet no comfort came to me, and now
the morn appears,
When he will tear me from your side, who
bought me for his slave;
This father pays his debt with me, and
weds me to my grave.   20

VI

What father, this or mine, was he, who, on
that summer day
When I had fallen from off the crag we
clamber'd up in play,
Found, fear'd me dead, and groan'd, and
took and kiss'd me, and again
He kiss'd me; and I loved him then; he
was my father then.

VII

No father now, the tyrant vassal of a ty-
rant vice !
The godless Jephtha vows his child . . .
to one cast of the dice.
These ancient woods, this Hall at last will
go — perhaps have gone,
Except his own meek daughter yield her
life, heart, soul to one —

VIII

To one who knows I scorn him. O, the
formal mocking bow,
The cruel smile, the courtly phrase that
masks his malice now —   30
But often in the sidelong eyes a gleam of all
things ill —
It is not Love but Hate that weds a bride
against her will;

IX

Hate, that would pluck from this true
breast the locket that I wear,
The precious crystal into which I braided
Edwin's hair !
The love that keeps this heart alive beats
on it night and day —
One golden curl, his golden gift, before he
past away.

X

He left us weeping in the woods; his boat
was on the sand;
How slowly down the rocks he went, how
loth to quit the land !
And all my life was darken'd, as I saw the
white sail run,
And darken, up that lane of light into the
setting sun.   40

XI

How often have we watch'd the sun fade
from us thro' the West,
And follow Edwin to those isles, those
Islands of the Blest !
Is *he* not there ? would I were there, the
friend, the bride, the wife,
With him, where summer never dies, with
Love, the sun of life !

XII

O, would I were in Edwin's arms — once
more — to feel his breath
Upon my cheek — on Edwin's ship, with
Edwin, even in death,
Tho' all about the shuddering wreck the
death-white sea should rave,
Or if lip were laid to lip on the pillows of
the wave !

XIII

Shall I take *him?* I kneel with *him?* I
swear and swear forsworn
To love him most whom most I loathe, to
honor whom I scorn ?   50
The Fiend would yell, the grave would
yawn, my mother's ghost would
rise —
To lie, to lie — in God's own house — the
blackest of all lies !

XIV

Why — rather than that hand in mine, tho'
every pulse would freeze,
I'd sooner fold an icy corpse dead of some
foul disease.
Wed him ? I will not wed him, let them
spurn me from the doors,
And I will wander till I die about the bar-
ren moors.

XV

The dear, mad bride who stabb'd her bride-
groom on her bridal night —

If mad, then I am mad, but sane if she
    were in the right.
My father's madness makes me mad — but
    words are only words !
I am not mad, not yet, not quite — There !
    listen how the birds   60

XVI

Begin to warble yonder in the budding
    orchard trees !
The lark has past from earth to heaven
    upon the morning breeze !
How gladly, were I one of those, how early
    would I wake !
And yet the sorrow that I bear is sorrow
    for *his* sake.

XVII

They love their mates, to whom they sing;
    or else their songs, that meet
The morning with such music, would never
    be so sweet !
And tho' these fathers will not hear, the
    blessed Heavens are just,
And Love is fire, and burns the feet would
    trample it to dust.

XVIII

A door was open'd in the house — who ?
    who ? my father sleeps !
A stealthy foot upon the stair ! he — some
    one — this way creeps !   70
If he ? yes, he — lurks, listens, fears his
    victim may have fled —
He ! where is some sharp-pointed thing ?
    he comes, and finds me dead.

XIX

Not he, not yet ! and time to act — but how
    my temples burn !
And idle fancies flutter me, I know not
    where to turn;
Speak to me, sister, counsel me; this mar-
    riage must not be.
You only know the love that makes the
    world a world to me !

XX

Our gentle mother, had *she* lived — but we
    were left alone.
That other left us to ourselves, he cared
    not for his own;
So all the summer long we roam'd in these
    wild woods of ours,
My Edwin loved to call us then 'his two
    wild woodland flowers.'   80

XXI

Wild flowers blowing side by side in God's
    free light and air,
Wild flowers of the secret woods, when
    Edwin found us there,
Wild woods in which we roved with him,
    and heard his passionate vow,
Wild woods in which we rove no more, if
    we be parted now !

XXII

You will not leave me thus in grief to wan-
    der forth forlorn;
We never changed a bitter word, not once
    since we were born;
Our dying mother join'd our hands; she
    knew this father well;
She bade us love, like souls in heaven, and
    now I fly from hell,

XXIII

And you with me; and we shall light upon
    some lonely shore,
Some lodge within the waste sea-dunes, and
    hear the waters roar,   90
And see the ships from out the West go
    dipping thro' the foam,
And sunshine on that sail at last which
    brings our Edwin home.

XXIV

But look, the morning grows apace, and
    lights the old church-tower,
And lights the clock ! the hand points five
    — O, me ! — it strikes the hour —
I bide no more, I meet my fate, whatever
    ills betide !
Arise, my own true sister, come forth ! the
    world is wide.

XXV

And yet my heart is ill at ease, my eyes are
    dim with dew,
I seem to see a new-dug grave up yonder
    by the yew !
If we should never more return, but wan-
    der hand in hand
With breaking hearts, without a friend,
    and in a distant land !   100

XXVI

O sweet, they tell me that the world is
    hard, and harsh of mind,
But can it be so hard, so harsh, as those
    that should be kind ?

That matters not. Let come what will; at
 last the end is sure,
And every heart that loves with truth is
 equal to endure.

TO-MORROW

Tennyson's one poem in Irish brogue;
founded on a story told him by Aubrey de
Vere.

I

HER, that yer Honor was spakin' to?
 Whin, yer Honor? last year —
Standin' here be the bridge, when last yer
 Honor was here?
An' yer Honor ye gev her the top of the
 mornin', 'To-morra,' says she.
What did they call her, yer Honor? They
 call'd her Molly Magee.
An' yer Honor's the thrue ould blood that
 always manes to be kind,
But there's rason in all things, yer Honor,
 for Molly was out of her mind.

II

Shure, an' meself remimbers wan night
 comin' down be the sthrame,
An' it seems to me now like a bit of yisther-
 day in a dhrame —
Here where yer Honor seen her — there
 was but a slip of a moon,
But I hard thim — Molly Magee wid her
 bachelor, Danny O'Roon —   10
'You've been takin' a dhrop o' the crathur,'
 an' Danny says, 'Troth, an' I been
Dhrinkin' yer health wid Shamus O'Shea
 at Katty's shebeen; [1]
But I must be lavin' ye soon.' 'Ochone,
 are ye goin' away?'
'Goin' to cut the Sassenach whate,' he says,
 'over the say' —
'An' whin will ye meet me agin?' an' I
 hard him, 'Molly asthore,
I'll meet you agin to-morra,' says he, 'be
 the chapel-door.'
'An' whin are ye goin' to lave me?' 'O'
 Monday mornin',' says he;
'An' shure thin ye'll meet me to-morra?'
 'To-morra, to-morra, machree!'
Thin Molly's ould mother, yer Honor, that
 had no likin' for Dan,

[1] Grog-shop.

Call'd from her cabin an' tould her to
 come away from the man,   20
An' Molly Magee kem flyin' acrass me, as
 light as a lark,
An' Dan stood there for a minute, an' thin
 wint into the dark.
But wirrah! the storm that night — the
 tundher, an' rain that fell,
An' the sthrames runnin' down at the back
 o' the glin 'ud 'a dhrownded hell.

III

But airth was at pace nixt mornin', an'
 hiven in its glory smiled,
As the Holy Mother o' Glory that smiles
 at her sleepin' child —
Ethen — she stept an the chapel-green, an'
 she turn'd herself roun'
Wid a diamond dhrop in her eye, for Danny
 was not to be foun',
An' many's the time that I watch'd her at
 mass lettin' down the tear,
For the divil a Danny was there, yer
 Honor, for forty year.   30

IV

Och, Molly Magee, wid the red o' the rose
 an' the white o' the may,
An' yer hair as black as the night, an' yer
 eyes as bright as the day!
Achora, yer laste little whishper was sweet
 as the lilt of a bird!
Acushla, ye set me heart batin' to music
 wid ivery word!
An' sorra the Queen wid her sceptre in
 sich an illigant han',
An' the fall of yer foot in the dance was as
 light as snow an the lan',
An' the sun kem out of a cloud whiniver
 ye walkt in the shtreet,
An' Shamus O'Shea was yer shadda, an' laid
 himself undher yer feet,
An' I loved ye meself wid a heart an' a
 half, me darlin', and be
'Ud 'a shot his own sowl dead for a kiss of
 ye, Molly Magee.   40

V

But shure we wor betther frinds whin I
 crack'd his skull for her sake,
An' he ped me back wid the best he could
 give at ould Donovan's wake —
For the boys wor about her agin whin Dan
 did n't come to the fore,

An' Shamus along wid the rest, but she put
   thim all to the door.
An', afther, I thried her meself av the bird
   'ud come to me call,
But Molly, begorrah, 'ud listhen to naither
   at all, at all.

VI

An' her nabors an' frinds 'ud consowl an'
   condowl wid her, airly an' late,
'Your Danny,' they says, ' niver crasst over
   say to the Sassenach whate;
He 's gone to the States, aroon, an' he 's
   married another wife,
An' ye 'll niver set eyes an the face of the
   thraithur agin in life !   50
An' to dhrame of a married man, death
   alive, is a mortial sin.'
But Molly says, ' I 'd his hand-promise, an'
   shure he 'll meet me agin.'

VII

An' afther her paärints had inter'd glory,
   an' both in wan day,
She began to spake to herself, the crathur,
   an' whishper, an' say,
' To-morra, to-morra !' an' Father Mo-
   lowny he tuk her in han',
'Molly, you 're manin',' he says, 'me dear,
   av I undherstan',
That ye 'll meet your paärints agin an' yer
   Danny O'Roon afore God
Wid his blessed Marthyrs an' Saints;' an'
   she gev him a frindly nod,
' To-morra, to-morra,' she says, an' she
   did n't intind to desave,
But her wits wor dead, an' her hair was as
   white as the snow an a grave.   60

VIII

Arrah now, here last month they wor dig-
   gin' the bog, an' they foun'
Dhrownded in black bog-wather a corp
   lyin' undher groun'.

IX

Yer Honor's own agint, he says to me
   wanst, at Katty's shebeen,
'The divil take all the black lan', for a
   blessin' 'ud come wid the green !'
An' where 'ud the poor man, thin, cut his
   bit o' turf for the fire ?
But och ! bad scran to the bogs whin they
   swallies the man intire !

An' sorra the bog that 's in hiven wid all
   the light an' the glow,
An' there 's hate enough, shure, widout
   thim in the divil's kitchen below.

X

Thim ould blind nagers in Agypt, I hard
   his Riverence say,
Could keep their haithen kings in the flesh
   for the Jidgmint day,   70
An', faix, be the piper o' Moses, they kep'
   the cat an' the dog,
But it 'ud 'a been aisier work av they lived
   be an Irish bog.

XI

How-an-iver they laid this body they foun'
   an the grass,
Be the chapel-door, an' the people 'ud see
   it that wint in to mass —
But a frish gineration had riz, an' most of
   the ould was few,
An' I did n't know him meself, an' nōne of
   the parish knew.

XII

But Molly kem limpin' up wid her stick, —
   she was lamed iv a knee, —
Thin a slip of a gossoon call'd, ' Div ye
   know him, Molly Magee ?'
An' she stood up strait as the queen of the
   world — she lifted her head —
' He said he would meet me to-morra !'
   an' dhropt down dead an the dead. 80

XIII

Och, Molly, we thought, machree, ye would
   start back agin into life,
Whin we laid yez, aich be aich, at yer wake
   like husban' an' wife,
Sorra the dhry eye thin but was wet for the
   frinds that was gone !
Sorra the silent throat but we hard it
   cryin', ' Ochone !'
An' Shamus O'Shea that has now ten
   childer, hansome an' tall,
Him an' his childer wor keenin' as if he
   had lost thim all.

XIV

Thin his Riverence buried thim both in
   wan grave be the dead boor-tree,[1]
The young man Danny O'Roon wid his ould
   woman, Molly Magee.

   [1] Elder-tree.

XV

May all the flowers o' Jeroosilim blossom
an' spring from the grass,
Imbrashin' an' kissin' aich other — as ye
did — over yer Crass ! 90
An' the lark fly out o' the flowers wid his
song to the sun an' the moon,
An' tell thim in hiven about Molly Magee
an' her Danny O'Roon,
Till Holy Saint Pether gets up wid his kays
an' opens the gate !
An' shure, be the Crass, that 's betther nor
cuttin' the Sassenach whate,
To be there wid the Blessed Mother an'
Saints an' Marthyrs galore,
An' singin' yer ' Aves ' an' ' Pathers ' for
iver an' ivermore.

XVI

An' now that I tould yer Honor whativer
I hard an' seen,
Yer Honor 'ill give me a thrifle to dhrink
yer health in potheen.

THE SPINSTER'S SWEET-ARTS

I

MILK for my sweet-arts, Bess ! fur it mun
be the time about now
When Molly cooms in fro' the far-end close
wi' her paäils fro' the cow.
Eh ! tha be new to the plaäce — thou 'rt
gaäpin' — does n't tha see
I calls 'em arter the fellers es once was
sweet upo' me ?

II

Naäy, to be sewer, it be past 'er time.
What maäkes 'er sa laäte ?
Goä to the laäne at the back, an' looök thruf
Maddison's gaäte !

III

Sweet-arts ! Molly belike may 'a lighted
to-night upo' one.
Sweet-arts ! thanks to the Lord that I niver
not listen'd to noän !
So I sits i' my oän armchair wi' my oän
kettle theere o' the hob,
An' Tommy the fust, an' Tommy the sec-
ond, an' Steevie an' Rob. 10

IV

Rob, coom oop 'ere o' my knee. Thou sees
that i' spite o' the men
I 'a kep' thruf thick an' thin my two
'oonderd a-year to mysen;
Yis ! thaw tha call'd me es pretty es ony
lass i' the Shere;
An' thou be es pretty a tabby, but Robby
I seed thruf ya theere.

V

Feyther 'ud saäy I wur ugly es sin, an' I
beänt not vaäin,
But I niver wur downright hugly, thaw
soom 'ud 'a thowt ma plaäin,
An' I was n't sa plaäin i' pink ribbons — ye
said I wur pretty i' pinks,
An' I liked to 'ear it I did, but I beänt
sich a fool as ye thinks;
Ye was stroäkin' ma down wi' the 'air, as I
be a-stroäkin' o' you,
But whiniver I loooäked i' the glass I wur
sewer that it could n't be true; 20
Niver wur pretty, not I, but ye knaw'd it
wur pleasant to 'ear,
Thaw it warn't not me es wur pretty, but
my two 'oonderd a-year.

VI

D' ya mind the murnin' when we was
a-walkin' togither, an' stood
By the claäy'd-oop pond, that the foälk be
sa scared at, i' Gigglesby wood,
Wheer the poor wench drowndid hersen,
black Sal, es 'ed been disgraäced ?
An' I feel'd thy arm es I stood wur
a-creeäpin' about my waäist;
An' me es wur allus afear'd of a man's git-
tin' ower fond,
I sidled awaäy an' awaäy till I plumpt foot
fust i' the pond;
And, Robby, I niver 'a liked tha sa well, as
I did that daäy,
Fur tha joompt in thysen, an' tha hoickt
my feet wi' a flop fro' the claäy. 30
Ay, stick oop thy back, an' set oop thy
taäil, tha may gie ma a kiss,
Fur I walk'd wi' tha all the way hoäm an'
wur niver sa nigh saäyin' Yis.
But wa boäth was i' sich a clat we was
shaämed to cross Gigglesby Greeän,
Fur a cat may looök at a king, thou knaws,
but the cat mun be cleän.

Sa we boäth on us kep' out o' sight o' the
   winders o' Gigglesby Hinn —
Naäy, but the claws o' tha ! quiet ! they
   pricks cleän thruf to the skin —
An' wa boäth slinkt 'oäm by the brokken
   shed i' the laäne at the back,
Wheer the poodle runn'd at tha once, an'
   thou runn'd oop o' the thack;
An' tha squeedg'd my 'and i' the shed, fur
   theere we was forced to 'ide,
Fur I seed that Steevie wur coomin', and
   one o' the Tommies beside.   40

VII

Theere now, what art 'a mewin' at, Stee-
   vie ? for owt I can tell —
Robby wur fust, to be sewer, or I mowt 'a
   liked tha as well.

VIII

But, Robby, I thowt o' tha all the while I
   wur chaängin' my gown,
An' I thowt, shall I chaänge my staäte ?
   but, O Lord, upo' coomin' down —
My bran-new carpet es fresh es a midder
   o' flowers i' Maäy —
Why 'ed n't tha wiped thy shoes ? it wur
   clatted all ower wi' claäy.
An' I could 'a cried ammost, fur I seed that
   it could n't be,
An', Robby, I gied tha a raätin' that sat-
   tled thy coortin' o' me.
An' Molly an' me was agreed, as we was
   a-cleänin' the floor,
That a man be a durty thing an' a trouble
   an' plague wi' indoor.   50
But I rued it arter a bit, fur I stuck to tha
   moor na the rest,
But I could n't 'a lived wi' a man, an' I
   knaws it be all fur the best.

IX

Naäy — let ma stroäk tha down till I
   maäkes tha es smooth es silk,
But if I 'ed married tha, Robby, thou 'd
   not 'a been worth thy milk,
Thou 'd niver 'a cotch'd ony mice but 'a
   left me the work to do,
And 'a taäen to the bottle beside, so es all
   that I 'ears be true;
But I loovs tha to maäke thysen 'appy, an'
   soä purr awaäy, my dear,
Thou 'ed wellnigh purr'd ma awaäy fro' my
   oän two 'oonderd a-year.

X

Sweärin' ageän, you Toms, as ye used to do
   twelve year sin' !
Ye niver eärd Steevie sweär 'cep' it wur at
   a dog coomin' in,   60
An' boäth o' ye mun be fools to be hallus
   a-shawin' your claws,
Fur I niver cared nothink for neither — an'
   one o' ye deäd, ye knaws !
Coom, give hoäver then, weänt ye ? I war-
   rant ye soom fine daäy —
Theere, lig down — I shall hev to gie one
   or tother awaäy.
Can't ye taäke pattern by Steevie ? ye
   shan't hev a drop fro' the paäil.
Steevie be right good manners bang thruf
   to the tip o' the taäil.

XI

Robby, git down wi' tha, wilt tha ? let
   Steevie coom oop o' my knee.
Steevie, my lad, thou 'ed very nigh been
   the Steevie fur me !
Robby wur fust, to be sewer, 'e wur burn
   an' bred i' the 'ouse,
But thou be es 'ansom a tabby es iver patted
   a mouse.   70

XII

An' I beänt not vaäin, but I knaws I 'ed
   led tha a quieter life
Nor her wi' the hepitaph yonder ! ' A
   faäithful an' loovin' wife ! '
An' 'cos o' thy farm by the beck, an' thy
   windmill oop o' the croft,
Tha thowt tha would marry ma, did tha ?
   but that wur a bit ower soft,
Thaw thou was es soäber es daäy, wi' a
   niced red faäce, an' es cleän
Es a shillin' fresh fro' the mint wi' a bran-
   new 'eäd o' the Queeän,
An' thy farmin' es cleän es thysen, fur,
   Steevie, tha kep' it sa neät
That I niver not spied sa much es a poppy
   along wi' the wheät,
An' the wool of a thistle a-flyin' an' seeädin'
   tha haäted to see;
'T wur es bad es a battle-twig [1] 'ere i' my
   oän blue chaumber to me.   80
Ay, roob thy whiskers ageän ma, fur I
   could 'a taäen to tha well,
But fur thy bairns, poor Steevie, a bouncin'
   boy an' a gell.

[1] Earwig.

XIII

An' thou was es fond o' thy bairns es I be
    mysen o' my cats,
But I niver not wish'd fur childer, I hev n't
    naw likin' fur brats;
Pretty anew when ya dresses 'em oop, an'
    they goäs fur a walk,
Or sits wi' their 'auds afoor 'em, an' does n't
    not 'inder the talk !
But their bottles o' pap, an' their mucky
    bibs, an' the clats an' the clouts,
An' their mashin' their toys to pieäces an'
    maäkin' ma deäf wi' their shouts,
An' hallus a-joompin' about ma as if they
    was set upo' springs,
An' a haxin' ma hawkard questions, an'
    saäyin' ondecent things,   90
An' a-callin' ma ' hugly ' mayhap to my
    faäce, or a-teärin' my gown —
Dear ! dear ! dear ! I mun part them
    Tommies — Steevie, git down.

XIV

Ye be wuss nor the men-tommies, you. I
    tell'd ya, na moor o' that !
Tom, lig theere o' the cushion, an' tother
    Tom 'ere o' the mat.

XV

Theere ! I ha' master'd *them !* Hed I mar-
    ried the Tommies — O Lord,
To loove an' obaäy the Tommies ! I could n't
    'a stuck by my word.
To be horder'd about, an' waäked, when
    Molly 'd put out the light,
By a man coomin' in wi' a hiccup at ony
    hour o' the night !
An' the taäble staäin'd wi' 'is aäle, an' the
    mud o' 'is boots o' the stairs,
An' the stink o' 'is pipe i' the 'ouse, an' the
    mark o' 'is 'eäd o' the chairs !   100
An' noän o' my four sweet-arts 'ud 'a let
    me 'a hed my oän waäy,
Sa I likes 'em best wi' taäils when they
    'ev n't a word to saäy.

XVI

An' I sits i' my oän little parlor, an' sarved
    by my oän little lass,
Wi' my oän little garden outside, an' my
    oän bed o' sparrow-grass,
An' my oän door-poorch wi' the woodbine
    an' jessmine a-dressin' it greeän,
An' my oän fine Jackman i' purple a
    roäbin' the 'ouse like a queeän.

XVII

An' the little gells bobs to ma hoffens es I
    be abroad i' the laänes,
When I goäs fur to coomfut the poor es be
    down wi' their haäches an' their
    paäins:
An' a haäf-pot o' jam, or a mossel o' meät
    when it beänt too dear,
They maäkes ma a graäter lady nor 'er i'
    the mansion theer,   110
Hes 'es hallus to hax of a man how much
    to spare or to spend;
An' a spinster I be an' I will be, if soä
    pleäse God, to the hend.

XVIII

Mew ! mew ! — Bess wi' the milk ! what
    ha maäde our Molly sa laäte ?
It should 'a been 'ere by seven, an' theere
    — it be strikin' height —
' Cushie wur craäzed fur 'er cauf,' well —
    I 'eärd 'er a-maäkin' 'er moän,
An' I thowt to mysen, ' thank God that I
    hev n't naw cauf o' my oän.'
Theere !
    Set it down !
            Now, Robby !
    You Tommies shall waäit to-night
Till Robby an' Steevie 'es 'ed their lap —
    an' it sarves ye right.

PROLOGUE

TO GENERAL HAMLEY

The poem introduced by this Prologue was
printed in ' Macmillan's Magazine ' for March,
1882. The Prologue and Epilogue were added
when it appeared in the ' Tiresias ' volume,
1885.

Sir Edward Bruce Hamley was born at Bod-
win in Cornwall, April 27, 1824. He entered
the army in 1843 ; served in the Crimean War ;
was successively professor of military history
and commandant at the Staff College, Sand-
hurst (1858–77) ; was chief of the commission
for the delimitation of the Balkan and Arme-
nian frontiers (1879–80) ; and commanded a
division in the Egyptian war of 1882. He was
also the author of several works on military
subjects. He died August 12, 1893.

Our birches yellowing and from each
    The light leaf falling fast,

While squirrels from our fiery beech
  Were bearing off the mast,
You came, and look'd and loved the view
  Long-known and loved by me,
Green Sussex fading into blue
  With one gray glimpse of sea;
And, gazing from this height alone,
  We spoke of what had been
Most marvellous in the wars your own
  Crimean eyes had seen;
And now — like old-world inns that take
  Some warrior for a sign
That therewithin a guest may make
  True cheer with honest wine —
Because you heard the lines I read
  Nor utter'd word of blame,
I dare without your leave to head
  These rhymings with your name,
Who know you but as one of those
  I fain would meet again,
Yet know you, as your England knows
  That you and all your men
Were soldiers to her heart's desire,
  When, in the vanish'd year,
You saw the league-long rampart-fire
  Flare from Tel-el-Kebir
Thro' darkness, and the foe was driven,
  And Wolseley overthrew
Arâbi, and the stars in heaven
  Paled, and the glory grew.

THE CHARGE OF THE HEAVY BRIGADE AT BALACLAVA

OCTOBER 25, 1854

I

THE charge of the gallant three hundred,
  the Heavy Brigade !
Down the hill, down the hill, thousands of
  Russians,
Thousands of horsemen, drew to the valley
  — and stay'd;
For Scarlett and Scarlett's three hundred
  were riding by
When the points of the Russian lances
  arose in the sky;
And he call'd, ' Left wheel into line ! ' and
  they wheel'd and obey'd.
Then he look'd at the host that had halted
  he knew not why,
And he turn'd half round, and he bade his
  trumpeter sound
To the charge, and he rode on ahead, as he
  waved his blade

To the gallant three hundred whose glory
  will never die —
' Follow,' and up the hill, up the hill, up
  the hill,
Follow'd the Heavy Brigade.

II

The trumpet, the gallop, the charge, and
  the might of the fight !
Thousands of horsemen had gather'd there
  on the height,
With a wing push'd out to the left and a
  wing to the right,
And who shall escape if they close ? but he
  dash'd up alone
Thro' the great gray slope of men,
Sway'd his sabre, and held his own
Like an Englishman there and then.
All in a moment follow'd with force
Three that were next in their fiery course,
Wedged themselves in between horse and
  horse,
Fought for their lives in the narrow gap
  they had made —
Four amid thousands ! and up the hill, up
  the hill,
Gallopt the gallant three hundred, the
  Heavy Brigade.

III

Fell like a cannon-shot,
Burst like a thunderbolt,
Crash'd like a hurricane,
Broke thro' the mass from below,
Drove thro' the midst of the foe,
Plunged up and down, to and fro,
Rode flashing blow upon blow,
Brave Inniskillens and Greys
Whirling their sabres in circles of light !
And some of us, all in amaze,
Who were held for a while from the fight,
And were only standing at gaze,
When the dark-muffled Russian crowd
Folded its wings from the left and the
  right,
And roll'd them around like a cloud, —
O, mad for the charge and the battle were
  we,
When our own good redcoats sank from
  sight,
Like drops of blood in a dark-gray sea,
And we turn'd to each other, whispering,
  all dismay'd,
' Lost are the gallant three hundred of
  Scarlett's Brigade ! '

IV

'Lost one and all' were the words
Mutter'd in our dismay;
But they rode like victors and lords
Thro' the forest of lances and swords
In the heart of the Russian hordes,
They rode, or they stood at bay —
Struck with the sword-hand and slew,
Down with the bridle-hand drew
The foe from the saddle and threw
Underfoot there in the fray —
Ranged like a storm or stood like a rock
In the wave of a stormy day;
Till suddenly shock upon shock
Stagger'd the mass from without,
Drove it in wild disarray,
For our men gallopt up with a cheer and
      a shout,
And the foeman surged, and waver'd, and
      reel'd
Up the hill, up the hill, up the hill, out of
      the field,
And over the brow and away.

V

Glory to each and to all, and the charge
      that they made !
Glory to all the three hundred, and all the
      Brigade !

NOTE. — The 'three hundred' of the 'Heavy
Brigade' who made this famous charge were
the Scots Greys and the 2d squadron of Innis-
killens ; the remainder of the 'Heavy Bri-
gade' subsequently dashing up to their sup-
port.
    The 'three' were Scarlett's aide-de-camp,
Elliot, and the trumpeter, and Shegog the
orderly, who had been close behind him.

EPILOGUE

IRENE.

NOT this way will you set your name
    A star among the stars.

POET.

What way ?

IRENE.

    You praise when you should blame
The barbarism of wars.
A juster epoch has begun.

POET.

    Yet tho' this cheek be gray,
And that bright hair the modern sun,
    Those eyes the blue to-day,
You wrong me, passionate little friend.
    I would that wars should cease,
I would the globe from end to end
    Might sow and reap in peace,
And some new Spirit o'erbear the old,
    Or Trade re-frain the Powers
From war with kindly links of gold,
    Or Love with wreaths of flowers.
Slav, Teuton, Kelt, I count them all
    My friends and brother souls,
With all the peoples, great and small,
    That wheel between the poles.
But since our mortal shadow, Ill,
    To waste this earth began —
Perchance from some abuse of Will
    In worlds before the man
Involving ours — he needs must fight
    To make true peace his own,
He needs must combat might with might,
    Or Might would rule alone;
And who loves war for war's own sake
    Is fool, or crazed, or worse;
But let the patriot-soldier take
    His meed of fame in verse;
Nay — tho' that realm were in the wrong
    For which her warriors bleed,
It still were right to crown with song
    The warrior's noble deed —
A crown the Singer hopes may last,
    For so the deed endures;
But Song will vanish in the Vast;
    And that large phrase of yours
'A star among the stars,' my dear,
    Is girlish talk at best;
For dare we dally with the sphere
    As he did half in jest,
Old Horace ? 'I will strike,' said he,
    'The stars with head sublime,'
But scarce could see, as now we see,
    The man in space and time,
So drew perchance a happier lot
    Than ours, who rhyme to-day.
The fires that arch this dusky dot —
    Yon myriad-worlded way —
The vast sun-clusters' gather'd blaze,
    World-isles in lonely skies,
Whole heavens within themselves, amaze
    Our brief humanities.
And so does Earth; for Homer's fame,
    Tho' carved in harder stone —

The falling drop will make his name
As mortal as my own.

IRENE.

No!

POET.

Let it live then — ay, till when?
Earth passes, all is lost
In what they prophesy, our wise men,
Sun-flame or sunless frost,
And deed and song alike are swept
Away, and all in vain
As far as man can see, except
The man himself remain;
And tho', in this lean age forlorn,
Too many a voice may cry
That man can have no after-morn,
Not yet of those am I.
The man remains, and whatsoe'er
He wrought of good or brave
Will mould him thro' the cycle-year
That dawns behind the grave.

And here the Singer for his art
Not all in vain may plead
' The song that nerves a nation's heart
Is in itself a deed.'

TO VIRGIL

WRITTEN AT THE REQUEST OF THE
MANTUANS FOR THE NINETEENTH
CENTENARY OF VIRGIL'S DEATH

First printed in ' The Nineteenth Century '
for November, 1882.

I

ROMAN VIRGIL, thou that singest
    Ilion's lofty temples robed in fire,
Ilion falling, Rome arising,
    wars, and filial faith, and Dido's
        pyre;

II

Landscape-lover, lord of language
    more than he that sang the ' Works
        and Days,'
All the chosen coin of fancy
    flashing out from many a golden
        phrase;

III

Thou that singest wheat and woodland,
    tilth and vineyard, hive and horse
        and herd;
All the charm of all the Muses
    often flowering in a lonely word;

IV

Poet of the happy Tityrus
    piping underneath his beechen bow-
        ers;
Poet of the poet-satyr
    whom the laughing shepherd bound
        with flowers;

V

Chanter of the Pollio, glorying
    in the blissful years again to be,
Summers of the snakeless meadow,
    unlaborious earth and oarless sea;

VI

Thou that seest Universal
    Nature moved by Universal Mind;
Thou majestic in thy sadness
    at the doubtful doom of human
        kind;

VII

Light among the vanish'd ages;
    star that gildest yet this phantom
        shore;
Golden branch amid the shadows,
    kings and realms that pass to rise no
        more;

VIII

Now thy Forum roars no longer,
    fallen every purple Cæsar's dome —
Tho' thine ocean-roll of rhythm
    sound forever of Imperial Rome —

IX

Now the Rome of slaves hath perish'd,
    and the Rome of freemen holds her
        place,
I, from out the Northern Island
    sunder'd once from all the human
        race.

X

I salute thee, Mantovano,
    I that loved thee since my day began,
Wielder of the stateliest measure
    ever moulded by the lips of man.

THE DEAD PROPHET

182–

Not referring to any particular prophet, or poet, as Tennyson himself declared.

I

DEAD !
  And the Muses cried with a stormy
      cry,
' Send them no more, for evermore.
  Let the people die.'

II

Dead !
  ' Is it *he* then brought so low ? '
And a careless people flock'd from the
      fields
  With a purse to pay for the show.

III

Dead, who had served his time,
  Was one of the people's kings,
Had labor'd in lifting them out of slime,
  And showing them, souls have wings !

IV

Dumb on the winter heath he lay.
  His friends had stript him bare,
And roll'd his nakedness everyway
  That all the crowd might stare.

V

A storm-worn signpost not to be read,
  And a tree with a moulder'd nest
On its barkless bones, stood stark by the
      dead;
  And behind him, low in the West,

VI

With shifting ladders of shadow and light,
  And blurr'd in color and form,
The sun hung over the gates of night,
  And glared at a coming storm.

VII

Then glided a vulturous beldam forth,
  That on dumb death had thriven;
They call'd her ' Reverence ' here upon
      earth,
  And ' The Curse of the Prophet ' in
      heaven.

VIII

She knelt — ' We worship him ' — all but
      wept —
  ' So great, so noble, was he ! '
She clear'd her sight, she arose, she swept
  The dust of earth from her knee.

IX

' Great ! for he spoke and the people heard,
  And his eloquence caught like a flame
From zone to zone of the world, till his
      word
  Had won him a noble name.

X

' Noble ! he sung, and the sweet sound
      ran
  Thro' palace and cottage door,
For he touch'd on the whole sad planet of
      man,
  The kings and the rich and the poor;

XI

' And he sung not alone of an old sun set,
  But a sun coming up in his youth !
Great and noble — O, yes — but yet —
  For man is a lover of truth,

XII

' And bound to follow, wherever she go
  Stark-naked, and up or down,
Thro' her high hill - passes of stainless
      snow,
  Or the foulest sewer of the town —

XIII

' Noble and great — O, ay — but then,
  Tho a prophet should have his due,
Was he noblier-fashion'd than other men ?
  Shall we see to it, I and you ?

XIV

' For since he would sit on a prophet's
      seat,
  As a lord of the human soul,
We needs must scan him from head to
      feet,
  Were it but for a wart or a mole ? '

XV

His wife and his child stood by him in
      tears,
  But she — she push'd them aside.

'Tho' a name may last for a thousand
      years,
  Yet a truth is a truth,' she cried.

XVI

And she that had haunted his pathway
      still,
  Had often truckled and cower'd
When he rose in his wrath, and had yielded
      her will
  To the master, as overpower'd,

XVII

She tumbled his helpless corpse about.
  'Small blemish upon the skin!
But I think we know what is fair with-
      out
  Is often as foul within.'

XVIII

She crouch'd, she tore him part from part,
  And out of his body she drew
The red 'blood-eagle'[1] of liver and heart;
  She held them up to the view;

XIX

She gabbled, as she groped in the dead,
  And all the people were pleased;
'See, what a little heart,' she said,
  ' And the liver is half-diseased!'

XX

She tore the prophet after death,
  And the people paid her well.
Lightnings flicker'd along the heath;
  One shriek'd, 'The fires of hell!'

EARLY SPRING

Contributed to 'The Youth's Companion'
(Boston) for December 13, 1883.

I

  ONCE more the Heavenly Power
    Makes all things new,
  And domes the red-plow'd hills
    With loving blue;
  The blackbirds have their wills,
    The throstles too.

[1] Old Viking term for lungs, liver, etc., when
torn by the conqueror out of the body of the
conquered.

II

  Opens a door in heaven;
    From skies of glass
  A Jacob's ladder falls
    On greening grass,
  And o'er the mountain-walls
    Young angels pass.

III

  Before them fleets the shower,
    And burst the buds,
  And shine the level lands,
    And flash the floods;
  The stars are from their hands
    Flung thro' the woods,

IV

  The woods with living airs
    How softly fann'd,
  Light airs from where the deep,
    All down the sand,
  Is breathing in his sleep,
    Heard by the land.

V

  O, follow, leaping blood,
    The season's lure!
  O heart, look down and up
    Serene, secure,
  Warm as the crocus cup,
    Like snowdrops, pure!

VI

  Past, Future glimpse and fade
    Thro' some slight spell,
  A gleam from yonder vale,
    Some far blue fell,
  And sympathies, how frail,
    In sound and smell!

VII

  Till at thy chuckled note,
    Thou twinkling bird,
  The fairy fancies range,
    And, lightly stirr'd,
  Ring little bells of change
    From word to word.

VIII

  For now the Heavenly Power
    Makes all things new,
  And thaws the cold, and fills
    The flower with dew;
  The blackbirds have their wills,
    The poets too.

PREFATORY POEM TO MY BROTHER'S SONNETS

MIDNIGHT, JUNE 30, 1879

The collected edition of Charles Tennyson Turner's 'Sonnets,' for which this poem was written, was published in 1880.

I

MIDNIGHT — in no midsummer tune
The breakers lash the shores;
The cuckoo of a joyless June
Is calling out of doors.

And thou hast vanish'd from thine own
To that which looks like rest,
True brother, only to be known
By those who love thee best.

II

Midnight — and joyless June gone by,
And from the deluged park
The cuckoo of a worse July
Is calling thro' the dark;

But thou art silent underground,
And o'er thee streams the rain,
True poet, surely to be found
When Truth is found again.

III

And, now to these unsummer'd skies
The summer bird is still,
Far off a phantom cuckoo cries
From out a phantom hill;

And thro' this midnight breaks the sun
Of sixty years away,
The light of days when life begun,
The days that seem to-day,

When all my griefs were shared with
    thee,
As all my hopes were thine —
As all thou wert was one with me,
May all thou art be mine !

'FRATER AVE ATQUE VALE'

First printed in 'The Nineteenth Century' for March, 1883.
Desenzano is a town at the southern end of Lake Garda, in Italy. The narrow peninsula of Sermione (the Latin *Sirmio*), where Catullus had his country house, is about three miles and a half to the east of Desenzano. There are some slight remains of an ancient building on the edge of the lake, said to belong to the poet's villa ; and on a hill near by are fragments of Roman baths.

Row us out from Desenzano, to your Sir-
    mione row !
So they row'd, and there we landed — 'O
    venusta Sirmio !'
There to me thro' all the groves of olive in
    the summer glow,
There beneath the Roman ruin where the
    purple flowers grow,
Came that 'Ave atque Vale' of the Poet's
    hopeless woe,
Tenderest of Roman poets nineteen hun-
    dred years ago,
'Frater Ave atque Vale'— as we wander'd
    to and fro
Gazing at the Lydian laughter of the Garda
    Lake below
Sweet Catullus's all-but-island, olive-sil-
    very Sirmio !

HELEN'S TOWER

[Written at the request of my friend, Lord Dufferin.]

Inscribed on the walls of a tower erected in 1860 by the Earl of Dufferin on his estate near Belfast, as a tribute to his mother, the late Countess of Gifford, and named after her. The fourth line refers to a poetical inscription on the tower, written by Lady Gifford to her son.
Later, in 1861, 'Helen's Tower' was privately printed by Lord Dufferin. It was also printed in 'Good Words' for January, 1884, before it appeared in the 'Tiresias' volume.

HELEN'S TOWER, here I stand,
Dominant over sea and land.
Son's love built me, and I hold
Mother's love in letter'd gold.
Love is in and out of time,
I am mortal stone and lime.
Would my granite girth were strong
As either love, to last as long !
I should wear my crown entire
To and thro' the Doomsday fire,
And be found of angel eyes
In earth's recurring Paradise.

EPITAPH ON LORD STRATFORD DE REDCLIFFE

IN WESTMINSTER ABBEY

This and the two following epitaphs were published in the 'Tirésias' volume.

THOU third great Canning, stand among our best
  And noblest, now thy long day's work hath ceased,
Here silent in our Minster of the West
  Who wert the voice of England in the East.

EPITAPH ON GENERAL GORDON

IN THE GORDON BOYS' NATIONAL MEMORIAL HOME NEAR WOKING

WARRIOR of God, man's friend, and tyrant's foe,
  Now somewhere dead far in the waste Soudan,
Thou livest in all hearts, for all men know
  This earth has never borne a nobler man.

EPITAPH ON CAXTON

IN ST. MARGARET'S, WESTMINSTER

Fiat Lux (his motto)

THY prayer was 'Light — more Light — while Time shall last !'
  Thou sawest a glory growing on the night,
But not the shadows which that light would cast,
  Till shadows vanish in the Light of Light.

TO THE DUKE OF ARGYLL

The Duke was an intimate friend of Tennyson, and visited him occasionally at Aldworth. This poem was probably suggested by the course of the Duke in resigning the Privy Seal in 1881, on account of his disagreement with Gladstone (who had appointed him to the office in 1880) on the Irish Bill. Tennyson himself said, in 1892: 'I love Mr. Gladstone, but hate his present Irish policy.'

O PATRIOT Statesman, be thou wise to know
The limits of resistance, and the bounds
Determining concession; still be bold
Not only to slight praise but suffer scorn;
And be thy heart a fortress to maintain
The day against the moment, and the year
Against the day; thy voice, a music heard
Thro' all the yells and counter-yells of feud
And faction, and thy will, a power to make
This ever-changing world of circumstance,
In changing, chime with never-changing Law.

HANDS ALL ROUND

For the first version of this song, which appeared in the London 'Examiner' for February 7, 1852, see the Notes.

FIRST pledge our Queen this solemn night,
  Then drink to England, every guest;
That man 's the best Cosmopolite
  Who loves his native country best.
May freedom's oak for ever live
  With stronger life from day to day;
That man 's the true Conservative
  Who lops the moulder'd branch away.
    Hands all round !
  God the traitor's hope confound !
To this great cause of Freedom drink, my friends,
  And the great name of England, round and round.

To all the loyal hearts who long
  To keep our English Empire whole !
To all our noble sons, the strong
  New England of the Southern Pole !
To England under Indian skies,
  To those dark millions of her realm !
To Canada whom we love and prize,
  Whatever statesman hold the helm.
    Hands all round !
  God the traitor's hope confound !
To this great name of England drink, my friends,
  And all her glorious empire, round and round.

To all our statesmen so they be
　True leaders of the land's desire !
To both our Houses, may they see
　Beyond the borough and the shire !
We sail'd wherever ship could sail,
　We founded many a mighty state;
Pray God our greatness may not fail
　Thro' craven fears of being great !
　　　　Hands all round !
God the traitor's hope confound !
To this great cause of Freedom drink, my
　　friends,
　And the great name of England, round
　　and round.

FREEDOM

First printed in this country in 1884, in the
New York 'Independent,' and in England in
'Macmillan's Magazine' for December, 1884;
afterwards included in the 'Tiresias' volume.

I

O THOU so fair in summers gone,
　While yet thy fresh and virgin soul
Inform'd the pillar'd Parthenon,
　The glittering Capitol;

II

So fair in southern sunshine bathed,
　But scarce of such majestic mien
As here with forehead vapor-swathed
　In meadows ever green;

III

For thou — when Athens reign'd and
　　Rome,
　Thy glorious eyes were dimm'd with
　　pain
To mark in many a freeman's home
　The slave, the scourge, the chain;

IV

O follower of the Vision, still
　In motion to the distant gleam
Howe'er blind force and brainless will
　May jar thy golden dream

V

Of Knowledge fusing class with class,
　Of civic Hate no more to be,
Of Love to leaven all the mass,
　Till every soul be free;

VI

Who yet, like Nature, wouldst not mar
　By changes all too fierce and fast
This order of her Human Star,
　This heritage of the past;

VII

O scorner of the party cry
　That wanders from the public good,
Thou — when the nations rear on high
　Their idol smear'd with blood,

VIII

And when they roll their idol down —
　Of saner worship sanely proud;
Thou loather of the lawless crown
　As of the lawless crowd;

IX

How long thine ever-growing mind
　Hath still'd the blast and strown the
　　wave,
Tho' some of late would raise a wind
　To sing thee to thy grave,

X

Men loud against all forms of power —
　Unfurnish'd brows, tempestuous tongues,
Expecting all things in an hour —
　Brass mouths and iron lungs !

POETS AND THEIR BIBLIOGRA-
PHIES

First published in the 'Tiresias' volume, but
without the present title, which was added in
1889.

OLD poets foster'd under friendlier skies,
　Old Virgil who would write ten lines,
　　they say,
　At dawn, and lavish all the golden day
To make them wealthier in his readers'
　　eyes;
And you, old popular Horace, you the wise
　Adviser of the nine-years-ponder'd lay,
　And you, that wear a wreath of sweeter
　　bay,
Catullus, whose dead songster never dies;
If, glancing downward on the kindly
　　sphere
　That once had roll'd you round and
　　round the sun,

You see your Art still shrined in human shelves,
You should be jubilant that you flourish'd here
Before the Love of Letters, overdone,
Had swampt the sacred poets with themselves.

TO H. R. H. PRINCESS BEATRICE

First printed in the London 'Times,' July 23, 1885.
The Princess was married to Prince Henry of Battenberg, on that day.

Two Suns of Love make day of human life,
Which else with all its pains, and griefs, and deaths,
Were utter darkness — one, the Sun of dawn
That brightens thro' the Mother's tender eyes,
And warms the child's awakening world — and one
The later-rising Sun of spousal Love,
Which from her household orbit draws the child
To move in other spheres.   The Mother weeps
At that white funeral of the single life,
Her maiden daughter's marriage; and her tears
Are half of pleasure, half of pain — the child
Is happy — even in leaving *her*! but thou,
True daughter, whose all-faithful, filial eyes
Have seen the loneliness of earthly thrones,
Wilt neither quit the widow'd Crown, nor let
This later light of Love have risen in vain,
But moving thro' the Mother's home, between
The two that love thee, lead a summer life,
Sway'd by each Love, and swaying to each Love,
Like some conjectured planet in mid heaven
Between two suns, and drawing down from both
The light and genial warmth of double day.

LOCKSLEY HALL SIXTY YEARS AFTER, ETC.

This was the title of the volume published late in 1886, containing the 'Locksley Hall,' 'The Fleet,' 'Opening of the Indian and Colonial Exhibition,' and 'The Promise of May.'   The book had the following dedication :

TO MY WIFE
I DEDICATE
THIS DRAMATIC MONOLOGUE
AND
THE POEMS WHICH FOLLOW

LOCKSLEY HALL SIXTY YEARS AFTER

Late, my grandson! half the morning have I paced these sandy tracts,
Watch'd again the hollow ridges roaring into cataracts,

Wander'd back to living boyhood while I heard the curlews call,
I myself so close on death, and death itself in Locksley Hall.

So — your happy suit was blasted — she the faultless, the divine;

And you liken — boyish babble — this boy-love of yours with mine.

I myself have often babbled doubtless of a foolish past;
Babble, babble; our old England may go down in babble at last.

'Curse him!' curse your fellow-victim? call him dotard in your rage?
Eyes that lured a doting boyhood well might fool a dotard's age.   10

Jilted for a wealthier! wealthier? yet perhaps she was not wise;

I remember how you kiss'd the miniature
with those sweet eyes.

In the hall there hangs a painting — Amy's
arms about my neck —
Happy children in a sunbeam sitting on the
ribs of wreck.

In my life there was a picture, she that
clasp'd my neck had flown;
I was left within the shadow sitting on the
wreck alone.

Yours has been a slighter ailment, will you
sicken for her sake ?
You, not you ! your modern amorist is of
easier, earthlier make.

Amy loved me, Amy fail'd me, Amy was a
timid child;
But your Judith — but your worldling —
she had never driven me wild.   20

She that holds the diamond necklace dearer
than the golden ring,
She that finds a winter sunset fairer than a
morn of spring.

She that in her heart is brooding on his
briefer lease of life,
While she vows ' till death shall part us,'
she the would-be-widow wife.

She the worldling born of worldlings — fa-
ther, mother — be content,
Even the homely farm can teach us there
is something in descent.

Yonder in that chapel, slowly sinking now
into the ground,
Lies the warrior, my forefather, with his
feet upon the hound.

Cross'd ! for once he sail'd the sea to crush
the Moslem in his pride;
Dead the warrior, dead his glory, dead the
cause in which he died.   30

Yet how often I and Amy in the moulder-
ing aisle have stood,
Gazing for one pensive moment on that
founder of our blood.

There again I stood to-day, and where of
old we knelt in prayer,

Close beneath the casement crimson with
the shield of Locksley — there,

All in white Italian marble, looking still as
if she smiled,
Lies my Amy dead in childbirth, dead the
mother, dead the child.

Dead — and sixty years ago, and dead her
aged husband now —
I, this old white-headed dreamer, stoopt
and kiss'd her marble brow.

Gone the fires of youth, the follies, furies,
curses, passionate tears,
Gone like fires and floods and earthquakes
of the planet's dawning years.   40

Fires that shook me once, but now to silent
ashes fallen away.
Cold upon the dead volcano sleeps the
gleam of dying day.

Gone the tyrant of my youth, and mute be-
low the chancel stones,
All his virtues — I forgive them — black in
white above his bones.

Gone the comrades of my bivouac, some in
fight against the foe,
Some thro' age and slow diseases, gone as
all on earth will go.

Gone with whom for forty years my life in
golden sequence ran,
She with all the charm of woman, she with
all the breadth of man,

Strong in will and rich in wisdom, Edith,
yet so lowly-sweet,
Woman to her inmost heart, and woman to
her tender feet,   50

Very woman of very woman, nurse of ail-
ing body and mind,
She that link'd again the broken chain that
bound me to my kind.

Here to-day was Amy with me, while I
wander'd down the coast,
Near us Edith's holy shadow, smiling at the
slighter ghost.

Gone our sailor son thy father, Leonard
early lost at sea;

Thou alone, my boy, of Amy's kin and mine art left to me.

Gone thy tender-natured mother, wearying to be left alone,
Pining for the stronger heart that once had beat beside her own.

Truth, for truth is truth, he worshipt, being true as he was brave;
Good, for good is good, he follow'd, yet he look'd beyond the grave, 60

Wiser there than you, that crowning barren Death as lord of all,
Deem this over-tragic drama's closing curtain is the pall !

Beautiful was death in him, who saw the death, but kept the deck,
Saving women and their babes, and sinking with the sinking wreck,

Gone for ever ! Ever ? no — for since our dying race began,
Ever, ever, and for ever was the leading light of man.

Those that in barbarian burials kill'd the slave, and slew the wife
Felt within themselves the sacred passion of the second life.

Indian warriors dream of ampler hunting grounds beyond the night;
Even the black Australian dying hopes he shall return, a white. 70

Truth for truth, and good for good ! The good, the true, the pure, the just —
Take the charm ' For ever ' from them, and they crumble into dust.

Gone the cry of ' Forward, Forward,' lost within a growing gloom;
Lost, or only heard in silence from the silence of a tomb.

Half the marvels of my morning, triumphs over time and space,
Staled by frequence, shrunk by usage into commonest commonplace !

' Forward ' rang the voices then, and of the many mine was one.

Let us hush this cry of ' Forward ' till ten thousand years have gone.

Far among the vanish'd races, old Assyrian kings would flay
Captives whom they caught in battle — iron-hearted victors they. 80

Ages after, while in Asia, he that led the wild Moguls,
Timur built his ghastly tower of eighty thousand human skulls;

Then, and here in Edward's time, an age of noblest English names,
Christian conquerors took and flung the conquer'd Christian into flames.

Love your enemy, bless your haters, said the Greatest of the great;
Christian love among the Churches look'd the twin of heathen hate.

From the golden alms of Blessing man had coin'd himself a curse:
Rome of Cæsar, Rome of Peter, which was crueller ? which was worse ?

France had shown a light to all men, preach'd a Gospel, all men's good;
Celtic Demos rose a Demon, shriek'd and slaked the light with blood. 90

Hope was ever on her mountain, watching till the day begun —
Crown'd with sunlight — over darkness — from the still unrisen sun.

Have we grown at last beyond the passions of the primal clan ?
' Kill your enemy, for you hate him,' still, ' your enemy ' was a man.

Have we sunk below them ? peasants maim the helpless horse, and drive
Innocent cattle under thatch, and burn the kindlier brutes alive.

Brutes, the brutes are not your wrongers — burnt at midnight, found at morn,
Twisted hard in mortal agony with their offspring, born-unborn,

Clinging to the silent mother ! Are we devils ? are we men ?

Sweet Saint Francis of Assisi, would that
   he were here again,   100

He that in his Catholic wholeness used to
   call the very flowers
Sisters, brothers — and the beasts — whose
   pains are hardly less than ours !

Chaos, Cosmos ! Cosmos, Chaos ! who can
   tell how all will end ?
Read the wide world's annals, you, and take
   their wisdom for your friend.

Hope the best, but hold the Present fatal
   daughter of the Past,
Shape your heart to front the hour, but
   dream not that the hour will last.

Ay, if dynamite and revolver leave you
   courage to be wise —
When was age so cramm'd with menace ?
   madness ? written, spoken lies ?

Envy wears the mask of Love, and, laugh-
   ing sober fact to scorn,
Cries to weakest as to strongest, ' Ye are
   equals, equal-born.'   110

Equal-born ? O, yes, if yonder hill be
   level with the flat.
Charm us, orator, till the lion look no larger
   than the cat,

Till the cat thro' that mirage of overheated
   language loom
Larger than the lion, — Demos end in
   working its own doom.

Russia bursts our Indian barrier, shall we
   fight her ? shall we yield ?
Pause ! before you sound the trumpet, hear
   the voices from the field.

Those three hundred millions under one
   Imperial sceptre now,
Shall we hold them ? shall we loose them ?
   take the suffrage of the plow.

Nay, but these would feel and follow
   Truth if only you and you,
Rivals of realm-ruining party, when you
   speak were wholly true.   120

Plowmen, shepherds, have I found, and
   more than once, and still could find,

Sons of God, and kings of men in utter no-
   bleness of mind,

Truthful, trustful, looking upward to the
   practised hustings-liar;
So the higher wields the lower, while the
   lower is the higher.

Here and there a cotter's babe is royal-born
   by right divine;
Here and there my lord is lower than his
   oxen or his swine.

Chaos, Cosmos ! Cosmos, Chaos ! once
   again the sickening game;
Freedom, free to slay herself, and dying
   while they shout her name.

Step by step we gain'd a freedom known
   to Europe, known to all;
Step by step we rose to greatness, — thro'
   the tonguesters we may fall.   130

You that woo the Voices — tell them ' old
   experience is a fool,'
Teach your flatter'd kings that only those
   who cannot read can rule.

Pluck the mighty from their seat, but set
   no meek ones in their place;
Pillory Wisdom in your markets, pelt your
   offal at her face.

Tumble Nature heel o'er head, and, yelling
   with the yelling street,
Set the feet above the brain and swear the
   brain is in the feet.

Bring the old dark ages back without the
   faith, without the hope,
Break the State, the Church, the Throne,
   and roll their ruins down the slope.

Authors — essayist, atheist, novelist, real-
   ist, rhymester, play your part,
Paint the mortal shame of nature with the
   living hues of art.   140

Rip your brothers' vices open, strip your
   own foul passions bare;
Down with Reticence, down with Reverence
   —forward—naked—let them stare.

Feed the budding rose of boyhood with the
   drainage of your sewer;

Send the drain into the fountain, lest the stream should issue pure.

Set the maiden fancies wallowing in the troughs of Zolaism, —
Forward, forward, ay, and backward, downward too into the abysm !

Do your best to charm the worst, to lower the rising race of men;
Have we risen from out the beast, then back into the beast again ?

Only ' dust to dust ' for me that sicken at your lawless din,
Dust in wholesome old-world dust before the newer world begin. 150

Heated am I ? you — you wonder — well, it scarce becomes mine age —
Patience ! let the dying actor mouth his last upon the stage.

Cries of unprogressive dotage ere the dotard fall asleep ?
Noises of a current narrowing, not the music of a deep ?

Ay, for doubtless I am old, and think gray thoughts, for I am gray;
After all the stormy changes shall we find a changeless May ?

After madness, after massacre, Jacobinism and Jacquerie,
Some diviner force to guide us thro' the days I shall not see ?

When the schemes and all the systems, kingdoms and republics fall,
Something kindlier, higher, holier — all for each and each for all ? 160

All the full-brain, half-brain races, led by Justice, Love, and Truth;
All the millions one at length with all the visions of my youth ?

All diseases quench'd by Science, no man halt, or deaf, or blind;
Stronger ever born of weaker, lustier body, larger mind ?

Earth at last a warless world, a single race, a single tongue —

I have seen her far away — for is not Earth as yet so young ? —

Every tiger madness muzzled, every serpent passion kill'd,
Every grim ravine a garden, every blazing desert till'd,

Robed in universal harvest up to either pole she smiles,
Universal ocean softly washing all her warless isles. 170

Warless ? when her tens are thousands, and her thousands millions, then —
All her harvest all too narrow — who can fancy warless men ?

Warless ? war will die out late then. Will it ever ? late or soon ?
Can it, till this outworn earth be dead as yon dead world the moon ?

Dead the new astronomy calls her. — On this day and at this hour,
In this gap between the sandhills, whence you see the Locksley tower,

Here we met, our latest meeting — Amy — sixty years ago —
She and I — the moon was falling greenish thro' a rosy glow,

Just above the gateway tower, and even where you see her now —
Here we stood and claspt each other, swore the seeming-deathless vow. —

Dead, but how her living glory lights the hall, the dune, the grass ! 181
Yet the moonlight is the sunlight, and the sun himself will pass.

Venus near her ! smiling downward at this earthlier earth of ours,
Closer on the sun, perhaps a world of never fading flowers.

Hesper, whom the poet call'd the Bringer home of all good things —
All good things may move in Hesper, perfect peoples, perfect kings.

Hesper — Venus — were we native to that splendor or in Mars,

We should see the globe we groan in,
    fairest of their evening stars.

Could we dream of wars and carnage, craft
    and madness, lust and spite,
Roaring London, raving Paris, in that point
    of peaceful light ?   190

Might we not in glancing heavenward on a
    star so silver-fair,
Yearn, and clasp the hands and murmur,
    ' Would to God that we were there ' ?

Forward, backward, backward, forward,
    in the immeasurable sea,
Sway'd by vaster ebbs and flows than can
    be known to you or me.

All the suns — are these but symbols of in-
    numerable man,
Man or Mind that sees a shadow of the
    planner or the plan ?

Is there evil but on earth ? or pain in every
    peopled sphere ?
Well, be grateful for the sounding watch-
    word ' Evolution ' here,

Evolution ever climbing after some ideal
    good,
And Reversion ever dragging Evolution in
    the mud.   200

What are men that He should heed us ?
    cried the king of sacred song;
Insects of an hour, that hourly work their
    brother insect wrong,

While the silent heavens roll, and suns
    along their fiery way,
All their planets whirling round them, flash
    a million miles a day.

Many an æon moulded earth before her
    highest, man, was born,
Many an æon too may pass when earth is
    manless and forlorn,

Earth so huge, and yet so bounded — pools
    of salt, and plots of land —
Shallow skin of green and azure — chains
    of mountain, grains of sand !

Only That which made us meant us to be
    mightier by and by,

Set the sphere of all the boundless heavens
    within the human eye,   210

Sent the shadow of Himself, the boundless,
    thro' the human soul;
Boundless inward in the atom, boundless
    outward in the Whole.

.   .   .   .

Here is Locksley Hall, my grandson, here
    the lion-guarded gate.
Not to-night in Locksley Hall — to-morrow
    — you, you come so late.

Wreck'd — your train — or all but
    wreck'd ? a shatter'd wheel ? a vi-
    cious boy !
Good, this forward, you that preach it, is it
    well to wish you joy ?

Is it well that while we range with Science,
    glorying in the Time,
City children soak and blacken soul and
    sense in city slime ?

There among the glooming alleys Progress
    halts on palsied feet,
Crime and hunger cast our maidens by the
    thousand on the street.   220

There the master scrimps his haggard
    sempstress of her daily bread,
There a single sordid attic holds the living
    and the dead.

There the smouldering fire of fever creeps
    across the rotted floor,
And the crowded couch of incest in the
    warrens of the poor.

Nay, your pardon, cry your ' Forward,'
    yours are hope and youth, but I —
Eighty winters leave the dog too lame to
    follow with the cry,

Lame and old, and past his time, and pass-
    ing now into the night;
Yet I would the rising race were half as
    eager for the light.

Light the fading gleam of even ? light the
    glimmer of the dawn ?
Aged eyes may take the growing glimmer
    for the gleam withdrawn.   230

Far away beyond her myriad coming
  changes earth will be
Something other than the wildest modern
  guess of you and me.

Earth may reach her earthly-worst, or if
  she gain her earthly-best,
Would she find her human offspring this
  ideal man at rest ?

Forward then, but still remember how the
  course of Time will swerve,
Crook and turn upon itself in many a back-
  ward streaming curve.

Not the Hall to-night, my grandson ! Death
  and Silence hold their own.
Leave the master in the first dark hour of
  his last sleep alone.

Worthier soul was he than I am, sound and
  honest, rustic Squire,
Kindly landlord, boon companion — youth-
  ful jealousy is a liar.   240

Cast the poison from your bosom, oust the
  madness from your brain.
Let the trampled serpent show you that you
  have not lived in vain.

Youthful ! youth and age are scholars yet
  but in the lower school,
Nor is he the wisest man who never proved
  himself a fool.

Yonder lies our young sea-village — Art
  and Grace are less and less:
Science grows and Beauty dwindles — roofs
  of slated hideousness !

There is one old hostel left us where they
  swing the Locksley shield,
Till the peasant cow shall butt the 'lion
  passant' from his field.

Poor old Heraldry, poor old History, poor
  old Poetry, passing hence,
In the common deluge drowning old politi-
  cal common-sense !   250

Poor old voice of eighty crying after voices
  that have fled !
All I loved are vanish'd voices, all my steps
  are on the dead.

All the world is ghost to me, and as the
  phantom disappears,
Forward far and far from here is all the
  hope of eighty years.

.   .   .   .

In this hostel — I remember — I repent it
  o'er his grave —
Like a clown — by chance he met me — I
  refused the hand he gave.

From that casement where the trailer man-
  tles all the mouldering bricks —
I was then in early boyhood, Edith but a
  child of six —

While I shelter'd in this archway from a
  day of driving showers —
Peept the winsome face of Edith like a
  flower among the flowers.   260

Here to-night ! the Hall to-morrow, when
  they toll the chapel bell !
Shall I hear in one dark room a wailing,
  'I have loved thee well' ?

Then a peal that shakes the portal — one
  has come to claim his bride,
Her that shrank, and put me from her,
  shriek'd, and started from my side —

Silent echoes ! You, my Leonard, use and
  not abuse your day,
Move among your people, know them, fol-
  low him who led the way,

Strove for sixty widow'd years to help his
  homelier brother men,
Served the poor, and built the cottage,
  raised the school, and drain'd the
  fen.

Hears he now the voice that wrong'd him ?
  who shall swear it cannot be ?
Earth would never touch her worst, were
  one in fifty such as he.   270

Ere she gain her heavenly-best, a God must
  mingle with the game.
Nay, there may be those about us whom we
  neither see nor name,

Felt within us as ourselves, the Powers of
  Good, the Powers of Ill,

Strowing balm, or shedding poison in the
fountains of the will.

Follow you the star that lights a desert
pathway, yours or mine.
Forward, till you see the Highest Human
Nature is divine.

Follow Light, and do the Right — for man
can half-control his doom —
Till you find the deathless Angel seated in
the vacant tomb.

Forward, let the stormy moment fly and
mingle with the past.
I that loathed have come to love him.
Love will conquer at the last.   280

Gone at eighty, mine own age, and I and
you will bear the pall;
Then I leave thee lord and master, latest
lord of Locksley Hall.

THE FLEET [1]

Contributed to the 'Times,' April 23, 1885.
The quotation from Sir Graham Berry's speech
was added in 1886, when the poem was re-
printed in the 'Locksley Hall' volume. Waugh
('Alfred Lord Tennyson,' 2d ed., London,
1893) says that the poem was 'suggested by
the speech,' which was not delivered until
more than a year after the poem was first
printed ; and others have made the same mis-
take.

I

You, you, if you shall fail to understand
　What England is, and what her all-in-all,
On you will come the curse of all the land,
　　Should this old England fall
　　Which Nelson left so great.

[1] The speaker said that 'he should like to
be assured that other outlying portions of the
Empire, the Crown colonies, and important
coaling stations were being as promptly and as
thoroughly fortified as the various capitals of
the self-governing colonies. He was credibly
informed this was not so. It was impossible,
also, not to feel some degree of anxiety about
the efficacy of present provision to defend and
protect, by means of swift well-armed cruisers,
the immense mercantile fleet of the Empire.
A third source of anxiety, so far as the colonies
were concerned, was the apparently insufficient
provision for the rapid manufacture of arma-

II

His isle, the mightiest Ocean-power on
　earth,
　Our own fair isle, the lord of every
　　sea —
Her fuller franchise — what would that be
　worth —
　Her ancient fame of Free —
　　Were she . . . a fallen state ?

III

Her dauntless army scatter'd, and so small,
　Her island - myriads fed from alien
　　lands —
The fleet of England is her all-in-all;
　Her fleet is in your hands,
　　And in her fleet her fate.

IV

You, you, that have the ordering of her
　fleet,
If you should only compass her disgrace,
When all men starve, the wild mob's mil-
　lion feet
　Will kick you from your place,
　　But then too late, too late.

ments and their prompt despatch when ordered
to their colonial destination. Hence the neces-
sity for manufacturing appliances equal to the
requirements, not of Great Britain alone, but
of the whole Empire. But the keystone of the
whole was the necessity for an overwhelmingly
powerful fleet and efficient defence for all
necessary coaling stations. This was as essen-
tial for the colonies as for Great Britain. It
was the one condition for the continuance of
the Empire. All that Continental Powers did
with respect to armies England should effect
with her navy. It was essentially a defensive
force, and could be moved rapidly from point
to point, but it should be equal to all that was
expected from it. It was to strengthen the
fleet that colonists would first readily tax them-
selves, because they realized how essential a
powerful fleet was to the safety, not only of
that extensive commerce sailing in every sea,
but ultimately to the security of the distant
portions of the Empire. Who could estimate
the loss involved in even a brief period of dis-
aster to the Imperial Navy ? Any amount of
money timely expended in preparation would
be quite insignificant when compared with the
possible calamity he had referred to.' — Ex-
tract from Sir Graham Berry's Speech at the
Colonial Institute, 9th November, 1886.

OPENING OF THE INDIAN AND COLONIAL EXHIBITION BY THE QUEEN

WRITTEN AT THE REQUEST OF THE PRINCE OF WALES

The exhibition was opened on the 4th of May, 1886, and the poem was printed in the newspapers of the time.

I

WELCOME, welcome with one voice !
In your welfare we rejoice,
Sons and brothers that have sent,
From isle and cape and continent,
Produce of your field and flood,
Mount and mine, and primal wood;
Works of subtle brain and hand,
And splendors of the morning land,
Gifts from every British zone;
    Britons, hold your own !

II

May we find, as ages run,
The mother featured in the son;
And may yours for ever be
That old strength and constancy
Which has made your fathers great
In our ancient island State,
And wherever her flag fly,
Glorying between sea and sky,
Makes the might of Britain known;
    Britons, hold your own !

III

Britain fought her sons of yore —
Britain fail'd; and never more,
Careless of our growing kin,
Shall we sin our fathers' sin,
Men that in a narrower day —
Unprophetic rulers they —
Drove from out the mother's nest
That young eagle of the West
To forage for herself alone;
    Britons, hold your own !

IV

Sharers of our glorious past,
Brothers, must we part at last ?
Shall we not thro' good and ill
Cleave to one another still ?
Britain's myriad voices call,
' Sons, be welded each and all
Into one imperial whole,
One with Britain, heart and soul !
One life, one flag, one fleet, one throne ! '
    Britons, hold your own !

TO W. C. MACREADY

1851

Written to be read at a dinner given to the actor, March 1, 1851, on his retirement from the stage ; but not included in the poet's collected works until 1891.

FAREWELL, Macready, since to-night we part;
  Full-handed thunders often have confessed
  Thy power, well-used to move the public breast.
We thank thee with our voice, and from the heart.
Farewell, Macready, since this night we part,
  Go, take thine honors home; rank with the best,
  Garrick and statelier Kemble, and the rest
Who made a nation purer through their art.
Thine is it that our drama did not die,
  Nor flicker down to brainless pantomime,
  And those gilt gauds men-children swarm to see.
  Farewell, Macready, moral, grave, sublime;
Our Shakespeare's bland and universal eye
  Dwells pleased, through twice a hundred years, on thee.

DEMETER

AND OTHER POEMS

The volume with this title was published in December, 1889, when Tennyson was eighty years old, and included the poems that follow, as far as 'In Memoriam: W. G. Ward,' and also 'Crossing the Bar,' which the poet afterwards requested to have printed at the end of all collected editions of his works. Twenty thousand copies of the book were sold during the week after it appeared.

TO THE MARQUIS OF DUFFERIN AND AVA

This dedication commemorates the death of the poet's son Lionel, which occurred on the voyage home from India, April 20, 1886. It was first printed in the 'Demeter' volume; as were the poems that follow, unless otherwise stated.

I

At times our Britain cannot rest,
  At times her steps are swift and rash;
  She moving, at her girdle clash
The golden keys of East and West.

II

Not swift or rash, when late she lent
  The sceptres of her West, her East,
  To one that ruling has increased
Her greatness and her self-content.

III

Your rule has made the people love
  Their ruler. Your viceregal days
  Have added fulness to the phrase
Of 'Gauntlet in the velvet glove.'

IV

But since your name will grow with time,
  Not all, as honoring your fair fame
  Of Statesman, have I made the name
A golden portal to my rhyme;

V

But more, that you and yours may know
  From me and mine, how dear a debt
  We owed you, and are owing yet
To you and yours, and still would owe.

VI

For he — your India was his Fate,
  And drew him over sea to you —

He fain had ranged her thro' and thro',
To serve her myriads and the State, —

VII

A soul that, watch'd from earliest youth,
  And on thro' many a brightening year,
  Had never swerved for craft or fear,
By one side-path, from simple truth;

VIII

Who might have chased and claspt Renown
  And caught her chaplet here — and there
  In haunts of jungle-poison'd air
The flame of life went wavering down;

IX

But ere he left your fatal shore,
  And lay on that funereal boat,
  Dying, 'Unspeakable,' he wrote,
'Their kindness,' and he wrote no more;

X

And sacred is the latest word;
  And now the Was, the Might-have-been,
  And those lone rites I have not seen,
And one drear sound I have not heard,

XI

Are dreams that scarce will let me be,
  Not there to bid my boy farewell,
  When That within the coffin fell,
Fell — and flash'd into the Red Sea,

XII

Beneath a hard Arabian moon
  And alien stars. To question why
  The sons before the fathers die,
Not mine! and I may meet him soon;

XIII

But while my life's late eve endures,
  Nor settles into hueless gray,
  My memories of his briefer day
Will mix with love for you and yours.

ON THE JUBILEE OF QUEEN VICTORIA

Written in commemoration of the fiftieth anniversary of the Queen's accession, 1887, and printed in 'Macmillan's Magazine' for April.

I

FIFTY times the rose has flower'd and faded,
Fifty times the golden harvest fallen,
Since our Queen assumed the globe, the sceptre.

II

She beloved for a kindliness
Rare in fable or history,
Queen, and Empress of India,
Crown'd so long with a diadem
Never worn by a worthier,
Now with prosperous auguries
Comes at last to the bounteous
Crowning year of her Jubilee.

III

Nothing of the lawless, of the despot,
Nothing of the vulgar, or vainglorious,
All is gracious, gentle, great and queenly.

IV

You then joyfully, all of you,
Set the mountain aflame to-night,
Shoot your stars to the firmament,
Deck your houses, illuminate
All your towns for a festival,
And in each let a multitude
Loyal, each, to the heart of it,
One full voice of allegiance,
Hail the fair Ceremonial
Of this year of her Jubilee.

V

Queen, as true to womanhood as Queen-hood,
Glorying in the glories of her people,
Sorrowing with the sorrows of the lowest!

VI

You, that wanton in affluence,
Spare not now to be bountiful,
Call your poor to regale with you,
All the lowly, the destitute,
Make their neighborhood healthfuller,
Give your gold to the hospital,
Let the weary be comforted,
Let the needy be banqueted,
Let the maim'd in his heart rejoice
At this glad Ceremonial,
And this year of her Jubilee.

VII

Henry's fifty years are all in shadow,
Gray with distance Edward's fifty summers,
Even her Grandsire's fifty half forgotten.

VIII

You, the Patriot Architect,
You that shape for eternity,
Raise a stately memorial,
Make it regally gorgeous,
Some Imperial Institute,
Rich in symbol, in ornament,
Which may speak to the centuries,
All the centuries after us,
Of this great Ceremonial,
And this year of her Jubilee.

IX

Fifty years of ever-broadening Commerce!
Fifty years of ever-brightening Science!
Fifty years of ever-widening Empire!

X

You, the Mighty, the Fortunate,
You, the Lord-territorial,
You, the Lord-manufacturer,
You, the hardy, laborious,
Patient children of Albion,
You, Canadian, Indian,
Australasian, African,
All your hearts be in harmony,
All your voices in unison,
Singing, 'Hail to the glorious
Golden year of her Jubilee!'

XI

Are there thunders moaning in the distance?
Are there spectres moving in the darkness?
Trust the Hand of Light will lead her people,
Till the thunders pass, the spectres vanish,
And the Light is Victor, and the darkness
Dawns into the Jubilee of the Ages.

TO PROFESSOR JEBB

WITH THE FOLLOWING POEM

Addressed to Richard Claverhouse Jebb, Professor of Greek at St. Andrews, Scotland, and afterwards at Cambridge, England, one of the most eminent Hellenists of our day. The footnotes are the poet's own.

FAIR things are slow to fade away,
Bear witness you, that yesterday [1]
   From out the Ghost of Pindar in you
Roll'd an Olympian; and they say [2]

That here the torpid mummy wheat
Of Egypt bore a grain as sweet
   As that which gilds the glebe of England,
Sunn'd with a summer of milder heat.

So may this legend for awhile,
If greeted by your classic smile,
   Tho' dead in its Trinacrian Enna,
Blossom again on a colder isle.

DEMETER AND PERSEPHONE

(IN ENNA)

The present Lord Tennyson says in the 'Memoir,' (vol. ii. p. 364) : 'The poem was written at my request, because I knew that he considered Demeter one of the most beautiful types of womanhood.'

FAINT as a climate-changing bird that flies
All night across the darkness, and at dawn
Falls on the threshold of her native land,
And can no more, thou camest, O my child,
Led upward by the God of ghosts and dreams,
Who laid thee at Eleusis, dazed and dumb
With passing thro' at once from state to state,
Until I brought thee hither, that the day,
When here thy hands let fall the gather'd flower,
Might break thro' clouded memories once again   10
On thy lost self. A sudden nightingale

[1] In Bologna.
[2] They say, for the fact is doubtful.

Saw thee, and flash'd into a frolic of song
And welcome; and a gleam as of the moon,
When first she peers along the tremulous deep,
Fled wavering o'er thy face, and chased away
That shadow of a likeness to the king
Of shadows, thy dark mate. Persephone !
Queen of the dead no more — my child !
Thine eyes
Again were human-godlike, and the Sun
Burst from a swimming fleece of winter gray,   20
And robed thee in his day from head to feet —
'Mother !' and I was folded in thine arms.

Child, those imperial, disimpassion'd eyes
Awed even me at first, thy mother — eyes
That oft had seen the serpent-wanded power
Draw downward into Hades with his drift
Of flickering spectres, lighted from below
By the red race of fiery Phlegethon;
But when before have Gods or men beheld
The Life that had descended re-arise,   30
And lighted from above him by the Sun ?
So mighty was the mother's childless cry,
A cry that rang thro' Hades, Earth, and Heaven !

So in this pleasant vale we stand again,
The field of Enna, now once more ablaze
With flowers that brighten as thy footstep falls,
All flowers — but for one black blur of earth
Left by that closing chasm, thro' which the car
Of dark Aïdoneus rising rapt thee hence.
And here, my child, tho' folded in thine arms,   40
I feel the deathless heart of motherhood
Within me shudder, lest the naked glebe
Should yawn once more into the gulf, and thence
The shrilly whinnyings of the team of Hell,
Ascending, pierce the glad and songful air,
And all at once their arch'd necks, midnight-maned,
Jet upward thro' the midday blossom. No !
For, see, thy foot has touch'd it; all the space

Of blank earth - baldness clothes itself
afresh,
And breaks into the crocus-purple hour 50
That saw thee vanish.

    Child, when thou wert gone,
I envied human wives, and nested birds,
Yea, the cubb'd lioness; went in search of
thee
Thro' many a palace, many a cot, and gave
Thy breast to ailing infants in the night,
And set the mother waking in amaze
To find her sick one whole; and forth again
Among the wail of midnight winds, and
cried,
'Where is my loved one ? Wherefore do
ye wail ? '
And out from all the night an answer
shrill'd,   60
'We know not, and we know not why we
wail.'
I climb'd on all the cliffs of all the seas,
And ask'd the waves that moan about the
world,
'Where ? do ye make your moaning for
my child ? '
And round from all the world the voices
came,
'We know not, and we know not why we
moan.'
'Where ? ' and I stared from every eagle-
peak,
I thridded the black heart of all the woods,
I peer'd thro' tomb and cave, and in the
storms   69
Of autumn swept across the city, and heard
The murmur of their temples chanting
me,
Me, me, the desolate mother ! 'Where ? '
—and turn'd,
And fled by many a waste, forlorn of
man,
And grieved for man thro' all my grief for
thee, —
The jungle rooted in his shatter'd hearth,
The serpent coil'd about his broken shaft,
The scorpion crawling over naked skulls; —
I saw the tiger in the ruin'd fane
Spring from his fallen God, but trace of
thee
I saw not; and far on, and, following
out   80
A league of labyrinthine darkness, came
On three gray heads beneath a gleaming
rift.

'Where ? ' and I heard one voice from all
the three,
'We know not, for we spin the lives of men,
And not of Gods, and know not why we
spin !
There is a Fate beyond us.' Nothing knew.

 Last as the likeness of a dying man,
Without his knowledge, from him flits to
warn
A far-off friendship that he comes no more,
So he, the God of dreams, who heard my
cry,   90
Drew from thyself the likeness of thyself
Without thy knowledge, and thy shadow
past
Before me, crying, 'The Bright one in the
highest
Is brother of the Dark one in the lowest,
And Bright and Dark have sworn that I,
the child
Of thee, the great Earth-Mother, thee, the
Power
That lifts her buried life from gloom to
bloom,
Should be for ever and for evermore
The Bride of Darkness.'

     So the Shadow wail'd.
Then I, Earth-Goddess, cursed the Gods of
heaven.   100
I would not mingle with their feasts; to me
Their nectar smack'd of hemlock on the
lips,
Their rich ambrosia tasted aconite.
The man, that only lives and loves an hour,
Seem'd nobler than their hard eternities.
My quick tears kill'd the flower, my rav-
ings hush'd
The bird, and lost in utter grief I fail'd
To send my life thro' olive-yard and vine
And golden-grain, my gift to helpless man.
Rain-rotten died the wheat, the barley-
spears   110
Were hollow-husk'd, the leaf fell, and the
Sun,
Pale at my grief, drew down before his
time
Sickening, and Ætna kept her winter snow.

 Then He, the brother of this Darkness,
He
Who still is highest, glancing from his
height
On earth a fruitless fallow, when he miss'd

The wonted steam of sacrifice, the praise
And prayer of men, decreed that thou
    shouldst dwell
For nine white moons of each whole year
    with me,
Three dark ones in the shadow with thy
    king.   120

Once more the reaper in the gleam of
    dawn
Will see me by the landmark far away,
Blessing his field, or seated in the dusk
Of even, by the lonely threshing-floor,
Rejoicing in the harvest and the grange.

Yet I, Earth-Goddess, am but ill-content
With them who still are highest. Those
    gray heads,
What meant they by their 'Fate beyond
    the Fates'
But younger kindlier Gods to bear us down,
As we bore down the Gods before us?
    Gods,   130
To quench, not hurl the thunderbolt, to
    stay,
Not spread the plague, the famine; Gods
    indeed,
To send the noon into the night and break
The sunless halls of Hades into Heaven?
Till thy dark lord accept and love the Sun,
And all the Shadow die into the Light,
When thou shalt dwell the whole bright
    year with me,
And souls of men, who grew beyond their
    race,
And made themselves as Gods against the
    fear
Of Death and Hell; and thou that hast
    from men,   140
As Queen of Death, that worship which is
    Fear,
Henceforth, as having risen from out the
    dead,
Shalt ever send thy life along with mine
From buried grain thro' springing blade,
    and bless
Their garner'd autumn also, reap with me,
Earth-mother, in the harvest hymns of
    Earth
The worship which is Love, and see no more
The Stone, the Wheel, the dimly-glimmer-
    ing lawns
Of that Elysium, all the hateful fires
Of torment, and the shadowy warrior glide
Along the silent field of Asphodel.   151

OWD ROÄ [1]

The footnotes are the poet's.

NAÄY, noä mander [2] o' use to be callin' 'im
    Roä, Roä, Roä,
Fur the dog 's stoän-deäf, an' 'e 's blind, 'e
    can naither stan' nor goä.

But I meäns fur to maäke 'is owd aäge as
    'appy as iver I can,
Fur I owäs owd Roäver moor nor I iver
    owäd mottal man.

Thou 's rode of 'is back when a babby,
    afoor thou was gotten too owd,
Fur 'e 'd fetch an' carry like owt, 'e was
    allus as good as gowd.

Eh, but 'e 'd fight wi' a will *when* 'e fowt;
    'e could howd [3] 'is oän,
An' Roä was the dog as knaw'd when an'
    wheere to bury his boäne.

An' 'e kep his heäd hoop like a king, an'
    'e 'd niver not down wi' 'is taäil,   9
Fur 'e 'd niver done nowt to be shaämed
    on, when we was i' Howlaby Daäle.

An' 'e sarved me sa well when 'e lived,
    that, Dick, when 'e cooms to be
    deäd,
I thinks as I 'd like fur to hev soom soort
    of a sarvice reäd.

Fur 'e 's moor good sense na the Parlia-
    ment man 'at stans fur us 'ere,
An' I 'd voät fur 'im, my oän sen, if 'e
    could but stan' for the Shere.

'Faäithful an' True' — them words be i'
    Scriptur — an' Faäithful an' True
Ull be fun' [4] upo' four short legs ten times
    fur one upo' two.

An' maäybe they 'll walk upo' two, but I
    knaws they runs upo' four, [5] —
Bedtime, Dicky! but waäit till tha 'eärs it
    be strikin' the hour.

Fur I wants to tell tha o' Roä when we
    lived i' Howlaby Daäle,

[1] Old Rover.   [2] Manner.
[3] Hold.   [4] Found.
[5] *ou* as in 'house.'

Ten year sin' — Naäy — naäy ! tha mun
nobbut hev' one glass of aäle.   20

Straänge an' owd-farran'd [1] the 'ouse, an'
belt [2] long afoor my daäy,
Wi' haäfe o' the chimleys a-twizzen'd [3] an'
twined like a band o' haäy.

The fellers as maäkes them picturs, 'ud
coom at the fall o' the year,
An' sattle their ends upo' stools to pictur
the door-poorch theere,

An' the Heagle 'as hed two heäds stannin'
theere o' the brokken stick; [4]
An' they niver 'ed seed sich ivin' [5] as
graw'd hall ower the brick;

An' theere i' the 'ouse one night — but it 's
down, an' all on it now
Goän into mangles an' tonups, [6] an' raäved
slick thruf by the plow —

Theere, when the 'ouse wur a house, one
night I wur sittin' aloän,
Wi' Roäver athurt my feeät, an' sleeäpin'
still as a stoän,   30

Of a Christmas Eäve, an' as cowd as this,
an' the midders [7] as white,
An' the fences all on 'em bolster'd oop wi'
the windle [8] that night;

An' the cat wur a-sleeäpin' alongside
Roäver, but I wur awaäke,
An' smoäkin' an' thinkin' o' things — Doänt
maäke thysen sick wi' the caäke.

Fur the men ater supper 'ed sung their
songs an' 'ed 'ed their beer,
An' 'ed goän their waäys; ther was nobbut
three, an' noän on 'em theere.

They was all on 'em fear'd o' the Ghoäst
an' duss n't not sleeäp i' the 'ouse,
But, Dicky, the Ghoäst moästlins [9] was
nobbut a rat or a mouse.

[1] ' Owd-farran'd,' old-fashioned.
[2] Built.
[3] ' Twizzen'd,' twisted.
[4] On a staff *ragulé.*   [5] Ivy.
[6] Mangolds and turnips.
[7] Meadows.
[8] Drifted snow.
[9] ' Moästlins,' for the most part, generally.

An' I looökt out wonst [1] at the night, an'
the daäle was all of a thaw,
Fur I seed the beck coomin' down like a
long black snaäke i' the snaw,   40

An' I heärd greät heäps o' the snaw slush-
in' down fro' the bank to the beck,
An' then as I stood i' the doorwaäy, I
feeäld it drip o' my neck.

Saw I turn'd in ageän, an' I thowt o' the
good owd times 'at was goan,
An' the munney they maäde by the war,
an' the times 'at was coomin' on;

Fur I thowt if the Staäte was a-gawin' to
let in furriners' wheät,
Howiver was British farmers to stan' ageän
o' their feeät ?

Howiver was I fur to find my rent an' to
paäy my men ?
An' all along o' the feller [2] as turn'd 'is
back of hissen.

Thou slep i' the chaumber above 'us, we
could n't ha' 'eärd tha call,
Sa moother 'ed tell'd ma to bring tha down,
an' thy craädle an' all;   50

Fur the gell o' the farm 'at slep wi' tha
then 'ed gotten wer leäve,
Fur to goä that night to 'er foälk by cause
o' the Christmas Eäve;

But I cleän forgot tha, my lad, when
moother 'ed gotten to bed,
An' I slep i' my chair hup-on-end, an' the
Freeä Traäde runn'd i' my 'ead,

Till I dreäm'd 'at Squire walkt in, an' I
says to him, ' Squire, ya 're laäte,'
Then I seed 'at 'is faäce wur as red as the
Yule-block theere i' the graäte.

An' 'e says, ' Can ya paäy me the rent to-
night ? ' an' I says to 'im, ' Noä,'
An' 'e cotch'd howd hard o' my hairm, [3]
' Then hout to-night tha shall goä.'

' Tha 'll niver,' says I, ' be a-turnin' ma
hout upo' Christmas Eäve ? '
Then I waäked an' I fun it was Roäver
a-tuggin' an' teärin' my sleäve.   60

[1] Once.   [2] Peel.   [3] Arm.

An' I thowt as 'e 'd goän cleän-wud,[1] fur I
  noäwaäys knaw'd 'is intent;
An' I says, 'Git awaäy, ya beast,' an' I
  fetcht 'im a kick, an' 'e went.

Then 'e tummled up stairs, fur I 'eärd 'im,
  as if 'e 'd 'a brokken 'is neck,
An' I 'd cleär forgot, little Dicky, thy
  chaumber door would n't sneck;[2]

An' I slep i' my chair ageän wi' my hairm
  hingin' down to the floor,
An' I thowt it was Roäver a-tuggin' an'
  teärin' me wuss nor afoor,

An' I thowt 'at I kick'd 'im ageän, but I
  kick'd thy moother istead.
'What arta snorin' theere fur? the house
  is afire,' she said.

Thy moother 'ed beän a-naggin' about the
  gell o' the farm,
She offens 'ud spy summut wrong when
  there warn't not a mossel o' harm; 70

An' she did n't not solidly meän I wur
  gawin' that waäy to the bad,
Fur the gell[3] was as howry a trollope as
  iver traäpes'd i' the squad.

But moother was free of 'er tongue, as I
  offens 'ev tell'd 'er mysen,
Sa I kep i' my chair, fur I thowt she was
  nobbut a-rilin' ma then.

An' I says, 'I 'd be good to tha, Bess, if
  tha'd onywaäys let ma be good,'
But she skelpt ma haäfe ower i' the chair,
  an' screeäd like a howl gone wud[4] —

'Ya mun run fur the lether.[5] Git oop, if
  ya 're onywaäys good for owt.'
And I says, 'If I beänt noäwaäys — not
  nowadaäys — good fur nowt —

[1] Mad.
[2] Latch.
[3] 'The girl was as dirty a slut as ever trudged in the mud,' but there is a sense of slatternliness in 'traäpes'd' which is not expressed in 'trudged.'
[4] 'She half overturned me and shrieked like an owl gone mad.'
[5] Ladder.

'Yit I beänt sich a nowt[1] of all nowts as
  'ull hallus do as 'e 's bid.'
'But the stairs is afire,' she said; then I
  seed 'er a-cryin', I did.   80

An' she beäld, 'Ya mun saäve little Dick,
  an' be sharp about it an' all,'
Sa I runs to the yard fur a lether, an' sets
  'im ageän the wall,

An' I claums an' I mashes the winder bin,
  when I gits to the top,
But the heät druv hout i' my heyes till I
  feäld mysen ready to drop.

Thy moother was howdin' the lether, an'
  tellin' me not to be skeärd,
An' I was n't afeärd, or I thinks leästwaäys
  as I was n't afeärd;

But I could n't see fur the smoäke wheere
  thou was a-liggin', my lad,
An' Roäver was theere i' the chaumber
  a-yowlin' an' yaupin' like mad;

An' thou was a-beälin' likewise, an'
  a-squeälin', as if tha was bit,
An' it was n't a bite but a burn, fur the
  merk 's[2] o' thy shou'der yit;   90

Then I call'd out, 'Roä, Roä, Roä,' thaw I
  did n't haäfe think as 'e 'd 'ear,
*But 'e coom'd thruf the fire wi' my bairn i' 'is
  mouth to the winder theere!*

He coom'd like a hangel o' marcy as soon
  as 'e 'eärd 'is naäme,
Or like tother hangel i' Scriptur 'at sum-
  mun seed i' the flaäme,

When summun 'ed hax'd fur a son, an' 'e
  promised a son to she,
An' Roä was as good as the hangel i'
  saävin' a son fur me.

Sa I browt tha down, an' I says, 'I mun
  gaw up ageän fur Roä.'
'Gaw up ageän fur the varmint?' I tell'd
  'er, 'Yeäs, I mun goä.'

An' I claumb'd up ageän to the winder, an'
  clemm'd[3] owd Roä by the 'eäd,

[1] A thoroughly insignificant or worthless person.   [2] Mark.   [3] Clutched.

An' 'is 'air coom'd off i' my 'ands an' I
    taäked 'im at fust fur deäd;   100

Fur 'e smell'd like a herse a-singein', an'
    seeäm'd as blind as a poop,
An' haäfe on 'im bare as a bublin'.[1] I
    could n't wakken 'im oop,

But I browt 'im down, an' we got to the
    barn, fur the barn would n't burn
Wi' the wind blawin' hard tother waäy, an'
    the wind was n't like to turn.

An' I kep a-callin' o' Roä till 'e waggled 'is
    taäil fur a bit,
But the cocks kep a-crawin' an' crawin' all
    night, an' I 'ears 'em yit;

An' the dogs was a-yowlin' all round, and
    thou was a-squeälin' thysen,
An' moother was naggin' an' groänin' an'
    moänin' an' naggin' ageän;

An' I 'eärd the bricks an' the baulks [2]
    rummle down when the roof gev
    waäy,
Fur the fire was a-raägin' an' raävin' an'
    roarin' like judgment daäy.   110

Warm enew theere sewer-ly, but the barn
    was as cowd as owt,
An' we cuddled and huddled togither, an'
    happt [3] wersens oop as we mowt.

An' I browt Roä round, but moother 'ed
    beän sa soäk'd wi' the thaw
'At she cotch'd 'er death o' cowd that night,
    poor soul, i' the straw.

Haäfe o' the parish runn'd oop when the
    rig-tree [4] was tummlin' in —
Too laäte — but it 's all ower now — hall
    hower — an' ten year sin';

Too laäte, tha mun git tha to bed, but I 'll
    coom an' I 'll squench the light,
Fur we moänt 'ev naw moor fires — and soä,
    little Dick, good-night.

---

[1] 'Bubbling,' a young unfledged bird.
[2] Beams.
[3] Wrapt ourselves.
[4] The beam that runs along the roof of the
house just beneath the ridge.

VASTNESS

First printed in 'The Nineteenth Century'
for November, 1885.

I

MANY a hearth upon our dark globe sighs
    after many a vanish'd face,
Many a planet by many a sun may roll
    with the dust of a vanish'd race.

II

Raving politics, never at rest — as this poor
    earth's pale history runs, —
What is it all but a trouble of ants in the
    gleam of a million million of suns?

III

Lies upon this side, lies upon that side,
    truthless violence mourn'd by the
    wise,
Thousands of voices drowning his own in a
    popular torrent of lies upon lies;

IV

Stately purposes, valor in battle, glorious
    annals of army and fleet,
Death for the right cause, death for the
    wrong cause, trumpets of victory,
    groans of defeat;

V

Innocence seethed in her mother's milk,
    and Charity setting the martyr
    aflame;
Thraldom who walks with the banner of
    Freedom, and recks not to ruin a
    realm in her name.

VI

Faith at her zenith, or all but lost in the
    gloom of doubts that darken the
    schools;
Craft with a bunch of all-heal in her hand,
    follow'd up by her vassal legion of
    fools;

VII

Trade flying over a thousand seas with her
    spice and her vintage, her silk and
    her corn;
Desolate offing, sailorless harbors, famish-
    ing populace, wharves forlorn;

VIII

Star of the morning, Hope in the sunrise;
  gloom of the evening, Life at a
  close;
Pleasure who flaunts on her wide downway
  with her flying robe and her poison'd
  rose;

IX

Pain, that has crawl'd from the corpse of
  Pleasure, a worm which writhes all
  day, and at night
Stirs up again in the heart of the sleeper,
  and stings him back to the curse of
  the light;

X

Wealth with his wines and his wedded har-
  lots; honest Poverty, bare to the
  bone;
Opulent Avarice, lean as Poverty; Flattery
  gilding the rift in a throne;

XI

Fame blowing out from her golden trum-
  pet a jubilant challenge to Time and
  to Fate;
Slander, her shadow, sowing the nettle on
  all the laurell'd graves of the great;

XII

Love for the maiden, crown'd with mar-
  riage, no regrets for aught that has
  been,
Household happiness, gracious children,
  debtless competence, golden mean;

XIII

National hatreds of whole generations, and
  pigmy spites of the village spire;
Vows that will last to the last death-ruckle,
  and vows that are snapt in a mo-
  ment of fire;

XIV

He that has lived for the lust of the min-
  ute, and died in the doing it, flesh
  without mind;
He that has nail'd all flesh to the Cross, till
  Self died out in the love of his kind;

XV

Spring and Summer and Autumn and Win-
  ter, and all these old revolutions of
  earth;

All new - old revolutions of Empire —
  change of the tide — what is all of
  it worth?

XVI

What the philosophies, all the sciences,
  poesy, varying voices of prayer,
All that is noblest, all that is basest, all
  that is filthy with all that is fair?

XVII

What is it all, if we all of us end but in
  being our own corpse - coffins at
  last?
Swallow'd in Vastness, lost in Silence,
  drown'd in the deeps of a meaning-
  less Past?

XVIII

What but a murmur of gnats in the gloom,
  or a moment's anger of bees in their
  hive? —

.   .   .   .
Peace, let it be! for I loved him, and love
  him for ever: the dead are not dead
  but alive.

THE RING

Dedicated to the Hon. J. Russell Lowell

Mr. Lowell told Tennyson the story, 'or
something like it, of a house near where he had
once lived' ('Memoir,' vol. ii. p. 365).

MIRIAM AND HER FATHER

MIRIAM (*singing*).

MELLOW moon of heaven,
  Bright in blue,
Moon of married hearts,
  Hear me, you!

Twelve times in the year
  Bring me bliss,
Globing honey moons
  Bright as this.

Moon, you fade at times
  From the night.   10
Young again you grow
  Out of sight.

Silver crescent-curve,
  Coming soon,

Globe again, and make
Honey moon.

Shall not *my* love last,
Moon, with you,
For ten thousand years
Old and new ? 20

FATHER.

And who was he with such love-drunken
eyes
They made a thousand honey moons of one ?

MIRIAM.

The prophet of his own, my Hubert — his
The words, and mine the setting. ' Air and
words,'
Said Hubert, when I sang the song, ' are
bride
And bridegroom.' Does it please you ?

FATHER.

Mainly, child,
Because I hear your mother's voice in
yours.
She —, why, you shiver tho' the wind is
west
With all the warmth of summer.

MIRIAM.

Well, I felt
On a sudden I know not what, a breath
that past 30
With all the cold of winter.

FATHER (*muttering to himself*).

Even so.
The Ghost in Man, the Ghost that once was
Man,
But cannot wholly free itself from Man,
Are calling to each other thro' a dawn
Stranger than earth has ever seen; the veil
Is rending, and the Voices of the day
Are heard across the Voices of the dark.
No sudden heaven, nor sudden hell, for
man,
But thro' the Will of One who knows and
rules —
And utter knowledge is but utter love —
Æonian Evolution, swift or slow, 41
Thro' all the spheres — an ever opening
height,
An ever lessening earth — and she per-
haps,
My Miriam, breaks her latest earthly link
With me to-day.

MIRIAM.

You speak so low; what is it ?
Your ' Miriam breaks ' — is making a new
link
Breaking an old one ?

FATHER.

No, for we, my child,
Have been till now each other's all-in-all.

MIRIAM.

And you the lifelong guardian of the child.

FATHER.

I, and one other whom you have not
known. 50

MIRIAM.

And who ? what other ?

FATHER.

Whither are you bound ?
For Naples which we only left in May ?

MIRIAM.

No, father, Spain, but Hubert brings me
home
With April and the swallow. Wish me joy !

FATHER.

What need to wish when Hubert weds in
you
The heart of love, and you the soul of
truth
In Hubert ?

MIRIAM.

Tho' you used to call me once
The lonely maiden princess of the wood,
Who meant to sleep her hundred summers
out 59
Before a kiss should wake her.

FATHER.

Ay, but now
Your fairy prince has found you, take this
ring.

MIRIAM.

' Io t' amo ' — and these diamonds — beau-
tiful !
' From Walter,' and for me from you then ?

FATHER.

Well,
One way for Miriam.

MIRIAM.
Miriam am I not ?

FATHER.
This ring bequeath'd you by your mother,
        child,
Was to be given you — such her dying
        wish —
Given on the morning when you came of
        age
Or on the day you married. Both the
        days
Now close in one. The ring is doubly
        yours.   69
Why do you look so gravely at the tower ?

MIRIAM.
I never saw it yet so all ablaze
With creepers crimsoning to the pinnacles,
As if perpetual sunset linger'd there,
And all ablaze too in the lake below !
And how the birds that circle round the
        tower
Are cheeping to each other of their flight
To summer lands !

FATHER.
                And that has made you grave ?
Fly — care not. Birds and brides must
        leave the nest.
Child, I am happier in your happiness   79
Than in mine own.

MIRIAM.
                It is not that !

FATHER.
                            What else ?
MIRIAM.
That chamber in the tower.

FATHER.
                        What chamber, child ?
Your nurse is here ?

MIRIAM.
                My mother's nurse and mine.
She comes to dress me in my bridal veil.

FATHER.
What did she say ?

MIRIAM.
                She said that you and I

Had been abroad for my poor health so
        long
She fear'd I had forgotten her, and I ask'd
About my mother, and she said, ' Thy hair
Is golden like thy mother's, not so fine.'

FATHER.
What then ? what more ?

MIRIAM.
                She said — perhaps indeed
She wander'd, having wander'd now so far
Beyond the common date of death — that
        you,   91
When I was smaller than the statuette
Of my dear mother on your bracket
        here —
You took me to that chamber in the tower,
The topmost — a chest there, by which you
        knelt —
And there were books and dresses — left
        to me,
A ring too which you kiss'd, and I, she
        said,
I babbled, ' Mother, mother ' — as I used
To prattle to her picture — stretch'd my
        hands
As if I saw her; then a woman came   100
And caught me from my nurse. I hear her
        yet —
A sound of anger like a distant storm.

FATHER.
Garrulous old crone !

MIRIAM.
                Poor nurse !

FATHER.
                            I bade her keep,
Like a seal'd book, all mention of the ring,
For I myself would tell you all to-day.

MIRIAM.
' She too might speak to-day,' she mumbled.
        Still,
I scarce have learnt the title of your book,
But you will turn the pages.

FATHER.
                            Ay, to-day !
I brought you to that chamber on your
        third
September birthday with your nurse, and
        felt   110

An icy breath play on me, while I stoopt
To take and kiss the ring.

MIRIAM.

This very ring,
' Io t' amo ' ?

FATHER.

Yes, for some wild hope was mine
That, in the misery of my married life,
Miriam your mother might appear to me.
She came to you, not me. The storm you hear
Far-off is Muriel — your stepmother's voice.

MIRIAM.

Vext, that you thought my mother came to me ?
Or at my crying, ' Mother ' ? or to find
My mother's diamonds hidden from her there, 120
Like worldly beauties in the cell, not shown
To dazzle all that see them ?

FATHER.

Wait a while.
Your mother and stepmother — Miriam Erne
And Muriel Erne — the two were cousins — lived
With Muriel's mother on the down, that sees
A thousand squares of corn and meadow, far
As the gray deep, a landscape which your eyes
Have many a time ranged over when a babe.

MIRIAM.

I climb'd the hill with Hubert, yesterday,
And from the thousand squares, one silent voice 130
Came on the wind, and seem'd to say, ' Again.'
We saw far off an old forsaken house,
Then home, and past the ruin'd mill.

FATHER.

And there
I found these cousins often by the brook,
For Miriam sketch'd and Muriel threw the fly ;
The girls of equal age, but one was fair,
And one was dark, and both were beautiful.
No voice for either spoke within my heart

Then, for the surface eye, that only dotes
On outward beauty, glancing from the one
To the other, knew not that which pleased it most, 141
The raven ringlet or the gold ; but both
Were dowerless, and myself, I used to walk
This terrace — morbid, melancholy ; mine
And yet not mine the hall, the farm, the field ;
For all that ample woodland whisper'd, ' Debt,'
The brook that feeds this lakelet murmur'd, ' Debt,'
And in yon arching avenue of old elms,
Tho' mine, not mine, I heard the sober rook
And carrion crow cry, ' Mortgage.'

MIRIAM.

Father's fault
Visited on the children !

FATHER.

Ay, but then
A kinsman, dying, summon'd me to Rome — 152
He left me wealth — and while I journey'd hence,
And saw the world fly by me like a dream,
And while I communed with my truest self,
I woke to all of truest in myself,
Till, in the gleam of those midsummer dawns,
The form of Muriel faded, and the face
Of Miriam grew upon me, till I knew ;
And past and future mixt in heaven and made 160
The rosy twilight of a perfect day.

MIRIAM.

So glad ? no tear for him who left you wealth,
Your kinsman ?

FATHER.

I had seen the man but once ;
He loved my name, not me ; and then I pass'd
Home, and thro' Venice, where a jeweller,
So far gone down, or so far up in life,
That he was nearing his own hundred, sold
This ring to me, then laugh'd, ' The ring is weird.'
And weird and worn and wizard-like was he.

'Why weird?' I ask'd him; and he said,
    'The souls   170
Of two repentant lovers guard the ring;'
Then with a ribald twinkle in his bleak
    eyes —
'And if you give the ring to any maid,
They still remember what it cost them
    here,
And bind the maid to love you by the ring;
And if the ring were stolen from the maid,
The theft were death or madness to the
    thief,
So sacred those ghost lovers hold the gift.'
And then he told their legend:
                              'Long ago
Two lovers parted by a scurrilous tale   180
Had quarrell'd, till the man repenting sent
This ring, "Io t' amo," to his best beloved,
And sent it on her birthday. She in wrath
Return'd it on her birthday, and that day
His death-day, when, half-frenzied by the
    ring,
He wildly fought a rival suitor, him
The causer of that scandal, fought and fell;
And she that came to part them all too late,
And found a corpse and silence, drew the
    ring
From his dead finger, wore it till her death,
Shrined him within the temple of her
    heart,   191
Made every moment of her after life
A virgin victim to his memory,
And dying rose, and rear'd her arms, and
    cried,
"I see him, Io t' amo, Io t' amo."'

MIRIAM.

Legend or true? so tender should be true!
Did *he* believe it? did you ask him?

FATHER.

                                      Ay!
But that half skeleton, like a barren ghost
From out the fleshless world of spirits,
    laugh'd —
A hollow laughter!

MIRIAM.

                Vile, so near the ghost
Himself, to laugh at love in death! But
    you?   201

FATHER.

Well, as the bygone lover thro' this ring
Had sent his cry for her forgiveness, I

Would call thro' this 'Io t' amo' to the
    heart
Of Miriam; then I bade the man engrave
'From Walter' on the ring, and sent it —
    wrote
Name, surname, all as clear as noon, but
    he —
Some younger hand must have engraven
    the ring —
His fingers were so stiffen'd by the frost
Of seven and ninety winters, that he
    scrawl'd   210
A 'Miriam' that might seem a 'Muriel;'
And Muriel claim'd and open'd what I
    meant
For Miriam, took the ring, and flaunted it
Before that other whom I loved and love.

A mountain stay'd me here, a minster
    there,
A galleried palace, or a battle-field,
Where stood the sheaf of Peace: but —
    coming home —
And on your mother's birthday — all but
    yours —
A week betwixt — and when the tower as
    now
Was all ablaze with crimson to the roof, 220
And all ablaze too plunging in the lake
Head-foremost — who were those that
    stood between
The tower and that rich phantom of the
    tower?
Muriel and Miriam, each in white, and
    like
May-blossoms in mid-autumn — was it
    they?
A light shot upward on them from the lake.
What sparkled there? whose hand was
    that? they stood
So close together. I am not keen of sight,
But coming nearer — Muriel had the
    ring —
'O Miriam! have you given your ring to
    her?   230
O Miriam!' Miriam redden'd, Muriel
    clench'd
The hand that wore it, till I cried again:
'O Miriam, if you love me take the ring!'
She glanced at me, at Muriel, and was
    mute.
'Nay, if you cannot love me, let it be.'
Then — Muriel standing ever statue-like —
She turn'd, and in her soft imperial way
And saying gently, 'Muriel, by your leave,'

Unclosed the hand and from it drew the
  ring,
And gave it me, who pass'd it down her
  own, 240
'Io t' amo, all is well then.' Muriel fled.

MIRIAM.

Poor Muriel !

FATHER.

Ay, poor Muriel, when you hear
What follows ! Miriam loved me from the
  first,
Not thro' the ring; but on her marriage-
  morn
This birthday, death-day, and betrothal
  ring,
Laid on her table overnight, was gone;
And after hours of search and doubt and
  threats,
And hubbub, Muriel enter'd with it,
  'See ! —
Found in a chink of that old moulder'd
  floor ! ' 249
My Miriam nodded with a pitying smile,
As who should say that 'those who lose
  can find.'
  Then I and she were married for a year,
One year without a storm, or even a cloud;
And you, my Miriam, born within the
  year;
And she, my Miriam, dead within the
  year.
  I sat beside her dying, and she gaspt:
'The books, the miniature, the lace are
  hers,
My ring too when she comes of age, or
  when
She marries; you — you loved me, kept
  your word.
You love me still, "Io t' amo." — Muriel
  — no — 260
She cannot love; she loves her own hard
  self,
Her firm will, her fix'd purpose. Promise
  me,
Miriam, not Muriel — she shall have the
  ring.'
And there the light of other life, which
  lives
Beyond our burial and our buried eyes,
Gleam'd for a moment in her own on earth.
I swore the vow, then with my latest kiss
Upon them, closed her eyes, which would
  not close,

But kept their watch upon the ring and
  you. 269
Your birthday was her death-day.

MIRIAM.

O poor mother !
And you, poor desolate father, and poor
  me,
The little senseless, worthless, wordless
  babe,
Saved when your life was wreck'd !'

FATHER

Desolate ? yes !
Desolate as that sailor whom the storm
Had parted from his comrade in the boat,
And dash'd half dead on barren sands,
  was I.
Nay, you were my one solace; only — you
Were always ailing. Muriel's mother,
  sent,
And sure am I, by Muriel, one day came
And saw you, shook her head, and patted
  yours, 280
And smiled, and making with a kindly
  pinch
Each poor pale cheek a momentary rose —
' That should be fix'd,' she said; your pretty
  bud,
So blighted here, would flower into full
  health
Among our heath and bracken. Let her
  come !
And we will feed her with our mountain
  air,
And send her home to you rejoicing.'
  No —
We could not part. And once, when you,
  my girl,
Rode on my shoulder home — the tiny fist
Had graspt a daisy from your mother's
  grave — 290
By the lych-gate was Muriel. 'Ay,' she
  said,
' Among the tombs in this damp vale of
  yours !
You scorn my mother's warning, but the
  child
Is paler than before. We often walk
In open sun, and see beneath our feet
The mist of autumn gather from your lake,
And shroud the tower; and once we only
  saw
Your gilded vane, a light above the
  mist ' —

Our old bright bird that still is veering
    there   299
Above his four gold letters — ' and the light,'
She said, ' was like that light ' — and there
    she paused,
And long; till I, believing that the girl's
Lean fancy, groping for it, could not find
One likeness, laugh'd a little and found her
    two —
' A warrior's crest above the cloud of
    war ' —
' A fiery phœnix rising from the smoke,
The pyre he burnt in.' — ' Nay,' she said,
    ' the light
That glimmers on the marsh and on the
    grave.'
And spoke no more, but turn'd and past
    away.
    Miriam, I am not surely one of those 310
Caught by the flower that closes on the
    fly,
But after ten slow weeks her fix'd intent,
In aiming at an all but hopeless mark
To strike it, struck. I took, I left you
    there;
I came, I went, was happier day by day;
For Muriel nursed you with a mother's
    care;
Till on that clear and heather - scented
    height
The rounder cheek had brighten'd into
    bloom.
She always came to meet me carrying you,
And all her talk was of the babe she
    loved;   320
So, following her old pastime of the brook,
She threw the fly for me; but oftener left
That angling to the mother. ' Muriel's
    health
Had weaken'd, nursing little Miriam.
    Strange !
She used to shun the wailing babe, and
    dotes
On this of yours.' But when the matron
    saw
That hinted love was only wasted bait,
Not risen to, she was bolder. ' Ever since
You sent the fatal ring ' — I told her ' sent
To Miriam,' ' Doubtless — ay, but ever
    since   330
In all the world my dear one sees but
    you —
In your sweet babe she finds but you — she.
    makes
Her heart a mirror that reflects but you.'

And then the tear fell, the voice broke.
    Her heart !
I gazed into the mirror, as a man
Who sees his face in water, and a stone,
That glances from the bottom of the pool,
Strike upward thro' the shadow; yet at
    last,
Gratitude — loneliness — desire to keep
So skilled a nurse about you always —
    nay !   340
Some half remorseful kind of pity too —
Well ! well, you know I married Muriel
    Erne.
    ' I take thee Muriel for my wedded
    wife ' —
I had forgotten it was your birthday,
    child —
When all at once with some electric thrill
A cold air pass'd between us, and the
    hands
Fell from each other, and were join'd
    again.
    No second cloudless honeymoon was
    mine.
For by and by she sicken'd of the farce,
She dropt the gracious mask of mother-
    hood,   350
She came no more to meet me, carrying
    you,
Nor ever cared to set you on her knee,
Nor ever let you gambol in her sight,
Nor ever cheer'd you with a kindly smile,
Nor ever ceased to clamor for the ring;
Why had I sent the ring at first to her ?
Why had I made her love me thro' the
    ring,
And then had changed ? so fickle are men
    — the best !
Not she — but now my love was hers
    again,
The ring by right, she said, was hers
    again.   360
At times too shrilling in her angrier moods,
' That weak and watery nature love you ?
    No !
" *Io* t' amo, *Io* t' amo " ! ' flung herself
Against my heart, but often while her lips
Were warm upon my cheek, an icy breath,
As from the grating of a sepulchre,
Past over both. I told her of my vow,
No pliable idiot I to break my vow;
But still she made her outcry for the ring;
For one monotonous fancy madden'd her,
Till I myself was madden'd with her
    cry,   371

And even that 'Io t' amo,' those three sweet
Italian words, became a weariness.
　My people too were scared with eerie sounds,
A footstep, a low throbbing in the walls,
A noise of falling weights that never fell,
Weird whispers, bells that rang without a hand,
Door-handles turn'd when none was at the door,
And bolted doors that open'd of themselves;
And one betwixt the dark and light had seen
Her, bending by the cradle of her babe. 381

MIRIAM.

And I remember once that being waked
By noises in the house — and no one near —
I cried for nurse, and felt a gentle hand
Fall on my forehead, and a sudden face
Look'd in upon me like a gleam and pass'd,
And I was quieted, and slept again.
Or is it some half memory of a dream ?

FATHER.

Your fifth September birthday.

MIRIAM.

　　　　　　　　And the face,
The hand, — my mother.

FATHER.

　　　　　　Miriam, on that day
Two lovers parted by no scurrilous tale —
Mere want of gold — and still for twenty years 392
Bound by the golden cord of their first love —
Had ask'd us to their marriage, and to share
Their marriage - banquet. Muriel, paler then
Than ever you were in your cradle, moan'd,
' I am fitter for my bed, or for my grave,
I cannot go, go you.' And then she rose,
She clung to me with such a hard embrace,
So lingeringly long, that half-amazed 400
I parted from her, and I went alone.
And when the bridegroom murmur'd,
　' With this ring,'
I felt for what I could not find, the key,
The guardian of her relics, of *her* ring.
I kept it as a sacred amulet
About me, — gone ! and gone in that embrace !

Then, hurrying home, I found her not in house
Or garden — up the tower — an icy air
Fled by me. — There, the chest was open — all 409
The sacred relics tost about the floor —
Among them Muriel lying on her face —
I raised her, call'd her, ' Muriel, Muriel, wake ! '
The fatal ring lay near her; the glazed eye
Glared at me as in horror. Dead ! I took
And chafed the freezing hand. A red mark ran
All round one finger pointed straight, the rest
Were crumpled inwards. Dead ! — and maybe stung
With some remorse, had stolen, worn the ring —
Then torn it from her finger, or as if — 419
For never had I seen her show remorse —
As if —

MIRIAM.

— those two ghost lovers —

FATHER.

　　　　　　　　Lovers yet —

MIRIAM.

Yes, yes !

FATHER.

— but dead so long, gone up so far,
That now their ever-rising life has dwarf'd
Or lost the moment of their past on earth,
As we forget our wail at being born —
As if —

MIRIAM.

—a dearer ghost had —

FATHER.

　　　　　　— wrench'd it away.

MIRIAM.

Had floated in with sad reproachful eyes,
Till from her own hand she had torn the ring 428
In fright, and fallen dead. And I myself
Am half afraid to wear it.

FATHER.

　　　　　　Well, no more !
No bridal music this ! but fear not you !
You have the ring she guarded; that poor link

With earth is broken, and has left her
    free,
Except that, still drawn downward for an
    hour,
Her spirit hovering by the church, where
    she
Was married too, may linger, till she sees
Her maiden coming like a queen, who
    leaves
Some colder province in the North to gain
Her capital city, where the loyal bells
Clash welcome — linger, till her own, the
    babe   440
She lean'd to from her spiritual sphere,
Her lonely maiden princess, crowned with
    flowers,
Has enter'd on the larger woman-world
Of wives and mothers.
              But the bridal veil —
Your nurse is waiting. Kiss me, child, and
    go.

FORLORN

I

'HE is fled — I wish him dead —
  He that wrought my ruin —
O, the flattery and the craft
  Which were my undoing —
  In the night, in the night,
  When the storms are blowing.

II

'Who was witness of the crime ?
  Who shall now reveal it ?
He is fled, or he is dead,
  Marriage will conceal it —
  In the night, in the night,
  While the gloom is growing.'

III

Catherine, Catherine, in the night,
  What is this you 're dreaming ?
There is laughter down in hell
  At your simple scheming —
  In the night, in the night,
  When the ghosts are fleeting.

IV

You to place a hand in his
  Like an honest woman's,
You that lie with wasted lungs
  Waiting for your summons —

In the night, O, the night !
O, the deathwatch beating !

V

There will come a witness soon
  Hard to be confuted,
All the world will hear a voice
  Scream you are polluted —
  In the night ! O, the night,
  When the owls are wailing !

VI

Shame and marriage, shame and marriage,
  Fright and foul dissembling,
Bantering bridesman, reddening priest,
  Tower and altar trembling —
  In the night, O, the night,
  When the mind is failing !

VII

Mother, dare you kill your child ?
  How your hand is shaking !
Daughter of the seed of Cain,
  What is this you 're taking ? —
  In the night, O, the night,
  While the house is sleeping.

VIII

Dreadful ! has it come to this,
  O unhappy creature ?
You that would not tread on a worm
  For your gentle nature —
  In the night, O, the night,
  O, the night of weeping !

IX

Murder would not veil your sin,
  Marriage will not hide it,
Earth and Hell will brand your name,
  Wretch, you must abide it —
  In the night, O, the night,
  Long before the dawning.

X

Up, get up, and tell him all,
  Tell him you were lying !
Do not die with a lie in your mouth,
  You that know you 're dying —
  In the night, O, the night,
  While the grave is yawning.

XI

No — you will not die before,
  Tho' you 'll ne'er be stronger;

You will live till *that* is born,
Then a little longer —
In the night, O, the night,
While the Fiend is prowling.

XII

Death and marriage, death and marriage!
Funeral hearses rolling!
Black with bridal favors mixt!
Bridal bells with tolling! —
In the night, O, the night,
When the wolves are howling.

XIII

Up, get up, the time is short,
Tell him now or never!
Tell him all before you die,
Lest you die for ever —
In the night, O, the night,
Where there's no forgetting.

XIV

Up she got, and wrote him all,
All her tale of sadness,
Blister'd every word with tears,
And eased her heart of madness —
In the night, and nigh the dawn,
And while the moon was setting.

HAPPY

THE LEPER'S BRIDE

Suggested by the quotation from an archæological letter by Rev. Bourchier James, appended to the poem by Tennyson.

I

WHY wail you, pretty plover? and what is
it that you fear?
Is he sick, your mate, like mine? have
you lost him, is he fled?
And there — the heron rises from his watch
beside the mere,
And flies above the leper's hut, where
lives the living-dead.

II

Come back, nor let me know it! would he
live and die alone?
And has he not forgiven me yet, his over-
jealous bride,

Who am, and was, and will be his, his own
and only own,
To share his living death with him, die
with him side by side?

III

Is that the leper's hut on the solitary moor,
Where noble Ulric dwells forlorn, and
wears the leper's weed? 10
The door is open. He! is he standing at
the door,
My soldier of the Cross? it is he, and
he indeed!

IV

My roses — will he take them *now* — mine,
his — from off the tree
We planted both together, happy in our
marriage morn?
O God, I could blaspheme, for he fought
Thy fight for Thee,
And Thou hast made him leper to com-
pass him with scorn —

V

Hast spared the flesh of thousands, the
coward and the base,
And set a crueller mark than Cain's on
him, the good and brave!
He sees me, waves me from him. I will
front him face to face.
You need not wave me from you. I
would leap into your grave. 20

.   .   .   .

VI

My warrior of the Holy Cross and of the
conquering sword,
The roses that you cast aside — once
more I bring you these.
No nearer? do you scorn me when you tell
me, O my lord,
You would not mar the beauty of your
bride with your disease.

VII

You say your body is so foul — then here
I stand apart,
Who yearn to lay my loving head upon
your leprous breast.
The leper plague may scale my skin, but
never taint my heart;
Your body is not foul to me, and body is
foul at best.

VIII

I loved you first when young and fair, but
    now I love you most;
  The fairest flesh at last is filth on which
    the worm will feast;   30
This poor rib-grated dungeon of the holy
    human ghost,
  This house with all its hateful needs no
    cleaner than the beast,

IX

This coarse diseaseful creature which in
    Eden was divine,
  This Satan-haunted ruin, this little city
    of sewers,
This wall of solid flesh that comes between
    your soul and mine,
  Will vanish and give place to the beauty
    that endures,

X

The beauty that endures on the Spiritual
    height,
  When we shall stand transfigured, like
    Christ on Hermon hill,
And moving each to music, soul in soul and
    light in light,
  Shall flash thro' one another in a moment
    as we will.   40

XI

Foul ! foul ! the word was yours not mine,
    I worship that right hand
  Which fell'd the foes before you as the
    woodman fells the wood,
And sway'd the sword that lighten'd back
    the sun of Holy Land,
  And clove the Moslem crescent moon,
    and changed it into blood.

XII

And once I worshipt all too well this crea-
    ture of decay,
  For age will chink the face, and death
    will freeze the supplest limbs —
Yet you in your mid manhood — O, the
    grief when yesterday
  They bore the Cross before you to the
    chant of funeral hymns !

XIII

'Libera me, Domine !' you sang the Psalm,
    and when
  The priest pronounced you dead, and
    flung the mould upon your feet,   50

A beauty came upon your face, not that of
    living men,
  But seen upon the silent brow when life
    has ceased to beat.

XIV

'Libera *nos*, Domine ' — you knew not one
    was there
  Who saw you kneel beside your bier, and
    weeping scarce could see;
May I come a little nearer, I that heard,
    and changed the prayer
  And sang the married 'nos' for the soli-
    tary 'me' ?

XV

My beauty marred by you ? by you ! so be
    it. All is well
  If I lose it and myself in the higher
    beauty, yours.
My beauty lured that falcon from his eyry
    on the fell,
  Who never caught one gleam of the
    beauty which endures —   60

XVI

The Count who sought to snap the bond
    that link'd us life to life,
  Who whisper'd me, 'Your Ulric loves'
    — a little nearer still —
He hiss'd, 'Let us revenge ourselves, your
    Ulric woos my wife' —
  A lie by which he thought he could sub-
    due me to his will.

XVII

I knew that you were near me when I let
    him kiss my brow;
  Did he touch me on the lips ? I was
    jealous, anger'd, vain,
And I meant to make *you* jealous. Are
    you jealous of me now ?
  Your pardon, O my love, if I ever gave
    you pain !

XVIII

You never once accused me, but I wept
    alone, and sigh'd
  In the winter of the present for the sum-
    mer of the past;   70
That icy winter silence — how it froze you
    from your bride,
  Tho' I made one barren effort to break it
    at the last !

XIX

I brought you, you remember, these roses,
  when I knew
  You were parting for the war, and you
    took them tho' you frown'd;
You frown'd and yet you kiss'd them. All
    at once the trumpet blew,
  And you spurr'd your fiery horse, and
    you hurl'd them to the ground.

XX

You parted for the Holy War without a
    word to me,
  And clear myself unask'd — not I. My
    nature was too proud.
And him I saw but once again, and far
    away was he,
  When I was praying in a storm — the
    crash was long and loud —   80

XXI

That God would ever slant His bolt from
    falling on your head —
  Then I lifted up my eyes, he was coming
    down the fell —
I clapt my hands. The sudden fire from
    heaven had dash'd him dead,
  And sent him charr'd and blasted to the
    deathless fire of hell.

XXII

See, I sinn'd but for a moment. I repented
    and repent,
  And trust myself forgiven by the God to
    whom I kneel.
A little nearer? Yes. I shall hardly be
    content
  Till I be leper like yourself, my love,
    from head to heel.

XXIII

O foolish dreams, that you, that I, would
    slight our marriage oath!
  I held you at that moment even dearer
    than before;   90
Now God has made you leper in His loving
    care for both,
  That we might cling together, never
    doubt each other more.

XXIV

The priest, who join'd you to the dead, has
    join'd our hands of old;
  If man and wife be but one flesh, let
    mine be leprous too,

As dead from all the human race as if be-
    neath the mould;
  If you be dead, then I am dead, who
    only live for you.

XXV

Would Earth tho' hid in cloud not be fol-
    low'd by the Moon?
  The leech forsake the dying bed for ter-
    ror of his life?
The shadow leave the Substance in the
    brooding light of noon?
  Or if *I* had been the leper would you
    have left the wife?   100

XXVI

Not take them? Still you wave me off —
    poor roses — must I go —
  I have worn them year by year — from
    the bush we both had set —
What? fling them to you? — well — that
    were hardly gracious. No!
  Your plague but passes by the touch. A
    little nearer yet!

XXVII

There, there! he buried you, the priest;
    the priest is not to blame,
  He joins us once again, to his either
    office true.
I thank him. I am happy, happy. Kiss
    me. In the name
  Of the everlasting God, I will live and die
    with you!

[Dean Milman has remarked that the pro-
tection and care afforded by the Church to this
blighted race of lepers was among the most
beautiful of its offices during the Middle Ages.
The leprosy of the thirteenth and fourteenth
centuries was supposed to be a legacy of the
Crusades, but was in all probability the off-
spring of meagre and unwholesome diet, miser-
able lodging and clothing, physical and moral
degradation. The services of the Church in
the seclusion of these unhappy sufferers were
most affecting. The stern duty of looking
to the public welfare is tempered with exqui-
site compassion for the victims of this loath-
some disease. The ritual for the sequestration
of the leprous differed little from the burial
service. After the leper had been sprinkled
with holy water, the priest conducted him into
the church, the leper singing the psalm 'Libera
me, Domine,' and the crucifix and bearer going
before. In the church a black cloth was
stretched over two trestles in front of the altar,

and the leper leaning at its side devoutly heard mass. The priest, taking up a little earth in his cloak, threw it on one of the leper's feet, and put him out of the church, if it did not rain too heavily ; took him to his hut in the midst of the fields, and then uttered the prohibitions: 'I forbid you entering the church ... or entering the company of others. I forbid you quitting your home without your leper's dress.' He concluded: 'Take this dress, and wear it in token of humility ; take these gloves, take this clapper, as a sign that you are forbidden to speak to any one. You are not to be indignant at being thus separated from others, and as to your little wants, good people will provide for you, and God will not desert you.' Then in this old ritual follow these sad words : 'When it shall come to pass that the leper shall pass out of this world, he shall be buried in his hut, and not in the churchyard.' At first there was a doubt whether wives should follow their husbands who had been leprous, or remain in the world and marry again. The Church decided that the marriage-tie was indissoluble, and so bestowed on these unhappy beings this immense source of consolation. With a love stronger than this living death, lepers were followed into banishment from the haunts of men by their faithful wives. Readers of Sir J. Stephen's 'Essays on Ecclesiastical Biography' will recollect the description of the founder of the Franciscan order, how, controlling his involuntary disgust, Saint Francis of Assisi washed the feet and dressed the sores of the lepers, once at least reverently applying his lips to their wounds. — BOURCHIER-JAMES.]

This ceremony of *quasi*-burial varied considerably at different times and in different places. In some cases a grave was dug, and the leper's face was often covered during the service.

TO ULYSSES[1]

Mr. W. G. Palgrave, to whom the poem was addressed, was a brother of Professor F. T. Palgrave. Tennyson once said to the latter, 'I think your brother is the cleverest man I ever saw.' Waugh, who records this, adds : 'He had, indeed, earned the title [of Ulysses], having been consul in 1866 at Sonkhoum Kale, in 1867 at Trebizond, in 1873 at St. Thomas, in 1876 at Manilla, and in 1878 consul-general in Bulgaria. To these he added, in 1879, the consulship at Bangkok, and in 1884 he was

[1] 'Ulysses,' the title of a number of essays by W. G. Palgrave. He died at Montevideo before seeing my poem.

consul-general of the Republic of Uruguay, a position which he still held at his death.'

I

ULYSSES, much-experienced man,
　Whose eyes have known this globe of ours,
　Her tribes of men, and trees, and flowers,
From Corrientes to Japan,

II

To you that bask below the Line,
　I soaking here in winter wet —
　The century's three strong eights have met
To drag me down to seventy-nine

III

In summer if I reach my day —
　To you,· yet young, who breathe the balm
　Of summer-winters by the palm
And orange grove of Paraguay,

IV

I, tolerant of the colder time,
　Who love the winter woods, to trace
　On paler heavens the branching grace
Of leafless elm, or naked lime,

V

And see my cedar green, and there
　My giant ilex keeping leaf
　When frost is keen and days are brief —
Or marvel how in English air

VI

My yucca, which no winter quells,
　Altho' the months have scarce begun,
　Has push'd toward our faintest sun
A spike of half-accomplish'd bells —

VII

Or watch the waving pine which here
　The warrior of Caprera set,[1]
　A name that earth will not forget
Till earth has roll'd her latest year —

VIII

I, once half-crazed for larger light
　On broader zones beyond the foam,

[1] Garibaldi said to me, alluding to his barren island, 'I wish I had your trees.'

But chaining fancy now at home
Among the quarried downs of Wight,

IX

Not less would yield full thanks to you
  For your rich gift, your tale of lands
  I know not,[1] your Arabian sands;
Your cane, your palm, tree-fern, bamboo,

X

The wealth of tropic bower and brake;
  Your Oriental Eden-isles,[2]
  Where man, nor only Nature smiles;
Your wonder of the boiling lake;[3]

XI

Phra-Chai, the Shadow of the Best,[4]
  Phra-bat[5] the step; your Pontic coast;
Crag-cloister;[6] Anatolian Ghost;[7]
  Hong-Kong,[8] Karnac,[9] and all the rest;

XII

Thro' which I follow'd line by line
  Your leading hand, and came, my friend,
  To prize your various book, and send
A gift of slenderer value, mine.

TO MARY BOYLE

WITH THE FOLLOWING POEM

For the poet's acquaintance with Mary Boyle,
see the 'Memoir,' vol. ii. p. 294.

I

'SPRING-FLOWERS'! While you still delay
    to take
  Your leave of town,
Our elm-tree's ruddy-hearted blossom-flake
  Is fluttering down.

[1] The tale of Nejd.
[2] The Philippines.
[3] In Dominica.
[4] The Shadow of the Lord. Certain obscure markings on a rock in Siam, which express the image of Buddha to the Buddhist more or less distinctly according to his faith and his moral worth.
[5] The footstep of the Lord on another rock.
[6] The monastery of Sumelas.
[7] Anatolian spectre stories.
[8] The three cities.
[9] Travels in Egypt.

II

Be truer to your promise. There! I heard
  Our cuckoo call.
Be needle to the magnet of your word,
  Nor wait, till all

III

Our vernal bloom from every vale and
    plain
  And garden pass,
And all the gold from each laburnum chain
  Drop to the grass.

IV

Is memory with your Marian gone to rest,
  Dead with the dead?
For ere she left us, when we met, you prest
  My hand, and said

V

'I come with your spring-flowers.' You
    came not, friend;
  My birds would sing,
You heard not. Take then this spring-
    flower I send,
  This song of spring,

VI

Found yesterday — forgotten mine own
    rhyme
  By mine old self,
As I shall be forgotten by old Time,
  Laid on the shelf —

VII

A rhyme that flower'd betwixt the whiten-
    ing sloe
  And kingcup blaze,
And more than half a hundred years ago,
  In rick-fire days,

VIII

When Dives loathed the times, and paced
    his land
  In fear of worse,
And sanguine Lazarus felt a vacant hand
  Fill with *his* purse.

IX

For lowly minds were madden'd to the
    height
  By tonguester tricks,
And once — I well remember that red night
  When thirty ricks,

X

All flaming, made an English homestead
    hell —
        These hands of mine
Have helpt to pass a bucket from the well
        Along the line,

XI

When this bare dome had not begun to
    gleam
        Thro' youthful curls,
And you were then a lover's fairy dream,
        His girl of girls;

XII

And you, that now are lonely, and with
    Grief
        Sit face to face,
Might find a flickering glimmer of relief
        In change of place.

XIII

What use to brood ?   This life of mingled
    pains
        And joys to me,
Despite of every Faith and Creed, remains
        The Mystery.

XIV

Let golden youth bewail the friend, the
    wife,
        For ever gone.
He dreams of that long walk thro' desert
    life
        Without the one.

XV

The silver year should cease to mourn and
    sigh —
        Not long to wait —
So close are we, dear Mary, you and I
        To that dim gate.

XVI

Take, read ! and be the faults your Poet
    makes
        Or many or few,
He rests content, if his young music wakes
        A wish in you

XVII

To change our dark Queen-city, all her
    realm
        Of sound and smoke,

For his clear heaven, and these few lanes
    of elm
        And whispering oak.

THE PROGRESS OF SPRING

Written more than fifty years before it was
printed in the ' Demeter' volume.   See stanza
vii. of the preceding poem.

I

THE ground-flame of the crocus breaks the
    mould,
    Fair Spring slides hither o'er the South-
        ern sea,
Wavers on her thin stem the snowdrop
    cold
    That trembles not to kisses of the bee.
Come, Spring, for now from all the drip-
    ping eaves
    The spear of ice has wept itself away,
And hour by hour unfolding woodbine
    leaves
    O'er his uncertain shadow droops the
        day.
She comes !   The loosen'd rivulets run;
    The frost-bead melts upon her golden
        hair;
Her mantle, slowly greening in the Sun,
    Now wraps her close, now arching leaves
        her bare
    To breaths of balmier air;

II

Up leaps the lark, gone wild to welcome
    her,
    About her glance the tits, and shriek the
        jays,
Before her skims the jubilant woodpecker
    The linnet's bosom blushes at her gaze,
While round her brows a woodland culver
    flits,
    Watching her large light eyes and gra-
        cious looks,
And in her open palm a halcyon sits
    Patient — the secret splendor of the
        brooks.
Come, Spring !   She comes on waste and
    wood,
    On farm and field; but enter also here,
Diffuse thyself at will thro' all my blood,
    And, tho' thy violet sicken into sere,
    Lodge with me all the year !

III

Once more a downy drift against the brakes,
　Self - darken'd in the sky, descending
　　slow !
But gladly see I thro' the wavering flakes
　Yon blanching apricot like snow in snow.
These will thine eyes not brook in forest-
　　paths,
　On their perpetual pine, nor round the
　　beech;
They fuse themselves to little spicy baths,
　Solved in the tender blushes of the
　　peach;
They lose themselves and die
　On that new life that gems the hawthorn
　　line;
Thy gay lent-lilies wave and put them by,
　And out once more in varnish'd glory
　　shine
　　Thy stars of celandine.

IV

She floats across the hamlet. Heaven
　　lours,
　But in the tearful splendor of her smiles
I see the slowly-thickening chestnut towers
　Fill out the spaces by the barren tiles.
Now past her feet the swallow circling
　　flies,
　A clamorous cuckoo stoops to meet her
　　hand;
Her light makes rainbows in my closing
　　eyes,
　I hear a charm of song thro' all the land.
Come, Spring ! She comes, and Earth is
　　glad
　To roll her North below thy deepening
　　dome,
But ere thy maiden birk be wholly clad,
　And these low bushes dip their twigs in
　　foam,
　　Make all true hearths thy home.

V

Across my garden ! and the thicket stirs,
　The fountain pulses high in sunnier jets,
The blackcap warbles, and the turtle purrs,
　The starling claps his tiny castanets.
Still round her forehead wheels the wood-
　　land dove,
　And scatters on her throat the sparks of
　　dew,
The kingcup fills her footprint, and above
　Broaden the glowing isles of vernal blue.

Hail, ample presence of a Queen,
　Bountiful, beautiful, apparell'd gay,
Whose mantle, every shade of glancing
　　green,
　Flies back in fragrant breezes to display
　A tunic white as May !

VI

She whispers, 'From the South I bring
　　you balm,
　For on a tropic mountain was I born,
While some dark dweller by the coco-palm
　Watch'd my far meadow zoned with airy
　　morn;
From under rose a muffled moan of floods;
　I sat beneath a solitude of snow;
There no one came, the turf was fresh, the
　　woods
　Plunged gulf on gulf thro' all their vales
　　below.
I saw beyond their silent tops
　The steaming marshes of the scarlet
　　cranes,
The slant seas leaning on the mangrove
　　copse,
　And summer basking in the sultry plains
　About a land of canes.

VII

' Then from my vapor-girdle soaring forth
　I scaled the buoyant highway of the
　　birds,
And drank the dews and drizzle of the
　　North,
　That I might mix with men, and hear
　　their words
On pathway'd plains; for — while my hand
　　exults
　Within the bloodless heart of lowly flow-
　　ers
To work old laws of Love to fresh results,
　Thro' manifold effect of simple pow-
　　ers —
I too would teach the man
　Beyond the darker hour to see the
　　bright,
That his fresh life may close as it began,
　The still-fulfilling promise of a light
　　Narrowing the bounds of night.'

VIII

So wed thee with my soul, that I may
　　mark
　The coming year's great good and varied
　　ills,

And new developments, whatever spark
  Be struck from out the clash of warring
      wills;
Or whether, since our nature cannot rest,
  The smoke of war's volcano burst again
From hoary deeps that belt the changeful
      West,
  Old Empires, dwellings of the kings of
      men;
Or should those fail that hold the helm,
  While the long day of knowledge grows
      and warms,
And in the heart of this most ancient realm
  A hateful voice be utter'd, and alarms
  Sounding 'To arms! to arms!'

IX

A simpler, saner lesson might he learn
  Who reads thy gradual process, Holy
      Spring.
Thy leaves possess the season in their turn,
  And in their time thy warblers rise on
      wing.
How surely glidest thou from March to
      May,
  And changest, breathing it, the sullen
      wind,
Thy scope of operation, day by day,
  Larger and fuller, like the human mind!
Thy warmths from bud to bud
Accomplish that blind model in the seed,
And men have hopes, which race the rest-
      less blood,
  That after many changes may succeed
  Life which is Life indeed.

MERLIN AND THE GLEAM

Compare 'The Voyage;' and see also 'Free-
dom' (1884):

  'O follower of the Vision, still
    In motion to the distant gleam,' etc.

Stopford Brooke says of this poem: 'It is as
lovely in form and rhythm and imagination, as
it is noble in thought and emotion. It speaks
to all poetic hearts in England; it tells them of
his coming death. It then recalls his past, his
youth, his manhood; his early poems, his crit-
ics, his central labor on Arthur's tale; and we
see through its verse clear into the inmost
chamber of his heart. What sits there upon
the throne, what has always sat thereon? It is
the undying longing and search after the ideal
light, the mother-passion of all the supreme
artists of the world. "I am Merlin, who fol-
low the Gleam." I know of no poem of Ten-
nyson's which more takes my heart with magic
and beauty.'

I

O young Mariner,
You from the haven
Under the sea-cliff,
You that are watching
The gray Magician
With eyes of wonder,
I am Merlin,
And *I* am dying,
I am Merlin
Who follow the Gleam.

II

Mighty the Wizard
Who found me at sunrise
Sleeping, and woke me
And learn'd me Magic!
Great the Master,
And sweet the Magic,
When over the valley,
In early summers,
Over the mountain,
On human faces,
And all around me,
Moving to melody,
Floated the Gleam.

III

Once at the croak of a Raven who crost it
A barbarous people,
Blind to the magic
And deaf to the melody,
Snarl'd at and cursed me.
A demon vext me,
The light retreated,
The landskip darken'd,
The melody deaden'd,
The Master whisper'd,
'Follow the Gleam.'

IV

Then to the melody,
Over a wilderness
Gliding, and glancing at
Elf of the woodland,
Gnome of the cavern,
Griffin and Giant,
And dancing of Fairies
In desolate hollows,
And wraiths of the mountain,
And rolling of dragons
By warble of water,

Or cataract music
Of falling torrents,
Flitted the Gleam.

V

Down from the mountain
And over the level,
And streaming and shining on
Silent river,
Silvery willow,
Pasture and plowland,
Innocent maidens,
Garrulous children,
Homestead and harvest,
Reaper and gleaner,
And rough-ruddy faces
Of lowly labor,
Slided the Gleam —

VI

Then, with a melody
Stronger and statelier,
Led me at length
To the city and palace
Of Arthur the King;
Touch'd at the golden
Cross of the churches,
Flash'd on the tournament,
Flicker'd and bicker'd
From helmet to helmet,
And last on the forehead
Of Arthur the blameless
Rested the Gleam.

VII

Clouds and darkness
Closed upon Camelot;
Arthur had vanish'd
I knew not whither,
The king who loved me,
And cannot die;
For out of the darkness
Silent and slowly
The Gleam, that had waned to a wintry
    glimmer
On icy fallow
And faded forest,
Drew to the valley
Named of the shadow,
And slowly brightening
Out of the glimmer,
And slowly moving again to a melody
    Yearningly tender,
Fell on the shadow,

No longer a shadow,
But clothed with the Gleam.

VIII

And broader and brighter
The Gleam flying onward,
Wed to the melody,
Sang thro' the world;
And slower and fainter,
Old and weary,
But eager to follow,
I saw, whenever
In passing it glanced upon
Hamlet or city,
That under the Crosses
The dead man's garden,
The mortal hillock,
Would break into blossom;
And so to the land's
Last limit I came —
And can no longer,
But die rejoicing,
For thro' the Magic
Of Him the Mighty,
Who taught me in childhood,
There on the border
Of boundless Ocean,
And all but in Heaven
Hovers the Gleam.

IX

Not of the sunlight,
Not of the moonlight,
Not of the starlight!
O young Mariner,
Down to the haven,
Call your companions,
Launch your vessel
And crowd your canvas,
And, ere it vanishes
Over the margin,
After it, follow it,
Follow the Gleam.

ROMNEY'S REMORSE

[I read Hayley's Life of Romney the other
day — Romney wanted but education and read-
ing to make him a very fine painter: but his
ideal was not high nor fixed. How touching
is the close of his life! He married at nine-
teen, and because Sir Joshua and others had
said that 'marriage spoilt an artist' almost
immediately left his wife in the North and

scarce saw her till the end of his life ; when
old, nearly mad, and quite desolate, he went
back to her and she received him and nursed
him till he died. This quiet act of hers is
worth all Romney's pictures ! even as a matter
of Art, I am sure. — EDWARD FITZGERALD,
'Letters and Literary Remains,' vol. i.]

'BEAT, little heart — I give you this and
   this.'
  Who are you ? What ! the Lady Ham-
   ilton ?
Good, I am never weary painting you.
To sit once more ? Cassandra, Hebe, Joan,
Or spinning at your wheel beside the
   vine —
Bacchante, what you will; and if I fail
To conjure and concentrate into form
And color all you are, the fault is less
In me than Art. What artist ever yet
Could make pure light live on the canvas ?
   Art !
Why should I so disrelish that short word ?
  Where am I ? snow on all the hills ! so
   hot,
So fever'd ! never colt would more delight
To roll himself in meadow grass than I
To wallow in that winter of the hills.
  Nurse, were you hired ? or came of your
   own will
To wait on one so broken, so forlorn ?
Have I not met you somewhere long ago ?
I am all but sure I have — in Kendal
   church —
O, yes ! I hired you for a season there,
And then we parted; but you look so kind
That you will not deny my sultry throat
One draught of icy water. There — you
   spill
The drops upon my forehead. Your hand
   shakes.
I am ashamed. I am a trouble to you,
Could kneel for your forgiveness. Are
   they tears ?
For me — they do me too much grace —
   for me ?
O Mary, Mary !
          Vexing you with words !
Words only, born of fever, or the fumes
Of that dark opiate dose you gave me, —
   words,
Wild babble. I have stumbled back again
Into the common day, the sounder self.
God stay me there, if only for your sake,
The truest, kindliest, noblest-hearted wife
That ever wore a Christian marriage-ring.

My curse upon the Master's apothegm,
That wife and children drag an artist
   down !
This seem'd my lodestar in the heaven of
   Art,
And lured me from the household fire on
   earth.
To you my days have been a lifelong lie,
Grafted on half a truth; and tho' you say,
  'Take comfort you have won the painter's
   fame,'
The best in me that sees the worst in me,
And groans to see it, finds no comfort
   there.
  What fame ? I am not Raphael, Titian,
   — no,
Nor even a Sir Joshua, some will cry.
Wrong there ! The painter's fame ? but
   mine, that grew
Blown into glittering by the popular breath,
May float awhile beneath the sun, may roll
The rainbow hues of heaven about it —
               There !
The color'd bubble bursts above the abyss
Of Darkness, utter Lethe.

               Is it so ?
Her sad eyes plead for my own fame with
   me
To make it dearer.

           Look, the sun has risen
To flame along another dreary day.
Your hand. How bright you keep your
   marriage-ring !
Raise me. I thank you.

          Has your opiate then
Bred this black mood ? or am I conscious,
   more
Than other Masters, of the chasm between
Work and Ideal ? Or does the gloom of
   age
And suffering cloud the height I stand
   upon
Even from myself ? stand ? stood — no
   more.
             And yet
The world would lose, if such a wife as you
Should vanish unrecorded. Might I crave
One favor ? I am bankrupt of all claim
On your obedience, and my strongest wish
Falls flat before your least unwillingness.
Still, would you — if it please you — sit to
   me ?

I dream'd last night of that clear sum-
mer noon,
When seated on a rock, and foot to foot
With your own shadow in the placid lake,
You claspt our infant daughter, heart to
heart.
I had been among the hills, and brought
you down
A length of staghorn-moss, and this you
twined
About her cap. I see the picture yet,
Mother and child. A sound from far away,
No louder than a bee among the flowers,
A fall of water lull'd the noon asleep.
You still'd it for the moment with a song
Which often echo'd in me, while I stood
Before the great Madonna-masterpieces
Of ancient Art in Paris, or in Rome.

Mary, my crayons! if I can, I will.
You should have been — I might have
made you once,
Had I but known you as I know you now —
The true Alcestis of the time. Your song —
Sit, listen! I remember it, a proof
That I — even I — at times remember'd
you.

'Beat upon mine, little heart! beat, beat!
Beat upon mine! you are mine, my sweet!
All mine from your pretty blue eyes to your feet,
My sweet.'

Less profile! turn to me — three-quarter
face.

'Sleep, little blossom, my honey, my bliss!
For I give you this, and I give you this!
And I blind your pretty blue eyes with a kiss!
Sleep!'

Too early blinded by the kiss of death —

'Father and Mother will watch you grow' —

You watch'd, not I; she did not grow, she
died.

'Father and Mother will watch you grow,
And gather the roses whenever they blow,
And find the white heather wherever you go,
My sweet.'

Ah, my white heather only blooms in hea-
ven
With Milton's amaranth. There, there,
there! a child
Had shamed me at it — Down, you idle
tools,

Stampt into dust — tremulous, all awry,
Blurr'd like a landskip in a ruffled pool, —
Not one stroke firm. This Art, that harlot-
like
Seduced me from you, leaves me harlot-
like,
Who love her still, and whimper, impotent
To win her back before I die — and then —
Then, in the loud world's bastard judg-
ment-day,
One truth will damn me with the mindless
mob,
Who feel no touch of my temptation, more
Than all the myriad lies that blacken round
The corpse of every man that gains a name;
'This model husband, this fine artist!'
Fool,
What matters? Six foot deep of burial
mould
Will dull their comments! Ay, but when
the shout
Of His descending peals from heaven, and
throbs
Thro' earth and all her graves, if *He* should
ask,
'Why left you wife and children? for my
sake,
According to my word?' and I replied,
'Nay, Lord, for *Art*,' why, that would
sound so mean
That all the dead, who wait the doom of
hell
For bolder sins than mine, adulteries,
Wife-murders, — nay, the ruthless Mussul-
man
Who flings his bowstrung harem in the
sea,
Would turn, and glare at me, and point
and jeer,
And gibber at the worm who, living, made
The wife of wives a widow-bride, and lost
Salvation for a sketch.
                    I am wild again!
The coals of fire you heap upon my head
Have crazed me. Some one knocking there
without?
No! Will my Indian brother come? to
find
Me or my coffin? Should I know the
man?
This worn-out Reason dying in her house
May leave the windows blinded, and if so,
Bid him farewell for me, and tell him —
                              Hope!
I hear a death-bed angel whisper, 'Hope.'

'The miserable have no medicine —
But only hope !' He said it — in the play.
His crime was of the senses; of the mind
Mine — worse, cold, calculated.
                Tell my son —
O, let me lean my head upon your breast.
'Beat, little heart' on this fool brain of
    mine.
I once had friends — and many — none
    like you.
I love you more than when we married.
    Hope !
O, yes, I hope, or fancy that, perhaps,
Human forgiveness touches heaven, and
    thence —
For you forgive me, you are sure of that —
Reflected, sends a light on the forgiven.

PARNASSUS

Exegi monumentum . . .
Quod non . . .
Possit diruere . . .
                . . . innumerabilis
Annorum series et fuga temporum.
                    HORACE.

I

WHAT be those crown'd forms high over
    the sacred fountain ?
Bards, that the mighty Muses have raised
    to the heights of the mountain,
And over the flight of the Ages ! O God-
    desses, help me up thither !
Lightning may shrivel the laurel of Cæsar,
    but mine would not wither.
Steep is the mountain, but you, you will
    help me to overcome it,
And stand with my head in the zenith, and
    roll my voice from the summit,
Sounding for ever and ever thro' Earth
    and her listening nations,
And mixt with the great sphere-music of
    stars and of constellations.

II

What be those two shapes high over the
    sacred fountain,
Taller than all the Muses, and huger than
    all the mountain ?
On those two known peaks they stand ever
    spreading and heightening;
Poet, that evergreen laurel is blasted by
    more than lightning !

Look, in their deep double shadow the
    crown'd ones all disappearing !
Sing like a bird and be happy, nor hope for
    a deathless hearing !
'Sounding for ever and ever ?' pass on !
    the sight confuses —
These are Astronomy and Geology, terrible
    Muses !

III

If the lips were touch'd with fire from off
    a pure Pierian altar,
Tho' their music here be mortal need the
    singer greatly care ?
Other songs for other worlds ! the fire
    within him would not falter;
Let the golden Iliad vanish, Homer here is
    Homer there.

BY AN EVOLUTIONIST

THE Lord let the house of a brute to the
    soul of a man,
And the man said, 'Am I your debtor ?'
And the Lord — 'Not yet; but make it as
    clean as you can,
And then I will let you a better.'

I

If my body come from brutes, my soul un-
    certain or a fable,
Why not bask amid the senses while the
    sun of morning shines,
I, the finer brute rejoicing in my hounds,
    and in my stable,
Youth and health, and birth and wealth,
    and choice of women and of wines ?

II

What hast thou done for me, grim Old
    Age, save breaking my bones on the
    rack ?
Would I had past in the morning that
    looks so bright from afar !

OLD AGE

Done for thee ? starved the wild beast that
    was linkt with thee eighty years
    back.
Less weight now for the ladder-of-heaven
    that hangs on a star.

I

If my body come from brutes, tho' some-
what finer than their own,
  I am heir, and this my kingdom. Shall
the royal voice be mute?
No, but if the rebel subject seek to drag
me from the throne,
  Hold the sceptre, Human Soul, and rule
thy province of the brute.

II

I have climb'd to the snows of Age, and I
gaze at a field in the Past,
  Where I sank with the body at times in
the sloughs of a low desire,
But I hear no yelp of the beast, and the
Man is quiet at last,
  As he stands on the heights of his life
with a glimpse of a height that is
higher.

FAR — FAR — AWAY

(FOR MUSIC)

WHAT sight so lured him thro' the fields
he knew
As where earth's green stole into heaven's
own hue,
        Far — far — away?

What sound was dearest in his native
dells?
The mellow lin-lan-lone of evening bells
        Far — far — away.

What vague world-whisper, mystic pain or
joy,
Thro' those three words would haunt him
when a boy,
        Far — far — away?

A whisper from his dawn of life? a
breath
From some fair dawn beyond the doors of
death
        Far — far — away?

Far, far, how far? from o'er the gates of
birth,
The faint horizons, all the bounds of earth,
        Far — far — away?

What charm in words, a charm no words
could give?
O dying words, can Music make you live
        Far — far — away?

POLITICS

WE move, the wheel must always move,
  Nor always on the plain,
And if we move to such a goal
  As Wisdom hopes to gain,
Then you that drive, and know your craft,
  Will firmly hold the rein,
Nor lend an'ear to random cries,
  Or you may drive in vain;
For some cry 'Quick' and some cry 'Slow,'
  But, while the hills remain,
Up hill 'Too-slow' will need the whip,
  Down hill 'Too-quick' the chain.

BEAUTIFUL CITY

BEAUTIFUL city, the centre and crater of
European confusion,
O you with your passionate shriek for the
rights of an equal humanity,
How often your Re-volution has proven but
E-volution
Roll'd again back on itself in the tides of a
civic insanity!

THE ROSES ON THE TERRACE

ROSE, on this terrace fifty years ago,
  When I was in my June, you in your May,
Two words, 'My Rose,' set all your face
aglow,
  And now that I am white and you are gray,
That blush of fifty years ago, my dear,
  Blooms in the past, but close to me to-day,
As this red rose, which on our terrace here
Glows in the blue of fifty miles away.

THE PLAY

ACT first, this Earth, a stage so gloom'd
with woe
You all but sicken at the shifting scenes.
And yet be patient. Our Playwright may
show
  In some fifth act what this wild Drama
means.

ON ONE WHO AFFECTED AN EFFEMINATE MANNER

WHILE man and woman still are incomplete,
I prize that soul where man and woman meet,
Which types all Nature's male and female plan,
But, friend, man - woman is not woman-man.

TO ONE WHO RAN DOWN THE ENGLISH

You make our faults too gross, and thence maintain
Our darker future. May your fears be vain !
At times the small black fly upon the pane
May seem the black ox of the distant plain.

THE SNOWDROP

MANY, many welcomes,
February fair-maid,
Ever as of old time,
Solitary firstling,
Coming in the cold time,
Prophet of the gay time,
Prophet of the May time,
Prophet of the roses,
Many, many welcomes,
February fair-maid !

THE THROSTLE

This poem, which had been printed in this country in the New York 'World,' was first published in England, 'to secure copyright, in an edition ultimately reduced to two copies, . . . a mere leaflet, consisting of a title and one page of text' (Waugh). It was subsequently printed in the 'New Review' for October, 1889, and was included in the 'Demeter' volume, published in December of the same year.

'SUMMER is coming, summer is coming.
I know it, I know it, I know it.
Light again, leaf again, life again, love again !'
Yes, my wild little Poet.

Sing the new year in under the blue.
Last year you sang it as gladly.
'New, new, new, new !' Is it then so new
That you should carol so madly ?

'Love again, song again, nest again, young again,'
Never a prophet so crazy !
And hardly a daisy as yet, little friend,
See, there is hardly a daisy.

'Here again, here, here, here, happy year !'
O warble unchidden, unbidden !
Summer is coming, is coming, my dear,
And all the winters are hidden.

THE OAK

This poem, as the 'Memoir' (vol. ii. p. 366) informs us, was one which, like 'Far — far — away,' the author liked, thinking it 'clean cut like a Greek epigram.'

LIVE thy Life,
Young and old,
Like yon oak,
Bright in spring,
Living gold;

Summer-rich
Then; and then
Autumn-changed,
Soberer-hued
Gold again.

All his leaves
Fallen at length,
Look, he stands,
Trunk and bough,
Naked strength.

IN MEMORIAM

W. G. WARD

William George Ward (1812-82) was prominent in the 'Tractarian' movement in the English Church during the second quarter of the present century. The London 'Times' of June 21, 1887, in its jubilee retrospect of the events of Queen Victoria's reign, referring to the ecclesiastical aspect of the period, says: 'The Catholic — or, as it is named from the accident of its method, the Tractarian — movement in the Church of England, is the first to arrest the attention of the observer;' and, after discussing its influence on the religion of England, adds that its originators 'found themselves stranded in an eddy of the stream they had set in motion, and while the Catholic revival vivified and transformed the English Church, itself being modified and transformed in the process, its distinguished pioneers, with Newman and Ward at their head, joined the Church of Rome.' The life of Ward, with special reference to his connection with this religious movement, has been written by his son, Mr. Wilfrid Ward, in the two volumes entitled 'William George Ward and the Oxford Movement' (London, 1889), which was reviewed by the present Lord Tennyson in the 'Nineteenth Century,' (vol. xxvi. p. 343), and 'William George Ward and the Catholic Revival in England' (London, 1893).

FAREWELL, whose like on earth I shall not find,
 Whose Faith and Work were bells of full accord,
My friend, the most unworldly of mankind,
 Most generous of all Ultramontanes, Ward,
How subtle at tierce and quart of mind with mind,
 How loyal in the following of thy Lord !

THE DEATH OF ŒNONE

JUNE BRACKEN AND HEATHER

TO ——

THERE on the top of the down,
The wild heather round me and over me
 June's high blue,
When I look'd at the bracken so bright and the heather so brown,
I thought to myself I would offer this book to you,
This, and my love together,
To you that are seventy-seven,
With a faith as clear as the heights of the June-blue heaven,
And a fancy as summer-new
As the green of the bracken amid the gloom of the heather.

TO THE MASTER OF BALLIOL

I

DEAR Master in our classic town,
You, loved by all the younger gown
 There at Balliol,
Lay your Plato for one minute down,

II

And read a Grecian tale re-told,
Which, cast in later Grecian mould,
 Quintus Calaber
Somewhat lazily handled of old;

III

And on this white midwinter day —
For have the far-off hymns of May,
 All her melodies,
All her harmonies echo'd away? —

IV

To-day, before you turn again
To thoughts that lift the soul of men,
 Hear my cataract's
Downward thunder in hollow and glen,

V

Till, led by dream and vague desire,
The woman, gliding toward the pyre,
 Find her warrior
Stark and dark in his funeral fire.

THE DEATH OF ŒNONE

ŒNONE sat within the cave from out
Whose ivy-matted mouth she used to gaze
Down at the Troad; but the goodly view
Was now one blank, and all the serpent vines
Which on the touch of heavenly feet had risen,
And gliding thro' the branches overbower'd

The naked Three, were wither'd long ago,
And thro' the sunless winter morning-mist
In silence wept upon the flowerless earth.
  And while she stared at those dead cords
      that ran
Dark thro' the mist, and linking tree to
      tree,
But once were gayer than a dawning sky
With many a pendent bell and fragrant
      star,
Her Past became her Present, and she saw
Him, climbing toward her with the golden
      fruit,
Him, happy to be chosen Judge of Gods,
Her husband in the flush of youth and
      dawn,
Paris, himself as beauteous as a God.
  Anon from out the long ravine below,
She heard a wailing cry, that seem'd at first
Thin as the batlike shrillings of the Dead
When driven to Hades, but, in coming
      near,
Across the downward thunder of the brook
Sounded 'Œnone'; and on a sudden he,
Paris, no longer beauteous as a God,
Struck by a poison'd arrow in the fight,
Lame, crooked, reeling, livid, thro' the
      mist
Rose, like the wraith of his dead self, and
      moan'd
'Œnone, *my* Œnone, while we dwelt
Together in this valley — happy then —
Too happy had I died within thine arms,
Before the feud of Gods had marr'd our
      peace,
And sunder'd each from each. I am dying
      now
Pierced by a poison'd dart. Save me.
      Thou knowest,
Taught by some God, whatever herb or
      balm
May clear the blood from poison, and thy
      fame
Is blown thro' all the Troad, and to thee
The shepherd brings his adder-bitten lamb,
The wounded warrior climbs from Troy to
      thee.
My life and death are in thy hand. The
      Gods
Avenge on stony hearts a fruitless prayer
For pity. Let me owe my life to thee.
I wrought thee bitter wrong, but thou
      forgive,
Forget it. Man is but the slave of Fate.
Œnone, by thy love which once was mine,

Help, heal me. I am poison'd to the heart.'
'And I to mine' she said 'Adulterer,
Go back to thine adulteress and die!'
  He groan'd, he turn'd, and in the mist at
      once
Became a shadow, sank and disappear'd,
But, ere the mountain rolls into the plain,
Fell headlong dead; and of the shepherds
      one
Their oldest, and the same who first had
      found
Paris, a naked babe, among the woods
Of Ida, following lighted on him there,
And shouted, and the shepherds heard and
      came.
  One raised the Prince, one sleek'd the
      squalid hair,
One kiss'd his hand, another closed his
      eyes,
And then, remembering the gay playmate
      rear'd
Among them, and forgetful of the man,
Whose crime had half unpeopled Ilion,
      these
All that day long labor'd, hewing the pines,
And built their shepherd-prince a funeral
      pile;
And, while the star of eve was drawing
      light
From the dead sun, kindled the pyre, and
      all
Stood round it, hush'd, or calling on his
      name.
  But when the white fog vanish'd like a
      ghost
Before the day, and every topmost pine
Spired into bluest heaven, still in her cave,
Amazed, and ever seeming stared upon
By ghastlier than the Gorgon head, a
      face, —
His face deform'd by lurid blotch and
      blain —
There, like a creature frozen to the heart
Beyond all hope of warmth, Œnone sat
Not moving, till in front of that ravine
Which drowsed in gloom, self-darken'd
      from the west,
The sunset blazed along the wall of Troy.
  Then her head sank, she slept, and thro'
      her dream
A ghostly murmur floated, 'Come to me,
Œnone! I can wrong thee now no more,
Œnone, my Œnone,' and the dream
Wail'd in her, when she woke beneath the
      stars.

What star could burn so low? not Ilion
yet.
What light was there? She rose and slowly
down,
By the long torrent's ever-deepen'd roar,
Paced, following, as in trance, the silent
cry.
She waked a bird of prey that scream'd
and past;
She roused a snake that hissing writhed
away;
A panther sprang across her path, she
heard
The shriek of some lost life among the
pines,
But when she gain'd the broader vale, and
saw
The ring of faces redden'd by the flames
Enfolding that dark body which had lain
Of old in her embrace, paused — and then
ask'd
Falteringly, 'Who lies on yonder pyre?'
But every man was mute for reverence.
Then moving quickly forward till the heat
Smote on her brow, she lifted up a voice
Of shrill command, 'Who burns upon the
pyre?'
Whereon their oldest and their boldest
said,
'He, whom thou wouldst not heal!' and all
at once
The morning light of happy marriage
broke
Thro' all the clouded years of widowhood,
And muffling up her comely head, and
crying
'Husband!' she leapt upon the funeral pile,
And mixt herself with *him* and past in fire.

SAINT TELEMACHUS

HAD the fierce ashes of some fiery peak
Been hurl'd so high they ranged about the
globe?
For day by day, thro' many a blood-red
eve,
In that four hundredth summer after
Christ,
The wrathful sunset glared against a cross
Rear'd on the tumbled ruins of an old fane
No longer sacred to the Sun, and flamed
On one huge slope beyond, where in his
cave

The man, whose pious hand had built the
cross,
A man who never changed a word with
men,
Fasted and pray'd, Telemachus the Saint.
Eve after eve that haggard anchorite
Would haunt the desolated fane, and there
Gaze at the ruin, often mutter low
'Vicisti Galilæe'; louder again,
Spurning a shatter'd fragment of the God,
'Vicisti Galilæe!' but — when now
Bathed in that lurid crimson — ask'd 'Is
earth
On fire to the West? or is the Demon-god
Wroth at his fall?' and heard an answer
'Wake
Thou deedless dreamer, lazying out a life
Of self-suppression, not of selfless love.'
And once a flight of shadowy fighters crost
The disk, and once, he thought, a shape
with wings
Came sweeping by him, and pointed to the
West,
And at his ear he heard a whisper 'Rome'
And in his heart he cried 'The call of God!'
And call'd arose, and, slowly plunging
down
Thro' that disastrous glory, set his face
By waste and field and town of alien
tongue,
Following a hundred sunsets, and the
sphere
Of westward-wheeling stars; and every
dawn
Struck from him his own shadow on to
Rome.
    Foot-sore, way-worn, at length he
touch'd his goal,
The Christian city. All her splendor fail'd
To lure those eyes that only yearn'd to see,
Fleeting betwixt her column'd palace-walls,
The shape with wings. Anon there past a
crowd
With shameless laughter, Pagan oath, and
jest,
Hard Romans brawling of their monstrous
games;
He, all but deaf thro' age and weariness,
And muttering to himself 'The call of God'
And borne along by that full stream of
men,
Like some old wreck on some indrawing
sea,
Gain'd their huge Colosseum. The caged
beast

Yell'd, as he yell'd of yore for Christian
blood.
Three slaves were trailing a dead lion
away,
One, a dead man. He stumbled in, and sat
Blinded; but when the momentary gloom,
Made by the noonday blaze without, had
left
His aged eyes, he raised them, and beheld
A blood-red awning waver overhead,
The dust send up a steam of human blood,
The gladiators moving toward their fight,
And eighty thousand Christian faces watch
Man murder man. A sudden strength from
heaven,
As some great shock may wake a palsied
limb,
Turn'd him again to boy, for up he sprang,
And glided lightly down the stairs, and
o'er
The barrier that divided beast from man
Slipt, and ran on, and flung himself
between
The gladiatorial swords, and call'd
'Forbear
In the great name of Him who died for
men,
Christ Jesus!' For one moment afterward
A silence follow'd as of death, and then
A hiss as from a wilderness of snakes,
Then one deep roar as of a breaking sea,
And then a shower of stones that stoned
him dead,
And then once more a silence as of death.
  His dream became a deed that woke the
world,
For while the frantic rabble in half-amaze
Stared at him dead, thro' all the nobler
hearts
In that vast Oval ran a shudder of shame.
The Baths, the Forum gabbled of his
death,
And preachers linger'd o'er his dying
words,
Which would not die, but echo'd on to
reach
Honorius, till he heard them, and decreed
That Rome no more should wallow in this
old lust
Of Paganism, and make her festal hour
Dark with the blood of man who murder'd
man.

(For Honorius, who succeeded to the
sovereignty over Europe, supprest the gladi-
atorial combats practised of old in Rome, on
occasion of the following event. There was
one Telemachus, embracing the ascetic mode
of life, who setting out from the East and
arriving at Rome for this very purpose, while
that accursed spectacle was being performed,
entered himself the circus, and descending
into the arena, attempted to hold back those
who wielded deadly weapons against each
other. The spectators of the murderous fray,
possest with the drunken glee of the demon
who delights in such bloodshed, stoned to
death the preacher of peace. The admirable
Emperor learning this put a stop to that
evil exhibition. — Theodoret's *Ecclesiastical
History*.)

AKBAR'S DREAM

AN INSCRIPTION BY ABUL FAZL

FOR A TEMPLE IN KASHMIR

(BLOCHMANN XXXII.)

O GOD in every temple I see people that see
thee, and in every language I hear spoken,
people praise thee.
  Polytheism and Islám feel after thee.
  Each religion says, 'Thou art one, without
equal.'
  If it be a mosque people murmur the
holy prayer, and if it be a Christian Church,
people ring the bell from love to Thee.
  Sometimes I frequent the Christian clois-
ter, and sometimes the mosque.
  But it is thou whom I search from temple
to temple.
  Thy elect have no dealings with either
heresy or orthodoxy; for neither of them
stands behind the screen of thy truth.
  Heresy to the heretic, and religion to
the orthodox,
  But the dust of the rose-petal belongs to
the heart of the perfume seller.

  AKBAR *and* ABUL FAZL *before the
  palace at Futehpur-Sikri at night.*

'LIGHT of the nations' ask'd his Chronicler
Of Akbar 'what has darken'd thee to-
night?'
Then, after one quick glance upon the
stars,
And turning slowly toward him, Akbar
said
'The shadow of a dream — an idle one

It may be. Still I raised my heart to heaven,
I pray'd against the dream. To pray, to do —
To pray, to do according to the prayer,
Are, both, to worship Alla, but the prayers,
That have no successor in deed, are faint
And pale in Alla's eyes, fair mothers they
Dying in childbirth of dead sons. I vow'd
Whate'er my dreams, I still would do the right
Thro' all the vast dominion which a sword,
That only conquers men to conquer peace,
Has won me. Alla be my guide!
                            But come,
My noble friend, my faithful counsellor,
Sit by my side. While thou art one with me,
I seem no longer like a lonely man
In the king's garden, gathering here and there
From each fair plant the blossom choicest-grown
To wreathe a crown not only for the king
But in due time for every Mussulmân,
Brahmin, and Buddhist, Christian, and Parsee,
Thro' all the warring world of Hindustan.
  Well spake thy brother in his hymn to heaven
"Thy glory baffles wisdom. All the tracks
Of science making toward Thy Perfectness
Are blinding desert sand; we scarce can spell
The Alif of Thine alphabet of Love."
  He knows Himself, men nor themselves nor Him,
For every splinter'd fraction of a sect
Will clamour "*I* am on the Perfect Way,
All else is to perdition."
                            Shall the rose
Cry to the lotus "No flower thou"? the palm
Call to the cypress "I alone am fair"?
The mango spurn the melon at his foot?
"Mine is the one fruit Alla made for man."
  Look how the living pulse of Alla beats
Thro' all His world. If every single star
Should shriek its claim "I only am in heaven"
Why that were such sphere-music as the Greek
Had hardly dream'd of. There is light in all,
And light, with more or less of shade, in all

Man-modes of worship; but our Ulama,
Who "sitting on green sofas contemplate
The torment of the damn'd" already, these
Are like wild brutes new-caged — the narrower
The cage, the more their fury. Me they front
With sullen brows. What wonder! I decreed
That even the dog was clean, that men may taste
Swine-flesh, drink wine; they know too that whene'er
In our free Hall, where each philosophy
And mood of faith may hold its own, they blurt
Their furious formalisms, I but hear
The clash of tides that meet in narrow seas, —
Not the Great Voice not the true Deep.
                            To drive
A people from their ancient fold of Faith,
And wall them up perforce in mine — unwise,
Unkinglike; — and the morning of my reign
Was redden'd by that cloud of shame when I . . .
  I hate the rancor of their castes and creeds,
I let men worship as they will, I reap
No revenue from the field of unbelief.
I cull from every faith and race the best
And bravest soul for counsellor and friend.
I loathe the very name of infidel.
I stagger at the Korân and the sword.
I shudder at the Christian and the stake;
Yet "Alla," says their sacred book, "is Love,"
And when the Goan Padre quoting Him,
Issa Ben Mariam, his own prophet, cried
"Love one another little ones" and "bless"
Whom? even "your persecutors"! there methought
The cloud was rifted by a purer gleam
Than glances from the sun of our Islâm.
  And thou rememberest what a fury shook
Those pillars of a moulder'd faith, when he,
That other, prophet of their fall, proclaimed
His Master as "the Sun of Righteousness,"
Yea, Alla here on earth, who caught and held

His people by the bridle-rein of Truth.
  What art thou saying? "And was not
    Alla call'd
In old Irân the Sun of Love? and Love
The net of truth?"
                    A voice from old Irân!
Nay, but I know it — *his*, the hoary Shiek,
On whom the women shrieking "Athiest"
    flung
Filth from the roof, the mystic melodist
Who all but lost himself in Alla, him
Abû Saîd ——
                  — a sun but dimly seen
Here, till the mortal morning mists of
    earth
Fade in the noon of heaven, when creed
    and race
Shall bear false witness, each of each, no
    more,
But find their limits by that larger light,
And overstep them, moving easily
Thro' after-ages in the love of Truth,
The truth of Love.
                  The sun, the sun! they rail
At me the Zoroastrian. Let the Sun,
Who heats our earth to yield us grain
    and fruit,
And laughs upon thy field as well as mine,
And warms the blood of Shiah and Sunnee,
Symbol the Eternal! Yea and may not
    kings
Express Him also by their warmth of love
For all they rule — by equal law for all?
By deeds a light to men?
                          But no such light
Glanced from our Presence on the face
    of one,
Who breaking in upon us yestermorn,
With all the Hells a-glare in either eye,
Yell'd "hast *thou* brought us down a new
    Korân
From heaven? art *thou* the Prophet? canst
    thou work
Miracles?" and the wild horse, anger,
    plunged
To fling me, and fail'd. Miracles! no, not I
Nor he, nor any. I can but lift the torch
Of Reason in the dusky cave of Life,
And gaze on this great miracle, the World,
Adoring That who made, and makes,
    and is,
And is not, what I gaze on — all else Form,
Ritual, varying with the tribes of men.
  Ay but, my friend, thou knowest I hold
    that forms

Are needful: only let the hand that rules,
With politic care, with utter gentleness,
Mould them for all his people.
                          And what are forms?
Fair garments, plain or rich, and fitting
    close
Or flying looselier, warm'd but by the
    heart
Within them, moved but by the living
    limb,
And cast aside, when old, for newer, —
    Forms!
The Spiritual in Nature's market-place —
The silent Alphabet-of-heaven-in-man
Made vocal — banners blazoning a Power
That is not seen and rules from far away —
A silken cord let down from Paradise,
When fine Philosophies would fail, to draw
The crowd from wallowing in the mire of
    earth,
And all the more, when these behold their
    Lord,
Who shaped the forms, obey them, and
    himself
Here on this bank in *some* way live the life
Beyond the bridge, and serve that Infinite
Within us, as without, that All-in-all,
And over all, the never-changing One
And ever-changing Many, in praise of
    Whom
The Christian bell, the cry from off the
    mosque,
And vaguer voices of Polytheism
Make but one music, harmonizing "Pray."
  There westward — under yon slow-fall-
    ing star,
The Christians own a Spiritual Head;
And following thy true counsel, by thine
    aid,
Myself am such in our Islâm, for no
Mirage of glory, but for power to fuse
My myriads into union under one;
To hunt the tiger of oppression out
From office; and to spread the Divine
    Faith
Like calming oil on all their stormy creeds,
And fill the hollows between wave and
    wave;
To nurse my children on the milk of Truth,
And alchemise old hates into the gold
Of Love, and make it current; and beat
    back
The menacing poison of intolerant priests,
Those cobras ever setting up their hoods —
One Alla! one Kalifa!

Still — at times
A doubt, a fear, — and yester afternoon
I dream'd, — thou knowest how deep a
    well of love
My heart is for my son, Saleem, mine
    heir, —
And yet so wild and wayward that my
    dream —
He glares askance at thee as one of those
Who mix the wines of heresy in the cup
Of counsel — so — I pray thee ——
                Well, I dream'd
That stone by stone I rear'd a sacred fane,
A temple, neither Pagod, Mosque, nor
    Church,
But loftier, simpler, always open-door'd
To every breath from heaven, and Truth
    and Peace
And Love and Justice came and dwelt
    therein;
But while we stood rejoicing, I and thou,
I heard a mocking laugh "the new Korân!"
And on the sudden, and with a cry
    "Saleem"
Thou, thou — I saw thee fall before me,
    and then
Me too the black-wing'd Azrael overcame,
But Death had ears and eyes; I watch'd
    my son,
And those that follow'd, loosen, stone from
    stone,
All my fair work; and from the ruin arose
The shriek and curse of trampled millions,
    even
As in the time before; but while I groan'd,
From out the sunset pour'd an alien race,
Who fitted stone to stone again, and Truth,
Peace, Love and Justice came and dwelt
    therein,
Nor in the field without were seen or heard
Fires of Súttee, nor wail of baby-wife,
Or Indian widow; and in sleep I said
"All praise to Alla by whatever hands
My mission be accomplish'd!" but we hear
Music: our palace is awake, and morn
Has lifted the dark eyelash of the Night
From off the rosy cheek of waking Day.
Our hymn to the sun. They sing it. Let
    us go.'

HYMN

I

Once again thou flamest heavenward, once
    again we see thee rise.

Every morning is thy birthday gladdening
    human hearts and eyes.
Every morning here we greet it,
    bowing lowly down before thee,
Thee the Godlike, thee the changeless in
    thine ever-changing skies.

II

Shadow-maker, shadow-slayer, arrowing
    light from clime to clime,
Hear thy myriad laureates hail thee mon-
    arch in their woodland rhyme.
    Warble bird, and open flower, and,
    men, below the dome of azure
Kneel adoring Him the Timeless in the
    flame that measures Time!

NOTES TO AKBAR'S DREAM

The great Mogul Emperor Akbar was born October 14, 1542, and died 1605. At 13 he succeeded his father Humayun; at 18 he himself assumed the sole charge of government. He subdued and ruled over fifteen large provinces; his empire included all India north of the Vindhya Mountains — in the south of India he was not so successful. His tolerance of religions and his abhorrence of religious persecution put our Tudors to shame. He invented a new eclectic religion by which he hoped to unite all creeds, castes and peoples: and his legislation was remarkable for vigour, justice and humanity.

'Thy glory baffles wisdom.' The Emperor quotes from a hymn to the Deity by Faizi, brother of Abul Fazl, Akbar's chief friend and minister, who write the *Ain i Akbari* (Annals of Akbar). His influence on his age was immense. It may be that he and his brother Faizi led Akbar's mind away from Islám and the Prophet — this charge is brought against him by every Muhammadan writer; but Abul Fazl also led his sovereign to a true appreciation of his duties, and from the moment that he entered Court, the problem of successfully ruling over mixed races, which Islám in few other countries had to solve, was carefully considered, and the policy of toleration was the result (Blochmann xxix).

Abul Fazl thus gives an account of himself 'The advice of my Father with difficulty kept me back from acts of folly; my mind had no rest and my heart felt itself drawn to the sages of Mongolia or to the hermits on Lebanon. I longed for interviews with the Llamás of Tibet or with the padres of

Portugal, and I would gladly sit with the priests of the Parsis and the learned of the Zendavesta. I was sick of the learned of my own land.'

He became the intimate friend and adviser of Akbar and helped him in his tolerant system of government. Professor Blochmann writes 'Impressed with a favourable idea of the value of his Hindu subjects, he (Akbar) had resolved when pensively sitting in the evenings on the solitary stone at Futehpur-Sikri to rule with an even hand all men in his dominions; but as the extreme views of the learned and the lawyers continually urged him to persecute instead of to heal, he instituted discussions, because, believing himself to be in error, he thought it his duty as ruler to inquire.' 'These discussions took place every Thursday night in the Ibadat-khana a building at Futehpur-Sikri, erected for the purpose' (Malleson).

In these discussions Abul Fazl became a great power, and he induced the chief of the disputants to draw up a document defining the 'divine Faith' as it was called, and assigning to Akbar the rank of a Mujahid, or supreme khalifah, the viceregent of the one true God.

Abul Fazl was finally murdered at the instigation of Akbar's son Salim, who in his Memoirs declares that it was Abul Fazl who had perverted his father's mind so that he denied the divine mission of Mahomet, and turned away his love from his son.

Faizi. When Akbar conquered the North-West Provinces of India, Faizi, then 20, began his life as a poet, and earned his living as a physician. He is reported to have been very generous and to have treated the poor for nothing. His fame reached Akbar's ears who commanded him to come to the camp at Chitor. Akbar was delighted with his varied knowledge and scholarship and made the poet teacher to his sons. Faizi at 33 was appointed Chief Poet (1588). He collected a fine library of 4300 MSS. and died at the age of 40 (1595) when Akbar incorporated his collection of rare books in the Imperial Library.

The warring world of Hindostan. Akbar's rapid conquests and the good government of his fifteen provinces with their complete military, civil and political systems make him conspicuous among the great kings of history.

The Goan Padre. Abul Fazl relates that 'one night the Ibadat-khana was brightened by the presence of Padre Rodolpho, who for intelligence and wisdom was unrivalled among Christian doctors. Several carping and bigoted men attacked him and this afforded an opportunity for the display of the calm judgment and justice of the assembly. These men brought forward the old received assertions, and did not attempt to arrive at truth by reasoning. Their statements were torn to pieces, and they were nearly put to shame, when they began to attack the contradictions of the Gospel, but they could not prove their assertions. With perfect calmness, and earnest conviction of the truth he replied to their arguments.'

Abû Sa'îd. 'Love is the net of Truth, Love is the noose of God' is a quotation from the great Sufee poet Abû Sa'îd — born A.D. 968, died at the age of 83. He is a mystical poet, and some of his expressions have been compared to our George Herbert. Of Shaikh Abû Sa'îd it is recorded that he said, 'when my affairs had reacht a certain pitch I buried under the dust my books and opened a shop on my own account (*i.e.* began to teach with authority), and verily men represented me as that which I was not, until it came to this, that they went to the Qâdhî and testified against me of unbelieverhood; and women got upon the roofs and cast unclean things upon me.' (*Vide* reprint from article in *National Review*, March 1891, by C. J. Pickering.)

Aziz. I am not aware that there is any record of such intrusion upon the king's privacy, but the expressions in the text occur in a letter sent by Akbar's foster brother Aziz, who refused to come to court when summoned and threw up his government, and 'after writing an insolent and reproachful letter to Akbar in which he asked him if he had received a book from heaven, or if he could work miracles like Mahomet that he presumed to introduce a new religion, warned him that he was on the way to eternal perdition, and concluded with a prayer to God to bring him back into the path of salvation' (Elphinstone).

'The Koran, the Old and New Testament, and the Psalms of David are called *books* by way of excellence, and their followers "People of the Book" ' (Elphinstone).

Akbar according to Abdel Kadir had his son Murad instructed in the Gospel, and used to make him begin his lessons 'In the name of Christ' instead of in the usual way 'In the name of God.'

> *To drive*
> *A people from their ancient fold of Truth,* etc.

Malleson says 'This must have happened because Akbar states it, but of the forced conversions I have found no record. This must have taken place whilst he was still a minor, and whilst the chief authority was wielded by Bairam.'

'*I reap no revenue from the field of unbelief*' The Hindus are fond of pilgrimages and Akbar removed a remunerative tax raised by his predecessors on pilgrimages. He also abolished the fezza or capitation tax on those who differed from the Mahomedan faith. He discouraged all *excessive* prayers, fasts and pilgrimages.

Suttee. Akbar decreed that every widow who showed the least desire not to be burnt on her husband's funeral pyre should be let go free and unharmed.

baby-wife. He forbad marriage before the age of puberty.

Indian widow. Akbar ordained that re-marriage was lawful.

Music. 'About a watch before daybreak,' says Abul Fazl, the musicians played to the king in the palace. 'His Majesty had such a knowledge of the science of music as trained musicians do not possess.'

'*The Divine Faith.*' The Divine Faith slowly passed away under the immediate successors of Akbar. An idea of what the Divine Faith was may be gathered from the inscription at the head of the poem. The document referred to, Abul Fazl says 'brought about excellent results (1) the Court became a gathering place of the sages and learned of all creeds; the good doctrines of all religious systems were recognized, and their defects were not allowed to obscure their good features; (2) perfect toleration or peace with all was established; and (3) the perverse and evil-minded were covered with shame on seeing the disinterested motives of His Majesty, and these stood in the pillory of disgrace.' Dated September 1579 — Ragab 987 (Blochmann xiv).

TO SIR WALTER SCOTT [1]

O great and gallant Scott,
True gentleman, heart, blood and bone,
I would it had been my lot
To have seen thee, and heard thee, and
known.

[1] I have adopted Sir Walter Scott's version of the following story as given in his last journal (Death of Il Bizarro) — but I have taken the liberty of making some slight alterations.

THE BANDIT'S DEATH

SIR, do you see this dagger? nay, why do
you start aside?
I was not going to stab you, tho' I *am* the
Bandit's bride.

You have set a price on his head: I may
claim it without a lie.
What have I here in the cloth? I will show
it you by-and-by.

Sir, I was once a wife. I had one brief
summer of bliss.
But the Bandit had woo'd me in vain, and
he stabb'd my Piero with this.

And he dragg'd me up there to his cave in
the mountain, and there one day
He had left his dagger behind him. I found
it. I hid it away.

For he reek'd with the blood of Piero; his
kisses were red with his crime,
And I cried to the Saints to avenge me.
They heard, they bided their time.

In a while I bore him a son, and he loved
to dandle the child,
And that was a link between us; but I —
to be reconciled? —

No, by the Mother of God, tho' I think I
hated him less,
And — well, if I sinn'd last night, I will
find the Priest and confess.

Listen! we three were alone in the dell at
the close of the day.
I was lilting a song to the babe, and it
laugh'd like a dawn in May.

Then on a sudden we saw your soldiers
crossing the ridge,
And he caught my little one from me: we
dipt down under the bridge

By the great dead pine — you know it —
and heard as we crouch'd below,
The clatter of arms, and voices, and men
passing to and fro.

Black was the night when we crept away —
not a star in the sky —

Hush'd as the heart of the grave, till the
little one utter'd a cry.

I whisper'd 'give it to me,' but he would
not answer me — then
He gript it so hard by the throat that the
boy never cried again.

We return'd to his cave — the link was
broken — he sobb'd and he wept,
And cursed himself; then he yawn'd, for
the wretch *could* sleep, and he slept

Ay, till dawn stole into the cave, and a ray
red as blood
Glanced on the strangled face — I could
make Sleep Death, if I would —

Glared on at the murder'd son, and the
murderous father at rest, . . .
I drove the blade that had slain my
husband thrice thro' his breast.

He was loved at least by his dog: it was
chain'd, but its horrible yell
'She has kill'd him, has kill'd him, has
kill'd him' rang out all down thro'
the dell,

Till I felt I could end myself too with the
dagger — so deafen'd and dazed —
Take it, and save me from it! I fled. I was
all but crazed

With the grief that gnaw'd at my heart,
and the weight that dragg'd at my
hand;
But thanks to the Blessed Saints that I
came on none of his band;

And the band will be scatter'd now their
gallant captain is dead,
For I with this dagger of his — do you
doubt me? Here is his head!

THE CHURCH WARDEN AND
THE CURATE

This is written in the dialect which was
current in my youth at Spilsby and in the
country about it.

I

Eн? good daäy! good daäy! thaw it bean't
not mooch of a daäy,

Nasty, casselty weather! an' mea haäfe
down wi' my haäy!

II

How be the farm gittin on? noäways.
Gittin on i'deeäd!
Why, tonups was haäfe on 'em fingers an'
toäs, an' the mare brokken-kneeäd,
An' pigs didn't sell at fall, an' wa lost wer
Haldeny cow,
An' it beäts ma to knaw wot she died on,
but wool's looking oop ony how.

III

An' soä they've maäde tha a parson, an'
thou'll git along, niver fear,
Fur I beän chuch-warden mysen i' the
parish fur fifteen year.
Well — sin ther beä chuch-wardens, ther
mun be parsons an' all,
An' if t'öne stick alongside t'uther the
chuch weänt happen a fall.

IV

Fur I wur a Baptis wonst, an' ageän the
toithe an' the raäte,
Till I fun that it warn't not the gaäinist
waäy to the narra Gaäte.
An' I can't abeär 'em, I can't, fur a lot
on 'em coom'd ta-year —
I wur down wi' the rheumatis then — to
my pond to wesh thessens theere —
Sa I sticks like the ivin as long as I lives to
the owd chuch now,
Fur they wesh'd their sins i' *my* pond, an'
I doubts they poison'd the cow.

V

Ay, an' ya seed the Bishop. They says 'at
he coom'd fra nowt —
Burn i' traäde. Sa I warrants 'e niver said
haäfe wot 'e thowt,
But 'e creeäpt an' 'e crawl'd along, till 'e
feeäld 'e could howd 'is oän,
Then 'e married a greät Yerl's darter, an'
sits o' the Bishop's throän.

VI

Now I'll gie tha a bit o' my mind an' tha
weant be taakin' offence,
Fur thou be a big scholard now wi' a
hoonderd haäcre o' sense —
But sich an obstropulous lad — naay,
naay — fur I minds tha sa well,
Tha'd niver not hopple thy tongue, an' the
tongue's sit afire o' Hell,

As I says to my missis to-daay, when she
  hurl'd a plaäte at the cat
An' anoother ageän my noäse. Ya was
  niver sa bad as that.

VII

But I minds when i' Howlaby beck won
  daäy ya was ticklin' o' trout,
An' keeäper 'e seed ya an roon'd, an' 'e
  beal'd to ya 'Lad coom hout'
An' ya stood oop naäkt i' the beck, an' ya
  tell'd 'im to knaw his awn plaäce
An' ya call'd 'im a clown, ya did, an' ya
  thraw'd the fish i' 'is faäce,
An' 'e torn'd as red as a stag-tuckey's
  wattles, but theer an' then
I coämb'd 'im down, fur I promised ya'd
  niver not do it ageän.

VIII

An' I cotch'd tha wonst i' my garden,
  when thou was a height-year-howd,
An' I fun thy pockets as full o' my pippins
  as iver they'd 'owd,
An' thou was as peärky as owt, an' tha
  maäde me as mad as mad,
But I says to tha 'keeap 'em, an' welcome'
  fur thou was the Parson's lad.

IX

An' Parson 'e 'ears on it all, an' then
  taäkes kindly to me,
An' then I wur chose Chuch-warden an'
  coom'd to the top o' the tree,
Fur Quoloty's hall my friends, an' they
  maäkes ma a help to the poor,
When I gits the plaäte fuller o' Soondays
  nor ony chuch-warden afoor,
Fur if iver thy feyther 'ed riled me I kep'
  mysen meeäk as a lamb,
An' saw by the Graäce o' the Lord, Mr.
  Harry, I ham wot I ham.

X

But Parson 'e *will* speäk out, saw, now 'e
  be sixty-seven,
He'll niver swap Owlby an' Scratby fur
  owt but the Kingdom o' Heaven;
An' thou'll be 'is Curate 'ere, but, if iver
  tha meäns to git 'igher,
Tha mun tackle the sins o' the Wo'ld, an'
  not the faults o' the Squire.
An' I reckons tha'll light of a livin'
  somewheers i' the Wowd or the Fen,

If tha cottons down to thy betters, an'
  keeäps thysen to thysen.
But niver not speäk plaain out, if tha
  wants to git forrards a bit,
But creeäp along the hedge-bottoms, an'
  thou'll be a Bishop yit.

XI

Naäy, but tha *mun* speäk hout to the
  Baptises here i' the town,
Fur moäst on 'em talks ageän tithe, an'
  I'd like tha to preäch 'em down,
Fur *they*'ve bin a-preächin' *mea* down, they
  heve, an' I haätes 'em now,
Fur they leäved their nasty sins i' *my*
  pond, an' it poison'd the cow.

GLOSSARY

'Casselty,' casualty, chance weather.
'Haäfe down wi' my haäy,' while my grass
is only half-mown.
'Fingers and toes,' a disease in turnips.
'Fall,' autumn.
'If t'ōne stick alongside t'uther,' if the one
hold by the other. One is pronounced like
'own.'
'Fun,' found.
'Gaäinist,' nearest.
'Ta-year,' this year.
'Ivin,' ivy.
'Obstropulous,' obstreperous — here the
Curate makes a sign of deprecation.
'Hopple' or 'hobble,' to tie the legs of a
skittish cow when she is being milked.
'Beal'd,' bellowed.
In such words as 'torned' (turned),
'hurled,' the r is hardly audible.
'Stag-tuckey,' turkey-cock.
'Height-year-howd,' eight-year-old.
' 'Owd,' hold.
'Pearky,' pert.
'Wo'ld,' the world. Short o.
'Wowd,' wold.

CHARITY

I

WHAT am I doing, you say to me, 'wasting
  the sweet summer hours'?
Haven't you eyes? I am dressing the grave
  of a woman with flowers.

II

For a woman ruin'd the world, as God's
  own scriptures tell,

And a man ruin'd mine, but a woman, God
   bless her, kept me from Hell.

III

Love me? O yes, no doubt — how long —
   till you threw me aside!
Dresses and laces and jewels and never a
   ring for the bride.

IV

All very well just now to be calling me
   darling and sweet,
And after a while would it matter so much
   if I came on the street?

V

You when I met you first — when *he*
   brought you! — I turn'd away
And the hard blue eyes have it still, that
   stare of a beast of prey.

VI

You were his friend — you — you — when
   he promised to make me his bride,
And you knew that he meant to betray me
   — you knew — you knew that he
   lied.

VII

He married an heiress, an orphan with half
   a shire of estate, —
I sent him a desolate wail and a curse,
   when I learn'd my fate.

VIII

For I used to play with the knife, creep
   down to the river-shore,
Moan to myself 'one plunge — then quiet
   for evermore.'

IX

Would the man have a touch of remorse
   when he heard what an end was
   mine?
Or brag to his fellow rakes of his conquest
   over their wine?

X

Money — my hire — *his* money — I sent
   him back what he gave, —
Will you move a little that way? your
   shadow falls on the grave.

XI

Two trains clash'd: then and there he was
   crush'd in a moment and died,

But the new-wedded wife was unharm'd,
   tho' sitting close at his side.

XII

She found my letter upon him, my wail of
   reproach and scorn;
I had cursed the woman he married, and
   him, and the day I was born.

XIII

They put him aside for ever, and after a
   week — no more —
A stranger as welcome as Satan — a
   widow came to my door:

XIV

So I turn'd my face to the wall, I was mad,
   I was raving-wild,
I was close on that hour of dishonor, the
   birth of a baseborn child.

XV

O you that can flatter your victims, and
   juggle, and lie and cajole,
Man, can you even guess at the love of a
   soul for a soul?

XVI

I had cursed her as woman and wife, and
   in wife and woman I found
The tenderest Christ-like creature that
   ever stept on the ground.

XVII

She watch'd me, she nursed me, she fed
   me, she sat day and night by my bed,
Till the joyless birthday came of a boy
   born happily dead.

XVIII

And her name? what was it? I ask'd her.
   She said with a sudden glow
On her patient face 'My dear, I will tell
   you before I go.'

XIX

And I when I learnt it at last, I shriek'd, I
   sprang from my seat,
I wept, and I kiss'd her hands, I flung
   myself down at her feet,

XX

And we pray'd together for *him*, for *him*
   who had given her the name.
She has left me enough to live on. I need
   no wages of shame.

XXI

She died of a fever caught when a nurse in
    a hospital ward.
She is high in the Heaven of Heavens, she
    is face to face with her Lord,

XXII

And He sees not her like anywhere in this
    pitiless world of ours!
I have told you my tale. Get you gone. I
    am dressing her grave with flowers.

KAPIOLANI

Kapiolani was a great chieftainess who
lived in the Sandwich Islands at the begin-
ning of this century. She won the cause of
Christianity by openly defying the priests of
the terrible goddess Peelè. In spite of their
threats of vengeance she ascended the vol-
cano Mauna-Loa, then clambered down over
a bank of cinders 400 feet high to the great
lake of fire (nine miles round) — Kilauëä —
the home and haunt of the goddess, and flung
into the boiling lava the consecrated berries
which it was sacrilege for a woman to handle.

I

WHEN from the terrors of Nature a people
    have fashion'd and worship a Spirit
    of Evil,
Blest be the Voice of the Teacher who calls
    to them
'Set yourselves free!'

II

Noble the Saxon who hurl'd at his Idol a
    valorous weapon in olden England!
Great and greater, and greatest of women,
    island heroine, Kapiolani
Clomb the mountain, and flung the berries,
    and dared the Goddess, and freed
    the people
Of Hawa-i-ee!

III

A people believing that Peelè the Goddess
    would wallow in fiery riot and revel
On Kilauëä,
Dance in a fountain of flame with her
    devils, or shake with her thunders
    and shatter her island,

Rolling her anger
Thro' blasted valley and flaring forest in
    blood-red cataracts down to the sea!

IV

Long as the lava-light
Glares from the lava-lake
Dazing the starlight,
Long as the silvery vapor in daylight
Over the mountain
Floats, will the glory of Kapiolani be
    mingled with either on Hawa-i-ee.

V

What said her Priesthood?
'Woe to this island if ever a woman should
    handle or gather the berries of Peelè!
Accursèd were she!
And woe to this island if ever a woman
    should climb to the dwelling of Peelè
    the Goddess!
Accursèd were she!'

VI

One from the Sunrise
Dawn'd on His people, and slowly before
    him
Vanish'd shadow-like
Gods and Goddesses,
None but the terrible Peelè remaining as
    Kapiolani ascended her mountain,
Baffled her priesthood,
Broke the Taboo,
Dipt to the crater,
Call'd on the Power adored by the
    Christian, and crying 'I dare her, let
    Peelè avenge herself'!
Into the flame-billow dash'd the berries,
    and drove the demon from Hawa-i-ee.

THE DAWN

"You are but children."
Egyptian Priest to Solon

I

RED of the Dawn!
Screams of a babe in the red-hot palms of a
    Moloch of Tyre,
    Man with his brotherless dinner on man
    in the tropical wood,
    Priests in the name of the Lord passing
    souls thro' fire to the fire,
Head-hunters and boats of Dahomey that
    float upon human blood!

II

Red of the Dawn!
Godless fury of peoples, and Christless
  frolic of kings,
  And the bolt of war dashing down upon
    cities and blazing farms,
  For Babylon was a child new-born, and
    Rome was a babe in arms,
And London and Paris and all the rest are
  as yet but in leading-strings.

III

Dawn not Day,
While scandal is mouthing a bloodless
  name at *her* cannibal feast,
And rake-ruin'd bodies and souls go down
  in a common wreck,
  And the press of a thousand cities is
    prized for it smells of the beast,
Or easily violates virgin Truth for a coin or
  a check.

IV

Dawn not Day!
Is it Shame, so few should have climb'd
  from the dens in the level below,
  Men, with a heart and a soul, no slaves
    of a four-footed will?
  But if twenty million of summers are
    stored in the sunlight still,
We are far from the noon of man, there is
  time for the race to grow.

V

Red of the Dawn!
Is it turning a fainter red? so be it, but
  when shall we lay
  The Ghost of the Brute that is walking
    and haunting us yet, and be free?
  In a hundred, a thousand winters? Ah,
    what will *our* children be,
The men of a hundred thousand, a million
  summers away?

THE MAKING OF MAN

WHERE is one that, born of woman,
  altogether can escape
From the lower world within him, moods
  of tiger, or of ape?
  Man as yet is being made, and ere the
    crowning Age of ages,
Shall not æon after æon pass and touch
  him into shape?

All about him shadow still, but, while the
  races flower and fade,
Prophet-eyes may catch a glory slowly
  gaining on the shade,
Till the peoples all are one, and all their
  voices blend in choric
Hallelujah to the Maker 'It is finish'd.
  Man is made.'

THE DREAMER

ON a midnight in midwinter when all but
  the winds were dead,
'The meek shall inherit the earth' was a
  Scripture that rang thro' his head,
Till he dream'd that a Voice of the Earth
  went wailingly past him and said:
'I am losing the light of my Youth
And the Vision that led me of old,
And I clash with an iron Truth,
When I make for an Age of gold,
And I would that my race were run,
For teeming with liars, and madmen,
    and knaves,
And wearied of Autocrats, Anarchs, and
    Slaves,
And darken'd with doubts of a Faith
    that saves,
And crimson with battles, and hollow
    with graves,
To the wail of my winds, and the moan
    of my waves
I whirl, and I follow the Sun.'

Was it only the wind of the Night shrilling
    out Desolation and wrong
Thro' a dream of the dark? Yet he thought
    that he answer'd her wail with a
    song —

Moaning your losses, O Earth,
    Heart-weary and overdone!
But all's well that ends well,
    Whirl, and follow the Sun!

He is racing from heaven to heaven
    And less will be lost than won,
For all's well that ends well,
    Whirl, and follow the Sun!

The Reign of the Meek upon earth,
    O weary one, has it begun?
But all's well that ends well,
    Whirl, and follow the Sun!

For moans will have grown sphere-music
  Or ever your race be run!
And all's well that ends well,
  Whirl, and follow the Sun!

MECHANOPHILUS

(In the time of the first railways)

Now first we stand and understand,
And sunder false from true,
And handle boldly with the hand,
  And see and shape and do.

Dash back that ocean with a pier,
  Strow yonder mountain flat,
A railway there, a tunnel here,
  Mix me this Zone with that!

Bring me my horse — my horse? my wings
  That I may soar the sky,
For Thought into the outward springs,
  I find her with the eye.

O will she, moonlike, sway the main,
  And bring or chase the storm,
Who was a shadow in the brain,
  And is a living form?

Far as the Future vaults her skies,
  From this my vantage ground
To those still-working energies
  I spy nor term nor bound.

As we surpass our fathers' skill,
  Our sons will shame our own;
A thousand things are hidden still
  And not a hundred known.

And had some prophet spoken true
  Of all we shall achieve,
The wonders were so wildly new
  That no man would believe.

Meanwhile, my brothers, work, and wield
  The forces of to-day,
And plow the Present like a field,
  And garner all you may!

You, what the cultured surface grows,
  Dispense with careful hands:
Deep under deep for ever goes,
  Heaven over heaven expands.

RIFLEMEN FORM!

THERE is a sound of thunder afar,
Storm in the South that darkens the day!
Storm of battle and thunder of war!
Well if it do not roll our way.
Storm, Storm, Riflemen form!
Ready, be ready against the storm!
Riflemen, Riflemen, Riflemen form!

Be not deaf to the sound that warns,
Be not gull'd by a despot's plea!
Are figs of thistles? or grapes of thorns?
How can a despot feel with the Free?
Form, Form, Riflemen Form!
Ready, be ready to meet the storm!
Riflemen, Riflemen, Riflemen form!

Let your reforms for a moment go!
Look to your butts, and take good aims!
Better a rotten borough or so
Than a rotten fleet and a city in flames!
Storm, Storm, Riflemen form!
Ready, be ready against the storm!
Riflemen, Riflemen, Riflemen form!

Form, be ready to do or die!
Form in Freedom's name and the Queen's!
True we have got — *such* a faithful ally
That only the Devil can tell what he
    means.
Form, Form, Riflemen Form!
Ready, be ready to meet the storm!
Riflemen, Riflemen, Riflemen form![1]

THE TOURNEY

RALPH would fight in Edith's sight,
  For Ralph was Edith's lover,
Ralph went down like a fire to the fight,
Struck to the left and struck to the right,
  Roll'd them over and over.
'Gallant Sir Ralph,' said the king.

Casques were crack'd and hauberks hack'd,
  Lances snapt in sunder,
Rang the stroke, and sprang the blood,

[1] I have been asked to republish this old poem, which was first published in 'The Times,' May 9, 1859, before the Volunteer movement began.

Knights were thwack'd and riven, and
   hew'd
Like broad oaks with thunder.
'O what an arm,' said the king.

Edith bow'd her stately head,
  Saw them lie confounded,
Edith Montfort bow'd her head,
Crown'd her knight's, and flush'd as red
  As poppies when she crown'd it.
'Take her Sir Ralph,' said the king.

THE WANDERER

THE gleam of household sunshine ends,
And here no longer can I rest;
Farewell! — You will not speak, my
   friends,
Unfriendly of your parted guest.

O well for him that finds a friend,
Or makes a friend where'er he come,
And loves the world from end to end,
And wanders on from home to home!

O happy he, and fit to live,
On whom a happy home has power
To make him trust his life, and give
His fealty to the halcyon hour!

I count you kind, I hold you true;
But what may follow who can tell?
Give me a hand — and you — and you —
And deem me grateful, and farewell!

POETS AND CRITICS

THIS thing, that thing is the rage,
Helter-skelter runs the age;
Minds on this round earth of ours
Vary like the leaves and flowers,
  Fashion'd after certain laws;
Sing thou low or loud or sweet,
All at all points thou canst not meet,
  Some will pass and some will pause.

What is true at last will tell:
Few at first will place thee well;
Some too low would have thee shine,
Some too high — no fault of thine —
  Hold thine own, and work thy will!
Year will graze the heel of year,

But seldom comes the poet here,
And the Critic's rarer still.

A VOICE SPAKE OUT OF THE SKIES

A VOICE spake out of the skies
To a just man and a wise —
'The world and all within it
Will only last a minute!'
And a beggar began to cry
'Food, food or I die'!
Is it worth his while to eat,
Or mine to give him meat,
If the world and all within it
Were nothing the next minute?

DOUBT AND PRAYER

THO' Sin too oft, when smitten by Thy rod,
Rail at 'Blind Fate' with many a vain
  'Alas!'
From sin thro' sorrow into Thee we pass
By that same path our true forefathers
  trod;
And let not Reason fail me, nor the sod
Draw from my death Thy living flower
  and grass,
Before I learn that Love, which is, and was
My Father, and my Brother, and my God!

Steel me with patience! soften me with
  grief!
Let blow the trumpet strongly while I
  pray,
Till this embattled wall of unbelief
My prison, not my fortress, fall away!
Then, if thou willest, let my day be brief,
So Thou wilt strike Thy glory thro' the
  day.

FAITH

I

DOUBT no longer that the Highest is the
  wisest and the best,
Let not all that saddens Nature blight thy
  hope or break thy rest,
  Quail not at the fiery mountain, at the
   shipwreck, or the rolling
Thunder, or the rending earthquake, or the
  famine, or the pest!

II

Neither mourn if human creeds be lower
    than the heart's desire!
Thro' the gates that bar the distance comes
    a gleam of what is higher.
Wait till Death has flung them open,
    when the man will make the Maker
Dark no more with human hatreds in the
    glare of deathless fire!

THE SILENT VOICES

WHEN the dumb Hour, clothed in black,
Brings the Dreams about my bed,
Call me not so often back,
Silent Voices of the dead,
Toward the lowland ways behind me,
And the sunlight that is gone!
Call me rather, silent voices,
Forward to the starry track
Glimmering up the heights beyond me
On, and always on!

GOD AND THE UNIVERSE

I

WILL my tiny spark of being wholly vanish
    in your deeps and heights?
Must my day be dark by reason, O ye
    Heavens, of your boundless nights,
Rush of Suns, and roll of systems, and
    your fiery clash of meteorites?

II

'Spirit, nearing yon dark portal at the limit
    of thy human state,

Fear not thou the hidden purpose of that
    Power which alone is great,
Nor the myriad world, His shadow, nor the
    silent Opener of the Gate.'

THE DEATH OF THE DUKE OF CLARENCE AND AVONDALE

TO THE MOURNERS

THE bridal garland falls upon the bier,
The shadow of a crown, that o'er him hung,
Has vanish'd in the shadow cast by Death.
    So princely, tender, truthful, reverent,
        pure —
Mourn! That a world-wide Empire mourns
    with you,
That all the Thrones are clouded by your
    loss,
Were slender solace. Yet be comforted;
For if this earth be ruled by Perfect Love,
Then, after his brief range of blameless
    days,
The toll of funeral in an Angel ear
Sounds happier than the merriest marriage-
    bell.
    The face of Death is toward the Sun of
        Life,
His shadow darkens earth: his truer name
Is 'Onward,' no discordance in the roll
And march of that Eternal Harmony
Whereto the worlds beat time, tho' faintly
    heard
Until the great Hereafter. Mourn in hope!

CROSSING THE BAR

This poem first appeared in the 'Demeter'
volume of 1889, but is placed here in accord-
ance with Lord Tennyson's request that it
might be put at the end of all editions of his
poems. See the 'Memoir,' vol. ii. p. 367.

SUNSET and evening star,
    And one clear call for me!
And may there be no moaning of the bar,
    When I put out to sea,

But such a tide as moving seems asleep,
    Too full for sound and foam,

When that which drew from out the bound-
    less deep
    Turns again home.

Twilight and evening bell,
    And after that the dark!
And may there be no sadness of farewell,
    When I embark;

For tho' from out our bourne of Time and
    Place
    The flood may bear me far,
I hope to see my Pilot face to face
    When I have crost the bar.

And gaiety, resulting
From conscious innocence?

All, all have past and fled,
And left me lorn and lonely;
All those dear hopes are dead,
Remembrance wakes them only!

I stand like some lone tower
Of former days remaining,
Within whose place of power
The midnight owl is plaining; —

Like oak-tree old and grey,
Whose trunk with age is failing,
Thro' whose dark boughs for aye
The winter winds are wailing.

Thus, Memory, thus thy light
O'er this worn soul is gleaming,
Like some far fire at night
Along the dun deep streaming.

THE EXILE'S HARP

I WILL hang thee, my Harp, by the side of the
fountain,
On the whispering branch of the lone-waving
willow:
Above thee shall rush the hoarse gale of the
mountain,
Below thee shall tumble the dark breaking
billow.
The winds shall blow by thee, abandon'd, for-
saken,
The wild gales alone shall arouse thy sad
strain;
For where is the heart or the hand to awaken
The sounds of thy soul-soothing sweetness
again?
Oh! Harp of my fathers!
Thy chords shall decay,
One by one with the strings
Shall thy notes fade away;
Till the fiercest of tempests
Around thee may yell,
And not waken one sound
Of thy desolate shell!

Yet, oh! yet, ere I go, will I fling a wreath
round thee,
With the richest of flowers in the green valley
springing;
Those that see shall remember the hand that
hath crown'd thee,
When, wither'd and dead, to thee still they
are clinging.
There! now I have wreath'd thee — the roses
are twining
Thy chords with their bright blossoms glow-
ing and red:
Though the lapse of one day see their freshness
declining,
Yet bloom for one day when thy ninstrel has
fled!

Oh! Harp of my fathers!
No more in the hall,
The souls of the chieftains
Thy strains shall enthral:
One sweep will I give thee,
And wake thy bold swell;
Then, thou friend of my bosom,
For ever farewell!

'WHY SHOULD WE WEEP FOR THOSE WHO DIE?'

I doubt whether this poem is rightly attri-
buted to Alfred.

'Quamobrem, si dolorum finem mors affert, si secu-
rioris et melioris initium vitæ: si futura mala avertit
— cur eam tantopere accusare, ex qua potius consola-
tionem et lætitiam haurire fas esset?' — CICERO.

WHY should we weep for those who die?
They fall — their dust returns to dust;
Their souls shall live eternally
Within the mansions of the just.

They die to live — they sink to rise,
They leave this wretched mortal shore;
But brighter suns and bluer skies
Shall smile on them for evermore.

Why should we sorrow for the dead?
Our life on earth is but a span;
They tread the path that all must tread,
They die the common death of man.

The noblest songster of the gale
Must cease, when Winter's frowns appear;
The reddest rose is wan and pale,
When Autumn tints the changing year.

The fairest flower on earth must fade,
The brightest hopes on earth must die:
Why should we mourn that man was made
To droop on earth, but dwell on high?

The soul, th' eternal soul, must reign
In worlds devoid of pain and strife;
Then why should mortal man complain
Of death, which leads to happier life?

REMORSE

The complex interlacing of the rhymes is
peculiar to Alfred. Compare 'Persia,' 'The
Fall of Jerusalem,' 'Time,' etc.

'— sudant tacita præcordia culpa.' — JUVENAL.

OH! 'tis a fearful thing to glance
Back on the gloom of mis-spent years:
What shadowy forms of guilt advance,
And fill me with a thousand fears!
The vices of my life arise,
Pourtray'd in shapes, alas! too true;
And not one beam of hope breaks through,
To cheer my old and aching eyes,

APPENDIX

I. SELECTIONS FROM 'POEMS BY TWO BROTHERS'

In 1893 the present Lord Tennyson published a facsimile reprint of the 'Poems by Two Brothers,' in which his uncle, Mr. Frederick Tennyson, had appended the initials of the authors to their contributions to the volume, so far as he remembered them. He was not certain of the authorship of every poem. Some he signs 'A. T. (?)' or 'C. T. (?),' and some 'A. T. or C. T.' I give here all that are probably Alfred's, with some about which (see prefatory notes) I have my doubts. I follow the spelling and pointing of the reprint except in the few instances mentioned in the Notes.

MEMORY

It is interesting to compare this poem with the 'Ode to Memory' published in 1830. Like several others of Alfred's it is longer than any of Charles's.

'The memory is perpetually looking back when we have nothing present to entertain us: it is like those repositories in animals that are filled with stores of food, on which they may ruminate when their present pasture fails.' — ADDISON.

MEMORY ! dear enchanter !
　Why bring back to view
Dreams of youth, which banter
　All that e'er was true ?

Why present before me
　Thoughts of years gone by,
Which, like shadows o'er me,
　Dim in distance fly ?

Days of youth, now shaded
　By twilight of long years,
Flowers of youth, now faded,
　Though bathed in sorrow's tears:

Thoughts of youth, which waken
　Mournful feelings now,
Fruits which time hath shaken
　From off their parent bough:

Memory ! why, oh why,
　This fond heart consuming,
Shew me years gone by,
　When those hopes were blooming ?

Hopes which now are parted,
　Hopes which then I priz'd,
Which this world, cold-hearted,
　Ne'er has realiz'd ?

I knew not then its strife,
　I knew not then its rancour;
In every rose of life,
　Alas ! there lurks a canker.

Round every palm-tree, springing
　With bright fruit in the waste,
A mournful asp is clinging,
　Which sours it to our taste.

O'er every fountain, pouring
　Its waters thro' the wild,
Which man imbibes, adoring,
　And deems it undefil'd,

The poison-shrubs are dropping
　Their dark dews day by day;
And Care is hourly lopping
　Our greenest boughs away !

Ah ! these are thoughts that grieve me
　Then, when others rest.
Memory ! why deceive me
　By thy visions blest?

Why lift the veil, dividing
　The brilliant courts of spring —
Where gilded shapes are gliding
　In fairy colouring —

From age's frosty mansion,
　So cheerless and so chill ?
Why bid the bleak expansion
　Of past life meet us still ?

Where 's now that peace of mind
　O'er youth's pure bosom stealing,
So sweet and so refin'd,
　So exquisite a feeling ?

Where 's now the heart exulting
　In pleasure's buoyant sense,

And gaiety, resulting
  From conscious innocence?

All, all have past and fled,
  And left me lorn and lonely;
All those dear hopes are dead,
  Remembrance wakes them only!

I stand like some lone tower
  Of former days remaining,
Within whose place of power
  The midnight owl is plaining; —

Like oak-tree old and grey,
  Whose trunk with age is failing,
Thro' whose dark boughs for aye
  The winter winds are wailing.

Thus, Memory, thus thy light
  O'er this worn soul is gleaming,
Like some far fire at night
  Along the dun deep streaming.

THE EXILE'S HARP

I WILL hang thee, my Harp, by the side of the
  fountain,
  On the whispering branch of the lone-waving
    willow:
Above thee shall rush the hoarse gale of the
  mountain,
  Below thee shall tumble the dark breaking
    billow.
The winds shall blow by thee, abandon'd, for-
  saken,
  The wild gales alone shall arouse thy sad
    strain;
For where is the heart or the hand to awaken
  The sounds of thy soul-soothing sweetness
    again?
    Oh! Harp of my fathers!
      Thy chords shall decay,
    One by one with the strings
      Shall thy notes fade away;
    Till the fiercest of tempests
      Around thee may yell,
    And not waken one sound
      Of thy desolate shell!

Yet, oh! yet, ere I go, will I fling a wreath
  round thee,
  With the richest of flowers in the green valley
    springing;
Those that see shall remember the hand that
  hath crown'd thee,
  When, wither'd and dead, to thee still they
    are clinging.
There! now I have wreath'd thee — the roses
  are twining
  Thy chords with their bright blossoms glow-
    ing and red:
Though the lapse of one day see their freshness
  declining,
  Yet bloom for one day when thy minstrel has
    fled!

    Oh! Harp of my fathers!
      No more in the hall,
    The souls of the chieftains
      Thy strains shall enthral:
    One sweep will I give thee,
      And wake thy bold swell;
    Then, thou friend of my bosom,
      For ever farewell!

'WHY SHOULD WE WEEP FOR THOSE WHO DIE?'

I doubt whether this poem is rightly attri-
buted to Alfred.

'Quamobrem, si dolorum finem mors affert, si secu-
rioris et melioris initium vitæ: si futura mala avertit
— cur eam tantopere accusare, ex qua potius consola-
tionem et lætitiam haurire fas esset?' — CICERO.

WHY should we weep for those who die?
  They fall — their dust returns to dust;
Their souls shall live eternally
  Within the mansions of the just.

They die to live — they sink to rise,
  They leave this wretched mortal shore;
But brighter suns and bluer skies
  Shall smile on them for evermore.

Why should we sorrow for the dead?
  Our life on earth is but a span;
They tread the path that all must tread,
  They die the common death of man.

The noblest songster of the gale
  Must cease, when Winter's frowns appear;
The reddest rose is wan and pale,
  When Autumn tints the changing year.

The fairest flower on earth must fade,
  The brightest hopes on earth must die:
Why should we mourn that man was made
  To droop on earth, but dwell on high?

The soul, th' eternal soul, must reign
  In worlds devoid of pain and strife;
Then why should mortal man complain
  Of death, which leads to happier life?

REMORSE

The complex interlacing of the rhymes is
peculiar to Alfred. Compare 'Persia,' 'The
Fall of Jerusalem,' 'Time,' etc.

'— sudant tacita præcordia culpa.' — JUVENAL.

OH! 'tis a fearful thing to glance
  Back on the gloom of mis-spent years:
What shadowy forms of guilt advance,
  And fill me with a thousand fears!
The vices of my life arise,
  Pourtray'd in shapes, alas! too true;
And not one beam of hope breaks through,
To cheer my old and aching eyes,

T' illume my night of wretchedness,
My age of anguish and distress.
If I am damn'd, why find I not
Some comfort in this earthly spot ?
But no ! this world and that to come
Are both to me one scene of gloom !
Lest ought of solace I should see,
   Or lose the thoughts of what I do,
Remorse, with soul-felt agony,
   Holds up the mirror to my view.
And I was cursed from my birth,
A reptile made to creep on earth,
An hopeless outcast, born to die
A living death eternally !
With too much conscience to have rest,
Too little to be ever blest,
To yon vast world of endless woe,
   Unlighted by the cheerful day,
   My soul shall wing her weary way;
      To those dread depths where aye the same,
Throughout the waste of darkness, glow
   The glimmerings of the boundless flame.
And yet I cannot here below
Take my full cup of guilt, as some,
And laugh away my doom to come.
I would I 'd been all-heartless ! then
I might have sinn'd like other men;
But all this side the grave is fear,
A wilderness so dank and drear,
That never wholesome plant would spring;
   And all behind — I dare not think !
I would not risk th' imagining —
   From the full view my spirits shrink;
And starting backwards, yet I cling
To life, whose every hour to me
Hath been increase of misery.
But yet I cling to it, for well
I know the pangs that rack me now
Are trifles, to the endless hell
   That waits me, when my burning brow
And my wrung eyes shall hope in vain
For one small drop to cool the pain,
The fury of that madd'ning flame
That then shall scorch my writhing frame !
Fiends ! who have goaded me to ill !
Distracting fiends, who goad me still !
If e'er I work'd a sinful deed,
   Ye know how bitter was the draught;
Ye know my inmost soul would bleed,
   And ye have look'd at me and laugh'd,
Triumphing that I could not free
My spirit from your slavery !
Yet is there that in me which says,
   Should these old feet their course retread
From out the portal of my days,
   That I should lead the life I 've led:
My agony, my torturing shame,
My guilt, my errors all the same !
Oh, God ! that thou wouldst grant that ne'er
   My soul its clay-cold bed forsake,
That I might sleep, and never wake
Unto the thrill of conscious fear;
   For when the trumpet's piercing cry
Shall burst upon my slumb'ring ear,
   And countless seraphs throng the sky,
How shall I cast my shroud away,
And come into the blaze of day ?

How shall I brook to hear each crime,
Here veil'd by secrecy and time,
Read out from thine eternal book ?
   How shall I stand before thy throne,
   While earth shall like a furnace burn ?
How shall I bear the with'ring look
   Of men and angels, who will turn
Their dreadful gaze on me alone ?

THE DELL OF E——

'Tantum ævi longinqua valet mutare vetustas !' —
VIRGIL.

THERE was a long, low, rushy dell, emboss'd
   With knolls of grass and clumps of copsewood
      green;
Mid-way a wandering burn the valley cross'd,
   And streak'd with silvery line the wood-land
      scene;
High hills on either side to heaven upsprung,
   Y-clad with groves of undulating pine,
Upon whose heads the hoary vapours hung,
   And far — far off the heights were seen to
      shine
In clear relief against the sapphire sky,
   And many a blue stream wander'd thro' the
      shade
Of those dark groves that clomb the mountains
      high,
   And glistening 'neath each lone entangled
      glade,
At length with brawling accent loudly fell
Within the limpid brook that wound along the
      dell.

How pleasant was the ever-varying light
   Beneath that emerald coverture of boughs !
How often, at th' approach of dewy night,
   Have those tall pine-trees heard the lover's
      vows !
How many a name was carv'd upon the trunk
   Of each old hollow willow-tree, that stoop'd
To lave its branches in the brook, and drunk
   Its freshening dew ! How many a cypress
      droop'd
From those fair banks, where bloom'd the ear-
      liest flowers,
   Which the young year from her abounding
      horn
Scatters profuse within her secret bowers !
   What rapturous gales from that wild dell
      were borne !
And, floating on the rich spring breezes, flung
Their incense o'er that wave on whose bright
      banks they sprung !

Long years had past, and there again I came,
   But man's rude hand had sorely scath'd the
      dell;
And though the cloud-capped mountains, still
      the same,
   Uprear'd each heaven-invading pinnacle;
Yet were the charms of that lone valley fled,
   And the grey - winding of the stream was
      gone;

The brook, once murmuring o'er its pebbly
bed,
Now deeply — straightly — noiselessly went
on.
Slow turn'd the sluggish wheel beneath its
force,
Where clattering mills disturb'd the solitude:
Where was the prattling of its former course?
Its shelving, sedgy sides y-crown'd with
wood?
The willow trunks were fell'd, the names eras'd
From one broad shattered pine, which still its
station grac'd.

Remnant of all its brethren, there it stood,
Braving the storms that swept the cliffs
above,
Where once, throughout th' impenetrable wood,
Were heard the plainings of the pensive dove.
But man had bid th' eternal forests bow
That bloom'd upon the earth-imbedded base
Of the strong mountain, and perchance they
now
Upon the billows were the dwelling-place
Of their destroyers, and bore terror round
The trembling earth: — ah! lovelier, had they
still
Whisper'd unto the breezes with low sound,
And greenly flourish'd on their native hill,
And flinging their proud arms in state on high,
Spread out beneath the sun their glorious can-
opy!

ANTONY TO CLEOPATRA

O, CLEOPATRA! fare thee well,
We two can meet no more;
This breaking heart alone can tell
The love to thee I bore.
But wear not thou the conqueror's chain
Upon thy race and thee;
And though we ne'er can meet again,
Yet still be true to me:
For I for thee have lost a throne,
To wear the crown of love alone.

Fair daughter of a regal line!
To thraldom bow not tame;
My every wish on earth was thine,
My every hope the same.
And I have mov'd within thy sphere,
And liv'd within thy light;
And oh! thou wert to me so dear,
I breath'd but in thy sight!
A subject world I lost for thee,
For thou wert all my world to me!

Then when the shriekings of the dying
Were heard along the wave,
Soul of my soul! I saw thee flying;
I follow'd thee, to save.
The thunder of the brazen prows
O'er Actium's ocean rung;
Fame's garland faded from my brows,
Her wreath away I flung.
I sought, I saw, I heard but thee:
For what to love was victory?

Thine on the earth, and on the throne,
And in the grave, am I;
And, dying, still I am thine own,
Thy bleeding Antony.
How shall my spirit joy to hear
That thou art ever true!
Nay — weep not — dry that burning tear,
That bathes thine eyes' dark hue.
Shades of my fathers! lo! I come;
I hear your voices from the tomb!

I WANDER IN DARKNESS AND SORROW'

Note the repetition in the last lines of each
stanza. Alfred was more given to these regu-
larities of *form* than his brother. He also tries
his hand at a greater variety of stanzas and
arrangements of rhymes.

I WANDER in darkness and sorrow,
Unfriended, and cold, and alone,
As dismally gurgles beside me
The bleak river's desolate moan.
The rise of the volleying thunder
The mountain's lone echoes repeat:
The roar of the wind is around me,
The leaves of the year at my feet.

I wander in darkness and sorrow,
Uncheer'd by the moon's placid ray;
Not a friend that I lov'd but is dead,
Not a hope but has faded away!
Oh! when shall I rest in the tomb,
Wrapt about with the chill winding sheet?
For the roar of the wind is around me,
The leaves of the year at my feet.

I heed not the blasts that sweep o'er me,
I blame not the tempests of night;
They are not the foes who have banish'd
The visions of youthful delight:
I hail the wild sound of their raving,
Their merciless presence I greet;
Though the roar of the wind be around me,
The leaves of the year at my feet.

In this waste of existence, for solace,
On whom shall my lone spirit call?
Shall I fly to the friends of my bosom?
My God! I have buried them all!
They are dead, they are gone, they are cold,
My embraces no longer they meet;
Let the roar of the wind be around me,
The leaves of the year at my feet!

Those eyes that glanc'd love unto mine,
With motionless slumbers are prest;
Those hearts which once throbb'd but for me,
Are chill as the earth where they rest.
Then around on my wan wither'd form
Let the pitiless hurricanes beat;
Let the roar of the wind be around me,
The leaves of the year at my feet!

Like the voice of the owl in the hall,
    Where the song and the banquet have ceas'd,
Where the green weeds have mantled the
        hearth,
    Whence arose the proud flame of the feast;
So I cry to the storm, whose dark wing
    Scatters on me the wild-driving sleet —
'*Let the roar of the wind be around me,*
    The fall of the leaves at my feet ! '

THE OLD SWORD

OLD Sword! tho' dim and rusted
    Be now thy sheeny blade,
Thy glitt'ring edge encrusted
    With cankers Time hath made;
        Yet once around thee swell'd the cry
            Of triumph's fierce delight,
        The shoutings of the victory,
            The thunders of the fight !

Tho' age hath past upon thee
    With still corroding breath,
Yet once stream'd redly on thee
    The purpling tide of death :
        What time amid the war of foes
            The dastard's cheek grew pale,
        As through the feudal field arose
            The ringing of the mail.

Old Sword ! what arm hath wielded
    Thy richly gleaming brand,
'Mid lordly forms who shielded
    The maidens of their land ?
        And who hath clov'n his foes in wrath
            With thy puissant fire,
        And scatter'd in his perilous path
            The victims of his ire ?

Old Sword ! whose fingers clasp'd thee
    Around thy carved hilt ?
And with that hand which grasp'd thee
    What heroes' blood was spilt ;
        When fearlessly, with open hearts,
            And lance to lance oppos'd,
        Beneath the shade of barbed darts
            The dark-ey'd warriors clos'd ?

Old Sword ! I would not burnish
    Thy venerable rust,
Nor sweep away the tarnish
    Of darkness and of dust !
        Lie there, in slow and still decay,
            Unfam'd in olden rhyme,
        The relic of a former day,
            A wreck of ancient time !

'WE MEET NO MORE'

The present Lord Tennyson agrees with me
that this is incorrectly assigned to Alfred.

WE meet no more — the die is cast,
    The chain is broke that tied us,

Our every hope on earth is past,
    And there 's no helm to guide us:
We meet no more — the roaring blast
    And angry seas divide us !

And I stand on a distant shore,
    The breakers round me swelling;
And lonely thoughts of days gone o'er
    Have made this breast their dwelling:
We meet no more — We meet no more:
    Farewell for ever, Ellen !

WRITTEN

BY AN EXILE OF BASSORAH,

WHILE SAILING DOWN THE EUPHRATES

THOU land of the Lily ! thy gay flowers are
        blooming
    In joy on thine hills, but they bloom not for
        me;
For a dark gulf of woe, all my fond hopes en-
        tombing,
    Has roll'd its black waves 'twixt this lone
        heart and thee.

The far-distant hills, and the groves of my
        childhood,
    Now stream in the light of the sun's setting
        ray;
And the tall-waving palms of my own native
        wildwood
    In the blue haze of distance are melting away.

I see thee, Bassorah ! in splendour retiring,
    Where thy waves and thy walls in their ma-
        jesty meet;
I see the bright glory thy pinnacles firing,
    And the broad vassal river that rolls at thy
        feet.

I see thee but faintly — thy tall towers are
        beaming
    On the dusky horizon so far and so blue;
And minaret and mosque in the distance are
        gleaming,
    While the coast of the stranger expands on
        my view.

I see thee no more : for the deep waves have
        parted
    The land of my birth from her desolate son;
And I am gone from thee, though half broken-
        hearted,
    To wander thro' climes where thy name is
        unknown.

Farewell to my harp, which I hung in my
        anguish
    On the lonely palmetto that nods to the gale;
For its sweet-breathing tones in forgetfulness
        languish,
    And around it the ivy shall weave a green
        veil.

Farewell to the days which so smoothly have
      glided
    With the maiden whose look was like Cama's
      young glance,
And the sheen of whose eyes was the load-star
      which guided
    My course on this earth thro' the storms of
      mischance !

THE VALE OF BONES

' Albis informem — ossibus agrum.' — HORACE.

ALONG yon vapour-mantled sky
The dark-red moon is riding high;
At times her beams in beauty break
Upon the broad and silv'ry lake;
At times more bright they clearly fall
On some white castle's ruin'd wall;
At times her partial splendour shines
Upon the grove of deep-black pines,
Through which the dreary night-breeze moans,
Above this Vale of scatter'd bones.

The low, dull gale can scarcely stir
The branches of that black'ning fir,
Which betwixt me and heav'n flings wido
Its shadowy boughs on either side,
And o'er yon granite rock uprears
Its giant form of many years.
And the shrill owlet's desolate wail
Comes to mine ear along the gale,
As, list'ning to its lengthen'd tones,
I dimly pace the Vale of Bones.

Dark Valley ! still the same art thou,
Unchang'd thy mountain's cloudy brow;
Still from yon cliffs, that part asunder,
Falls down the torrent's echoing thunder;
Still from this mound of reeds and rushes
With bubbling sound the fountain gushes;
Thence, winding thro' the whisp'ring ranks
Of sedges on the willowy banks,
Still brawling, chafes the rugged stones
That strew this dismal Vale of Bones.

Unchang'd art thou ! no storm hath rent
Thy rude and rocky battlement;
Thy rioting mountains sternly pil'd,
The screen of nature, wide and wild:
But who were they, whose bones bestrew
The heather, cold with midnight dew,
Upon whose slowly-rotting clay
The raven long hath ceas'd to prey,
But, mould'ring in the moon-light air,
Their wan, white skulls show bleak and bare ?
And, aye, the dreary night-breeze moans
Above them in this Vale of Bones!

I knew them all — a gallant band,
The glory of their native land,
And on each lordly brow elate
Sate valour and contempt of fate,
Fierceness of youth, and scorn of foe,
And pride to render blow for blow.
In the strong war's tumultuous crash,

How darkly did their keen eyes flash !
How fearlessly each arm was rais'd !
How dazzlingly each broad-sword blaz'd !
Though now the dreary night-breeze moans
Above them in this Vale of Bones.

What lapse of time shall sweep away
The memory of that gallant day,
When on to battle proudly going,
Your plumage to the wild winds blowing,
Your tartans far behind ye flowing,
Your pennons rais'd, your clarions sounding,
Fiercely your steeds beneath ye bounding,
Ye mix'd the strife of warring foes
In fiery shock and deadly close ?
What stampings in the madd'ning strife,
What thrusts, what stabs, with brand and knife,
What desp'rate strokes for death or life,
Were there ! What cries, what thrilling groans,
Re-echo'd thro' the Vale of Bones !

Thou peaceful Vale, whose mountains lonely,
Sound to the torrent's chiding only,
Or wild-goat's cry from rocky ledge,
Or bull-frog from the rustling sedge,
Or eagle from her airy cairn,
Or screaming of the startled hern —
How did thy million echoes waken
Amid thy caverns deeply shaken !
How with the red dew o'er thee rain'd
Thine emerald turf was darkly stain'd !
How did each innocent flower, that sprung
Thy greenly-tangl'd glades among,
Blush with the big and purple drops
That dribbled from the leafy copse!
I pac'd the valley, when the yell
Of triumph's voice had ceas'd to swell:
When battle's brazen throat no more
Rais'd its annihilating roar.
There lay ye on each other pil'd,
Your brows with noble dust defil'd;[1]
There, by the loudly-gushing water,
Lay man and horse in mingled slaughter.
Then wept I not, thrice gallant band;
For though no more each dauntless hand
The thunder of the combat hurl'd,
Yet still with pride your lips were curl'd;
And e'en in death's o'erwhelming shade
Your fingers linger'd round the blade !
I deem'd, when gazing proudly there
Upon the fix'd and haughty air
That mark'd each warrior's bloodless face,
Ye would not change the narrow space
Which each cold form of breathless clay
Then cover'd, as on earth ye lay,
For realms, for sceptres, or for thrones —
I dream'd not on this Vale of Bones !

But years have thrown their veil between,
And alter'd is that lonely scene;
And dreadful emblems of thy might,
Stern Dissolution ! meet my sight:
The eyeless socket, dark and dull,
The hideous grinning of the skull,
Are sights which Memory disowns,
Thou melancholy Vale of Bones !

[1] ' Non indecoro pulvere sordidos.' — HOR.

'DID NOT THY ROSEATE LIPS OUTVIE'

In this poem, as in 'Persia,' 'Midnight,' and others, the long sentences are to be noted. One finds very few of these in Charles's poems.

> 'Ulla si juris tibi pejerati
> Pœna, Barine, nocuisset unquam;
> Dente si nigro fieres, vel uno
>   Turpior ungui
> Crederem.'
>   HORACE.

DID not thy roseate lips outvie
  The gay Anana's spicy bloom; [1]
Had not thy breath the luxury,
  The richness of its deep perfume —

Were not the pearls it fans more clear
  Than those which grace the valved shell;
Thy foot more airy than the deer,
  When startled from his lonely dell —

Were not thy bosom's stainless whiteness,
  Where angel loves their vigils keep,
More heavenly than the dazzling brightness
  Of the cold crescent on the deep —

Were not thine eye a star might grace
  Yon sapphire concave beaming clear,
Or fill the vanish'd Pleiad's place,
  And shine for aye as brightly there —

Had not thy locks the golden glow
  That robes the gay and early east,
Thus falling in luxuriant flow
  Around thy fair but faithless breast:

I might have deem'd that thou wert she
  Of the Cumæan cave, who wrote
Each fate-involving mystery,
  Upon the feathery leaves that float,

Borne thro' the boundless waste of air,
  Wherever chance might drive along.
But she was wrinkled — thou art fair:
  And she was old — but thou art young.

Her years were as the sands that strew
  The fretted ocean-beach; but thou —
Triumphant in that eye of blue,
  Beneath thy smoothly-marble brow;

Exulting in thy form thus moulded,
  By nature's tenderest touch design'd;
Proud of the fetters thou hast folded
  Around this fond deluded mind —

Deceivest still with practis'd look,
  With fickle vow, and well-feign'd sigh.
I tell thee, that I will not brook
  Reiterated perjury !

[1] Ulloa says, that the blossom of the West-Indian Anana is of so elegant a crimson as even to dazzle the eye, and that the fragrancy of the fruit discovers the

Alas ! I feel thy deep control,
  E'en now when I would break thy chain:
But while I seek to gain thy soul,
  Ah ! say — hast thou a soul to gain ?

PERSIA

One of the most notable of these juvenile poems. The familiarity with Persian history and geography is remarkable in one so young; and proper names are managed with much skill.

> 'The flower and choice
> Of many provinces from bound to bound.'
>   MILTON.

LAND of bright eye and lofty brow !
  Whose every gale is balmy breath
Of incense from some sunny flower,
  Which on tall hill or valley low,
    In clustering maze or circling wreath,
    Sheds perfume; or in blooming bower
Of Schiraz or of Ispahan,
In bower untrod by foot of man,
Clasps round the green and fragrant stem
  Of lotos, fair and fresh and blue,
And crowns it with a diadem
Of blossoms, ever young and new;
Oh ! lives there yet within thy soul
  Ought of the fire of him who led
Thy troops, and bade thy thunder roll
  O'er lone Assyria's crownless head ?
I tell thee, had that conqueror red
  From Thymbria's plain beheld thy fall,
When stormy Macedonia swept
  Thine honours from thee one and all,
He would have wail'd, he would have wept,
That thy proud spirit should have bow'd
To Alexander, doubly proud.
Oh ! Iran ! Iran ! had he known
The downfall of his mighty throne,
Or had he seen that fatal night,
  When the young king of Macedon
In madness led his veterans on,
And Thais held the funeral light,
  Around that noble pile which rose
  Irradiant with the pomp of gold,
  In high Persepolis of old,
Encompass'd with its frenzied foes;
He would have groan'd, he would have spread
The dust upon his laurell'd head,
To view the setting of that star,
Which beam'd so gorgeously and far
O'er Anatolia, and the fane
Of Belus, and Caïster's plain,
  And Sardis, and the glittering sands
  Of bright Pactolus, and the lands
Where Crœsus held his rich domain:
On fair Diarbeck's land of spice, [2]
Adiabene's plains of rice,
Where down th' Euphrates, swift and strong,

plant though concealed from sight. — See Ulloa's *Voyages*, vol. i. p. 72.
[2] Xenophon says, that every shrub in these wilds had an aromatic odour.

The shield-like kuphars bound along; [1]
And sad Cunaxa's field, where, mixing
    With host to adverse host oppos'd,
'Mid clashing shield and spear transfixing,
    The rival brothers sternly clos'd.
And further east, where, broadly roll'd,
Old Indus pours his stream of gold;
And there, where tumbling deep and hoarse,
Blue Ganga leaves her vaccine source; [2]
Loveliest of all the lovely streams
That meet immortal Titan's beams,
And smile upon their fruitful way
Beneath his golden orient ray:
And southward to Cilicia's shore,
Where Cydnus meets the billows' roar,
And where the Syrian gates divide
The meeting realms on either side; [3]
E'en to the land of Nile, whose crops
    Bloom rich beneath his bounteous swell,
    To hot Syene's wondrous well,
Nigh to the long-liv'd Æthiops.
And northward far to Trebizonde,
    Renown'd for kings of chivalry,
    Near where old Hyssus, from the strand,
    Disgorges in the Euxine sea —
The Euxine, falsely nam'd, which whelms
    The mariner in the heaving tide,
To high Sinope's distant realms,
    Whence cynics rail'd at human pride.

EGYPT

'Egypt's palmy groves,
Her grots, and sepulchres of kings.'
MOORE'S *Lalla Rookh.*

THE sombre pencil of the dim-grey dawn
Draws a faint sketch of Egypt to mine eye,
As yet uncolour'd by the brilliant morn,
    And her gay orb careering up the sky.

And see ! at last he comes in radiant pride,
    Life in his eye, and glory in his ray;
No veiling mists his growing splendour hide,
    And hang their gloom around his golden way.

The flowery region brightens in his smile,
    Her lap of blossoms freights the passing gale,
That robs the odours of each balmy isle,
    Each fragrant field and aromatic vale.

But the first glitter of his rising beam
    Falls on the broad-bas'd pyramids sublime,
As proud to show us with his earliest gleam,
    Those vast and hoary enemies of time.

E'en History's self, whose certain scrutiny
    Few eras in the list of Time beguile,

Pauses, and scans them with astonish'd eye,
    As unfamiliar with their aged pile.

Awful, august, magnificent, they tower
    Amid the waste of shifting sands around;
The lapse of year and month and day and hour,
    Alike unfelt, perform th' unwearied round.

How often hath yon day-god's burning light,
    From the clear sapphire of his stainless heaven,
Bath'd their high peaks in noontide brilliance bright,
    Gilded at morn, and purpled them at even ! [4]

THE DRUID'S PROPHECIES [5]

Perhaps suggested by Cowper's ' Boadicea,'
but longer and more elaborate, and here and
there hardly inferior to that poem.

MONA ! with flame thine oaks are streaming,
    Those sacred oaks we rear'd on high :
Lo ! Mona, Lo ! the swords are gleaming
    Adown thine hills confusedly.

Hark ! Mona, Hark ! the chargers' neighing !
    The clang of arms and helmets bright !
The crash of steel, the dreadful braying
    Of trumpets thro' the madd'ning fight !

Exalt your torches, raise your voices;
    Your thread is spun — your day is brief;
Yea ! Howl for sorrow ! Rome rejoices,
    But Mona — Mona bends in grief !

But woe to Rome, though now she raises
    Yon eagles of her haughty power;
Though now her sun of conquest blazes,
    Yet soon shall come her darkening hour !

Woe, woe to him who sits in glory,
    Enthroned on thine hills of pride !
Can he not see the poignard gory,
    With his best heart's-blood deeply dyed ?

Ah ! what avails his gilded palace,
    Whose wings the seven-hill'd town enfold ? [6]
The costly bath, the chrystal chalice ?
    The pomp of gems — the glare of gold ?

See where, by heartless anguish driven,
    Crownless he creeps 'mid circling thorns; [7]
Around him flash the bolts of heaven,
    And angry earth before him yawns. [8]

---

[1] See Rennel on Herodotus.
[2] The cavern in the ridge of Himmalah, whence the
Ganges seems to derive its original springs, has been
moulded, by the mind of Hindoo superstition, into the
head of a cow.
[3] See Xenophon's *Expeditio Cyri.*
[4] See Savary's *Letters.*
[5] ' Stabat pro littore diversa acies, densa armis virisque, intercursantibus feminis in modum Furiarum, quæ

---

veste ferali, crinibus dejectis, faces præferebant. Druidæque circum, preces diras, sublatis ad cœlum manibus,
fundentes,' etc. — TACIT. *Annal.* xiv. c. 30.
[6] Pliny says, that the golden palace of Nero extended
all round the city.
[7] ' Ut ad diverticulum ventum est, dimissis equis inter
fruticeta ac vepres, per arundineti semitam ægre, nec
nisi strata sub pedibus veste, ad adversum villæ parietem evasit.' — SUETON. *Vit. Cæsar.*
[8] ' Statimque tremore terræ, et fulgure adverso pavefactus, audiit ex proximis castris clamorem,' etc. — *Ibid.*

Then, from his pinnacle of splendour,
  The feeble king,[1] with locks of grey,
Shall fall, and sovereign Rome shall render
  Her sceptre to the usurper's [2] sway.

Who comes with sounds of mirth and gladness,
  Triumphing o'er the prostrate dead ? [3]
Ay, me ! thy mirth shall change to sadness,
  When Vengeance strikes thy guilty head.

Above thy noon-day feast suspended,
  High hangs in air a naked sword:
Thy days are gone, thy joys are ended,
  The cup, the song, the festal board.

Then shall the eagle's shadowy pinion
  Be spread beneath the eastern skies; [4]
And dazzling far with wide dominion,
  Five brilliant stars shall brightly rise.[5]

Then, coward king ! [6] the helpless aged
  Shall bow beneath thy dastard blow;
But reckless hands and hearts, enraged,
  By double fate shall lay thee low.[7]

And two,[8] with death-wounds deeply mangled,
  Low on their parent-earth shall lie;
Fond wretches ! ah ! too soon entangled
  Within the snares of royalty.

Then comes that mighty one victorious
  In triumph o'er this earthly ball,[9]
Exulting in his conquests glorious —
  Ah ! glorious to his country's fall !

But thou shalt see the Romans flying,
  O Albyn ! with yon dauntless ranks; [10]
And thou shalt view the Romans dying,
  Blue Carun ! on thy mossy banks.

But lo ! what dreadful visions o'er me
  Are bursting on this aged eye !
What length of bloody train before me,
  In slow succession passes by ! [11]

Thy hapless monarchs fall together,
  Like leaves in winter's stormy ire;
Some by the sword, and some shall wither
  By light'ning's flame and fever's fire.[12]

They come ! they leave their frozen regions,
  Where Scandinavia's wilds extend;
And Rome, though girt with dazzling legions,
  Beneath their blasting power shall bend.

Woe, woe to Rome ! though tall and ample
  She rears her domes of high renown;
Yet fiery Goths shall fiercely trample
  The grandeur of her temples down !

She sinks to dust; and who shall pity
  Her dark despair and hopeless groans ?
There is a wailing in her city —
  Her babes are dash'd against the stones !

Then, Mona ! then, though wan and blighted
  Thy hopes be now by Sorrow's dearth,
Then all thy wrongs shall be requited —
  The Queen of Nations bows to earth !

THE EXPEDITION OF NADIR SHAH INTO HINDOSTAN

' Quoi ! vous allez combattre un roi, dont la puissance
Semble forcer le ciel de prendre sa défense,
Sous qui toute l'Asie a vu tomber ses rois
Et qui tient la fortune attachée à ses lois ! '
                    RACINE's *Alexandre.*

' Squallent populatibus agri.' — CLAUDIAN.

As the host of the locusts in numbers, in might
As the flames of the forest that redden the
    night,
They approach: but the eye may not dwell on
    the glare
Of standard and sabre that sparkle in air.

Like the fiends of destruction they rush on their
    way,
The vulture behind them is wild for his prey;
And the spirits of death, and the demons of
    wrath,
Wave the gloom of their wings o'er their deso-
    late path.

Earth trembles beneath them, the dauntless,
    the bold.
Oh ! weep for thy children, thou region of
    gold; [18]
For thy thousands are bow'd to the dust of the
    plain,
And all Delhi runs red with the blood of her
    slain.

---

[1] Galba.   [2] Otho.
[3] ' Utque campos, in quibus pugnatum est, adiit (*i. e.*
Vitellius) plurimum meri propalam hausit,' etc.— SUET.
[4] At the siege of Jerusalem.
[5] The five good Emperors: Nerva, Trajan, Adrian,
Antoninus Pius, and Marcus Aurelius, or Antoninus the
Philosopher. Perhaps the best commentary on the life
and virtues of the last, is his own volume of *Medita-
tions.*
[6] ' Debiles pedibus, et eos, qui ambulare non possent,
in gigantum modum, ita ut a genibus de pannis et lin-
teis quasi dracones digererentur; eosdemque sagittis
confecit.' — ÆL. LAMPRID. *in Vita Comm.* — Such were
the laudable amusements of Commodus !
[7] He was first poisoned; but the operation not fully
answering the wishes of his beloved, he was afterwards
strangled by a robust wrestler.
[8] Pertinax and Didius Julian.
[9] Severus, who was equally victorious in the Eastern
and Western World: but those conquests, however glo-

rious, were conducive to the ruin of the Roman Empire.
— See GIBBON, vol. vi. chap. v. p. 203.
[10] In allusion to the real or feigned victory obtained
by Fingal over Caracul or Caracalla. — See OSSIAN.
[11] Very few of the Emperors after Severus escaped
assassination.
[12] Macrinus, Heliogabalus, Alexander, Maximin Pu-
pienus, Balbinus, Gordian, Philip, etc., were assassi-
nated; Claudius died of a pestilential fever; and Carus
was struck dead by lightning in his tent.
[13] This invader required as a ransom for Mohammed
Shah no less than thirty millions, and amassed in the
rich city of Delhi the enormous sum of two hundred
and thirty-one millions sterling. Others, however, dif-
fer considerably in their account of this treasure.

For thy glory is past, and thy splendour is dim,
And the cup of thy sorrow is full to the brim;
And where is the chief in thy realms to abide,
The 'Monarch of Nations,' [1] the strength of his
    pride?

Like a thousand dark streams from the moun-
    tain they throng,
With the fife and the horn and the war-beating
    gong:
The land like an Eden before them is fair,
But behind them a wilderness dreary and bare.[2]

The shrieks of the orphan, the lone widow's
    wail,
The groans of the childless, are loud on the
    gale;
For the star of thy glory is blasted and wan,
And wither'd the flower of thy fame, Hindo-
    stan!

THE MAID OF SAVOY

Down Savoy's hills of stainless white
    A thousand currents run,
And sparkle bright in the early light
    Of the slowly-rising sun:
        But brighter far,
        Like the glance of a star
        From regions above,
        Is the look of love
            In the eye of the Maid of Savoy!

Down Savoy's hills of lucid snow
    A thousand roebucks leap,
And headlong they go when the bugles blow,
    And sound from steep to steep:
        But lighter far,
        Like the motion of air
        On the smooth river's bed,
        Is the noiseless tread
            Of the foot of the Maid of Savoy!

In Savoy's vales, with green array'd,
    A thousand blossoms flower,
'Neath the odorous shade by the larches made,
    In their own ambrosial bower:
        But sweeter still,
        Like the cedars which rise
        On Lebanon's hill
        To the pure blue skies,
            Is the breath of the Maid of Savoy!

In Savoy's groves full merrily sing
    A thousand songsters gay,
When the breath of spring calls them forth on
    the wing,
    To sport in the sun's mild ray:

[1] Such pompous epithets the Oriental writers are
accustomed to bestow on their monarchs; of which suf-
ficient specimens may be seen in Sir William Jones's
translation of the History of Nadir Shah. We can
scarcely read one page of this work without meeting
with such sentences as these: 'Le roi de rois;' 'Les
étendards qui subjuguent le monde;' 'L'âme rayon-

But softer far,
Like the holy song
Of angels in air,
When they sweep along,
    Is the voice of the Maid of Savoy!

MIDNIGHT

'T is midnight o'er the dim mere's lonely bosom,
    Dark, dusky, windy midnight: swift are
        driven
The swelling vapours onward: every blossom
    Bathes its bright petals in the tears of heaven.
Imperfect, half-seen objects meet the sight,
    The other half our fancy must pourtray;
A wan, dull, lengthen'd sheet of swimming
    light
Lies the broad lake: the moon conceals her ray,
Sketch'd faintly by a pale and lurid gleam
    Shot thro' the glimmering clouds: the lovely
        planet
Is shrouded in obscurity; the scream
    Of owl is silenc'd; and the rocks of granite
Rise tall and drearily, while damp and dank
    Hang the thick willows on the reedy bank.
Beneath, the gurgling eddies slowly creep,
    Blacken'd by foliage; and the glutting wave,
That saps eternally the cold grey steep,
    Sounds heavily within the hollow cave.
All earth is restless — from his glossy wing [3]
    The heath-fowl lifts his head at intervals;
Wet, driving, rainy, come the bursting squalls;
All nature wears her dun dead covering.
Tempest is gather'd, and the brooding storm
Spreads its black mantle o'er the mountain's
    form;
And, mingled with the rising roar, is swelling,
From the far hunter's booth, the blood hound's
    yelling.
The water-falls in various cadence chiming,
    Or in one loud unbroken sheet descending,
        Salute each other thro' the night's dark
            womb;
        The moaning pine-trees to the wild blast
            bending,
        Are pictured faintly thro' the chequer'd
            gloom;
The forests, half-way up the mountain climbing,
    Resound with crash of falling branches;
        quiver
        Their aged mossy trunks: the startled doe
Leaps from her leafy lair: the swelling river
    Winds his broad stream majestic, deep,
        and slow.

SCOTCH SONG

In the reprint this is marked ' (?) ' but it is
probably Alfred's. It is the only experiment
in Scottish verse in the volume.

nante de sa majesté;' 'Le rayonnant monarque du
monde;' 'Sa majesté conquérante du monde;' etc.
[2] 'The land is as the garden of Eden before them,
and behind them a desolate wilderness.' — JOEL.
[3] The succeeding lines are a paraphrase of Ossian.

THERE are tears o' pity, an' tears o' wae,
  An' tears for excess o' joy will fa' ;
Yet the tears o' luve are sweeter than a' !

There are sighs o' pity, an' sighs o' wae,
  An' sighs o' regret frae the saul will gae;
Yet the sighs o' luve are sweeter than a' !

There 's the look o' pity, the look o' wae,
  The look o' frien', an' the look o' fae;
Yet the look o' luve is sweeter than a' !

There 's the smile o' friends when they come
    frae far,
  There 's the smile o' joy in the festive ha' ;
Yet the smile o' luve is sweeter than a' !

SONG

IT is the solemn even-time,
  And the holy organ 's pealing:
And the vesper chime, oh ! the vesper chime !
  O'er the clear blue wave is stealing.

It is the solemn mingled swell
  Of the monks in chorus singing:
And the vesper bell, oh ! the vesper bell !
  To the gale is its soft note flinging.

'T is the sound of the voices sweeping along,
  Like the wind thro' a grove of larches:
And the vesper song, oh ! the vesper song !
  Echoes sad thro' the cloister'd arches.

FRIENDSHIP

'Neque ego nunc de vulgari aut de mediocri, quæ
tamen ipsa et delectat et prodest, sed de vera et per-
fecta loquor (amicitia) qualis eorum, qui pauci nomi-
nantur, fuit.' — CICERO.

O THOU most holy Friendship ! wheresoe'er
  Thy dwelling be — for in the courts of man
But seldom thine all-heavenly voice we hear,
  Sweet'ning the moments of our narrow span ;
And seldom thy bright foot-steps do we scan
  Along the weary waste of life unblest,
For faithless is its frail and wayward plan,
  And perfidy is man's eternal guest,
With dark suspicion link'd and shameless in-
    terest ! —

'T is thine, when life has reach'd its final goal,
  Ere the last sigh that frees the mind be giv'n,
To speak sweet solace to the parting soul,
  And pave the bitter path that leads to heav'n:
'T is thine, whene'er the heart is rack'd and
    riv'n
By the hot shafts of baleful calumny,
When the dark spirit to despair is driv'n,
  To teach its lonely grief to lean on thee,
And pour within thine ear the tale of misery.

But where art thou, thou comet of an age,
  Thou phœnix of a century ? Perchance
Thou art but of those fables which engage
  And hold the minds of men in giddy trance.
Yet, be it so, and be it all romance,
  The thought of thine existence is so bright
With beautiful imaginings — the glance
  Upon thy fancied being such delight,
That I will deem thee Truth, so lovely is thy
    might !

'AND ASK YE WHY THESE SAD TEARS STREAM?'

'Te somnia nostra reducunt.'
OVID.

AND ask ye why these sad tears stream ?
  Why these wan eyes are dim with weep-
    ing?
I had a dream — a lovely dream,
  Of her that in the grave is sleeping.

I saw her as 't was yesterday,
  The bloom upon her cheek still glowing;
And round her play'd a golden ray,
  And on her brows were gay flowers blowing.

With angel-hand she swept a lyre,
  A garland red with roses bound it;
Its strings were wreath'd with lambent fire
  And amaranth was woven round it.

I saw her mid the realms of light,
  In everlasting radiance gleaming;
Co-equal with the seraphs bright,
  Mid thousand thousand angels beaming.

I strove to reach her, when, behold,
  Those fairy forms of bliss Elysian,
And all that rich scene wrapt in gold,
  Faded in air — a lovely vision !

And I awoke, but oh ! to me
  That waking hour was doubly weary;
And yet I could not envy thee,
  Although so blest, and I so dreary.

ON SUBLIMITY

One of the best of Alfred's early efforts.
Here, as in ' Persia,' the metrical management
of proper names is noteworthy.

' The sublime always dwells on great objects and ter-
rible.'
BURKE.

O TELL me not of vales in tenderest green,
  The poplar's shade, the plantane's graceful
    tree;
Give me the wild cascade, the rugged scene,
  The loud surge bursting o'er the purple sea:

On such sad views my soul delights to pore,
By Teneriffe's peak, or Kilda's giant height,
Or dark Loffoden's melancholy shore,
  What time grey eve is fading into night;
When by that twilight beam I scarce descry
The mingled shades of earth and sea and sky.

Give me to wander at midnight alone,
  Through some august cathedral, where, from high,
The cold, clear moon on the mosaic stone
  Comes glancing in gay colours gloriously,
Through windows rich with gorgeous blazonry,
  Gilding the niches dim, where, side by side,
Stand antique mitred prelates, whose bones lie
  Beneath the pavement, where their deeds of pride
Were graven, but long since are worn away
By constant feet of ages day by day.

Then, as Imagination aids, I hear
  Wild heavenly voices sounding from the quoir,
And more than mortal music meets mine ear,
  Whose long, long notes among the tombs expire,
With solemn rustling of cherubic wings,
  Round those vast columns which the roof upbear;
While sad and undistinguishable things
  Do flit athwart the moonlit windows there;
And my blood curdles at the chilling sound
Of lone, unearthly steps, that pace the hallow'd ground!

I love the starry spangled heav'n, resembling
  A canopy with fiery gems o'erspread,
When the wide loch with silvery sheen is trembling,
  Far stretch'd beneath the mountain's hoary head.
But most I love that sky, when, dark with storms,
  It frowns terrific o'er this wilder'd earth,
While the black clouds, in strange and uncouth forms,
  Come hurrying onward in their ruinous wrath;
And shrouding in their deep and gloomy robe
The burning eyes of heav'n and Dian's lucid globe!

I love your voice, ye echoing winds, that sweep
  Thro' the wide womb of midnight, when the veil
Of darkness rests upon the mighty deep,
  The labouring vessel, and the shatter'd sail —
Save when the forked bolts of lightning leap
  On flashing pinions, and the mariner pale

Raises his eyes to heaven. Oh! who would sleep
What time the rushing of the angry gale
Is loud upon the waters? — Hail, all hail!
Tempest and clouds and night and thunder's rending peal!

All hail, Sublimity! thou lofty one,
  For thou dost walk upon the blast, and gird
Thy majesty with terrors, and thy throne
Is on the whirlwind, and thy voice is heard
In thunders and in shakings: thy delight
Is in the secret wood, the blasted heath,
The ruin'd fortress, and the dizzy height,
  The grave, the ghastly charnel - house of death,
In vaults, in cloisters, and in gloomy piles,
Long corridors and towers and solitary aisles!

Thy joy is in obscurity, and plain
  Is nought with thee; and on thy steps attend
Shadows but half-distinguish'd; the thin train
  Of hovering spirits round thy pathway bend,
With their low tremulous voice and airy tread,[1]
  What time the tomb above them yawns and gapes:
For thou dost hold communion with the dead
  Phantoms and phantasies and grisly shapes;
And shades and headless spectres of Saint Mark,[2]
Seen by a lurid light, formless and still and dark!

What joy to view the varied rainbow smile
  On Niagara's flood of matchless might,
Where all around the melancholy isle[3]
  The billows sparkle with their hues of light!
While, as the restless surges roar and rave,
  The arrowy stream descends with awful sound,
Wheeling and whirling with each breathless wave,[4]
Immense, sublime, magnificent, profound!
If thou hast seen all this, and could'st not feel,
Then know, thine heart is fram'd of marble or of steel.

The hurricane fair earth to darkness changing,
  Kentucky's chambers of eternal gloom,[5]
The swift-pac'd columns of the desert ranging
  Th' uneven waste, the violent Simoom,
Thy snow-clad peaks, stupendous Gungotree!
  Whence springs the hallow'd Jumna's echoing tide,
Hoar Cotopaxi's cloud-capt majesty,
  Enormous Chimborazo's naked pride,
The dizzy Cape of winds that cleaves the sky,[6]
Whence we look down into eternity,

---

[1] According to Burke, a low tremulous intermitted sound is conducive to the sublime.
[2] It is a received opinion, that on St. Mark's Eve all the persons who are to die on the following year make their appearances without their heads in the churches of their respective parishes. — See DR. LANGHORNE's Notes to Collins.
[3] This island, on both sides of which the waters rush with astonishing swiftness, is 900 or 800 feet long, and its lower edge is just at the perpendicular edge of the fall.
[4] 'Undis Phlegethon perlustrat ANHELIS.' — CLAUDIAN.
[5] See Dr. Nahum Ward's account of the great Kentucky Cavern, in the Monthly Magazine, October, 1816.
[6] In the Ukraine.

The pillar'd cave of Morven's giant king,[1]
  The Yanar,[2] and the Geyser's boiling foun-
    tain,
The deep volcano's inward murmuring,
  The shadowy Colossus of the mountain; [3]
Antiparos, where sun-beams never enter;
  Loud Stromboli, amid the quaking isles;
The terrible Maelstroom, around his centre
  Wheeling his circuit of unnumber'd miles:
These, these are sights and sounds that freeze
    the blood,
Yet charm the awe-struck soul which doats on
    solitude.

Blest be the bard, whose willing feet rejoice
  To tread the emerald green of Fancy's vales,
Who hears the music of her heavenly voice,
  And breathes the rapture of her nectar'd
    gales!
Blest be the bard, whom golden Fancy loves,
He strays for ever thro' her blooming bowers,
  Amid the rich profusion of her groves,
  And wreathes his forehead with her spicy
    flowers
Of sunny radiance; but how blest is he
Who feels the genuine force of high Sublimity!

THE DEITY

Signed 'A. T. or C. T.' in the reprint, but
Lord Tennyson believes, as I do, that Charles
wrote it.

'Immutable — immortal — infinite!' — MILTON.

WHERE is the wonderful abode,
  The holy, secret, searchless shrine,
Where dwells the immaterial God,
  The all-pervading and benign?

O! that he were reveal'd to me,
  Fully and palpably display'd
In all the awful majesty
  Of heaven's consummate pomp array'd —

How would the overwhelming light
  Of his tremendous presence beam!
And how insufferably bright
  Would the broad glow of glory stream!

What tho' this flesh would fade like grass,
  Before th' intensity of day?
One glance at Him who always was,
  The fiercest pangs would well repay.

When Moses on the mountain's brow
  Had met th' Eternal face to face,
While anxious Israel stood below,
  Wond'ring and trembling at its base;

His visage, as he downward trod,
  Shone starlike on the shrinking crowd,
With lustre borrow'd from his God:
  They could not brook it, and they bow'd.

The mere reflection of the blaze
  That lighten'd round creation's Lord,
Was too puissant for their gaze;
  And he that caught it was ador'd.

Then how ineffably august,
  How passing wond'rous must He be,
Whose presence lent to earthly dust
  Such permanence of brilliancy!

Thron'd in sequester'd sanctity,
  And with transcendant glories crown'd;
With all his works beneath his eye,
  And suns and systems burning round, —

How shall I hymn him? How aspire
  His holy Name with song to blend,
And bid my rash and feeble lyre
  To such an awless flight ascend?

TIME: AN ODE

Remarkable for imagination and for versifi-
cation as the work of a boy of sixteen.

I SEE the chariot, where,
Throughout the purple air,
  The forelock'd monarch rides:
Arm'd like some antique vehicle for war,
Time, hoary Time! I see thy scythed car,
In voiceless majesty,
Cleaving the clouds of ages that float by,
  And change their many-colour'd sides,
    Now dark, now dun, now richly bright,
    In an ever-varying light.
The great, the lowly, and the brave
    Bow down before the rushing force
    Of thine unconquerable course;
Thy wheels are noiseless as the grave,
Yet fleet as Heaven's red bolt they hurry on,
They pass above us, and are gone!

Clear is the track which thou hast past;
  Strew'd with the wrecks of frail renown,
  Robe, sceptre, banner, wreath, and crown,
  The pathway that before thee lies,
An undistinguishable waste,
    Invisible to human eyes,
Which fain would scan the various shapes
    which glide
    In dusky cavalcade,
Imperfectly descried,
    Through that intense, impenetrable
    shade.

[1] Fingal's Cave in the Island of Staffa. If the Colos-
sus of Rhodes bestrid a harbour, Fingal's powers were
certainly far from despicable: —

    A chos air Cromleach druim-ard
    Chos eile air Crommeal dubh
    Thoga Fion le lamh mhoir
    An d'uisge o Lubhair na fruth.

    With one foot on Cromleach his brow,
    The other on Crommeal the dark,
    Fion took up with his large hand
    The water from Lubhair of streams.

See the Dissertations prefixed to Ossian's *Poems*.
[2] Or, perpetual fire.
[3] Alias, the Spectre of the Broken.

Four grey steeds thy chariot draw;
In th' obdurate, tameless jaw
  Their rusted iron bits they sternly champ;
Ye may not hear the echoing tramp
  Of their light-bounding, windy feet,
  Upon that cloudy pavement beat.
Four wings have each, which, far outspread,
Receive the many blasts of heav'n,
As with unwearied speed,
  Throughout the long extent of ether driven,
Onward they rush for ever and for aye:
  Thy voice, thou mighty Charioteer!
  Always sounding in their ear,
Throughout the gloom of night and heat of day.

Fast behind thee follows Death,
  Thro' the ranks of wan and weeping,
That yield their miserable breath,
  On with his pallid courser proudly sweeping.
Arm'd is he in full mail,[1]
  Bright breast-plate and high crest,
    Nor is the trenchant falchion wanting:
So fiercely does he ride the gale,
  On Time's dark car, before him, rest
    The dew-drops of his charger's panting.

On, on they go along the boundless skies,
  All human grandeur fades away
Before their flashing, fiery, hollow eyes;
    Beneath the terrible control
    Of those vast armed orbs, which roll
Oblivion on the creatures of a day.
Those splendid monuments alone he spares,
  Which, to her deathless votaries,
Bright Fame, with glowing hand, uprears
Amid the waste of countless years.

' Live ye!' to these he crieth; ' live!
To ye eternity I give —
Ye, upon whose blessed birth
  The noblest star of heaven hath shone;
Live, when the ponderous pyramids of earth
  Are crumbling in oblivion!
Live, when, wrapt in sullen shade,
The golden hosts of heaven shall fade;
Live, when yon gorgeous sun on high
Shall veil the sparkling of his eye!
Live, when imperial Time and Death himself
  shall die!'

GOD'S DENUNCIATIONS AGAINST PHARAOH-HOPHRA, OR APRIES

THOU beast of the flood, who hast said in thy
  soul,
'I have made me a stream that for ever shall
  roll!'[2]

[1] I am indebted for the idea of Death's Armour to that famous Chorus in Caractacus beginning with —

  ' Hark! heard ye not that footstep dread?'

[2] 'Pliny's reproach to the Egyptians, for their vain and foolish pride with regard to the inundations of the Nile, points out one of their most distinguishing char-

Thy strength is the flower that shall last but a
  day,
And thy might is the snow in the sun's burning
  ray.

Arm, arm from the east, Babylonia's son!
Arm, arm for the battle — the Lord leads thee
  on!
With the shield of thy fame, and the power of
  thy pride,
Arm, arm in thy glory — the Lord is thy guide.

Thou shalt come like a storm when the moon-
  light is dim,
And the lake's gloomy bosom is full to the
  brim;
Thou shalt come like the flash in the darkness
  of night,
When the wolves of the forest shall howl for
  affright.

Woe, woe to thee, Tanis![3] thy babes shall be
  thrown
By the barbarous hands on the cold marble-
  stone:
Woe, woe to thee, Nile! for thy stream shall
  be red
With the blood that shall gush o'er thy billowy
  bed!

Woe, woe to thee, Memphis! the war-cry is
  near,
And the child shall be toss'd on the murderer's
  spear;
For fiercely he comes in the day of his ire,
With wheels like a whirlwind, and chariots of
  fire!

THE GRAVE OF A SUICIDE

Perhaps incorrectly assigned to Alfred.

HARK! how the gale, in mournful notes and
  stern,
Sighs thro' yon grove of aged oaks, that wave
(While down these solitary walks I turn)
  Their mingled branches o'er yon lonely
  grave!

Poor soul! the dawning of thy life was dim;
  Frown'd the dark clouds upon thy natal day;
Soon rose thy cup of sorrow to the brim,
  And hope itself but shed a doubtful ray.

That hope h~d fled, and all within was gloom;
  That hope had fled — thy woe to phrenzy
  grew;

acteristics, and recalls to my mind a fine passage of Ezekiel, where God thus speaks to Pharaoh, one of their kings: " Behold, I am against thee, Pharaoh king of Egypt, the great dragon that lieth in the midst of his rivers, that hath said, MY RIVER IS MINE OWN, AND I HAVE MADE IT FOR MYSELF." ' — ROLLIN, vol. i. p. 216.

[3] The Scriptural appellations are ' Zoan ' and ' Noph.'

For thou, wed to misery from the womb —
  Scarce one bright scene thy night of darkness
    knew !

Oft when the moon-beam on the cold bank
  sleeps,
  Where 'neath the dewy turf thy form is laid,
In silent woe thy wretched mother weeps,
  By this lone tomb, and by this oak-tree's
    shade.

' Oh ! softly tread : in death he slumbers here;
  'T is here,' she cries, ' within his narrow
    cell ! ' —
The bitter sob, the wildly-starting tear,
  The quivering lip, proclaim the rest too well !

THE WALK AT MIDNIGHT

' Tremulo sub lumine.' — VIRGIL.

SOFT, shadowy moon-beam ! by thy light
  Sleeps the wide meer serenely pale :
How various are the sounds of night,
  Borne on the scarcely-rising gale !

The swell of distant brook is heard,
  Whose far-off waters faintly roll;
And piping of the shrill small bird,
  Arrested by the wand'ring owl.

Come hither ! let us thread with care
  The maze of this green path, which binds
The beauties of the broad parterre,
  And thro' yon fragrant alley winds.

Or on this old bench will we sit,
  Round which the clust'ring woodbine
    wreathes;
While birds of night around us flit;
  And thro' each lavish wood-walk breathes,

Unto my ravish'd senses, brought
  From yon thick-woven odorous bowers,
The still rich breeze, with incense fraught
  Of glowing fruits and spangled flowers.

The whispering leaves, the gushing stream,
  Where trembles the uncertain moon,
Suit more the poet's pensive dream,
  Than all the jarring notes of noon.

Then, to the thickly-crowded mart
  The eager sons of interest press;
Then, shine the tinsel works of art —
  Now, all is Nature's loneliness !

Then, wealth aloft in state displays
  The glittering of her gilded cars;
Now, dimly stream the mingled rays
  Of yon far-twinkling, silver stars.

Yon church, whose cold grey spire appears
  In the black outline of the trees,
Conceals the object of my tears,
  Whose form in dreams my spirit sees.

There in the chilling bed of earth,
  The chancel's letter'd stone above —
There sleepeth she who gave me birth,
  Who taught my lips the hymn of love !

Yon mossy stems of ancient oak,
  So widely crown'd with sombre shade,
Those ne'er have heard the woodman's stroke
  Their solemn, secret depths invade.

How oft the grassy way I 've trod
  That winds their knotty boles between,
And gather'd from the blooming sod
  The flowers that flourish'd there unseen !

Rise ! let us trace that path once more,
  While o'er our track the cold beams shine;
Down this low shingly vale, and o'er
  Yon rude rough bridge of prostrate pine.

MITHRIDATES PRESENTING BERE-NICE WITH THE CUP OF POISON

OH ! Berenice, lorn and lost,
  This wretched soul with shame is bleed-
    ing :
Oh ! Berenice, I am tost
  By griefs, like wave to wave succeeding.

Fall'n Pontus ! all her fame is gone,
  And dim the splendour of her glory;
Low in the west her evening sun,
  And dark the lustre of her story.

Dead is the wreath that round her brow
  The glowing hands of Honour braided;
What change of fate can wait her now,
  Her sceptre spoil'd, her throne degraded ?

And wilt thou, wilt thou basely go,
  My love, thy life, thy country shaming,
In all the agonies of woe,
  Mid madd'ning shouts, and standards flam-
    ing ?

And wilt thou, wilt thou basely go,
  Proud Rome's triumphal car adorning ?
Hark ! hark ! I hear thee answer ' No ! '
  The proffer'd life of thraldom scorning.

Lone, crownless, destitute, and poor,
  My heart with bitter pain is burning;
So thick a cloud of night hangs o'er,
  My daylight into darkness turning.

Yet though my spirit, bow'd with ill,
  Small hope from future fortune borrows;
One glorious thought shall cheer me still,
  That thou art free from abject sorrows —

Art free for ever from the strife
  Of slavery's pangs and tearful anguish;
For life is death, and death is life,
  To those whose limbs in fetters languish.

Fill high the bowl! the draught is thine!
  The Romans! — now thou need'st not heed
    them!
'T is nobler than the noblest wine —
  It gives thee back to fame and freedom!

The scalding tears my cheek bedew;
  My life, my love, my all — we sever!
One last embrace, one long adieu,
  And then farewell — farewell for ever!

In reality Mithridates had no personal interview with
Monima and Berenice before the deaths of those prin-
cesses, but only sent his eunuch Bacchidas to signify
his intention that they should die. I have chosen
Berenice as the more general name, though Monima
was his peculiar favourite.

THE OLD CHIEFTAIN

'And said I, that my limbs were old!' — SCOTT.

RAISE, raise the song of the hundred shells!
  Though my hair is grey and my limbs are
    cold;
Yet in my bosom proudly dwells
  The memory of the days of old;

When my voice was high, and my arm was
    strong,
  And the foeman before my stroke would bow,
And I could have rais'd the sounding song
  As loudly as I hear ye now.

For when I have chanted the bold song of
    death,
  Not a page would have stay'd in the hall,
Not a lance in the rest, not a sword in the
    sheath,
  Not a shield on the dim grey wall.

And who might resist the united powers
  Of battle and music that day,
When, all martiall'd in arms on the heaven-
    kissing towers,
  Stood the chieftains in peerless array?

When our enemies sunk from our eyes as the
    snow
  Which falls down the stream in the dell,
When each word that I spake was the death of
    a foe,
  And each note of my harp was his knell?

So raise ye the song of the hundred shells;
  Though my hair is grey and my limbs are
    cold,
Yet in my bosom proudly dwells
  The memory of the days of old!

THE FALL OF JERUSALEM

JERUSALEM! Jerusalem!
  Thou art low! thou mighty one,
How is the brilliance of thy diadem,
  How is the lustre of thy throne

Rent from thee, and thy sun of fame
Darken'd by the shadowy pinion
  Of the Roman bird, whose sway
  All the tribes of earth obey,
Crouching 'neath his dread dominion,
And the terrors of his name!

How is thy royal seat — whereon
  Sate in days of yore
Lowly Jesse's godlike son,
And the strength of Solomon,
  In those rich and happy times
    When the ships from Tarshish bore
    Incense, and from Ophir's land,
    With silken sail and cedar oar,
      Wafting to Judea's strand
All the wealth of foreign climes —
How is thy royal seat o'erthrown!
  Gone is all thy majesty:
    Salem! Salem! city of kings,
  Thou sittest desolate and lone,
    Where once the glory of the Most High
    Dwelt visibly enshrin'd between the wings
Of Cherubims, within whose bright embrace
  The golden mercy-seat remain'd:
Land of Jehovah! view that sacred place
  Abandon'd and profan'd!

Wail! fallen Salem! Wail:
  Mohammed's votaries pollute thy fane;
The dark division of thine holy veil
  Is rent in twain!
Thrice hath Sion's crowned rock
  Seen thy temple's marble state,
  Awfully, serenely great,
  Towering on his sainted brow,
  Rear its pinnacles of snow:
Thrice, with desolating shock,
  Down to earth hath seen it driv'n
  From his heights, which reach to heaven!

Wail, fallen Salem! Wail:
  Though not one stone above another
There was left to tell the tale
  Of the greatness of thy story,
  Yet the long lapse of ages cannot smother
  The blaze of thine abounding glory;
Which thro' the mist of rolling years,
O'er history's darken'd page appears,
Like the morning star, whose gleam
  Gazeth thro' the waste of night,
What time old ocean's purple stream
  In his cold surge hath deeply lav'd
  Its ardent front of dewy light.
    Oh! who shall e'er forget thy bands,
      which brav'd
The terrors of the desert's barren reign,
And that strong arm which broke the chain
  Wherein ye foully lay enslav'd,
  Or that sublime Theocracy which pav'd
Your way thro' ocean's vast domain,
And on, far on to Canaan's emerald plain
  Led the Israelitish crowd
  With a pillar and a cloud?

Signs on earth and signs on high
Prophesied thy destiny;

A trumpet's voice above thee rung,
A starry sabre o'er thee hung;
Visions of fiery armies, redly flashing
In the many-colour'd glare
Of the setting orb of day;
And flaming chariots, fiercely dashing,
Swept along the peopled air,
In magnificent array:
The temple doors, on brazen hinges crashing,
Burst open with appalling sound,
A wond'rous radiance streaming round!

'Our blood be on our heads!' ye said:
Such your awless imprecation:
Full bitterly at length 't was paid
Upon your captive nation!
Arms of adverse legions bound thee,
Plague and pestilence stood round thee;
Seven weary suns had brighten'd Syria's
sky,
Yet still was heard th' unceasing cry —
From south, north, east, and west, a voice,
'Woe unto thy sons and daughters!
Woe to Salem! thou art lost!'
A sound divine
Came from the sainted, secret, inmost shrine:
'Let us go hence!' — and then a noise —
The thunders of the parting Deity,
Like the rush of countless waters,
Like the murmur of a host!

Though now each glorious hope be blighted,
Yet an hour shall come, when ye,
Though scatter'd like the chaff, shall be
Beneath one standard once again united;
When your wandering race shall own,
Prostrate at the dazzling throne
Of your high Almighty Lord,
The wonders of his searchless word,
Th' unfading splendours of his Son!

LAMENTATION OF THE PERU-VIANS

THE foes of the east have come down on our
shore,
And the state and the strength of Peru are no
more:
Oh! curs'd, doubly curs'd, was that desolate
hour,
When they spread o'er our land in the pride of
their power!
Lament for the Inca, the son of the Sun;
Ataliba 's fallen — Peru is undone!

Pizarro! Pizarro! though conquest may wing
Her course round thy banners that wanton in
air;
Yet remorse to thy grief-stricken conscience
shall cling,
And shriek o'er thy banquets in sounds of
despair.
It shall tell thee, that he who beholds from his
throne
The blood thou hast spilt and the deeds thou
hast done,

Shall mock at thy fear, and rejoice at thy
groan,
And arise in his wrath for the death of his
son!
Why blew ye, ye gales, when the murderer
came?
Why fann'd ye the fire, and why fed ye the
flame?
Why sped ye his sails o'er the ocean so blue?
Are ye also combin'd for the fall of Peru?
And thou, whom no prayers, no entreaties can
bend,
Thy crimes and thy murders to heav'n shall as-
cend:
For vengeance the ghosts of our forefathers
call;
At thy threshold, Pizarro, in death shalt thou
fall!
Ay there — even there in the halls of thy pride,
With the blood of thine heart shall thy portals
be dyed!

Lo! dark as the tempests that frown from the
north,
From the cloud of past time Manco Capac looks
forth —
Great Inca! to whom the gay day-star gave
birth,
Whose throne is the heaven, and whose foot-
stool the earth —
His visage is sad as the vapours that rise
From the desolate mountain of fire to the skies;
But his eye flashes flame as the lightnings that
streak
Those volumes that shroud the volcano's high
peak.
Hark! he speaks — bids us fly to our moun-
tains, and cherish
Bold freedom's last spark ere for ever it per-
ish;
Bids us leave these wild condors to prey on each
other,
Each to bathe his fierce beak in the gore of his
brother!
This symbol we take of our godhead the Sun,
And curse thee and thine for the deeds thou
hast done.
May the curses pursue thee of those thou hast
slain,
Of those that have fallen in war on the plain,
When we went forth to greet ye — but foully
ye threw
Your dark shots of death on the sons of Peru.
May the curse of the widow — the curse of the
brave —
The curse of the fatherless, cleave to thy grave!
And the words which they spake with their last
dying breath,
Embitter the pangs and the tortures of death!

May he that assists thee be childless and poor,
With famine behind him, and death at his door:
May his nights be all sleepless, his days spent
alone,
And ne'er may he list to a voice but his own!
Or, if he shall sleep, in his dreams may he view
The ghost of our Inca, the fiends of Peru:

May the flames of destruction that here he has
   spread
Be tenfold return'd on his murderous head!

'THE SUN GOES DOWN IN THE DARK BLUE MAIN'

' Irreparabile tempus.' — VIRGIL.

THE sun goes down in the dark blue main,
   To rise the brighter to-morrow;
But oh! what charm can restore again
   Those days now consign'd to sorrow?

The moon goes down on the calm still night,
   To rise sweeter than when she parted;
But oh! what charm can restore the light
   Of joy to the broken-hearted?

The blossoms depart in the wintry hour,
   To rise in vernal glory;
But oh! what charm can restore the flower
   Of youth to the old and hoary?

ON A DEAD ENEMY

' Non odi mortuum.' — CICERO.

I CAME in haste with cursing breath,
   And heart of hardest steel;
But when I saw thee cold in death,
   I felt as man should feel.

For when I look upon that face,
   That cold, unheeding, frigid brow,
Where neither rage nor fear has place,
   By Heaven! I cannot hate thee now!

THE DUKE OF ALVA'S OBSERVATION ON KINGS [1]

KINGS, when to private audience they descend,
   And make the baffled courtier their prey,
Do use an orange, as they treat a friend —
   Extract the juice, and cast the rind away.

When thou art favour'd by thy sovereign's eye,
   Let not his glance thine inmost thoughts discover;
Or he will scan thee through, and lay thee by,
   Like some old book which he has read all over.

'AH! YES, THE LIP MAY FAINTLY SMILE'

Signed ' A. T. (?) ' in the reprint, and probably not Alfred's.

[1] See D'Israeli's *Curiosities of Literature.*
[2] A simile elicited from the songs of Jayadeva, the Horace of India.
[3] Vide Horace's ODE — ' Pulchris EXCUBAT in genis.'

AH! yes, the lip may faintly smile,
   The eye may sparkle for a while;
But never from that wither'd heart
   The consciousness of ill shall part!

That glance, that smile of passing light,
   Are as the rainbow of the night;
But seldom seen, it dares to bloom
   Upon the bosom of the gloom.

Its tints are sad and coldly pale,
   Dim-glimmering thro' their misty veil;
Unlike the ardent hues which play
   Along the flowery bow of day.

The moon-beams sink in dark-rob'd shades,
   Too soon the airy vision fades;
And double night returns, to shroud
   The volumes of the showery cloud.

'THOU CAMEST TO THY BOWER, MY LOVE, ACROSS THE MUSKY GROVE'

' Virgo egregia forma.' — TERENCE.

THOU camest to thy bower, my love, across the
   musky grove,
To fan thy blooming charms within the coolness
   of the shade;
Thy locks were like a midnight cloud with silver moon-beams wove,[2]
And o'er thy face the varying tints of youthful
   passion play'd.

Thy breath was like the sandal-wood that casts
   a rich perfume,
Thy blue eyes mock'd the lotos in the noon-day
   of his bloom;
Thy cheeks were like the beamy flush that gilds
   the breaking day,
And in th' ambrosia of thy smiles the god of
   rapture lay.[3]

Fair as the cairba-stone art thou, that stone of
   dazzling white,[4]
Ere yet unholy fingers chang'd its milk-white
   hue to night;
And lovelier than the loveliest glance from
   Even's placid star,
And brighter than the sea of gold,[5] the gorgeous
   Himsagar.

In high Mohammed's boundless heaven Al Cawthor's stream may play,
The fount of youth may sparkling gush beneath the western ray;[6]
And Tasnim's wave in chrystal cups may glow
   with musk and wine,
But oh! their lustre could not match one beauteous tear of thine!

[4] Vide Sale's *Koran.*
[5] See Sir William Jones on Eastern Plants.
[6] The fabled fountain of youth in the Bahamas, in search of which Juan Ponce de Leon discovered Florida.

THE PASSIONS

'You have passions in your heart—scorpions; they sleep now—beware how you awaken them! they will sting you even to death!'—*Mysteries of Udolpho*, vol. iii.

BEWARE, beware, ere thou takest
  The draught of misery!
Beware, beware, e'er thou wakest
  The scorpions that sleep in thee!

The woes which thou canst not number,
  As yet are wrapt in sleep;
Yet oh! yet they slumber,
  But their slumbers are not deep.

Yet oh! yet while the rancour
  Of hate has no place in thee,
While thy buoyant soul has an anchor
  In youth's bright tranquil sea:

Yet oh! yet while the blossom
  Of hope is blooming fair,
While the beam of bliss lights thy bosom—
  O! rouse not the serpent there!

For bitter thy tears will trickle
  'Neath misery's heavy load,
When the world has put in its sickle
  To the crop which fancy sow'd.

When the world has rent the cable
  That bound thee to the shore,
And launched thee weak and unable
  To bear the billow's roar;

Then the slightest touch will waken
  Those pangs that will always grieve thee,
And thy soul will be fiercely shaken
  With storms that will never leave thee!

So beware, beware, ere thou takest
  The draught of misery!
Beware, beware, ere thou wakest
  The scorpions that sleep in thee!

THE HIGH-PRIEST TO ALEXANDER

'Derrame en todo el orbe de la tierra
Las armas, el furor, y nueva guerra.'
      La Araucana, cant. xvi.

Go forth, thou man of force!
  The world is all thine own;
Before thy dreadful course
  Shall totter every throne.
Let India's jewels glow
  Upon thy diadem:
Go, forth to conquest go,
  But spare Jerusalem.
    For the God of gods, which liveth
      Through all eternity,
    'T is he alone which giveth
      And taketh victory:

'T is he the bow that blasteth,
  And breaketh the proud one's quiver;
And the Lord of armies resteth
  In his Holy of Holies for ever!

For God is Salem's spear,
  And God is Salem's sword;
What mortal man shall dare
  To combat with the Lord?
Every knee shall bow
  Before his awful sight;
Every thought sink low
  Before the Lord of might.
    For the God of gods, which liveth
      Through all eternity,
    'T is he alone which giveth
      And taketh victory:
    'T is he the bow that blasteth,
      And breaketh the proud one's quiver;
    And the Lord of armies resteth
      In his Holy of Holies for ever!

ON THE MOON-LIGHT SHINING UPON A FRIEND'S GRAVE

Signed 'A. T. (?),' and probably Charles's.

SHOW not, O Moon! with pure and liquid beam,
  That mournful spot, where Memory fears to tread;
Glance on the grove, or quiver in the stream,
  Or tip the hills—but shine not on the dead:
It wounds the lonely hearts that still survive,
And after bury'd friends are doom'd to live.

A CONTRAST

DOST ask why Laura's soul is riven
  By pangs her prudence can't command?
To one who heeds not she has giv'n
  Her *heart*, alas! *without her hand.*

But Chloe claims our sympathy,
  To wealth a martyr and a slave;
For when the knot she dar'd to tie,
  Her hand without her heart she gave.

THE DYING CHRISTIAN

Signed 'A. T. or C. T.,' but quite certainly Charles's, as Lord Tennyson tells me that he also thinks.

'It cannot die, it cannot stay,
But leaves its darken'd dust behind.'
      BYRON.

I DIE—my limbs with icy feeling
  Bespeak that Death is near;
His frozen hand each pulse is stealing;
  Yet still I do not fear!

There is a hope—not frail as that
  Which rests on human things—

The hope of an immortal state,
And with the King of kings!

And ye may gaze upon my brow,
Which is not sad, tho' pale;
These hope-illumin'd features show
But little to bewail.

Death should not chase the wonted bloom
From off the Christian's face;
Ill prelude of the bliss to come,
Prepar'd by heavenly grace.

Lament no more — no longer weep
That I depart from men;
Brief is the intermediate sleep,
And bliss awaits me then!

HOW GAILY SINKS THE GOR-GEOUS SUN WITHIN HIS GOLD-EN BED'

These lines are signed ' A. T. (?),' and may be safely assigned to Charles.

> ' Tu fais naître la lumière
> Du sein de l'obscurité.'
> ROUSSEAU.

How gaily sinks the gorgeous sun within his golden bed,
As heaven's immortal azure glows and deepens into red!
How gaily shines the burnish'd main beneath that living light,
And trembles with his million waves magnificently bright!
But ah! how soon that orb of day must close his burning eye,
And night, in sable pall array'd, involve yon lovely sky!
E'en thus in life our fairest scenes are preludes to our woe;
For fleeting as that glorious beam is happiness below.
But what? though evil fates may frown upon our mortal birth,
Yet Hope shall be the star that lights our night of grief on earth:
And she shall point to sweeter morns, when brighter suns shall rise,
And spread the radiance of their rays o'er earth, and sea, and skies!

'OH! YE WILD WINDS, THAT ROAR AND RAVE'

' It is the great army of the dead returning on the northern blast.'
SONG OF THE FIVE BARDS IN OSSIAN.

OH! ye wild winds, that roar and rave
Around the headland's stormy brow,
That toss and heave the Baltic wave,
And bid the sounding forest bow,

Whence is your course? and do ye bear
The sighs of other worlds along,
When through the dark immense of air
Ye rush in tempests loud and strong?

Methinks, upon your moaning course
I hear the army of the dead;
Each on his own invisible horse,
Triumphing in his trackless tread.

For when the moon conceals her ray,
And midnight spreads her darkest veil,
Borne on the air, and far away,
Upon the eddying blasts they sail.

Then, then their thin and feeble bands
Along the echoing winds are roll'd;
The bodyless tribes of other lands!
The formless, misty sons of old!

And then at times their wailings rise,
The shrilly wailings of the grave!
And mingle with the madden'd skies,
The rush of wind, and roar of wave.

Heard you that sound? It was the hum
Of the innumerable host,
As down the northern sky they come,
Lamenting o'er their glories lost.

Now for a space each shadowy king,
Who sway'd of old some mighty realm,
Mounts on the tempest's squally wing,
And grimly frowns thro' barred helm.

Now each dim ghost, with awful yells,
Uprears on high his cloudy form;
And with his feeble accent swells
The hundred voices of the storm.

Why leave ye thus the narrow cell,
Ye lords of night and anarchy!
Your robes the vapours of the dell,
Your swords the meteors of the sky?

Your bones are whitening on the heath;
Your fame is in the minds of men:
And would ye break the sleep of death,
That ye might live to war again?

SWITZERLAND

Signed ' A. T. (?),' and I am inclined to believe the poem Charles's, though Mr. Shepherd, in his ' Tennysoniana,' compares the closing lines with ' The red fool-fury of the Seine' in ' In Memoriam.'

> ' Tous les objets de mon amour,
> Nos clairs ruisseaux,
> Nos hameaux,
> Nos coteaux,
> Nos montagnes?'
> RANZ DES VACHES.

WITH Memory's eye,
Thou land of joy!
I view thy cliffs once more;

And tho' thy plains
Red slaughter stains,
  'T is Freedom's blessed gore.

Thy woody dells,
And shadowy fells,
  Exceed a monarch's halls;
Thy pine-clad hills,
And gushing rills,
  And foaming water-falls.

The Gallic foe
Has work'd thee woe,
  But trumpet never scar'd thee;
How could he think
That thou would'st shrink,
  With all thy rocks to guard thee?

E'en now the Gaul,
That wrought thy fall,
  At his own triumph wonders;
So long the strife
For death and life,
  So loud our rival thunders!

O! when shall Time
Avenge the crime,
  And to our rights restore us?
And bid the Seine
Be chok'd with slain,
  And Paris quake before us?

BABYLON

'Come down, and sit in the dust, O virgin daughter of Babylon; sit on the ground: there is no throne.' — ISAIAH xlvii. 1.

Bow, daughter of Babylon, bow thee to dust!
Thine heart shall be quell'd, and thy pride shall be crush'd:
Weep, Babylon, weep! for thy splendour is past;
And they come like the storm in the day of the blast.

Howl, desolate Babylon, lost one and lone!
And bind thee in sack-cloth — for where is thy throne?
Like a wine-press in wrath will I trample thee down,
And rend from thy temples the pride of thy crown.

Though thy streets be a hundred, thy gates be all brass,
Yet thy proud ones of war shall be wither'd like grass;
Thy gates shall be broken, thy strength be laid low,
And thy streets shall resound to the shouts of the foe!

---

[1] 'Arise, ye princes, and anoint the shield.' — ISAIAH xxi. 5.
[2] 'I will make drunk her princes.' — JEREMIAH li. 57.
[3] 'The mountains melted from before the Lord.' — JUDG. v. 5. 'Oh! that the mountains might flow down

Though thy chariots of power on thy battlements bound,
And the grandeur of waters encompass thee round;
Yet thy walls shall be shaken, thy waters shall fail,
Thy matrons shall shriek, and thy king shall be pale.

The terrible day of thy fall is at hand,
When my rage shall descend on the face of thy land;
The lances are pointed, the keen sword is bar'd,
The shields are anointed,[1] the helmets prepar'd.

I call upon Cyrus! He comes from afar,
And the armies of nations are gather'd to war;
With the blood of thy children his path shall be red,
And the bright sun of conquest shall blaze o'er his head!

Thou glory of kingdoms! thy princes are drunk,[2]
But their loins shall be loos'd, and their hearts shall be sunk;
They shall crouch to the dust, and be counted as slaves,
At the roll of his wheels, like the rushing of waves!

For I am the Lord, who have mightily spann'd
The breadth of the heavens, and the sea and the land;
And the mountains shall flow at my presence,[3] and earth
Shall reel to and fro in the glance of my wrath!

Your proud domes of cedar on earth shall be thrown,
And the rank grass shall wave o'er the lonely hearthstone;
And your sons and your sires and your daughters shall bleed
By the barbarous hands of the murdering Mede!

I will sweep ye away in destruction and death,
As the whirlwind that scatters the chaff with its breath;
And the fanes of your gods shall be sprinkled with gore,
And the course of your stream shall be heard of no more![4]

There the wandering Arab shall ne'er pitch his tent,
But the beasts of the desert shall wail and lament;
In their desolate houses the dragons shall lie,
And the satyrs shall dance, and the bittern shall cry![5]

---

at thy presence.' — ISAIAH lxiv. 1. And again, ver. 3, 'The mountains flowed down at thy presence.'
[4] 'A drought is upon her waters.' — JEREMIAH l. 38.
[5] Vide ISAIAH xiii. 20.

LOVE

I

ALMIGHTY Love! whose nameless power
This glowing heart defines too well,
Whose presence cheers each fleeting hour,
Whose silken bonds our souls compel,
Diffusing such a sainted spell,

As gilds our being with the light
Of transport and of rapturous bliss,
And almost seeming to unite
The joys of other worlds to this,
The heavenly smile, the rosy kiss; —

Before whose blaze my spirits shrink,
My senses all are wrapt in thee,
Thy force I own too much, to think
(So full, so great thine ecstacy)
That thou art less than deity!

Thy golden chains embrace the land,
The starry sky, the dark blue main;
And at the voice of thy command,
(So vast, so boundless is thy reign)
All nature springs to life again!

II

The glittering fly, the wondrous things
That microscopic art descries;
The lion of the waste, which springs,
Bounding upon his enemies;
The mighty sea-snake of the storm,
The vorticella's viewless form,[1]

The vast leviathan, which takes
His pastime in the sounding floods;
The crafty elephant, which makes
His haunts in Ceylon's spicy woods —
Alike confess thy magic sway,
Thy soul-enchanting voice obey!

O! whether thou, as bards have said,
Of bliss or pain the partial giver,
Wingest thy shaft of pleasing dread
From out thy well-stor'd golden quiver,
O'er earth thy cherub wings extending,
Thy sea-born mother's side attending; —

Or else, as Indian fables say,
Upon thine emerald lory riding,
Through gardens, mid the restless play
Of fountains, in the moon-beam gliding,
Mid sylph-like shapes of maidens dancing,
Thy scarlet standard high advancing; —

Thy fragrant bow of cane thou bendest,[2]
Twanging the string of honey'd bees,
And thence the flower-tipp'd arrow sendest,
Which gives or robs the heart of ease;
Camdeo, or Cupid, O be near,
To listen, and to grant my prayer!

[1] See BAKER on Animalculæ.
[2] See Sir WILLIAM JONES's WORKS, vol. vi. p. 313.

SONG

To sit beside a chrystal spring,
Cool'd by the passing zephyr's wing,
And bend my every thought to thee,
Is life, is bliss, is ecstacy!

And as within that spring I trace
Each line, each feature of my face;
The faithful mirror tells me true —
It tells me that I think of *you!*

EXHORTATION TO THE GREEKS

'En illa, illa quam sæpe optastis, libertas!'
SALLUST.

AROUSE thee, O Greece! and remember the
day,
When the millions of Xerxes were quell'd on
their way!
Arouse thee, O Greece! let the pride of thy
name
Awake in thy bosom the light of thy fame!
Why hast thou shone in the temple of glory?
Why hast thou blaz'd in those annals of fame?
For know, that the former bright page of thy
story
Proclaims but thy bondage and tells but thy
shame:
Proclaims from how high thou art fallen — how
low
Thou art plung'd in the dark gulf of thraldom
and woe!
Arouse thee, O Greece! from the weight of thy
slumbers!
The chains are upon thee! — arise from thy
sleep!
Remember the time, when nor nations nor num-
bers
Could break thy thick phalanx embodied and
deep.
Old Athens and Sparta remember the morning,
When the swords of the Grecians were red to
the hilt:
And, the bright gem of conquest her chaplet
adorning,
Platæa rejoic'd at the blood that ye spilt!
Remember the night, when, in shrieks of af-
fright,
The fleets of the East in your ocean were
sunk:
Remember each day, when, in battle array,
From the fountain of glory how largely ye
drunk!
For there is not ought that a freeman can fear,
As the fetters of insult, the name of a slave;
And there is not a voice to a nation so dear,
As the war-song of freedom that calls on the
brave.

'He bends the luscious cane, and twists the string;
With bees how sweet, but ah! how keen the sting!
He with five flowrets tips thy ruthless darts,
Which thro' five senses pierce enraptur'd hearts.'

KING CHARLES'S VISION

[A Vision somewhat resembling the following, and prophetic of the Northern Alexander, is said to have been witnessed by Charles XI. of Sweden, the antagonist of Sigismund. The reader will exclaim, 'Credat Judæus Apella ! ']

KING CHARLES was sitting all alone,
    In his lonely palace-tower,
When there came on his ears a heavy groan,
    At the silent midnight hour.

He turn'd him round where he heard the sound,
    But nothing might he see;
And he only heard the nightly bird
    That shriek'd right fearfully.

He turn'd him round where he heard the sound,
    To his casement's arched frame;
' And he was aware of a light that was there,' [1]
    But he wist not whence it came.

He looked forth into the night,
    'Twas calm as night might be;
But broad and bright the flashing light
    Stream'd red and radiantly.

From ivory sheath his trusty brand
    Of stalwart steel he drew;
And he rais'd the lamp in his better hand,
    But its flame was dim and blue.

And he open'd the door of that palace-tower,
    But harsh turn'd the jarring key:
' By the Virgin's might,' cried the king that
        night,
' All is not as it should be ! '

Slow turn'd the door of the crazy tower,
    And slowly again did it close;
And within and without, and all about,
    A sound of voices rose.

The king he stood in dreamy mood,
    For the voices his name did call;
Then on he past, till he came at last
    To the pillar'd audience-hall.

Eight and forty columns wide,
    Many and carv'd and tall,

---

[1] ' And he was aware of a Grey-friar.'
            The Grey Brother.
' And he was aware of a knight that was there.'
            The Baron of Smalhome.

[2] ' A hideous rock is PIGHT
Of mighty magnes-stone.'
            SPENSER.
' You vile abominable tents,
Thus proudly PIGHT upon our Phrygian plains ! '
            SHAKESPEARE.

[3] This is, perhaps, an unpardonable falsehood, since it is well known that Charles was so great an enemy to finery as even to object to the appearance of the Duke of Marlborough on that account. Let those readers, therefore, whose critical nicety this passage offends,

---

(Four and twenty on each side)
    Stand in that lordly hall.

The king had been pight [2] in the mortal fight,
    And struck the deadly blow;
The king he had strode in the red red blood,
    Often, afore, and now:

Yet his heart had ne'er been so harrow'd with
        fear
    As it was this fearful hour;
For his eyes were not dry, and his hair stood on
        high,
    And his soul had lost its power.

For a blue livid flame, round the hall where he
        came,
    In fiery circles ran;
And sounds of death, and chattering teeth,
    And gibbering tongues began.

He saw four and twenty statesmen old
    Round a lofty table sit;
And each in his hand did a volume hold,
    Wherein mighty things were writ.

In burning steel were their limbs all cas'd;
    On their cheeks was the flush of ire:
Their armour was brac'd, and their helmets
        were lac'd,
    And their hollow eyes darted fire.

With sceptre of might, and with gold crown
        bright,
    And locks like the raven's wing,
And in regal state at that board there sate
    The likeness of a king.

With crimson ting'd, and with ermine fring'd
    And with jewels spangled o'er,
And rich as the beam of the sun on the stream,
    A sparkling robe he wore.[3]

Yet though fair shone the gem on his proud
        diadem,
    Though his robe was jewell'd o'er,
Though brilliant the vest on his mailed breast,
    Yet they all were stain'd with gore !

And his eye darted ire, and his glance shot fire,
    And his look was high command;

substitute the following stanza, which is ' the whole truth, and nothing but the truth ' :

With buttons of brass that glitter'd like glass,
    And brows that were crown'd with bays,
With large blue coat, and with black jack-boot,
    The theme of his constant praise.

Nothing indeed could exceed Charles's affection for his boots: he eat, drank, and slept in them; nay, he never went on a bootless errand. When the dethroned monarch Augustus waited upon him with proposals of peace, Charles entertained him with a long dissertation on his unparalleled aforesaid jack-boots: he even went so far as to threaten (according to Voltaire), in an authoritative epistle to the senate at Stockholm, that unless they proved less refractory, he would send them one of his boots as regent ! Now this, we must allow, was a step beyond Caligula's consul.

And each, when he spoke, struck his mighty
    book,
And rais'd his shadowy hand.

And a headman stood by, with his axe on high,
    And quick was his ceaseless stroke;
And loud was the shock on the echoing block,
    As the steel shook the solid oak.

While short and thick came the mingled shriek
    Of the wretches who died by his blow;
And fast fell each head on the pavement red,
    And warm did the life-blood flow.

Said the earthly king to the ghostly king,
    'What fearful sights are those?'
Said the ghostly king to the earthly king,
    'They are signs of future woes!'

Said the earthly king to the ghostly king,
    'By Saint Peter, who art thou?'
Said the ghostly king to the earthly king,
    'I shall be, but I am not now.'

Said the earthly king to the ghostly king,
    'But when will thy time draw nigh?'
'Oh! the sixth after thee will a warrior be,
    And that warrior am I.

'And the lords of the earth shall be pale at my
    birth,
    And conquest shall hover o'er me;
And the kingdoms shall shake, and the nations
        shall quake,
    And the thrones fall down before me.

'And Cracow shall bend to my majesty,
    And the haughty Dane shall bow;
And the Pole shall fly from my piercing eye,
    And the scowl of my clouded brow.

'And around my way shall the hot balls play,
    And the red-tongued flames arise;
And my pathway shall be on the midnight sea,
    'Neath the frown of the wintry skies.

'Thro' narrow pass, over dark morass,
    And the waste of the weary plain,
Over ice and snow, where the dark streams
        flow,
    Thro' the woods of the wild Ukraine.

'And though sad be the close of my life and
        my woes,
    And the hand that shall slay me unshown;
Yet in every clime, thro' the lapse of all time,
    Shall my glorious conquests be known.

'And blood shall be shed, and the earth shall
        be red
    With the gore of misery;
And swift as this flame shall the light of my
        fame
    O'er the world as brightly fly.'

As the monarch spoke, crew the morning cock,
    When all that pageant bright,

And the glitter of gold, and the statesmen old,
    Fled into the gloom of night!

II. TIMBUCTOO

Church, in 'The Laureate's Country' (London, 1891), says : —

'The poet tells a curious story of the way in which this English verse prize came to be won. His father imagined, not, it may be, wholly without reason, that his son was doing very little at the university, and, knowing that he had a certain gift for writing verse, told him that he ought to compete for the Chancellor's medal. Alfred Tennyson had composed, two years before, a poem on "The Battle of Armageddon." This he took, furnished it with a new beginning and a new end, and sent it in for the theme of "Timbuctoo."'

This is confirmed by the 'Memoir' (vol. i. p. 46), where other interesting information concerning the poem may be found.

The poem was printed in the 'Prolusiones Academicæ' at Cambridge in 1829, and was reprinted several times afterwards in the collection of 'Cambridge Prize Poems.' It was never reprinted by the author, but his son appends it to the 1893 edition of 'Poems by Two Brothers.'

Arthur Hallam was one of the unsuccessful competitors for this prize. His poem, written in the *terza rima* of Dante, was privately printed in pamphlet form, and is included in the 'Remains' of 1834, edited by his father.

TIMBUCTOO

'Deep in that lion-haunted inland lies
    A mystic city, goal of high emprise.'
                                CHAPMAN.

I STOOD upon the Mountain which o'erlooks
The narrow seas, whose rapid interval
Parts Afric from green Europe, when the Sun
Had fall'n below th' Atlantic, and above
The silent heavens were blench'd with faery
        light,
Uncertain whether faery light or cloud,
Flowing Southward, and the chasms of deep,
        deep blue
Slumber'd unfathomable, and the stars
Were flooded over with clear glory and pale.
I gazed upon the sheeny coast beyond,
There where the Giant of old Time infix'd
The limits of his prowess, pillars high
Long time erased from earth: even as the Sea
When weary of wild inroad buildeth up
Huge mounds whereby to stay his yeasty waves.
And much I mused on legends quaint and old
Which whilome won the hearts of all on earth
Toward their brightness, ev'n as flame draws
        air;
But had their being in the heart of man

As air is th' life of flame: and thou wert then
A center'd glory-circled memory,
Divinest Atalantis, whom the waves
Have buried deep, and thou of later name,
Imperial Eldorado, roof'd with gold:
Shadows to which, despite all shocks of change,
All on-set of capricious accident,
Men clung with yearning hope which would not
    die.
As when in some great city where the walls
Shake, and the streets with ghastly faces
    throng'd,
Do utter forth a subterranean voice,
Among the inner columns far retired
At midnight, in the lone Acropolis,
Before the awful Genius of the place
Kneels the pale Priestess in deep faith, the
    while
Above her head the weak lamp dips and winks
Unto the fearful summoning without:
Nathless she ever clasps the marble knees,
Bathes the cold hands with tears, and gazeth on
Those eyes which wear no light but that where-
    with
Her phantasy informs them.
                            Where are ye,
Thrones of the Western wave, fair Islands
    green?
Where are your moonlight halls, your cedarn
    glooms,
The blossoming abysses of your hills?
Your flowering capes, and your gold-sanded
    bays
Blown round with happy airs of odorous winds?
Where are the infinite ways, which, seraph-trod,
Wound thro' your great Elysian solitudes,
Whose lowest deeps were, as with visible love,
Fill'd with Divine effulgence, circumfused,
Flowing between the clear and polish'd stems,
And ever circling round their emerald cones
In coronals and glories, such as gird
The unfading foreheads of the Saints in Hea-
    ven?
For nothing visible, they say, had birth
In that blest ground, but it was play'd about
With its peculiar glory.   Then I raised
My voice and cried, 'Wide Afric, doth thy Sun
Lighten, thy hills enfold a city as fair
As those which starr'd the night o' the elder
    world?
Or is the rumour of thy Timbuctoo
A dream as frail as those of ancient time?'
    A curve of whitening, flashing, ebbing light!
A rustling of white wings! the bright descent
Of a young Seraph! and he stood beside me
There on the ridge, and look'd into my face
With his unutterable, shining orbs.
So that with hasty motion I did veil
My vision with both hands, and saw before me
Such colour'd spots as dance athwart the eyes
Of those that gaze upon the noonday Sun.
Girt with a zone of flashing gold beneath
His breast, and compass'd round about his brow
With triple arch of ever-changing bows,
And circled with the glory of living light
And alternation of all hues, he stood.
    'O child of man, why muse you here alone

Upon the Mountain, on the dreams of old
Which fill'd the earth with passing loveliness,
Which flung strange music on the howling
    winds,
And odours rapt from remote Paradise?
Thy sense is clogg'd with dull mortality;
Thy spirit fetter'd with the bond of clay:
Open thine eyes and see.'
                        I look'd, but not
Upon his face, for it was wonderful
With its exceeding brightness, and the light
Of the great Angel Mind which look'd from out
The starry glowing of his restless eyes.
I felt my soul grow mighty, and my spirit
With supernatural excitation bound
Within me, and my mental eye grew large
With such a vast circumference of thought,
That in my vanity I seem'd to stand
Upon the outward verge and bound alone
Of full beatitude.   Each failing sense,
As with a momentary flash of light,
Grew thrillingly distinct and keen.   I saw
The smallest grain that dappled the dark earth,
The indistinctest atom in deep air,
The Moon's white cities, and the opal width
Of her small glowing lakes, her silver heights
Unvisited with dew of vagrant cloud,
And the unsounded, undescended depth
Of her black hollows.   The clear galaxy
Shorn of its hoary lustre, wonderful,
Distinct and vivid with sharp points of light,
Blaze within blaze, an unimagin'd depth
And harmony of planet-girded suns
And moon-encircled planets, wheel in wheel,
Arch'd the wan sapphire.   Nay — the hum of
    men,
Or other things talking in unknown tongues,
And notes of busy life in distant worlds
Beat like a far wave on my anxious ear.
    A maze of piercing, trackless, thrilling
    thoughts,
Involving and embracing each with each,
Rapid as fire, inextricably link'd,
Expanding momently with every sight
And sound which struck the palpitating sense,
The issue of strong impulse, hurried through
The riven rapt brain; as when in some large
    lake
From pressure of descendant crags, which lapse
Disjointed, crumbling from their parent slope
At slender interval, the level calm
Is ridg'd with restless and increasing spheres
Which break upon each other, each th' effect
Of separate impulse, but more fleet and strong
Than its precursor, till the eye in vain
Amid the wild unrest of swimming shade
Dappled with hollow and alternate rise
Of interpenetrated arc, would scan
Definite round.
                    I know not if I shape
These things with accurate similitude
From visible objects, for but dimly now,
Less vivid than a half-forgotten dream,
The memory of that mental excellence
Comes o'er me, and it may be I entwine
The indecision of my present mind
With its past clearness, yet it seems to me

As even then the torrent of quick thought
Absorbed me from the nature of itself
With its own fleetness. Where is he that,
    borne
Adown the sloping of an arrowy stream,
Could link his shallop to the fleeting edge,
And muse midway with philosophic calm
Upon the wondrous laws which regulate
The fierceness of the bounding element?
  My thoughts which long had grovell'd in the
    slime
Of this dull world, like dusky worms which
    house
Beneath unshaken waters, but at once
Upon some earth-awakening day of Spring
Do pass from gloom to glory, and aloft
Winnow the purple, bearing on both sides
Double display of star-lit wings, which burn
Fan-like and fibred with intensest bloom;
Ev'n so my thoughts, erewhile so low, now felt
Unutterable buoyancy and strength
To bear them upward through the trackless
    fields
Of undefin'd existence far and free.
  Then first within the South methought I saw
A wilderness of spires, and chrystal pile
Of rampart upon rampart, dome on dome,
Illimitable range of battlement
On battlement, and the imperial height
Of canopy o'ercanopied.
               Behind
In diamond light upsprung the dazzling peaks
Of Pyramids, as far surpassing earth's
As heaven than earth is fairer. Each aloft
Upon his narrow'd eminence bore globes
Of wheeling suns, or stars, or semblances
Of either, showering circular abyss
Of radiance. But the glory of the place
Stood out a pillar'd front of burnish'd gold,
Interminably high, if gold it were
Or metal more etherial, and beneath
Two doors of blinding brilliance, where no gaze
Might rest, stood open, and the eye could scan,
Through length of porch and valve and bound-
    less hall,
Part of a throne of fiery flame, wherefrom
The snowy skirting of a garment hung,
And glimpse of multitudes of multitudes
That minister'd around it — if I saw
These things distinctly, for my human brain
Stagger'd beneath the vision, and thick night
Came down upon my eyelids, and I fell.
  With ministering hand he raised me up:
Then with a mournful and ineffable smile,
Which but to look on for a moment fill'd
My eyes with irresistible sweet tears,
In accents of majestic melody,
Like a swoln river's gushings in still night
Mingled with floating music, thus he spake:
  ' There is no mightier Spirit than I to sway
The heart of man: and teach him to attain
By shadowing forth the Unattainable;
And step by step to scale that mighty stair
Whose landing-place is wrapt about with clouds

Of glory of heaven.[1] With earliest light of
    Spring,
And in the glow of sallow Summertide,
And in red Autumn when the winds are wild
With gambols, and when full-voiced Winter
    roofs
The headland with inviolate white snow,
I play about his heart a thousand ways,
Visit his eyes with visions, and his ears
With harmonies of wind and wave and wood, —
Of winds which tell of waters, and of waters
Betraying the close kisses of the wind —
And win him unto me: and few there be
So gross of heart who have not felt and known
A higher than they see: They with dim eyes
Behold me darkling. Lo! I have given thee
To understand my presence, and to feel
My fulness; I have fill'd thy lips with power.
I have raised thee nigher to the spheres of hea-
    ven,
Man's first, last home: and thou with ravish'd
    sense
Listenest the lordly music flowing from
Th' illimitable years. I am the Spirit,
The permeating life which courseth through
All th' intricate and labyrinthine veins
Of the great vine of Fable, which, outspread
With growth of shadowing leaf and clusters
    rare,
Reacheth to every corner under heaven,
Deep-rooted in the living soil of truth;
So that men's hopes and fears take refuge in
The fragrance of its complicated glooms,
And cool impleachèd twilights. Child of man,
See'st thou yon river, whose translucent wave,
Forth issuing from the darkness, windeth
    through
The argent streets o' th' city, imaging
The soft inversion of her tremulous domes,
Her gardens frequent with the stately palm,
Her pagods hung with music of sweet bells,
Her obelisks of rangèd chrysolite,
Minarets and towers? Lo! how he passeth
    by,
And gulphs himself in sands, as not enduring
To carry through the world those waves, which
    bore
The reflex of my city in their depths.
Oh city! oh latest throne! where I was raised
To be a mystery of loveliness
Unto all eyes, the time is well-nigh come
When I must render up this glorious home
To keen Discovery: soon yon brilliant towers
Shall darken with the waving of her wand;
Darken, and shrink and shiver into huts,
Black specks amid a waste of dreary sand,
Low-built, mud-wall'd, barbarian settlements.
How chang'd from this fair city!'
              Thus far the Spirit:
Then parted heaven-ward on the wing: and I
Was left alone on Calpe, and the moon
Had fallen from the night, and all was dark!

[1] ' Be ye perfect even as your Father in heaven is
perfect.'

III. POEMS PUBLISHED IN THE EDITION OF 1830, AND OMITTED IN LATER EDITIONS

Of the fifty-three poems in the 1830 volume, thirty-two were suppressed in 1842; but nine of these (as explained in the prefatory notes) were afterwards included in the collected editions.

THE 'HOW' AND THE 'WHY'

?

I AM any man's suitor,
If any will be my tutor:
Some say this life is pleasant,
　Some think it speedeth fast,
In time there is no present,
In eternity no future,
　In eternity no past.
We laugh, we cry, we are born, we die,
Who will riddle me the *how* and the *why*?

The bulrush nods unto its brother.
The wheatears whisper to each other:
What is it they say? what do they there?
Why two and two make four? why round is
　not square?
Why the rock stands still, and the light clouds
　fly?
Why the heavy oak groans, and the white wil-
　lows sigh?
Why deep is not high, and high is not deep?
Whether we wake, or whether we sleep?
Whether we sleep, or whether we die?
How you are you? why I am I?
Who will riddle me the *how* and the *why*?

The world is somewhat; it goes on somehow:
But what is the meaning of *then* and *now*?
I feel there is something; but how and what?
I know there is somewhat: but what and why?
I cannot tell if that somewhat be I.
　The little bird pipeth — 'why? why?'
In the summer woods when the sun falls low,
And the great bird sits on the opposite bough,
And stares in his face, and shouts 'how?
　how?'
And the black owl scuds down the mellow twi-
　light,
And chants 'how? how?' the whole of the
　night.

Why the life goes when the blood is spilt?
　What the life is? where the soul may lie?
Why a church is with a steeple built:
And a house with a chimney-pot?
Who will riddle me the how and the what?
Who will riddle me the what and the why?

THE BURIAL OF LOVE

HIS eyes in eclipse,
Pale-cold his lips,
The light of his hopes unfed,
Mute his tongue,
His bow unstrung
With the tears he hath shed,
Backward drooping his graceful head,
　Love is dead:
His last arrow is sped;
He hath not another dart;
Go — carry him to his dark deathbed;
Bury him in the cold, cold heart —
　Love is dead.

O truest love! art thou forlorn,
And unrevenged? thy pleasant wiles
　Forgotten, and thine innocent joy?
Shall hollow-hearted apathy,
The cruellest form of perfect scorn,
　With languor of most hateful smiles,
　For ever write,
　In the withered light
Of the tearless eye,
An epitaph that all may spy?
No! sooner she herself shall die.

For her the showers shall not fall,
Nor the round sun shine that shineth to all;
Her light shall into darkness change;
For her the green grass shall not spring,
Nor the rivers flow, nor the sweet birds sing,
Till Love have his full revenge.

TO ——

SAINTED Juliet! dearest name!
If to love be life alone,
　Divinest Juliet,
　I love thee, and live; and yet
Love unreturned is like the fragrant flame
Folding the slaughter of the sacrifice
　Offered to gods upon an altar-throne;
My heart is lighted at thine eyes,
Changed into fire, and blown about with sighs.

SONG

I

I' THE glooming light
Of middle night
So cold and white,
Worn Sorrow sits by the moaning wave,
　Beside her are laid
　Her mattock and spade,
For she hath half delved her own deep grave.
　Alone she is there:
The white clouds drizzle: her hair falls loose:
　Her shoulders are bare;
Her tears are mixed with the beaded dews.

II

Death standeth by;
She will not die;
With glazéd eye
She looks at her grave: she cannot sleep;
　Ever alone
She maketh her moan:

She cannot speak: she can only weep,
    For she will not hope.
The thick snow falls on her flake by flake,
    The dull wave mourns down the slope,
The world will not change, and her heart will
    not break.

SONG

I

THE lintwhite and the throstlecock
Have voices sweet and clear;
    All in the blooméd May.
They from the blosmy brere
Call to the fleeting year,
If that he would them hear
    And stay.
Alas! that one so beautiful
Should have so dull an ear!

II

Fair year, fair year, thy children call,
But thou art deaf as death;
    All in the blooméd May.
When thy light perisheth
That from thee issueth,
Our life evanisheth:
    O, stay!
Alas! that lips so cruel-dumb
Should have so sweet a breath!

III

Fair year, with brows of royal love
Thou comest, as a king,
    All in the blooméd May.
Thy golden largess fling,
And longer hear us sing;
Though thou art fleet of wing,
    Yet stay.
Alas! that eyes so full of light
Should be so wandering!

IV

Thy locks are all of sunny sheen
In rings of gold yronne,[1]
    All in the blooméd May.
We pri'thee pass not on;
If thou dost leave the sun,
Delight is with thee gone.
    O, stay!
Thou art the fairest of thy feres,
We pri'thee pass not on.

SONG

I

EVERY day hath its night:
Every night its morn:
Thorough dark and bright
    Wingéd hours are borne;
      Ah! welaway!

[1] 'His crispè hair in ringis was yronne.'
          CHAUCER, *Knightes Tale.*

Seasons flower and fade;
Golden calm and storm
    Mingle day by day.
There is no bright form
Doth not cast a shade —
    Ah! welaway!

II

When we laugh, and our mirth
Apes the happy vein,
We 're so kin to earth,
    Pleasaunce fathers pain —
      Ah! welaway!
Madness laugheth loud:
    Laughter bringeth tears:
    Eyes are worn away
Till the end of fears
Cometh in the shroud,
      Ah! welaway!

III

All is change, woe or weal;
Joy is Sorrow's brother;
Grief and gladness steal
    Symbols of each other:
      Ah! welaway!
Larks in heaven's cope
Sing: the culvers mourn
    All the livelong day.
Be not all forlorn:
Let us weep in hope —
      Ah! welaway!

HERO TO LEANDER

Included by Emerson in his 'Parnassus'
(1874).

O GO not yet, my love!
    The night is dark and vast;
The white moon is hid in her heaven above,
    And the waves climb high and fast.
O, kiss me, kiss me, once again,
    Lest thy kiss should be the last!
O kiss me ere we part;
Grow closer to my heart!
My heart is warmer surely than the bosom of
    the main.
O joy! O bliss of blisses!
    My heart of hearts art thou.
Come bathe me with thy kisses,
    My eyelids and my brow.
Hark how the wild rain hisses,
    And the loud sea roars below.

Thy heart beats through thy rosy limbs,
    So gladly doth it stir;
Thine eye in drops of gladness swims.
I have bathed thee with the pleasant myrrh;
Thy locks are dripping balm;
Thou shalt not wander hence to-night,
I 'll stay thee with my kisses.
To-night the roaring brine
    Will rend thy golden tresses;
The ocean with the morrow light
Will be both blue and calm;

And the billow will embrace thee with a kiss as
 soft as mine.
No Western odors wander
 On the black and moaning sea,
And when thou art dead, Leander,
 My soul must follow thee !
O go not yet, my love !
 Thy voice is sweet and low;
The deep salt wave breaks in above
 Those marble steps below.
The turret-stairs are wet
 That lead into the sea.
Leander ! go not yet.
The pleasant stars have set:
O, go not, go not yet,
 Or I will follow thee !

THE MYSTIC

ANGELS have talked with him, and showed
 him thrones:
Ye knew him not; he was not one of ye,
Ye scorned him with an undiscerning scorn:
Ye could not read the marvel in his eye,
The still serene abstraction: he hath felt
The vanities of after and before;
Albeit, his spirit and his secret heart
The stern experiences of converse lives,
The linkèd woes of many a fiery change
Had purified, and chastened, and made free.
Always there stood before him, night and day,
Of wayward vary-colored circumstance
The imperishable presences serene,
Colossal, without form, or sense, or sound,
Dim shadows but unwaning presences
Fourfacèd to four corners of the sky:
And yet again, three shadows, fronting one,
One forward, one respectant, three but one;
And yet again, again and evermore,
For the two first were not, but only seemed,
One shadow in the midst of a great light,
One reflex from eternity on time,
One mighty countenance of perfect calm,
Awful with most invariable eyes.
For him the silent congregated hours,
Daughters of time, divinely tall, beneath
Severe and youthful brows, with shining eyes
Smiling a godlike smile (the innocent light
Of earliest youth pierced through and through
 with all
Keen knowledges of low-embowèd eld)
Upheld, and ever hold aloft the cloud
Which droops low-hung on either gate of life,
Both birth and death: he in the centre fixt,
Saw far on each side through the grated gates
Most pale and clear and lovely distances.
He often lying broad awake, and yet
Remaining from the body, and apart
In intellect and power and will, hath heard
Time flowing in the middle of the night,
And all things creeping to a day of doom.
How could ye know him ? Ye were yet within
The narrower circle: he had wellnigh reached
The last, which with a region of white flame,
Pure without heat, into a larger air
Upburning, and an ether of black blue,
Investeth and ingirds all other lives.

THE GRASSHOPPER

I

VOICE of the summer wind,
Joy of the summer plain,
Life of the summer hours,
Carol clearly, bound along.
No Tithon thou as poets feign
(Shame fall 'em, they are deaf and blind),
But an insect lithe and strong,
Bowing the seeded summer flowers.
Prove their falsehood and thy quarrel,
 Vaulting on thine airy feet.
Clap thy shielded sides and carol,
 Carol clearly, chirrup sweet.
Thou art a mailèd warrior in youth and
 strength complete;
  Armed cap-a-pie
  Full fair to see;
  Unknowing fear,
  Undreading loss,
  A gallant cavalier,
  Sans peur et sans reproche,
  In sunlight and in shadow,
  The Bayard of the meadow.

II

I would dwell with thee,
 Merry grasshopper,
Thou art so glad and free,
 And as light as air;
Thou hast no sorrow or tears,
Thou hast no compt of years,
No withered immortality,
But a short youth sunny and free.
Carol clearly, bound along,
 Soon thy joy is over,
A summer of loud song,
 And slumbers in the clover.
What hast thou to do with evil
In thine hour of love and revel,
 In thy heat of summer pride,
Pushing the thick roots aside
Of the singing flowerèd grasses,
That brush thee with their silken tresses ?
What hast thou to do with evil,
Shooting, singing, ever springing
 In and out the emerald glooms,
Ever leaping, ever singing,
 Lighting on the golden blooms ?

LOVE, PRIDE, AND FORGETFUL-NESS

ERE yet my heart was sweet Love's tomb,
Love labored honey busily.
I was the hive, and Love the bee,
My heart the honeycomb.
One very dark and chilly night
Pride came beneath and held a light.

The cruel vapors went through all,
Sweet Love was withered in his cell:
Pride took Love's sweets, and by a spell
Did change them into gall ;

And Memory, though fed by Pride,
Did wax so thin on gall,
Awhile she scarcely lived at all.
What marvel that she died ?

CHORUS

IN AN UNPUBLISHED DRAMA, WRITTEN
VERY EARLY

THE varied earth, the moving heaven,
  The rapid waste of roving sea,
The fountain-pregnant mountains riven
  To shapes of wildest anarchy,
By secret fire and midnight storms
  That wander round their windy cones,
The subtle life, the countless forms
  Of living things, the wondrous tones
  Of man and beast are full of strange
    Astonishment and boundless change.

The day, the diamonded night,
  The echo, feeble child of sound,
The heavy thunder's griding might,
  The herald lightning's starry bound,
The vocal spring of bursting bloom,
  The naked summer's glowing birth,
The troublous autumn's sallow gloom,
  The hoarhead winter paving earth
    With sheeny white, are full of strange
    Astonishment and boundless change.

Each sun which from the centre flings
  Grand music and redundant fire,
The burning belts, the mighty rings,
  The murm'rous planets' rolling choir,
The globe-filled arch that, cleaving air,
  Lost in its own effulgence sleeps,
The lawless comets as they glare,
  And thunder through the sapphire deeps
    In wayward strength, are full of strange
    Astonishment and boundless change.

LOST HOPE

YOU cast to ground the hope which once was
    mine:
But did the while your harsh decree deplore,
Embalming with sweet tears the vacant shrine,
My heart, where Hope had been and was no
    more.

  So on an oaken sprout
    A goodly acorn grew;
But winds from heaven shook the acorn out,
    And filled the cup with dew.

THE TEARS OF HEAVEN

HEAVEN weeps above the earth all night till
    morn,
In darkness weeps as all ashamed to weep,
Because the earth hath made her state forlorn
With self-wrought evil of unnumbered years,

And doth the fruit of her dishonor reap.
And all the day heaven gathers back her tears
Into her own blue eyes so clear and deep,
And showering down the glory of lightsome
    day,
Smiles on the earth's worn brow to win her if
    she may.

LOVE AND SORROW

O MAIDEN, fresher than the first green leaf
With which the fearful springtide flecks the
    lea,
Weep not, Almeida, that I said to thee
That thou hast half my heart, for bitter grief
Doth hold the other half in sovranty.
Thou art my heart's sun in love's crystalline:
Yet on both sides at once thou canst not shine:
Thine is the bright side of my heart, and thine
My heart's day, but the shadow of my heart,
Issue of its own substance, my heart's night
Thou canst not lighten even with *thy* light,
All-powerful in beauty as thou art.
Almeida, if my heart were substanceless,
Then might thy rays pass through to the other
    side,
So swiftly, that they nowhere would abide,
But lose themselves in utter emptiness.
Half-light, half-shadow, let my spirit sleep;
They never learned to love who never knew to
    weep.

TO A LADY SLEEPING

O THOU whose fringéd lids I gaze upon,
Through whose dim brain the wingéd dreams
    are borne,
Unroof the shrines of clearest vision,
In honor of the silver-fleckéd morn;
Long hath the white wave of the virgin light
Driven back the billow of the dreamful dark.
Thou all unwittingly prolongest night,
Though long ago listening the poiséd lark,
With eyes dropt downward through the blue
    serene,
Over heaven's parapet the angels lean.

SONNET

COULD I outwear my present state of woe
With one brief winter, and indue i' the spring
Hues of fresh youth, and mightily outgrow
The wan dark coil of faded suffering —
Forth in the pride of beauty issuing
A sheeny snake, the light of vernal bowers,
Moving his crest to all sweet plots of flowers
And watered valleys where the young birds
    sing;
Could I thus hope my lost delight's renewing,
I straightly would command the tears to creep
From my charged lids; but inwardly I weep;
Some vital heat as yet my heart is wooing:
That to itself hath drawn the frozen rain
From my cold eyes, and melted it again.

SONNET

Though Night hath climbed her peak of high-
    est noon,
And bitter blasts the screaming autumn whirl,
All night through archways of the bridgéd
    pearl,
And portals of pure silver, walks the moon.
Walk on, my soul, nor crouch to agony,
Turn cloud to light, and bitterness to joy,
And dross to gold with glorious alchemy,
Basing thy throne above the world's annoy.
Reign thou above the storms of sorrow and
    ruth
That roar beneath; unshaken peace hath won
    thee;
So shalt thou pierce the woven glooms of truth;
So shall the blessing of the meek be on thee;
So in thine hour of dawn, the body's youth,
An honorable eld shall come upon thee.

SONNET

Shall the hag Evil die with child of Good,
Or propagate again her loathéd kind,
Thronging the cells of the diseaséd mind,
Hateful with hanging cheeks, a withered brood,
Though hourly pastured on the salient blood?
Oh! that the wind which bloweth cold or heat
Would shatter and o'erbear the brazen beat
Of their broad vans, and in the solitude
Of middle space confound them, and blow back
Their wild cries down their cavern throats, and
    slake
With points of blast-borne hail their heated
    eyne!
So their wan limbs no more might come be-
    tween
The moon and the moon's reflex in the night,
Nor blot with floating shades the solar light.

SONNET

The pallid thunder-stricken sigh for gain,
Down an ideal stream they ever float,
And sailing on Pactolus in a boat,
Drown soul and sense, while wistfully they strain
Weak eyes upon the glistering sands that robe
The understream. The wise, could he behold
Cathedraled caverns of thick-ribbéd gold
And branching silvers of the central globe,
Would marvel from so beautiful a sight
How scorn and ruin, pain and hate could flow:
But Hatred in a gold cave sits below;
Pleached with her hair, in mail of argent light
Shot into gold, a snake her forehead clips,
And skins the color from her trembling lips.

LOVE

I

Thou, from the first, unborn, undying Love,
Albeit we gaze not on thy glories near,
Before the face of God didst breathe and move,
Though night and pain and ruin and death
    reign here.
Thou foldest, like a golden atmosphere,
The very throne of the eternal God:
Passing through thee the edicts of his fear
Are mellowed into music, borne abroad
By the loud winds, though they uprend the sea.
Even from its central deeps: thine empery
Is over all; thou wilt not brook eclipse;
Thou goest and returnest to His lips
Like lightning: thou dost ever brood above
The silence of all hearts, unutterable Love.

II

To know thee is all wisdom, and old age
Is but to know thee: dimly we behold thee
Athwart the veils of evils which infold thee.
We beat upon our aching hearts in rage;
We cry for thee; we deem the world thy tomb.
As dwellers in lone planets look upon
The mighty disk of their majestic sun,
Hollowed in awful chasms of wheeling gloom,
Making their day dim, so we gaze on thee.
Come, thou of many crowns, white-robéd Love,
Oh! rend the veil in twain: all men adore thee;
Heaven crieth after thee; earth waiteth for
    thee;
Breathe on thy wingéd throne, and it shall
    move
In music and in light o'er land and sea.

III

And now — methinks I gaze upon thee now,
As on a serpent in his agonies
Awe-stricken Indians; what time laid low
And crushing the thick fragrant reeds he lies,
When the new year warm-breathéd on the
    Earth,
Waiting to light him with her purple skies,
Calls to him by the fountain to uprise.
Already with the pangs of a new birth
Strain the hot spheres of his convulséd eyes,
And in his writhings awful hues begin
To wander down his sable-sheeny sides,
Like light on troubled waters: from within
Anon he rusheth forth with merry din,
And in him light and joy and strength abides;
And from his brows a crown of living light
Looks through the thick-stemmed woods by
    day and night.

ENGLISH WAR-SONG

Who fears to die? Who fears to die?
Is there any here who fears to die?
He shall find what he fears; and none shall
    grieve
For the man who fears to die;
But the withering scorn of the many shall
    cleave
To the man who fears to die.

CHORUS.

Shout for England!
Ho! for England!

George for England !
Merry England !
England for aye !

The hollow at heart shall crouch forlorn,
He shall eat the bread of common scorn;
It shall be steeped in the salt, salt tear,
Shall be steeped in his own salt tear:
Far better, far better he never were born
Than to shame merry England here.
        CHO. — Shout for England ! etc.

There standeth our ancient enemy;
Hark ! he shouteth — the ancient enemy !
On the ridge of the hill his banners rise;
They stream like fire in the skies;
Hold up the Lion of England on high
Till it dazzle and blind his eyes.
        CHO. — Shout for England ! etc.

Come along ! we alone of the earth are free;
The child in our cradles is bolder than he;
For where is the heart and strength of slaves ?
Oh ! where is the strength of slaves ?
He is weak ! we are strong: he a slave, we are
        free;
Come along ! we will dig their graves.
        CHO. — Shout for England ! etc.

There standeth our ancient enemy;
Will he dare to battle with the free ?
Spur along ! spur amain ! charge to the fight:
Charge ! charge to the fight !
Hold up the Lion of England on high !
Shout for God and our right !
        CHO. — Shout for England ! etc.

NATIONAL SONG

Reprinted in ' The Foresters ' in 1892. See
Notes.

THERE is no land like England
    Where'er the light of day be;
There are no hearts like English hearts,
    Such hearts of oak as they be.
There is no land like England
    Where'er the light of day be;
There are no men like Englishmen,
    So tall and bold as they be.

CHORUS.

For the French the Pope may shrive 'em,
For the devil a whit we heed 'em:
As for the French, God speed 'em
    Unto their heart's desire,
And the merry devil drive 'em
    Through the water and the fire.

FULL CHORUS.

Our glory is our freedom,
    We lord it o'er the sea;
We are the sons of freedom,
    We are free.

There is no land like England,
    Where'er the light of day be;
There are no wives like English wives,
    So fair and chaste as they be.
There is no land like England,
    Where'er the light of day be;
There are no maids like English maids,
    So beautiful as they be.
        CHO. — For the French, etc.

DUALISMS

Two bees within a crystal flowerbell rockéd,
    Hum a love-lay to the west-wind at noontide.
Both alike, they buzz together,
Both alike, they hum together,
    Through and through the flowered heather.
Where in a creeping cove the wave unshockéd
    Lays itself calm and wide.
Over a stream two birds of glancing feather
Do woo each other, carolling together.
Both alike, they glide together,
        Side by side;
Both alike, they sing together,
Arching blue-glosséd necks beneath the purple
    weather.

Two children lovelier than Love adown the lea
    are singing,
As they gambol, lily-garlands ever stringing:
    Both in blosm-white silk are frockéd:
Like, unlike, they roam together
Under a summer vault of golden weather:
Like, unlike, they sing together
        Side by side,
    Mid-May's darling golden-lockéd,
    Summer's tanling diamond-eyed.

THE SEA FAIRIES

This poem (see p. 15 above) was so much
altered when it was included in the edition of
1853 that I give the original form in full here.

SLOW sailed the weary mariners, and saw
Between the green brink and the running foam
White limbs unrobéd in a crystal air,
Sweet faces, rounded arms, and bosoms prest
To little harps of gold : and while they mused,
Whispering to each other half in fear,
Shrill music reached them on the middle sea.

SONG

Whither away, whither away, whither
    away ? Fly no more:
Whither away wi' the singing sail ? whither
    away wi' the oar ?
Whither away from the high green field and the
    happy blossoming shore ?
Weary mariners, hither away,
    One and all, one and all,
Weary mariners, come and play;
We will sing to you all the day;

Furl the sail and the foam will fall
From the prow !   One and all,
Furl the sail !   Drop the oar !
    Leap ashore,
Know danger and trouble and toil no more.
Whither away wi' the sail and the oar ?

    Drop the oar,
    Leap ashore,
    Fly no more !
Whither away wi' the sail ? whither away wi'
    the oar ?
Day and night to the billow the fountain
    calls:
Down shower the gambolling waterfalls
    From wandering over the lea;
They freshen the silvery-crimson shells,
And thick with white bells the clover-hill
    swells
    High over the full-toned sea.
Merrily carol the revelling gales
    Over the islands free:
From the green seabanks the rose down-trails
    To the happy brimméd sea.

Come hither, come hither and be our lords,
    For merry brides are we:
We will kiss sweet kisses, and speak sweet
    words.
    Oh listen, listen, your eyes shall glisten
    With pleasure and love and revelry;
    Oh listen, listen, your eyes shall glisten
When the clear sharp twang of the golden
    chords
    Runs up the ridgéd sea.
Ye will not find so happy a shore,
Weary mariners ! all the world o'er;
    Oh ! fly no more !
Hearken ye, hearken ye, sorrow shall darken
    ye,
    Danger and trouble and toil no more;
        Whither away ?
        Drop the oar;
    Hither away,
    Leap ashore;
    Oh fly no more — no more:
Whither away, whither away, whither away
    with the sail and the oar ?

Οἱ ῥέοντες

I

ALL thoughts, all creeds, all dreams are true,
    All visions wild and strange;
Man is the measure of all truth
    Unto himself.   All truth is change.
All men do walk in sleep, and all
    Have faith in that they dream:
For all things are as they seem to all,
    And all things flow like a stream.

II

There is no rest, no calm, no pause,
    Nor good nor ill, nor light nor shade,
Nor essence nor eternal laws:
    For nothing is, but all is made.

But if I dream that all these are,
    They are to me for that I dream;
For all things are as they seem to all,
    And all things flow like a stream.

Argal — this very opinion is only true relatively to
the flowing philosophers.

IV. POEMS PUBLISHED IN THE EDITION OF 1833, AND OMITTED IN LATER EDITIONS

Of the thirty poems in the 1833 volume,
fourteen were omitted in 1842 ; but eight of
these (including ' Kate,' restored since the
poet's death) were afterwards given a place in
the collected editions, as explained in the pre-
fatory notes.

SONNET

O BEAUTY, passing beauty ! sweetest Sweet !
    How canst thou let me waste my youth in
        sighs ?
I only ask to sit beside thy feet.
    Thou knowest I dare not look into thine eyes.
Might I but kiss thy hand !   I dare not fold
    My arms about thee — scarcely dare to speak.
And nothing seems to me so wild and bold,
    As with one kiss to touch thy blesséd cheek.
Methinks if I should kiss thee, no control
    Within the thrilling brain could keep afloat
The subtle spirit.   Even while I spoke,
The bare word KISS hath made my inner soul
    To tremble like a lutestring, ere the note
Hath melted in the silence that it broke.

THE HESPERIDES

This poem is reprinted in the ' Memoir '
(vol. i. p. 61) with the following note : —
    ' Published and suppressed by my father,
and republished by me here (with accents
written by him) in consequence of a talk that I
had with him, in which he regretted that he
had done away with it from among his " Juve-
nilia." '
    The author of the ' Memoir ' has since added
' Kate ' (which he does not mention) to the
' Juvenilia ' in the collected editions (see p. 23
above), but he has not restored this poem.

    " Hesperus and his daughters three,
    That sing about the golden tree."
                                Comus.

THE North-wind fall'n, in the new-starréd
        night
Zidonian Hanno, voyaging beyond
The hoary promontory of Soloë
Past Thymiaterion, in calméd bays,
Between the southern and the western Horn,

Heard neither warbling of the nightingale,
Nor melody of the Libyan lotus flute
Blown seaward from the shore; but from a
    slope
That ran bloom-bright into the Atlantic blue,
Beneath a highland leaning down a weight
Of cliffs, and zoned below with cedar shade,
Came voices, like the voices in a dream,
Continuous, till he reached the outer sea.

SONG

I

The golden apple, the golden apple, the hal-
    lowed fruit,
Guard it well, guard it warily,
Singing airily,
Standing about the charméd root.
Round about all is mute,
As the snow-field on the mountain-peaks,
As the sand-field at the mountain-foot.
Crocodiles in briny creeks
Sleep and stir not: all is mute.
If ye sing not, if ye make false measure,
We shall lose eternal pleasure,
Worth eternal want of rest.
Laugh not loudly: watch the treasure
Of the wisdom of the West.
In a corner wisdom whispers.   Five and three
(Let it not be preached abroad) make an awful
    mystery.
For the blossom unto threefold music bloweth;
Evermore it is born anew;
And the sap to threefold music floweth,
From the root
Drawn in the dark,
Up to the fruit,
Creeping under the fragrant bark,
Liquid gold, honeysweet, thro' and thro'.
Keen-eyed Sisters, singing airily,
Looking warily
Every way,
Guard the apple night and day,
Lest one from the East come and take it away.

II

Father Hesper, Father Hesper, watch, watch,
    ever and aye,
Looking under silver hair with a silver eye.
Father, twinkle not thy steadfast sight;
Kingdoms lapse, and climates change, and races
    die;
Honor comes with mystery;
Hoarded wisdom brings delight.
Number, tell them over and number
How many the mystic fruit-tree holds
Lest the red-combed dragon slumber
Rolled together in purple folds.
Look to him, father, lest he wink, and the
    golden apple be stol'n away,
For his ancient heart is drunk with overwatch-
    ings night and day,
Round about the hallowed fruit-tree curled —
Sing away, sing aloud evermore in the wind,
    without stop,
Lest his scaléd eyelid drop,

For he is older than the world.
If he waken, we waken,
Rapidly levelling eager eyes.
If he sleep, we sleep,
Dropping the eyelid over the eyes.
If the golden apple be taken,
The world will be overwise.
Five links, a golden chain, are we,
Hesper, the dragon, and sisters three,
Bound about the golden tree.

III

Father Hesper, Father Hesper, watch, watch,
    night and day,
Lest the old wound of the world be healéd,
The glory unsealéd,
The golden apple stolén away,
And the ancient secret revealéd.
Look from west to east along:
Father, old Himala weakens, Caucasus is bold
    and strong.
Wandering waters unto wandering waters call;
Let them clash together, foam and fall.
Out of watchings, out of wiles,
Comes the bliss of secret smiles.
All things are not told to all.
Half-round the mantling night is drawn,
Purple fringéd with even and dawn.
Hesper hateth Phosphor, evening hateth morn.

IV

Every flower and every fruit the redolent breath
Of this warm sea-wind ripeneth,
Arching the billow in his sleep;
But the land-wind wandereth,
Broken by the highland-steep,
Two streams upon the violet deep;
For the western sun and the western star,
And the low west-wind, breathing afar,
The end of day and beginning of night
Make the apple holy and bright;
Holy and bright, round and full, bright and
    blest,
Mellowed in a land of rest;
Watch it warily day and night;
All good things are in the west.
Till mid noon the cool east light
Is shut out by the tall hillbrow;
But when the full-faced sunset yellowly
Stays on the flowering arch of the bough,
The luscious fruitage clustereth mellowly,
Golden-kernelled, golden-cored,
Sunset-ripened above on the tree.
The world is wasted with fire and sword,
But the apple of gold hangs over the sea.
Five links, a golden chain are we,
Hesper, the dragon, and sisters three,
Daughters three,
Bound about
The gnarléd bole of the charméd tree.
The golden apple, the golden apple, the hal-
    lowed fruit,
Guard it well, guard it warily,
Watch it warily,
Singing airily,
Standing about the charméd root.

ROSALIND

This poem (see p. 21 above) has been restored, but *without* the following note, which is appended to it in the 1833 volume : —

AUTHOR'S NOTE. — Perhaps the following lines may be allowed to stand as a separate poem ; originally they made part of the text, where they were manifestly superfluous.

My Rosalind, my Rosalind,
Bold, subtle, careless Rosalind,
Is one of those who know no strife
Of inward woe or outward fear;
To whom the slope and stream of Life,
The life before, the life behind,
In the ear, from far and near,
Chimeth musically clear.
My falcon-hearted Rosalind,
Full-sailed before a vigorous wind,
Is one of those who cannot weep
For others' woes, but overleap
All the petty shocks and fears
That trouble life in early years,
With a flash of frolic scorn
And keen delight, that never falls
Away from freshness, self-upborne
With such gladness as, whenever
The fresh-flushing springtime calls
To the flooding waters cool,
Young fishes, on an April morn,
Up and down a rapid river,
Leap the little waterfalls
That sing into the pebbled pool.
My happy falcon, Rosalind,
Hath daring fancies of her own,
Fresh as the dawn before the day,
Fresh as the early sea-smell blown
Through vineyards from an inland bay.
My Rosalind, my Rosalind,
Because no shadow on you falls,
Think you hearts are tennisballs
To play with, wanton Rosalind ?

SONG

Who can say
Why To-day
To-morrow will be yesterday ?
Who can tell
Why to smell
The violet recalls the dewy prime
Of youth and buried time ?
The cause is nowhere found in rhyme.

SONNET

WRITTEN ON HEARING OF THE OUTBREAK OF THE POLISH INSURRECTION

Blow ye the trumpet, gather from afar
The hosts to battle: be not bought and sold.
Arise, brave Poles, the boldest of the bold;
Break through your iron shackles — fling them far.
O for those days of Piast, ere the Czar
Grew to his strength among his deserts cold;
When even to Moscow's cupolas were rolled
The growing murmurs of the Polish war !
Now must your noble anger blaze out more
Than when from Sobieski, clan by clan,
The Moslem myriads fell, and fled before —
Than when Zamoysky smote the Tartar Khan;
Than earlier, when on the Baltic shore
Boleslas drove the Pomeranian.

O DARLING ROOM

I

O DARLING room, my heart's delight,
Dear room, the apple of my sight,
With thy two couches soft and white,
There is no room so exquisite,
No little room so warm and bright,
Wherein to read, wherein to write.

II

For I the Nonnenwerth have seen,
And Oberwinter's vineyards green,
Musical Lurlei; and between
The hills to Bingen have I been,
Bingen in Darmstadt, where the Rhene
Curves toward Mentz, a woody scene.

III

Yet never did there meet my sight,
In any town to left or right,
A little room so exquisite,
With two such couches soft and white,
Not any room so warm and bright,
Wherein to read, wherein to write.

TO CHRISTOPHER NORTH

You did late review my lays,
    Crusty Christopher;
You did mingle blame and praise,
    Rusty Christopher.
When I learnt from whom it came,
I forgave you all the blame,
    Musty Christopher;
I could *not* forgive the praise,
    Fusty Christopher.

V. OTHER DISCARDED AND UNCOLLECTED POEMS

ON CAMBRIDGE UNIVERSITY

Written in 1830. See Notes.

Therefore your Halls, your ancient Colleges,
Your portals statued with old kings and queens,
Your gardens, myriad-volumed libraries,
Wax-lighted chapels, and rich carven screens,

Your doctors and your proctors, and your
      deans
Shall not avail you, when the Daybeam sports
New-risen o'er awaken'd Albion — No!
Nor yet your solemn organ-pipes that blow
Melodious thunders thro' your vacant courts
At morn and eve — because your manner sorts
Not with this age wherefrom ye stand apart —
Because the lips of little children preach
Against you, you that do profess to teach
And teach us nothing, feeding not the heart.

NO MORE

This and the two following poems were con-
tributed to 'The Gem, a Literary Annual'
(London, 1831).

O SAD *No More!* O sweet *No More!*
    O strange *No More!*
By a mossed brookbank on a stone
I smelt a wildweed flower alone;
There was a ringing in my ears,
    And both my eyes gushed out with tears.
Surely all pleasant things had gone before,
Low-buried fathom deep beneath with thee,
    No MORE!

ANACREONTICS

WITH roses musky-breathed,
And drooping daffodilly,
And silver-leaved lily,
And ivy darkly-wreathed,
I wove a crown before her,
For her I love so dearly,
A garland for Lenora.
With a silken cord I bound it.
Lenora, laughing clearly
A light and thrilling laughter,
About her forehead wound it,
And loved me ever after.

A FRAGMENT

WHERE is the Giant of the Sun, which stood
In the midnoon the glory of old Rhodes,
A perfect Idol with profulgent brows
Far-sheening down the purple seas to those
Who sailed from Mizraim underneath the star
Named of the Dragon — and between whose
      limbs
Of brassy vastness broad-blown Argosies
Drave into haven? Yet endure unscathed
Of changeful cycles the great Pyramids
Broad-based amid the fleeting sands, and sloped
Into the slumberous summer noon; but where,
Mysterious Egypt, are thine obelisks
Graven with gorgeous emblems undiscerned?
Thy placid Sphinxes brooding o'er the Nile?
Thy shadowing Idols in the solitudes,
Awful Memnonian countenances calm
Looking athwart the burning flats, far off

Seen by the high-necked camel on the verge
Journeying southward? Where are thy monu-
      ments
Piled by the strong and sunborn Anakim
Over their crowned brethren ON and OPH?
Thy Memnon when his peaceful lips are kist
With earliest rays, that from his mother's eyes
Flow over the Arabian bay, no more
Breathes low into the charmed ears of morn
Clear melody flattering the crisped Nile
By columned Thebes. Old Memphis hath gone
      down:
The Pharaohs are no more: somewhere in death
They sleep with staring eyes and gilded lips,
Wrapped round with spiced cerements in old
      grots
Rock-hewn and sealed for ever.

SONNET

Contributed to 'Friendship's Offering,' an
annual, 1832.

ME my own fate to lasting sorrow doometh:
    Thy woes are birds of passage, transitory:
    Thy spirit, circled with a living glory,
In summer still a summer joy resumeth.
Alone my hopeless melancholy gloometh,
    Like a lone cypress, through the twilight
      hoary,
From an old garden where no flower bloom-
      eth,
    One cypress on an island promontory.
But yet my lonely spirit follows thine,
    As round the rolling earth night follows day:
But yet thy lights on my horizon shine
    Into my night, when thou art far away.
I am so dark, alas! and thou so bright,
When we two meet there 's never perfect light.

SONNET

Contributed to 'The Englishman's Maga-
zine' for August, 1831; and reprinted in
Friendship's Offering,' 1833.

CHECK every outflash, every ruder sally
    Of thought and speech; speak low, and give
      up wholly
Thy spirit to mild-minded Melancholy;
This is the place. Through yonder poplar
      alley
Below the blue-green river windeth slowly;
But in the middle of the sombre valley
The crispéd waters whisper musically,
    And all the haunted place is dark and holy.
The nightingale, with long and low preamble,
    Warbled from yonder knoll of solemn larches,
    And in and out the woodbine's flowery arches
The summer midges wove their wanton gam-
      bol,
    And all the white-stemmed pinewood slept
      above —
When in this valley first I told my love.

SONNET

Contributed to 'the Yorkshire Literary Annual,' 1832.

THERE are three things which fill my heart
        with sighs,
And steep my soul in laughter (when I view
Fair maiden-forms moving like melodies) —
Dimples, roselips, and eyes of any hue.
There are three things beneath the blessed skies
For which I live — black eyes and brown and
        blue:
I hold them all most dear; but oh! black eyes,
I live and die, and only die in you.
Of late such eyes looked at me — while I
        mused,
At sunset, underneath a shadowy plane,
In old Bayona nigh the southern sea —
From an half-open lattice looked at *me*.
I saw no more — only those eyes — confused
And dazzled to the heart with glorious pain.

THE SKIPPING-ROPE

Printed in 1842, but omitted in all editions
after 1850.

SURE never yet was antelope
    Could skip so lightly by.
Stand off, or else my skipping-rope
    Will hit you in the eye.
How lightly whirls the skipping-rope!
    How fairy-like you fly!
Go, get you gone, you muse and mope —
    I hate that silly sigh.
Nay, dearest, teach me how to hope,
    Or tell me how to die.
There, take it, take my skipping-rope,
    And hang yourself thereby.

THE NEW TIMON AND THE POETS

Published in 'Punch,' February 28, 1846,
signed 'Alcibiades'; and followed in the next
number (March 7, 1846) by the lines entitled
'Afterthought,' afterwards included as 'Literary Squabbles' in the collected edition of
1872. See p. xv. above.

WE know him, out of Shakespeare's art,
    And those fine curses which he spoke;
The old Timon, with his noble heart,
    That, strongly loathing, greatly broke.

So died the Old: here comes the New.
    Regard him: a familiar face:
I thought we knew him: What, it 's you,
    The padded man — that wears the stays —

Who killed the girls and thrilled the boys
    With dandy pathos when you wrote!

A Lion, you, that made a noise,
    And shook a mane *en papillotes*.

And once you tried the Muses too;
    You failed, Sir: therefore now you turn,
To fall on those who are to you
    As Captain is to Subaltern.

But men of long-enduring hopes,
    And careless what this hour may bring,
Can pardon little would-be POPES
    And BRUMMELS, when they try to sting.

An Artist, Sir, should rest in Art,
    And waive a little of his claim;
To have the deep Poetic heart
    Is more than all poetic fame.

But you, Sir, you are hard to please;
    You never look but half content;
Nor like a gentleman at ease,
    With moral breadth of temperament.

And what with spites and what with fears,
    You cannot let a body be:
It 's always ringing in your ears,
    'They call this man as good as *me*.'

What profits now to understand
    The merits of a spotless shirt —
A dapper boot — a little hand —
    If half the little soul is dirt?

You talk of tinsel! why, we see
    The old mark of rouge upon your cheeks.
You prate of Nature! you are he
    That spilt his life about the cliques.

A TIMON you! Nay, nay, for shame:
    It looks too arrogant a jest —
The fierce old man — to take his name,
    You bandbox. Off, and let him rest.

LINES

Contributed to 'The Manchester Athenæum
Album,' 1850.

HERE often, when a child I lay reclined,
    I took delight in this locality.
Here stood the infant Ilion of the mind,
    And here the Grecian ships did seem to be.
And here again I come, and only find
    The drain-cut levels of the marshy lea, —
Gray sea-banks and pale sunsets, — dreary
        wind,
    Dim shores, dense rains, and heavy-clouded
        sea!

STANZAS

Contributed to 'The Keepsake,' an illustrated annual, 1851.

WHAT time I wasted youthful hours,
One of the shining wingéd powers,
Show'd me vast cliffs with crown of towers.

As towards the gracious light I bow'd,
They seem'd high palaces and proud,
Hid now and then with sliding cloud.

He said, ' The labor is not small;
Yet winds the pathway free to all: —
Take care thou dost not fear to fall ! '

BRITONS, GUARD YOUR OWN

Contributed to ' The Examiner,' January 31, 1852.

RISE, Britons, rise, if manhood be not dead;
The world's last tempest darkens overhead;
 The Pope has bless'd him;
 The Church caress'd him;
He triumphs; maybe we shall stand alone.
 Britons, guard your own.

His ruthless host is bought with plunder'd gold,
By lying priests the peasants' votes controll'd.
 All freedom vanish'd,
 The true men banish'd,
He triumphs; maybe we shall stand alone.
 Britons, guard your own.

Peace-lovers we — sweet Peace we all desire —
Peace-lovers we — but who can trust a liar ? —
 Peace-lovers, haters
 Of shameless traitors,
We hate not France, but this man's heart of stone.
 Britons, guard your own.

We hate not France, but France has lost her voice.
This man is France, the man they call her choice.
 By tricks and spying,
 By craft and lying,
And murder was her freedom overthrown.
 Britons, guard your own.

'Vive l'Empereur' may follow by and by;
'God save the Queen' is here a truer cry.
 God save the Nation,
 The toleràtion,
And the free speech that makes a Briton known.
 Britons, guard your own.

Rome's dearest daughter now is captive France,
The Jesuit laughs, and reckoning on his chance,
 Would, unrelenting,
 Kill all dissenting,
Till we were left to fight for truth alone.
 Britons, guard your own.

Call home your ships across Biscayan tides,
To blow the battle from their oaken sides.
 Why waste they yonder
 Their idle thunder ?

Why stay they there to guard a foreign throne ?
 Seamen, guard your own.

We were the best of marksmen long ago,
We won old battles with our strength, the bow.
 Now practise, yeomen,
 Like those bowmen,
Till your balls fly as their true shafts have flown.
 Yeomen, guard your own.

His soldier-ridden Highness might incline
To take Sardinia, Belgium, or the Rhine:
 Shall we stand idle,
 Nor seek to bridle
His rude aggressions, till we stand alone ?
 Make their cause your own.

Should he land here, and for one hour prevail,
There must no man go back to bear the tale:
 No man to bear it —
 Swear it ! we swear it !
Although we fight the banded world alone,
 We swear to guard our own.

ADDITIONAL VERSES

To ' God Save the Queen ! ' written for the marriage of the Princess Royal of England with the Crown Prince of Prussia, January 25, 1858.

GOD bless our Prince and Bride !
God keep their lands allied,
 God save the Queen !
Clothe them with righteousness,
Crown them with happiness,
Them with all blessings bless,
 God save the Queen !

Fair fall this hallow'd hour,
Farewell, our England's flower,
 God save the Queen !
Farewell, first rose of May !
Let both the peoples say,
God bless thy marriage-day,
 God bless the Queen !

THE WAR

Printed in the ' London Times,' May 9, 1859; reprinted in the ' Death of Œnone ' volume, 1892, with the title, ' Riflemen, Form.'

THERE is a sound of thunder afar,
 Storm in the South that darkens the day !
Storm of battle and thunder of war !
 Well if it do not roll our way.
 Form ! form ! Riflemen, form !
 Ready, be ready to meet the storm !
 Riflemen, Riflemen, Riflemen, form !

Be not deaf to the sound that warns !
Be not gull'd by a despot's plea !
Are figs of thistles, or grapes of thorns ?
How should a despot set men Free ?
 Form ! form ! Riflemen, form !

Ready, be ready to meet the storm !
Riflemen, Riflemen, Riflemen, form !

Let your reforms for a moment go !
Look to your butts, and take good aims !
Better a rotten borough or so
Than a rotten fleet or a city in flames !
Form ! form ! Riflemen, form !
Ready, be ready to meet the storm !
Riflemen, Riflemen, Riflemen, form !

Form, be ready to do or die !
Form in Freedom's name and the Queen's !
True that we have a faithful ally,
But only the devil can tell what he means.
Form ! form ! Riflemen, form !
Ready, be ready to meet the storm !
Riflemen, Riflemen, Riflemen, form !

THE RINGLET

Printed in the ' Enoch Arden ' volume, 1864,
but afterwards suppressed.

' YOUR ringlets, your ringlets,
  That look so golden-gay,
If you will give me one, but one,
  To kiss it night and day,
Then never chilling touch of Time
  Will turn it silver-gray;
And then shall I know it is all true gold
To flame and sparkle and stream as of old.
Till all the comets in heaven are cold,
  And all her stars decay.'
' Then take it, love, and put it by;
This cannot change, nor yet can I.'

2

' My ringlet, my ringlet,
  That art so golden-gay,
Now never chilling touch of Time
  Can turn thee silver-gray;
And a lad may wink, and a girl may hint,
  And a fool may say his say;
For my doubts and fears were all amiss,
And I swear henceforth by this and this,
That a doubt will only come for a kiss,
  And a fear to be kiss'd away.'
' Then kiss it, love, and put it by:
If this can change, why so can I.'

II

O Ringlet, O Ringlet,
  I kiss'd you night and day,
And Ringlet, O Ringlet,
  You still are golden-gay,
But Ringlet, O Ringlet,
  You should be silver-gray:
For what is this which now I 'm told,
I that took you for true gold,
She that gave you 's bought and sold,
  Sold, sold.

2

O Ringlet, O Ringlet,
  She blush'd a rosy red,

When Ringlet, O Ringlet,
  She clipt you from her head,
And Ringlet, O Ringlet,
  She gave you me, and said,
' Come, kiss it, love, and put it by:
If this can change, why so can I.'
O fie, you golden nothing, fie,
  You golden lie.

3

O Ringlet, O Ringlet,
  I count you much to blame,
For Ringlet, O Ringlet,
  You put me much to shame,
So Ringlet, O Ringlet,
  I doom you to the flame.
For what is this which now I learn,
Has given all my faith a turn ?
Burn, you glossy heretic, burn,
  Burn, burn.

LINES

Written in 1864, at the request of the Queen,
for inscription on the statue of the Duchess of
Kent at Frogmore ; printed in ' The Court
Journal,' March 19, 1864.

LONG as the heart beats life within her breast,
  Thy child will bless thee, guardian mother
    mild,
And far away thy memory will be blest
  By children of the children of thy child.

1865–1866

Contributed to ' Good Words,' March, 1868.

I STOOD on a tower in the wet,
And New Year and Old Year met,
And winds were roaring and blowing,
And I said, ' O years that meet in tears,
Have ye aught that is worth the knowing ?
Science enough and exploring,
Wanderers coming and going,
Matter enough for deploring,
But aught that is worth the knowing ? '
Seas at my feet were flowing,
Waves on the shingle pouring,
Old Year roaring and blowing,
And New Year blowing and roaring.

STANZA

Contributed to the ' Shakespearean Show-
Book,' printed in March, 1884, for a fair got
up for the Chelsea Hospital for Women.

NOT he that breaks the dams, but he
  That thro' the channels of the State
  Convoys the people's wish, is great ;
His name is pure, his fame is free.

COMPROMISE

Addressed to Mr. Gladstone, then Prime
Minister, in November, 1884, when the Fran-

chise Bill was being discussed in the House of
Lords; and afterwards printed in the 'Pall
Mall Gazette.'

STEERSMAN, be not precipitate in thy act
  Of steering, for the river here, my friend,
  Parts in two channels, moving to one end.
This goes straight forward to the cataract,
  That streams about the bend;
But tho' the cataract seem the nearer way,
Whate'er the crowd on either bank may say,
Take thou the bend, 't will save thee many a
  day.

EXPERIMENT IN SAPPHIC METRE

Contributed to Professor Jebb's 'Primer of
Greek Literature,' 1877.

> Faded every violet, all the roses;
> Gone the glorious promise, and the victim
> Broken in the anger of Aphrodite
>   Yields to the victor.

The following 'unpublished fragment' was
printed in 'Ros Rosarum,' an anthology edited
by Hon. Mrs. Boyle, 1885: —

> The night with sudden odor reel'd,
> The southern stars a music peal'd,
> Warm beams across the meadow stole;
> For Love flew over grove and field,
> Said, 'Open, Rosebud, open, yield
>   Thy fragrant soul.'

The following prefatory stanza was contri-
buted in 1891 to 'Pearl,' an English poem of
the 14th century, edited by Mr. Israel Gol-
lancz: —

> We lost you for how long a time,
> True Pearl of our poetic prime!
> We found you, and you gleam reset
> In Britain's lyric coronet.

[Other poems by Tennyson mentioned by
Shepherd and Luce in their Bibliographies
(neither of which is invariably accurate) as
printed, but omitted in the collected editions,
are the following: a stanza in the volume of
his poems presented to the Princess Louise of
Schleswig-Holstein by representatives of the
nurses of England; lines on the christening of
the daughter of the Duchess of Fife; and lines
to the memory of J. R. Lowell. These are
not referred to in the 'Memoir,' and I have
not been able to find copies of them.]

VI. NOTES AND ILLUSTRA-
TIONS

Page 1. TO THE QUEEN.
The following is the stanza referring to the
Crystal Palace Exhibition of 1851, which origi-
nally followed the 6th: —

> She brought a vast design to pass,
>   When Europe and the scattered ends
>   Of our fierce world were mixt as friends
> And brethren in her halls of glass.

For an early version of the poem (from a MS.
in the Library of the Drexel Institute, Phila-
delphia), see Jones's 'The Growth of the Idylls
of the King,' p. 152. Nine of the thirteen
stanzas are entirely unlike the poem as finally
published.

  Page 2. *And statesmen at her councils met*, etc.
This stanza was once quoted by Mr. Gladstone
in the House of Commons with remarkable
effect. Lord John Manners, in an argument
against political change, had quoted the poet's
description of England as

> A land of old and wide renown
> Where Freedom slowly broadens down.

The retort was none the less effective because
the passage was taken from a different poem.
  Page 4. LEONINE ELEGIACS.
The title in 1830 was simply 'Elegiacs.' In
line 6 'wood-dove' was 'turtle,' and in 15 'or'
was 'and.'
  For the allusion in 'The ancient poetess sing-
eth,' etc., compare 'Locksley Hall Sixty Years
After': 'Hesper, whom the poet call'd the
Bringer home of all good things.' The refer-
ence is to the fragment of Sappho: —

> Ἔσπερε, πάντα φέρεις·
>   Φέρεις οἶνον, φέρεις αἶγα,
>   Φέρεις ματέρι παῖδα.

Byron paraphrases it in 'Don Juan' (iii. 107):—

> O Hesperus! thou bringest all good things —
>   Home to the weary, to the hungry cheer,
> To the young bird the parent's brooding wings,
>   The welcome stall to the o'er-labor'd steer;
> Whate'er of peace about our hearth-stone clings,
>   Whate'er our household gods protect of dear,
> Are gather'd round us by thy look of rest;
> Thou bring'st the child, too, to the mother's breast.

  SUPPOSED CONFESSIONS, etc.
The original title was 'Supposed Confessions
of a Second-rate Sensitive Mind not in Unity
with Itself.' In the poem as restored the fol-
lowing lines, after line 39, were omitted: —

> A grief not uninformed, and dull,
> Hearted with hope, of hope as full
> As is the blood with life, or night
> And a dark cloud with rich moonlight.
> To stand beside a grave, and see
> The red small atoms wherewith we
> Are built, and smile in calm, and say —
> 'These little motes and grains shall be
> Clothed on with immortality
> More glorious than the noon of day.
> All that is pass'd into the flowers,
> And into beasts and other men,
> And all the Norland whirlwind showers
> From open vaults, and all the sea
> O'erwashes with sharp salts, again
> Shall fleet together all, and be
> Indued with immortality.'

The only other changes are 'rosy fingers' for
'waxen fingers' in 42, and 'man' for 'men' in
169.

The 'Westminster Review' (January, 1831) recognized in this poem 'an extraordinary combination of deep reflection, metaphysical analysis, picturesque description, dramatic transition, and strong emotion.' Arthur Hallam, in the 'Englishman's Magazine' (August, 1831), said of it: 'The "Confessions of a Second-rate Sensitive Mind" are full of deep insight into human nature, and into those particular trials which are sure to beset men who think and feel for themselves at this epoch of social development. The title is perhaps ill chosen; not only has it an appearance of quaintness, which has no sufficient reason, but it seems to us incorrect. The mood portrayed in this poem, unless the admirable skill of delineation has deceived us, is rather the clouded season of a strong mind than the habitual condition of one feeble and second-rate.'

Page 7. ISABEL.
In 1842 'wifehood' (line 16) was changed to 'marriage,' and 'blenched' (a misprint?) to 'blanched.'

Page 8. MARIANA.
In the 4th line the first reading was 'the peach to the garden-wall.' Bayard Taylor, writing in 1877 (in 'International Review,' vol. iv.), quotes the poet as saying: 'There is my "Mariana," for example. A line in it is wrong, and I cannot possibly change it, because it has been so long published; yet it always annoys me. I wrote "That held the peach to the garden-wall." Now this is not a characteristic of the scenery I had in mind. The line should be "That held the pear to the gable-wall."' Whether this conversation occurred during Taylor's visit to Tennyson in 1857 I cannot say; but the line was changed in the printed poem in 1860, or seventeen years before the review was written.

In line 43, the original reading was 'did dark;' retained in 1842, but changed in 1845.

In line 50, 'up and away' was at first 'up an' away' (changed in 1842). In line 63, the original 'sung i' the pane' was retained down to 1850. Line 80 was originally, 'Downsloped[1] was westering in his bower' (changed in 1842).

Page 9. To ——.
The 1830 reading in the 3d and 4th lines was

> The knotted lies of human creeds,
> The wounding cords which bind and strain.

MADELINE.
Printed in 1830 without the division into stanzas, which was made in 1842. The only other change (except the spelling 'airy' for 'aery') is 'amorously' for 'three times three' in the last stanza (in the *errata* of the 1830 volume).

Page 10. RECOLLECTIONS OF THE ARABIAN NIGHTS.
In line 29 the 1830 volume has 'Of breaded blosms'; in 78 'Blackgreen' for 'Black'; in

[1] In the volumes of 1830 and 1833, compound words are, with rare exceptions, printed without the hyphen; as 'silverchiming,' 'gardenbowers,' 'mountainstreams,' etc.

90 'unrayed' for 'inlaid'; in 100 'I was borne'; in 125 'wreathed silvers'; and in 140 'Flowing beneath.'

Page 13. ODE TO MEMORY.
In line 68, 'waken'd' was at first 'waked'; 103 was 'Emblems or glimpses of infinity'; in 117 'And those' was 'The few'; and 119–121 were: —

> My friend, with thee to live alone,
> Methinks were better than to own
> A crown, a sceptre, and a throne!

Page 14. THE POET.
In 1830 the 12th stanza read thus: —

> And in the bordure of her robe was writ
> WISDOM, a name to shake
> Hoar anarchies, as with a thunderfit,
> And when she spake, etc.

The 9th had 'a' for 'one'; and the 14th 'hurl'd' for 'whirl'd.'
In the 1st stanza, 'the hate of hate,' etc., clearly means the hatred of hate, etc. Rev. F. W. Robertson explains it thus: 'That is, the Prophet of Truth receives for his dower the scorn of men in whom scorn dwells, hatred from men who hate, while his reward is the gratitude and affection of men who seek the truth which they love, more eagerly than the faults which their acuteness can blame.' A very intelligent lady once told me that she had always understood 'hate of hate' to mean the utmost intensity of hate, etc., the poet's passions and sensibilities being to those of ordinary men 'as moonlight unto sunlight, and as water unto wine.'

THE POET'S MIND.
Reprinted in 1842 with the omission of the following passage after line 7: —

> Clear as summer mountainstreams,
> Bright as the inwoven beams,
> Which beneath their crisping sapphire
> In the midday, floating o'er
> The golden sands, make evermore
> To a blossomstarrèd shore.
> Hence away, unhallowed laugher!

The 9th line in 1830 was 'The poet's mind is holy ground'; and the 35th had 'would never.'

Page 15. THE SEA-FAIRIES.
For the original form of this poem, see p. 786.

Page 16. THE DYING SWAN.
Reprinted in 1842 with 'And loudly did lament' for 'Which loudly,' etc.; and in 1850 with 'Above in the wind was the swallow' for 'sung the swallow.'

Page 18. CIRCUMSTANCE.
The last line originally began, 'Fill up the round,' etc.

Page 20. ADELINE.
The only changes since 1842 are in the 5th stanza: 'the side of the morn' for 'the side o' the morn,' and 'locks a-drooping' for 'locks a-dropping.'

MARGARET.
In the 3d stanza the first reading was 'The

lion-souled Plantagenet ' (Richard I.). ' Chate-
let ' was proscribed in the Reign of Terror, and
executed in December, 1793.

In the 4th stanza, the 1830 volume has ' And
more aerially blue,' with ' And ' instead of
' But ' in the next line.

Page 21. ROSALIND.

The only change in 1884 was the omission of
the ' Note ' printed on p. 789 above.

Page 22. ELEÄNORE.

Line 99 was originally, ' Did roof noonday
with doubt and fear.' The reading of 108–111
was: —

> As waves that from the outer deep
> Roll into a quiet cove,
> There fall away, and lying still,
> Having glorious dreams in sleep,
> Shadow forth the banks at will:
> Or sometimes they swell and move, etc.

In 123 ' While ' was originally ' When.' For
127 the reading was : —

> I gaze on thee the cloudless noon
> Of mortal beauty: in its place, etc.

That of 134 was ' Floweth; then I faint, I
swoon.'

Page 23. KATE.

This poem, after being included in the one-
volume English edition of 1897, has been omit-
ted in the ' Globe ' edition of 1898. On second
thought, Lord Tennyson appears to have de-
cided to add nothing to the collected works as
last arranged by his father.

Page 24. ' MY LIFE IS FULL OF WEARY
DAYS.'

The reading of the first two stanzas in 1833
was as follows: —

I

> All good things have not kept aloof,
> Nor wander'd into other ways:
> I have not lacked thy mild reproof,
> Nor golden largess of thy praise,
> But life is full of weary days.

II

> Shake hands, my friend, across the brink
> Of that deep grave to which I go.
> Shake hands once more: I cannot sink
> So far — far down, but I shall know
> Thy voice, and answer from below.

The only changes in the next three stanzas
were ' scritches of the jay ' for ' laughters of the
jay,' and ' darnel ' for ' darnels.'

The following stanzas, with which the poem
originally ended (connected closely with the
preceding, there being only a comma after ' the
woodbines blow '), have not been restored: —

VI

> If thou art blest, my mother's smile
> Undimmed, if bees are on the wing:
> Then cease, my friend, a little while,
> That I may hear the throstle sing
> His bridal song, the boast of spring.

VII

> Sweet as the noise in parchèd plains
> Of bubbling wells that fret the stones
> (If any sense in me remains),
> Thy words will be; thy cheerful tones
> As welcome to my crumbling bones.

The ' Quarterly Review ' for July, 1833, had
its fling at the line, ' If any sense in me re-
mains.' ' This doubt,' it says, is ' inconsistent
with the opening stanza of the piece, and, in
fact, too modest; we take upon ourselves to re-
assure Mr. Tennyson that, even after he shall
be dead and buried, as much " sense " will still
remain as he has now the good fortune to pos-
sess.'

In the 4th stanza ' may ' refers to the blos-
soms of the hawthorn. Compare ' The Miller's
Daughter: ' ' The lanes, you know, were white
with may.' Here, as there, some of the Ameri-
can reprints put ' May ' for ' may.'

EARLY SONNETS.

I. The original version has ' a confused dream '
in the 3d line; ' Altho' I knew not ' in the 12th;
and for the 14th ' And each had lived in the
other's mind and speech.' In the 8th ' hath ' is
italicized.

III. In the 1st line ' full ' was originally
' fierce '; and in the 12th ' warm ' was ' great.'

VI. The 10th line was originally ' How long
shall the icy-hearted Muscovite.'

VII. The 1st line had originally ' dainty ' for
' slender.'

VIII. The 5th line had ' waltzing-circle ' for
' whirling dances.'

X. The first line originally began ' But were
I loved,' etc.

XI. The ' bridesmaid ' was Emily Sellwood,
who afterwards became the poet's wife; and
the marriage was that of his brother Charles to
Louisa Sellwood, May 24, 1836. See the ' Me-
moir,' vol. i. p. 148.

Page 27. THE LADY OF SHALOTT.

The last four lines of the 1st stanza were
originally as follows: —

> The yellowleavèd waterlily,
> The greensheathèd daffodilly,
> Tremble in the water chilly,
> Round about Shalott.

The next stanza began thus: —

> Willows whiten, aspens shiver.
> The sunbeam-showers break and quiver
> In the stream that runneth ever, etc.

The first reading of the 3d and 4th stanzas
was: —

> Underneath the bearded barley,
> The reaper, reaping late and early,
> Hears her ever chanting cheerly,
> Like an angel, singing clearly,
> 　　O'er the stream of Camelot.
> Piling the sheaves in furrows airy,
> Beneath the moon, the reaper weary
> Listening whispers, ' 't is the fairy,
> 　　Lady of Shalott.'

> The little isle is all inrailed
> With a rose-fence, and overtrailed

With roses: by the marge unhailed
The shallop flitteth silkensailed,
      Skimming down to Camelot.
A pearlgarland winds her head:
She leaneth on a velvet bed,
Full royally apparellèd,
      The Lady of Shalott.

Part II. goes on thus: —

No time hath she to sport and play:
A charmèd web she weaves alway.
A curse is on her, if she stay
Her weaving, either night or day,
      To look down to Camelot.
She knows not what the curse may be;
Therefore she weaveth steadily,
Therefore no other care hath she,
      The Lady of Shalott.

She lives with little joy or fear.
Over the water, running near,
The sheepbell tinkles in her ear.
Before her hangs a mirror clear,
      Reflecting towered Camelot.
And as the mazy web she whirls,
She sees the surly village churls, etc.

The next stanza (' Sometimes a troop,' etc.) is unchanged; and the only alteration in the next is ' went to Camelot ' for ' came from Camelot.'
In Part III. the 5th line of the 2d and 3d stanzas had ' down from Camelot; ' the last line of the 3d had ' over green Shalott; ' the 8th line of the 4th was ' Tirra lirra, tirra lirra; ' and the 3d line of the 5th had ' water-flower.'
In Part IV. the latter part of the 1st stanza was as follows: —

Outside the isle a shallow boat
Beneath a willow lay afloat,
Below the carven stern she wrote,
    The Lady of Shalott.

Then followed this stanza: —

A cloudwhite crown of pearl she dight.
All raimented in snowy white
That loosely flew (her zone in sight,
Clasped with one blinding diamond bright)
    Her wide eyes fixed on Camelot,
Though the squally eastwind keenly
Blew, with folded arms serenely
By the water stood the queenly
    Lady of Shalott.

The next stanza opened thus: —

With a steady stony glance —
Like some bold seer in a trance,
Beholding all his own mischance,
Mute, with a glassy countenance —
    She looked down to Camelot.
It was the closing, etc.

The remaining stanzas were as follows: —

As when to sailors while they roam,
By creeks and outfalls far from home,
Rising and dropping with the foam,
From dying swans wild warblings come,
    Blown shoreward; so to Camelot
Still as the boathead wound along
The willowy hills and fields among,
They heard her chanting her deathsong,
    The Lady of Shalott.

A longdrawn carol, mournful, holy,
She chanted loudly, chanted lowly,

Till her eyes were darkened wholly,
And her smooth face sharpened slowly,
    Turned to towered Camelot:
For ere she reached, etc.

Under tower and balcony,
By gardenwall and gallery,
A pale, pale corpse she floated by,
Deadcold, between the houses high,
    Dead into towered Camelot.
Knight and burgher, lord and dame,
To the plankèd wharfage came:
Below the stern they read her name,
    ' The Lady of Shalott.'

They crossed themselves, their stars they blest,
Knight, minstrel, abbot, squire, and guest.
There lay a parchment on her breast,
That puzzled more than all the rest,
    The wellfed wits at Camelot.
' *The web was woven curiously,*
  The charm is broken utterly,
Draw near and fear not — this is I,
    The Lady of Shalott.'

The ending of the poem is much improved by the revision. The ' wellfed wits ' (the epithet seems out of keeping here) might well be ' puzzled ' by the parchment, which is as pointless as it is enigmatical; but the new ending, with its introduction of Lancelot, is most pathetic and suggestive.
In line 157 the reading in 1842 (and down to 1873) was ' A corse between,' etc.
According to Palgrave (' Lyrical Poems by Tennyson '), the poem was suggested by ' an Italian romance upon the *Donna di Scalotta,* in which Camelot, unlike the Celtic tradition, was placed near the sea.' It is in a very different form that the legend reappears in the ' Idylls of the King.'
Page 29. MARIANA.
The original form was as follows: —

Behind the barren hill upsprung
  With pointed rocks against the light,
The crag sharpshadowed overhung
  Each glaring creek and inlet bright.
Far, far, one lightblue ridge was seen,
  Looming like baseless fairyland;
  Eastward a slip of burning sand,
Dark-rimmed with sea, and bare of green.
Down in the dry salt-marshes stood
  That house darklatticed. Not a breath
  Swayed the sick vineyard underneath,
Or moved the dusty southernwood.
    ' Madonna,' with melodious moan
    Sang Mariana, night and morn,
    ' Madonna ! lo ! I am all alone,
    Love-forgotten and love-forlorn.'

She, as her carol sadder grew,
  From her warm brow and bosom down
Through rosy taper fingers drew
  Her streaming curls of deepest brown
On either side, and made appear,
  Still-lighted in a secret shrine,
  Her melancholy eyes divine,
The home of woe without a tear.
    ' Madonna,' with melodious moan
    Sang Mariana, night and morn,
    ' Madonna ! lo ! I am all alone,
    Love-forgotten and love-forlorn.'

When the dawncrimson changed, and past
  Into deep orange o'er the sea,

Low on her knees herself she cast,
 Unto our lady prayèd she.
She moved her lips, she prayed alone,
 She praying disarrayed and warm
 From slumber, deep her wavy form
In the darklustrous mirror shone.
 'Madonna,' in a low clear tone
 Said Mariana, night and morn,
 Low she mourned, 'I am all alone,
 Love-forgotten and love-forlorn.'

At noon she slumbered. All along
 The silvery field, the large leaves talked
With one another, as among
 The spikèd maize in dreams she walked.
The lizard leapt: the sunlight played:
 She heard the callow nestling lisp,
 And brimful meadow-runnels crisp,
In the full-leavèd platan-shade.
 In sleep she breathed in a lower tone,
 Murmuring as at night and morn,
 'Madonna! lo! I am all alone,
 Love-forgotten and love-forlorn.'

Dreaming, she knew it was a dream
 Most false: *he* was and was not there.
She woke: the babble of the stream
 Fell, and without the steady glare
Shrank the sick olive sere and small.
 The riverbed was dusty-white;
 From the bald rock the blinding light
Beat ever on the sunwhite wall.
 She whispered, with a stifled moan
 More inward than at night or morn,
 'Madonna, leave me not all alone,
 To die forgotten and live forlorn.'

One dry cicala's summer song
 At night filled all the gallery,
Backward the latticeblind she flung,
 And leaned upon the balcony.
Ever the low wave seemed to roll
 Up to the coast: far on, alone
 In the East, large Hesper overshone
The mourning gulf, and on her soul
 Poured divine solace, or the rise
Of moonlight from the margin gleamed,
Volcano-like, afar, and streamed
 On her white arm, and heavenward eyes.
 Not all alone she made her moan,
 Yet ever sang she, night and morn,
 'Madonna! lo! I am all alone,
 Love-forgotten and love-forlorn.'

The only change since 1842 is in line 53, which in that edition retains the original 'Shrank the sick olive,' etc.

Page 30. THE TWO VOICES.
Unaltered except in line 457, which was originally 'So variously seem'd all things wrought.'
The poem, according to Palgrave (who unquestionably writes 'with authority'), describes 'the conflict in a soul between Scepticism and Faith.'
Lines 8–15 have been variously interpreted. Peter Bayne (who is followed by Professor Corson) understands the passage to mean 'that the shuffling off of this mortal coil may open to him new spheres of energy and happiness;' and that 'the reply of the poet is that man is nature's highest product, — the obvious suggestion being that there is no splendid dragon-fly into which the human grub, released by death, is likely to develop.' But (as I remarked in my 'Select

Poems of Tennyson,' in 1884) this 'suggestion,' so far from being 'obvious,' seems to me merely a desperate attempt to make the reference to the higher nature of man a 'reply' to what the critic assumes that the Voice means to say. For myself, I had no hesitation in adopting Tainsh's interpretation of the passage: 'A dragon-fly is more wonderful than you;' and Lord Tennyson afterwards explained it to me in almost the same words: 'The dragon-fly is as wonderful as you.'
In line 228, the allusion is to the old notion that man was composed of the four elements, earth, air, fire, and water, and that the well-balanced mixture of these produced the perfection of humanity. Compare Shakespeare, 'Julius Cæsar,' v. 5. 73: —

 His life was gentle, and the elements
 So mix'd in him that Nature might stand up
 And say to all the world, 'This was a man!'

Page 35. THE MILLER'S DAUGHTER.
The poem originally began with this stanza: —

 I met in all the close green ways,
 While walking with my line and rod,
 The wealthy miller's mealy face,
 Like the moon in an ivy-tod.
 He look'd so jolly and so good,
 While fishing in the mill-dam water,
 I laugh'd to see him as he stood,
 And dreamt not of the miller's daughter.

The 2d stanza, now the 1st, remains unaltered, and the only change in the next is 'can make' for 'makes' in the last line. In the next (3d) stanza, the original reading in the 2d line was 'My darling Alice,' and 'my own sweet wife' in the 6th line.
The 4th stanza ('Have I not found,' etc.) was added in 1842.
The 5th stanza originally stood thus: —

 My father's mansion, mounted high,
 Looked down upon the village spire.
 I was a long and listless boy,
 And son and heir unto the squire.
 In these dear walls, where I and you
 Have lived and loved alone so long,
 Each morn my sleep, etc.

The 6th stanza began: —

 I often heard the cooing dove
 In firry woodlands mourn alone;
 But ere I saw, etc.

The last line had 'the long' for 'those long.'
The 7th stanza was as follows: —

 Sometimes I whistled in the wind,
 Sometimes I angled, thought and deed
 Torpid, as swallows left behind
 That winter 'neath the floating weed:
 At will to wander everyway
 From brook to brook my sole delight,
 As lithe eels over meadows gray
 Oft shift their glimmering pool by night.

The 8th stanza was the one now made the 13th, and the first quatrain read thus: —

 How dear to me in youth, my love,
 Was everything about the mill —

The black and silent pool above,
The pool beneath that ne'er stood still, etc.

The 9th and 10th were as follows: —

I loved from off the bridge to hear
The rushing sound the water made,
And see the fish that everywhere
In the backcurrent glanced and played:
Low down the tall flagflower that sprung
Beside the noisy steppingstones,
And the massed chestnutboughs that hung
Thickstudded over with white cones.

Remember you that pleasant day
When, after roving in the woods,
('T was April then) I came and lay
Beneath those gummy chestnutbuds
That glistened in the April blue
Upon the slope so smooth and cool,
I lay and never thought of *you*,
But angled in the deep millpool.

The stanza beginning ' A love-song,' etc., was not in the original version, which continued thus: —

A water-rat from off the bank
Plunged in the stream. With idle care,
Downlooking through the sedges rank,
I saw your troubled image there.
Upon the dark and dimpled beck
It wandered like a floating light,
A full fair form, a warm white neck,
And two white arms — how rosy white !

If you remember, you had set
Upon the narrow casement-edge
A long green box of mignonette,
And you were leaning from the ledge.
I raised my eyes at once: above
They met two eyes so blue and bright,
Such eyes ! I swear to you, my love, .
That they have never lost their light.

The next (13th) stanza, now suppressed, was as follows: —

That slope beneath the chestnut tall,
Is wooed with choicest breaths of air;
Methinks that I could tell you all
The cowslips and the kingcups there;
Each coltsfoot down the grassy bent,
Whose round leaves hold the gathered shower,
Each quaintly-folded cuckoo-pint,
And silver-paly cuckoo flower.

The 14th was: —

In rambling on the eastern wold,
When thro' the showery April nights
Their hueless crescent glimmered cold,
From all the other village lights
I knew your taper far away.
My heart was full of trembling hope,
Down from the wold I came and lay
Upon the dewy swarded slope.

The 15th was as follows: —

The white chalkquarry from the hill
Upon the broken ripple gleamed,
I murmured lowly, sitting still,
While round my feet the eddy streamed:
' Oh ! that I were the wreath she wears,
The mirror where her sight she feeds,
The song she sings, the air she breathes,
The letters of the book she reads.'

The 16th was identical with the present 16th, 'Sometimes I saw you sit and spin,' etc.
The 17th was:

I loved, but when I dared to speak
My love, the lawns were white with **May;**
Your ripe lips moved not, but your cheek
Flushed like the coming of the day:
Rosecheekt, roselipt, half-sly, half-shy,
You would, etc.

' May,' which must have been a misprint, was changed to ' may ' in 1842.

The 18th and 19th (afterwards omitted to make room for the three new ones, in which Alice is brought to visit his mother, — the present 18th, 19th, and 20th) were as follows: —

Remember you the clear moonlight
That whitened all the eastern ridge,
When o'er the water, dancing white,
I stept upon the old mill-bridge ?
I heard you whisper from above
A lute-toned whisper, ' I am here; '
I murmured, ' Speak again, my love,
The stream is loud; I cannot hear.'

I heard, as I have seemed to hear,
When all the under air was still,
The low voice of the glad new year
Call to the freshly-flowered hill.
I heard, as I have often heard,
The nightingale in leafy woods
Call to its mate, when nothing stirred
To left or right but falling floods.

The 20th stanza was as follows: —

Come, Alice, sing to me the song
I made you on our marriageday,
When, arm in arm, we went along
Half-tearfully, and you were gay
With brooch and ring: for I shall seem,
The while you sing that song, to hear
The millwheel turning in the stream,
And the green chestnut whisper near.

The ' Song ' was originally this: —

I wish I were her earring
Ambushed in auburn ringlets sleek,
(So might my shadow tremble
Over her downy cheek)
Hid in her hair, all day and night,
Touching her neck so warm and white.

I wish I were the girdle
Buckled about her dainty waist,
That her heart might beat against me
In sorrow and in rest.
I should know well if it beat right,
I'd clasp it round so close and tight.

I wish I were her necklace,
So might I ever fall and rise
Upon her balmy bosom
With her laughter or her sighs.
I would lie round so warm and light
I would not be unclasped at night.

The next stanzas (21st and 22d) were: —

A trifle, sweet, which true love spells —
True love interprets right alone;
For o'er each letter broods and dwells
(Like light from running waters thrown
On flowery swaths) the blissful flame
Of his sweet eyes, that, day and night,

With pulses thrilling thro' his frame
Do inly tremble, starrybright.

How I waste language — yet in truth
   You must blame love, whose early rage
Made me a rhymester in my youth,
   And over-garrulous in age.
Sing me that other song I made,
   Half-angered with my happy lot,
When in the breezy limewood-shade
   I found the blue forget-me-not.

This was the second 'Song': —

All yesternight you met me not.
   My ladylove, forget me not.
When I am gone, regret me not,
   But, here or there, forget me not.
With your arched eyebrow threat me not,
   And tremulous eyes, like April skies,
      That seem to say, 'forget me not.'
   I pray you, love, forget me not.

In idle sorrow set me not;
   Regret me not: forget me not:
Oh ! leave me not; oh, let me not
   Wear quite away; — forget me not.
With roguish laughter fret me not
   From dewy eyes, like April skies,
      That ever *look*, 'forget me not,'
   Blue as the blue forget-me-not.

The 23d stanza is unaltered from the one beginning 'Look thro' mine eyes with thine,' etc.; and the 24th and last is the same that now ends the poem, except that the first quatrain reads thus: —

I 've half a mind to walk, my love,
   To the old mill across the wolds,
For look ! the sunset from above
   Winds all the vale in rosy folds, etc.

The present 25th and 26th stanzas ('Yet tears they shed,' etc.) were added in 1842. In the 7th line of the 25th all the American editions that I have seen (from 1842 down) have 'the loss *that* brought' instead of 'had brought.'
Page 38. FATIMA.
The 2d stanza was added in 1842. The 2d line of the poem had originally 'at' for 'from.'
ŒNONE.
The poem originally began thus: —

There is a dale in Ida, lovelier
Than any in old Ionia, beautiful
With emerald slopes of sunny sward, that lean
Above the loud glenriver, which hath worn
A path thro' steepdown granite walls below
Mantled with flowering tendriltwine. In front
The cedarshadowy valleys open wide.
Far-seen, high over all the Godbuilt wall
And many a snowycolumned range divine,
Mounted with awful sculptures — men and Gods,
The work of Gods — bright on the darkblue sky
The windy citadel of Ilion
Shone, like the crown of Troas. Hither came
Mournful Œnone, wandering forlorn
Of Paris, once her playmate. Round her neck,
Her neck all marblewhite and marblecold,
Floated her hair or seemed to float in rest.
She, leaning on a vine-entwinèd stone,
Sang to the stillness, till the mountain-shadow
Sloped downward to her seat from the upper cliff.

[1] In the Pyrenees, where part of this poem was written, I saw a very beautiful species of Cicala, which had

O mother Ida, manyfountained Ida,
Dear mother Ida, hearken ere I die.
The grasshopper is silent in the grass,
The lizard with his shadow on the stone
Sleeps like a shadow, and the scarletwinged [1]
Cicala in the noonday leapeth not.
Along the water-rounded granite-rock
The purple flower droops: the golden bee, etc.

The text then goes on without change (except the insertion of line 46, 'I waited underneath the dawning hills,' which is not in the first version) to line 51, 'Came up from reedy Simois all alone.' It then proceeds as follows: —

O mother Ida, hearken ere I die.
I sate alone: the goldensandalled morn
Rosehued the scornful hills: I sate alone
With downdropt eyes: whitebreasted like a star
Fronting the dawn he came: a leopard skin
From his white shoulder drooped: his sunny hair
Clustered about his temples like a God's:
And his cheek brightened, as the foambow brightens
When the wind blows the foam; and I called out,
'Welcome, Apollo, welcome home, Apollo,
Apollo, my Apollo, loved Apollo.'

Dear mother Ida, hearken ere I die.
He, mildly smiling, in his milkwhite palm
Close-held a golden apple, lightningbright
With changeful flashes, dropt with dew of Heaven
Ambrosially smelling. From his lip,
Curved crimson, the fullflowing river of speech
Came down upon my heart.
                 'My own Œnone,
Beautifulbrowed Œnone, mine own soul,
Behold this fruit, whose gleaming rind ingrav'-
"For the most fair" in aftertime may breed
Deep evilwilledness of heaven and sere
Heartburning toward hallowed Ilion;
And all the colour of my afterlife
Will be the shadow of today. Today
Here and Pallas and the floating grace
Of laughterloving Aphrodite meet
In manyfolded Ida to receive
This meed of beauty, she to whom my hand
Award the palm. Within the green hillside,
Under yon whispering tuft of oldest pine,
Is an ingoing grotto, strown with spar
And ivymatted at the mouth, wherein
Thou unbeholden may'st behold, unheard
Hear all, and see thy Paris judge of Gods.'

Dear mother Ida, hearken ere I die.
It was the deep midnoon: one silvery cloud
Had lost his way between the piney hills.
They came — all three — the Olympian goddesses:
Naked they came to the smoothswarded bower,
Lustrous with lilyflower, violeteyed
Both white and blue, with lotetree-fruit thickset,
Shadowed with singing pine; and all the while,
Above, the overwandering ivy and vine
This way and that in many a wild festoon
Ran riot, garlanding the gnarlèd boughs
With bunch and berry and flower thro' and thro'.
On the treetops a golden glorious cloud
Leaned, slowly dropping down ambrosial dew.
How beautiful they were, too beautiful
To look upon ! but Paris was to me
More lovelier than all the world beside.

O mother Ida, hearken ere I die.
First spake the imperial Olympian

scarlet wings spotted with black. Probably nothing of the kind exists in Mount Ida.

With archèd eyebrow smiling sovranly,
Fulleyèd Here. She to Paris made
Proffer of royal power, ample rule
Unquestioned, overflowing revenue
Wherewith to embellish state 'from many a vale
And riversundered champaign clothed with corn,
Or upland glebe wealthy in oil and wine —
Honour and homage, tribute, tax and toll
From many an inland town and haven large,
Mast-thronged below her shadowing citadel
In glassy bays among her tallest towers.'

O mother Ida, hearken ere I die.
Still she spake on and still she spake of power
' Which in all action is the end of all.
Power fitted to the season, measured by
The height of the general feeling, wisdomborn
And throned of wisdom — from all neighbour crowns
Alliance and allegiance evermore.
Such boon from me Heaven's Queen to thee king-
  born,' etc.

The next six lines (126-131) follow without
change, and the speech of Juno ends with these
two lines, afterwards suppressed: —

The changeless calm of undisputed right,
The highest height and topmost strength of power.

There is no change in the next ten lines
(132-141) except ' Flattered his spirit ' for ' Flat-
ter'd his heart.'
The speech of Pallas (142-164) originally stood
thus : —

' Selfreverence, selfknowledge, selfcontrol
Are the three hinges of the gates of Life,
That open into power, everyway
Without horizon, bound or shadow or cloud.
Yet not for power (power of herself
Will come uncalled-for) but to live by law,
Acting the law we live by without fear,
And because right is right, to follow right
Were wisdom, in the scorn of consequence.
(Dear mother Ida, hearken ere I die.)
Not as men value gold because it tricks
And blazons outward Life with ornament,
But rather as the miser, for itself.
Good for selfgood doth half destroy selfgood.
The means and end, like two coiled snakes, infect
Each other, bound in one with hateful love.
So both into the fountain and the stream
A drop of poison falls. Come hearken to me,
And look upon me and consider me,
So shalt thou find me fairest, so endurance,
Like to an athlete's arm, shall still become
Sinew'd with motion, till thine active will
(As the dark body of the Sun robed round
With his own ever-emanating lights)
Be flooded o'er with her own effluences,
And thereby grow to freedom.'
                              Here she ceased, etc.

The next five lines (165-169) are unchanged,
and the poem then goes on thus : —

Idalian Aphrodite oceanborn,
Fresh as the foam, newbathed in Paphian wells,
With rosy slender fingers upward drew
From her warm brow and bosom her dark hair
Fragrant and thick, and on her head upbound
In a purple band: below her lucid neck
Shone ivorylike, and from the ground her foot
Gleamed rosywhite, and o'er her rounded form
Between the shadows of the vinebunches
Floated the glowing sunlights, as she moved.

There is no change in the next twenty-four
lines (179-202) except that, instead of the *three*
lines beginning ' She spoke and laugh'd,' the
first version has these *two :* —

I only saw my Paris raise his arm:
I only saw great Here's angry eyes, etc.

In the remainder of the poem the changes are
few and slight. In line 203 the earlier reading
is ' Dear mother Ida, hearken ere I die; ' and so
also in 252. Line 226 was ' Oh ! mother Ida,
hearken ere I die; ' and 241 was ' Yet, mother
Ida, hear me ere I die.' For 205-208 the origi-
nal reading was: —

My dark tall pines, that plumed the craggy ledge
High over the blue gorge, or lower down
Filling greengulphèd Ida, all between
The snowy peak and snowwhite cataract
Fostered the callow eaglet — from beneath, etc.

Lines 216-225 were inserted in 1842; and for
249-251 the original version has only the line,
' Ere it is born. I will not die alone.'
In line 27 all the editions I have seen down to
that of 1884 have ' and the cicala sleeps; ' and
in the next line ' The purple flowers droop.' It
probably occurred to the poet that the intro-
duction of the *cicala*, or *cicada* (the *Greek* ci-
cada, not our insect so called), was too nearly a
repetition of that of the grasshopper.
For lines 39, 40, compare ' Tithonus ' : —

Like that strange song I heard Apollo sing
While Ilion like a mist rose into towers.

For the myth, see Ovid, ' Heroides,' xv. 179;
and for a similar legend concerning the origin
of Camelot, see ' Gareth and Lynette.'
Page 42. To ——.
In the 1833 volume this introduction to ' The
Palace of Art ' began thus: —

I send you, Friend, a sort of allegory,
(You are an artist and will understand
Its many lesser meanings) of a soul, etc.

In 1842 it was reprinted with no change ex-
cept in these lines.
THE PALACE OF ART.
In the 2d stanza the original reading was: —

I chose, whose ranged ramparts bright
From great broad meadow-bases of deep grass, etc.

The 4th stanza originally began thus: ' While
the great world runs round,' etc.
Between the 4th and 5th stanzas (the latter is
unchanged) was the following, suppressed in
1842: —

And richly feast within thy palacehall,
  Like to the dainty bird that sups,
Lodged in the lustrous crown-imperial,
  Draining the honeycups.

Then came these stanzas, which have been
more or less altered and transposed: —

Full of long sounding corridors it was
  That overvaulted grateful glooms,
Roofed with thick plates of green and orange glass
  Ending in stately rooms.

Full of great rooms and small the palace stood,
All various, all beautiful,
Looking all ways, fitted to every mood
And change of my still soul.

'For some were hung,' etc. (the present 16th stanza,
unaltered).

'One showed an English home,' etc. (the present 22d
stanza, with no further change).

Some were all dark and red, a glimmering land
Lit with a low round moon,
Among brown rocks a man upon the sand
Went weeping all alone.

One seemed a foreground black with stones and slags,
Below sunsmitten icy spires
Rose striped with long white cloud the scornful crags,
Deeptrenched with thunderfires.

Some showed far-off thick woods mounted with towers.
Nearer, a flood of mild sunshine
Poured on long walks and lawns and beds and bowers
Trellised with bunchy vine.[1]

Or the maidmother by a crucifix,
In yellow pastures sunnywarm, etc.

Or Venus in a snowy shell alone,
Deepshadowed in the glassy brine,
Moonlike glowed double on the blue, and shone
A naked shape divine.

'Or in a clearwalled city,' etc. (now 25th stanza).

Or that deepwounded child of Pendragon
Mid misty woods on sloping greens
Dozed in the valley of Avilion
Tended by crowned queens.

Or blue-eyed Kriemhilt from a craggy hold,
Athwart the light-green rows of vine,
Pour'd blazing hoards of Nibelungen gold,
Down to the gulfy Rhine.

Europa's scarf blew in an arch, unclasped,
From her bare shoulder backward borne;
From one hand drooped a crocus: one hand grasped
The mild bull's golden horn.

He thro' the streaming crystal swam, and rolled
Ambrosial breaths that seemed to float
In lightwreathed curls. She from the ripple cold
Updrew her sandalled foot.[2]

'Or else flushed Ganymede,' etc. (as now, except 'Over'
for 'Above' in 4th line).

Not these alone: but many a legend fair,
Which the supreme Caucasian mind
Carved out of nature for itself, was there
Broidered in screen and blind.

So that my soul, beholding in her pride
All these, from room to room did pass;
And all things that she saw, she multiplied,
A manyfacèd glass.

And being both the sower and the seed,
Remaining in herself became
All that she saw, Madonna, Ganymede,
Or the Asiatic dame —

Still changing, as a lighthouse in the night
Changeth athwart the gleaming main,

[1] This stanza, like the next but one, was omitted in
1842. The hyphen in 'far-off,' as in occasional in-
stances before and after, is in the original edition.

From red to yellow, yellow to pale white,
Then back to red again.

'From change to change four times within the womb
The brain is moulded,' she began,
'So through all phases of all thought I come
Into the perfect man.'

In 1842 this last stanza was altered as fol-
lows: —

'From shape to shape at first within the womb
The brain is modell'd,' she began,
'And thro' all phases of all thought I come
Into the perfect man.'

The next stanza in the 1833 volume was as
follows: —

'All Nature widens upward. Evermore
The simpler essence lower lies:
More complex is more perfect, owning more
Discourse, more widely wise.'

This was retained in 1842 and in the subse-
quent editions down to 1853, when the present
three stanzas were substituted for this and the
preceding one.

The next stanza in 1833, and until 1853, was
as follows: —

I take possession of men's minds and deeds.
I live in all things great and small.
I sit apart holding no forms of creeds,
But contemplating all.

The 1833 version then continued thus: —

Four ample courts there were, East, West, South,
North,
In each a squarèd lawn wherefrom
A golden-gorgèd dragon spouted forth
The fountain's diamond foam.

'All round the cool green courts,' etc. (the present
7th stanza, with no further change).

From those four jets four currents in one swell
Over the black rock streamed below
In steamy folds, that, floating as they fell,
Lit up a torrentbow;

And round the roofs ran gilded galleries,
That gave large view to distant lands,
Tall towns [_sic_] and mounds, and close beneath the
skies
Long lines of amber sands.

Huge incense-urns along the balustrade,
Hollowed of solid amethyst,
Each with a different odour fuming, made
The air a silver mist.

Far-off 't was wonderful to look upon
Those sumptuous towers between the gleam
Of that great foambow trembling in the sun,
And the argent incense-steam;

And round the terraces and round the walls,
While day sank lower or rose higher,
To see those rails with all their knobs and balls,
Burn like a fringe of fire.

Likewise the deepset windows, stained and traced,
Burned, like slowflaming crimson fires,
From shadowed grots of arches interlaced,
And topped with frostlike spires.

[2] Omitted in 1842, like the 3d, 4th, and 5th stanzas
below.

Up in the towers I placed great bells,' etc. (33d stanza,
  otherwise unchanged).

There deephaired Milton like an angel tall
  Stood limnèd, Shakespeare bland and mild,
Grim Dante pressed his lips, and from the wall
  The bald blind Homer smiled.

And underneath freshcarved in cedarwood,
  Somewhat alike in form and face,
The Genii of every climate stood,
  All brothers of one race: [1]

Angels who sway the seasons by their art,
  And mould all shapes in earth and sea;
And with great effort build the human heart
  From earliest infancy.

And in the sunpierced Oriel's coloured flame
  Immortal Michael Angelo
Looked down, bold Luther, largebrowed Verulam,
  The king of those who know.

Cervantes, the bright face of Calderon,
  Robed David touching holy strings,
The Halicarnasseän, and alone,
  Alfred the flower of kings,

Isaïah with fierce Ezekiel,
  Swarth Moses by the Coptic sea,
Plato, Petrarca, Livy, and Raphaël,
  And eastern Confutzee:

And many more that in their lifetime were
  Fullwelling fountainheads of Change,
Between the stone shafts glimmered, blazoned fair
  In divers raiment strange.

' Thro' which the lights,' etc. (43d stanza, unchanged).

' No nightingale,' etc. (44th stanza, unchanged).

' Singing and murmuring,' etc. (45th unchanged).

As some rich tropic mountain, that infolds
  All change, from flats of scattered palms
Sloping through five great zones of climate, holds
  His head in snows and calms —

Full of her own delight and nothing else
  My vainglorious, gorgeous soul [sic]
Sat throned between the shining oriels,
  In pomp beyond control; [2]

With piles of flavorous fruits in basket-twine
  Of gold, upheapèd, crushing down
Muskscented blooms — all taste — grape, gourd or
  pine —
  In bunch, or singlegrown —

Our growths, and such as brooding Indian heats
  Make out of crimson blossoms deep,
Ambrosial pulps and juices, sweets from sweets
  Sunchanged, when seawinds sleep.

With graceful chalices of curious wine,
  Wonders of art — and costly jars,
And bossèd salvers. Ere young night divine
  Crowned dying day with stars,

Making sweet close of his delicious toils,
  She lit white streams of dazzling gas,
And soft and fragrant flames of precious oils
  In moons of purple glass

[1] This stanza and the next one omitted in 1842, as
were the 2d and 3d below.
[2] These two stanzas, with those describing the sensu-

Ranged on the fretted woodwork to the ground.
  Thus her intense untold delight
In deep or vivid colour, smell and sound,
  Was flattered day and night.

' Sometimes the riddle,' etc. (the present 54th stanza,
  otherwise unchanged).

Of full-sphered contemplation. So three years
  She throve, but on the fourth she fell, etc.

The remaining twenty stanzas of the poem
(57th to 76th), except for the omission of one
stanza, are the same as the 56th to 74th that
now end it, with the following slight changes: —
  In line 247 ' onward-sloping ' has been put for
' downward-sloping; ' in 281, ' a sound ' for ' the
sound,' and ' rocks ' (retained until 1853) for
' stones; ' and in 288, ' And save me lest I die '
for ' Dying the death I die.'
  The omitted stanza followed the present 58th
(' Deep dread,' etc.) and read thus: —

Who hath drawn dry the fountains of delight,
  That from my deep heart everywhere
Moved in my blood and dwelt, as power and might
  Abode in Sampson's hair?

  In the 1833 volume the following foot-note
(suppressed in 1842) appeared: —
  ' When I first conceived the plan of the Pal-
ace of Art, I intended to have introduced both
sculptures and paintings into it; but it is the
most difficult of all things to *devise* a statue in
verse. Judge whether I have succeeded in the
statues of Elijah and Olympias: —

One was the Tishbite whom the raven fed,
  As when he stood on Carmel-steeps
With one arm stretch'd out bare, and mock'd and said,
  ' Come, cry aloud — he sleeps ! '

Tall, eager, lean, and strong, his cloak wind-borne
  Behind, his forehead heavenly-bright
From the clear marble pouring glorious scorn,
  Lit as with inner light.

One was Olympias: the floating snake
  Roll'd round her ankles, round her waist
Knotted, and folded once about her neck,
  Her perfect lips to taste

Round by the shoulder moved: she seeming blithe
  Declined her head: on every side
The dragon's curves melted and mingled with
  The woman's youthful pride

Of rounded limbs.

  Another foot-note gave the following stanzas,
' expressive of the joy wherewith the soul con-
templated the results of astronomical experi-
ment: ' —

Hither, when all the deep unsounded skies
  Shuddered with silent stars, she clomb,
And as with optic glasses her keen eyes
  Pierced through the mystic dome,

Regions of lucid matter taking forms,
  Brushes of fire, hazy gleams,

ous delights of the palate that follow, were struck out
in 1842. Compare the suppression of the similar refer-
ence in the 5th stanza (' And richly feast,' etc.) of the
first version. The poet wisely decided to allow his lux-
urious ' soul ' none but intellectual joys.

Clusters and beds of worlds, and bee-like swarms
    Of suns, and starry streams.

She saw the snowy poles of moonless Mars,
    That marvellous round of milky light
Below Orion, and those double stars
    Whereof the one more bright

Is circled by the other, etc.

In Mr. Palgrave's 'Lyrical Poems by Lord Tennyson' these stanzas are reprinted in the notes by the permission of the author; but the closing stanzas are revised thus: —

She saw the snowy poles and moons of Mars,
    That marvellous field of drifted light
In mid Orion, and the married stars —

The two moons of Mars had been discovered since the preceding stanzas were written; and the position of the great nebula in Orion is more accurately given. It will be understood that the two passages are given as printed in the edition of 1833 (and in Mr. Palgrave's book), the stanzas being incomplete there as here.

Line 80. *And hoary to the wind.* When the whitish-gray underside of the olive-tree leaves is turned up by the wind.

Line 96. *Babe in arm.* The reviewers of the 1833 volume ridiculed this phrase, comparing it with the 'lance in rest' of the romances of chivalry; but the poet has not only retained it here, but repeated it in 'The Princess' (vi.): —

But high upon the palace Ida stood
With Psyche's babe in arm.

Line 111. *The Ausonian King.* Numa Pompilius. The 1833 reading was 'the Tuscan king.'

Line 115. *Indian Cama.* The Hindu god of love, the Indian Cupid, who is sometimes represented as riding by night on a parrot, or lory. Compare Alfred's poem, ' Love,' in ' Poems by Two Brothers' (8th and 9th stanzas, p. 776 above).

Line 117. *Sweet Europa's mantle blew.* Some editions misprint ' blue ' for ' blew.'

Line 137. *The Ionian father of the rest.* Homer.

Line 164. *The first of those who know.* The edition of 1833 has the foot-note: ' Il maestro di color chi sanno. *Dante. Inf.* iii.'

Line 174. Here the poet (as in ' The Princess,' i. 218: ' Rapt in her song ') follows ancient fable rather than modern ornithology in making the musical bird feminine; but in ' The Gardener's Daughter ' he is true to the latter: —

The redcap whistled; and the nightingale
Sang loud, as tho' he were the bird of day.

Line 222. *God, before whom ever lie bare, etc.* This is borrowed from an essay by Arthur Hallam, entitled ' Theodicæa Novissima ' (see his ' Remains,' p. 363): ' I believe that redemption is universal in so far as it left no obstacle between man and God but man's own will; that indeed is in the power of God's election, with

whom alone rest the abysmal secrets of personality.'

Line 242. *With dim-fretted foreheads all.* ' Dim-fretted ' has been variously explained, but I have the poet's authority for stating that it means ' worm-eaten.'

Page 46. LADY CLARA VERE DE VERE.
In the 7th stanza the line ' The gardener Adam and his wife ' was changed in many subsequent editions to ' The grand old gardener and his wife,' but the original reading has been restored, and the poem now stands exactly as it appeared in 1842.

Page 47. THE MAY QUEEN.
Only a few slight changes have been made in this poem. The 2d line had originally ' the blythe New Year.' In the 3d stanza ' ye ' was used for ' you,' as in a dozen or more places in the ' New-Year's Eve.' Line 52 began at first with ' The may upon the blackthorn;' line 77 was ' Ye 'll kiss me, my own mother, upon my cheek and brow;' and line 93 was ' Goodnight, sweet mother: call me when it begins to dawn.' In the ' Conclusion,' lines 107, 108 were originally: —

But still it can't be long, mother, before I find release;
And that good man, the clergyman, he preaches words of peace.

In line 113 ' taught ' and ' show'd ' have been transposed; line 134 had ' comes ' for ' come;' and 142 had ' many worthier.'

Page 51. THE LOTOS-EATERS.
Line 7th was originally ' Above the valley burned the golden moon;' and line 16 was ' Three thundercloven thrones of oldest snow.' The 6th stanza in the ' Choric Song ' was added in 1842; and line 86 had at first ' worn out with many wars.' The next stanza began ' Or propt on lavish beds of amaranth and moly;' line 90 had ' eyelids ' for ' eyelid;' and line 98 had ' Only to watch and see,' etc. The 1st line of the next stanza (100) had ' the flowery peak ' for ' the barren peak.'

From ' We have had enough of action,' etc. (105) to the end, the original reading was as follows: —

We have had enough of motion,
Weariness and wild alarm,
Tossing on the tossing ocean,
Where the tuskèd seahorse walloweth
In a stripe of grassgreen calm,
At noon tide beneath the lee;
And the monstrous narwhale swalloweth
His foamfountains in the sea.
Long enough the winedark wave our weary bark did
    carry.
This is lovelier and sweeter,
Men of Ithaca, this is meeter,
In the hollow rosy vale to tarry,
Like a dreamy Lotos-eater, a delirious Lotos-eater!
We will eat the Lotos, sweet
As the yellow honeycomb,
In the valley some, and some
On the ancient heights divine;
And no more roam,
On the loud hoar foam,
To the melancholy home

At the limit of the brine,
The little isle of Ithaca, beneath the day's decline.
We 'll lift no more the shattered oar,
No more unfurl the straining sail;
With the blissful Lotos-eaters pale
We will abide in the golden vale
Of the Lotos-land, till the Lotos fail;
We will not wander more.
Hark! how sweet the horned ewes bleat
On the solitary steeps,
And the merry lizard leaps,
And the foamwhite waters pour;
And the dark pine weeps,
And the lithe vine creeps,
And the heavy melon sleeps
On the level of the shore:
Oh! islanders of Ithaca, we will not wander more.
Surely, surely slumber is more sweet than toil, the
  shore
Than labour in the ocean, and rowing with the oar.
Oh! islanders of Ithaca, we will return no more.'

On the line (11 of the introduction), 'Slow-dropping veils of thinnest lawn,' the poet, in a letter to Mr. S. E. Dawson (printed in his 'Study of The Princess,' 2d ed., Montreal, 1884) says: —

  ' When I was about twenty or twenty-one I went on a tour to the Pyrenees. Lying among those mountains before a waterfall that comes down one thousand or twelve hundred feet, I sketched it (according to my custom then) in these words: —

Slow-dropping veils of thinnest lawn.

When I printed this, a critic informed me that "lawn was the material used in theatres to imitate a waterfall," and graciously added, "Mr. T. should not go to the boards of a theatre, but to nature herself for his suggestions." And I *had* gone to nature herself.
  ' I think it is a moot point whether — if I had known how that effect was produced on the stage — I should have ventured to publish the line.'
  Peter Bayne ('Lessons from My Masters,' American ed., 1879) remarks: 'Whoever has seen a stream in its midsummer slenderness of volume, falling down a front of rock divided into steps or ledges, will admit that no words could possibly surpass these in descriptive precision. The Falling Foss, for example — a small cascade on one of the affluents of the Esk, near Whitby — affords a realization so exact of the "slow-dropping veil of thinnest lawn," that it at once, when I saw it last summer, reminded me of the poem; nor could an officer of the Geological Survey, writing with purely scientific intent, devise a more literal or a more expressive description.'
  In line 6 of the 'Choric Song' ('Than tired eyelids upon tired eyes') all the English editions print 'tir'd' in both places, contrary to the poet's rule not to use the apostrophe when the verb ends in *e*. This might suggest that he meant to have the word pronounced as a monosyllable, but nobody with an ear for rhythm would read it so. I asked Lord Tennyson why he printed it with the apostrophe, and he replied, 'That people might not pronounce it *ti-red* instead of *ti-erd*.' I told him that no American would ever think of reading it in the former way, and I doubted whether any Englishman would; but he said he was not sure of that.

Page 53. A DREAM OF FAIR WOMEN.
In the 1833 volume the poem began with these four stanzas, omitted in 1842: —

As when a man, that sails in a balloon,
  Downlooking sees the solid shining ground
Stream from beneath him in the broad blue noon, —
  Tilth, hamlet, mead and mound:

And takes his flags and waves them to the mob,
  That shout below, all faces turned to where
Glows rubylike the far-up crimson globe,
  Filled with a finer air:

So, lifted high, the Poet at his will
  Lets the great world flit from him, seeing all,
Higher thro' secret splendours mounting still,
  Selfpoised, nor fears to fall,

Hearing apart the echoes of his fame.
  While I spoke thus, the seedsman, memory,
Sowed my deepfurrowed thought with many a name
  Whose glory will not die.

The next four stanzas are the four that now begin the poem, and have not been altered.
  Then follow these two stanzas, omitted in 1842: —

In every land I thought that, more or less,
  The stronger sterner nature overbore
The softer, uncontrolled by gentleness
  And selfish evermore:

And whether there were any means whereby,
  In some far aftertime, the gentler mind
Might reassume its just and full degree
  Of rule among mankind.

In the next thirty-one stanzas the only changes are the following: —
In line 23 'pass'd' was at first 'scream'd;' in 69-71 'Growths of' was 'Clasping,' and 'Their humid' was 'Its twined.'
Line 106 until 1884 was 'Which yet to name my spirit loathes and fears.'
The 28th stanza was originally: —

The tall masts quiver'd as they lay afloat,
  The temples and the people and the shore,
One drew a sharp knife thro' my tender throat
  Slowly, — and nothing more.

This was ridiculed by Lockhart (Scott's son-in-law) in the 'Quarterly Review,' July, 1833: 'What touching simplicity! What genuine pathos! *He cut my throat — nothing more!* One might indeed ask *what more she would have.*' Some critics have supposed that this led the poet to alter the stanza; but he allowed it to stand in 1842 and for at least ten years more. It is more likely that the alteration was made in order to conform to the classical story. It is not now said that Iphigenia's throat *was* cut; we may assume that she was snatched away just as the knife touched it. However that may be, the critics are divided on the question whether the alteration is for the better. For myself I must confess that I was troubled by the change from the first person to the third in 'The bright death quiver'd at the victim's throat,' until the poet explained it to me thus: 'The high masts flickered, the crowds, the shore, the whole landskip shook, the bright death quivered, everything reeled before her — even, perhaps, her own personality.'

After 140 the early version goes on thus: —

By him great Pompey dwarfs and suffers pain,
  A mortal man before immortal Mars;
The glories of great Julius lapse and wane,
  And shrink from suns to stars.

That man, of all the men I ever knew,
  Most touched my fancy. O! what days and nights
We had in Egypt, ever reaping new
  Harvest of ripe delights,

Realmdraining revels! Life was one long feast.
  What wit! what words! what sweet words, only made
Less sweet by the kiss that broke 'em, liking best
  To be so richly stayed!

What dainty strifes, when fresh from war's alarms,
  My Hercules, my gallant Antony,
My mailed captain, leapt into my arms,
  Contented there to die.

And in those arms he died; I heard my name
  Sigh'd forth with life: then I shook off all fear;
O what a little snake stole Cæsar's fame!
  What else was left? look here.

All this portion of the poem remained without alteration until 1845.

Stanzas 40–72 (lines 157–288) stand as in 1833, except that line 166 had originally 'Touch'd' for 'Struck;' line 22 had 'in his den;' and the reading in 267, 268 was: —

Ere I saw her that in her latest trance
Clasped her dead father's heart [*sic*], or Joan of Arc,
  etc.

Line 27. *The tortoise creeping to the wall.* That is, the *testudo* of ancient warfare.

Line 54. *In an old wood.* This is like Dante's 'selva oscura,' and, as Palgrave notes, is 'an image of the past.'

Line 85. *A lady.* Helen, 'the Greek woman' of 'Œnone.'

Line 100. *One that stood beside.* Iphigenia.

Line 127. *A queen, with swarthy cheeks.* The poet describes her, as Shakespeare does ('Antony and Cleopatra,' i. 5. 28), 'with Phœbus' amorous pinches black;' but the reference to 'the polished argent of her breast' below (158) shows that he did not forget her Hellenic origin. She was the daughter of Ptolemy Auletes and a lady of Pontus.

Line 155. *Of the other.* That is, Octavius.

Line 259. *To Fulvia's waist.* Cleopatra puts the name of the wife of her paramour Antony for that of Eleanor, the wife of Rosamond's paramour.

Line 263. *The captain of my dreams.* Venus, the morning star, — the leader or inspirer of the poet's dreams of fair women, herself the fairest of her sex. This interpretation, given in my 'Select Poems of Tennyson,' in 1884, was disputed by some critics, who supposed the sun to be meant; but Lord Tennyson assured me that I was right. The sun has not risen, but the morning star is up, and the dawn is broadening and brightening in the east.

Line 266. *Her who clasp'd in her last trance, etc.* Margaret Roper, the daughter of Sir Thomas More. After his execution his head was exposed on London Bridge, but she obtained permission to take it down, and, after preserving it as a precious relic till her death, was buried with it in her arms.

Line 269. *Or her who knew that Love can vanquish Death, etc.* Eleanor, queen of Edward I. of England, who accompanied her husband to the Holy Land in 1269. There he was stabbed in the arm with a dagger which was believed to have been poisoned; and Eleanor instantly applied her lips to the wound and sucked the blood until the surgeons were ready to dress it.

Page 58. THE BLACKBIRD.
The only changes from the earlier version are in the 1st line of the 3d stanza, which originally was 'Yet tho' I spared thee kith and kin,' with 'jennetin' in the rhyme; in the 1st line of the 5th stanza, originally, 'I better brook the brawling stares,' and in the 3d line 'Not hearing thee at all,' etc.

THE DEATH OF THE OLD YEAR.
Unchanged except in the 1st line, which originally had 'winter's snow,' and the 5th line of the 5th stanza, which had 'one o'clock,'— a curious slip. Of course the poet knew that the year ends at midnight; but for the moment he seems to have thought of *one o'clock* as the beginning instead of the end of the *first hour* in the new year.

Page 59. TO J. S.
Addressed to James Spedding. The 2d stanza originally began 'My heart this knowledge,' etc., with 'it' for 'I' in the next line. The 8th stanza had 'mild' for 'bold;' the 13th had 'sunken' for 'fallen;' the 14th, 'my tablets' for 'the letters;' the 16th, 'holy' for 'only;' and the 17th, 'Although to calm you I would take.'

Page 60. ON A MOURNER.
The 2d stanza had at first 'hums' for 'humm'd.'

'YOU ASK ME WHY,' etc.
A writer in the 'British Quarterly Review' for October, 1880 (vol. 72, p. 282), says that this and the two following poems were based upon a speech delivered by a friend of the poet's (James Spedding, according to others who have told the story) before the Cambridge Union when the young men were at the University. Lord Tennyson, however, wrote me: 'The speech at the Cambridge Union is purely mythical; at least I never heard it, and no poem of mine was ever founded upon it.'

In line 11 the original reading was, 'Where freedom broadens slowly down.' The change was evidently made to avoid the juxtaposition of sibilants, which Tennyson particularly disliked. See note on 'In Memoriam,' xl. line 5.

'OF OLD SAT FREEDOM ON THE HEIGHTS.'
In the 4th stanza 'Who, Godlike, grasps the triple forks' does not allude to Neptune with his trident, but to Jove with his thunderbolts ('trisulca fulmina'), — an explanation confirmed by Lord Tennyson.

Page 61. 'LOVE THOU THY LAND,' etc.
The first reading in line 71 was ' the boasting words we said.'

Page 62. ENGLAND AND AMERICA IN 1782.
According to Mr. R. H. Shepherd (' Bibliography of Tennyson,' 1896), this poem was ' contributed to an American newspaper in 1872.'

Page 63. THE EPIC: MORTE D'ARTHUR.
Slightly retouched since 1842. The 'Morte d'Arthur ' has been incorporated, with no other change than the omission of a single line ('Sir Bedivere, the last of all his knights '), in 'The Passing of Arthur,' the last of the 'Idylls of the King;' but it has continued to be included, with the original introduction and conclusion, in the complete editions of Tennyson.

The poem was written as early as 1833, as allusions to it in the correspondence of that year (' Memoir,' vol. i. pp. 129, 131) clearly prove. This is two years earlier than the mention of it by Landor, quoted on p. 302 above.

Line 27. ' What came of that ? ' ' You know,' said Frank, etc. The original reading was : —

What came of that ? ' ' You know,' said Frank, ' he flung
His epic of King Arthur in the fire '—
And then to me, etc.

Line 38. Remodel models ? these twelve books of mine, etc. Originally thus: —

Remodel models rather than the life ?
And these twelve books of mine (to say the truth)
Were faint Homeric echoes, etc.

Line 107. With diamond sparks. The reading until 1853 was ' diamond studs.'
Line 111. This way and that dividing the swift mind. Compare Virgil, ' Æneid,' iv. 285: ' Atque animum nunc huc celerem, nunc dividit illuc.'

Page 65. Line 134. Across the ridge, and paced beside the mere. This line was added in 1853.

Page 68. THE GARDENER'S DAUGHTER.
The only change since 1842 is ' faltering ' for ' lisping ' in line 230.

Page 72. DORA.
This poem is remarkable for the complete absence of figurative language and every form of ' poetic diction,' — unless possibly the repetition of

The reapers reaped,
And the sun fell, and all the land was dark,

may be so called.

Page 75. WALKING TO THE MAIL.
In 1842 the poem began thus: —

John. I 'm glad I walk'd. How fresh the country looks !
Is yonder planting where this byway joins
The turnpike ?

James.   Yes.
John.   And when does this come by ?
James. The mail ? at one o'clock.
John.   What is it now ?
James. A quarter to.
John.   Whose house is that I see
Beyond the water mills ?
James.   Sir Edward Head's:
But he 's abroad; the place is to be sold.

Line 22. You saw the man, etc. Until 1851 the reading was as follows: —

James. You saw the man but yesterday:
He pick'd the pebble from your horse's foot.
His house was haunted by a jolly ghost
That rummaged like a rat. No servant stay'd.

Line 72. I myself. Originally, ' I that am.'
Line 78. We paid in person, etc. The reading in 1842 was: —

We paid in person, scored upon the part
Which cherubs want. He had a sow, sir.

Page 77. EDWIN MORRIS.
For line 22, ' finished to the finger-nail,' compare Horace, ' Satires,' i. v. 32: —

Capitoque simul Fonteius, ad unguem
Factus homo.

Line 78. Shall not Love to me, etc. Compare Catullus, ' Carmina,' xlv.: —

Hoc ut dixit, Amor, sinistram ut ante,
Dextram sternuit approbationem.

Line 110. The sweet-gale. The Myrica Gale, a shrub growing in marshes in Northern Europe, called ' sweet-gale ' from its aromatic odor.

Page 82. THE TALKING OAK.
Since 1842 only two slight changes have been made: ' For ah ! my friend, the days were brief ' (line 84) instead of ' For oh ! the Dryad-days were brief; ' and ' The murmurs of the drum and fife ' (line 215) for ' The whispers of the drum and fife.'

Line 47. Bluff Harry. Henry VIII.; his daughter Elizabeth being the ' man-minded offset ' of the next stanza.

Line 54. Till that wild wind made work, etc. The violent storm of the night when Cromwell died. The oak, as an old Tory, sneers at Cromwell, who, as some say, was a brewer.

Line 63. In teacup-times of hood and hoop, etc. The days of Queen Anne, when the affected pastoral poetry hit off in the next stanza was in vogue.

Line 181. I, rooted here among the groves, etc. Only a botanist can appreciate the blended poetry and science of this stanza.

Line 291. That Thessalian growth, etc. The oak grove at Dodona (in Epirus, not in the neighboring Thessaly), where the black dove, flying from Thebes in Egypt, alighted and proclaimed that an oracle of Jupiter should be established.

Page 85. LOVE AND DUTY.
The only change since 1842 (except ' who ' for ' that ' in line 75) is in 85–90, which then read: —

Should my shadow cross thy thoughts
Too sadly for their peace, so put it back
For calmer hours in memory's darkest hold,

If unforgotten ! should it cross thy dreams,
So might it come like one that looks content, etc.

Page 87. THE GOLDEN YEAR.
The original reading in lines 5-8 was: —

And found him in Llanberis; and that same song
He told me; for I banter'd him, etc.

Llanberis, a village to the northwest of Snowdon, is one of the points from which the mountain is ascended. On 'the counter side,' or the opposite side of the valley, are the 'lakes,' Llyn Padarn and Llyn Peris, and beyond them the heights of Elidyr-fach (2550 feet) and Elidyr-fawr (3033 feet).
Line 18. *Catch me who can, etc.* Alluding to a familiar children's game.
Line 29. *Seas that daily gain upon the shore.* Compare Shakespeare, 'Sonnet' 64. 5: —

When I have seen the hungry ocean gain
Advantage on the kingdom of the shore, etc.

Line 45. *Clear of toll.* There is to be universal 'free trade' in this 'good time coming.'
Line 63. *O'erflourish'd with the hoary clematis.* Covered with the flowers of the *Clematis vitalba*, the 'traveller's joy' of 'Aylmer's Field.'
Line 76. *From bluff to bluff.* In a letter received from Lord Tennyson, commenting on this and other passages, he says : '*Uff*, *uff* gives almost exactly the echo of the blasting as I heard it from the counter side to that of Snowdon.'
Page 88. ULYSSES.
When reading 'In Memoriam' to Mr. Knowles, the poet said: 'It is a very impersonal poem as well as personal. There is more about myself in "Ulysses," which was written under the sense of loss and that all had gone by, but that still life must be fought out to the end. It was more written with the feeling of his loss upon me than many poems in "In Memoriam."'
Line 10. *The rainy Hyades.* Compare Virgil, 'Æneid,' i. 748: 'Arcturum, pluviasque Hyadas, geminosque Triones.'
Line 16. *Delight of battle.* Peter Bayne refers to this as 'a superb translation of the *certaminis gaudia* of the Latin poet.'
Page 89. TITHONUS.
When it was published in the 'Cornhill Magazine' Thackeray was the editor, and was very proud of having secured the poem. The first line was originally 'Ay me ! ay me ! the woods decay and fall;' and line 39 had 'and that wild team.'
Line 25. *The silver star.* The morning-star.
Line 62. *Like that strange song I heard Apollo sing, etc.* See note on 'Œnone,' lines 39, 40.
Page 90. LOCKSLEY HALL.
In line 3 the original reading was 'and round the gables.'
Line 4. *Dreary gleams about the moorland, etc.* The construction of 'gleams' has been much disputed. I always regarded it as referring to the curlews, which in flying over the hall might seem like dreary gleams in the sky; and I was

gratified when this explanation (printed in my 'Select Poems of Tennyson' in 1884) was confirmed and aptly illustrated by Dr. Horace Howard Furness, who says (in a private letter which he permits me to quote here): 'The curlews have dusky backs, indistinguishable at twilight, but white breasts, and as they fly in coveys are not noticed until on wheeling they show for a moment these "gleaming" breasts. I saw them first when I was riding at sunset across the dreary plain of La Mancha in Spain, and I could n't imagine what these momentary flashes of light were until I happened to see a flock near at hand, when I involuntarily exclaimed "Locksley Hall !" and the line which had long puzzled me was explained.' But Lord Tennyson afterwards wrote me that the *gleams* are not curlews at all, and that '*dreary gleams flying* is put absolutely — while dreary gleams are flying.'
Dr. Furness also sent me two unpublished stanzas of 'Locksley Hall' which Mrs. Kemble transcribed many years ago into his copy of the edition of 1842. They were inserted after the 19th stanza ('And our spirits rush'd together,' etc.), and were as follows: —

In the hall there is a picture, Amy's arms are round my neck,
Happy children, in a sunbeam, sitting on the ribs of wreck.

In my life there is a picture, she who clasp'd my neck is flown.
I am left within the shadow, sitting on the wreck alone.

Since these were first printed in the 2d edition of the 'Select Poems,' the poet has introduced them, with slight changes, in 'Locksley Hall Sixty Years After.'
Line 9. *Locksley Hall, that in the distance overlooks the sandy tracts.* This is the original reading, altered in the 'Selections' of 1845 to 'Locksley Hall, that half in ruins overlooks,' etc.
Line 76. *That a sorrow's crown of sorrow, etc.* This is from Dante, 'Inferno,' v. 121: —

Nessun maggior dolore
Che ricordarsi del tempo felice
Nella miseria.

Line 162. *Swings the trailer from the crag.* Originally 'droops the trailer,' etc.
Line 182. *Let the great world spin for ever, etc.* Originally, 'Let the peoples spin,' etc. The next line had 'the world' for 'the globe.'
Line 184. *A cycle of Cathay.* 'Cycle' is used of course for an indefinitely long period, or an age; but some criticaster has plumed himself upon the discovery that a Chinese 'cycle' is less than fifty years (I forget the precise length); and somebody else takes the cycle to be the Platonic 'great year.'
Page 95. GODIVA.
The old story on which the poem is founded is thus told by Sir William Dugdale in his 'Antiquities of Warwickshire,' 1656 : 'The Countess Godiva, bearing an extraordinary affection to this place [Coventry], often and earnestly be-

sought her husband that, for the love of God
and the Blessed Virgin, he would free it from
that grievous servitude whereunto it was sub-
ject; but he, rebuking her for importuning him
in a manner so inconsistent with his profit, com-
manded that she should thenceforward forbear
to move therein ; yet she, out of her womanish
pertinacity, continued to solicit him, insomuch
that he told her if she would ride on horseback
naked from one end of the town to the other,
in sight of all the people, he would grant her
request. Whereunto she replied, " But will ye
give me leave to do so ? " And he replying
" Yes," the noble lady, upon an appointed day,
got on horseback naked, with her hair loose, so
that it covered all her body but her legs; and
thus performing her journey, she returned with
joy to her husband, who thereupon granted to
the inhabitants a charter of freedom. . . . In
memory whereof the picture of him and his
lady was set up in a south window of Trinity
Church in this city, about Richard II.'s time,
his right hand holding a charter with these
words written thereon : —

𝔍, 𝔏uriche, for 𝔏obe of thee
𝔇oe make 𝔠obentrp 𝔠ol-free.'

It is said that the inhabitants all withdrew
from the streets and from their windows while
the lady was passing through the city; but one
man, a tailor, could not resist the temptation
to look forth. He was struck blind at the mo-
ment, and to this day the effigy of ' Peeping
Tom ' may be seen in the upper part of a house
at the corner of Hertford Street as a monument
of his disgrace.

The ' Procession of Lady Godiva,' said to
have been instituted to commemorate the ser-
vice she rendered Coventry, has been satisfac-
torily proved to have originated in the reign of
Charles II. It was kept up annually until 1826,
and has been reproduced several times since.
In its palmy days it was graced by the presence
of the civic authorities, and was attended with
great pomp and display. Lady Godiva was
represented by a beautiful woman dressed in
a closely fitting suit of flesh-coloured material.
She was preceded by the city guards in old
armor with a band of music, and followed by
the mayor, aldermen, and sheriffs, the ancient
companies and benefit societies of the city with
their insignia and decorations, other bands of
music, and various historical and mythological
characters.

Line 3. *The three tall spires.* That of St. Mi-
chael's Church, 303 feet high (built 1373–1395),
that of Trinity Church, 237 feet high (built
1664-1667, to replace one blown down in 1664),
and that of Christ Church, which originally be-
longed to the Grey-friars' Monastery, founded
in the fourteenth century. The monastic build-
ings were destroyed in the time of Henry VIII.;
but the beautiful spire escaped, and was made
part of the present edifice built in 1832.

Line 11. *A thousand summers back.* Not to
be taken literally, Earl Leofric having flour-
ished in the first half of the eleventh century,

if we accept the tradition that he founded the
Benedictine Priory in Coventry in 1043. It is
said that both he and his lady were buried in a
porch of the monastery, of which some frag-
ments still remain.

Page 96. THE DAY-DREAM.

Line 15. *Then take the broidery-frame, etc.*
Originally, ' So take,' etc.

Line 78. *She lying on her couch alone, etc.*
The reading in 1830 was : —

> The while she slumbereth alone,
> Over the purpled coverlet
> The maiden's jet-black hair had grown.

' Purpled ' was retained in 1842. The first line
of the next stanza had in 1830 ' star-braided '
for ' star-broider'd.'

Line 81. *On either side.* The 1830 reading
was ' on either hand.'

Line 112. *Or scatter'd blanching on the grass.*
The early reading was ' in the grass.'

Line 126. *The Magic Music in his heart.*
Compare ' The Princess,' prol. 190 : —

> She remember'd that:
> A pleasant game, she thought: she liked it more
> Than magic music, forfeits, all the rest.

Line 129. *His spirit flutters, etc.* Misprinted
' The spirit flutters ' in the English one-volume
edition of 1884.

Line 149. *And last with these the king awoke.*
Originally, ' And last of all,' etc.

Line 158. *My joints are somewhat stiff.* The
early reading was ' something stiff.'

Page 99. AMPHION.

Line 33. *The linden broke her ranks, etc.*
Until 1853 this reading was : —

> The birch-tree swang her fragrant hair,
> The bramble cast her berry,
> The gin within the juniper
> Began to make him merry.

Line 92. *The spindlings.* Until 1850 the
reading was ' The poor things.'

Page 102. WILL WATERPROOF'S LYRICAL
MONOLOGUE.

The Cock tavern in Fleet Street, just inside
Temple Bar, was a favorite resort of the poet
and some of his friends during his early years
in London. The building was torn down sev-
eral years ago, but some of the furniture of the
grill-room, including a fine old oak fireplace,
was transferred to a new tavern with the old
name, on the other side of the street, opposite
Chancery Lane. One of the ancient tankards,
with the inscription, ' A pint-pot neatly graven,'
was presented by the proprietors to the poet,
who, in his letter of acknowledgment, said that
he would keep it as an heirloom in his family,
in memory of the vanished tavern.

Line 24. ' In ' was originally ' To.'

Line 35. *Against its fountain upward runs, etc.*
The reading until 1853 was this : —

> Like Hezekiah's, backward runs
> The shadow of my days.

Compare Isaiah, xxxviii. 8.

Line 142. *Till where the street, etc.* Origi-
nally ' With motion less or greater.'

Page 105. LADY CLARE.
Until 1851 the poem began thus: —

Lord Ronald courted Lady Clare,
    I trow they did not part in scorn;
Lord Ronald, her cousin, courted her,
    And they will wed the morrow morn.

The 16th stanza ('The lily-white doe Lord Ronald had brought,' etc.) was added in 1851.
Line 7. *They two will wed, etc.* Both the one-volume and the seven-volume editions of 1884 misprint 'They too.'
Page 107. THE LORD OF BURLEIGH.
The ballad is 'a narrative in verse, with the usual poetic licenses, of the wooing and romantic marriage of the tenth Earl and first Marquis of Exeter.' See Napier, 'Homes and Haunts of Tennyson,' pp. 103–111.
Page 109. SIR LAUNCELOT AND QUEEN GUINEVERE.
Line 34. *By night to eery warblings.* 'Warblings' is here a trisyllable (war-ble-ings), being lengthened after an Elizabethan fashion. Compare 'assembly,' 'resembleth,' 'fiddler,' 're-membrance,' etc. in Shakespeare.
Page 110. THE BEGGAR MAID.
For the old ballad on which the poem is founded, see Percy's 'Reliques.'
Page 114. To E. L. ON HIS TRAVELS IN GREECE.
Edward Lear was also the author of those classics of the nursery, the 'Nonsense Books.'
Page 115. THE PRINCESS.
The poem was at first received with little favor by the critics. 'It was thought scarce worthy of the author. The abundant grace, descriptive beauty, and human sentiment were evident; but the medley was thought somewhat incongruous, and the main web of the tale too weak to sustain the embroidery raised upon it' (Wace). Even so late as 1855, when the poem had received its last touches, the 'Edinburgh Review' said of it: 'The subject of "The Princess," so far from being great, in a poetical point of view, is partly even of transitory interest. . . . This piece, though full of meanings of abiding value, is ostensibly a brilliant serio-comic *jeu d'esprit* upon the noise about "women's rights," which even now ceases to make itself heard anywhere but in the refuge of exploded European absurdities beyond the Atlantic. A carefully elaborated construction, a "wholeness," arising out of distinct and well-contrasted parts, which is another condition of a great poem, would have been worse than thrown away on such a subject. . . . In reading the poem, the mind is palled and wearied with wasted splendor and beauty.'
On the other hand, there were a few eminent critics who were prompt to recognize the true merit of the poem. Professor James Hadley, of Yale College, wrote a long and appreciative review of it for the 'New Englander' (May, 1849), which has been reprinted in a revised form in his 'Essays, Philological and Critical.'
Charles Kingsley, in 'Fraser's Magazine' (September, 1850), said of the poem: 'In this work Mr. Tennyson shows himself more than ever the poet of the day. In it, more than ever, the old is interpenetrated with the new; the domestic and scientific with the ideal and sentimental. He dares, in every page, to make use of modern words and notions from which the mingled clumsiness and archaism of his compeers shrinks, as unpoetical. Though his stage is an ideal fairy-land, yet he has reached the ideal by the only true method — by bringing the Middle Age forward to the present one, and not by ignoring the present to fall back on a cold and galvanized Mediævalism; and thus he makes the "Medley" a mirror of the nineteenth century, possessed of its own new art and science, its own new temptations and aspirations, and yet grounded on, and continually striving to reproduce, the forms and experiences of all past time. The idea, too, of "The Princess" is an essentially modern one. In every age women have been tempted, by the possession of superior beauty, intellect, or strength of will, to deny their own womanhood, and attempt to stand alone as men, whether on the ground of political intrigue, ascetic saintship, or philosophic pride. Cleopatra and St. Hedwiga, Madame de Staël and the Princess, are merely different manifestations of the same self-willed and proud longing of woman to unsex herself, and realize, single and self-sustained, some distorted and partial notion of her own as to what the "angelic life" should be. Cleopatra acted out the pagan ideal of an angel; St. Hedwiga, the mediæval one; Madame de Staël hers, with the peculiar notions of her time as to what "spiritual" might mean; and in "The Princess" Mr. Tennyson has embodied the ideal of that nobler, wider, purer, yet equally fallacious, because equally unnatural analogue, which we may now meet too often up and down England. He shows us the woman, when she takes her stand on the false masculine ground of intellect, working out her own moral punishment; by destroying in herself the tender heart of flesh: not even her vast purposes of philanthropy can preserve her, for they are built up, not on the womanhood which God has given her, but on her own self-will; they change, they fall, they become inconsistent, even as she does herself, till at last she loses all feminine sensibility; scornfully and stupidly she rejects and misunderstands the heart of man; and then, falling from pride to sternness, from sternness to sheer inhumanity, she punishes sisterly love as a crime, robs the mother of her child, and becomes all but a vengeful fury, with all the peculiar faults of woman, and none of the peculiar excellences of man. . . . How Mr. Tennyson can have attained the prodigal fulness of thought and imagery which distinguishes this poem, and especially the last canto, without his style ever becoming overloaded, seldom even confused, is perhaps one of the greatest marvels of the whole production. The songs themselves, which have been inserted between the cantos in the last edition, seem, perfect as they are, wasted and smothered among the surrounding

fertility, — till we discover that they stand there, not merely for the sake of their intrinsic beauty, but serve to call the reader's mind, at every pause in the tale of the Princess's folly, to that very healthy ideal of womanhood which she has spurned.'

Mr. Dawson, in his 'Study of The Princess' (Montreal, 1884), remarks that the following extract from Rev. F. W. Robertson 'is perhaps the most justly appreciative criticism of Tennyson which has ever appeared.' It is from a lecture upon English Poetry, delivered to the workingmen of Brighton in 1852: —

'I ranked Tennyson in the first order,[1] because with great mastery over his material, — words, great plastic power of versification, and a rare gift of harmony, — he has also vision or insight; and because, feeling intensely the great questions of the day, — not as a mere man of letters, but as a man, — he is to some extent the interpreter of his age, not only in its mysticism, which I tried to show you is the necessary reaction from the rigid formulas of science and the earthliness of an age of work into the vagueness which belongs to infinitude, but also in his poetic and almost prophetic solution of some of its great questions.

'Thus in "The Princess," . . . he has with exquisite taste disposed of the question — which has its burlesque and comic as well as its tragic side — of woman's present place and future destinies. And if any one wishes to see this subject treated with a masterly and delicate hand, in protest alike against the theories which would make her as the man, which she could only be by becoming masculine, not manly, and those which would have her to remain the toy, or the slave, or the slight thing of sentimental and frivolous accomplishment which education has hitherto aimed at making her, I would recommend him to study the few last pages of "The Princess," where the poet brings the question back, as a poet should, to nature; develops the ideal out of the actual woman, and reads out of what she is, on the one hand, what her Creator intended her to be, and on the other, what she never can or ought to be.'

Mr. Dawson says well that 'Psyche's baby is the conquering heroine of the epic.' He adds: 'Ridiculous in the lecture-room, the babe, in the poem, as in the songs, is made the central point upon which the plot turns; for the unconscious child is the concrete embodiment of Nature herself, clearing away all merely intellectual theories by her silent influence. Ida feels the power of the child. The postscript of the despatch sent to her brother in the height of her indignation, contains, as is fitting, the kernel of the matter. She says: —

I took it for an hour in mine own bed
This morning; there the tender orphan hands
Felt at my heart, and seemed to charm from thence
The wrath I nursed against the world.

[1] The lecturer had divided poets into 'two orders; those in whom the vision and the faculty divine of imagination exists, and those in whom the plastic power

'Rash princess! that fatal hour dashed "the hopes of half the world." Alas for these hopes! The cause, the great cause, totters to the fall when the Head confesses —

I felt
Thy helpless warmth about my barren breast
In the dead prime.

Whenever the plot thickens the babe appears. It is with Ida on her judgment-seat. In the topmost height of the storm the wail of the "lost lamb at her feet" reduces her eloquent anger into incoherence. She carries it when she sings her song of triumph. When she goes to tend her wounded brothers on the battlefield she carries it. Through it, and for it, Cyril pleads his successful suit, and wins it for the mother. For its sake the mother is pardoned. O fatal babe! more fatal to the hopes of woman than the doomful horse to the proud towers of Ilion; for through thee the walls of pride are breached, and all the conquering affections flock in.'

While reading the poem with a class of girls many years ago, I remarked that the babe might almost be called its heroine. I was gratified to find my opinion confirmed by Mr. Dawson's; and more so to find it indorsed by the author, in the interesting letter to Mr. Dawson printed in the preface to the 2d edition of the 'Study.' Tennyson there says: —

'I may tell you that the songs were not an after-thought. Before the first edition came out I deliberated with myself whether I should put songs in between the separate divisions of the poem: again, I thought, the poem will explain itself; but the public did not see that the child, as you say, was the heroine of the piece, and at last I conquered my laziness, and inserted them. You would be still more certain that the child was the heroine, if, instead of the first song as it now stands,

As thro' the land at eve we went,

I had printed the first song which I wrote, — "The Losing of the Child." The child is sitting on the bank of a river, and playing with flowers: a flood comes down — a dam has been broken thro' — the child is borne down by the flood — the whole village distracted; after a time the flood has subsided — the child is thrown safe and sound again upon the bank, and all the women are in raptures. I quite forget the words of the ballad, but I think I may have it somewhere.'

There are also some admirable comments on 'The Princess' in Mr. E. C. Stedman's 'Victorian Poets.' 'Other works of our poet,' he says, 'are greater, but none is so fascinating as this romantic tale, — English throughout, yet combining the England of Cœur-de-Lion with that of Victoria in one bewitching picture.'

The Prologue. The scene of the Prologue was suggested by Park House, the residence of Mr. Edmund Lushington, who had married the

of shaping predominates, — the men of poetic inspiration, and the men of poetic taste.'

poet's sister Cecilia. In some reminiscences contributed to the ' Memoir ' (vol. i. p. 203), Mr. Lushington says: ' He was present on July 6th, 1842, at a festival of the Maidstone Mechanics' Institute held in our Park, of which he has introduced a lively description in the beginning of " The Princess." '

Line 9. *Five others: we were seven at Vivianplace.* Added in the 3d edition.

Line 20. *Laborious orient ivory, sphere in sphere.* Referring to Chinese ivory balls within balls. The line is a striking example of the correspondence of sound and sense, the words seeming to roll round like the ' sphere in sphere.'

Lines 35-49. *O miracle of women . . . the gallant glorious chronicle.* Added in the 5th edition of the poem.

Line 69. *Whom the electric shock.* The 1st American edition misprints ' from the electric shock.'

Line 80. *Went hand in hand with science.* The early editions [1] have ' With science hand in hand went.'

Lines 131-138. *Ah, were I something great ! . . . with her curls.* For these eight lines the early editions have only the following: —

O, were I some great Princess, I would build
Far off from men a college of my own,
And I would teach them all things: you should see.

Lines 176-179. *We seven stay'd at Christmas up to read.* The early editions read: ' We seven took one tutor. Never man,' etc.

Lines 190-194. *She remember'd that . . . by themselves.* The early editions have: —

' I remember that:
A pleasant game,' she said; ' I liked it more
Than magic music, forfeits, all the rest.
But these — what kind of tales do men tell men,
I wonder, by themselves.'

Lines 197-208. *The rest would follow . . . Grave, solemn !* The early editions read thus: —

' The rest would follow; so we tost the ball:
What kind of tales ? Why, such as served to kill
Time by the fire in winter.' ' Kill him now !
Tell one,' she said: ' kill him in summer, too.'
And ' tell one,' cried the solemn maiden aunt.
' Why not a summer's as a winter's tale ?
A tale for summer as befits the time;
And something it should be to suit the place,
Grave, moral, solemn, like the mouldering walls
About us.'

Line 211. *Like a ghostly woodpecker.* The first four editions have: ' an April woodpecker.'

Lines 214-239. *Turn'd to me, . . . the story and the songs.* In the early editions the remainder of the Prologue reads thus: —

turn'd to me: ' Well — as you will —
Just as you will,' she said; ' be, if you will,
Yourself your hero.' ' Look, then,' added he,
' Since Lilia would be princess, that you stoop
No lower than a prince.' To which I said,
' Take care then that my tale be follow'd out

[1] By the ' early editions ' I mean the 1st and 2d, unless otherwise stated.

By all the lieges in my royal vein:
But one that really suited time and place
Were such a medley, we should have him back
Who told the Winter's Tale to do it for us:
A Gothic ruin, and a Grecian house,
A talk of college and of ladies' rights,
A feudal knight in silken masquerade,
And there with shrieks and strange experiments,
For which the good Sir Ralph had burnt them all,
The nineteenth century gambols on the grass.
No matter; we will say whatever comes:
Here are we seven: if each man takes his turn
We make a sevenfold story:' then began.

Line 222 was added in the 5th edition.

Part I. Line 2 is not in the early editions.

Lines 5-21. *There lived an ancient legend, etc.* This passage, like all the others referring to the ' weird seizures,' was added in the 5th edition. For ' mutter'd epilepsy ' the original reading was ' call'd it catalepsy.'

I am inclined to agree with Dawson that ' these additions seem not only unnecessary and uncalled for, but are actually injurious to the unity of the work.' He adds: ' They confuse the simple conception of his character, and graft on to his personality the foreign and somewhat derogatory idea of catalepsy; for in that light does the court doctor regard them. The poet must have had some definite object in inserting them. Can it be that they are to indicate the weakness and incompleteness of the poet side of the Prince's character until he has found rest in his ideal ? Then only can he say: —

My doubts are dead,
My haunting sense of hollow shows; the change,
This truthful change, in thee has killed it.

' The dreamy Prince, haunted by doubts, and living in shadow-land, by the healing influence of a happy love, wakes up to the purpose and dignity of life.'

Line 23. *Half-canoniz'd by all that look'd on her.* The early editions read: ' And nearly canoniz'd by all she knew.'

Line 26. *He cared not for the affection of the house.* This line is not in the early editions.

Line 33. *Proxy-wedded with a bootless calf.* Marriage by proxy was common in the Middle Ages. For another instance in poetry — an historical one — compare Longfellow's ' Belfry of Bruges ' : —

I beheld proud Maximilian, kneeling humbly on the ground;
I beheld the gentle Mary hunting with her hawk and hound;
And her lighted bridal chamber, where a duke slept with the queen,
And the armed guard around them, and the sword unsheathed between.

The author's note on the passage says: ' Marie de Valois, Duchess of Burgundy, was left by the death of her father, Charles-le-Téméraire, at the age of twenty, the richest heiress of Europe. She came to Bruges, as Countess of Flanders, in 1477, and in the same year was married by proxy to the Archduke Maximilian. According to the custom of the time, the Duke of Bavaria, Maximilian's substitute, slept with the princess. They were both in complete dress, separated by a naked sword, and attended by four armed guards.'

Bacon, in his 'Henry VII.,' tells of the proxy marriage of this Maximilian, when King of the Romans, with Anne, the heiress of Brittany, in 1489: 'The king having thus upheld the reputation of Maximilian, advised him now to press on his marriage with Britain to a conclusion, which Maximilian accordingly did; and so far forth prevailed, both with the young lady and with the principal persons about her, as the marriage was consummated by proxy, with a ceremony at that time in those parts new. For she was not only publicly contracted, but stated, as a bride, and solemnly bedded; and after she was laid, there came in Maximilian's ambassador, with letters of procuration, and in the presence of sundry noble personages, men and women, put *his leg, stript naked to the knee*, between the espousal sheets; to the end, that the ceremony might be thought to amount to a consummation and actual knowledge.'

In the present instance, as Ida afterwards urged (p. 124), the marriage was 'invalid,' since her 'will sealed not the bond.' According to both canon and civil law, consent was the only basis of marriage; and it was necessary, moreover, that the parties should have arrived at years of discretion. There were different opinions as to this age, but it was never assumed to be as early as 'eight years.'

Line 36. *Youths of puissance.* The reading of the first five editions is 'knights of puissance.'

Line 55. *And almost my half-self, etc.* The early editions read: —

My shadow, my half-self, for still we moved
Together, kin as horse's eye and ear.

Line 65. *Cook'd his spleen.* Compare the figurative use of the Latin *coquere* in Plautus, Livy, Cicero, etc.

Line 80. *And Cyril whisper'd.* The early editions have 'Then whisper'd Cyril.' Of course they do not contain the next three lines. In 84 they have 'Trust me' for 'Take me;' in 86, 'Replied the king, "You shall not; I myself;"' and in 87 'these pretty maiden fancies.'

Line 96. *A wind arose and rush'd upon the South.* Wace ('Alfred Tennyson,' Edinburgh, 1881) compares Shelley, 'Prometheus Unbound,' ii. 1: —

A wind arose among the pines; it shook
The clinging music from their boughs, and then
Low, sweet, faint sounds, like the farewell of ghosts,
Were heard; 'O, follow, follow, follow me!'

Dawson remarks that the passage 'must have, consciously or unconsciously, dwelt in Tennyson's memory when writing these lines;' but the poet, in the letter to Dawson elsewhere quoted, says: 'I was walking in the New Forest. A wind did arise and —

Shake the songs, the whispers, and the shrieks
Of the wild wood together.

The wind, I believe, was a west wind; but, because I wished the Prince to go south, I turned the wind to the south, and the wind said, "Follow." I believe the resemblance which you note is just a chance one. Shelley's lines are not familiar to me, tho', of course, if they occur in the Prometheus, I must have read them.

'I could multiply instances, but I will not bore you, and far indeed am I from asserting that books, as well as nature, are not, and ought not to be, suggestive to the poet. I am sure that I myself, and many others, find a peculiar charm in those passages of such great masters as Virgil or Milton where they adopt the creation of a by-gone poet, and re-clothe it, more or less, according to their fancy. But there is, I fear, a prosaic set growing up among us, editors of booklets, book-worms, index-hunters, or men of great memories and no imagination, who *impute themselves* to the poet, and so believe that *he*, too, has no imagination, but is forever poking his nose between the pages of some old volume in order to see what he can appropriate. They will not allow one to say "Ring the bells," without finding that we have taken it from Sir P. Sydney, — or even to use such a simple expression as the ocean "roars," without finding out the precise verse in Homer or Horace from which we have plagiarized it (fact!).

'I have known an old fish-wife, who had lost two sons at sea, clench her fist at the advancing tide on a stormy day, and cry out, "Ay! roar, do! how I hates to see thee show thy white teeth!" Now, if I had adopted her exclamation and put it into the mouth of some old woman in one of my poems, I daresay the critics would have thought it original enough, but would most likely have advised me to go to nature for my old woman, and not to my own imagination; and indeed it is a strong figure.'

Then follows the passage quoted from the same letter on page 805 above.

Lines 103–105. *Cat-footed through the town, etc.* These three lines are not in the early editions. The next two read thus in the first two editions: —

Down from the bastion'd walls we dropt by night,
And flying reach'd the frontier: then we crost, etc.

The 3d edition (1850) has: —

Down from the bastion'd wall, suspense by night,
Like threaded spiders from a balk, we dropt,
And flying reach'd, etc.

Line 109. *Tilth and grange.* The early editions have: 'town and thorpe;' with 'tilth' for 'vines' in the next line.

Line 113. *Crack'd and small his voice.* The reading of 1st, 3d, and later editions. The 2d has: 'in voice,' — probably a misprint.

Lines 114, 115. *But bland the smile, etc.* These lines are not in the first two editions. The 3d has: 'But bland the smile that pucker'd up his cheeks.'

Line 121. *We remember love ourself.* All the editions, including that of 1898, have 'ourselves;' but as the poet has elsewhere changed the form to 'ourself' and in this very expression in v. 198, I have no doubt that he intended to do it here.

Line 133. *My very ears were hot To hear them.* The early editions omit from this point down to 145, reading thus: 'To hear them. Last, my daughter begg'd a boon,' etc.

Line 134. *Knowledge, so my daughter said, was all in all.* Some have thought this — and the idea of the poem — borrowed from Johnson's 'Rasselas': 'The Princess thought that of all sublunary things knowledge was the best; she desired, first, to learn all sciences, and then proposed to found a college of learned women, in which she would preside, that, by conversing with the old, and educating the young, she might divide her time between the acquisition and communication of wisdom, and raise up for the next age models of prudence and patterns of piety.'

Line 151. *We know not, — only this: they see no man.* The early editions read: 'We know not, — have not been; they see no men.'

Lines 163–172. *Our formal compact, etc.* The pointing and reading of the early editions are as follows: —

Our formal compact, yet not less all frets
But chafing me on fire to find my bride,
Set out once more with those two gallant boys;
Then pushing onward under sun and stars
Many a long league back to the North, we came,
When the first fern-owl whirr'd about the copse,
Upon a little town within a wood
Close at the boundary of the liberties:
There entering in an hostel call'd mine host, etc.

Lines 183–185. *She once had past that way, etc.* These three lines are not in the early editions, which go on thus: 'For him, he reverenced,' etc. Lines 183 and 185 were inserted in the 3d edition, but 184 not until the 5th.

Line 196. *We sent mine host to purchase female gear.* The early editions go on as follows: —

Which brought and clapt upon us, we tweezer'd out
What slender blossom lived on lip and cheek
Of manhood, gave mine host a costly bribe, etc.

Line 203. *We follow'd up the river, etc.* The early editions read: —

We rode till midnight when the college lights
Began to glitter firefly-like in copse
And linden alley; and then we past an arch
Inscribed too dark for legible, and gain'd
A little street half garden and half house;
But could not hear each other speak for noise, etc.

Line 213. *Clocks and chimes, etc.* Dawson remarks: 'The love of precise punctuality, so deeply implanted in the female breast, has full scope at last, as far as pretty clocks go. . . . Very properly, also, the path of knowledge, thorny to the tyrannous male, is made comfortable there. The ladies drink in science "leaning deep in broidered down," as is befitting. . . . Due attention is paid to dress also; the doctors are violet-hooded, and the girls all uniformly in white — gregarious, though, even there as in the outer world.'

Lord Tennyson, in a letter dated October 12, 1884, called my attention to this statement that the girls are 'uniformly in white.' He said: 'They were in white at chapel as we Cantabs were at our Trinity College Chapel in Cambridge; but . . . Lady Psyche's "side" (that is a Cambridge equivalent of "pupils") wore lilac robes and Lady Blanche's robes of daffodil colour. These two made the "long hall glitter like a bed of flowers." Dawson has lost half the splendour of the picture.'

Line 218. *Rapt in her song.* It is only the male bird that sings; but the poets generally follow the mythic ornithology which regards the nightingale as the transformed Philomela. See, however, 'The Gardener's Daughter': —

The redcap whistled; and the nightingale
Sang loud, as tho' he were the bird of day.

In the 'Recollections of the Arabian Nights,' the *bulbul* is made masculine, as in the Persian: 'the bulbul as he sang.'

Line 222. *Above an entry.* The early reading is 'Above an archway.'

Lines 237–241. *This I seal'd . . . Venus hung.* The early editions read: —

This I seal'd
(A Cupid reading) to be sent with dawn.

Line 239. *Uranian Venus.* The allusion is to Plato's 'Symposium': 'And am I not right in asserting that there are two goddesses? The elder one having no mother, who is called the heavenly Aphrodite — she is the daughter of Uranus; the younger who is the daughter of Zeus and Dione — her we call Common; and the Love, who is her fellow-worker, may and must also have the name of common, as the other love is called heavenly' (Jowett, 'Dialogues of Plato,' vol. ii.).

Line 244. *A full sea glazed with muffled moonlight.* The poet, in the letter to Mr. Dawson already referred to, says: —

'There was a period in my life when, as an artist, Turner, for instance, takes rough sketches of landskip, &c., in order to work them eventually into some great picture, so I was in the habit of chronicling, in four or five words or more, whatever might strike me as picturesque in nature. I never put these down, and many and many a line has gone away on the north wind, but some remain, e. g.:

'A full sea glazed with muffled moonlight. *Suggestion:* The sea one night at Torquay, when Torquay was the most lovely sea-village in England, tho' now a smoky town. The sky was covered with thin vapour, and the moon was behind it.'

Page 122. *Song.* The 3d edition has 'I went' for 'we went' in the 1st line. Lines 6–10 were omitted in the 4th edition, but restored in the 5th. The last line but one is not in the 3d edition.

Part II. Line 19. *Couch'd beside her throne.* The 1st American edition misprints 'crouch'd.'

Line 29. *Of use and glory to yourselves.* The early editions have: 'Of fame and profit unto yourselves.'

Line 38. *She replied.* The early editions have 'and she replied.'

Line 39. *We scarcely thought.* The early editions read: 'We did not think;' and six lines below: 'We think not of him.' They do not have lines 42–44.

Line 44. *Indeed.* The 3d edition has 'For us' instead of 'Indeed,' which was adopted in the 5th.

Lines 65–71. *That taught the Sabine how to rule.* The nymph Egeria, who was said to have given laws to Numa Pompilius. Compare 'The Palace of Art': —

> Or hollowing one hand against his ear,
> To list a footfall, ere he saw
> The wood-nymph, stay'd the Ausonian king to hear
> Of wisdom and of law.

The foundress of the Babylonian wall. Semiramis.

The Carian Artemisia. The queen of Caria who was an ally of Xerxes, and who fought so well at Salamis that the Persian monarch said his women had become men and his men women.

The Rhodope that built the pyramid. A famous courtesan of Greece who was said to have built a pyramid near Memphis with a part of the fortune she had acquired. According to Ælian, she afterwards married Psammetichus, King of Egypt. Compare Shakespeare, '1 Henry VI.' i. 6. 22: —

> A statelier pyramis to her I'll rear
> Than Rhodope's of Memphis ever was.

Clelia was a Roman girl, who, having been given as a hostage to Porsenna, escaped by swimming the Tiber on horseback. *Cornelia* is, of course, the mother of the Gracchi, and *the Palmyrene* is Zenobia. *Agrippina*, the granddaughter of Augustus, accompanied her husband Germanicus on his German campaigns.

Lines 71–80. *Dwell with these, etc.* This passage is not in the early editions, which read: 'Of Agrippina. Leave us: you may go.' The first part ('Dwell with these . . . which is higher') was added in the 3d edition, the remainder in the 5th.

Line 84. *She spoke and bowing waved.* The early editions read: 'So saying, she bowed and waved,' etc.

Line 98. *That whisper'd 'Asses' ears' among the sedge.* Tennyson follows Chaucer, who ('Wife of Bath's Tale') makes Midas confide the secret of his asses' ears only to his wife. Chaucer professes to follow Ovid, but, according to the Latin poet, it was Midas's barber that could not keep the secret.

Line 101. *This world was once a fluid haze of light, etc.* It would be impossible to summarize the nebular hypothesis more concisely or precisely than the poet has done it here.

On the lecture as a whole, compare Prior, 'Alma': —

> She kindly talked, at least three hours,
> Of plastic forms and mental powers,

> Described our pre-existing station
> Before this vile terrene creation:
> And lest we should grow weary, Madam,
> To cut things short, came down to Adam;
> From thence, as fast as she was able,
> She drowns the world and builds up Babel;
> Thro' Syria, Persia, Greece, she goes,
> And takes the Romans in the close.

Line 112. *The Lycian custom.* According to Herodotus, the Lycians differed from all other nations in taking their names from their mothers instead of their fathers, and in tracing their ancestry in the feminine rather than the masculine line.

Line 113. *That lay at wine with Lar and Lucumo.* That is, the Etruscan women, who, in the paintings at Volterra, are depicted as sharing the banquets with their husbands. 'Lar' or 'Lars' was an honorary appellation in Etruria, equivalent to the English *Lord*; and 'Lucumo' was a title given to the Etruscan princes and priests, like the Roman *patricius*.

Line 144. *Plato, Verulam.* Compare 'The Palace of Art': 'Plato the wise, and large-brow'd Verulam.'

Line 149. *And, last not least, she who had left her place.* The early editions have: 'And she, tho' last not least, who left her place.'

Line 169. *The slacken'd sail.* The early editions have 'her' for 'the.'

Line 184. *My vow binds me to speak, etc.* The early editions read: —

> I am bound
> To tell her. O, she has an iron will,
> An axelike edge unturnable, etc.

Line 224. *Bestrode my grandsire.* To defend him. Compare Shakespeare, 'Comedy of Errors,' v. 1. 192: —

> When I bestrid thee in the wars, and took
> Deep scars to save thy life;

and '1 Henry IV.' v. 1. 122: 'Hal, if thou see me down in the battle, and bestride me, so; 'tis a point of friendship.'

Line 240. *Woman, if I might sit beside your feet.* The early editions have: 'A woman,' etc.

Line 285. *I knew you at the first . . . to see you, Florian.* The early editions read: —

> You are grown, and yet I knew you at the first.
> I am very glad, and I am very vext
> To see you, Florian.

Line 291. *Then, a moment after.* The early editions have: 'and a moment after.'

Line 303. *April daffodilly.* The 'Quarterly Review' (vol. 82, March, 1848) says that daffodils are 'not April guests, but "take the winds of *March* with beauty"' ['Winter's Tale,' iv. 4. 120]. Commenting on this in a letter to me, Tennyson said: 'Daffodils in the North of England belong as much to April as to March. I myself remember a man presenting me in the streets of Dublin the finest bunch of daffodils I almost ever saw on the 15th of April. It amused me at the time, for I had just been reading the Quarterly article.' I may add that *ten days* of Shakespeare's *March* properly belonged to *April*, as we now reckon it.

Line 306. *Seen to wave and float.* The early editions have: 'seem to wave and float.'

Line 311. *Did not wish.* The early editions have: 'did not mean;' and in the next line, '*I* pray you,' etc.

Line 319. *The Danaïd of a leaky vase.* The allusion to the myth of the daughters of Danaus, condemned eternally to the hopeless task of filling a leaky vessel with water, seems a little pedantic here; but perhaps not more so than Melissa's reply. Both teacher and pupil are crammed with ancient lore.

Line 326. *That we still may lead.* The early editions have: 'that we may live to lead.'

Line 332. *Tho', madam, you should answer.* All the English editions down to 1890 point thus: 'Tho' madam *you* should answer,' etc. Even the small *m* in 'madam' (which in those editions is elsewhere printed with a capital) was not changed until 1884.

Line 333. *If you came.* The early editions have 'if e'er you came.'

Lines 347, 348. *For half the day, etc.* The early editions have: 'From room to room: in each we sat,' etc.

Lines 386–393. *What think you, etc.* The early editions have only the line, 'What think you of it, Florian? Will it hold?'

Lines 419–426. *Intent on her, etc.* The early editions read thus: —

Intent upon the Princess, where she sat
Among her grave Professors, scattering gems
Of Art and Science: only Lady Blanche,
A double-rouged and treble-wrinkled Dame,
With all her faded Autumns falsely brown, etc.

Line 402. *But thou.* The early editions have 'but come.'

Lines 442, 443. *Men hated learned women, etc.* The early editions read: 'Men hated learned women: and to us came;' and three lines below: —

That harm'd not: so we sat; and now when day
Droop'd, and the chapel tinkled, mixt with those, etc.

In the 6th line of the 'Song' that follows, the 3d edition has 'dropping moon' for 'dying moon.'

Part III. Line 7. *There while we stood beside the fount.* The early editions have: 'And while,' etc.; in line 10 'Or sorrow' for 'Or grief'; and in line 13 'and we demanding' for 'and when I ask'd her.'

Lines 33–41. *If they had been men, etc.* The early editions read: —

                    if they had been men,
And in their fulsome fashion woo'd you, child,
You need not take so deep a rouge: like men —
And so they are, — very like men indeed—
And closeted with her for hours. Aha!
Then came these dreadful words out, etc.

Line 34. *Set your thoughts in rubric.* That is, in *red*, like the rubrics in a prayer-book.

Line 55. *They mounted, Ganymedes.* Compare the picture in 'The Palace of Art': —

Or else flushed Ganymede, his rosy thigh
Half-buried in the Eagle's down,

Sole as a flying star shot through the sky,
Above the pillar'd town.

Line 67. *God help her!* The early editions have: 'God pardon her!' and below, 'the love of the Princess' for 'the heart of Ida.'

Line 75. *Yet my mother still.* The early editions have: 'only Lady Blanche' (the poet forgot who was speaking), and below, 'the Royal heart,' for 'her pupil's love.'

Line 90. *To the sphere.* That is, to the upper air. Milton, in 'Comus,' 241, calls Echo 'Sweet queen of parley, daughter of the sphere,' which has puzzled the commentators and given rise to sundry far-fetched explanations. In my opinion, 'daughter of the sphere' means daughter of the *air;* and the 'sphere-born harmonious sisters, Voice and Verse' of the same poet ('At a Solemn Music,' 2) are the *air*-born sisters. The dictionaries do not recognize this meaning of *sphere* (equivalent to *atmosphere*), but it is a Grecism of a simple sort, and furnishes an easy explanation of these otherwise perplexing passages.

Line 92. *But in her own grand way: being herself.* The early editions read: 'For being and wise in knowing that she is,' etc.

Line 97. *Hebes are they to hand ambrosia.* The early reading is: 'They are Hebes meet to hand ambrosia,' etc.

Line 99. *The Samian Herè.* Juno, or the Greek *Hera.* The island Samos was one of her favorite seats.

Line 101. *From the court.* The early editions have: 'from out the court.'

Line 103. *Balusters.* The accent on the second syllable is peculiar.

Lines 109, 110. *No fighting shadows, etc.* These two lines are not in the early editions.

Line 114. *I knock'd, and, bidden, enter'd; found her there.* The early editions have: 'I knock'd and bidden went in; I found,' etc. In the next line they have 'sally,' for 'move.'

Line 118. *As man's could be.* The early editions have: 'As man could be,' — connected of course with 'courteous' instead of 'phrase.'

Line 120. *Fabled nothing fair.* Told no plausible falsehoods; or 'minted nothing false,' as it reads in the early editions.

Line 126. *True — we had limed ourselves.* The early reading is: 'She said we had limed ourselves.'

Line 146. *Some palace in our land.* The early reading was 'A palace in our own land.'

Line 153. *That afternoon.* The early editions have: 'In the afternoon.'

Line 158. *Furrowy forks.* The early editions have: 'dark-blue forks,' and 'full-leaved' in the next line.

Lines 167–173. *I gazed, etc.* One of the passages added in the 4th edition.

Line 175. *Then from my breast.* The early editions have 'And' for 'Then,' and 'clomb' for 'got' in line 178.

Line 179. *Retinue.* Accented on the second syllable; as in 'Guinevere': 'Of his and her retinue moving they;' and in 'Aylmer's Field': 'The dark retinue reverencing death.' So

Milton, in the two instances in which he uses the word: 'Paradise Lost,' v. 355: 'On princes, when their rich retinue long;' and 'Paradise Regained,' ii. 419: 'What followers, what retinue canst thou gain?' and Shakespeare (the only instance in verse), 'Lear,' i. 4. 221: 'But other of your insolent retinue.'

Line 203. *As we ourself have been.* 'Ourselves' in the early editions, as elsewhere in the poem. I shall not refer to the other instances.

Line 207. *To lift the woman's fallen divinity.* The early editions have: 'To uplift,' etc.

Line 215. *Breathes full East.* Breathes the proud and defiant spirit of the Eastern queen. Dawson takes it to refer (as it may, incidentally) to 'the dry and unpleasant east-winds prevalent in England.'

Line 216. *On that which leans to you.* In regard to what suits your purpose, or favors your theories.

Line 246. *The one* POU STO. Alluding to the oft-quoted saying of Archimedes, 'Give me *where I may stand*, and I will move the world' (δὸς ποῦ στῶ, καὶ κόσμον κινήσω).

Line 250. *By frail successors.* The early editions have: 'Of frail successors.'

Line 256. *If that same poet-princess, etc.* The early editions read: 'If that strange maiden could,' etc.

Line 262. *Gynœceum.* The portion of the Greek house where the women had their quarters.

Line 285. *Diotima.* A wise woman of Mantinea, whom Socrates, in Plato's 'Symposium,' calls his instructress.

Line 293. *Those monstrous males that carve the living hound, etc.* Referring to vivisection, and the assertion that dogs have sometimes been fed with the fragments of the dissecting-room. The poet was one of the signers of the petition to Parliament against vivisection. Compare The Children's Hospital':

I could think he was one of those who would break their jests on the dead,
And mangle the living dog that had loved him and fawned at his knee —
Drenched with the hellish oorali — that ever such things should be!

Line 298. *Encarnalize.* Make carnal, sensualize; apparently the poet's own coinage, but since used by Hartley Coleridge, Canon Farrar, and others.

Line 316. *We rode a league beyond, etc.* The early editions read: —

we rode a little higher
To cross the flood by a narrow bridge, and came, etc.

Line 319. *O how sweet, etc.* The early editions have: 'And O how sweet,' etc.

Line 324. *The Elysian lawns.* Dawson takes these to be the plains of Troy, and 'built to the sun' to refer to the origin of the city, ascribed by Ovid to the music of Apollo's lyre. Compare 'Œnone,' 39. But the poet writes to me thus: 'The "Elysian lawns" are the lawns of

Elysium, and have nothing to do with Troy — or perhaps they rather refer to the Islands of the Blest (Pindar, *Olymp.* 2d).' 'Built to the sun' must then mean simply 'rising sunward, lofty.'

Line 331. *Fair Corinna's triumph.* Over Pindar, 'the bearded Victor of ten thousand hymns.'

Line 337. *With Psyche, with Melissa Florian, I.* The early editions read: 'With Psyche, Florian with the other, and I,' etc.

The 'Song' that follows was suggested by the bugle music of the boatmen on Lake Killarney; and Mrs. Anne Thackeray Ritchie ('Records of Tennyson, etc.' 1892) says: 'Here is a reminiscence of Tennyson's about the echo at Killarney, where he said to the boatman, "When I last was here I heard eight echoes, and now I only hear one." To which the man, who had heard people quoting the bugle song, replied, "Why, you must be the gentleman that brought all the money to the place."'

It may be noted that some of the most musical lines in the song are composed entirely of monosyllables.

Part IV. Line 1. *The nebulous star we call the Sun.* Dawson says: 'The Princess, with the accuracy taught only recently by the spectroscope, calls the sun *a nebulous star;*' but the expression implies no more than was taught by the nebular hypothesis of Laplace, to which reference has been made by Psyche above. This is the 'hypothesis' of the next line.

Line 17. *Fruit, blossom, viand, amber wine, and gold.* The early editions have: 'Fruit, viand, blossom, and amber wine and gold.'

Line 21. *Tears, idle tears, etc.* Mrs. Anne Thackeray Ritchie says ('Records of Tennyson, etc.'): 'One of my family remembers hearing Tennyson say that "Tears, idle Tears" was suggested by Tintern Abbey: who shall say by what mysterious wonder of beauty and regret, by what sense of the "transient with the abiding"?'

Line 47. *Cram our ears with wool.* No doubt suggested by the story of Ulysses stopping the ears of his companions with wax, that they might not hear the song of the Sirens.

Line 50. *A true occasion lost.* The early editions have: 'gone' for 'lost;' and the next two lines read thus: —

But trim our sails, and let the old proverb serve
While down the streams that buoy each separate craft, etc.

One might not guess 'the old proverb' here.

Line 59. *Kex.* A provincial word for the dry stalks of hemlock; here put for any wild growth springing up in the crevices of the mosaic pavement and breaking the beautiful work.

Line 60. *The beard-blown goat.* As the poet explains, in his letter to Dawson, this refers to 'the wind blowing the beard on the height of the ruined pillar.' The early editions read: —

The starr'd mosaic, and the wild goat hang
Upon the pillar, and the wild fig-tree split, etc.

Line 61. *The wild fig-tree.* Often referred to by the Roman poets as rending asunder ruined buildings and monuments. Compare Martial (**x.** 2): 'Marmora Messalæ findit caprificus.' See also Juvenal, **x.** 147.

'Ramage in his "Nooks and By-ways of Italy" (p. 69) is reminded of this passage by noticing a wild fig springing out of, and splitting a rock in the Apennines' (Dawson).

Line 65. *Then to me.* The first edition has: 'and then to me.'

Line 69. *A death's-head at the wine.* According to the Egyptian custom mentioned by Herodotus (i. 78): 'At their convivial banquets, among the wealthy classes, when they have finished supper, a man carries round in a coffin the image of a dead body carved in wood, made as like as possible in color and workmanship, and in size generally about one or two cubits in length; and showing this to each of the company, he says, "Look upon this, then drink and enjoy yourself; for when dead you will be like this."'

Line 85. *And her heart would rock the snowy cradle till I died.* Compare Shakespeare, 'Venus and Adonis,' 1185: —

Lo, in this hollow cradle take thy rest,
My throbbing heart shall rock thee day and night.

Line 88. *The tender ash delays To clothe herself, when all the woods are green.* This is botanically true, and is one of the many passages that show the poet's close obser̄ .tion of nature.

Line 100. *Like the Ithacensia.ι suitors in old time.* That is, like the suitors of Penelope, who do not recognize the disguised Ulysses, and laugh in a constrained way, they know not why. Compare 'Odyssey,' **xx.** 347: οἱ δ' ἤδη γναθμοισι γελώων ἀλλοτρίοισιν (literally, 'laughed with other men's jaws').

Line 104. *O Bulbul, any rose of Gulistan, etc.* The love of the nightingale for the rose is a favorite theme with Saadi and his brother poets. 'Gulistan' is Persian for rose-garden, and Saadi takes it as the title of his book of poems.

The 'marsh-diver' (or water-rail) and the 'meadow-crake' (corn-crake, or land-rail) are unmusical birds. Wood (quoted by Dawson) says of the latter that its cry 'may be exactly imitated by drawing a quill or a piece of stick smartly over the large teeth of a comb, or by rubbing together two jagged strips of bone.'

Lines 115-124. *Poor soul! etc.* These ten lines are not in the early editions.

Line 121. *Valkyrian hymns.* Such as were sung by the Valkyrs, or Valkyrias, 'the choosers of the slain,' or fatal sisters of Odin in the Northern mythology.

Line 125. *Would this same mock-love, etc.* The early editions have: 'I would.'

Line 130. *Owed to none.* The early editions have: 'due to none.'

Line 137. *Cyril, with whom the bell-mouth'd glass had wrought.* The early editions have: 'Did Cyril;' and 'begin' for 'began' in the next line.

Line 149. *Said Ida, 'home! to horse!' and fled.* The early editions read: 'Said Lady Ida; and fled at once, as flies,' etc.

Line 172. *Her maidens glimmeringly group'd.* The 2d edition misprints 'group.'

Line 174. *They cried, 'she lives.'* The early editions have: 'and crying.'

Line 180. *Across the woods.* The 1st edition reads: 'Across the thicket.'

Line 182. *The garden portals.* The early reading was 'The gates of the garden.'

Line 185. *The hunter.* Actæon. The 1st edition has: 'Of open metal, in which the old hunter rued,' etc.

Line 194. *The Bear.* The constellation *Ursa Major,* the 'seven slow suns' being of course the stars that form 'Charles's Wain,' or the 'Dipper.' The early editions print 'the bear.'

Line 196. *Then a loftier form.* The 1st edition has: 'and then.'

Line 202. '*How came you here?' I told him: 'I,' said he.* The early editions read: 'I found the key in the doors: how came you here?'

Line 215. *Or Psyche, she affirm'd not, or denied.* The first reading was: 'Or Lady Psyche, affirm'd not, or denied.'

Line 236. *But as the water-lily, etc.* Critics have compared Wordsworth, 'Excursion,' book v., where Moral Truth is said to be

a thing
Subject, you deem, to vital accidents,
And, like the water-lily, lives and thrives,
Whose root is fix'd in stable earth, whose head
Floats on the tossing waves.

Tennyson, in his letter to Dawson, gives as the 'suggestion' of this passage: 'Water-lilies in my own pond, seen on a gusty day with my own eyes. They did start and slide in the sudden puffs of wind, till caught and stayed by the tether of their own stalks — quite as *true* as Wordsworth's simile, and more in detail.' Dawson had said that Wordsworth's was 'the truer picture.'

Line 242. *Musky-circled mazes.* The early editions read: 'To thrid thro' all the musky mazes, wind,' etc.

Line 247. *Bubbled the nightingale.* Most aptly descriptive of the bird's warbling. Mrs. Anne Thackeray Ritchie says: 'Once, when Mr. Tennyson was in Yorkshire, so he told me, as he was walking at night in a friend's garden, he heard a nightingale singing with such a frenzy of passion that it was unconscious of everything else, and not frightened though he came and stood quite close beside it; he could see its eye flashing, and feel the air bubble in his ear through the vibration.'

Line 249. *Hook'd my ankle in a vine.* The early editions have 'took' for 'hook'd.'

Line 255. *The mystic fire on a mast-head.* The electrical phenomenon known to Italian and other sailors as 'St. Elmo's fires.' Compare Longfellow, 'Golden Legend': —

Last night I saw Saint Elmo's stars,
With their glimmering lanterns, all at play

On the tops of the masts and the tips of the spars,
And I knew we should have foul weather to-day.

Line 263. *Wail'd about with mews.* The early editions have: ' clang'd about with mews.'

Line 273. *In old days.* The early editions have: ' in the old days.'

Line 283. *To me you froze.* The early editions have: ' you froze to me.'

Line 323. *I came to tell you ; found that you had gone.* The early editions read: ' I judged it best to speak; but you had gone; ' in line 325 ' tell you ' for ' speak;' and in line 330 ' the merit ' for ' some sense.'

Line 343. *We take it to ourself.* The early editions have: ' assume it.'

Line 352. *A Niobean daughter.* The poet has another allusion to Niobe in ' Walking to the Mail ' : ' the Niobe of swine,'

Line 355. *And on a sudden rush'd.* The 1st edition has: ' ran in ' for ' rush'd.'

Line 356. *Out of breath, as one pursued.* The early editions have: ' all out of breath, as pursued.'

Line 366. *When the wild peasant rights himself, etc.* Referring to the incendiary fires so common in the troubles with the English agricultural laborers some years before the poem was written. The early editions have ' and the rick ' for ' the rick.'

Line 389. *Render him up.* The early editions have: ' deliver him up.'

Line 401. *Regal compact.* The 1st American edition misprints ' legal.'

Line 403. *Zealous it should be.* The early editions have: ' and willing it should be.'

Line 409. *Vague brightness.* The ' Quarterly Review,' (vol. 82), commenting on this, says: that ' no brightness can be more distinct than that of the moon ; ' but the purblind critic does not see that the poet describes it as it appears *to the baby.* The comparison is as true as it is apt.

Line 411. *Inmost south.* The early editions have: ' the inmost south; ' and in the next line, ' the inmost north.' In line 417 they have: ' tho' you had been' for ' had you been.' It will be noticed that these changes, like many before and after, are made to get rid of an extra unaccented syllable in the measure. Tennyson uses this ' license ' freely, to give variety to his verse (see Professor Hadley's criticism quoted in my edition of ' The Princess,' pp. 142-145). but he appears to have decided that in the early editions of the poem he had used it too often.

Line 426. *Landskip.* The earlier and better form of ' landscape.'

Line 430. *My boyish dream.* The early editions have: ' Mine old ideal.'

Line 450. *At her feet.* The early editions have: ' on the marble.'

Line 472. *Fixt like a beacon tower above the waves, etc.* Compare ' Enoch Arden ' : —

Allured him as the beacon-blaze allures
The bird of passage, till he madly strikes
Against it, and beats out his weary life.

Line 473. *The crimson-rolling eye.* It is a red

' revolving ' light. In the next line the 1st edition has: ' wild sea-birds ' for ' wild birds.'

Line 490. *We hold a great convention.* The early editions read: ' We meet to elect new tutors.'

Line 510. *You saved our life.* The early editions have: ' You have saved; ' and in the following lines: ' the wholesome ' for ' our good,' and ' tutors ' for ' servants.'

Line 524. *Your falsehood and yourself are hateful to us.* The early editions have: ' your face ' for ' yourself,' and ' loathsome ' for ' hateful.'

Lines 537-550. *While I listen'd, etc.* The early editions read: —

The voices murmuring; till upon my spirits
Settled a gentle cloud of melancholy,
Which I shook off, for I was young, and one
To whom the shadow of all mischance but came, etc.

Interlude. This was added in the 3d edition. There the song begins thus: —

When all among the thundering drums
Thy soldier in the battle stands;

and ends with

Strikes them dead for thine and thee.
Tara ta tantara.

In the 4th edition it was changed to its present form.

The following is another version of the song, printed in the ' Selections ' of 1865, but not included in the collected works : —

Lady, let the rolling drums
Beat to battle where thy warrior stands:
Now thy face across his fancy comes,
And gives the battle to his hands.

Lady, let the trumpets blow,
Clasp thy little babes about thy knee:
Now their warrior father meets the foe,
And strikes him dead for thine and thee.

Part V. Line 7. *Till we heard.* The early editions have ' until.'

Line 15. *There brake.* The early editions have ' out-brake.'

Line 23. *King, you are free.* The early editions have: ' You are free, O king.'

Line 28. *More crumpled than a poppy from the sheath.* This simile, like so many others, illustrates the poet's minute observation of nature. No flower that blows has a more crumpled and generally unpromising look when it first opens than the poppy.

Lines 30-35. *Then some one, etc.* The early editions read: —

' But hence,' he said, ' indue yourselves like men.
Your Cyril told us all.' As boys that slink, etc.

Line 42. *Here Cyril met us.* All the recent editions (down to 1898) have a period after ' us,' but this is clearly a misprint.

Line 70. *From brows as pale and smooth, etc.* Probably referring to Michael Angelo's *Pietà* in St. Peter's at Rome.

Line 110. ' *Look you,' cried my father, etc.* The early editions read here: —

'Look to it,' cried
My father, 'that our compact is perform'd.
You have spoilt this girl; she laughs at you and man:
She shall not legislate for Nature, king,
But yields, or war,' etc.

Line 117. *Our strange girl.* The early editions have 'child' for 'girl.'

Line 126. *At him that mars her plan.* The early editions have: 'At the enemy of her plan.'

Line 129. *More soluble is this knot.* The early editions add the line: 'Like almost all the rest, if men were wise;' and 'And dusted down your domes with mangonels' after line 132, 'Your cities into shards,' etc.

Line 136. *Flitting chance.* The first four editions have: 'little chance.'

Lines 145–151. *Boy, when . . . for shame!* For these seven lines the early editions have only the line: 'They prize hard knocks, and to be won by force.'

Line 188. *Pure as lines of green that streak the white, etc.* Another illustration of the poet's keen observation of nature. Most writers would have taken the *white* of the snowdrop as the emblem of purity (as Tennyson himself does in 'Saint Agnes'), but that delicate *green* seems more exquisitely pure, even beside the white.

Line 190. *Not like the piebald miscellany, man.* The early editions read: —

Not like strong bursts of sample among men,
But all one piece; and take them all in all, etc.

Line 195. *As frankly theirs.* The early editions have: 'as easily theirs.'

Line 215. *Our royal word.* The 1st American edition misprints 'loyal.'

Line 250. *The airy Giant's zone.* The belt of Orion.

Line 252. *And as the fiery Sirius alters hue, etc.* Dawson quotes Proctor's 'Myths and Marvels of Astronomy': 'Every bright star when close to the horizon shows these colors, and so much the more distinctly as the star is the brighter. Sirius, which surpasses the brightest stars of the northern hemisphere full four times in lustre, shows these changes of color so conspicuously that they were regarded as specially characteristic of this star, insomuch that Homer speaks of Sirius (not by name, but as the "Star of Autumn") shining most beautifully "when laved of ocean's wave," — that is, when close to the horizon.'

Dawson adds: 'The expression "laved of ocean's wave" explains the "washed with morning" of our poet. The glitter of the early morning sun on the bright helmets of the brothers, and the glance of light upon their armor as they rode, are vividly realized in this beautiful simile.' The passage of Homer is 'Iliad,' v. 5, thus rendered by Merivale: —

Flashed from his helm and buckler a bright incessant gleam,
Like summer star that burns afar, new bathed in ocean's stream.

Lines 262–300. *And, ere the windy jest . . . three to three.* The early editions read thus: —

and Arac turning said:
'Our land invaded, life and soul! himself
Your captive, yet my father wills not war:
But, Prince, the question of your troth remains;
And there 's a downright honest meaning in her:
She ask'd but space and fairplay for her scheme;
She prest and prest it on me; life! I felt
That she was half right talking of her wrongs:
And I 'll stand by her. Waive your claim, or else
Decide it here; why not ? we are three to three.'

I lagg'd in answer, loth to strike her kin,
And cleave the rift of difference deeper yet;
Till one of those two brothers, half aside,
And fingering at the hair about his lip,
To prick us on to combat, 'Three to three ?'
But such a three to three were three to one.'
A boast that clenched his purpose like a blow!
For fiery-short was Cyril's counter-scoff,
And sharp I answer'd, touch'd upon the sense
Where idle boys are cowards to their shame,
And tipt with sportive malice to and fro
Like pointed arrows leapt the taunts and hit.

The passage now stands as in the 5th edition. The 3d does not contain lines 268 and 276–279. In 268 it has 'But, Prince, the' for 'But then this'; in 280 'Yet' for 'And'; and in 282 and 288 (also in 314) 'Life !' for ''Sdeath !'

Line 284. *Her that talk'd down the fifty wisest men.* St. Catherine of Alexandria, daughter of Costis (half-brother to Constantine the Great) and Sabinella, Queen of Egypt. Maxentius during his persecution sent fifty learned men to dispute with her, but she confuted and converted them all.

Line 314. *'Sdeath ! but we will send to her, etc.* The early editions read: —

'We will send to her,' Arac said,
'A score of worthy reasons why she should
Bide by this issue,' etc.

Line 333. *Thro' open doors.* The early editions have: 'Thro' the open doors.'

Line 336. *Like a stately pine, etc.* The following is from the 'Remains of Arthur Hugh Clough,' dated in the Valley of Cauterets, Sept. 7, 1861: 'I have been out for a walk with A. T. to a sort of island between two waterfalls, with pines on it, of which he retained a recollection from his visit of thirty-one years ago, and which, moreover, furnished a simile to "The Princess." He is very fond of this place, evidently.'

Line 355. *Tomyris.* The queen of the Massagetæ, who, according to Herodotus (i. 214), defeated Cyrus the Great in battle, B. C. 529, and afterwards insulted his dead body.

Line 364. *O brother, you have known, etc.* The early editions read: —

You have known, O brother, all the pangs we felt,
What heats of moral anger when we heard, etc.

Line 367. *Of lands in which at the altar the poor bride, etc.* It was a Russian custom in the seventeenth century for the bride, on her wedding-day, to present her husband, in token of submission, with a whip made by her own hands.

Line 371. *Mothers . . . fling their pretty maids in the running flood, etc.* The reference is to the throwing of female infants into the Ganges, where the vultures are often seen to swoop down upon them before they sink.

Line 375. *That equal baseness lived in sleeker times.* The early editions have: 'That it was little better in better times.'

Line 380. *I built a fold for them.* The early editions have: 'we built' (but 'I set' just above); and the plural pronoun also in the following thirteen lines.

Line 384. *Rout of saucy boys.* The early editions have 'set' for 'rout;' and in 388 'old affiance' for 'baby troth.'

Line 391. *Since you think me touch'd.* The early editions have: 'think we are touch'd;' and 'nay' for 'what' in the next line.

Lines 395-397. *You failing, I abide, etc.* The early editions read: —

We abide what end soe'er,
You failing; but we know you will not. Still,
You must not slay him: he risk'd his life for ours, etc.

Lines 407-410. *Till she Whose name is yoked with children . . . following, etc.* The early editions read: —

till she
The woman-phantom, she that seem'd no more
Than the man's shadow in a glass, her name
Yoked in his mouth with children's, know herself,
And knowledge liberate her, nor only here,
But ever following, etc.

Line 419. *I think Our chiefest comfort, etc.* The early editions have: 'we think;' and in 424-427 they read: —

We took it for an hour this morning to us,
In our own bed: the tender orphan hands
Felt at our heart, and seem'd to charm from thence
The wrath we nursed against the world: farewell.

Line 441. *Look you!* The early editions have: 'Look to it.'

Lines 445-448. *But you — she's yet a colt . . . and brawl, etc.* The early reading is: —

but take and break her, you!
She's yet a colt: well groom'd and strongly curb'd,
She might not rank with those detestable
That to the hireling leave their babe, and brawl, etc.

Line 457. *For it was nearly noon.* The early editions have: 'it was the point of noon.' After omitting the next fourteen lines, 458-471, they go on thus: —

The lists were ready. Empanoplied and plumed
We enter'd in, and waited, fifty there
To fifty, till the terrible trumpet blared
At the barrier, — yet a moment, and once more, etc.

Line 480. *In conflict with the crash, etc.* The early editions have: 'In the middle with the crash,' etc. Of course, they do not contain the sentence, 'Yet it seem'd a dream; I dream'd Of fighting.'

Line 484. *And out of stricken helmets sprang the fire.* After this line, the 4th edition has the line (afterwards omitted): 'A noble dream! What was it else I saw?'

Line 491. *Mellay.* An anglicized spelling of the French *mêlée.*

Line 496. *And in my dream, etc.* The early editions read: —

and thinking thus
I glanced to the left, and saw, etc.

Line 506. *Let me see her fall.* The early editions have 'die' for 'fall.' They do not contain the sentence: 'Yea, let me make my dream All that I would;' nor line 510, 'His visage all agrin as at a wake.'

Line 514. *Flaying.* The early editions add 'off;' and in 517 they read: 'that the earth.'

Line 525. *Heavier.* The early editions have 'suppler;' and in line 530 below, 'life and love' for 'dream and truth.'

Song. In the 1st line the original reading was 'the warrior' for 'her warrior;' and in the last line but one, 'Like a summer,' etc.

A song first published in the 'Selections (1865), and not included in the latest editions of Tennyson's collected works, seems like an early draft of this one. It reads thus: —

Home they brought him slain with spears.
They brought him home at even-fall;
All alone she sits and hears
Echoes in his empty hall,
Sounding on the morrow.

The sun peeped in from open field,
The boy began to leap and prance,
Rode upon his father's lance,
Beat upon his father's shield —
'O, hush, my joy, my sorrow!'

Part VI. Lines 1-5. In place of these lines the early editions have only this: —

What follow'd, tho' I saw not, yet I heard
So often that I speak as having seen;

and for the next three lines: 'For when our side was vanquish'd and my cause.'

Line 15. *Babe in arm.* Compare 'The Palace of Art': 'Sat smiling, babe in arm;' and see note on the passage.

Line 16. *That great dame of Lapidoth.* See Judges, iv. 4 and v. 1 fol.

Line 40. *Growing breeze.* The early editions have: 'Æonian breeze.'

Line 47. *Blanch'd in our annals.* That is, fortunate, propitious; as the Latin *albus* was sometimes used.

Line 65. *The tremulous isles of light.* 'Spots of sunshine coming through the leaves, and seeming to slide from one to the other, as the procession of girls "moves under shade "' (Tennyson's letter to Dawson).

Slided occurs again (for the sake of the metre, as here) in 'Merlin and Vivien': 'Writhed toward him, slided up his knee and sat.'

Line 68. *Thro' open field.* The early editions have: 'Thro' the open field.'

Line 91. *And her hue.* The early editions have 'and all her hue.'

Line 110. *This great clog of thanks, that make.* The early editions have 'makes.'

Line 137. *But he that lay Beside us, etc.* The early editions read: —

but Cyril, who lay
Bruised, where he fell, not far off, much in pain,
Trail'd himself, etc.

Line 161. *Fixt in yourself.* All the editions have 'fix'd,' but elsewhere 'fixt.'

Line 166. *One port of sense.* Portal; as in Shakespeare, '2 Henry IV.' iv. 5. 24: 'That keep'st the ports of slumber open wide,' etc. The first four editions have 'part' for 'port,' perhaps a misprint. Wallace's edition of 'The Princess' explains 'port' as 'haven, from Latin *portus*,' and this is endorsed by the present Lord Tennyson; but I nevertheless feel confident that the poet had the Shakespearian use of the word in mind. The figure of the gate (*porta*) seems to me both more natural and more appropriate than the other. The reader can take his choice.

Line 171. *I will give it her.* The early editions have: 'and I will.'

Line 179. *No purple in the distance.* Compare 'In Memoriam,' xxxvii.: —

> With weary steps I loiter on,
> Tho' always under alter'd skies
> The purple from the distance dies,
> My prospect and horizon gone.

Line 185. *Helpless . . . barren.* The early editions have: 'waxen . . . milkless.'

Line 204. *Then Arac, etc.* The early editions read: 'Then Arac: "Soul and life!"' etc. They have the line: 'I am your brother; I advise you well' after line 206.

Line 209. *'Sdeath! I would sooner fight.* The early editions have: 'Life! I would sooner fight.'

Line 225. *I trust that there is no one hurt to death.* This line is not in the early editions.

Line 304. *Amazed am I to hear.* The early editions have: 'I am all amaze to hear.'

Line 313. *Rang ruin, answered, etc.* The speech that follows has been much abridged, the early editions reading thus: —

> Rang ruin, answered full of grief and scorn:
> 'What! in our time of glory when the cause
> Now stands up, first, a trophied pillar — now
> So clipt, so stinted in our triumph — barred
> Even from our free heart-thanks, and every way
> Thwarted and vext, and lastly catechised
> By our own creature! one that made our laws!
> Our great she-Solon! her that built the nest
> To hatch the cuckoo! whom we called our friend!
> But we will crush the lie that glances at us
> As cloaking in the larger charities
> Some baby predilection; all amazed!
> We must amaze this legislator more.
> Fling our doors wide!' etc.

Below (321) the reading was: —

> Pass and mingle with your likes.
> Go, help the half-brain'd dwarf, Society,
> To find low motives unto noble deeds,
> To fix all doubt upon the darker side;
> Go, fitter thou for narrowest neighborhoods,
> Old talker, haunt where gossip breeds and seethes
> And festers in provincial sloth! and you,
> That think we sought to practise on a life
> Risk'd for our own and trusted to our hands,
> What say you, Sir? you hear us; deem ye not

'T is all too like that even now we scheme,
In one broad death confounding friend and foe,
To drug them all? revolve it: you are man,
And therefore no doubt wise; but after this
We brook no further insult, but are gone.

The omissions here are the most important in the whole poem, and are certainly for the better. The briefer speech is the more dignified.

Line 332. *And on they moved.* The early editions have: 'And they moved on.'

Line 340. *Amazed they glared.* The early editions have 'amaze,' which, if not a misprint, is used as in the early reading of 304 above.

Song. This song is equally musical and monosyllabic. Of one hundred and twenty-five words in it all are monosyllables except *seven*, and those are dissyllables.

Part VII. Line 19. *Void was her use.* Her occupation was gone, like Othello's. Dawson quotes 'Aylmer's Field': —

> So that the gentle creature, *shut from all
> Her charitable use*, and face to face
> With twenty months of silence, slowly lost,
> Nor greatly cared to lose her hold on life.

Line 21. *A great black cloud, etc.* The poet, in his letter to Dawson, says that this was suggested by 'a coming storm as seen from the top of Snowdon.'

Line 23. *Verge.* Horizon; as iv. 29 above: 'below the verge.' Compare 'The Gardener's Daughter': 'and May from verge to verge.' The *slope* is an optical illusion.

Line 36. *Deeper than those weird doubts, etc.* This line is not in the early editions, the next beginning 'Lay sundered,' etc.

Line 60. *Upon the babe restored.* The early editions have: 'on what she said of the child' (see v. 101 above); and in the next line, 'would she yield' for 'yielded she.'

Line 68. *Were at peace.* The construction is confused; as if 'each' had been 'both.'

Line 96. *Flourished up.* 'Blossomed up' (ii. 292 above) the etymological sense of 'flourished.'

Line 109. *The Oppian law.* A sumptuary law passed when Hannibal was almost at the gates of Rome. It enacted that no woman should wear a gay-colored dress, or have more than half an ounce of gold ornaments, and that none should approach within a mile of any city or town in a car drawn by horses. After the war the women demanded the repeal of the law. They gained one consul, but Cato, the other one, resisted. The women harassed the magistrates until the law was repealed.

Line 111. *Dwarf-like.* The early editions have 'little.'

Line 112. *Hortensia spoke against the tax.* A heavy tax imposed on Roman matrons by the second triumvirate. No man was found bold enough to oppose it; but Hortensia, daughter of Hortensius the orator, spoke so eloquently against it that it was repealed.

Line 118. *I saw the forms, etc.* The early editions read: —

I saw the forms: I knew not where I was:
Sad phantoms conjured out of circumstance,
Ghosts of the fading brain they seem'd; nor more
Sweet Ida, etc.

In 122 below they have ' show'd ' for ' seem'd.'
Line 140. *She stoop'd, etc.* The 1st edition reads thus : —

She stoop'd ; and with a great shock of the heart
Our mouths met : out of languor leapt a cry,
Crown'd Passion from the brinks of death, and up
Along the shuddering senses struck the soul,
And closed on fire with Ida's at the lips.

The 2d edition changes ' Crown'd ' to ' Leapt.'
Line 148. *That other when she came, etc.* Bayard Taylor calls the passage ' an exquisite rapid picture of Aphrodite floating along the wave to her home at Paphos; but,' he adds, ' what must we think of the lover, who, in relating the supreme moment of his passion, could turn aside to interpolate it ? Its very loveliness emphasizes his utter forgetfulness of the governing theme.' It seems to me natural enough in the ' relating,' especially as it leads up to the impassioned

nor end of mine,
Stateliest, for thee !

which shows that he has dwelt upon the picture of the goddess because he half-identifies her with Ida.
Line 165. *The milk-white peacock.* Darwin (' Animals and Plants under Domestication ') speaks of a white variety of peacock.
Line 177. *Come down, O maid, etc.* This ' small sweet idyl,' like the exquisite song, ' Tears, idle tears,' was perfect from the first, and has undergone no revision at the author's hands. ' It transfers,' says Symonds in his ' Greek Poets,' ' with perfect taste, the Greek Idyllic feeling to Swiss scenery; it is a fine instance of new wine being successfully poured into old bottles, for nothing could be fresher, and not even the " Thalysia " is sweeter.'
All the editions have ' idyl ' here, as in the heading ' ENGLISH IDYLS AND OTHER POEMS.'
Line 189. *With Death and Morning on the Silver Horns.* In the early editions we find ' Silver Horns,' but all the more recent ones print ' silver horns.' The former is, of course, to be preferred, on account of the obvious reference to the Silberhorn, one of the peaks or spurs of the Jungfrau, and markedly the most silvery-white part of the summit, as seen from Interlachen and its vicinity.
The ' Memoir ' (vol. i. p. 252) tells us that this ' idyl ' was ' written in Switzerland (chiefly at Lauterbrunnen and Grindelwald),' and that the poet considered it among his ' most successful work.'
Morning walks on the mountains here, as ' o'er the dew of yon high eastern hill ' in ' Hamlet ' (i. 1. 167); and *Death* is her companion because life has no home on those ' Alpine summits cold,' or must face Death in attempting to scale them.
Line 191. *Firths of ice, etc.* Bayard Taylor

remarks that this would be ' almost incomprehensible to one who has not looked with his own bodily eyes upon the Mer de Glace.'
Line 198. *Water-smoke.* Compare ' The Lotos-Eaters : ' —

And, like a downward smoke, the slender stream
Along the cliff to fall and pause did seem.

Line 245. *Out of Lethe.* The poet may have been thinking of Wordsworth's ' Our birth is but a sleep and a forgetting; ' or of Virgil, ' Æneid,' vi. 748 : —

Has omnes, ubi mille rotam volvere per annos,
Lethaeum ad fluvium deus evocat agmine magno;
Scilicet immemores supera ut convexa revisant
Rursus, et incipiant in corpora velle reverti.

Lines 250–256. *How shall men grow ? . . . her own.* The early editions read : —

How shall men grow ? We two will serve them both
In aiding her strip off, as in us lies,
(Our place is much) the parasitic forms
That seem to keep her up but drag her down —
Will leave her field to burgeon and to bloom
From all within her, make herself her own, etc.

Line 261. *His dearest bond.* The early editions have ' whose ' for ' his.'
Line 268. *Nor lose the childlike, etc.* In place of this line the early editions have : ' More as the double-natured Poet each.'
Lines 313–320. *Said Ida, tremulously, etc.* The early editions read : —

Said Ida, ' so unlike, so all unlike —
It seems you love to cheat yourself with words:
This mother is your model. Never, Prince;
You cannot love me.' ' Nay, but thee,' I said,
' From yearlong poring on thy pictured eyes,
Or some mysterious or magnetic touch,
Ere seen I loved,' etc.

Lines 327–330. *Lift thine eyes, etc.* The early reading is : —

lift thine eyes; doubt me no more;
Look up, and let thy nature strike on mine, etc.

Line 335. *Is morn to more, etc.* The early editions have : ' I scarce believe, and all the rich to-come; ' and in 337, ' flowers ' for ' weeds.'
Bayard Taylor was troubled at this latter change, the first reading having suggested to him ' a more delicate fancy than the poet seems to have intended.' It gave him, not the view of an ' ordinary piece of farm-work,' but ' a vision of the autumnal haze slowly gathering from myriads of flowers as they burn away in the last ardors of summer.' This is a good illustration of the manner in which a person of lively imagination may ' read into ' poetry a meaning which is not there. Of course, all that Tennyson had in mind was the burning up of weeds in autumn, and the apparent wavering of the landscape as seen through the rising currents of heated and smoky air.
Conclusion. This part of the poem was almost entirely rewritten in the 3d edition. In place of the first thirty-two lines, the 1st edition has only the following : —

Here closed our compound story, which at first
Had only meant to banter little maids
With mock heroics and with parody:
But slipt in some strange way, crost with burlesque,
From mock to earnest, even into tones
Of tragic, and with less and less of jest,
To such a serious end, that Lilia fixt, etc.

The 2d edition changed 'Had only' in the second line to 'Perhaps, but.'
Lines 34–80. *Who might have told . . . garden rails.* For these forty-six lines the early editions have: —

who there began
A treatise, growing with it, and might have flow'd
In axiom worthier to be graven on rock
Than all that lasts of old-world hieroglyph,
Or lichen-fretted Rune and arrowhead;
But that there rose a shout: the gates were closed
At sundown, and the crowd were swarming now,
To take their leave, about the garden rails,
And I and some went out, and mingled with them.

The reference to the French Revolution seems out of place; and yet one would be sorry to spare the eight lines that follow ('Have patience,' etc.).
Line 102. *Why should not, etc.* The early editions read: —

Why don't these acred Sirs
Throw up their parks some dozen times a year,
And let the people breathe?

Line 108. *But spoke not.* The early editions have: 'Saying little;' and in 116, 'without sound' for 'quietly.'
Page 162. IN MEMORIAM.
Of the commentaries on the poem Professor John F. Genung's ('In Memoriam; its Purpose and its Structure,' 2d ed. Boston, 1884) seems to me the most satisfactory. Other valuable works are 'A Key to Lord Tennyson's In Memoriam,' by Rev. Alfred Gatty, D. D. (3d edition, London, 1885), for which the poet himself furnished some corrections and comments, which in this edition are printed in italics; 'Prolegomena to In Memoriam,' by Thomas Davidson (Boston, 1889); 'A Companion to In Memoriam,' by Elizabeth R. Chapman (London, 1888); and 'Tennyson and In Memoriam,' by Joseph Jacobs (London, 1892). See also the admirable studies of the poem in 'Phases of Thought and Criticism,' by Brother Azarias (Boston, 1892), pages 183–268; and in Rev. Stopford A. Brooke's 'Tennyson: His Art and Relation to Modern Life' (New York, 1894), pages 188–228. The 'Memoir' (vol. i. pp. 295–327) has much interesting matter not to be found elsewhere.
According to Professor Genung, the fundamental idea of the poem may be thus stated: —

'THAT LOVE IS INTRINSICALLY IMMORTAL.

'All the achievements of thought which make "In Memoriam" so victorious a poem are simply this idea raised to a higher power, with its interpretation for life and history.'
The 'framework' of the poem is tabulated by the same critic thus: —

PROLOGUE.

Introductory Stage. I.-XXVII.

PROSPECT	I.-VI.
DEFINING-POINT — BEGINNING	VII.
ARRIVAL AND BURIAL OF THE DEAD	XVII.-XX.

First Cycle. XXVIII.-LXXVII.

CHRISTMAS-TIDE	XXVIII.-XXX.
SPRINGTIDE	XXXVIII., XXXIX.
FIRST ANNIVERSARY OF THE DEATH	LXXII.

Second Cycle. LXXVIII.-CIII.

CHRISTMAS-TIDE	LXXVIII.
NEW YEAR	LXXXIII.
SECOND ANNIVERSARY OF THE DEATH	XCIX.

Third Cycle. CIV.-CXXXI.

CHRISTMAS-TIDE	CIV., CV.
NEW YEAR	CVI.
BIRTHDAY OF DECEASED (FEB. 1)	CVII.
SPRINGTIDE	CXV., CXVI.
DEFINING-POINT — END	CXIX.
RETROSPECT AND CONCLUSION	CXX.-CXXXI.

EPILOGUE.

Prologue. The form of stanza had been used by Lord Herbert of Cherbury and by Ben Jonson in his 'Underwoods.' Rossetti 'claimed to have rediscovered the metre in 1844' (Jacobs); but Tennyson had already used it in two poems written in 1833, though not published until 1842 ('You ask me why' and 'Love thou thy land'); and Jennings ('Lord Tennyson,' page 125) says: 'We have excellent authority for saying that, as far as Tennyson knew then, he thought he had invented the metre.' This is confirmed by the 'Memoir' (vol. i. p. 305).
Strong Son of God, immortal love. 'Immortal Love is recognized not only as an affection within us, but as an entity above us, . . . as a divine Object of faith and love, to be worshipped and obeyed, to be recognized as at the same time the source and the goal of our noblest life' (Genung).
I. 1.[1] *I held it truth, with him who sings, etc.* 'It may be stated, on the highest authority, that the special passage alluded to cannot be identified, but *it is Goethe's creed*' (Gatty). Brother Azarias remarks: 'Faust, in Goethe's great life-poem, emerges from the ruins of his dead self to a higher life and a broader assertion of selfhood. It is still the same self trampling upon the narrower and lower experiences of life.' Compare Longfellow, 'The Ladder of St. Augustine.' The passage of St. Augustine is in 'Serm.' iii.: 'De vitiis nostris scalam nobis facimus si vitia calcamus.'
'The "dead selves" of Tennyson are neither our vices nor our calamities; but, rather, our general experiences, which all perish as they happen' (Gatty).
II. 1. *Old yew, which graspest at the stones, etc.* When the poet wrote this he supposed that Arthur was buried in the churchyard, though a

[1] The references in these notes on 'In Memoriam' are to *sections* (or 'poems,' as Tennyson calls them) and *stanzas*, not to *lines*.

tablet to his memory was placed inside the church (lxvii.). Compare xxi. and xxxix.

3. *O, not for thee the glow, the bloom.* Some have foolishly inferred from this that the poet was not aware the yew blossoms, and that xxxix. was afterwards inserted to correct the error; but, as an italicized note in Gatty states, 'of course, the poet always knew that a tree which bears a berry must have a blossom; but sorrow only saw the winter gloom of the foliage.' The blossoming of the yew and the 'smoke' of its abundant pollen are referred to in the opening lines of 'The Holy Grail.'

4. *And gazing on thee, sullen tree.* The 1st edition misprints 'the sullen tree.'

III. 1. *What whispers from thy lying lip?* Sorrow 'clothes all nature in her own phantom hollowness, her own mourning garb; she blurs the truth, and it may well be that she should be stifled rather than cherished' (Chapman). I may state here that Miss Chapman's comments on the poem were cordially approved by the poet.

3. *With all the music in her tone.* The 1st edition has 'her music.'

IV. 3. *That grief hath shaken into frost.* Water may be cooled below the freezing-point if it is kept perfectly still; but if disturbed it becomes ice at once, and the sudden expansion may break the vessel containing it.

4. *Thou shalt not be the fool of loss.* The 1st edition misprints 'Thou shall.'

V. 2. *A use in measured language lies.* 'There is some negative relief in the exercise of expressing sorrow in metrical language. Poesy shall therefore be cherished for its practical office' (Genung).

VI. 5. *Ye know no more than I who wrought, etc.* Tennyson was writing to Arthur in the very hour his friend died.

VII. 1. *The long unlovely street.* Wimpole Street in London, where Arthur had lodgings at No. 67 (see page 162 above) while he was studying at Lincoln's Inn. There are many longer streets in the metropolis than Wimpole Street, which, even with its continuation as Devonshire Street, is barely half a mile from end to end; but it somehow got a local notoriety for its length. 'It is said of a celebrated clerical wit, that almost his last words were, "All things come to an end" — a pause — "except Wimpole Street"' (Gatty).

IX. 1. *Fair ship, that from the Italian shore, etc.* 'Many have been the endeavors to discover the name of the "fair ship" which brought home Hallam's remains, and thus trace her after-history, but all in vain. It seems, however, that she landed her precious freight at Dover, though the poet till a few years ago always believed that she had put in to Bristol' (Napier).

5. *Till all my widow'd race be run.* The line is repeated at the end of xvii. ; and 'More than my brothers are to me' in lxxix. 1.

X. 4. *Or where the kneeling hamlet, etc.* That is, in the chancel of the village church, near the altar rails.

5. *Should toss with tangle and with shells.* 'Tangle,' or 'oarweed' (*Laminaria digitata*), grows at extreme tide-limits, where its fronds rise and dip in the water.

XI. 1. *Calm is the morn, etc.* As the poet explained to Dr. Gatty, the scenery described 'does not refer to Clevedon, but to some Lincolnshire wold, from which the whole range from marsh to the sea was visible.'

XV. 5. *To-night the winds begin to rise.* The 1st edition has 'began.'

Stopford Brooke remarks here: 'The tempest begins with what is close at hand — the wood by which he stands at sunset: —

> The last red leaf is whirl'd away,
> The rooks are blown about the skies.

And then, after that last admirable line which fills the whole sky with the gale, he lifts his eyes, and we see with him the whole world below painted also in four lines [as in xi. 3.] — the forest, the waters, the meadows, struck out, each in one word; and the wildness of the wind and the width of the landscape given, as Turner would have given them, by the low shaft of storm-shaken sunlight dashed from the west right across to the east. Lastly, to heighten the impression of tempest, to show the power it will have when the night is come, to add a far horizon to the solemn world, he paints the rising wrath of the storm in the cloud above the ocean rim, all aflame with warlike sunset. It is well done, but whosoever reads the whole will feel that the storm of the human heart is higher than the storm of Nature.'

XVI. 1. *Calm despair and wild unrest.* The former expressed in xi., the latter in xv. He asks whether such alternations of feeling are possible. 'Is his sorrow variable? Or do these changes affect the surface merely of his deep-seated grief? Or, again, has his reason been unhinged by grief?' (Chapman).

XVIII. 1. *The violet of his native land.* Compare 'Hamlet,' v. 1. 262: —

> And from her fair and unpolluted flesh
> May violets spring!

3. *Come then, pure hands, and bear the head, etc.* The bearers at the funeral of Arthur were the tenant farmers on the Clevedon estate. The Rev. William Newland Pedder, who was vicar of Clevedon for forty years and died in 1871, read the burial service.

XIX. 1. *They laid him by the pleasant shore, etc.* Clevedon Church, where Arthur was buried, overlooks a broad expanse of water, where the Severn flows into the Bristol Channel. The church, which is dedicated to St. Andrew, is quaint and picturesque, though not architecturally noteworthy. The chancel was the original fishermen's church, to which additions have been made from time to time. It stands half a mile to the south of Clevedon, and is so secluded that —

> A stranger here
> Might wondering ask, 'Where stands the house of God?'

She sought it o'er the fields, and found at last
An old and lonely church, beside the sea,
In a green hollow, 'twixt two headlands green.

These heights, known as Church Hill and Wains Hill, seem to guard and shelter the edifice with its surrounding churchyard.

XXI. 1. *Since the grasses round me wave.* See note on ii. 1 above.

5. *The latest moon.* Mr. Jacobs thinks that this must allude to the discovery of the satellite of Neptune in 1846, and that this part of this poem was therefore written very late; but the reference to astronomical discoveries may be less specific.

7. *And one is glad.* The 1st edition has ' And unto one; ' and the same, two lines below, instead of ' And one is sad.'

XXII. 1. *Thro' four sweet years.* From 1828, the ' fifth autumnal slope ' referring to September, 1833, when Arthur died.

XXIII. 1. *Breaking into song by fits.* Here Gatty has the italicized note: ' It is a fact that the poem was written at both various times and places — through a course of years, and where the author happened to be, in Lincolnshire, London, Essex, Gloucestershire, Wales, anywhere, as the spirit moved him.'

2. *Who keeps the keys of all the creeds.* Death will solve all questions concerning the world beyond the grave.

Critics have complained that ' the notion of a Shadow keeping keys is a very halting metaphor '; and Mr. Tainsh says that he cannot defend the figure, though he ' nevertheless likes the line.' It is a sufficient defence to remind the critics that the keys are as shadowy and insubstantial as the phantom who keeps them.

XXIV. 1. *Wandering isles of light.* The spots on the sun.

2. *Since our first sun arose and set.* The 1st edition reads: ' Since Adam left his garden yet.'

3. *Makes former gladness loom so great.* The reading in the 1st edition was: ' Hath stretch'd my former joy so great.'

XXVI. 4. *Then might I find, etc.* The 1st edition has: ' So might I find; ' and in the last line of the stanza, ' To cloak me from my proper scorn.' For ' proper ' in the sense of ' own,' compare ' The Princess,' vi.: ' each to her proper hearth,' etc.

XXVII. 4. *I feel it, when I sorrow most, etc.* These three lines are repeated in the 1st stanza of lxxxv.

XXVIII. 1. *The time draws near the birth of Christ.* The critics, as we shall see, have made sundry mistakes concerning the date of the three Christmases referred to in the poem. Gatty says here that this first Christmas is ' possibly at the end of the year 1833 '; but in a note on the ' Last year ' of xxx. 4 he says: ' This seems to identify the time to be Christmas, 1834, as Hallam died on 15th September, 1833, and was buried in January, 1834.' On the contrary, the ' last year ' must refer to the Christmas of 1832, when Arthur was living; and *this* Christmas must be that of 1833.

Some, however, have been puzzled to reconcile this date with the preceding poem xxi., which, they say, implies that Arthur was buried *before* the Christmas of xxviii.–xxx. But, as Tennyson himself has told us (see on xxiii. 1 above), the poem was written at various times and places; and, in arranging the parts for publication, some were probably inserted before others that had been written earlier. If xxi. was written before xxviii., the poet, residing in a remote and secluded part of Lincolnshire, might have taken it for granted that the remains of his friend had already reached Clevedon and been laid in their last resting-place, several months having elapsed since his death. What Mrs. Ritchie says of Somersby in the childhood of the poet was still true of it in 1833: —

' It was so far away from the world, so behindhand in its echoes (which must have come there softened through all manner of green and tranquil things, and, as it were, hushed into pastoral silence), that though the early part of the century was stirring with the clang of legions, few of its rumors seem to have reached the children. They never heard, at the time, of the battle of Waterloo.' In 1833, when railways were just beginning to be built, Somersby was farther from London than the remotest corner of the kingdom is now.

The Christmas bells from hill to hill, etc. ' The churches are not to be identified. Those in the neighborhood [of Somersby] probably have too small belfries to allow of change-ringing. The sounds may have been only in the poet's mind ' (Gatty).

3. *Peace and good-will, etc.* The rhythm is like the chiming of bells.

XXXI. 1. *That Evangelist.* St. John, the only one who records the raising of Lazarus.

XXXIII. 3. *O thou that after toil and storm, etc.* ' Regarding the relation of one who knows to one who believes. Lazarus and Mary illustrate two phases of Christian life: those whose ripened reason and spiritual insight make their view of unseen things approach the character of knowledge; and those whose faith, without knowledge, supports itself by forms. Each life has a blessedness of its own; and " faith through form," which produces practical good deeds, is not to be despised, even by the most advanced in spiritual things ' (Genung).

' Let those who have not such simplicity of trust, who deem perhaps that they have reached a higher standpoint, fought their way to a purer creed, beware of troubling the Mary-spirits that they know. It may be that their faith, which has outgrown all form, is a subtler thing, but is it as fruitful of good works as the childlike faith of the Marys ? And let them beware lest, in a world of sin, it fail them in the hour of need ' (Chapman).

XXXV. 3. *Æonian hills.* The ' everlasting hills.' Compare xcv. 11 below: ' Æonian music.'

According to Mr. James Knowles (' Nineteenth Century,' January, 1893), the poet explains this stanza as referring to ' the vastness of the future — the enormity of the ages to come after your little life would act against that love.'

XXXVI. 1. *Tho' truths in manhood darkly join, etc.* 'What our holiest intuitions require finds its fitting expression in the revealed Word of God; especially in the Word made flesh, who appeals to all, and expresses an inner idea which is too deep-seated for men unaided to utter, and yet which every one, even the most unlettered, may read ' (Genung).

XXXVII. 1. *Urania speaks with darken'd brow, etc.* ' But how shall his muse dare to profane these holy mysteries ? She is of earth, and not for her is it to treat of things revealed. The song of human love and human loss alone is hers. These loftier themes pertain to Urania, not Melpomene. Yet Arthur loved to speak of things divine, and so the poet is fain to mingle some whisper of them in his song ' (Chapman).

3. *I am not worthy even to speak.* The 1st edition has ' but to speak.'

5. *And dear to me as sacred wine.* The first reading was: ' And dear as sacramental wine.' Gatty suggests that the poet made the change ' that the reader should see that he spoke only for himself,' which the addition of ' to me ' makes clear.

XXXIX. *Old warder of these buried bones, etc.* Added to the poem in 1871 (see page 162 above). 'Some acute critics have quite failed to comprehend the poet's purpose in introducing it. Considered in its connection, however, and with its allusions resolved, it supplies a very important link in the thought. It alludes, as does the other inserted poem, to poem iii., together with ii., and adds another link in the same chain of references to sorrow and nature, by showing how the heart, which sorrow has deadened into despair in the face of nature, is yet touched and cheered by the awaking life of springtide ' (Genung).

XL. 2. *Make April of her tender eyes.* Compare Shakespeare, ' Antony and Cleopatra,' iii. 2. 43: —

The April 's in her eyes; it is love's spring,
And these the showers to bring it on.

5. *In those great offices that suit.* The 1st edition reads: ' In such great offices as suit.' Mr. Knowles quotes the poet as saying: ' I hate that — I should not write so now — I 'd almost rather sacrifice a meaning than let two *s's* come together.' This occurs, however, in cxi. 2, where he might have written ' fashion sake,' as in Elizabethan English.

XLIII. 3. *So that still garden of the souls.* The 1st edition has ' But ' for ' So; ' and ' would last ' for ' will last ' in the next stanza.

XLIV. 1. *But he forgets the days, etc.* That is, his earliest infancy, before the sutures of the skull had closed. Mr. B. Kellogg, in an American edition of selections from ' In Memoriam,' strangely takes the allusion to be to extreme old age, the ' doorways of the head ' being ' the senses.'

3. *If death so taste Lethean springs.* Gatty says that ' The poet here makes Lethe produce remembrance, instead of forgetfulness, which is its normal effect.' Not so; he merely suggests, as Wordsworth does in his famous Ode, that the forgetfulness is not absolutely complete.

XLV. 1. *The baby new to earth and sky, etc.* ' The grand result of this earthly life, as it advances from infancy to maturity, is the development of self-conscious personality, and with it the possibility of memory. Unless we suppose all this life's highest achievement is lost, this self-conscious personality and memory continue in heaven ' (Genung).

XLVI. 1. *We, ranging down this lower track, etc.* ' In this life we experience "thorn and flower," grief and joy; and the past becomes mercifully shaded as time goes on, otherwise the retrospect would be intolerable. But hereafter all shadow on what has happened will be removed, and all will be clear "from marge to marge;" and the five years of earthly friendship will be the "richest field " in the " eternal landscape " ' (Gatty).

4. *Love, a brooding star, etc.* ' As if Lord of the whole life ' (Tennyson, as quoted by Knowles).

XLVII. 1. *That each, who seems a separate, etc.* The theory that the individual being will, in another state of existence, be merged in ' the general soul,' is repudiated by the poet. 'St. Paul is not more distinct and emphatic upon our individuality hereafter ' (Gatty).

4. *Before the spirits fade away, etc.* ' Into the Universal Spirit — but at least one last parting ! and would always want it again — of course ' (Tennyson, quoted by Knowles).

XLVIII. 1. *If these brief lays, of sorrow born, etc.* ' The office of the song is not to give logically conclusive answers, but Love's answer, making doubts yield her service ' (Genung).

XLIX. 1. *From art, from nature, etc.* ' Let no man think that the fancied hopes and fears with which he toys touch more than the surface of the mourner's grief. He hails every random influence that art, nature, philosophy, may shed upon that sullen surface, chequering and dimpling it, like shafts of light and tender breezes playing upon a pool. Beneath, in the depths, the very springs of life are tears ' (Chapman).

LI. 1. *Do we indeed desire the dead, etc.* The dead, if near us, must see all our ' inner vileness.' But ' they see as God sees, and make gracious allowance.'

LIII. 2. *And dare we to this fancy given.* The 1st edition has ' doctrine ' for ' fancy; ' ' had not ' for ' scarce had '; and ' Oh ! ' for ' Or.'

The poet's comment on this stanza, as Mr. Knowles tells us, was: ' There 's a passionate heat of nature in a rake sometimes — the nature that yields emotionally may come straighter than a prig's.' He added, on the next two stanzas: ' Yet don't you be making excuses for this kind of thing — it 's unsafe. You must set a rule before youth. There 's need of rule to men also — though no particular one that I know of — it may be arbitrary.'

LIV. 5. *An infant crying in the night.* Compare cxxiv. 5 below: 'Then was I as a child that cries,' etc.

LVI. 1. *'So careful of the type?' but no, etc.* Genung remarks: 'It is worthy of notice that in an earlier work this same question of man's destiny has presented itself to the poet, and in the same manner has been left unanswered. At the close of "The Vision of Sin," where discussion has been made concerning sin's ravages, whether avenged by sense, or also disintegrating the spirit, the lines occur:—

> At last I heard a voice upon the slope
> Cry to the summit, 'Is there any hope?'
> To which an answer peal'd from that high land,
> But in a tongue no man could understand;
> And on the glimmering limit far withdrawn
> God made Himself an awful rose of dawn.

In the poem under discussion, however, the thought is greatly ripened under the agency of Faith. From all deepest doubts suggested by Nature, she rises, and flees from Nature to God, in whose hands she tremblingly leaves the answer.'

LVII. 1. *Peace: come away, etc.* 'Possibly addressed to his sister, whom he now calls away from the sad subject which his earthly song had treated' (Gatty).

2. *Methinks my friend is richly shrined, etc.* Gatty gives (italicized) as the poet's comment: 'The author speaks of these poems — "methinks I have built a rich shrine for my friend, but it will not last."'

LIX. *O Sorrow, wilt thou live with me, etc.* Added in the 4th edition, 1851.

LXI. 3. *The soul of Shakespeare love thee more.* 'Perhaps he might — if he were a greater soul' (Tennyson, quoted by Knowles).

LXII. 1. *Then be my love an idle tale.* The 1st edition has 'So' for 'Then.'

LXIII. 1. *In its assumptions up to heaven.* The word *assumption* is used as in its ecclesiastical application to the 'taking up' of the Virgin to heaven.

LXVII. 1. *I know that in thy place of rest, etc.* Clevedon Church, where Hallam was laid to rest. See page 163 above.

4. *And in the dark church, etc.* The 1st edition reads: 'And in the chancel;' but the tablet is not in the chancel of the church, as the elder Hallam stated in the memoir of his son, but on the west wall of the south transept, or the 'manor aisle,' as Napier calls it. When the moon is high in the heavens, it shines through the large south window upon the tablet, as the poet here imagines.

The inscription on the tablet is as follows:—

To the Memory of
ARTHUR HENRY HALLAM,
of Trinity College, Cambridge, B. A.,
Eldest son of HENRY HALLAM, Esquire,
and of JULIA MARIA his wife,
Daughter of Sir ABRAHAM ELTON, Bart.,
of Clevedon Court,

Who was snatched away by sudden death,
at Vienna, on September 15th, 1833,
In the 23rd year of his age.

And now in this obscure and solitary Church
repose the mortal remains of
one too early lost for public fame,
but already conspicuous among his contemporaries
for the brightness of his genius,
the depth of his understanding,
the nobleness of his disposition,
the fervor of his piety,
and the purity of his life.

VALE DULCISSIME
VALE DILECTISSIME DESIDERATISSIME
REQUIESCAS IN PACE
PATER AC MATER HIC POSTHAC REQUIESCAMUS TECUM
USQUE AD TUBAM.

LXIX. 3. *I met with scoffs, etc.* 'I tried to make my grief into a crown of these poems — but it is not to be taken too closely. To write verses about sorrow, grief, and death is to wear a crown of thorns which ought to be put by, as people say' (Tennyson, quoted by Knowles). The 'angel of the night' in the next stanza was explained by the poet as 'the divine Thing in the gloom.'

LXXI. 1. *We went thro' summer France.* In the summer of 1830. To this journey he refers in the lines 'In the Valley of Cauteretz.' See the notes on that poem.

2. *Then bring an opiate.* The 1st edition has 'So' for 'Then;' and the last line of the stanza reads: 'That thus my pleasure might be whole.'

LXXII. 1. *Rises thou thus, dim dawn, etc.* The anniversary of Arthur's death, September 15th.

4. *Along the hills.* The 1st edition reads: 'From hill to hill.'

LXXVI. 3. *The matin songs, etc.* The songs of the great early poets.

LXXVIII. 1. *Again at Christmas, etc.* Compare xxx. above. Genung remarks that this Christmas is 'an occasion characterized by calmness. The lapse of time has brought a change in the spirit of its observance, in this respect, that the merriments and pleasures peculiar to Christmas are accepted and enjoyed no longer under querulous protest but for their own sake. At the same time, "the quiet sense of something lost" is a reminder that the occasion is not what it was before bereavement.'

3. *Hoodman-blind.* Blindman's buff. Compare 'Hamlet,' iii. 4. 77: 'That thus hath cozen'd you at hoodman-blind.'

4. *No mark of pain.* The 1st edition has: 'no type of pain.'

LXXIX. 1. *More than my brothers are to me.* Compare ix. 5, above.

This poem is evidently addressed to Charles, the brother nearest his own age, and associated with him in the production of 'Poems by Two Brothers.'

3. *For us the same cold streamlet curl'd.* The brook near Somersby to which reference is made in the early 'Ode to Memory':—

> And chiefly from the brook that loves
> To purl o'er matted cress and ribbed sand,

Or dimple in the dark of rushy coves,
Drawing into his narrow earthen urn,
   In every elbow and turn,
The filtered tribute of the rough woodland.

LXXX. 2. *Then fancy shapes, as fancy can,* etc. 'If places were changed and he the mourner, I know that he would turn his sorrow into gain, by being stayed in peace with God and man. So let me do, and thus honor his influence' (Genung).

LXXXIII. 1. *O sweet new year, etc.* Genung remarks here: 'As in the preceding cycle Springtide added to the thought of immortality the suggestiveness of a new awaking season, so in this broader field of thought New Year heralds a new round of seasons. The spirit of the thought too has changed, — has become more wholesome and free. Frozen in the past sorrow as the mind was in the preceding cycle, the Springtide must thrust its cheer from without on a reluctant mood; but here the new year illustrates the greater health of spirit, in that now the mood answers to the promise of the season, and goes forth congenially to meet it.'

LXXXIV. 3. *When thou shouldst link thy life with one,* etc. Referring to young Hallam's engagement to the poet's sister Emily.

LXXXV. 1. *'T is better to have loved and lost,* etc. Compare xxvii. 4 above.

2. *O true in word and tried in deed, etc.* This, as the poet explained to Gatty, is addressed to Mr. E. L. Lushington, like the epithalamium at the close of the poem.

LXXXVI. 1. *Sweet after showers, etc.* The four stanzas form a single sentence. Compare the early poem on 'The Poet' for a fine passage similarly sustained. Tennyson told Knowles that this was one of the poems he liked. It was written at Bournemouth, and the 'ambrosial air' was 'the west wind,' which, in the last stanza, is represented as 'rolling to the Eastern seas till it meets the evening star.' In the 3d stanza, 'the fancy' means 'imagination — *the* fancy — no particular fancy.'

LXXXVII. 1. *I past beside the reverend walls,* etc. Referring to a visit to Cambridge.

4. *That long walk of limes.* In the grounds of Trinity College.

6. *Where once we held debate.* Referring, as the poet told Mr. Knowles, to the 'Water Club,' so called 'because there was no wine.' He added: 'They used to make speeches — I never did.'

10. *The bar of Michael Angelo.* 'Michael Angelo had a strong bar of bone over his eyes' (Tennyson to Gatty).

LXXXVIII. 1. *Wild bird, whose warble, liquid sweet, etc.* The nightingale.

2. *The darkening leaf.* The 1st edition has 'the dusking leaf.'

LXXXIX. 1. *This flat lawn, etc.* The lawn of Somersby Rectory. The poet tells Gatty that 'the "towering sycamore" is cut down, and the four poplars are gone, and the lawn is no longer a flat one.'

3. *Dusty purlieus of the law.* The 1st edition has 'dusky purlieus.'

6. *The Tuscan poets.* Compare page 162 above. The following sonnet was addressed by Arthur to Tennyson's sister Emily (to whom he was betrothed at the time), when he began to teach her Italian : [1] —

Lady, I bid thee to a sunny dome,
  Ringing with echoes of Italian song;
  Henceforth to thee these magic halls belong,
And all the pleasant place is like a home.
Hark, on the right, with full piano tone,
  Old Dante's voice encircles all the air;
  Hark yet again, like flute-tones mingling rare,
Comes the keen sweetness of Petrarca's moan.
Pass thou the lintel freely ; without fear
  Feast on the music. I do better know thee
Than to suspect this pleasure thou dost owe me
  Will wrong thy gentle spirit, or make less dear
That element whence thou must draw thy life —
An English maiden and an English wife.

Again he addresses her thus (compare lxxxix. 6): —

Sometimes I dream thee leaning o'er
  The harp I used to love so well;
Again I tremble and adore
  The soul of its delicious swell;
Again the very air is dim
  With eddies of harmonious might,
And all my brain and senses swim
  In a keen madness of delight.

12. *The crimson - circled star.* The planet Venus. The next line, as the poet explained, refers to the evolution of the planet from the sun, according to the nebular hypothesis of La Place.

XCI. 1. *The sea-blue bird of March.* The kingfisher, as the poet himself explained. Gatty quotes, as a parallel passage : —

The fields made golden with the flower of March,
The throstle singing in the feather'd larch,
And down the river, like a flame of blue,
Keen as an arrow flies the water-king.

XCII. 4. *And such refraction of events, etc.* An allusion to the effect of atmospheric refraction in making objects appear above the horizon when they are actually below it.

Compare Coleridge, 'Death of Wallenstein,' v. 1 : —

        As the sun,
Ere it is risen, sometimes paints its image
In the atmosphere, so often do the spirits
Of great events stride on before the events,
And in to-day already walks to-morrow.

XCIV. 3. *They haunt the silence of the breast,* etc. 'I figure myself in this rather' (Tennyson, quoted by Knowles).

XCV. *By night we linger'd on the lawn, etc.* Another family scene at Somersby.

2. *The fluttering urn.* The adjective is very descriptive.

3. *The filmy shapes, etc.* Night moths (*Arctica menthrasti*), as the poet explained to Gatty.

9. *The living soul.* 'Perchance the Deity. The first reading (in 1st edition) was "His liv-

[1] Mrs. Ritchie says that Emily was 'scarcely seventeen' at the time of Arthur's death in 1833 ; but she was born on the 25th of October, 1811.

ing soul '' — but my conscience was troubled by '' his.'' I've often had a strange feeling of being wound and wrapped in the Great Soul ' (Tennyson, quoted by Knowles).

11. *Æonian music.* Compare xxxv. 3, above.

XCVI. 2. *One indeed I knew, etc.* Genung remarks: ' It is generally supposed that this poem narrates the spiritual experience of Arthur Hallam himself. . . . The passage where Tennyson recognizes in Arthur

> The faith, the vigor, bold to dwell
> On doubts that drive the coward back,

and the one where he describes Arthur's as a character of

> Seraphic intellect and force
> To seize and throw the doubts of man,

would seem to indicate much more calmness of assured strength than the poem before us; but at the same time this calmness may have been reached through severe struggle. Would not this passage, from Arthur Hallam's '' Remains,'' indicate such spiritual conflict ? —

> I do but mock me with these questionings.
> Dark, dark, yea, ' irrecoverably dark,'
> Is the soul's eye: yet how it strives and battles
> Thorough th' impenetrable gloom to fix
> That master light, the secret truth of things,
> Which is the body of the infinite God !

One of Arthur's early friends also writes: '' Perhaps I ought to mention that when I first knew him he was subject to occasional fits of mental depression, which gradually grew fewer and fainter, and had at length, I thought, disappeared, or merged in a peaceful Christian faith. I have witnessed the same in other ardent and adventurous minds, and have always looked upon them as the symptom, indeed, of an imperfect moral state, but one to which the finest spirits, during the process of their purification, are most subject.'' '

XCVII. 1. *My love has talk'd with rocks and trees, etc.* Gatty remarks that ' this is highly mystical,' and he appears not to have explained it correctly at first. A note of the poet's informs him that it is intended to describe ' the relation of one on earth to one in the other and higher world — not the author's relation to him here. He certainly looked up to the author, fully as much as the author to him.'

XCVIII. 1. *You leave us: you will see the Rhine, etc.* Addressed to his brother Charles, who, in 1836, made a wedding tour to the Continent and expected to visit Vienna. See the ' Memoir,' vol. i. p. 148.

6. *Any mother town.* Any metropolis. The poet was fond of translating a classical term into the vernacular. Compare ' the tortoise [*testudo*] creeping to the wall,' in the ' Dream of Fair Women;' ' the northern morn ' (*aurora borealis*) in ' Morte d'Arthur,' etc. In ' The Princess,' i. we have ' mother-city ' for metropolis.

XCIX. 1. *Risest thou thus, dim morn, again, etc.* Another return of the anniversary of Arthur's death. Compare lxxii. 1, above.

C. 1. *I climb the hill.* The 1st edition reads: ' I wake, I rise.'

CI. 1. *Unwatch'd, the garden bough shall sway, etc.* The poet's farewell to Somersby. The date has been often given as 1835, but Napier is right in putting it early in 1837. The three Christmases of the poem are not in three successive years. See on xxviii. 1, above.

3. *The Lesser Wain.* The constellation *Ursa Minor*, the ' polar star ' being at the end of the tail.

CII. 2. *Two spirits of a diverse love.* As the poet explained to Gatty, these do not represent persons: ' the first is the love of the native place; the second, the same love enhanced by the memory of the friend.'

CIII. 1. *I dream'd a vision of the dead.* An intimate friend of the poet says that this was a real dream. Tennyson furnished Gatty with this note: ' I rather believe that the maidens are the Muses, Arts, etc. Everything that made life beautiful here, we may hope may pass on with us beyond the grave.'

To Mr. Knowles he said that the maidens are ' all the human powers and talents that do not pass with life but go along with it.' The ' river ' is ' life,' and the ' hidden summits ' are ' the high — the divine — the origin of life.' The ' sea ' in the 4th stanza is ' eternity.' The 7th stanza refers to ' the great progress of the age, as well as the opening of another world; ' and the 9th to ' all the great hopes of science and men.'

12. *I did them wrong.* ' He was wrong to drop his earthly hopes and powers — they will be still of use to him ' (Tennyson, quoted by Knowles).

CIV. 1. *A single church below the hill.* Waltham Abbey, as the poet himself explained. The family resided for a time at High Beech, Epping Forest. The mansion, known as Beech Hill House, has since been torn down and rebuilt. It stood on high ground, from which there is a fine view of Waltham Abbey, about two and a half miles distant.

CV. 1. *To-night ungather'd let us leave, etc.* The 1st edition reads: —

> This holly by the cottage-eave,
> To-night, ungather'd shall it stand.

Genung remarks here: ' In the second Christmas-tide the lapse of time had made Christmas observances pleasant for their own sake; now the '' change of place, like growth of time,'' has wrought to cause the interest of the usual customs to die; as was indeed predicted at the first Christmas-tide. But in this dying of use and wont after they have been once revived there is no sign of retrogression in the thought; rather, the usual customs have lost their life because the *spirit* of Christmas hope has become so settled and significant that the ancient form can no more express its meaning. The cheer of this season not only eclipses the grief, but rejects all formal demonstrations of joy as unnecessary and meaningless.'

6. *What lightens in the lucid east, etc.* The

poet explained to Gatty that this ' refers to the scintillation of the stars rising.'

CVII. 1. *It is the day when he was born.* The 1st of February. Genung remarks: 'In the first cycle Springtide brought the cheer of a new season: in the second, New Year heralded a new round of seasons, and now this characterizing occasion of the third cycle suggests a new life, a noble life, which, having been lived once, may furnish the model for noble lives to come. The present anniversary illustrates, as has already been intimated in the Christmastide, how in this cycle the spirit of hope has overcome. In the first cycle the suggestiveness of the blooming season must make its way from without into a reluctant mood; in the second cycle the calmer mood and the promising season answer spontaneously to each other; but here in the closing cycle the hopeful mood has so overcome the influences of season and weather that even the bitter wintry day can have no disturbing effect on the confirmed cheer within, — the mind's peace is sufficient to itself, and not dependent.'

3. *All the brakes and thorns.* The ' brakes,' as Tennyson explained, are ' bushes.'

CIX. 4. *The blind hysterics of the Celt.* Compare cxxvii. 2 below, and the ' Conclusion ' of ' The Princess.'

CX. 1. *The men of rathe and riper years.* ' Rathe,' of which ' rather ' is the comparative, means early. The poet uses it again, adverbially, in ' Lancelot and Elaine ': ' Till rathe she rose.' Compare Milton, ' Lycidas,' 142: ' Bring the rathe primrose that forsaken dies.' For an instance of the word in recent *prose,* see J. A. Symonds's ' Sketches and Studies in Southern Europe ' (Essay on ' Rimini '): ' Whether it be the rathe loveliness of an art still immature, or the beauty of an art in its wane,' etc.

2. *His double tongue.* The 1st edition has ' treble tongue; ' and in 4 below, ' dearest ' for ' nearest.'

To him who grasps, etc. The 1st edition reads: ' To who may grasp.'

CXI. 4. *Best seem'd the thing he was.* The 1st edition has: ' So wore his outward best.'

CXII. 2. *The lesser lords of doom.* ' Those that have free will but less intellect ' (Tennyson's note to Gatty).

CXIII. 1. *'T is held that sorrow makes us wise, etc.* Compare cviii. 4 above.

3. *In civic action.* The 1st edition has 'in.' but some later ones have 'of ' — perhaps a misprint.

5. *With thousand shocks that come and go.* The 1st edition has ' many shocks.'

CXIV. 7. *But by year and hour.* The 1st edition reads: ' but from hour to hour.'

CXV. 1. *Now fades the last long streak of snow, etc.* ' The last note of time in the poem. Standing immediately after those poems in which is defined, in terms of Arthur's character, the greatness which the world needs, it adds to them the suggestiveness of the budding year. The special object of this Springtide seems to be to indicate the permanent mood in which the foregoing thought has left the poet; and thus it

corresponds to the groups of poems, lxvi.-lxxi., in the first cycle, and xcvi.-xcviii., in the second cycle. It also introduces the final application and conclusion of the whole thought; and so with Springtide the poem leaves us passing on into a new era of hope ' (Genung).

CXVI. 3. *And that dear voice.* The 1st edition has ' The dear, dear voice that I have known; ' and in the next line ' Will' for ' Still.'

CXVII. 3. *Every kiss of toothed wheels.* In the mechanism of clocks and watches.

CXVIII. In this poem we have a striking illustration of Tennyson's treatment of modern scientific theories and discoveries. The succession of the geological ages and the evolution of man from lower types are admirably ' moralized.'

1. *Dying Nature's earth and lime.* The inorganic elements of the human body.

5. *Or, crown'd with attributes of woe.* The 1st edition has ' And ' for ' Or.'

CXIX. 1. *Doors, where my heart was used to beat, etc.* Referring to another visit to the ' long unlovely' Wimpole Street. Compare vii. 1 above. ' No longer in confused despair, but in peaceful hope, the poet comes, thinking on the departed friend with blessings; and all surroundings of weather and scenery answer to the calm within ' (Genung).

CXX. 3. *Let him, the wiser man, etc.* Gatty remarks that ' this is spoken ironically, and is a strong protest against materialism;' but, as the poet adds, ' not against evolution.'

CXXI. 1. *Sad Hesper, o'er the buried sun, etc.* The evening-star, as ' Phosphor ' is the morning-star, ' double-name for what is one ' — the same planet Venus. Compare lxxxix. 12 above.

5. *Thou, like my present and my past, etc.* Gatty took this to be a reference to Arthur; but Tennyson says, ' No — the writer is rather referring to himself.'

CXXII. 1. *O, wast thou with me, dearest, etc.* Tennyson said to Mr. Knowles: ' If anybody thinks I ever called him "dearest " in his life they are much mistaken, for I never even called him " dear." ' The ' doom ' in the next line is that ' of grief.'

And yearn'd to burst the folded gloom. The 1st edition has ' strove ' for ' yearn'd.'

CXXIII. 1. *There rolls the deep where grew the tree, etc.* Referring to the changes in the limits of the ocean, and the upheaval of hills and mountains, in the past history of our planet. Compare Shakespeare's allusion to comparatively recent changes of the sea-line (as on the east coast of England) in Sonnet lxiv.: —

> When I have seen the hungry ocean gain
> Advantage on the kingdom of the shore,
> And the firm soil win of the watery main,
> Increasing store with loss and loss with store, etc.

CXXIV. 6. *And what I am beheld again, etc.* The 1st edition has: ' And what-I-seem beheld again; ' and, in the next line, ' What-is, and no-man-understands.'

CXXV. 3. *And if the song were full of care,*

etc. ' In his deepest self the poet has never lost hope; he has merely used the song to guide thought and feeling to a hopeful end ' (Genung).

CXXVI. 3. *Who moves about from place to place, etc.* The 1st edition reads: —

> That moves about from place to place,
> And whispers to the vast of space
> Among the worlds, that all is well.

CXXVII. 2. *The red fool-fury of the Seine, etc.* This has been supposed to refer to the Revolution of 1848, but the poet informed Gatty that it was ' probably written long before '48.'

3. *But ill for him that wears a crown.* The 1st edition reads: ' But woe to him; ' and, in the next stanza, ' the vast Æon.'

CXXVIII. 2. *O ye mysteries of good.* The 1st edition has ' ministers of good; ' and, in the 5th stanza, ' baseness ' for ' bareness.'

CXXXI. 1. *O living will, etc.* ' Free will in man,' as the poet explained to Gatty.

2. *Out of dust.* The 1st edition has ' out the dust.'

The Epilogue. O true and tried, etc. ' The poem that began with death, over which in its long course it has found love triumphant, now ends with marriage, that highest earthly illustration of crowned and completed love.' (Genung).

The epithalamium celebrates the marriage of the poet's younger sister, Cecilia, to Edmund Law Lushington, October 10th, 1842.

Gatty said that this marriage song ' scarcely harmonizes with the lofty solemnity ' of ' In Memoriam; ' but Tennyson replied that the poem ' was meant to be a kind of Divina Commedia, ending cheerfully.'

2. *Since first he told me that he loved, etc.* Referring to Arthur's betrothal to Emily Tennyson.

9. *He too foretold the perfect rose.* Also referring to Arthur.

12. *For I that danced her on my knee, etc.* As Cecilia was born October 10, 1817, she was eight years younger than the poet.

13. *Her feet, my darling, on the dead.* Referring to the graves beneath the chancel floor, as the next line does to the memorial tablets on the walls.

14. *Her sweet 'I will' has made you one.* The 1st edition has ' ye ' for ' you.'

As Genung remarks, this closing poem ' affords occasion to bring in review before us the leading features and influences of " In Memoriam," ' namely: —

' 1. Love, which survives regret and the grave, has recovered her peace in this world, has grown greater and holier, and yet by no means less loyal to the dead; and now, no more disturbed by the past, she devotes herself to the innocent joys of the present.

' 2. Remembrance of the dead is cherished, not sacrificed; the dead is thought of as living, and perhaps present on this occasion, shedding unseen blessings on this coronation of love.

' 3. The living present is suggested by the marriage-bells and festivities; a present in which love finds its purest expression.

' 4. The greater future is suggested in the thought of the new life that may rise from this union, a new-born soul, who will look on a race more advanced than this, and contribute to its greatness, and so be a link between us and the perfect future.

' 5. Finally, a view of the far future perfected. Its character: the view of knowledge eye to eye, the complete subjugation in our nature of all that is brutish, the flower and fruit of which the present contains the seed. Its type: the life of Arthur, who appeared in advance of his time. Its culmination: life in God.'

When reading ' In Memoriam ' to Mr. Knowles, the poet said: ' It is rather the cry of the whole human race than mine. In the poem altogether private grief swells out into thought of, and hope for, the whole world. It begins with a funeral and ends with a marriage — begins with death and ends in promise of a new life — a sort of Divine Comedy, cheerful at the close. . . . It 's too hopeful, this poem, more than I am myself. . . . The general way of its being written was so queer that if there were a blank space I would put in a poem. . . . I think of adding another to it, a speculative one, bringing out the thoughts of the " Higher Pantheism," and showing that all the arguments are about as good on one side as the other, and thus throw man back more on the primitive impulses and feelings.'

The poet also explained to Mr. Knowles that there were ' nine natural groups or divisions ' in ' In Memoriam,' as follows: from i. to viii.; from ix. to xx.; from xxi. to xxvii.; from xxviii. to xlix.; from l. to lviii.; from lix. to lxxi.; from lxxii. to xcviii.; from xcix. to ciii.; and from civ. to cxxxi.

For fuller notes on the poem, the reader may be referred to Rolfe's edition (Boston, 1895).

Page 198. MAUD.

' The Tribute,' in which the poem appeared that eighteen years later became the germ of ' Maud,' was a collection of miscellaneous poems by various authors, edited by Lord Northampton. Swinburne, in 1876 (in ' The Academy ' for January 29), refers to it as ' the poem of deepest charm and fullest delight of pathos and melody ever written by Mr. Tennyson; since recast into new form and refreshed with new beauty to fit it for reappearance among the crowning passages of " Maud." '

This poem is also interesting as having been the subject of the first notice that Tennyson received from the ' Edinburgh Review ' (October, 1837). The writer says: —

We do not profess to understand the somewhat mysterious contribution of Mr. Alfred Tennyson, entitled ' Stanzas ; ' but amidst some quaintness, and some occasional absurdities of expression, it is not difficult to detect the hand of a true poet — such as the author of ' Mariana ' and the lines on the ' Arabian Nights ' undoubtedly is — in those stanzas which describe the appearance of a visionary form, by which the writer is supposed to be haunted amidst the streets of a crowded city.

Part I. The division into Parts was not made in the early editions.

Line 2. *Dabbled with blood-red heath.* When I heard Tennyson read the poem he paused here and said, ' Blood-red heath ! The critics might have known by *that* that the man was mad; there 's no such thing.'

9. *A vast speculation.* The 1st edition has ' great ' for ' vast.'

12. *And the flying gold of the ruin'd woodlands drove thro' the air.* Ruskin, in ' Modern Painters ' (vol. iii. chap. 12), cites this as an ' exquisite ' illustration of what he calls ' pathetic fallacy.'

21. *Why do they prate of the blessings of Peace?* This and the stanzas that follow, as well as those on war at the end of the poem, were particularly criticised by the early reviewers, who made the stupid mistake, to which I have already referred, of interpreting the morbid utterances of the hero as the poet's own. There were protests in verse also; as in a poor travesty entitled ' Anti-Maud,' of which this may serve as a specimen : —

Who is it clamours for War ? Is it one who is ready to fight ?

Is it one who will grasp the sword, and rush on the foe with a shout ?

Far from it: — 't is one of the musing mind who merely intends to write —

He sits at home by his own snug hearth, and hears the storm howl without.

44. *To pestle a poison'd poison behind his crimson lights.* Even the drugs of the apothecary are adulterated.

53. *What ! am I raging alone, etc.* This and the two following stanzas were not in the 1st edition.

65. *Workmen up at the Hall !* The 1st edition has: ' There are workmen up at the Hall.'

76. *I will bury myself in myself.* The 1st edition has: ' I will bury myself in my books.' Peter Bayne (' Lessons from My Masters,' 1879) says: ' No change could be more expressive. Of all the graves in which a man can bury himself, self is the worst — haunted with the ghostliest visions, tormented with the loathliest worms. Accordingly, the recluse now sinks into a mood of contented and cynical Epicureanism, more venomously bad than that in which he had invoked Mars to shame Belial and Mammon. He will let the world have its way. . . . This is his point of deepest degradation; henceforward he ascends.'

87. *From which I escaped, heartfree.* Not quite, or he would not have said so.

102. *A million emeralds break from the ruby-budded lime.* The green leaves bursting from their crimson sheath.

115. *I met her to-day with her brother.* The 1st edition has ' abroad ' for ' to-day.'

178. *Till I well could weep, etc.* ' The meanness and the sordid spirit of the world now begin to call forth *tears* instead of sarcasm and raillery; and he could weep, too, for *his own inactivity and baseness,* as well as for its meanness. The change of the measure beautifully expresses the character of the transformation the voice and its mistress are working in the hearer ' (Mann).

This quotation is from ' Tennyson's " Maud " Vindicated: an Explanatory Essay,' by Robert James Mann, M. D., published in 1856. The poet, acknowledging the receipt of the pamphlet, said: ' No one with this essay before him can in future pretend to misunderstand my dramatic poem " Maud." Your commentary is as true as it is full.' In replying to another gentleman who had sent him a copy of a favorable review, he wrote thus: —

' I am much obliged to you for sending me your critique on my poem; and happy to find that you approve of it, and, unlike most of the critics (so-called), have taken some pains to look into it and see what it means. There has been from many quarters a torrent of abuse against it; and I have even had insulting anonymous letters: indeed, I am quite at a loss to account for the bitterness of feeling which this poor little work of mine has excited.'

212. *What if with her sunny hair, etc.* ' The natural reaction of doubt following upon exalted hope ' (Mann).

233. *That oil'd and curl'd Assyrian bull.* Bayne considers this ' one of the crudest lines Tennyson ever penned, . . . grotesque, without being expressive.' It is true that ' the last thing the winged bull from Nineveh suggests is a dandy; ' but that is just what it might suggest to a morbid imagination which, at the moment, recalls only the abundant curls of the majestic figure. It is the hero's metaphor, not Tennyson's.

264. *Till a morbid hate and horror have grown, etc.* ' The cynic now begins really to understand his own cynicism; he not only feels his languor and deficiency, but comprehends much concerning their cause. This is a beautiful indication of the better state of things that is already initiated for him, through the healthy operation of his affections ' (Mann).

285-300. *Did I hear it half in a doze, etc.* These stanzas, which sorely puzzled the critics at first, are now made clear by the 19th poem of Part I. (pp. 209-210) which was not in the 1st edition.

328. *Then returns the dark.* The 1st edition reads: ' And back returns the dark.'

363, 364. *A wounded thing, etc.* These two lines were not in the 1st edition.

366-381. *Last week came one to the county town, etc.* This stanza was foolishly supposed by some to be the poet's own ' attack upon peace-advocates in general; ' and one journalist considered it a personal allusion to a certain prominent member of the Society of Friends.

382-388. *I wish I could hear again, etc.* This stanza was not in the 1st edition; nor the two lines that end the poem below — ' And ah for a man to arise in me.' etc. The former, as Bayne remarks, 'greatly strengthens the poem at this point;' and the 'two lines, set by themselves, are like a jewelled clasp knitting the earlier to the later portions of the first Part.'

412–415. *Birds in the high Hall-garden, etc.* When reading the poem Tennyson would ask his listeners what birds these were that cried, 'Maud, Maud, Maud;' and Mrs. Ritchie tells of a lady who replied, 'Nightingales, sir?' 'Pooh!' said the poet, 'what a cockney you are! Nightingales don't say Maud. Rooks do, or something like it — Caw, caw, caw, caw.' He asked the same question when he read the poem to my wife and myself.

421. *Ringing through the valleys.* 'Lilies' is a very imperfect rhyme to 'valleys;' but Tennyson not unfrequently indulges in such license. For a list of the imperfect rhymes in 'In Memoriam,' see Mr. Joseph Jacobs's 'Tennyson and In Memoriam' (London, 1892). He, however, includes many rhymes that are unobjectionable; like *prayer, air; moods, woods; hours, flowers,* etc.

434, 435. *For her feet have touch'd the meadows,* etc. Because, as the poet said to Knowles (and to me also) when reading the passage, 'if you tread on daisies they turn up underfoot and get rosy.'

441. *And little King Charley snarling!* The 1st edition reads: 'And little King Charles is snarling.'

557. *My yet young life.* Bayne says: 'These words are more curiously expressive of a brooding inward-looking habit of mind than any I know of in literature.' He doubts whether the young man 'ought to have been represented as still so morbidly self-conscious' as this implies. To my thinking, it is not unnatural that even at this stage of his experience he should occasionally lapse into the old unhealthy introspectiveness. Later than this — after 'the happy Yes' has faltered from the maiden's lips — it would be impossible.

582. *Over glowing ships.* The 1st edition has 'O'er the blowing ships.'

599. *I have led her home, my love, etc.* 'The one feature that dwells, soul-like, within the delicious lines of these subtle stanzas — the all-pervading inspiration of their richly varied movements — is the sustained sense of absolute content and calm. There is joyous rapture within them everywhere, but the rapture is still and deep. The very first line is, in its smooth, long measure, the audible symbol of perfect rest' (Mann).

616. *Dark cedar.* The same under which he heard Maud singing the 'passionate ballad gallant and gay' (page 202). These cedars of Lebanon are not uncommon in old English gardens.

634. *A sad astrology.* Not the old astrology which made human destiny dependent on the stars, but 'the sadder astrology of modern astronomy, which shows that the celestial bodies follow their own courses, and have nothing to do with human affairs.' The science of our day has removed them to such inconceivable dis-

tance that they only make man feel 'his nothingness.'

656. *That long, loving kiss.* The 1st edition has 'long lover's kiss.'

663. *In bridal white.* Prophetic of the coming bridal; or, as Mann explains, 'fresh in the history of his joy.'

681. *Some dark undercurrent woe.* A presentiment of coming misfortune, which he nevertheless refuses to dwell upon.

684–786. *Her brother is coming back to-night,* etc. As already mentioned, this poem is not in the 1st edition. It clears up the obscurities of the story, 'varies the interest and deepens the pathos,' and makes the love of Maud for the hero less improbable. We learn, among other things, that 'Maud had always nursed the idea that it was her duty, for her mother's sake, to be reconciled to the son of the suicide, and while he was gloomily cursing the family of his father's destroyer, Maud was kneeling in foreign churches praying that they might be friends' (Bayne).

757. *That he left his wine, etc.* No doubt he was better than this prejudiced witness had represented; and we have stronger reason for thinking so later.

845. *My Maud has sent it by thee.* At least, he flatters his fancy that she did.

850–923. *Come into the garden, Maud.* This lovely song abounds in illustrations of what Ruskin calls 'the pathetic fallacy' (see on line 12 above). 'The lover transfers all the passion of his heart to the flowers, and the flowers become part of his heart' (Stopford Brooke).

Part II. Lines 49–77. *See what a lovely shell,* etc. 'This is unquestionably true to nature. The merest trifles commonly catch the eye of persons who are intensely occupied with grief, and then lead them out from themselves, until they are able to find some relief for the internal pressure through words' (Mann).

131–140. *Courage, poor heart of stone, etc.* These lines were not in the 1st edition. As Bayne remarks, they tell us that Maud dies, — a fact that previously we could only guess at.

141–238. *O, that 't were possible, etc.* For the history of this poem, see page 198 above. The changes from the version of 1837 are many.

146. *By the home that gave me birth.* Originally, 'Of the land that gave me birth.' In the next stanza (153) 'God' has been changed to 'Christ.'

164, 165. *Half in dreams . . . early skies.* These two lines are not in the 1837 poem, which below (168) has 'to-morrow' for 'the morrow.'

171–195. *'T is a morning, pure and sweet, etc.* This stanza and the next (vi. and vii.) take the place of the following: —

> Do I hear the pleasant ditty
> That I heard her chant of old?
> But I wake — my dream is fled,
> Without knowledge, without pity —
> In the shuddering dawn behold,
> By the curtains of my bed,
> That abiding phantom cold.

196–201. *Get thee hence, etc.* In the 1837

poem this stanza comes before the present xii.
as explained below.

202–220. *Then I rise, etc.* There is no change
in ix., x., and xi. except 'crosses' for 'cross-
eth' (twice) in x. They are followed by the
present xiii. which originally read thus: —

> *Then* the broad light glares and beats,
> And the *sunk eye* flits and fleets,
> And will not let me be.
> I loathe the squares and streets
> And the faces that one meets,
> Hearts with no love for me;
> Always I long to creep
> *To* some still cavern deep,
> *And* to weep, and weep, and weep,
> My whole soul out to thee.

This is followed by the present viii. and xii., to
the latter of which the 2d and 6th lines have
been added. The poem then concludes with
the following stanzas, which do not appear in
'Maud': —

> But she tarries in her place,
> And I paint the beauteous face
> Of the maiden, that I lost,
> In my inner eyes again,
> Lest my heart be overborne
> By the thing I hold in scorn,
> By a dull mechanic ghost
> And a juggle of the brain.
> I can shadow forth my bride
> As I knew her fair and kind,
> As I woo'd her for my wife;
> She is lovely by my side
> In the silence of my life —
> 'T is a phantom of the mind.
>
> 'T is a phantom fair and good;
> I can call it to my side,
> So to guard my life from ill,
> Tho' its ghastly sister glide
> And be moved around me still
> With the moving of the blood,
> That is moved not of the will.
>
> Let it pass, the dreary brow,
> Let the dismal face go by.
> Will it lead me to the grave?
> Then I lose it: it will fly:
> Can it overlast the nerves?
> Can it overlie the eye ?
> But the other, like the star,
> Thro' the channel windeth far
> Till it fade and fail and die,
> To its Archetype that waits,
> Clad in light by golden gates —
> Clad in light the Spirit waits
> To embrace me in the sky.

239–342. *Dead, long dead, etc.* 'The reason
of the long-tasked sufferer has at last yielded
to the continued strain, and he is now a maniac,
confined in one of the London asylums for the
insane, where he can hear the muffled sound
and confusion of the vast metropolitan traffic
surging around him in an interminable whirl'
(Mann).

The critics have generally agreed that the
delineation of insanity here is surprisingly true
to nature; but Stopford Brooke thinks there is
too much method in the madness. The whole
of this part of the poem, he says, 'falls almost
into a logical order, as if at the bottom of his
madness the man was not mad at all. We can
trace, then, the elaborate argumentative way in
which Tennyson has worked it out — a thing
we cannot do, for example, in the madness of
Ophelia — a similar madness of love and sorrow
and death. The picture is also carefully made
up of scattered impressions recorded in the first
part of the poem. These are apparently huddled
together in the disorder of madness, but it is
not really so. They have a connection, and the
stitches which unite them are too clear. The
interspersed reflections are also too sane — as
for instance, " Friend, to be struck by the
public foe," etc. A madman might think a
part of it, but not the whole, and not in that
way.' But later Mr. Brooke says: 'I have
made certain criticisms on " Maud," and I am
troubled by having made them. . . . The criti-
cisms may be all wrong. When we approach
a great poet's work, our proper position is hu-
mility.'

The poet said to Mr. Knowles: 'The whole of
the stanzas where he is mad in Bedlam, from
" Dead, long dead," to " Deeper, ever so little
deeper," were written in twenty minutes, and
some mad doctor wrote to me that nothing since
Shakespeare has been so good for madness as
this.'

I recollect, by the by, that when Tennyson
was reading 'Maud,' and referring at intervals
to his treatment of the hero's madness, he inci-
dentally made a remark or two in disparage-
ment of Shakespeare's delineations of insanity.
The gist of the criticism was that the talk of
the dramatist's crazy people was of too ran-
dom a character, lacking the 'method' which
professional observers detect in madness — the
connection, by disordered association, of ideas
that to ordinary folk appear disconnected.
This was in the summer of 1891, and Stopford
Brooke's book was not published until 1894.

Part III. My life has crept so long, etc. 'In
Part III. he is sane and calm, capable of sym-
pathizing with the high ambition of a people
resolute to do justice, and glad that England,
in the Crimean war, has undertaken to wreak
God's wrath " on a giant liar." . . . Last of
all, six lines (54–59) are added in which the
meaning and moral of the poem are grandly
summed up.' These last six lines are not in
the 1st edition.

Page 217. THE BROOK.
Certain critics have attempted to identify the
brook of this poem with the one near Ten-
nyson's birthplace at Somersby; but the two
differ in some particulars, and this one, as he
himself said, was an imaginary brook.

Line 6. *How money breeds.* Compare 'The
Merchant of Venice,' i. 3. 95: —

> *Antonio.* Was this inserted to make interest good?
> Or is your gold and silver ewes and rams?
> *Shylock.* I cannot tell; I make it breed as fast.

See also Bacon, ' Essay on Usury ': ' That it is
against nature for money to beget money.'

17. *Or even the sweet, half-English Neilgherry
air.* The cool and salubrious Neilgherry Hills

in India, a favorite summer resort of the English residents.

46. *Willow-weed.* The *Epilobium hirsutum* of Linnæus.

92. *Nor of those.* Originally, ' neither one.'

118. *Meadow-sweet.* Also called ' meadow-wort,' the *Spiræa ulmaria* of the botanists.

189. *The dome Of Brunelleschi.* The Duomo, or Cathedral of Florence, the dome of which is the masterpiece of Brunelleschi.

194. *By the long wash of Australasian seas.* The poet is said to have specially prided himself on the sustained rhythmical quality of this line, as well he might.

196. *And breathes in April-autumns.* I find this reading first in the edition of 1890. All the earlier ones that I have seen have: ' And breathes in converse seasons.' The change was probably made to avoid the succession of *s*'s. Compare note on ' In Memoriam,' xl. 5.

Page 221. THE DAISY.

Line 5. *Turbia.* A village two miles from Monaco. Near by is the ' Tower of Augustus,' one of the trophies erected to commemorate the subjection of the Ligurians.

23. *Cogoletto.* More properly, *Cogoleto*, the supposed birthplace of Columbus, about fifteen miles from Genoa. A monument was erected to him here in 1888.

37. *We loved that hall, etc.* According to Palgrave (who got his notes of this kind from the poet) this refers to the hall of the Ducal Palace in Genoa, which contains (or did at that time) plaster statues of celebrated citizens; but I suspect that it was the much finer hall in the ancient Bank of St. George, which is adorned with twenty or more marble statues of the ' grave, severe Genovese of old.' It is one of the noblest monumental halls in the world. Tennyson, after the lapse of thirty-five years, may have confounded the two.

43. *The fresh Cascinè.* The park of Florence, on the bank of the Arno. *Boboli's ducal bowers* are the Boboli Gardens in the rear of the Pitti Palace, commanding beautiful views of the city.

75. *Of Lari Maxume.* See Virgil, ' Georgics,' ii. 159: —

Anne lacus tantos ? te, Lari maxume, teque,
Fluctibus et fremitu adsurgens, Benace, marino ?

Lake Como was the *Lacus Larius* of the Romans. There is always a ' Lariano ' among the steamers on the lake.

79. *To that fair port below the castle, etc.* Varenna, with the picturesque ruins of an old castle on the height behind it, associated by popular tradition with Queen Theodolinde.

93. *So dear a life your arms enfold.* Referring to the poet's son Hallam, then an infant. He was born August 11, 1852.

Page 222. TO THE REV. F. D. MAURICE.

Maurice was an intimate friend of the poet, and stood godfather to his son Hallam. In 1854, the year of this visit to Tennyson, Maurice prefixed the following dedication to his volume of ' Theological Essays ': —

To Alfred Tennyson, Esq., Poet-Laureate.

MY DEAR SIR, — I have maintained in these Essays that a theology which does not correspond to the deepest thoughts and feelings of human beings cannot be a true theology. Your writings have taught me to enter into many of those thoughts and feelings. Will you forgive me the presumption of offering you a book which at least acknowledges them and does them homage ?

As the hopes which I have expressed in this volume are more likely to be fulfilled to our children than to ourselves, I might perhaps ask you to accept it as a present to one of your name, in whom you have given me a very sacred interest. Many years, I trust, will elapse before he knows that there are any controversies in the world into which he has entered. Would to God that in a few more he may find that they have ceased ! At all events, if he should ever look into these Essays, they may tell him what meaning some of the former generation attached to words which will be familiar and dear to his generation, and to those that follow his, — how there were some who longed that the bells of our churches might indeed

> Ring out the darkness of the land,
> Ring in the Christ that is to be.

Believe me, my dear Sir,
Yours very truly and gratefully,
F. D. MAURICE.

Page 223. ODE ON THE DEATH OF THE DUKE OF WELLINGTON.

Line 1. *Bury.* The 1st edition has ' Let us bury; ' as in 3 below.

5. *Mourning, etc.* The 1st edition reads: —

> When laurel-garlanded leaders fall,
> And warriors carry, etc.

8. *Where shall we lay, etc.* After this line the edition of 1853 has the following line, since suppressed: ' He died on Walmer's lonely shore.' The next line begins ' But here,' etc.
The reading of the 1st edition was this: —

> Where shall we lay the man whom we deplore ?
> Let the sound of those he wrought for, etc.

20. *Remembering, etc.* The 1st edition reads: ' Our sorrow draws but on the golden Past; ' and it does not contain the next two lines.

28. *Clearest of.* The 1st edition has ' freest from.'

42. *World-victor's victor.* The conqueror of Napoleon.

49. *The cross of gold.* On St. Paul's Cathedral, in the crypt of which the Duke is buried.

59. *Knoll'd.* This line is not in the 1st edition. Compare *Macbeth,* v. 8. 50: ' And so his knell is knoll'd.'

79. *Ever-echoing.* The reading down to 1873 was ' ever-ringing.'

80-82. *Who is he, etc.* The question is asked by the *mighty seaman*, Nelson, who is also buried in St. Paul's.

91. *His foes were thine, etc.* The 1st edition reads: ' His martial wisdom kept us free; ' and the following lines are: —

> O warrior-seaman, this is he,
> This is England's greatest son,
> Worthy of our gorgeous rites,
> And worthy to be laid by thee;
> He that gain'd a hundred fights,
> And never lost an English gun;
> He that in his earlier day
> Against the myriads of Assaye
> Clash'd with his fiery few and won:
> And underneath another sun
> Made the soldier, led him on,
> And ever great and greater grew,
> Beating from the wasted vines
> All their marshals' bandit swarms
> Back to France with countless blows;
> Till their host of eagles flew
> Past the Pyrenean pines,
> Follow'd up, etc.

99. *Assaye.* A small town in Hindostan, memorable as the place where Wellington (then General Wellesley) began his career of victory, September 23, 1803, by defeating an army of thirty thousand with a force of less than five thousand.

101. *Underneath another sun.* In Spain. The allusions to the famous campaign there need no comment.

118. *Such a war, etc.* After this line the 1st edition has ' He withdrew to brief repose; ' and then goes on with 119 as in the text.

123. *That loud Sabbath.* The day of Waterloo.

154, 155. *Thank Him who isled us here . . . storming showers.* This couplet is not in the 1st edition.

157. *Of boundless love and reverence.* The 1st edition has: ' Of most unbounded reverence,' etc. It does not contain the next line but one.

166. *For saving that, ye help to save mankind.* The 1st edition reads: ' for saving that, ye save mankind;' two lines below: 'And help the march of human mind;' and in the next line: ' Till crowds be sane and crowns be just.'

170. *But wink no more, etc.* After this line the 1st edition has the following, omitted in all subsequent editions: —

> Perchance our greatness will increase;
> Perchance a darkening future yields
> Some reverse from worse to worse,
> The blood of men in quiet fields,
> And sprinkled on the sheaves of peace.

It goes on thus : —

> And O remember him who led your hosts;
> Respect his sacred warning; guard your coasts;
> His voice is silent, etc.

181–185. *Who let the turbid streams, etc.* These five lines are not in the 1st edition, which goes on with: ' His eighty winters,' etc.

195–217. *He on whom . . . is moon and sun.* This fine passage of twenty-three lines is unaltered from the 1st edition.

218. *Such was he: his work is done, etc.* The 1st edition reads : —

> He has not fail'd; he hath prevail'd:
> So let the men whose hearths he saved from shame
> Thro' many and many an age proclaim
> At civic revel, etc.

241. *Ours the pain, be his the gain.* The line is not in the 1st edition.

251. *We revere, and while we hear, etc.* The 1st edition reads thus: —

> For solemn, too, this day are we.
> O friends, we doubt not that for one so true
> There must be other nobler work to do
> Than when he fought at Waterloo,
> And Victor he must ever be.
> Though worlds on worlds in myriad myriads roll
> Round us, etc.

266–270. *On God and Godlike men, etc.* These five lines are not in the 1st edition.

271. *He is gone who seem'd so great.* The 1st edition has: ' The man is gone,' etc.

278. *Speak no more, etc.* The 1st edition has: ' But speak no more,' etc.

Page 226. THE CHARGE OF THE LIGHT BRIGADE.

The first version of the poem appeared in the London ' Examiner,' December 9, 1854, and was as follows: —

> Half a league, half a league,
>   Half a league onward,
> All in the valley of Death
>   Rode the six hundred.
>
> Into the valley of Death
>   Rode the six hundred,
> For up came an order which
>   Some one had blunder'd.
> ' Forward, the Light Brigade !
> Take the guns,' Nolan said:
> Into the valley of Death
>   Rode the six hundred.
>
> ' Forward, the Light Brigade !'
> No man was there dismay'd,
> Not tho' the soldier knew
>   Some one had blunder'd:
> Theirs not to make reply,
> Theirs not to reason why,
> Theirs but to do and die,
> Into the valley of Death
>   Rode the six hundred.
>
> Cannon to right of them,
> Cannon to left of them,
> Cannon in front of them
>   Volley'd and thunder'd;
> Storm'd at with shot and shell,
> Boldly they rode and well,
> Into the jaws of Death,
> Into the mouth of Hell
>   Rode the six hundred.
>
> Flash'd all their sabres bare,
> Flash'd all at once in air,
> Sabring the gunners there,
> Charging an army, while
>   All the world wonder'd:
> Plunged in the battery smoke,
> With many a desperate stroke
> The Russian line they broke;
> Then they rode back, but not,
>   Not the six hundred.

Cannon to right of them,
Cannon to left of them,
Cannon behind them
   Volley'd and thunder'd;
Storm'd at with shot and shell,
While horse and hero fell,
Those that had fought so well
Came from the jaws of Death
Back from the mouth of Hell,
All that was left of them,
   Left of six hundred.

When can their glory fade?
O the wild charge they made!
   All the world wonder'd.
Honor the charge they made!
Honor the Light Brigade,
   Noble six hundred!

This note is prefixed to the poem: 'Written after reading the first report of the "Times" correspondent, where only six hundred and seven sabres are mentioned as having taken part in the charge.'

The poem was next printed in the 'Maud' volume, in the summer of 1855, as follows: —

Half a league, half a league,
  Half a league onward,
All in the valley of Death
   Rode the six hundred.
'Charge,' was the captain's cry;
Theirs not to reason why,
Theirs not to make reply,
Theirs but to do and die,
Into the valley of Death
   Rode the six hundred.

Cannon to right of them,
Cannon to left of them,
Cannon behind them
   Volley'd and thunder'd;
Storm'd at with shot and shell,
Boldly they rode and well;
Into the jaws of Death,
Into the mouth of Hell
   Rode the six hundred.

Flash'd all their sabres bare,
Flash'd all at once in air,
Sabring the gunners there,
Charging an army, while
   All the world wonder'd:
Plunged in the battery smoke,
Fiercely the line they broke;
Strong was the sabre-stroke,
Making an army reel
   Shaken and sunder'd.
Then they rode back, but not,
   Not the six hundred.

Cannon to right of them,
Cannon to left of them,
Cannon behind them
   Volley'd and thunder'd;
Storm'd at with shot and shell,
They that had struck so well
Rode thro' the jaws of Death,
Half a league back again,
Up from the mouth of Hell,
All that was left of them,
   Left of six hundred.

Honor the brave and bold!
Long shall the tale be told,
Yea, when our babes are old—
   How they rode onward.

The poet was severely criticised for the alterations he had made in this version, and a few weeks later the poem was printed in its present form on a quarto sheet of four pages, with the following note: —

Having heard that the brave soldiers at Sebastopol, whom I am proud to call my countrymen, have a liking for my ballad on the charge of the Light Brigade at Balaclava, I have ordered a thousand copies of it to be printed for them. No writing of mine can add to the glory they have acquired in the Crimea; but if what I heard be true, they will not be displeased to receive these copies of the ballad from me, and to know that those who sit at home love and honour them.   ALFRED TENNYSON.
8th August, 1855.

Page 227. ENOCH ARDEN.
The title of the 'Enoch Arden' volume, in the first proofs, was 'Idylls of the Hearth.' For interesting reviews of this poem, see 'Blackwood,' vol. xcvi. p. 555; the 'Quarterly Review,' vol. cxix. p. 58; the 'Westminster Review,' vol. lxxxii. p. 396; the 'London Quarterly Review,' vol. xxiii. p. 153; and 'Chambers's Journal,' vol. xli. p. 620. See also the 'Memoir,' vol. ii. pp. 5–9.

Line 1. *Long lines of cliff*, etc. It is said that this description was suggested by the scenery of Clovelly in Devonshire; but the poet had not then seen Clovelly, and as the writer in the 'Quarterly Review' remarks, such quaint little fishing villages are to be found elsewhere in England. Mr. J. Cuming Walters ('Tennyson; Poet, Philosopher, Idealist,' London, 1893) says that Deal is the place; but his identification of the localities of the poems, as Tennyson himself declared, is seldom to be trusted.

7. *Danish barrows.* These ancient sepulchral mounds, some of which are supposed to be older than the Danish, or even the Roman conquest, are common in Great Britain, especially in Wilts and Dorset. Compare 'Tithonus': 'And grassy barrows of the happier dead.'

8. *By autumn nutters haunted, flourishes.* A line somewhat harsh, as the reader who gives every word its full enunciation will perceive. Tennyson rarely errs in that way.

32. *The helpless wrath of tears.* A good example of the poet's felicitous condensation of phrase.

55. *From the dread sweep of the down-streaming seas.* An admirably graphic line.

71. *All kindled by a still and sacred fire,* etc. 'How could the high devotion of Enoch's love be brought more strikingly before us than in these few words?' ('Quarterly Review').

112. *Altho' a grave and staid God-fearing man.* Peter Bayne remarks: 'Very notable is the stress which the poet lays upon the religion of Enoch.' Compare what the 'Quarterly' reviewer says: 'We would pause here for a moment to point out the skill and judgment which Mr. Tennyson has shown in giving intensity and sinew to the passion of his tale by the slight leaven of a Puritan faith. The want of moral

grandeur in modern life is one of the chief difficulties with which a modern poet has to deal; nor can he longer fill this want by use of those supernatural systems which are now fitly called "machineries." This difficulty the Laureate has successfully evaded by laying the scene of his action in a secluded fishing port, where a stern creed had grown up under the changeful northern sky and the mysterious perils of the sea; and where the traditional superstitions of a sailor life were woven in with an intense and living belief handed down from a Puritan ancestry. The occasional use of supernatural means, such as Annie's dream, so falls evenly upon the reader's mind, and certain superstitious observances are justified; while a moral sublimity is also gained which gives depth and unity to the tone of the poem.'

131. *Isles a light in the offing.* The cloud on the horizon seems like an island with a light upon it. The line has been misinterpreted by some critics.

142. *This voyage more than once.* 'Voyage' is here metrically a dissyllable, as in several lines further on. Compare 'Julius Cæsar,' iv. 3, 20. 'Omitted, all the voyage of their life,' etc. The word is oftener monosyllabic in modern verse, and even in Shakespeare.

196. *Nay, for I love him, etc.* This is said in reply to a *look* from Annie.

220. *Keep everything shipshape.* The critic in 'Blackwood' ' strongly objects' to this nautical phrase. He adds: ' In real life men do not delight in the slang of the calling as much as books make them do — least of all in their solemn moments. We hope to see *shipshape* omitted in future editions. But who can fail to admire the rest of the speech?' The objection to *shipshape* is hypercritical. The word is not 'slang,' but a nautical figure in keeping with the character, like 'Will bring fair weather yet' above, etc.

For the Scriptural allusions in the passage, see Psalms, xcv. 5, cxxxix. 9; Hebrews, vi. 19, and 1 Peter, v. 7.

267-269. *After a lingering, etc.* The reviewer in 'Blackwood' remarks: 'The "flitting" soul recalls to our mind Mr. Merivale's admirable translation of the dying emperor's address to his own. We may earn some reader's thanks by quoting it here: —

> Animula, vagula, blandula,
> Hospes comesque corporis,
> Quae nunc abibis in loca —
> Pallidula, rigida, nudula —
> Nec, ut soles, dabis jocos?

> Soul of mine, pretty one, flitting one,
> Guest and partner of my clay,
> Whither wilt thou hie away —
> Pallid one, rigid one, naked one —
> Never to play again, never to play?

The 'Quarterly' reviewer says of the same passage: 'Wonderful as are many of Mr. Tennyson's descriptive rhythms, perhaps none have shown such marvellous and subtle skill as these three lines, which, catching the reader "ere he is aware" by their quickened flight and the sudden hurry of their cadence, leave him with parted lips.'

340. *From his tall mill that whistled on the waste.* The verb is aptly chosen to express the sound of the mill.

491. *Then desperately seized the holy Book, etc.* A favorite mode of divination among the ancients was that of *stichomancy*, or by lines of poetry. A number of verses were selected from a poet, mixed together in an urn, and one drawn out at random from which the good or evil fortune was inferred. The 'Æneid' of Virgil came to be especially used for this purpose, and hence the name *Sortes Virgilianæ* subsequently given to the method. After the introduction of Christianity the Bible was used in a similar way, the book being opened at random, as here by Annie, and the first passage touched by the finger or catching the eye being taken as the response of the oracle. The custom was in vogue among the Puritans, and still lingers among the common people in England and Scotland.

494. *Under the palm-tree.* The 1st edition had ' Under a palm-tree.' See Judges, iv. 5. 'She beholds Enoch seated "Under a palmtree, over him the sun;" ' as he doubtless was at that moment in the island on which he had been wrecked, and where the ghostly echo of her wedding-bells is so soon to torment his ear. But the true vision is but a lying dream to his wife. In her simplicity she cannot think of palms as real trees growing in foreign lands. Her mind flies to Scriptural associations, ... and the last obstacle to her marriage with Philip is removed ' (' Blackwood ').

523. *Prosperously sail'd, etc.* The ten lines that follow are noteworthy as a word-picture of the vicissitudes of the voyage — the rough seas of the Bay of Biscay, the smooth sailing before the tropical trade-winds on either side of the African continent, and the variable weather about the Cape of Good Hope. The description of the 'home-voyage' just below is no less admirable. Tennyson excels in his sea-pictures.

609-617. *Once likewise, in the ringing of his ears, etc.* 'How well is the unity of interest kept up by this simple infusion of a supernatural sympathy — a sympathy used by other imaginative writers with similar success, as by Hawthorne in " Transformation " [the infelicitous name under which ' The Marble Faun ' is published in England] and by Miss Brontë in " Jane Eyre " ' (' Quarterly Review '). Compare ' Aylmer's Field ': —

> Star to star vibrates light: may soul to soul
> Strike thro' a finer element of her own?

635. *Muttering and mumbling, etc.* The ' Quarterly Review ' says here: ' Arden, all due allowance made, must have passed at least full seven years of solitary life upon his isle; and it is a serious question whether any human being, much more a man of his intensity of nature, could have passed through this ordeal and kept his wits. The awful consequences of much

shorter periods of utter solitude are well known, although we admit, on the other hand, that in the present state of psychology it is difficult to pronounce either way with certainty. We have little science to guide us, but against the imaginative insight of Mr. Tennyson we have the declaration of Wordsworth ("Excursion," book iv.) that

> the innocent sufferer often sees
> Too clearly; feels too vividly; and longs
> To realize the vision, with intense
> And over-constant yearning; there — there lies
> The excess by which the balance is destroyed.'

But Wordsworth is not really 'against' Tennyson, for he only says that the sufferer 'often' becomes insane — which is unquestionably true; and, as the reviewer himself admits, even scientific men do not settle the question either way. The poet may therefore claim the benefit of the doubt in Enoch's case.

Although the poor fellow has not lost his wits, he has lost the power of speech, and recovers it only by degrees. Tennyson's 'imaginative insight' is doubtless true to nature in this, and I am willing to believe it so in the rest.

638. *To where the rivulets of sweet water ran.* That is, fresh water; like the 'dulces aquae' of Virgil ('Æneid,' i. 167). Compare line 799 below: 'Like fountains of sweet water in the sea.'

657. *Of England, blown across her ghostly wall.* The chalk cliffs of the southern coast.

667. *Either haven.* The one where he landed, and that in which his native village lay. Compare line 102 above.

711. *Repeated muttering, 'cast away and lost.'* 'We may briefly record our admiration for the sustained power and absence of maudlin sensibility with which the last scenes of "Enoch Arden" are put before us. They are very pathetic; and they are never foolishly sentimental. The way in which Enoch is stunned by the news of his wife's second marriage; his longing to see her, and assure himself that she is happy; the picture of peace and comfort *within* Philip's house, which throws into stronger relief the anguish of the wretched husband and father as he stands *without;* Enoch's grand (if not strictly just) self-sacrifice, as, recovering from the shock of *seeing* what only to *hear* of had been woe sufficient, he repeats his resolution to himself, "Not to tell *her,* never to let her know:" all these things in the hands of a French writer, aiming at the *déchirant* and the *larmoyant,* would have been morbidly painful. Mr. Tennyson so tells them that they elevate our minds by the sight of a spirit refining to its highest perfection in the purgatorial fires of earth' ('Blackwood').

866. *See your bairns before you go.* The word *bairns* is used in the dialects of the North of England as well as in Scotland. Harrison, in his 'Description of England' (1577), says: 'The common sort doo call their male children *barnes* here in England, especiallie in the North countrie, where that word is still accustomablie in use.'

870. *Woman, disturb me not, etc.* 'The dying man's last victory over selfishness (when, forbidding the woman to fetch his children, he sends to them and to his wife the loving messages which it might grieve them too much to hear from his own lips) bespeaks not merely our pity for him, but our reverence. There is also something profoundly sad in the way in which that desolate heart, after half-claiming back the living children, feels that, in real fact, only the dead little one is left it' (Blackwood').

904. *There came so loud a calling of the sea, etc.* In the English illustrated edition there is here a cut, from a drawing by Arthur Hughes, representing a stormy sea dashing against the wharves of the port. This cut was reproduced in my annotated edition of 'Enoch Arden and Other Poems' (Boston, 1887). Lord Tennyson afterwards wrote to me: 'The illustration of the "calling of the sea," by Arthur Hughes, is wrong. The "calling of the sea" is an expression for the sound of a ground swell, not of a storm. The timber of old houses would never have rung to such a sound except upon a still night when the calling of the sea is often heard for miles inland.'

908. *And so fell back and spoke no more.* And here the critic of 'Blackwood,' like others of his class, thinks that the poem should have ended: 'What need to *tell* us that the noble fisherman was strong and heroic, when the poet has just completed his fine delineation of his strength and heroism? . . . The costly funeral sounds an impertinent intrusion. We cannot doubt for a moment that Philip gave honorable burial to the man whom he had so deeply, though so unwittingly, wronged. But the atonement is such a poor one that it looks like a mockery; and we would rather hear nothing of it. Why disturb in our minds the image which what went before had left there? — the humble bed on which the form, so often tempest-tossed, reposes in its last sleep; the white face, serene in death, waiting for the kisses which it might not receive in life.'

The poet may, however, have felt that such an ending, though perhaps more rhetorically effective, was less in keeping with the simplicity of the narrative. This ends, as it began, like a plain story of humble village life; and the costly funeral — something more than mere 'honorable burial,' a loving tribute to the sailor hero rather than a poor attempt at 'atonement' for the wrong he had suffered — is, after all, if we let our imaginations fill out the picture of which the poet gives this single hint, a most touching and most appropriate conclusion.

To the critical comments on the poem already cited, I may add that of Mr. E. C. Stedman, in his 'Victorian Poets' (page 181): '"Enoch Arden," in sustained beauty, bears a relation to his shorter pastorals similar to that existing between the epic and his minor heroic-verse. Coming within the average range of emotions, it has been very widely read. This poem is in its author's purest idyllic style; noticeable for evenness of tone, clearness of diction, successful description of coast and ocean, — finally, for the loveliness and fidelity of its *genre* scenes. In study of a class below him, hearts "centred in the sphere of common duties," the Laureate is unsurpassed.'

Nor can I refrain from quoting one more tribute to the poem, — that of Mr. George William Curtis in 'Harper's Magazine' for October, 1864 (vol. xxix. p. 676): 'The fascinating fancy which Hawthorne elaborated under the title "Wakefield," of a man withdrawing from his home and severing himself for many years from his family, yet stealing to the windows in the darkness to see wife and children, and the changes time works in his familiar circle, is reproduced in "Enoch Arden," except that the separation is involuntary, and the unbetrayed looking in upon the change of years is not a mere psychological diversion, but an act of the highest moral heroism. Indeed, the tale is profoundly tragical, and like the last Idyll of the King is a rare tribute to the master passion of the human heart. It is not the most subtle selfishness, whispers the poet; it is the perfection of self-denial. Xavier de Maistre says that the Fornarina loved her love more than her lover. Not so would Raphael's Madonna have loved. Not so loved Enoch Arden. There is no nobler tale of true love than his.

'It is told with that consummate elegance in which Tennyson has no peer. The English language has a burnished beauty in his use of it which is marvellous. In his earlier verses it was too dainty, too conspicuously fastidious, and the words were chosen too much for themselves and their special suggestions and individual melody. But his mastery of them now is manly. It is as striking as Milton's, although entirely different. There are a Miltonic and a Tennysonian blank verse in English literature — is there any other? . . .

'This volume, with all the others of Tennyson, are an invaluable study to every literary aspirant and neophyte; for as his poems are the most striking illustrations of the fondness of the literary spirit of the age for the most gorgeous verbiage, so they are the most noble examples of a luxuriant tendency constantly restrained and tempered by the truest taste. He has gained severity and simplicity without losing richness, and force without losing fire. Literature is not the record of thought only — it is thought *and* the vehicle of thought. Gold is very precious; but gold carved by Benvenuto is priceless.'

Page 240. AYLMER'S FIELD.
Line 3. *Like that long-buried body, etc.* Tennyson undoubtedly refers to the opening of an Etruscan tomb at the ancient city of Tarquinii, near Corneto, in Italy. The discovery was made by Carlo Avvolta, a native of Corneto, and was the first that directed the attention of archæologists to this interesting necropolis, in which more than two thousand sepulchres have since been explored. While digging into a tumulus for stones to mend a road, Signor Avvolta

broke into the tomb of an Etruscan Lucumo, or prince. 'I beheld,' he says, 'a warrior stretched on a couch of rock, and in a few minutes I saw him vanish, as it were, under my eyes, for as the atmosphere entered the sepulchre, the armor, thoroughly oxidized, crumbled away into most minute particles; so that in a short time scarcely a vestige of what I had seen was left on the couch.' The golden crown worn by the dead prince was so fragile that all but a small portion of it crumbled into dust on its way to Rome.

6. *Slipt into ashes.* A good illustration of the poet's felicity in the choice of words.

12. *And been himself a part of what he told.* A reminiscence of Æneas's 'quorum pars magna fui' (' Æneid,' ii. 6).

13. *That almighty man, etc.* The 'Quarterly' critic is troubled by this, and asks: 'Now what do we gain by this profanation of words which immemorial usage has consecrated to one purpose only? They overweight by their exaggeration the satire they were designed to point.'

17. *Whose blazing wyvern, etc.* The heraldic dragon-like creature so called, — evidently a prominent figure in the Aylmer arms. Compare line 516 below.

39. *An immemorial intimacy.* The phrase is repeated in line 136 below.

44. *Sons of men, etc.* See Genesis, vi. 2.

53. *Not proven.* A Scottish law phrase. *Proven* is an illegitimate form (as *approven* — which Tennyson has once in the 'Idylls of the King' — or *reproven* would be), but is now often used instead of *proved.*

65. *That islet in the chestnut-bloom.* That spot of red.

72. *Shone like a mystic star, etc.* A 'variable star,' like Algol in the constellation Perseus.

82. *A decad.* The spelling *decade* is more common in America, though the analogy of *triad, pentad,* etc. favors the other.

90. *The fairy footings on the grass.* The 'fairy rings,' or circles on the grass, supposed to be made by the elves in their nightly dances. Compare 'The Tempest,' v. 1. 36: —

> You demi-puppets that
> By moonshine do the green sour ringlets make,
> Whereof the ewe not bites, etc.

92. *The petty mare's-tail forest.* The *Hippuris vulgaris,* a plant native to Britain, but found in other temperate and cold regions.

93. *Or from the tiny pitted target blew, etc.* Referring to the dandelion. Compare 'The Poet': 'the arrow-seeds of the field-flower;' and 'Gareth and Lynette': —

> The flower
> That blows a globe of after arrowlets.

102. *The music of the moon.* The reviewer in 'Blackwood' says, somewhat hypercritically: 'We do not think such an equivocal expression as "the music of the moon," so inevitably suggesting the "music of the spheres," should have been employed to designate that with

which Philomel salutes the goddess of the night.'

105. *Temple-eaten terms.* Terms spent as a law-student at the Temple in London.

110. *The tented winter-field, etc.* The hop-field as it looks in winter, when the poles are put together in tent-like stacks. The military figure is well carried out in the description of summer. when the poles are set up again to support the vines that will cover them with garlands of ripened cones in autumn.

121. *And mighty courteous in the main.* In the use of 'mighty' there is something approaching to a play upon the word.

135. *Nor by plight or broken ring, etc.* Lovers used sometimes to break a ring in two, each keeping one of the pieces in token of betrothal.

147. *By sallowy rims.* Its banks bordered with sallows, or willows.

152. *One that, summer-blanch'd, etc.* One whose walls were in summer all white with the profuse blossoms of the ' traveller's joy ' (*Clematis vitalba*), and in autumn covered partly with its feathery and silky tufts, partly with ivy. Compare ' The Golden Year ': ' O'erflourish'd with the hoary clematis.'

160. *A milky-way on earth.* A path white with borders of lilies. Compare Wordsworth, ' The Daffodils ': —

> Continuous as the stars that shine
> And twinkle on the milky way,
> They stretch'd in never-ending line.

161. *Like visions in the Northern dreamer's heavens.* The allusion is to Swedenborg.

168. *For she, etc.* The verb is eleven lines below: ' was adored.'

171. *Not sowing hedgerow texts, etc.* Not merely scattering tracts among the peasantry.

191. *With half a score of swarthy faces.* His Indian servants.

193. *The close ecliptic.* The tropical sun.

202. *Unawares they flitted off.* That is, her thoughts wandered off.

221. *Gold that branch'd itself, etc.* An apt description of the exquisite Indian work in metal.

233. *The costly Sahib.* The critic in ' Blackwood ' says: ' We must own we are much puzzled to understand in what sense the Indian kinsman who presents Edith with the fatal dagger is called " the *costly* Sahib." A man who made such handsome gifts to his relatives was anything but costly to them; and large as they may have been his pension, we cannot think the poet meant to allude to it as a burden on the East Indian Company.' We wonder that the reviewer was not equally troubled by the *wealthy scabbard* three lines below, and that he did not suggest transposing the adjectives, like his brother Scotchman who was inclined to believe that Shakespeare really wrote in ' As You Like It ': —

> Stones in the running brooks,
> Sermons in books, etc.

What would the prosaic reviewer make of the similar use of *costly* in ' The Merchant of Venice,' ii. 9. 94 ?

> A day in April never came so sweet
> To show how costly summer was at hand, etc.

251. *Blues and reds.* The colors of rival political parties, like Whigs and Tories.

256. *That great pock - pitten fellow.* Some poacher for whom they had been on the watch.

263. *This blacksmith border - marriage.* A ' Gretna Green marriage.' This Scotch village was the first convenient halting-place for run-away couples from England, who could be married here without the publication of bans and certain other formalities prescribed by the English law, nothing being required in Scotland but a mutual declaration of marriage in presence of witnesses, — a ceremony which could be performed instantly, even in the case of minors. For some years a *blacksmith* was the person who officiated at these extempore marriages. Owing to changes in both the English and the Scotch laws, Gretna Green is no longer famous for such matches.

265. *That cursed France, with her egalities !* It will be remembered that the time of the poem is supposed to be 1793.

277. *And Sir Aylmer Aylmer watch'd.* Acting on the neighbor's hint, though too haughty to let him know it.

280. *Pale as the Jephtha's daughter.* A prophetic picture here.

321. *As the wind-hover hangs in balance.* A species of hawk (*Falco tinnunculus*), so called from its hovering in the wind, or ' hanging in balance.'

405. *His richest bee's-wing from a bin reserved.* His oldest and choicest port. The ' bee's-wing ' is a peculiar film in this wine, so called from its resemblance to the wing of a bee. It is much esteemed by connoisseurs as a mark of age. ' The waning red ' in the next line is an allusion to the gradual change from red to a permanent brown which takes place in port wine.

428–431. *The rain of heaven, and their own bitter tears, etc.* The complimentary ' pretty ' of ' Blackwood ' is ' faint praise ' for this fine passage.

435–437. *The lawless science of our law, etc.* The labyrinthic complexity of English law is aptly described in these lines.

455. *The gardens of that rival rose, etc.* The Temple Gardens in London, where Plantagenet plucked the white rose and Somerset the red. Compare ' 1 Henry VI.' ii. 4.

463. *Ran a Malayan amuck against the times.* Made a furious and indiscriminate attack, like those Malays who sometimes rush out in a frantic state with dagger in hand, yelling ' Amuck ! amuck ! ' and attacking all who come in their way. We often meet with the incorrect expression ' run a muck; ' and the first reading of the text here was ' a Malayan muck.'

490. *The nightly wirer of their innocent hare.* A poacher, using snares of wire to entrap the hares.

509. *The brand of John.* That is, a mark

burnt into the bark of the tree in the reign of King John, covered from view by bark growing for centuries, but never adhering to the part branded, and finally disclosed by the falling-off of this outer growth. Major Rooke (quoted in 'Notes and Queries' for September 25, 1880) tells us that 'in cutting down some timber in Birkland and Billagh, in Sherwood Forest, letters have been found cut or stamped in the body of the trees, denoting the King's reign in which they were so marked. The ciphers were of the reigns of James I., of William and Mary, and one of King John. The mark of John was eighteen inches within the tree, and something more than a foot from the centre; it was cut down in 1791.' Several other instances of trees bearing 'the brand of John' are cited by correspondents of the same journal.

516. *Burst his own wyvern on the seal.* The seal bore the Aylmer arms. See on line 17 above.

529. *The black republic on his elms.* The flock of rooks. Compare 'Locksley Hall': 'the clanging rookery.'

530. *Sweeping the frothfly from the fescue.* The 'frothfly' (*Aphrophora spumaria*) is also known as the 'froth-insect,' 'froth-worm,' 'froghopper,' etc. 'Fescue' is the name of many kinds of grass in the genus *Festuca*.

539. *Babyisms.* Lovers' baby-talk; a word dating back only to 1836, according to the 'New English Dictionary.' The 'Blackwood' critic doubts whether the description is true to the time. He says: 'In the last century letter-writing was a stately, grave, and formal thing, even amongst near relations. And we have no doubt that a gentleman of ancient family like Leolin, and the heiress of the good-breeding, though not of the pride, of the Aylmers, could write to one another without forgetting the established proprieties of their day.'

560. *A Martin's summer.* The mild weather coming near Martinmas, or St. Martin's Day, the 11th of November, corresponding to the 'Indian Summer' of New England. Compare '1 Henry VI.' i. 2, 131: 'Expect Saint Martin's summer, halcyon days,' etc.

571–573. *Like flies that haunt a wound, or deer, or men, etc.* 'The simile is at once new and appropriate, and the divine beauty of the exception stands out in stronger relief from the dark background' ('Blackwood').

578. *Star to star vibrates light, etc.* Compare the illustrations of the same mysterious sympathy of souls widely sundered in 'Enoch Arden.'

585. *With a weird bright eye, etc.* The line should be scanned thus: 'With a weird | bright eye | sweating | and trem- | ble-ing;' making 'trembling' a trisyllable, as many similar words are lengthened in Elizabethan poets. Compare Shakespeare, 'Two Gentlemen of Verona,' i. 3. 84: 'O, how this spring of love *resembleth;*' 'Coriolanus,' i. 1. 159: 'You, the great toe of this *assembly,*' etc.

618. *Their own gray tower, or plain-faced*

tabernacle. The neighboring church (of England) or chapel (of Dissenters). The people from the former, supposed to be of the better class, are 'all in mourning;' while the humbler folk from the latter can afford only some bit of black as a badge of sorrow.

628. *The verse, 'Behold,' etc.* See Matthew, xxiii. 38, or Luke, xiii. 35.

644. *Gash thyself, priest, and honor thy brute Baal.* Compare 1 Kings, xviii. 28.

648. *The babe shall lead the lion.* Compare Isaiah, xi. 6; and for the next line, Isaiah, xxxv. 1.

651. *No coarse and blockish god of acreage.* The Roman god Terminus, who presided over the boundaries of private property. So Lord Tennyson explained it in a letter to me.

671. *Not passing through the fire, etc.* As in the worship of Moloch. Compare Leviticus, xviii. 21, 2 Kings, xxiii. 10, Jeremiah, xxxii. 35, etc.

681. *The angel that said 'Hail!'* See Luke, i. 28.

698. *The hand that robed your cottage-walls with flowers.* See 151 fol. above.

716. *May wreck itself without the pilot's guilt.* Alluding to his brother's suicide, which he suggests may have been in a moment of frenzy, and therefore without the guilt of deliberate self-murder.

724. *That knit themselves for summer-shadow.* That contract the brow instinctively in the glare of sunshine.

728. *Anger-charm'd from sorrow.* His wrath overpowering his grief, as if by a magic spell.

742. *Or in the waste, 'Repent.'* Like John the Baptist in the wilderness. See Matthew, iii. 1, 2; and for what precedes, Daniel, iv. 25, v. 26, etc.

759. *Sent like the twelve-divided concubine, etc.* See Judges, xix. 29.

760. *Out yonder.* That is, in France. See on 265 above.

771. *May Pharaoh's darkness, etc.* See Exodus, x. 21, and Matthew, xxvii. 45.

824. *Yet to the lychgate, etc.* A churchyard gate with a porch under which a bier was formerly placed while the introductory part of the burial-service was read. It is also called a *corpse-gate,* which means the same, *lich* (Anglo-Saxon *lic*) being an old word for a dead body. These gates are still to be seen in some parts of England.

842. *The dark retinue reverencing death.* 'Retinue' is accented on the second syllable, as in 'The Princess,' iii.: 'Went forth in long retinue following up;' and 'Guinevere': 'Of his and her retinue moving they.' This is the accent of Shakespeare and Milton, in the only instances in which they use the word in verse.

849. *The hawk's cast.* Indigestible matter ejected from the stomach by the hawk or other bird of prey.

851. *The rabbit fondles his own harmless face.* As the timid creature does this only when absolutely at ease, nothing could better indicate the

complete desolation of the scene; but all the details of the picture are in keeping.

A correspondent of ' Notes and Queries ' says that the scene of ' Aylmer's Field ' is ' Aylmerston in Norfolk.' I presume he refers to *Aylmerton*, a parish twenty miles north of Norwich, and about three miles from the coast. Rye's ' Guide to Norfolk ' mentions it as ' interesting from the open pits or earth dwellings . . . which are locally called "shrieking pits," from the local belief that the wraith of a woman is always wandering about looking into them at night-time, wringing her hands and shrieking.'

Page 252. SEA DREAMS.

' Poor Esther Johnson said of Swift that he could write beautifully on a broomstick; but even a broomstick, if one were permitted to wander in thought to the woods in which it grew, might seem a likelier subject for poetry than the pecuniary loss of a city clerk, on which Tennyson has contrived to hang a powerful and beautiful poem' (Bayne).

' The grace of the poem,' says the ' Quarterly Review,' ' is equalled by the winning kindliness of it.' Stedman calls it ' a poem of measureless satire and much idyllic beauty.'

Line 4. *Her clear germander eye.* ' Some might call this a touch of Pre-Raphaelite conceit or affectation, but I think a poet has a right to invent color-words for himself when he wants them, provided only that they are expressive, picturesque, and not too far-fetched. There is no word in the language that will define the particular tint of blue which you see not unfrequently in the eye of an ailing child so well as that which is here applied by Tennyson. It is the faintly mottled blue of the germander speedwell (*Veronica chamædrys*) — nothing else. As the little flower can be seen in summer in every English lane, the reference to it can hardly be called far-fetched ' (Bayne). I believe, however, that *germander* is here applied to the color of the child's eye in health, not when ' ailing.'

8. *Small were his gains.* The first reading was: ' His gains were small.'

15. *To buy strange shares.* At first, ' wild shares.'

19. *Variers from the church.* That is, Dissenters.

23. *The Scarlet Woman.* The Church of Rome; his interpretation of Revelation, xvii. 3. For the ' Apocalyptic millstone,' see Revelation, xviii. 21.

32. *They came and paced the shore.* At first, ' moved and paced the shore.'

34. *The large air.* Compare Virgil, ' Æneid,' vi. 640. ' Largior hic campos aether et lumine vestit.'

39. *Till all the sails were darken'd in the east, etc.* ' There is another reading, fresh and bright, from nature's own page ! You stand by the sea, on a southward-looking coast, as the sun goes down. Westward, where the sails come between you and the sunset, they show simply as spots of shade; eastward, where they are farther from the sun than you, they catch the gleam from the west,' and every sail is a speck of rose-light. I call that a proper illustration of our Alfred's " truth of *touch* " ' (Bayne).

For ' Till all ' the first reading was ' Until.'

44. *Let not the sun go down upon your wrath.* See Ephesians, iv. 26.

47. *Remembering her dear Lord.* Originally, ' our dear Lord.'

65, 66. *Is it so true that second thoughts are best ?* The first reading was: —

> It is not true that second thoughts are best,
> But first, and third, which are a riper first.

Tainsh considers the alteration an unfortunate one; but the interrogative form seems to me to add a bitter emphasis to the statement, not to weaken it by the expression of doubt, as he understands it.

70. *When first I fronted him.* At first, ' I lighted on him.'

84. *Had you ill dreams ?* In the dream that follows, the results of speculation are contrasted with those of honest work.

130. *I thought I could have died to save it.* This is true to the intensity of feeling we often experience in dreams.

148. *See Daniel seven and ten.* At first, ' seven, the tenth.'

154. *And all things work together for the good, etc.* See Romans, viii. 28.

176–194. *With all his conscience and one eye askew, etc.* ' A masterly imitation of our Old English satiric style. I am not sure whether it was Dryden or Cowper that Tennyson had in mind, and I cannot help thinking that he must have been influenced, in composing the lines, by Crabbe. The first line will recall Dryden's " With two left legs and Judas-colored hair " ' (Bayne). The critic in ' Blackwood ' says that the first two lines ' might be sworn to as Pope's any day.'

186. *Made Him his catspaw, and the Cross his tool.* This line and the next were not in the first version.

195. *I loathe it: he had never kindly heart, etc.* ' Her answer honors Tennyson, and is, by implication, one of the noblest tributes ever paid to the heart-wisdom of woman' (Bayne).

201. *But round the North, etc.* The indirect quotation passes into direct in line 231: ' Then I fixt,' etc. The first reading here was: —

> Still
> It awed me. *Well — I* dream'd *that* round the North
> A light, a belt of luminous vapor, lay,
> And ever in it a low musical note
> Swell'd up and died; and, as it swell'd, a ridge
> Of breaker *came from out* the belt, and still
> Grew with the growing note, and when the note
> Had reach'd a thunderous fulness, on *these* cliffs
> Broke, mixt with awful light (the same as that
> *Which lived* within the belt) *by which* I saw, etc.

The ' Quarterly Review ' remarks: ' If we have a fault to find, it is with the mother's dream. This dream is vague and something too ponderous for the piece. It labors under the double obscurity of being both dream and allegory, and it remains with us a doubt to this day whether we have hit upon the true meaning of it, or whether the poet will rise up in judgment against our interpretation. We had almost said with Bottom that it is " past the wit of man to say what dream it was." Not that this is all a fault, for, as the husband tells her, Boanerges the pulpiteer and the unfamiliar ocean roar were likely parents of such a fantasy.'

Bayne says that the dream 'seems to be an imaginative shadowing forth of the general revolutionary movement of those times, and of the battle of churches and sects, of creeds and scepticisms, through all which — an echo, shall we say? of the indestructible harmony in her own heart — she hears a note of Divine music. Readers will find much food for musing in these dreams.'

215–218. *And past into the belt, etc.* The first reading was: —

> And past into the belt, and swell'd again
> *To music;* ever when it broke *I saw*
> The statues, *saint or king* or founder, *fall;*
> Then from *the gaps of ruin which it* left, etc.

222. *And she grieved, etc.* Originally: —

> And *I* grieved
> In *my* strange dream, *I* knew not why, etc.

225. *As their shrieks, etc.* At first, 'when their shrieks,' etc.

227. *While none mark'd it.* Originally, 'tho' none mark'd it.'

231. *To the waste deeps together, etc.* The first reading was : ' To the waste deeps together: and I fixt,' etc.

243. *Our Boanerges with his threats of doom.* Compare Mark, iii. 17.

246. *But if there were, etc.* Originally, 'But were there such,' etc.

257. *The dimpled flounce of the sea-furbelow.* I did not understand this when editing the poem in 1887, and Lord Tennyson explained it in a letter thus: ' The reference is to a long dark-green seaweed, one of the *Laminaria,* called the " sea-furbelow," with dimpled, flounce-like edges. Boys sometimes running along the sand against the wind with this seaweed in their hands make it flap for sport. I should have put a note to this in my book. The name " sea-furbelow " is not generally known.' A similar seaweed is known on our New England coast as the ' Devil's apron-string.'

259–261. *Why were you silent when I spoke to-night ?* In place of this and the two next lines, the first version had the following: —

> I would not tell you then to spoil your day,
> But he at whom you rail so much is dead.

280. *This baby song.* 'An exquisite lullaby, a song which all mothers may learn, for it is what household songs should be, tender, simple, graceful, and picturesque' ('Quarterly Review ').

Page 257. Ode Sung at the Opening of the International Exhibition.

Line 7. *O silent father of our kings to be.* Prince Albert. Compare p. xv. above.

10. *The world-compelling plan.* *Compelling* is used in the etymological sense of ' bringing together.'

A Welcome to Alexandra.

Lines 20–24. *Rush to the roof . . . when he welcomes the land.* These five lines were not in the first version.

Page 258. The Grandmother.

For the suggestion of this poem, see the ' Memoir,' vol. i. p. 432.

Page 260. Northern Farmer, Old Style.

I add a few additional glossarial notes from Palgrave's ' Lyrical Poems by Lord Tennyson ' (London, 1885).

Page 261. *'asta beän*, hast thou been; *thoort*, thou art; *moänt*, may not have; *point*, pint; *'issén*, himself; *towd*, told; *boy*, by; *Larn'd a ma' beä*, learned he may be (*a* stands for *he* in this dialect); *a cast oop*, he cast up against me; *owt*, ought; *'Siver*, howsoever; *boy um*, by him; *stubb'd*, broken up for cultivation; *moind*, remember; *boggle*, bogle, haunting spirit; *the lot*, piece of waste; *raäved and rembled*, tore up and threw away; *Keäper's it wur*, it was the game-keeper's ghost; *at 'soize*, at the assizes; *Dubbut*, do but; *yows*, ewes.

Page 262. *ta-year*, this year; *thruff*, through; *haäte oonderd*, eight hundred; *thutty*, thirty; *a moost*, he must; *cauve*, calve; *hoälms*, holms, mounds of slightly rising ground; *quoloty*, quality, the gentry; *thessèn*, themselves; *sewerloy*, surely; *howd*, hold; *Sartin-sewer*, certain sure; *kittle*, kettle, boiler; *Huzzin' an' maäzin'*, worrying with a hiss and astonishing; *atta*, art thou; *'toättler*, teetotaler; *a's hallus i' the owd taäle*, is always telling the same old story; *floy*, fly.

Northern Farmer, New Style.

The following notes are added by Palgrave: —

Page 262. *craw to pluck*, crow to pluck, matter to dispute; *lass*, daughter.

Page 263. *as 'ant nowt*, as has nothing; *weänt 'a*, will not have; *shut on*, clear of; *i' the grip*, in the little draining-ditch; *tued an' moil'd*, put himself in a stew and toiled; *run oop*, his land run up.

Page 265. The Sailor Boy.

Line 12. *And in thy heart the scrawl shall play.* In the Lincolnshire dialect, ' the young of the dog-crab ' is known as the ' scrawl ' (Halliwell, ' Archaic Dictionary ').

Page 266. Boadicea.

Written in 1859 (' Memoir,' vol. i. p. 436), the metre being ' an echo of the metre in the " Atys " of Catullus.' The poet ' wished that it were musically annotated so that it might be read with proper quantity and force.' He found that people would not understand the rhythm; but he said that ' if they would only read it straight like prose just as it is written, it would come all right.'

Page 268. Specimen of a Translation of the Iliad in Blank Verse.

The first line of the translation originally read thus: ' So Hector said, and sea-like roar'd his host;' and this was retained in the 'Enoch Arden' reprint.

The last two lines were as follows in the magazine: —

> And champing golden grain their horses stood
> Hard by the chariots, waiting for the dawn;

and the following foot-note was appended: —
'Or, if something like the spondaic close of the line be required,

> And waited — by their chariots — the fair dawn.

Or, more literally,

> And champing the white barley and spelt, their steeds
> Stood by the cars, waiting the thronèd morn.'

There was also the following foot-note to 'honey-hearted':
'Or "wine sweet· to the mind," but I use this epithet simply as a synonym of "sweet."'
In the 'Enoch Arden' volume, the reading in the text was: —

> And champing golden grain, the horses stood
> Hard by their chariots, waiting for the dawn;

with this foot-note: —
'Or more literally —

> And eating hoary grain and pulse the steeds
> Stood by their cars, waiting the thronèd morn.'

Page 269. THE THIRD OF FEBRUARY, 1852.
No changes have been made in the poem; but some reprints have 'It might safe be' in the 2d stanza, and 'And flung the burthen' in the 5th.

Page 271. THE SPITEFUL LETTER.
In the 2d stanza, 'little bard' was originally 'foolish bard.' The 3d and 4th stanzas were as follows: —

> This fallen leaf, is n't fame as brief?
> My rhymes may have been the stronger,
> Yet hate me not, but abide your lot;
> I last but a moment longer.
>
> O faded leaf, is n't fame as brief?
> What room is here for a hater?
> Yet the yellow leaf hates the greener leaf,
> For it hangs one moment later.

The 5th had 'is n't that your cry?' and the next line was 'And I shall live to see it.' The last stanza read thus: —

> O summer leaf, is n't life as brief?
> But this is the time of hollies,
> And my heart, my heart is an evergreen;
> I hate the spites and follies.

Page 272. LITERARY SQUABBLES.
For the history of this poem, see p. xv. above.
In the 2d stanza, the reading in 'Punch' was 'That hate each other,' and brothers' for 'brethren.' In the 3d stanza, 'strain' was 'strive'; the last line of the 4th was 'Like those that cried Diana great'; and the last line of the 5th had 'kindly silence' for 'perfect stillness.'

Page 274. LUCRETIUS.
'The poem is Roman, not Greek, and it bears

the impress of the Roman race. In Tennyson's Greek poems, the Greek's grave beauty shines through the modern thought, through the modern description of Nature. Even in speeches like those of Athena and of Ulysses, beauty sits hand in hand with the experience of life. But in "Lucretius," stern, robust, rigid duty to self-chosen, self-approved law is first; the sense of the beautiful as a part of life does not appear in the poem. Lucretius has no religion save that of acceptance of Nature, but to that he is faithful. He has no duty to the gods, but he has duty to his own philosophic honor. He dies rather than be mastered by lustful visions which a Greek, even in the noble time when beauty meant pure harmony, would have gone through, smiled at, and forgotten.

'The philosophy also is a Greek philosophy, but Lucretius has made it Roman in temper; and one of the noble excellences of this poem is that Tennyson has never deviated in a single word from the Roman basis of the soul. Moreover, it takes a great poet to assimilate, as Tennyson does, the essence of Lucretius as a thinker and a poet in the space of about 300 lines; and to combine this with the representation of a man in an hour of doom and madness, such as an inferior poet, overloading it with frenzied ornament, would have made intemperate. Tennyson's masterly reticence, rigid restraint only to the absolutely necessary, are supreme in this poem' (Stopford Brooke).

Line 13. *Left by the Teacher, whom he held divine.* Epicurus, who, according to Diogenes Laertius, wrote three hundred volumes.

37. *A void was made in Nature, etc.* 'The possibility, or rather ultimate certainty, of this dissolution is repeated over and over again in Lucretius' (J. C. Collins's 'Illustrations of Tennyson': London, 1891).

40. *Ruining along the illimitable inane.* Compare Milton, 'Paradise Lost,' vi. 867: —

> Hell saw
> Heaven ruining from Heaven.

On the lines that follow, compare 'Lucretius,' ii. 999–1022, and v. 828–836.

52. *But girls, Hetairai, etc.* That is, harlots (the Greek ἑταῖραι).

54. *The mulberry-faced Dictator's orgies.* Referring to Sulla in his latter years.

55. *The quiet gods.* Compare the last stanza of 'The Lotos-Eaters,' and 'Œnone': —

> Gods, who have attain'd
> Rest in a happy place and quiet seats
> Above the thunder, etc.

See also lines 76–79 and 104–110 below.

82. *Thy Mavors.* Mars.

88. *The Trojan.* Anchises; as 'the wounded hunter' is Adonis, and 'the beardless apple-arbiter' (see 'Œnone') is Paris. 'The great Sicilian' is Empedocles.

95. *Kypris.* The Greek Κύπρις, as Aphrodite (Venus) was called, from the island of Cyprus, her favorite seat.

97. *The all-generating powers and genial*

heat, etc. 'In these lines Tennyson has caught the one joyous note of Lucretius, his intense and keen delight in Nature, as rapturous as Shelley's' (Collins).

119. *My Memmius.* Caius Memmius Gemellus, to whom Lucretius dedicated his 'De Rerum Natura.'

147. *Or lend an ear to Plato where he says, etc.* The reference is to the 'Phædo,' vi.: ὡς ἔν τινι φρουρᾷ ἐσμὲν οἱ ἄνθρωποι καὶ οὐ δεῖ δὴ ἑαυτὸν ἐκ ταύτης λύειν οὐδ' ἀποδιδράσκειν (we men are as it were on guard, and a man ought not to free himself from it, nor to run away). As Mr. Collins notes, Jowett takes φρουρά to mean a prison; but Tennyson's interpretation may be correct. Plato seems to be alluding to a saying of Pythagoras, to which Cicero refers ('De Senectute,' 73): 'Vetatque Pythagoras injussu imperatoris, id est Dei, de praesidio et statione vitae decedere.'

164. *How should the mind, except it loved them, clasp, etc.* 'These lines contain, with the passage that follows, an allusion to the images or emanations which, according to Lucretius, matter is always throwing off' (Collins).

181. *But who was he that in the garden snared, etc.* Compare Ovid, 'Fasti,' iii. 291–328, 'where Egeria instructs Numa to ensnare Picus and Faunus, that they may show him how the thunderbolts of Jupiter may be averted' (Collins).

235. *Not he, who bears one name with her, etc.* That is, with *Lucretia.*

273. *Thus — thus: the soul flies out and dies in the air.* The repetition of 'thus' marks the successive stabs of the dagger. Collins compares the 'Æneid,' iv. 660. 'Sic, sic, juvat ire sub umbras.'

'How the whole poem is wrought, how nobly the character of Lucretius emerges line after line, with what poetic strength and sculpturing power his masculine passion clears its way to death till the brief close shuts up the tragedy, is for every reader to grasp as he has capacity' (Stopford Brooke).

Page 281. THE LOVER'S TALE.

'The lover's sorrow is mingled up with Nature. Every natural description illustrates and reflects the changing moods of the characters. . . . The one charm of the poem is its youthfulness. The lavishness, the want of temperance, the inability to stop when enough has been said, the welling-over of words, the boyishness of sentiment, the playing at sorrow — while they prove that Tennyson was right in withdrawing the poem from publication — nevertheless give us pleasure, the pleasure of touching youth' (Stopford Brooke).

'With "The Golden Supper" there comes a change. The treatment is more dramatic, the grasp on the subject more confident. Event follows event with spirited rapidity. The pictures are not less vivid, but they are sketched with bolder, clearer touches' (Waugh).

Page 302. IDYLLS OF THE KING.

Dedication. This was first inserted in the edition of 1862. It is not merely a tribute to Prince Albert, ' but strikes the key-note of the poem very artistically as well, by introducing the idea of chivalry that Arthur set before his knights' (Littledale).

Line 6. *Scarce other than my king's ideal knight.* The first reading was ' my own ideal knight.'

12. *Commingled with the gloom of imminent war.* Alluding to the threatened war with the United States on account of the 'Trent' affair. It was largely through Prince Albert's influence that the danger was averted.

13. *The shadow of his loss drew like eclipse.* The first version had ' moved' for ' drew.'

33. *Thou noble Father of her Kings to be.* Compare the ' Ode Sung at the Opening of the International Exhibition' (1862): 'O silent father of our Kings to be,' etc.

37. *To fruitful strifes and rivalries of peace.* Referring to the International Exhibitions of 1851 and 1862. The Prince was engaged in planning the latter at the time of his death.

Page 304. THE COMING OF ARTHUR.

The story is from Malory's ' Morte Darthur' (book i.), with many variations, particularly in dealing with the coarser features of the old romance.

5. *For many a petty king, etc.* Among those enumerated by Geoffrey of Monmouth, whom the poet follows here, are Brutus, or ' Brute,' and Locrine, mentioned by Milton in 'Comus' (827, 828), Leir (the Lear of Shakespeare) and Cassibelaunus (the Cassibelan of ' Cymbeline,' i. 1. 30, etc.).

13. *Aurelius.* Aurelius Ambrosius (or Emrys), ' a descendant of the last Roman general who claimed the purple as an Emperor in Britain' (Green, ' Making of England'). He met his death by poison, as related by Geoffrey: ' For there was near the court a spring of very clear water which the King used to drink of. . . . This the detestable conspirators made use of to destroy him, by so poisoning the whole mass of water which sprang up, that the next time the King drank of it he was seized with sudden death, as were also a hundred other persons after him.' Uther, who succeeded him, was his brother.

32. *They grew up to wolf-like men.* The reader will recall the story of Romulus and Remus, the *lycanthropi* of Greek and Roman fable, the *loup-garous* and were-wolves of France and Germany, etc. Compare ' Geraint and Enid,' 94: ' The three dead wolves of woman born.'

34. *Groan'd for the Roman legions here again.* Probably, as Littledale suggests, an allusion to the famous ' Groans of the Britons' of Gildas, who says that the Britons wrote to the Roman senate: ' The barbarians drive us into the sea; the sea throws us back on the barbarians: thus two modes of death await us, we are either slain or drowned.'

36. *Urien, assail'd him.* The 1869 edition had ' Rience' for ' Urien.' According to Geoffrey, Urien was the brother of Lot; and Malory makes him the husband of Arthur's sister,

Morgan le Fay. Rience was the King of North Wales, who 'made great war upon King Leodegrance of Cameliard' (Malory).

58. *Then he drave, etc.* The 1st edition reads here: —

And he drave
The heathen, and he slew the beast, and fell'd
The forest, and let in the sun.

66. *Colleaguing with a score of petty kings.* This line was not in the 1st edition.

94–133. *Thereafter — as he speaks who tells the tale, etc.* This passage is not in the 1st edition.

111. *Carádos, Urien, Cradlemont of Wales, etc.* This list of conquered kings is from Malory.

132. *Man's word is God in man.* Repeated in 'Balin and Balan,' 8. Littledale paraphrases it thus: 'A man's promise is a divine thing, therefore it must be regarded as especially sacred.'

134. *Then quickly from the foughten field.* The first reading was: 'Then Arthur from the field of battle sent,' etc. 'Foughten field,' which Tennyson has several times elsewhere (in 'The Princess,' 'The Holy Grail,' etc.) is a reminiscence of Shakespeare, 'Henry V.' iv. 6. 18: 'this glorious and well-foughten field.'

207. *Should go to wrack.* 'Wrack' is the one form of 'wreck' in Shakespeare and other Elizabethan writers.

247–253. *A doubtful throne . . . to hold his foemen down.* For these six lines the 1st edition has only these four: —

A doubtful throne is ice on summer seas —
Ye come from Arthur's court: think ye this king —
So few his knights, however brave they be —
Hath body enow to beat his foemen down?

275. *Three fair queens.* According to Elsdale, these denote Faith, Hope, and Charity. Littledale thinks they are rather 'Charity, Abstinence, and Truth — the three virtues noted by Malory as deficient in the Knights.' When Boyd Carpenter asked Tennyson if those who made them Faith, Hope, and Charity were right, he answered: 'They are right, and they are not right. They mean that and they do not. They are three of the noblest of women. They are also those three Graces, but they are much more. I hate to be tied down to say "*This* means *that*," because the thought within the image is much more than any one interpretation' ('Memoir,' vol. ii. p. 127).

The Lady of the Lake. She symbolizes Religion, as is denoted by the sacred fish on her breast, and the great emblematic figure of her at the gate of Arthur's palace.

284. *Clothed in white samite.* A rich heavy silk, originally with thread twisted of six fibres (*hexamitum*, of which *samite* is a corruption).

298. *Jewels, elfin Urim.* For the 'Urim' of the Jewish High Priest, which many authorities believe to have been precious stones, see Exodus, xxviii. 30, Numbers, xxvii. 21, etc.

302. *Turn the blade, and ye shall see.* The 1st edition has 'you' for 'ye.'

312. *The swallow and the swift are near akin.* Littledale says that 'Leodogran's ornithology is open to question.' An ornithologist might object to the 'near' in a scientific description; but the swallows and the swifts are groups of the same family, and in some parts of England the common swift is popularly known as the 'black swallow.' Tennyson was probably as familiar with the strict classification of the birds as Littledale, who elsewhere (page 98) pays a tribute to the poet's knowledge in that line. See on 'Gareth and Lynette,' 779.

362. *Shrunk like a fairy changeling lay the mage.* The elves that fairies were supposed to leave in exchange for the human babies they stole could sometimes be recognized as 'changelings' by their shrivelled and shrunken appearance — 'like little old men,' as the stories have it. Compare 'Gareth and Lynette,' 200: 'But only changeling out of Fairyland.'

379. *Till last, a ninth one, etc.* The old Welsh poets make the ninth wave larger than its predecessors, as the Romans did the tenth.

401. *Riddling triplets of old time.* 'The tercet rhymes in which many of the bardic poems, as well as the later Breton songs, are written' (Littledale).

431. *The hind fell, the herd was driven off.* The peasant was slain, and his cattle carried off as plunder.

442. *But the King stood out in heaven.* The 1st edition has 'and' for 'but.'

452. *Dubric, the high saint.* Archbishop of Caerleon-upon-Usk, primate of Britain and legate of the Pope.

459–469. *Far shone the fields of May. . . . I love thee to the death.* These eleven lines were not in the 1st edition.

475–505. *So Dubric said; . . . as of yore.* For these thirty-one lines the 1st edition had only three: —

Then at the marriage feast came in from Rome,
The slowly-fading mistress of the world,
Great lords, who claim'd the tribute as of yore.

481–501. *Blow trumpet, etc.* Stopford Brooke calls this marriage and coronation song 'a piece of glorious literature.' He adds: 'It embodies the thought of the poem, grips the whole meaning of it together. And its sound is the sound of martial triumph, of victorious weapons in battle, and of knights in arms. We hear in the carefully varied chorus, in the very rattle and shattering of the vowels in the words, the beating of axe on helm and shield on shield. Rugged, clanging, clashing lines — it is a splendid effort of art. King Olaf might have sung it.

'We hear its contrast in Merlin's song [402–410], as soft and flowing as the other was braying and broken, and we think with gratitude of the artist who could do both with equal ease. The graciousness of the rivulet-music and soft play of Nature is in the lines of this delicate song, and the gaiety of youth; and mingled with these the deep and favorite thought of Tennyson of the pre-existence of the soul.'

507. *To wage my wars, etc.* The 1st edition had 'fight' for 'wage.'

Page 311. GARETH AND LYNETTE.

A note in the 1st edition (1872) says : —
'With this poem the Author concludes THE IDYLLS OF THE KING.

'GARETH follows THE COMING OF ARTHUR, and THE LAST TOURNAMENT precedes GUINEVERE.'

The addition of ' Balin and Balan' in 1885 was evidently an afterthought. In 1872 the 'Enid' had not been divided, and the author's plan then included only ten poems instead of the present twelve, which fulfil the suggestion in the introduction to the 'Morte d'Arthur' of 1842: 'His epic, his King Arthur, some twelve books.' He once said to Mr. Knowles: 'When I was twenty-four I meant to write a whole great poem on it, and began it in the "Morte d'Arthur." I said I should do it in twenty years; but the Reviews stopped me. . . . By King Arthur I always meant the soul, and by the Round Table the passions and capacities of a man. There is no grander subject in the world than King Arthur.'

3. *Stared at the spate.* At the river in flood or freshet. *Spate* is of Celtic origin. Compare Burns, 'The Brigs of Ayr' : —

> While crashing ice, borne on the roaring spate,
> Sweeps dams an' mills an' brigs a' to the gate.

It is used figuratively in 'Jock o' the Side' ('Border Minstrelsy') : —

> And down the water wi' speed she ran,
> While tears in spates fa' fast frae her e'e.

18. *Heaven yield her for it.* For 'yield' in the sense of 'reward,' compare 'Antony and Cleopatra,' iv. 2. 33: 'And the gods yield you for 't!' and 'Hamlet,' iv. 5. 41: 'God 'ield you!'

40. *The goose and golden eggs.* Compare Tennyson's early poem, 'The Goose.'

46. *As glitters gilded in thy Book of Hours.* An illuminated prayer-book.

84. *Red berries charm the bird.* That is, allure the bird; a proverbial saying. Compare Goldsmith, 'She Stoops to Conquer' : 'he would charm the bird from the tree.'

198. *We have heard from our wise man at home.* The 1st edition has 'men' for 'man.'

229. *The dragon-boughts.* The coils of the dragons' tails.

249. *I have seen the good ship sail, etc.* Referring to the effects of mirage.

258. *And built it to the music of their harps.* Compare 'Œnone' : —

> As yonder walls
> Rose slowly to a music slowly breathed;

and see note on that passage.

280. *The Riddling of the Bards.* Compare 'The Coming of Arthur,' 401: 'riddling triplets of old time;' and see note.

293. *Let love be blamed for it, not she, nor I.* As Littledale remarks, 'Gareth's grammar becomes a little confused.'

359. *Sir Kay.* 'The Thersites of the Romance-writers.'

362. *The wholesome boon of gyve and gag.*

Alluding to the ducking-stool and branks of the olden time, with which scolds were disciplined.

386. *His goodly cousin, Tristram.* 'Cousin' is here used, as in Malory and other old writers, in the sense of kinsman. Shakespeare applies it to nephew, niece, brother-in-law, grandchild, etc. Tristram was the son of Mark's sister.

422. *Lest we should lap him up in cloth of lead.* Alluding to the use of lead for coffins. Compare Richard Barnfield's verses, ascribed to Shakespeare in 'The Passionate Pilgrim': 'All thy friends are lapp'd in lead.' For 'lap' (wrap, enfold) compare 'The Princess,' vi.: 'Half-lapt in glowing gauze and golden brede.'

441. *But, so thou wilt no goodlier, etc.* The 1st edition has 'an' for 'so.'

455. *And hands Large, fair, and fine.* According to Malory, he was 'the fairest and largest handed that ever man saw;' and Kay says: 'Since he hath no other name, I shall give him a name that shall be Beaumains, that is Fairhands.'

490. *On Caer-Eryri's highest found the King.* On the summit of Snowdon; referring to another legend concerning the birth of Arthur. 'Caer-Eryri literally means, in Welsh, Snowdon Field' (Littledale).

492. *The Isle Avilion.* The 'Isle of Apples' — the 'Avalon' of 'The Palace of Art' : —

> Or mythic Uther's deeply-wounded son
> In some fair space of sloping greens
> Lay, dozing in the vale of Avalon,
> And watch'd by weeping queens.

642. *The may-white.* All the English editions print 'the May-white.' See on 'Guinevere,' 22.

675. *Then as he donn'd the helm, etc.* The 1st edition has 'while' for 'as;' and, four lines below, 'and' for 'while.'

710. *Kay, wherefore wilt thou go against the King?* The 1st edition has 'will ye.'

729. *A foul-flesh'd agaric in the holt.* An ill-smelling fungus in the wood. Compare 'Edwin Morris': 'Long learned names of agaric, moss, and fern.'

779. *Round as the red eye of an eagle-owl.* 'The comparison between the pool gleaming red in the twilight and the eye of an eagle-owl, burning round and bright in the darkness, may have the fault of being too uncommon to really illustrate the description, but it is a simile that an ornithologist can appreciate. Indeed, a book might be written on the bird-lore of Tennyson, as has been well done by Mr. Harting in the case of Shakespeare' (Littledale). Compare the note on 'the swallow and the swift,' in 'The Coming of Arthur' (312).

In the next line the 1st edition has 'cries' for 'shouts.'

806. *Flickering in a grimly light.* 'Grimly' (grim, hideous) is rare as an adjective. Compare 'Marmion,' iv. 440: 'So grimly and so ghast.'

807. *Good now, ye have saved a life.* For the vocative use of 'good' (my good fellow), with or without now,' compare 'Hamlet,' i. 1. 70: 'Good now, sit down and tell me, he who

knows; ' ' The Tempest,' i. 1. 3: ' Good, speak to the mariners,' etc.

813. *But wilt thou yield this damsel harborage?* The 1st edition has ' will ye yield.' Two lines below, it has ' Ye ' for ' You,' as in some passages further on; but oftener ' you ' in the early editions is changed to ' ye.'

829. *And there they placed a peacock in his pride, etc.* ' Lynette is to be reminded by the peacock in his pride that ladies should be loving and gentle to their champions — a lesson she stands rather in need of ' (Littledale). The bird was constantly the object of the solemn vows of the knights; and when it was served at table, ' all the guests, male and female, took a solemn vow; the knights vowing bravery, and the ladies engaging to be loving and faithful ' (Stanley, ' History of Birds ').

852. *Whether thou be kitchen-knave or not, etc.* The 1st edition has ' ye ' for ' thou.'

889. *Lent-lily in hue.* The daffodil is called the ' Lent-lily,' because it blossoms about the time of Lent.

894. *The champion thou hast brought.* The 1st edition has ' ye have brought.'

908. *The stone Avanturine.* A kind of quartz with spangles of mica in it. A better spelling is ' aventurine,' on account of the derivation of the word.

928. *When mounted.* The editions, down to 1884 at least, have ' being mounted.'

970. *And then she sang, etc.* ' Lynette has now seen that he is a gentleman and no knave, and admiration of his valor awakens a different feeling in her heart. Her songs conceal rather than reveal this dawning love; maiden modesty will not permit her to abate one jot of her missayings and revilings. Her first song indicates the sudden light that has dawned upon her: her morning dream has once proved true, that her love would smile on her that day. . . . After the Sun has been overthrown, her love has smiled on her twice; her dream that she would find a victorious champion that day — a knight who would achieve her quest and become her love — has been twice proved true. . . . Thrice [after the victory over the Evening Star] hath her dream come true — or rather three omens have now proved her dream true — her dream of a victorious and loving champion ' (Littledale).

996. *Fair damsel, you should worship me the more.* The 1st edition has ' ye ' for ' you.'

1002. *The flower That blows a globe of after arrowlets.* The dandelion. Compare ' The Poet ': ' like the arrow-seeds of the field-flower;' and ' Aylmer's Field ': —

> Or from the tiny pitted target blew
> What look'd a flight of fairy arrows.

1023. *But he that fought no more.* The 1st edition reads: ' that would not fight.'

1142. *Damsel, he said, you be not all to blame, etc.* The 1st edition has ' ye ' for ' you ' here and in the next line; also ' yield thee,' ' thy quest,' and ' Ye said ' in the following lines.

1163. *Anon they pass a narrow comb.* A

' comb ' (Celtic) is a hollow in a ' hillside,' or ' the head of a valley.'

1172. *In letters like to those the vexillary, etc.* Referring to the Latin inscription carved by the vexillary, or standard-bearer, of the second legion upon a cliff overhanging the little river Gelt near Brampton in Cumberland. A detachment of this legion appears to have been stationed there in 207 A. D.

1227. *O damsel, be you wise, etc.* Here again, as in several places below, ' ye ' has been changed to ' you.'

1281. *Arthur's Harp.* According to Littledale, this ' denotes a star that lies near the Pole-star and Arcturus, the three forming a triangle like a harp.' Arcturus is so far from the Pole-star that no star could well be ' near ' both of them; and from the allusion in ' The Last Tournament ' we should infer that a single star, and not a constellation, was meant: —

> ' Dost thou know the star
> We call the Harp of Arthur up in heaven ? '
> And Tristram, ' Ay, Sir Fool, for when our King
> Was victor wellnigh day by day, the knights,
> Glorying in each new glory, set his name
> High on all hills, and in the signs of heaven.'

1366. *And Death's dark war-horse bounded, etc.* The 1st edition reads: ' At once the black horse bounded,' etc.

1386. *Then sprang the happier day from underground.* The poet seems to write ' underground ' and ' under ground ' interchangeably, both forms being found several times in the English editions.

1392. *He that told the tale in older times.* Malory: ' he that told it later ' being Tennyson himself.

Page 333. THE MARRIAGE OF GERAINT. The story of this and the following Idyll is from the ' Mabinogion ' of Lady Charlotte Guest, a collection of ancient Welsh tales (London, 1838–1849). As Littledale states, ' a French translation from the same source that Lady Guest has followed — the " Llyfr Coch o Hergest " — will be found in M. de Villemarqué's " Table Ronde," pp. 239–320, under the title of " Ghérent, ou Le Chevalier au Faucon." '

39. *To cleanse this common sewer of all his realm.* Repeated in the next Idyll, 894.

70. *They sleeping each by either.* The reading of 1859 is ' each by other.'

124. *At this he hurl'd his huge limbs out of bed.* The 1859 edition has ' snatch'd ' for ' hurl'd.'

130. *And thou, put on thy worst and meanest dress.* The pronouns in 1859 were ' you ' and ' your;' and, three lines below, ' you ' for ' thee.'

146. *Held court at old Caerleon upon Usk.* ' The romances very frequently mention these " plenary courts " (*cours plenières*) which were customarily held by the monarchs of France and England at the principal feasts of Easter, Whitsuntide, and Christmas. The Forest of Dean, in Gloucestershire, was anciently a very extensive tract of country west of the Severn; it now comprises about 22,000 acres and belongs to the Crown ' (Littledale).

202. *Whereat Geraint, etc.* The 1859 edition

has 'at which' for 'whereat,' as also on page 130 below: 'Whereat the armorer,' etc. Similarly on page 128, 'of which' has been changed to 'whereof.'

217. *I will track this vermin to their earths.* The use of 'vermin' as at once collective and plural is archaic.

274. *A thousand pips eat up your sparrow-hawk!* Littledale says that 'the disease called the *pip*, which attacks young fowls, seems to be confused with another disease called *gapes*.' He adds: 'As pips are not insects, they cannot eat up sparrow-hawks.' But 'eat' need not be taken literally, and 'thousand' is merely intensive. The meaning apparently is, May the worst kind of pip destroy your sparrow-hawk!

347. *Turn, Fortune, turn thy wheel*, etc. 'The metrical structure of the song is original, but seems intended to convey a suggestion or reminiscence of the troubadour rondels and villanelles, such as a high-born maiden might have sung in an old baronial bower' (Littledale).

386. *A costrel.* A flagon, flask, or bottle, made of leather or earthenware, sometimes called 'pilgrim's bottle.' Here it holds the 'wine,' not the 'flesh,' which is brought, though it is possible (as Littledale thinks) that the poet forgot it was a vessel for holding liquids only.

389. *Manchet bread.* The finest kind of white bread. Compare Drayton, 'Polyolbion': —

No manchet can so well the courtly palate please
As that made of the meal fetched from my fertile leas;
The finest of that kind, compared with my wheat,
For fineness of the bread, doth look like common cheat.

Cheat, or *cheat-bread*, was a coarser kind of wheaten bread.

421. *But if ye know*, etc. The 1859 edition has 'you know.'

475. *That if the sparrow-hawk, this nephew, fight.* The 1859 reading was: 'That if, as I suppose, your nephew fight,' etc. In 479, 'your' and 'yours' have been changed to 'thine.'

483. *And over these is placed*, etc. The 1859 edition has 'laid' for 'placed;' and, in the next line: 'And over that is placed the sparrow-hawk.'

493. *But thou, that hast no lady.* Originally, 'you that have;' and, just below, 'Your leave!'

507. *Had stolen away.* Originally, 'had slipt away.'

543. *The Chair of Idris.* The mountain, Cader-Idris, in Merionethshire, the highest in Wales (2914 feet) next to Snowdon. Idris, according to the old legends, was one of the three Primitive Bards (Eidiol and Beli being the others) and the inventor of the harp.

550. *And over that the golden sparrow-hawk.* The 1859 edition has 'a' for 'the.'

576. *Edyrn, son of Nudd.* He appears again in the next Idyll (780 fol.).

581. *First, thou thyself, with damsel and with dwarf.* The early reading was 'thou thyself, thy lady and thy dwarf;' and, in the next line, 'being' for 'coming.'

593. *And, being young, he changed*, etc. The early reading was: —

And, being young, he changed himself and grew
To hate the sin, that seem'd so like his own,
Of Modred, Arthur's nephew, and fell at last
In the great battle fighting for the King.

615. *And still she look'd and still the terror grew.* This recalls Goldsmith's 'And still they gazed, and still the wonder grew,' etc.

641. *Which being sold and sold*, etc. That is, sold one after another.

661. *A turkis.* One of the old spellings of *turquoise*, indicating what is still one of the authorized pronunciations.

714. *But since our fortune swerved from sun to shade.* The early editions have 'slipt' for 'swerved.'

742. *That maiden in the tale*, etc. The tale is in the 'Mabinogion.' Math says to Gwydion: 'Well, we will seek, I and thou, by charms and illusion, to form a wife for him out of flowers . . . so they took the blossoms of the oak, and the blossoms of the broom, and the blossoms of the meadow-sweet, and produced from them a maiden, the fairest and most graceful that man ever saw. And they baptized her, and gave her the name of Blodenwedd.'

744. *The bride of Cassivelaun*, etc. According to the Welsh tradition, it was the love of a British maiden named Flur, who was betrothed to Casswallaun (or Cassivelaunus), that led Cæsar to invade Britain. She was carried off by a Gallic prince, an ally of Cæsar, who thus got possession of her; but she was recaptured by Casswallawn after a battle in which six thousand of Cæsar's army were slain.

764. *Flaws in summer.* Sudden gusts of wind. Compare 'Hamlet,' v. i. 239: 'the winter's flaw.'

774. *As careful robins eye the delver's toil.* The simile is repeated in the next Idyll (431).

780. *Thy new son.* Originally 'your new son.'

785. *This ruin'd hall.* Originally, 'this ruin'd hold;' and, two lines below, 'kind Queen' for 'fair Queen.'

791. *Fain I would*, etc. Originally, 'for I wish'd,' etc. The next two lines had 'To love' for 'Should love,' 'should' for 'can,' and 'I had' for 'was mine.'

797. *I doubted whether daughter's tenderness.* Originally 'filial tenderness;' and, in the next line 'did' for 'might.'

804. *And all its perilous glories.* Originally 'dangerous glories;' and below (811) 'intermitted custom' for 'intermitted usage.'

818. *Some gaudy-day.* Some holiday; especially an English University festival. Compare Middleton, 'The Black Book': 'Never passing beyond the confines of a farthing, nor once munching commons but only upon gaudy-days.'

Page 344. GERAINT AND ENID.

1. *O purblind race of miserable men*, etc. Compare 'Lucretius,' ii. 14: —

O miseras hominum mentes, O pectora caeca,
Qualibus in tenebris vitae, quantisque periclis,
Degitur hoc aevi quodcumquest.

9. *When they both had got to horse.* Originally 'had both.'

14. *I charge thee ride before.* Originally, ' you ' for ' thee; ' as also two lines below.

49. *The great plover's human whistle.* ' The shrill call of the stone curlew, or Norfolk plover, which thus often deceives wanderers on the wolds ' (Littledale).

77. *Your warning or your silence.* Originally, ' Your silence or your warning.' Professor Jones (see p. 303 above) suggests that the first reading was due to the influence of the ' Mabinogion,' which has, ' I wish but for silence, and not for warning.' The poet apparently did not see at the moment of writing that the change from the declarative to the interrogative form required a transposition of the nouns. The correction was made in 1869. In the second and third lines below ' you ' has been changed to ' ye.'

94. *Wolves of woman born.* Compare ' The Coming of Arthur,' 32; and see note.

163. *That had a sapling growing on it, slide, etc.* Originally, ' slip ' for ' slide.'

213. *Less having stomach for it.* The American 1859 edition reads: ' having a stomach.' This is not in any English edition, and may be a misprint.

221. *Ye will be all the wealthier.* Originally, ' You will; ' and a few lines below, ' you are ' for ' thou art,' and ' you ' (twice) for ' thee.'

301. *She doth not speak to me.* Originally, ' does ' for ' doth; ' as in ' doth he love you,' on the next page. Similarly, ' has ' has been changed to ' hath ' in ' hath turn'd me wild ' (line 308) and elsewhere. I shall not hereafter note all these little changes, nor those of ' you ' to ' ye ' or ' thee,' which occur frequently.

338. *Nay; I do not mean blood.* The ' nay ' was originally ' no.'

340. *My malice is no deeper than a moat, etc.* That is, I mean only to imprison Geraint, not to kill him.

344. *The one true lover whom you ever own'd.* Originally, ' which you ever had.'

426. *Not all mismated, etc.* Originally, ' Not quite mismated.'

475. *The cressy islets.* Masses of water-cress. Compare the ' Ode to Memory: ' ' To purl o'er matted cress and ribbed sand.'

582. *Till at the last he waken'd from his swoon.* Originally, ' And at the last.'

762. *And never yet, since high in Paradise, etc.* Stopford Brooke refers to these as ' some of the loveliest lines the poet ever wrote of womanhood.'

770. *Before the useful trouble of the rain.* ' This seems to imply that the " useful *trouble* of the rain " only came after man's departure from Paradise. This is not exactly stated in Genesis ii., where we read that *before* the plantation of Eden " the Lord God had not caused it to rain upon the earth. . . . But there went up a mist from the earth," etc. Milton makes Eve in Eden speak of " the fertile earth after soft showers " ' (Littledale).

902. *The vicious quitch.* A kind of worthless grass, hard to eradicate from cultivated fields. In New England it is often called ' witch-grass.'

Browning, in ' Sordello,' speaks of ' Docks, quitch-grass, loathly mallows no man plants.'

914. *Then if some knight of mine, etc.* Originally ' a knight.'

932. *On each of all whom Uther left in charge.* Originally, ' On whom his father Uther left in charge.'

935. *The White Horse on the Berkshire hills.* The English editions print ' the white horse,' See Thomas Hughes's ' Scouring of the White Horse,' — a figure of a horse cut in the turf on the side of a chalk-hill near Wantage in Berkshire, to commemorate Alfred's victory over the Danes in the time of Ethelred.

961. *Enid, whom her ladies loved to call, etc.* Originally, ' the ladies.'

Page 357. BALIN AND BALAN.

The story is abridged from the second book of Malory's ' Morte Darthur,' with the addition of incidents and details that are Tennyson's own.

8. *Man's word is God in man.* Compare ' The Coming of Arthur,' 132.

24. *A plume of lady-fern.* A species of fern (*Asplenium Filix-femina*) so called, according to some authorities, because dedicated to the Virgin Mary.

226. *Thus, as a hearth, etc.* The 1st edition has ' Then ' for ' Thus.'

256. *The maiden Saint who stands with lily in hand.* The Virgin Mary.

361. *And one was rough with wattling, and the walls, etc.* The 1st edition has: ' rough with pole and scaffoldage.'

The goblet is embossed with two scenes from the legend of Joseph of Arimathea, — his voyage, and the little church he built at Glastonbury. Compare ' The Holy Grail,' 63: —

And there he built with wattles from the marsh
A little lonely church in days of yore.

410. *The blindfold rummage.* Compare ' Hamlet,' i. 1. 107: ' Of this post-haste and romage in the land.'

425. *I have shamed thee so that now thou shamest me.* ' Apparently the killing of Garlon was feloniously done, for Garlon was unarmed and unprepared ' (Littledale).

434. *The fire of heaven has kill'd the barren cold, etc.* Stopford Brooke remarks that this song, glorifying the fire of the appetites and senses, ' might have been written for the worship of Astarte, and it is splendidly imagined by Tennyson: it sets the sensual side of pagan Nature-worship into the keenest contrast with the self-control of Christianity. The fire from heaven she speaks of is not the holy fire of the pure spirit; it is the fire of that heaven which some have conceived, and which consists in the full enjoyment of desire. It is this blaze of desire which she sees in all Nature as well as in man, and it creates, she thinks, the real beauty of the world. Tennyson got to the heart of the thing in this exultant pagan song.' It shows us Vivien ' as she is — honest, true, and bold, confessing evil and rejoicing in it. The whole sketch of her in " Balin and Balan " is

of this strain of triumphant daring. Her tale of slander about the Queen is there delivered with a ring of conquest in it. Her mocking of her boy squire and of Balan has the bravery of a queen of sin.'

Page 366. MERLIN AND VIVIEN.

The hint of the story is from Malory, who simply tells 'how Merlin fell in a dotage about one of the damsels of the lake, whose name was Nimue.'

2. *The wild woods of Broceliande.* In Brittany, and famous in legendary lore.

4. *A tower of ivied mason-work.* The 1st edition (1859) has 'ruin'd mason-work.' After the next line that edition goes on with 'The wily Vivien stole from Arthur's court' (line 147 below). The long passage that intervenes was first inserted in 1874, when it began thus: —

Whence came she ? One that bore in bitter grudge
The scorn of Arthur and his Table, Mark,
The Cornish King, had heard a wandering voice,
A minstrel of Caerleon by strong storm
Blown into shelter by Tintagil, say,

and so on to 146 below.

42. *My father died in battle against the King.* To the Queen she says (line 71), 'for thy King.'

52. *Saith not Holy Writ the same ?* See Job, xxv. 5, 6.

108. *That gray cricket.* The 'minstrel of Caerleon.' See line 9 above.

123. *Diet and seeling, jesses, leash, and lure, etc.* The 'diet,' or feeding, of the hawks was regulated strictly.

'Seeling' was partly sewing up the eyelids of a young hawk, to prevent it seeing men, etc., in front of it, and so becoming alarmed. Hoods came in time to be used instead of seeling.

'Jesses' were two narrow strips of leather, fastened one to each leg, and attached to a swivel, from which hung the 'leash,' or thong.

The 'lure' was sometimes a live pigeon, but more usually a piece of iron or wood, generally in the shape of a heart or a horseshoe, to which were attached the wings of some bird, with a piece of raw meat fixed between them. The falconer swung this round his head or threw it to a distance by a thong, and the hawk flew down to it.

'She is too noble.' — The 'falcon' was the female; the 'tercel' was the male.

'Check at pies.' — Either, leave pursuing a game-bird to follow a magpie that crosses her flight; or, as more usually, fly at worthless birds such as magpies.

'Towered.' — Rose spirally to a height.

'Pounced.' — Swooped down on.

'Quarry.' — The game flown at.

Her 'bells' were globular, of brass or silver, and attached to each leg by 'bewits.'

These 'terms of art' are from Harting's 'Ornithology of Shakespeare.'

125. *Nor will she rake.* That is, 'fly wide at game.'

148. *She hated all the knights, etc.* The 1859 *American* edition reads : —

She loathed the knights, and ever seem'd to hear
Their laughing comment when her name was named.

For once, when Arthur walking all alone,
Vexed at a rumor rife about the Queen,
Had met her, etc.

This reading is found nowhere else. The American edition was evidently printed from advance sheets, but the poet must have altered the passage before the English edition of 1859 was printed.

The 1857 reading was : —

She hated all the knights because she deem'd
They wink'd and jested when her name was named.

187. *Then fell on Merlin a great melancholy.* The 1859 reading was 'fell upon him.' The next seven lines are not in that edition, but were added in 1873; and the next line began, 'And leaving Arthur's court,' etc.

196. *There found a little boat, etc.* As Littledale notes, these little boats in the romances (compare 'The Holy Grail') are generally independent of sail or oar, and this one drives with 'a sudden wind' across the deeps; 'not a wind raised by enchantment — the poet does not directly say that — but there is just a subtle suggestion of glamour, of something more than natural, in this sudden wind, which sustains the sense of spirit-daunting mystery.'

219. *A twist of gold was round her hair.* The 1st *American* (1859) edition, like 'The True and the False' (1859), has 'snake' for 'twist;' but the *English* 1859 edition has 'twist.' The poet must have made the change from 'snake' to 'twist' after the advance sheets were sent to the American publishers, as he did in 148 fol.

233. *O Merlin, do ye love me ?* The early reading was 'you' for 'ye,' as in sundry other places that I shall not take space to note.

285. *Boon ? ay, there was a boon.* The 1859 edition has 'yea' for 'ay.'

311. *Not yet so strange as you yourself are strange.* Originally, 'Nor yet.'

338. *That I should prove it on you unawares.* After this line the 1859 edition has the line, 'To make you lose your use and name and fame' (omitted in 1873); and, in the next line, 'most indignant' for 'passing wrathful.'

385. *In Love, if Love be Love, etc.* The song of the lover to his lady. The 5th stanza (444-447) is her reply.

430. *It buzzes fiercely round the point.* The early reading was 'buzzes wildly.'

459. *Yea ! Love, though Love were of the grossest, etc.* The early reading was 'True !' for 'Yea !'

472. *Fancied arms.* These may be 'described in unheraldic language as an eagle of gold soaring upon a blue surface to a golden sun depicted on the right hand of the upper part of the shield (*dexter*, that is, on the left hand of any one *facing* the shield; the *right hand* of the bearer of the shield who is supposed to be sheltered behind it).

'As the picture that Merlin substituted is blazoned *proper*, that is, in the natural colors of the objects represented, it is allowable in strict heraldry to place it upon a field azure, in spite of the fundamental heraldic law that forbids metal to be charged on metal or color on color' (Littledale).

494. *Because I fain had given them greater wits.* In 1859, 'Because I wish'd to give them greater minds.' In 501 below, 'Broke' has been changed to 'Brake.'

507. *The second in a line of stars, etc.* The star in the sword of Orion which is surrounded by the great nebula. It is just below the well-known 'belt of three' stars.

571. *Magnet-like she drew, etc.* Littledale sees here 'a suggestion of Sindbad's magnet-mountain;' but why assume that the attractive maid is compared to the mountain? The general suggestion of magnetism is sufficient.

601. *The lady never made unwilling war, etc.* Littledale remarks that Vivien's criticism exactly parallels the remark made to Dr. Johnson by a lady 'of great beauty and excellence,' after reading the fourth line of Pope's epitaph on Mrs. Corbet. The line in question states that Mrs. Corbet 'no arts essayed but not to be admired;' and the lady considered that it contained 'an unnatural and incredible panegyric.' In fact, Mrs. Corbet never made unwilling war with those fine eyes! 'Of this,' adds the doctor, 'let the ladies judge.'

652. *For keep it like a puzzle chest in chest, etc.* Littledale sees here an allusion to those Chinese puzzles of 'laborious orient ivory, sphere in sphere,' mentioned in the prologue to 'The Princess;' but those are not 'chests,' nor are they 'locked,' and they cannot be opened, the inner spheres having been carved and detached through the openings in the carving of the outer ones. The reference in the present passage is to sets of chests, or boxes, made to fit one within another, each with its own lock.

707. *There lay the reckling.* 'Reckling' is properly the smallest and weakest in a litter, as of puppies or kittens; here used contemptuously for the puny infant.

763. *The holy king, whose hymns, etc.* David.

779. *Man! is he man at all, etc.* The 1859 edition has 'Him!' for 'Man!' In the next line, 'winks' is used in its old sense of shutting one's eyes. Compare Shakespeare, Sonnet 43. 1: 'When most I wink [in sleep], then do my eyes best see,' etc.

816. *She cloaks the scar of some repulse with lies, etc.* The 1859 edition reads: —

I think she cloaks the wounds of loss with lies;
I do believe she tempted them and fail'd,
She is so bitter.

In 822 below, it has: 'Face-flatterers and back-biters are the same.'

842. *Leapt from her session on his lap.* This use of 'session' is archaic. Compare Hooker, 'Ecclesiastical Polity,' v. 55: 'his ascension into heaven and his session at the right hand of God,' etc.

867. *Seethed like the kid, etc.* See Exodus, xxxiv. 26; Deuteronomy, xiv. 21.

921. *Lo! what was once to me, etc.* The 1859 edition has 'Oh!' for 'Lo;' and below (924) it reads: —

Farewell; think kindly of me, for I fear
My fate or fault, omitting gayer youth
For one so old, must be to love you still.
But ere I leave you, etc.

Page 380. LANCELOT AND ELAINE.

The outline of the story is from Malory (book xviii. chapters 7 to 21), whom the poet has followed very closely in many passages, of which I give occasional illustrations. For a fuller account of the poet's indebtedness to the 'Morte Darthur,' as also of the points in which he has varied from it, see Littledale, or consult the editions of Malory mentioned on p. 303 above.

2. *The lily maid of Astolat.* 'Elaine le Blank' (*blanche*, or white), as Malory calls her.

7. *Fearing rust or soilure.* Knights usually kept their shields covered, to prevent 'rust or soilure,' and doubtless many a fair damsel wrought a cover for her warrior's shield.

34. *For Arthur, long before they crown'd him king, etc.* The 1859 edition reads: —

For Arthur when none knew from whence he came,
Long ere the people chose him for their king,
Roving the trackless realms, etc.

45. *And he that once was king had on a crown.* Originally, 'And one of these, the king, had on a crown.'

75. *The place which now Is this world's hugest.* That is, London.

78. *Spake — for she had been sick — to Guinevere, etc.* Compare Malory (xviii. 8): 'So King Arthur made him ready to depart to those jousts, and would have had the queen with him; but at that time she would not, she said, for she was sick and might not ride at that time. . . . And many deemed the queen would not be there because of Sir Launcelot du Lake, for Sir Launcelot would not ride with the King; for he said that he was not whole of the wound the which Sir Mador had given him. Wherefore the King was heavy and passing wroth,' etc.

80. *'Yea, lord,' she said, 'ye know it.'* The 1859 edition has 'you' for 'ye,' as in the next line and in 83; also in about forty other places in the idyll of which I shall make no note.

97. *To blame, my lord Sir Lancelot, much to blame!* Compare Malory (xviii. 8): 'Sir Launcelot, ye are greatly to blame, thus to hold you behind my lord; what trow ye, what will your enemies and mine say and deem? nought else but see how Sir Launcelot holdeth him ever behind the king and so doth the queen, for that they would be together: and thus will they say, said the queen to Launcelot, have ye no doubt thereof.'

168. *Thither he made, and blew the gateway horn.* Originally, 'wound' for 'blew.'

288. *And in the four loud battles by the shore.* The 1859 reading was 'wild battles.' The list of the twelve great battles, as Littledale notes, is first found in Nennius, whom Tennyson follows. Compare the translation of Nennius in Bohn's 'Six Chronicles,' p. 408: 'Then it was that the magnanimous Arthur, with all the kings and military force of Britain, fought against the Saxons. And though there

were many more noble than himself, yet he was twelve times chosen their commander, and was as often conqueror. The first battle in which he was engaged, was at the mouth of the river Gleni. The second, third, fourth, and fifth, were on another river, by the Britons called Duglas, in the region Linius. The sixth, on the river Bassas. The seventh in the wood Celidon, which the Britains call Cat Coit Celidon. The eighth was near Gurnion Castle, where Arthur bore the image of the Holy Virgin, mother of God, upon his shoulders, and through the power of our Lord Jesus Christ, and the holy Mary, put the Saxons to flight, and pursued them the whole day with great slaughter. The ninth was at the City of Legion, which is called Caer Leon. The tenth was on the banks of the river Trat Treuroit. The eleventh was on the mountain Breguoin, which we call Cat Bregion. The twelfth was a most severe contest, when Arthur penetrated to the hill of Badon. In this engagement, nine hundred and forty fell by his hand alone, no one but the Lord affording him assistance. In all these engagements the Britons were successful. For no strength can avail against the will of the Almighty.'

338. *Till rathe she rose.* For 'rathe,' see 'In Memoriam,' cx. 1 and note.

392. *Paused by the gateway, standing near the shield.* Originally, 'Paused in the gateway, standing by the shield.'

474. *A fury seized them all.* Originally, 'seized on them.'

498. *Then the trumpets blew.* The 1859 edition has 'heralds' for 'trumpets.'

509. '*Draw the lance-head,*' etc. Compare Malory (xviii. 12): 'O gentle knight Sir Lavaine, help me that this truncheon were out of my side, for it sticketh so sore that it nigh slayeth me. O mine own lord, said Sir Lavaine, I would fain do that might please you, but I dread me sore, and I draw out the truncheon, that ye shall be in peril of death. I charge you, said Sir Launcelot, as ye love me draw it out. And therewithal he descended from his horse, and right so did Sir Lavaine, and forthwith Sir Lavaine drew the truncheon out of his side. And he gave a great shriek, and a marvellous grisly groan, and his blood brast out nigh a pint at once, that at last he sank down, and so swooned pale and deadly.'

513. *And Sir Lancelot gave, etc.* The 1859 edition has 'that other' for 'Sir Lancelot.'

534. *He must not pass uncared for, etc.* The 1859 edition reads: —

He must not pass uncared for. Gawain, arise,
My nephew, and ride forth and find the knight.

543. *Rise and take, etc.* Originally, 'Wherefore take,' etc.

545. *And bring us where he is.* Originally, 'what' for 'where.'

555. *And Gareth, a good knight.* Originally 'Lamorack' for 'Gareth;' and, in the next line, 'of a crafty house' for 'and the child of Lot.'

595. *Ill news, my Queen, for all who love him, this!* Originally, 'these' for 'this.'

605. *Past to her chamber.* Originally, 'moved to her chamber.'

626. *The victor, but had ridden a random round, etc.* The 1859 edition reads: —

The victor, that had ridden wildly round,
To seek him, and was wearied of the search.
To whom the Lord of Astolat, 'Bide with us,
And ride no longer wildly, noble Prince!'

653. *Who lost the hern we slipt her at.* Originally, 'him' for 'her,' which was a slip, as the male bird was seldom used in the sport, the female being larger and stronger.

658. *And when the shield was brought, etc.* Compare Malory (xviii. 14): 'Ah, mercy, said Sir Gawaine, now is my heart more heavier than ever it was tofore. Why? said Elaine. For I have great cause, said Sir Gawaine; is that knight that owneth this shield your love? Yea truly, said she, my love he is, God would I were his love. Truly, said Sir Gawaine, fair damsel, ye have right, for, and he be your love, ye love the most honorable knight of the world, and the man of most worship. So me thought ever, said the damsel, for never, or that time, for no knight that ever I saw loved I never none erst. God grant, said Sir Gawaine, that either of you may rejoice other, but that is in a great adventure. But truly, said Sir Gawaine unto the damsel, ye may say ye have a fair grace, for why, I have known that noble knight this four and twenty year, and never or that day I nor none other knight, I dare make it good, saw nor heard say that ever he bare token or sign of no lady, gentlewoman, nor maiden, at no justs nor tournament. And therefore, fair maiden, said Sir Gawaine, ye are much beholden to him to give him thanks. But I dread me, said Sir Gawaine, that ye shall never see him in this world, and that is great pity that ever was of earthly knight. Alas, said she, how may this be? Is he slain? I say not so, said Sir Gawaine, but wit ye well, he is grievously wounded, by all manner of signs, and by men's sight more likely to be dead then to be on live; and wit ye well he is the noble knight Sir Launcelot, for by this shield I know him. Alas, said the fair maiden of Astolat, how may this be, and what was his hurt? Truly, said Sir Gawaine, the man in the world that loved him best hurt him so, and I dare say, said Sir Gawaine, and that knight that hurt him knew the very certainty that he had hurt Sir Launcelot, it would be the most sorrow that ever came to his heart. Now, fair father, said then Elaine, I require you give me leave to ride and to seek him, or else I wot well I shall go out of my mind, for I shall never stint till that I find him and my brother Sir Lavaine. Do as it liketh you, said her father, for me right sore repenteth of the hurt of that noble knight. Right so the maid made her ready, and before Sir Gawaine making great dole. Then on the morn Sir Gawaine came to king Arthur, and told him how he had found Sir Launcelot's shield in the keeping of the fair maiden of Astolat. All

that knew I aforehand, said king Arthur, and that caused me I would not suffer you to have ado at the great justs: for I espied, said king Arthur, when he came in till his lodging, full late in the evening in Astolat. But marvel have I, said Arthur, that ever he would bear any sign of any damsel: for, or now, I never heard say nor knew that ever he bare any token of none earthly woman. By my head, said Sir Gawaine, the fair maiden of Astolat loveth him marvellously well; what it meaneth I cannot say; and she is ridden after to seek him. So the king and all came to London, and there Sir Gawaine openly disclosed to all the court that it was Sir Launcelot that justed best.'

674. *I know there is none other I can love.* Originally, 'Methinks there is,' etc.

683. *Nay — like enow.* Originally, 'May it be so?'

728. *Marr'd her friend's aim.* Originally, 'point' for 'aim.'

806. *The cell wherein he slept.* Originally, 'in which he slept.'

810. *Then she that saw him lying unsleek, unshorn, etc.* Compare Malory (xviii. 15): 'And when she saw him lie so sick and pale in his bed, she might not speak, but suddenly she fell to the earth down suddenly in a swoon, and there she lay a great while. And when she was relieved she sighed, and said, My lord Sir Launcelot, alas, why be ye in this plight? and then she swooned again. And then Sir Launcelot prayed Sir Lavaine to take her up, — And bring her to me. And when she came to herself, Sir Launcelot kissed her, and said, Fair maiden, why fare ye thus? Ye put me to pain; wherefore make ye no more such cheer, for, and ye be come to comfort me, ye be right welcome, and of this little hurt that I have, I shall be right hastily whole, by the grace of God. But I marvel, said Sir Launcelot, who told you my name.'

826. '*Your ride hath wearied you.*' Originally, 'has wearied you.'

839. *The weirdly-sculptured gates.* Originally, 'wildly-sculptured.'

877. *The bright image of one face.* Originally, 'the sweet image.'

920. *Seeing I go to-day.* Originally, 'Seeing I must go to-day.'

924. *Then suddenly and passionately she spoke, etc.* Compare Malory (xviii. 19): 'My lord Sir Launcelot, now I see ye will depart, now, fair knight and courteous knight, have mercy upon me, and suffer me not to die for thy love. What would ye that I did? said Sir Launcelot. I would have you to my husband, said Elaine. Fair damsel, I thank you, said Sir Launcelot, but truly, said he, I cast me never to be wedded man. Then, fair knight, said she, will ye be my love? Jesu defend me, said Sir Launcelot, for then I rewarded to your father and your brother full evil for their great goodness. Alas, said she, then must I die for your love. Ye shall not so, said Sir Launcelot, for wit ye well, fair maiden, I might have been married and I had would, but I never applied

me to be married yet. But because, fair damsel, that ye love me as ye say ye do, I will, for your good will and kindness, shew you some goodness, and that is this; that wheresoever ye will beset your heart upon some good knight that will wed you, I shall give you together a thousand pound yearly, to you and to your heirs. Thus much will I give you, fair maiden, for your kindness, and always while I live to do your own knight. Of all this, said the maiden, I will none, for, but if ye will wed me, or else be my lover, wit you well, Sir Launcelot, my good days are done. Fair damsel, said Sir Launcelot, of these two things ye must pardon me. Then she shrieked shrilly, and fell down in a swoon.'

Stopford Brooke remarks here: 'She rises to the very verge of innocent maidenliness in passionate love, but she does not go over the verge. And to be on the verge, and not pass beyond it, is the very peak of innocent girlhood when seized by overmastering love. It was as difficult to represent Elaine as to represent Juliet; and Tennyson has succeeded well where Shakespeare has succeeded beautifully. It is great praise, but it is well deserved.'

1015. *Hark the Phantom of the house, etc.* As Littledale remarks, this phantom is described in Croker's stories of the Banshee ('Fairy Legends,' pages 103, 119). Compare Scott's 'Rosabelle,' and see Baring Gould's 'Curious Myths' (2d series, pages 215, 225).

1060. *To whom the gentle sister made reply.* The 1859 edition has 'which' for 'whom.'

1147. *Oar'd by the dumb.* Originally, 'Steer'd by the dumb.'

1167. *The shadow of some piece of pointed lace.* Originally, 'of a piece.'

1230. *In half disdain.* Originally, 'half disgust.'

1264. *Most noble lord, Sir Lancelot of the Lake, etc.* Compare Malory (xviii. 20): 'And this was the intent of the letter: — Most noble knight, Sir Launcelot, now hath death made us two at debate for your love; I was your lover, that men called the fair maiden of Astolat; therefore unto all ladies I make my moan; yet pray for my soul, and bury me at the least, and offer ye my mass-penny. This is my last request. And a clean maiden I died, I take God to witness. Pray for my soul, Sir Launcelot, as thou art peerless. — This was all the substance in the letter. And when it was read the king, the queen, and all the knights wept for pity of the doleful complaints. Then was Sir Launcelot sent for. And when he was come, king Arthur made the letter to be read to him; and when Sir Launcelot heard it word by word, he said, My lord Arthur, wit ye well I am right heavy of the death of this fair damsel. God knoweth I was never causer of her death by my willing, and that will I report me to her own brother; here he is, Sir Lavaine. I will not say nay, said Sir Launcelot, but that she was both fair and good, and much I was beholden unto her, but she loved me out of measure. Ye might have shewed her, said the queen, some bounty and gentleness, that might have preserved her life. Madam, said Sir Launcelot, she would none other way be answered, but that she would be my wife, or else my love, and of these two I would not grant her; but I proffered her, for her good love that she shewed me, a thousand pound yearly to her and to her heirs, and to wed any manner knight that she could find best to love in her heart. For, madam, said Sir Launcelot, I love not to be constrained to love; for love must arise of the heart, and not by no constraint. That is truth, said the king, and many knights: love is free in himself, and never will be bounden; for where he is bounden he loseth himself. Then said the king unto Sir Launcelot, It will be your worship that ye oversee that she be interred worshipfully. Sir, said Sir Launcelot, that shall be done as I can best devise. And so many knights went thither to behold that fair maiden. And so upon the morn she was interred richly, and Sir Launcelot offered her mass-penny, and all the knights of the Table Round that were there at that time offered with Sir Launcelot. And then the poor man went again with the barget. Then the queen sent for Sir Launcelot, and prayed him of mercy, for why she had been wroth with him causeless. This is not the first time, said Sir Launcelot, that ye have been displeased with me causeless; but, madam, ever I must suffer you, but what sorrow I endure I take no force.'

1343. *But Arthur, who beheld his clouded brows, etc.* The 1859 edition reads: —

> But Arthur, who beheld his clouded brows,
> Approach'd him, and with full affection flung
> One arm about his neck, and spake and said,
> 'Lancelot, my Lancelot, thou in whom I have
> Most love and most affiance,' etc.

1354. *Seeing the homeless trouble in thine eyes.* For this line the 1859 edition has: 'For the wild people say wild things of thee.'

1393. *Lancelot, whom the Lady of the Lake, etc.* The edition of 1859 reads: —

> Lancelot, whom the Lady of the lake [*sic*]
> Stole from his mother — as the story runs —
> She chanted snatches of mysterious song, etc.

Page 400. THE HOLY GRAIL.
The story is found in Malory, books xi. to xvii., *preceding* the story of Elaine, in xviii. The poet follows his original closely here and there, but omits much that Malory gives and often varies from him.

15. *That puff'd the swaying branches into smoke.* For another allusion to the abundant pollen of the yew, scattered into 'smoke' by the wind, see 'In Memoriam,' xxxix: —

> Old warder of these buried bones,
> And answering now my random stroke
> With fruitful cloud and living smoke,
> Dark yew, that graspest at the stones, etc.

48. *The blessed land of Aromat.* 'Aromat —a name suggestive of Sabæan spicery and sweet Eastern balms — is used for Arimathea, a town in Palestine, probably the modern Ramleh, and the home of the "honorable counsellor, which also waited for the kingdom of God." Joseph, who placed Christ in the sepulchre that had been made for himself. The mediæval legend added that Joseph had received in the Grail the blood that flowed from the Saviour's side' (Littledale).

49. *When the dead Went wandering o'er Moriah.* See Matthew, xxvii. 50 fol.

52. *To Glastonbury, where the winter thorn, etc.* There is a variety of hawthorn which puts forth leaves and flowers about the time of Christmas. It is said to have originated at Glastonbury Abbey, and the original thorn was believed to have been the staff with which Joseph of Arimathea aided his steps on his wanderings from the Holy Land to Glastonbury, where he is said to have founded the celebrated Abbey. The first church, according to the legend, was ' built of wattles,' and interwoven twigs. Compare ' Balin and Balan ': —

> And one was rough with wattling, and the walls
> Of that low church he built at Glastonbury.

In A. D. 439 St. Patrick is said to have visited the place, and to have founded the monastery, of which he became the abbot. In 542 King Arthur was buried here. The abbey was several times repaired and rebuilt before the reign of Henry II., when it was destroyed by fire, and the large and splendid structure the ruins of which still remain was erected. It was the wealthiest abbey in England, except Westminster.

182. *And all at once, as there we sat, etc.* Compare Malory (xiii. 7): ' And every knight sat in his own place as they were toforehand. Then anon they heard cracking and crying of thunder, that them thought that the place should all to-drive. In the midst of this blast entered a sun-beam more clearer by seven times than ever they saw day, and all they were alighted of the grace of the Holy Ghost. Then began every knight to behold other, and either saw other by their seeming fairer than ever they saw afore. Not for then there was no knight might speak one word a great while, and so they looked every man on other, as they had been dumb. Then there entered into the hall the holy Graile covered with white samite, but there was none might see it, nor who bare it. And there was all the hall full filled with good odors, and every knight had such meats and drinks as he best loved in this world: and when the holy Graile had been borne through the hall, then the holy vessel departed suddenly, that they wist not where it became. Then had they all breath to speak. Then the king yielded thankings unto God of his good grace that he had sent them. Certes, said the king, we ought to thank our Lord Jesu greatly, for that he hath showed us this day at the reverence of this high feast of Pentecost. Now, said Sir Gawaine, we have been served this day of what meats and drinks we thought on, but one thing beguiled us, we might not see the holy Graile, it was so preciously covered: wherefore I will make here avow, that to-morn, without

longer abiding, I shall labor in the quest of the Sancgreal, that I shall hold me out a twelvemonth and a day, or more if need be, and never shall I return again unto the court till I have seen it more openly than it hath been seen here: and if I may not speed, I shall return again as he that may not be against the will of our Lord Jesu Christ. When they of the Table Round heard Sir Gawaine say so, they arose up the most party, and made such avows as Sir Gawaine had made.

'Anon as king Arthur heard this he was greatly displeased, for he wist well that they might not againsay their avows. Alas! said king Arthur unto Sir Gawaine, ye have nigh slain me with the avow and promise that ye have made. For through you ye have bereft me of the fairest fellowship and the truest of knighthood that ever were seen together in any realm of the world. For when they depart from hence, I am sure they all shall never meet more in this world, for they shall die many in the quest. And so it forethinketh me a little, for I have loved them as well as my life, wherefore it shall grieve me right sore the departition of this fellowship. For I have had an old custom to have them in my fellowship.'

256. *O, there, perchance, when all our wars are done.* The 1869 edition has 'then' for 'there.'

298. *But ye, that follow but the leader's bell.* Originally, 'you' for 'ye.'

300. *Taliessin is our fullest throat of song.* The name means 'the radiant brow.' He was 'the prince of British singers, and flourished in the seventh century' (Littledale). Compare Gray, 'The Bard': 'Hear from the grave, great Taliessin, hear!'

312. *The strong White Horse.* Referring to the banner of Hengist.

318. *This chance of noble deeds.* Originally, 'The chance,' etc.

350. *On wyvern, lion, dragon, griffin, swan.* Heraldic devices. The 'wyvern' is a dragonlike creature. Compare 'Aylmer's Field': 'Whose blazing wyvern weathercock'd the spire,' etc.

352. *But in the ways below.* The 1869 edition has 'street' for 'ways;' and in 355 it reads: 'For sorrow, and in the middle street the Queen.' In 358, 359 it reads: —

And then we reach'd the weirdly-sculptured gates
Where Arthur's wars were render'd mystically.

421. *And I rode on and found a mighty hill, etc.* The 1869 reading was: 'And on I rode;' and, in the preceding line, 'wearied' for 'wearying.'

433. *That so cried out upon me.* The 1869 edition omits 'out' — probably a misprint.

466. *I saw the fiery face as of a child, etc.* Compare Malory (xvii. 20): 'And then he took an ubbly [sacramental cake], which was made in likeness of bread; and at the lifting up there came a figure in likeness of a child, and the visage was as red and as bright as any fire, and smote himself into the bread, so that they all

saw it, that the bread was formed of a fleshly man, and then he put it into the holy vessel again.'

489. *There rose a hill, etc.* Originally, 'Then rose,' etc.

574. *Thither I made, etc.* Originally, 'Whither I made,' etc.

648. *For Lancelot's kith and kin so worship him.* The 1869 edition reads: 'For Lancelot's kith and kin adore him so.'

681. *The seven clear stars of Arthur's Table Round.* The seven stars of the Great Bear, or 'Charles's Wain.'

792. *But such a blast, my King, began to blow, etc.* Compare Malory (xvii. 14): 'And the wind arose, and drove Launcelot more than a month throughout the sea, where he slept but little, but prayed to God that he might see some tidings of the Sancgreal. So it befell on a night, at midnight he arrived afore a castle, on the back side, which was rich and fair. And there was a postern opened towards the sea, and was open without any keeping, save two lions kept the entry; and the moon shone clear. Anon Sir Launcelot heard a voice that said, Launcelot, go out of this ship, and enter into the castle, where thou shalt see a great part of thy desire. Then he ran to his arms, and so armed him, and so he went to the gate, and saw the lions. Then set he hand to his sword, and drew it. Then there came a dwarf suddenly, and smote him on the arm so sore that the sword fell out of his hand. Then heard he a voice say, Oh man of evil faith and poor belief, wherefore trowest thou more on thy harness than in thy Maker? for He might more avail thee than thine armor, in whose service thou art set. Then said Launcelot, Fair Father, Jesu Christ, I thank thee of thy great mercy, that thou reprovest me of my misdeed. Now see I well that ye hold me for your servant. Then took he again his sword, and put it up in his sheath, and made a cross in his forehead, and came to the lions, and they made semblant to do him harm. Notwithstanding he passed by them without hurt, and entered into the castle to the chief fortress, and there were they all at rest. Then Launcelot entered in so armed, for he found no gate nor door but it was open. And at the last he found a chamber whereof the door was shut, and he set his hand thereto to have opened it, but he might not.'

Stopford Brooke says of this part of the poem: 'Its basis is to be found in the old tale; but whoever reads it in Malory's "Morte Darthur" will see how imaginatively it has been re-conceived. It is full of the true romantic element; it is close to the essence of the story of the Holy Grail; there is nothing in the "Idylls" more beautiful in vision and in sound; and the art with which it is worked is as finished as the conception is majestic.'

810. *The enchanted towers of Carbonek.* The name is from Malory (xvii. 16). After Lancelot had lain 'four and twenty days, and also many nights, . . . still as a dead man,' he recovered from the long swoon. 'Then they

asked him how it stood with him. Forsooth, said he, I am whole of body, thanked be our Lord; therefore, sirs, for God's love tell me where that I am? Then said they all that he was in the castle of Carbonek.'

862. *Deafer than the blue-eyed cat.* Compare Darwin, ' Origin of Species,' chap. i.: ' Thus cats which are entirely white and have blue eyes are generally deaf; but it has lately been pointed out by Mr. Tait that this is confined to the males.'

Page 413. PELLEAS AND ETTARRE.
Little altered since its first appearance in 1869 except for the insertion of a passage of seventeen lines (386–403). The story is from Malory (iv. 20–23), but the poet modifies many of the details and changes the *dénoûment.*

20. *The forest call'd of Dean.* See on ' The Marriage of Geraint,' 146.

65. *Pelleas gazing thought, etc.* The 1869 edition reads: ' And Pelleas gazing thought,' etc.

342. *Prowest knight.* That is, bravest, most valiant. Compare Spenser, ' Faërie Queene,' ii. 3. 15: ' For they be two the prowest knights on grownd.'

379. ' *Ay,*' thought Gawain, ' *and you be fair enow.*' The 1869 edition has ' ye ' for ' you.'

386–404. *Hot was the night . . . and bound his horse, etc.* For these nineteen lines the 1869 edition has only the following: —

The night was hot: he could not rest but rode
Ere midnight to her walls, and bound his horse, etc.

409. *Then he crost the court, etc.* The 1869 edition reads: —

Then he crost the court,
And saw the postern portal also wide
Yawning; and up a slope of garden, all
Of roses white and red, and wild ones mixt, etc.

419. *Then was he ware of three pavilions rear'd, etc.* The 1869 edition reads: —

Then was he ware that white pavilions rose,
Three from the bushes, gilden-peakt.

421. *Her lurdane knights.* Her stupid, worthless knights. ' Lurdane ' (really from the Old French *lourdin,* dull, blockish, from *lourd*) was supposed by some of our old authors to be a corruption of ' lord Dane,' formed in derision of the Danes. It was used as both adjective and noun. Compare the ' Mirror for Magistrates ': —

In every house *lord Dane* did then rule all,
Whence laysie lozels *lurdanes* now we call.

455. *Huge, solid, etc.* The 1869 edition has ' So solid,' etc.

553. ' *No name, no name,*' he shouted. The 1869 edition reads: ' I have no name,' etc.

560. *Yell'd the youth.* The 1869 edition reads: ' yell'd the other.'

565. *Yea, between thy lips — and sharp.* Littledale remarks: ' The metaphor of the slanderous tongue, that sharp weapon between the lips, is no doubt nearly as old as the human race itself.'

594. *And all talk died, etc.* Compare ' Sir Lancelot and Queen Guinevere ' : —

Sometimes the sparhawk wheel'd along
Hush'd all the groves for fear of wrong.

Page 422. THE LAST TOURNAMENT.
Few changes have been made in this Idyll since its appearance in the ' Contemporary Review ' for December, 1871. The outline of the story of Tristram and his two Isolts and the vengeance of Mark is taken from Malory, but the rest is Tennyson's own.

Littledale gives the following abstract of the Tristram story: —

' Tristram, having been wounded by an Irish spear, can only be healed by an Irish hand, so he goes to Ireland, and is treated by La Beale Isoud or Isolt, daughter of the Irish king. On his return he gives a glowing description of her to his uncle Mark, who sends him back as his envoy to ask for her hand. On the voyage from Ireland they innocently drink the potent philtre, and their fatal love for each other begins. Long after, when the effects of the philtre have become exhausted, Tristram is hurt by a poisoned arrow, and goes to Brittany to be cured by King Hoel's daughter, Isolt of the White Hands (Isoud la blanche Maynys), whom he loves and marries. Lancelot reproaches him for his inconstancy to La Beale Isoud, and the lady herself writes sadly to him. Tristram's old love revives, and he resolves to go to Cornwall to see his old love. There is a quarrel, and Tristram reproaches Isolt for her unfaithfulness to him. He goes mad, and throws Dagonet into a well. After many adventures Arthur knights him, and he runs away with Isolt, but is wounded in a tournament. Mark undertakes to nurse him, which he does by putting him into a dungeon. Tristram and Isolt again escape, and live in Lancelot's castle of Joyous Gard; he goes out riding with Isolt, both of them being clad in green attire, when probably the bower mentioned by Tennyson is constructed. He fights with many knights; but we need not go into the rest of his story, of which enough has been given to show its affinity to the Lancelot story, and to illustrate the love-scene with Isolt in the Idyll. We may, however, quote Malory's last words about them: " That traitor king Mark slew the noble knight Sir Tristram, as he sat harping afore his lady La Beale Isoud, with a trenchant glaive, for whose death was much bewailing of every knight that ever was in Arthur's days . . . and La Beale Isoud died, swooning upon the cross of Sir Tristram, whereof was great pity." '

10. *For Arthur and Sir Lancelot riding once, etc.* Tennyson has apparently based his story of the ruby necklace on an incident in the life of Alfred, quoted in Stanley's ' Book of Birds,' where it is credited to the ' Monast. Anglic.,' vol. i.: ' Alfred, King of the West Saxons, went out one day a-hunting, and passing by a certain wood heard, as he supposed, the cry of an infant from the top of a tree, and forthwith diligently inquiring of the huntsmen what that doleful sound could be, commanded one of them to climb the tree, when on the top of it was found an eagle's nest, and lo ! therein a sweet-

faced infant, wrapped up in a purple mantle, and upon each arm a bracelet of gold, a clear sign that he was born of noble parents. Whereupon the king took charge of him, and caused him to be baptized; and, because he was found in a nest, he gave him the name of *Nestingum*, and, in aftertime, having nobly educated him, he advanced him to the dignity of an earl.'

37. *Those diamonds that I rescued from the tarn.* See 'Lancelot and Elaine,' 34 fol.

39. *Would rather you had let them fall.* Originally, ' ye ' for ' you.'

51. *A great jousts.* This use of ' jousts ' in the singular is peculiar, and is not mentioned in the dictionaries.

150. *And vail'd his eyes again.* Cast down his eyes. Compare 'Guinevere,' line 657 below: 'made her vail her eyes.' This word 'vail' has no connection with 'veil,' though often confounded with it. It is contracted from 'avail,' or 'avale,' the French 'avaler' (Latin, 'ad vallem'). Compare 'Hamlet,' i. 2. 70: —

> Do not forever with thy vailed lids
> Seek for thy noble father in the dust.

'Avail' occurs in Malory (v. 12): 'Then the King availed his visor, with a meek and lowly countenance,' etc.

216. *A swarthy one.* Originally, 'a swarthy dame.'

222. *Come — let us gladden their sad eyes.* Originally, 'comfort their sad eyes.'

252. *And while he twangled, little Dagonet stood, etc.* Littledale says that 'Dagonet's standing still is doubtless meant to recall St. Matthew, xi. 17: "We have piped unto you, and ye have not danced," etc.' It may or may not remind us of that passage, but I doubt whether it was 'meant' to do so.

256. *And being ask'd, ' Why skipt ye not, Sir Fool ? '* Originally, 'Then being ask'd,' etc.

259. *Than any broken music thou canst make.* Originally, 'ye can make.' 'Properly speaking, "broken music" meant either (as Chappell explains) short unsustained notes, such as are made on stringed instruments when played without a bow; or concerted music, played by several instruments in combination' (Littledale).

322. *A Paynim harper.* The allusion to Orpheus is obvious.

333. *The Harp of Arthur.* See on 'Gareth and Lynette,' 1281.

343. *The black king's highway.* The 'broad road leading to destruction.'

357. *Burning spurge.* A plant of the genus *Euphorbia*, which burns with an acrid smoke.

371. *But at the slot or fewmets of a deer.* 'Slot' and 'fewmets' (footprints and droppings) are old terms of 'venerie,' or woodcraft (Littledale).

373. *From lawn to lawn.* For 'lawn' as an open place in a forest, compare 'A Dream of Fair Women': —

> On those long, rank, dark wood-walks drench'd in dew,
>   Leading from lawn to lawn.

Malory (iv. 19) has the word in this sense: 'So

on the morn they rode into the forest of adventure till they came to a lawn, and thereby they found a cross,' etc.

450. *The scorpion-worm that twists itself in hell, etc.* A legendary creature, evidently suggested by the old notion (long since proved false by naturalists) that the scorpion, if surrounded by fire, will sting itself to death. The use of *worm* is suggested by the obsolete sense of snake, dragon, etc. Compare Shakespeare, 'Measure for Measure,' iii. 1. 17 : —

> For thou dost fear the soft and tender fork
> Of a poor worm.

It is in a similar sense that Venus (' Venus and Adonis,' 933) calls Death 'grim-grinning ghost, earth's worm.'

461. *Fall, as the crest of some slow-arching wave.* The elaborate simile seems out of keeping with the fall of the drunken knight from his horse; but it is an 'Homeric echo,' like not a few others in the Idylls.

467. *Then the knights, etc.* Originally, 'while' for 'then.'

477. *Then, echoing yell with yell.* Originally, 'Then, yell with yell echoing.'

479. *Alioth and Alcor.* Stars in the Great Bear. Alcor is really a fifth-magnitude star close to Mizar, and distinguishable only by good eyes. For the reference to the Aurora borealis, compare 'The Passing of Arthur,' 307.

481. *As the water Moab saw, etc.* See 2 Kings, iii. 22.

483. *Lazy-plunging sea.* Compare 'The Palace of Art': —

> that hears all night
> The plunging seas draw backward from the land
>   Their moon-led waters white;

and 'A Dream of Fair Women': —

> I would the white cold heavy-plunging foam,
> Whirl'd by the wind, had roll'd me deep below,
>   Then when I left my home.

495. *What if she hate me now?* Originally, 'an' for 'if,' as also in the next line.

501. *Last in a roky hollow, belling, etc.* 'Roky' (associated with 'reek') means misty, foggy. For 'belling' as applied to hounds, compare 'A Midsummer-Night's Dream,' iv. 1. 128: —

> Slow in pursuit, but match'd in mouth like bells,
> Each under each;

that is, like a chime of bells.

502. *Felt the goodly hounds Yelp at his heart.* Littledale thinks this may mean that 'the belling of the hounds set the hunter's heart throbbing in harmony — he longed to follow the chase, but turned aside to Tintagil;' but I prefer Elsdale's explanation, that it is a presentiment of coming disaster.

504. *Tintagil, half in sea and high on land.* The ruins of the castle are still to be seen ' by the Cornish sea,' six miles from Camelford. The keep, the oldest part of the structure, is probably Norman, but there may have been a Saxon, and perhaps also a British, stronghold on the same site.

509. *The spiring stone.* The spiral stairway of stone. The dictionaries do not recognize this sense of 'spiring,' but I have no doubt that it was what Tennyson had in mind, rather than rising like a spire.

570. *To sin in leading-strings.* Referring to what he had just said about the sin of Guinevere.

588. *The King was all fulfill'd with gratefulness.* For 'fulfil' in the old sense of fill full, compare Shakespeare, Sonnet 136. 5: —

'Will' will fulfil the treasure of thy love,
Ay, fill it full with wills, and my will one.

Wiclif has in Matthew, v. 6: 'Blessid be thei that hungren and thirsten rigtwisnesse; for thei schal be fulfillid.'

627. *The swineherd's malkin in the mast.* Compare 'The Princess,' v.: —

If this be he, — or a draggled mawkin, thou,
That tends her bristled grunters in the sludge!

'Mawkin' is merely a phonetic spelling of 'malkin,' which is probably a diminutive of 'Mall,' or 'Mary,' though it was also connected with 'Matilda.' The 'Promptorium Parvulorum' has: 'Malkyne, or Mawt, proper name *Matildis.*'

629. *Far other was the Tristram, Arthur's knight!* This line is not in the 1st edition.

650. *Vows! did you keep the vow you made to Mark?* The 1st edition has 'ye' for 'you.'

690. *The wide world laughs at it.* The 1st edition has 'great world.'

692. *The ptarmigan that whitens ere his hour, etc.* 'The color of this bird varies, being brownish-gray in summer and white in winter. The changes of plumage enable it to harmonize with its surroundings at the various seasons. If the ptarmigan's feathers were to turn white before the winter snows began, it would be seen by the eagle-owls and falcons, and would 'soon be killed' (Littledale).

695. *The garnet-headed yaffingale.* The green woodpecker, *Gecinus viridis;* so called from its loud laughing notes. It is also known as the 'yaffle' (or 'yaffil') and 'yaffler.'

743. *He spoke, he turn'd, then flinging round her neck, etc.* The 1st edition reads: —

He rose, he turn'd, and, flinging round her neck,
Claspt it; but while he bow'd himself to lay
Warm kisses in the hollow of her throat,
Out of the dark, etc.

752. *The great Queen's bower was dark.* She had fled, as the next Idyll explains.

Page 433. GUINEVERE.
The poet is indebted to Malory for only a few hints of the story — Arthur's discovery of the guilt of Lancelot and Guinevere; her condemnation to be burnt alive; her escape from the stake through Lancelot, who carries her off to his castle of La Joyeuse Gard; the siege of the castle by Arthur, who compels Lancelot to give up the Queen; and her retirement — but not until after Arthur's death — to Almesbury, where she 'was ruler and abbess as reason would.'

9. *For hither had she fled, etc.* The 1859 reading was: —

For hither had she fled, her cause of flight
Sir Modred; he the nearest to the King,
His nephew, ever like a subtle beast,
Lay couchant, etc.

Littledale notes that 'by a curious coincidence, this is the very simile that Arthur Hallam used to describe Tennyson's fame waiting to come upon him': —

A being full of clearest insight,
. . . whose fame
Is couching now with panther eyes intent,
As who shall say, 'I 'll spring to him anon,
And have him for my own.'

'Almesbury;' now Amesbury, is about eight miles from Salisbury, and the old Abbey Church is still standing.

15. *Lords of the White Horse* See on 'Lancelot and Elaine,' 297.

22. *Plumes that mock'd the may.* That is, white as the hawthorn blossoms. Compare 'The Miller's Daughter': 'The lanes, you know, were white with may;' and see note on 'Gareth and Lynette,' 642.

97, 98. *And part for ever. Vivien, lurking, heard, etc.* The 1859 ed. reads: 'And part for ever. Passion-pale they met,' etc. The addition is not in the ed. of 1884, but I find it in that of 1890. 'They met' is now ambiguous.

147. *For housel or for shrift.* For receiving the Eucharist, or for confession.

166. *Late, late, so late!* It is hardly necessary to say that the song is founded on the parable of the wise and foolish virgins (Matthew, xxv.).

289. *Bude and Bos.* Districts of Cornwall.

292. *Of dark Tintagil.* See page 860, note on 504. The 1859 edition has 'Dundagil.'

400. *Came to that point where first she saw the King.* The 1859 edition has 'when first.'

470. *To honor his own word as if his God's.* This line is not in the 1859 edition.

481. *Before I wedded thee.* The 1859 edition has 'until I wedded.'

535. *The flaming death.* Being burned at the stake, a punishment for unfaithful wives mentioned several times by Malory.

569. *Where I must strike against the man they call, etc.* The 1859 edition reads: —

Where I must strike against my sister's son,
Leagued with the lords of the White Horse and knights
Once mine, and strike him dead, etc.

601. *Moving ghostlike to his doom.* 'That doom is told in "The Passing of Arthur," but that he is already enwound by its misty pall, and himself a ghost in it, is nobly conceived, and as splendidly expressed '(Stopford Brooke).

642. *I yearn'd for warmth and color.* The 1859 edition has: 'I wanted warmth,' etc.

657. *Made her vail her eyes.* See on 'The Last Tournament,' 150.

Page 443. THE PASSING OF ARTHUR.
This Idyll in its present form was first published in the 'Holy Grail' volume, 1869; but, with the exception of 169 lines at the beginning and 30 at the close, it was printed in 1842 in 'The Epic,' which is still included in the col-

lected poems. See the notes on that poem, and also p. 302 above.

The following notice appears in the 'Holy Grail' volume, opposite the titlepage: —

'These four "Idylls of the King" are printed in their present form for the convenience of those who possess the former volume.

'The whole series should be read, and is to-day published, in the following order: —

THE COMING OF ARTHUR.

The Round Table.

GERAINT AND ENID.

MERLIN AND VIVIEN.

LANCELOT AND ELAINE.

THE HOLY GRAIL.

PELLEAS AND ETTARRE.

GUINEVERE.

THE PASSING OF ARTHUR.[1]

[1] This last, the earliest written of the poems, is here connected with the rest in accordance with an early project of the author's.

Apparently the addition of 'Gareth and Lynette' and 'The Last Tournament' was an afterthought; and later the poet decided to divide 'Geraint and Enid,' and to add 'Balin and Balan,' making 'twelve books' in all.

The story of 'The Passing of Arthur' is taken from Malory (xxi. 5).

6–28. *For on their march to westward, . . . I pass, but shall not die.* These twenty-three lines are not in the 1869 edition, which goes on thus: 'Before that last weird battle in the west,' etc.

61. *Once thine whom thou hast loved, etc.* The reading of 1869 was: —

Once thine, whom thou hast loved, but baser now
Than heathen scoffing at their vows and thee.

68. *And brake the petty kings, and fought with Rome.* This line is not in the 1869 edition, in which the next line begins with 'And thrust,' etc.

85. *And the long mountains, etc.* Originally, 'the long mountain.'

129. *Only the wan wave.* Originally, 'waste wave.'

170. *So all day long the noise of battle roll'd.* With this sonorous line the early 'Morte d'Arthur' begins.

175. *The bold Sir Bedivere uplifted him.* After this line, the 'Morte d'Arthur' of 1842 has the line, 'Sir Bedivere, the last of all his knights;' omitted here, of course, because the fact is mentioned in line 2 of the new matter.

195. *Thou therefore take my brand Excalibur, etc.* Compare Malory (xxi. 5): 'But my time hieth fast, said the king. Therefore said Arthur, take thou Excalibur, my good sword, and go with it to yonder water side, and when thou comest there, I charge thee throw my sword in that water, and come again, and tell me what thou there seest. My lord, said Bedivere, your commandment shall be done, and lightly bring you word again. So Sir Bedivere departed, and by the way he beheld that noble sword, that the pommel and haft were all of precious stones, and then he said to himself, If I throw this rich sword in the water, thereof shall never come good, but harm and loss. And then Sir Bedivere hid Excalibur under a tree. And as soon as he might he came again unto the king, and said he had been at the water, and had thrown the sword into the water. What sawest thou there? said the king. Sir, he said, I saw nothing but waves and winds. That is untruly said of thee, said the king; therefore go thou lightly again, and do my command as thou art to me lief and dear, spare not, but throw it in. Then Sir Bedivere returned again, and took the sword in his hand; and then him thought sin and shame to throw away that noble sword; and so eft he hid the sword, and returned again, and told to the king that he had been at the water, and done his commandment. What saw thou there? said the king. Sir, he said, I saw nothing but the waters wap and the waves wan. Ah traitor, untrue, said king Arthur, now hast thou betrayed me twice. Who would have wend that thou that hast been to me so lief and dear, and thou art named a noble knight, and would betray me for the riches of the sword. But now go again lightly, for thy long tarrying putteth me in great jeopardy of my life, for I have taken cold. And but if thou do now as I bid thee, if ever I may see thee, I shall slay thee with mine own hands, for thou wouldest for my rich sword see me dead. Then Sir Bedivere departed, and went to the sword, and lightly took it up, and went to the water side, and there he bound the girdle about the hilts, and then he threw the sword as far into the water as he might, and there came an arm and an hand above the water, and met it, and caught it, and so shook it thrice and brandished, and then vanished away the hand with the sword in the water. So Sir Bedivere came again to the king, and told him what he saw. Alas, said the king, help me hence, for I dread me I have tarried over long. Then Sir Bedivere took the king upon his back, and so went with him to that water side. And when they were at the water side, even fast by the bank hoved a little barge, with many fair ladies in it, and among them all was a queen, and all they had black hoods, and all they wept and shrieked when they saw king Arthur. Now put me into the barge, said the king: and so he did softly. And there received him three queens with great mourning, and so they set him down, and in one of their laps king Arthur laid his head, and then that queen said, Ah, dear brother, why have ye tarried so long from me? Alas, this wound on your head hath caught over much cold. And so then they rowed from the land; and Sir

Bedivere beheld all those ladies go from him. Then Sir Bedivere cried, Ah, my lord Arthur, what shall become of me now ye go from me, and leave me here alone among mine enemies. Comfort thyself, said the king, and do as well as thou mayest, for in me is no trust for to trust in. For I will into the vale of Avilion, to heal me of my grievous wound. And if thou hear never more of me, pray for my soul. But ever the queens and the ladies wept and shrieked, that it was pity to hear. And as soon as Sir Bedivere had lost the sight of the barge, he wept and wailed, and so took the forest, and so he went all that night, and in the morning he was ware betwixt two holts hoar of a chapel and an hermitage.'

354. *Dry clash'd his harness in the icy caves, etc.* 'We hear all the changes on the vowel *a* — every sound of it used to give the impression — and then, in a moment, the verse runs into breadth, smoothness, and vastness; for Bedivere comes to the shore and sees the great water: —

> And on a sudden, lo ! the level lake
> And the long glories of the winter moon.

in which the vowel *o* in its changes is used as the vowel *a* has been used before' (Stopford Brooke).

379. *And dropping bitter tears against a brow.* The 1869 edition has 'his brow.'

435. *Like some full-breasted swan.* Compare 'The Dying Swan.'

440. *And on the mere the wailing died away.* Here the original 'Morte d'Arthur' ends. The next five lines are not in the 1869 edition, which goes on thus: —

> At length he groan'd, and turning slowly clomb
> The last hard footstep of that iron crag.

445. *Even to the highest he could climb.* The 1869 edition has 'E'en,' for which the printer is probably responsible, as Tennyson never uses it.

To the Queen. This epilogue has not been altered since it first appeared in the 'Library Edition,' 1872–73.

3. *That rememberable day.* Referring to the public thanksgiving in February, 1872, on the recovery of the Prince of Wales from typhoid fever.

12. *Thunderless lightnings striking under sea, etc.* Congratulatory despatches by submarine telegraph.

14. *That true North, etc.* When Manitoba was added to the Dominion of Canada, complaint was made in England of the cost of maintaining the colonial possessions in North America. Mr. Justin McCarthy, in his 'History of Our Own Times,' says: 'For some years a feeling was spreading in England which began to find expression in repeated and very distinct suggestions that the Canadians had better begin to think of looking out for themselves. Many Englishmen complained of this country being expected to undertake the principal cost. of the defences of Canada, and to guarantee her railway schemes, especially when the commer-

cial policy which Canada adopted towards England was one of a strictly protective character.'

20. *The roar of Hougoumont.* The battle of Waterloo. The *Château of Hougoumont*, with its massive buildings, its gardens and plantations, was occupied by the Allies, and 'formed the key to the British position.' It is computed that 'during the day the attacks of nearly 12,000 men were launched against this miniature fortress, notwithstanding which the garrison held out to the last.'

35. *For one to whom I made it, etc.* Referring to the dedication of the 'Idylls' to the memory of Prince Albert.

38. *Ideal manhood closed in real man.* This line does not appear in any English or American edition up to the present time (1898); but the 'Memoir' (vol. ii. p. 129) states that the poet, thinking that 'perhaps he had not made the real humanity of the King sufficiently clear in his epilogue,' inserted this line 'in 1891, as his last correction.' It is probably through mere oversight that it has not been inserted in the editions published since 1891.

41. *Geoffrey's book, or him of Malleor's.* Geoffrey of Monmouth and Malory, whose name was also written Malorye, Maleore, and Malleor.

55. *With poisonous honey stolen from France.* Compare 'Locksley Hall Sixty Years After,' 145: 'Set the maiden fancies wallowing in the troughs of Zolaism,' etc. Littledale quotes Goldwin Smith, 'Essays': 'As to French novels, Carlyle says of one of the most famous of the last century that after reading it you ought to wash seven times in Jordan; but after reading the French novels of the present day, in which lewdness is sprinkled with sentimental rosewater, and deodorized, but not disinfected, your washings had better be seventy times seven.'

Page 452. THE FIRST QUARREL.

The poem is 'an idyll of the hearth inspired with life: Nelly and Harry are lifelike in the very respect in which Annie and Philip in "Enoch Arden" are idealized. They speak the rough, genuine language of the fisherfolk' (Waugh).

Page 454. RIZPAH.

A reviewer in 'Macmillan's Magazine' for January, 1881, says of the poem: 'As the recital in lyric form of a weird tale of misery and madness, this poem is unmatched in Mr. Tennyson's work. An old woman, in her fierce and at the same time trembling dotage, tells a lady who has come to visit her how her boy had long ago been hung in chains, under the old laws of England, for robbing the mail; how he had done it not in wickedness but in recklessness, but how her plea to that effect had availed him nothing; how, when she had gone to visit him in prison, she had been forced from him by the jailer, with his cry of "mother, mother!" ringing in her ears; how the same cry rang afterwards in her brain while she lay bound and beaten in a madhouse; and how, when she was at last set free, she used to steal out on stormy nights, and gather together his bones from beneath the gallows, until she had gathered them every one and buried them in consecrated ground beside the churchyard wall. It is as terrible a tale as could well be imagined, and is told with a plain and classic force, a freedom from shrillness or emphasis, which leaves the terror all the more piercing and unescapable.'

The 'Edinburgh Review' for October, 1881, refers to the poem as one in which Tennyson 'has broken on the world with a new strength and splendor,' and 'has achieved a new reputation.' The writer adds: 'Of this astonishing production it has been said that, were all the rest of the author's works destroyed, this alone would at once place him among the first of the world's poets. Such was the verdict pronounced by Mr. Swinburne. It has all his characteristic generosity, and not much of his characteristic exaggeration. . . . A work of this order can never be done justice to by quotations; but we have used them with no further end than to indicate baldly the outline of the poet's subject. For his sublime treatment of it, for the tenderness and the terror of his pathos, we must refer the reader to the poem itself in its entirety. Nothing in " Maud," nothing in " Guinevere," can approach in power to " Rizpah." This fact can, we conceive, be accounted for by the special nature of the subject. Of all the affections of human nature that are least subject to change, either in the way of contraction or development, is the passion of mother for child. It asks least aid either from faith or reason. And something may be said of the three other poems that we have associated with " Rizpah " ['The First Quarrel,' 'The Northern Cobbler,' and 'The Village Wife']. These three deal all of them with the life of the common people, and touch our feelings and principles in their rudest and simplest form. They take us below the reach of either conscious faith or philosophy; and they elude, they do not meet, the problems of human destiny. Thus Mr. Tennyson's genius has escaped, in these cases, from the external circumstances that have been depressing it; and, once supplied with a fitting theme to handle, it has shown itself as strong, if not stronger than ever.'

For the suggestion of the title of 'Rizpah,' see 2 Samuel, xxi. 1–14.

Line 7. *The creak of the chain.* It was formerly the custom in England to hang the bodies of certain malefactors in chains after execution. The bodies of pirates were so hanged on the banks of the Thames.

54. *They had moved in my side.* For the use of 'side,' compare 'Comus,' 1009 : —

And from her fair unspotted side
Two blissful twins are to be born,
Youth and Joy; so Jove hath sworn.

Page 456. THE NORTHERN COBBLER.
'The general lines of the Northern Cobbler's position are the same as of many reformed drinkers, but no one but himself could have set the bottle up in the window, or declared that he would take it with him after death, like a Norse warrior his sword, before the throne' (Stopford Brooke).

Line 6. *The line.* The equator.

13. *I could fettle and clump, etc.* Repair and put new soles to old boots and shoes. Shakespeare uses 'fettle' once, in 'Romeo and Juliet,' iii. 5. 154: —

But fettle your fine joints 'gainst Thursday next,
To go with Paris to Saint Peter's Church;

where it means to prepare, make ready.

19. *I slither'd.* That is, slipped.

20. *Slaäpe down i' the squad.* Suddenly down in the slush.

22. *Scrawm'd and scratted.* Clawed and scratched.

32. *Weär'd it o' liquor.* Spent it for liquor.

53. *All in a tew.* All in a fluster.

78. *Snaggy.* Snappish, ill-tempered.

108. *Feät.* Trim; used by Shakespeare several times.

110. *A codlin.* A codling, or unripe apple. Compare 'Twelfth Night,' i. 5. 167: 'a codling when 't is almost an apple.'

Page 458. THE REVENGE.

Line 51. *Having that within her womb, etc.* 'Womb' is here used in its original sense of belly. Compare Wiclif's Bible, Luke, xv. 16: 'And he coveitide to fille his wombe of the coddis that the hoggis eaten,' etc.

118. *And the little Revenge herself went down, etc.* Markham, in a postscript to his poem, says: 'What became of the *Reuenge* after Sir *Richards* death, diuers report diuersly, but the most probable and sufficient proofe sayth, that within fewe dayes after the Knights death, there arose a great storme from the VVest and North-west, that all the Fleet was disperced, aswell the *Indian* Fleet, which were then come vnto them, as all the rest of the *Armada*, which attended their ariuall; of vvhich fourteene sayle, together with the *Reuenge*, and in her two hundred *Spanyards*, were cast away vppon the Ile of *S. Michaels;* so it pleased them to honour the buriall of that renowned Ship the *Reuenge*, not suffering her to perrish alone, for the great horour shee atchiued in her life time.'

Page 461. THE SISTERS.

Line 91. *Lake Llanberis.* In North Wales. Compare 'The Golden Year' : —

And found him in Llanberis: then we crost
Between the lakes, etc.

The lakes are Llyn Padarn and Llyn Peris; but they are often called the 'Llanberis Lakes.'

111. *Of our New Forest.* An ancient royal hunting demesne, extending westward from Southampton Water. There are about 140 square miles in the district, little more than two thirds of which now belongs to the crown.

117. *My Rosalind in this Arden.* The allusion to 'As You Like It' is obvious.

Page 465. THE VILLAGE WIFE.

Line 19. *Can tha tell ony harm on 'im, lass?* All the English editions omit the comma before 'lass.'

64. *The 'Ouse.* That is, the poorhouse: a colloquial use of the word in England.

80. *White wi' the maäy.* That is, with the blossoms of the white hawthorn. See note on ' The Miller's Daughter,' line 130. All the English editions have ' Maäy ' in the present passage.

88. *Fur he ca'd 'is 'erse Billy-rough-un.* For he called his horse Bellerophon. Similarly, the name of the warship Bellerophon is said to have been corrupted by the sailors into ' Billy-ruffian.'

99. *Siver the mou'ds rattled down upo' poor owd Squire i' the wood.* Howsoever (however) the mould (earth) rattled down on the poor old Squire's coffin.

107. *Hes fur Miss Hannie the heldest hes now, etc.* This is the reading of the English editions; but elsewhere in the poem we have ' Miss Annie ' and ' es ' (for ' as ') except in the preceding line, where it is misprinted ' as.'

121. *Hugger-mugger they lived.* They lived in a slovenly way (Century Dict.). The word, whether as noun or adjective, often means in privacy or secrecy. Compare ' Hamlet,' iv. 5. 84: —

> and we have done but greenly,
> In hugger-mugger to inter him.

126. *Roomlin' by.* Rumbling by (in his coach).

Page 468. IN THE CHILDREN'S HOSPITAL.

Line 10. *Drench'd with the hellish oorali.* A drug, also known as ' woorali ' and ' curari ' (or ' curara '), extracted from the *Strychnos toxifera.* It acts by paralyzing the nerves of motion without impairing the sensibility. It is used by the South American Indians for poisoning their arrows. The reference here is to the practice of vivisection for purposes of physiological investigation. Tennyson evidently sympathized with the criticisms, not wholly groundless, which have been urged against it, and which have led in England to the enactment of laws restricting and regulating it.

Page 470. DEDICATORY POEM TO THE PRINCESS ALICE.

Line 7. *Thy soldier-brother's bridal orange-bloom, etc.* Prince Arthur, Duke of Connaught, was married at Windsor, on the 13th of March, 1879, to Louise-Marguerite, Princess of Prussia.

Page 470. THE DEFENCE OF LUCKNOW.

Line 20. *The brute bullet.* The senseless bullet; antithetical to the sentient ' brain.'

25. *Mine ? yes, a mine !* Sir James Outram, describing the siege, says: ' I am aware of no parallel to our series of mines in modern war. Twenty-one shafts, aggregating two hundred feet in depth, and 3291 feet of gallery have been executed. The enemy advanced twenty mines against the palaces and outposts; of these they exploded three which caused us loss of life, and two which did no injury; seven have been blown in; and out of seven others the enemy have been driven and their galleries taken possession of by our miners.'

Page 472. SIR JOHN OLDCASTLE.

Line 5. *Scribbled or carved upon the pitiless stone.* Like the carvings by prisoners of state still to be seen on the walls of the Beauchamp Tower in the Tower of London.

16. *The proud Archbishop Arundel.* Thomas Arundel, Archbishop of Canterbury, a zealous persecutor of the Lollards.

19. *Bara.* Bread (Welsh).

20. *Vailing a sudden eyelid.* The ' vailing ' is the obsolete word meaning to lower or let fall.

21. *Dim Saesneg.* No English; that is, I do not speak English.

24. *Not least art thou, thou little Bethlehem, etc.* See Micah, v. 2.

26. *Little Lutterworth.* Lutterworth, the parish in Leicestershire of which Wiclif was rector.

77. *Sir Roger Acton.* A prominent Lollard.

78. *Beverley.* John of Beverley, who was martyred January 19, 1413–14.

79. *Thy two witnesses.* See Revelation, xi. 3.

84. *Him, who should bear the sword, etc.* Henry V. The poet seems here to identify the speaker with the Sir John Oldcastle who appears as one of Prince Henry's wild companions in the old play of ' The Famous Victories of Henry the Fifth,' on which Shakespeare founded his ' Henry IV.' and ' Henry V.; ' and it is well known that ' Sir John Oldcastle ' was originally the name of Falstaff in the ' Henry IV.' plays. The dramatist changed the name to avoid offending the Protestants and gratifying the Roman Catholics. See the epilogue to ' 2 Henry IV.': ' Falstaff shall die of a sweat, unless already a' be killed with your hard opinions; for Oldcastle died a martyr, and this is not the man.' Fuller, in his ' Church History ' (lib. iv.), says: ' Stage poets have themselves been very bold with, and others very merry at, the memory of Sir John Oldcastle, whom they have fancied a boon companion, a jovial royster, and yet a coward to boot. . . . The best is, Sir John Falstaff hath relieved the memory of Sir John Oldcastle, and of late is substituted buffoon in his place.'

93. *Or Amurath of the East.* A Turkish Sultan. Compare ' 2 Henry IV.' v. 2. 48: —

> This is the English, not the Turkish court;
> Not Amurath an Amurath succeeds,
> But Harry Harry.

159. *Sylvester.* Sylvester II., who became Pope A. D. 999.

Page 476. COLUMBUS.

When Columbus returned to San Domingo on his third expedition, the colony was in a deplorable condition. Things went from bad to worse, and the Spanish monarchs sent an officer of the royal household, Francis de Bobadilla, to make investigations, with authority to send back to Spain ' any cavaliers or other persons ' whom he thought proper. It is not probable that the intention was to include Columbus in the list of persons subject to arrest; but Bobadilla, soon after his arrival in the island, put the great admiral in chains, and sent him to Spain, where he arrived in November, 1499.

Line 18. *The great ' Laudamus.'* The Te Deum.

25. *The Dragon's Mouth.* The name (*Bocca*

del Drago) which Columbus gave to a channel between the island of Trinidad and the mainland of South America.

26. *The Mountain of the World.* The 'Mountain of Adam,' or 'Mountain of the Gods,' the highest peak in Ceylon, on the summit of which the print of Buddha's foot is supposed to be visible.

46. *King David call'd the heavens a hide, a tent.* See Psalms, civ. 2.

48. *Some cited old Lactantius.* An eminent Christian author, who flourished early in the 4th century. The 1st edition of his works, one of the oldest of printed books, was brought out at Subiaco in 1465.

74. *Guanahani.* The native name of the first island discovered by Columbus.

107. *The belting wall of Cambalu, etc.* The royal residence of the Khan of Cathay. Compare Milton, 'Paradise Lost,' xi. 388: 'Cambalu, seat of Cathayan Can.'

109. *Prester John* was a mythical Christian king of India. Compare 'Much Ado About Nothing,' ii. 1. 274: 'I will fetch you a toothpicker now from the furthest inch of Asia, bring you the length of Prester John's foot.'

117. *Howl'd me from Hispaniola.* The name which Columbus gave to the island of Hayti.

125. *Fonseca, my main enemy at their court.* Juan Rodriguez Fonseca, a bigoted Spanish prelate, who called Columbus a visionary and treated him with persistent malignity.

126. *Bovadilla.* The Francisco de Bobadilla mentioned above.

144. *Veragua.* A province of New Granada in South America.

190. *The Catalonian Minorite.* Bernardo Buil (Boyle), a Benedictine monk, according to the best authorities (not a *Minorite*, or Franciscan), who was sent by the Pope to the new Indies in June, 1493, as apostolical vicar. He hated Columbus, but there seems to be no evidence that he *excommunicated* him.

206. *Colón.* The Spanish form of 'Columbus.'

Page 479. THE VOYAGE OF MAELDUNE.

Line 22. *Fainter than any flittermouse-shriek.* The cry of the bat, which in England is popularly called 'flittermouse' (fluttering-mouse), 'flickermouse,' or 'flindermouse.' Compare Ben Jonson, 'Sad Shepherd,' ii. 8: 'And giddy flittermice, with leather wings,' etc.

26. *They almost fell on each other.* This idea, which occurs so often in the poem, is not to be found in the old legend.

48. *The triumph of Finn.* Finn, the son of Cumal, was the most renowned of all the heroes of ancient Ireland. He was commander of the Feni, or 'Feni of Erin,' a sort of standing army maintained by the monarch for the support of the throne. Each province had its own soldiers under a local captain, but all were under one commander-in-chief. Finn was equally brave and sagacious. His foresight was, indeed, so extraordinary that the people believed it to be a preternatural gift, and a legend was invented to account for it. He was killed at a place

called Athbrea, on the Boyne, A. D. 284. Ossian, or Oisin, the famous hero-poet, to whom the bards attribute many poems still extant, was the son of Finn.

55. *The Isle of Fruits.* The poet may have got the hint of this island from the 'isle of intoxicating wine-fruits' in the Celtic tale; but the rich details of the picture are all his own.

77. *That undersea isle.* The description here is developed from the simple statement in the old legend that 'they could see, beneath the clear water, a beautiful country, with many mansions surrounded by groves and woods.' So far from being tempted to dive down to the place, the sight of 'an animal fierce and terrible' which infests it makes them tremble lest they may 'not be able to cross the sea over the monster, on account of the extreme thinness of the water; but after much difficulty and danger they get across it safely.'

105. *The Isle of the Double Towers.* If I had not read the old tale, I should have said that this quaint and wild conception must have been taken from it; but, though it seems so thoroughly like a Celtic fancy, there is nothing in the legend that could have suggested it.

115. *Saint Brendan.* One of the most famous of the ancient Celtic legends is that of 'The Voyage of Saint Brendan,' undertaken in the sixth century. He set out from Kerry, sailed westward into the Atlantic, and, as some believed, landed on the shore of America. The adventures he met with were as varied and surprising as those of Maeldune.

Page 484. PREFATORY SONNET TO 'THE NINETEENTH CENTURY.'

Line 3. *Their old craft, seaworthy still.* 'The Contemporary Review.'

7. *This roaring moon of daffodil.* Compare 'The Winter's Tale,' iv. 4. 118: —

daffodils
That come before the swallow dares, and take
The winds of March with beauty.

Page 484. TO THE REV. W. H. BROOKFIELD.

Line 6. *We paced that walk of limes.* Compare 'In Memoriam,' lxxxvii.: —

Up that long walk of limes I past
To see the rooms in which he dwelt.

11. *Our kindlier, trustier Jaques.* The allusion to 'As You Like It' needs no explanation.

Page 484. MONTENEGRO.

Line 12. *Great Tsernogora!* Or *Tzernagora*, the native name of Montenegro.

Page 488. TO E. FITZGERALD.

Line 15. *Your table of Pythagoras.* For the allusion to the vegetarianism of the old philosopher, based on the doctrine of metempsychosis, compare 'Twelfth Night,' iv. 2. 54: —

Clown. What is the opinion of Pythagoras concerning wild-fowl?
Malvolio. That the soul of our grandam might haply inhabit a bird.
Clown. What thinkest thou of his opinion?
Malvolio. I think nobly of the soul, and no way approve his opinion.

Clown. Fare thee well. Remain thou still in darkness. Thou shalt hold the opinion of Pythagoras ere I will allow of thy wits, and fear to kill a woodcock lest thou dispossess the soul of thy grandam.

For the poet's account of the vegetarian dream, see the 'Memoir,' vol. ii. p. 317. The visit to Fitzgerald was made in 1876.

16. *A thing enskied.* See 'Measure for Measure,' i. 4. 34: 'I hold you as a thing enskied and sainted.'

28. *Of Eschol hugeness.* See Numbers, xiii. 23.

32. *Your golden Eastern lay.* The 'Rubáiyát' of Omar Kayyam, translated by Fitzgerald in 1859.

46. *My son.* Hallam, the present Lord Tennyson.

Page 489. TIRESIAS.

Line 9. *My son.* Used in a familiar figurative way. Menœceus, whom he addresses below, was the son of Creon, and directly descended from Cadmus, who had offended Ares (Mars) by killing the dragon guarding a spring sacred to the god.

25. *Subjected to the Heliconian ridge.* 'Subjected' is used in its etymological sense of lying below.

38. *There in a secret olive-glade I saw, etc.* The description of the goddess is nowise inferior to that of the same goddess and her companion deities in 'Œnone.'

96. *The song-built towers and gates.* The walls of Thebes rose to the music of Amphion's harp, as those of Troy to Apollo's. Compare 'Œnone.'

147. *A wiser than herself.* Œdipus.

164. *Their ocean-islets.* The Isles of the Blest.

192. *Find the gate Is bolted, and the master gone.* For the figure, compare 'The Deserted House.'

Page 495. DESPAIR.

Line 21. *In the drear nightfold of your fatalist.* The 1881 reading was 'dark nightfold.'

75. *Tho' glory and shame dying out for ever, etc.* The 1881 reading was: 'Tho' name and fame dying out,' etc.

Page 504. TO-MORROW.

Line 31. *The white o' the may.* All the English editions have 'May;' but I have no doubt that the reference is to the blossoms of the white hawthorn, as in 'The Village Wife,' line 80. See note on that passage.

48. *The Sassenach whate.* The Saxon (English) wheat.

Page 508. PROLOGUE TO GENERAL HAMLEY.

Line 5. *You came, and look'd, and loved the view, etc.* The view from the poet's summer residence at Aldworth.

28. *Tel-el-Kebir.* A village in Lower Egypt, about fifty miles northeast of Cairo. Here, on the 13th of September, 1882, the English under General Wolseley defeated the Egyptian insurgents under Arabi Pasha, whose surrender soon followed.

Page 509. THE CHARGE OF THE HEAVY BRIGADE AT BALACLAVA.

Line 5. *When the points of the Russian lances arose on the sky.* Originally, 'broke in on the sky.'

14–21. *Thousands of horsemen had gather'd there on the height, etc.* For these eight lines the first version had: —

Down the hill slowly thousands of Russians
Drew to the valley, and halted at last on the height,
With a wing push'd out to the left, and a wing to the right —
But Scarlett was far on ahead, and he dashed up alone
Thro' the great gray slope of men,
And he wheel'd his sabre, he held his own
Like an Englishman there and then;
And the three that were nearest him follow'd with force, etc.

45. *'Lost are the gallant three hundred of Scarlett's Brigade!'* Originally, 'the gallant three hundred, the Heavy Brigade!' In the preceding line, 'whispering' was 'muttering.'

46. *'Lost one and all!' were the words.* This line and the next were not in the first version.

60. *Drove it in wild dismay.* Not in the first version.

66. *And all the Brigade.* Originally, 'the Heavy Brigade.'

Page 510. EPILOGUE.

Irene. The name, which is the Greek word for 'peace,' is in keeping with the character.

Line 14. *Or Trade re-frain the Powers, etc.* The hyphen is apparently intended to call attention to the derivation of 're-frain' from the late Latin *refrenare*, to bridle or hold in with a bit (*frenum*).

17. *Kelt.* Elsewhere the poet uses the form 'Celt.' Compare 'In Memoriam,' cix.: 'The blind hysterics of the Celt;' 'A Welcome to Alexandra': 'Teuton or Celt, or whatever we be,' etc.

45. *'I will strike,' said he, etc.* See his Ode (i. 1. 35, 36): —

Quod si me lyricis vatibus inseres,
Sublimi feriam sidera vertice.

52. *Yon myriad-worlded way.* The Galaxy.

59. *The falling drop will make his name As mortal as my own.* That is, by finally obliterating the record; apparently suggested by Ovid's 'Gutta cavat lapidem non vi sed saepe cadendo.'

Page 511. TO VIRGIL.

The allusions to the 'Æneid,' the 'Georgics,' and certain 'Eclogues' need no explanation.

Line 3. *He that sang the Works and Days.* Hesiod.

18. *The Northern Island sunder'd once from all the human race.* Compare the first 'Eclogue,' 67: 'Et penitus toto divisos orbe Britannos.'

Page 513. EARLY SPRING.

Line 19. *The woods with living airs.* Originally, 'by living airs.'

33. *A gleam from yonder vale.* Originally, 'Some gleam,' etc.

Page 514. *Frater Ave Atque Vale.* The Latin quotations in the poem are from Catullus, the 'Frater ave atque vale' being the end of his lament for the loss of his brother (101.10).

Page 514. HELEN'S TOWER.

Line 4. *Mother's love in letter'd gold.* The

original reading (on the tower and in 'Good
Words') was: 'Mother's love engraved in
gold.' In the 'Tiresias' volume 'engraved'
was changed to 'engrav'n.' The present read-
ing was adopted in 1889.

The reading in the 8th line was originally
' to last so long,' changed in the 'Tiresias'. vol-
ume.

Page 515.　HANDS ALL ROUND.

The version of this song in the 'Examiner'
was as follows: —

First drink a health, this solemn night,
　A health to England, every guest;
That man 's the best cosmopolite
　Who loves his native country best.
May Freedom's oak for ever live
　With stronger life from day to day;
That man 's the true Conservative
　Who lops the moulder'd branch away.
　　　Hands all round !
　God the tyrant's hope confound !
To this great cause of Freedom drink, my friends,
　And the great name of England, round and round.

A health to Europe's honest men !
　Heaven guard them from her tyrants' jails !
From wronged Poerio's noisome den,
　From iron'd limbs and tortured nails !
We curse the crimes of Southern kings,
　The Russian whips and Austrian rods —
We likewise have our evil things;
　Too much we make our Ledgers, Gods.
　　　Yet hands all round !
　God the tyrant's cause confound !
To Europe's better health we drink, my friends,
　And the great name of England, round and round !

What health to France, if France be she,
　Whom martial prowess only charms ?
Yet tell her — better to be free
　Than vanquish all the world in arms.
Her frantic city's flashing heats
　But fire, to blast, the hopes of men.
Why change the titles of your streets ?
　You fools, you 'll want them all again.
　　　Yet hands all round !
　God their tyrant's cause confound !
To France, the wiser France, we drink, my friends,
　And the great name of England, round and round.

Gigantic daughter of the West,
　We drink to thee across the flood,
We know thee most, we love thee best,
　For art thou not of British blood ?
Should war's mad blast again be blown,
　Permit not thou the tyrant powers
To fight thy mother here alone,
　But let thy broadsides roar with ours.
　　　Hands all round !
　God the tyrant's cause confound !
To our great kinsmen of the West, my friends,
　And the great name of England, round and round.

O rise, our strong Atlantic sons,
　When war against our freedom springs !
O speak to Europe through your guns !
　They can be understood by kings.
You must not mix our Queen with those
　That wish to keep their people fools;
Our freedom's foemen are her foes,
　She comprehends the race she rules.
　　　Hands all round !
　God the tyrant's cause confound !
To our dear kinsmen of the West, my friends,
　And the great cause of Freedom, round and round.

All the reprints (not excepting that in the
'Memoir,' which has ' the tyrant's ' in the 3d
stanza, and 'great kinsmen ' in the last) are
more or less inaccurate. Only the first stanza
of this version appears in the present song,
which was written to be sung by Mr. Santley,
at St. James's Hall, London, on the Queen's
birthday, May 24, 1882.

The 6th line then had 'larger' for 'stron-
ger,' and the 11th line had ' the great,' as also
in the 11th line of the other two stanzas.

This new version as printed in the 'Tiresias'
volume had 'true Cosmopolite ' and ' best Con-
servative.' In 1889 it took its present form.

Page 516.　FREEDOM.

Line 3. *The pillar'd Parthenon.* Sometimes
printed (without authority, as Lord Tennyson
told me) ' the column'd Parthenon.'

17–20. *Of Knowledge fusing class with class,*
etc. This stanza was not in the poem as first
printed.

21. *Who yet, like Nature, etc.* Originally,
'Who, like great Nature,' etc. The next line
had ' our Human Star.'

Page 516.　POETS AND THEIR BIBLIOGRA-
PHIES.

Line 6. *Adviser of the nine-years ponder'd*
lay. See Horace, ' Ars Poetica,' 388.

8. *Catullus, whose dead songster never dies.*
Lesbia's sparrow.

Page 517.　LOCKSLEY HALL SIXTY YEARS
AFTER.

For a long review of the poem by Mr. W. E.
Gladstone, see 'The Nineteenth Century' for
January, 1887. In the closing paragraph there
is a reference to a criticism in the 'Spectator'
(of December 18, 1886) ' bearing the signs of a
master hand,' and finding ' a perfect harmony,
a true equation, between the two "Locksley
Halls; " the warmer picture due to the ample
vitality of the prophet's youth, and the colder
one not less due to the stinted vitality of his
age.' I add a portion of the article to which
Mr. Gladstone alludes: —

' The critics hitherto have done no justice to
Tennyson's "Locksley Hall," if, indeed, they
have carefully read it. We venture to say that
it is at least as fine a picture of age reviewing
the phenomena of life, and reviewing them with
an insight impossible to youth into all that
threatens man with defeat and degradation,
though of course without any of that irrepres-
sible elasticity of feeling which shows even
by the very wildness and tumult of its despair
that despair is, for it, ultimately impossible; as
Tennyson's earlier poem was of youth passion-
ately resenting the failure of its first bright
hope, and yet utterly unable to repress the
"promise and potency" of its buoyant vitality.
The difference between the "Locksley Hall"
of Tennyson's early poems and the "Locksley
Hall" of his latest is this — that in the former
all the melancholy is attributed to personal
grief, while all the sanguine visionariness which
really springs out of overflowing vitality justifies
itself by dwelling on the cumulative resources
of science and the arts; — in the latter, the mel-

ancholy in the man, a result of ebbing vitality, justifies itself by the failure of knowledge and science to cope with the moral horrors which experience has brought to light, while the set-off against that melancholy is to be found in a real personal experience of true nobility in man and woman. Hence those who call the new "Locksley Hall" pessimist seem to us to do injustice to that fine poem. No one can expect age to be full of the irrepressible buoyancy of youth. Age is conscious of a dwindling power to meet the evils which loom larger as experience widens. What the noblest old age has to set off against this consciousness of rapidly diminishing buoyancy is a larger and more solid experience of human goodness, as well as a deeper faith in the power which guides youth and age alike. Now Tennyson's poem shows us these happier aspects of age, though it shows us also that exaggerated despondency in counting up the moral evils of life which is one of the consequences of dwindling vitality. Nothing could well be finer than Tennyson's picture of the despair which his hero would feel if he had nothing but "evolution" to depend on, or than the rebuke which the speaker himself gives to that despondency when he remembers how much more than evolution there is to depend on, — how surely that has been already "evolved" in the heart of man which, itself inexplicable, yet promises an evolution far richer and more boundless than is suggested by any physical law. The final upshot of the swaying tides of progress and retrogression, in their periodic advance and retreat, is, he tells us, quite incalculable by us — the complexity of the forward and backward movements of the wave being beyond our grasp; — and yet he is sure that there is that in us which supplies an ultimate solution of the riddle. . . .

' On the whole, we have here the natural pessimism of age in all its melancholy, alternating with that highest mood like "old experience" which, in Milton's phrase, "doth attain to something like prophetic strain." The various eddies caused by these positive and negative currents seem to us delineated with at least as firm a hand as that which painted the tumultuous ebb and flow of angry despair and angrier hope in the bosom of the deceived and resentful lover of sixty years since. The later "Locksley Hall " is in the highest sense worthy of its predecessor.'

Line 1. *Half the morning have I paced these sandy tracts, etc.* Compare the opening lines of the first 'Locksley Hall.'

13–16. *In the hall there hangs a painting, etc.* These two couplets were originally written for the first 'Locksley Hall.' See the notes on that poem.

29. *Cross'd ! for once he sail'd the sea, etc.* The crossed feet indicate that the knight was a Crusader.

42. *Cold upon the dead volcano, etc.* Compare Lowell, ' The Vision of Sir Launfal ': —

The soul partakes the season's youth,
And the sulphurous rifts of passion and woe

Lie deep 'neath a silence pure and smooth,
Like burnt-out craters healed with snow.

55. *Gone our sailor son thy father.* Evidently an only son, as the grandson also is.

67–72. *Gone for ever ! Ever ? no, etc.* The 'Spectator' says: 'As an illustration of the strong grasp which age gets of the convictions which are products neither of hope nor of fear, take the following on the significance of the belief in eternity as moulding and shaping to new meanings the life of man: —

Gone for ever ! Ever ? no — for since our dying race began

Ever, ever, and for ever was the leading light of man.

Those that in barbarian burials kill'd the slave and slew the wife

Felt within themselves the sacred passion of the second life.

.   .   .   .   .   .

Truth for truth and good for good ! The good, the true, the pure, the just —

Take the charm "For ever" from them, and they crumble into dust.

Has Tennyson ever written anything which concentrates into a single line more of the wisdom of maturity than the last line here quoted ? '

73. *Gone the cry of 'Forward, Forward!'* Compare the first 'Locksley Hall': 'Forward, forward let us range,' etc.

78. *Let us hush this cry of 'Forward !' till ten thousand years have gone.* Compare ' The Golden Year ': —

Ah, folly ! for it lies so far away,
Not in our time, nor in our children's time,
'T is like the second world to us that live;
'T were all as one to fix our hopes on heaven
As on the vision of the golden year.

89. *France had shown a light to all men, etc.* Referring to the French Revolution. 'Demos' (δῆμος) is the Greek name for the common people.

95. *Peasants maim the helpless horse.* The allusion, as Lord Tennyson wrote me, is to 'modern Irish doings.' The next couplet refers to an actual instance of wanton cruelty reported in the newspapers at the time.

103. *Cosmos.* Order and harmony as opposed to ' chaos.' ' The fabric of the external universe first received the title of *cosmos*, or " beautiful " ' (Trench).

110. *Equal-born ? oh, yes, if yonder hill be level with the flat.* The critic of the London ' Academy ' (January 1, 1887) asks: 'Is it defensible to twist the Radical's demand for " equality " of rights into a statement that all men are " equal-born " in order to pour a very natural contempt upon it ? ' It is this equality of 'inalienable rights,' not equality of rank or endowments, which the Declaration of Independence claims for all men.

116. *The voices from the field.* The vote of the laboring classes.

130. *Thro' the tonguesters we may fall.* Tennyson has 'tonguesters' (which he may have coined) again in ' Harold,' v. 1.: —

The simple, silent, selfless man
Is worth a world of tonguesters.

131. *You that woo the Voices.* Compare
' Coriolanus,' ii. 3. 132: —

Here come moe voices. —
Your voices: for your voices I have fought;
Watch'd for your voices; for your voices bear
Of wounds two dozen odd; battles thrice six
I have seen, and heard of; for your voices have
Done many things, some less, some more: your voices.
Indeed, I would be consul.

133. *Pluck the mighty from their seat, etc.*
Compare Luke, i. 52, and Psalms, cxlvii. 6.

145. *Wallowing in the troughs of Zolaism.*
Alluding to the ' realistic ' French novelist.

157. *Jacobinism and Jacquerie.* Mad oppo-
sition to legitimate government, like that of
the ' Jacobins,' a club of violent Republicans
in the French Revolution of 1789, who got their
name from the Jacobin monastery where their
secret meetings were held. ' Jacquerie,' origi-
nally the name given to a revolt of the peasants
of Picardy against the nobles in 1358, came to
be applied to any similar insurrection of the
lower classes.

162. *All the millions one at length with all the
visions of my youth.* Compare the first ' Locks-
ley Hall ': —

Till the war-drum throbb'd no longer, and the battle-
flags were furl'd
In the Parliament of man, the Federation of the world.

185. *Hesper, whom the poet call'd the Bringer
home of all good things.* See note on ' Leonine
Elegiacs ' above.

201–212. *What are men that he should heed
us?* This passage ' takes for its text the 8th
Psalm, which, beginning with the same dismay
at the smallness of man's material significance,
sees, nevertheless, that in his apprehension of
the world he is proved " little lower than the
angels " ' (' The Academy ').

226. *The dog too lame to follow with the cry.*
That is, with the rest of the pack. Compare
' Othello,' ii. 3. 370: ' Not like a hound that
hunts, but one that fills up the cry; ' and ' Co-
riolanus,' iii. 3. 120: ' You common cry of curs ! '

240. *Youthful jealousy is a liar.* Alluding to
the earlier poem, where he is described as a
' clown,' etc.

246. *Roofs of slated hideousness.* The ' model
houses ' to be seen in many English towns and
villages, built on scientific principles, but with
none of the picturesque charm of the old do-
mestic architecture — better to live in, though
not to look at.

276. *Forward, till you see the Highest Human
Nature is divine, etc.* The youthful cry is
taken up again in these closing lines, in which
there is surely no pessimism.

278. *The deathless Angel seated in the vacant
tomb.* See Mark, xxi. 5, and compare John,
xx. 12.

Page 525. OPENING OF THE INDIAN AND
COLONIAL EXHIBITION.

Line 17. *And wherever her flag fly.* The ori-
ginal reading, as printed in the newspapers at

the time, was: ' And — where'er her flag may
fly —; ' and the poem ended thus : —

Britons, hold your own !
And God guard all !

Page 525. To W. C. MACREADY.

At the banquet the sonnet was read to the
guests by John Forster. It was printed at the
time in ' The Household Narrative of Current
Events ' and other periodicals.

Page 526. TO THE MARQUIS OF DUFFERIN
AND AVA.

On the 20th of April, 1886, the poet's younger
son, Lionel, died on the voyage home from
India. A monument was erected to his mem-
ory in Freshwater Church on the Isle of Wight
— a beautiful statue of St. John, from the chisel
of Miss Mary Grant. A tribute more enduring
than brass or marble, and more beautiful than
sculptor could carve, is built in lofty and tender
rhyme in these lines addressed by his father to
the Marquis of Dufferin and Ava.

Page 527. ON THE JUBILEE OF QUEEN VIC-
TORIA.

Line 39. *Henry's fifty years are all in shadow.*
Henry III., who came to the throne in 1216, and
died in 1272. The other sovereigns referred to
are Edward III., who reigned fifty-one years,
and George III., who reigned sixty years.

Page 528. DEMETER AND PERSEPHONE.

Line 5. *The God of ghosts and dreams.* Her-
mes (Mercury), the ' serpent-wanded power ' of
line 25.

39. *Aïdoneus.* Dis (Pluto).

82. *Three gray heads.* The Fates.

114. *The brother of this Darkness.* Zeus (Jupi-
ter).

119. *For nine white moons.* The earlier classi-
cal authorities made it *eight* months, the later
ones *six* months.

148. *The Stone, the Wheel.* The stone of Sisy-
phus and the wheel of Ixion.

Page 530. OWD ROÄ.

Line 6. *Like owt.* Like anything (aught).

15. *Faäithful an' True.* See Revelation,
xix. 11.

61. *Cleän-wud.* The *wud* is the old English
wode or *wood*, meaning mad, frantic. Compare
the play upon the word in the ' Midsummer-
Night's Dream,' ii. 1. 192: —

And here am I, and wode within this wood,
Because I cannot meet my Helena.

94. *Tother Hangel i' Scriptur.* See Judges,
xiii. 20.

Page 533. VASTNESS.

Mr. W. E. Henley remarks: ' In " Vastness "
the insight into essentials, the command of
primordial matter, the capacity of vital sug-
gestion, are gloriously in evidence from the first
to the last. Here is no touch of ingenuity, no
trace of " originality," no sign of cleverness,
. . . nothing is antic, peculiar, superfluous; but
here is epic unity and completeness, here is a
sublimation of experience expressed by means
of a sublimation of style. It is unique in Eng-
lish, and, for all that one can see, it is likely to
remain unique this good while yet.'

Line 9. *Innocence seethed in her mother's milk.*
Compare Exodus, xxiii. 19, or xxxiv. 26.

Page 534. THE RING.
Line 58. *The lonely maiden Princess of the wood.* Compare Tennyson's version of the story in 'The Day Dream.'

62. *Io t' amo.* I love thee (Italian).

159. *Till I knew.* Referring to the 'knew not that which pleased it most,' in line 141 above.

Page 546. TO ULYSSES.
Line 4. *Corrientes.* The capital of the province of the same name in the Argentine Republic.

7. *The century's three strong eights.* This fixes the date of the composition of the poem.

26. *The warrior of Caprera.* Garibaldi, so called from the town which was his home from 1854 to 1882. It was in April, 1864, that the Italian hero planted the 'waving pine' — a *Wellingtonia gigantea* — in the garden at Farringford.

Page 547. TO MARY BOYLE.
Of the poems of friendship which occur so frequently in the later volumes of Tennyson, Stopford Brooke says: 'They ought to be read together when we desire to feel his grace and power in this special kind of poetry, which no one, I think, has ever done so well. They are revelations of character, and of a character made braver and kindlier by old age. No trace of cynicism deforms them, and their little sadness is balanced by a soft and sunny clearness, by tenderness in memory and magnanimity of hope. Each of them is also tinged by the individuality of the person to whom it is written. The poems to Edward Fitzgerald, to his brother, to Mary Boyle, to Lord Dufferin, possess these qualities, and are drenched, as it were, with the dew of this delicate sentiment peculiar to old age. They look backward, therefore, but they also look forward; and not only friends on earth, but those also who have found their life in death enter into their hour of prospect and retrospect.'

Line 28. *In rick-fire days.* Referring to the troublous times of 1830-33, when the irritation of the agricultural laborers of England against their employers was at its height, and for months together the burning of stacks, farmbuildings, and other property was of nightly occurrence. Compare 'The Princess,' iv.: —

As of some fire against a stormy cloud,
When the wild peasant rights himself, the rick
Flames, and his anger reddens in the heavens.

Page 550. MERLIN AND THE GLEAM.
Line 14. *And learn'd me Magic.* The use of 'learn'd' for 'taught' is an archaism. Compare 'Much Ado About Nothing,' iv. 1. 31. 'Sweet prince, you learn me noble thankfulness.'

Page 551. ROMNEY'S REMORSE.
Line 104. *With Milton's amaranth.* See 'Paradise Lost,' iii. 353: —

Immortal amaranth, a flower which once
In Paradise, fast by the Tree of Life,
Began to bloom, but, soon for man's offence
To Heaven removed where first it grew, there grows
And flowers aloft, shading the Fount of Life,
And where the River of Bliss through midst of Heaven
Rolls o'er Elysian flowers her amber stream.

142. *He said it . . . in the play.* See 'Measure for Measure,' iii. 1. 2: —

The miserable have no other medicine
But only hope.

Page 555. FAR — FAR — AWAY.
The 'Memoir' (vol. ii. p. 366) says: 'Distant bells always charmed him with their "lin-lan-lone," and, when heard over the sea or a lake, he was never tired of listening to them.'

Page 556. THE THROSTLE.
Stopford Brooke, after referring to the poems of friendship in the later volumes of Tennyson (see note on lines 'To Mary Boyle,' above), remarks: 'There is another kind of poetry which is naturally written in old age, and recurs to those motives of youth which arise out of the happiness of the world and of the poet in the awakening of life in Spring. This poetry is born out of the memories of that early joy, and is also touched with a distinctive sentiment native only to old age, delicately clear, having a breath of the color and warmth of youth, and flushed with the hope of its re-awakening. Its poems are like those February days which enter from time to time into the wintry world, so genial in their misty sunlight that the earth seems then to breathe like a sleeping woman, and her bosom to heave with a dream of coming pleasure. They recall the past, and prophesy the immortal Spring. Old age often feels this sentiment, but is rarely able to shape it; but when, by good fortune, it can be shaped, the poem has a unique charm. Of such poems, "The Throstle" is one, and "Early Spring" is another. They may have been originally conceived, or even written, in earlier days, but I am sure that they were rewritten in old age, and in its evening air.'

VII. BIBLIOGRAPHICAL NOTE

THE STANDARD EDITION is now *The Poems of Tennyson*, edited by Christopher Ricks, London, 1969. Sir Charles Tennyson's *Alfred Tennyson* (1949) is a biography which supplements but does not supersede Hallam Tennyson's *Alfred Lord Tennyson: A Memoir* (two volumes in 1897, later one volume), which, in spite of its excessive filial piety, is indispensable for the letters and conversations and the large amount of contemporary comment which it reprints. The best short biographical and critical study is Christopher Ricks's *Tennyson* (1972). A. C. Bradley's *Commentary on Tennyson's "In Memoriam"* (1901) is still a classic. *Tennyson: The Critical Heritage*, edited by J. D. Jump (1967), anthologizes the most valuable criticism written by Tennyson's contemporaries. W. H. Auden's introduction to his *Selections from the Poems of Alfred Lord Tennyson* (1944) has a special interest. The best representation of the criticism of recent years (including T. S. Eliot's two essays) is found in *Critical Essays on the Poetry of Tennyson*, edited by John Killham (1961).

INDEX OF FIRST LINES

INDEX OF TITLES